HISTORY OF THE CHRISTIAN CHURCH

IMPERIUM ROMANORUM

latissime patens

Milliara 50 0 50 100 200 350 Romana
Milliara 50 0 50 100 200 350 Anglica

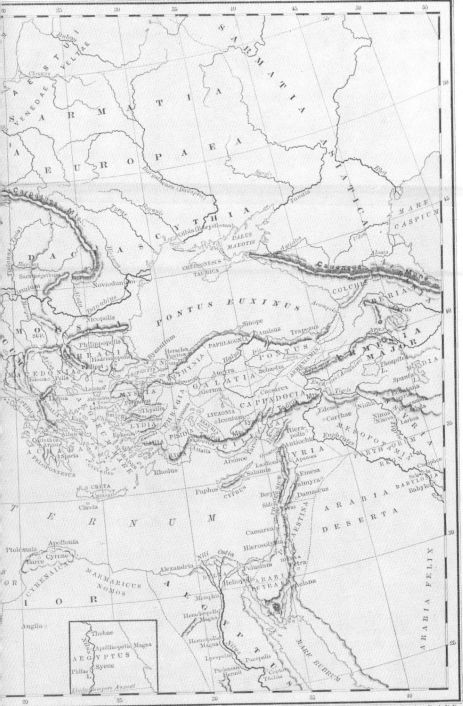

HISTORY

OF THE

CHRISTIAN CHURCH

BY

PHILIP SCHAFF

Christianus sum. Christiani nihil a me alienum puto

VOLUME I

APOSTOLIC CHRISTIANITY

A.D. 1–100

WM. B. EERDMANS PUBLISHING COMPANY

GRAND RAPIDS   MICHIGAN

PHOTOLITHOPRINTED BY CUSHING - MALLOY, INC.
ANN ARBOR, MICHIGAN, UNITED STATES OF AMERICA
1978

PREFACE TO THE THIRD REVISION

The continued demand for my Church History lays upon me the grateful duty of keeping it abreast of the times. I have, therefore, submitted this and the other volumes (especially the second) to another revision and brought the literature down to the latest date, as the reader will see by glancing at pages 2, 35, 45, 51–53, 193, 411, 484, 569, 570, etc. The changes have been effected by omissions and condensations, without enlarging the size. The second volume is now passing through the fifth edition, and the other volumes will follow rapidly.

This is my last revision. If any further improvements should be necessary during my life-time, I shall add them in a separate appendix.

I feel under great obligation to the reading public which enables me to perfect my work. The interest in Church History is steadily increasing in our theological schools and among the rising generation of scholars, and promises good results for the advancement of our common Christianity.

THE AUTHOR

New York, January, 1890.

PREFACE TO THE REVISED EDITION

As I appear before the public with a new edition of my Church History, I feel more than ever the difficulty and responsibility of a task which is well worthy to occupy the whole time and strength of a long life, and which carries in it its own rich reward. The true historian of Christianity is yet to come. But short as I have fallen of my own ideal, I have done my best, and shall rejoice if my efforts stimulate others to better and more enduring work.

History should be written from the original sources of friend and foe, in the spirit of truth and love, "sine ira et studio," "with malice towards none, with charity for all," in clear, fresh, vigorous style, under the guidance of the twin parables of the mustard-seed and leaven, as a book of life for instruction, correction, encouragement, as the best exposition and vindication of Christianity. The great and good Neander, "the father of church history"—first an Israelite without guile hoping for the Messiah, then a Platonist longing for the realization of his ideal of righteousness, last a Christian in head and heart—made such a history his life-work, but before reaching the Reformation he was interrupted by sickness, and said to his faithful sister: "Hannchen, I am weary; let us go home; good night!" And thus he fell gently asleep, like a child, to awake in the land where all problems of history are solved.

When, after a long interruption caused by a change of professional duties and literary labors, I returned to the favorite studies of my youth, I felt the necessity, before continuing the History to more recent times, of subjecting the first volume to a thorough revision, in order to bring it up to the present state of investigation. We live in a stirring and restless age of discovery, criticism, and reconstruction. During the thirty years which have elapsed since the publication of my separate "History of the Apostolic Church," there has been an incessant activity in this field, not only in Germany, the great workshop of critical research, but in all other Protestant countries. Almost every inch of ground has been disputed and defended with a degree of learning, acumen, and skill such as were never spent before on the solution of historical problems.

In this process of reconstruction the first volume has been more than doubled in size and grown into two volumes. The first embraces Apostolic, the second post-Apostolic or ante-Nicene Christianity. This first volume is larger than my separate "History of the Apostolic Church," but differs from it in that it is chiefly devoted to the theology and literature, the other to the mission work and spiritual life of that period. I have studiously avoided repetition and seldom looked into the older book. On two points I have changed my opinion—the second Roman captivity of Paul (which I am disposed to admit in the interest of the Pastoral Epistles), and the date of the Apocalypse (which I now assign, with the majority of modern critics, to the year 68 or 69 instead of 95, as before).[1]

I express my deep obligation to my friend, Dr. Ezra Abbot, a scholar of rare learning and microscopic accuracy, for his kind and valuable assistance in reading the proof and suggesting many improvements.

The second volume, likewise thoroughly revised and partly rewritten, is in the hands of the printer; the third requires very few changes. Two new volumes, one on the History of Mediæval Christianity, and one on the Reformation (to the Westphalian Treaty and the Westminster Assembly, 1648), are in an advanced stage of preparation.

May the work in this remodelled shape find as kind and indulgent readers as when it first appeared. My highest ambition in this sceptical age is to strengthen the faith in the immovable historical foundations of Christianity and its victory over the world.

Philip Schaff.

Union Theological Seminary, New York,
        October, 1882.

---

[1] My "History of the Apostolic Church" (which bears a relation to my "History of the Christian Church," similar to that which Neander's "History of the Planting and Training of the Christian Church by the Apostles" bears to his "General History of the Christian Religion and Church") appeared in German at Mercersburg, Pa., 1851, then in a revised edition, Leipzig, 1854, in an English translation by the late Dr. Yeomans, New York, 1853, at Edinburgh, 1854 (in 2 vols.), and several times since without change. Should there be a demand for a new edition, I intend to make a number of improvements, which are ready in manuscript, especially in the General Introduction, which covers 134 pages. The first volume of my Church History (from A.D. 1 to 311) was first published in New York, 1858 (and in German at Leipzig, 1867); but when I began the revision, I withdrew it from sale. The Apostolic Age there occupies only 140, the whole volume 535 pages.

FROM THE PREFACE TO THE FIRST EDITION

ENCOURAGED by the favorable reception of my "History of the Apostolic Church," I now offer to the public a History of the Primitive Church from the birth of Christ to the reign of Constantine, as an independent and complete work in itself, and at the same time as the first volume of a general history of Christianity, which I hope, with the help of God, to bring down to the present age.

The church of the first three centuries, or the ante-Nicene age, possesses a peculiar interest for Christians of all denominations, and has often been separately treated, by Eusebius, Mosheim, Milman, Kaye, Baur, Hagenbach, and other distinguished historians. It is the daughter of Apostolic Christianity, which itself constitutes the first and by far the most important chapter in its history, and the common mother of Catholicism and Protestantism, though materially differing from both. It presents a state of primitive simplicity and purity unsullied by contact with the secular power, but with this also, the fundamental forms of heresy and corruption, which reappear from time to time under new names and aspects, but must serve, in the overruling providence of God, to promote the cause of truth and righteousness. It is the heroic age of the church, and unfolds before us the sublime spectacle of our holy religion in intellectual and moral conflict with the combined superstition, policy, and wisdom of ancient Judaism and Paganism; yet growing in persecution, conquering in death, and amidst the severest trials giving birth to principles and institutions which, in more matured form, still control the greater part of Christendom.

Without the least disposition to detract from the merits of my numerous predecessors, to several of whom I feel deeply indebted, I have reason to hope that this new attempt at a historical reproduction of ancient Christianity will meet a want in our theological literature and commend itself, both by its spirit and method, and by presenting with the author's own labors the results of the latest German and English research, to the respectful attention of the American student. Having no sectarian ends to serve, I have confined myself to the duty of a witness—to tell the truth, the whole truth, and nothing but the truth; always remembering, however, that history has a soul as well as a body, and that the ruling ideas and general principles must be represented no less than the outward facts and dates.   A church history without the life of Christ glowing through its pages could give us at best only the picture of a temple stately and imposing from without, but vacant and dreary within, a mummy in praying posture perhaps and covered with trophies, but withered and unclean : such a history is not worth the trouble of writing or reading.   Let the dead bury their dead ; we prefer to live among the living, and to record the immortal thoughts and deeds of Christ in and through his people, rather than dwell upon the outer hulls, the trifling accidents and temporary scaffolding of history, or give too much promi nence to Satan and his infernal tribe, whose works Christ came to destroy.

The account of the apostolic period, which forms the divine-human basis of the whole structure of history, or the ever-living fountain of the unbroken stream of the church, is here necessarily short and not intended to supersede my larger work, although it presents more than a mere summary of it, and views the subject in part under new aspects. For the history of the second period, which constitutes the body of this volume, large use has been made of the new sources of information recently brought to light, such as the Syriac and Armenian Ignatius, and especially the Philosophoumena of Hippolytus. The bold and searching criticism of modern German historians as applied to the apostolic and post-apostolic literature, though often arbitrary and untenable in its results, has nevertheless done good service by removing old prejudices, placing many things in a new light, and conducing to a comprehensive and organic view of the living process and gradual growth of ancient Christianity in its distinctive character, both in its unity with, and difference from, the preceding age of the apostles and the succeeding systems of Catholicism and Protestantism.

And now I commit this work to the great Head of the church with the prayer that, under his blessing, it may aid in promoting a correct knowledge of his heavenly kingdom on earth, and in setting forth its history as a book of life, a storehouse of wisdom and piety, and the surest test of his own promise to his people : "Lo, I am with you alway, even unto the end of the world."

P. S.

THEOLOGICAL SEMINARY, Mercersburg, Pennsylvania,
November 8, 1858.

CONTENTS

GENERAL INTRODUCTION

FIRST PERIOD

APOSTOLIC CHRISTIANITY

A.D. 1-100.

CHAPTER I

PREPARATION FOR CHRISTIANITY

CHAPTER II.

JESUS CHRIST.

CHAPTER III

THE APOSTOLIC AGE.

CHAPTER IV

ST. PETER AND THE CONVERSION OF THE JEWS

(Map of Palestine.)

CHAPTER V

ST. PAUL AND THE CONVERSION OF THE GENTILES

(Map of Paul's Journeys.)

CHAPTER VI

THE GREAT TRIBULATION.

CHAPTER VII

ST. JOHN AND THE LAST STADIUM OF THE APOSTOLIC PERIOD—THE CONSOLIDATION OF JEWISH AND GENTILE CHRISTIANITY.

(Map of Asia Minor.)

CHAPTER VIII

CHRISTIAN LIFE IN THE APOSTOLIC CHURCH.

CHAPTER IX

WORSHIP IN THE APOSTOLIC AGE

CHAPTER X

ORGANIZATION OF THE APOSTOLIC CHURCH

CHAPTER XI.

THEOLOGY OF THE APOSTOLIC CHURCH

CHAPTER XII

THE NEW TESTAMENT.

LIST OF MAPS

ADDENDA

(Fifth Edition.)

Since the third revision of this volume in 1889, the following works deserving notice have appeared till September, 1893. (P. S.)

Page 2. After "Nirschl" add:

E. BERNHEIM : *Lehrbuch der historischen Methode. Mit Nachweis der wichtigsten Quellen und Hilfsmittel zum Studium der Geschichte.* Leipzig, 1889.

EDWARD BRATKE : *Wegweiser zur Quellen- und Literaturkunde der Kirchengeschichte.* Gotha, 1890 (282 pp.).

Page 35, line 9 :

H. BRÜCK (Mainz, 5th ed., 1890).

Page 45 :

Of the Church History of KURTZ (who died at Marburg, 1890), an 11th revised edition appeared in 1891.

WILHELM MÖLLER (d. at Kiel, 1891): *Lehrbuch der Kirchengeschichte.* Freiburg, 1891. 2 vols., down to the Reformation. Vol. III. to be added by Kawerau. Vol. I. translated by Rutherford. London, 1892.

KARL MÜLLER (Professor in Breslau): *Kirchengeschichte.* Freiburg, 1892. A second volume will complete the work. An excellent manual from the school of Ritschl-Harnack.

HARNACK's large *Lehrbuch der Dogmengeschichte* was completed in 1890 in 3 vols. Of his *Grundriss*, a 2d ed. appeared in 1893 (386 pp.); translated by Edwin K. Mitchell, of Hartford, Conn. : *Outlines of the History of Dogma.* New York, 1893.

FRIEDRICH LOOFS (Professor of Church History in Halle, of the Ritschl-Harnack school) : *Leitfaden zum Studium der Dogmengeschichte.* Halle, 1889 ; 3d ed., 1893.

Page 51. After "Schaff" add:

5th revision, 1889–93, 7 vols. (including vol. v., which is in press).

Page 51. After "Fisher" add :

JOHN FLETCHER HURST (Bishop of the Methodist Episcopal Church): *Short History of the Christian Church.* New York, 1893.

Page 61.   After " Kittel " add :

FRANZ DELITZSCH (d. 1890) : *Messianische Weissagungen in geschicht-licher Folge.* Leipzig, 1890. His last work. Translated by Sam. Ives Curtiss (of Chicago), Edinb. and New York, 1892.

Page 97 :

SAMUEL J. ANDREWS: *Life of our Lord.* "A new and wholly revised edition." New York, 1891 (651 pp.). With maps and illustrations. Maintains the quadri-paschal theory. Modest, reverent, accurate, devoted chiefly to the chronological and topographical relations.

Page 183 add :

On the Apocryphal Traditions of Christ, comp. throughout

ALFRED RESCH : *Agrapha.   Aussercanonische Evangelienfragmente ge-sammelt und untersucht.* With an appendix of HARNACK on the Gospel Fragment of Tajjum. Leipzig, 1889 (520 pp.). By far the most complete and critical work on the extra-canonical sayings of our Lord, of which he collects and examines 63 (see p. 80), in-cluding many doubtful ones, *e.g.*, the much-discussed passage of the *Didache* (I. 6) on the sweating of aloes.

Page 247 :

Abbé CONSTANT FOUARD : *Saint Peter and the First Years of Christianity.* Translated from the second French edition with the author's sanc-tion, by George F. X. Griffith. With an Introduction by Cardinal Gibbons. New York and London, 1892 (pp. xxvi, 422). The most learned work in favor of the traditional Roman theory of a twenty-five years' pontificate of Peter in Rome from 42 to 67.

The *apocryphal* literature of *Peter* has received an important addition by the discovery of fragments of the Greek Gospel and Apocalypse of Peter in a tomb at Akhmim in Egypt. See Harnack's ed. of the Greek text with a German translation and commentary, Berlin, 1892 (revised, 1893) ; Zahn's edition and discussion, Leipzig, 1893; and O. von Gebhardt's facsimile ed., Leipzig, 1893; also the English translation by J. Rendel Harris, London, 1893.

Page 284.   Add to lit. on the life of Paul :

W. H. RAMSEY (Professor of Humanity in the University of Aberdeen) : *The Church in the Roman Empire before* A. D. 170. With Maps and Illustrations. London and New York, 1893 (494 pp.). An impor-tant work, for which the author received a gold medal from Pope Leo XIII. The first part (pp. 3–168) treats of the missionary journeys of Paul in Asia Minor, on the ground of careful topo-graphical exploration and with a full knowledge of Roman history at that time. He comes to the conclusion that nearly all the books of the New Testament can no more be forgeries of the second cen-tury than the works of Horace and Virgil can be forgeries of the time of Nero. He assumes a "travel-document," which was written down under the immediate influence of Paul, and underlies the account in The Acts of the Apostles (chs. 13–21), which he calls "an authority of the highest character for an historian of Asia Minor" (p. 168). He affirms the genuineness of the Pastoral Epistles, which suit the close of the Neronian period (246 *sqq.*), and combats Holtzmann. He puts II Peter to the age of "The Shepherd of Hermas" before 130 (p. 432). As to the First Epistle of Peter, he assumes that it was written about 80, soon after Vespasian's resumption of the Neronian policy (279 *sqq.*). If this date is correct, it would follow either that Peter cannot have been the author, or that he must have long outlived the Neronian persecution. The tradition that he died a martyr in Rome is early and universal, but the exact date of his death is uncertain.

Page 285 insert:

Of Weizsäcker's *Das Apostolische Zeitalter*, which is chiefly devoted to Paul, a second edition has appeared in 1892, slightly revised and provided with an alphabetical index (770 pp.). It is the best critical history of the Apostolic age from the school of Dr. Baur, whom Dr. Weizsäcker succeeded as professor of Church history in Tübingen, but gives no references to literature and other opinions.

CHARLES CARROLL EVERETT: *The Gospel of Paul.* New York, 1893.

Page 360:

RODOLFO LANCIANI: *Pagan and Christian Rome.* New York, 1893 (pp. x, 374). A very important work which shows from recent explorations that Christianity entered more deeply into Roman Society in the first century than is usually supposed.

Page 401 add:

HENRY WILLIAM WATKINS: *Modern Criticism in its relation to the Fourth Gospel; being the Bampton Lectures for* 1890. London, 1890. Only the external evidence, but with a history of opinions since Breitschneider's *Probabilia.*

PATON J. GLOAG: *Introduction to the Johannine Writings.* London, 1891 (pp. 440). Discusses the critical questions connected with the Gospel, the Epistles, and the Apocalypse of John from a liberal conservative standpoint.

E. SCHÜRER: *On the Genuineness of the Fourth Gospel.* In the "Contemporary Review" for September, 1891.

Page 484:

E. LOENING: *Die Gemeindeverfassung des Urchristenthums.* Halle, 1889 —CH. DE SMEDT: *L'organisation des églises chrétiennes jusqu'au milieu du 3e siècle.* 1889.

Page 569. Add to literature :

GREGORY : *Prolegomena to Tischendorf*, Pt. II., 1890. (Pt. III. will complete this work.)

SCHAFF : *Companion to the Greek Testament*, 4th ed. revised, 1892.

SALMON : *Introduction to the New Testament*, 5th ed., 1890.

HOLTZMANN : *Introduction to the New Testament*, 3d ed., 1892.

F. GODET : *Introduction au Nouveau Testament*. Neuchatel, 1893. The first volume contains the Introduction to the Pauline Epistles; the second and third will contain the Introduction to the Gospels, the Catholic Epp. and the Revelation. To be translated.

Page 576 :

Robinson's *Harmony*, revised edition, by M. B. RIDDLE (Professor in Allegheny Theological Seminary), New York, 1885.

Page 724 :

FRIEDRICH SPITTA : *Die Apostelgeschichte, ihre Quellen und ihr historischer Wert*. Halle, 1891 (pp. 380). It is briefly criticised by Ramsey.

GENERAL INTRODUCTION

LITERATURE

C. SAGITTARIUS : *Introductio in historiam ecclesiasticam.* Jen. 1694.

F. WALCH : *Grundsätze der zur K. Gesch. nöthigen Vorbereitungslehren u. Bücherkenntnisse.* 3d ed. Giessen, 1793.

FLÜGGE : *Einleitung in das Studium u. die Liter. der K. G.* Gött. 1801.

JOHN G. DOWLING : *An Introduction to the Critical Study of Ecclesiastical History, attempted in an account of the progress, and a short notice of the sources of the history of the Church.* London, 1838.

MÖHLER (R. C.) : *Einleitung in die K. G.* 1839 ("Verm. Schriften," ed. Döllinger, II. 261 sqq.).

KLIEFOTH : *Einleitung in die Dogmengeschichte.* Parchim & Ludwigslust, 1839.

PHILIP SCHAFF : *What is Church History? A Vindication of the Idea of Historical Development.* Philad. 1846.

H. B. SMITH : *Nature and Worth of the Science of Church History.* Andover, 1851.

E. P. HUMPHREY : *Inaugural Address, delivered at the Danville Theol. Seminary.* Cincinnati, 1854.

R. TURNBULL : *Christ in History; or, the Central Power among Men.* Bost. 1854, 2d ed. 1860.

W. G. T. SHEDD : *Lectures on the Philosophy of History.* Andover, Mass., 1856.

R. D. HITCHCOCK : *The True Idea and Uses of Church History.* N. York, 1856.

C. BUNSEN : *Gott in der Geschichte oder der Fortschritt des Glaubens an eine sittliche Weltordnung.* Bd. I. Leipz. 1857. (Erstes Buch. Allg. Einleit. p. 1–134.) Engl. Transl. : *God in History.* By S. Winkworth. Lond. 1868. 3 vols.

A. P. STANLEY : *Three Introductory Lectures on the Study of Eccles. History.* Lond. 1857. (Also incorporated in his *History of the Eastern Church*, 1861.)

GOLDWIN SMITH: *Lectures on the Study of History, delivered in Oxford,* 1859–'61. Oxf. and Lond. (republished in N. York) 1866.

J. GUST. DROYSEN: *Grundriss der Historik.* Leipz. 1868 ; new ed. 1882.

C. DE SMEDT (R. C.) : *Introductio generalis ad historiam ecclesiasticam critice tractandam.* Gandavi (Ghent), 1876 (533 pp.).

E. A. FREEMAN : *The Methods of Historical Study.* Lond. 1886.

O. LORENZ : *Geschichtswissenschaft.* Berlin, 1886.

JOS. NIRSCHL (R. C.) : *Propädeutik der Kirchengeschichte.* Mainz, 1888 (352 pp.).

On the philosophy of history in general, see the works of HERDER (*Ideen zur Philosophie der Gesch. der Menschheit*), FRED. SCHLEGEL, HEGEL (1840, transl. by Sibree, 1870), HERMANN (1870), ROCHOLL (1878), FLINT (*The Philosophy of History in Europe.* Edinb., 1874, etc.), LOTZE (*Mikrokosmus,* Bk. viith ; 4th ed. 1884 ; Eng. transl. by Elizabeth Hamilton and E. E. C. Jones, 1885, 3d ed. 1888). A philosophy of *church history* is a desideratum. Herder and Lotze come nearest to it.

A fuller introduction, see in SCHAFF : *History of the Apostolic Church ; with a General Introduction to Ch. H.* (N. York, 1853), pp. 1–134.

§ 1. *Nature of Church History.*

HISTORY has two sides, a divine and a human. On the part of God, it is his revelation in the order of time (as the creation is his revelation in the order of space), and the successive unfolding of a plan of infinite wisdom, justice, and mercy, looking to his glory and the eternal happiness of mankind. On the part of man, history is the biography of the human race, and the gradual development, both normal and abnormal, of all its physical, intellectual, and moral forces to the final consummation at the general judgment, with its eternal rewards and punishments. The idea of universal history presupposes the Christian idea of the unity of God, and the unity and common destiny of men, and was unknown to ancient Greece and Rome. A view of history which overlooks or undervalues the divine factor starts from deism and consistently runs into atheism ; while the opposite view, which overlooks the free agency of man and his moral responsibility and guilt, is essentially fatalistic and pantheistic.

From the human agency we may distinguish the Satanic, which enters as a third power into the history of the race. In the temptation of Adam in Paradise, the temptation of Christ in the wilderness, and at every great epoch, Satan appears as the antagonist of God, endeavoring to defeat the plan of redemption and the progress of Christ's kingdom, and using weak and wicked men for his schemes, but is always defeated in the end by the superior wisdom of God.

The central current and ultimate aim of universal history is the KINGDOM OF GOD established by JESUS CHRIST. This is the grandest and most comprehensive institution in the world, as vast as humanity and as enduring as eternity. All other institutions are made subservient to it, and in its interest the whole world is governed. It is no after-thought of God, no subsequent emendation of the plan of creation, but it is the eternal forethought, the controlling idea, the beginning, the middle, and the end of all his ways and works. The first Adam is a type of the second Adam; creation looks to redemption as the solution of its problems. Secular history, far from controlling sacred history, is controlled by it, must directly or indirectly subserve its ends, and can only be fully understood in the central light of Christian truth and the plan of salvation. The Father, who directs the history of the world, "draws to the Son," who rules the history of the church, and the Son leads back to the Father, that "God may be all in all." "All things," says St. Paul, "were created through Christ and unto Christ: and He is before all things, and in Him all things hold together. And He is the head of the body, the Church: who is the beginning, the firstborn from the dead, that in all things He may have the pre-eminence." Col. 1: 16–18. "The Gospel," says John von Müller, summing up the final result of his life-long studies in history, "is the fulfilment of all hopes, the perfection of all philosophy, the interpreter of all revolutions, the key of all seeming contradictions of the physical and moral worlds; it is life—it is immortality."

The history of the church is the rise and progress of the kingdom of heaven upon earth, for the glory of God and the salvation of the world. It begins with the creation of Adam, and with that promise of the serpent-bruiser, which relieved the loss of the paradise of innocence by the hope of future redemption from the curse of sin. It comes down through the preparatory revelations under the patriarchs, Moses, and the prophets, to the immediate forerunner of the Saviour, who pointed his followers to the Lamb of God, which taketh away the sin of the world. But this part of its course was only introduction. Its proper starting-point is the incarnation of the Eternal Word, who dwelt among us and revealed his glory, the glory as of the only-begotten of the Father, full of grace and truth ; and next to this, the miracle of the first Pentecost, when the Church took her place as a Christian institution, filled with the Spirit of the glorified Redeemer and entrusted with the conversion of all nations. Jesus Christ, the God-Man and Saviour of the world, is the author of the new creation, the soul and the head of the church, which is his body and his bride. In his person and work lies all the fulness of the Godhead and of renewed humanity, the whole plan of redemption, and the key of all history from the creation of man in the image of God to the resurrection of the body unto everlasting life.

This is the objective conception of church history.

In the subjective sense of the word, considered as theological science and art, church history is the faithful and life-like description of the origin and progress of this heavenly kingdom. It aims to reproduce in thought and to embody in language its outward and inward development down to the present time. It is a continuous commentary on the Lord's twin parables of the mustard-seed and of the leaven. It shows at once how Christianity spreads over the world, and how it penetrates, transforms, and sanctifies the individual and all the departments and institutions of social life. It thus embraces not only the external fortunes of Christendom, but more especially her inward experience, her religious life, her mental and moral activity, her conflicts with the ungodly world, her sorrows and sufferings, her joys and her triumphs over sin and error. It records the deeds of those heroes of faith "who subdued kingdoms, wrought righteousness, obtained promises, stopped the mouths of lions, quenched the violence of fire, escaped the edge of the sword, out of weakness were made strong, waxed valiant in fight, turned to flight the armies of aliens."

From Jesus Christ, since his manifestation in the flesh, an unbroken stream of divine light and life has been and is still flowing, and will continue to flow, in ever-growing volume, through the waste of our fallen race; and all that is truly great and good and holy in the annals of church history is due, ultimately, to the impulse of his spirit. He is the fly-wheel in the world's progress. But he works upon the world through sinful and fallible men, who, while as self-conscious and free agents they are accountable for all their actions, must still, willing or unwilling, serve the great purpose of God. As Christ, in the days of his flesh, was hated, mocked, and crucified, his church likewise is assailed and persecuted by the powers of darkness The history of Christianity includes therefore a history of Antichrist. With an unending succession of works of saving power and manifestations of divine truth and holiness, it uncovers also a fearful mass of corruption and error. The church militant must, from its very nature, be at perpetual warfare with the world, the flesh, and the devil, both without and within. For as Judas sat among the apostles, so "the man of sin" sits in the temple of God; and as even a Peter denied the Lord, though he afterwards wept bitterly and regained his holy office, so do many disciples in all ages deny him in word and in deed.

But, on the other hand, church history shows that God is ever stronger than Satan, and that his kingdom of light puts the kingdom of darkness to shame. The Lion of the tribe of Judah has bruised the head of the serpent. With the crucifixion of Christ his resurrection also is repeated ever anew in the history of his church on earth; and there has never yet been a day without a witness of his presence and power ordering all things according to his holy will. For he has received all power in heaven and in earth for the good of his people, and from his heavenly throne he rules even his foes. The infallible word of promise, confirmed by experience, assures us that all corruptions, heresies, and schisms must, under the guidance of divine wisdom and love, subserve the cause of truth, holiness, and peace; till, at the last judgment, Christ shall make his enemies his footstool, and rule undisputed with the sceptre of righteousness and peace, and his church shall realize her idea and destiny as " the fullness of him that filleth all in all."

Then will history itself, in its present form, as a struggling and changeful development, give place to perfection, and the stream of time come to rest in the ocean of eternity, but this rest will be the highest form of life and activity in God and for God.

§ 2. *Branches of Church History.*

The kingdom of Christ, in its principle and aim, is as comprehensive as humanity. It is truly catholic or universal, designed and adapted for all nations and ages, for all the powers of the soul, and all classes of society. It breathes into the mind, the heart, and the will a higher, supernatural life, and consecrates the family, the state, science, literature, art, and commerce to holy ends, till finally God becomes all in all. Even the body, and the whole visible creation, which groans for redemption from its bondage to vanity and for the glorious liberty of the children of God, shall share in this universal transformation; for we look for the resurrection of the body, and for the new earth, wherein dwelleth righteousness. But we must not identify the kingdom of God with the visible church or churches, which are only its temporary organs and agencies, more or less inadequate, while the kingdom itself is more comprehensive, and will last for ever.

Accordingly, church history has various departments, corresponding to the different branches of secular history and of natural life. The principal divisions are :

I. The history of MISSIONS, or of the spread of Christianity among unconverted nations, whether barbarous or civilized. This work must continue, till " the fullness of the Gentiles shall come in," and " Israel shall be saved." The law of the missionary progress is expressed in the two parables of the grain of mustard-seed which grows into a tree, and of the leaven which gradually pervades the whole lump. The first parable illustrates the outward expansion, the second the all-penetrating and transforming power of Christianity. It is difficult to convert a nation; it is more difficult to train it to the high standard of the gospel; it is most difficult to revive and reform a dead or apostate church.

The foreign mission work has achieved three great conquests: first, the conversion of the elect remnant of the Jews, and of civilized Greeks and Romans, in the first three centuries; then the conversion of the barbarians of Northern and Western Europe, in the middle ages; and last, the combined efforts of various churches and societies for the conversion of the savage races in America, Africa, and Australia, and the semi-civilized nations of Eastern Asia, in our own time. The whole non-Christian world is now open to missionary labor, except the Mohammedan, which will likewise become accessible at no distant day.

The domestic or home mission work embraces the revival of Christian life in corrupt or neglected portions of the church in old countries, the supply of emigrants in new countries with the means of grace, and the labors among the semi-heathenish populations of large cities. Here we may mention the planting of a purer Christianity among the petrified sects in Bible Lands, the labors of the Gustavus Adolphus Society, and the Inner Mission of Germany, the American Home Missionary Societies for the western states and territories, the City Mission Societies in London, New York, and other fast-growing cities.

II. The history of PERSECUTION by hostile powers; as by Judaism and Heathenism in the first three centuries, and by Mohammedanism in the middle age. This apparent repression of the church proves a purifying process, brings out the moral heroism of martyrdom, and thus works in the end for the spread and establishment of Christianity. " The blood of martyrs is the seed of the church." [1] There are cases, however, where systematic and persistent persecution has crushed out the church or reduced it to a mere shadow, as in Palestine, Egypt, and North Africa, under the despotism of the Moslems.

Persecution, like missions, is both foreign and domestic. Besides being assailed from without by the followers of false religions, the church suffers also from intestine wars and violence. Witness the religious wars in France, Holland, and England, the Thirty Years' War in Germany, all of which grew out of the Protestant Reformation and the Papal Reaction ; the crusade against the Albigenses and Waldenses, the horrors of the Spanish Inquisition, the massacre of the Huguenots, the dragonnades of Louis XIV., the crushing out of the Reformation in Bohemia, Belgium, and Southern Europe ; but also, on the Protestant side, the persecution of Anabaptists, the burning of Servetus in Geneva, the penal laws of the reign of Elizabeth against Catholic and Puritan Dissenters, the hanging of witches and Quakers in New England. More Christian blood has been shed by Christians than by heathens and Mohammedans.

The persecutions of Christians by Christians form the satanic chapters, the fiendish midnight scenes, in the history of the church. But they show also the gradual progress of the truly Christian spirit of religious toleration and freedom. Persecution exhausted ends in toleration, and toleration is a step to freedom. The blood of patriots is the price of civil, the blood of martyrs the price of religious liberty. The conquest is dear, the progress slow and often interrupted, but steady and irresistible. The principle of intolerance is now almost universally disowned in the Christian world, except by ultramontane Ro-

---

[1] A well-known saying of Tertullian, who lived in the midst of persecution. A very different estimate of martyrdom is suggested by the Arabic proverb : " The ink of the scholar is more precious than the blood of the martyr." The just estimate depends on the quality of the scholar and the quality of the martyr, and the cause for which the one lives and the other dies.

manism (which indirectly reasserts it in the Papal Syllabus of 1864); but a ruling church, allied to the state, under the influ-ence of selfish human nature, and relying on the arm of flesh rather than the power of truth, is always tempted to impose or retain unjust restrictions on dissenting sects, however innocent and useful they may have proved to be.

In the United States all Christian denominations and sects are placed on a basis of equality before the law, and alike pro-tected by the government in their property and right of public worship, yet self-supporting and self-governing; and, in turn, they strengthen the moral foundations of society by training loyal and virtuous citizens. Freedom of religion must be recog-nized as one of the inalienable rights of man, which lies in the sacred domain of conscience, beyond the restraint and control of politics, and which the government is bound to protect as much as any other fundamental right. Freedom is liable to abuse, and abuse may be punished. But Christianity is itself the parent of true freedom from the bondage of sin and error, and is the best protector and regulator of freedom.

III. The history of CHURCH GOVERNMENT and DISCIPLINE. The church is not only an invisible communion of saints, but at the same time a visible body, needing organs, laws, and forms, to regulate its activity. Into this department of history fall the various forms of church polity: the apostolic, the primitive episcopal, the patriarchal, the papal, the consistorial, the pres-byterial, the congregational, etc.; and the history of the law and discipline of the church, and her relation to the state, under all these forms.

IV. The history of WORSHIP, or divine service, by which the church celebrates, revives, and strengthens her fellowship with her divine head. This falls into such subdivisions as the his-tory of preaching, of catechisms, of liturgy, of rites and cere-monies, and of religious art, particularly sacred poetry and music.

The history of church government and the history of worship are often put together under the title of Ecclesiastical Antiquities or Archæology, and commonly confined to the patristic age, whence most of the catholic institutions and usages of the church date their origin.   But they may as well be extended to the formative period of Protestantism.

V. The history of CHRISTIAN LIFE, or practical morality and religion: the exhibition of the distinguishing virtues and vices of different ages, of the development of Christian philanthropy, the regeneration of domestic life, the gradual abatement and abolition of slavery and other social evils, the mitigation and diminution of the horrors of war, the reform of civil law and of government, the spread of civil and religious liberty, and the whole progress of civilization, under the influence of Christianity.

VI. The history of THEOLOGY, or of Christian learning and literature.   Each branch of theology—exegetical, doctrinal, ethical, historical, and practical—has a history of its own.

The history of doctrines or dogmas is here the most important, and is therefore frequently treated by itself.   Its object is to show how the mind of the church has gradually apprehended and unfolded the divine truths of revelation, how the teachings of scripture have been formulated and shaped into dogmas, and grown into creeds and confessions of faith, or systems of doctrine stamped with public authority.   This growth of the church in the knowledge of the infallible word of God is a constant struggle against error, misbelief, and unbelief; and the history of heresies is an essential part of the history of doctrines.

Every important dogma now professed by the Christian church is the result of a severe conflict with error.   The doctrine of the holy Trinity, for instance, was believed from the beginning, but it required, in addition to the preparatory labors of the ante-Nicene age, fifty years of controversy, in which the strongest intellects were absorbed, until it was brought to the clear expression of the Niceno-Constantinopolitan Creed.   The Christological conflict was equally long and intense, until it was brought to a settlement by the council of Chalcedon.   The

Reformation of the sixteenth century was a continual warfare with popery.   The doctrinal symbols of the various
churches, from the Apostles' Creed down to the confessions of
Dort and Westminster, and more recent standards, embody the
results of the theological battles of the militant church.

The various departments of church history have not a merely
external and mechanical, but an organic relation to each other,
and form one living whole, and this relation the historian must
show.   Each period also is entitled to a peculiar arrangement,
according to its character.   The number, order, and extent of
the different divisions must be determined by their actual importance at a given time.

§ 3. *Sources of Church History.*

The sources of church history, the data on which we rely for
our knowledge, are partly divine, partly human.   For the history of the kingdom of God from the creation to the close of
the apostolic age, we have the inspired writings of the Old and
New Testaments.   But after the death of the apostles we have
only human authorities, which of course cannot claim to be infallible.   These human sources are partly written, partly unwritten.

I. The WRITTEN sources include:

(a) Official documents of ecclesiastical and civil authorities:
acts of councils and synods, confessions of faith, liturgies,
church laws, and the official letters of popes, patriarchs, bishops,
and representative bodies.

(b) Private writings of personal actors in the history: the
works of the church fathers, heretics, and heathen authors, for
the first six centuries; of the missionaries, scholastic and mystic divines, for the middle age; and of the reformers and their
opponents, for the sixteenth century.   These documents are the
richest mines for the historian.   They give history in its birth
and actual movement.   But they must be carefully sifted and
weighed; especially the controversial writings, where fact is

generally more or less adulterated with party spirit, heretical and orthodox.

(c) Accounts of chroniclers and historians, whether friends or enemies, who were eye-witnesses of what they relate. The value of these depends, of course, on the capacity and credibility of the authors, to be determined by careful criticism. Subsequent historians can be counted among the direct or immediate sources only so far as they have drawn from reliable and contemporary documents, which have either been wholly or partially lost, like many of Eusebius' authorities for the period before Constantine, or are inaccessible to historians generally, as are the papal *regesta* and other documents of the Vatican library.

(d) Inscriptions, especially those on tombs and catacombs, revealing the faith and hope of Christians in times of persecution. Among the ruins of Egypt and Babylonia whole libraries have been disentombed and deciphered, containing mythological and religious records, royal proclamations, historical, astronomical, and poetical compositions, revealing an extinct civilization and shedding light on some parts of Old Testament history.

II. The UNWRITTEN sources are far less numerous: church edifices, works of sculpture and painting, and other monuments, religious customs and ceremonies, very important for the history of worship and ecclesiastical art, and significant of the spirit of their age.[1]

The works of art are symbolical embodiments of the various types of Christianity. The plain symbols and crude sculptures of the catacombs correspond to the period of persecution; the basilicas to the Nicene age; the Byzantine churches to the genius of the Byzantine state-churchism; the Gothic cathedrals to the Romano-Germanic catholicism of the middle ages; the renaissance style to the revival of letters.

To come down to more recent times, the spirit of Romanism

---

[1] Comp. F. Piper: *Einleitung in die monumentale Theologie.* Gotha, 1867

can be best appreciated amidst the dead and living monuments of Rome, Italy, and Spain. Lutheranism must be studied in Wittenberg, Northern Germany, and Scandinavia; Calvinism in Geneva, France, Holland, and Scotland; Anglicanism at Oxford, Cambridge, and London; Presbyterianism in Scotland and the United States; Congregationalism in England and New England. For in the mother countries of these denominations we generally find not only the largest printed and manuscript sources, but also the architectural, sculptural, sepulchral, and other monumental remains, the natural associations, oral traditions, and living representatives of the past, who, however they may have departed from the faith of their ancestors, still exhibit their national genius, social condition, habits, and customs—often in a far more instructive manner than ponderous printed volumes.

§ 4. *Periods of Church History.*

The purely chronological or annalistic method, though pursued by the learned Baronius and his continuators, is now generally abandoned. It breaks the natural flow of events, separates things which belong together, and degrades history to a mere chronicle.

The centurial plan, which prevailed from Flacius to Mosheim, is an improvement. It allows a much better view of the progress and connection of things. But it still imposes on the history a forced and mechanical arrangement; for the salient points or epochs very seldom coincide with the limits of our centuries. The rise of Constantine, for example, together with the union of church and state, dates from the year 311; that of the absolute papacy, in Hildebrand, from 1049; the Reformation from 1517; the peace of Westphalia took place in 1648; the landing of the Pilgrim Fathers of New England in 1620; the American emancipation in 1776; the French revolution in 1789; the revival of religious life in Germany began in 1817.

The true division must grow out of the actual course of the

history itself, and present the different phases of its development or stages of its life. These we call periods or ages. The
beginning of a new period is called an epoch, or a stopping and
starting point.

In regard to the number and length of periods there is,
indeed, no unanimity; the less, on account of the various denominational differences establishing different points of view,
especially since the sixteenth century. The Reformation, for
instance, has less importance for the Roman church than for
the Protestant, and almost none for the Greek; and while the
edict of Nantes forms a resting-place in the history of French
Protestantism, and the treaty of Westphalia in that of German,
neither of these events had as much to do with English Protestantism as the accession of Elizabeth, the rise of Cromwell,
the restoration of the Stuarts, and the revolution of 1688.

But, in spite of all confusion and difficulty in regard to
details, it is generally agreed to divide the history of Christianity into three principal parts—ancient, mediæval, and modern; though there is not a like agreement as to the dividing
epochs, or points of departure and points of termination.

I. The history of ANCIENT CHRISTIANITY, from the birth of
Christ to Gregory the Great. A.D. 1–590.

This is the age of the Græco-Latin church, or of the Christian Fathers. Its field is the countries around the Mediterranean—Western Asia, Northern Africa, and Southern Europe—
just the theatre of the old Roman empire and of classic heathendom. This age lays the foundation, in doctrine, government,
and worship, for all the subsequent history. It is the common
progenitor of all the various confessions.

The Life of Christ and the Apostolic Church are by far the
most important sections, and require separate treatment. They
form the divine-human groundwork of the church, and inspire,
regulate, and correct all subsequent periods.

Then, at the beginning of the fourth century, the accession
of Constantine, the first Christian emperor, marks a decisive
turn; Christianity rising from a persecuted sect to the prevail-

ing religion of the Græco-Roman empire. In the history of doctrines, the first œumenical council of Nicæa, falling in the midst of Constantine's reign, A.D. 325, has the prominence of an epoch.

Here, then, are three periods within the first or patristic era, which we may severally designate as the period of the Apostles, the period of the Martyrs, and the period of the Christian Emperors and Patriarchs.

II. MEDIÆVAL CHRISTIANITY, from Gregory I to the Reformation. A.D. 590–1517.

The middle age is variously reckoned — from Constantine, 306 or 311; from the fall of the West Roman empire, 476; from Gregory the Great, 590; from Charlemagne, 800. But it is very generally regarded as closing at the beginning of the sixteenth century, and more precisely, at the outbreak of the Reformation in 1517. Gregory the Great seems to us to form the most proper ecclesiastical point of division. With him, the author of the Anglo-Saxon mission, the last of the church fathers, and the first of the proper popes, begins in earnest, and with decisive success, the conversion of the barbarian tribes, and, at the same time, the development of the absolute papacy, and the alienation of the eastern and western churches.

This suggests the distinctive character of the middle age: the transition of the church from Asia and Africa to Middle and Western Europe, from the Græco-Roman nationality to that of the Germanic, Celtic, and Slavonic races, and from the culture of the ancient classic world to the modern civilization. The great work of the church then was the conversion and education of the heathen barbarians, who conquered and demolished the Roman empire, indeed, but were themselves conquered and transformed by its Christianity. This work was performed mainly by the Latin church, under a firm hierarchical constitution, culminating in the bishop of Rome. The Greek church, though she made some conquests among the Slavic tribes of Eastern Europe, particularly in the Russian empire, since grown so important, was in turn sorely pressed and reduced by Mohammedanism in Asia and Africa, the very seat of primitive Christianity, and at last in Constantinople itself; and in doctrine, worship, and organization, she stopped at the position of the œumenical councils and the patriarchal constitution of the fifth century.

In the middle age the development of the hierarchy occupies the foreground, so that it may be called the church of the Popes, as distinct from the ancient church of the Fathers, and the modern church of the Reformers.

In the growth and decay of the Roman hierarchy three popes stand out as representatives of as many epochs: Gregory I., or the Great (590), marks the rise of absolute papacy; Gregory VII., or Hildebrand (1049), its summit; and Boniface VIII. (1294), its decline. We thus have again three periods in mediæval church history. We may briefly distinguish them as the Missionary, the Papal, and the pre- or ante-Reformatory[1] ages of Catholicism.

III. MODERN CHRISTIANITY, from the Reformation of the sixteenth century to the present time. A.D. 1517–1880.

Modern history moves chiefly among the nations of Europe, and from the seventeenth century finds a vast new theatre in North America. Western Christendom now splits into two hostile parts—one remaining on the old path, the other striking out a new one; while the eastern church withdraws still further from the stage of history, and presents a scene of almost undisturbed stagnation, except in modern Russia and Greece. Modern church history is the age of Protestantism in conflict with Romanism, of religious liberty and independence in conflict with the principle of authority and tutelage, of individual and personal Christianity against an objective and traditional church system.

---

[1] This new word is coined after the analogy of *ante-Nicene*, and in imitation of the German *vor-reformatorisch*. It is the age of the forerunners of the Reformation, or reformers before the Reformation, as Ullmann calls such men as Wicklyffe, Huss, Savonarola, Wessel, etc. The term presents only one view of the period from Boniface VIII. to Luther. But this is the case with every other single term we may choose.

Here again three different periods appear, which may be denoted briefly by the terms, Reformation, Revolution, and Revival.

The sixteenth century, next to the apostolic age the most fruitful and interesting period of church history, is the century of the evangelical renovation of the Church, and the papal counter-reform. It is the cradle of all Protestant denominations and sects, and of modern Romanism.

The seventeenth century is the period of scholastic orthodoxy, polemic confessionalism, and comparative stagnation. The reformatory motion ceases on the continent, but goes on in the mighty Puritanic struggle in England, and extends even into the primitive forests of the American colonies. The seventeenth century is the most fruitful in the church history of England, and gave rise to the various nonconformist or dissenting denominations which were transplanted to North America, and have outgrown some of the older historic churches. Then comes, in the eighteenth century, the Pietistic and Methodistic revival of practical religion in opposition to dead orthodoxy and stiff formalism. In the Roman church Jesuitism prevails, but opposed by the half-evangelical Jansenism, and the quasi-liberal Gallicanism.

In the second half of the eighteenth century begins the vast overturning of traditional ideas and institutions, leading to revolution in state, and infidelity in church, especially in Roman Catholic France and Protestant Germany. Deism in England, atheism in France, rationalism in Germany, represent the various degrees of the great modern apostasy from the orthodox creeds.

The nineteenth century presents, in part, the further development of these negative and destructive tendencies, but with it also the revival of Christian faith and church life, and the beginnings of a new creation by the everlasting gospel. The revival may be dated from the third centenary of the Reformation, in 1817.

In the same period North America, English and Protestant

in its prevailing character, but presenting an asylum for all the nations, churches, and sects of the old world, with a peaceful separation of the temporal and the spiritual power, comes upon the stage like a young giant full of vigor and promise.

Thus we have, in all, nine periods of church history, as follows :

FIRST PERIOD :
    The Life of Christ, and the Apostolic church.
    From the Incarnation to the death of St. John. A.D. 1–100.

SECOND PERIOD :
    Christianity under persecution in the Roman empire.
    From the death of St. John to Constantine, the first Christian emperor. A.D. 100–311.

THIRD PERIOD :
    Christianity in union with the Græco-Roman empire, and amidst the storms of the great migration of nations.
    From Constantine the Great to Pope Gregory I. A.D. 311–590.

FOURTH PERIOD :
    Christianity planted among the Teutonic, Celtic, and Slavonic nations.
    From Gregory I. to Hildebrand, or Gregory VII. A.D. 590–1049.

FIFTH PERIOD :
    The Church under the papal hierarchy, and the scholastic theology.
    From Gregory VII. to Boniface VIII. A.D. 1049–1294.

SIXTH PERIOD :
    The decay of mediæval Catholicism, and the preparatory movements for the Reformation.
    From Boniface VIII. to Luther. A.D. 1294–1517.

SEVENTH PERIOD:
> The evangelical Reformation, and the Roman Catholic Reaction.
>
> From Luther to the Treaty of Westphalia. A.D. 1517–1648.

EIGHTH PERIOD:
> The age of polemic orthodoxy and exclusive confessionalism, with reactionary and progressive movements.
>
> From the Treaty of Westphalia to the French Revolution. A.D. 1648–1790.

NINTH PERIOD:
> The spread of infidelity, and the revival of Christianity in Europe and America, with missionary efforts encircling the globe.
>
> From the French Revolution to the present time. A.D. 1790–1880.

Christianity has thus passed through many stages of its earthly life, and yet has hardly reached the period of full manhood in Christ Jesus. During this long succession of centuries it has outlived the destruction of Jerusalem, the dissolution of the Roman empire, fierce persecutions from without, and heretical corruptions from within, the barbarian invasion, the confusion of the dark ages, the papal tyranny, the shock of infidelity, the ravages of revolution, the attacks of enemies and the errors of friends, the rise and fall of proud kingdoms, empires, and republics, philosophical systems, and social organizations without number. And, behold, it still lives, and lives in greater strength and wider extent than ever; controlling the progress of civilization, and the destinies of the world; marching over the ruins of human wisdom and folly, ever forward and onward; spreading silently its heavenly blessings from generation to generation, and from country to country, to the ends of the earth. It can never die; it will never see the decrepitude of old age; but, like its divine founder, it will live in the unfading freshness of self-renewing youth and the unbroken vigor of manhood to the end of time, and will outlive time itself. Single denominations and sects, human forms of doctrine, government, and worship, after having served their purpose, may disappear and go the way of all flesh; but the Church Universal of Christ, in her divine life and substance, is too strong for the gates of hell. She will only exchange her earthly garments for the festal dress of the Lamb's Bride, and rise from the state of humiliation to the state of exaltation and glory. Then at the coming of Christ she will reap the final harvest of history, and as the church triumphant in heaven celebrate and enjoy the eternal sabbath of holiness and peace. This will be the endless end of history, as it was foreshadowed already at the beginning of its course in the holy rest of God after the completion of his work of creation.

§ 5. *Uses of Church History.*

Church history is the most extensive, and, including the sacred history of the Old and New Testaments, the most important branch of theology. It is the backbone of theology or. which it rests, and the storehouse from which it derives its supplies. It is the best commentary of Christianity itself, under all its aspects and in all its bearings. The fulness of the stream is the glory of the fountain from which it flows.

Church history has, in the first place, a general interest for every cultivated mind, as showing the moral and religious development of our race, and the gradual execution of the divine plan of redemption.

It has special value for the theologian and minister of the gospel, as the key to the present condition of Christendom and the guide to successful labor in her cause. The present is the fruit of the past, and the germ of the future. No work can stand unless it grow out of the real wants of the age and strike firm root in the soil of history. No one who tramples on the rights of a past generation can claim the regard of its posterity. Church history is no mere curiosity shop. Its facts are not dry bones, but embody living realities, the general principles and laws for our own guidance and action. Who studies church history studies Christianity itself in all its phases, and human nature under the influence of Christianity as it now is, and will be to the end of time.

Finally, the history of the church has practical value for every Christian, as a storehouse of warning and encouragement, of consolation and counsel. It is the philosophy of facts, Christianity in living examples. If history in general be, as Cicero describes it, "*testis temporum, lux veritatis, et magistra vitæ*," or, as Diodorus calls it, "the handmaid of providence, the priestess of truth, and the mother of wisdom," the history of the kingdom of heaven is all these in the highest degree. Next to the holy scriptures, which are themselves a history and depository of divine revelation, there is no stronger proof of the continual presence of Christ with his people, no more thorough vindication of Christianity, no richer source of spiritual wisdom and experience, no deeper incentive to virtue and piety, than the history of Christ's kingdom. Every age has a message from God to man, which it is of the greatest importance for man to understand.

The Epistle to the Hebrews describes, in stirring eloquence, the cloud of witnesses from the Old dispensation for the encouragement of the Christians. Why should not the greater cloud of apostles, evangelists, martyrs, confessors, fathers, reformers, and saints of every age and tongue, since the coming of Christ, be held up for the same purpose? They were the heroes of Christian faith and love, the living epistles of Christ, the salt of the earth, the benefactors and glory of our race; and it is impossible rightly to study their thoughts and deeds, their lives and deaths, without being elevated, edified, comforted, and encouraged to follow their holy example, that we at last, by the grace of God, be received into their fellowship, to spend with them a blessed eternity in the praise and enjoyment of the same God and Saviour.

§ 6. *Duty of the Historian.*

The first duty of the historian, which comprehends all others, is fidelity and justice. He must reproduce the history itself, making it live again in his representation. His highest and only aim should be, like a witness, to tell the truth, the whole truth, and nothing but the truth, and, like a judge, to do full justice to every person and event which comes under his review.

To be thus faithful and just he needs a threefold qualification—scientific, artistic, and religious.

1. He must master the sources. For this purpose he must be acquainted with such auxiliary sciences as ecclesiastical philology (especially the Greek and Latin languages, in which most of the earliest documents are written), secular history, geography, and chronology. Then, in making use of the sources, he must thoroughly and impartially examine their genuineness and integrity, and the credibility and capacity of the witnesses. Thus only can he duly separate fact from fiction, truth from error.

The number of sources for general history is so large and increasing so rapidly, that it is, of course, impossible to read and digest them all in a short lifetime. Every historian rests on the shoulders of his predecessors. He must take some things on trust even after the most conscientious search, and avail himself of the invaluable aid of documentary collections and digests, ample indexes, and exhaustive monographs, where he cannot examine all the primary sources in detail. Only he should always carefully indicate his authorities and verify facts, dates, and quotations. A want of accuracy is fatal to the reputation of an historical work.

2. Then comes the composition. This is an art. It must not simply recount events, but reproduce the development of the church in living process. History is not a heap of skeletons, but an organism filled and ruled by a reasonable soul.

One of the greatest difficulties here lies in arranging the material. The best method is to combine judiciously the chronological and topical principles of division; presenting at once the succession of events and the several parallel (and, indeed, interwoven) departments of the history in due proportion. Accordingly, we first divide the whole history into periods, not arbitrary, but determined by the actual course of events; and then we present each of these periods in as many parallel sections or chapters as the material itself requires. As to the number of the periods and chapters, and as to the arrangement of the chapters, there are indeed conflicting opinions, and in the application of our principle, as in our whole representation, we can only make approaches to perfection. But the principle itself is, nevertheless, the only true one.

The ancient classical historians, and most of the English and French, generally present their subject in one homogeneous composition of successive books or chapters, without rubrical division. This method might seem to bring out better the living unity and variety of the history at every point. Yet it really does not. Language, unlike the pencil and the chisel, can exhibit only the succession in time, not the local concomitance. And then this method, rigidly pursued, never gives a complete view of any one subject, of doctrine, worship, or practical life. It constantly mixes the various topics, breaking off from one to bring up another, even by the most sudden transitions, till the alternation is exhausted. The German method of periodical and rubrical arrangement has great practical advantages for the student, in bringing to view the order of subjects as well as the order of time. But it should not be made a uniform and monotonous mechanism, as is done in the Magdeburg Centuries and many subsequent works. For, while history has its order, both of subject and of time, it is yet, like all life, full of variety. The period of the Reformation requires a very different arrangement from the middle age; and in modern history the rubrical division must be combined with and made subject to a division by confessions and countries, as the Roman Catholic, Lutheran, Reformed churches in Germany, France, England, and America.

The historian should aim then to reproduce both the unity and the variety of history, presenting the different topics in their separate completeness, without overlooking their organic connection. The scheme must not be arbitrarily made, and then pedantically applied, as a Procrustean framework, to the history; but it must be deduced from the history itself, and varied as the facts require.

Another difficulty even greater than the arrangement of the material consists in the combination of brevity and fulness. A general church history should give a complete view of the progress of Christ's kingdom in all its departments. But the material is so vast and constantly increasing, that the utmost condensation should be studied by a judicious selection of the salient points, which really make up the main body of history. There is no use in writing books unless they are read. But who has time in this busy age to weary through the forty folios of Baronius and his continuators, or the thirteen folios of Flacius, or the forty-five octavos of Schroeckh? The student of ecclesiastical history, it is true, wants not miniature pictures only (as in Hase's admirable compend), but full-length portraits. Yet much space may be gained by omitting the processes and unessential details, which may be left to monographs and special treatises. Brevity is a virtue in the historian, unless it makes him obscure and enigmatic.[1]

---

[1] The German poet, Friedrich Rückert, thus admirably enjoins the duty of condensation:

> " Wie die Welt läuft immer weiter,
> Wird stets die Geschichte breiter ;
> Und uns wird je mehr je länger
> Nöthig ein Zusammendränger :
>
> Nicht der aus dem Schutt der Zeiten
> Wühle mehr Erbärmlichkeiten,
> Sondern der den Plunder sichte
> Und zum Bau die Steine schichte ;

The historian, moreover, must make his work readable and interesting, without violating truth.   Some parts of history are dull and wearisome; but, upon the whole, the truth of history is "stranger than fiction."   It is God's own epos.   It needs no embellishment.   It speaks for itself if told with earnestness, vivacity, and freshness.   Unfortunately, church historians, with very few exceptions, are behind the great secular historians in point of style, and represent the past as a dead corpse rather than as a living and working power of abiding interest.   Hence church histories are so little read outside of professional circles.

3. Both scientific research and artistic representation must be guided by a sound moral and religious, that is, a truly Christian spirit.   The secular historian should be filled with universal human sympathy, the church historian with universal Christian sympathy.   The motto of the former is: "*Homo sum, nihil humani a me alienum puto*"; the motto of the latter: "*Christianus sum, nihil Christiani a me alienum puto.*"

The historian must first lay aside all prejudice and party zeal, and proceed in the pure love of truth.   Not that he must become a tabula rasa.   No man is able, or should attempt, to cast off the educational influences which have made him what he is.   But the historian of the church of Christ must in every thing be as true as possible to the objective fact, "*sine ira et studio*"; do justice to every person and event; and stand in the centre of Christianity, whence he may see all points in the

Nicht das Einzle unterdrückend,
Noch damit willkührlich schmückend,
Sondern in des Einzlen Hülle
Legend allgemeine Fülle;

Der gelesen Alles habe,
Und besitze Dichtergabe,
Klar zu schildern mir das Wesen,
Der ich nicht ein Wort gelesen.

Sagt mir nichts von Resultaten!
Denn die will ich selber ziehen.
Lasst Begebenheiten, Thaten,
Helden, rasch vorüberziehen."

circumference, all individual persons and events, all confessions, denominations, and sects, in their true relations to each other and to the glorious whole. The famous threefold test of catholic truth—universality of time (*semper*), place (*ubique*), and number (*ab omnibus*)—in its literal sense, is indeed untrue and inapplicable. Nevertheless, there is a common Christianity in the Church, as well as a common humanity in the world, which no Christian can disregard with impunity. Christ is the divine harmony of all the discordant human creeds and sects. It is the duty and the privilege of the historian to trace the image of Christ in the various physiognomies of his disciples, and to act as a mediator between the different sections of his kingdom.

Then he must be in thorough sympathy with his subject, and enthusiastically devoted thereto. As no one can interpret a poet without poetic feeling and taste, or a philosopher without speculative talent, so no one can rightly comprehend and exhibit the history of Christianity without a Christian spirit. An unbeliever could produce only a repulsive caricature, or at best a lifeless statue. The higher the historian stands on Christian ground, the larger is his horizon, and the more full and clear his view of single regions below, and of their mutual bearings. Even error can be fairly seen only from the position of truth. " *Verum est index sui et falsi.*" Christianity is the absolute truth, which, like the sun, both reveals itself and enlightens all that is dark. Church history, like the Bible, is its own best interpreter.

So far as the historian combines these three qualifications, he fulfils his office. In this life we can, of course, only distantly approach perfection in this or in any other branch of study. Absolute success would require infallibility; and this is denied to mortal man. It is the exclusive privilege of the Divine mind to see the end from the beginning, and to view events from all sides and in all their bearings; while the human mind can only take up things consecutively and view them partially or in fragments.

The full solution of the mysteries of history is reserved for that heavenly state, when we shall see no longer through a glass darkly, but face to face, and shall survey the developments of time from the heights of eternity. What St. Augustine so aptly says of the mutual relation of the Old and New Testament, " *Novum Testamentum in Vetere latet, Vetus in Novo patet*," may be applied also to the relation of this world and the world to come. The history of the church militant is but a type and a prophecy of the triumphant kingdom of God in heaven—a prophecy which will be perfectly understood only in the light of its fulfilment.

§ 7. *Literature of Church History.*

STÄUDLIN : *Geschichte u. Literatur der K. Geschichte.* Hann. 1827.

J. G. DOWLING : *An Introduction to the Critical Study of Eccles. History.* London, 1838. Quoted p. 1. The work is chiefly an account of the ecclesiastical historians. pp. 1–212.

F. C. BAUR : *Die Epochen der kirchlichen Geschichtschreibung.* Tüb. 1852.

PHILIP SCHAFF : Introduction to *History of the Apost. Church* (N. York, 1853), pp. 51–134.

ENGELHARDT : *Uebersicht der kirchengeschichtlichen Literatur vom Jahre 1825–1850.* In Niedner's "Zeitschrift für historische Theologie," 1851.

G. UHLHORN : *Die kirchenhist. Arbeiten von* 1851–1860. In Niedner's "Zeitschrift für histor. Theologie," for 1866, Gotha, pp. 3–160. The same : *Die ältere Kirchengesch. in ihren neueren Darstellungen.* In "Jahrbücher für deutsche Theol." Vol. II. 648 sqq.

BRIEGER's "Zeitschrift für Kirchengeschichte " (begun in 1877 and published in Gotha) contains bibliographical articles of AD. HARNACK, MÖLLER, and others, on the latest literature.

CH. K. ADAMS: *A Manual of Historical Literature.* N. York, 3d ed. 1888.

Like every other science and art, church historiography has a history of development toward its true perfection. This history exhibits not only a continual growth of material, but also a gradual, though sometimes long interrupted, improvement of method, from the mere collection of names and dates in a Christian chronicle, to critical research and discrimination, pragmatic reference to causes and motives, scientific command

of material, philosophical generalization, and artistic reproduc·
tion of the actual history itself.   In this progress also are
marked the various confessional and denominational phases of
Christianity, giving different points of view, and consequently
different conceptions and representations of the several periods
and divisions of Christendom ; so that the development of the
Church itself is mirrored in the development of church historiography.

We can here do no more than mention the leading works
which mark the successive epochs in the growth of our science.

I. The APOSTOLIC Church.

The first works on church history are the canonical Gospels
of MATTHEW, MARK, LUKE, and JOHN, the inspired biographical
memoirs of Jesus Christ, who is the theanthropic head of the
Church universal.

These are followed by LUKE's Acts of the Apostles, which
describes the planting of Christianity among Jews and Gentiles
from Jerusalem to Rome, by the labors of the apostles, especially Peter and Paul.

II. The GREEK Church historians.

The first post-apostolic works on church history, as indeed all
branches of theological literature, take their rise in the Greek
Church.

EUSEBIUS, bishop of Cæsarea, in Palestine, and contemporary
with Constantine the Great, composed a church history in ten
books (ἐκκλησιαστικὴ ἱστορία, from the incarnation of the
Logos to the year 324), by which he has won the title of the
Father of church history, or the Christian Herodotus.   Though
by no means very critical and discerning, and far inferior in
literary talent and execution to the works of the great classical
historians, this ante-Nicene church history is invaluable for its
learning, moderation, and love of truth ; for its use of sources
since totally or partially lost; and for its interesting position of
personal observation between the last persecutions of the church
and her establishment in the Byzantine empire.

Eusebius was followed in similar spirit and on the same plan by SOCRATES, SOZOMEN, and THEODORET in the fifth century, and THEODORUS and EVAGRIUS in the sixth, each taking up the thread of the narrative where his predecessor had dropped it, and covering in part the same ground, from Constantine the Great till toward the middle of the fifth century.[1]

Of the later Greek historians, from the seventh century to the fifteenth, the "Scriptores Byzantini," as they are called, NICEPHORUS CALLISTI (son of Callistus, about A.D. 1333) deserves special regard.   His Ecclesiastical History was written with the use of the large library of the church of St. Sophia in Constantinople, and dedicated to the emperor Andronicus Palæologus (d. 1327).   It extends in eighteen books (each of which begins with a letter of his name) from the birth of Christ to the death of Phocas, A.D. 610, and gives in the preface a summary of five books more, which would have brought it down to 911.   He was an industrious and eloquent, but uncritical and superstitious writer.[2]

III.   LATIN Church historians of the middle ages.

The Latin Church, before the Reformation, was, in church history, as in all other theological studies, at first wholly dependent on the Greek, and long content with mere translations and extracts from Eusebius and his continuators.

The most popular of these was the *Historia Tripartita*, composed by CASSIODORUS, prime minister of Theodoric, and afterwards abbot of a convent in Calabria (d. about A.D. 562).   It is a compilation from the histories of Socrates, Sozomen, and

---

[1] These Greek historians have been best edited by Henri de Valois (Valesius), in Greek and Latin with notes, in 3 folios, Paris, 1659–73 ; also Amsterd., 1695, and, with additional notes by W. Reading, Cambridge, 1720. Eusebius has been often separately published in several languages.

[2] Νικηφόρου Καλλίστου τοῦ Ξανθοπούλου Ἐκκλησιαστικῆς Ἱστορίας Βιβλία ιή. Edited by the Jesuit, Fronton le Duc (Fronto-Ducæus), Par. 1630, 2 fol. This is the only Greek edition from the only extant MS., which belonged to the King of Hungary, then came into the possession of the Turks, and last into the imperial library of Vienna.   But a Latin version by John Lang was published at Basle as early as 1561.

Theodoret, abridging and harmonizing them, and supplied—together with the translation of Eusebius by Rufinus—the West for several centuries with its knowledge of the fortunes of the ancient church.

The middle age produced no general church history of consequence, but a host of chronicles, and histories of particular nations, monastic orders, eminent popes, bishops, missionaries, saints, etc. Though rarely worth much as compositions, these are yet of great value as material, after a careful sifting of truth from legendary fiction.

The principal mediæval historians are GREGORY OF TOURS (d. 595), who wrote a church history of the Franks; the VENERABLE BEDE (d. 735), the father of English church history; PAULUS DIACONUS (d. 799), the historian of the Lombards; ADAM OF BREMEN, the chief authority for Scandinavian church history from A.D. 788–1072; HAIMO (or Haymo, Aimo, a monk of Fulda, afterwards bishop of Halberstadt, d. 853), who described in ten books, mostly from Rufinus, the history of the first four centuries (*Historiæ Sacræ Epitome*); ANASTASIUS (about 872), the author in part of the *Liber Pontificalis*, i. e., biographies of the Popes till Stephen VI. (who died 891); BARTHOLOMÆUS OF LUCCA (about 1312), who composed a general church history from Christ to A.D. 1312; ST. ANTONINUS (Antonio Pierozzi), archbishop of Florence (d. 1459), the author of the largest mediæval work on secular and sacred history (*Summa Historialis*), from the creation to A.D. 1457.

Historical criticism began with the revival of letters, and revealed itself first in the doubts of Laurentius Valla (d. 1457) and Nicolaus of Cusa (d. 1464) concerning the genuineness of the donation of Constantine, the Isidorian Decretals, and other spurious documents, which are now as universally rejected as they were once universally accepted.

IV. ROMAN CATHOLIC historians.

The Roman Catholic Church was roused by the shock of the Reformation, in the sixteenth century, to great activity in this

and other departments of theology, and produced some works
of immense learning and antiquarian research, but generally
characterized rather by zeal for the papacy, and against Protestantism, than by the purely historical spirit. Her best historians are either Italians, and ultramontane in spirit, or
Frenchmen, mostly on the side of the more liberal but less
consistent Gallicanism.

(a) Italians :

First stands the Cardinal CÆSAR BARONIUS (d. 1607), with his
Annales Ecclesiastici (Rom. 1588 sqq.), in 12 folio volumes, on
which he spent thirty years of unwearied study. They come
down only to the year 1198, but are continued by RAYNALDI
(to 1565), LADERCHI (to 1571), and THEINER (to 1584).[1]

This truly colossal and monumental work is even to this day
an invaluable storehouse of information from the Vatican library and other archives, and will always be consulted by professional scholars. It is written in dry, ever broken, unreadable
style, and contains many spurious documents. It stands wholly
on the ground of absolute papacy, and is designed as a positive
refutation of the Magdeburg Centuries, though it does not
condescend directly to notice them. It gave immense aid and
comfort to the cause of Romanism, and was often epitomized
and popularized in several languages. But it was also severely
criticized, and in part refuted, not only by such Protestants
as Casaubon, Spanheim, and Samuel Basnage, but by Roman
Catholic scholars also, especially two French Franciscans, An-
toine and François Pagi, who corrected the chronology.

[1] We omit the inferior continuations of the Polish Dominican, ABR. BZO-
VIUS, from 1198 to 1565, in 8 vols., and of HENR. SPONDÉ, bishop of Pamiers,
from 1197 to 1647, 2 vols.   The best of the older editions, including the continuation of Raynaldi (but not of Laderchi) and the learned criticisms of Pagi
and his nephew, was arranged by Archbishop MANSI, in 38 folios, Lucca,
1738–'57.   A hundred years later, a German scholar in Rome, AUGUSTIN
THEINER, prefect of the Vatican Archives, resumed the continuation in 3
vols., embracing the pontificate of Gregory XIII. (A.D. 1572–'84), Rome and
Paris, 1856, 3 vols. fol., and hoped to bring the history down to the pontifi-

Far less known and used than the Annals of Baronius is the *Historia Ecclesiastica* of CASPAR SACHARELLI, which comes down to A.D. 1185, and was published in Rome, 1771–1796, in 25 quarto volumes.

Invaluable contributions to historical collections and special researches have been made by other Italian scholars, as MURATORI, ZACCAGNI, ZACCARIA, MANSI, GALLANDI, PAOLO SARPI, PALLAVICINI (the last two on the Council of Trent), the three ASSEMANI, and ANGELO MAI.

(b) French Catholic historians.

NATALIS (NOEL) ALEXANDER, Professor and Provincial of the Dominican order (d. 1724), wrote his *Historia Ecclesiastica Veteris et Nova Testamenti* to the year 1600 (Paris, 1676, 2d ed. 1699 sqq. 8 vols. fol.) in the spirit of Gallicanism, with great learning, but in dry scholastic style. Innocent XI. put it in the Index (1684). This gave rise to the corrected editions.

The abbot CLAUDE FLEURY (d. 1723), in his *Histoire ecclésiastique* (Par. 1691–1720, in 20 vols. quarto, down to A.D. 1414, continued by CLAUDE FABRE, a very decided Gallican, to A.D. 1595), furnished a much more popular work, commended by mildness of spirit and fluency of style, and as useful for edification as for instruction. It is a minute and, upon the whole, accurate narrative of the course of events as they occurred, but without system and philosophical generalization, and hence tedious and wearisome. When Fleury was asked why he unnecessarily darkened his pages with so many discreditable facts, he properly replied that the survival and progress of Christianity, notwithstanding the vices and crimes of its

cate of Pius VII., A.D. 1800, in 12 folios ; but he interrupted the continuation, and began, in 1864, a new edition of the whole work (including Raynaldi and Laderchi), which is to be completed in 45 or 50 volumes, at Bar-le-Duc, France. Theiner was first a liberal Catholic, then an Ultramontanist, last an Old Catholic (in correspondence with Döllinger), excluded from the Vatican (1870), but pardoned by the pope, and died suddenly, 1874. His elder brother, Johann Anton, became a Protestant.

professors and preachers, was the best proof of its divine origin.[1]

JACQUES BÉNIGNE BOSSUET, the distinguished bishop of Meaux (d. 1704), an advocate of Romanism on the one hand against Protestantism, but of Gallicanism on the other against Ultramontanism, wrote with brilliant eloquence, and in the spirit of the Catholic church, a universal history, in bold outlines for popular effect.[2] This was continued in the German language by the Protestant Cramer, with less elegance but more thoroughness, and with special reference to the doctrine history of the middle age.

SEBASTIEN LE NAIN DE TILLEMONT (d. 1698), a French nobleman and priest, without office and devoted exclusively to study and prayer—a pupil and friend of the Jansenists and in partial sympathy with Gallicanism—composed a most learned and useful history of the first six centuries (till 513), in a series of minute biographies, with great skill and conscientiousness, almost entirely in the words of the original authorities, from which he carefully distinguishes his own additions. It is, as far as it goes, the most valuable church history produced by Roman Catholic industry and learning.[3]

Contemporaneously with Tillemont, the Gallican, L. ELLIES DUPIN (d. 1719), furnished a biographical and bibliographical church history down to the seventeenth century.[4] REMI CEIL-

---

[1] A portion of Fleury's *History*, from the second œcumenical Council to the end of the fourth century (A.D. 381–400), was published in English at Oxford, 1842, in three volumes, on the basis of Herbert's translation (London, 1728), carefully revised by John H. Newman, who was at that time the theological leader of the Oxford Tractarian movement, and subsequently (1879) became a cardinal in the Roman Catholic Church.

[2] *Discours sur l'histoire universelle depuis le commencement du monde jusqu'à l'empire de Charlemagne.* Paris, 1681, and other editions.

[3] *Mémoires pour servir à l'histoire ecclésiastique des six premiers siècles, justifiés par les citations des auteurs originaux.* Paris, 1693–1712, 16 vols. quarto. Reprinted at Venice, 1732 sqq. His *Histoire des empereurs*, Paris, 1690–1738, in 6 vols., gives the secular history down to emperor Anastasius.

[4] Under the title : *Nouvelle Bibliothèque des auteurs ecclésiastiques, contenant l'histoire de leur vie, le catalogue, la critique et la chronologie de leurs ouvrages.* Paris and Amsterdam, 1693–1715, 19 vols. ; 9th ed., Par., 1698 sqq.,

LIER (d. 1761) followed with a similar work, which has the advantage of greater completeness and accuracy.[1]

The French Benedictines of the congregation of St. Maur, in the seventeenth and eighteenth century, did immense service to historical theology by the best critical editions of the fathers and extensive archæological works. We can only mention the names of MABILLON, MASSUET, MONTFAUCON, D'ACHERY, RUINART, MARTÈNE, DURAND. Among the Jesuits, SIRMOND and PETAU occupy a prominent place.

The Abbé ROHRBACHER (Professor of Church History at Nancy, d. 1856) wrote an extensive *Universal History of the Church*, including that of the Old Testament, down to 1848. It is less liberal than the great Gallican writers of the seventeenth century, but shows familiarity with German literature.[2]

(c) German Catholic historians.

The pioneer of modern German Catholic historians of note is a poet and an ex-Protestant, Count LEOPOLD VON STOLBERG (d. 1819). With the enthusiasm of an honest, noble, and devout, but credulous convert, he began, in 1806, a very full *Geschichte der Religion Jesu Christi*, and brought it down in 15 volumes to the year 430. It was continued by F. KERZ (vols. 16–45, to A.D. 1192) and J. N. BRISCHAR (vols. 45–53, to A.D. 1245).

THEOD. KATERKAMP (d. at Münster, 1834) wrote a church history, in the same spirit and pleasing style, down to A.D. 1153.[3] It remained unfinished, like the work of LOCHERER (d. 1837), which extends to 1073.[4]

Bishop HEFELE's *History of the Councils (Conciliengeschichte,*

with the continuations of Goujet, Petit-Didier, to the 18th cent., and the critique of R. Simon, 61 vols. The work was condemned by Rome for its free criticism of the fathers.

[1] *Histoire générale des auteurs sacrés et ecclésiastiques.* Paris, 1729–'63, in 23 vols. 4to. New ed. begun 1858.

[2] *Histoire universelle de l'église catholique.* Nancy and Paris, 1842–'49 ; 3d ed., 1856–'61, in 29 vols. oct. ; 4th ed. by Chantral, 1864 sqq. A German translation by HÜLSKAMP, RUMP and others appeared at Münster, 1860 sqq.

[3] Münster, 1819–'34, 5 vols. 8vo.   [4] Ravensburg, 1824 sqq., 9 vols.

1855–'86; revised edition and continuation, 1873 sqq.) is a most valuable contribution to the history of doctrine and discipline down to the Council of Trent.[1]

The best compendious histories from the pens of German Romanists are produced by Jos. IGN. RITTER, Professor in Bonn and afterward in Breslau (d. 1857);[2] JOH. ADAM MÖHLER, formerly Professor in Tubingen, and then in Munich, the author of the famous *Symbolik* (d. 1838);[3] JOH. ALZOG (d. 1878);[4] H. BRÜCK (Mayence, 2d ed., 1877); F. X. KRAUS (Treves, 1873; 3d ed., 1882); Card. HERGENRÖTHER (Freiburg, 3d ed., 1886, 3 vols.); F. X. FUNK (Tubingen, 1886; 2d ed., 1890).

A. F. GFRÖRER (d. 1861) began his learned *General Church History* as a Protestant, or rather as a Rationalist (1841–'46, 4 vols., till A.D. 1056), and continued it from Gregory VII. on as a Romanist (1859–'61).

Dr. JOHN JOSEPH IGNATIUS DÖLLINGER (Professor in Munich, born 1799), the most learned historian of the Roman Church in the nineteenth century, represents the opposite course from popery to anti-popery. He began, but never finished, a *Handbook of Christian Church History* (Landshut, 1833, 2 vols.) till A.D. 680, and a *Manual of Church History* (1836, 2d ed., 1843, 2 vols.) to the fifteenth century, and in part to 1517.[5]

---

[1] The first two volumes of the first ed. were translated by *W. R. Clark* and *H. N. Oxenham*, and published by T. & T. Clark, Edinburgh, 1871 and 1876.

[2] *Handbuch der K. G.* Bonn, 3d ed., 1846; 6th ed., 1862, 2 vols.

[3] His *Kirchengeschichte* was published from his lectures by PIUS BONIFACE GAMS. Regensburg, 1867–'68, in 3 vols. It is very unequal and lacks the author's own finish. We have from Möhler also a monograph on *Athanasius* (1827), and a *Patrologie* (covering the first three centuries, and published after his death, 1840).

[4] *Handbuch der Universal-Kirchengeschichte.* 9th ed., Mainz, 1872, 2 vols.; 10th ed., 1882. Alzog aims to be the Roman Catholic Hase as to brevity and condensation. A French translation from the 5th ed. was prepared by GOESCHLER and AUDLEY, 1849 (4th ed. by Abbé Sabatier, 1874); an English translation by F. J. PABISCH and THOS. BYRNE, Cincinnati, O., 1874 sqq., in 3 vols. The Am. translators censure the French translators for the liberties they have taken with Alzog, but they have taken similar liberties, and, by sundry additions, made the author more Romish than he was.

[5] English translation by Dr. *Edw. Cox*, Lond. 1840–'42, in 4 vols. This combines Döllinger's *Handbuch* and *Lehrbuch* as far as they supplement each other.

He wrote also learned works against the Reformation (*Die Reformation*, 1846–'48, in 3 vols.), on *Hippolytus and Callistus*, (1853), on the preparation for Christianity (*Heidenthum und Judenthum*, 1857), *Christianity and the Church in the time of its Founding* (1860), *The Church and the Churches* (1862), *Papal Fables of the Middle Age* (1865), *The Pope and the Council* (under the assumed name of "Janus," 1869), etc.

During the Vatican Council in 1870 Döllinger broke with Rome, became the theological leader of the Old Catholic secession, and was excommunicated by the Archbishop of Munich (his former pupil), April 17, 1871, as being guilty of "the crime of open and formal heresy." He knows too much of church history to believe in the infallibility of the pope. He solemnly declared (March 28, 1871) that, "as a Christian, as a theologian, as a historian, and as a citizen," he could not accept the Vatican decrees, because they contradict the spirit of the gospel and the genuine tradition of the church, and, if carried out, must involve church and state, the clergy and the laity, in irreconcilable conflict.[1]

V. The PROTESTANT Church historians.

The Reformation of the sixteenth century is the mother of church history as a science and art in the proper sense of the term. It seemed at first to break off from the past and to depreciate church history, by going back directly to the Bible as the only rule of faith and practice, and especially to look most unfavorably on the Catholic middle age, as a progressive corruption of the apostolic doctrine and discipline. But, on the other hand, it exalted primitive Christianity, and awakened a new and enthusiastic interest in all the documents of the apostolic church, with an energetic effort to reproduce its spirit and institutions. It really repudiated only the later tradition in favor of the older, taking its stand upon the primitive historical basis of Christianity. Then again, in the course of controversy with Rome, Protestantism found it desirable and necessary to

[1] See Schaff's *Creeds of Christendom*, Vol. I., 195 sq.; Von Schulte: *Der Altkatholicismus* (Giessen, 1887), 109 sqq.

wrest from its opponent not only the scriptural argument, but also the historical, and to turn it as far as possible to the side of the evangelical cause. For the Protestants could never deny that the true Church of Christ is built on a rock, and has the promise of indestructible permanence. Finally, the Reformation, by liberating the mind from the yoke of a despotic ecclesiastical authority, gave an entirely new impulse, directly or indirectly, to free investigation in every department, and produced that historical criticism which claims to clear fact from the accretions of fiction, and to bring out the truth, the whole truth, and nothing but the truth, of history. Of course this criticism may run to the extreme of rationalism and scepticism, which oppose the authority of the apostles and of Christ himself; as it actually did for a time, especially in Germany. But the abuse of free investigation proves nothing against the right use of it; and is to be regarded only as a temporary aberration, from which all sound minds will return to a due appreciation of history, as a truly rational unfolding of the plan of redemption, and a standing witness for the all-ruling providence of God, and the divine character of the Christian religion.

(a) German, Swiss, and Dutch historians.

Protestant church historiography has thus far flourished most on German soil. A patient and painstaking industry and conscientious love of truth and justice qualify German scholars for the mining operations of research which bring forth the raw material for the manufacturer; while French and English historians know best how to utilize and popularize the material for the general reader.

The following are the principal works :

MATTHIAS FLACIUS (d. 1575), surnamed ILLYRICUS, a zealous Lutheran, and an unsparing enemy of Papists, Calvinists, and Melancthonians, heads the list of Protestant historians with his great *Ecclesiastica Historia Novi Testamenti*, commonly called *Centuriæ Magdeburgenses* (Basle, 1560–'74), covering thirteen centuries of the Christian era in as many folio volumes. He began the work in Magdeburg, in connection with ten other scholars of like spirit and zeal, and in the face of innumerable difficulties, for the purpose of exposing the corruptions and errors of the papacy, and of proving the doctrines of the Lutheran Reformation orthodox by the "witnesses of the truth" in all ages. The tone is therefore controversial throughout, and quite as partial as that of the Annals of Baronius on the papal side. The style is tasteless and repulsive, but the amount of persevering labor, the immense, though ill-digested and un wieldy mass of material, and the boldness of the criticism, are imposing and astonishing. The "Centuries" broke the path of free historical study, and are the first general church history deserving of the name. They introduced also a new method. They divide the material by centuries, and each century by a uniform Procrustean scheme of not less than sixteen rubrics: " de loco et propagatione ecclesiae ; de persecutione et tranquillitate ecclesiae ; de doctrina ; de haeresibus ; de ceremoniis ; de politia ; de schismatibus ; de conciliis ; de vitis episcoporum ; de haereticis ; de martyribus ; de miraculis et prodigiis ; de rebus Judaicis ; de aliis religionibus ; de mutationibus politicis." This plan destroys all symmetry, and occasions wearisome diffuseness and repetition. Yet, in spite of its mechanical uniformity and stiffness, it is more scientific than the annalistic or chronicle method, and, with material improvements and considerable curtailment of rubrics, it has been followed to this day.

The Swiss, J. H. HOTTINGER (d. 1667), in his *Historia Ecclesiastica N. Testamenti* (Zurich, 1655-'67, 9 vols. fol.), furnished a Reformed counterpart to the Magdeburg Centuries. It is less original and vigorous, but more sober and moderate. It comes down to the sixteenth century, to which alone five volumes are devoted.

From FRED. SPANHEIM of Holland (d. 1649) we have a *Summa Historiae Ecclesiasticae* (Lugd. Bat. 1689), coming down to the sixteenth century. It is based on a thorough and critical knowledge of the sources, and serves at the same time as a refutation of Baronius.

A new path was broken by GOTTFRIED ARNOLD (d. 1714), in his *Impartial History of the Church and Heretics* to A.D. 1688.[1] He is the historian of the pietistic and mystic school. He made subjective piety the test of the true faith, and the persecuted sects the main channel of true Christianity; while the reigning church from Constantine down, and indeed not the Catholic church only, but the orthodox Lutheran with it, he represented as a progressive apostasy, a Babylon full of corruption and abomination. In this way he boldly and effectually broke down the walls of ecclesiastical exclusiveness and bigotry; but at the same time, without intending or suspecting it, he opened the way to a rationalistic and sceptical treatment of history. While, in his zeal for impartiality and personal piety, he endeavored to do justice to all possible heretics and sectaries, he did great injustice to the supporters of orthodoxy and ecclesiastical order. Arnold was also the first to use the German language instead of the Latin in learned history; but his style is tasteless and insipid.

J. L. VON MOSHEIM (Chancellor of the University at Göttingen, d. 1755), a moderate and impartial Lutheran, is the father of church historiography as an *art*, unless we prefer to concede this merit to Bossuet. In skilful construction, clear, though mechanical and monotonous arrangement, critical sagacity, pragmatic combination, freedom from passion, almost bordering on cool indifferentism, and in easy elegance of Latin style, he surpasses all his predecessors. His well-known *Institutiones Historiae Ecclesiasticae antiquae et recentioris* (Helmstädt, 1755) follows the centurial plan of Flacius, but in simpler form, and, as translated and supplemented by Maclaine, and Murdock, is still used extensively as a text-book in England and America.[2]

---

[1] *Unpartheiische Kirchen- und Ketzerhistorie.* Frankfurt, 1699 sqq. 4 vol.i fol.

[2] Best edition : *Institutes of Ecclesiastical History ancient and modern, by* JOHN LAWRENCE VON MOSHEIM. *A new and literal translation from the original Latin, with copious additional Notes, original and selected. By James Murdock, D.D.* 1832 ; 5th ed., New York. 1854, 3 vols. Murdock was Professor of Ecclesiastical History at Andover, Mass. (d. 1856), and translated

J. M. Schröckh (d. 1808), a pupil of Mosheim, but already touched with the neological spirit which Semler (d. 1791) intro- duced into the historical theology of Germany, wrote with un- wearied industry the largest Protestant church history after the Magdeburg Centuries. He very properly forsook the centurial plan still followed by Mosheim, and adopted the periodic. His *Christian Church History* comprises forty-five volumes, and reaches to the end of the eighteenth century. It is written in diffuse but clear and easy style, with reliable knowledge of sources, and in a mild and candid spirit, and is still a rich store- house of historical matter.[1]

The very learned *Institutiones Historiae Ecclesiasticae V. et N. Testamenti* of the Dutch Reformed divine, H. Venema (d. 1787), contain the history of the Jewish and Christian Church down to the end of the sixteenth century (Lugd. Bat. 1777–'83, in seven parts).

H. P. C. Henke (d. 1809) is the leading representative of the rationalistic church historiography, which ignores Christ in history. In his spirited and able *Allgemeine Geschichte der christlichen Kirche*, continued by Vater (Braunschweig, 1788– 1820, 9 vols.), the church appears not as the temple of God on earth, but as a great infirmary and bedlam.

August Neander (Professor of Church History in Berlin, d. 1850), the "father of modern church history," a child in spirit, a giant in learning, and a saint in piety, led back the study of history from the dry heath of rationalism to the fresh fountain of divine life in Christ, and made it a grand source of edification as well as instruction for readers of every creed. His *General History of the Christian Religion and*

---

also Münscher's *Dogmengeschichte*. Mosheim's special history of the ante- Nicene period (1733) was translated from the Latin by Vidal (1813), and *Murdock* (1851), new ed., N. York, 1853, 2 vols.

[1] *Christliche Kirchengeschichte.* Leipzig, 1768–1812, 45 vols. 8vo, including 10 vols. of the History after the Reformation (the last two by Tzschirner). Nobody ever read Schroeckh through (except the author and the proof-reader), and the very name is rather *abschreckend*, but he is as valuable for reference as Baronius, and far more impartial.

Church begins after the apostolic age (which he treated in a separate work), and comes down to the Council of Basle in 1430, the continuation being interrupted by his death.[1] It is distinguished for thorough and conscientious use of the sources, critical research, ingenious combination, tender love of truth and justice, evangelical catholicity, hearty piety, and by masterly analysis of the doctrinal systems and the subjective Christian life of men of God in past ages. The edifying character is not introduced from without, but naturally grows out of his conception of church history, viewed as a continuous revelation of Christ's presence and power in humanity, and as an illustration of the parable of the leaven which gradually pervades and transforms the whole lump. The political and artistic sections, and the outward machinery of history, were not congenial to the humble, guileless simplicity of Neander. His style is monotonous, involved, and diffuse, but unpretending, natural, and warmed by a genial glow of sympathy and enthusiasm. It illustrates his motto : *Pectus est quod theologum facit.*

Torrey's excellent translation (Rose translated only the first three centuries), published in Boston, Edinburgh, and London, in multiplied editions, has given Neander's immortal work even a much larger circulation in England and America than it has in Germany itself.

Besides this general history, Neander's indefatigable industry produced also special works on the Life of Christ (1837, 4th ed. 1845), the Apostolic Age (1832, 4th ed. 1842, translated by J. E. Ryland, Edinburgh, 1842, and again by E. G. Robinson, N. York, 1865), Memorials of Christian Life (1823, 3d ed. 1845, 3 vols.), the Gnostic Heresies (1818), and biographies of representative characters, as Julian the Apostate (1812), St. Bernard (1813, 2d ed. 1848), St. Chrysostom (1822, 3d ed.

---

[1] *Allgemeine Geschichte der christlichen Religion und Kirche.* Hamburg, 1825–'52, 11 parts; 3d ed. 1856, in 4 large vols., with an excellent introduction by *Dr. Ullmann.* The translation of Prof. *Joseph Torrey* (of Burlington, Vt., d. 1867) was published in Boston in 5 vols., 12th ed., 1881, with a model Index of 239 pages.

1848), and Tertullian (1825, 2d ed. 1849). His History of
Christian Doctrines was published after his death by Jacobi
(1855), and translated by J. E. Ryland (Lond., 1858).[1]

From J. C. L. GIESELER (Professor of Church History in
Göttingen, d. 1854), a profoundly learned, acute, calm, impartial, conscientious, but cold and dry scholar, we have a *Text
book of Church History* from the birth of Christ to 1854.[2] He
takes Tillemont's method of giving the history in the very
words of the sources; only he does not form the text from
them, but throws them into notes. The chief excellence of
this invaluable and indispensable work is in its very carefully
selected and critically elucidated extracts from the original
authorities down to the year 1648 (as far as he edited the work
himself). The skeleton-like text presents, indeed, the leading
facts clearly and concisely, but does not reach the inward life
and spiritual marrow of the church of Christ. The theological
views of Gieseler hardly rise above the jejune rationalism of
Wegscheider, to whom he dedicated a portion of his history;
and with all his attempt at impartiality he cannot altogether
conceal the negative effect of a rationalistic conception of Christianity, which acts like a chill upon the narrative of its history,
and substitutes a skeleton of dry bones for a living organism.

Neander and Gieseler matured their works in respectful and
friendly rivalry, during the same period of thirty years of slow,
but solid and steady growth. The former is perfectly subjective, and reproduces the original sources in a continuous

---

[1] I have given a fuller account of the life and writings of Neander, my
beloved teacher, in my "Kirchenfreund" for 1851, pp. 20 sqq. and 283 sqq.,
and in *Aug. Neander, Erinnerungen*, Gotha, 1886 (76 pp.). Comp. also Harnack's oration at the centennial of Neander's birth, Berlin, Jan 17, 1889, and
A. Wiegand, *Aug. Neander*, Erfurt, 1889.

[2] *Lehrbuch der Kirchengeschichte.* Bonn, 1824–'56 (4th ed. 1844 sqq.), in 5
volumes, the last two published from his lectures after his death by *Redepenning.* Translated into English first by *Cunningham*, in Philadelphia, 1846,
then by *Davidson* and *Hull*, in England, and last and best, on the basis of the
former, by *Henry B. Smith*, New York (Harpers), in 5 vols., 1857–1880. The
fifth and last volume of this edition was completed after Dr. Smith's death
(1877) by Prof. Stearns and Miss Mary A. Robinson, with an introductory notice
by Philip Schaff. Gieseler's *Dogmengeschichte* appeared separately in 1855.

warm and sympathetic composition, which reflects at the same time the author's own mind and heart; the latter is purely objective, and speaks with the indifference of an outside spectator, through the *ipsissima verba* of the same sources, arranged as notes, and strung together simply by a slender thread of narrative. The one gives the history ready-made, and full of life and instruction; the other furnishes the material and leaves the reader to animate and improve it for himself. With the one, the text is everything; with the other, the notes. But both admirably complete each other, and exhibit together the ripest fruit of German scholarship in general church history in the first half of the nineteenth century.

FERDINAND CHRISTIAN BAUR (Prof. of Church History in Tübingen, d. 1860) must be named alongside with Neander and Gieseler in the front rank of German church historians. He was equal to both in independent and thorough scholarship, superior in constructive criticism and philosophical generalization, but inferior in well-balanced judgment and solid merit. He over-estimated theories and tendencies, and undervalued persons and facts. He was an indefatigable investigator and bold innovator. He completely revolutionized the history of apostolic and post-apostolic Christianity, and resolved its rich spiritual life of faith and love into a purely speculative process of conflicting tendencies, which started from an antagonism of Petrinism and Paulinism, and were ultimately reconciled in the compromise of ancient Catholicism. He fully brought to light, by a keen critical analysis, the profound intellectual fermentation of the primitive church, but eliminated from it the supernatural and miraculous element; yet as an honest and serious sceptic he had to confess at last a psychological miracle in the conversion of St. Paul, and to bow before the greater miracle of the resurrection of Christ, without which the former is an inexplicable enigma. His critical researches and speculations gave a powerful stimulus to a reconsideration and modification of the traditional views on early Christianity.

We have from his fertile pen a general *History of the Chris-*

tian Church, in five volumes (1853–1863), three of which were published after his death and lack the originality and careful finish of the first and second, which cover the first six centuries; *Lectures on Christian Doctrine History* (*Dogmengeschichte*), published by his son (1865–'67, in 3 volumes), and a brief *Lehrbuch der Dogmengeschichte*, edited by himself (1847, 2d ed. 1858). Even more valuable are his monographs: on *St. Paul*, for whom he had a profound veneration, although he recognized only four of his Epistles as genuine (1845, 2d ed. by E. Zeller, 1867, 2 vols., translated into English, 1875); on *Gnosticism*, with which he had a strong spiritual affinity (*Die christliche Gnosis, oder die christliche Religionsphilosophie*, 1835); the history of the Doctrine of the *Atonement* (1838, 1 vol.), and of the *Trinity* and *Incarnation* (1841–'43, in 3 vols.), and his masterly vindication of Protestantism against Möhler's *Symbolik* (2d ed. 1836).[1]

KARL RUDOLPH HAGENBACH (Professor of Church History at Basel, d. 1874) wrote, in the mild and impartial spirit of Neander, with poetic taste and good judgment, and in pleasing popular style, a general *History of the Christian Church*, in seven volumes (4th ed. 1868–'72),[2] and a *History of Christian Doctrines*, in two volumes (1841, 4th ed. 1857).[3]

Protestant Germany is richer than any other country in manuals and compends of church history for the use of students. We mention ENGELHARDT (1834), NIEDNER (*Geschichte der christl. Kirche*, 1846, and *Lehrbuch*, 1866), HASE (11th ed.

---

[1] Comp. Landerer's *Worte der Erinnerung an Dr. Baur*, 1860, the article "Baur und die Tübinger Schule," in Herzog and Plitt, "Theol. Encykl.," Vol. II., 163–184 (2d ed.), and R. W. Mackay: *The Tübingen School and its Antecedents.* London, 1863. See also Zeller, *Vorträge* (1865), pp. 267 sqq.

[2] Portions of Hagenbach's History have been translated, namely, the *History of the Church in the 18th and 19th Centuries* by Dr. John F. Hurst (President of Drew Theol. Seminary, Madison, N. J.), N. York, 1869, 2 vols., and the *History of the Reformation* by Miss EVELINA MOORE (of Newark, N. J.), Edinburgh, 1879, 2 vols. A new ed. with literature by *Nippold*, 1885 sqq.

[3] English translation by C. W. *Buch*, Edinburgh, 1846, revised from the 4th ed., and enlarged from Neander, Gieseler, Baur, etc., by *Henry B. Smith*, N. York, 1861, in 2 vols. ; 6th Germ. ed. by K. *Benrath*, Leipz. 1888.

1886), GUERICKE (9th ed. 1866, 3 vols.), LINDNER (1848-'54),
JACOBI (1850, unfinished), FRICKE (1850), KURTZ (*Lehrbuch*,
10th ed. 1887, in 2 vols., the larger *Handbuch*, unfinished),
HASSE (edited by Köhler, 1864, in 3 small vols.), KÖLLNER
(1864), EBRARD (1866, 2 vols.), ROTHE (lectures edited by WEIN-
GARTEN, 1875, 2 vols.), HERZOG (1876-'82, 3 vols.), H. SCHMID
(1881, 2 vols.). Niedner's *Lehrbuch* (1866) stands first for
independent and thorough scholarship, but is heavy. Hase's
Compend is unsurpassed for condensation, wit, point, and artistic taste, as a miniature picture.[1] Herzog's *Abriss* keeps the
medium between voluminous fulness and enigmatic brevity, and
is written in a candid Christian spirit. Kurtz is clear, concise,
and evangelical.[2] A new manual was begun by MÖLLER, 1889.

The best works on doctrine history (*Dogmengeschichte*) are by
MÜNSCHER, GIESELER, NEANDER, BAUR, HAGENBACH, THOMASIUS,
H. SCHMID, NITZSCH, and HARNACK (1887).

It is impossible to do justice here to the immense service
which Protestant Germany has done to special departments of
church history. Most of the fathers, popes, schoolmen and
reformers, and the principal doctrines of Christianity have been
made the subject of minute and exhaustive historical treatment. We have already mentioned the monographs of Neander and Baur, and fully equal to them are such masterly and
enduring works as ROTHE's *Beginnings of the Christian Church*,
ULLMANN's *Reformers before the Reformation*, HASSE's *Anselm
of Canterbury*, and DORNER's *History of Christology*.

(b) French works.

Dr. ETIENNE L. CHASTEL (Professor of Church History in the
National Church at Geneva, d. 1886) wrote a complete *Histoire
du Christianisme* (Paris, 1881-'85, 5 vols.).

Dr. MERLE D'AUBIGNÉ (Professor of Church History in the
independent Reformed Seminary at Geneva, d. 1872) reproduced in elegant and eloquent French an extensive history both
of the Lutheran and Calvinistic Reformation, with an evan-

---

[1] In 1885 Hase began the publication of his *Lectures on Ch. Hist.*, 3 vols.
[2] English translation from the 9th ed. by J. Macpherson, 1889, 3 vols.

gelical enthusiasm and a dramatic vivacity which secured it an extraordinary circulation in England and America (far greater than on the Continent), and made it the most popular work on that important period. Its value as a history is somewhat diminished by polemical bias and the occasional want of accuracy. Dr. Merle conceived the idea of the work during the celebration of the third centenary of the German Reformation in 1817, in the Wartburg at Eisenach, where Luther translated the New Testament and threw his inkstand at the devil. He labored on it till the year of his death.[1]

Dr. EDMUND DE PRESSENSÉ (pastor of a free church in Paris, member of the National Assembly, then senator of France), an able scholar, with evangelical Protestant convictions similar to those of Dr. Merle, wrote a Life of Christ against Renan, and a History of Ancient Christianity, both of which are translated into English.[2]

ERNEST RENAN, the celebrated Orientalist and member of the French Academy, prepared from the opposite standpoint of sceptical criticism, and mixing history with romance, but in brilliant and fascinating style, the Life of Christ, and the history of the Beginnings of Christianity to the middle of the second century.[3]

---

[1] *Histoire de la Réformation du 16 siècle.* Paris, 1835 sqq., 4th ed. 1861 sqq., 5 vols. *Histoire de la Réformation en Europe au temps de Calvin.* Paris, 1863 sqq. German translation of both works, Stuttgart (Steinkopf), 1861 and 1863 sqq. English translation repeatedly published in England and the United States by the Amer. Tract Society (with sundry changes), and by Carter & Brothers. The Carter ed. (N. York, 1863–1879) is in 5 vols. for the Lutheran Reformation, and in 8 vols. for the Reformation in the time of Calvin. The last three vols. of the second series were translated and published after the author's death by *W. L. Cates.* By a singular mistake Dr. Merle goes in England and America by the name of D'Aubigné, which is merely an assumed by-name from his Huguenot ancestors.

[2] *Jésus Christ, son temps, sa vie, son œuvre.* Paris, 1866. *Histoire des trois premiers siècles de l'église chrétienne.* Paris, 1858 sqq. German translation by *Fabarius* (Leipzig, 1862–65), English translation by *Annie Harwood.* Lond. and N. York, 1870 sqq., 4 vols. Superseded by a revised ed. of the original, Paris, 1887 sqq.

[3] *Vie de Jésus.* Paris, 1863, and in many editions in different languages. This book created even a greater sensation than the *Leben Jesu* of Strauss, but is very superficial and turns the gospel history into a novel with a self-contradictory and impossible hero. It forms the first volume of his *Histoire des origines du christianisme.* The other volumes are: 2. *Les Apôtres,* Paris,

(c) English works.

English literature is rich in works on Christian antiquity, English church history, and other special departments, but poor in general histories of Christianity.

The first place among English historians, perhaps, is due to EDWARD GIBBON (d. 1794). In his monumental *History of the Decline and Fall of the Roman Empire* (finished after twenty years' labor, at Lausanne, June 27, 1787), he notices throughout the chief events in ecclesiastical history from the introduction of the Christian religion to the times of the crusades and the capture of Constantinople (1453), with an accurate knowledge of the chief sources and the consummate skill of a master in the art of composition, with occasional admiration for heroic characters like Athanasius and Chrysostom, but with a keener eye to the failings of Christians and the imperfections of the visible church, and unfortunately without sympathy and understanding of the spirit of Christianity which runs like a golden thread even through the darkest centuries. He conceived the idea of his magnificent work in papal Rome, among the ruins of the Capitol, and in tracing the gradual decline and fall of imperial Rome, which he calls "the greatest, perhaps, and most awful scene in the history of mankind," he has involuntarily become a witness to the gradual growth and triumph of the religion of the cross, of which no historian of the future will ever record a history of decline and fall, though some "lonely traveller from New Zealand," taking his stand on "a broken arch" of the bridge of St. Angelo, may sketch the ruins of St. Peter's.[1]

1866; 3. *St. Paul*, 1869; 4. *L'Antechrist*, 1873; 5. *Les évangiles et la seconde génération des chrétiens*, 1877; 6. *L'église chrétienne*, 1879; *Marc-Aurèle et la fin du monde antique*, 1882. The work of twenty years. Renan wrote, he says, "without any other passion than a very keen curiosity."

[1] Cardinal Newman, shortly before his transition from Oxford Tractarianism to Romanism (in his essay on *Development of Christian Doctrine*, 1845), declared "the infidel Gibbon to be the chief, perhaps the only English writer who has any claim to be considered an ecclesiastical historian." This is certainly not true any longer. Dr. McDonald, in an essay, "Was Gibbon an infidel?" (in the "Bibliotheca Sacra" for July, 1868, Andover, Mass.), tried to

JOSEPH MILNER (Vicar of Hull, d. 1797) wrote a *History of the Church of Christ* for popular edification, selecting those portions which best suited his standard of evangelical orthodoxy and piety. "Nothing," he says in the preface, "but what appears to me to belong to Christ's kingdom shall be admitted; genuine piety is the only thing I intend to celebrate." He may be called the English Arnold, less learned, but free from polemics and far more readable and useful than the German pietist. His work was corrected and continued by his brother, *Isaac Milner* (d. 1820), by *Thomas Grantham* and Dr. *Stebbing*.[1]

Dr. WADDINGTON (Dean of Durham) prepared three volumes on the history of the Church before the Reformation (1835) and three volumes on the Continental Reformation (1841). Evangelical.

Canon JAMES C. ROBERTSON of Canterbury (Prof. of Church History in King's College, d. 1882) brings his *History of the Christian Church* from the Apostolic Age down to the Reformation (A.D. 64–1517). The work was first published in four octavo volumes (1854 sqq.) and then in eight duodecimo volumes (Lond. 1874), and is the best, as it is the latest, general church history written by an Episcopalian. It deserves praise for its candor, moderation, and careful indication of authorities.

From CHARLES HARDWICK (Archdeacon of Ely, d. 1859) we have a useful manual of the Church History of the *Middle Age* (1853, 3d ed. by Prof. *W. Stubbs*, 1872), and another on the *Reformation* (1856, 3d ed. by *W. Stubbs*, London, 1873). His

vindicate him against the charge of infidelity. But Gibbon was undoubtedly a Deist and deeply affected by the skepticism of Hume and Voltaire. While a student at Oxford he was converted to Romanism by reading Bossuet's *Variations of Protestantism*, and afterwards passed over to infidelity, with scarcely a ray of hope of any immortality but that of fame. See his *Autobiography*, Ch. VIII., and his letter to Lord Sheffield of April 27, 1793, where he says that his "only consolation" in view of death and the trials of life was "the presence of a friend." Best ed. of Gibbon, by W. Smith.

[1] London, 1794–1812; new ed. by Grantham, 1847, 4 vols., 1860, and other ed. A German translation by *Mortimer*, Gnadau, 5 vols.

History of the Anglican Articles of Religion (1859) is a valuable contribution to English church history.

Dr. TRENCH, Archbishop of Dublin, has published his *Lectures on Mediæval Church History* (Lond. 1877), delivered before the girls of Queen's College, London. They are conceived in a spirit of devout churchly piety and interspersed with judicious reflections.

PHILIP SMITH's *History of the Christian Church during the First Ten Centuries* (1879), and *during the Middle Ages* (1885), in 2 vols., is a skilful and useful manual for students.[1]

The most popular and successful modern church historians in the English or any other language are Dean MILMAN of St. Paul's, Dean STANLEY of Westminster Abbey, and Archdeacon FARRAR of Westminster. They belong to the broad church school of the Church of England, are familiar with Continental learning, and adorn their chosen themes with all the charms of elegant, eloquent, and picturesque diction. HENRY HART MILMAN (d. 1868) describes, with the stately march of Gibbon and as a counterpart of his decline and fall of Paganism, the rise and progress of Ancient and Latin Christianity, with special reference to its bearing on the progress of civilization.[2] ARTHUR PENRHYN STANLEY (d. 1881) unrolls a picture gallery of great men and events in the Jewish theocracy, from Abraham to the Christian era, and in the Greek church, from Constantine the Great to Peter the Great.[3] FREDERIC W. FARRAR (b.

---

[1] Republished by Harper & Brothers, New York, 1885. The author has transferred verbatim a large portion of his Manual from my church history, but with proper acknowledgment. Another church history by a writer nearer home has made even larger, but less honest use of my book.

[2] *The History of Christianity from the Birth of Christ to the Abolition of Paganism in the Roman Empire.* Lond. 1840, revised ed., Lond. and N. York (Middleton), 1866, 3 vols. More important is his *History of Latin Christianity to the Pontificate of Nicholas V.* (A.D. 1455), Lond. and N. York, 1854 sqq., in 8 vols. Milman wrote also a *History of the Jews*, 1829 (revised 1862, 3 vols.), and published an edition of Gibbon's *Decline and Fall* with useful annotations. A complete edition of his historical works appeared, Lond. 1866–'67, in 15 vols. 8vo.

[3] *Lectures on the History of the Eastern Church* (delivered in Oxford), Lond. and N. York, 1862. No complete history, but a series of picturesque de-

1831) illuminates with classical and rabbinical learning, and with exuberant rhetoric the Life of Christ, and of the great Apostle of the Gentiles, and the Early Days of Christianity.[1]

(d) American works.

American literature is still in its early youth, but rapidly growing in every department of knowledge. PRESCOTT, WASHINGTON IRVING, MOTLEY, and BANCROFT have cultivated interesting portions of the history of Spain, Holland, and the United States, and have taken rank among the classical historians in the English language.

In ecclesiastical history the Americans have naturally so far been mostly in the attitude of learners and translators, but with every prospect of becoming producers. They have, as already noticed, furnished the best translations of Mosheim, Neander, and Gieseler.

HENRY B. SMITH (late Professor in the Union Theol. Seminary, New York, d. 1877) has prepared the best Chronological Tables of Church History, which present in parallel columns a synopsis of the external and internal history of Christianity, including that of America, down to 1858, with lists of Councils, Popes, Patriarchs, Archbishops, Bishops, and Moderators of General Assemblies.[2]

---

scriptions of the most interesting characters and scenes in the Eastern church. *Lectures on the History of the Jewish Church*, Lond. and N. York, 1862–'76, in 3 vols. An independent and skilful adaptation of the views and results of Ewald's *Geschichte Israel's*, to which Stanley pays a fine tribute in the Prefaces to the first and third vols. His *Historical Memorials of Canterbury Cathedral* (1855, 5th ed. 1869), and of *Westminster Abbey* (1867, 4th ed. 1874), are important for English church history. His *Lectures on the History of the Church of Scotland* (1872) have delighted the moderate and liberal, but displeased the orthodox Presbyterians of the land of Knox and Walter Scott.

[1] Farrar's *Life of Christ* appeared first in London, 1874, in 2 vols., and has up to 1879 gone through about thirty editions, including the American reprints. His *Life and Work of St. Paul*, Lond. and N. York, 1879, in 2 vols. *The Early Days of Christianity*, London and New York, 1882, 2 vols.; and *Lives of the Fathers*, Lond. and N. Y. 1889, 2 vols.

[2] *History of the Church of Christ in* (16) *Chronological Tables*. N. York (Charles Scribner), 1860. Weingarten's *Zeittafeln zur Kirchengeschichte*, 3d ed., 1888, are less complete, but more convenient in size.

W. G. T. Shedd (Professor in the same institution, b. 1820) wrote from the standpoint of Calvinistic orthodoxy an eminently readable *History of Christian Doctrine* (N. York, 1863, 2 vols.), in clear, fresh, and vigorous English, dwelling chiefly on theology, anthropology, and soteriology, and briefly touching on eschatology, but entirely omitting the doctrine of the Church and the sacraments, with the connected controversies.

Philip Schaff is the author of a special *History of the Apostolic Church*, in English and German (N. York, 1853, etc., and Leipzig, 1854), of a *History of the Creeds of Christendom* (N. York, 4th ed., 1884, 3 vols., with documents original and translated), and of a general *History of the Christian Church* (N. York and Edinb., 1859–'67, in 3 vols.; also in German, Leipzig, 1867; rewritten and enlarged, N. Y. and Edinb., 1882–'88; third revision, 1889, 5 vols.; to be continued).

George P. Fisher (Professor in New Haven, b. 1827) has written the best manual in the English language: *History of the Christian Church, with Maps.* N. York, 1887. He has also published a *History of the Reformation* (1873); *Beginnings of Christianity* (1877), and *Outlines of Universal History* (1885),—all in a calm, amiable, and judicious spirit, and a clear, chaste style.

Contributions to interesting chapters in the history of Protestantism are numerous. Dr. E. H. Gillett (d. 1875) wrote a monograph on *John Hus* (N. York, 1864, 2 vols.), a *History of the Presbyterian Church in the United States of America* (Philad. 1864, 2 vols.), and a History of Natural Theology (*God in Human Thought*, N. York, 1874, 2 vols.); Dr. Abel Stevens, a *History of Methodism*, viewed as the great religious revival of the eighteenth century, down to the centenary celebration of 1839 (N. York, 1858–'61, 3 vols.), and a *History of the Methodist Episcopal Church in the United States* (1864–'67, 4 vols.); Henry M. Baird, a *History of the Rise and Progress of the Huguenots in France* (N. York, 1879, 2 vols.), and *The Huguenots and Henry of Navarre* (1886, 2 vols.).

The denominational and sectarian divisions of American

Christianity seem to be unfavorable to the study and cultivation
of general church history, which requires a large-hearted catholic spirit.   But, on the other hand, the social and national in-
termingling of ecclesiastical organizations of every variety of
doctrine and discipline, on a basis of perfect freedom and
equality before the law, widens the horizon, and facilitates
comparison and appreciation of variety in unity and unity in
variety; while the growth and prosperity of the churches on
the principle of self-support and self-government encourages a
hopeful view of the future.   America falls heir to the whole
wealth of European Christianity and civilization, and is in a
favorable position to review and reproduce in due time the
entire course of Christ's kingdom in the old world with the
faith and freedom of the new.[1]

(e) Finally, we must mention biblical and ecclesiastical Ency-
clopædias which contain a large number of valuable contributions to church history from leading scholars of the age, viz.:
   1. The *Bible Dictionaries* of WINER (Leipzig, 1820, 3d ed.
1847, 2 vols.); SCHENKEL (Leipzig, 1869–'75, 5 vols.); RIEHM
(Leipzig, 1877 sqq., illustrated); KITTO (Edinb., 1845, third revised ed. by W. L. ALEXANDER, 1862–'65, 3 vols.); WM. SMITH
(London, 1860–'64, in 3 vols., American edition much enlarged
and improved by H. HACKETT and E. ABBOT, N. York, 1870,
in 4 vols.); PH. SCHAFF (Philadelphia, 1880, with maps and
illustrations; 4th ed., revised, 1887).
   2. The *Biblical* and *Historical Dictionaries* of HERZOG (*Real-
Encyklopädie für Protestantische Theologie und Kirche*, Gotha.
1854 to 1868, in 22 vols., new ed. thoroughly revised by
HERZOG, PLITT and HAUCK, Leipzig, 1877–'88, in 18 vols.);
SCHAFF-HERZOG (*Religious Encyclopædia*, based on Herzog,
but condensed, supplemented, and adapted to English and
American students, edited by Philip Schaff in connection with

---

[1] Comp. the author's *Christianity in the United States of America* (a report
prepared for the seventh General Conference of the Evang. Alliance, held at
Basle, Sept., 1879), printed in the Proceedings of that Conference, and his
Church and State in the U. S., N. York, 1888.

Samuel M. Jackson and D. S. Schaff, N. York and Edinburgh, revised ed., 1887, in 3 vols., with a supplementary vol. on *Living Divines and Christian Workers*, 1887); WETZER and WELTE (Roman Catholic *Kirchenlexicon*, Freiburg i. Breisgau, 1847–1860, in 12 vols.; second ed. newly elaborated by Cardinal JOSEPH HERGENRÖTHER and Dr. FRANZ KAULEN, 1880 sqq., promised in 10 vols.) ; LICHTENBERGER (*Encyclopédie des sciences religieuses*, Paris, 1877–'82, in 13 vols., with supplement); McCLINTOCK and STRONG (*Cyclopædia of Biblical, Theological, and Ecclesiastical Literature*, New York, 1867–'81, 10 vols. and two supplementary volumes, 1885 and 1887, largely illustrated).   The *Encyclopædia Britannica* (9th ed., completed 1889 in 25 vols.) contains also many elaborate articles on biblical and ecclesiastical topics.

3. For ancient church history down to the age of Charlemagne: SMITH and CHEETHAM, *Dictionary of Christian Antiquities* (London and Boston, 1875, 2 vols.); SMITH and WACE, *Dictionary of Christian Biography, Literature, Sects and Doctrines during the first eight centuries* (London and Boston, 1877–'87, 4 vols.).   The articles in these two works are written mostly by scholars of the Church of England, and are very valuable for fulness and accuracy of information.

NOTE.—The study of church history is reviving in the Greek Church where it began.   PHILARET BAPHEIDOS has issued a compendious church history under the title : Ἐκκλησιαστικὴ ἱστορία ἀπὸ τοῦ κυρίου ἡμῶν Ἰησοῦ Χριστοῦ μέχρι τῶν καθ᾽ ἡμᾶς χρόνων ὑπὸ Φιλαρετοῦ Βαψείδου, ἀρχιμανδρίτου Δ. Φ. καὶ καθηγητοῦ τῆς Θεολογίας ἐν τῇ ἐν Χάλκη Θεολογικῇ Σχολῇ. Τόμος πρῶτος.   Ἀρχαία ἐκκλησ᾽ ἱστορία.   A. D. 1–700.   Ἐν Κωνσταντινοπόλει, 1884 (Lorentz & Keil, libraires de S. M. I. le Sultan), 380 pp.   The second vol. embraces the mediæval church to the fall of Constantinople, 1453, and has 459 pp.   The work is dedicated to Dr. Philotheos Bryennios, Metropolitan of Nicomedia, the discoverer of the famous Jerusalem Codex.   Nearly all the literature quoted is German Protestant; no English, very few Latin, and still fewer Greek works are mentioned.   Another compend of Church History in Greek by DIOMEDES KYRIAKOS appeared at Athens, 1881, in 2 vols.

FIRST PERIOD

THE CHURCH UNDER THE APOSTLES

FROM THE BIRTH OF CHRIST TO THE DEATH OF ST. JOHN,

A.D. 1–100

CHAPTER I

PREPARATION FOR CHRISTIANITY IN THE HISTORY OF THE JEWISH AND HEATHEN WORLD.

Literature.

J. L. von Mosheim : *Historical Commentaries on the State of Christianity in the first three centuries.* 1753. Transl. by *Vidal* and *Murdock*, vol. i. chs. 1 and 2 (pp. 9–82, of the N. York ed. 1853).

Neander : *Allg. Gesch. der christl. Religion und Kirche.* Vol. 1st (1842). Einleit. (p. 1–116).

J. P. Lange : *Das apost. Zeitalter.* 1853, I. pp. 224–318.

Schaff : *Hist. of the Apostolic Church.* pp. 137–188 (New York ed.).

Lutterbeck (R. C.) : *Die N. Testamentlichen Lehrbegriffe, oder Untersuchungen über das Zeitalter der Religionswende, die Vorstufen des Christenthums und die erste Gestaltung desselben.* Mainz, 1852, 2 vols.

Döllinger (R. C.) : *Heidenthum und Judenthum. Vorhalle zur Geschichte des Christenthums.* Regensb. 1857. Engl. transl. by *N. Darnell* under the title : *The Gentile and the Jew in the courts of the Temple of Christ : an Introduction to the History of Christianity.* Lond. 1862, 2 vols.

Charles Hardwick (d. 1859) : *Christ and other Masters.* London, 4th ed. by *Procter*, 1875.

M. Schneckenburger (d. 1848) : *Vorlesungen über N. Testamentliche Zeit-geschichte, aus dessen Nachlass herausgegeben von Löhlein, mit Vorwort von Hundeshagen.* Frankf. a M. 1862.

A. Hausrath : *N. Testamentliche Zeitgeschichte.* Heidelb. 1868 sqq., 2d ed. 1873–'77, 4 vols. The first vol. appeared in a third ed. 1879. The work includes the state of Judaism and heathenism in the time of Christ, the apostolic and the post-apostolic age to Hadrian (A.D. 117). English translation by *Poynting* and *Guenzer*, Lond. 1878 sqq.

E. Schürer : *Lehrbuch der N. Testamentlichen Zeitgeschichte.* Leipz. 1874. Revised and enlarged under the title : *Gesch. des jüd. Volkes im Zeitalter Christi.* 1886, 2 vols. Engl. translation, Edinb. and N. Y.

H. Schiller : *Geschichte des römischen Kaiserreichs unter der Regierung des Nero.* Berlin, 1872.

L. Friedländer : *Darstellungen aus der Sittengeschichte Roms in der Zeit von Augustus bis zum Ausgang der Antonine.* Leipzig, 5th ed., revised, 1881, 3 vols. A standard work.

Geo. P. Fisher (of Yale College, New Haven) : *The Beginnings of Christianity.* N. York, 1877. Chs. II.–VII.

Gerhard Uhlhorn : *The Conflict of Christianity with Heathenism.* Transl. by *Egbert C. Smyth* and *C. J. H. Ropes.* N. York, 1879. Book I. chs. 1 and 2. The German original appeared in a 4th ed., 1884.

§ 8. *Central Position of Christ in the History of the World.*

To see clearly the relation of the Christian religion to the preceding history of mankind, and to appreciate its vast influence upon all future ages, we must first glance at the preparation which existed in the political, moral, and religious condition of the world for the advent of our Saviour.

As religion is the deepest and holiest concern of man, the entrance of the Christian religion into history is the most momentous of all events. It is the end of the old world and the beginning of the new. It was a great idea of Dionysius " the Little" to date our era from the birth of our Saviour. Jesus Christ, the God-Man, the prophet, priest, and king of mankind, is, in fact, the centre and turning-point not only of chronology, but of all history, and the key to all its mysteries. Around him, as the sun of the moral universe, revolve at their several distances, all nations and all important events, in the religious life of the world ; and all must, directly or indirectly, consciously or unconsciously, contribute to glorify his name and advance his cause. The history of mankind before his birth must be viewed as a preparation for his coming, and the history after his birth as a gradual diffusion of his spirit and progress of his kingdom. " All things were created by him, and for him." He is " the desire of all nations." He appeared in the " fulness of time," [1] when the process of preparation was finished, and the world's need of redemption fully disclosed.

This preparation for Christianity began properly with the very creation of man, who was made in the image of God, and destined for communion with him through the eternal Son; and with the promise of salvation which God gave to our first parents as a star of hope to guide them through the darkness of sin and error. [2] Vague memories of a primitive paradise and subsequent fall, and hopes of a future redemption, survive even in the heathen religions.

With Abraham, about nineteen hundred years before Christ, the religious development of humanity separates into the two independent, and, in their compass, very unequal branches of Judaism and heathenism. These meet and unite .at last in Christ as the common Saviour, the fulfiller of the types and prophecies, desires and hopes of the ancient world ; while at the same time the ungodly elements of both league in deadly hostility against him, and thus draw forth the full revelation of his all-conquering power of truth and love.

As Christianity is the reconciliation and union of God and man in and through Jesus Christ, the God-Man, it must have been preceded by a twofold process of preparation, an approach of God to man, and an approach of man to God. In Judaism the preparation is direct and positive, proceeding from above downwards, and ending with the birth of the Messiah. In heathenism it is indirect and mainly, though not entirely, negative, proceeding from below upwards, and ending with a help-

[1] Mark 1 : 15 ; Gal. 4 : 4.   [2] Gen. 3 : 15.

less cry of mankind for redemption. There we have a special revelation or self-communication of the only true God by word and deed, ever growing clearer and plainer, till at last the divine Logos appears in human nature, to raise it to communion with himself; here men, guided indeed by the general providence of God, and lighted by the glimmer of the Logos shining in the darkness,[1] yet unaided by direct revelation, and left to "walk in their own ways,"[2] "that they should seek God, if haply they might feel after him, and find him."[3] In Judaism the true religion is prepared for man; in heathenism man is prepared for the true religion. There the divine substance is begotten; here the human forms are moulded to receive it. The former is like the elder son in the parable, who abode in his father's house; the latter like the prodigal, who squandered his portion, yet at last shuddered before the gaping abyss of perdition, and penitently returned to the bosom of his father's compassionate love.[4] Heathenism is the starry night, full of darkness and fear, but of mysterious presage also, and of anxious waiting for the light of day; Judaism, the dawn, full of the fresh hope and promise of the rising sun; both lose themselves in the sunlight of Christianity, and attest its claim to be the only true and the perfect religion for mankind.

The heathen preparation again was partly intellectual and literary, partly political and social. The former is represented by the Greeks, the latter by the Romans.

Jerusalem, the holy city, Athens, the city of culture, and Rome, the city of power, may stand for the three factors in that preparatory history which ended in the birth of Christianity.

This process of preparation for redemption in the history of the world, the groping of heathenism after the "unknown God"[5] and inward peace, and the legal struggle and comfort-

---

[1] John 1 : 5 ; Rom. 1 : 19, 20 ; 2 :14, 15.
[2] Acts 14: 16. [3] Acts 17 : 26, 27.
[4] Luke 15 : 11–32. [5] Acts 17 : 23.

ing hope of Judaism, repeat themselves in every individual
believer; for man is made for Christ, and " his heart is restless,
till it rests in Christ."[1]

§ 9. *Judaism.*

Literature.

I. SOURCES.

1. The CANONICAL Books of the O. and N. TESTAMENTS.
2. The Jewish APOCRYPHA. Best edition by *Otto Frid. Fritzsche: Libri
   Apocryphi Veteris Testamenti Graece.* Lips. 1871. German Commentary by *Fritzsche* and *Grimm,* Leipz. 1851-'60 (in the "Exeget.
   Handbuch zum A. T."); English Com. by Dr. *E. C. Bissell,* N. York,
   1880 (vol. xxv. in Schaff's ed. of Lange's Bible-Work).
3. JOSEPHUS (a Jewish scholar, priest, and historian, patronized by Vespasian and Titus, b. A.D. 37, d. about 103) : *Antiquitates Judaicae*
   (Ἀρχαιολογία Ἰουδαϊκή), in 20 books, written first (but not preserved)
   in Aramaic, and then reproduced in Greek, A.D. 94, beginning with
   the creation and coming down to the outbreak of the rebellion
   against the Romans, A.D. 66, important for the post-exilian period.
   Bellum Judaicum (περὶ τοῦ Ἰουδαϊκοῦ πολέμου), in 7 books, written
   about 75, from his own personal observation (as Jewish general in
   Galilee, then as Roman captive, and Roman agent), and coming down
   to the destruction of Jerusalem, A.D. 70. *Contra Apionem,* a defence
   of the Jewish nation against the calumnies of the grammarian Apion.
   His *Vita* or Autobiography was written after A.D. 100.—Editions of
   Josephus by *Hudson,* Oxon. 1720, 2 vols. fol. ; *Havercamp,* Amst.
   1726, 2 fol. ; *Oberthür,* Lips. 1785, 3 vols. ; *Richter,* Lips. 1827, 6 vols. ;
   Dindorf, Par. 1849, 2 vols. ; *Imm. Bekker,* Lips. 1855, 6 vols. The
   editions of Havercamp and Dindorf are the best. English translations by *Whiston* and *Traill,* often edited, in London, New York,
   Philadelphia. German translations by *Hedio, Ott, Cotta, Demme.*
4. PHILO of Alexandria (d. after A.D. 40) represents the learned and philosophical (Platonic) Judaism. Best ed. by *Mangey,* Lond. 1742, 2
   fol., and *Richter,* Lips. 1828, 2 vols. English translation by *C. D.
   Yonge,* London, 1854, 4 vols. (in Bohn's "Ecclesiastical Library ").
5. The TALMUD (תַּלְמוּד, i. e. Doctrine) represents the traditional, post-
   exilian, and anti-Christian Judaism. It consists of the *Mishna* (מִשְׁנָה,
   δευτέρωσις, Repetition of the Law), from the end of the second century, and the *Gemara* (גְּמָרָא, i. e. Perfect Doctrine, from גְּמַר, to
   bring to an end). The latter exists in two forms, the Palestinian

---

[1] St. Augustine, *Conf.* I. 1 : " *Fecisti nos ad Te, et inquietum est cor nos-
trum, donec requiescat in Te.*"

Gemara, completed at Tiberias about A.D. 350, and the Babylonian Gemara of the sixth century. Best eds. of the Talmud by *Bomberg*, Ven. 1520 sqq. 12 vols. fol., and *Sittenfeld*, Berlin, 1862–'68, 12 vols. fol. Latin version of the Mishna by *G. Surenhusius*, Amst. 1698–1703, 6 vols. fol.; German by J. J. Rabe, Onolzbach, 1760–'63.

6. MONUMENTAL Sources: of Egypt (see the works of Champollion, Young, Rosellini, Wilkinson, Birch, Mariette, Lepsius, Bunsen, Ebers, Brugsch, etc.); of Babylon and Assyria (see Botta, Layard, George Smith, Sayce, Schrader, etc.).

7. GREEK and ROMAN authors: POLYBIUS (d. B.C. 125), DIODORUS SICULUS (contemporary of Cæsar), STRABO (d. A.D. 24), TACITUS (d. about 117), SUETONIUS (d. about 130), JUSTINUS (d. after A.D. 160). Their accounts are mostly incidental, and either simply derived from Josephus, or full of error and prejudice, and hence of very little value.

II. HISTORIES.

(a) By Christian authors.

PRIDEAUX (Dean of Norwich, d. 1724): *The Old and New Testament Connected in the History of the Jews and neighboring nations, from the declension of the kingdoms of Israel and Judah to the time of Christ.* Lond. 1715; 11th ed. 1749, 4 vols. (and later eds.). The same in French and German.

J. J. HESS (d. 1828): *Geschichte der Israeliten vor den Zeiten Jesu.* Zür. 1766 sqq., 12 vols.

WARBURTON (Bishop of Gloucester, d. 1779): *The Divine Legation of Moses demonstrated.* 5th ed. Lond. 1766; 10th ed. by *James Nichols*, Lond. 1846, 3 vols. 8vo.

MILMAN (Dean of St. Paul's, d. 1868): *History of the Jews.* Lond. 1829, 3 vols.; revised ed. Lond. and N. York, 1865, 3 vols.

J. C. K. HOFMANN (Prof. in Erlangen, d. 1878): *Weissagung und Erfüllung.* Nördl. 1841, 2 vols.

ARCHIBALD ALEXANDER (d. at Princeton, 1851): *A History of the Israelitish Nation.* Philadelphia, 1853. (Popular.)

H. EWALD (d. 1874): *Geschichte des Volkes Israel bis Christus.* Gött. 1843 sqq. 3d ed. 1864–'68, 7 vols. A work of rare genius and learning, but full of bold conjectures. Engl. transl. by *Russell Martineau* and *J. E. Carpenter.* Lond. 1871–'76, 5 vols. Comp. also Ewald's *Prophets*, and *Poetical Books of the O. T.*

E. W. HENGSTENBERG (d. 1869): *Geschichte des Reiches Gottes unter dem Alten Bunde.* Berl. 1869–'71, 2 vols. (Posthumous publication.) English transl., Edinburgh (T. & T. Clark), 1871–'72, 2 vols. (Name of the translator not given.)

J. H. KURTZ: *Geschichte des Alten Bundes.* Berlin, 1848–'55, 2 vols. (unfinished). Engl. transl. by *Edersheim*, Edinb. 1859, in 3 vols. The same: *Lehrbuch der heil. Geschichte.* Königsb. 6th ed. 1853; also in English, by *C. F. Schäffer.* Phil. 1855.

P. Cassel : *Israel in der Weltgeschichte.*   Berlin, 1865 (32 pp.).

Joseph Langen (R. C.) : *Das Judenthum in Palästina zur Zeit Christi.*
Freiburg i. B. 1866.

G. Weber and **H. Holtzmann** : *Geschichte des Volkes Israel und der
Gründung des Christenthums.*   Leipzig, 1867, 2 vols. (the first vol.
by Weber, the second by Holtzmann).

H. Holtzmann : *Die Messiasidee zur Zeit Christi,* in the "Jahrbücher für
Deutsche Theologie," Gotha, 1867 (vol. xii. pp. 389–411).

F. Hitzig : *Geschichte des Volkes Israel von Anbeginn bis zur Eroberung
Masada's im J. 72 nach Chr.*   Heidelb. 1869, 2 vols.

A. Kuenen (Prof. in Leyden) : *De godsdienst van Israël tot den ondergang
van den joodschen staat.*   Haarlem, 1870, 2 vols.   Transl. into English : *The Religion of Israel to the Fall of the Jewish State,* by *A. H.
May.*   Lond. (Williams & Norgate), 1874–'75, 3 vols.   Represents
the advanced rationalism of Holland.

A. P. Stanley (Dean of Westminster) : *Lectures on the History of the
Jewish Church.*   Lond. and N. York, 1863–'76, 3 vols.   Based on Ewald.

W. Wellhausen : *Geschichte Israels.*   Berlin, 1878, 3d ed. 1886.   Transl.
by *Black* and *Menzies : Prolegomena to the History of Israel.*   Edinb. 1885.

E. Schürer : *Geschichte des jüd. Volkes im Zeitalter Christi.*   1886 sq.   2 vols.

A. Edersheim : *Prophecy and History in relation to the Messiah.*   Lond. 1885.

A. Köhler : *Lehrbuch der bibl. Geschichte des A. T.*   Erlangen, 1875–'88.

C. A. Briggs : *Messianic Prophecy.*   N. York and Edinb. 1886.

V. H. Stanton : *The Jewish, and the Christian Messiah.*   Lond. 1886.

B. Stade : *Gesch. des Volkes Israel.*   Berlin, 1888, 2 vols.   Radical.

E. Renan : *Hist. du peuple d'Israel.*   Paris, 1887 sqq., 3 vols.   Engl.
translation, London, 1888 sqq.   Radical.

R. Kittel : *Gesch. der Hebräer.*   Gotha, 1888 sqq.   Moderate.

(b) By Jewish authors.

J. M. Jost : *Geschichte der Israeliten seit der Zeit der Maccabäer bis auf
unsere Tage.*   Leipz. 1820–'28, 9 vols.   By the same : *Geschichte des
Judenthums und seiner Secten.*   1857–'59, 3 vols.

Salvador : *Histoire de la domination Romaine en Judée et de la ruine de
Jérusalem.*   Par. 1847, 2 vols.

Raphall : *Post-biblical History of the Jews from the close of the O. T. about
the year 420 till the destruction of the second Temple in the year 70.*
Lond. 1856, 2 vols.

Abraham Geiger (a liberal Rabbi at Frankfort on the M.) : *Das Judenthum und seine Geschichte.*   Breslau; 2d ed. 1865–'71, 3 vols.   With
an appendix on Strauss and Renan.   Comes down to the 16th century.   English transl. by *Maurice Mayer.*   N. York, 1865.

L. Herzfeld : *Geschichte des Volkes Jizrael.*   Nordhausen, 1847–'57, 3
vols.   The same work, abridged in one vol.   Leipz. 1870.

H. Grätz (Prof. in Breslau) : *Geschichte der Juden von den ältesten Zeiten
bis auf die Gegenwart.*   Leipz. 1854–'70, 11 vols. (to 1848).

"Salvation is of the Jews."[1] This wonderful people, whose
fit symbol is the burning bush, was chosen by sovereign grace
to stand amidst the surrounding idolatry as the bearer of the
knowledge of the only true God, his holy law, and cheering promise, and thus to become the cradle of the Messiah. It arose with
the calling of Abraham, and the covenant of Jehovah with him
in Canaan, the land of promise; grew to a nation in Egypt, the
land of bondage; was delivered and organized into a theocratic
state on the basis of the law of Sinai by Moses in the wilderness; was led back into Palestine by Joshua; became, after the
Judges, a monarchy, reaching the height of its glory in David
and Solomon; split into two hostile kingdoms, and, in punishment for internal discord and growing apostasy to idolatry, was
carried captive by heathen conquerors; was restored after seventy years' humiliation to the land of its fathers, but fell again
under the yoke of heathen foes; yet in its deepest abasement
fulfilled its highest mission by giving birth to the Saviour of
the world. "The history of the Hebrew people," says Ewald,
"is, at the foundation, the history of the true religion growing
through all the stages of progress unto its consummation;
the religion which, on its narrow national territory, advances
through all struggles to the highest victory, and at length reveals itself in its full glory and might, to the end that, spreading abroad by its own irresistible energy, it may never vanish
away, but may become the eternal heritage and blessing of all
nations. The whole ancient world had for its object to seek
the true religion; but this people alone finds its being and
honor on earth exclusively in the true religion, and thus it
enters upon the stage of history."[2]

Judaism, in sharp contrast with the idolatrous nations of
antiquity, was like an oasis in a desert, clearly defined and isolated; separated and enclosed by a rigid moral and ceremonial
law. The holy land itself, though in the midst of the three
Continents of the ancient world, and surrounded by the great

[1] John 4 : 22. Comp. Luke 24 : 47 ; Rom. 9 : 4, 5.
[2] *Geschichte des Volkes Israel*, Vol. I. p. 9 (3d ed.).

nations of ancient culture, was separated from them by deserts south and east, by sea on the west, and by mountain on the north; thus securing to the Mosaic religion freedom to unfold itself and to fulfil its great work without disturbing influences from abroad. But Israel carried in its bosom from the first the large promise, that in Abraham's seed all the nations of the earth should be blessed. Abraham, the father of the faithful, Moses, the lawgiver, David, the heroic king and sacred psalmist, Isaiah, the evangelist among the prophets, Elijah the Tishbite, who reappeared with Moses on the Mount of Transfiguration to do homage to Jesus, and John the Baptist, the impersonation of the whole Old Testament, are the most conspicuous links in the golden chain of the ancient revelation.

The outward circumstances and the moral and religious condition of the Jews at the birth of Christ would indeed seem at first and on the whole to be in glaring contradiction with their divine destiny. But, in the first place, their very degeneracy proved the need of divine help. In the second place, the redemption through Christ appeared by contrast in the greater glory, as a creative act of God. And finally, amidst the mass of corruption, as a preventive of putrefaction, lived the succession of the true children of Abraham, longing for the salvation of Israel, and ready to embrace Jesus of Nazareth as the promised Messiah and Saviour of the world.

Since the conquest of Jerusalem by Pompey, B.C. 63 (the year made memorable by the consulship of Cicero, the conspiracy of Catiline, and the birth of Cæsar Augustus), the Jews had been subject to the heathen Romans, who heartlessly governed them by the Idumean Herod and his sons, and afterwards by procurators. Under this hated yoke their Messianic hopes were powerfully raised, but carnally distorted. They longed chiefly for a political deliverer, who should restore the temporal dominion of David on a still more splendid scale; and they were offended with the servant form of Jesus, and with his spiritual kingdom. Their morals were outwardly far better than those of the heathen; but under the garb of strict obedience to their law, they concealed great corruption. They are pictured in the New Testament as a stiff-necked, ungrateful, and impenitent race, the seed of the serpent, a generation of vipers. Their own priest and historian, Josephus, who generally endeavored to present his countrymen to the Greeks and Romans in the most favorable light, describes them as at that time a debased and wicked people, well deserving their fearful punishment in the destruction of Jerusalem.

As to religion, the Jews, especially after the Babylonish captivity, adhered most tenaciously to the letter of the law, and to their traditions and ceremonies, but without knowing the spirit and power of the Scriptures. They cherished a bigoted horror of the heathen, and were therefore despised and hated by them as misanthropic, though by their judgment, industry, and tact, they were able to gain wealth and consideration in all the larger cities of the Roman empire.

After the time of the Maccabees (B.C. 150), they fell into three mutually hostile sects or parties, which respectively represent the three tendencies of formalism, skepticism, and mysticism ; all indicating the approaching dissolution of the old religion and the dawn of the new. We may compare them to the three prevailing schools of Greek philosophy—the Stoic, the Epicurean, and the Platonic, and also to the three sects of Mohammedanism—the Sunnis, who are traditionalists, the Sheas, who adhere to the Koran, and the Sufis or mystics, who seek true religion in " internal divine sensation."

1. The PHARISEES, the "separate," [1] were, so to speak, the Jewish Stoics. They represented the traditional orthodoxy and stiff formalism, the legal self-righteousness and the fanatical bigotry of Judaism. They had most influence with the people and the women, and controlled the public worship. They

---

[1] From פָּרַשׁ. They were separated from ordinary persons and all foreign and contaminating influences by the supposed correctness of their creed and the superior holiness of their life. Ewald (IV. 482): " Pharisäer bezeichnet GESONDERTE oder BESONDERE, nämlich Leute die vor andern durch Frömmigkeit ausgezeichnet und gleichsam mehr oder heiliger als andere sein wollen."

confounded piety with theoretical orthodoxy. They overloaded the holy Scriptures with the traditions of the elders so as to make the Scriptures " of none effect." They analyzed the Mosaic law to death, and substituted a labyrinth of casuistry for a living code. " They laid heavy burdens and grievous to be borne on men's shoulders," and yet they themselves would " not move them with their fingers." In the New Testament they bear particularly the reproach of hypocrisy; with, of course, illustrious exceptions, like Nicodemus, Gamaliel, and his disciple, Paul.

2. The less numerous SADDUCEES [1] were skeptical, rationalistic, and worldly-minded, and held about the same position in Judaism as the Epicureans and the followers of the New Academy in Greek and Roman heathendom. They accepted the written Scriptures (especially the Pentateuch), but rejected the oral traditions, denied the resurrection of the body and the immortality of the soul, the existence of angels and spirits, and the doctrine of an all-ruling providence. They numbered their followers among the rich, and had for some time possession of the office of the high-priest. Caiaphas belonged to their party.

The difference between the Pharisees and Sadducees reappears among modern Jews, who are divided into the orthodox and the liberal or rationalistic parties.

3. The ESSENES (whom we know only from Philo and Josephus) were not a party, but a mystic and ascetic order or brotherhood, and lived mostly in monkish seclusion in villages and in the desert Engedi on the Dead Sea.[2] They numbered about

---

[1] So called either from their supposed founder, Zadoc (so Ewald, IV. 358), or from צָדִּיק, " just."

[2] The name is variously written ('Εσσηνοί, 'Εσσαῖοι, 'Οσσαῖοι) and derived from proper names, or from the Greek, or from the Hebrew and Aramaic. The most plausible derivations are from חסיד, ὅσιος, holy ; from אביא, physician (comp. the corresponding term of Philo, θεραπευτής, which, however, means worshipper, devotee) ; from חזיא, seer ; from the rabbinical חזן, watchman, keeper (Ewald, formerly) ; from חשא, to be silent (Jost, Lightfoot) ; from the Syriac chasi or chasyo, pious, which is of the same root with the Hebrew chasid, chasidim (De Sacy, Ewald, IV. 484, 3d ed., and

4,000 members.   With an arbitrary, allegorical interpretation of the Old Testament, they combined some foreign theosophic elements, which strongly resemble the tenets of the new Pythagorean and Platonic schools, but were probably derived (like the Gnostic and Manichæan theories) from eastern religions, especially from Parsism.   They practised communion of goods, wore white garments, rejected animal food, bloody sacrifices, oaths, slavery, and (with few exceptions) marriage, and lived in the utmost simplicity, hoping thereby to attain a higher degree of holiness.   They were the forerunners of Christian monasticism.

The sect of the Essenes came seldom or never into contact with Christianity under the Apostles, except in the shape of a heresy at Colossæ.   But the Pharisees and Sadducees, particularly the former, meet us everywhere in the Gospels as bitter enemies of Jesus, and hostile as they are to each other, unite in condemning him to that death of the cross, which ended in the glorious resurrection, and became the foundation of spiritual life to believing Gentiles as well as Jews.

§ 10. *The Law, and the Prophecy.*

Degenerate and corrupt though the mass of Judaism was, yet the Old Testament economy was the divine institution preparatory to the Christian redemption, and as such received deepest reverence from Christ and his apostles, while they sought by terrible rebuke to lead its unworthy representatives to repentance.   It therefore could not fail of its saving effect on those hearts which yielded to its discipline, and conscientiously searched the Scriptures of Moses and the prophets.

Law and prophecy are the two great elements of the Jewish religion, and make it a direct divine introduction to Christiani-

Hitzig).   See Schürer, *N. T. Zeitgesch.* pp. 599 sqq., and Lightfoot's instructive Excursus on the Essenes and the Colossian heresy, in *Com. on Coloss.* (1875), pp. 73, 114–179.   Lightfoot again refutes the exploded derivation of Christianity from Essenic sources.

ty, "the voice of him that crieth in the wilderness, Prepare ye the way of the Lord; make straight in the desert a highway for our God."

1. The law of Moses was the clearest expression of the holy will of God before the advent of Christ. The Decalogue is a marvel of ancient legislation, and in its two tables enjoins the sum and substance of all true piety and morality—supreme love to God, and love to our neighbor. It set forth the ideal of righteousness, and was thus fitted most effectually to awaken the sense of man's great departure from it, the knowledge of sin and guilt.[1] It acted as a schoolmaster to lead men to Christ[2] that they might be justified by faith.[3]

The same sense of guilt and of the need of reconciliation was constantly kept alive by daily sacrifices, at first in the tabernacle and afterwards in the temple, and by the whole ceremonial law, which, as a wonderful system of types and shadows, perpetually pointed to the realities of the new covenant, especially to the one all-sufficient atoning sacrifice of Christ on the cross.

God in his justice requires absolute obedience and purity of heart under promise of life and penalty of death. Yet he cannot cruelly sport with man; he is the truthful, faithful, and merciful God. In the moral and ritual law, therefore, as in a shell, is hidden the sweet kernel of a promise, that he will one day exhibit the ideal of righteousness in living form, and give the penitent sinner pardon for all his transgressions and the power to fulfil the law. Without such assurance the law were bitter irony.

As regards the law, the Jewish economy was a religion of repentance.

2. But it was at the same time, as already hinted, the vehicle of the divine promise of redemption, and, as such, a religion of hope. While the Greeks and Romans put their golden age in the past, the Jews looked for theirs in the future. Their whole

---

[1] Rom. 3 : 20 : Διὰ νόμου ἐπίγνωσις ἁμαρτίας.
[2] Παιδαγωγὸς εἰς Χριστόν.   [3] Gal. 3 : 24.

history, their religious, political, and social institutions and cus‑
toms pointed to the coming of the Messiah, and the establish‑
ment of his kingdom on earth.

Prophecy, or the gospel under the covenant of the law, is
really older than the law, which was added afterwards and
came in between the promise and its fulfilment, between sin
and redemption, between the disease and the cure.[1] Prophecy
begins in paradise with the promise of the serpent-bruiser im‑
mediately after the fall. It predominates in the patriarchal
age, especially in the life of Abraham, whose piety has the
corresponding character of trust and faith ; and Moses, the
lawgiver, was at the same time a prophet pointing the people
to a greater successor.[2] Without the comfort of the Messianic
promise, the law must have driven the earnest soul to despair.
From the time of Samuel, some eleven centuries before Christ,
prophecy, hitherto sporadic, took an organized form in a per‑
manent prophetical office and order. In this form it accom‑
panied the Levitical priesthood and the Davidic dynasty down
to the Babylonish captivity, survived this catastrophe, and
directed the return of the people and the rebuilding of the
temple ; interpreting and applying the law, reproving abuses
in church and state, predicting the terrible judgments and the
redeeming grace of God, warning and punishing, comforting and
encouraging, with an ever plainer reference to the coming Mes‑
siah, who should redeem Israel and the world from sin and misery,
and establish a kingdom of peace and righteousness on earth.

The victorious reign of David and the peaceful reign of
Solomon furnish, for Isaiah and his successors, the historical
and typical ground for a prophetic picture of a far more glori‑
ous future, which, unless thus attached to living memories and
present circumstances, could not have been understood. The
subsequent catastrophe and the sufferings of the captivity

---

[1] Νόμος παρεισῆλθεν, came in besides, was added as an accessory arrange‑
ment, Rom. 5: 20; comp. προσετέθη, the law was "superadded" to the
promise given to Abraham, Gal. 3 : 19.

[2] Deut. 18 : 15.

served to develop the idea of a Messiah atoning for the sins of the people and entering through suffering into glory.

The prophetic was an extraordinary office, serving partly to complete, partly to correct the regular, hereditary priesthood, to prevent it from stiffening into monotonous formality, and keep it in living flow. The prophets were, so to speak, the Protestants of the ancient covenant, the ministers of the spirit and of immediate communion with God, in distinction from the ministers of the letter and of traditional and ceremonial mediation.

The flourishing period of our canonical prophecy began with the eighth century before Christ, some seven centuries after Moses, when Israel was suffering under Assyrian oppression. In this period before the captivity, Isaiah ("the salvation of God"), who appeared in the last years of king Uzziah, about ten years before the founding of Rome, is the leading figure; and around him Micah, Joel, and Obadiah in the kingdom of Judah, and Hosea, Amos, and Jonah in the kingdom of Israel, are grouped. Isaiah reached the highest elevation of prophecy, and unfolds feature by feature a picture of the Messiah— springing from the house of David, preaching the glad tidings to the poor, healing the broken-hearted, opening the eyes to the blind, setting at liberty the captives, offering himself as a lamb to the slaughter, bearing the sins of the people, dying the just for the unjust, triumphing over death and ruling as king of peace over all nations—a picture which came to its complete fulfilment in one person, and one only, Jesus of Nazareth. He makes the nearest approach to the cross, and his book is the Gospel of the Old Testament. In the period of the Babylonian exile, Jeremiah (i. e. "the Lord casts down") stands chief. He is the prophet of sorrow, and yet of the new covenant of the Spirit. In his denunciations of priests and false prophets, his lamentations over Jerusalem, his holy grief, his bitter persecution, he resembles the mission and life of Christ. He remained in the land of his fathers, and sang his lamentation on the ruins of Jerusalem; while Ezekiel warned the exiles on the river

Chebar against false prophets and carnal hopes, urged them to repentance, and depicted the new Jerusalem and the revival of the dry bones of the people by the breath of God; and Daniel at the court of Nebuchadnezzar in Babylon saw in the spirit the succession of the four empires and the final triumph of the eternal kingdom of the Son of Man. The prophets of the restoration are Haggai, Zechariah, and Malachi. With Malachi, who lived to the time of Nehemiah, the Old Testament prophecy ceased, and Israel was left to himself four hundred years, to digest during this period of expectation the rich substance of that revelation, and to prepare the birth-place for the approaching redemption.

3. Immediately before the advent of the Messiah the whole Old Testament, the law and the prophets, Moses and Isaiah together, reappeared for a short season embodied in John the Baptist, and then in unrivalled humility disappeared as the red dawn in the splendor of the rising sun of the new covenant. This remarkable man, earnestly preaching repentance in the wilderness and laying the axe at the root of the tree, and at the same time comforting with prophecy and pointing to the atoning Lamb of God, was indeed, as the immediate forerunner of the New Testament economy, and the personal friend of the heavenly Bridegroom, the greatest of them that were born of woman; yet in his official character as the representative of the ancient preparatory economy he stands lower than the least in that kingdom of Christ, which is infinitely more glorious than all its types and shadows in the past.

This is the Jewish religion, as it flowed from the fountain of divine revelation and lived in the true Israel, the spiritual children of Abraham, in John the Baptist, his parents and disciples, in the mother of Jesus, her kindred and friends, in the venerable Simeon, and the prophetess Anna, in Lazarus and his pious sisters, in the apostles and the first disciples, who embraced Jesus of Nazareth as the fulfiller of the law and the prophets, the Son of God and the Saviour of the world, and who were the first fruits of the Christian Church.

§ 11. Heathenism.

Literature.

I. Sources.

The works of the Greek and Roman Classics from Homer to Virgil and the age of the Antonines.

The monuments of Antiquity.

The writings of the early Christian Apologists, especially Justin Martyr: *Apologia* I. and II.; Tertullian: *Apologeticus;* Minucius Felix: *Octavius;* Eusebius: *Praeparatio Evangelica;* and Augustine (d. 430): *De Civitate Dei* (the first ten books).

II. Later Works.

Is. Vossius: *De theologia gentili et physiolog. Christ.* Frcf. 1675, 2 vols.

Creuzer (d. 1858): *Symbolik und Mythologie der alten Völker.* Leipz. 3d ed. 1837 sqq. 3 vols.

Tholuck (d. 1877): *Das Wesen und der sittliche Einfluss des Heidenthums, besonders unter den Griechen und Römern, mit Hinsicht auf das Christenthum.* Berlin, 1823. In Neander's *Denkwürdigkeiten,* vol. i. of the 1st ed. Afterwards separately printed. English translation by *Emerson* in "Am. Bibl. Repository" for 1832.

Tzschirner (d. 1828): *Der Fall des Heidenthums,* ed. by *Niedner.* Leipz. 1829, 1st vol.

O. Müller (d. 1840): *Prolegomena zu einer wissenschaftl. Mythologie.* Gött. 1825. Transl. into English by *J. Leitch.* Lond. 1844.

Hegel (d. 1831): *Philosophie der Religion.* Berl. 1837, 2 vols.

Stuhr: *Allgem. Gesch. der Religionsformen der heidnischen Völker.* Berl. 1836, 1837, 2 vols. (vol. 2d on the Hellenic Religion).

Hartung: *Die Religion der Römer.* Erl. 1836, 2 vols.

C. F. Nägelsbach: *Homerische Theologie.* Nürnb. 1840; 2d ed. 1861. The same: *Die nach-homerische Theologie des Griechischen Volksglaubens bis auf Alexander.* Nürnb. 1857.

Sepp (R. C.): *Das Heidenthum und dessen Bedeutung für das Christenthum.* Regensb. 1853, 3 vols.

Wuttke: *Geschichte des Heidenthums in Beziehung auf Religion, Wissen, Kunst, Sittlichkeit und Staatsleben.* Bresl. 1852 sqq. 2 vols.

Schelling (d. 1854): *Einleitung in die Philosophie der Mythologie.* Stuttg. 1856; and *Philosophie der Mythologie.* Stuttg. 1857.

Maurice (d. 1872): *The Religions of the World in their Relations to Christianity.* Lond. 1854 (reprinted in Boston).

Trench: *Hulsean Lectures* for 1845-'46. No. 2: *Christ the Desire of all Nations, or the Unconscious Prophecies of Heathendom* (a commentary on the star of the wise men, Matt. ii.). Cambr. 4th ed. 1854 (also Philad. 1850).

L. Preller: *Griechische Mythologie.* Berlin, 1854, 3d ed. 1875, 2 vols.

By the same ; *Römische Mythologie.* Berlin, 1858; 3d ed., by H. JORDAN, 1881–83, 2 vols.

M. W. HEFFTER : *Griech. und Röm. Mythologie.* Leipzig, 1854.

DÖLLINGER : *Heidenthum und Judenthum,* quoted in § 8.

C. SCHMIDT : *Essai historique sur la société civil dans le monde romain et sur sa transformation par le christianisme.* Paris, 1853.

C. G. SEIBERT : *Griechenthum und Christenthum, oder der Vorhof des Schönen und das Heiligthum der Wahrheit.* Barmen, 1857.

FR. FABRI : *Die Entstehung des Heidenthums und die Aufgabe der Heidenmission.* Barmen, 1859.

W. E. GLADSTONE (the English statesman) : *Studies on Homer and the Homeric Age.* Oxf. 1858, 3 vols. (vol. ii. Olympus ; or the Religion of the Homeric Age). The same : *Juventus Mundi : the Gods and Men of the Heroic Age.* 2d ed. Lond. 1870. (Embodies the results of the larger work, with several modifications in the ethnological and mythological portions.)

W. S. TYLER (Prof. in Amherst Coll., Mass.) : *The Theology of the Greek Poets.* Boston, 1867.

B. F. COCKER : *Christianity and Greek Philosophy ; or the Relation between Reflective Thought in Greece and the Positive Teaching of Christ and his Apostles.* N. York, 1870.

EDM. SPIESS : *Logos spermaticós. Parallelstellen zum N. Test. aus den Schriften der alten Griechen. Ein Beitrag zur christl. Apologetik und zur vergleichenden Religionsforschung.* Leipz. 1871.

G. BOISSIER : *La religion romaine d'Auguste aux Antonins.* Paris, 1884, 2 vols.

J. REVILLE : *La religion à Rome sous les Sévères.* Paris, 1886.

Comp. the histories of Greece by THIRLWALL, GROTE, and CURTIUS ; the histories of Rome by GIBBON, NIEBUHR, ARNOLD, MERIVALE, SCHWEGLER, IHNE, DURUY (transl. from the French by W. J. Clarke), and MOMMSEN. RANKE'S *Weltgeschichte.* Th. iii. 1882. SCHILLER'S *Gesch. der römischen Kaiserzeit.* 1882.

Heathenism is religion in its wild growth on the soil of fallen human nature, a darkening of the original consciousness of God, a deification of the rational and irrational creature, and a corresponding corruption of the moral sense, giving the sanction of religion to natural and unnatural vices.[1]

Even the religion of Greece, which, as an artistic product of the imagination, has been justly styled the religion of beauty, is deformed by this moral distortion. It utterly lacks the true conception of sin, and consequently the true conception of holiness. It regards sin, not as a perverseness of will and an

---

[1] Comp. Paul's picture of heathen immorality, Rom. 1 : 19–32.

offence against the gods, but as a folly of the understanding and an offence against men, often even proceeding from the gods themselves; for "Infatuation," or Moral Blindness (᾽Ατη), is a "daughter of Jove," and a goddess, though cast from Olympus, and the source of all mischief upon earth. Homer knows no devil, but he puts a devilish element into his deities. The Greek gods, and also the Roman gods, who were copied from the former, are mere men and women, in whom Homer and the popular faith saw and worshipped the weaknesses and vices of the Grecian character, as well as its virtues, in magnified forms. The gods are born, but never die. They have bodies and senses, like mortals, only in colossal proportions. They eat and drink, though only nectar and ambrosia. They are awake and fall asleep. They travel, but with the swiftness of thought. They mingle in battle. They cohabit with human beings, producing heroes or demigods. They are limited to time and space. Though sometimes honored with the attributes of omnipotence and omniscience, and called holy and just, yet they are subject to an iron fate (Moira), fall under delusion, and reproach each other with folly and crime. Their heavenly happiness is disturbed by all the troubles of earthly life. Even Zeus or Jupiter, the patriarch of the Olympian family, is cheated by his sister and wife Hera (Juno), with whom he had lived three hundred years in secret marriage before he proclaimed her his consort and queen of the gods, and is kept in ignorance of the events before Troy. He threatens his fellows with blows and death, and makes Olympus tremble when he shakes his locks in anger. The gentle Aphrodite or Venus bleeds from a spear-wound on her finger. Mars is felled with a stone by Diomedes. Neptune and Apollo have to serve for hire and are cheated. Hephaestus limps and provokes an uproarious laughter. The gods are involved by their marriages in perpetual jealousies and quarrels. They are full of envy and wrath, hatred and lust, prompt men to crime, and provoke each other to lying and cruelty, perjury and adultery. The Iliad and Odyssey, the most popular poems of the Hellenic genius, are a chronique scandaleuse of the gods. Hence Plato banished them from his ideal Republic. Pindar, Aeschylos, and Sophocles also rose to loftier ideas of the gods and breathed a purer moral atmosphere; but they represented the exceptional creed of a few, while Homer expressed the popular belief. Truly we have no cause to long with Schiller for the return of the "gods of Greece," but would rather join the poet in his joyful thanksgiving:

> " *Einen zu bereichern unter allen,*
> *Musste diese Götterwelt vergehn.*"

Notwithstanding this essential apostasy from truth and holiness, heathenism was religion, a groping after "the unknown God." By its superstition it betrayed the need of faith. Its polytheism rested on a dim monotheistic background; it subjected all the gods to Jupiter, and Jupiter himself to a mysterious fate. It had at bottom the feeling of dependence on higher powers and reverence for divine things. It preserved the memory of a golden age and of a fall. It had the voice of conscience, and a sense, obscure though it was, of guilt. It felt the need of reconciliation with deity, and sought that reconciliation by prayer, penance, and sacrifice. Many of its religious traditions and usages were faint echoes of the primal religion; and its mythological dreams of the mingling of the gods with men, of demigods, of Prometheus delivered by Hercules from his helpless sufferings, were unconscious prophecies and fleshly anticipations of Christian truths.

This alone explains the great readiness with which heathens embraced the gospel, to the shame of the Jews.[1]

There was a spiritual Israel scattered throughout the heathen world, that never received the circumcision of the flesh, but the unseen circumcision of the heart by the hand of that Spirit which bloweth where it listeth, and is not bound to any human laws and to ordinary means. The Old Testament furnishes several

---

[1] Comp. Matt. 8 : 10 ; 15 : 28.   Luke 7 : 9.   Acts 10 : 35.

examples of true piety outside of the visible communion with
the Jewish church, in the persons of Melchisedec, the friend
of Abraham, the royal priest, the type of Christ; Jethro, the
priest of Midian; Rahab, the Canaanite woman and hostess of
Joshua and Caleb; Ruth, the Moabitess and ancestress of our
Saviour; King Hiram, the friend of David; the queen of
Sheba, who came to admire the wisdom of Solomon; Naaman
the Syrian; and especially Job, the sublime sufferer, who rejoiced in the hope of his Redeemer.[1]

The elements of truth, morality, and piety scattered throughout ancient heathenism, may be ascribed to three sources. In
the first place, man, even in his fallen state, retains some traces
of the divine image, a knowledge of God,[2] however weak, a
moral sense or conscience,[3] and a longing for union with the
Godhead, for truth and for righteousness.[4] In this view we
may, with Tertullian, call the beautiful and true sentences of a
Socrates, a Plato, an Aristotle, of Pindar, Sophocles, Cicero, Virgil, Seneca, Plutarch, "the testimonies of a soul constitution-
ally Christian,"[5] of a nature predestined to Christianity. Secondly, some account must be made of traditions and recollections, however faint, coming down from the general primal
revelations to Adam and Noah. But the third and most important source of the heathen anticipations of truth is the all-
ruling providence of God, who has never left himself without a
witness. Particularly must we consider, with the ancient Greek
fathers, the influence of the divine Logos before his incarnation,[6]

---

[1] Even Augustine, exclusive as he was, adduces the case of Job in proof of
the assertion that the kingdom of God under the Old dispensation was not
confined to the Jews, and then adds: "*Divinitus autem provisum fuisse non
dubito, ut ex hoc uno sciremus, etiam per alias gentes esse potuisse, qui secundum Deum vixerunt, eique placuerunt, pertinentes ad spiritualem Hierusalem.*"
De Civit. Dei, xviii. 47.

[2] Rom. 1 : 19, τὸ γνωστὸν τοῦ θεοῦ. Comp. my annotations on Lange *in loc.*

[3] Rom. 2 : 14, 15. Comp. Lange *in loc.*

[4] Comp. Acts 17 : 23, 27, 28. and my remarks on the altar to the θεὸς ἄγνωστος
in the *History of the Apost. Church,* § 73, p. 269 sqq.

[5] *Testimonia animae naturaliter Christianae.*

[6] Λόγος ἄσαρκος, Λόγος σπερματικός.

who was the tutor of mankind, the original light of reason, shining in the darkness and lighting every man, the sower scattering
in the soil of heathendom the seeds of truth, beauty, and virtue.[1]

The flower of paganism, with which we are concerned here,
appears in the two great nations of classic antiquity, Greece and
Rome. With the language, morality, literature, and religion
of these nations, the apostles came directly into contact, and
through the whole first age the church moves on the basis of
these nationalities. These, together with the Jews, were the
chosen nations of the ancient world, and shared the earth
among them. The Jews were chosen for things eternal, to
keep the sanctuary of the true religion. The Greeks prepared
the elements of natural culture, of science and art, for the use
of the church. The Romans developed the idea of law, and
organized the civilized world in a universal empire, ready to
serve the spiritual universality of the gospel. Both Greeks and
Romans were unconscious servants of Jesus Christ, "the unknown God."

These three nations, by nature at bitter enmity among themselves, joined hands in the superscription on the cross, where
the holy name and the royal title of the Redeemer stood written, by the command of the heathen Pilate, "in Hebrew and
Greek and Latin."[2]

§ 12. *Grecian Literature, and the Roman Empire.*

The literature of the ancient Greeks and the universal empire of the Romans were, next to the Mosaic religion, the chief
agents in preparing the world for Christianity. They furnished the human forms, in which the divine substance of the
gospel, thoroughly prepared in the bosom of the Jewish theocracy, was moulded. They laid the natural foundation for the
supernatural edifice of the kingdom of heaven. God endowed
the Greeks and Romans with the richest natural gifts, that they

---

[1] Comp. John 1 : 4, 5, 9, 10.   [2] John 19 : 20.

might reach the highest civilization possible without the aid of Christianity, and thus both provide the instruments of human science, art, and law for the use of the church, and yet at the same time show the utter impotence of these alone to bless and save the world.

The GREEKS, few in number, like the Jews, but vastly more important in history than the numberless hordes of the Asiatic empires, were called to the noble task of bringing out, under a sunny sky and with a clear mind, the idea of humanity in its natural vigor and beauty, but also in its natural imperfection. They developed the principles of science and art. They liberated the mind from the dark powers of nature and the gloomy broodings of the eastern mysticism. They rose to the clear and free consciousness of manhood, boldly investigated the laws of nature and of spirit, and carried out the idea of beauty in all sorts of artistic forms. In poetry, sculpture, architecture, painting, philosophy, rhetoric, historiography, they left true master-pieces, which are to this day admired and studied as models of form and taste.

All these works became truly valuable and useful only in the hands of the Christian church, to which they ultimately fell. Greece gave the apostles the most copious and beautiful language to express the divine truth of the Gospel, and Providence had long before so ordered political movements as to spread that language over the world and to make it the organ of civilization and international intercourse, as the Latin was in the middle ages, as the French was in the eighteenth century, and as the English is coming to be in the nineteenth. "Greek," says Cicero, "is read in almost all nations; Latin is confined by its own narrow boundaries." Greek schoolmasters and artists followed the conquering legions of Rome to Gaul and Spain. The youthful hero Alexander the Great, a Macedonian indeed by birth, yet an enthusiastic admirer of Homer, an emulator of Achilles, a disciple of the philosophic world-conqueror, Aristotle, and thus the truest Greek of his age, conceived the sublime thought of making Babylon the seat of a Grecian empire

of the world; and though his empire fell to pieces at his untimely death, yet it had already carried Greek letters to the
borders of India, and made them a common possession of all
civilized nations.   What Alexander had begun Julius Cæsar
completed.   Under the protection of the Roman law the apostles could travel everywhere and make themselves understood
through the Greek language in every city of the Roman domain.

The Grecian philosophy, particularly the systems of Plato
and Aristotle, formed the natural basis for scientific theology ;
Grecian eloquence, for sacred oratory ; Grecian art, for that of
the Christian church.   Indeed, not a few ideas and maxims of
the classics tread on the threshold of revelation, and sound like
prophecies of Christian truth ; especially the spiritual soarings
of Plato,[1] the deep religious reflections of Plutarch,[2] the sometimes almost Pauline moral precepts of Seneca.[3]   To many of
the greatest church fathers, Justin Martyr, Clement of Alexandria, Origen, and in some measure even to Augustine, Greek
philosophy was a bridge to the Christian faith, a scientific
schoolmaster leading them to Christ.   Nay, the whole ancient
Greek church rose on the foundation of the Greek language
and nationality, and is inexplicable without them.

Here lies the real reason why the classical literature is to this
day made the basis of liberal education throughout the Christian world.   Youth are introduced to the elementary forms of
science and art, to models of clear, tasteful style, and to self-
made humanity at the summit of intellectual and artistic culture, and thus they are at the same time trained to the scientific
apprehension of the Christian religion, which appeared when

---

[1] Compare C. Ackermann, *The Christian Element in Plato and the Platonic
Philosophy*, 1835, transl. from the German by S. R. Asbury, *with an introductory note by Dr. Shedd.*   Edinburgh, 1861.

[2] As in his excellent treatise : *De sera numinis vindicta.*   It is strange that
this philosopher, whose moral sentiments come nearest to Christianity, never
alludes to it.   Epictetus and Marcus Aurelius do mention it, but only once.

[3] On the relation of Paul and Seneca comp. an elaborate dissertation of
Bishop Lightfoot in his *Commentary on the Philippians*, pp. 268–331 (3d ed.
1873).

the development of Greek and Roman civilization had reached its culmination and began already to decay. The Greek and Latin languages, as the Sanskrit and Hebrew, died in their youth and were embalmed and preserved from decay in the immortal works of the classics. They still furnish the best scientific terms for every branch of learning and art and every new invention. The primitive records of Christianity have been protected against the uncertainties of interpretation incident upon the constant changes of a living language.

But aside from the permanent value of the Grecian literature, the glory of its native land had, at the birth of Christ, already irrecoverably departed. Civil liberty and independence had been destroyed by internal discord and corruption. Philosophy had run down into skepticism and refined materialism. Art had been degraded to the service of levity and sensuality. Infidelity or superstition had supplanted sound religious sentiment. Dishonesty and licentiousness reigned among high and low.

This hopeless state of things could not but impress the more earnest and noble souls with the emptiness of all science and art, and the utter insufficiency of this natural culture to meet the deeper wants of the heart. It must fill them with longings for a new religion.

The ROMANS were the practical and political nation of antiquity. Their calling was to carry out the idea of the state and of civil law, and to unite the nations of the world in a colossal empire, stretching from the Euphrates to the Atlantic, and from the Libyan desert to the banks of the Rhine. This empire embraced the most fertile and civilized countries of Asia, Africa, and Europe, and about one hundred millions of human beings, perhaps one-third of the whole race at the time of the introduction of Christianity.[1] To this outward extent corre-

---

[1] Charles Merivale, in his *History of the Romans under the Empire* (Lond. 1856), vol. iv. p. 450 and 451, estimates the population of the Roman empire in the age of Augustus at 85 millions, namely, 40 millions for Europe, 28 millions for Asia, and 17 millions for Africa, but he does not include Palestine. Greswell and others raise the estimate of the whole population to 120 millions.

sponds its historical significance. The history of every ancient nation ends, says Niebuhr, as the history of every modern nation begins, in that of Rome. Its history has therefore a universal interest; it is a vast storehouse of the legacies of antiquity. If the Greeks had, of all nations, the deepest mind, and in literature even gave laws to their conquerors, the Romans had the strongest character, and were born to rule the world without. This difference of course reached even into the moral and religious life of the two nations. Was the Greek mythology the work of artistic fantasy and a religion of poesy, so was the Roman the work of calculation adapted to state purposes, political and utilitarian, but at the same time solemn, earnest, and energetic. "The Romans had no love of beauty, like the Greeks. They held no communion with nature, like the Germans. Their one idea was Rome—not ancient, fabulous, poetical Rome, but Rome warring and conquering; and *orbis terrarum domina. S. P. Q. R.* is inscribed on almost every page of their literature." [1]

The Romans from the first believed themselves called to govern the world. They looked upon all foreigners—not as barbarians, like the cultured Greeks, but—as enemies to be conquered and reduced to servitude. War and triumph were their highest conception of human glory and happiness. The

" Tu, regere imperio populos, Romane, memento !"

had been their motto, in fact, long before Virgil thus gave it form. The very name of the *urbs æterna*, and the characteristic legend of its founding, prophesied its future. In their greatest straits the Romans never for a moment despaired of the commonwealth. With vast energy, profound policy, unwavering consistency, and wolf-like rapacity, they pursued their ambitious schemes, and became indeed the lords, but also, as their greatest historian, Tacitus, says, the insatiable robbers of the world. [2]

[1] Hare, *Guesses at Truth*, p. 432 (Lond. ed. 1867).
[2] *Raptores orbis, quos non oriens, non occidens satiaverit.*

Having conquered the world by the sword, they organized it by law, before whose majesty every people had to bow, and beautified it by the arts of peace. Philosophy, eloquence, history, and poetry enjoyed a golden age under the setting sun of the republic and the rising sun of the empire, and extended their civilizing influence to the borders of barbarianism. Although not creative in letters and fine arts, the Roman authors were successful imitators of Greek philosophers, orators, historians, and poets. Rome was converted by Augustus from a city of brick huts into a city of marble palaces.[1] The finest paintings and sculptures were imported from Greece, triumphal arches and columns were erected on public places, and the treasures of all parts of the world were made tributary to the pride, beauty, and luxury of the capital. The provinces caught the spirit of improvement, populous cities sprung up, and the magnificent temple of Jerusalem was rebuilt by the ambitious extravagance of Herod. The rights of persons and property were well protected. The conquered nations, though often and justly complaining of the rapacity of provincial governors, yet, on the whole, enjoyed greater security against domestic feuds and foreign invasion, a larger share of social comfort, and rose to a higher degree of secular civilization. The ends of the empire were brought into military, commercial, and literary communication by carefully constructed roads, the traces of which still exist in Syria, on the Alps, on the banks of the Rhine. The facilities and security of travel were greater in the reign of the Cæsars than in any subsequent period before the nineteenth century. Five main lines went out from Rome to the extremities of the empire, and were connected at seaports with maritime routes. "We may travel," says a Roman writer, "at all hours, and sail from east to west." Merchants brought diamonds from the East, ambers from the shores of the Baltic, precious metals from Spain, wild animals from Africa, works of art from Greece, and every article of luxury, to the market

[1] So the nephew of the modern Cæsar transformed Paris into a city of straight and broad streets and magnificent palaces.

on the banks of the Tiber, as they now do to the banks of the Thames. The Apocalyptic seer, in his prophetic picture of the downfall of the imperial mistress of the world, gives prominence to her vast commerce: "And the merchants of the earth," he says, "weep and mourn over her; for no man buyeth their merchandise any more: merchandise of gold, and silver, and precious stone, and pearls, and fine linen, and purple, and silk, and scarlet; and all thyine wood, and every vessel of ivory, and every vessel made of most precious wood, and of brass, and iron, and marble; and cinnamon, and spice, and incense, and ointment, and frankincense, and wine, and oil, and fine flour, and wheat, and cattle, and sheep; and merchandise of horses and chariots and slaves; and souls of men. And the fruits that thy soul desired are departed from thee, and all things which were dainty and sumptuous are perished from thee, and men shall find them no more at all." [1]

Heathen Rome lived a good while after this prediction, but the causes of decay were already at work in the first century. The immense extension and outward prosperity brought with it a diminution of those domestic and civil virtues which at first so highly distinguished the Romans above the Greeks. The race of patriots and deliverers, who came from their ploughs to the public service, and humbly returned again to the plough or the kitchen, was extinct. Their worship of the gods, which was the root of their virtue, had sunk to mere form, running either into the most absurd superstitions, or giving place to unbelief, till the very priests laughed each other in the face when they met in the street. Not unfrequently we find unbelief and superstition united in the same persons, according to the maxim that all extremes touch each other. Man must believe something, and worship either God or the devil.[2]

---

[1] Rev. 18: 11–14.

[2] "Unbelief and superstition, different hues of the same historical phenomenon, went in the Roman world of that day hand in hand, and there was no lack of individuals who in themselves combined both—who denied the gods with Epicurus, and yet prayed and sacrificed before every shrine."

Magicians and necromancers abounded, and were liberally pat·
ronized. The ancient simplicity and contentment were exchanged for boundless avarice and prodigality. Morality and
chastity, so beautifully symbolized in the household ministry of
the virgin Vesta, yielded to vice and debauchery. Amusement
came to be sought in barbarous fights of beasts and gladiators,
which not rarely consumed twenty thousand human lives in a
single month. The lower classes had lost all nobler feeling,
cared for nothing but "*panem et circenses*," and made the
proud imperial city on the Tiber a slave of slaves. The huge
empire of Tiberius and of Nero was but a giant body without a
soul, going, with steps slow but sure, to final dissolution. Some
of the emperors were fiendish tyrants and monsters of iniquity ;
and yet they were enthroned among the gods by a vote of the
Senate, and altars and temples were erected for their worship.
This characteristic custom began with Cæsar, who even during
his lifetime was honored as "Divus Julius" for his brilliant
victories, although they cost more than a million of lives slain
and another million made captives and slaves.[1] The dark picture which St. Paul, in addressing the Romans, draws of the
heathenism of his day, is fully sustained by Seneca, Tacitus,

Theod. Mommsen, *History of Rome*, transl. by Dickson, Lond. 1867, vol. iv.
p. 560.
[1] " In the excess of their adoration, the Roman Senate desired even to place
his image in the Temple of Quirinus himself, with an inscription to him as
ϑεὸς ἀνίκητος, the invincible God. Golden chairs, gilt chariots, triumphal
robes, were piled one upon another, with laurelled fasces and laurelled
wreaths. His birthday was made a perpetual holiday, and the month Quinctilis was renamed, in honor of him, July. A temple to Concord was to be
erected in commemoration of his clemency. His person was declared sacred,
and to injure him by word or deed was to be counted sacrilege. The Fortune
of Cæsar was introduced into the constitutional oath, and the Senate took a
solemn pledge to maintain his acts inviolate. Finally, they arrived at a conclusion that he was not a man at all ; no longer Caius Julius, but Divus
Julius, a God or the Son of God. A temple was to be built to Cæsar as another Quirinus, and Antony was to be his priest." J. A. Froude, *Cæsar*
(1879), Ch. XXVI. p. 491. The insincerity of these adulations shortly before
the senatorial conspiracy makes them all the worse. " One obsequious senator proposed that every woman in Rome should be at the disposition of
Cæsar." *Ibid.*, p 492.

Juvenal, Persius, and other heathen writers of that age, and shows the absolute need of redemption. "The world," says Seneca, in a famous passage, "is full of crimes and vices. More are committed than can be cured by force. There is an immense struggle for iniquity. Crimes are no longer hidden, but open before the eyes. Innocence is not only rare, but nowhere." [1]

Thus far the negative. On the other hand, the universal empire of Rome was a positive groundwork for the universal empire of the gospel. It served as a crucible, in which all contradictory and irreconcilable peculiarities of the ancient nations and religions were dissolved into the chaos of a new creation. The Roman legions razed the partition-walls among the ancient nations, brought the extremes of the civilized world together in free intercourse, and united north and south and east and west in the bonds of a common language and culture, of common laws and customs. Thus they evidently, though unconsciously, opened the way for the rapid and general spread of that religion which unites all nations in one family of God by the spiritual bond of faith and love.

The idea of a common humanity, which underlies all the distinctions of race, society and education, began to dawn in the heathen mind, and found expression in the famous line of Terentius, which was received with applause in the theatre:

> "*Homo sum: humani nihil a me alienum puto.*"

This spirit of humanity breathes in Cicero and Virgil. Hence the veneration paid to the poet of the Æneid by the fathers and throughout the middle ages. Augustine calls him the noblest of poets, and Dante, "the glory and light of other poets," and "his master," who guided him through the regions of hell and purgatory to the very gates of Paradise. It was believed that in his fourth Eclogue he had prophesied the advent of Christ. This interpretation is erroneous; but "there is in

[1] *De Ira*, II. 8.

Virgil," says an accomplished scholar,[1] " a vein of thought and sentiment more devout, more humane, more akin to the Christian, than is to be found in any other ancient poet, whether Greek or Roman. He was a spirit prepared and waiting, though he knew it not, for some better thing to be revealed."

The civil laws and institutions, also, and the great administrative wisdom of Rome did much for the outward organization of the Christian church. As the Greek church rose on the basis of the Grecian nationality, so the Latin church rose on that of ancient Rome, and reproduced in higher forms both its virtues and its defects. Roman Catholicism is pagan Rome baptized, a Christian reproduction of the universal empire seated of old in the city of the seven hills.

§ 13. *Judaism and Heathenism in Contact.*

The Roman empire, though directly establishing no more than an outward political union, still promoted indirectly a mutual intellectual and moral approach of the hostile religions of the Jews and Gentiles, who were to be reconciled in one divine brotherhood by the supernatural power of the cross of Christ.

1. The Jews, since the Babylonish captivity, had been scattered over all the world. They were as ubiquitous in the Roman empire in the first century as they are now throughout Christendom. According to Josephus and Strabo, there was no country where they did not make up a part of the population.[2]

---

[1] Principal Shairp, in an article on " Virgil as a Precursor of Christianity," in the " Princeton Review" for Sept., 1879, pp. 403–420. Comp. the learned essay of Professor Piper, in Berlin, on "Virgil als Theologe und Prophet," in his " Evang. Kalender " for 1862.

[2] Jos., *Bell. Jud.*, VII. c. 3, § 3 : " As the Jewish nation is widely dispersed over all the habitable earth," etc. *Antiqu.*, XIV. 7, 2 : " Let no one wonder that there was so much wealth in our temple, since all the Jews throughout the habitable earth, and those that worship God, nay, even those of Asia and Europe, sent their contributions to it." Then, quoting from Strabo, he says : " These Jews are already gotten into all cities, and it is hard to find a

Among the witnesses of the miracle of Pentecost were " Jews
from every nation under heaven . . . Parthians and Medes
and Elamites, and the dwellers of Mesopotamia, in Judæa and
Cappadocia, in Pontus and Asia, in Phrygia and Pamphylia, in
Egypt and the parts of Libya about Cyrene, and sojourners
from Rome, both Jews and proselytes, Cretans and Arabians." [1]
In spite of the antipathy of the Gentiles, they had, by talent
and industry, risen to wealth, influence, and every privilege,
and had built their synagogues in all the commercial cities of
the Roman empire.   Pompey brought a considerable number
of Jewish captives from Jerusalem to the capital (B.C. 63), and
settled them on the right bank of the Tiber (Trastevere).   By
establishing this community he furnished, without knowing it,
the chief material for the Roman church.   Julius Cæsar was
the great protector of the Jews ; and they showed their gratitude by collecting for many nights to lament his death on the
forum where his murdered body was burnt on a funeral pile.[2]
He granted them the liberty of public worship, and thus
gave them a legal status as a religious society.   Augustus
confirmed these privileges.   Under his reign they were numbered already by thousands in the city.   A reaction followed ;
Tiberius and Claudius expelled them from Rome ; but they
soon returned, and succeeded in securing the free exercise of
their rites and customs.   The frequent satirical allusions to them
prove their influence as well as the aversion and contempt in
which they were held by the Romans.   Their petitions reached
the ear of Nero through his wife Poppæa, who seems to have
inclined to their faith ; and Josephus, their most distinguished
scholar, enjoyed the favor of three emperors—Vespasian, Titus,
and Domitian.   In the language of Seneca (as quoted by Augustin) "the conquered Jews gave laws to their Roman conquerors."

place in the habitable earth that has not admitted this tribe of men, and is
not possessed by it ; and it has come to pass that Egypt and Cyrene . . .
and a great number of other nations imitate their way of living, and maintain
great bodies of these Jews in a peculiar manner, and grow up to greater prosperity with them, and make use also of the same laws with that nation."

[1] Acts 2 : 5, 9–11.   [2] Sueton., *Cæs.*, c. 84.

By this dispersion of the Jews the seeds of the knowledge of the true God and the Messianic hope were sown in the field of the idolatrous world. The Old Testament Scriptures were translated into Greek two centuries before Christ, and were read and expounded in the public worship of God, which was open to all. Every synagogue was a mission-station of monotheism, and furnished the apostles an admirable place and a natural introduction for their preaching of Jesus Christ as the fulfiller of the law and the prophets.

Then, as the heathen religions had been hopelessly undermined by skeptical philosophy and popular infidelity, many earnest Gentiles, especially multitudes of women, came over to Judaism either wholly or in part. The thorough converts, called "proselytes of righteousness," [1] were commonly still more bigoted and fanatical than the native Jews. The half-converts, "proselytes of the gate" [2] or "fearers of God," [3] who adopted only the monotheism, the principal moral laws, and the Messianic hopes of the Jews, without being circumcised, appear in the New Testament as the most susceptible hearers of the gospel, and formed the nucleus of many of the first Christian churches. Of this class were the centurion of Capernaum, Cornelius of Cæsarea, Lydia of Philippi, Timothy, and many other prominent disciples.

2. On the other hand, the Græco-Roman heathenism, through its language, philosophy, and literature, exerted no inconsiderable influence to soften the fanatical bigotry of the higher and more cultivated classes of the Jews. Generally the Jews of the dispersion, who spoke the Greek language—the "Hellenists," as they were called—were much more liberal than the proper "Hebrews," or Palestinian Jews, who kept their mother tongue. This is evident in the Gentile missionaries, Barnabas of Cyprus and Paul of Tarsus, and in the whole church of Antioch, in contrast with that at Jerusalem. The Hellenistic form of Christianity was the natural bridge to the Gentile.

---

[1] גֵּרֵי הַצֶּדֶק.   [2] גֵּרֵי הַשַּׁעַר, Ex. 20: 10; Deut. 5: 14.

[3] Οἱ εὐσεβεῖς, οἱ φοβούμενοι τὸν θεόν, Acts 10: 2; 13: 16, etc., and Josephus.

The most remarkable example of a transitional, though very
fantastic and Gnostic-like combination of Jewish and heathen
elements meets us in the educated circles of the Egyptian metropolis, Alexandria, and in the system of PHILO, who was born
about B.C. 20, and lived till after A.D. 40, though he never
came in contact with Christ or the apostles. This Jewish
divine sought to harmonize the religion of Moses with the
philosophy of Plato by the help of an ingenious but arbitrary
allegorical interpretation of the Old Testament; and from the
books of Proverbs and of Wisdom he deduced a doctrine of the
Logos so strikingly like that of John's Gospel, that many expositors think it necessary to impute to the apostle an acquaintance with the writings, or at least with the terminology
of Philo. But Philo's speculation is to the apostle's "Word
made flesh" as a shadow to the body, or a dream to the reality.
He leaves no room for an incarnation, but the coincidence of
his speculation with the great fact is very remarkable.[1]

The THERAPEUTÆ, or Worshippers, a mystic and ascetic sect
in Egypt, akin to the Essenes in Judæa, carried this Platonic
Judaism into practical life; but were, of course, equally unsuccessful in uniting the two religions in a vital and permanent
way. Such a union could only be effected by a new religion
revealed from Heaven.[2]

Quite independent of the philosophical Judaism of Alexandria were the SAMARITANS, a mixed race, which also combined,
though in a different way, the elements of Jewish and Gentile
religion.[3] They date from the period of the exile. They held

---

[1] The system of Philo has been very thoroughly investigated, both independently, and in connection with John's Logos-doctrine, by Grossmann
(1829), Gfrörer (1831), Dähne (1834), Lücke, Baur, Zeller, Dorner, Ueberweg,
Ewald, J. G. Müller (*Die Messian. Erwartungen des Juden Philo*, Basel,
1870), Keim, Lipsius, Hausrath, Schürer, etc. See the literature in Schürer,
N. T. Zeitgesch., p. 648.

[2] P. E. LUCIUS: *Die Therapeuten und ihre Stellung in der Geschichte der
Askese.* Strassburg, 1880.

[3] A remnant of the Samaritans (about 140 souls) still live in Nablous, the
ancient Shechem, occupy a special quarter, have a synagogue of their own,
with a very ancient copy of the Pentateuch, and celebrate annually on the

to the Pentateuch, to circumcision, and to carnal Messianic hopes; but they had a temple of their own on Mount Gerizim, and mortally hated the proper Jews.   Among these Christianity, as would appear from the interview of Jesus with the woman of Samaria,[1] and the preaching of Philip,[2] found ready access, but, as among the Essenes and Therapeutæ, fell easily into a heretical form.   Simon Magus, for example, and some other Samaritan arch-heretics, are represented by the early Christian writers as the principal originators of Gnosticism.

3. Thus was the way for Christianity prepared on every side, positively and negatively, directly and indirectly, in theory and in practice, by truth and by error, by false belief and by unbelief—those hostile brothers, which yet cannot live apart—by Jewish religion, by Grecian culture, and by Roman conquest; by the vainly attempted amalgamation of Jewish and heathen thought, by the exposed impotence of natural civilization, philosophy, art, and political power, by the decay of the old religions, by the universal distraction and hopeless misery of the age, and by the yearnings of all earnest and noble souls for the religion of salvation.

" In the fulness of the time," when the fairest flowers of science and art had withered, and the world was on the verge of despair, the Virgin's Son was born to heal the infirmities of mankind.   Christ entered a dying world as the author of a new and imperishable life.

---

top of Mount Gerizim the Jewish Passover, Pentecost, and Feast of Tabernacles.   It is the only spot on earth where the paschal sacrifice is perpetuated according to the Mosaic prescription in the twelfth chapter of Exodus.   See Schaff, *Through Bible Lands* (N. York and Lond. 1878), pp. 314 sqq. ; and Hausrath, *l.c.* I. 17 sqq.

[1] John 4.   [2] Acts 8.

CHAPTER II.

JESUS CHRIST.

§ 14. *Sources and Literature.*

A. SOURCES.

Christ himself wrote nothing, but furnished endless material for books
and songs of gratitude and praise. The living Church of the redeemed is his book. He founded a religion of the living spirit, not
of a written code, like the Mosaic law. (His letter to King Abgarus
of Edessa, in Euseb., *Hist. Eccl.*, I. 13, is a worthless fabrication.)
Yet his words and deeds are recorded by as honest and reliable witnesses as ever put pen to paper.

I. Authentic Christian Sources.

(1) The four CANONICAL GOSPELS. Whatever their origin and date, they
exhibit essentially the same divine-human life and character of
Christ, which stands out in sharp contrast with the fictitious Christ
of the Apocryphal Gospels, and cannot possibly have been invented,
least of all by illiterate Galileans. They would never have thought
of writing books without the inspiration of their Master.

(2) The ACTS OF LUKE, the APOSTOLIC EPISTLES, and the APOCALYPSE OF
JOHN. They presuppose, independently of the written Gospels,
the main facts of the gospel-history, especially the crucifixion and
the resurrection, and abound in allusions to these facts. Four of
the Pauline Epistles (Romans, 1 and 2 Corinthians, Galatians) are
admitted as genuine by the most extreme of liberal critics (Baur
and the Tübingen School), and from them alone a great part of the
life of Christ might be reconstructed. (See the admissions of Keim,
Gesch. Jesu v. Naz., I. 35 sqq.)

II. The APOCRYPHAL GOSPELS are very numerous (about 50), some of
them only known by name, others in fragments, and date from the
second and later centuries. They are partly heretical (Gnostic and
Ebionite) perversions or mutilations of the real history, partly innocent compositions of fancy, or religious novels intended to link together the disconnected periods of Christ's biography, to satisfy the
curiosity concerning his relations, his childhood, his last days, and
to promote the glorification of the Virgin Mary. They may be

divided into four classes : (1) Heretical Gospels (as the *Evangelium Cerinthi, Ev. Marcionis, Ev. Judae Ischariotae, Ev. secundum Hebraeos,* etc.) ; (2) Gospels of Joseph and Mary, and the birth of Christ (*Protevangelium Jacobi, Evang. Pseudo-Mathaei sive liber de Ortu Beatae Mariae et Infantia Salvatoris, Evang. de Nativitate Mariae, Historia Josephi Fabri lignarii,* etc.) ; (3) Gospels of the childhood of Jesus from the flight to Egypt till his eighth or twelfth year (*Evang. Thomae,* of Gnostic origin, *Evang. Infantiae Arabicum,* etc.) ; (4) Gospels of the passion and the mysterious triduum in Hades (*Evang. Nicodemi,* including the *Gesta* or *Acta Pilati* and the *Descensus ad Inferos, Epistola Pilati,* a report of Christ's passion to the emperor Tiberius, *Paradosis Pilati, Epistolae Herodis ad Pilatum* and *Pilati ad Herodem, Responsum Tiberii ad Pilatum, Narratio Josephi Arimathiensis,* etc.). It is quite probable that Pilate sent an account of the trial and crucifixion of Jesus to his master in Rome (as Justin Martyr and Tertullian confidentially assert), but the various documents bearing his name are obviously spurious, including the one recently published by Geo. Sluter (*The Acta Pilati,* Shelbyville, Ind. 1879), who professes to give a translation from the supposed authentic Latin copy in the Vatican Library.

These apocryphal productions have no historical, but considerable apologetic value ; for they furnish by their contrast with the genuine Gospels a very strong negative testimony to the historical truthfulness of the Evangelists, as a shadow presupposes the light, a counterfeit the real coin, and a caricature the original picture. They have contributed largely to mediæval art (e. g., the ox and the ass in the history of the nativity), and to the traditional Mariology and Mariolatry of the Greek and Roman churches, and have supplied Mohammed with his scanty knowledge of Jesus and Mary.

See the collections of the apocryphal Gospels by FABRICIUS (*Codex Apocryphus Novi Testamenti,* Hamburg, 1703, 2d ed. 1719), THILO (*Cod. Apocr. N. Ti.,* Lips. 1832), TISCHENDORF (*Evangelia Apocrypha,* Lips. 1853), W. WRIGHT (*Contributions to the Apocr. Lit. of the N. T. from Syrian MSS. in the British Museum,* Lond. 1865), B. HARRIS COWPER (*The Apocryphal Gospels, translated,* London, 1867), and ALEX. WALKER (Engl. transl. in Roberts & Donaldson's "Ante-Nicene Library," vol. xvi., Edinb. 1870 ; vol. viii. of Am. ed., N. Y. 1886).

Comp. the dissertations of TISCHENDORF : *De Evang. apocr. origine et usu* (Hagae, 1851), and *Pilati circa Christum judicio quid lucis offeratur ex Actis Pilati* (Lips. 1855). RUD. HOFMANN : *Das Leben Jesu nach den Apokryphen* (Leipz. 1851), and his art., *Apokryphen des N. T.,* in Herzog & Plitt, "R. Encykl.," vol. i. (1877), p. 511. G. BRUNET : *Les évangiles apocryphes,* Paris, 1863. MICHEL NICOLAS : *Études sur les évangiles apocryphes,* Paris, 1866. LIPSIUS : *Die Pilatus-Acten,* Kiel, 1871 ; *Die edessenische Abgar-Sage,* 1880 ; GOSPELS, APOCR., in Smith & Wace, I. 700 sqq. ; HOLTZMANN : *Einl. in's N. T.,* pp. 534–'54.

III. Jewish Sources.

The O. Test. Scriptures are, in type and prophecy, a preparatory history of Christ, and become fully intelligible only in Him who came "to fulfill the law and the prophets."

The Apocryphal and post-Christian Jewish writings give us a full view of the outward framework of society and religion in which the life of Christ moved, and in this way they illustrate and confirm the Gospel accounts.

IV. The famous testimony of the Jewish historian JOSEPHUS (d. after A.D. 103) deserves special consideration. In his *Antiqu. Jud.*, l. xviii. cap. 3, § 3, he gives the following striking summary of the life of Jesus :

"Now there rose about this time Jesus, a wise man, if it be lawful to call him a man ; for he was a doer of wonderful works (παραδόξων ἔργων ποιητής), a teacher of such men as receive the truth with gladness. He carried away with him many of the Jews and also many of the Greeks. He was the Christ (ὁ Χριστὸς οὗτος ἦν). And after Pilate, at the suggestion of the principal men among us, had condemned him to the cross, his first adherents did not forsake him. For he appeared to them alive again the third day (ἐφάνη γὰρ αὐτοῖς τρίτην ἔχων ἡμέραν πάλιν ζῶν) ; the divine prophets having foretold these and ten thousand other wonderful things (ἄλλα μυρία 3αυμάσια) concerning him. And the tribe of those called Christians, after him, is not extinct to this day."

This testimony is first quoted by Eusebius, twice, without a misgiving (*Hist. Eccl.*, I. 11 ; and *Demonstr. Evang.*, III. 5), and was considered genuine down to the 16th century, but has been disputed ever since. We have added the most doubtful words in Greek.

The following are the arguments for the genuineness :

(1) The testimony is found in all the MSS. of Josephus.

But these MSS. were written by Christians, and we have none older than from the 11th century.

(2) It agrees with the style of Josephus.

(3) It is extremely improbable that Josephus, in writing a history of the Jews coming down to A.D. 66, should have ignored Jesus ; all the more since he makes favorable mention of John the Baptist (*Antiqu.*, XVIII. 5, 2), and of the martyrdom of James "the Brother of Jesus called the Christ" (*Antiqu.*, XX. 9, 1 : τὸν ἀδελφὸν Ἰησοῦ τοῦ λεγομένου Χριστοῦ, Ἰάκωβος ὄνομα αὐτῷ). Both passages are generally accepted as genuine, unless the words τοῦ λεγομένου Χριστοῦ should be an interpolation.

Against this may be said that Josephus may have had prudential reasons for ignoring Christianity altogether.

Arguments against the genuineness :

(1) The passage interrupts the connection.

But not necessarily. Josephus had just recorded a calamity which befell the Jews under Pontius Pilate, in consequence of a sedition, and he may have regarded the crucifixion of Jesus as an additional calamity. He then goes on (§ 4 and 5) to record another calamity, the expulsion of the Jews from Rome under Tiberius.

(2) It betrays a Christian, and is utterly inconsistent with the known profession of Josephus as a Jewish priest of the sect of the Pharisees. We would rather expect him to have represented Jesus as an impostor, or as an enthusiast.

But it may be urged, on the other hand, that Josephus, with all his great literary merits, is also known as a vain and utterly un-principled man, as a renegade and sycophant who glorified and betrayed his nation, who served as a Jewish general in the revolt against Rome, and then, after having been taken prisoner, flattered the Roman conquerors, by whom he was richly rewarded. History furnishes many examples of similar inconsistencies. Remember Pontius Pilate who regarded Christ as innocent, and yet condemned him to death, the striking testimonies of Rousseau and Napoleon I. to the divinity of Christ, and also the concessions of Renan, which contradict his position.

(3) It is strange that the testimony should not have been quoted by such men as Justin Martyr, Clement of Alexandria, Tertullian, or any other writer before Eusebius (d. 340), especially by Origen, who expressly refers to the passages of Josephus on John the Baptist and James (*Contra Cels.*, I. 35, 47). Even Chrysostom (d. 407), who repeatedly mentions Josephus, seems to have been ignorant of this testimony.

In view of these conflicting reasons, there are different opinions:

(1) The passage is entirely genuine. This old view is defended by Hauteville, Oberthür, Bretschneider, Böhmert, Whiston, Schoedel (1840), Böttger (*Das Zeugniss des Jos.*, Dresden, 1865).

(2) It is wholly interpolated by a Christian hand. Bekker (in his ed. of Jos., 1855), Hase (1865 and 1876), Keim (1867), Schürer (1874).

(3) It is partly genuine, partly interpolated. Josephus probably wrote Χριστὸς οὗτος ἐλέγετο (as in the passage on James), but not ἦν, and all other Christian sentences were added by a transcriber before Eusebius, for apologetic purposes. So Paulus, Heinichen, Gieseler (I. § 24, p. 81, 4th Germ. ed.), Weizsäcker, Renan, Farrar. In the introduction to his *Vie de Jésus* (p. xii.), Renan says: "*Je crois le passage sur Jésus authentique. Il est parfaitement dans le goût de Joseph, et si cet historien a fait mention de Jésus, c'est bien comme cela qu'il a dû en parler. On sent seulement qu'une main chrétienne a retouché le morceau, y a ajouté quelques mots sans lesquels il eût été presque blasphématoire, a peut-être retranché ou modifié quelques ex-pressions.*"

(4) It is radically changed from a Jewish calumny into its present Christian form. Josephus originally described Jesus as a pseudo-Messiah, a magician, and seducer of the people, who was justly crucified. So Paret and Ewald (*Gesch. Christus'*, p. 183, 3d ed.).

It is difficult to resist the conclusion that Josephus must have taken some notice of the greatest event in Jewish history (as he certainly did of John the Baptist and of James), but that his statement—whether non-committal or hostile—was skilfully enlarged or altered by a Christian hand, and thereby deprived of its historical value.

In other respects, the writings of Josephus contain, indirectly, much valuable testimony to the truth of the gospel history. His *History of the Jewish War* is undesignedly a striking commentary on the predictions of our Saviour concerning the destruction of the city and the temple of Jerusalem ; the great distress and affliction of the Jewish people at that time ; the famine, pestilence, and earthquake ; the rise of false prophets and impostors, and the flight of his disciples at the approach of these calamities. All these coincidences have been traced out in full by the learned Dr. Lardner, in his *Collection of Ancient Jewish and Heathen Testimonies to the Truth of the Christian Religion*, first published 1764–'67, also in vol. vi. of his *Works*, ed. by Kippis, Lond. 1838.

V. Heathen testimonies are few and meagre. This fact must be accounted for by the mysterious origin, the short duration and the unworldly character of the life and work of Christ, which was exclusively devoted to the kingdom of heaven, and was enacted in a retired country and among a people despised by the proud Greeks and Romans.

The oldest heathen testimony is probably in the Syriac letter of MARA, a philosopher, to his son Serapion, about A.D. 74, first published by Cureton, in *Spicilegium Syriacum*, Lond. 1855, and translated by Pratten in the "Ante-Nicene Library," Edinb. vol. xxiv. (1872), 104–114. Here Christ is compared to Socrates and Pythagoras, and called "the wise king of the Jews," who were justly punished for murdering him. Ewald (*l. c.* p. 180) calls this testimony "very remarkable for its simplicity and originality as well as its antiquity."

Roman authors of the 1st and 2d centuries make only brief and incidental mention of Christ as the founder of the Christian religion, and of his crucifixion under Pontius Pilate, in the reign of Tiberius. TACITUS, *Annales*, l. xv. cap. 44, notices him in connection with his account of the conflagration at Rome and the Neronian persecution, in the words : " *Auctor nominis ejus [Christiani] Christus Tiberio imperitante per procuratorem Pontium Pilatum supplicio affectus erat,*" and calls the Christian religion an *exitiabilis superstitio.* Comp. his equally contemptuous misrepresentation of the Jews in *Hist.*, v. c. 3–5. Other

notices are found in SUETONIUS : *Vita Claudii*, c. 25 ; *Vita Neronis*, c.
16 ; PLINIUS, jun. : *Epist.*, X. 97, 98 ; LUCIAN : *De morte Peregr.*, c.
11 ; LAMPRIDIUS : *Vita Alexandri Severi*, c. 29, 43.
The heathen opponents of Christianity, LUCIAN, CELSUS, PORPHYRY,
JULIAN the APOSTATE, etc., presuppose the principal facts of the gospel-history, even the miracles of Jesus, but they mostly derive them,
like the Jewish adversaries, from evil spirits. Comp. my book on
the *Person of Christ*, Appendix, and Dr. NATH. LARDNER's *Credibility*, and *Collection of Testimonies*.

B. BIOGRAPHICAL AND CRITICAL.

The numerous Harmonies of the Gospels began already A.D. 170, with
TATIAN's τὸ διὰ τεσσάρων (on which Ephraem Syrus, in the fourth
century, wrote a commentary, published in Latin from an Armenian
version in the Armenian convent at Venice, 1876). The first biographies of Christ were ascetic or poetic, and partly legendary. See
Hase, *Leben Jesu*, § 17–19. The critical period began with the infidel and infamous attacks of Reimarus, Bahrdt, and Venturini, and
the noble apologetic works of Hess, Herder, and Reinhard. But a
still greater activity was stimulated by the *Leben Jesu* of Strauss, 1835,
and again by Renan's *Vie de Jésus*, 1863.

J. J. HESS (Antistes at Zürich, d. 1828) : *Lebensgeschichte Jesu*. Zürich,
1774 ; 8th ed. 1823, 3 vols. Translated into Dutch and Danish. He
introduced the psychological and pragmatic treatment.

F. V. REINHARD (d. 1812) : *Versuch über den Plan Jesu*. Wittenberg,
1781 ; 5th ed. by *Heubner*, 1830. English translation, N. York, 1831.
Reinhard proved the originality and superiority of the plan of Christ
above all the conceptions of previous sages and benefactors of the
race.

J. G. HERDER (d. 1803) : *Vom Erlöser der Menschen nach unsern 3 ersten
Evang.* Riga, 1796. The same : *Von Gottes Sohn, der Welt Heiland,
nach Joh. Evang.* Riga, 1797.

H. E. G. PAULUS (Prof. in Heidelberg, d. 1851) : *Leben Jesu als Grundlage einer reinen Geschichte des Urchristenthums.* Heidelb. 1828, 2
vols. Represents the " vulgar " rationalism, superseded afterwards
by the speculative rationalism of Strauss.

C. ULLMANN (d. 1865) : *Die Sündlosigkeit Jesu*. Hamb. 1828 ; 7th ed.
1864. Eng. translation (of 7th ed.) by *Sophia Taylor*, Edinb. 1870.
The best work on the sinlessness of Jesus. Comp. also his essay
(against Strauss), *Historisch oder Mythisch?* Gotha, 1838.

KARL HASE : *Das Leben Jesu*. Leipz. 1829 ; 5th ed. 1865. The same :
Geschichte Jesu. Leipz. 1876.

SCHLEIERMACHER (d. 1834) : *Vorlesungen über das Leben Jesu, herausgeg. von
Rütenik.* Berlin, 1864. The lectures were delivered 1832, and published from imperfect manuscripts. " Eine Stimme aus vergangenen

Tagen." Comp. the critique of D. F. Strauss in *Der Christus des Glaubens und der Jesus der Geschichte*. Berlin, 1865.

D. F. STRAUSS (d. 1874) : *Das Leben Jesu kritisch bearbeitet*. Tübingen, 1835–'36 ; 4th ed. 1840, 2 vols. French transl. by *Emile Littré,* Par. 1856 (2d ed.) ; Engl. transl. by Miss *Marian Evans* (better known under the assumed name *George Eliot*), Lond. 1846, in 3 vols., republ. in N. York, 1850. The same : *Das Leben Jesu für das deutsche Volk bearbeitet*. Leipz. 1864 ; 3d ed. 1875. In both these famous works Strauss represents the mythical theory. It has been popularized in the third volume of *The Bible for Learners* by OORT and HOOYKAAS, Engl. transl., Boston ed. 1879.

A. NEANDER (d. 1850) : *Das Leben Jesu*. Hamb. 1837 ; 5th ed. 1852. A positive refutation of Strauss. The same in English by *McClintock and Blumenthal*, N. York, 1848.

JOH. NEP. SEPP (R. C.) : *Das Leben Jesu Christi*. Regensb. 1843 sqq. ; 2d ed. 1865, 6 vols. Much legendary matter.

JORDAN BUCHER (R. C.) : *Das Leben Jesu Christi*. Stuttgart, 1859.

A. EBRARD : *Wissenschaftliche Kritik der evangelischen Geschichte*. Erl. 1842 ; 3d ed. 1868. Against Strauss, Bruno Bauer, etc. Condensed English translation, Edinb. 1869.

J. P. LANGE : *Das Leben Jesu*. Heidelb. 1844–'47, 3 parts in 5 vols. Engl. transl. by *Marcus Dods* and others, in 6 vols., Edinb. 1864. Rich and suggestive.

J. J. VAN OOSTERZEE : *Leven van Jesus*. First publ. in 1846–'51, 3 vols. ; 2d ed. 1863–'65. Comp. his *Christologie*, Rotterdam, 1855–'61, 3 vols., which describe the Son of God before his incarnation, the Son of God in the flesh, and the Son of God in glory. The third part is translated into German by *F. Meyering : Das Bild Christi nach der Schrift*, Hamburg, 1864.

CHR. FR. SCHMID : *Biblische Theologie des N. Testaments*. Ed. by *Weizsäcker*. Stuttgart, 1853 (3d ed. 1854), 2 vols. The first volume contains the life and doctrine of Christ. The English translation by *G. H. Venables* (Edinb. 1870) is an abridgment.

H. EWALD : *Geschichte Christus' und seiner Zeit*. Gött. 1854 ; 3d ed. 1867 (vol. v. of his Hist. of Israel). Transl. into Engl. by *O. Glover*, Cambridge, 1865.

J. YOUNG : *The Christ of History*. Lond. and N. York, 1855. 5th ed., 1868.

P. LICHTENSTEIN : *Lebensgeschichte Jesu in chronolog. Uebersicht*. Erlangen, 1856.

C. J. RIGGENBACH : *Vorlesungen über das Leben Jesu*. Basel, 1858.

M. BAUMGARTEN : *Die Geschichte Jesu für das Verständniss der Gegenwart*. Braunschweig, 1859.

W. F. GESS : *Christi Person und Werk nach Christi Selbstzeugniss und den Zeugnissen der Apostel*. Basel, 1878, in several parts. (This supersedes his first work on the same subject, publ. 1856.)

HORACE BUSHNELL (d. 1878): *The Character of Jesus: forbidding his possible classification with men.* N. York, 1861. (A reprint of the tenth chapter of his work on "Nature and the Supernatural," N. York, 1859.) It is the best and most useful product of his genius.

C. J. ELLICOTT (Bishop): *Historical Lectures on the Life of our Lord Jesus Christ, being the Hulsean Lect. for* 1859. 5th ed. Lond. 1869; republ. in Boston, 1862.

SAMUEL J. ANDREWS: *The Life of our Lord upon the earth, considered in its historical, chronological, and geographical relations.* N. York, 1863; 4th ed. 1879.

ERNEST RENAN: *Vie de Jésus.* Par. 1863, and often publ. since (13th ed. 1867) and in several translations. Strauss popularized and Frenchi-fied. The legendary theory. Eloquent, fascinating, superficial, and contradictory.

DANIEL SCHENKEL: *Das Charakterbild Jesu.* Wiesbaden, 1864; 4th ed. revised 1873. English transl. by *W. H. Furness.* Boston, 1867, 2 vols. By the same: *Das Christusbild der Apostel und der nach-apostolischen Zeit.* Leipz. 1879. See also his art., *Jesus Christus,* in Schenkel's "Bibel-Lexikon," III. 257 sqq. Semi-mythical theory. Comp. the sharp critique of Strauss on the *Characterbild: Die Hal-ben und die Ganzen.* Berlin, 1865.

PHILIP SCHAFF: *The Person of Christ: the Perfection of his Humanity viewed as a Proof of his Divinity. With a Collection of Impartial Testimonies.* Boston and N. York, 1865; 12th ed., revised, New York, 1882. The same work in German, Gotha, 1865; revised ed., N. York (Am. Tract Soc.), 1871; in Dutch by *Cordes,* with an introduction by *J. J. van Oosterzee.* Groningen, 1866; in French by Prof. *Sardinoux,* Toulouse, 1866, and in other languages. By the same: *Die Christusfrage.* N. York and Berlin, 1871.

Ecce Homo: A Survey of the Life and Work of Jesus Christ. [By Prof. J. R. SEELEY, of Cambridge.] Lond. 1864, and several editions and translations. It gave rise also to works on *Ecce Deus, Ecce Deus Homo,* and a number of reviews and essays (one by Gladstone).

CHARLES HARDWICK (d. 1859): *Christ and other Masters.* Lond., 4th ed., 1875. (An extension of the work of Reinhard; Christ compared with the founders of the Eastern religions.)

E. H. PLUMPTRE: *Christ and Christendom.* Boyle Lectures. Lond. 1866.

E. DE PRESSENSÉ: *Jésus Christ, son temps, sa vie, son œuvre.* Paris, 1866. (Against Renan.) The same transl. into English by *Annie Harwood* (Lond., 7th ed. 1879), and into German by *Fabarius* (Halle, 1866).

F. DELITZSCH: *Jesus und Hillel.* Erlangen, 1867; 3rd ed. revised, 1879.

THEOD. KEIM (Prof. in Zürich, and then in Giessen, d. 1879); *Geschichte Jesu von Nazara.* Zürich, 1867–'72, 3 vols. Also an abridgment in one volume, 1873, 2d ed. 1875. (This 2d ed. has important addi-tions, particularly a critical Appendix.) The large work is trans-

lated into English by *Geldart* and *Ransom.* Lond. (Williams &
Norgate), 1873–'82, 6 vols. By the same author : *Der geschichtliche
Christus.* Zürich, 3d ed. 1866. Keim attempts to reconstruct a
historical Christ from the Synoptical Gospels, especially Matthew,
but without John.

Wм. HANNA : *The Life of our Lord.* Edinb. 1868–'69, 6 vols.

Bishop DUPANLOUP (R. C.) : *Histoire de notre Sauveur Jésus Christ.*
Paris, 1870.

FR. W. FARRAR (Canon of Westminster) : *The Life of Christ.* Lond.
and N. York, 1874, 2 vols. (in many editions, one with illustrations).

C. GEIKIE : *The Life and Words of Christ.* Lond. and N. York, 1878,
2 vols. (Illustrated. Several editions.)

BERNHARD WEISS (Prof. in Berlin) : *Das Leben Jesu.* Berlin, 1882,
2 vols., 3d ed. 1888. English transl. Edinb. 1885, 3 vols.

ALFRED EDERSHEIM : *The Life and Times of Jesus the Messiah.* London
and N. Y. 1884, 2 vols. Strictly orthodox. Valuable for rabbinical
illustrations.

W. BEYSCHLAG : *Das Leben Jesu.* Halle, 1885–'86, 2 vols. ; 2d ed. 1888.

The works of PAULUS, STRAUSS, and RENAN (also JOSEPH SALVADOR,
a learned Jew in France, author of *Jésus Christ et sa doctrine,* Par.
1838) represent the various phases of rationalism and destructive
criticism, but have called forth also a copious and valuable apologetic literature. See the bibliography in Hase's *Leben Jesu,* 5th ed.
p. 44 sqq., and in his *Geschichte Jesu,* p. 124 sqq. SCHLEIERMACHER,
GFRÖRER, WEISSE, EWALD, SCHENKEL, HASE, and KEIM occupy, in
various degrees and with many differences, a middle position. The
great Schleiermacher almost perished in the sea of scepticism, but,
like Peter, he caught the saving arm of Jesus extended to him
(Matt. 14 : 30, 31). Hase is very valuable for the bibliography and
suggestive sketches, Ewald and Keim for independent research and
careful use of Josephus and the contemporary history. Keim rejects,
Ewald accepts, the Gospel of John as authentic ; both admit the
sinless perfection of Jesus, and Keim, from his purely critical and
synoptical standpoint, goes so far as to say (vol. iii. 662) that Christ,
in his gigantic elevation above his own and succeeding ages, "makes
the impression of mysterious loneliness, superhuman miracle, divine
creation (*den Eindruck geheimnissvoller Einsamkeit, übermenschlichen
Wunders, göttlicher Schöpfung*)." Weiss and Beyschlag mark a still
greater advance, and triumphantly defend the genuineness of John's
Gospel, but make concessions to criticism in minor details.

C. CHRONOLOGICAL.

KEPLER : *De Jesu Christi Servatoris nostri vero anno natalicio.* Frankf.
1606. *De vero anno quo æternus Dei Filius humanam naturam in
utero benedictæ Virginis Mariæ assumpsit.* Frcf. 1614.

J. A. BENGEL : *Ordo Temporum.* Stuttgart, 1741, and 1770.

HENR. SANCLEMENTE : *De Vulgaris Aeræ Emendatione libri quatuor.*

C. IDELER : *Handbuch der Chronologie.* Berlin, 1825-'26, 2 vols. By the same : *Lehrbuch der Chronologie,* 1831.

FR. MÜNTER : *Der Stern der Weisen.* Kopenhagen, 1827.

K. WIESELER : *Chronolog. Synopse der vier Evangelien.* Hamb. 1843. Eng. trans. by *Venables,* 2d ed., 1877. Supplemented by his *Beiträge zur richtigen Würdigung der Evangelien.* Gotha, 1869.

HENRY BROWNE : *Ordo Sæclorum.* London, 1844. Comp. his art. *Chronology,* in the 3d ed. of Kitto's "Cycl. of Bib. Lit."

SAM. F. JARVIS (historiographer of the Prot. Episc. Ch. in the U. S., d. 1851) : *A Chronological Introduction to the History of the Church.* N. York, 1845.

G. SEYFFARTH : *Chronologia sacra, Untersuchungen über das Geburtsjahr des Herrn.* Leipzig, 1846.

RUD. ANGER : *Der Stern der Weisen und das Geburtsjahr Christi.* Leipz. 1847. By the same. *Zur Chronologie des Lehramtes Christi.* Leipz. 1848.

HENRY F. CLINTON : *Fasti Romani.* Oxford, 1845-'50, 2 vols.

THOMAS LEWIN : *Essay on the Chronology of the New Testament.* Oxford, 1854. The same : *Fasti Sacri* (from B.C. 70 to A.D. 70). Lond. 1865.

F. PIPER : *Das Datum der Geburt Christi,* in his "Evangel. Kalender" for 1856, pp. 41 sqq.

HENRI LUTTEROTH : *Le recensement de Quirinius en Judée.* Paris, 1865 (134 pp.).

GUST. RÖSCH : *Zum Geburtsjahr Jesu,* in the "Jahrbücher für Deutsche Theol." Gotha, 1866, pp. 3-48.

CH. ED. CASPARI : *Chronologisch-Geographische Einleitung in das Leben J. C.* Hamb. 1869 (263 pp.). English translation by *M. J. Evans.* Edinburgh (T. Clark), 1876.

FRANCIS W. UPHAM : *The Wise Men.* N. York, 1869 (ch. viii., 145, on Kepler's Discovery). *Star of Our Lord,* by the same author. N. Y., 1873.

A. W. ZUMPT : *Das Geburtsjahr Christi.* Leipz. 1869 (306 pp.). He makes much account of the double governorship of Quirinius, Luke 2 : 2. Comp. Pres. WOOLSEY in *Bibl. Sacra,* April, 1870.

HERM. SEVIN : *Chronologie des Lebens Jesu.* Tübingen, 2d. ed., 1874.

FLORIAN RIESS (Jesuit) : *Das Geburtsjahr Christi.* Freiburg i. Br. 1880.

PETER SCHEGG (R. C.) : *Das Todesjahr des Königs Herodes und das Todesjahr Jesu Christi.* Against Riess. München, 1882.

FLORIAN RIESS : *Nochmals das Geburtsjahr Jesu Christi.* Reply to Schegg. Freib. im Br. 1883.

BERNHARD MATTHIAS : *Die römische Grundsteuer und das Vectigalrecht.* Erlangen, 1882.

H. LECOULTRE : *De censu Quiriniano et anno nativitatis Christi secundum Lucam evangelistam Dissertatio.* Lausanne, 1883.

§ 15. *The Founder of Christianity.*

When "the fulness of the time" was come, God sent forth his only-begotten Son, "the Desire of all nations," to redeem the world from the curse of sin, and to establish an everlasting kingdom of truth, love, and peace for all who should believe on his name.

In JESUS CHRIST a preparatory history both divine and human comes to its close. In him culminate all the previous revelations of God to Jews and Gentiles; and in him are fulfilled the deepest desires and efforts of both Gentiles and Jews for redemption. In his divine nature, as Logos, he is, according to St. John, the eternal Son of the Father, and the agent in the creation and preservation of the world, and in all those preparatory manifestations of God, which were completed in the incarnation. In his human nature, as Jesus of Nazareth, he is the ripe fruit of the religious growth of humanity, with an earthly ancestry, which St. Matthew (the evangelist of Israel) traces to Abraham, the patriarch of the Jews, and St. Luke (the evangelist of the Gentiles), to Adam, the father of all men. In him dwells all the fulness of the Godhead bodily; and in him also is realized the ideal of human virtue and piety. He is the eternal Truth, and the divine Life itself, personally joined with our nature; he is our Lord and our God; yet at the same time flesh of our flesh and bone of our bone. In him is solved the problem of religion, the reconciliation and fellowship of man with God; and we must expect no clearer revelation of God, nor any higher religious attainment of man, than is already guaranteed and actualized in his person.

But as Jesus Christ thus closes all previous history, so, on the other hand, he begins an endless future. He is the author of a new creation, the second Adam, the father of regenerate humanity, the head of the church, "which is his body, the fulness of him, that filleth all in all." He is the pure fountain of that stream of light and life, which has since flowed unbroken through nations and ages, and will continue to flow, till the earth shall be full of his praise, and every tongue shall confess that he is Lord, to the glory of God the Father. The universal diffusion and absolute dominion of the spirit and life of Christ will be also the completion of the human race, the end of history, and the beginning of a glorious eternity.

It is the great and difficult task of the biographer of Jesus to show how he, by external and internal development, under the conditions of a particular people, age, and country, came to be in fact what he was in idea and destination, and what he will continue to be for the faith of Christendom, the God-Man and Saviour of the world. Being divine from eternity, he could not become God; but as man he was subject to the laws of human life and gradual growth. "He advanced in wisdom and stature, and in favor with God and man."[1] Though he was the Son of God, "yet he learned obedience by the things which he suffered; and having been made perfect, he became the author of eternal salvation unto all them that obey him."[2] There is no conflict between the historical Jesus of Nazareth and the ideal Christ of faith. The full understanding of his truly human life, by its very perfection and elevation above all other men before and after him, will necessarily lead to an admission of his own testimony concerning his divinity.

> " Deep strike thy roots, O heavenly Vine,
>   Within our earthly sod !
> Most human and yet most divine,
>   The flower of man and God ! "

JESUS CHRIST came into the world under Cæsar Augustus, the first Roman emperor, before the death of king Herod the Great, four years before the traditional date of our Dionysian æra. He was born at Bethlehem of Judæa, in the royal line of David, from Mary, " the wedded Maid and Virgin Mother." The world was at peace, and the gates of Janus were closed for only the second time in the history of Rome. There

---

[1] Luke 2 : 52.   [2] Hebr. 5 : 8, 9.

is a poetic and moral fitness in this coincidence : it secured a hearing for the gentle message of peace which might have been drowned in the passions of war and the clamor of arms. Angels from heaven proclaimed the good tidings of his birth with songs of praise; Jewish shepherds from the neighboring fields, and heathen sages from the far east greeted the new-born king and Saviour with the homage of believing hearts. Heaven and earth gathered in joyful adoration around the Christ-child, and the blessing of this event is renewed from year to year among high and low, rich and poor, old and young, throughout the civilized world.

The idea of a perfect childhood, sinless and holy, yet truly human and natural, had never entered the mind of poet or historian before; and when the legendary fancy of the Apocryphal Gospels attempted to fill out the chaste silence of the Evangelists, it painted an unnatural prodigy of a child to whom wild animals, trees, and dumb idols bowed, and who changed balls of clay into flying birds for the amusement of his playmates.

The youth of Jesus is veiled in mystery. We know only one, but a very significant fact. When a boy of twelve years he astonished the doctors in the temple by his questions and answers, without repelling them by immodesty and premature wisdom, and filled his parents with reverence and awe by his absorption in the things of his heavenly Father, and yet was subject and obedient to them in all things. Here, too, there is a clear line of distinction between the supernatural miracle of history and the unnatural prodigy of apocryphal fiction, which represents Jesus as returning most learned answers to perplexing questions of the doctors about astronomy, medicine, physics, metaphysics, and hyperphysics.[1]

The external condition and surroundings of his youth are in sharp contrast with the amazing result of his public life. He grew up quietly and unnoticed in a retired Galilean mountain village of proverbial insignificance, and in a lowly carpen-

---

[1] See Cowper, *l. c.* pp. 212–214.

ter-shop, far away from the city of Jerusalem, from schools and libraries, with no means of instruction save those which were open to the humblest Jew—the care of godly parents, the beauties of nature, the services of the synagogue, the secret communion of the soul with God, and the Scriptures of the Old Testament, which recorded in type and prophecy his own character and mission. All attempts to derive his doctrine from any of the existing schools and sects have utterly failed. He never referred to the traditions of the elders except to oppose them. From the Pharisees and Sadducees he differed alike, and provoked their deadly hostility. With the Essenes he never came in contact. He was independent of human learning and literature, of schools and parties. He taught the world as one who owed nothing to the world. He came down from heaven and spoke out of the fulness of his personal intercourse with the great Jehovah. He was no scholar, no artist, no orator; yet was he wiser than all sages, he spake as never man spake, and made an impression on his age and all ages after him such as no man ever made or can make. Hence the natural surprise of his countrymen as expressed in the question: "From whence hath this man these things?" "How knoweth this man letters, having never learned?"[1]

He began his public ministry in the thirtieth year of his age, after the Messianic inauguration by the baptism of John, and after the Messianic probation in the wilderness—the counterpart of the temptation of the first Adam in Paradise. That ministry lasted only three years—and yet in these three years is condensed the deepest meaning of the history of religion. No great life ever passed so swiftly, so quietly, so humbly, so far removed from the noise and commotion of the world; and no great life after its close excited such universal and lasting interest. He was aware of this contrast: he predicted his deepest humiliation even to the death on the cross, and the subsequent irresistible attraction of this cross, which may be

---

[1] Mark 6 : 2, 3; Matt. 13 : 54–56; John 7 : 15.

witnessed from day to day wherever his name is known. He who could say, " If I be lifted up from the earth, I will draw all men unto myself," [1] knew more of the course of history and of the human heart than all the sages and legislators before and after him.

He chose twelve apostles for the Jews and seventy disciples for the Gentiles, not from among the scholars and leaders, but from among the illiterate fishermen of Galilee. He had no home, no earthly possessions, no friends among the mighty and the rich. A few pious women from time to time filled his purse ; and this purse was in the hands of a thief and a traitor. He associated with publicans and sinners, to raise them up to a higher and nobler life, and began his reformation among the lower classes, which were despised and neglected by the proud hierarchy of the day. He never courted the favor of the great, but incurred their hatred and persecution. He never flattered the prejudices of the age, but rebuked sin and vice among the high and the low, aiming his severest words at the blind leaders of the blind, the self-righteous hypocrites who sat on Moses' seat. He never encouraged the carnal Messianic hopes of the people, but withdrew when they wished to make him a king, and declared before the representative of the Roman empire that his kingdom was not of this world. He announced to his disciples his own martyrdom, and promised to them in this life only the same baptism of blood. He went about in Palestine, often weary of travel, but never weary of his work of love, doing good to the souls and bodies of men, speaking words of spirit and life, and working miracles of power and mercy.

He taught the purest doctrine, as a direct revelation of his heavenly Father, from his own intuition and experience, and with a power and authority which commanded unconditional trust and obedience. He rose above the prejudices of party and sect, above the superstitions of his age and nation. He addressed the naked heart of man and touched the quick of the conscience. He announced the founding of a spiritual kingdom which should grow from the smallest seed to a mighty tree, and, working like leaven from within, should gradually pervade all nations and countries. This colossal idea, the like of which had never entered the imagination of men, he held fast even in the darkest hour of humiliation, before the tribunal of the Jewish high-priest and the Roman governor, and when suspended as a malefactor on the cross; and the truth of this idea is illustrated by every page of church history and in every mission station on earth.

The miracles or signs which accompanied his teaching are supernatural, but not unnatural, exhibitions of his power over man and nature; no violations of law, but manifestations of a higher law, the superiority of mind over matter, the superiority of spirit over mind, the superiority of divine grace over human nature. They are all of the highest moral and of a profoundly symbolical significance, prompted by pure benevolence, and intended for the good of men; in striking contrast with deceptive juggler works and the useless and absurd miracles of apocryphal fiction. They were performed without any ostentation, with such simplicity and ease as to be called simply his "works." They were the practical proof of his doctrine and the natural reflex of his wonderful person. The absence of wonderful works in such a wonderful man would be the greatest wonder.

His doctrine and miracles were sealed by the purest and holiest life in private and public. He could challenge his bitterest opponents with the question: "Which of you convicteth me of sin?" well knowing that they could not point to a single spot.

At last he completed his active obedience by the passive obedience of suffering in cheerful resignation to the holy will of God. Hated and persecuted by the Jewish hierarchy, betrayed into their hands by Judas, accused by false witnesses, condemned by the Sanhedrin, rejected by the people, denied by Peter, but declared innocent by the representative of the

Roman law and justice, surrounded by his weeping mother and faithful disciples, revealing in those dark hours by word and silence the gentleness of a lamb and the dignity of a God, praying for his murderers, dispensing to the penitent thief a place in paradise, committing his soul to his heavenly Father, he died, with the exclamation: " It is finished ! " He died before he had reached the prime of manhood. The Saviour of the world a youth! He died the shameful death of the cross, the just for the unjust, the innocent for the guilty, a free self-sacrifice of infinite love, to reconcile the world unto God. He conquered sin and death on their own ground, and thus redeemed and sanctified all who are willing to accept his benefits and to follow his example. He instituted the Lord's Supper, to perpetuate the memory of his death and the cleansing and atoning power of his blood till the end of time.

The third day he rose from the grave, the conqueror of death and hell, the prince of life and resurrection. He repeatedly appeared to his disciples; he commissioned them to preach the gospel of the resurrection to every creature; he took possession of his heavenly throne, and by the outpouring of the Holy Spirit he established the church, which he has ever since protected, nourished, and comforted, and with which he has promised to abide, till he shall come again in glory to judge the quick and the dead.

This is a meagre outline of the story which the evangelists tell us with childlike simplicity, and yet with more general and lasting effect than could be produced by the highest art of historical composition. They modestly abstained from adding their own impressions to the record of the words and acts of the Master whose " glory they beheld, the glory as of the only-begotten from the Father, full of grace and truth."

Who would not shrink from the attempt to describe the moral character of Jesus, or, having attempted it, be not dissatisfied with the result ? Who can empty the ocean into a bucket ? Who (we may ask with Lavater) "can paint the glory of the rising sun with a charcoal ? " No artist's ideal comes up to the reality in this case, though his ideals may surpass every other reality. The better and holier a man is, the more he feels his need of pardon, and how far he falls short of his own imperfect standard of excellence. But Jesus, with the same nature as ours and tempted as we are, never yielded to temptation; never had cause for regretting any thought, word, or action; he never needed pardon, or conversion, or reform; he never fell out of harmony with his heavenly Father. His whole life was one unbroken act of self-consecration to the glory of God and the eternal welfare of his fellow-men. A catalogue of virtues and graces, however complete, would give us but a mechanical view. It is the spotless purity and sinlessness of Jesus as acknowledged by friend and foe; it is the even harmony and symmetry of all graces, of love to God and love to man, of dignity and humility, of strength and tenderness, of greatness and simplicity, of self-control and submission, of active and passive virtue; it is, in one word, the absolute perfection which raises his character high above the reach of all other men and makes it an exception to a universal rule, a moral miracle in history. It is idle to institute comparisons with saints and sages, ancient or modern. Even the infidel Rousseau was forced to exclaim: "If Socrates lived and died like a sage, Jesus lived and died like a God." Here is more than the starry heaven above us, and the moral law within us, which filled the soul of Kant with ever-growing reverence and awe. Here is the holy of holies of humanity, here is the very gate of heaven.

Going so far in admitting the human perfection of Christ—and how can the historian do otherwise?—we are driven a step farther, to the acknowledgment of his amazing claims, which must either be true, or else destroy all foundation for admiration and reverence in which he is universally held. It is impossible to construct a life of Christ without admitting its supernatural and miraculous character.

The divinity of Christ, and his whole mission as Redeemer, is an article of faith, and, as such, above logical or mathemati-

cal demonstration. The incarnation or the union of the infi·
nite divinity and finite humanity in one person is indeed the
mystery of mysteries. "What can be more glorious than God?
What more vile than flesh? What more wonderful than God
in the flesh?"[1] Yet aside from all dogmatizing which lies outside of the province of the historian, the divinity of Christ has
a self-evidencing power which forces itself irresistibly upon the
reflecting mind and historical inquirer; while the denial of it
makes his person an inexplicable enigma.

It is inseparable from his own express testimony respecting
himself, as it appears in every Gospel, with but a slight difference of degree between the Synoptists and St. John. Only
ponder over it! He claims to be the long-promised Messiah
who fulfilled the law and the prophets, the founder and lawgiver of a new and universal kingdom, the light of the world,
the teacher of all nations and ages, from whose authority there
is no appeal. He claims to have come into this world for the
purpose to save the world from sin—which no merely human
being can possibly do. He claims the power to forgive sins on
earth ; he frequently exercised that power, and it was for the
sins of mankind, as he foretold, that he shed his own blood.
He invites all men to follow him, and promises peace and life
eternal to every one that believes in him. He claims pre-existence before Abraham and the world, divine names, attributes,
and worship. He disposes from the cross of places in Paradise. In directing his disciples to baptize all nations, he co-
ordinates himself with the eternal Father and the Divine Spirit,
and promises to be with them to the consummation of the world
and to come again in glory as the Judge of all men. He, the
humblest and meekest of men, makes these astounding pretensions in the most easy and natural way ; he never falters,
never apologizes, never explains ; he proclaims them as self-
evident truths. We read them again and again, and never feel
any incongruity nor think of arrogance and presumption.

---

[1] Augustine : " *Deus ; quid gloriosius ? Caro ; quid vilius ? Deus in carne ;
quid mirabilius ?* "

And yet this testimony, if not true, must be downright blasphemy or madness. The former hypothesis cannot stand a moment before the moral purity and dignity of Jesus, revealed in his every word and work, and acknowledged by universal consent. Self-deception in a matter so momentous, and with an intellect in all respects so clear and so sound, is equally out of the question. How could He be an enthusiast or a madman who never lost the even balance of his mind, who sailed serenely over all the troubles and persecutions, as the sun above the clouds, who always returned the wisest answer to tempting questions, who calmly and deliberately predicted his death on the cross, his resurrection on the third day, the outpouring of the Holy Spirit, the founding of his Church, the destruction of Jerusalem—predictions which have been literally fulfilled? A character so original, so complete, so uniformly consistent, so perfect, so human and yet so high above all human greatness, can be neither a fraud nor a fiction. The poet, as has been well said, would in this case be greater than the hero. It would take more than a Jesus to invent a Jesus.

We are shut up then to the recognition of the divinity of Christ; and reason itself must bow in silent awe before the tremendous word: "I and the Father are one!" and respond with skeptical Thomas: "My Lord and my God!"

This conclusion is confirmed by the effects of the manifestation of Jesus, which far transcend all merely human capacity and power. The history of Christianity, with its countless fruits of a higher and purer life of truth and love than was ever known before or is now known outside of its influence, is a continuous commentary on the life of Christ, and testifies on every page to the inspiration of his holy example. His power is felt on every Lord's Day from ten thousand pulpits, in the palaces of kings and the huts of beggars, in universities and colleges, in every school where the sermon on the Mount is read, in prisons, in almshouses, in orphan asylums, as well as in happy homes, in learned works and simple tracts in endless succession. If this history of ours has any value at all, it is a new evidence that Christ is the light and life of a fallen world.

And there is no sign that his power is waning. His kingdom is more widely spread than ever before, and has the fairest prospect of final triumph in all the earth. Napoleon at St. Helena is reported to have been struck with the reflection that millions are now ready to die for the crucified Nazarene who founded a spiritual empire by love, while no one would die for Alexander, or Cæsar, or himself, who founded temporal empires by force. He saw in this contrast a convincing argument for the divinity of Christ, saying: "I know men, and I tell you, Christ was not a man. Everything about Christ astonishes me. His spirit overwhelms and confounds me. There is no comparison between him and any other being. He stands single and alone."[1] And Gœthe, another commanding genius, of very different character, but equally above suspicion of partiality for religion, looking in the last years of his life over the vast field of history, was constrained to confess that "if ever the Divine appeared on earth, it was in the Person of Christ," and that "the human mind, no matter how far it may advance in every other department, will never transcend the height and moral culture of Christianity as it shines and glows in the Gospels."

The rationalistic, mythical, and legendary attempts to explain the life of Christ on purely human and natural grounds, and to resolve the miraculous elements either into common events, or into innocent fictions, split on the rock of Christ's character and testimony. The ablest of the infidel biographers of Jesus now profess the profoundest regard for his character, and laud

---

[1] On the testimony of Napoleon to the divinity of Christ see the letters of Bersier and Lutteroth appended to the twelfth ed. of my book on the *Person of Christ* (1882), p. 284, and pp. 219 sqq. Napoleon is reported to have asked the poet Wieland at a court-ball in Weimar, during the Congress of Erfurt, whether he doubted that Jesus ever lived; to which Wieland promptly and emphatically replied in the negative, adding that with equal right a thousand years hence men might deny the existence of Napoleon or the battle of Jena. The emperor smiled and said, *très-bien!* The question was designed not to express doubt, but to test the poet's faith. So Dr. Hase reports from the mouth of Chancellor Müller, who heard the conversation. *Geschichte Jesu*, p. 9.

him as the greatest sage and saint that ever appeared on earth. But, by rejecting his testimony concerning his divine origin and mission, they turn him into a liar; and, by rejecting the miracle of the resurrection, they make the great fact of Christianity a stream without a source, a house without a foundation, an effect without a cause.   Denying the physical miracles, they expect us to believe even greater psychological miracles; yea, they substitute for the supernatural miracle of history an unnatural prodigy and incredible absurdity of their imagination.   They moreover refute and supersede each other.   The history of error in the nineteenth century is a history of self-destruction.   A hypothesis was scarcely matured before another was invented and substituted, to meet the same fate in its turn; while the old truth and faith of Christendom remains unshaken, and marches on in its peaceful conquest against sin and error.

Truly, Jesus Christ, the Christ of the Gospels, the Christ of history, the crucified and risen Christ, the divine-human Christ, is the most real, the most certain, the most blessed of all facts. And this fact is an ever-present and growing power which pervades the Church and conquers the world, and is its own best evidence, as the sun shining in the heavens.   This fact is the only solution of the terrible mystery of sin and death, the only inspiration to a holy life of love to God and man, the only guide to happiness and peace.   Systems of human wisdom will come and go, kingdoms and empires will rise and fall, but for all time to come Christ will remain "the Way, the Truth, and the Life."

§ 16. *Chronology of the Life of Christ.*

See the Lit. in ¿ 14, p. 98, especially BROWNE, WIESELER, ZUMPT, ANDREWS, and KEIM.

We briefly consider the chronological dates of the life of Christ.

I. THE YEAR OF THE NATIVITY.—This must be ascertained by historical and chronological research, since there is no cer-

tain and harmonious tradition on the subject.   Our Christian æra,
which was introduced by the Roman abbot Dionysius Exiguus, in
the sixth century, and came into general use two centuries later,
during the reign of Charlemagne, puts the Nativity Dec. 25, 754
Anno Urbis, that is, after the founding of the city of Rome.[1]
Nearly all chronologers agree that this is wrong by at least four
years.   Christ was born A.U. 750 (or B.C. 4), if not earlier.

This is evident from the following chronological hints in the
Gospels, as compared with and confirmed by Josephus and
contemporary writers, and by astronomical calculations.

The Death of Herod.

(1) According to Matthew 2 : 1 (comp. Luke 1 : 5, 26), Christ
was born "in the days of king Herod" I. or the Great, who
died, according to Josephus, at Jericho, A.U. 750, just before
the Passover, being nearly seventy years of age, after a reign
of thirty-seven years.[2]   This date has been verified by the
astronomical calculation of the eclipse of the moon, which took
place March 13, A.U. 750, a few days before Herod's death.[3]
Allowing two months or more for the events between the birth
of Christ and the murder of the Innocents by Herod, the
Nativity must be put back at least to February or January, A.U.
750 (or B.C. 4), if not earlier.

Some infer from the slaughter of the male children in Bethlehem, "from two years old and under,"[4] that Christ must have

---

[1] The fathers distinguish between the Nativity (γένεσις, Matt. 1 : 18) and the
Incarnation (σάρκωσις), and identify the Incarnation with the Conception or
Annunciation.   Since the time of Charlemagne the two terms seem to have
been used synonymously.   See Ideler, *Chronol.*, ii. 383, and Gieseler, i. 70
(4th Germ. ed.).

[2] Jos., *Antiqu.*, xvii. 8, 1 : "Herod died . . . having reigned since he had
procured Antigonus to be slain [A.U. 717, or B.C. 37], thirty-four years, but since
he had been declared king by the Romans [A.U. 714, or B.C. 40], thirty-seven."
Comp. the same statement in *Bell. Jud.*, i. 33, 8, and other passages.

[3] According to Josephus, *Antiqu.*, xvii. 6, 4 : "And that night there was
an eclipse of the moon."   It is worthy of note that Josephus mentions no
other eclipse in any of his works.

[4] Matt. 2 : 16 : πάντας τοὺς παῖδας . . . ἀπὸ διετοῦς καὶ κατωτέρω κατὰ τὸν
χρόνον ὃν ἠκρίβωσεν παρὰ τῶν μάγων.

been born two years before Herod's death; but he counted from the time when the star was first seen by the Magi (2 : 7), and wished to make sure of his object.   There is no good reason to doubt the fact itself, and the flight of the holy family to Egypt, which is inseparably connected with it.   For, although the horrible deed is ignored by Josephus, it is in keeping with the well-known cruelty of Herod, who from jealousy murdered Hyrcanus, the grandfather of his favorite wife, Mariamne; then Mariamne herself, to whom he was passionately attached; her two sons, Alexander and Aristobulus, and, only five days before his death, his oldest son, Antipater; and who ordered all the nobles assembled around him in his last moments to be executed after his decease, so that at least his death might be attended by universal mourning.   For such a monster the murder of one or two dozen infants in a little town [1] was a very small matter, which might easily have been overlooked, or, owing to its connection with the Messiah, purposely ignored by the Jewish historian.   But a confused remembrance of it is preserved in the anecdote related by Macrobius (a Roman grammarian and probably a heathen, about A.D. 410), that Augustus, on hearing of Herod's murder of "boys under two years" and of his own son, remarked "that it was better to be Herod's swine than his son." [2]   The cruel persecution of Herod and the flight into Egypt were a significant sign of the experience of the early church, and a source of comfort in every period of martyrdom.

THE STAR OF THE MAGI.

(2) Another chronological hint of Matthew, ch. 2 : 1–4, 9, which has been verified by astronomy, is the Star of the Wise Men,

---

[1] Tradition has here most absurdly swelled the number of Innocents to 20,000, as indicated on the massive column, which marks the spot of their supposed martyrdom in the Church of the Nativity at Bethlehem. XX *M* [*artyres*], i. e. martyrs, have become XX *M* [*ilia*], i. e. twenty thousands.

[2] Macrob., *Sat.*, ii. 4 : "*Augustus, cum audisset, inter pueros, quos in Syria Herodes, rex Judæorum, intra bimatum* [perhaps taken from Matt. 2 : 16, Vulg. : *a bimatu et infra*] *jussit interfici, filium quoque eius occisum, ait : melius est Herodis porcum esse quam filium.*"   It is a pun on the similar sounding

which appeared before the death of Herod, and which would naturally attract the attention of the astrological sages of the East, in connection with the expectation of the advent of a great king among the Jews. Such a belief naturally arose from Balaam's prophecy of "the star that was to rise out of Jacob" (Num. 24 : 17), and from the Messianic prophecies of Isaiah and Daniel, and widely prevailed in the East since the dispersion of the Jews.[1]

The older interpretation of that star made it either a passing meteor, or a strictly miraculous phenomenon, which lies beyond astronomical calculation, and was perhaps visible to the Magi alone. But Providence usually works through natural agencies, and that God did so in this case is made at least very probable by a remarkable discovery in astronomy. The great and devout Kepler observed in the years 1603 and 1604 a conjunction of Jupiter and Saturn, which was made more rare and luminous by the addition of Mars in the month of March, 1604. In the autumn of the same year (Oct. 10) he observed near the planets Saturn, Jupiter and Mars a new (fixed) star of uncommon brilliancy, which appeared "in triumphal pomp, like some all-powerful monarch on a visit to the metropolis of his realm." It was

Greek terms for sow and son ($\tilde{v}s$ and $vi\delta s$). Kepler already quoted this passage in confirmation of Matthew.

[1] Tacitus (*Hist.*, v. 13) and Suetonius (*Vespas.*, c. 4) speak of a widespread expectation of that kind at the time of the Jewish war and before (Suetonius calls it a *vetus et constans opinio*), but falsely refer it to the Roman emperors Vespasianus and Titus. In this the heathen historians followed Josephus, who well knew and believed the Messianic hopes of his people (comp. *Ant.*, iv. 6, 5 ; x. 10, 4 ; 11, 7), and yet was not ashamed basely to betray and pervert them, saying (*Bell. Jud.*, vi. 5, 4) : "What did the most to elevate the Jews in undertaking this war, was an *ambiguous* oracle that was found also in their sacred writings, how 'about that time, one from their country should become governor of the habitable earth.' The Jews took this prediction to belong to themselves in particular, and many of the wise men were thereby deceived in their determination. Now, *this oracle certainly denoted the government of Vespasian*, who was appointed emperor in Judæa." Comp. Hausrath, *N. T. Ztgesch.*, I. 173. The Messianic hopes continued long after the destruction of Jerusalem. The false Messiah, who led the rebellion under the reign of Hadrian (A.D. 135), called himself *Bar-Cocheba*, i. e. "Son of the Star," and issued coins with a star, in allusion probably to Num. 24 : 17. When his real character was revealed, his name was turned into *Bar-Coziba*, "Son of Falsehood."

blazing and glittering "like the most beautiful and glorious torch ever seen when driven by a strong wind," and seemed to him to be "an exceedingly wonderful work of God."[1] His genius perceived that this phenomenon must lead to the determination of the year of Christ's birth, and by careful calculation he ascertained that a similar conjunction of Jupiter and Saturn, with the later addition of Mars, and probably some extraordinary star, took place repeatedly A.U. 747 and 748 in the sign of the Pisces.

It is worthy of note that Jewish astrologers ascribe a special signification to the conjunction of the planets Jupiter and Saturn in the sign of the Pisces, and connect it with the advent of the Messiah.[2]

The discovery of Kepler was almost forgotten till the nineteenth century, when it was independently confirmed by several eminent astronomers, Schubert of Petersburg, Ideler and Encke of Berlin, and Pritchard of London.   It is pronounced by Pritchard to be "as certain as any celestial phenomenon of ancient

[1] In the beginning of his *Bericht vom Geburtsjahr Christi* (*Opera*, IV. 204), he describes this new star in these words : " *Ein ungewöhnlicher, sehr heller und schöner Stern . . . der wie die schönste, herrlichste Fackel so jemahl mit Augen gesehen worden, wenn sie von einem starken Wind getrieben wird, geflammet und gefunkelt, gerad neben den drey höchsten Planeten Saturno, Jove und Marte.*"   He calls this phenomenon "*ein überaus grosses Wunderwerk Gottes.*"   A fuller description of the whole phenomenon he gives in his work *De Stella Nova* (*Opera*, II. 575 sqq. and 801 sqq., ed. Frisch).   Upham (*The Wise Men*, N. Y. 1869, p. 145) says : "Tycho de Brahe had observed a similar wonder in the constellation Cassiopeia, on the night of the 11th of October, in the year 1572.   These were not luminous bodies within our atmosphere ; were not within, or near, the solar system ; they were in the region of the fixed stars.   Each grew more and more brilliant, till it shone like a planet.   Then its lustre waned until it ceased to be visible,—the one in March, 1574, the other in February, 1606.   The light was white, then yellow, then red, then dull, and so went out."   On Temporary Stars, see Herschel's *Astronomy*, Chap. XII.

[2] The learned Jewish Rabbi Abarbanel, in his Commentary on Daniel (called *Ma'jne hajeshuah*, i. e. "Wells of Salvation," Isa. 12 : 3), which was published 1547, more than fifty years before Kepler's calculation, says that such a conjunction took place three years before the birth of Moses (A.M. 2365), and would reappear before the birth of the Messiah, A.M. 5224 (or A.D. 1463). Ideler and Wieseler conjecture that this astrological belief existed among the Jews already at the time of Christ.

date." It certainly makes the pilgrimage of the Magi to Jerusalem and Bethlehem more intelligible. "The star of astrology
has thus become a torch of chronology" (as Ideler says), and an
argument for the truthfulness of the first Gospel.[1]

It is objected that Matthew seems to mean a single star (ἀστήρ,
comp. ver. 9) rather than a combination of stars (ἄστρον).
Hence Dr. Wieseler supplements the calculation of Kepler and
Ideler by calling to aid a single comet which appeared from
February to April, A.U. 750, according to the Chinese astronomical tables, which Pingré and Humboldt acknowledge as historical. But this is rather far-fetched and hardly necessary; for
that extraordinary star described by Kepler, or Jupiter at its
most luminous appearance, as described by Pritchard, in that
memorable conjunction, would sufficiently answer the description of a single star by Matthew, which must at all events not
be pressed too literally; for the language of Scripture on the
heavenly bodies is not scientific, but phenomenal and popular.
God condescended to the astrological faith of the Magi, and
probably made also an internal revelation to them before, as
well as after the appearance of the star (comp. 2 : 12).

If we accept the result of these calculations of astronomers
we are brought to within two years of the year of the Nativity,
namely, between A.U. 748 (Kepler) and 750 (Wieseler). The
difference arises, of course, from the uncertainty of the time of
departure and the length of the journey of the Magi.

As this astronomical argument is often very carelessly and erroneously
stated, and as the works of Kepler and Ideler are not easy of access, at
least in America (I found them in the Astor Library), I may be permitted
to state the case more at length. John Kepler wrote three treatises on
the year of Christ's birth, two in Latin (1606 and 1614), one in German
(1613), in which he discusses with remarkable learning the various pas-

---

[1] It has been so accepted by Dean Alford and others. See the note in 6th
ed. of his Com. on Matt. 2 : 2 (1868), with the corrections furnished by Rev. C.
Pritchard. McClellan (*New Test.*, I. 402) assumes that the conjunction of
Jupiter and Saturn was premonitory and coincided with the conception of the
birth of John the Baptist, Oct. 748, and that Kepler's *new* star was Messiah's
star appearing a year later.

sages and facts bearing on that subject. They are reprinted in Dr. Ch. Frisch's edition of his *Opera Omnia* (Frcf. et Erlang. 1858-'70, 8 vols.), vol. IV. pp. 175 sqq. ; 201 sqq. ; 279 sqq. His astronomical observations on the constellation which led him to this investigation are fully described in his treatises *De Stella Nova in Pede Serpentarii* (*Opera,* vol. II. 575 sqq.), and *Phenomenon singulare seu Mercurius in Sole* (*ibid.* II. 801 sqq.). Prof. Ideler, who was himself an astronomer and chronologist, in his *Handbuch der mathemat. und technischen Chronologie* (Berlin, 1826, vol. II. 400 sqq.), gives the following clear summary of Kepler's and of his own observations :

"It is usually supposed that the star of the Magi was, if not a fiction of the imagination, some meteor which arose accidentally, or *ad hoc.* We will belong neither to the unbelievers nor the hyper-believers (*weder zu den Ungläubigen noch zu den Uebergläubigen*), and regard this starry phenomenon with Kepler to be real and well ascertainable by calculation, namely, as a *conjunction of the Planets Jupiter and Saturn.* That Matthew speaks only of a star (ἀστήρ), not a constellation (ἄστρον), need not trouble us, for the two words are not unfrequently confounded. The just named great astronomer, who was well acquainted with the astrology of his and former times, and who used it occasionally as a means for commending astronomy to the attention and respect of the laity, first conceived this idea when he observed the conjunction of the two planets mentioned at the close of the year 1603. It took place Dec. 17. In the spring following Mars joined their company, and in autumn 1604 still another star, one of those fixed star-like bodies (*einer jener fixstern-artigen Körper*) which grow to a considerable degree of brightness, and then gradually disappear without leaving a trace behind. This star stood near the two planets at the eastern foot of Serpentarius (*Schlangenträger*), and appeared when last seen as a star of the first magnitude with uncommon splendor. From month to month it waned in brightness, and at the end of 1605 was withdrawn from the eyes which at that time could not yet be aided by good optical instruments. Kepler wrote a special work on this *Stella nova in pede Serpentarii* (Prague, 1606), and there he first set forth the view that the star of the Magi consisted in a conjunction of Saturn, Jupiter and some other extraordinary star, the nature of which he does not explain more fully." Ideler then goes on to report (p. 404) that Kepler, with the imperfect tables at his disposal, discovered the same conjunction of Jupiter and Saturn A.U. 747 in June, August and December, in the sign of the Pisces ; in the next year, February and March, Mars was added, and probably another extraordinary star, which must have excited the astrologers of Chaldæa to the highest degree. They probably saw the new star first, and then the constellation.

Dr. Münter, bishop of Seeland, in 1821 directed new attention to this remarkable discovery, and also to the rabbinical commentary of Abarbanel on Daniel, according to which the Jewish astrologers expected a conjunction of the planets Jupiter and Saturn in the sign of the Pisces before the advent of the Messiah, and asked the astronomers to reinvestigate this point. Since then Schubert of Petersburg (1823), Ideler and Encke of Berlin (1826 and 1830), and more recently Pritchard of London, have verified Kepler's calculations.

Ideler describes the result of his calculation (vol. II. 405) thus: "I have made the calculation with every care. . . . The results are sufficiently remarkable. Both planets [Jupiter and Saturn] came in conjunction for the first time A.U. 747, May 20, in the 20th degree of Pisces. They stood then on the heaven before sunrise and were only one degree apart. Jupiter passed Saturn to the north. In the middle of September both came in opposition to the sun at midnight in the south. The difference in longitude was one degree and a half. Both were retrograde and again approached each other. On the 27th of October a second conjunction took place in the sixteenth degree of the Pisces, and on the 12th of November, when Jupiter moved again eastward, a third in the fifteenth degree of the same sign. In the last two constellations also the difference in longitude was only about one degree, so that to a weak eye both planets might appear as one star. If the Jewish astrologers attached great expectations to a conjunction of the two upper planets in the sign of the Pisces, this one must above all have appeared to them as most significant."

In his shorter *Lehrbuch der Chronologie*, which appeared Berlin 1831 in one vol., pp. 424–431, Ideler gives substantially the same account somewhat abridged, but with slight changes of the figures on the basis of a new calculation with still better tables made by the celebrated astronomer Encke, who puts the first conjunction of Jupiter and Saturn A.U. 747, May 29th, the second Sept. 30th, the third Dec. 5th. See the full table of Encke, p. 429.

We supplement this account by an extract from an article on the Star of the Wise Men, by the Rev. Charles Pritchard, M.A., Hon. Secretary of the Royal Astronomical Society, who made a fresh calculation of the constellation in A.U. 747, from May to December, and published the results in *Memoirs of Royal Ast. Society*, vol. xxv., and in Smith's "Bible Dictionary," p. 3108, Am. ed., where he says: "At that time [end of Sept., B.C. 7] there can be no doubt Jupiter would present to astronomers, especially in so clear an atmosphere, a magnificent spectacle. It was then at its most brilliant apparition, for it was at its nearest approach both to the sun and to the earth. Not far from it would be seen its duller and much less conspicuous companion, Saturn. This glorious spectacle continued almost unaltered for several days, when the planets again slowly separated, then came to a halt, when, by reassuming a direct motion, Jupiter again approached to a conjunction for the third time with Saturn, just as the Magi may be supposed to have entered the Holy City. And, to complete the fascination of the tale, about an hour and a half after sunset, the two planets might be seen from Jerusalem, hanging as it were in the meridian, and suspended over Bethlehem in the distance.   These celestial phenomena thus described are, it will be seen, beyond the reach of question, and at the first impression they assuredly appear to fulfil the conditions of the Star of the Magi." If Pritchard, nevertheless, rejects the identity of the constellation with the single star of Matthew, it is because of a too literal understanding of Matthew's language, that the star προῆγεν αὐτούς and ἐστάϑη ἐπάνω, which would make it miraculous in either case.

THE FIFTEENTH YEAR OF TIBERIUS.

(3) Luke, ch. 3 : 1, 23, gives us an important and evidently careful indication of the reigning powers at the time when John the Baptist and Christ entered upon their public ministry, which, according to Levitical custom, was at the age of thirty.[1]   John the Baptist began his ministry "in the fifteenth year of the reign of Tiberius,"[2] and Jesus, who was only about six months younger than John (comp. Luke 1 : 5, 26), was baptized and began to teach when he was "about thirty years of age."[3]

Tiberius began to reign jointly with Augustus, as "collega imperii," A.U. 764 (or, at all events, in the beginning of 765), and independently, Aug. 19, A.U. 767 (A.D. 14); consequently, the fifteenth year of his reign was either A.U. 779, if we count from the joint reign (as Luke probably did, using the more general term ἡγεμονία rather than μοναρχία or βασιλεία),[4] or

[1] Comp. Num. 4 : 3, 35, 39, 43, 47.

[2] In the new revision the passage, 3 : 1, 2, is thus translated : "Now in the fifteenth year of the reign (ἡγεμονίας) of Tiberius Cæsar, Pontius Pilate being governor (ἡγεμονεύοντος) of Judæa, and Herod being tetrarch of Galilee, and his brother Philip tetrarch of the region of Ituræa and Trachonitis, and Lysanias tetrarch of Abilene, in the high-priesthood of Annas and Caiaphas, the word of God came unto John the son of Zacharias in the wilderness."   The statement must have been quite intelligible to the educated readers of that time.

[3] The different interpretations of αὐτὸς ἦν ἀρχόμενος ὡσεὶ ἐτῶν τριάκοντα do not alter the result much, but the ὡσεί leaves a margin for a few months more or less.   Comp. McClellan, I. 404.

[4] He uses the same term of Pontius Pilate (ἡγεμονεύοντος).   Zumpt, l. c. p. 296, says : "Eigentlich verstanden, bezeichnet ἡγεμονία die Würde des militär-ischen Befehlshabers und des Regenten über die Provinzen.   Hätte Lucas 'Augustus Kaiser' (αὐτοκράτωρ) oder auch nur 'Herrscher' (ἄρχων) gesagt, so würde man an eine Zählung von Tiberius' Provincialverwaltung weniger denken können."

782, if we reckon from the independent reign (as was the usual Roman method).[1]

Now, if we reckon back thirty years from A.U. 779 or 782, we come to A.U. 749 or 752 as the year of John's birth, which preceded that of Christ about six months. The former date (749) is undoubtedly to be preferred, and agrees with Luke's own statement that Christ was born under Herod (1 : 5, 26).[2]

Dionysius probably (for we have no certainty on the subject) calculated from the independent reign of Tiberius; but even that would not bring us to 754, and would involve Luke in contradiction with Matthew and with himself.[3]

The other dates in Luke 3 : 1 generally agree with this result,

---

[1] Different modes of counting were not unusual, regarding the early Roman emperors, and Herod I. See above, p. 112, Zumpt, *l. c.* 282 sqq., and Andrews, p. 27. Suetonius (*Tib.*, 23) and Tacitus (*Annal.*, vi. 51) say that Tiberius died in the 23d year of his reign, meaning his sole reign ; but there are indications also of the other counting, at least in Egypt and the provinces, where the authority of Tiberius as the active emperor was more felt than in Rome. There are coins from Antioch in Syria of the date A. U. 765, with the head of Tiberius and the inscription, Καισαρ. Σεβαστος (*Augustus*). In favor of the computation from the colleagueship are Ussher, Bengel, Lardner, Greswell, Andrews, Zumpt, Wieseler, McClellan; in favor of the computation from the sole reign are Lightfoot, Ewald, Browne. Wieseler formerly held that Luke refers to the imprisonment, and not the beginning of the ministry, of John, but he changed his view ; see his art. in Herzog's "Encykl.," xxi. 547.

[2] Andrews, *l. c.* p. 28, thus sums up his investigations upon this point: "We find three solutions of the chronological difficulties which the statements of Luke present : 1st. That the 15th year of Tiberius is to be reckoned from the death of Augustus, and extends from August, 781, to August, 782. In this year the Baptist, whose labors began some time previous, was imprisoned ; but the Lord's ministry began in 780, before this imprisonment, and when he was about thirty years of age. 2d. That the 15th year is to be reckoned from the death of Augustus, but that the statement, the Lord was about thirty years of age, is to be taken in a large sense, and that he may have been of any age from thirty to thirty-five when he began his labors. 3d. That the 15th year is to be reckoned from the year when Tiberius was associated with Augustus in the empire, and is therefore the year 779. In this case the language, 'he was about thirty,' may be strictly taken, and the statement, 'the word of God came unto John,' may be referred to the beginning of his ministry."

[3] Hase (*Gesch. Jesu*, p. 209) strangely defends the Dionysian æra, but sacrifices the date of Matthew, together with the whole history of the childhood of Jesus. Against the view of Keim see Schürer, p. 242.

but are less definite. Pontius Pilate was ten years governor of
Judæa, from A.D. 26 to 36. Herod Antipas was deposed by
Caligula, A.D. 39. Philip, his brother, died A.D. 34. Consequently, Christ must have died before A.D. 34, at an age of
thirty-three, if we allow three years for his public ministry.

THE CENSUS OF QUIRINIUS.

(4) The Census of Quirinius, Luke, ch. 2 : 2.[1] Luke gives us
another chronological date by the incidental remark that Christ
was born about the time of that census or enrolment, which
was ordered by Cæsar Augustus, and which was "the first
[enrolment] made when Quirinius (Cyrenius) was governor
of Syria."[2] He mentions this fact as the reason for the
journey of Joseph and Mary to Bethlehem. The journey of
Mary makes no difficulty, for (aside from the intrinsic propriety of his company for protection) all women over twelve
years of age (and slaves also) were subject in the Roman empire to a head-tax, as well as men over fourteen, till the age of

---

[1] See the literature till 1874 in Schürer, p. 262, who devotes 24 pages to
this subject. The most important writers on the census of Quirinius are
Huschke (a learned jurist, in 2 treatises, 1840 and 1847), Wieseler (1843 and
1869), and Zumpt (1854 and 1869). Comp. also the article "Taxing," by Dr.
Plumptre, supplemented by Dr. Woolsey, in Smith's "Bible Dictionary"
(Hackett and Abbot's ed.), IV. 3185, and J. B. McClellan, *New Test.*, I. 392.

[2] This is the proper meaning of the original (according to the last text of
Tischendorf, Westcott and Hort, who with B D omit the article ἡ): αὕτη
ἀπογραφὴ πρώτη ἐγένετο ἡγεμονεύοντος τῆς Συρίας Κυρηνίου. Vulg. : *Hæc de-
scriptio prima facta est a præside Syriæ Cyrino.* The English version, "this
taxing was *first* made when," is ungrammatical, and would require πρῶτον or
πρῶτα. instead of πρώτη. Luke either meant to say that there was no previous enrolment in Judæa, or, more probably, he had in his mind a *second* enrolment made under Quirinius at his second governorship, which is noticed by
him in Acts 5 : 37, and was well known to his readers. See below. *Quirinius*
(Κυρήνιος) is the proper spelling (Strabo, Josephus, Tacitus, Justin M.)—
not *Quirinus*, which was also a Roman name ; hence the confusion. (See
Weiss, in the 6th ed. of Meyer on *Luke*, p. 286.) His full name was *Publius
Sulpicius Quirinius* (Tacitus, *Annal.*, iii. 48 ; Suetonius, *Tiber.*, 49). He
was consul A.U. 742, at the head of an army in Africa, 747, and died in Rome,
A.D. 21. Josephus speaks of him at the close of the 17th and the beginning
of the 18th book of his *Archæol.* See a full account of him in Zumpt, pp.
43–71.

sixty-five.[1] There is some significance in the coincidence of the
birth of the King of Israel with the deepest humiliation of Israel,
and its incorporation in the great historical empire of Rome.
But the statement of Luke seems to be in direct conflict with
the fact that the governorship and census of Quirinius began
A.D. 6, i. e., ten years *after* the birth of Christ.[2] Hence many
artificial interpretations.[3] But this difficulty is now, if not entirely removed, at least greatly diminished by archæological
and philological research independent of theology. It has been
proved almost to a demonstration by Bergmann, Mommsen,
and especially by Zumpt, that Quirinius was *twice* governor of
Syria—first, A.U. 750 to 753, or B.C. 4 to 1 (when there happens
to be a gap in our list of governors of Syria), and again, A.U
760–765 (A.D. 6–11). This double legation is based upon a
passage in Tacitus,[4] and confirmed by an old monumental in-

---

[1] Ulpian, quoted by Zumpt, *Geburtsjahr Christi*, p. 203 sq.

[2] Josephus, *Antiqu.*, xvii. 13, 5 ; xviii. 1, 1. The census here referred to
is evidently the same which Luke means in Acts 5 : 37: "After this man
arose Judas the Galilæan in the days of the enrolment." Josephus calls him
"Judas, a Gaulanite," because he was of Gamala in lower Gaulanitis; but in
Ant., xx. 5, 2, and *Bell. Jud.*, ii. 8, 1, he calls him likewise a Galilæan. In
this case, then, Luke is entirely correct, and it is extremely improbable that
a writer otherwise so well informed as Luke should have confounded two enrolments which were ten years apart.

[3] The usual solution of the difficulty is to give πρώτη the sense of προτέρα,
before Quirinius was governor ; as πρῶτός τινος is used (though not in connection with a participle) in the sense of *prior to*, John 1 : 15, 30 ; 15 : 18. So
Ussher, Huschke, Tholuck, Wieseler, Caspari, Ewald. But this would have
been more naturally and clearly expressed by πρίν or πρὸ τοῦ ἡγεμονεύειν (as in
Luke 2 : 21 ; 12 : 15 ; Acts 23 : 15). Paulus, Ebrard, Lange, Godet, and others
accentuate αὐτή (*ipsa*) and explain : The *decree* of the census was issued at
the time of Christ's birth, but the so-called first *census itself* did not take
place till the governorship of Quirinius (ten years later). Impossible on
account of ver. 3, which reports the execution of the decree, ver. 1. Browne
(p. 46) and others understand ἡγεμονεύειν in a wider sense, so as to include an
extraordinary commission of Quirinius as *legatus Cæsaris*.

[4] *Annal.*, iii. 48, as interpreted by A. W. Zumpt in a Latin dissertation .
De Syria Romanorum provincia ab Cæsare Augusto ad T. Vespasianum, in
Comment. Epigraph., Berol. 1854, vol. ii. 88–125, and approved by Mommsen
in *Res gestæ divi Augusti*, 121–124. Zumpt has developed his views more
fully in *Das Geburtsjahr Christi*, 1869, pp. 1–90. Ussher, Sanclemente, Ideler
(II. 397), and Browne (p. 46) had understood Tacitus in the same way.

scription discovered between the Villa Hadriani and the Via Tiburtina.[1] Hence Luke might very properly call the census about the time of Christ's birth "the first" (πρώτη) under Quirinius, to distinguish it from the second and better known, which he himself mentions in his second treatise on the history of the origin of Christianity (Acts 5 : 37). Perhaps the experience of Quirinius as the superintendent of the first census was the reason why he was sent to Syria a second time for the same purpose.

There still remain, however, three difficulties not easily solved : (a) Quirinius cannot have been governor of Syria before autumn A.U. 750 (B.C. 4), several months *after* Herod's death (which occurred in March, 750), and consequently *after* Christ's birth ; for we know from coins that Quintilius Varus was governor from A.U. 748 to 750 (B.C. 6–4), and left his post *after* the death of Herod.[2] (b) A census during the first governorship of Quirinius is nowhere mentioned but in Luke. (c) A Syrian governor could not well carry out a census in Judæa during the lifetime of Herod, before it was made a Roman province (i. e., A.U. 759).

In reply to these objections we may say : (a) Luke did not intend to give an exact, but only an approximate chronological statement, and may have connected the census with the well-

---

[1] First published at Florence, 1765, then by Sanclemente (*De vulg. ærae Emendat.* Rom. 1793), and more correctly by Bergmann and Mommsen : *De inscriptione Latina, ad P. Sulpicium Quirinium referenda,* Berol. 1851. Mommsen discussed it again in an appendix to *Res gestæ Augusti,* Berol. 1865, pp. 111–126. The inscription is defective, and reads : ". . . Pro. Consul. Asiam. Provinciam. OP[tinuit legatus]. Divi. Augusti. [i]terum [i. e., again, a second time]. Syriam. Et. Ph[oenicem administravit, or, obtinuit]. The name is obliterated. Zumpt refers it to C. Sentius Saturninus (who preceded Quirinius, but is not known to have been *twice* governor of Syria), Bergmann, Mommsen, and Merivale to Quirinius (as was done by Sanclemente in 1793, and by Ideler, 1826). Nevertheless Mommsen denies any favorable bearing of the discovery on the solution of the difficulty in Luke, while Zumpt defends the substantial accuracy of the evangelist.

[2] Josephus, *Antiqu.,* xvii. 11, 1 ; Tacitus, *Hist.,* v. 9 : "*post mortem Herodis* . . . *Simo quidam regium nomen invaserat ; is a Quintilio Vare obtinente Syriam punitus,*" etc.

known name of Quirinius because he completed it, although it was begun under a previous administration. (b) Augustus ordered several *census populi* between A.U. 726 and 767, partly for taxation, partly for military and statistical purposes;[1] and, as a good statesman and financier, he himself prepared a *rationarium* or *breviarium totius imperii*, that is, a list of all the resources of the empire, which was read, after his death, in the Senate.[2] (c) Herod was only a tributary king (*rex socius*), who could exercise no act of sovereignty without authority from the emperor. Judæa was subject to taxation from the time of Pompey, and it seems not to have ceased with the accession of Herod. Moreover, towards the end of his life he lost the favor of Augustus, who wrote him in anger that "whereas of old he had used him as his friend, he would now use him as his subject."[3]

It cannot, indeed, be proven by direct testimony of Josephus or the Roman historians, that Augustus issued a decree for a universal census, embracing all the Provinces ("that all the world," i. e., the Roman world, "should be taxed," Luke 2 : 1), but it is in itself by no means improbable, and was necessary to enable him to prepare his *breviarium totius imperii.*[4]

---

[1] Three censuses, held A.U. 726, 748, and 767, are mentioned on the monument of Ancyra; one in Italy, 757, by Dion Cassius; others in Gaul are assigned to 727, 741, 767; Tertullian, who was a learned lawyer, speaks of one in Judæa under Sentius Saturninus, A.U. 749; and this would be the one which must be meant by Luke.   See Gruter, Huschke, Zumpt, Plumptre, *l. c.*

[2] Suetonius, *Aug.* 28, 101; Tacitus, *Annal.*, i. 11; Dio Cassius, lii. 30; lvi. 33.   The breviarium contained, according to Tacitus: "*opes publicæ, quantum civium sociorumque in armis* [which would include Herod], *quot classes, regna, provinciæ, tributa aut vectigalia, et necessitates ac largitiones. Quæ cuncta sua manu perscripserat Augustus, addideratque consilium coërcendi intra terminos imperii, incertum metu an per invidiam.*"

[3] Joseph. *Ant.* xvi. 9, § 4.   Comp. Marquardt, *Röm. Staatsverwaltung*, I. 249.

[4] Such a decree has been often inferred from the passages of Suetonius and Tacitus just quoted.   The silence of Josephus is not very difficult to explain, for he does not profess to give a history of the empire, is nearly silent on the period from A.U. 750–760, and is not as impartial a historian as Luke, nor worthy of more credit.   Cassiodorus (*Variarum*, iii. 52) and Suidas (*s. v.*, ἀπογραφή) expressly assert the fact of a general census, and add several particulars which are not derived from Luke ; e. g. Suidas says that Augustus elected twenty commissioners of high character and sent them to all parts of the empire to

In the nature of the case, it would take several years to carry out such a decree, and its execution in the provinces would be modified according to national customs.   Zumpt assumes that Sentius Saturninus,[1] who was sent as governor to Syria A.U. 746 (B.C. 9), and remained there till 749 (B.C. 6), began a census in Judæa with a view to substitute a head tax in money for the former customary tribute in produce ; that his successor, Quintilius Varus (B.C. 0–4), continued it, and that Quirinius (B.C. 4) completed the census.   This would explain the confident statement of Tertullian, which he must have derived from some good source, that enrolments were held under Augustus by Sentius Saturninus in Judæa.[2]   Another, but less probable view is that Quirinius was sent to the East as special commissioner for the census during the administration of his predecessor.   In either case Luke might call the census "the first" under Quirinius, considering that he finished the census for personal taxation or registration according to the Jewish custom of family registers, and that afterwards he alone executed the second census for the taxation of property according to the Roman fashion.

The problem is not quite solved ; but the establishment of the fact that Quirinius was prominently connected with the Roman government in the East about the time of the Nativity, is a considerable step towards the solution, and encourages the hope of a still better solution in the future.[3]

collect statistics of population as well as of property, and to return a portion to the national treasury.   Hence Huschke, Wieseler, Zumpt, Plumptre and McClellan accept their testimony as historically correct (while Schürer derives it simply from Luke, without being able to account for these particulars). Wieseler quotes also John Malala, the historian of Antioch, as saying, probably on earlier authorities, that "Augustus, in the 39th year and 10th month of his reign [i. e. B.C. 5 or 6], issued a decree for a general registration throughout the empire."   Julius Cæsar had begun a measurement of the whole empire, and Augustus completed it.

[1] Not to be confounded with L. Volusius Saturninus, who is known, from coins, to have been governor of Syria A.U. 758 (A.D. 4).

[2] *Adv. Marc.* iv. 19 : "*Sed et census constat actos sub Augusto tunc in Judæa per Sentium Saturninum, apud quos genus ejus inquirere potuissent.*"

[3] Zumpt, the classical scholar and archæologist, concludes (p. 223) that there is nothing in Luke's account which does not receive, from modern research,

THE FORTY-SIX YEARS OF THE BUILDING OF HEROD'S TEMPLE.

(5) St. John, ch. 2 : 20, furnishes us a date in the remark of the Jews, in the first year of Christ's ministry : "Forty and six years was this temple in building, and wilt thou raise it up in three days?"

We learn from Josephus that Herod began the reconstruction of the temple in Jerusalem in the eighteenth year of his reign, i. e., A.U. 732, if we reckon from his appointment by the Romans (714), or A.U. 735, if we reckon from the death of Antigonus and the conquest of Jerusalem (717).[1] The latter is the correct view; otherwise Josephus would contradict himself, since, in another passage, he dates the building from the fifteenth year of Herod's reign.[2] Adding forty-six years to 735, we have the year A.U. 781 (A.D. 27) for the first year of Christ's ministry; and deducting thirty and a half or thirty-one years from 781, we come back to A.U. 750 (B.C. 4) as the year of the Nativity.

THE TIME OF THE CRUCIFIXION.

(6) Christ was crucified under the consulate of the two Gemini (i. e., C. Rubellius Geminus and C. Fufius Geminus), who were consuls A.U. 782 to 783 (A.D. 28 to 29). This statement is made by Tertullian, in connection with an elaborate calculation of the time of Christ's birth and passion from the seventy weeks

"full historical probability" ("*volle historische Wahrscheinlichkeit*"); while Schürer, the theologian, still doubts (Matt. 28 : 17). Dr. Woolsey (*s. v.* "Cyrenius," in "Smith's Bible Dict.," Hackett and Abbot's ed., p. 526), decides that "something is gained." In the art. "Taxing" he says that a registration of Judæa made under the direction of the president of Syria by Jewish officers would not greatly differ from a similar registration made by Herod, and need not have alarmed the Jews if carefully managed.

[1] *Antiqu.* xv. 11, 1 : "And now Herod, in the eighteenth year of his reign (ὀκτωκαιδεκάτου τῆς Ἡρώδου βασιλείας ἐνιαυτοῦ) . . . undertook a very great work, that is, to build of himself the temple of God, and to raise it to a most magnificent altitude, as esteeming it to be the most glorious of all his actions, as it really was, to bring it to perfection, and that this would be sufficient for an everlasting memorial of him."

[2] *Bell. Jua* I. 21, 1, πεντεκαιδεκάτῳ ἔτει τῆς βασιλείας αὐτὸν δὲ τὸν ναὸς ἐπεσκεύασε.

of Daniel.[1] He may possibly have derived it from some public record in Rome. He erred in identifying the year of Christ's passion with the first year of his ministry (the 15th year of Tiberius, Luke 3 : 1). Allowing, as we must, two or three years for his public ministry, and thirty-three years for his life, we reach the year 750 or 749 as the year of the Nativity.

Thus we arrive from these various incidental notices of three Evangelists, and the statement of Tertullian essentially at the same conclusion, which contributes its share towards establishing the credibility of the gospel history against the mythical theory. Yet in the absence of a *precise* date, and in view of uncertainties in calculation, there is still room for difference of opinion between the years A.U. 747 (B.C. 7), as the earliest, and A.U. 750 (B.C. 4), as the latest, possible date for the year of Christ's birth. The French Benedictines, Sanclemente, Münter, Wurm, Ebrard, Jarvis, Alford, Jos. A. Alexander, Zumpt, Keim, decide for A.U. 747 ; Kepler (reckoning from the conjunction of Jupiter, Saturn and Mars in that year), Lardner, Ideler, Ewald, for 748 ; Petavius, Ussher, Tillemont, Browne, Angus, Robinson, Andrews, McClellan, for 749 ; Bengel, Wieseler, Lange, Lichtenstein, Anger, Greswell, Ellicott, Plumptre, Merivale, for 750.

II. The Day of the Nativity.—The only indication of the season of our Saviour's birth is the fact that the Shepherds were watching their flocks in the field at that time, Luke 2 : 8. This fact points to any other season rather than winter, and is therefore not favorable to the traditional date, though not conclusive against it. The time of pasturing in Palestine (which has

---

[1] *Adv. Jud.* c. 8 : "*Huius* [*Tiberii*] *quinto decimo anno imperii passus est Christus, annos habens quasi triginta, cum pateretur* . . . . *Quæ passio huius exterminii intra tempora* LXX *hebdomadarum perfecta est sub Tiberio Cæsare,* CONSULIBUS RUBELLIO GEMINO ET FUFIO GEMINO, *mense Martio, temporibus paschæ, die* VIII *Kalendarum Aprilium, die prima azymorum, quo agnum occi- derunt ad vesperam, sicuti a Moyse fuerat præceptum.*" Lactantius (*De Mort. Persec.* 2 ; *De Vera Sap.* 10) and Augustine make the same statement (*De Civit. Dei*, I. xviii. c. 54 : "*Mortuus est Christus duobus Geminis Consulibus, octavo Kalendas Aprilis* "). Zumpt assigns much weight to this tradition, pp. 268 sqq.

but two seasons, the dry and the wet, or summer and winter)
begins, according to the Talmudists, in March, and lasts till
November, when the herds are brought in from the fields, and
kept under shelter till the close of February. But this refers
chiefly to pastures in the wilderness, far away from towns and
villages,[1] and admits of frequent exceptions in the close neighborhood of towns, according to the character of the season. A succession of bright days in December and January is of frequent
occurrence in the East, as in Western countries. Tobler, an
experienced traveller in the Holy Land, says that in Bethlehem
the weather about Christmas is favorable to the feeding of flocks
and often most beautiful. On the other hand strong and cold
winds often prevail in April, and explain the fire mentioned John
18 : 18.

No certain conclusion can be drawn from the journey of
Joseph and Mary to Bethlehem, and to Egypt; nor from the
journey of the Magi. As a rule February is the best time
for travelling in Egypt, March the best in the Sinaitic Peninsula, April and May, and next to it autumn, the best in Palestine ; but necessity knows no rule.

The ancient tradition is of no account here, as it varied down
to the fourth century. Clement of Alexandria relates that some
regarded the 25th Pachon (i. e. May 20), others the 24th or 25th
Pharmuthi (April 19 or 20), as the day of Nativity.

(1) The traditional 25th of December is defended by Jerome,
Chrysostom, Baronius, Lamy, Ussher, Petavius, Bengel (Ideler),
Seyffarth and Jarvis. It has no historical authority beyond the
fourth century, when the Christmas festival was introduced first
in Rome (before A.D. 360), on the basis of several Roman festivals (the *Saturnalia, Sigillaria, Juvenalia, Brumalia,* or *Dies
natalis Invicti Solis*), which were held in the latter part of December in commemoration of the golden age of liberty and
equality, and in honor of the sun, who in the winter solstice is,
as it were, born anew and begins his conquering march. This

---

[1] As in Switzerland the herds are driven to the mountain pastures in May
and brought home in August or September.

phenomenon in nature was regarded as an appropriate symbol of the appearance of the Sun of Righteousness dispelling the long night of sin and error. For the same reason the summer solstice (June 24) was afterwards selected for the festival of John the Baptist, as the fittest reminder of his own humble self-estimate that he must decrease, while Christ must increase (John 3 : 30). Accordingly the 25th of March was chosen for the commemoration of the Annunciation of the Virgin Mary, and the 24th of September for that of the conception of Elizabeth.[1]

(2) The 6th of January has in its favor an older tradition (according to Epiphanius and Cassianus), and is sustained by Eusebius. It was celebrated in the East from the third century as the feast of the Epiphany, in commemoration of the Nativity as well as of Christ's baptism, and afterwards of his manifestation to the Gentiles (represented by the Magi).

(3) Other writers have selected some day in February (Hug, Wieseler, Ellicott), or March (Paulus, Winer), or April (Greswell), or August (Lewin), or September (Lightfoot, who assumes, on chronological grounds, that Christ was born on the feast of Tabernacles, as he died on the Passover and sent the Spirit on Pentecost), or October (Newcome). Lardner puts the birth between the middle of August and the middle of November; Browne December 8 ; Lichtenstein in summer ; Robinson leaves it altogether uncertain.

III. THE DURATION OF CHRIST'S LIFE.—This is now generally confined to thirty-two or three years. The difference of one or two years arises from the different views on the length of his public ministry. Christ died and rose again in the full vigor of early manhood, and so continues to live in the memory of the church. The decline and weakness of old age is inconsistent with his position as the Renovator and Saviour of mankind.

Irenæus, otherwise (as a disciple of Polycarp, who was a dis-

[1] The latest learned advocate of the traditional date is John Brown McClellan, who tries to prove that Christ was born Dec. 25, A.U. 749 (B.C. 5). See his *New Test.*, etc. vol. I. 390 sqq.

ciple of St. John) the most trustworthy witness of apostolic traditions among the fathers, held the untenable opinion that
Christ attained to the ripe age of forty or fifty years and taught
over ten years (beginning with the thirtieth), and that he thus
passed through all the stages of human life, to save and sanctify
"old men" as well as "infants and children and boys and
youths." [1] He appeals for this view to tradition dating from
St. John, [2] and supports it by an unwarranted inference from
the loose conjecture of the Jews when, surprised at the claim of
Jesus to have existed before Abraham was born, they asked
him: "Thou art not yet fifty years old, and hast thou seen
Abraham?" [3] A similar inference from another passage, where
the Jews speak of the "forty-six years" since the temple of
Herod began to be constructed, while Christ spoke of the temple
his body (John 2 : 20), is of course still less conclusive.

IV. DURATION OF CHRIST'S PUBLIC MINISTRY.—It began with
the baptism by John and ended with the crucifixion. About
the length of the intervening time there are (besides the isolated
and decidedly erroneous view of Irenæus) three theories, allowing respectively one, two, or three years and a few months, and
designated as the bipaschal, tripaschal, and quadripaschal schemes,
according to the number of Passovers. The Synoptists mention
only the last Passover during the public ministry of our Lord,
at which he was crucified, but they intimate that he was in
Judæa more than once. [4] John certainly mentions three Passo-

---

[1] *Adv. Hær.* II. c. 22, § 4–6.

[2] This shows conclusively how uncertain patristic traditions are as to mere
facts.

[3] John 8 : 57. Irenæus reasons that the Jews made the nearest approach
to the real age, either from mere observation or from knowledge of the public records, and thus concludes · " Christ did not therefore preach only for one
year, nor did he suffer in the twelfth month of the year; for the period included
between the thirtieth and the fiftieth year can never be regarded as one
year, unless indeed, among their æons [he speaks of the Gnostics] there be
such long years assigned to those who sit in their ranks with Bythos in the
Pleroma."

[4] Comp. Matt. 4 : 12 ; 23 : 37 ; Mark 1 : 14 ; Luke 4 : 14 ; 10 : 38 ; 13 : 34.

overs, two of which (the first and the last) Christ did attend,[1] and *perhaps* a fourth, which he also attended.[2]

(1) The bipaschal scheme confines the public ministry to one year and a few weeks or months. This was first held by the Gnostic sect of the Valentinians (who connected it with their fancy about thirty æons), and by several fathers, Clement of Alexandria, Tertullian, and perhaps by Origen and Augustine (who express themselves doubtfully). The chief argument of the fathers and those harmonists who follow them, is derived from the prophecy of "the acceptable year of the Lord," as quoted by Christ,[3] and from the typical meaning of the paschal lamb, which must be of "one year" and without blemish.[4] Far more important is the argument drawn by some modern critics from the silence of the synoptical Gospels concerning the other Passovers.[5] But this silence is not in itself conclusive, and must yield to the positive testimony of John, which cannot be conformed to the bipaschal scheme.[6] Moreover, it is simply impossible to crowd the events of Christ's life, the training of the Twelve, and the development of the hostility of the Jews, into one short year.

(2) The choice therefore lies between the tripaschal and the quadripaschal schemes. The decision depends chiefly on the interpretation of the unnamed "feast of the Jews," John 5 : 1, whether it was a Passover, or another feast ; and this again depends much (though not exclusively) on a difference of reading

---

[1] John 2 : 13, 23 ; 6 : 4 ; 11 : 55 ; 12 : 1 ; 13 : 1. The Passover mentioned 6 : 4 Christ did not attend, because the Jews sought to kill him (7 : 1 ; comp. 5: 18).

[2] John 5 : 1 if we read the article ἡ before ἑορτὴ τῶν Ἰουδαίων. See below.

[3] Isa. 61 : 2 ; comp. Luke 4 : 14.

[4] Exod. 12 : 5.   [5] Keim, I. 130.

[6] Henry Browne who, in his *Ordo Sæclorum* (pp. 80 sqq.), likewise defends the one year's ministry, in part by astronomical calculations, is constrained to eliminate without any MSS. authority τὸ πάσχα from John 6 : 4, and to make the ἑορτή there mentioned to be the same as that in 7 : 2, so that John would give the feasts of one year only, in regular chronological order, namely, the Passover 2 : 13 in March, the Pentecost 5 : 1 in May, the Feast of Tabernacles 6 : 4 ; 7 : 2 in September, the Feast of Dedication 10 : 22 in December, the Passover of the Crucifixion in March.

(*the* feast, or *a* feast).[1] The parable of the barren fig-tree, which represents the Jewish people, has been used as an argument in favor of a three years' ministry: "Behold, these three years I come seeking fruit on this fig-tree, and find none."[2] The three years are certainly significant; but according to Jewish reckoning two and a half years would be called three years. More remote is the reference to the prophetic announcement of Daniel 9 : 27: "And he shall confirm the covenant with many for one week, and in the midst of the week he shall cause the sacrifice and the oblation to cease." The tripaschal theory is more easily reconciled with the synoptical Gospels, while the quadripaschal theory leaves more room for arranging the discourses and miracles of our Lord, and has been adopted by the majority of harmonists.[3]

But even if we extend the public ministry to three years, it presents a disproportion between duration and effect without a parallel in history and inexplicable on purely natural grounds. In the language of an impartial historian, "the simple record of three short years of active life has done more to regenerate

---

[1] The definite article before "feast" (ἡ ἑορτή), which is supported by the Sinaitic MS. and adopted by Tischendorf (ed. viii.), favors the view that the feast was the Passover, *the* great feast of the Jews. The reading without the article, which has the weight of the more critical Vatican MS., and is preferred by Lachmann, Tregelles, Westcott and Hort, and by the Revision of the E. V., favors the view that it was Pentecost, or Purim, or some other subordinate feast. (On the grammatical question comp. Thayer's Winer, p. 125, and Moulton's Winer, p. 155.) In all other passages John gives the name of the feast (τὸ πάσχα 2 : 13 ; 6 : 4 ; 11 : 55 ; ἡ σκηνοπηγία 7 : 2 ; τὰ ἐγκαίνια 10 : 22). It is objected that Jesus would not be likely to attend the patriotic and secular feast of Purim, which was not a temple feast and required no journey to Jerusalem, while he omitted the next Passover (John 6 : 4) which was of divine appointment and much more solemn ; but the objection is not conclusive, since he attended other minor festivals (John 7 : 2 ; 10 : 22) merely for the purpose of doing good.

[2] Luke 13 : 6-9. Bengel, Hengstenberg, Wieseler, Weizsäcker, Alford, Wordsworth, Andrews, McClellan.

[3] By Eusebius (*H. E.*, I. 10), Theodoret (*in Dan.* ix.), Robinson, Andrews, McClellan, Gardiner, and many others. On the other hand Jerome, Wieseler, and Tischendorf hold the tripaschal theory. Jerome says (on Isaiah, ch. 29, in Migne's ed. of the *Opera*, IV. 330): "*Scriptum est in Evangelio secundum Joannem, per tria Pascha Dominum venisse in Jerusalem, quæ duos annos efficiunt.*"

and soften mankind than all the disquisitions of philosophers and all the exhortations of moralists.   This has indeed been the wellspring of whatever is best and purest in the Christian life." [1]

V. The Date of the Lord's Death.—The day of the week on which Christ suffered on the cross was a Friday,[2] during the week of the Passover, in the month of Nisan, which was the first of the twelve lunar months of the Jewish year, and included the vernal equinox.   But the question is whether this Friday was the 14th, or the 15th of Nisan, that is, the day before the feast or the first day of the feast, which lasted a week.   The Synoptical Gospels clearly decide for the 15th, for they all say (independently) that our Lord partook of the paschal supper on the legal day, called the "first day of unleavened bread," [3] that is on the evening of the 14th, or rather at the beginning of the 15th (the paschal lambs being slain "between the two evenings," i. e. before and after sunset, between 3 and 5 P.M. of the 14th). [4] John, on the other hand, seems at first sight to point to the 14th, so that the death of our Lord would very nearly have coincided with the slaying of the paschal lamb.[5]   But the three or four passages which look in that direction can, and, on closer examination, must

[1] W. E. H. Lecky : *History of European Morals from Augustus to Charlemagne* (1869) vol. II. p. 9.   He adds: "Amid all the sins and failings, amid all the priestcraft and persecution and fanaticism that have defaced the Church, it has preserved, in the character and example of its Founder, an enduring principle of regeneration."

[2] Mark 15 : 42 ; Matt. 27 : 62 ; Luke 23 : 54 ; John 19 : 14.   Friday is called Preparation-day ($\pi\alpha\rho\alpha\sigma\kappa\epsilon\nu\acute{\eta}$), because the meals for the Sabbath were prepared on the sixth day, as no fires were allowed to be kindled on the Sabbath (Ex. 16 : 5).

[3] Matt. 26 : 17, 20 ; Mark 14 : 12 ; Luke 22 : 7, 15.   Comp. John 18 : 39, 40.

[4] Ex. 12 : 6 ; Lev. 23 : 5 ; Num. 9 : 3, 5.   If the phrase "between the two evenings " (הָעַרְבַּיִם בֵּין) could be taken to mean between the evening of the 14th and the evening of the 15th of Nisan, we should have twenty-four hours for the slaying and eating of the paschal lambs, and the whole difficulty between John and the Synoptists would disappear.   We could easier conceive also the enormous number of 270,000 lambs which, according to the statement of Josephus, had to be sacrificed.   But that interpretation is excluded by the fact that the same expression is used in the rules about the daily evening sacrifice (Ex. 29 : 39, 41 ; Num. 28 : 4).

[5] John 13 : 1 ; 13 : 29 ; 18 : 28 ; 19 : 14.

be harmonized with the Synoptical statement, which admits only of one natural interpretation.[1] It seems strange, indeed, that

---

[1] John 13 : 1 "*before* the feast of the Passover" does not mean a day before (which would have been so expressed, comp. 12 : 1), but a short time before, and refers to the commencement of the 15th of Nisan. The passage, 13 : 29 : "Buy what things we have need of for the feast," causes no difficulty if we remember that Jesus sat down with his disciples before the regular hour of the Passover (13 : 1), so that there was time yet for the necessary purchases. The passage on the contrary affords a strong argument against the supposition that the supper described by John took place a full day before the Passover; for then there would have been no need of such haste for purchases as the apostles understood Christ to mean when he said to Judas, "That thou doest, do quickly" (13 : 27). In John 18 : 28 it is said that the Jews went not into the Prætorium of the heathen Pilate "that they might not be defiled, but might eat the *Passover;*" but this was said early in the morning, at about 3 A.M., when the regular paschal meal was not yet finished in the city; others take the word "Passover" here in an unusual sense so as to embrace the *chagigah* (הֲגִיגָה) or festive thank-offerings during the Passover week, especially on the fifteenth day of Nisan (comp. 2 Chr. 30 : 22); at all events it cannot apply to the paschal supper on the evening of the fifteenth of Nisan, for the defilement would have ceased *after sunset*, and could therefore have been no bar to eating the paschal supper (Lev. 15 : 1–18; 22 : 1–7). "The Preparation of the Passover," ἡ παρασκευὴ τοῦ πάσχα, 19 : 14, is not the day preceding the Passover (*Passover-Eve*), but, as clearly in vers. 31 and 42, the Preparation day of the Passover week, i. e. the Paschal Friday; παρασκευή being the technical term for Friday as the preparation day for the Sabbath, the fore-Sabbath, προσάββατον, Mark 15 : 42 (comp. the German *Sonnabend* for Saturday, *Sabbath-eve*, etc.). For a fuller examination of the respective passages, see my edition of Lange on *Matthew* (pp. 454 sqq.), and on *John* (pp. 406, 415, 562, 569). Lightfoot, Wieseler, Lichtenstein, Hengstenberg, Ebrard (in the *third* ed. of his *Kritik*, 1868), Lange, Kirchner, Keil, Robinson, Andrews, Milligan, Plumptre and McClellan take the same view; while Lücke, Bleek, DeWette, Meyer, Ewald, Stier, Beyschlag, Greswell, Ellicott, Farrar, Mansel and Westcott maintain that Christ was crucified on the fourteenth of Nisan, and either assume a contradiction between John and the Synoptists (which in this case seems quite impossible), or transfer the paschal supper of Christ to the preceding day, contrary to law and custom. John himself clearly points to the fifteenth of Nisan as the day of the crucifixion, when he reports that the customary release of a prisoner " at the Passover" (ἐν τῷ πάσχα) was granted by Pilate on the day of crucifixion, 18 : 39, 40. The critical and cautious Dr. Robinson says (*Harmony*, p. 222) : "After repeated and calm consideration, there rests upon my own mind a clear conviction, that there is nothing in the language of John, or in the attendant circumstances, which upon fair interpretation requires or permits us to believe, that the beloved disciple either intended to correct, or has in fact corrected or contradicted, the explicit and unquestionable testimony of Matthew, Mark and Luke." Comp. also among the more recent discussions Mor. Kirchner : *Die*

the Jewish priests should have matured their bloody counsel in the solemn night of the Passover, and urged a crucifixion on a great festival, but it agrees with the satanic wickedness of their crime.[1] Moreover it is on the other hand equally difficult to explain that they, together with the people, should have remained about the cross till late in the afternoon of the fourteenth, when, according to the law, they were to kill the paschal lamb and prepare for the feast; and that Nicodemus and Joseph of Arimathæa, with the pious women, should have buried the body of Jesus and so incurred defilement at that solemn hour.

The view here advocated is strengthened by astronomical calculation, which shows that in A.D. 30, the probable year of the crucifixion, the 15th of Nisan actually fell on a Friday (April 7); and this was the case only once more between the years A.D. 28 and 36, except perhaps also in 33. Consequently Christ must have been crucified A.D. 30.[2]

To sum up the results, the following appear to us the most probable dates in the earthly life of our Lord:

Birth................A.U. 750 (Jan. ?) or 749 (Dec. ?) B.C. 4 or 5.
Baptism .............A.U. 780 (Jan. ?)   A.D. 27.
Length of Public Ministry
    (three years and three or
    four months)........A.U. 780–783   A.D. 27–30.
Crucifixion...........A.U. 783 (15th of Nisan)   A.D. 30 (April 7).

jüd. Passahfeier und Jesu letztes Mahl (Gotha, 1870); McClellan : *N. Test.* (1875), I. 473 sqq., 482 sqq.; Keil : *Evang. des Matt.* (Leipz. 1877), pp. 513 sqq.

[1] The answer to this objection is well presented by Dr. Robinson, *Harmony*, p. 222, and Keil, *Evang. des Matt.*, pp. 522 sqq. The Mishna prescribes that "on Sabbaths and festival days no trial or judgment may be held;" but on the other hand it contains directions and regulations for the meetings and actions of the Sanhedrin on the Sabbaths, and executions of criminals were purposely reserved to great festivals for the sake of stronger example. In our case, the Sanhedrin on the day after the crucifixion, which was a Sabbath and "a great day," applied to Pilate for a watch and caused the sepulchre to be sealed, Matt. 27 : 62 sq.

[2] See Wieseler, *Chronol. Synopse*, p. 446, and in Herzog, vol. XXI. 550; and especially the carefully prepared astronomical tables of new and full moons by Prof. Adams, in McClellan, I. 493, who devoutly exults in the result of the crucial test of astronomical calculation which makes the very heavens, after the roll of centuries, bear witness to the harmony of the Gospels.

§ 17.   *The Land and the People.*

Literature.

I. The geographical and descriptive works on the Holy Land by RELAND
(1714), ROBINSON (1838 and 1856), RITTER (1850–1855), RAUMER (4th
ed. 1860), TOBLER (several monographs from 1849 to 1869), W. M.
THOMSON (revised ed. 1880), STANLEY (1853, 6th ed. 1866), TRISTRAM
(1864), SCHAFF (1878 ; enlarged ed. 1889), GUÉRIN (1869, 1875, 1880).
See TOBLER's *Bibliographia geographica Palæstinæ* (Leipz. 1867),
and the supplementary lists of more recent works by PH. WOLFF in
the "Jahrbücher für deutsche Theologie," 1868 and 1872, and by
SOCIN in the "Zeitschrift des deutschen Palästina-Vereins," 1878,
p. 40, etc.

II. The "Histories of New Testament Times" (*Neutestamentliche Zeitgeschichte*, a special department of historical theology recently introduced), by SCHNECKENBURGER (1862), HAUSRATH (1868 sqq.), and
SCHÜRER (1874).
See Lit. in ? 8, p. 56.

There is a wonderful harmony between the life of our Lord
as described by the Evangelists, and his geographical and historical environment as known to us from contemporary writers,
and illustrated and confirmed by modern discovery and research.
This harmony contributes not a little to the credibility of the
gospel history. The more we come to understand the age and
country in which Jesus lived, the more we feel, in reading the
Gospels, that we are treading on the solid ground of real history illuminated by the highest revelation from heaven. The
poetry of the canonical Gospels, if we may so call their prose,
which in spiritual beauty excels all poetry, is not (like that of
the Apocryphal Gospels) the poetry of human fiction—"no
fable old, no mythic lore, nor dream of bards and seers ; " it is
the poetry of revealed truth, the poetry of the sublimest facts,
the poetry of the infinite wisdom and love of God which never
before had entered the imagination of man, but which assumed
human flesh and blood in Jesus of Nazareth and solved through
his life and work the deepest problem of our existence.

The stationary character of Oriental countries and peoples
enables us to infer from their present aspect and condition what

they were two thousand years ago. And in this we are aided
by the multiplying discoveries which make even stones and
mummies eloquent witnesses of the past. Monumental evidence
appeals to the senses and overrules the critical conjectures and
combinations of unbelieving skepticism, however ingenious and
acute they may be. Who will doubt the history of the Phara-
ohs when it can be read in the pyramids and sphinxes, in the
ruins of temples and rock-tombs, in hieroglyphic inscriptions
and papyrus rolls which antedate the founding of Rome and the
exodus of Moses and the Israelites ? Who will deny the biblical records of Babylon and Nineveh after these cities have risen
from the grave of centuries to tell their own story through
cuneiform inscriptions, eagle-winged lions and human-headed
bulls, ruins of temples and palaces disentombed from beneath
the earth ? We might as well erase Palestine from the map
and remove it to fairy-land, as to blot out the Old and New
Testament from history and resolve them into airy myths and
legends.[1]

The Land.

Jesus spent his life in Palestine. It is a country of about
the size of Maryland, smaller than Switzerland, and not half as
large as Scotland,[2] but favored with a healthy climate, beautiful
scenery, and great variety and fertility of soil, capable of producing fruits of all lands from the snowy north to the tropical south ; isolated from other countries by desert, mountain

---

[1] Well says Hausrath (Preface to 2nd ed. of vol. I. p. ix) against the mythical theory : " *Für die poëtische Welt der religiösen Sage ist innerhalb einer rein
historischen Darstellung kein Raum ; ihre Gebilde verbleichen vor einem geschichtlich hellen Hintergrund . . . Wenn wir die heilige Geschichte als Bruch-
stück einer allgemeinen Geschichte nachweisen und zeigen können, wie die Ränder
passen, wenn wir die abgerissenen Fäden, die sie mit der profanen Welt verbanden,
wieder aufzufinden vermögen, dann ist die Meinung ausgeschlossen, diese Geschichte sei der schöne Traum eines späteren Geschlechtes gewesen.*"

[2] The average length of Palestine is 150 miles, the average breadth east and
west of the Jordan to the Mediterranean, from 80 to 90 miles, the number of
square miles from 12,000 to 13,000.   The State of Maryland has 11,124,
Switzerland 15,992, Scotland 30,695 English square miles.

and sea, yet lying in the centre of the three continents of the
eastern hemisphere and bordering on the Mediterranean highway of the historic nations of antiquity, and therefore providentially adapted to develop not only the particularism of Judaism, but also the universalism of Christianity.   From little
Phœnicia the world has derived the alphabet, from little Greece
philosophy and art, from little Palestine the best of all—the
true religion and the cosmopolitan Bible.   Jesus could not have
been born at any other time than in the reign of Cæsar Augustus, after the Jewish religion, the Greek civilization, and the
Roman government had reached their maturity; nor in any
other land than Palestine, the classical soil of revelation, nor
among any other people than the Jews, who were predestinated
and educated for centuries to prepare the way for the coming of
the Messiah and the fulfilment of the law and the prophets.   In
his infancy, a fugitive from the wrath of Herod, He passed
through the Desert (probably by the short route along the Mediterranean coast) to Egypt and back again; and often may his
mother have spoken to him of their brief sojourn in "the land of
bondage," out of which Jehovah had led his people, by the mighty
arm of Moses, across the Red Sea and through "the great and
terrible wilderness" into the land of promise.   During his forty
days of fasting "in the wilderness" he was, perhaps, on Mount
Sinai communing with the spirits of Moses and Elijah, and preparing himself in the awfully eloquent silence of that region for the
personal conflict with the Tempter of the human race, and for the
new legislation of liberty from the Mount of Beatitudes.[1]   Thus
the three lands of the Bible, Egypt, the cradle of Israel, the Desert, its school and playground, and Canaan, its final home, were
touched and consecrated by "those blessed feet which, *eighteen*
centuries ago, were nailed for our advantage on the bitter cross."
   He travelled on his mission of love through Judæa, Samaria,

---

[1] The tradition, which locates the Temptation on the barren and dreary
mount Quarantania, a few miles northwest of Jericho, is of late date.   Paul
also probably went, after his conversion, as far as Mount Sinai during the
three years of repose and preparation "in Arabia," Gal. 1:17, comp. 4:24.

Galilee, and Peræa; he came as far north as mount Hermon, and once he crossed beyond the land of Israel to the Phœnician border and healed the demonized daughter of that heathen mother to whom he said, "O woman, great is thy faith: be it done unto thee even as thou wilt."

We can easily follow him from place to place, on foot or on horseback, twenty or thirty miles a day, over green fields and barren rocks, over hill and dale, among flowers and thistles, under olive and fig-trees, pitching our tent for the night's rest, ignoring the comforts of modern civilization, but delighting in the unfading beauties of God's nature, reminded at every step of his wonderful dealings with his people, and singing the psalms of his servants of old.

We may kneel at his manger in Bethlehem, the town of Judæa where Jacob buried his beloved Rachel, and a pillar, now a white mosque, marks her grave; where Ruth was rewarded for her filial devotion, and children may still be seen gleaning after the reapers in the grainfields, as she did in the field of Boaz; where his ancestor, the poet-king, was born and called from his father's flocks to the throne of Israel; where shepherds are still watching the sheep as in that solemn night when the angelic host thrilled their hearts with the heavenly anthem of glory to God, and peace on earth to men of his good pleasure; where the sages from the far East offered their sacrifices in the name of future generations of heathen converts; where Christian gratitude has erected the oldest church in Christendom, the "Church of the Nativity," and inscribed on the solid rock in the "Holy Crypt," in letters of silver, the simple but pregnant inscription: "*Hic de Virgine Maria Jesus Christus natus est.*" When all the surroundings correspond with the Scripture narrative, it is of small account whether the traditional grotto of the Nativity is the identical spot—though pointed out as such it would seem already in the middle of the second century.[1]

---

[1] W. Hepworth Dixon (*The Holy Land*, ch. 14) ingeniously pleads for the traditional cave, and the identity of the inn of the Nativity with the patrimony of Boaz and the home of David.

We accompany him in a three days' journey from Bethlehem
to Nazareth, his proper home, where he spent thirty silent
years of his life in quiet preparation for his public work, unknown in his divine character to his neighbors and even the
members of his own household (John 7 : 5), except his saintly
parents. Nazareth is still there, a secluded, but charmingly
located mountain village, with narrow, crooked and dirty streets,
with primitive stone houses where men, donkeys and camels are
huddled together, surrounded by cactus hedges and fruitful
gardens of vines, olive, fig, and pomegranates, and favorably
distinguished from the wretched villages of modern Palestine
by comparative industry, thrift, and female beauty ; the never
failing "Virgin's Fountain," whither Jesus must often have
accompanied his mother for the daily supply of water, is still
there near the Greek Church of the Annunciation, and is the
evening rendezvous of the women and maidens, with their water-
jars gracefully poised on the head or shoulder, and a row of
silver coins adorning their forehead ; and behind the village still
rises the hill, fragrant with heather and thyme, from which he
may often have cast his eye eastward to Gilboa, where Jonathan
fell, and to the graceful, cone-like Tabor—the Righi of Palestine—northward to the lofty Mount Hermon—the Mont Blanc
of Palestine—southward to the fertile plain of Esdraëlon—the
classic battle-ground of Israel—and westward to the ridge of
Carmel, the coast of Tyre and Sidon and the blue waters of the
Mediterranean sea—the future highway of his gospel of peace
to mankind.   There he could feast upon the rich memories of
David and Jonathan, Elijah and Elisha, and gather images of
beauty for his lessons of wisdom.   We can afford to smile at
the silly superstition which points out the kitchen of the Virgin Mary beneath the Latin Church of the Annunciation, the
suspended column where she received the angel's message, the
carpenter shop of Joseph and Jesus, the synagogue in which he
preached on the acceptable year of the Lord, the stone table at
which he ate with his disciples, the Mount of Precipitation two
miles off, and the stupendous monstrosity of the removal of the

dwelling-house of Mary by angels in the air across the sea to
Loretto in Italy! These are childish fables, in striking contrast with the modest silence of the Gospels, and neutralized by
the rival traditions of Greek and Latin monks ; but nature in its
beauty is still the same as Jesus saw and interpreted it in his
incomparable parables, which point from nature to nature's God
and from visible symbols to eternal truths.[1]

Jesus was inaugurated into his public ministry by his baptism
in the fast-flowing river Jordan, which connects the Old and
New Covenant. The traditional spot, a few miles from Jericho,
is still visited by thousands of Christian pilgrims from all parts of

[1] We add the vivid description of Renan (*Vie de Jésus*, Ch. II. p. 25) from
personal observation : " Nazareth was a small town, situated in a fold of land
broadly open at the summit of the group of mountains which closes on the
north the plain of Esdraëlon. The population is now from three to four
[probably five to six] thousand, and it cannot have changed very much. It
is quite cold in winter and the climate is very healthy. The town, like all the
Jewish villages of the time, was a mass of dwellings built without style, and
must have presented the same poor and uninteresting appearance as the villages
in Semitic countries. The houses, from all that appears, did not differ much
from those cubes of stone, without interior or exterior elegance, which now
cover the richest portion of the Lebanon, and which, in the midst of vines and
fig-trees, are nevertheless very pleasant. The environs, moreover, are charming, and no place in the world was so well adapted to dreams of absolute happiness (*nul endroit du monde ne fut si bien fait pour les rêves de l'absolu bon-
heur*). Even in our days, Nazareth is a delightful sojourn, the only place perhaps in Palestine where the soul feels a little relieved of the burden which
weighs upon it in the midst of this unequalled desolation. The people are
friendly and good-natured ; the gardens are fresh and green. Antonius Martyr, at the end of the sixth century, draws an enchanting picture of the fertility of the environs, which he compares to paradise. Some valleys on the
western side fully justify his description. The fountain about which the life
and gayety of the little town formerly centered, has been destroyed ; its broken
channels now give but a turbid water. But the beauty of the women who
gathered there at night, this beauty which was already remarked in the sixth
century, and in which was seen the gift of the Virgin Mary, has been surpris-
ingly well preserved. It is the Syrian type in all its languishing grace.
There is no doubt that Mary was there nearly every day and took her place,
with her urn upon her shoulder, in the same line with her unremembered
countrywomen. Antonius Martyr remarks that the Jewish women, elsewhere
disdainful to Christians, are here full of affability. Even at this day religious
animosities are less intense at Nazareth than elsewhere." Comp. also the
more elaborate description in Keim, I. 318 sqq., and Tobler's monograph on
Nazareth, Berlin, 1868.

the world at the Easter season, who repeat the spectacle of the multitudinous baptisms of John, when the people came "from Jerusalem and all Judæa and all the region round about the Jordan" to confess their sins and to receive his water-baptism of repentance.

The ruins of Jacob's well still mark the spot where Jesus sat down weary of travel, but not of his work of mercy, and opened to the poor woman of Samaria the well of the water of life and instructed her in the true spiritual worship of God; and the surrounding landscape, Mount Gerizim, and Mount Ebal, the town of Shechem, the grain-fields whitening to the harvest, all illustrate and confirm the narrative in the fourth chapter of John; while the fossil remnant of the Samaritans at Nablous (the modern Shechem) still perpetuates the memory of the paschal sacrifice according to the Mosaic prescription, and their traditional hatred of the Jews.

We proceed northward to Galilee where Jesus spent the most popular part of his public ministry and spoke so many of his undying words of wisdom and love to the astonished multitudes. That province was once thickly covered with forests, cultivated fields, plants and trees of different climes, prosperous villages and an industrious population.[1] The rejection of the Messiah and the Moslem invasion have long since turned that paradise of nature into a desolate wilderness, yet could not efface the holy memories and the illustrations of the gospel history. There is the lake with its clear blue waters, once whitened with ships sailing from shore to shore, and the scene of a naval battle between the Romans and the Jews, now utterly forsaken, but still abounding in fish, and subject to sudden violent storms, such as the one which

---

[1] Josephus no doubt greatly exaggerates when he states that there were no less than two hundred and four towns and villages in Galilee (*Vita*, c. 45, διακόσιαι καὶ τέσσαρες κατὰ τὴν Γαλιλαίαν εἰσὶ πόλεις καὶ κῶμαι), and that the smallest of those villages contained above fifteen thousand inhabitants (*Bell. Jud.* III. 3, 2). This would give us a population of over three millions for that province alone, while the present population of all Palestine and Syria scarcely amounts to two millions, or forty persons to the square mile (according to Bädeker, *Pal. and Syria*, 1876, p. 86).

Jesus commanded to cease; there are the hills from which he proclaimed the Sermon on the Mount, the Magna Charta of his kingdom, and to which he often retired for prayer; there on the western shore is the plain of Gennesaret, which still exhibits its natural fertility by the luxuriant growth of briers and thistles and the bright red magnolias overtopping them; there is the dirty city of Tiberias, built by Herod Antipas, where Jewish rabbis still scrupulously search the letter of the Scriptures without finding Christ in them; a few wretched Moslem huts called Mejdel still indicate the birth-place of Mary Magdalene, whose penitential tears and resurrection joys are a precious legacy of Christendom. And although the cities of Capernaum, Bethsaida and Chorazim, "where most of his mighty works were done," have utterly disappeared from the face of the earth, and their very sites are disputed among scholars, thus verifying to the letter the fearful prophecy of the Son of Man,[1] yet the ruins of Tell Hum and Kerazeh bear their eloquent testimony to the judgment of God for neglected privileges, and the broken columns and friezes with a pot of manna at Tell Hum are probably the remains of the very synagogue which the good Roman centurion built for the people of Capernaum, and in which Christ delivered his wonderful discourse on the bread of life from heaven.[2]

Cæsarea Philippi, formerly and now called Banias (or Paneas, Paneion, from the heathen sanctuary of Pan), at the foot of Hermon, marks the northern termination of the Holy Land and of the travels of the Lord, and the boundary-line between the Jews and the Gentiles; and that Swiss-like, picturesque landscape, the most beautiful in Palestine, in full view of the fresh, gushing source of the Jordan, and at the foot of the snow-crowned

[1] Matt. 11 : 20–24 ; Luke 10 : 13–15.
[2] Comp. Fr. Delitzsch: *Ein Tag in Capernaum*, 2d ed. 1873; Furrer: *Die Ortschaften am See Genezareth*, in the "Zeitschrift des deutschen Palæstina-Vereins," 1879, pp. 52 sqq. ; my article on Capernaum, *ibid.* 1878, pp. 216 sqq. ; and in the "Quarterly Statement of the Palestine Exploration Fund" for July, 1879, pp. 131 sqq., with the observations thereon by Lieut. Kitchener, who agrees with Dr. Robinson in locating Capernaum at Khan Minyeh, although there are no ruins there at all to be compared with those of Tell Hum.

monarch of Syrian mountains seated on a throne of rocks, seems to give additional force to Peter's fundamental confession and Christ's prophecy of his Church universal built upon the im-movable rock of his eternal divinity.

The closing scenes of the earthly life of our Lord and the be-ginning of his heavenly life took place in Jerusalem and the immediate neighborhood, where every spot calls to mind the most important events that ever occurred or can occur in this world. Jerusalem, often besieged and destroyed, and as often rebuilt "on her own heap," is indeed no more the Jerusalem of Herod, which lies buried many feet beneath the rubbish and filth of centuries; even the site of Calvary is disputed, and superstition has sadly disfigured and obscured the historic asso-ciations.[1] "Christ is not there, He is risen."[2] There is no more melancholy sight in the world than the present Jerusalem as contrasted with its former glory, and with the teeming life of Western cities; and yet so many are the sacred memories clustering around it and perfuming the very air, that even Rome must yield the palm of interest to the city which witnessed the crucifixion and the resurrection. The Herodian temple on Mount Moriah, once the gathering place of pious Jews from all the earth, and enriched with treasures of gold and silver which excited the avarice of the conquerors, has wholly disappeared, and "not one stone is left upon another," in literal fulfilment of Christ's prophecy;[3] but the massive foundations of Solomon's structure around the temple area still bear the marks of the Phœnician workmen; the "wall of wailing" is moistened with the tears of the Jews who assemble there every Friday to mourn

---

[1] The present mongrel population of Jerusalem—Moslems, Jews, and Chris-tians of all denominations, though mostly Greek—scarcely exceeds 30,000, while at the time of Christ it must have exceeded 100,000, even if we make a large deduction from the figures of Josephus, who states that on a passover under the governorship of Cestius Gallus 256,500 paschal lambs were slain, and that at the destruction of the city, A.D. 70, 1,100,000 Jews perished and 97,000 were sold into slavery (including 600,000 strangers who had crowded into the doomed city). *Bell. Jud.* vi. 9, 3.

[2] Matt. 28 : 6.   [3] Matt. 24 : 2 ; Mark 13 : 2 ; Luke 19 : 44.

over the sins and misfortunes of their forefathers; and if we look down from Mount Olivet upon Mount Moriah and the Moslem Dome of the Rock, the city even now presents one of the most imposing as well as most profoundly affecting sights on earth. The brook Kedron, which Jesus crossed in that solemn night after the last Passover, and Gethsemane with its venerable olive-trees and reminiscences of the agony, and Mount Olivet from which he rose to heaven, are still there, and behind it the remnant of Bethany, that home of peace and holy friendship which sheltered him the last nights before the crucifixion. Standing on that mountain with its magnificent view, or at the turning point of the road from Jericho and Bethany, and looking over Mount Moriah and the holy city, we fully understand why the Saviour wept and exclaimed, "Jerusalem, Jerusalem, thou that killest the prophets, and stonest them that are sent unto thee, how often would I have gathered thy children together even as a hen gathereth her chickens under her wings, and ye would not! Behold, your house is left unto you desolate!"

Thus the Land and the Book illustrate and confirm each other. The Book is still full of life and omnipresent in the civilized world; the Land is groaning under the irreformable despotism of the "unspeakable" Turk, which acts like a blast of the Sirocco from the desert. Palestine lies under the curse of God. It is at best a venerable ruin "in all the imploring beauty of decay," yet not without hope of some future resurrection in God's own good time. But in its very desolation it furnishes evidence for the truth of the Bible. It is "a fifth Gospel," engraven upon rocks.[1]

---

[1] Renan sums up the results of his personal observations as director of the scientific commission for the exploration of ancient Phœnicia in 1860 and 1861, in the following memorable confession (*Vie de Jésus*, Introd. p. liii.): *"J'ai traversé dans tous les sens la province évangélique ; j'ai visité Jérusalem, Hébron et la Samarie ; presque aucune localité importante de l'histoire de Jésus ne m'a échappé. Toute cette histoire qui, à distance, semble flotter dans les nuages d'un monde sans réalité, prit ainsi un corps, une solidité qui m'étonnèrent. L'accord frappant des textes et des lieux, la merveilleuse harmonie de l'idéal évangélique avec le paysage qui lui servit de cadre furent pour moi comme une révélation. J'eus devant les yeux un cinquième évangile, lacéré, mais lisible*

The People.

Is there a better argument for Christianity than the Jews? Is there a more patent and a more stubborn fact in history than that intense and unchangeable Semitic nationality with its equally intense religiosity? Is it not truly symbolized by the bush in the desert ever burning and never consumed? Nebuchadnezzar, Antiochus Epiphanes, Titus, Hadrian exerted their despotic power for the extermination of the Jews; Hadrian's edict forbade circumcision and all the rites of their religion; the intolerance of Christian rulers treated them for ages with a sort of revengeful cruelty, as if every Jew were personally responsible for the crime of the crucifixion. And, behold, the race still lives as tenaciously as ever, unchanged and unchangeable in its national traits, an omnipresent power in Christendom. It still produces, in its old age, remarkable men of commanding influence for good or evil in the commercial, political, and literary world; we need only recall such names as Spinoza, Rothschild, Disraeli, Mendelssohn, Heine, Neander. If we read the accounts of the historians and satirists of imperial Rome about the Jews in their filthy quarter across the Tiber, we are struck by the identity of that people with their descendants in the ghettos of modern Rome, Frankfurt, and New York. Then they excited as much as they do now the mingled contempt and wonder of the world; they were as remarkable then for contrasts of intellectual beauty and striking ugliness, wretched poverty and princely wealth; they liked onions and garlic, and dealt in old clothes, broken glass, and sulphur matches, but knew how to push themselves from poverty and filth into wealth and influence; they were rigid monotheists and scrupulous legalists who would strain out a gnat and swallow a camel; then as now they were temper-

encore, et désormais, à travers les récits de Matthieu et de Marc, au lieu d'un être abstrait, qu'on dirait n'avoir jamais existé, je vis une admirable figure humaine vivre, se mouvoir." His familiarity with the Orient accounts for the fact that this brilliant writer leaves much more historical foundation for the gospel history than his predecessor Strauss, who never saw Palestine.

ate, sober, industrious, well regulated and affectionate in their domestic relations, and careful for the religious education of their children. The majority were then, as they are now, car nal descendants of Jacob, the Supplanter, a small minority spirit- ual children of Abraham, the friend of God and father of the faithful. Out of this gifted race have come, at the time of Jesus and often since, the bitterest foes and the warmest friends of Christianity.

Among that peculiar people Jesus spent his earthly life, a Jew of the Jews, yet in the highest sense the Son of Man, the second Adam, the representative Head and Regenerator of the whole race. For thirty years of reserve and preparation he hid his divine glory and restrained his own desire to do good, quietly waiting till the voice of prophecy after centuries of silence an- nounced, in the wilderness of Judæa and on the banks of the Jordan, the coming of the kingdom of God, and startled the conscience of the people with the call to repent. Then for three years he mingled freely with his countrymen. Occasionally he met and healed Gentiles also, who were numerous in Galilee; he praised their faith the like of which he had not found in Israel, and prophesied that many shall come from the east and the west and shall sit down with Abraham, Isaac and Jacob in the kingdom of heaven, while the children of the kingdom shall be cast out into outer darkness.[1] He conversed with a woman of Samaria, to the surprise of his disciples, on the sublimest theme, and rebuked the national prejudice of the Jews by hold- ing up a good Samaritan as a model for imitation.[2] It was on the occasion of a visit from some "Greeks," shortly before the crucifixion, that he uttered the remarkable prophecy of the uni- versal attraction of his cross.[3] But these were exceptions. His mission, before the resurrection, was to the lost sheep of Israel.[4]

He associated with all ranks of Jewish society, attracting the

[1] Matt. 8 : 5–13 ; 15 : 21–28 ; Luke 7 : 1–9.
[2] John 4 : 5–42 ; Luke 10 : 30–37.
[3] John 12 : 20–32.
[4] Matt. 10 : 5, 6 ; 15 : 14.

good and repelling the bad, rebuking vice and relieving misery, but most of his time he spent among the middle classes who constituted the bone and sinew of the nation, the farmers and workingmen of Galilee, who are described to us as an industrious, brave and courageous race, taking the lead in seditious political movements, and holding out to the last moment in the defence of Jerusalem.[1] At the same time they were looked upon by the stricter Jews of Judæa as semi-heathens and semi-barbarians; hence the question, "Can any good come out of Nazareth," and "Out of Galilee ariseth no prophet."[2] He selected his apostles from plain, honest, unsophisticated fishermen, who became fishers of men and teachers of future ages. In Judæa he came in contact with the religious leaders, and it was proper that he should close his ministry and establish his church in the capital of the nation.

He moved among the people as a Rabbi (my Lord) or a Teacher, and under this name he is usually addressed.[3] The

---

[1] Josephus, *Bell. Jud.* III. c. 3, § 2: "These two Galilees, of so great largeness, and encompassed with so many nations of foreigners, have been always able to make a strong resistance on all occasions of war; for the Galileans are inured to war from their infancy, and have been always very numerous; nor hath the country ever been destitute of men of courage, or wanted a numerous set of them: for their soil is universally rich and fruitful, and full of the plantations of trees of all sorts, insomuch that it invites the most slothful to take pains in its cultivation by its fruitfulness: accordingly it is all cultivated by its inhabitants, and no part of it lies idle. Moreover, the cities lie here very thick, and the very many villages there are so full of people, by the richness of their soil, that the very least of them contained above fifteen thousand inhabitants (?)."

[2] John 1 : 46 ; 7 : 52 ; Matt. 4 : 16. The Sanhedrists forgot in their blind passion that Jonah was from Galilee. After the fall of Jerusalem Tiberias became the headquarters of Hebrew learning and the birthplace of the Talmud.

[3] ῥαββί (from רַב, or with the suff. רַבִּי, my prince, lord, κύριος) sixteen times in the N. T., ῥαββονί or ῥαββουνί twice; διδάσκαλος (variously rendered in the E. V. *teacher*, *doctor*, and mostly *master*) about forty times; ἐπιστάτης (rendered *master*) six times, καθηγητής (rendered *master*) once in Matt. 23 : 10 (the text rec. also in ver. 8, where διδάσκαλος is the correct reading). Other designations of these teachers in the N. T. are γραμματεῖς, νομικοί, νομοδιδάσκαλοι. Josephus calls them σοφισταί, ἱερογραμματεῖς, πατρίων ἐξηγηταὶ νόμων, the Mishna חֲכָמִים and סוֹפְרִים, *scholars*. See Schürer, p. 441.

Rabbis were the intellectual and moral leaders of the nation, theologians, lawyers, and preachers, the expounders of the law, the keepers of the conscience, the regulators of the daily life and conduct ; they were classed with Moses and the prophets, and claimed equal reverence. They stood higher than the priests who owed their position to the accident of birth, and not to personal merit. They coveted the chief seats in the synagogues and at feasts; they loved to be greeted in the markets and to be called of men, "Rabbi, Rabbi." Hence our Lord's warning: "Be not ye called 'Rabbi': for one is your Master, *even* Christ; and all ye are brethren."[1] They taught in the temple, in the synagogue, and in the school-house (Beth-hamidrash), and introduced their pupils, sitting on the floor at their feet, by asking and answering questions, into the intricacies of Jewish casuistry. They accumulated those oral traditions which were afterwards embodied in the Talmud, that huge repository of Jewish wisdom and folly. They performed official acts gratuitously.[2] They derived their support from an honorable trade or free gifts of their pupils, or they married into rich families. Rabbi Hillel warned against making gain of the crown (of the law), but also against excess of labor, saying, "Who is too much given to trade, will not become wise." In the book of Jesus Son of Sirach (which was written about 200 B.C.) a trade is represented as incompatible with the vocation of a student and teacher,[3] but the prevailing sentiment at the time of Christ favored a combination of intellectual and physical labor as beneficial to health and character. One-third of the day should be given to study, one-third to prayer, one-third to work. "Love manual labor," was the motto of She-

---

[1] Matt. 23 : 8; comp. Mark 12 : 38, 39 ; Luke 11 : 43 ; 20 : 46.

[2] The same, however, was the case with Greek and Roman teachers before Vespasian, who was the first to introduce a regular salary. I was told in Cairo that the professors of the great Mohammedan University likewise teach gratuitously.

[3] Ecclesiasticus 38 : 24–34 : " The wisdom of a learned man *cometh* by opportunity of leisure ; and he that hath little business shall become wise. How can he get wisdom that holdeth the plough," etc.

maja, a teacher of Hillel. "He who does not teach his son a
trade," said Rabbi Jehuda, "is much the same as if he taught
him to be a robber." "There is no trade," says the Talmud.
"which can be dispensed with; but happy is he who has in
his parents the example of a trade of the more excellent sort." [1]

Jesus himself was not only the son of a carpenter, but during
his youth he worked at that trade himself. [2] When he entered
upon his public ministry the zeal for God's house claimed all
his time and strength, and his modest wants were more than
supplied by a few grateful disciples from Galilee, so that something was left for the benefit of the poor. [3] St. Paul learned
the trade of tentmaking, which was congenial to his native
Cilicia, and derived from it his support even as an apostle, that
he might relieve his congregations and maintain a noble independence. [4]

Jesus availed himself of the usual places of public instruction
in the synagogue and the temple, but preached also out of

---

[1] See Fr. Delitzsch : *Jüdisches Handwerkerleben zur Zeit Jesu.* Erlangen,
third ed. revised, 1879. He states (p. 77) that more than one hundred Rabbis
who figure in the Talmud carried on a trade and were known by it, as R. Oshaja
the shoemaker, R. Abba the tailor, R. Juda the baker, R. Abba Josef the
architect, R. Chana the banker, R. Abba Shaul the grave-digger, R. Abba
Oshaja the fuller, R. Abin the carpenter, etc. He remarks (p. 23) : " The Jews
have always been an industrious people and behind no other in impulse, ability
and inventiveness for restless activity ; agriculture and trade were their chief
occupations before the dissolution of their political independence; only in
consequence of their dispersion and the contraction of their energies have
they become a people of sharpers and peddlers and taken the place of the
old Phœnicians." But the talent and disposition for sharp bargains was inherited from their father Jacob, and turned the temple of God into " a house
of merchandise." Christ charges the Pharisees with avarice which led them
to "devour widows' houses." Comp. Matt. 23 : 14; Mark 12 : 40; Luke
16 : 14 ; 20 : 47.

[2] Mark 6 : 3 Jesus is called, by his neighbors, "the carpenter" (ὁ τέκτων),
Matt. 13 : 55 "the carpenter's son."

[3] Luke 8 : 3 ; Matt. 27 : 55 ; Mark 15 : 41 ; John 13 : 29. Among the pious
women who ministered to Jesus was also Joanna, the wife of Chuzas, King
Herod's steward. To her may be traced the vivid circumstantial description
of the dancing scene at Herod's feast and the execution of John the Baptist,
Mark 6 : 14–29.

[4] Acts 18 : 3; 20 : 33–35 ; 1 Thess. 2 : 9; 2 Thess. 3 : 8; 2 Cor. 11 : 7–9.

doors, on the mountain, at the sea-side, and wherever the people assembled to hear him. "I have spoken openly to the world; I ever taught in synagogues and in the temple, where all the Jews come together; and in secret spake I nothing."[1] Paul likewise taught in the synagogue wherever he had an opportunity on his missionary journeys.[2] The familiar mode of teaching was by disputation, by asking and answering questions on knotty points of the law, by parables and sententious sayings, which easily lodged in the memory; the Rabbi sat on a chair, the pupils stood or sat on the floor at his feet.[3] Knowledge of the Law of God was general among the Jews and considered the most important possession. They remembered the commandments better than their own name.[4] Instruction began in early childhood in the family and was carried on in the school and the synagogue. Timothy learned the sacred Scriptures on the knees of his mother and grandmother.[5] Josephus boasts, at the expense of his superiors, that when only fourteen years of age he had such an exact knowledge of the law that he was consulted by the high priest and the first men of Jerusalem.[6] Schoolmasters were appointed in every town, and children were taught to read in their sixth or seventh year, but writing was probably a rare accomplishment.[7]

The synagogue was the local, the temple the national centre of religious and social life; the former on the weekly Sabbath (and also on Monday and Thursday), the latter on the Passover

---

[1] John 18 : 20.   Comp. Matt. 4 : 23 ; 9 : 35 ; 21 : 23 ; 26 : 55 ; Mark 1 : 21, 39 ; 14 : 49 ; Luke 2 : 46 ; 4 : 14–16, 31, 44 ; 13 : 10 ; 21 : 37.

[2] Acts 13 : 14–16 ; 16 : 13 ; 17 : 2, 3.

[3] Luke 2 : 46 ; 5 : 17 ; Matt. 5 : 1 ; 26 : 55 ; John 8 : 2 ; Acts 22 : 3 ("at the feet of Gamaliel").

[4] Josephus often speaks of this.   C. Ap. I. 12 : "More than all we are concerned for the education of our youth (παιδοτροφία), and we consider the keeping of the laws (τὸ φυλάττειν τοὺς νόμους) and the corresponding piety (τὴν κατὰ τούτους παραδεδομένην εὐσέβειαν) to be the most necessary work of life."   Comp. II. 18 ; Ant. IV. 8, 12.   To the same effect is the testimony of Philo, Legat. ad Cajum, § 16, 31, quoted by Schürer, p. 467.

[5] 2 Tim. 1 : 5 ; 3 : 15 ; comp. Eph. 6 : 4.   [6] Vita, § 2.

[7] Schürer, p. 468 ; and Ginsburg, art. Education, in Kitto's " Cyc. of Bibl. Liter.," 3d ed.

and the other annual festivals. Every town had a synagogue, large cities had many, especially Alexandria and Jerusalem.[1] The worship was very simple: it consisted of prayers, singing, the reading of sections from the Law and the Prophets in Hebrew, followed by a commentary and homily in the vernacular Aramaic. There was a certain democratic liberty of prophesying, especially outside of Jerusalem. Any Jew of age could read the Scripture lessons and make comments on invitation of the ruler of the synagogue. This custom suggested to Jesus the most natural way of opening his public ministry. When he returned from his baptism to Nazareth, " he entered, as his custom was, into the synagogue on the Sabbath day, and stood up to read. And there was delivered unto him the roll of the prophet Isaiah. And he opened the roll and found the place where it was written (61 : 1, 2) ' The Spirit of the Lord is upon me, because he anointed me to preach good tidings to the poor; he hath sent me to proclaim release to the captives, and recovering of sight to the blind, to set at liberty them that are bruised, to proclaim the acceptable year of the Lord.' And he closed the book, and gave it back to the attendant, and sat down : and the eyes of all in the synagogue were fastened on him. And he began to say unto them, ' To-day hath this scripture been fulfilled in your ears.' And all bare witness unto him, and wondered at the words of grace which proceeded out of his mouth : and they said, Is not this Joseph's son ? "[2]

On the great festivals he visited from his twelfth year the capital of the nation where the Jewish religion unfolded all its splendor and attraction. Large caravans with trains of camels and asses loaded with provisions and rich offerings to the temple, were set in motion from the North and the South, the East and the West for the holy city, " the joy of the whole earth;" and these yearly pilgrimages, singing the beautiful Pil-

---

[1] Acts 6 : 9 for the freedmen and the Hellenists and proselytes from different countries. Rabbinical writers estimate the number of synagogues in Jerusalem as high as 480 (i. e. $4 \times 10 \times 12$), which seems incredible.

[2] Luke 4 : 16–22.

grim Psalms (Ps. 120 to 134), contributed immensely to the
preservation and promotion of the common faith, as the Moslem
pilgrimages to Mecca keep up the life of Islam. We may
greatly reduce the enormous figures of Josephus, who on one
single Passover reckoned the number of strangers and residents
in Jerusalem at 2,700,000 and the number of slaughtered lambs
at 256,500, but there still remains the fact of the vast extent and
solemnity of the occasion. Even now in her decay, Jerusalem
(like other Oriental cities) presents a striking picturesque appearance at Easter, when Christian pilgrims from the far West mingle with the many-colored Arabs, Turks, Greeks, Latins, Spanish and Polish Jews, and crowd to suffocation the Church of the
Holy Sepulchre. How much more grand and dazzling must this
cosmopolitan spectacle have been when the priests (whose number Josephus estimates at 20,000) with the broidered tunic, the
fine linen girdle, the showy turban, the high priests with the
ephod of blue and purple and scarlet, the breastplate and the
mitre, the Levites with their pointed caps, the Pharisees with
their broad phylacteries and fringes, the Essenes in white dresses
and with prophetic mien, Roman soldiers with proud bearing,
Herodian courtiers in oriental pomposity, contrasted with beggars
and cripples in rags, when pilgrims innumerable, Jews and proselytes from all parts of the empire, " Parthians and Medes and
Elamites, and the dwellers in Mesopotamia, in Judæa and Cappadocia, in Pontus and Asia, in Phrygia and Pamphylia, in
Egypt and parts of Libya about Cyrene, and sojourners from
Rome, both Jews and proselytes, Cretans and Arabians," [1] all
wearing their national costume and speaking a Babel of tongues,
surged through the streets, and pressed up to Mount Moriah,
where " the glorious temple rear'd her pile, far off appearing
like a mount of alabaster, topp'd with golden spires," and where
on the fourteenth day of the first month columns of sacrificial
smoke arose from tens of thousands of paschal lambs, in historical commemoration of the great deliverance from the land

---

[1] Acts 2 : 8-12.

of bondage, and in typical prefiguration of the still greater re
demption from the slavery of sin and death.[1]

To the outside observer the Jews at that time were the most
religious people on earth, and in some sense this is true. Never
was a nation so ruled by the written law of God; never did a
nation so carefully and scrupulously study its sacred books, and
pay greater reverence to its priests and teachers. The leaders
of the nation looked with horror and contempt upon the unclean,
uncircumcised Gentiles, and confirmed the people in their spiritual pride and conceit. No wonder that the Romans charged
the Jews with the *odium generis humani*.

Yet, after all, this intense religiosity was but a shadow of true
religion. It was a praying corpse rather than a living body.
Alas! the Christian Church in some ages and sections presents
a similar sad spectacle of the deceptive form of godliness without its power. The rabbinical learning and piety bore the same
relation to the living oracles of God as sophistic scholasticism
to Scriptural theology, and Jesuitical casuistry to Christian
ethics. The Rabbis spent all their energies in "fencing" the
law so as to make it inaccessible. They analyzed it to death.
They surrounded it with so many hair-splitting distinctions and
refinements that the people could not see the forest for the trees
or the roof for the tiles, and mistook the shell for the kernel.[2]
Thus they made void the Word of God by the traditions of men.[3]
A slavish formalism and mechanical ritualism was substituted
for spiritual piety, an ostentatious sanctimoniousness for holiness

---

[1] Comp. the description of King Josiah's Passover, 2 Chr. 35 : 1–19.

[2] The Rabbinical scholasticism reminds one of the admirable description of
logic in Goethe's *Faust:*

> "*Wer will was Lebendig's erkennen und beschreiben,*
> *Sucht erst den Geist hinauszutreiben;*
> *Dann hat er die Theile in seiner Hand,*
> *Fehlt leider! nur das geistige Band.*"

[3] Matt. 15 : 2, 3, 6 ; Mark 7 : 3, 5, 8, 9, 13. It is significant that Christ
uses the word παράδοσις always in a bad sense of such human doctrines and
usages as obscure and virtually set aside the sacred Scriptures. Precisely the
same charge was applied by the Reformers to the doctrines of the monks and
schoolmen of their day.

of character, scrupulous casuistry for genuine morality, the killing letter for the life-giving spirit, and the temple of God was turned into a house of merchandise.

The profanation and perversion of the spiritual into the carnal, and of the inward into the outward, invaded even the holy of holies of the religion of Israel, the Messianic promises and hopes which run like a golden thread from the protevangelium in paradise lost to the voice of John the Baptist pointing to the Lamb of God. The idea of a spiritual Messiah who should crush the serpent's head and redeem Israel from the bondage of sin, was changed into the conception of a political deliverer who should re-establish the throne of David in Jerusalem, and from that centre rule over the Gentiles to the ends of the earth. The Jews of that time could not separate David's Son, as they called the Messiah, from David's sword, sceptre and crown. Even the apostles were affected by this false notion, and hoped to secure the chief places of honor in that great revolution; hence they could not understand the Master when he spoke to them of his approaching passion and death.[1]

The state of public opinion concerning the Messianic expectations as set forth in the Gospels is fully confirmed by the preceding and contemporary Jewish literature, as the Sibylline Books (about b.c. 140), the remarkable Book of Enoch (of uncertain date, probably from b.c. 130–30), the Psalter of Solomon (b.c. 63–48), the Assumption of Moses, Philo and Josephus, the Apocalypse of Baruch, and the Fourth Book of Esdras.[2] In all of them the Messianic kingdom, or the kingdom of God, is represented as an earthly paradise of the Jews, as a kingdom of this world, with Jerusalem for its capital. It was this popular idol of a pseudo-Messiah with which Satan tempted Jesus in the wilderness, when he showed him all the kingdoms of the world; well knowing that if he could convert him to this carnal creed,

---

[1] Matt. 16 : 21–23; Mark 8 : 31–33; Luke 9 : 22, 44, 45; 18 : 34; 24 : 21; John 12 : 34.

[2] See, of older works, Schöttgen, *Horæ Hebraicæ et Talmudicæ*, tom. II. (*De Messia*), of modern works, Schürer, *l. c.* pp. 563–599, with the literature there quoted; also James Drummond, *The Jewish Messiah*, Lond. 1877.

and induce him to abuse his miraculous power for selfish grati-
fication, vain ostentation, and secular ambition, he would most
effectually defeat the scheme of redemption.   The same political aspiration was a powerful lever of the rebellion against the
Roman yoke which terminated in the destruction of Jerusalem,
and it revived again in the rebellion of Bar-Cocheba only to end
in a similar disaster.

Such was the Jewish religion at the time of Christ.   He was
the only teacher in Israel who saw through the hypocritical mask
to the rotten heart.   None of the great Rabbis, no Hillel, no
Shammai, no Gamaliel attempted or even conceived of a reformation; on the contrary, they heaped tradition upon tradition
and accumulated the talmudic rubbish of twelve large folios and
2947 leaves, which represents the anti-Christian petrifaction of
Judaism; while the four Gospels have regenerated humanity
and are the life and the light of the civilized world to this day.

Jesus, while moving within the outward forms of the Jewish
religion of his age, was far above it and revealed a new world
of ideas.   He, too, honored the law of God, but by unfolding
its deepest spiritual meaning and fulfilling it in precept and example.   Himself a Rabbi, he taught as one having direct authority from God, and not as the scribes.   How he arraigned those
hypocrites seated on Moses' seat, those blind leaders of the blind,
who lay heavy burdens on men's shoulders without touching
them with their finger; who shut the kingdom of heaven against
men, and will not enter themselves; who tithe the mint and
the anise and the cumin, and leave undone the weightier matters of the law, justice and mercy and faith; who strain out the
gnat and swallow the camel; who are like unto whited sepulchres which outwardly appear beautiful indeed, but inwardly
are full of dead men's bones, and of all uncleanness.   But
while he thus stung the pride of the leaders, he cheered and
elevated the humble and lowly.   He blessed little children, he
encouraged the poor, he invited the weary, he fed the hungry,
he healed the sick, he converted publicans and sinners, and laid
the foundation strong and deep, in God's eternal love, for a new

society and a new humanity. It was one of the sublimest as well as loveliest moments in the life of Jesus when the disciples asked him, Who is the greatest in the kingdom of heaven? and when he called a little child, set him in the midst of them and said, " Verily I say unto you, Except ye be converted and become as little children, ye shall in no wise enter into the kingdom of heaven. Whosoever therefore shall humble, himself as this little child, the same is greatest in the kingdom of heaven. And whoso shall receive one such little child in my name receiveth me." [1] And that other moment when he thanked his heavenly Father for revealing unto babes the things of the kingdom which were hid from the wise, and invited all that labor and are heavy laden to come to him for rest. [2]

He knew from the beginning that he was the Messiah of God and the King of Israel. This consciousness reached its maturity at his baptism when he received the Holy Spirit without measure. [3] To this conviction he clung unwaveringly, even in those dark hours of the apparent failure of his cause, after Judas had betrayed him, after Peter, the confessor and rock-apostle, had denied him, and everybody had forsaken him. He solemnly affirmed his Messiahship before the tribunal of the Jewish high-priest; he assured the heathen representative of the Roman empire that he was a king, though not of this world, and when hanging on the cross he assigned to the dying robber a place in his kingdom. [4] But before that time and in the days of his greatest popularity he carefully avoided every publication and demonstration which might have encouraged the prevailing idea of a political Messiah and an uprising of the people. He chose for himself the humblest of the Messianic titles which represents his condescension to our common lot, while at the same time it

---

[1] Matt. 18 : 1–6 ; comp. Mark 10 : 13–16 ; Luke 18 : 15–17.

[2] Matt. 11 : 25–30. This passage, which is found only in Matthew and (in part) in Luke 10 : 21, 22, is equal to any passage in John. It is a genuine echo of this word when Schiller sings :

" *Was kein Verstand der Verständigen sieht,*
   Das übet in Einfalt ein kindlich Gemüth."

[3] John 1 : 32–34 ; comp. 3 : 34.   [4] Matt. 26 : 64 ; John 18 : 37 ; Luke 23 : 43.

implies his unique position as the representative head of the human family, as the ideal, the perfect, the universal, the archetypal Man.   He calls himself habitually "the Son of Man" who "hath not where to lay his head," who "came not to be ministered unto but to minister, and to give his life a ransom for many," who "hath power to forgive sins," who "came to seek and to save that which was lost."[1]   When Peter made the great confession at Cæsarea Philippi, Christ accepted it, but immediately warned him of his approaching passion and death, from which the disciple shrunk in dismay.[2]   And with the certain expectation of his crucifixion, but also of his triumphant resurrection on the third day, he entered in calm and sublime fortitude on his last journey to Jerusalem which "killeth the prophets," and nailed him to the cross as a false Messiah and blasphemer. But in the infinite wisdom and mercy of God the greatest crime in history was turned into the greatest blessing to man kind.

We must conclude then that the life and work of Christ, while admirably adapted to the condition and wants of his age and people, and receiving illustration and confirmation from his environment, cannot be explained from any contemporary or preceding intellectual or moral resources.   He learned nothing from human teachers.   His wisdom was not of this world.   He needed no visions and revelations like the prophets and apostles. He came directly from his great Father in heaven, and when he spoke of heaven he spoke of his familiar home.   He spoke from the fullness of God dwelling in him.   And his words were verified by deeds.   Example is stronger than precept.   The wisest sayings remain powerless until they are incarnate in a living person.   It is the life which is the light of men.   In purity of doctrine and holiness of character combined in perfect harmony, Jesus stands alone, unapproached and unapproachable.   He

---

[1] Luke 9:58; 19:10; Matt. 18:11; 20:17, 28; Mark 2:10, 28; John 1:51; 6:53, and many other passages.   The term ὁ υἱὸς τοῦ ἀνθρώπου occurs about 80 times in the Gospels.   On its meaning comp. my book on the *Person of Christ*, pp. 83 sqq. (ed. of 1880).

[2] Matt. 16:20–23; Mark 8:30–33; Luke 9:21–27.

breathed a fresh life from heaven into his and all subsequent ages. He is the author of a new moral creation.

JESUS AND HILLEL.—The infinite elevation of Christ above the men of his time and nation, and his deadly conflict with the Pharisees and scribes are so evident that it seems preposterous and absurd to draw a parallel between him and Hillel or any other Rabbi. And yet this has been done by some modern Jewish Rabbis, as Geiger, Grätz, Friedländer, who boldly affirm, without a shadow of historical proof, that Jesus was a Pharisee, a pupil of Hillel, and indebted to him for his highest moral principles. By this left-handed compliment they mean to depreciate his originality. Abraham Geiger (d. 1874) says, in his *Das Judenthum und seine Geschichte* (Breslau, 2d ed. 1865, vol. I. p. 117) : *"Jesus war ein Jude, ein pharisäischer Jude mit galiläischer Färbung, ein Mann der die Hoffnungen der Zeit theilte und diese Hoffnungen in sich erfüllt glaubte. Einen neuen Gedanken sprach er keineswegs aus* [!], *auch brach er nicht etwa die Schranken der Nationalität . . . . Er hob nicht im Entferntesten etwas vom Judenthum auf; er war ein Pharisäer, der auch in den Wegen Hillels ging."* This view is repeated by Rabbi Dr. M. H. Friedländer, in his *Geschichtsbilder aus der Zeit der Tanaiten und Amoräer. Ein Beitrag zur Geschichte des Talmuds* (Brünn, 1879, p. 32) : *"Jesus, oder Jeschu, war der Sohn eines Zimmermeisters, Namens Josef, aus Nazareth. Seine Mutter hiess Mirjam oder Maria. Selbst der als conservativer Katholik* [sic *!*] *wie als bedeutender Gelehrter bekannte Ewald nennt ihn ' Jesus den Sohn Josefs ' . . . . Wenn auch Jesus' Gelehrsamkeit nicht riesig war, da die Galiläer auf keiner hohen Stufe der Cultur standen, so zeichnete er sich doch durch Seelenadel, Gemüthlichkeit und Herzensgüte vortheilhaft aus. Hillel I. scheint sein Vorbild und Musterbild gewesen zu sein; denn der hillelianische Grundsatz: ' Was dir nicht recht ist, füge deinem Nebenmenschen nicht zu,' war das Grundprincip seiner Lehren."* Renan makes a similar assertion in his *Vie de Jésus* (Chap. III. p. 35), but with considerable qualifications : *"Par sa pauvreté humblement supportée, par la douceur de son caractère, par l'opposition qu'il faisait aux hypocrites et aux prêtres, Hillel fut le vrai maître de Jésus, s'il est permis de parler de maître, quand il s'agit d'une si haute originalité."* This comparison has been effectually disposed of by such able scholars as Dr. Delitzsch, in his valuable pamphlet *Jesus und Hillel* (Erlangen, 3d revised ed. 1879, 40 pp.) ; Ewald, V. 12–48 (*Die Schule Hillel's und deren Gegner*); Keim I. 268–272 ; Schürer, p. 456 ; and Farrar, *Life of Christ*, II. 453–460. All these writers come to the same conclusion of the perfect independence and originality of Jesus. Nevertheless it is interesting to examine the facts in the case.

Hillel and Shammai are the most distinguished among the Jewish Rabbis. They were contemporary founders of two rival schools of rabbinical theology (as Thomas Aquinas and Duns Scotus of two schools of scholastic theology). It is strange that Josephus does not mention them, unless he refers to them under the Hellenized names of *Sameas* and *Pol-lion ;* but these names agree better with *Shemaja* and *Abtalion*, two cele-brated Pharisees and teachers of Hillel and Shammai; moreover he designates Sameas as a disciple of Pollion. (See Ewald, v. 22–26; Schürer, p. 455). The Talmudic tradition has obscured their history and embellished it with many fables.

Hillel I. or the Great was a descendant of the royal family of David, and born at Babylon. He removed to Jerusalem in great poverty, and died about A.D. 10. He is said to have lived 120 years, like Moses, 40 years without learning, 40 years as a student, 40 years as a teacher. He was the grandfather of the wise Gamaliel in whose family the presidency of the Sanhedrin was hereditary for several generations. By his burning zeal for knowledge, and his pure, gentle and amiable character, he at-tained the highest renown. He is said to have understood all languages, even the unknown tongues of mountains, hills, valleys, trees, wild and tame beasts, and demons. He was called "the gentle, the holy, the scholar of Ezra." There was a proverb: "Man should be always as meek as Hillel, and not quick-tempered as Shammai." He differed from Rabbi Shammai by a milder interpretation of the law, but on some points, as the mighty question whether it was right or wrong to eat an egg laid on a Sabbath day, he took the more rigid view. A talmudic tract is called *Beza, The Egg*, after this famous dispute. What a distance from him who said: "The Sabbath was made for man, and not man for the Sabbath : so then the Son of Man is Lord even of the Sabbath."

Many wise sayings, though partly obscure and of doubtful interpreta-tion, are attributed to Hillel in the tract Pirke Aboth (which is embodied in the Mishna and enumerates, in ch. 1, the pillars of the legal traditions from Moses down to the destruction of Jerusalem). The following are the best :

"Be a disciple of Aaron, peace-loving and peace-making; love men, and draw them to the law."

"Whoever abuses a good name (or, is ambitious of aggrandizing his name) destroys it."

"Whoever does not increase his knowledge diminishes it."

"Separate not thyself from the congregation, and have no confidence in thyself till the day of thy death."

"If I do not care for my soul, who will do it for me? If I care only for my own soul, what am I? If not now, when then?"

"Judge not thy neighbor till thou art in his situation."

"Say not, I will repent when I have leisure, lest that leisure should never be thine."

"The passionate man will never be a teacher."

"In the place where there is not a man, be thou a man."

Yet his haughty Pharisaism is clearly seen in this utterance: "No uneducated man easily avoids sin; no common person is pious." The enemies of Christ in the Sanhedrin said the same (John 7 : 49) : " This multitude that knoweth not the law are accursed." Some of his teachings are of doubtful morality, e. g. his decision that, in view of a vague expression in Deut. 24 : 1, a man might put away his wife "even if she cooked his dinner badly." This is, however, softened down by modern Rabbis so as to mean : "if she brings discredit on his home."

Once a heathen came to Rabbi Shammai and promised to become a proselyte if he could teach him the whole law while he stood on one leg. Shammai got angry and drove him away with a stick. The heathen went with the same request to Rabbi Hillel, who never lost his temper, received him courteously and gave him, while standing on one leg, the following effective answer :

"Do not to thy neighbor what is disagreeable to thee. This is the whole Law ; all the rest is commentary : go and do that." (See Delitzsch, p. 17 ; Ewald, V. 31, comp. IV. 270).

This is the wisest word of Hillel and the chief ground of a comparison with Jesus. But

1. It is only the negative expression of the positive precept of the gospel, "Thou shalt love thy neighbor as thyself," and of the golden rule, "All things whatsoever ye would that men should do to you, even so do ye also to them" (Matt. 7 : 12 ; Luke 6 : 31). There is a great difference between not doing any harm, and doing good. The former is consistent with selfishness and every sin which does not injure our neighbor. The Saviour, by presenting God's benevolence (Matt. 7 : 11) as the guide of duty, directs us to do to our neighbor all the good we can, and he himself set the highest example of self-denying love by sacrificing his life for sinners.

2. It is disconnected from the greater law of supreme love to God, without which true love to our neighbor is impossible. "On these *two* commandments," combined and inseparable, "hang all the law and the prophets" (Matt. 22 : 37–40).

3. Similar sayings are found long before Hillel, not only in the Pentateuch and the Book of Tobith (4 : 15 : ὁ μισεῖς μηδενὶ ποιήσῃς, "Do that to no man which thou hatest"), but substantially even among the heathen (Confucius, Buddha, Herodotus, Isocrates, Seneca, Quintilian), but always either in the negative form, or with reference to a particular case or class ; e. g. Isocrates, *Ad Demonic.* c. 4 : "Be such towards your parents as thou shalt pray thy children shall be towards thyself ;" and the same *In Æginet.* c. 23 : "That you would be such judges to me as you would desire to obtain for yourselves." See Wetstein on Matt. 7 : 12 (*Nov. Test.* I. 341 sq.). Parallels to this and other biblical maxims have been gathered in considerable number from the Talmud and the classics by Lightfoot, Grotius, Wetstein, Deutsch, Spiess, Ramage ; but what are they all compared with the Sermon on the Mount? Moreover, *si duo idem dicunt, non est idem.* As to the rabbinical parallels, we must remember that they

were not committed to writing before the second century, and that, as Delitzsch says (*Ein Tag in Capernaum*, p. 137), "not a few sayings of Christ, circulated by Jewish Christians, reappeared anonymously or under false names in the Talmuds and Midrashim."

4. No amount of detached words of wisdom constitute an organic system of ethics any more than a heap of marble blocks constitute a palace or temple; and the best system of ethics is unable to produce a holy life, and is worthless without it.

We may admit without hesitation that Hillel was "the greatest and best of all Pharisees" (Ewald), but he was far inferior to John the Baptist; and to compare him with Christ is sheer blindness or folly. Ewald calls such comparison "utterly perverse" (*grundverkehrt*, v. 48). Farrar remarks that the distance between Hillel and Jesus is "a distance absolutely immeasurable, and the resemblance of his teaching to that of Jesus is the resemblance of a glow-worm to the sun" (II. 455). "The fundamental tendencies of both," says Delitzsch (p. 23), "are as widely apart as heaven and earth. That of Hillel is legalistic, casuistic, and nationally contracted; that of Jesus is universally religious, moral and human. Hillel lives and moves in the externals, Jesus in the spirit of the law." He was not even a reformer, as Geiger and Friedländer would make him, for what they adduce as proofs are mere trifles of interpretation, and involve no new principle or idea.

Viewed as a mere human teacher, the absolute originality of Jesus consists in this, "that his words have touched the hearts of all men in all ages, and have regenerated the moral life of the world" (Farrar, II. 454). But Jesus is far more than a Rabbi, more than a sage and saint, more than a reformer, more than a benefactor; he is the author of the true religion, the prophet, priest and king, the renovator, the Saviour of men, the founder of a spiritual kingdom as vast as the race and as long as eternity.

§ 18. *Apocryphal Traditions.*

We add some notes of minor interest connected with the history of Christ outside of the only authentic record in the Gospels.

I. The Apocryphal Sayings of our Lord.—The canonical Gospels contain all that is necessary for us to know about the words and deeds of our Lord, although many more might have been recorded (John 20 : 30 ; 21 : 25). Their early composition and reception in the church precluded the possibility of a successful rivalry of oral tradition. The extrabiblical sayings of our Lord are mere fragments, few in number, and with one exception rather unimportant, or simply variations of genuine words.

They have been collected by FABRICIUS, in *Codex Apocr. N. T.*, I. pp. 321–335 ; GRABE : *Spicilegium SS. Patrum*, ed. alt. I. 12 sqq., 326 sq. ; KOERNER : *De sermonibus Christi ἀγράφοις* (Lips. 1776) ; ROUTH, in *Reliq. Sacræ*, vol. I. 9–12, etc. ; RUD. HOFMANN, in *Das Leben Jesu nach den Apokryphen* (Leipz. 1851, § 75, pp. 317–334) ; BUNSEN, in *Anal. ante-Nic.* I. 29 sqq. ; ANGER, in *Synops. Evang.* (1852) ; WESTCOTT : *Introd. to the Study of the Gospels*, Append. C. (pp. 446 sqq. of the Boston ed. by Hackett) ; PLUMPTRE, in Ellicott's *Com. for English Readers*, I. p. xxxiii. ; J. T. DODD : *Sayings ascribed to our Lord by the Fathers* (1874) ; E. B. NICHOLSON : *The Gospel according to the Hebrews* (Lond. 1879, pp. 143–162). Comp. an essay of Ewald in his "Jahrbücher der Bibl. Wissenschaft," VI. 40 and 54 sqq., and *Geschichte Christus'*, p. 288. We avail ourselves chiefly of the collections of Hofmann, Westcott, Plumptre, and Nicholson.

(1) *"It is more blessed to give than to receive."* Quoted by Paul, Acts 20 : 35. Comp. Luke 6 : 30, 31 ; also Clement of Rome, *Ad Cor.* c. 2, ἥδιον διδόντες ἢ λαμβάνοντες, "more gladly giving than receiving." This is unquestionably authentic, pregnant with rich meaning, and shining out like a lone star all the more brilliantly. It is true in the highest sense of the love of God and Christ. The somewhat similar sentences of Aristotle, Seneca, and Epicurus, as quoted by Plutarch (see the passages in Wetstein on Acts 20 : 35), savor of aristocratic pride, and are neutralized by the opposite heathen maxim of mean selfishness : "Foolish is the giver, happy the receiver." Shakespeare may have had the sentence in his mind when he put into the mouth of Portia the golden words :

> " The quality of mercy is not strained,
> It droppeth as the gentle rain from heaven
> Upon the place beneath : it is twice blessed ;
> It blesseth him that gives and him that takes ;
> 'Tis mightiest in the mightiest ; it becomes
> The throned monarch better than his crown."

(2) "And on the same day Jesus saw a man working at his craft on the Sabbath-day, and He said unto him, '*O man, if thou knowest what thou doest, then art thou blessed ; but if thou knowest not, then art thou accursed, and art a transgressor of the Law.*'" An addition to Luke 6 : 4, in Codex D. or Bezæ (in the University library at Cambridge), which contains several remarkable additions. See Tischendorf's apparatus in ed. VIII. Luc. 6 : 4, and Scrivener, *Introd. to Criticism of the N. T.* p. 8. ἐπικατάρατος is used John 7 : 49 (text. rec.) by the Pharisees of the people who know not the law (also Gal. 3 : 10, 13 in quotations from the O. T.) ; παραβάτης τοῦ νόμου by Paul (Rom. 2 : 25, 27 ; Gal. 2 : 18) and James (2 : 9, 11). Plumptre regards the narrative as authentic, and remarks that "it brings out with a marvellous force the distinction between the conscious transgression of a law recognized as still binding, and the assertion of a higher law as superseding the lower." Comp. also the remarks of Hofmann, *l. c.* p. 318.

(3) *"But ye seek* (or, in the imperative, *seek ye,* ζητεῖτε) *to increase from little, and (not) from greater to be less."* An addition in Codex D. to Matt 20 : 28. See Tischendorf. Comp. Luke 14 : 11 ; John 5 : 44. Westcott regards this as a genuine fragment. Nicholson inserts "not," with the Curetonian Syriac, D ; all other authorities omit it. Juvencus has in· corporated the passage in his poetic *Hist. Evang.* III. 613 sqq., quoted by Hofmann, p. 319.

(4) *"Be ye trustworthy money-changers,* or, *proved bankers* (τραπεζῖται δόκιμοι) ; i. e. expert in distinguishing the genuine coin from the counterfeit. Quoted by Clement of Alexandria (several times), Origen (*in Joann.* xix.), Eusebius, Epiphanius, Cyril of Alexandria, and many others. Comp. 1 Thess. 5 : 21 : "Prove all things, hold fast the good," and the parable of the talents, Matt. 25 : 27. Delitzsch, who with many others regards this maxim as genuine, gives it the meaning : Exchange the less valuable for the more valuable, esteem sacred coin higher than common coin, and highest of all the one precious pearl of the gospel. (*Ein Tag in Capernaum,* p. 136.) Renan likewise adopts it as historical, but explains it in an Ebionite and monastic sense as an advice of voluntary poverty. "Be ye good bankers (*soyez de bons banquiers*), that is to say : Make good investments for the kingdom of God, by giving your goods to the poor, according to the ancient proverb (Prov. 19 : 17) : 'He that hath pity upon the poor, lendeth to the Lord'" (*Vie de Jésus,* ch. XI. p. 180, 5th Par. ed.).

[(5) "The Son of God says, (?) *'Let us resist all iniquity, and hold it in abhorrence.'* " From the Epistle of Barnabas, c. 4. This Epistle, though incorporated in the Codex Sinaiticus, is probably not a work of the apostolic Barnabas. Westcott and Plumptre quote the passage from the Latin version, which introduces the sentence with the words : *sicut dicit Filius Dei.* But this seems to be a mistake for *sicut decet filios Dei,* "as becometh the sons of God." This is evident from the Greek original (brought to light by the discovery of the Codex Sinaiticus), which reads, ὡς πρέπει υἱοῖς ᵹεοῦ, and connects the words with the preceding sentence. See the edition of *Barnabæ Epistula* by Gebhardt and Harnack in *Patr. Apost. Op.* I. 14. For the sense comp. 2 Tim. 2 : 19 : ἀποστήτω ἀπὸ ἀδικίας, James 4 : 7 : ἀντίστητε τῷ διαβόλῳ, Ps. 119 : 163 : ἀδικίαν ἐμίσησα.]

(6) *"They who wish to see me, and to lay hold on my kingdom, must receive me with affliction and suffering."* From the Epistle of Barnabas, c. 7, where the words are introduced by "Thus he [Jesus] saith," φησίν. But it is doubtful whether they are meant as a quotation or rather as a conclusion of the former remarks and a general reminiscence of several passages. Comp. Matt. 16 : 24 ; 20 : 23 ; Acts 14 : 22 : "We must through much tribulation enter into the kingdom of God."

(7) *"He that wonders* [ὁ ᵹαυμάσας, with the wonder of reverential faith] *shall reign, and he that reigns shall be made to rest."* From the "Gospel of the Hebrews," quoted by Clement of Alexandria (*Strom.* II. 9, § 45).

The Alexandrian divine quotes this and the following sentence to show, as Plumptre finely says, "that in the teaching of Christ, as in that of Plato, wonder is at once the beginning and the end of knowledge."

(8) "*Look with wonder at the things that are before thee* (Ʒαύμασον τὰ παρόντα)." From Clement of Alexandria (*Strom.* II. 9, § 45.).

(9) "*I came to abolish sacrifices, and unless ye cease from sacrificing, the wrath [of God] will not cease from you.*" From the Gospel of the Ebionites (or rather Essæan Judaizers), quoted by Epiphanius (*Hær.* xxx. 16). Comp. Matt. 9 : 13, "I will have mercy and not sacrifice."

(10) "*Ask great things, and the small shall be added to you : ask heavenly things, and there shall be added unto you earthly things.*" Quoted by Clement of Alexandria (*Strom.* I. 24, § 154 ; comp. IV. 6, § 34) and Origen (*de Oratione*, c. 2), with slight differences. Comp. Matt. 6 : 33, of which it is probably a free quotation from memory. Ambrose also quotes the sentence (*Ep.* xxxvi. 3) : "Denique scriptum est : '*Petite magna, et parva adjicientur vobis. Petite cœlestia, et terrena adjicientur.*'"

(11) "*In the things wherein I find you, in them will I judge you.*" Quoted by Justin Martyr (*Dial. c. Tryph.* c. 47), and Clement of Alexandria (*Quis dives*, § 40). Somewhat different Nilus : "Such as I find thee, I will judge thee, saith the Lord." The parallel passages in Ezekiel 7 : 3, 8 ; 18 : 30 ; 24 : 14 ; 33 : 20 are not sufficient to account for this sentence. It is probably taken from an apocryphal Gospel. See Hofmann, p. 323.

(12) "*He who is nigh unto me is nigh unto the fire : he who is far from me is far from the kingdom.*" From Origen (*Comm. in Jer.* III. p. 778), and Didymus of Alexandria (*in Ps.* 88 : 8). Comp. Luke 12 : 49. Ignatius (*Ad Smyrn.* c. 4) has a similar saying, but not as a quotation, "To be near the sword is to be near God" (ἐγγὺς μαχαίρας ἐγγὺς Ʒεοῦ).

(13) "*If ye kept not that which is little, who will give you that which is great ? For I say unto you, he that is faithful in the least is faithful also in much.*" From the homily of Pseudo-Clement of Rome (ch. 8). Comp. Luke 16 : 10–12 and Matt. 25 : 21, 23. Irenæus (II. 34, 3) quotes similarly, probably from memory : "*Si in modico fideles non fuistis, quod magnum est quis dabit nobis ?*"

(14) "*Keep the flesh pure, and the seal* [probably baptism] *without stain that we (ye) may receive eternal life.*" From Pseudo-Clement, ch. 8. But as this is connected with the former sentence by ἄρα οὖν τοῦτο λέγει, it seems to be only an explanation ("he means this") not a separate quotation. See Lightfoot, *St. Clement of Rome*, pp. 200 and 201, and his *Appendix containing the newly recovered Portions*, p. 384. On the sense comp. 2 Tim. 2 : 19 ; Rom. 4 : 11 ; Eph. 1 : 13 ; 4 : 30.

(15) Our Lord, being asked by Salome when His kingdom should come, and the things which he had spoken be accomplished, answered, "*When the two shall be one, and the outward as the inward, and the male with the female, neither male nor female.*" From Clement of Alexandria, as a quotation from "the Gospel according to the Egyptians" (*Strom.*

III. 13, § 92), and the homily of Pseudo-Clement of Rome (ch. 12). Comp. Matt. 22 : 30 ; Gal. 3 : 28 ; 1 Cor. 7 : 29. The sentence has a mystical color‧ ing which is alien to the genuine Gospels, but suited the Gnostic taste.

(16) " *For those that are infirm was I infirm, and for those that hunger did I hunger, and for those that thirst did I thirst.*" From Origen (*in Matt.* xiii. 2). Comp. Matt. 25 : 35, 36 ; 1 Cor. 9 : 20–22.

·(17) " *Never be ye joyful, except when ye have seen your brother* [*dwelling*] *in love.*" Quoted from the Hebrew Gospel by Jerome (*in Eph.* v. 3).

(18) " *Take hold, handle me, and see that I am not a bodiless demon* [*i. e. spirit*]." From Ignatius (*Ad Smyrn.* c. 3), and Jerome, who quotes it from the Nazarene Gospel (*De Viris illustr.* 16). Words said to have been spoken to Peter and the apostles after the resurrection. Comp. Luke 24 : 39 ; John 20 : 27.

(19) "*Good must needs come, but blessed is he through whom it cometh ; in like manner evil must needs come, but woe to him through whom it cometh.*" From the "Clementine Homilies," xii. 29. For the second clause comp. Matt. 18 : 7 ; Luke 17 : 1.

(20) " *My mystery is for me, and for the sons of my house.*" From Clement of Alexandria (*Strom.* V. 10, § 64), the Clementine Homilies (xix. 20), and Alexander of Alexandria (*Ep. ad Alex.* c. 5, where the words are ascribed to the Father). Comp. Isa. 24 : 16 (Sept.) ; Matt. 13 : 11 ; Mark 4 : 11.

(21) " *If you do not make your low things high and your crooked things straight, ye shall not enter into my kingdom.*" From the *Acta Philippi* in Tischendorf's *Acta Apost. Apocr.* p. 90, quoted by Ewald, *Gesch. Christus,'* p. 288, who calls these words a weak echo of more excellent sayings.

(22) " *I will choose these things to myself. Very excellent are those whom my Father that is in heaven hath given to me.*" From the Hebrew Gospel, quoted by Eusebius (*Theophan.* iv. 13).

(23) "The Lord said, speaking of His kingdom, '*The days will come in which vines will spring up, each having ten thousand stocks, and on each stock ten thousand branches, and on each branch ten thousand shoots, and on each shoot ten thousand bunches, and on each bunch ten thousand grapes, and each grape when pressed shall give five-and-twenty measures of wine. And when any saint shall have laid hold on one bunch, another shall cry, I am a better bunch, take me ; through me bless the Lord.*' Likewise also [he said], '*that a grain of wheat shall produce ten thousand ears of corn, and each grain ten pounds of fine pure flour ; and so all other fruits and seeds and each herb according to its proper nature. And that all animals, using for food what is received from the earth, shall live in peace and concord with one another, subject to men with all subjection.*'" To this description Papias adds : "These things are credible to those who believe. And when Judas the traitor believed not and asked, ' How shall such products come from the Lord? ' the Lord said, ' *They shall see who come to me in these times.*'" From the "weak-minded" Papias (quoted by Irenæus, *Adv. Hær.* V. 33, 3). Comp. Isa. 11 : 6-9.

This is a strongly figurative description of the millennium. Westcott thinks it is based on a real discourse, but to me it sounds fabulous, and borrowed from the Apocalypse of Baruch which has a similar passage (cap. 29, first published in *Monumenta Sacra et Profana opera Collegii Doctorum Bibliothecæ Ambrosianæ*, Tom. I. Fasc. II. Mediol. 1866, p. 80, and then in Fritzsche's ed. of *Libri Apocryphi Veteris Test.* Lips. 1871, p. 666):

"*Etiam terra dabit fructus suos unum in decem millia, et in vite una erunt mille palmites, et unus palmes faciet mille botros, et botrus unus faciet mille acinos, et unus acinus faciet corum vini.   Et qui esurierunt jucundabuntur, iterum autem videbunt prodigia quotidie . . . . Et erit in illo tempore, descendet iterum desuper thesaurus manna, et comedent ex eo in istis annis.*"

Westcott quotes eleven other apocryphal sayings which are only loose quotations or perversions of genuine words of Christ, and may therefore be omitted.   Nicholson has gathered the probable or possible fragments of the Gospel according to the Hebrews, which correspond more or less to passages in the canonical Gospels.

Mohammedan tradition has preserved in the Koran and in other writings several striking words of Christ, which Hofmann, *l. c.* pp. 327–329, has collected. The following is the best:

"Jesus, the Son of Mary, said, '*He who longs to be rich is like a man who drinks sea-water; the more he drinks the more thirsty he becomes, and never leaves off drinking till he perishes.*'"

II. PERSONAL APPEARANCE OF JESUS.—None of the Evangelists, not even the beloved disciple and bosom-friend of Jesus, gives us the least hint of his countenance and stature, or of his voice, his manner, his food, his dress, his mode of daily life. In this respect our instincts of natural affection have been wisely overruled. He who is the Saviour of all and the perfect exemplar for all should not be identified with the particular lineaments of one race or nationality or type of beauty. We should cling to the Christ in spirit and in glory rather than to the Christ in the flesh So St. Paul thought (2 Cor. 5 : 16; comp. 1 Pet. 1:8). Though unseen, he is loved beyond all human beings.

> " I see Thee not, I hear Thee not,
>   Yet art Thou oft with me;
>   And earth hath ne'er so dear a spot,
>   As when I meet with Thee."

Jesus no doubt accommodated himself in dress and general appearance to the customs of his age and people, and avoided all ostentation. He probably passed unnoticed through busy crowds. But to the closer observer he must have revealed a spiritual beauty and an overawing majesty in his countenance and personal bearing. This helps to explain the readiness with which the disciples, forsaking all things, followed him in boundless reverence and devotion. He had not the physiognomy of a sinner. He had more than the physiognomy of a saint. He reflected from his eyes and countenance the serene peace and celestial purity of a sinless soul in blessed harmony with God. His presence commanded reverence, confidence and affection.

In the absence of authentic representation, Christian art in its irrepress- ible desire to exhibit in visible form the fairest among the children of men, was left to its own imperfect conception of ideal beauty. The church under persecution in the first three centuries, was averse to pic- torial representations of Christ, and associated with him in his state of humiliation (but not in his state of exaltation) the idea of uncomeliness, taking too literally the prophetic description of the suffering Messiah in the twenty-second Psalm and the fifty-third chapter of Isaiah. The vic- torious church after Constantine, starting from the Messianic picture in the forty-fifth Psalm and the Song of Solomon, saw the same Lord in heavenly glory, "fairer than the children of men" and "altogether lovely." Yet the difference was not so great as it is sometimes repre- sented. For even the ante-Nicene fathers (especially Clement of Alexan- dria), besides expressly distinguishing between the first appearance of Christ in lowliness and humility, and his second appearance in glory and majesty, did not mean to deny to the Saviour even in the days of his flesh a higher order of spiritual beauty, "the glory of the only-begotten of the Father full of grace and truth," which shone through the veil of his humanity, and which at times, as on the mount of transfiguration, anticipated his future glory. "Certainly," says Jerome, "a flame of fire and starry brightness flashed from his eye, and the majesty of the God head shone in his face."

The earliest pictures of Christ, in the Catacombs, are purely symbolic, and represent him under the figures of the Lamb, the good Shepherd, the Fish. The last has reference to the Greek word *Ichthys*, which con- tains the initials of the words Ἰησοῦς Χριστὸς Θεοῦ Ὑιὸς Σωτήρ, "Jesus Christ, Son of God, Saviour." Real pictures of Christ in the early church would have been an offence to the Jewish, and a temptation and snare to the heathen converts.

The first formal description of the personal appearance of Christ, which, though not authentic and certainly not older than the fourth cen- tury, exerted great influence on the pictorial representations, is ascribed to the heathen PUBLIUS LENTULUS, a supposed contemporary of Pilate and "President of the people of Jerusalem" (there was no such office), in an apocryphal Latin letter to the Roman Senate, which was first discov- ered in a MS. copy of the writings of Anselm of Canterbury in the twelfth century, and published with slight variations by Fabricius, Carpzov, Gabler, etc. It is as follows :

"In this time appeared a man, who lives till now, a man endowed with great powers. Men call him a great prophet ; his own disciples term Him the Son of God. His name is Jesus Christ. He restores the dead to life, and cures the sick of all manner of diseases. This man is of noble and well-proportioned stature, with a face full of kindness and yet firmness, so that the beholders both love Him and fear Him. His hair is of the color of wine, and golden at the root; straight, and without lustre, but from the level of the ears curling and glossy, and divided down the centre after the fashion of the Nazarenes [Nazarites?] His forehead is even and smooth, his face without wrinkle or blemish, and glowing with a delicate bloom. His countenance is frank and kind. Nose and mouth are in no way faulty. His beard is full, of the same hazel color as his hair, not long, but forked. His eyes are blue, and extremely brilliant. In reproof and rebuke he is formidable; in exhortation and teaching, gentle and amiable. He has never been seen to laugh, but oftentimes to weep (*numquam visus est ridere, flere autem sæpe*). His person is tall and erect; his hands and limbs beautiful and straight. In speaking he is deliberate and grave, and little given to loquacity. In beauty he surpasses the children of men."

Another description is found in the works of the Greek theologian, JOHN OF DAMASCUS, of the 8th century (*Epist. ad Theoph. Imp. de venerandis Imag.*, spurious), and a similar one in the Church History of NICEPHORUS (I. 40), of the 14th century. They represent Christ as resembling his mother, and ascribe to him a stately person though slightly stooping, beautiful eyes, blond, long, and curly hair, pale, olive complexion, long fingers, and a look expressive of nobility, wisdom, and patience.

On the ground of these descriptions, and of the Abgar and the Veronica legends, arose a vast number of pictures of Christ, which are divided into two classes: the *Salvator* pictures, with the expression of calm serenity and dignity, without the faintest mark of grief, and the *Ecce Homo* pictures of the suffering Saviour with the crown of thorns. The greatest painters and sculptors have exhausted the resources of their genius in representations of Christ; but neither color nor chisel nor pen can do more than produce a feeble reflection of the beauty and glory of Him who is the Son of God and the Son of Man.

Among modern biographers of Christ, Dr. Sepp (Rom. Cath., *Das Leben Jesu Christi*, 1865, vol. VI. 312 sqq.) defends the legend of St. Veronica of the Herodian family, and the genuineness of the picture of the suffering Saviour with the crown of thorns which he impressed on her silken veil. He rejects the philological explanation of the legend from "the true image" (*vera εἰκών* = Veronica), and derives the name from φερενίκη (Berenice), the Victorious. But Bishop Hefele (Art. *Christusbilder*, in the Cath. *Kirchen-Lexikon* of Wetzer and Welte, II. 519–524) is inclined, with Grimm, to identify Veronica with the Berenice who is said to have erected a statue to Christ at Cæsarea Philippi (Euseb. VII. 18), and to see in the Veronica legend only the Latin version of the Abgar legend of the Greek Church. Dr. Hase (*Leben Jesu*, p. 79) ascribes to Christ manly beauty, firm health, and delicate, yet not very characteristic features. He quotes John 20 : 14 and Luke 24 : 16, where it is said that his friends did not recognize him, but these passages refer only to the mysterious appearances of the risen Lord. Renan (*Vie de Jésus*, ch. XXIV. p. 403) describes him in the frivolous style of a novelist, as a *doux Galiléen*, of calm and dignified attitude, as a *beau jeune homme* who made a deep impression upon women, especially Mary of Magdala ; even a proud Roman lady, the wife of Pontius Pilate, when she caught a glimpse of him from the window (?), was enchanted, dreamed of him in the night and was frightened at the prospect of his death. Dr. Keim (I. 463) infers from his character, as described in the Synoptical Gospels, that he was perhaps not strikingly handsome, yet certainly noble, lovely, manly, healthy and vigorous, looking like a prophet, commanding reverence, making men, women, children, sick and poor people feel happy in his presence. Canon Farrar (1. 150) adopts the view of Jerome and Augustine, and speaks of Christ as "full of mingled majesty and tenderness in—

> 'That face
> How beautiful, if sorrow had not made
> Sorrow more beautiful than beauty's self.' "

On artistic representations of Christ see J. B. Carpzov : *De oris et corporis J. Christi forma Pseudo-Lentuli, J. Damasceni et Nicephori prosopographiæ.* Helmst. 1777. P. E. Jablonski : *De origine imaginum Christi Domini.* Lugd. Batav. 1804. W. Grimm : *Die Sage vom Ursprung der Christusbilder.* Berlin, 1843. Dr. Legis Glückselig : *Christus-Archäologie ; Das Buch von Jesus Christus und seinem wahren Ebenbilde.* Prag, 1863. 4to. Mrs. Jameson and Lady Eastlake : *The History of our Lord as exemplified in Works of Art* (with illustrations). Lond., 2d ed. 1865, 2 vols. Cowper : *Apocr. Gospels.* Lond. 1867, pp. 217-226. Hase : *Leben Jesu*, pp. 76-80 (5th ed.). Keim : *Gesch. Jesu von Naz.* I. 459-464. Farrar : *Life of Christ.* Lond. 1874, I. 148-150, 312-313 ; II. 464.

III. The Testimony of Josephus on John the Baptist.—*Antiq. Jud.* xviii. c. 5, ¿ 2. Whatever may be thought of the more famous passage of Christ which we have discussed in ¿ 14 (p. 92), the passage on John is undoubtedly genuine and so accepted by most scholars. It fully and independently confirms the account of the Gospels on John's work and martyrdom, and furnishes, indirectly, an argument in favor of the historical character of their account of Christ, for whom he merely prepared the way. We give it in Whiston's translation : "Now some of the Jews thought that the destruction of Herod's army came from God, and that very justly, as a punishment of what he did against John, who was called the Baptist ; for Herod slew him, who was a good man (ἀγαθὸν ἄνδρα), and commanded the Jews to exercise virtue, both as to righteousness towards one another, and piety towards God, and so to come to baptism ;

for that the washing [with water] would be acceptable to him, if they made use of it, not in order to the putting away [or the remission] of some sins [only], but for the purification of the body : supposing still that the soul was thoroughly purified beforehand by righteousness. Now when [many] others came in crowds about him, for they were greatly moved [or pleased] by hearing his words, Herod, who feared lest the great influence John had over the people might put it into his power and inclination to raise a rebellion (for they seemed ready to do any thing he should advise), thought it best, by putting him to death, to prevent any mischief he might cause, and not bring himself into difficulties, by sparing a man who might make him repent of it when it should be too late. Accordingly he was sent a prisoner, out of Herod's suspicious temper, to Machærus, the castle I before mentioned, and was there put to death. Now the Jews had an opinion that the destruction of this army was sent as a punishment upon Herod, and a mark of God's displeasure to him."

IV. The Testimony of Mara to Christ, a.d. 74.—This extra-biblical notice of Christ, made known first in 1865, and referred to above (§ 14, p. 94) reads as follows (as translated from the Syriac by Cureton and Pratten) :

" What are we to say, when the wise are dragged by force by hands of tyrants, and their wisdom is deprived of its freedom by slander, and they are plundered for their [superior] intelligence, without [the opportunity of making] a defence ? [They are not wholly to be pitied.] For what benefit did the Athenians obtain by putting Socrates to death, seeing that they received [as] retribution for it famine and pestilence ? Or the people of Samos by the burning of Pythagoras, seeing that in one hour the whole of their country was covered with sand ? Or the Jews [by the murder] of their Wise King, seeing that from that very time their kingdom was driven away [from them] ? For with justice did God grant a recompense to the wisdom of [all] three of them. For the Athenians died by famine ; and the people of Samos were covered by the sea without remedy ; and the Jews, brought to destruction and expelled from their kingdom, are driven away into every land. [Nay], Socrates did not die, because of Plato ; nor yet Pythagoras, because of the statue of Hera ; nor yet the Wise King, because of the new laws which he enacted."

The nationality and position of Mara are unknown. Dr. Payne Smith supposes him to have been a Persian. He wrote from prison and wished to die, " by what kind of death concerns me not." In the beginning of his letter Mara says : " On this account, lo, I have written for thee this record, [touching] that which I have by careful observation discovered in the world. For the kind of life men lead has been carefully observed by me. I tread the path of learning, and from the study of Greek philosophy have I found out all these things, although they suffered shipwreck when the birth of life took place." The birth of life may refer to the appearance of Christianity in the world, or to Mara's own conversion. But there is no other indication that he was a Christian. The advice he gives to his son is simply to "devote himself to wisdom, the fount of all things good, the treasure that fails not."

§ 19. *The Resurrection of Christ.*

The resurrection of Christ from the dead is reported by the four Gospels, taught in the Epistles, believed throughout Christendom, and celebrated on every " Lord's Day," as an historical fact, as the crowning miracle and divine seal of his whole work, as the foundation of the hopes of believers, as the pledge of their own future resurrection. It is represented in the New Testament both as an act of the Almighty Father who raised his Son from the dead,[1] and as an act of Christ himself, who had the power to lay down his life and to take it again.[2] The ascension was the proper conclusion of the resurrection: the risen life of our Lord, who is " the Resurrection and the Life," could not end in another death on earth, but must continue in eternal glory in heaven. Hence St. Paul says, ' Christ being raised from the dead dieth no more; death no more hath dominion over him. For the death that he died he died unto sin once: but the life that he liveth, he liveth unto God." [3]

The Christian church rests on the resurrection of its Founder. Without this fact the church could never have been born, or if born, it would soon have died a natural death. The miracle of the resurrection and the existence of Christianity are so closely

---

[1] Acts 2 : 24, 32; Rom. 6 : 4 ; 10 : 9; 1 Cor. 15 : 15 ; Eph. 1 : 20; 1 Pet. 1 : 21.

[2] John 2 : 19; 10 : 17, 18. In like manner the first advent of the Lord is represented as his own voluntary act and as a mission from the Father, John 8 : 42 : ἐγὼ ἐκ τοῦ θεοῦ ἐξῆλθεν καὶ ἥκω· οὐδὲ γὰρ ἀπ᾽ ἐμαυτοῦ ἐλήλυθα, ἀλλ᾽ ἐκεῖνός με ἀπέστειλεν.

[3] Rom. 6 . 9, 10. Neander (*Leben Jesu*, pp. 596 and 597 of the 6th Germ. ed.) makes some excellent remarks on this inseparable connection between the resurrection and the ascension, and says that the ascension would stand fast as a supernatural fact even if Luke had not said a word about it. A temporary resurrection followed by another death could never have become the foundation of a church.

connected that they must stand or fall together. If Christ was
raised from the dead, then all his other miracles are sure, and
our faith is impregnable; if he was not raised, he died in vain,
and our faith is vain. It was only his resurrection that made
his death available for our atonement, justification and salvation; without the resurrection, his death would be the grave of
our hopes; we should be still unredeemed and under the power
of our sins. A gospel of a dead Saviour would be a contradiction and wretched delusion. This is the reasoning of St.
Paul, and its force is irresistible. [1]

The resurrection of Christ is therefore emphatically a test
question upon which depends the truth or falsehood of the
Christian religion. It is either the greatest miracle or the
greatest delusion which history records.[2]

Christ had predicted both his crucifixion and his resurrection,
but the former was a stumbling-block to the disciples, the latter
a mystery which they could not understand till after the event.[3]
They no doubt expected that he would soon establish his Messianic kingdom on earth. Hence their utter disappointment and
downheartedness after the crucifixion. The treason of one of
their own number, the triumph of the hierarchy, the fickleness
of the people, the death and burial of the beloved Master, had
in a few hours rudely blasted their Messianic hopes and exposed
them to the contempt and ridicule of their enemies. For two
days they were trembling on the brink of despair. But on the
third day, behold, the same disciples underwent a complete revolution from despondency to hope, from timidity to courage,
from doubt to faith, and began to proclaim the gospel of the

---

[1] 1 Cor. 15 : 13-19 ; comp. Rom. 4 : 25, where Paul represents Christ's death
and resurrection in inseparable connection, as the sum and substance of the
whole gospel.

[2] Ewald makes the striking remark (VI. 90) that the resurrection is " the
culmination of all the miraculous events which are conceivable from the
beginning of history to its close."

[3] Matt. 16 : 21-23 ; 17 : 9, 22, 23 ; 20 : 17-20 ; Mark 8 : 31 ; 9 : 9, 10, 31, 32
(" they understood not that saying, and were afraid to ask him "); Luke 9 : 22,
44, 45 ; 18 : 31-34 ; 24 : 6-8 ; John 2 : 21, 22 ; 3 : 14 ; 8 : 28 ; 10 : 17, 18 ;
12 : 32.

resurrection in the face of an unbelieving world and at the peril of their lives. This revolution was not isolated, but general among them ; it was not the result of an easy credulity, but brought about in spite of doubt and hesitation ;[1] it was not superficial and momentary, but radical and lasting ; it affected not only the apostles, but the whole history of the world. It reached even the leader of the persecution, Saul of Tarsus, one of the clearest and strongest intellects, and converted him into the most devoted and faithful champion of this very gospel to the hour of his martyrdom.

This is a fact patent to every reader of the closing chapters of the Gospels, and is freely admitted even by the most advanced skeptics.[2]

The question now rises whether this inner revolution in the life of the disciples, with its incalculable effects upon the fortunes of mankind, can be rationally explained without a corresponding outward revolution in the history of Christ; in other

---

[1] The devoted women went to the sepulchre on the first Christian Sabbath, not to see it empty but to embalm the body with spices for its long rest, Mark 16 : 1 ; Luke 23 : 56 ; and when they told the eleven what they saw, their words seemed to them "as idle talk," and "they disbelieved them," Luke 24 : 11. Comp. Matt. 28 : 17 ("some doubted"); Mark 16 : 8 ("they were afraid") ; John 20 : 25.

[2] Dr. Baur states the contrast tersely thus : "*Zwischen dem Tod [Jesu] und seiner Auferstehung liegt ein so tiefes undurchdringliches Dunkel, dass man nach so gewaltsam zerrissenem und so wundervoll wiederhergestelltem Zusammenhange sich gleichsam auf einem neuen Schauplatz der Geschichte sieht.*" Compare his remarks at the close of this section. Dr. Ewald describes the depression and sudden exaltation of the disciples more fully with his usual force (vol. vi. 54 sqq.). I will quote also the description of Renan, at the beginning of the first chapter of his work, *Les Apôtres :* "*Jésus, quoique parlant sans cesse de résurrection, de nouvelle vie, n'avait jamais dit bien clairement qu'il ressusciterait en sa chair. Les disciples, dans les premières heures qui suivirent sa mort, n'avaient à cet égard aucune espérance arrêtée. Les sentiments dont ils nous font la naïve confidence supposent même qu'ils croyaient tout fini. Ils pleurent et enterrent leur ami, sinon comme un mort vulgaire, du moins comme une personne dont la perte est irréparable* (Marc 16 : 10 ; Luc 24 : 17, 21) ; *ils sont tristes et abattus ; l'espoir qu'ils avaient eu de le voir réaliser le salut d'Israël est convaincu de vanité ; on dirait des hommes qui ont perdu une grande et chère illusion. Mais l'enthousiasme et l'amour ne connaissent par les situations sans issue. Ils se jouent de l'impossible, et plutôt que d'abdiquer l'espérance, ils font violence à toute réalité,*" etc.

words, whether the professed faith of the disciples in the risen
Christ was true and real, or a hypocritical lie, or an honest self-
delusion.

There are four possible theories which have been tried again
and again, and defended with as much learning and ingenuity as
can be summoned to their aid.   Historical questions are not like
mathematical problems.   No argument in favor of the resurrection will avail with those critics who start with the philosophical assumption that miracles are impossible, and still less with
those who deny not only the resurrection of the body, but even
the immortality of the soul.   But facts are stubborn, and if a
critical hypothesis can be proven to be psychologically and historically impossible and unreasonable, the result is fatal to the
philosophy which underlies the critical hypothesis.   It is not
the business of the historian to construct a history from precon-
ceived notions and to adjust it to his own liking, but to reproduce it from the best evidence and to let it speak for itself.

1. The HISTORICAL view, presented by the Gospels and believed
in the Christian church of every denomination and sect.   The
resurrection of Christ was an actual though miraculous event,
in harmony with his previous history and character, and in fulfilment of his own prediction.   It was a re-animation of the
dead body of Jesus by a return of his soul from the spirit-world,
and a rising of body and soul from the grave to a new life,
which after repeated manifestations to believers during a short
period of forty days entered into glory by the ascension to
heaven.   The object of the manifestations was not only to convince the apostles personally of the resurrection, but to make
them witnesses of the resurrection and heralds of salvation to
all the world.[1]

Truth compels us to admit that there are serious difficulties
in harmonizing the accounts of the evangelists, and in forming a
consistent conception of the nature of Christ's resurrection-body,
hovering as it were between heaven and earth, and oscillating for

[1] Matt. 28 : 18-20; Mark 16 : 15, 16; Luke 24 : 46-48; John 20 : 21-23;
Acts 1 : 8.

forty days between a natural and a supernatural state, of a body clothed with flesh and blood and bearing the wound-prints, and yet so spiritual as to appear and disappear through closed doors and to ascend visibly to heaven. But these difficulties are not so great as those which are created by a denial of the fact itself. The former can be measurably solved, the latter cannot. We do not know all the details and circumstances which might enable us to clearly trace the order of events. But among all the variations the great central fact of the resurrection itself and its principal features "stand out all the more sure." [1] The period

---

[1] So Meyer says, who is one of the fairest as well as most careful exegetes (*Com. on John*, 5th Germ. ed., p. 643). I will add the observations of Canon Farrar (*Life of Christ*, vol. II. 432) : "The *lacunæ*, the compressions, the variations, the actual differences, the subjectivity of the narrators as affected by spiritual revelations, render all harmonies at the best uncertain. Our belief in the resurrection, as an historic fact, as absolutely well attested to us by subsequent and contemporary circumstances as any other event in history, rests on grounds far deeper, wider, more spiritual, more eternal, than can be shaken by divergences of which we can only say that they are not necessarily contradictions, but of which the true solution is no longer attainable. Hence the 'ten discrepancies' which have been dwelt on since the days of Celsus, have never for one hour shaken the faith of Christendom. The phenomena presented by the narratives are exactly such as we should expect, derived as they are from different witnesses, preserved at first in oral tradition only, and written 1,800 years ago at a period when *minute circumstantial accuracy*, as distinguished from perfect truthfulness, was little regarded. St. Paul, surely no imbecile or credulous enthusiast, vouches, both for the reality of the appearances, and also for the fact that the vision by which he was himself converted came, at a long interval after the rest, to him as to the 'abortive-born' of the apostolic family (1 Cor. 15 : 4–8). If the narratives of Christ's appearance to his disciples were *inventions*, how came they to possess the severe and simple character which shows no tinge of religious excitement? If those appearances were purely *subjective*, how can we account for their sudden, rapid, and total cessation ? As Lange finely says, the great fugue of the first Easter tidings has not come to us as a 'monotonous chorale,' and mere boyish verbal criticism cannot understand the common feeling and harmony which inspire the individual vibrations of those enthusiastic and multitudinous voices (vol. V. 61). Professor Westcott, with his usual profundity and insight, points out the differences of purpose in the narrative of the four Evangelists. St. Matthew dwells chiefly on the majesty and glory of the Resurrection ; St. Mark, both in the original part and in the addition (Mark 16 : 9–20), insists upon it as a fact; St. Luke, as a *spiritual necessity ;* St. John, as a *touchstone of character* (*Introd.* 310–315)."

of the forty days is in the nature of the case the most mysterious in the life of Christ, and transcends all ordinary Christian
experience.   The Christophanies resemble in some respects the
theophanies of the Old Testament, which were granted only to
few believers, yet for the general benefit.   At all events the
fact of the resurrection furnishes the only key for the solution
of the psychological problem of the sudden, radical, and permanent change in the mind and conduct of the disciples; it is the
necessary link in the chain which connects their history before
and after that event.   Their faith in the resurrection was too
clear, too strong, too steady, too effective to be explained in any
other way.   They showed the strength and boldness of their
conviction by soon returning to Jerusalem, the post of danger,
and founding there, in the very face of the hostile Sanhedrin,
the mother-church of Christendom.

2. The THEORY OF FRAUD.   The apostles stole and hid the body
of Jesus, and deceived the world.[1]

This infamous lie carries its refutation on its face: for if
the Roman soldiers who watched the grave at the express request of the priests and Pharisees, were asleep, they could not
see the thieves, nor would they have proclaimed their military
crime; if they, or only some of them, were awake, they would
have prevented the theft.   As to the disciples, they were too

---

[1] This theory was invented by the Jewish priests who crucified the Lord, and
knew it to be false, Matt. 27 : 62–66 ; 28 : 12–15.   The lie was repeated and
believed, like many other lies, by credulous infidels, first by malignant Jews at
the time of Justin Martyr, then by Celsus, who learned it from them, but
wavered between it and the vision-theory, and was renewed in the eighteenth
century by Reimarus in the Wolfenbüttel Fragments.   Salvador, a French Jew,
has again revived and modified it by assuming (according to Hase, *Geschichte
Jesu*, p. 132) that Jesus was justly crucified, and was saved by the wife of
Pilate through Joseph of Arimathæa or some Galilean women ; that he retired
among the Essenes and appeared secretly to a few of his disciples.   (See his
Jésus Christ et sa doctrine, Par. 1838.)   Strauss formerly defended the vision-
hypothesis (see below), but at the close of his life, when he exchanged his
idealism and pantheism for materialism and atheism, he seems to have relapsed
into this disgraceful theory of fraud ; for in his *Old and New Faith* (1873)
he was not ashamed to call the resurrection of Christ "a world-historical
humbug."   Truth or falsehood : there is no middle ground.

timid and desponding at the time to venture on such a daring act, and too honest to cheat the world. And finally a self-invented falsehood could not give them the courage and constancy of faith for the proclamation of the resurrection at the peril of their lives. The whole theory is a wicked absurdity, an insult to the common sense and honor of mankind.

3. The SWOON-THEORY. The physical life of Jesus was not extinct, but only exhausted, and was restored by the tender care of his friends and disciples, or (as some absurdly add) by his own medical skill; and after a brief period he quietly died a natural death.[1]

Josephus, Valerius Maximus, psychological and medical authorities have been searched and appealed to for examples of such apparent resurrections from a trance or asphyxy, especially on the third day, which is supposed to be a critical turning-point for life or putrefaction.

But besides insuperable physical difficulties—as the wounds and loss of blood from the very heart pierced by the spear of the Roman soldier—this theory utterly fails to account for the moral effect. A brief sickly existence of Jesus in need of medical care, and terminating in his natural death and final burial, without even the glory of martyrdom which attended the crucifixion, far from restoring the faith of the apostles, would have only in the end deepened their gloom and driven them to utter despair.[2]

---

[1] The *Scheintod-Hypothese* (as the Germans call it) was ably advocated by Paulus of Heidelberg (1800), and modified by Gfrörer (1838), who afterwards became a Roman Catholic. We are pained to add Dr. Hase (*Gesch. Jesu*, 1876, p. 601), who finds it necessary, however, to call to aid a "special providence," to maintain some sort of consistency with his former advocacy of the miracle of the resurrection, when he truly said (*Leben Jesu*, p. 269, 5th ed. 1865): "*Sonach ruht die Wahrheit der Auferstehung unerschütterlich auf dem Zeugnisse, ja auf dem Dasein der apostolischen Kirche.*"

[2] Dr. Strauss (in his second *Leben Jesu*, 1864, p. 298) thus strikingly and conclusively refutes the swoon-theory: "*Ein halbtodt aus dem Grabe Hervorgekrochener, siech Umherschleichender, der ärztlichen Pflege, des Verbandes, der Stärkung und Schonung Bedürftiger, und am Ende doch dem Leiden Erliegender konnte auf die Jünger unmöglich den Eindruck des Siegers über Tod und*"

4. The VISION-THEORY. Christ rose merely in the imagination of his friends, who mistook a subjective vision or dream
for actual reality, and were thereby encouraged to proclaim their
faith in the resurrection at the risk of death. Their wish was
father to the belief, their belief was father to the fact, and the
belief, once started, spread with the power of a religious epidemic
from person to person and from place to place. The Christian
society wrought the miracle by its intense love for Christ. Accordingly the resurrection does not belong to the history of Christ
at all, but to the inner life of his disciples. It is merely the embodiment of their reviving faith.

This hypothesis was invented by a heathen adversary in the
second century and soon buried out of sight, but rose to new
life in the nineteenth, and spread with epidemical rapidity among
skeptical critics in Germany, France, Holland and England.[1]

*Grab, des Lebensfürsten machen, der ihrem spätern Auftreten zu Grunde lag.
Ein solches Wiederaufleben hätte den Eindruck, den er im Leben und Tode auf
sie gemacht hatte, nur schwächen, denselben höchstens elegisch ausklingen lassen,
unmöglich aber ihre Trauer in Beigeisterung verwandeln, ihre Verehrung zur An-
betung steigern können.*" Dr. Hase (p. 603) unjustly calls this exposure of the
absurdity of his own view, "*Straussische Tendenzmalerei.*" Even more effective
is the refutation of the swoon-theory by Dr. Keim (*Leben Jesu v. Naz.* III. 576):
"*Und dann das Unmöglichste: der arme, schwache, kranke, mühsam auf den
Füssen erhaltene, versteckte, verkleidete, schliesslich hinsterbende Jesus ein Gegen-
stand des Glaubens, des Hochgefühles, des Triumphes seiner Anhänger, ein aufer-
standener Sieger und Gottessohn! In der That hier beginnt die Theorie armselig,
abgeschmackt, ja verwerflich zu werden, indem sie die Apostel als arme Betrogene,
oder gar mit Jesus selber als Betrüger zeigt. Denn vom Scheintod hatte man
auch damals einen Begriff, und die Lage Jesu musste zeigen, dass hier von Auferstehung nicht die Rede war; hielt man ihn doch für auferstanden, gab er sich
selbst als auferstanden, so fehlte das nüchterne Denken, und hütete er sich gar,
seinen Zustand zu verrathen, so fehlte am Ende auch die Ehrlichkeit. Aus
allen diesen Gründen ist der Scheintod von der Neuzeit fast ausnahmslos verworfen worden.*"

[1] The vision-hypothesis (*Visions-Hypothese*) was first suggested by the heathen Celsus (see Keim, III. 577), and in a more respectful form by the Jewish
philosopher Spinoza, and elaborately carried out by Strauss and Renan, with
the characteristic difference, however, that Strauss traces the resurrection
dream to the apostles in Galilee, Renan (after Celsus) to Mary Magdalene in
Jerusalem, saying, in his *Life of Jesus* (almost blasphemously), that "the
passion of a hallucinated woman gave to the world a risen God!" In his
work on the *Apostles*, Renan enters more fully into the question and again

The advocates of this hypothesis appeal first and chiefly to the vision of St. Paul on the way to Damascus, which occurred several years later, and is nevertheless put on a level with the former appearances to the older apostles (1 Cor. 15 : 8); next to supposed analogies in the history of religious enthusiasm and mysticism, such as the individual visions of St. Francis of Assisi, the Maid of Orleans, St. Theresa (who believed that she had seen Jesus in person with the eyes of the soul more distinctly than she could have seen him with the eyes of the body), Swedenborg, even Mohammed, and the collective visions of the Montanists in Asia Minor, the Camisards in France, the spectral resurrections of the martyred Thomas à Becket of Canterbury and Savonarola of Florence in the excited imagination of their admirers, and the apparitions of the Immaculate Virgin at Lourdes.[1]

emphasizes, in the genuine style of a French novelist, the part of the Magdalene. "*La gloire de la résurrection* (he says, p. 13) *appartient à Marie de Magdala. Après Jésus, c'est Marie qui a le plus fait pour la fondation du christianisme. L'ombre créée par les sens délicats de Madeleine plane encore sur le monde . . . . Sa grande affirmation de femme : 'Il est resuscité!' a été la base de la foi de l'humanité.*" The vision-theory has also been adopted and defended by Zeller, Holsten (in an able treatise on the *Gospel of Paul and Peter*, 1868), Lang, Volkmar, Réville, Scholten, Meijboom, Kuenen, Hooykaas. Comp. Keim, III. 579 sqq. Among English writers the anonymous author of *Supernatural Religion* is its chief champion, and states it in these words (vol. III. 526, Lond. ed. of 1879): "The explanation which we offer, and which has long been adopted in various forms by able critics" [among whom, in a foot-note, he falsely quotes Ewald] "is, that doubtless Jesus was seen (ὤφθη), but the vision was not real and objective, but illusory and subjective; that is to say, Jesus was not himself seen, but only a representation of Jesus within the minds of the beholders."

On the other hand Ewald, Schenkel, Alex. Schweizer, and Keim have essentially modified the theory by giving the resurrection-visions an *objective* character and representing them as real though purely spiritual manifestations of the exalted Christ from *heaven*. Hase calls this view happily a *Verhimmelung der Visionshypothese* (*Gesch. Jesu*, p. 597). It is certainly a great improvement and a more than half-way approach to the truth, but it breaks on the rock of the empty sepulchre. It does not and cannot tell us what became of the body of Christ.

[1] The author of *Supernatural Religion* (III. 530), calls to aid even Luther's vision of the devil on the Wartburg, and especially the apparition of Lord Byron after his death to Sir Walter Scott in clear moonshine ; and he fancies that in the first century it would have been mistaken for reality.

Nobody will deny that subjective fancies and impressions are often mistaken for objective realities.   But, with the exception of the case of St. Paul—which we shall consider in its proper place, and which turns out to be, even according to the admission of the leaders of skeptical criticism, a powerful argument against the mythical or visionary theory—these supposed analogies are entirely irrelevant; for, not to speak of other differences, they were isolated and passing phenomena which left no mark on history; while the faith in the resurrection of Christ has revolutionized the whole world.   It must therefore be treated on its own merits as an altogether unique case.

(a) The first insuperable argument against the visionary nature, and in favor of the objective reality, of the resurrection is the empty tomb of Christ.   If he did not rise, his body must either have been removed, or remained in the tomb.   If removed by the disciples, they were guilty of a deliberate falsehood in preaching the resurrection, and then the vision-hypothesis gives way to the exploded theory of fraud.   If removed by the enemies, then these enemies had the best evidence against the resurrection, and would not have failed to produce it and thus to expose the baselessness of the vision.   The same is true, of course, if the body had remained in the tomb.   The murderers of Christ would certainly not have missed such an opportunity to destroy the very foundation of the hated sect.

To escape this difficulty, Strauss removes the origin of the illusion away off to Galilee, whither the disciples fled; but this does not help the matter, for they returned in a few weeks to Jerusalem, where we find them all assembled on the day of Pentecost.

This argument is fatal even to the highest form of the vision hypothesis, which admits a spiritual manifestation of Christ from heaven, but denies the resurrection of his body.

(b) If Christ did not really rise, then the words which he spoke to Mary Magdalene, to the disciples of Emmaus, to doubting Thomas, to Peter on the lake of Tiberias, to all the disciples on Mount Olivet, were likewise pious fictions.   But who

can believe that words of such dignity and majesty, so befitting
the solemn moment of the departure to the throne of glory, as
the commandment to preach the gospel to every creature, to
baptize the nations in the name of the Father, the Son, and the
Holy Spirit, and the promise to be with his disciples alway to
the end of the world—a promise abundantly verified in the daily
experience of the church—could proceed from dreamy and self-
deluded enthusiasts or crazy fanatics any more than the Sermon
on the Mount or the Sacerdotal Prayer! And who, with any
spark of historical sense, can suppose that Jesus never instituted
baptism, which has been performed in his name ever since the
day of Pentecost, and which, like the celebration of the Lord's
Supper, bears testimony to him every day as the sunlight does
to the sun!

(c) If the visions of the resurrection were the product of an
excited imagination, it is unaccountable that they should suddenly have ceased on the fortieth day (Acts 1 : 15), and not
have occurred to any of the disciples afterwards, with the single
exception of Paul, who expressly represents his vision of Christ
as "the last." Even on the day of Pentecost Christ did not
appear to them, but, according to his promise, "the other Paraclete" descended upon them ; and Stephen saw Christ in heaven,
not on earth.[1]

(d) The chief objection to the vision-hypothesis is its intrinsic
impossibility. It makes the most exorbitant claim upon our
credulity. It requires us to believe that many persons, singly
and collectively, at different times, and in different places, from
Jerusalem to Damascus, had the same vision and dreamed the
same dream ; that the women at the open sepulchre early in the
morning, Peter and John soon afterwards, the two disciples
journeying to Emmaus on the afternoon of the resurrection day,

---

[1] It is utterly baseless when Ewald and Renan extend these visions of Christ
for months and years. " Ces grands rêves mélancoliques," says Renan (Les
Apôtres, 34, 36), "ces entretiens sans cesse interrompus et recommencés avec le
mort chéri remplissaient les jours et les mois . . . . Près d'un an s'écoula dans
cette vie suspendue entre le ciel et la terre. Le charme, loin de décroître, aug-
mentait," etc. Even Keim, III. 598, protests against this view.

the assembled apostles on the evening in the absence of Thomas, and again on the next Lord's Day in the presence of the skeptical Thomas, seven apostles at the lake of Tiberias, on one occasion five hundred brethren at once most of whom were still alive when Paul reported the fact, then James, the brother of the Lord, who formerly did not believe in him, again all the apostles on Mount Olivet at the ascension, and at last the clear-headed, strong-minded persecutor on the way to Damascus— that all these men and women on these different occasions vainly imagined they saw and heard the self-same Jesus in bodily shape and form; and that they were by this baseless vision raised all at once from the deepest gloom in which the crucifixion of their Lord had left them, to the boldest faith and strongest hope which impelled them to proclaim the gospel of the resurrection from Jerusalem to Rome to the end of their lives! And this illusion of the early disciples created the greatest revolution not only in their own views and conduct, but among Jews and Gentiles and in the subsequent history of mankind! This illusion, we are expected to believe by these unbelievers, gave birth to the most real and most mighty of all facts, the Christian Church which has lasted these eighteen hundred years and is now spread all over the civilized world, embracing more members than ever and exercising more moral power than all the kingdoms and all other religions combined!

The vision-hypothesis, instead of getting rid of the miracle, only shifts it from fact to fiction; it makes an empty delusion more powerful than the truth, or turns all history itself at last into a delusion. Before we can reason the resurrection of Christ out of history we must reason the apostles and Christianity itself out of existence. We must either admit the miracle, or frankly confess that we stand here before an inexplicable mystery.

REMARKABLE CONCESSIONS.—The ablest advocates of the vision-theory are driven against their wish and will to admit some unexplained objecive reality in the visions of the risen or ascended Christ.

Dr. BAUR, of Tübingen (d. 1860), the master-critic among sceptical church historians, and the corypheus of the Tübingen school, came at

last to the conclusion (as stated in the revised edition of his Church History of the First Three Centuries, published shortly before his death,
1860) that "nothing but the miracle of the resurrection could disperse
the doubts which threatened to drive faith itself into the eternal night of
death (*Nur das Wunder der Auferstehung konnte die Zweifel zerstreuen,
welche den Glauben selbst in die ewige Nacht des Todes verstossen zu müssen
schienen*)." *Geschichte der christlichen Kirche*, I. 39.   It is true he adds that
the nature of the resurrection itself lies outside of historical investigation ("*Was die Auferstehung an sich ist, liegt ausserhalb des Kreises der
geschichtlichen Untersuchung*"), but also, that "for the faith of the disciples
the resurrection of Jesus became the most solid and most irrefutable certainty.   In this faith only Christianity gained a firm foothold of its historical development.   (*In diesem Glauben hat erst das Christenthum den
festen Grund seiner geschichtlichen Entwicklung gewonnen.*)   What history
requires as the necessary prerequisite of all that follows is not so much
the fact of the resurrection itself [?] as the faith in that fact.   In whatever light we may consider the resurrection of Jesus, whether as an
actual objective miracle or as a subjective psychological one (*als ein
objectiv geschehenes Wunder, oder als ein subjectiv psychologisches*), even
granting the possibility of such a miracle, no psychological analysis can
penetrate the inner spiritual process by which in the consciousness of the
disciples their unbelief at the death of Jesus was transformed into a belief of his resurrection . . . .   We must rest satisfied with this, that for
them the resurrection of Christ was a fact of their consciousness, and had
for them all the reality of an historical event." (*Ibid.*, pp. 39, 40.)   Baur's
remarkable conclusion concerning the conversion of St. Paul (*ibid.*, pp.
44, 45) we shall consider in its proper place.

Dr. EWALD, of Göttingen (d. 1874), the great orientalist and historian
of Israel, antagonistic to Baur, his equal in profound scholarship and
bold, independent, often arbitrary criticism, but superior in religious
sympathy with the genius of the Bible, discusses the resurrection of
Christ in his *History of the Apostolic Age* (*Gesch. des Volkes Israel*, vol. VI.
52 sqq.), instead of his *Life of Christ*, and resolves it into a purely spiritual, though long continued manifestation from heaven.   Nevertheless he
makes the strong statement (p. 69) that "nothing is historically more certain than that Christ rose from the dead and appeared to his own, and that
this their vision was the beginning of their new higher faith and of all
their Christian labors."   "*Nichts steht geschichtlich fester,*" he says, "*als
dass Christus aus den Todten auferstanden den Seinigen wiedererschien und
dass dieses ihr wiedersehen der anfang ihres neuen höhern glaubens und alles
ihres christlichen wirkens selbst war.   Es ist aber ebenso gewiss dass sie ihn
nicht wie einen gewöhnlichen menschen oder wie einen aus dem grabe auf-
steigenden schatten oder gespenst wie die sage von solchen meldet, sondern
wie den einzigen Sohn Gottes, wie ein durchaus schon übermächtiges und
übermenschliches wesen wiedersahen und sich bei späteren zurückerinner-*

ungen nichts anderes denken konnten als dass jeder welcher ihn wieder-
zusehen gewürdigt sei auch sogleich unmittelbar seine einzige göttliche würde
erkannt und seitdem felsenfest daran geglaubt habe. Als den ächten König
und Sohn Gottes hatten ihn aber die Zwölfe und andre schon im leben zu
erkennen gelernt : der unterschied ist nur der dass sie ihn jetzt auch nach
seiner rein göttlichen seite und damit auch als den über den tod siegreichen
erkannt zu haben sich erinnerten. Zwischen jenem gemeinen schauen des
irdischen Christus wie er ihnen sowohl bekannt war und diesem höhern tief-
erregten entzückten schauen des himmlischen ist also doch ein innerer zusam-
menhang, so dass sie ihn auch jezt in diesen ersten tagen und wochen nach
seinem tode nie als den himmlischen Messias geschauet hätten wenn sie ihn
nicht schon vorher als den irdischen so wohl gekannt hätten."

Dr. KEIM, of Zürich (d. at Giessen, 1879), an independent pupil of
Baur, and author of the most elaborate and valuable Life of Christ which
the liberal critical school has produced, after giving every possible advantage to the mythical view of the resurrection, confesses that it is, after
all, a mere hypothesis and fails to explain the main point.   He says
(*Geschichte Jesu von Nazara*, III. 600) : "*Nach allen diesen Ueberlegungen*
wird man zugestehen müssen, dass auch die neuerdings beliebt gewordene
Theorie nur eine Hypothese ist, welche Einiges erklärt, die Hauptsache nicht
erklärt, ja im Ganzen und Grossen das geschichtlich Bezeugte schiefen und
hinfälligen Gesichtspunkten unterstellt. Misslingt aber gleichmässig der
Versuch, die überlieferte Auferstehungsgeschichte festzuhalten, wie das Unter-
nehmen, mit Hilfe der paulinischen Visionen eine natürliche Erklärung des
Geschehenen aufzubauen, so bleibt für die Geschichte zunächst kein Weg
übrig als der des Eingeständnisses, dass die Sagenhaftigkeit der redseligen
Geschichte und die dunkle Kürze der glaubwürdigen Geschichte es nicht
gestattet, über die räthselhaften Ausgänge des Lebens Jesu, so wichtig sie
an und für sich und in der Einwirkung auf die Weltgeschichte gewesen
sind, ein sicheres unumstössliches Resultat zu geben. Für die Geschichte,
sofern sie nur mit benannten evidenten Zahlen und mit Reihen greifbarer
anerkannter Ursachen und Wirkungen rechnet, existirt als das Thatsäch-
liche und Zweifellose lediglich der feste Glaube der Apostel, dass Jesus aufer-
standen, und die ungeheure Wirkung dieses Glaubens, die Christianisirung
der Menschheit."   On p. 601 he expresses the conviction that "it was
the crucified and living Christ who, not as the risen one, but rather as
the divinely glorified one (*als der wenn nicht Auferstandene, so doch*
vielmehr himmlisch Verherrlichte), gave visions to his disciples and revealed himself to his society."   In his last word on the great problem,
Keim, in view of the exhaustion and failure of the natural explanations,
comes to the conclusion, that we must either, with Dr. Baur, humbly
confess our ignorance, or return to the faith of the apostles who "have
seen the Lord" (John 20 : 25).   See the third and last edition of his
abridged *Geschichte Jesu*, Zürich, 1875, p. 362.

Dr. SCHENKEL, of Heidelberg, who in his *Charakterbild Jesu* (third ed.

1864, pp. 231 sqq.) had adopted the vision-theory in its higher form as a purely spiritual, though real manifestation from heaven, confesses in his latest work, *Das Christusbild der Apostel* (1879, p. 18), his inability to solve the problem of the resurrection of Christ, and says : "*Niemals wird es der Forschung gelingen, das Räthsel des Auferstehungsglaubens zu ergründen. Nichts aber steht fester in der Geschichte* ALS DIE THATSACHE DIESES GLAUBENS *; auf ihm beruht die Stiftung der christlichen Gemeinschaft* . . . *Der Visionshypothese, welche die Christuserscheinungen der Jünger aus Sinnestäuschungen erklären will, die in einer Steigerung des 'Gemüths- und Nervenlebens' ihre physische und darum auch psychische Ursache hatten,* . . . . *steht vor allem die Grundfarbe der Stimmung in den Jüngern, namentlich in Petrus, im Wege: die tiefe Trauer, das gesunkene Selbstvertrauen, die nagende Gewissenspein, der verlorne Lebensmuth. Wie soll aus einer solchen Stimmung das verklärte Bild des Auferstandenen hervorgehen, mit dieser unverwüstlichen Sicherheit und unzerstörbaren Freudigkeit, durch welche der Auferstehungsglaube die Christengemeinde in allen Stürmen und Verfolgungen aufrecht zu erhalten vermochte?*"

CHAPTER III.

THE APOSTOLIC AGE.

§ 20. *Sources and Literature of the Apostolic Age.*

I. SOURCES.

1. THE CANONICAL BOOKS OF THE NEW TESTAMENT.—The twenty-seven books of the New Testament are better supported than any ancient classic, both by a chain of external testimonies which reaches up almost to the close of the apostolic age, and by the internal evidence of a spiritual depth and unction which raises them far above the best productions of the second century. The church has undoubtedly been guided by the Holy Spirit in the selection and final determination of the Christian canon. But this does, of course, not supersede the necessity of criticism, nor is the evidence equally strong in the case of the seven Eusebian Antilegomena. The Tübingen and Leyden schools recognized at first only five books of the New Testament as authentic, namely, four Epistles of Paul—Romans, First and Second Corinthians, and Galatians—and the Revelation of John. But the progress of research leads more and more to positive results, and nearly all the Epistles of Paul now find advocates among liberal critics. (Hilgenfeld and Lipsius admit seven, adding First Thessalonians, Philippians, and Philemon ; Renan concedes also Second Thessalonians, and Colossians to be Pauline, thus swelling the number of genuine Epistles to nine.) The chief facts and doctrines of apostolic Christianity are sufficiently guaranteed even by those five documents, which are admitted by the extreme left of modern criticism.

The ACTS OF THE APOSTLES give us the external, the EPISTLES the internal history of primitive Christianity. They are independent contemporaneous compositions and never refer to each other ; probably Luke never read the Epistles of Paul, and Paul never read the Acts of Luke, although he no doubt supplied much valuable information to Luke. But indirectly they illustrate and confirm each other by a number of coincidences which have great evidential value, all the more as these coincidences are undesigned and incidental. Had they been composed by post-apostolic writers, the agreement would have been more complete, minor disagreements would have been avoided, and the lacunæ in the Acts supplied, especially in regard to the closing labors and death of Peter and Paul.

The ACTS bear on the face all the marks of an original, fresh, and trustworthy narrative of contemporaneous events derived from the best sources of information, and in great part from personal observation and experience. The authorship of Luke, the companion of Paul, is conceded by a majority of the best modern scholars, even by Ewald. And this fact alone establishes the credibility. Renan (in his *St. Paul,* ch. 1) admirably calls the Acts "a book of joy, of serene ardor. Since the Homeric poems no book has been seen full of such fresh sensations. A breeze of morning, an odor of the sea, if I dare express it so, inspiring something joyful and strong, penetrates the whole book, and makes it an excellent *compagnon de voyage,* the exquisite breviary for him who is searching for ancient remains on the seas of the south. This is the second idyl of Christianity. The Lake of Tiberias and its fishing barks had furnished the first. Now, a more powerful breeze, aspirations toward more distant lands, draw us out into the open sea."

2. The POST-APOSTOLIC and PATRISTIC writings are full of reminiscences of, and references to, the apostolic books, and as dependent on them as the river is upon its fountain.

3. The APOCRYPHAL and HERETICAL literature. The numerous Apocryphal *Acts, Epistles,* and *Apocalypses* were prompted by the same motives of curiosity and dogmatic interest as the Apocryphal *Gospels,* and have a similar apologetic, though very little historical, value. The heretical character is, however, more strongly marked. They have not yet been sufficiently investigated. Lipsius (in Smith and Wace's "Dict. of Christ. Biog." vol. I. p. 27) divides the Apocryphal Acts into four classes : (1) Ebionitic ; (2) Gnostic ; (3) originally Catholic ; (4) Catholic adaptations or recensions of heretical documents. The last class is the most numerous, rarely older than the fifth century, but mostly resting on documents from the second and third centuries.

(a) Apocryphal Acts : *Acta Petri et Pauli* (of Ebionite origin, but recast), *Acta Pauli et Theclæ* (mentioned by Tertullian at the end of the second century, of Gnostic origin), *Acta Thomæ* (Gnostic), *Acta Matthæi, Acta Thaddæi, Martyrium Bartholomæi, Acta Barnabæ, Acta Andreæ, Acta Andreæ et Matthiæ, Acta Philippi, Acta Johannis, Acta Simonis et Judæ, Acta Thaddæi, The Doctrine of Addai, the Apostle* (ed. in Syriac and English by Dr. G. Phillips, London, 1876).

(b) Apocryphal Epistles : the correspondence between *Paul* and *Seneca* (six by Paul and eight by Seneca, mentioned by Jerome and Augustine), the *third* Epistle of *Paul* to the *Corinthians, Epistolæ Mariæ, Epistolæ Petri ad Jacobum.*

(c) Apocryphal Apocalypses : *Apocalypsis Johannis, Apocalypsis Petri, Apocalypsis Pauli* (or ἀναβατικὸν Παύλου, based on the report of his rapture into Paradise, 2 Cor. 12 : 2–4), *Apocalypsis Thomæ, Apoc. Stephani, Apoc. Mariæ, Apoc. Mosis, Apoc. Esdræ.*

Editions and Collections :

FABRICIUS : *Codex Apocryphus Novi Testamenti.* Hamburg, 1703, 2d ed. 1719, 1743, 3 parts in 2 vols. (vol. II.)

GRABE : *Spicilegium Patrum et Hæreticorum.* Oxford, 1698, ed. II. 1714.

BIRCH : *Auctarium Cod. Apoc. N. Ti Fabrician.* Copenh. 1804 (Fasc. I.). Contains the pseudo-Apocalypse of John.

THILO : *Acta Apost. Petri et Pauli.* Halis, 1838. *Acta Thomæ.* Lips. 1823.

TISCHENDORF : *Acta Apostolorum Apocrypha.* Lips. 1851.

TISCHENDORF : *Apocalypses Apocryphæ Mosis, Esdræ, Pauli, Joannis, item Mariæ Dormitio.* Lips. 1866.

R. A. LIPSIUS : *Die apokryph. Apostel geschichten und Apostel legenden.* Leipz. 1883 sq. 2 vols.

4. JEWISH sources : PHILO and JOSEPHUS, see § 14, p. 92. Josephus is all-important for the history of the Jewish war and the destruction of Jerusalem, A.D. 70, which marks the complete rupture of the Christian Church with the Jewish synagogue and temple. The apocryphal Jewish, and the Talmudic literature supplies information and illustrations of the training of the Apostles and the form of their teaching, and the discipline and worship of the primitive church. Lightfoot, Schöttgen, Castelli, Delitzsch, Wünsche, Siegfried, Schürer, and a few others have made those sources available for the exegete and historian. Comp. here also the Jewish works of JOST, GRAETZ, and GEIGER, mentioned § 9, p. 61, and HAMBURGER's *Real-Encyclopädie des Judenthums (für Bibel und Talmud),* in course of publication.

5. HEATHEN writers : TACITUS, PLINY, SUETONIUS, LUCIAN, CELSUS, PORPHYRY, JULIAN. They furnish only fragmentary, mostly incidental, distorted and hostile information, but of considerable apologetic value.

Comp. NATH. LARDNER (d. 1768) : *Collection of Ancient Jewish and Heathen Testimonies to the Truth of the Christian Religion.* Originally published in 4 vols. Lond. 1764–'67, and then in the several editions of his *Works* (vol. VI. 365–649, ed. Kippis).

II. HISTORIES OF THE APOSTOLIC AGE.

WILLIAM CAVE (Anglican, d. 1713) : *Lives of the Apostles, and the two Evangelists, St. Mark and St. Luke.* Lond. 1675, new ed. revised by H. Cary, Oxford, 1840 (reprinted in New York, 1857). Comp. also CAVE's *Primitive Christianity,* 4th ed. Lond. 1862.

JOH. FR. BUDDEUS (Luth., d. at Jena, 1729) : *Ecclesia Apostolica.* Jen. 1729.

GEORGE BENSON (d. 1763) : *History of the First Planting of the Christian*

Religion. Lond. 1756, 3 vols. 4to (in German by *Bamberger*, Halle, 1768).

J. J. HESS (d. at Zurich, 1828) : *Geschichte der Apostel Jesu.* Zür. 1788 ; 4th ed. 1820.

GOTTL. JAC. PLANCK (d. in Göttingen, 1833) : *Geschichte des Christenthums in der Periode seiner Einführung in die Welt durch Jesum und die Apostel.* Göttingen, 1818, 2 vols.

*AUG. NEANDER (d. in Berlin, 1850) : *Geschichte der Pflanzung und Leitung der christlichen Kirche durch die Apostel.* Hamb. 1832. 2 vols.; 4th ed. revised 1847. The same in English (*History of the Planting and Training of the Christ. Church*), by *J. E. Ryland*, Edinb. 1842, and in Bohn's Standard Library, Lond. 1851 ; reprinted in Philad. 1844 ; revised by *E. G. Robinson*, N. York, 1865. This book marks an epoch and is still valuable.

F. C. ALBERT SCHWEGLER (d. at Tübingen, 1857) : *Das nachapostolische Zeitalter in den Hauptmomenten seiner Entwicklung.* Tübingen, 1845, 1846, 2 vols. An ultra-critical attempt to transpose the apostolic literature (with the exception of five books) into the post-apostolic age.

*FERD. CHRIST. BAUR (d. 1860) : *Das Christenthum und die christliche Kirche der drei ersten Jahrhunderte.* Tübingen, 1853, 2d revised ed. 1860 (536 pp.). The third edition is a mere reprint or title edition of the second and forms the first volume of his General Church History, edited by his son, in 5 vols. 1863. It is the last and ablest exposition of the Tübingen reconstruction of the apostolic history from the pen of the master of that school. See vol. I. pp. 1–174. English translation by *Allen Menzies*, in 2 vols. Lond. 1878 and 1879. Comp. also Baur's *Paul*, second ed. by *Ed. Zeller*, 1866 and 1867, and translated by *A. Menzies*, 2 vols. 1873, 1875. Baur's critical researches have compelled a thorough revision of the traditional views on the apostolic age, and have so far been very useful, notwithstanding their fundamental errors.

A. P. STANLEY (Dean of Westminster) : *Sermons and Essays on the Apostolic Age.* Oxford, 1847. 3d ed. 1874.

*HEINRICH W. J. THIERSCH (Irvingite, died 1885 in Basle) : *Die Kirche im apostolischen Zeitalter.* Francf. a. M. 1852 ; 3d ed. Augsburg, 1879, "improved," but very slightly. (The same in English from the first ed. by *Th. Carlyle.* Lond. 1852.)

*J. P. LANGE (d. 1884) : *Das apostolische Zeitalter.* Braunschw. 1854. 2 vols.

*PHILIP SCHAFF : *History of the Apostolic Church*, first in German, Mercersburg, Penns. 1851 ; 2d ed. enlarged, Leipzig, 1854 ; English translation by Dr. *E. D. Yeomans*, N. York, 1853, in 1 vol. ; Edinb. 1854, in 2 vols. ; several editions without change. (Dutch translation from the second Germ. ed. by *J. W. Th. Lublink Weddik*, Tiel, 1857.)

*G. V. LECHLER (Prof. in Leipzig) : *Das apostolische und das nacha-

postolische Zeitalter. 2d ed. 1857; 3d ed. thoroughly revised, Leipzig, 1885. Engl. trsl. by Miss *Davidson,* Edinb. 1887. Conservative.
*ALBRECHT RITSCHL (d. in Göttingen, 1889) : *Die Entstehung der altkatholischen Kirche.* 2d ed. Bonn, 1857. The first edition was in harmony with the Tübingen School; but the second is materially improved, and laid the foundation for the Ritschl School.
*HEINRICH EWALD (d. at Göttingen, 1874) : *Geschichte des Volkes Israel,* vols. VI. and VII. 2d ed. Göttingen, 1858 and 1859. Vol. VI. of this great work contains the History of the Apostolic Age to the destruction of Jerusalem; vol. VII. the History of the post-Apostolic Age to the reign of Hadrian. English translation of the *History of Israel* by R. *Martineau* and J. E. *Carpenter.* Lond. 1869 sqq. A trans. of vols. VI. and VII. is not intended. Ewald (the *" Urvogel von Göttingen "*) pursued an independent path in opposition both to the traditional orthodoxy and to the Tübingen school, which he denounced as worse than heathenish. See Preface to vol. VII.
*E. DE PRESSENSÉ : *Histoire des trois premiers siècles de l'église chrétienne.* Par. 1858 sqq. 4 vols. German translation by E. *Fabarius* (Leipz. 1862–'65) ; English translation by *Annie Harwood-Holmden* (Lond. and N. York, 1870, new ed. Lond. 1879). The first volume contains the first century under the title *Le siècle apostolique;* rev. ed. 1887.
*JOH. JOS. IGN. VON DÖLLINGER (Rom. Cath., since 1870 Old Cath.) : *Christenthum und Kirche in der Zeit der Gründung.* Regensburg, 1860. 2d ed. 1868. The same translated into English by H. N. *Oxenham.* London, 1867.
C. S. VAUGHAN : *The Church of the First Days.* Lond. 1864–'65. 3 vols. Lectures on the Acts of the Apostles.
J. N. SEPP (Rom. Cath.) : *Geschichte der Apostel Jesu bis zur Zerstörung Jerusalems.* Schaffhausen, 1866.
C. HOLSTEN : *Zum Evangelium des Paulus und des Petrus.* Rostock, 1868 (447 pp.).
PAUL WILH. SCHMIDT *und* FRANZ V. HOLTZENDORF : *Protestanten-Bibel Neuen Testaments.* Zweite, revid. Auflage. Leipzig, 1874. A popular exegetical summary of the Tübingen views with contributions from BRUCH, HILGENFELD, HOLSTEN, LIPSIUS, PFLEIDERER and others.
A. B. BRUCE (Professor in Glasgow) : *The Training of the Twelve.* Edinburgh, 1871, second ed. 1877.
*ERNEST RENAN (de l'Académie Française) : *Histoire des origines du Christianisme.* Paris, 1863 sqq. The first volume is *Vie de Jésus,* 1863, noticed in § 14 (pp. 97 and 98) ; then followed II. *Les Apôtres,* 1866 ; III. *St. Paul,* 1869 ; IV. *L'Antechrist,* 1873 ; V. *Les Évangiles,* 1877 ; VI. *L'Église Chrétienne,* 1879 ; VII. and last volume, *Marc-Aurèle,* 1882. The II., III., IV., and V. volumes belong to the Apostolic age ; the last two to the next. The work of a sceptical outsider, of brilliant genius, eloquence, and secular learning. It increases

in value as it advances. The *Life of Jesus* is the most interesting and popular, but also by far the most objectionable volume, because it deals almost profanely with the most sacred theme.

EMILE FERRIÈRE : *Les Apôtres.* Paris, 1875.

SUPERNATURAL RELIGION. *An Inquiry into the Reality of Divine Revelation.* Lond. 1873, (seventh) "complete ed., carefully revised," 1879, 3 vols. This anonymous work is an English reproduction and repository of the critical speculations of the Tübingen School of Baur, Strauss, Zeller, Schwegler, Hilgenfeld, Volkmar, etc. It may be called an enlargement of Schwegler's *Nachapostolisches Zeitalter.* The first volume is mostly taken up with a philosophical discussion of the question of miracles ; the remainder of vol. I. (pp. 212–485) and vol. II. contain an historical inquiry into the apostolic origin of the canonical Gospels, with a negative result. The third volume discusses the Acts, the Epistles and the Apocalypse, and the evidence for the Resurrection and Ascension, which are resolved into hallucinations or myths. Starting with the affirmation of the antecedent incredibility of miracles, the author arrives at the conclusion of their impossibility ; and this philosophical conclusion determines the historical investigation throughout. Dr. Schürer, in the "Theol. Literaturzeitung" for 1879, No. 26 (p. 622), denies to this work scientific value for Germany, but gives it credit for extraordinary familiarity with recent German literature and great industry in collecting historical details. Drs. Lightfoot, Sanday, Ezra Abbot, and others have exposed the defects of its scholarship, and the false premises from which the writer reasons. The rapid sale of the work indicates the extensive spread of skepticism and the necessity of fighting over again, on Anglo-American ground, the theological battles of Germany and Holland ; it is to be hoped with more triumphant success.

*J. B. LIGHTFOOT (Bishop of Durham since 1879) : A series of elaborate articles against " *Supernatural Religion,*" in the "Contemporary Review" for 1875 to 1877. They should be republished in book form. Comp. also the reply of the anonymous author in the lengthy preface to the sixth edition. Lightfoot's Commentaries on Pauline Epistles contain valuable Excursuses on several historical questions of the apostolic age, especially *St. Paul and the Three,* in the Com. on the *Galatians,* pp. 283–355.

W. SANDAY : *The Gospels in the Second Century.* London, 1876. This is directed against the critical part of "Supernatural Religion." The eighth chapter on Marcion's Gnostic mutilation and reconstruction of St. Luke's Gospel (pp. 204 sqq.) had previously appeared in the "Fortnightly Review" for June, 1875, and finishes on English soil, a controversy which had previously been fought out on German soil, in the circle of the Tübingen School. The preposterous hypothesis of the priority of Marcion's Gospel was advocated by Ritschl,

Baur and Schwegler, but refuted by Volkmar and Hilgenfeld, of the same school; whereupon Baur and Ritschl honorably abandoned their error. The anonymous author of "Supernatural Religion," in his seventh edition, has followed their example. The Germans conducted the controversy chiefly under its historic and dogmatic aspects; Sanday has added the philological and textual argument with the aid of Holtzmann's analysis of the style and vocabulary of Luke.

A. HAUSRATH (Prof. in Heidelberg) : *Neutestamentliche Zeitgeschichte.* Heidelberg, 1873 sqq. Parts II. and III. (second ed. 1875) embrace the apostolic times, Part IV. (1877) the post-apostolic times. English translation by *Poynting* and *Quenzer.* Lond. 1878 sqq. H. belongs to the School of Tübingen.

DAN. SCHENKEL (Prof. in Heidelberg) : *Das Christusbild der Apostel und der nachapostolischen Zeit.* Leipz. 1879. Comp. the review by *H. Holtzmann* in Hilgenfeld's "Zeitschrift für wissensch. Theol." 1879, p. 392.

H. OORT and I. HOOYKAAS : *The Bible for Learners,* translated from the Dutch by *Philip H. Wicksteed,* vol. III. (the New Test., by Hooykaas), Book II. pp. 463–693 of the Boston ed. 1879. (In the Engl. ed. it is vol. VI.) This is a popular digest of the rationalistic Tübingen and Leyden criticism under the inspiration of Dr. *A. Kuenen,* Professor of Theology at Leyden. It agrees substantially with the *Protestanten-Bibel* noticed above.

*GEORGE P. FISHER (Prof. in Yale College, New Haven) : *The Beginnings of Christianity.* N. York, 1877. Comp. also the author's former work : *Essays on the Supernatural Origin of Christianity, with special reference to the Theories of Renan, Strauss, and the Tübingen School.* New York, 1865. New ed. enlarged, 1877.

*C. WEIZSÄCKER (successor of Baur in Tübingen) : *Das Apostolische Zeitalter.* Freiburg, 1886. Critical and very able.

*O. PFLEIDERER (Prof. in Berlin) : *Das Urchristenthum, seine Schriften und Lehren.* Berlin, 1887. (Tübingen School.)

III. THE CHRONOLOGY OF THE APOSTOLIC AGE.

RUDOLPH ANGER : *De temporum in Actis Apostolorum ratione.* Lips. 1833 (208 pp.).

HENRY BROWNE : *Ordo Sœclorum. A Treatise on the Chronology of the Holy Scriptures.* Lond. 1844. Pp. 95–163.

*KARL WIESELER : *Chronologie des apostolischen Zeitalters.* Göttingen, 1848 (606 pp.).

The older and special works are noticed in Wieseler, pp. 6–9. See also the elaborate Synopsis of the dates of the Apostolic Age in

Schäffer's translation of Lechler on *Acts* (in the Am. ed. of Lange's
Commentary); Henry B. Smith's *Chronological Tables of Church History* (1860); and WEINGARTEN : *Zeittafeln zur K-Gesch.* 3d ed. 1888.

§ 21. *General Character of the Apostolic Age.*

" Der Schlachtruf, der St. PAULI Brust entsprungen,
Rief nicht sein Echo auf zu tausend Streiten ?
Und welch' ein Friedensecho hat geklungen
Durch tausend Herzen von JOHANNIS Saiten !
Wie viele rasche Feuer sind entglommen
Als Wiederschein von PETRI Funkensprühen !
Und sieht man Andre still mit Opfern kommen,
Ist's, weil sie in JAKOBI Schul' gediehen :—
Ein Satz ist's, der in Variationen
Vom ersten Anfang forttönt durch Æonen."

                       (THOLUCK.)

EXTENT AND ENVIRONMENT OF THE APOSTOLIC AGE.

The apostolic period extends from the Day of Pentecost to the
death of St. John, and covers about seventy years, from A.D. 30
to 100. The field of action is Palestine, and gradually extends
over Syria, Asia Minor, Greece, and Italy. The most prominent centres are Jerusalem, Antioch, and Rome, which represent respectively the mother churches of Jewish, Gentile, and
United Catholic Christianity. Next to them are Ephesus and
Corinth. Ephesus acquired a special importance by the residence and labors of John, which made themselves felt during
the second century through Polycarp and Irenæus. Samaria,
Damascus, Joppa, Cæsarea, Tyre, Cyprus, the provinces of Asia
Minor, Troas, Philippi, Thessalonica, Berœa, Athens, Crete,
Patmos, Malta, Puteoli, come also into view as points where
the Christian faith was planted. Through the eunuch converted
by Philip, it reached Candace, the queen of the Ethiopians.[1]
As early as A.D. 58 Paul could say : " From Jerusalem and round
about even unto Illyricum, I have fully preached the gospel of
Christ."[2] He afterwards carried it to Rome, where it had already

---

[1] Acts 8 : 27.   [2] Rom. 15 : 19.

been known before, and possibly as far as Spain, the western
boundary of the empire.[1]

The nationalities reached by the gospel in the first century
were the Jews, the Greeks, and the Romans, and the languages
used were the Hebrew or Aramaic, and especially the Greek,
which was at that time the organ of civilization and of international intercourse within the Roman empire.

The contemporary secular history includes the reigns of the
Roman Emperors from Tiberius to Nero and Domitian, who
either ignored or persecuted Christianity. We are brought
directly into contact with King Herod Agrippa I. (grandson of
Herod the Great), the murderer of the apostle, James the Elder;
with his son King Agrippa II. (the last of the Herodian house),
who with his sister Bernice (a most corrupt woman) listened
to Paul's defense; with two Roman governors, Felix and Festus; with Pharisees and Sadducees; with Stoics and Epicureans;
with the temple and theatre at Ephesus, with the court of the
Areopagus at Athens, and with Cæsar's palace in Rome.

SOURCES OF INFORMATION.

The author of Acts records the heroic march of Christianity
from the capital of Judaism to the capital of heathenism with
the same artless simplicity and serene faith as the Evangelists
tell the story of Jesus; well knowing that it needs no embellishment, no apology, no subjective reflections, and that it will
surely triumph by its inherent spiritual power.

The Acts and the Pauline Epistles accompany us with reliable information down to the year 63. Peter and Paul are lost
out of sight in the lurid fires of the Neronian persecution which
seemed to consume Christianity itself. We know nothing certain of that satanic spectacle from authentic sources beyond the

---

[1] Rom. 15 : 24. Comp. Clement of Rome, *Ad Cor.* c. 5, ἐπὶ τὸ τέρμα τῆς
δύσεως ἐλθών. This passage, however, does not necessarily mean Spain, and
Paul's journey to Spain stands or falls with the hypothesis of his second
Roman captivity.

information of heathen historians.[1] A few years afterwards
followed the destruction of Jerusalem, which must have made an
overpowering impression and broken the last ties which bound
Jewish Christianity to the old theocracy. The event is indeed
brought before us in the prophecy of Christ as recorded in the
Gospels, but for the terrible fulfilment we are dependent on the
account of an unbelieving Jew, which, as the testimony of an
enemy, is all the more impressive.

The remaining thirty years of the first century are involved
in mysterious darkness, illuminated only by the writings of
John. This is a period of church history about which we know
least and would like to know most. This period is the favorite
field for ecclesiastical fables and critical conjectures. How
thankfully would the historian hail the discovery of any new
authentic documents between the martyrdom of Peter and Paul
and the death of John, and again between the death of John
and the age of Justin Martyr and Irenæus.

CAUSES OF SUCCESS.

As to the numerical strength of Christianity at the close of
the first century, we have no information whatever. Statistical
reports were unknown in those days. The estimate of half a
million among the one hundred millions or more inhabitants of
the Roman empire is probably exaggerated. The pentecostal
conversion of three thousand in one day at Jerusalem,[2] and the
"immense multitude" of martyrs under Nero,[3] favor a high estimate. The churches in Antioch also, Ephesus, and Corinth were
strong enough to bear the strain of controversy and division into
parties.[4] But the majority of congregations were no doubt small,

---

[1] Unless we find allusions to it in the Revelation of John, 6 : 9–11 ; 17 : 6 ;
18 : 24, comp. ver. 20 (" ye holy apostles and prophets "). See Bleek, *Vorlesungen über die Apokalypse*, Berlin, 1862, p. 120.

[2] Acts 2 : 41.

[3] Tacitus, *Anal.* XV. 44, speaks of a "*multitudo ingens*" who were convicted of the "*odium generis humani*," i. e. of Christianity (regarded as a
Jewish sect), and cruelly executed under Nero in 64.

[4] Gal. 2 : 1 sqq. ; 1 Cor. 3 : 3 sqq.

often a mere handful of poor people. In the country districts paganism (as the name indicates) lingered longest, even beyond the age of Constantine. The Christian converts belonged mostly to the middle and lower classes of society, such as fishermen, peasants, mechanics, traders, freedmen, slaves. St. Paul says: " Not many wise after the flesh, not many mighty, not many noble were called, but God chose the foolish things of the world, that he might put to shame them that are wise ; and God chose the weak things of the world that he might put to shame the things that are strong; and the base things of the world, and the things that are despised, did God choose, yea, and the things that are not, that he might bring to naught the things that are : that no flesh should glory before God." [1] And yet these poor, illiterate churches were the recipients of the noblest gifts, and alive to the deepest problems and highest thoughts which can challenge the attention of an immortal mind. Christianity built from the foundation upward. From the lower ranks come the rising men of the future, who constantly reinforce the higher ranks and prevent their decay.

At the time of the conversion of Constantine, in the beginning of the fourth century, the number of Christians may have reached ten or twelve millions, that is about one-tenth of the total population of the Roman empire. Some estimate it higher.

The rapid success of Christianity under the most unfavorable circumstances is surprising and its own best vindication. It was achieved in the face of an indifferent or hostile world, and by purely spiritual and moral means, without shedding a drop of blood except that of its own innocent martyrs. Gibbon, in the famous fifteenth chapter of his " History," attributes the rapid spread to five causes, namely : (1) the intolerant but enlarged religious zeal of the Christians inherited from the Jews; (2) the doctrine of the immortality of the soul, concerning which the ancient philosophers had but vague and dreamy ideas; (3) the miraculous powers attributed to the primitive church; (4) the

---

[1] 1 Cor. 1 : 26–29.

purer but austere morality of the first Christians; (5) the unity
and discipline of the church, which gradually formed a growing
commonwealth in the heart of the empire. But every one of
these causes, properly understood, points to the superior excellency and to the divine origin of the Christian religion, and this
is the chief cause, which the Deistic historian omits.

SIGNIFICANCE OF THE APOSTOLIC AGE.

The life of Christ is the divine-human fountain-head of the
Christian religion; the apostolic age is the fountain-head of the
Christian church, as an organized society separate and distinct
from the Jewish synagogue. It is the age of the Holy Spirit,
the age of inspiration and legislation for all subsequent ages.

Here springs, in its original freshness and purity, the living
water of the new creation. Christianity comes down from
heaven as a supernatural fact, yet long predicted and prepared
for, and adapted to the deepest wants of human nature. Signs
and wonders and extraordinary demonstrations of the Spirit, for
the conversion of unbelieving Jews and heathens, attend its entrance into the world of sin. It takes up its permanent abode
with our fallen race, to transform it gradually, without war or
bloodshed, by a quiet, leaven-like process, into a kingdom of
truth and righteousness. Modest and humble, lowly and un-
seemly in outward appearance, but steadily conscious of its
divine origin and its eternal destiny; without silver or gold, but
rich in supernatural gifts and powers, strong in faith, fervent
in love, and joyful in hope; bearing in earthen vessels the imperishable treasures of heaven, it presents itself upon the stage
of history as the only true, the perfect religion, for all the nations of the earth. At first an insignificant and even contemptible sect in the eyes of the carnal mind, hated and persecuted by
Jews and heathens, it confounds the wisdom of Greece and the
power of Rome, soon plants the standard of the cross in the
great cities of Asia, Africa, and Europe, and proves itself the
hope of the world.

In virtue of this original purity, vigor, and beauty, and the per manent success of primitive Christianity, the canonical authority of the single but inexhaustible volume of its literature, and the character of the apostles, those inspired organs of the Holy Spirit, those untaught teachers of mankind, the apostolic age has an incomparable interest and importance in the history of the church.   It is the immovable groundwork of the whole.   It has the same regulative force for all the subsequent developments of the church as the inspired writings of the apostles have for the works of all later Christian authors.

Furthermore, the apostolic Christianity is preformative, and contains the living germs of all the following periods, personages, and tendencies.   It holds up the highest standard of doctrine and discipline; it is the inspiring genius of all true progress; it suggests to every age its peculiar problem with the power to solve it.   Christianity can never outgrow Christ, but it grows in Christ; theology cannot go beyond the word of God, but it must ever progress in the understanding and application of the word of God.   The three leading apostles represent not only the three stages of the apostolic church, but also as many ages and types of Christianity, and yet they are all present in every age and every type.[1]

The Representative Apostles.

Peter, Paul, and John stand out most prominently as the chosen Three who accomplished the great work of the apostolic age, and exerted, by their writings and example, a controlling influence on all subsequent ages.   To them correspond three centres of influence, Jerusalem, Antioch, and Rome.

Our Lord himself had chosen Three out of the Twelve for his most intimate companions, who alone witnessed the Transfiguration and the agony in Gethsemane.   They fulfilled all the expectations, Peter and John by their long and successful labors, James the Elder by drinking early the bitter cup of his Master,

---

[1] On the typical import of apostolic Christianity compare the concluding section of my *History of the Apostolic Church*, pp. 674 sqq.

as the proto-martyr of the Twelve.[1] Since his death, A.D. 44, James, " the brother of the Lord," seems to have succeeded him, as one of the three " pillars " of the church of the circumcision, although he did not belong to the apostles in the strict sense of the term, and his influence, as the head of the church at Jerusalem, was more local than œcumenical.[2]

Paul was called last and out of the regular order, by the personal appearance of the exalted Lord from heaven, and in authority and importance he was equal to any of the three pillars, but filled a place of his own, as the independent apostle of the Gentiles. He had around him a small band of co-laborers and pupils, such as Barnabas, Silas, Titus, Timothy, Luke.

Nine of the original Twelve, including Matthias, who was chosen in the place of Judas, labored no doubt faithfully and effectively, in preaching the gospel throughout the Roman empire and to the borders of the barbarians, but in subordinate positions, and their labors are known to us only from vague and uncertain traditions.[3]

The labors of James and Peter we can follow in the Acts to the Council of Jerusalem, A.D. 50, and a little beyond; those of Paul to his first imprisonment in Rome, A.D. 61–63; John lived to the close of the first century. As to their last labors we have no authentic information in the New Testament, but the unanimous testimony of antiquity that Peter and Paul suffered martyrdom in Rome during or after the Neronian persecution, and

---

[1] Matt. 22 : 23 ; Acts 12 : 2.

[2] Gal. 2 : 9. James is even named before Cephas and John, and throughout the Acts from the Council of Jerusalem, at which he presided, he appears as the most prominent man in the churches of Palestine. In the Ebionite tradition he figures as the first universal bishop or pope.

[3] The apocryphal tradition of the second and later centuries assigns to Peter, Andrew, Matthew, and Bartholomew, as their field of missionary labor, the regions north and northwest of Palestine (Syria, Galatia, Pontus, Scythia, and the coasts of the Black Sea); to Thaddæus, Thomas, and Simon Cananites the eastern countries (Mesopotamia, Parthia, especially Edessa and Babylon, and even as far as India); to John and Philip Asia Minor (Ephesus and Hierapolis). Comp. the *Acta Sanctorum ;* Tischendorf's *Acta Apostolorum Apocrypha* (1851); and for a brief summary my *History of the Apost Church*, § 97, pp. 385 sqq.

that John died a natural death at Ephesus. The Acts breaks off abruptly with Paul still living and working, a prisoner in Rome, "preaching the kingdom of God and teaching the things concerning the Lord Jesus Christ, with all boldness, none forbidding him." A significant conclusion.

It would be difficult to find three men equally great and good, equally endowed with genius sanctified by grace, bound together by deep and strong love to the common Master, and laboring for the same cause, yet so different in temper and constitution, as Peter, Paul, and John. Peter stands out in history as the main pillar of the primitive church, as the Rock-apostle, as the chief of the twelve foundation-stones of the new Jerusalem; John as the bosom-friend of the Saviour, as the son of thunder, as the soaring eagle, as the apostle of love; Paul as the champion of Christian freedom and progress, as the greatest missionary, with "the care of all the churches" upon his heart, as the expounder of the Christian system of doctrine, as the father of Christian theology. Peter was a man of action, always in haste and ready to take the lead, the first to confess Christ, and the first to preach Christ on the day of Pentecost; Paul a man equally potent in word and deed; John a man of mystic contemplation. Peter was unlearned and altogether practical; Paul a scholar and thinker as well as a worker; John a theosophist and seer. Peter was sanguine, ardent, impulsive, hopeful, kind-hearted, given to sudden changes, "consistently inconsistent" (to use an Aristotelian phrase); Paul was choleric, ener- getic, bold, noble, independent, uncompromising; John somewhat melancholic, introverted, reserved, burning within of love to Christ and hatred of Antichrist. Peter's Epistles are full of sweet grace and comfort, the result of deep humiliation and rich experience; those of Paul abound in severe thought and logical argument, but rising at times to the heights of celestial eloquence, as in the seraphic description of love and the triumphant pæan of the eighth chapter of the Romans; John's writings are simple, serene, profound, intuitive, sublime, inexhaustible.

We would like to know more about the personal relations of

these pillar-apostles, but must be satisfied with a few hints. They labored in different fields and seldom met face to face in their busy life. Time was too precious, their work too serious, for sentimental enjoyments of friendship. Paul went to Jerusalem A.D. 40, three years after his conversion, for the express purpose of making the personal acquaintance of Peter, and spent two weeks with him; he saw none of the other apostles, but only James, the Lord's brother.[1] He met the pillar-apostles at the Conference in Jerusalem, A.D. 50, and concluded with them the peaceful concordat concerning the division of labor, and the question of circumcision; the older apostles gave him and Barnabas "the right hands of fellowship" in token of brotherhood and fidelity.[2] Not long afterwards Paul met Peter a third time, at Antioch, but came into open collision with him on the great question of Christian freedom and the union of Jewish and Gentile converts.[3] The collision was merely temporary, but significantly reveals the profound commotion and fermentation of the apostolic age, and foreshadowed future antagonisms and reconciliations in the church. Several years later (A.D. 57) Paul refers the last time to Cephas, and the brethren of the Lord, for the right to marry and to take a wife with him on his missionary journeys.[4] Peter, in his first Epistle to Pauline churches, confirms them in their Pauline faith, and in his second Epistle, his last will and testament, he affectionately commends the letters of his "beloved brother Paul," adding, however, the characteristic remark, which all commentators must admit to be true, that (even beside the account of the scene in Antioch) there are in them "some things hard to be understood."[5] According to tra-

---

[1] Gal. 1 : 18, 19. The εἰ μή in this connection rather excludes James from the number of the Twelve, but implies that he was an apostle in a wider sense, and a leader of apostolic dignity and authority. Comp. the εἰ μή (sed tantum) Luke 4 : 26, 27; Rom. 14 : 14; Gal. 2 : 16.

[2] Acts 15; Gal 2 : 1–10.

[3] Gal. 2 : 11–21.

[4] 1 Cor. 9 : 5; comp. Matt. 8 : 14.

[5] 2 Pet. 3 : 15, 16, δυσνόητά τινα. This passage, and the equally significant remark of Peter (1 : 20) that "no prophecy of Scripture is of *private* interpretation," or solution, have often been abused by the popes as a pretext for

dition (which varies considerably as to details), the great leaders of Jewish and Gentile Christianity met at Rome, were tried
and condemned together, Paul, the Roman citizen, to the death
by the sword on the Ostian road at Tre Fontane; Peter, the
Galilean apostle, to the more degrading death of the cross on
the hill of Janiculum. John mentions Peter frequently in his
Gospel, especially in the appendix,[1] but never names Paul; he
met him, as it seems, only once, at Jerusalem, gave him the right
hand of fellowship, became his successor in the fruitful field of
Asia Minor, and built on his foundation.

Peter was the chief actor in the first stage of apostolic Christianity and fulfilled the prophecy of his name in laying the foundation of the church among the Jews and the Gentiles. In the
second stage he is overshadowed by the mighty labors of Paul;
but after the apostolic age he stands out again most prominent
in the memory of the church. He is chosen by the Roman
communion as its special patron saint and as the first pope. He
is always named before Paul. To him most of the churches are
dedicated. In the name of this poor fisherman of Galilee, who
had neither gold nor silver, and was crucified like a malefactor
and a slave, the triple-crowned popes deposed kings, shook empires, dispensed blessings and curses on earth and in purgatory,
and even now claim the power to settle infallibly all questions
of Christian doctrine and discipline for the Catholic world.

Paul was the chief actor in the second stage of the apostolic
church, the apostle of the Gentiles, the founder of Christianity
in Asia Minor and Greece, the emancipator of the new religion
from the yoke of Judaism, the herald of evangelical freedom,
the standard-bearer of reform and progress. His controlling
influence was felt also in Rome, and is clearly seen in the genu-

---

withholding the Scriptures from the people and insisting on the necessity of an
authoritative interpretation. The passage refers to the prophecies of the
Old Testament, which are not the productions of the human mind, but inspired by the Holy Ghost (ver. 21), and cannot be properly understood except
as divinely inspired.

[1] John 21 : 15–23. The last word of the Lord about Peter and John is very
mysterious.

ine Epistle of Clement, who makes more account of him than of Peter. But soon afterwards he is almost forgotten, except by name. He is indeed associated with Peter as the founder of the church of Rome, but in a secondary line; his Epistle to the Romans is little read and understood by the Romans even to this day; his church lies outside of the walls of the eternal city, while St. Peter's is its chief ornament and glory. In Africa alone he was appreciated, first by the rugged and racy Tertullian, more fully by the profound Augustine, who passed through similar contrasts in his religious experience; but Augustine's Pauline doctrines of sin and grace had no effect whatever on the Eastern church, and were practically overpowered in the Western church by Pelagian tendencies. For a long time Paul's name was used and abused outside of the ruling orthodoxy and hierarchy by anti-catholic heretics and sectaries in their protest against the new yoke of traditionalism and ceremonialism. But in the sixteenth century he celebrated a real resurrection and inspired the evangelical reformation. Then his Epistles to the Galatians and Romans were republished, explained, and applied with trumpet tongues by Luther and Calvin. Then his protest against Judaizing bigotry and legal bondage was renewed, and the rights of Christian liberty asserted on the largest scale. Of all men in church history, St. Augustine not excepted, Martin Luther, once a contracted monk, then a prophet of freedom, has most affinity in word and work with the apostle of the Gentiles, and ever since Paul's genius has ruled the theology and religion of Protestantism. As the gospel of Christ was cast out from Jerusalem to bless the Gentiles, so Paul's Epistle to the Romans was expelled from Rome to enlighten and to emancipate Protestant nations in the distant North and far West.

St. John, the most intimate companion of Jesus, the apostle of love, the seer who looked back to the ante-mundane beginning and forward to the post-mundane end of all things, and who is to tarry till the coming of the Lord, kept aloof from active part in the controversies between Jewish and Gentile Christianity. He appears prominent in the Acts and the Epistle to the Galatians, as one of the pillar-apostles, but not a word of his is reported. He was waiting in mysterious silence, with a reserved force, for his proper time, which did not come till Peter and Paul had finished their mission. Then, after their departure, he revealed the hidden depths of his genius in his marvellous writings, which represent the last and crowning work of the apostolic church. John has never been fully fathomed, but it has been felt throughout all the periods of church history that he has best understood and portrayed the Master, and may yet speak the last word in the conflict of ages and usher in an era of harmony and peace. Paul is the heroic captain of the church militant, John the mystic prophet of the church triumphant.

Far above them all, throughout the apostolic age and all subsequent ages, stands the one great Master from whom Peter, Paul, and John drew their inspiration, to whom they bowed in holy adoration, whom alone they served and glorified in life and in death, and to whom they still point in their writings as the perfect image of God, as the Saviour from sin and death, as the Giver of eternal life, as the divine harmony of conflicting creeds and schools, as the Alpha and Omega of the Christian faith.

§ 22. *The Critical Reconstruction of the History of the Apostolic Age.*

"*Die Botschaft hör' ich wohl, allein mir fehlt der Glaube.*"
(Goethe.)

Never before in the history of the church has the origin of Christianity, with its original documents, been so thoroughly examined from standpoints entirely opposite as in the present generation. It has engaged the time and energy of many of the ablest scholars and critics. Such is the importance and the power of that little book which "contains the wisdom of the whole world," that it demands ever new investigation and sets serious minds of all shades of belief and unbelief in motion, as if their very life depended upon its acceptance or rejection. There is not a fact or doctrine which has not been thoroughly searched. The whole life of Christ, and the labors and writings of the apostles with their tendencies, antagonisms, and reconciliations are theoretically reproduced among scholars and reviewed under all possible aspects. The post-apostolic age has by necessary connection been drawn into the process of investigation and placed in a new light.

The great biblical scholars among the Fathers were chiefly concerned in drawing from the sacred records the catholic doctrines of salvation, and the precepts for a holy life; the Reformers and older Protestant divines studied them afresh with special zeal for the evangelical tenets which separated them from the Roman church; but all stood on the common ground of a reverential belief in the divine inspiration and authority of the Scriptures. The present age is preëminently historical and critical. The Scriptures are subjected to the same process of investigation and analysis as any other literary production of antiquity, with no other purpose than to ascertain the real facts in the case. We want to know the precise origin, gradual growth, and final completion of Christianity as an historical phenomenon in organic connection with contemporary events and currents of thought. The whole process through which it passed from the manger in Bethlehem to the cross of Calvary, and from the upper room in Jerusalem to the throne of the Cæsars is to be reproduced, explained and understood according to the laws of regular historical development. And in this critical process the very foundations of the Christian faith have been assailed and undermined, so that the question now is, "to be or not to be." The remark of Goethe is as profound as it is true : "The conflict of faith and unbelief remains the proper, the only, the deepest theme of the history of the world and mankind, to which all others are subordinated."

The modern critical movement began, we may say, about 1830, is still in full progress, and is likely to continue to the end of the nineteenth century, as the apostolic church itself extended over a period of seventy years before it had developed its resources. It was at first confined to Germany (Strauss, Baur, and the Tübingen School), then spread to France (Renan) and Holland (Scholten, Kuenen), and last to England ("Supernatural Religion") and America, so that the battle now extends along the whole line of Protestantism.

There are two kinds of biblical criticism, verbal and historical.

TEXTUAL CRITICISM.

The verbal or textual criticism has for its object to restore as far as possible the original text of the Greek Testament from the oldest and most trustworthy sources, namely, the uncial manuscripts (especially the Vatican and Sinaitic), the ante-Nicene versions, and the patristic quotations. In this respect our age has been very successful, with the aid of most important discoveries of ancient manuscripts. By the invaluable labors of Lachmann, who broke the path for the correct theory (*Novum Testament. Gr.*, 1831, large Græco-Latin edition, 1842–50, 2 vols.), Tischendorf (8th critical ed., 1869–72, 2 vols.), Tregelles (1857, completed

1879), Westcott and Hort (1881, 2 vols.), we have now in the place of the comparatively late and corrupt *textus receptus* of Erasmus and his followers (Stephens, Beza, and the Elzevirs), which is the basis of all Protestant versions in common use, a much older and purer text, which must henceforth be made the basis of all revised translations. After a severe struggle between the traditional and the progressive schools there is now in this basal department of biblical learning a remarkable degree of harmony among critics. The new text is in fact the older text, and the reformers are in this case the restorers. Far from unsettling the faith in the New Testament, the results have established the substantial integrity of the text, notwithstanding the one hundred and fifty thousand readings which have been gradually gathered from all sources. It is a noteworthy fact that the greatest textual critics of the nineteenth century are believers, not indeed in a mechanical or magical inspiration, which is untenable and not worth defending, but in the divine origin and authority of the canonical writings, which rest on far stronger grounds than any particular human theory of inspiration.

HISTORICAL CRITICISM.

The historical or inner criticism (which the Germans call the "higher criticism," *höhere Kritik*) deals with the origin, spirit, and aim of the New Testament writings, their historical environments, and organic place in the great intellectual and religious process which resulted in the triumphant establishment of the catholic church of the second century. It assumed two very distinct shapes under the lead of Dr. NEANDER in Berlin (d. 1850), and Dr. BAUR in Tübingen (d. 1860), who labored in the mines of church history at a respectful distance from each other and never came into personal contact. Neander and Baur were giants, equal in genius and learning, honesty and earnestness, but widely different in spirit. They gave a mighty impulse to historical study and left a long line of pupils and independent followers who carry on the historico-critical reconstruction of primitive Christianity. Their influence is felt in France, Holland and England. Neander published the first edition of his *Apostolic Age* in 1832, his *Life of Jesus* (against Strauss) in 1837 (the first volume of his General Church History had appeared already in 1825, revised ed. 1842) ; Baur wrote his essay on the *Corinthian Parties* in 1831, his critical investigations on the canonical Gospels in 1844 and 1847, his "*Paul*" in 1845 (second ed. by Zeller, 1867), and his "*Church History of the First Three Centuries*" in 1853 (revised 1860). His pupil Strauss had preceded him with his first *Leben Jesu* (1835), which created a greater sensation than any of the works mentioned, surpassed only by that of Renan's *Vie de Jésus*, nearly thirty years later (1863). Renan reproduces and popularizes Strauss and Baur for the French public with independent learning and brilliant genius, and the author of "Supernatural Religion" reëchoes the Tübingen and Leyden speculations

In England.   On the other hand Bishop Lightfoot, the leader of conservative criticism, declares that he has learnt more from the German Neander than from any recent theologian ("Contemp. Review" for 1875,
p. 866).   Matthew Arnold says (*Literature and Dogma*, Preface, p. xix.):
"To get the facts, the data, in all matters of science, but notably in theology and Biblical learning, one goes to Germany.   Germany, and it is
her high honor, has searched out the facts and exhibited them.   And
without knowledge of the facts, no clearness or fairness of mind can in
any study do anything ; this cannot be laid down too rigidly."   But he
denies to the Germans "quickness and delicacy of perception."   Something more is necessary than learning and perception to draw the right
conclusions from the facts :   sound common sense and well-balanced judgment.   And when we deal with sacred and supernatural facts, we need
first and last a reverential spirit and that faith which is the organ of the
supernatural.   It is here where the two schools depart, without difference of nationality ; for faith is not a national but an individual gift.

The Two Antagonistic Schools.

The two theories of the apostolic history, introduced by Neander and
Baur, are antagonistic in principle and aim, and united only by the moral
bond of an honest search for truth.   The one is conservative and recon-
structive, the other radical and destructive.   The former accepts the
canonical Gospels and Acts as honest, truthful, and credible memoirs of
the life of Christ and the labors of the apostles ; the latter rejects a great
part of their contents as unhistorical myths or legends of the post-apostolic age, and on the other hand gives undue credit to wild heretical
romances of the second century.   The one draws an essential line of distinction between truth as maintained by the orthodox church, and error
as held by heretical parties ; the other obliterates the lines and puts the
heresy into the inner camp of the apostolic church itself.   The one proceeds on the basis of faith in God and Christ, which implies faith in the
supernatural and miraculous wherever it is well attested ; the other proceeds from disbelief in the supernatural and miraculous as a philosophical
impossibility, and tries to explain the gospel history and the apostolic
history from purely natural causes like every other history.   The one has
a moral and spiritual as well as intellectual interest in the New Testament, the other a purely intellectual and critical interest.   The one
approaches the historical investigation with the subjective experience of
the divine truth in the heart and conscience, and knows and feels Christianity to be a power of salvation from sin and error ; the other views it
simply as the best among the many religions which are destined to give
way at last to the sovereignty of reason and philosophy.   The controversy turns on the question whether there is a God in History or not ; as
the contemporaneous struggle in natural science turns on the question
whether there is a God in nature or not.   Belief in a personal God

almighty and omnipresent in history and in nature, implies the possibility of supernatural and miraculous revelation. Absolute freedom from pre-possession (*Voraussetzungslosigkeit* such as Strauss demanded) is absolutely impossible, " *ex nihilo nihil fit.*" There is prepossession on either side of the controversy, the one positive, the other negative, and history itself must decide between them. The facts must rule philosophy, not philosophy the facts. If it can be made out that the life of Christ and the apostolic church can be psychologically and historically explained only by the admission of the supernatural element which they claim, while every other explanation only increases the difficulty of the problem and substitutes an unnatural miracle for a supernatural one, the historian has gained the case, and it is for the philosopher to adjust his theory to history. The duty of the historian is not to make the facts, but to discover them, and then to construct his theory wide enough to give them all comfortable room.

The Alleged Antagonism in the Apostolic Church.

The theory of the Tübingen school starts from the assumption of a fundamental antagonism between Jewish or primitive Christianity represented by Peter, and Gentile or progressive Christianity represented by Paul, and resolves all the writings of the New Testament into tendency writings (*Tendenzschriften*), which give us not history pure and simple, but adjust it to a doctrinal and practical aim in the interest of one or the other party, or of a compromise between the two.[1] The Epistles of Paul to the Galatians, Romans, First and Second Corinthians—which are admitted to be genuine beyond any doubt, exhibit the anti-Jewish and universal Christianity, of which Paul himself must be regarded as the chief founder. The Apocalypse, which was composed by the apostle John in 69, exhibits the original Jewish and contracted Christianity, in accordance with his position as one of the "pillar"-apostles of the circumcision (Gal. 2 : 9), and it is the only authentic document of the older apostles.

Baur (*Gesch. der christl. Kirche*, I., 80 sqq.) and Renan (*St. Paul*, ch. x.) go so far as to assert that this genuine John excludes Paul from the list of the apostles (Apoc. 21 : 14, which leaves no room for more than twelve),

[1] In this respect Baur differs from the standpoint of Strauss, who in his first *Leben Jesu* (1835) had represented the gospel history as an innocent and unconscious myth or poem of the religious imagination of the second generation of Christians; but in his second *Leben Jesu* (1864) he somewhat modified his view, and at last (1873) he gave up the whole problem as a bad job. A tendency writing implies more or less conscious fiction and falsification of history. The Tübingen critics, however, try to relieve this fictitious literature of the odious feature by referring us to the Jewish and Christian apocryphal literature which was passed off under honored names without giving any special offence on that score.

and indirectly attacks him as a "false Jew" (Apoc. 2 : 9; 3 : 9), a "false apostle" (2 : 2), a "false prophet" (2 : 20), as "Balaam" (2 : 2, 6, 14, 15; comp. Jude 11; 2 Pet. 2 : 15); just as the Clementine Homilies assail him under the name of Simon the Magician and arch-heretic. Renan interprets also the whole Epistle of Jude, a brother of James, as an attack upon Paul, issued from Jerusalem in connection with the Jewish counter-mission organized by James, which nearly ruined the work of Paul.

The other writings of the New Testament are post-apostolic productions and exhibit the various phases of a unionistic movement, which resulted in the formation of the orthodox church of the second and third centuries. The Acts of the Apostles is a Catholic Irenicon which harmonizes Jewish and Gentile Christianity by liberalizing Peter and contracting or Judaizing Paul, and concealing the difference between them ; and though probably based on an earlier narrative of Luke, it was not put into its present shape before the close of the first century. The canonical Gospels, whatever may have been the earlier records on which they are based, are likewise post-apostolic, and hence untrustworthy as historical narratives. The Gospel of John is a purely ideal composition of some unknown Gnostic or mystic of profound religious genius, who dealt with the historical Jesus as freely as Plato in his Dialogues dealt with Socrates, and who completed with consummate literary skill this unifying process in the age of Hadrian, certainly not before the third decade of the second century. Baur brought it down as late as 170 ; Hilgenfeld put it further back to 140, Keim to 130, Renan to the age of Hadrian.

Thus the whole literature of the New Testament is represented as the living growth of a century, as a collection of polemical and irenical tracts of the apostolic and post-apostolic ages. Instead of contemporaneous, reliable history we have a series of intellectual movements and literary fictions. Divine revelation gives way to subjective visions and delusions, inspiration is replaced by development, truth by a mixture of truth and error. The apostolic literature is put on a par with the controversial literature of the Nicene age, which resulted in the Nicene orthodoxy, or with the literature of the Reformation period, which led to the formation of the Protestant system of doctrine.

History never repeats itself, yet the same laws and tendencies reappear in ever-changing forms. This modern criticism is a remarkable renewal of the views held by heretical schools in the second century. The Ebionite author of the pseudo-Clementine Homilies and the Gnostic Marcion likewise assumed an irreconcilable antagonism between Jewish and Gentile Christianity, with this difference, that the former opposed Paul as the arch-heretic and defamer of Peter, while Marcion (about 140) regarded Paul as the only true apostle, and the older apostles as Jewish perverters of Christianity ; consequently he rejected the whole Old Testament and such books of the New Testament as he considered Judaizing, retaining in his canon only a mutilated Gospel of Luke and ten of the Pauline Epistles (excluding the Pastoral Epistles and the Epistle to the Hebrews). In the eyes of modern criticism these wild heretics are better historians of the apostolic age than the author of the Acts of the Apostles.

The Gnostic heresy, with all its destructive tendency, had an important mission as a propelling force in the ancient church and left its effects upon patristic theology. So also this modern gnosticism must be allowed to have done great service to biblical and historical learning by removing old prejudices, opening new avenues of thought, bringing to light the immense fermentation of the first century, stimulating research, and compelling an entire scientific reconstruction of the history of the origin of Christianity and the church. The result will be a deeper and fuller knowledge, not to the weakening, but to the strengthening of our faith.

REACTION.

There is considerable difference among the scholars of this higher criticism, and while some pupils of Baur (e. g. Strauss, Volkmar) have gone even beyond his positions, others make concessions to the traditional views. A most important change took place in Baur's own mind as regards the conversion of Paul, which he confessed at last, shortly before his death (1860), to be to him an insolvable psychological problem amounting to a miracle. Ritschl, Holtzmann, Lipsius, Pfleiderer, and especially Reuss, Weizsäcker, and Keim (who are as free from orthodox prejudices as the most advanced critics) have modified and corrected many of the extreme views of the Tübingen school. Even Hilgenfeld, with all his zeal for the "Fortschrittstheologie" and against the "Rückschrittstheologie," admits seven instead of four Pauline Epistles as genuine, assigns an earlier date to the Synoptical Gospels and the Epistle to the Hebrews (which he supposes to have been written by Apollos before 70), and says : "It cannot be denied that Baur's criticism went beyond the bounds of moderation and inflicted too deep wounds on the faith of the church " (*Hist. Krit. Einleitung in das N. T.* 1875, p. 197). Renan admits nine Pauline Epistles, the essential genuineness of the Acts, and even the narrative portions of John, while he rejects the discourses as pretentious, inflated, metaphysical, obscure, and tiresome ! (See his last discussion of the subject in *L'église chrétienne*, ch. IV. pp. 45 sqq.) Matthew Arnold and other critics reverse the proposition and accept the discourses as the sublimest of all human compositions, full of "heavenly glories" (*himmlische Herrlichkeiten*, to use an expression of Keim, who, however, rejects the fourth Gospel altogether). Schenkel (in his *Christusbild der Apostel*, 1879) considerably moderates the antagonism between Petrinism and Paulinism, and confesses (Preface, p. xi.) that in the progress of his investigations he has been "forced to the conviction that the Acts of the Apostles is a more trustworthy source of information than is

commonly allowed on the part of the modern criticism ; that older documents worthy of credit, besides the well known *We*-source (*Wirquelle*) are
contained in it ; and that the Paulinist who composed it has not intentionally distorted the facts, but only placed them in the light in which
they appeared to him and must have appeared to him from the time
and circumstances under which he wrote. He has not, in my opinion,
artificially brought upon the stage either a Paulinized Peter, or a Petri-
nized Paul, in order to mislead his readers, but has portrayed the two
apostles just as he actually conceived of them on the basis of his incomplete information." Keim, in his last work (*Aus dem Urchristenthum*, 1878, a year before his death), has come to a similar conclusion,
and proves (in a critical essay on the *Apostelkonvent*, pp. 64-89) in opposition to Baur, Schwegler, and Zeller, yet from the same standpoint of
liberal criticism, and allowing later additions, the substantial harmony
between the Acts and the Epistle to the Galatians as regards the apostolic conference and concordat of Jerusalem. Ewald always pursued his
own way and equalled Baur in bold and arbitrary criticism, but violently
opposed him and defended the Acts and the Gospel of John.

To these German voices we may add the testimony of Matthew Arnold,
one of the boldest and broadest of the broad-school divines and critics,
who with all his admiration for Baur represents him as an "unsafe
guide," and protests against his assumption of a bitter hatred of Paul
and the pillar-apostles as entirely inconsistent with the conceded religious greatness of Paul and with the nearness of the pillar-apostles to
Jesus (*God and the Bible*, 1875, Preface, vii-xii). As to the fourth Gospel,
which is now the most burning spot of this burning controversy, the
same author, after viewing it from without and from within, comes to the
conclusion that it is "no fancy-piece, but a serious and invaluable document, full of incidents given by tradition and genuine 'sayings of the
Lord'" (p. 370), and that "after the most free criticism has been fairly
and strictly applied, ... there is yet left an authentic residue comprising all the profoundest, most important, and most beautiful things in the
fourth Gospel" (p. 372 sq.).

The Positive School.

While there are signs of disintegration in the ranks of destructive
criticism, the historic truth and genuineness of the New Testament
writings have found learned and able defenders from different standpoints, such as Neander, Ullmann, C. F. Schmid (the colleague of Baur
in Tübingen), Rothe, Dorner, Ebrard, Lechler, Lange, Thiersch, Wieseler,
Hofmann (of Erlangen), Luthardt, Christlieb, Beyschlag, Uhlhorn, Weiss,
Godet, Edm. de Pressensé.

The English and American mind also has fairly begun to grapple man-
fully and successfully with these questions in such scholars as Lightfoot,
Plumptre, Westcott, Sanday, Farrar, G. P. Fisher, Ezra Abbot (on the
Authorship of the Fourth Gospel, 1880). English and American theology

is not likely to be extensively demoralized by these hyper-critical speculations of the Continent.   It has a firmer foothold in an active church
life and the convictions and affections of the people.   The German and
French mind, like the Athenian, is always bent upon telling and hearing
something new, while the Anglo-American mind cares more for what is
true, whether it be old or new.   And the truth must ultimately prevail.

St. Paul's Testimony to Historical Christianity.

Fortunately even the most exacting school of modern criticism leaves
us a fixed fulcrum from which we can argue the truth of Christianity,
namely, the four Pauline Epistles to the Galatians, Romans, and Corinthians, which are pronounced to be unquestionably genuine and made
the Archimedean point of assault upon the other parts of the New Testament.   We propose to confine ourselves to them.   They are of the
utmost historical as well as doctrinal importance ; they represent the
first Christian generation, and were written between 54 and 58, that is
within a quarter of the century after the crucifixion, when the older
apostles and most of the principal eye-witnesses of the life of Christ
were still alive.   The writer himself was a contemporary of Christ ; he
lived in Jerusalem at the time of the great events on which Christianity
rests ; he was intimate with the Sanhedrin and the murderers of Christ ;
he was not blinded by favorable prejudice, but was a violent persecutor,
who had every motive to justify his hostility ; and after his radical conversion (A.D. 37) he associated with the original disciples and could learn
their personal experience from their own lips (Gal. 1 : 18 ; 2 : 1–11).

Now in these admitted documents of the best educated of the apostles
we have the clearest evidence of all the great events and truths of primitive Christianity, and a satisfactory answer to the chief objections and
difficulties of modern skepticism.[1]

They prove

1. The leading facts in the life of Christ, his divine mission, his
birth from a woman, of the royal house of David, his holy life and example, his betrayal, passion, and death for the sins of the world, his
resurrection on the third day, his repeated manifestations to the disciples, his ascension and exaltation to the right hand of God, whence he
will return to judge mankind, the adoration of Christ as the Messiah,
the Lord and Saviour from sin, the eternal Son of God ; also the election of the Twelve, the institution of baptism and the Lord's Supper,
the mission of the Holy Spirit, the founding of the church.   Paul frequently alludes to these facts, especially the crucifixion and resurrection,
not in the way of a detailed narrative, but incidentally and in connection
with doctrinal expositions and exhortations as addressed to men already

---

[1] Comp. here a valuable article of J. Oswald Dykes, in the "Brit. and For.
Evang. Review," Lond. 1880, pp. 51 sqq.

familiar with them from oral preaching and instruction. Comp. Gal
3 : 13 ; 4 : 4–6 ; 6 : 14 ; Rom. 1 : 3 ; 4 : 24, 25 ; 5 : 8–21 ; 6 : 3–10 ; 8 : 3
11, 26, 39 ; 9 : 5 ; 10 : 6, 7 ; 14 : 15 ; 15 : 3 ; 1 Cor. 1 : 23 ; 2 : 2, 12 ; 5 : 7 ;
6 : 14 ; 10 : 16 ; 11 : 23–26 ; 15 : 3–8, 45–49 ; 2 Cor. 5 : 21.

2. Paul's own conversion and call to the apostleship by the personal
appearance to him of the exalted Redeemer from heaven. Gal. 1 : 1,
15, 16 ; 1 Cor. 9 : 1 ; 15 : 8.

3. The origin and rapid progress of the Christian church in all parts of
the Roman empire, from Jerusalem to Antioch and Rome, in Judæa, in
Syria, in Asia Minor, in Macedonia and Achaia. The faith of the Roman
church, he says, was known "throughout the world," and "in every
place" there were worshippers of Jesus as their Lord. And these little
churches maintained a lively and active intercourse with each other, and
though founded by different teachers and distracted by differences of
opinion and practice, they worshipped the same divine Lord, and formed
one brotherhood of believers. Gal. 1 : 2, 22 ; 2 : 1, 11 ; Rom. 1 : 8 ;
10 : 18 ; 16 : 26 ; 1 Cor. 1 : 12 ; 8 : 1 ; 16 : 19, etc.

4. The presence of miraculous powers in the church at that time.
Paul himself wrought the signs and mighty deeds of an apostle. Rom.
15 : 18, 19 ; 1 Cor. 2 : 4 ; 9 : 2 ; 2 Cor. 12 : 12. He lays, however, no great
stress on the outer sensible miracles, and makes more account of the
inner moral miracles and the constant manifestations of the power of
the Holy Spirit in regenerating and sanctifying sinful men in an utterly
corrupt state of society. 1 Cor. chs. 12 to 14 ; 6 : 9–11 ; Gal. 5 : 16–26 ;
Rom. chs. 6 and 8.

5. The existence of much earnest controversy in these young churches,
not indeed about the great facts on which their faith was based, and
which were fully admitted on both sides, but about doctrinal and ritual
inferences from these facts, especially the question of the continued
obligation of circumcision and the Mosaic law, and the personal question
of the apostolic authority of Paul. The Judaizers maintained the superior
claims of the older apostles and charged him with a radical departure
from the venerable religion of their fathers ; while Paul used against
them the argument that the expiatory death of Christ and his resurrection were needless and useless if justification came from the law. Gal.
2 : 21 ; 5 : 2–4.

6. The essential doctrinal and spiritual harmony of Paul with the
elder apostles, notwithstanding their differences of standpoint and field
of labor. Here the testimony of the Epistle to the Galatians, ch. 2 : 1–10,
which is the very bulwark of the skeptical school, bears strongly against
it. For Paul expressly states that the "pillar"-apostles of the circumcision, James, Peter, and John, at the conference in Jerusalem A.D. 50,
approved the gospel he had been preaching during the preceding fourteen years ; that they "imparted nothing" to him, gave him no new instruction, imposed on him no new terms, nor burden of any kind, but

that, on the contrary, they recognized the grace of God in him and his special mission to the Gentiles, and gave him and Barnabas "the right hands of fellowship" in token of their brotherhood and fidelity. He makes a clear and sharp distinction between the apostles and "the false brethren privily brought in, who came to spy out our liberty which we have in Christ Jesus, that they might bring us into bondage," and to whom he would not yield, "no, not for an hour." The hardest words he has for the Jewish apostles are epithets of honor; he calls them "the pillars" of the church, "the men in high repute" (οἱ στῦλοι, οἱ δοκοῦντες, Gal. 2 : 6, 9); while he considered himself in sincere humility "the least of the apostles," because he persecuted the church of God (1 Cor. 15 : 9).

This statement of Paul makes it simply impossible and absurd to suppose (with Baur, Schwegler, Zeller, and Renan) that John should have so contradicted and stultified himself as to attack, in the Apocalypse, the same Paul whom he had recognized as a brother during his life, as a false apostle and chief of the synagogue of Satan after his death. Such a reckless and monstrous assertion turns either Paul or John into a liar. The antinomian and antichristian heretics of the Apocalypse who plunged into all sorts of moral and ceremonial pollutions (Apoc. 2 : 14, 15) would have been condemned by Paul as much as by John; yea, he himself, in his parting address to the Ephesian elders, had prophetically foreannounced and described such teachers as "grievous wolves" that would after his departure enter in among them or rise from the midst of them, not sparing the flock (Acts 20 : 29, 30). On the question of fornication he was in entire harmony with the teaching of the Apocalypse (1 Cor. 3 : 15, 16 ; 6 : 15-20); and as to the question of eating meat offered in sacrifice to idols (τὰ εἰδωλόθυτα), though he regarded it as a thing indifferent in itself, considering the vanity of idols, yet he condemned it whenever it gave offence to the weak consciences of the more scrupulous Jewish converts (1 Cor. 8 : 7-13; 10 : 23-33; Rom. 14 : 2, 21); and this was in accord with the decree of the Apostolic Council (Acts 15 : 29).

7. Paul's collision with Peter at Antioch, Gal. 2 : 11-14, which is made the very bulwark of the Tübingen theory, proves the very reverse. For it was not a difference in principle and doctrine; on the contrary, Paul expressly asserts that Peter at first freely and habitually (mark the imperfect συνήσθιεν, Gal. 2 : 12) associated with the Gentile converts as brethren in Christ, but was intimidated by emissaries from the bigoted Jewish converts in Jerusalem and acted against his better conviction which he had entertained ever since the vision at Joppa (Acts 10 : 10-16), and which he had so boldly confessed at the Council in Jerusalem (Acts 15 : 7-11) and carried out in Antioch. We have here the same impulsive, impressible, changeable disciple, the first to confess and the first to deny his Master, yet quickly returning to him in bitter repentance and sincere humility. It is for this inconsistency of conduct, which Paul called by the strong term of dissimulation or hypocrisy, that he, in his uncompro-

mising zeal for the great principle of Christian liberty, reproved him pub licly before the church. A public wrong had to be publicly rectified. According to the Tübingen hypothesis the hypocrisy would have been in the very opposite conduct of Peter. The silent submission of Peter on the occasion proves his regard for his younger colleague, and speaks as much to his praise as his weakness to his blame. That the alienation was only temporary and did not break up their fraternal relation is apparent from the respectful though frank manner in which, several years after the occurrence, they allude to each other as fellow apostles, comp. Gal. 1 : 18, 19 ; 2 : 8, 9 ; 1 Cor. 9 : 5 ; 2 Pet. 3 : 15, 16, and from the fact that Mark and Silas were connecting links between them and alternately served them both.[1]

The Epistle to the Galatians then furnishes the proper solution of the difficulty, and essentially confirms the account of the Acts. It proves the harmony as well as the difference between Paul and the older apos- tles. It explodes the hypothesis that they stood related to each other like the Marcionites and Ebionites in the second century. These were the descendants of the *heretics* of the apostolic age, of the "*false* breth- ren insidiously brought in" (ψευδάδελφοι παρείσακτοι, Gal. 2 : 4) ; while the true apostles recognized and continued to recognize the same grace of God which wrought effectually through Peter for the conversion of the Jews, and through Paul for the conversion of the Gentiles. That the Judaizers should have appealed to the Jewish apostles, and the anti- nomian Gnostics to Paul, as their authority, is not more surprising than the appeal of the modern rationalists to Luther and the Reformation.

We have thus discussed at the outset, and at some length, the fundamen- tal difference of the two standpoints from which the history of the apos- tolic church is now viewed, and have vindicated our own general position in this controversy.

It is not to be supposed that all the obscure points have already been satisfactorily cleared up, or ever will be solved beyond the possibility

---

[1] It is amusing to read Renan's account of this dispute (*St. Paul*, ch. **x.**). He sympathizes rather with Peter, whom he calls a " man profoundly kind and upright and desiring peace above all things," though he admits him to have been amiably weak and inconsistent on that as on other occasions; while he charges Paul with stubbornness and rudeness ; but what is the most important point, he denies the Tübingen exegesis when he says : " Modern critics who infer from certain passages of the Epistle to the Galatians that the rupture between Peter and Paul was absolute, put themselves in contra- diction not only to the Acts, but to other passages of the Epistle to the Gala- tians (1 : 18 ; 2 : 2). Fervent men pass their lives disputing together without ever falling out. We must not judge these characters after the manner of things which take place in our day between people well-bred and susceptible in a point of honor. This last word especially never had much significance with the Jews ! "

of dispute. There must be some room left for faith in that God who has revealed himself clearly enough in nature and in history to strengthen our faith, and who is concealed enough to try our faith. Certain interstellar spaces will always be vacant in the firmament of the apostolic age that men may gaze all the more intensely at the bright stars, before which the post-apostolic books disappear like torches. A careful study of the ecclesiastical writers of the second and third centuries, and especially of the numerous Apocryphal Acts, Epistles, and Apocalypses, leaves on the mind a strong impression of the immeasurable superiority of the New Testament in purity and truthfulness, simplicity and majesty; and this superiority points to a special agency of the Spirit of God, without which that book of books is an inexplicable mystery.

§ 23. *Chronology of the Apostolic Age.*

See the works quoted in § 20, pp. 193, 194, especially WIESELER.   Comp. also HACKETT on *Acts*, pp. 22 to 30 (third ed.).

The chronology of the apostolic age is partly certain, at least within a few years, partly conjectural: certain as to the principal events from A.D. 30 to 70, conjectural as to intervening points and the last thirty years of the first century. The sources are the New Testament (especially the Acts and the Pauline Epistles), Josephus, and the Roman historians. Josephus (b. 37, d. 103) is especially valuable here, as he wrote the Jewish history down to the destruction of Jerusalem.

The following dates are more or less certain and accepted by most historians:

1. The founding of the Christian Church on the feast of Pentecost in May A.D. 30.   This is on the assumption that Christ was born B.C. 4 or 5, and was crucified in April A.D. 30, at an age of thirty-three.

2. The death of King Herod Agrippa I. A.D. 44 (according to Josephus).   This settles the date of the preceding martyrdom of James the elder, Peter's imprisonment and release (Acts 12 : 2, 23).

3. The Apostolic Council in Jerusalem, A.D. 50 (Acts 15 : 1 sqq.; Gal. 2 : 1–10). This date is ascertained by reckoning backwards to Paul's conversion, and forward to the Cæsarean cap-

tivity. Paul was probably converted in 37, and "fourteen years" elapsed from that event to the Council. But chronologists differ on the year of Paul's conversion, between 31 and 40.[1]

4. The dates of the Epistles to the Galatians, Corinthians, and Romans, between 56 and 58. The date of the Epistle to the Romans can be fixed almost to the month from its own indications combined with the statements of the Acts. It was written before the apostle had been in Rome, but when he was on the point of departure for Jerusalem and Rome on the way to Spain,[2] after having finished his collections in Macedonia and Achaia for the poor brethren in Judæa;[3] and he sent the epistle through Phebe, a deaconess of the congregation in the eastern port of Corinth, where he was at that time.[4] These indications point clearly to the spring of the year 58, for in that year he was taken prisoner in Jerusalem and carried to Cæsarea.

5. Paul's captivity in Cæsarea, A.D. 58 to 60, during the procuratorship of Felix and Festus, who changed places in 60 or 61, probably in 60. This important date we can ascertain by combination from several passages in Josephus, and Tacitus.[5] It enables us at the same time, by reckoning backward, to fix some preceding events in the life of the apostle.

6. Paul's first captivity in Rome, A.D. 61 to 63. This follows from the former date in connection with the statement in Acts 28 : 30.

7. The Epistles of the Roman captivity, Philippians, Ephesians, Colossians, and Philemon, A.D. 61–63.

---

[1] See *Hist. Apost. Ch.* § 63, p. 235, and § 67, p. 265. The allusion to the governorship of Aretas in Damascus, 2 Cor. 11 : 32, 33, furnishes no certain date, owing to the defects of our knowledge of that period ; but other indications combined lead to the year 37. Wieseler puts Paul's conversion in the year 40, but this follows from his erroneous view of the journey mentioned in Gal. 2 : 1, which he identifies with Paul's fourth journey to Jerusalem in 54, instead of his third journey to the Council four years earlier.

[2] Rom. 1 : 13, 15, 22 ; 15 : 23–28 ; comp. Acts 19 : 21 ; 20 : 16 ; 23 : 11 ; 1 Cor. 16 : 3.

[3] Rom. 15 : 25–27 ; 1 Cor. 16 : 1, 2 ; 2 Cor. chs. 8 and 9 ; Acts 24 : 17.

[4] Rom. 16 : 1, 23 ; comp. Acts 19 : 22 ; 2 Tim. 4 : 20 ; 1 Cor. 1 : 14.

[5] See Wieseler, l. c., pp. 67 sqq.

8. The Neronian persecution, A.D. 64 (the tenth year of Nero, according to Tacitus). The martyrdom of Paul and Peter occurred either then, or (according to tradition) a few years later. The question depends on the second Roman captivity of Paul.

9. The destruction of Jerusalem by Titus, A.D. 70 (according to Josephus and Tacitus).

10. The death of John after the accession of Trajan, A.D. 98 (according to general ecclesiastical tradition).

The dates of the Synoptical Gospels, the Acts, the Pastoral Epistles, the Hebrews, and the Epistles of Peter, James, and Jude cannot be accurately ascertained except that they were composed before the destruction of Jerusalem, mostly between 60 and 70. The writings of John were written after that date and towards the close of the first century, except the Apocalypse, which some of the best scholars, from internal indications, assign to the year 68 or 69, between the death of Nero and the destruction of Jerusalem.

The details are given in the following table:

CHRONOLOGICAL TABLE OF THE APOSTOLIC AGE.

A.D.	SCRIPTURE HISTORY.	EVENTS IN PALESTINE.	EVENTS IN THE ROMAN EMPIRE.	A.D.
B.C. 5 or 4	Birth of Christ	Death of Herod I., or the Great (A.U. 750. or B.C. 4). ARCHELAUS in Judæa, Samaria, and Idumea; HEROD ANTIPAS in Galilee and Peræa, and PHILIP in Auranitis, Trachonitis, Paneas, and Batanæa, ARCHELAUS deposed, and Judæa made a Roman province..................	AUGUSTUS Emperor of Rome, B.C. 27–A.D. 14.	
A.D. 8	His visit to the Temple at twelve years of age	CYRENIUS (Quirinius), Governor of Syria (for the second time). The registration, or "taxing." Acts 5:37. Revolt of "Judas of Galilee." COPONIUS Procurator of Judæa. MARCUS AMBIVIUS Procurator....................	-------------------------	6
			TIBERIUS colleague of Augustus............	9
				12
		ANNIUS RUFUS Procurator (about)	....	13

A.D.	SCRIPTURE HISTORY.	EVENTS IN PALESTINE.	EVENTS IN THE ROMAN EMPIRE.	A.D.
		VALERIUS GRATUS Procurator...................	....	14
			Augustus dies. TIBERIUS sole Emperor (14–37)...	14
		PONTIUS PILATE Procurator from A.D. 26.........	....	26
27	Christ's Baptism.	CAIAPHAS high-priest from		
27–30	His three years' ministry.	A.D. 25.		
30	His Crucifixion, Resurrection (April), and Ascension (May).			
	Descent of the Holy Spirit at Pentecost. Birthday of the Church (May). Acts, ch. 2.	MARCELLUS Procurator..... PILATE sent to Rome by the Prefect of Syria..........	....	36 36
37	Martyrdom of Stephen. Acts, ch. 7.	MARYLLUS appointed Hipparch.	CALIGULA Emperor (37–41)....................	37
	Peter and John in Samaria. Acts, ch. 8. Conversion of Saul. Acts, ch. 9, comp. 22 and 26, and Gal. 1 : 16 ; 1 Cor. 15 : 8.	HEROD AGRIPPA I., King of of Judæa and Samaria...	....	37
40	Saul's escape from Damascus, and first visit to Jerusalem (after his conversion). Gal. 1 : 18.		Philo at Rome...........	40
	Admission of Cornelius into the Church. Acts, chs. 10 and 11.		CLAUDIUS Emperor (41–54)....................	41
44	Persecution of the Church in Jerusalem. James the Elder, the son of Zebedee, beheaded. Peter imprisoned and delivered. He leaves Palestine. Acts 12 : 2–23.	HEROD AGRIPPA I. dies at Cæsarea	....	44
	Paul's second visit to Jerusalem, with alms from the church at Antioch. Acts 11 : 30.		Conquest of Britain, 43–51.	
45	Paul is set apart as an apostle. Acts 13 : 2.	CUSPIUS FADUS Procurator of Judæa.		
		TIBERIUS ALEXANDER Procurator.................	....	46
		VENTIDIUS CUMANUS Procurator....	....	47
50	Pa u l's first missionary journey with Barnabas and Mark, Cyprus, Pisidia, Lystra, Derbe. Return to Antioch. Acts chs. 13 and 14.			
	The *Epistle* of James (variously dated from 44 to 62).			
	The apostolic council of Jerusalem. Conflict between Jewish and Gentile Christianity. Paul's third visit to Jerusalem with Barnabas and Titus. Peaceful adjustment of the question of circumcision. Acts, ch. 15 and Gal. 2 : 1–10.			
	Temporary collision with Peter and Barnabas at Antioch. Gal. 2 : 11–14.			
51	Paul sets out on his second missionary journey from Antioch to Asia Minor (Cilicia, Lycaonia, Gala-			

A.D.	SCRIPTURE HISTORY.	EVENTS IN PALESTINE.	EVENTS IN THE ROMAN EMPIRE.	A.D.
	tia, Troas) and Greece (Philippi, Thessalonica, Berœa, Athens, Corinth). The Christianization of Europe. Acts, 15 : 36 to 18 : 22.	ANTONIUS FELIX Procurator..................	....	51
52-53	Paul at Corinth a year and a half. Writes *First* and *Second Epistles to the Thessalonians* from Corinth.	The Tetrarchy of Trachonitis given to HEROD AGRIPPA II. (the last of the Herodian family).	Decree of CLAUDIUS banishing the Jews from Rome..................	52
54	Paul's fourth visit to Jerusalem (spring). Short stay at Antioch. Enters (autumn, 54) on his third missionary journey, occupying about four years. Paul at Ephesus, 54 to 57. Acts, ch. 19.	Revolt of the Sicarii, headed by an Egyptian (Acts, 21 : 38)................	NERO Emperor (54-68)...	54
56	Paul writes to the *Galatians* (?) from Ephesus, or from some part of Greece on his journey to Corinth (57). Acts, ch. 20.		....	55
57	Paul writes *First Epistle to the Corinthians* from E p h e s u s ; starts for Macedonia and writes *Second Epistle* to the *Corinthians* from Macedonia.			
58	*Epistle* to the *Romans* from Corinth, where he spent three months. He visits (the fifth time) Jerusalem ; is apprehended, brought before Felix, and imprisoned at Cæsarea for two years. Acts, 21 : 17 to 26 : 32.			
60	Paul appears before Festus, appeals to Cæsar, is sent to Italy (in autumn). Shipwreck at Malta. Acts, chs. 27 and 28.	PORCIUS FESTUS Procurator	....	60
61	Arrives a prisoner at Rome (in spring).	Embassy from Jerusalem to Rome respecting the wall.	War with Boadicea in Britain..................	61
61-63	Paul writes to the *Philippians, Ephesians, Colossians, Philemon*, from his prison in Rome.		Apollonius of Tyana at the Olympic games.	
62	Martyrdom of James, the Lord's brother, at Jerusalem (according to Josephus, or 69 according to Hegesippus).		Josephus at Rome.......	62
63	Paul is supposed to have been released. Acts, 28 : 30.	ALBINUS Procurator.......	....	63
64	*Epistle to the Hebrews*, written from Italy after the release of Timothy (ch. 13 : 23).			
64-67	*First Epistle* of Peter. *Epistle* of Jude (?). *Second Epistle* of Peter (?)	GESSIUS FLORUS Procurator.	Great fire at Rome (in July); first imperial persecution of the Christians (martyrdom of Peter and Paul)........	64
60-70	The Synoptical *Gospels*, and *Acts*.	Beginning of the great war between the Romans and Jews................	Seneca and Lucan put to death by Nero.........	65 66

A.D.	SCRIPTURE HISTORY.	EVENTS IN PALESTINE.	EVENTS IN THE ROMAN EMPIRE.	A.D.
64–67	Paul visits Crete and Macedonia, and writes *First Epistle to Timothy*, and *Epistle to Titus* (?).[1] Paul writes *Second Epistle to Timothy* (?).	VESPASIAN General in Palestine...................	....	67
85–67	Paul's and Peter's martyrdom in Rome (?).			
68–69	The *Revelation* of John (?)		GALBA Emperor.........	68
			OTHO and VITELLIUS Emperors.............	69
			VESPASIAN Emperor.....	69
		Destruction of Jerusalem by Titus.................. .	....	70
		(Josephus released.)	Coliseum begun.........	76
			Destruction of Pompeii and Herculaneum	79
80–90	John writes his *Gospel* and *Epistles* (?).		TITUS Emperor..........	79
95	John writes the *Revelation* (?).		DOMITIAN Emperor......	91
			Persecution of Christians.	95
			NERVA Emperor.........	96
98–100	Death of John.		Death of Apollonius......	97
			TRAJAN Emperor........	98

[1] Those who deny a second imprisonment of Paul assign these Epistles to the period of Paul's residence in Ephesus, A.D. 54–57, and 2 Timothy to A.D. 63 or 64.

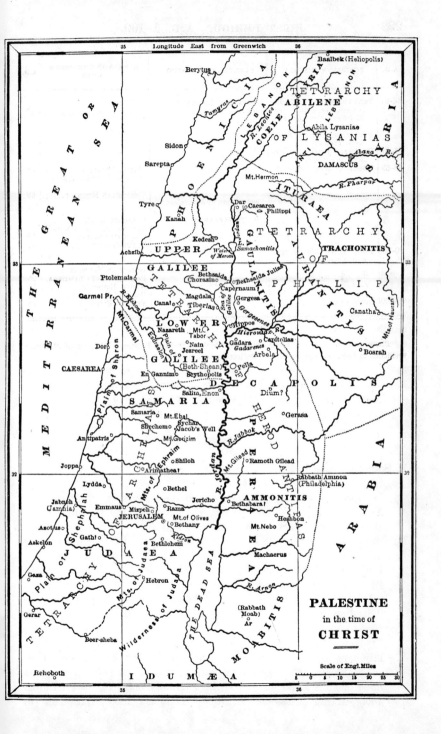

PALESTINE

in the time of

CHRIST

CHAPTER IV.

ST. PETER AND THE CONVERSION OF THE JEWS

§ 24.   *The Miracle of Pentecost and the Birthday of the Christian Church.*   A.D. 30.

Καὶ ἐπλήσθησαν πάντες πνεύματος ἁγίου, καὶ ἤρξαντο λαλεῖν ἑτέραις γλώσσαις, καθὼς τὸ πνεῦμα ἐδίδου ἀποφθέγγεσθαι αὐτοῖς.—Acts 2 : 4.

"The first Pentecost which the disciples celebrated after the ascension of our Saviour, is, next to the appearance of the Son of God on earth, the most significant event. It is the starting-point of the apostolic church and of that new spiritual life in humanity which proceeded from Him, and which since has been spreading and working, and will continue to work until the whole humanity is transformed into the image of Christ."—NEANDER (*Geschichte der Pflanzung und Leitung der christlichen Kirche durch die Apostel.*, I. 3, 4).

Literature.

I. SOURCES : Acts 2 : 1–47.   Comp. 1 Cor. chs. 12 and 14.   See Commentaries on the Acts by OLSHAUSEN, DE WETTE, MEYER, LECHLER, HACKETT, ALEXANDER, GLOAG, ALFORD, WORDSWORTH, PLUMPTRE, JACOBSON, HOWSON and SPENCE, etc., and on the Corinthians by BILLROTH, KLING, STANLEY, HEINRICI, EDWARDS, GODET, ELLICOTT.

II. Special treatises on the Pentecostal Miracle and the Gift of Tongues (glossolalia) by HERDER (*Die Gabe der Sprachen*, Riga, 1794) HASE (in Winer's "Zeitschrift für wissenschaftl. Theol." 1827), BLEEK in "Studien und Kritiken" for 1829 and 1830), BAUR in the "Tübinger Zeitschrift für Theol." for 1830 and 1831, and in the "Studien und Krit." 1838), SCHNECKENBURGER (in his *Beiträge zur Einleitung in das N. T.* 1832), BÄUMLEIN (1834), DAV. SCHULZ (1836), ZINSLER (1847), ZELLER (*Acts of the Apostles*, I. 171, of the E. translation by J. Dare), BÖHM (Irvingite, *Reden mit Zungen und Weissagen*, Berlin, 1848), ROSSTEUSCHER (Irvingite, *Gabe der Sprachen im apost. Zeitalter*, Marburg, 1855), AD. HILGENFELD (*Glossolalie*, Leipz. 1850), MAIER (*Glossolalie des apost. Zeitalters*, 1855), WIESELER (in

"Stud. u. Krit." 1838 and 1860), SCHENKEL (art. *Zungenreden* in his
"Bibel-Lex." V. 732), VAN HENGEL (*De gave der talen*, Leiden, 1864),
PLUMPTRE (art. *Gift of Tongues* in Smith's "B. D." IV. 3305, Am.
ed.), DELITZSCH (art. *Pfingsten* in Riehm's "H. B. A." 1880, p.
1184); K. SCHMIDT (in Herzog, 2d ed., xvii., 570 sqq.).

Comp. also NEANDER (I. 1), LANGE (II. 13), EWALD (VI. 106),
THIERSCH (p. 65, 3d ed.), SCHAFF (191 and 469), FARRAR (*St. Paul*,
ch. V. vol. I. 83).

The ascension of Christ to heaven was followed ten days
afterwards by the descent of the Holy Spirit upon earth and
the birth of the Christian Church. The Pentecostal event was
the necessary result of the Passover event. It could never have
taken place without the preceding resurrection and ascension.
It was the first act of the mediatorial reign of the exalted Redeemer in heaven, and the beginning of an unbroken series of
manifestations in fulfilment of his promise to be with his people
"alway, even unto the end of the world." For his ascension was
only a withdrawal of his visible local presence, and the beginning of his spiritual omnipresence in the church which is "his
body, the fulness of him that filleth all in all." The Easter
miracle and the Pentecostal miracle are continued and verified
by the daily moral miracles of regeneration and sanctification
throughout Christendom.

We have but one authentic account of that epoch-making
event, in the second chapter of Acts, but in the parting addresses
of our Lord to his disciples the promise of the Paraclete who
should lead them into the whole truth is very prominent,[1] and
the entire history of the apostolic church is illuminated and
heated by the Pentecostal fire.[2]

Pentecost, i. e. the fiftieth day after the Passover-Sabbath,[3]

[1] John 14:16, 26; 15:26; 16:7. The preparatory communication of the
Spirit is related in John 20:22.
[2] Comp. especially the classical chapters on the gifts of the Spirit, 1 Cor.
12, 13, and 14, and Rom. 12.
[3] The Greek name ἡ πεντηκοστή (ἡμέρα) is used (like *quinquagesima*) as a
substantive, Tob. 2:1; 2 Macc. 12:32; Acts 2:1; 20:16; 1 Cor. 16:3, and
by Josephus, *Ant.* III. 10, 6, etc. It survives not only in all the Romanic languages, but also in the German *Pfingsten*. The English *Whit-Sunday* is

was a feast of joy and gladness, in the loveliest season of the year, and attracted a very large number of visitors to Jerusalem from foreign lands.[1] It was one of the three great annual festivals of the Jews in which all the males were required to appear before the Lord. Passover was the first, and the feast of Tabernacles the third. Pentecost lasted one day, but the foreign Jews, after the period of the captivity, prolonged it to two days. It was the "feast of harvest," or "of the first fruits," and also (according to rabbinical tradition) the anniversary celebration of the Sinaitic legislation, which is supposed to have taken place on the fiftieth day after the Exodus from the land of bondage.[2]

This festival was admirably adapted for the opening event in

usually derived from the *white* garments of the candidates for baptism worn on that day (hence *Dominica alba*); others connect it with *wit*, the gift of wisdom from above. The Hebrew names of the festival are חַג הַקָּצִיר, ἑορτὴ θερισμοῦ, *the feast of harvest* (Ex. 23 : 16), יוֹם הַבִּכּוּרִים, ἡμέρα τῶν νέων, *day of the first fruits* (Num. 28 : 26), חַג שָׁבֻעֹת, ἑορτὴ ἑβδομάδων, ἀγία ἑπτὰ ἑβδομάδων, *festival of (seven) weeks*, as the harvest continued for seven weeks (Deut. 16 : 9, 10; Lev. 23 : 15; Tob. 2 : 1). It began directly after the Passover with the offering of the first sheaf of the barley-harvest, and ended at Pentecost with the offering of the first two loaves from the wheat-harvest.

[1] Josephus speaks of "many tens of thousands being gathered together about the temple" on Pentecost, *Ant.* xiv. 13, 4; comp. xvii. 10, 2; *Bell Jud.* II. 3, 1. The Passover, of course, was more numerously attended by Jews from Palestine; but distant foreigners were often prevented by the dangers of travel in the early spring. Paul twice went to Jerusalem on Pentecost, Acts 18 : 21; 20 : 16. Many Passover pilgrims would naturally remain till the second festival.

[2] Hence called *the feast of the joy of the Law* (שִׂמְחַת הַתּוֹרָה). The date of the Sinaitic legislation is based on a comparison of Ex. 12 : 2 with 19 : 1 (comp. my *Hist. of the Ap. Ch.*, p. 192, note 5). The legislation on Pentecost, Deut. 16 : 9–12, represents it as a feast of rejoicing, and concludes with a reference to the bondage in Egypt and the commandments of Jehovah. Otherwise there is no allusion in the Bible, nor in Philo nor Josephus, to the *historical* significance of Pentecost. But there was a Jewish custom which Schöttgen (*Hor. Heb.* in Act. 2 : 1) traces to apostolic times, of spending the night before Pentecost in thanksgiving to God for the gift of the law. In the present Jewish observance the commemoration of the Sinaitic legislation is made prominent. Some Jews "adorn their houses with flowers and wear wreaths on their heads, with the declared purpose of testifying their joy in the possession of the Law."

the history of the apostolic church. It pointed typically to the first Christian harvest, and the establishment of the new theocracy in Christ; as the sacrifice of the paschal lamb and the exodus from Egypt foreshadowed the redemption of the world by the crucifixion of the Lamb of God. On no other day could the effusion of the Spirit of the exalted Redeemer produce such rich results and become at once so widely known. We may trace to this day not only the origin of the mother church at Jerusalem, but also the conversion of visitors from other cities, as Damascus, Antioch, Alexandria, and Rome, who on their return would carry the glad tidings to their distant homes. For the strangers enumerated by Luke as witnesses of the great event, represented nearly all the countries in which Christianity was planted by the labors of the apostles.[1]

The Pentecost in the year of the Resurrection was the last Jewish (i. e. typical) and the first Christian Pentecost. It became the spiritual harvest feast of redemption from sin, and the birthday of the visible kingdom of Christ on earth. It marks the beginning of the dispensation of the Spirit, the third era in the history of the revelation of the triune God. On this day the Holy Spirit, who had hitherto wrought only sporadically and transiently, took up his permanent abode in mankind as the Spirit of truth and holiness, with the fulness of saving grace, to apply that grace thenceforth to believers, and to reveal and glorify Christ in their hearts, as Christ had revealed and glorified the Father.

While the apostles and disciples, about one hundred and twenty (ten times twelve) in number, no doubt mostly Galilæans,[2] were assembled before the morning devotions of the festal

---

[1] The list of nations, Acts 2 : 8-11, gives a bird's eye view of the Roman empire from the East and North southward and westward as far as Rome, and then again eastward to Arabia. Cyprus and Greece are omitted. There were Christians in Damascus before the conversion of Paul (9 : 2), and a large congregation at Rome long before he wrote his Epistle (Rom. 1 : 8).

[2] Acts 1 : 15; 2 : 7. Ten times the number of tribes of Israel. These were, however, not all the disciples; Paul mentions five hundred brethren to whom the risen Lord appeared at once, 1 Cor. 15 : 6.

day, and were waiting in prayer for the fulfilment of the promise, the exalted Saviour sent from his heavenly throne the Holy
Spirit upon them, and founded his church upon earth.   The
Sinaitic legislation was accompanied by "thunder and lightning, and a thick cloud upon the mount, and the voice of the
trumpet exceeding loud, and all the people that was in the camp
trembled." [1]   The church of the new covenant was ushered into
existence with startling signs which filled the spectators with
wonder and fear.   It is quite natural, as Neander remarks, that
"the greatest miracle in the inner life of mankind should have
been accompanied by extraordinary outward phenomena as sensible indications of its presence."   A supernatural sound resembling that of a rushing mighty wind,[2] came down from heaven
and filled the whole house in which they were assembled ; and
tongues like flames of fire, distributed themselves among them,
alighting for a while on each head.[3]   It is not said that these
phenomena were really wind and fire, they are only compared
to these elements,[4] as the form which the Holy Spirit assumed
at the baptism of Christ is compared to a dove.[5]   The tongues
of flame were gleaming, but neither burning nor consuming ;
they appeared and disappeared like electric sparks or meteoric
flashes.   But these audible and visible signs were appropriate

---

[1] Exod. 19 : 16 ; comp. Hebr. 12 : 18, 19.

[2] ἦχος ὥσπερ φερομένης πνοῆς βιαίας, *ein Getöse wie von einem dahinfahrenden
häftigen Wehen* (Meyer).   The term φερομένη, *borne on*, is the same which
Peter uses of the inspiration of the prophets, 2 Pet. 1 : 21.

[3] διαμεριζόμεναι γλῶσσαι ὡσεὶ πυρός, 2 : 3, are not parted or "cloven" tongues
(E. V.)—resembling the fork-like shape of the episcopal mitre—but distributed
tongues, spreading from one to another.   This is the meaning of διαμερίζειν in
ver. 45 ; Luke 22 : 17 ; 23 : 34 ; John 19 : 24 ; Matt. 27 : 35.   The distributive
idea explains the change of number in ver. 3, γλῶσσαι—ἐκάθισεν, i. e., one
tongue sat on each disciple.

[4] Hence ὥσπερ and ὡσεί.   John Lightfoot : " *Sonus ventus vehementis, sed
absque vento ; sic etiam linguæ igneæ, sed absque igne.*"

[5] Luke 3 : 22 (ὡς περιστεράν) ; Matt. 3 : 16 (ὡσεί) ; Mark 1 : 10 ; John 1 : 32.
The Rabbinical comment on Gen. 1 : 2 makes the same comparison, that "the
Spirit of God moved on the face of the waters *like a dove,*" and Milton sings
(*Parad. Lost*, i. 20) :

> " With mighty wings outspread
> *Dove-like* sat'st brooding on the vast abyss."

symbols of the purifying, enlightening, and quickening power of the Divine Spirit, and announced a new spiritual creation. The form of tongues referred to the glossolalia, and the apostolic eloquence as a gift of inspiration.

"AND THEY WERE ALL FILLED WITH THE HOLY SPIRIT." This is the real inward miracle, the main fact, the central idea of the Pentecostal narrative. To the apostles it was their baptism, confirmation, and ordination, all in one, for they received no other.[1] To them it was the great inspiration which enabled them hereafter to be authoritative teachers of the gospel by tongue and pen. Not that it superseded subsequent growth in knowledge, or special revelations on particular points (as Peter received at Joppa, and Paul on several occasions); but they were endowed with such an understanding of Christ's words and plan of salvation as they never had before. What was dark and mysterious became now clear and full of meaning to them. The Spirit revealed to them the person and work of the Redeemer in the light of his resurrection and exaltation, and took full possession of their mind and heart. They were raised, as it were, to the mount of transfiguration, and saw Moses and Elijah and Jesus above them, face to face, swimming in heavenly light. They had now but one desire to gratify, but one object to live for, namely, to be witnesses of Christ and instruments of the salvation of their fellow-men, that they too might become partakers of their "inheritance incorruptible, and undefiled, and that fadeth not away, reserved in heaven."[2]

But the communication of the Holy Spirit was not confined to the Twelve. It extended to the brethren of the Lord, the mother of Jesus, the pious women who had attended his ministry, and the whole brotherhood of a hundred and twenty souls who were assembled in that chamber.[3] They were "all" filled with the Spirit, and all spoke with tongues;[4] and Peter saw in

[1] They were baptized with water by John; but *Christian* baptism was first administered by them on the day of Pentecost. Christ himself did not baptize, John 4 : 2.

[2] 1 Pet. 1 : 3, 4.

[3] Comp. Acts 1 : 13, 14.

[4] Acts 2 : 3: "it (a tongue of fire) sat upon each of them."

the event the promised outpouring of the Spirit upon "all flesh," sons and daughters, young men and old men, servants and handmaidens.[1] It is characteristic that in this spring season of the church the women were sitting with the men, not in a separate court as in the temple, nor divided by a partition as in the synagogue and the decayed churches of the East to this day, but in the same room as equal sharers in the spiritual blessings. The beginning was a prophetic anticipation of the end, and a manifestation of the universal priesthood and brotherhood of believers in Christ, in whom all are one, whether Jew or Greek, bond or free, male or female.[2]

This new spiritual life, illuminated, controlled, and directed by the Holy Spirit, manifested itself first in the speaking with tongues towards God, and then in the prophetic testimony towards the people. The former consisted of rapturous prayers and anthems of praise, the latter of sober teaching and exhortation. From the Mount of Transfiguration the disciples, like their Master, descended to the valley below to heal the sick and to call sinners to repentance.

The mysterious gift of tongues, or glossolalia, appears here for the first time, but became, with other extraordinary gifts of the Spirit, a frequent phenomenon in the apostolic churches, especially at Corinth, and is fully described by Paul. The distribution of the flaming tongues to each of the disciples caused the speaking with tongues. A new experience expresses itself always in appropriate language. The supernatural experience of the disciples broke through the confines of ordinary speech and burst out in ecstatic language of praise and thanksgiving to God for the great works he did among them.[3] It was the Spirit himself who gave them utterance and played on their tongues, as on new tuned harps, unearthly melodies of praise. The glossolalia was here, as in all cases where it is mentioned, an act of worship and adoration, not an act of teaching and instruction,

---

[1] Acts 2 : 3, 4, 17, 18.

[2] Gal. 3 : 28.

[3] τὰ μεγαλεῖα τοῦ θεοῦ. Acts 2 : 11; comp. the same term Luke 1 : 69, and the μεγαλύνειν τὸν θεόν, Acts 10 : 46.

which followed afterwards in the sermon of Peter. It was the first *Te Deum* of the new-born church. It expressed itself in unusual, poetic, dithyrambic style and with a peculiar musical intonation. It was intelligible only to those who were in sympathy with the speaker; while unbelievers scoffingly ascribed it to madness or excess of wine. Nevertheless it served as a significant sign to all and arrested their attention to the presence of a supernatural power.[1]

So far we may say that the Pentecostal glossolalia was the same as that in the household of Cornelius in Cæsarea after his conversion, which may be called a Gentile Pentecost,[2] as that of the twelve disciples of John the Baptist at Ephesus, where it appears in connection with prophesying,[3] and as that in the Christian congregation at Corinth.[4]

But at its first appearance the speaking with tongues differed in its effect upon the hearers by coming home to them at once *in their own mother-tongues;* while in Corinth it required an interpretation to be understood. The foreign spectators, at least a number of them, believed that the unlettered Galilæans spoke intelligibly in the different dialects represented on the occasion.[5] We must therefore suppose either that the speakers themselves were endowed, at least temporarily, and for the particular purpose of proving their divine mission, with the gift of foreign languages not learned by them before, or that the Holy Spirit who distributed the tongues acted also as interpreter of the tongues, and applied the utterances of the speakers to the susceptible among the hearers.

The former is the most natural interpretation of Luke's language. Nevertheless I suggest the other alternative as preferable, for the following reasons: 1. The temporary endowment with a supernatural knowledge of foreign languages in-

---

[1] Comp. 1 Cor. 14 : 22.
[2] Acts 10 : 46.
[3] Acts 19 : 6.
[4] 1 Cor. chs. 12 and 14.
[5] Acts 2 : 8 : ἕκαστος τῇ ἰδίᾳ διαλέκτῳ ἡμῶν ἐν ᾗ ἐγεννήθημεν. Comp. ver. 11 : ἀκούομεν λαλούντων αὐτῶν ταῖς ἡμετέραις γλώσσαις τὰ μεγαλεῖα τοῦ θεοῦ.

volves nearly all the difficulties of a permanent endowment, which is now generally abandoned, as going far beyond the data of the New Testament and known facts of the early spread of the gospel. 2. The speaking with tongues began before the spectators arrived, that is before there was any motive for the employment of foreign languages.[1] 3. The intervening agency of the Spirit harmonizes the three accounts of Luke, and Luke and Paul, or the Pentecostal and the Corinthian glossolalia; the only difference remaining is that in Corinth the interpretation of tongues was made by men in audible speech,[2] in Jerusalem by the Holy Spirit in inward illumination and application. 4. The Holy Spirit was certainly at work among the hearers as well as the speakers, and brought about the conversion of three thousand on that memorable day. If he applied and made effective the sermon of Peter, why not also the preceding doxologies and benedictions? 5. Peter makes no allusion to foreign languages, nor does the prophecy of Joel which he quotes. 6. This view best explains the opposite effect upon the spectators. They did by no means all understand the miracle, but the mockers, like those at Corinth,[3] thought the disciples were out of their right mind and talked not intelligible words in their native dialects, but unintelligible nonsense. The speaking in a foreign language could not have been a proof of drunkenness. It may be objected to this view that it implies a mistake on the part of the hearers who traced the use of their mother-tongues directly to the speakers; but the mistake referred not to the fact itself, but only to the mode. It was the same Spirit who inspired the tongues of the speakers and the hearts of the susceptible hearers, and raised both above the ordinary level of consciousness.

Whichever view we take of this peculiar feature of the Pentecostal glossolalia, in this diversified application to the cosmopolitan multitude of spectators, it was a symbolical anticipation

---

[1] Comp. vers. 4 and 6.
[2] 1 Cor. 14 : 5, 13, 27, 28 ; comp. 1 Cor. 12 : 10, 30.
[3] Comp. 1 Cor. 14 : 23.

and prophetic announcement of the universalness of the Christian religion, which was to be proclaimed in all the languages of the earth and to unite all nations in one kingdom of Christ. The humility and love of the church united what the pride and hatred of Babel had scattered. In this sense we may say that the Pentecostal harmony of tongues was the counterpart of the Babylonian confusion of tongues.[1]

The speaking with tongues was followed by the sermon of Peter; the act of devotion, by an act of teaching; the rapturous language of the soul in converse with God, by the sober words of ordinary self-possession for the benefit of the people.

While the assembled multitude wondered at this miracle with widely various emotions, St. Peter, the Rock-man, appeared in the name of all the disciples, and addressed them with remarkable clearness and force, probably in his own vernacular Aramaic, which would be most familiar to the inhabitants of Jerusalem, possibly in Greek, which would be better understood by the foreign visitors.[2] He humbly condescended to refute the charge of intoxication by reminding them of the early hour of the day, when even drunkards are sober, and explained from the prophecies of Joel and the sixteenth Psalm of David the meaning of the supernatural phenomenon, as the work of that Jesus of Nazareth, whom the Jews had crucified, but who was by word and deed, by his resurrection from the dead, his exaltation to the right hand of God, and the effusion of the Holy Ghost, accredited as the promised Messiah, according to the express prediction of the Scripture. Then he called upon his hearers to repent and be baptized in the name of Jesus, as the founder and head of the heavenly kingdom, that even they, though they had crucified him, the Lord and the Messiah, might

---

[1] Grotius (*in loc.*): "*Pœna linguarum dispersit homines, donum linguarum dispersos in unum populum collegit.*" See note on Glossolalia.

[2] The former is the usual view, the latter is maintained by Stanley, Plumptre, and Farrar. Paul addressed the excited multitude in Jerusalem in the Hebrew tongue, which commanded greater silence, Acts 22 : 2. This implies that they would not have understood him in Greek as well, or listened as attentively.

receive the forgiveness of sins and the gift of the Holy Ghost, whose wonderful workings they saw and heard in the disciples. This was the first independent testimony of the apostles, the first Christian sermon: simple, unadorned, but full of Scripture truth, natural, suitable, pointed, and more effective than any other sermon has been since, though fraught with learning and burning with eloquence. It resulted in the conversion and baptism of three thousand persons, gathered as first-fruits into the garners of the church.

In these first-fruits of the glorified Redeemer, and in this founding of the new economy of Spirit and gospel, instead of the old theocracy of letter and law, the typical meaning of the Jewish Pentecost was gloriously fulfilled. But this birth-day of the Christian church is in its turn only the beginning, the type and pledge, of a still greater spiritual harvest and a universal feast of thanksgiving, when, in the full sense of the prophecy of Joel, the Holy Spirit shall be poured out on all flesh, when all the sons and daughters of men shall walk in his light, and God shall be praised with new tongues of fire for the completion of his wonderful work of redeeming love.

NOTES.

I. GLOSSOLALIA.—The Gift of Tongues is the most difficult feature of the Pentecostal miracle. Our only direct source of information is the second chapter in Acts, but the gift itself is mentioned in two other passages, ch. 10 : 46 and 19 : 6, in the concluding section of Mark (of disputed genuineness), and fully described by Paul in the 12th and 14th chapters of the First Epistle to the Corinthians. There can be no doubt as to the existence of that gift in the apostolic age, and if we had only either the account of Pentecost, or only the account of Paul, we would not hesitate to decide as to its nature, but the difficulty is in harmonizing the two.

(1) The *terms* employed for the strange tongues are "*new* tongues" (καιναὶ γλῶσσαι, Mark 16 : 17, where Christ promises the gift), "*other* tongues," differing from ordinary tongues (ἕτεραι γλ. Acts 2 : 4, but nowhere else), "kinds" or "diversities of tongues" (γένη γλωσσῶν, 1 Cor. 12 : 28), or simply "tongues" (γλῶσσαι, 1 Cor. 14 : 22), and in the singular, "tongue" (γλῶσσα, vers. 2, 13, 19, 27, in which passages the E. V. inserts the interpolation "*unknown* tongue "). To speak in tongues is called γλώσσαις or γλώσσῃ λαλεῖν (Acts 2 : 4 ; 10 : 46 ; 19 : 6 ; 1 Cor. 14 : 2, 4, 13,

14, 19, 27). Paul uses also the phrase to "pray with the tongue" προσεύχεσθαι γλώσσῃ), as equivalent to "praying and singing with the spirit" (προσεύχεσθαι and ψάλλειν τῷ πνεύματι, and as distinct from προσεύχεσθαι and ψάλλειν τῷ νοΐ, 1 Cor. 14:14, 15). The plural and the term "diversities" of tongues, as well as the distinction between tongues of "angels" and tongues of "men" (1 Cor. 13:1) point to different manifestations (speaking, praying, singing), according to the individuality, education, and mood of the speaker, but not to various *foreign* languages, which are excluded by Paul's description.

The term tongue has been differently explained.

(a) Wieseler (and Van Hengel) : the organ of speech, used as a pas‑ sive instrument ; speaking with the tongue *alone*, inarticulately, and in a low whisper. But this does not explain the plural, nor the terms "new" and "other" tongues ; the organ of speech remaining the same.

(b) Bleek : rare, provincial, archaic, poetic words, or glosses (whence our "glossary"). But this technical meaning of γλῶσσαι occurs only in classical writers (as Aristotle, Plutarch, etc.) and among grammarians, not in Hellenistic Greek, and the interpretation does not suit the singular γλῶσσα and γλώσσῃ λαλεῖν, as γλῶσσα could only mean a single gloss.

(c) Most commentators : language or dialect (διάλεκτος, comp. Acts 1:19 ; 2:6, 8 ; 21:40 ; 26:14). This is the correct view. "Tongue" is an abridgment for "*new* tongue" (which was the original term, Mark 16:17). It does not necessarily mean one of the known languages of the earth, but may mean a peculiar handling of the vernacular dialect of the speaker, or a new spiritual language never known before, a language of immediate inspiration in a state of ecstasy. The "tongues" were individual varieties of this language of inspiration.

(2) The glossolalia in the *Corinthian* church, with which that at Cæsarea in Acts 10:46, and that at Ephesus, 19:6, are evidently identical, we know very well from the description of Paul. It occurred in the first glow of enthusiasm after conversion and continued for some time. It was not a speaking in *foreign* languages, which would have been entirely useless in a devotional meeting of converts, but a speaking in a language differing from all known languages, and required an interpreter to be intelligible to foreigners. It had nothing to do with the *spread* of the gospel, although it may, like other devotional acts, have become a means of conversion to susceptible unbelievers if such were present. It was an act of *self-devotion*, an act of thanksgiving, praying, and sing‑ ing, within the Christian congregation, by individuals who were wholly absorbed in communion with God, and gave utterance to their raptur‑ ous feelings in broken, abrupt, rhapsodic, unintelligible words. It was emotional rather than intellectual, the language of the excited imagina‑ tion, not of cool reflection. It was the language of the spirit (πνεῦμα) or of ecstasy, as distinct from the language of the understanding (νοῦς). We might almost illustrate the difference by a comparison of the style

of the Apocalypse which was conceived ἐν πνεύματι (Apoc. 1 : 10) with
that of the Gospel of John, which was written ἐν νοΐ. The speaker
in tongues was in a state of spiritual intoxication, if we may use this
term, analogous to the poetic "frenzy" described by Shakespeare and
Goethe. His tongue was a lyre on which the divine Spirit played celestial tunes. He was unconscious or only half conscious, and scarcely
knew whether he was "in the body or out of the body." No one could
understand this unpremeditated religious rhapsody unless he was in a
similar trance. To an unbelieving outsider it sounded like a barbarous
tongue, like the uncertain sound of a trumpet, like the raving of a maniac
(1 Cor. 14 : 23), or the incoherent talk of a drunken man (Acts 2 : 13, 15).
"He that speaketh in a tongue speaketh *not to men*, but *to God;* for no
one understandeth ; and in the spirit he speaketh mysteries ; but he
that prophesieth speaketh *unto men* edification, and encouragement, and
comfort. He that speaketh in a tongue edifieth *himself;* but he that
prophesieth edifieth *the church*" (1 Cor. 14 : 2–4 ; comp. 26–33).

The Corinthians evidently overrated the glossolalia, as a showy display
of divine power ; but it was more ornamental than useful, and vanished
away with the bridal season of the church. It is a mark of the great
wisdom of Paul who was himself a master in the glossolalia (1 Cor. 14 : 18),
that he assigned to it a subordinate and transient position, restrained its
exercise, demanded an interpretation of it, and gave the preference to
the gifts of permanent usefulness in which God displays his goodness
and love for the general benefit. Speaking with tongues is good, but prophesying and teaching in intelligible speech for the edification of the
congregation is better, and love to God and men in active exercise is
best of all (1 Cor. ch. 13).

We do not know how long the glossolalia, as thus described by Paul,
continued. It passed away gradually with the other extraordinary or
strictly supernatural gifts of the apostolic age. It is not mentioned in
the Pastoral, nor in the Catholic Epistles. We have but a few allusions to it at the close of the second century. Irenæus (*Adv. Haer.* l. v.
c. 6, § 1) speaks of "many brethren" whom he heard in the church having the gift of prophecy and of speaking in "*diverse* tongues" (παντοδα-
παῖς γλώσσαις), bringing the hidden things of men (τὰ κρύφια τῶν ἀνϑρώπων)
to light and expounding the mysteries of God (τὰ μυστήρια τοῦ ϑεοῦ). It
is not clear whether by the term "diverse," which does not elsewhere
occur, he means a speaking in foreign languages, or in diversities of
tongues altogether peculiar, like those meant by Paul. The latter
is more probable. Irenæus himself had to learn the language of Gaul.
Tertullian (*Adv. Marc.* V. 8 ; comp. *De Anima,* c. 9) obscurely speaks of
the spiritual gifts, including the gift of tongues, as being still manifest
among the Montanists to whom he belonged. At the time of Chrysostom it had entirely disappeared ; at least he accounts for the obscurity
of the gift from our ignorance of the fact. From that time on the glos-

solalia was usually misunderstood as a miraculous and permanent gift of *foreign* languages for *missionary* purposes. But the whole history of missions furnishes no clear example of such a gift for such a purpose.

Analogous phenomena, of an inferior kind, and not miraculous, yet serving as illustrations, either by approximation or as counterfeits, reappeared from time to time in seasons of special religious excitement, as among the Camisards and the prophets of the Cevennes in France, among the early Quakers and Methodists, the Mormons, the Readers ("Läsare") in Sweden in 1841 to 1843, in the Irish revivals of 1859, and especially in the "Catholic Apostolic Church," commonly called Irvingites, from 1831 to 1833, and even to this day. See Ed. Irving's articles on *Gifts of the Holy Ghost called Supernatural*, in his "Works," vol. V., p. 509, etc. ; Mrs. Oliphant's *Life of Irving*, vol. II. ; the descriptions quoted in my *Hist. Ap. Ch.* § 55, p. 198 ; and from friend and foe in Stanley's *Com. on Corinth.*, p. 252, 4th ed. ; also Plumptre in Smith's "Bible Dict.," IV. 3311, Am. ed. The Irvingites who have written on the subject (Thiersch, Böhm, and Rossteuscher) make a marked distinction between the Pentecostal glossolalia in foreign languages and the Corinthian glossolalia in devotional meetings ; and it is the latter only which they compare to their own experience. Several years ago I witnessed this phenomenon in an Irvingite congregation in New York ; the words were broken, ejaculatory and unintelligible, but uttered in abnormal, startling, impressive sounds, in a state of apparent unconsciousness and rapture, and without any control over the tongue, which was seized as it were by a foreign power. A friend and colleague (Dr. Briggs), who witnessed it in 1879 in the principal Irvingite church at London, received the same impression.

(3) The *Pentecostal* glossolalia cannot have been *essentially* different from the Corinthian : it was likewise an ecstatic act of worship, of thanksgiving and praise for the great deeds of God in Christ, a dialogue of the soul with God. It was the purest and the highest utterance of the jubilant enthusiasm of the new-born church of Christ in the possession of the Holy Spirit. It began before the spectators arrived (comp. vers. 4 and 6), and was followed by a missionary discourse of Peter in plain, ordinary language. Luke mentions the same gift twice again (chs. 10 and 19) evidently as an act of devotion, and not of teaching.

Nevertheless, according to the evident meaning of Luke's narrative, the Pentecostal glossolalia differed from the Corinthian not only by its intensity, but also by coming home to the hearers then present in their *own vernacular dialects*, without the medium of a human interpreter. Hence the term "different" tongues, which Paul does not use, nor Luke in any other passage ; hence the astonishment of the foreigners at hearing each his own peculiar idiom from the lips of those unlettered Galilæans. It is this *heteroglossolalia*, as I may term it, which causes the chief diffi-

culty. I will give the various views which either deny, or shift, or inten-
sify, or try to explain this foreign element.

(a) The rationalistic interpretation cuts the Gordian knot by denying
the miracle, as a mistake of the narrator or of the early Christian tradition. Even Meyer surrenders the heteroglossolalia, as far as it differs
from the Corinthian glossolalia, as an unhistorical tradition which originated in a mistake, because he considers the sudden communication of
the facility of speaking foreign languages as "logically impossible, and
psychologically and morally inconceivable" (Com. on Acts 2 : 4, 4th ed.).
But Luke, the companion of Paul, must have been familiar with the
glossolalia in the apostolic churches, and in the two other passages where
he mentions it he evidently means the same phenomenon as that described by Paul.

(b) The heteroglossolalia was a mistake of the hearers (a *Hörwunder*),
who in the state of extraordinary excitement and profound sympathy
imagined that they heard their own language from the disciples ; while
Luke simply narrates their impression without correcting it. This view
was mentioned (though not adopted) by Gregory of Nyssa, and held by
Pseudo-Cyprian, the venerable Bede, Erasmus, Schneckenburger and
others. If the pentecostal language was the Hellenistic dialect, it could,
with its composite character, its Hebraisms and Latinisms, the more
easily produce such an effect when spoken by persons stirred in the inmost depth of their hearts and lifted out of themselves. St. Xavier is
said to have made himself understood by the Hindoos without knowing
their language, and St. Bernard, St. Anthony of Padua, St. Vincent
Ferrer were able, by the spiritual power of their eloquence, to kindle
the enthusiasm and sway the passions of multitudes who were ignorant
of their language. Olshausen and Bäumlein call to aid the phenomena
of magnetism and somnambulism, by which people are brought into
mysterious rapport.

(c) The glossolalia was speaking in archaic, poetic glosses, with an
admixture of foreign words. This view, learnedly defended by Bleek
(1829), and adopted with modifications by Baur (1838), has already been
mentioned above (p. 233), as inconsistent with Hellenistic usage, and the
natural meaning of Luke.

(d) The mystical explanation regards the Pentecostal Gift of Tongues
in some way as a counterpart of the Confusion of Tongues, either as a
temporary restoration of the original language of Paradise, or as a prophetic anticipation of the language of heaven in which all languages are
united. This theory, which is more deep than clear, turns the heteroglossolalia into a homoglossolalia, and puts the miracle into the language itself and its temporary restoration or anticipation. Schelling calls
the Pentecostal miracle "Babel reversed" (*das umgekehrte Babel*), and
says : "*Dem Ereigniss der Sprachenverwirrung lässt sich in der ganzen
Folge der religiösen Geschichte nur Eines an die Seite stellen, die momen-*

tan wiederhergestellte Spracheinheit (ὁμογλωσσία) *am Pfingstfeste, mit dem das Christenthum, bestimmt das ganze Menschengeschlecht durch die Erkenntniss des Einen wahren Gottes wieder zur Einheit zu verknüpfen, seinen grossen Weg beginnt.*" (*Einl. in d. Philos. der Mythologie*, p. 109). A similar view was defended by Billroth (in his *Com.* on 1 Cor. ch. 14, p. 177), who suggests that the primitive language combined elements of the different derived languages, so that each listener heard fragments of his own. Lange (II. 38) sees here the normal language of the inner spiritual life which unites the redeemed, and which runs through all ages of the church as the leaven of languages, regenerating, transforming, and consecrating them to sacred uses, but he assumes also, like Olshausen, a sympathetic rapport between speakers and hearers. Delitzsch (*l. c.* p. 1186) says : "*Die apostolische Verkündigung erging damals in einer Sprache des Geistes, welche das Gegenbild der in Babel zerschellten* EINEN *Menschheitssprache war und von allen ohne Unterschied der Sprachen gleichmässig verstanden wurde. Wie das weisse Licht alle Farben aus sich erschliesst, so fiel die geistgewirkte Apostelsprache wie in prismatischer Brechung verständlich in aller Ohren und ergreifend in aller Herzen. Es war ein Vorspiel der Einigung, in welcher die von Babel datirende Veruneinigung sich aufheben wird. Dem Sivan-Tag des steinernen Buchstabens trat ein Sivan-Tag des lebendigmachenden Geistes entgegen. Es war der Geburtstag der Kirche, der Geistesgemeinde im Unterschiede von der alttestamentlichen Volksgemeinde; darum nennt Chrysostomus in einer Pfingsthomilie die Pentekoste die Metropole der Feste.*" Ewald's view (VI. 116 sqq.) is likewise mystical, but original and expressed with his usual confidence. He calls the glossolalia an "*Auflallen und Aufjauchzen der christlichen Begeisterung, ein stürmisches Hervorbrechen aller der verborgenen Gefühle und Gedanken in ihrer vollsten Unmittelbarkeit und Gewalt.*" He says that on the day of Pentecost the most unusual expressions and synonyms of different languages (as ἀββὰ ὁ πατήρ, Gal. 4 : 6 ; Rom. 8 : 15, and μαρὰν ἀϑά, 1 Cor. 16 : 22), with reminiscences of words of Christ as resounding from heaven, commingled in the vortex of a new language of the Spirit, and gave utterance to the exuberant joy of the young Christianity in stammering hymns of praise never heard before or since except in the weaker manifestations of the same gift in the Corinthian and other apostolic churches.

(e) The Pentecostal glossolalia was a *permanent* endowment of the apostles with a miraculous knowledge of all those *foreign* languages in which they were to preach the gospel. As they were sent to preach to all nations, they were gifted with the tongues of all nations. This theory was first clearly brought out by the fathers in the fourth and fifth centuries, long after the gift of tongues had disappeared, and was held by most of the older divines, though with different modifications, but is now abandoned by nearly all Protestant commentators except Bishop Wordsworth, who defends it with patristic quotations. Chrysostom supposed that each disciple was assigned the particular language which he needed for his evangelistic work (*Hom.* on Acts 2). Augustine went much further, saying (*De Civ. Dei*, XVIII. c. 49) : "*Every one* of them spoke in the tongues of *all* nations ; thus signifying that the unity of the catholic church would embrace all nations, and would in like manner speak in all tongues." Some confined the number of languages to the number of foreign nations and countries mentioned by Luke (Chrysostom), others extended it to 70 or 72 (Augustine and Epiphanius), or 75, after the number of the sons of Noah (Gen. ch. 10), or even to 120 (Pacianus), after the number of the disciples present. Baronius mentions these opinions in *Annal. ad ann.* 34, vol. I. 197. The feast of languages in the Roman Propaganda perpetuates this theory, but turns the moral miracle of spiritual enthusiasm into a mechanical miracle of acquired learning in unknown tongues. Were all the speakers to speak at once, as on the day of Pentecost, it would be a more than Babylonian confusion of tongues.

Such a stupendous miracle as is here supposed might be justified by the far-reaching importance of that creative epoch, but it is without a parallel and surrounded by insuperable difficulties. The theory ignores the fact that the glossolalia began before the spectators arrived, that is, before there was any necessity of using foreign languages. It isolates the Pentecostal glossolalia and brings Luke into conflict with Paul and with himself ; for in all other cases the gift of tongues appears, as already remarked, not as a missionary agency, but as an exercise of devotion. It implies that all the one hundred disciples present, including the women —for a tongue as of fire "sat upon each of them"—were called to be traveling evangelists. A miracle of that kind was superfluous (a *Luxuswunder*) ; for since the conquest of Alexander the Great the Greek language was so generally understood throughout the Roman empire that the apostles scarcely needed any other—unless it was Latin and their native Aramæan—for evangelistic purposes ; and the Greek was used in fact by all the writers of the New Testament, even by James of Jerusalem, and in a way which shows that they had learnt it like other people, by early training and practice. Moreover there is no trace of such a miraculous knowledge, nor any such use of it after Pentecost.[1] On the

---

[1] What may be claimed for St. Bernard, St. Vincent Ferrer, and St. Francis Xavier is not a miraculous heteroglossolalia, but an eloquence so ardent, earnest, and intense, that the rude nations which they addressed in Latin or Spanish imagined they heard them in their mother tongue. St. Bernard (d. 1153) fired the Germans in *Latin* to the second crusade, and made a greater impression on them by his very appearance than the translation of the same speech by his interpreter. See Neander, *Der heil. Bernhard*, p. 338 (2d ed.). Alban Butler (*Lives of the Saints*, sub April 5) reports of St. Vincent Ferrer (died 1419) : "Spondanus and many others say, the saint was

contrary, we must infer that Paul did not understand the Lycaonian dialect (Acts 14 : 11–14), and we learn from early ecclesiastical tradition that Peter used Mark as an interpreter (ἑρμηνεύς or ἑρμηνευτής, *interpres*, according to Papias, Irenæus, and Tertullian). God does not supersede by miracle the learning of foreign languages and other kinds of knowledge which can be attained by the ordinary use of our mental faculties and opportunities.

(f) It was a *temporary* speaking in foreign languages confined to the day of Pentecost and passing away with the flame-like tongues. The exception was justified by the object, namely, to attest the divine mission of the apostles and to foreshadow the universalness of the gospel. This view is taken by most modern commentators who accept the account of Luke, as Olshausen (who combines with it the theory b), Baumgarten, Thiersch, Rossteuscher, Lechler, Hackett, Gloag, Plumptre (in his *Com. on Acts*), and myself (in *H. Ap. Ch.*), and accords best with the plain sense of the narrative. But it likewise makes an essential distinction between the Pentecostal and the Corinthian glossolalia, which is extremely improbable. A temporary endowment with the knowledge of foreign languages unknown before is as great if not a greater miracle than a permanent endowment, and was just as superfluous at that time in Jerusalem as afterwards at Corinth ; for the missionary sermon of Peter, which was in one language only, was intelligible to all.

(g) The Pentecostal glossolalia was essentially the same as the Corinthian glossolalia, namely, an act of worship, and not of teaching ; with only a slight difference in the medium of interpretation : it was at once internally interpreted and applied by the Holy Spirit himself to those hearers who believed and were converted, to each in his own vernacular dialect ; while in Corinth the interpretation was made either by the speaker in tongues, or by one endowed with the gift of interpretation.

I can find no authority for this theory, and therefore suggest it with modesty, but it seems to me to avoid most of the difficulties of the other theories, and it brings Luke into harmony with himself and with Paul. It is certain that the Holy Spirit moved the hearts of the hearers as well

honored with the gift of tongues, and that, preaching *in his own*, he was understood by men of different languages ; which is also affirmed by Lanzano, who says, that Greeks, Germans, Sardes, Hungarians, and people of other nations, declared they understood every word he spoke, though he preached *in Latin*, or *in his mother-tongue*, as spoken at Valentia." This account clearly implies that Ferrer did *not* understand Greek, German, and Hungarian. As to Francis Xavier (d. 1552), Alban Butler says (sub Dec. 3) that the gift of tongues was " a *transient* favor," and that he learned the Malabar tongue and the Japanese " by unwearied application ; " from which we may infer that his impression upon the heathen was independent of the language. Not one of these saints claimed the gift of tongues or other miraculous powers, but only their disciples or later writers.

as the tongues of the speakers on that first day of the new creation in Christ. In a natural form the Pentecostal heteroglossolalia is continued in the preaching of the gospel in all tongues, and in more than three hundred translations of the Bible.

II. FALSE INTERPRETATIONS OF THE PENTECOSTAL MIRACLE.

(1) The older rationalistic interpretation resolves the wind into a thunderstorm or a hurricane surcharged with electricity, the tongues of fire into flashes of lightning falling into the assembly, or electric sparks from a sultry atmosphere, and the glossolalia into a praying of each in his own vernacular, instead of the sacred old Hebrew, or assumes that some of the disciples knew several foreign dialects before and used them on the occasion. So Paulus, Thiess, Schulthess, Kuinöl, Schrader, Fritzsche, substantially also Renan, who dwells on the violence of Oriental thunderstorms, but explains the glossolalia differently, according to analogous phenomena of later times. This view makes the wonder of the spectators and hearers at such an ordinary occurrence a miracle. It robs them of common sense, or charges dishonesty on the narrator. It is entirely inapplicable to the glossolalia in Corinth, which must certainly be admitted as an historical phenomenon of frequent occurrence in the apostolic church. It is contradicted by the comparative ὥσπερ and ὡσεί of the narrative, which distinguishes the sound from ordinary wind and the tongues of flame from ordinary fire; just as the words, "like a dove," to which all the Gospels compare the appearance of the Holy Spirit at Christ's baptism, indicate that no real dove is intended.

(2) The modern rationalistic or mythical theory resolves the miracle into a subjective vision which was mistaken by the early Christians for an objective external fact. The glossolalia of Pentecost (not that in Corinth, which is acknowledged as historical) symbolizes the true idea of the universalness of the gospel and the Messianic unification of languages and nationalities (εἶς λαὸς Κυρίου καὶ γλῶσσα μία, as the Testament of the Twelve Patriarchs expresses it). It is an imitation of the rabbinical fiction (found already in Philo) that the Sinaitic legislation was proclaimed through the *bath-kol*, the echo of the voice of God, to all nations in the seventy languages of the world. So Zeller (*Contents and Origin of the Acts*, I. 203-205), who thinks that the whole pentecostal fact, if it occurred at all, "must have been distorted beyond recognition in our record." But his chief argument is " the impossibility and incredibility of miracles," which he declares (p. 175, note) to be "an axiom" of the historian; thus acknowledging the negative presupposition or philosophical prejudice which underlies his historical criticism. We hold, on the contrary, that the historian must accept the facts as he finds them, and if he cannot explain them satisfactorily from natural causes or subjective illusions, he must trace them to supernatural forces. Now the Christian church, which is certainly a most palpable and undeniable fact,

must have originated in a certain place, at a certain time, and in a certain manner, and we can imagine no more appropriate and satisfactory account of its origin than that given by Luke. Baur and Zeller think it impossible that three thousand persons should have been converted in one day and in one place. They forget that the majority of the hearers were no skeptics, but believers in a supernatural revelation, and needed only to be convinced that Jesus of Nazareth was the promised Messiah. Ewald says against Zeller, without naming him (VI. 119): "Nothing can be more perverse than to deny the historical truth of the event related in Acts 2." We hold with Rothe (*Vorlesungen über Kirchengeschichte* I. 33) that the Pentecostal event was a real miracle (*"ein eigentliches Wunder"*), which the Holy Spirit wrought on the disciples and which endowed them with the power to perform miracles (according to the promise, Mark 16 : 17, 18). Without these miraculous powers Christianity could not have taken hold on the world as it then stood. The Christian church itself, with its daily experiences of regeneration and conversion at home and in heathen lands, is the best living and omnipresent proof of its supernatural origin.

III. TIME and PLACE of Pentecost. Did it occur on a Lord's Day (the eighth after Easter), or on a Jewish Sabbath? In a private house, or in the temple? We decide for the Lord's Day, and for a private house. But opinions are much divided, and the arguments almost equally balanced.

(1) The choice of the *day* in the week depends partly on the interpretation of "the morrow after the (Passover) Sabbath" from which the fiftieth day was to be counted, according to the legislative prescription in Lev. 23 : 11, 15, 16—namely, whether it was the morrow following the *first day* of the Passover, i. e. the 16th of Nisan, or the day after the *regular Sabbath* in the Passover week; partly on the date of Christ's crucifixion, which took place on a Friday, namely, whether this was the 14th or 15th of Nisan. If we assume that the Friday of Christ's death was the 14th of Nisan, then the 15th was a Sabbath, and Pentecost in that year fell on a *Sunday;* but if the Friday of the crucifixion was the 15th of Nisan (as I hold myself, see ₰ 16, p. 133), then Pentecost fell on a Jewish *Sabbath* (so Wieseler, who fixes it on Saturday, May 27, A.D. 30), unless we count from the *end* of the 16th of Nisan (as Wordsworth and Plumptre do, who put Pentecost on a Sunday). But if we take the "Sabbath" in Lev. 23 in the usual sense of the weekly Sabbath (as the Sadducees and Karaites did), then the Jewish Pentecost fell *always* on a *Sunday.* At all events the Christian church has uniformly observed Whit-Sunday on the eighth Lord's Day after Easter, adhering in this case, as well as in the festivals of the resurrection (Sunday) and of the ascension (Thursday), to the old tradition as to the *day* of the *week* when the event occurred. This view would furnish an additional reason for

the substitution of Sunday, as the day of the Lord's resurrection and the descent of the Holy Spirit, for the Jewish Sabbath.   Wordsworth : "Thus the first day of the week has been consecrated to all the three Persons of the ever-blessed and undivided Trinity ; and the blessings of Creation, Redemption, and Sanctification are commemorated on the Christian Sunday." Wieseler assumes, without good reason, that the ancient church deliberately changed the day from opposition to the Jewish Sabbath ; but the celebration of Pentecost together with that of the Resurrection seems to be as old as the Christian church and has its precedent in the example of Paul, Acts 18 : 21 ; 20 : 16.—Lightfoot (*Horæ Hebr. in Acta Ap.* 2 : 1 ; *Opera* II. 692) counts Pentecost from the 16th of Nisan, but nevertheless puts the first Christian Pentecost on a Sunday by an unusual and questionable interpretation of Acts 2 : 1 ἐν τῷ συνπληροῦσθαι τὴν ἡμέραν τῆς Πεντηκοστῆς, which he makes to mean " when the day of Pentecost was *fully gone,*" instead of "*was fully come.*"   But whether Pentecost fell on a Jewish Sabbath or on a Lord's Day, the coincidence in either case was significant.

(2) As to the *place*, Luke calls it simply a " house" (οἶκος, 2 : 2), which can hardly mean the temple (not mentioned till ver. 46).   It was probably the same " upper room " or chamber which he had mentioned in the preceding chapter, as the well known usual meeting place of the disciples after the ascension, τὸ ὑπερῷον . . . οὗ ἦσαν καταμένοντες, 1 : 13).   So Neander, Meyer, Ewald, Wordsworth, Plumptre, Farrar, and others. Perhaps it was the same chamber in which our Lord partook of the Paschal Supper with them (Mark 14 : 14, 15 ; Matt. 26 : 28).   Tradition locates both events in the " Cœnaculum," a room in an irregular building called "David's Tomb," which lies outside of Zion Gate some distance from Mt. Moriah.   (See William M. Thomson, *The Land and the Book,* new ed. 1880, vol. I. p. 535 sq.)   But Cyril of Jerusalem (*Catech.* XVI. 4) states that the apartment where the Holy Spirit descended was afterwards converted into a church.   The uppermost room under the flat roof of Oriental houses (ὑπερῷον, עֲלִיָּה) was often used as a place of devotion (comp. Acts 20 : 8).   But as a private house could not possibly hold so great a multitude, we must suppose that Peter addressed the people in the street from the roof or from the outer staircase.

Many of the older divines, as also Olshausen, Baumgarten, Wieseler, Lange, Thiersch (and myself in first ed. of *Ap. Ch.,* p. 194), locate the Pentecostal scene in the temple, or rather in one of the thirty side buildings around it, which Josephus calls " houses " (οἴκους) in his description of Solomon's temple (*Ant.* VIII. 3, 2), or in Solomon's porch, which remained from the first temple, and where the disciples assembled afterwards (Acts 5 : 12, comp. 3 : 11).   In favor of this view may be said, that it better agrees with the custom of the apostles (Luke 24 : 53 ; Acts 2 : 46 ; 5 : 12, 42), with the time of the miracle (the morning hour of prayer), and with the assembling of a large multitude of at least three thousand hearers, and also that it seems to give additional solemnity to the event when it took place in the symbolical and typical sanctuary of the old dispensation. But it is difficult to conceive that the hostile Jews should have allowed the poor disciples to occupy one of those temple buildings and not interfered with the scene. In the dispensation of the Spirit which now began, the meanest dwelling, and the body of the humblest Christian becomes a temple of God. Comp. John 4 : 24.

IV. EFFECTS of the Day of Pentecost. From Farrar's *Life and Work of St. Paul* (I. 93) : " That this first Pentecost marked an eternal moment in the destiny of mankind, no reader of history will surely deny. Undoubtedly in every age since then the sons of God have, to an extent unknown before, been taught by the Spirit of God. Undoubtedly since then, to an extent unrealized before, we may know that the Spirit of Christ dwelleth in us. Undoubtedly we may enjoy a nearer sense of union with God in Christ than was accorded to the saints of the Old Dispensation, and a thankful certainty that we see the days which kings and prophets desired to see and did not see them, and hear the truths which they desired to hear and did not hear them. And this New Dispensation began henceforth in all its fulness. It was no exclusive consecration to a separated priesthood, no isolated endowment of a narrow apostolate. It was the consecration of a whole church—its men, its women, its children—to be all of them 'a chosen generation, a royal priesthood, a holy nation, a peculiar people ;' it was an endowment, of which the full free offer was meant ultimately to be extended to all mankind. Each one of that hundred and twenty was not the exceptional recipient of a blessing and witness of a revelation, but the forerunner and representative of myriads more. And this miracle was not merely transient, but is continuously renewed. It is not a rushing sound and gleaming light, seen perhaps for a moment, but it is a living energy and an unceasing inspiration. It is not a visible symbol to a gathered handful of human souls in the upper room of a Jewish house, but a vivifying wind which shall henceforth breathe in all ages of the world's history ; a tide of light which is rolling, and shall roll, from shore to shore until the earth is full of the knowledge of the Lord as the waters cover the sea."

§ 25. *The Church of Jerusalem and the Labors of Peter.*

Σὺ εἶ Πέτρος, καὶ ἐπὶ ταύτῃ τῇ πέτρᾳ οἰκοδομήσω μου τὴν ἐκκλησίαν, καὶ πύλαι ᾅδου οὐ κατισχύσουσιν αὐτῆς.—Matt. 16 : 18.

Literature.

I. *Genuine* sources : Acts, chs. 2 to 12 ; Gal. ch. 2 ; and two Epistles of Peter.

Comp. the Commentaries on Acts, and the Petrine Epistles.

Among the commentators of Peter's Epp. I mention Archbishop
LEIGHTON (in many editions, not critical, but devout and spiritual),
STEIGER (1832, translated by Fairbairn, 1836), JOHN BROWN (1849,
2 vols.), WIESINGER (1856 and 1862, in Olshausen's *Com.*), SCHOTT
(1861 and 1863), DE WETTE (3d ed. by Brückner, 1865), HUTHER (in
Meyer's *Com.*, 4th ed. 1877), FRONMÜLLER (in Lange's *Bibelwerk*,
transl. by Mombert, 1867), ALFORD (3d ed. 1864), JOHN LILLIE (ed.
by Schaff, 1869), DEMAREST (*Cath. Epp.* 1879), MASON and PLUMMER
(in Ellicott's *Com.*, 1879), PLUMPTRE (in the "Cambridge Bible," 1879,
with a very full introduction, pp. 1–83), SALMOND (in Schaff's *Pop.
Com.* 1883). Comp. also the corresponding sections in the works on
the Apostolic Age mentioned in § 20, and my *H. Ap. Ch.* pp. 348–377.

II. *Apocryphal* sources : Εὐαγγέλιον κατὰ Πέτρον, of Ebionite origin,
Κήρυγμα Πέτρου, Πράξεις Πέτρου, Ἀποκάλυψις Πέτρου, Περίοδοι Πέτρου
(*Itinerarium Petri*), Πράξεις τῶν ἁγίων ἀποστόλων Πέτρου καὶ Παύλου
(*Acta Petri et Pauli*). See Tischendorf's *Acta Apost. Apocr.* 1–39,
and Hilgenfeld's *Novum Testamentum extra canonem receptum* (1866),
IV. 52 sqq. The Pseudo-Clementine "Homilies" are a glorification
of Peter at the expense of Paul ; the "Recognitions" are a Catholic
recension and modification of the "Homilies." The pseudo-Clementine literature will be noticed in the second Period.

III. Special works on Peter :

E. TH. MAYERHOFF : *Historisch-Kritische Einleitung in die Petrinischen
Schriften.* Hamb. 1835.

WINDISCHMANN (R. C.) : *Vindiciæ Petrinæ.* Ratisb. 1836.

STENGLEIN (R. C.) : *Ueber den 25 jährigen Aufenthalt des heil. Petrus in
Rom.* In the "Tübinger Theol. Quartalschrift," 1840.

J. ELLENDORF : *Ist Petrus in Rom und Bischof der römischen Gemeinde
gewesen ?* Darmstadt, 1841. Transl. in the "Bibliotheca Sacra,"
Andover, 1858, No. 3. The author, a liberal R. Cath., comes to the
conclusion that Peter's presence in Rome can never be proven.

CARLO PASSAGLIA (Jesuit) : *De Prærogativis Beati Petri, Apostolorum
Principis.* Ratisbon, 1850.

THOMAS W. ALLIES (R. C.) : *St. Peter, his Name and his Office as set forth
in Holy Scripture.* London, 1852. Based upon the preceding work
of Father Passaglia.

BERNH. WEISS : *Der Petrinische Lehrbegriff.* Berlin, 1855. Comp. his
Bibl. Theol. des N. T., 3d ed. 1880, and his essay, *Die petrinische
Frage* in "Studien und Kritiken," 1865, pp. 619–657, 1866, pp. 255–
308, and 1873, pp. 539–546.

THOS. GREENWOOD : *Cathedra Petri.* Lond., vol. I. 1859, chs. I. and II.
pp. 1–50.

PERRONE (R. C.) : *S. Pietro in Roma.* Rome, 1864.

C. HOLSTEN (of the Tübingen School) : *Zum Evangelium des Paulus und
des Petrus.* Rostock, 1868.

R. A. LIPSIUS : *Die Quellen der röm. Petrussage.* Kiel, 1872. By the
same : *Chronologie der röm. Bischöfe.* Kiel, 1869. Lipsius examines carefully the heretical sources of the Roman Peter-legend, and
regards it as a fiction from beginning to end. A summary of his
view is given by

SAMUEL M. JACKSON : *Lipsius on the Roman Peter-Legend.* In the
"Presbyterian Quarterly and Princeton Review" (N. York) for 1876,
pp. 265 sqq.

G. VOLKMAR : *Die römische Papstmythe.* Zürich, 1873.

A. HILGENFELD : *Petrus in Rom und Johannes in Kleinasien.* In his
"Zeitschrift für wissenschaftliche Theol." for 1872. Also his *Einleitung in das N. T.*, 1875, pp. 618 sqq.

W. KRAFFT : *Petrus in Rom.* Bonn, 1877. In the "Theol. Arbeiten des
rhein. wissenschaftl. Predigervereins," III. 185–193.

JOH. FRIEDRICH (Old Cath.) : *Zur ältesten Gesch. des Primates in der
Kirche.* Bonn, 1879.

WILLIAM M. TAYLOR : *Peter the Apostle.* N. York, 1879.

The congregation of Jerusalem became the mother church of
Jewish Christianity, and thus of all Christendom. It grew both
inwardly and outwardly under the personal direction of the
apostles, chiefly of Peter, to whom the Lord had early assigned
a peculiar prominence in the work of building his visible church
on earth. The apostles were assisted by a number of presbyters,
and seven deacons or persons appointed to care for the poor and
the sick. But the Spirit moved in the whole congregation,
bound to no particular office. The preaching of the gospel, the
working of miracles in the name of Jesus, and the attractive
power of a holy walk in faith and love, were the instruments of
progress. The number of the Christians, or, as they at first
called themselves, disciples, believers, brethren, saints, soon rose
to five thousand. They continued steadfastly under the instruction and in the fellowship of the apostles, in the daily worship
of God and celebration of the holy Supper with their agapæ or
love-feasts. They felt themselves to be one family of God,
members of one body under one head, Jesus Christ; and this
fraternal unity expressed itself even in a voluntary community
of goods—an anticipation, as it were, of an ideal state at the
end of history, but without binding force upon any other con-

gregation. They adhered as closely to the temple worship and the Jewish observances as the new life admitted and as long as there was any hope of the conversion of Israel as a nation. They went daily to the temple to teach, as their Master had done, but held their devotional meetings in private houses.[1]

The addresses of Peter to the people and the Sanhedrin[2] are remarkable for their natural simplicity and adaptation. They are full of fire and vigor, yet full of wisdom and persuasion, and always to the point. More practical and effective sermons were never preached. They are testimonies of an eye-witness so timid a few weeks before, and now so bold and ready at any moment to suffer and die for the cause. They are an expansion of his confession that Jesus is the Christ the Son of the living God, the Saviour. He preached no subtle theological doctrines, but a few great facts and truths: the crucifixion and resurrection of Jesus the Messiah, already known to his hearers for his mighty signs and wonders, his exaltation to the right hand of Almighty God, the descent and power of the Holy Spirit, the fulfilment of prophecy, the approaching judgment and glorious restitution of all things, the paramount importance of conversion and faith in Jesus as the only name whereby we can be saved. There breathes in them an air of serene joy and certain triumph.

We can form no clear conception of this bridal season of the Christian church when no dust of earth soiled her shining garments, when she was wholly absorbed in the contemplation and love of her divine Lord, when he smiled down upon her from his throne in heaven, and added daily to the number of the saved. It was a continued Pentecost, it was paradise restored. "They did take their food with gladness and singleness of heart, praising God, and having favor with all the people."[3]

---

[1] Acts 2 : 46; 3 : 1; 5 : 42.

[2] Acts 2 : 14 sqq. ; 3 : 12 sqq. ; 5 : 29 sqq. ; 10 : 34 sqq. ; 11 : 5 sqq. ; 15 : 7 sqq.

[3] Acts 2 : 46, 47. Renan says, with reference to this period (*Les apôtres,* ch. v.), that in no literary work does the word "joy" so often occur as in the New Testament, and quotes 1 Thess. 1 : 6; 5 : 16; Rom. 14 : 17; 15 : 13; Gal. 5 : 22; Phil. 1 : 25; 3 : 1; 4 : 4; 1 John 1 : 4. Many other passages might be added.

Yet even in this primitive apostolic community inward corruption early appeared, and with it also the severity of discipline and self-purification, in the terrible sentence of Peter on
the hypocritical Ananias and Sapphira.

At first Christianity found favor with the people. Soon,
however, it had to encounter the same persecution as its divine
founder had undergone, but only, as before, to transform it into
a blessing and a means of growth.

The persecution was begun by the skeptical sect of the Sad
ducees, who took offence at the doctrine of the resurrection of
Christ, the centre of all the apostolic preaching.

When Stephen, one of the seven deacons of the church at
Jerusalem, a man full of faith and zeal, the forerunner of the
apostle Paul, boldly assailed the perverse and obstinate spirit of
Judaism, and declared the approaching downfall of the Mosaic
economy, the Pharisees made common cause with the Sadducees
against the gospel. Thus began the emancipation of Christianity from the temple-worship of Judaism, with which it had till
then remained at least outwardly connected. Stephen himself was
falsely accused of blaspheming Moses, and after a remarkable
address in his own defence, he was stoned by a mob (A.D. 37),
and thus became the worthy leader of the sacred host of martyrs,
whose blood was thenceforth to fertilize the soil of the church.
From the blood of his martyrdom soon sprang the great apostle
of the Gentiles, now his bitterest persecutor, and an eye-witness
of his heroism and of the glory of Christ in his dying face.[1]

The stoning of Stephen was the signal for a general persecution, and thus at the same time for the spread of Christianity
over all Palestine and the region around. And it was soon followed by the conversion of Cornelius of Cæsarea, which opened
the door for the mission to the Gentiles. In this important
event Peter likewise was the prominent actor.

[1] On Stephen comp. Thiersch: *De Stephani protomartyris oratione commen-
tatio exegetica*, Marb. 1849; Baur: *Paul*, ch. II.; my *Hist. of the Apost.
Church*, pp. 211 sqq.; and the commentaries of Meyer, Lechler, Hackett,
Wordsworth, Plumptre, Howson and Spence, on Acts, chs. 6 and 7.

After some seven years of repose the church at Jerusalem suffered a new persecution under king Herod Agrippa (A.D. 44). James the elder, the brother of John, was beheaded. Peter was imprisoned and condemned to the same fate; but he was miraculously liberated, and then forsook Jerusalem, leaving the church to the care of James the "brother of the Lord." Eusebius, Jerome, and the Roman Catholic historians assume that he went at that early period to Rome, at least on a temporary visit, if not for permanent residence. But the book of Acts (12 : 17) says only : "He departed, and went *into another place*." The indefiniteness of this expression, in connection with a remark of Paul, 1 Cor. 9 : 5, is best explained on the supposition that he had hereafter no settled home, but led the life of a travelling missionary like most of the apostles.

THE LATER LABORS OF PETER.

Afterwards we find Peter again in Jerusalem at the apostolic council (A.D. 50);[1] then at Antioch (51), where he came into temporary collision with Paul;[2] then upon missionary tours, accompanied by his wife (57);[3] perhaps among the dispersed Jews in Babylon or in Asia Minor, to whom he addressed his epistles.[4] Of a residence of Peter in Rome the New Testament contains no trace, unless, as the church fathers and many modern expositors think, Rome is intended by the mystic "Babylon" mentioned in 1 Pet. 5 : 13 (as in the Apocalypse), but others think of Babylon on the Euphrates, and still others of Babylon on the Nile (near the present Cairo, according to the Coptic tradition). The entire silence of the Acts of the Apostles, in ch. 28, respecting Peter, as well as the silence of Paul in his epistle to the Romans, and the epistles written from Rome during his imprisonment there, in which Peter is not once named in the salutations, is decisive proof that he was absent from that city during most of the time between the years 58 and 63. A casual visit before 58 is possible, but extremely doubtful, in view of

---

[1] A.D. 50 : Acts ch. 15.
[2] Gal. 2 : 11 sqq.
[3] 1 Cor. 9 : 5.
[4] 1 Pet. 1 : 1.

the fact that Paul labored independently and never built on the foundation of others;[1] hence he would probably not have written his epistle to the Romans at all, certainly not without some allusion to Peter if he had been in any proper sense the founder of the church of Rome. After the year 63 we have no data from the New Testament, as the Acts close with that year, and the interpretation of " Babylon " at the end of the first Epistle of Peter is doubtful, though probably meant for Rome. The martyrdom of Peter by crucifixion was predicted by our Lord, John 21 : 18, 19, but no place is mentioned.

We conclude then that Peter's presence in Rome before 63 is made extremely doubtful, if not impossible, by the silence of Luke and Paul, when speaking of Rome and writing from Rome, and that his presence after 63 can neither be proved nor disproved from the New Testament, and must be decided by post-biblical testimonies.

It is the uniform tradition of the eastern and western churches that Peter preached the gospel in Rome, and suffered martyrdom there in the Neronian persecution. So say more or less clearly, yet not without admixture of error, Clement of Rome (who mentions the martyrdom, but not the place), at the close of the first century ; Ignatius of Antioch (indistinctly), Dionysius of Corinth, Irenæus of Lyons, Caius of Rome, in the second century ; Clement of Alexandria, Origen, Hippolytus, Tertullian, in the third; Lactantius, Eusebius, Jerome, and others, in the fourth. To these patristic testimonies may be added the apocryphal testimonies of the pseudo-Petrine and pseudo-Clementine fictions, which somehow connect Peter's name with the founding of the churches of Antioch, Alexandria, Corinth, and Rome. However these testimonies from various men and countries may differ in particular circumstances, they can only be accounted for on the supposition of some fact at the bottom; for they were previous to any use or abuse of this tradition for heretical or for orthodox and hierarchical purposes.

---

[1] Rom. 15 : 20; 2 Cor. 10 : 16.

The chief error of the witnesses from Dionysius and Irenæus onward is that Peter is associated with Paul as "founder" of the church of Rome; but this may be explained from the very *probable* fact that some of the "strangers from Rome" who witnessed the Pentecostal miracle and heard the sermon of Peter, as also some disciples who were scattered abroad by the persecution after the martyrdom of Stephen, carried the seed of the gospel to Rome, and that these converts of Peter became the real founders of the Jewish-Christian congregation in the metropolis. Thus the indirect agency of Peter was naturally changed into a direct agency by tradition which forgot the names of the pupils in the glorification of the teacher.

The time of Peter's arrival in Rome, and the length of his residence there, cannot possibly be ascertained. The abovementioned silence of the Acts and of Paul's Epistles allows him only a short period of labor there, after 63. The Roman tradition of a twenty or twenty-five years' episcopate of Peter in Rome is unquestionably a colossal chronological mistake.[1] Nor can we fix the year of his martyrdom, except that it must have taken place after July, 64, when the Neronian persecution broke out (according to Tacitus). It is variously assigned to every year between 64 and 69. We shall return to it again below, and in connection with the martyrdom of Paul, with which it is associated in tradition.[2]

---

[1] Alzog (§ 48), and other modern Roman church historians try to reconcile the tradition with the silence of the Scripture by assuming two visits of Peter to Rome with a great interval.

[2] For particulars see my *H. Ap. Ch.* pp. 362–372. The presence of Peter in Rome was the universal belief of Christendom till the Reformation, and is so still in the Roman Catholic communion. It was denied first in the interest of orthodox Protestantism against Romanism by U. Velenus (1520), M. Flacius (1554), Blondel (1641), Salmasius (1645), and especially by Fr. Spanheim (*De ficta Profectione Petri in urbem Romam*, Lugd. B. 1679); more recently in the interest of historical criticism by Baur (in special essays, 1831 and 1836, and in his work on *Paul*, ch. IX.), K. Hase (1862, doubtful in the 10th ed. of his *Kirchengesch.* 1877, p. 34), Mayerhoff, De Wette, Greenwood (1856), Lipsius (1869), Volkmar (1873), Zeller (1876). Volkmar denies even the martyrdom of Paul, and fancies that he died quietly in a villa near Rome. Zeller (in Hilgenfeld's "Zeitschrift," for 1876, p. 46 sq.) was disposed to sub-

§ 26. THE PETER OF HISTORY AND THE PETER OF FICTION.

No character in the New Testament is brought before us in such life-like colors, with all his virtues and faults, as that of Peter. He was frank and transparent, and always gave himself as he was, without any reserve. We may distinguish three stages in his development. In the Gospels, the human nature of Simon appears most prominent : the Acts unfold the divine mission of Peter in the founding of the church, with a temporary relapse at Antioch (recorded by Paul); in his Epistles we see the complete triumph of divine grace. He was the strongest and the weakest of the Twelve. He had all the excellences and all the defects of a sanguine temperament. He was kind-hearted, quick, ardent, hopeful,

stitute " James " for the defective name " Peter " in the testimony of Clemens Rom., *Ad Cor.* c. 5, but this is now set aside by the edition of Bryennios from a more complete manuscript, which clearly reads Πέτρον ὃς in full. On the other hand the presence and martyrdom of Peter in Rome is affirmed not only by all the Roman Catholic, but also by many eminent Protestant historians and critics, as Bleek, Credner, Olshausen, Gieseler, Neander, Niedner, Rothe, Thiersch, Krafft, Ewald, Plumptre, and even by Hilgenfeld, who justly remarks (*Einleitung in das N. T.* 1875 p. 624): "*Man kann ein guter Protestant sein, wenn man den Märtyrertod des Petrus in Rom festhält.*" Renan (in an appendix to his *L'Antechrist*, 551 sqq.) likewise asserts that Peter came to Rome, though not before 63, and was among the victims of the Neronian persecution in 64, whom Tacitus describes as *crucibus affixi.* He understands " Babylon," 1 Pet. 5 : 13, of Rome, according to the secret style of the Christians of those days.

In February, 1872, after the downfall of the temporal power of the papacy, a disputation was held in Rome between Protestant ministers (Gavazzi, Sciarelli, and Ribetto) and Roman divines (Guidi, and Canon Fabiani) on Peter's presence in that city ; the former denying, the latter affirming it. The disputation was published in several languages, and although destitute of critical value, it derives a sort of historical significance from the place where it was held, within a short distance from the residence of Pius IX., the first infallible pope. See *Racconto autentico della disputa,* etc., Roma, 1872 ; *Authentic Report of the Discussion held in Rome, February 9 and 10, 1872, between Catholic Priests and Evangelical Ministers, concerning the Coming of St. Peter to Rome. Translated by William Arthur,* London, 1872 ; and *Römische Disputation zwischen Katholiken und Protestanten über die These : War Petrus in Rom ? Nach den stenographischen Berichten. Deutsche Ausg.* Münster, 1872. Comp. the review of Lipsius in the " Jahrbücher für Protest. Theologie," 1876, Heft 4.

impulsive, changeable, and apt to run from one extreme to another. He received from Christ the highest praise and the severest censure. He was the first to confess him as the Messiah of God, for which he received his new name of Peter, in prophetic anticipation of his commanding position in church history; but he was also the first to dissuade him from entering the path of the cross to the crown, for which he brought upon himself the rebuke, " Get thee behind me, Satan." The rock of the church had become a rock of offence and a stumbling-block. He protested, in presumptive modesty, when Christ would wash his feet; and then, suddenly changing his mind, he wished not his feet only, but his hands and head to be washed. He cut off the ear of Malchus in carnal zeal for his Master; and in a few minutes afterwards he forsook him and fled. He solemnly promised to be faithful to Christ, though all should forsake him ; and yet in the same night he betrayed him thrice. He was the first to cast off the Jewish prejudices against the unclean heathen and to fraternize with the Gentile converts at Cæsarea and at Antioch ; and he was the first to withdraw from them in cowardly fear of the narrow-minded Judaizers from Jerusalem, for which inconsistency he had to submit to a humiliating rebuke of Paul.[1]

---

[1] The old legend of Peter's flight from the Mamertine prison in Rome, which seems to antedate the hierarchical glorification of Peter, would prove that his " consistent inconsistency " overtook him once more at the close of his life. A few days before his execution, it is said, he bribed the jailor and escaped from prison, but when he reached a spot outside the Porta San Sebastiano, now marked by a chapel, the Lord appeared to him with a cross, and Peter asked in surprise : " Lord, whither goest thou (*Domine quo vadis*) ? " Jesus replied : " I go to Rome to be crucified again (*venio Romam iterum crucifigi*)." The disciple returned deeply humbled, and delivered himself to the jailor to be crucified head-downwards. The footprint of the Lord is still shown (or was shown in 1841, when I saw it) in the little chapel called " Domine quo vadis," and a rude fresco on the wall represents the encounter. The legend is first alluded to by Origen (quoting from the Πράξεις Παύλου or Πέτρου, the words of the Saviour : Ἄνωθεν μέλλω σταυρωϑῆναι, see *Opera* IV. 332, and Hilgenfeld, *l. c.* IV. 72), then fully told in the apocryphal *Acts of Peter and Paul*, c. 82 (Tischendorf, *l. c.* p. 36, where Peter asks, Κύριε, ποῦ πορεύῃ ; and the Lord answers : ἐν Ῥώμῃ ἀπέρχομαι σταυρωϑῆναι), and by Ambrose in *Sermo de basilicis non tradendis hæreticis contra Auxentium* (quoted by Lipsius, *Petrus-Sage*, p. 134 sq.).

But Peter was as quick in returning to his right position as in turning away from it. He most sincerely loved the Lord from the start and had no rest nor peace till he found forgiveness. With all his weakness he was a noble, generous soul, and of the greatest service in the church. God overruled his very sins and inconsistencies for his humiliation and spiritual progress. And in his Epistles we find the mature result of the work of purification, a spirit most humble, meek, gentle, tender, loving, and lovely. Almost every word and incident in the gospel history connected with Peter left its impress upon his Epistles in the way of humble or thankful reminiscence and allusion. His new name, " Rock," appears simply as a " stone " among other living stones in the temple of God, built upon Christ, " the chief corner-stone." [1] His charge to his fellow-presbyters is the same which Christ gave to him after the resurrection, that they should be faithful " shepherds of the flock " under Christ, the chief " shepherd and bishop of their souls." [2] The record of his denial of Christ is as prominent in all the four Gospels, as Paul's persecution of the church is in the Acts, and it is most prominent—as it would seem under his own direction—in the Gospel of his pupil and " interpreter" Mark, which alone mentions the two cock-crows, thus doubling the guilt of the denial, [3] and which records Christ's words of censure (" Satan "), but omits Christ's praise (" Rock "). [4] Peter made as little effort to conceal his great sin, as Paul. It served as a thorn in his flesh, and the remembrance kept him near the cross ; while his recovery from the fall was a standing proof of

[1] 1 Pet. 2 : 4–8. A striking instance of the impression of Christ's word without a trace of boastfulness and assumption of authority.

[2] 1 Pet. 5 : 2 ; 2 : 25 ; comp. John 21 : 15–17.

[3] Mark 14 : 72. " And straightway the second time the cock crew. And Peter called to mind the word how that Jesus said unto him, Before the cock crow twice, thou shalt deny me thrice (comp. ver. 30) ; and when he thought thereon he wept."

[4] Comp. Mark 8 : 27–33 with Matt. 16 : 13–23. The omission of the famous passage, " Thou art Rock," etc., can only be satisfactorily explained from the humility of Peter. An enemy or rival might have omitted them, but Mark was his faithful pupil, and would have mentioned them had he followed his own impulse, or had he been a papist.

the power and mercy of Christ and a perpetual call to gratitude. To the Christian Church the double story of Peter's denial and recovery has been ever since an unfailing source of warning and comfort. Having turned again to his Lord, who prayed for him that his personal faith fail not, he is still strengthening the brethren.[1]

As to his official position in the church, Peter stood from the beginning at the head of the Jewish apostles, not in a partisan sense, but in a large-hearted spirit of moderation and comprehension. He never was a narrow, contracted, exclusive sectarian. After the vision at Joppa and the conversion of Cornelius he promptly changed his inherited view of the necessity of circumcision, and openly professed the change at Jerusalem, proclaiming the broad principle " that God is no respecter of persons, but in every nation he that feareth him and worketh righteousness is acceptable to him ; " and " that Jews and Gentiles alike are saved only through the grace of the Lord Jesus Christ." [2] He continued to be the head of the Jewish Christian church at large, and Paul himself represents him as the first among the three " pillar "-apostles of the circumcision.[3] But he stood mediating between James, who represented the right wing of conservatism, and Paul, who commanded the left wing of the apostolic army. And this is precisely the position which Peter occupies in his Epistles, which reproduce to a great extent the teaching of both Paul and James, and have therefore the character of a doctrinal Irenicum ; as the Acts are a historical Irenicum, without violation of truth or fact.

The Peter of Fiction.

No character of the Bible, we may say, no personage in all history, has been so much magnified, misrepresented and mis-

---

[1] Luke 22 : 31, 32, spoken in view of the approaching denial. This is the proper meaning of the passage which has been distorted by the Vatican Council into an argument for papal infallibility. Such application would logically imply also that every pope must deny Christ, and be converted in order to strengthen the brethren.

[2] Acts 10 : 34, 35 ; 15 : 11.

[3] Gal. 2 : 8, 9 ; comp. 1 : 18 ; 1 Cor. 15 : 5.

used for doctrinal and hierarchical ends as the plain fisherman of Galilee who stands at the head of the apostolic college. Among the women of the Bible the Virgin Mary has undergone a similar transformation for purposes of devotion, and raised to the dignity of the queen of heaven. Peter as the Vicar of Christ, and Mary as the mother of Christ, have in this idealized shape become and are still the ruling powers in the polity and worship of the largest branch of Christendom.

In both cases the work of fiction began among the Judaizing heretical sects of the second and third centuries, but was modified and carried forward by the Catholic, especially the Roman church, in the third and fourth centuries.

1. *The Peter of the Ebionite fiction.* The historical basis is Peter's encounter with Simon Magus in Samaria,[1] Paul's rebuke of Peter at Antioch,[2] and the intense distrust and dislike of the Judaizing party to Paul.[3] These three undoubted facts, together with a singular confusion of *Simon Magus* with an old Sabine deity, *Semo Sancus*, in Rome,[4] furnished the material and prompted the motive to religious tendency-novels written about and after the middle of the second century by ingenious semi-Gnostic Ebionites, either anonymously or under the fictitious

---

[1] Acts 8 : 9–24. It is quite probable that in the description of the heretics in his second Epistle, Peter had in mind Simon Magus. Plumptre (*l. c.* p. 44) sees in the "great swelling words of vanity," 2 Pet. 2 : 18, an allusion to Simon's boast that he was "the Great Power of God" (Acts 8 : 9, 10), and in the words "having eyes full of an *adulteress*," etc. 2 Pet. 2 : 12–14, an allusion to Helena, the mistress of Simon, who is said to have accompanied him.

[2] Gal. 2 : 11–14.

[3] This is clear from the Epistles of Paul, especially the Galatians and Corinthians, and from the 21st ch. of Acts.

[4] Justin Martyr (*Apol.* I. c. 26 and 56) reports that Simon Magus went to Rome under Claudius and received divine honors there, as was shown by a statue erected to him on an island in the Tiber. Such a statue was actually discovered in 1574, but with the inscription *Semoni Sanco Deo Fidio sacrum*, [not *Simoni Deo sancto*]. With reference to this supposed worship, Simon boasts in the pseudo-Clementine *Recogn.* II. 9 : "*Adorabor ut deus, publicis divinis donabor honoribus, ita ut simulacrum mihi statuentes tanquam deum colant et adorent.*"

name of Clement of Rome, the reputed successor of Peter.[1]
In these productions Simon Peter appears as the great apostle of truth in conflict with Simon Magus, the pseudo-apostle
of falsehood, the father of all heresies, the Samaritan possessed by a demon; and Peter follows him step by step from
Cæsarea Stratonis to Tyre, Sidon, Berytus, Antioch, and Rome,
and before the tribunal of Nero, disputing with him, and
refuting his errors, until at last the impostor, in the daring
act of mocking Christ's ascension to heaven, meets a miserable
end.

In the pseudo-Clementine Homilies the name of Simon represents among other heresies also the free gospel of Paul, who is
assailed as a false apostle and hated rebel against the authority
of the Mosaic law. The same charges which the Judaizers
brought against Paul, are here brought by Peter against Simon
Magus, especially the assertion that one may be saved by grace
alone. His boasted vision of Christ by which he professed to
have been converted, is traced to a deceptive vision of the
devil. The very words of Paul against Peter at Antioch, that
he was "self-condemned" (Gal. 2 : 11), are quoted as an accusation against God. In one word, Simon Magus is, in part at
least, a malignant Judaizing caricature of the apostle of the
Gentiles.

2. *The Peter of the Papacy.* The orthodox version of the
Peter-legend, as we find it partly in patristic notices of Irenæus,
Origen, Tertullian, and Eusebius, partly in apocryphal produc-

---

[1] The chief of these productions are the twenty Greek pseudo-Clementine
Homilies, which are based upon the older Κήρυγμα Πέτρου and other Jewish-
Christian documents. See the ed. of Dressel : *Clementis Romani quæ ferun-
tur Homiliæ viginti nunc prinum integræ*, Gött. 1853 (429 pages), and of De
Lagarde, *Clementina*, 1865. The Clementine literature has been thoroughly
investigated by Baur, Hilgenfeld, Ritschl, Schliemann, Uhlhorn, Volkmar,
and Lipsius. See a brief résumé in Baur's *Kirchengesch.* vol. I. 85–94. Baur
first tried to prove the identity of Simon Magus with Paul, in his essay on
the *Christuspartei in der Korinthischen Gemeinde*, Tübingen, 1831. But Simon
is a more comprehensive representative of all anti-Jewish and Gnostic heresies, especially that of Marcion. If he were meant to represent Paul alone, the
author would not have retained the historic features from Acts, ch. 8, which
are entirely irreconcilable with Paul's well known history.

tions,[1] retains the general story of a conflict of Peter with Simon
Magus in Antioch and Rome, but extracts from it its anti-Pauline poison, associates Paul at the end of his life with Peter as
the joint, though secondary, founder of the Roman church, and
honors both with the martyr's crown in the Neronian persecution on the same day (the 29th of June), and in the same year
or a year apart, but in different localities and in a different manner.[2] Peter was crucified like his Master (though head-downwards[3]), either on the hill of Janiculum (where the church S.
Pietro in Montorio stands), or more probably on the Vatican hill
(the scene of the Neronian circus and persecution);[4] Paul, being
a Roman citizen, was beheaded on the Ostian way at the Three
Fountains (Tre Fontane), outside of the city. They even walked
together a part of the Appian way to the place of execution.
Caius (or Gaius), a Roman presbyter at the close of the second
century, pointed to their monuments or trophies[5] on the Vatican, and in the via Ostia. The solemn burial of the remains of
Peter in the catacombs of San Sebastiano, and of Paul on the Via
Ostia, took place June 29, 258, according to the Kalendarium of
the Roman church from the time of Liberius. A hundred

---

[1] Such as the lost Κήρυγμα Πέτρου ἐν Ῥώμῃ, and the *Prædicatio Pauli* (probably one book), used by Clement of Alexandria ; the Syriac *Sermon of Peter in
Rome* (in Curston's "Ancient Syriac Doc.," Lond. 1864) ; the *Acta Pauli*, used
by Origen and Eusebius ; the *Acts of Peter and Paul*, of a later date, published by Thilo and Tischendorf. The last book has a conciliatory tendency,
like the canonical Acts. Comp. Lipsius, *l. c.* pp. 47 sqq., and the fragments
collected by Hilgenfeld, *l. c.* IV. 52 sqq.

[2] The month is given in the *Acta Petri et Pauli* at the close: Ἐτελειώθησαν
οἱ ἅγιοι ἔνδοξοι ἀπόστολοι Πέτρος καὶ Παῦλος μηνὶ Ἰουνίῳ κθ. But different MSS.
give July second or eighth. See Tischendorf, *l. c.* p. 39. According to Prudentius (*Hymn.* 12) the two apostles suffered on the same day, but a year
apart :
"*Unus utrumque dies, pleno tamen innovatus anno,
Vidit superba morte laureatum.*"

[3] A bishop of the Vatican Council used this as an argument for papal absolutism and infallibility, inasmuch as Peter's head supported his body, and not
the body the head !

[4] Baronius, *Ad ann.* 69 (in Theiner's ed. vol. I. 594 sq.) reconciles this difference by making the Janiculum and the Vatican one hill extending to the
Milvian bridge.

[5] τροπαῖα, Euseb. *H. E.* II. 25.

years later the remains of Peter were permanently transferred
to the Basilica of St. Peter on the Vatican, those of St. Paul to
the Basilica of St. Paul (San Paolo fuori le mura) outside of
the Porta Ostiensis (now Porta San Paolo).[1]

The tradition of a twenty-five years' episcopate in Rome (preceded by a seven years' episcopate in Antioch) cannot be traced
beyond the fourth century (Jerome), and arose, as already remarked, from chronological miscalculations in connection with
the questionable statement of Justin Martyr concerning the arrival of Simon Magus in Rome under the reign of Claudius (41–
54). The "Catalogus Liberianus," the oldest list of popes
(supposed to have been written before 366), extends the pontificate of Peter to 25 years, 1 month, 9 days, and puts his death
on June 29, 65 (during the consulate of Nerva and Vestinus),
which would date his arrival in Rome back to A.D. 40. Eusebius, in his Greek Chronicle as far as it is preserved, does not
fix the number of years, but says, in his Church History, that
Peter came to Rome in the reign of Claudius to preach against
the pestilential errors of Simon Magus.[2] The Armenian translation of his Chronicle mentions "twenty" years;[3] Jerome, in
his translation or paraphrase rather, "twenty-five" years, assuming, without warrant, that Peter left Jerusalem for Antioch and
Rome in the second year of Claudius (42; but Acts 12:17
would rather point to the year 44), and died in the fourteenth
or last year of Nero (68).[4] Among modern Roman Catholic

---

[1] See Lipsius, *l. c.* pp. 96 sqq., and his *Chronologie der röm. Päpste*, pp.
49 sqq.

[2] *Hist. Eccl.* II. 14. His statement is merely an inference from Justin Martyr s story about Simon Magus, which he quotes in ch. 13. But Justin M.
says nothing about Simon Peter in that connection.

[3] " *Petrus apostolus, cum primum Antiochenam ecclesiam fundasset, Romanorum urbem proficiscitur, ibique evangelium prædicat, et commoratur illic antistes
ecclesiæ annis* VIGINTI."

[4] *Chr.*, ad ann. 44 : " *Petrus . . . cum primum Antiochenam ecclesiam fundasset, Romam proficiscitur, ubi evangelium prædicans* 25 *annis ejusdem urbis
episcopus perseverat.*" In *De viris illustr.* cap. I., Jerome omits Antioch and
says : " *Simon Petrus . . . secundo Claudii imperatoris anno, ad expugnandum
Simonem Magum, Romam pergit, ibique* VIGINTI QUINQUE *annis Cathedram
Sacerdotalem tenuit, usque ad* ULTIMUM *annum Neronis, id est, decimum quar-*

historians there is no agreement as to the year of Peter's martyrdom: Baronius puts it in 69;[1] Pagi and Alban Butler in 65; Möhler, Gams, and Alzog indefinitely between 66 and 68. In all these cases it must be assumed that the Neronian persecution was continued or renewed after 64, of which we have no historical evidence. It must also be assumed that Peter was conspicuously absent from his flock during most of the time, to superintend the churches in Asia Minor and in Syria, to preside at the Council of Jerusalem, to meet with Paul in Antioch, to travel about with his wife, and that he made very little impression there till 58, and even till 63, when Paul, writing to and from Rome, still entirely ignores him. Thus a chronological error is made to overrule stubborn facts. The famous saying that " no pope shall see the (twenty-five) years of Peter," which had hitherto almost the force of law, has been falsified by the thirty-two years' reign of the first infallible pope, Pius IX., who ruled from 1846 to 1878.

NOTE.—ON THE CLAIMS OF THE PAPACY.

On this tradition and on the indisputable preëminence of Peter in the Gospels and the Acts, especially the words of Christ to him after the great confession (Matt. 16 : 18), is built the colossal fabric of the papacy with all its amazing pretensions to be the legitimate succession of a permanent primacy of honor and supremacy of jurisdiction in the church of Christ, and—since 1870—with the additional claim of papal infallibility in all official utterances, doctrinal or moral. The validity of this claim requires three premises :

1. The presence of Peter in Rome. This may be admitted as an historical fact, and I for my part cannot believe it possible that such a rock-firm and world-wide structure as the papacy could rest on the sand of mere fraud and error. It is the underlying fact which gives to fiction its vitality, and error is dangerous in proportion to the amount of truth which it embodies. But the fact of Peter's presence in Rome, whether of one year or twenty-five, cannot be of such fundamental importance as the

---

tum. A quo et affixus cruci, martyrio coronatus est, capite ad terram verso, et in sublime pedibus elevatis: asserens se indignum qui sic crucifigeretur ut Dominus suus. "

[1] *Annal.* ad ann. 69. Tom. I. 590, comp. I. 272, ed. Theiner.

papacy assumes it to be : otherwise we would certainly have some allusion to it in the New Testament. Moreover, if Peter was in Rome, so was Paul, and shared with him on equal terms the apostolic supervision of the Roman congregation, as is very evident from his Epistle to the Romans.

2. The transferability of Peter's preëminence on a successor. This is derived by inference from the words of Christ : "Thou art Rock, and on this rock I will build my church, and the gates of Hades shall not prevail against it." [1] This passage, recorded only by Matthew, is the exegetical rock of Romanism, and more frequently quoted by popes and papists than any other passage of the Scriptures. But admitting the obvious reference of *petra* to *Peter*, the significance of this prophetic name evidently refers to the peculiar mission of Peter in laying the foundation of the church once and for all time to come. He fulfilled it on the day of Pentecost and in the conversion of Cornelius ; and in this pioneer work Peter can have no successor any more than St. Paul in the conversion of the Gentiles, and John in the consolidation of the two branches of the apostolic church.

3. The actual transfer of this prerogative of Peter—not upon the bishops of Jerusalem, or Antioch, where he undoubtedly resided—but upon the bishop of Rome, where he cannot be proven to have been from the New Testament. Of such a transfer history knows absolutely nothing. Clement, bishop of Rome, who first, about A.D. 95, makes mention of Peter's martyrdom, and Ignatius of Antioch, who a few years later alludes to Peter and Paul as exhorting the Romans, have not a word to say about the transfer. The very chronology and succession of the first popes is uncertain.

If the claims of the papacy cannot be proven from what we know of the historical Peter, there are, on the other hand, several undoubted facts in the real history of Peter which bear heavily upon those claims, namely :

1. That Peter was married, Matt. 8 : 14, took his wife with him on his missionary tours, 1 Cor. 9 : 5, and, according to a possible interpretation of the "coëlect" (sister), mentions her in his first Epistle (5 : 13). Patristic tradition ascribes to him children, or at least a daughter (Petronilla). His wife is said to have suffered martyrdom in Rome before him. What right have the popes, in view of this example, to forbid clerical

---

[1] Some Protestant writers press, in Matt. 16 : 18, the distinction between Πέτρος, *stone*, and πέτρα, *rock*, which disappears in the translations, but this does not apply to the Aramaic *Cepha*, which was used by Christ, comp. John 1 : 42 ; Gal. 2 : 9 ; 1 Cor. 1 : 12 ; 3 : 22 ; 9 : 5 ; 15 : 5 (and which, by the way, has analogies not only in Semitic but also in Aryan languages, as the Sanskrit *kap-ala*, the Greek κεφ-αλή, the Latin *cap-ut*, the German *Kopf* and *Gipfel*). On the interpretation of the famous passage in Matthew, see my annotations to Lange on *Matthew*, pp. 293 sqq., and my *H. Ap. Ch.*, pp. 351 sqq.

marriage? We pass by the equally striking contrast between the poverty of Peter, who had no silver nor gold (Acts 3 : 6) and the gorgeous display of the triple-crowned papacy in the middle ages and down to the recent collapse of the temporal power.

2. That in the Council at Jerusalem (Acts 15 : 1–11), Peter appears simply as the first speaker and debater, not as president and judge (James presided), and assumes no special prerogative, least of all an infallibility of judgment. According to the Vatican theory the whole question of circumcision ought to have been submitted to Peter rather than to a Council, and the decision ought to have gone out from him rather than from "the apostles and elders, brethren" (or "the elder brethren," ver. 23).

3. That Peter was openly rebuked for inconsistency by a younger apostle at Antioch (Gal. 2 : 11–14). Peter's conduct on that occasion is irreconcilable with his infallibility as to discipline; Paul's conduct is irreconcilable with Peter's alleged supremacy; and the whole scene, though perfectly plain, is so inconvenient to Roman and Romanizing views, that it has been variously distorted by patristic and Jesuit commentators, even into a theatrical farce gotten up by the apostles for the more effectual refutation of the Judaizers!

4. That, while the greatest of popes, from Leo I. down to Leo XIII. never cease to speak of their authority over all the bishops and all the churches, Peter, in his speeches in the Acts, never does so. And his Epistles, far from assuming any superiority over his "fellow-elders" and over "the clergy" (by which he means the Christian people), breathe the spirit of the sincerest humility and contain a prophetic warning against the besetting sins of the papacy, filthy avarice and lordly ambition (1 Pet. 5 : 1–3). Love of money and love of power are twin-sisters, and either of them is "a root of all evil."

It is certainly very significant that the weaknesses even more than the virtues of the natural Peter—his boldness and presumption, his dread of the cross, his love for secular glory, his carnal zeal, his use of the sword, his sleepiness in Gethsemane—are faithfully reproduced in the history of the papacy; while the addresses and epistles of the converted and inspired Peter contain the most emphatic protest against the hierarchical pretensions and worldly vices of the papacy, and enjoin truly evangelical principles—the general priesthood and royalty of believers, apostolic poverty before the rich temple, obedience to God rather than man, yet with proper regard for the civil authorities, honorable marriage, condemnation of mental reservation in Ananias and Sapphira, and of simony in Simon Magus, liberal appreciation of heathen piety in Cornelius, opposition to the yoke of legal bondage, salvation in no other name but that of Jesus Christ.

§ 27.   *James, the Brother of the Lord.*

'Η πίστις χωρὶς ἔργων νεκρά ἐστιν.—James 2 : 26.

SOURCES.

I. Genuine sources : Acts 12 : 17 ; 15 : 13 ; 21 : 18 ; 1 Cor. 15 : 7 ; Gal. 1 : 19 ; 2 : 9, 12.   Comp. James "the brother of the Lord," Matt. 13 : 55 ; Mark 6 : 3 ; Gal. 1 : 19. The Epistle of James.

II. Post-apostolic : JOSEPHUS : *Ant.* XX. 9, 1.—HEGESIPPUS in Euseb. *Hist. Ecc.* II. ch. 23.—JEROME : *Catal. vir. ill.* c. 2, under "Jacobus." EPIPHANIUS, *Hær.* XXIX. 4 ; XXX. 16 ; LXXVIII. 13 sq.

III. Apocryphal : *Protevangelium Jacobi,* ed. in Greek by *Tischendorf,* in "Evangelia Apocrypha," pp. 1–49, comp. the Prolegg. pp. xii–xxv.   James is honorably mentioned in several other apocryphal Gospels.—Epiphanius, *Hær.* XXX. 16, alludes to an Ebionite and strongly anti-Pauline book, the *Ascents of James* ('Αναβαᾳμοὶ 'Ιακώβου), descriptions of his ascension to heaven, which are lost.—*The Liturgy of James,* ed. by *W. Trollope,* Edinb. 1848.   Composed in the third century, after the Council of Nicæa (as it contains the terms ὁμοούσιος and ᾳεοτόκος), but resting on some older traditions.   It was intended for the church of Jerusalem, which is styled "the mother of all churches."   It is still used once a year on the festival of St. James, Oct. 23, in the Greek Church at Jerusalem.   (See vol. II. 527 sqq.)

EXEGETICAL AND DOCTRINAL.

Commentaries on *the Epistle of James* by HERDER (1775), STORR (1784), GEBSER (1828), SCHNECKENBURGER (1832), THEILE (1833), KERN (1838), DE WETTE (1849, 3d ed. by BRÜCKNER, 1865), CELLERIER (1850), WIESINGER (in Olshausen's *Com.*, 1854), STIER (1845), HUTHER and BEYSCHLAG (in Meyer's *Com.*, 1858, 4th ed. 1882), LANGE and VAN OOSTERZEE (in Lange's *Bibelwerk,* 1862, Engl. transl. enlarged by MOMBERT, 1867), ALFORD, WORDSWORTH, BASSETT (1876, ascribes the Ep. to James of Zebedee), PLUMPTRE (in the Cambridge series, 1878), PUNCHARD (in Ellicott's *Com.* 1878), ERDMANN (1882), GLOAG (1883). WOLDEMAR G. SCHMIDT : *Der Lehrgehalt des Jakobusbriefes.* Leipzig, 1869.

W. BEYSCHLAG : *Der Jakobusbrief als urchristliches Geschichtsdenkmal.* In the "Stud. u. Kritiken," 1874, No. 1, pp. 105–166. See his *Com.* Comp. also the expositions of the doctrinal type of James in NEANDER, SCHMID, SCHAFF, WEISS (pp. 176–194, third ed.).

HISTORICAL AND CRITICAL.

BLOM : *De* τοῖς ἀδελφοῖς *et* ταῖς ἀδελφαῖς τοῦ Κυρίου. Leyden, 1839.   (I have not seen this tract, which advocates the brother-theory.   Lightfoot says of it : "Blom gives the most satisfactory statement of the patristic authorities, and Schaff discusses the scriptural arguments most carefully.")

SCHAFF : *Jakobus Alphäi, und Jakobus der Bruder des Herrn.* Berlin, 1842 (101 pages).

MILL : *The Accounts of our Lord's Brethren in the New Test. vindicated.* Cambridge, 1843. (Advocates the cousin-theory of the Latin church.)

LIGHTFOOT : *The Brethren of the Lord.* Excursus in his *Com. on Galatians.* Lond. 2d ed. 1866, pp. 247–282. (The ablest defence of the step-brother-theory of the Greek Church.)

H. HOLTZMANN : *Jakobus der Gerechte und seine Namensbrüder*, in Hilgenfeld's "Zeitschrift für wissenschaftl. Theol." Leipz. 1880, No. 2.

Next to Peter, who was the œcumenical leader of Jewish Christianity, stands JAMES, THE BROTHER OF THE LORD (also called by post-apostolic writers "James the Just," and "Bishop of Jerusalem"), as the local head of the oldest church and the leader of the most conservative portion of Jewish Christianity. He seems to have taken the place of James the son of Zebedee, after his martyrdom, A.D. 44. He became, with Peter and John, one of the three "pillars" of the church of the circumcision. And after the departure of Peter from Jerusalem James presided over the mother church of Christendom until his death. Though not one of the Twelve, he enjoyed, owing to his relationship to our Lord and his commanding piety, almost apostolic authority, especially in Judæa and among the Jewish converts.[1] On one occasion even Peter yielded to his influence or that of his representatives, and was misled into his uncharitable conduct towards the Gentile brethren.[2]

James was not a believer before the resurrection of our Lord. He was the oldest of the four "brethren" (James, Joseph, Judas, Simon), of whom John reports with touching sadness : "Even his brethren did not believe in him."[3] It was one of the early and constant trials of our Lord in the days of his humiliation that he was without honor among his fellow-townsmen, yea,

---

[1] On his relation to the Twelve and to Jesus, see the first note at the end of this section.

[2] Gal. 2 : 12.

[3] Mark 6 : 3 ; Matt. 13 : 55 ; John 7 : 5.

"among his own kin, and in his own house."[1] James was no doubt imbued with the temporal and carnal Messianic misconceptions of the Jews, and impatient at the delay and unworldliness of his divine brother. Hence the taunting and almost disrespectful language: "Depart hence and go into Judæa . . . . If thou doest these things, manifest thyself to the world." The crucifixion could only deepen his doubt and sadness.

But a special personal appearance of the risen Lord brought about his conversion, as also that of his brothers, who after the resurrection appear in the company of the apostles.[2] This turning-point in his life is briefly but significantly alluded to by Paul, who himself was converted by a personal appearance of Christ.[3] It is more fully reported in an interesting fragment of the "Gospel according to the Hebrews" (one of the oldest and least fabulous of the apocryphal Gospels), which shows the sincerity and earnestness of James even before his conversion.[4] He had sworn, we are here told, "that he would not eat bread from that hour wherein the Lord had drunk the cup [of his passion][5] until he should see him rising from the dead." The Lord appeared to him and communed with him, giving bread to James the Just and saying: "My brother, eat thy bread, for the Son of man is risen from them that sleep."

---

[1] Mark 6 : 4 ; Matt. 13 : 57 ; Luke 4 : 24 ; John 4 : 44.

[2] Acts 1 : 13 ; comp. 1 Cor. 9 : 5.

[3] 1 Cor. 15 : 7 : ἔπειτα ὤφθη Ἰακώβῳ.

[4] The fragment is preserved by Jerome, De vir. ill. cap. 2. Comp. Hilgenfeld, Nov. Test. extra can. rec. IV. 17 and 29 ; and Nicholson, The Gospel according to the Hebrews (1879), pp. 63 sqq.

[5] I follow here with Credner and Lightfoot the reading Dominus for Domini, corresponding to the Greek translation, which reads ὁ κύριος, and with the context, which points to the Lord's death rather than the Lord's Supper as the starting-point of the vow. See Lightfoot, Ep. to the Gal., p. 266. If we read "hora qua biberat calicem DOMINI," the author of the Gospel of the Hebrews must have assumed either that James was one with James of Alphæus, or that the Lord's Supper was not confined to the twelve apostles. Neither of these is probable. James is immediately afterwards called "the Just." Gregory of Tours (Histor. Francorum, I. 21), relating this story, adds, in accordance with the Greek tradition : "Hic est Jacobus Justus, quem fratrem Domini nuncupant, pro eo quod Josephi fuerit filius ex alia uxore progenitus." See Nicholson, p. 64.

In the Acts and in the Epistle to the Galatians, James appears as the most conservative of the Jewish converts, at the head of the extreme right wing ; yet recognizing Paul as the apostle of the Gentiles, giving him the right hand of fellowship, as Paul himself reports, and unwilling to impose upon the Gentile Christians the yoke of circumcision. He must therefore not be identified with the heretical Judaizers (the forerunners of the Ebionites), who hated and opposed Paul, and made circumcision a condition of justification and church membership. He presided at the Council of Jerusalem and proposed the compromise which saved a split in the church. He probably prepared the synodical letter which agrees with his style and has the same greeting formula peculiar to him.[1]

He was an honest, conscientious, eminently practical, conciliatory Jewish Christian saint, the right man in the right place and at the right time, although contracted in his mental vision as in his local sphere of labor.

From an incidental remark of Paul we may infer that James, like Peter and the other brothers of the Lord, was married.[2]

The mission of James was evidently to stand in the breach between the synagogue and the church, and to lead the disciples of Moses gently to Christ. He was the only man that could do it in that critical time of the approaching judgment of the holy city. As long as there was any hope of a conversion of the Jews as a nation, he prayed for it and made the transition as easy as possible. When that hope vanished his mission was fulfilled.

According to Josephus he was, at the instigation of the younger Ananus, the high priest, of the sect of the Sadducees, whom he calls "the most unmerciful of all the Jews in the execution of judgment," stoned to death with some others, as "breakers of the law," i. e. Christians, in the interval between the procuratorship of Festus and that of Albinus, that is, in the year 63.

---

[1] "Greeting," χαίρειν, Acts 15 : 23, and James 1 : 1, instead of the specific Christian χάρις καὶ εἰρήνη.

[2] 1 Cor. 9 : 5.

The Jewish historian adds that this act of injustice created great indignation among those most devoted to the law (the Pharisees), and that they induced Albinus and King Agrippa to depose Ananus (a son of the Annas mentioned in Luke 3 : 2 ; John 18 : 13). He thus furnishes an impartial testimony to the high standing of James even among the Jews.[1]

Hegesippus, a Jewish Christian historian about A.D. 170, puts the martyrdom a few years later, shortly before the destruction of Jerusalem (69).[2] He relates that James was first thrown down from the pinnacle of the temple by the Jews and then stoned to death. His last prayer was an echo of that of his brother and Lord on the cross : " God, Father, forgive them ; for they know not what they do."

The dramatic account of James by Hegesippus [3] is an over-drawn picture from the middle of the second century, colored by Judaizing traits which may have been derived from the " Ascents of James " and other apocryphal sources. He turns James into a Jewish priest and Nazarite saint (comp. his advice to Paul, Acts 21 : 23, 24), who drank no wine, ate no flesh, never shaved, nor took a bath, and wore only linen. But the biblical James is Pharisaic and legalistic rather than Essenic and ascetic. In the pseudo-Clementine writings, he is raised even above Peter as the head of the holy church of the Hebrews, as " the lord and bishop of bishops," as " the prince of priests." According to tradition, mentioned by Epiphanius. James, like St. John at Ephesus, wore the high-priestly petalon, or golden plate on the forehead, with the inscription : " Holiness to the Lord " (Ex. 28 : 36). And in the *Liturgy of St. James*, the brother of Jesus is raised to the dignity of " the brother of the very God " (ἀδελφόθεος). Legends gather around the memory of great

---

[1] Josephus calls James "the brother of Jesus *the so-called Christ*" (τὸν ἀδελφὸν Ἰησοῦ τοῦ λεγομένου Χριστοῦ, Ἰάκωβος ὄνομα αὐτῷ), but these words are regarded by some critics (Lardner, Credner, and others) as a Christian interpolation.

[2] Neander, Ewald, and Renan give the preference to the date of Josephus. But according to the pseudo-Clementine literature James survived Peter.

[3] See below, Note II.

men, and reveal the deep impression they made upon their
friends and followers. The character which shines through
these James-legends is that of a loyal, zealous, devout, consistent Hebrew Christian, who by his personal purity and holiness
secured the reverence and affection of all around him.

But we must carefully distinguish between the Jewish-Christian, yet orthodox, overestimate of James in the Eastern church,
as we find it in the fragments of Hegesippus and in the Liturgy of
St. James, and the heretical perversion of James into an enemy
of Paul and the gospel of freedom, as he appears in apocryphal
fictions. We have here the same phenomenon as in the case of
Peter and Paul. Every leading apostle has his apocryphal
shadow and caricature both in the primitive church and in the
modern critical reconstruction of its history. The name and
authority of James was abused by the Judaizing party in under-
mining the work of Paul, notwithstanding the fraternal agreement of the two at Jerusalem.[1] The Ebionites in the second
century continued this malignant assault upon the memory of
Paul under cover of the honored names of James and Peter;
while a certain class of modern critics (though usually from the
opposite ultra- or pseudo-Pauline point of view) endeavor to
prove the same antagonism from the Epistle of James (as far as
they admit it to be genuine at all).[2]

The Epistle in our canon, which purports to be written by
"James, a bond-servant of God and of Jesus Christ, to the twelve
tribes of the dispersion," though not generally acknowledged at
the time of Eusebius and Jerome, has strong internal evidence
of genuineness. It precisely suits the character and position of
the historical James as we know him from Paul and the Acts,

---

[1] Gal. 2 : 12. How far the unnamed messengers of James from Jerusalem,
who intimidated Peter and Barnabas at Antioch, acted under authority from
James, does not appear; but it is certain from ver. 9, as well as from the
Acts, that James recognized the peculiar divine grace and success of Paul and
Barnabas in the conversion of the Gentiles; he could therefore not without
gross inconsistency make common cause with his adversaries.

[2] Even Luther, in an unguarded moment (1524), called the epistle of James
an "epistle of straw," because he could not harmonize it with Paul's doctrine
of justification by faith.

and differs widely from the apocryphal James of the Ebionite fictions.[1] It hails undoubtedly from Jerusalem, the theocratic metropolis, amid the scenery of Palestine. The Christian communities appear not as churches, but as synagogues, consisting mostly of poor people, oppressed and persecuted by the rich and powerful Jews. There is no trace of Gentile Christians or of any controversy between them and the Jewish Christians. The Epistle was perhaps a companion to the original Gospel of Matthew for the Hebrews, as the first Epistle of John was such a companion to his Gospel. It is probably the oldest of the epistles of the New Testament.[2] It represents, at all events, the earliest and meagerest, yet an eminently practical and necessary type of Christianity, with prophetic earnestness, proverbial sententiousness, great freshness, and in fine Greek. It is not dogmatic but ethical. It has a strong resemblance to the addresses of John the Baptist and the Lord's Sermon on the Mount, and also to the book of Ecclesiasticus and the Wisdom of Solomon.[3] It never attacks the Jews directly, but still less St. Paul, at least not his genuine doctrine. It characteristically calls the gospel the " perfect *law* of liberty," [4] thus connecting it very closely with the Mosaic dispensation, yet raising it by implica-

---

[1] Ewald (vi. 608) remarks that it is just such a letter as we may expect from the centre of Christianity in that period, when most Christians were poor and oppressed by rich Jews.

[2] The date of composition is as yet an unsolved problem, and critics vary between A.D. 45 and 62. Schneckenburger, Neander, Thiersch, Huther, Hofmann, Weiss, and Beyschlag, and among English divines, Alford, Bassett (who, however, wrongly vindicates the Epistle to James the son of Zebedee), and Plumptre assign it a very early date before the Council of Jerusalem (50) and the circumcision controversy, to which there is no allusion. On the other hand Lardner, De Wette, Wiesinger, Lange, Ewald, and also those commentators who see in the Epistle a polemical reference to Paul and his teaching, bring it down to 62. At all events, it was written before the destruction of Jerusalem, which would have been noticed by a later writer. The Tübingen school (Baur, Schwegler, Hilgenfeld) deny its genuineness and assign it to A.D. 80 or 90. Renan admits the genuineness of the Epistles of James and Jude, as counter-manifestoes of Jewish Christianity against Paulinism, and accounts for the good Greek style by the aid of a Greek secretary.

[3] See the lists of parallel passages in Plumptre, pp. 7–9 and 33.

[4] James 1 : 25. ὁ παρακύψας εἰς νόμον τέλειον τὸν τῆς ἐλευθερίας.

tion far above the *imperfect* law of *bondage*. The author has very little to say about Christ and the deeper mysteries of redemption, but evidently presupposes a knowledge of the gospel history, and reverently calls Christ "the Lord of glory," and himself humbly his "bond-servant."[1] He represents religion throughout in its practical aspect as an exhibition of faith by good works. He undoubtedly differs widely from Paul, yet does not contradict, but supplements him, and fills an important place in the Christian system of truth which comprehends all types of genuine piety. There are multitudes of sincere, earnest, and faithful Christian workers who never rise above the level of James to the sublime heights of Paul or John. The Christian church would never have given to the Epistle of James a place in the canon if she had felt that it was irreconcilable with the doctrine of Paul. Even the Lutheran church did not follow her great leader in his unfavorable judgment, but still retains James among the canonical books.

After the martyrdom of James he was succeeded by Symeon, a son of Clopas and a cousin of Jesus (and of James). He continued to guide the church at Jerusalem till the reign of Trajan, when he died a martyr at the great age of a hundred and twenty years.[2] The next thirteen bishops of Jerusalem, who came, however, in rapid succession, were likewise of Jewish descent.

Throughout this period the church of Jerusalem preserved its strongly Israelitish type, but joined with it "the genuine knowledge of Christ," and stood in communion with the Catholic church, from which the Ebionites, as heretical Jewish Christians, were excluded. After the line of the fifteen circumcised bishops had run out, and Jerusalem was a second time laid waste under Hadrian, the mass of the Jewish Christians gradually merged in the orthodox Greek Church.

---

[1] 2:1 ἔχετε τὴν πίστιν τοῦ κυρίου ἡμῶν Ἰησοῦ Χριστοῦ τῆς δόξης. In the inscription, 1 : 1, the Lord Jesus Christ is associated with God.

[2] Hegesippus *apud* Euseb. *H. E.* III., 11, 22, 32 ; IV., 5, 22. *Const. Apost.* VII. 46. Hegesippus assumes that Clopas, the father of Symeon, was a brother of Joseph and an uncle of Jesus. He never calls Symeon "brother of the Lord," but only James and Jude (II. 23 ; III. 20).

NOTES.

I. JAMES AND THE BROTHERS OF THE LORD.—There are three, perhaps four, eminent persons in the New Testament bearing the name of JAMES (abridged from JACOB, which from patriarchal memories was a more common name among the Jews than any other except Symeon or Simon, and Joseph or Joses) :

1. JAMES (the son) OF ZEBEDEE, the brother of John and one of the three favorite apostles, the proto-martyr among the Twelve (beheaded A.D. 44, see Acts 12 : 2), as his brother John was the survivor of all the apostles. They were called the "sons of thunder."

2. JAMES (the son) OF ALPHÆUS, who was likewise one of the Twelve, and is mentioned in the four apostle-catalogues, Matt. 10 : 3 ; Mark 3 : 10 ; Luke 6 : 15 ; Acts 1 : 13.

3. JAMES THE LITTLE, Mark 15 : 40 (ὁ μικρός, not "the Less," as in the E. V.), probably so called from his small stature (as Zacchæus, Luke 19 : 3), the son of a certain Mary and brother of Joseph, Matt. 27 : 56 (Μαρία ἡ τοῦ Ἰακώβου καὶ Ἰωσὴφ μήτηρ) ; Mark 15 : 40, 47 ; 16 : 1 ; Luke 24 : 10. He is usually identified with James the son of Alphæus, on the assumption that his mother Mary was the wife of Clopas, mentioned John 19 : 25, and that Clopas was the same person as Alphæus. But this identification is at least very problematical.

4. JAMES, simply so called, as the most distinguished after the early death of James the Elder, or with the honorable epithet BROTHER OF THE LORD (ὁ ἀδελφὸς τοῦ Κυρίου), and among post-apostolic writers, the JUST, also BISHOP OF JERUSALEM. The title connects him at once with the four brothers and the unnamed sisters of our Lord, who are repeatedly mentioned in the Gospels, and he as the first among them. Hence the complicated question of the nature of this relationship. Although I have fully discussed this intricate subject nearly forty years ago (1842) in the German essay above mentioned, and then again in my annotations to Lange on *Matthew* (Am. ed. 1864, pp. 256–260), I will briefly sum up once more the chief points with reference to the most recent discussions (of Lightfoot and Renan).

There are three theories on James and the brothers of Jesus. I would call them the *brother*-theory, the *half-brother*-theory, and the *cousin*-theory. Bishop Lightfoot (and Canon Farrar) calls them after their chief advocates, the *Helvidian* (an invidious designation), the *Epiphanian*, and the *Hieronymian* theories. The first is now confined to Protestants, the second is the Greek, the third the Roman view.

(1) The BROTHER-theory takes the term ἀδελφοί in the usual sense, and regards the brothers as younger children of Joseph and Mary, consequently as full brothers of Jesus in the eyes of the law and the opinion of the people, though really only half-brothers, in view of his supernatural conception. This is exegetically the most natural view and favored

by the meaning of ἀδελφός (especially when used as a standing designation), the constant companionship of these brethren with Mary (John 2 : 12 ; Matt. 12 : 46 ; 13 : 55), and by the obvious meaning of Matt. 1 : 25 (οὐκ ἐγίνωσκεν αὐτὴν ἕως οὗ, comp. 1 : 18 πρὶν ἢ συνελθεῖν αὐτούς), and Luke 2 : 7 (πρωτότοκος), as explained from the *standpoint of the evangelists*, who used these terms in full view of the *subsequent history* of Mary and Jesus. The only serious objection to it is of a doctrinal and ethical nature, viz., the assumed perpetual virginity of the mother of our Lord and Saviour, and the committal of her at the cross to John rather than her own sons and daughters (John 19 : 25). If it were not for these two obstacles the brother-theory would probably be adopted by every fair and honest exegete. The first of these objections dates from the post-apostolic ascetic overestimate of virginity, and cannot have been felt by Matthew and Luke, else they would have avoided those ambiguous terms just noticed. The second difficulty presses also on the other two theories, only in a less degree. It must therefore be solved on other grounds, namely, the profound spiritual sympathy and congeniality of John with Jesus and Mary, which rose above carnal relationships, the probable cousinship of John (based upon the proper interpretation of the same passage, John 19 : 25), and the unbelief of the real brethren at the time of the committal.

This theory was held by Tertullian (whom Jerome summarily disposes of as not being a "homo ecclesiæ," i. e. a schismatic), defended by Helvidius at Rome about 380 (violently attacked as a heretic by Jerome), and by several individuals and sects opposed to the incipient worship of the Virgin Mary ; and recently by the majority of German Protestant exegetes since Herder, such as Stier, De Wette, Meyer, Weiss, Ewald, Wieseler, Keim, also by Dean Alford, and Canon Farrar (*Life of Christ*, I. 97 sq.). I advocated the same theory in my German tract, but admitted afterwards in my *Hist. of Ap. Ch.*, p. 378, that I did not give sufficient weight to the second theory.

(2) The HALF-BROTHER-theory regards the brethren and sisters of Jesus as children of Joseph by a *former* wife, consequently as no blood-relations at all, but so designated simply as Joseph was called the father of Jesus, by an exceptional use of the term adapted to the exceptional fact of the miraculous incarnation. This has the dogmatic advantage of saving the perpetual virginity of the mother of our Lord and Saviour ; it lessens the moral difficulty implied in John 19 : 25 ; and it has a strong traditional support in the apocryphal Gospels and in the Eastern church. It also would seem to explain more easily the patronizing tone in which the brethren speak to our Lord in John 7 : 3, 4. But it does not so naturally account for the constant companionship of these brethren with Mary ; it assumes a former marriage of Joseph nowhere alluded to in the Gospels, and makes Joseph an old man and protector rather than husband of Mary ; and finally it is not free from suspicion of an ascetic bias, as being the first step towards the dogma of the perpetual virginity.

To these objections may be added, with Farrar, that if the brethren
had been elder sons of Joseph, Jesus would not have been regarded as
legal heir of the throne of David (Matt. 1 : 16 ; Luke 1 : 27 ; Rom. 1 : 3 ;
2 Tim. 2 : 8 ; Rev. 22 : 16).

This theory is found first in the apocryphal writings of James (the
Protevangelium Jacobi, the Ascents of James, etc.), and then among the
leading Greek fathers (Clement of Alexandria, Origen, Eusebius, Gregory
of Nyssa, Epiphanius, Cyril of Alexandria) ; it is embodied in the Greek,
Syrian, and Coptic services, which assign different dates to the commemoration of James the son of Alphæus (Oct. 9), and of James the
Lord's brother (Oct. 23).   It may therefore be called the theory of the
Eastern church.   It was also held by some Latin fathers before Jerome
(Hilary of Poitiers and Ambrose), and has recently been ably advocated
by Bishop Lightfoot (*l. c.*), followed by Dr. Plumptre (in the introduction to his *Com.* on the *Ep. of James*).

(3) The COUSIN-theory regards the brethren as more distant relatives,
namely, as children of Mary, the wife of Alphæus and sister of the Virgin Mary, and identifies James, the brother of the Lord, with James the
son of Alphæus and James the Little, thus making him (as well as also
Simon and Jude) an apostle.   The exceptive εἰ μή, Gal. 1 : 19 (but I
saw only James), does not prove this, but rather excludes James from
the apostles proper (comp. εἰ μή in Gal. 2 : 16 ; Luke 4 : 26, 27).

This theory was first advanced by Jerome in 383, in a youthful polemic
tract against Helvidius, without any traditional support,[1] but with the
professed dogmatic and ascetic aim to save the virginity of both *Mary* and
Joseph, and to reduce their marriage relation to a merely nominal and
barren connection.   In his later writings, however, after his residence in
Palestine, he treats the question with less confidence (see Lightfoot, p.
253).   By his authority and the still greater weight of St. Augustin, who
at first (394) wavered between the second and third theories, but afterwards
adopted that of Jerome, it became the established theory of the Latin
church and was embodied in the Western services, which acknowledge
only two saints by the name of James.   But it is the least tenable of all
and must be abandoned, chiefly for the following reasons :

(a) It contradicts the natural meaning of the word " brother," when
the New Testament has the proper term for cousin (ἀνεψιός, Col. 4 : 10,
comp. also συγγενής, Luke 2 : 44 ; 21 : 16 ; Mark 6 : 4, etc.), and the
obvious sense of the passages where the brothers and sisters of Jesus
appear as members of the holy family.

(b) It assumes that two sisters had the same name, Mary, which is
extremely improbable.

[1] The passage quoted from Papias · " *Maria Cleophæ sive Alphæi uxor, quæ
fuit mater Jacobi episcopi et apostoli,*" is taken from Jerome and belongs not to
the sub-apostolic Papias of Hierapolis (as has been supposed even by Mill and
Wordsworth), but to a mediæval Papias, the writer of an *Elementarium* or
Dictionary in the 11th century.   See Lightfoot, p. 265 sq.

(c) It assumes the identity of Clopas and Alphæus, which is equally doubtful; for Ἀλφαῖος is a Hebrew name (חלפי), while Κλωπᾶς, like Κλεόπας, Luke 24 : 18, is an abbreviation of the Greek Κλεόπατρος, as Antipas is contracted from Antipatros.

(d) It is absolutely irreconcilable with the fact that the brethren of Jesus, James among them, were before the resurrection unbelievers, John 7 : 5, and consequently none of them could have been an apostle, as this theory assumes of two or three.

RENAN'S theory.—I notice, in conclusion, an original combination of the second and third theories by Renan, who discusses the question of the brothers and cousins of Jesus in an appendix to his *Les évangiles*, 537–540. He assumes *four* Jameses, and distinguishes the son of Alphæus from the son of Clopas. He holds that Joseph was twice married, and that Jesus had several older brothers and cousins as follows :

1. Children of *Joseph* from the *first* marriage, and *older brothers* of Jesus :
    a. JAMES, the brother of the Lord, or Just, or Obliam. This is the one mentioned Matt. 13 : 55; Mark 6 : 3; Gal. 1 : 19; 2 : 9, 12; 1 Cor. 15 : 7; Acts 12 : 17, etc. ; James 1 : 1; Jude 1 : 1, and in Josephus and Hegesippus.
    b. JUDE, mentioned Matt. 13 : 55; Mark 6 : 3; Jude 1 : 1; Hegesippus in Eusebius' *Hist. Eccl.* III. 19, 20, 32. From him were descended those two grandsons, bishops of different churches, who were presented to the emperor Domitian as descendants of David and relations of Jesus. Hegesippus in Euseb. III. 19, 20, 32.
    c. Other sons and daughters unknown. Matt. 13 : 56; Mark 6 : 3 ; 1 Cor. 9 : 5.
2. Children of Joseph (?) from the marriage with *Mary* : JESUS.
3. Children of *Clopas*, and *cousins* of Jesus, probably from the father's side, since Clopas, according to Hegesippus, was a brother of Joseph, and may have married also a woman by the name of Mary (John 19 : 25).
    a. JAMES THE LITTLE (ὁ μικρός), so called to distinguish him from his older cousin of that name. Mentioned Matt. 27 : 56; Mark 15 : 40; 16 : 1; Luke 24 : 10; otherwise unknown.
    b. JOSES, Matt. 27 : 56; Mark 15 : 40, 47, but erroneously (?) numbered among the brothers of Jesus : Matt. 13 : 55 ; Mark 6 : 3; otherwise unknown.
    c. SYMEON, the second bishop of Jerusalem (Hegesippus in Eus. III. 11, 22, 32 ; IV. 5, 22), also erroneously (?) put among the brothers of Jesus by Matt. 13 : 55; Mark 6 : 3.
    d. Perhaps other sons and daughters unknown.

II. The description of James by Hegesippus (from Eusebius, *H. E.* II. 23). "Hegesippus also, who flourished nearest the days of the apostles, gives (in the fifth book of his *Memorials*) this most accurate account of him :

" 'Now James, the brother of the Lord, who (as there are many of this name) was surnamed the *Just* by all (ὁ ἀδελφὸς τοῦ Κυρίου ᾽Ιάκωβος, ὁ ὀνομασ3εὶς ὑπὸ πάντων δίκαιος), from the Lord's time even to our own, received the government of the church with (or from) the apostles [μετά, in conjunction with, or according to another reading, παρὰ τῶν ἀποστύλων, which would more clearly distinguish him from the apostles]. This man [οὗτος, not this *apostle*] was consecrated from his mother's womb. He drank neither wine nor strong drink, and abstained from animal food. No razor came upon his head, he never anointed himself with oil, and never used a bath [probably the luxury of the Roman bath, with its *sudatorium, frigidarium*, etc., but not excluding the usual ablutions practised by all devout Jews]. He alone was allowed to enter the sanctuary [not the holy of holies, but the court of priests]. He wore no woolen, but linen garments only. He was in the habit of entering the temple alone, and was often found upon his bended knees, and interceding for the forgiveness of the people ; so that his knees became as hard as a camel's, on account of his constant supplication and kneeling before God. And indeed, on account of his exceeding great piety, he was called the *Just* [Zaddik] and *Oblias* [δίκαιος καὶ ὠβλίας, probably a corruption of the Hebrew *Ophel am, Tower of the People*], which signifies justice and the bulwark of the people (περιοχὴ τοῦ λαοῦ) ; as the prophets declare concerning him. Some of the seven sects of the people, mentioned by me above in my *Memoirs*, used to ask him what was the door, [probably the estimate or doctrine] of Jesus? and he answered that he was the Saviour. And of these some believed that Jesus is the Christ. But the aforesaid sects did not believe either a resurrection, or that he was coming to give to every one according to his works ; as many, however, as did believe, did so on account of James. And when many of the rulers also believed, there arose a tumult among the Jews, Scribes, and Pharisees, saying that the whole people were in danger of looking for Jesus as the Messiah. They came therefore together, and said to James : We entreat thee, restrain the people, who are led astray after Jesus, as though he were the Christ. We entreat thee to persuade all that are coming to the feast of the Passover rightly concerning Jesus ; for we all have confidence in thee. For we and all the people bear thee testimony that thou art just, and art no respecter of persons. Persuade therefore the people not to be led astray by Jesus, for we and all the people have great confidence in thee. Stand therefore upon the pinnacle of the temple, that thou mayest be conspicuous on high, and thy words may be easily heard by all the people ; for all the tribes have come together on account of the Passover, with some of the Gentiles also.

The aforesaid Scribes and Pharisees, therefore, placed James upon the pinnacle of the temple, and cried out to him : "O thou just man, whom we ought all to believe, since the people are led astray after Jesus that was crucified, declare to us what is the door of Jesus that was crucified." And he answered with a loud voice : "Why do ye ask me respecting Jesus the Son of Man? He is now sitting in the heavens, on the right hand of the great Power, and is about to come on the clouds of heaven." And as many were confirmed, and gloried in this testimony of James, and said : "Hosanna to the Son of David," these same priests and Pharisees said to one another : "We have done badly in affording such testimony to Jesus, but let us go up and cast him down, that they may dread to believe in him." And they cried out : "Ho, ho, the Just himself is deceived." And they fulfilled that which is written in Isaiah, "Let us take away the Just, because he is offensive to us ; wherefore they shall eat the fruit of their doings." [Comp. Is. 3 : 10.]

And going up, they cast down the just man, saying to one another : "Let us stone James the Just." And they began to stone him, as he did not die immediately when cast down ; but turning round, he knelt down, saying : "I entreat thee, O Lord God and Father, forgive them, for they know not what they do." Thus they were stoning him, when one of the priests of the sons of Rechab, a son of the Rechabites, spoken of by Jeremiah the prophet (35 : 2), cried out, saying : "Cease, what are you doing? The Just is praying for you." And one of them, a fuller, beat out the brains of the Just with the club that he used to beat out clothes. Thus he suffered martyrdom, and they buried him on the spot where his tombstone is still remaining, by the temple. He became a faithful witness, both to the Jews and Greeks, that Jesus is the Christ. Immediately after this, Vespasian invaded and took Judæa.' "

"Such," adds Eusebius, "is the more ample testimony of Hegesippus, in which he fully coincides with Clement. So admirable a man indeed was James, and so celebrated among all for his justice, that even the wiser part of the Jews were of opinion that this was the cause of the immediate siege of Jerusalem, which happened to them for no other reason than the crime against him. Josephus also has not hesitated to superadd this testimony in his works : 'These things,' says he, 'happened to the Jews to avenge James the Just, who was the brother of him that is called Christ and whom the Jews had slain, notwithstanding his preeminent justice.' The same writer also relates his death, in the twentieth book of his *Antiquities*, in the following words,'" etc.

Then Eusebius gives the account of Josephus.

§ 28. *Preparation for the Mission to the Gentiles.*

The planting of the church among the Gentiles is mainly the work of Paul; but Providence prepared the way for it by several steps, before this apostle entered upon his sublime mission.

1. By the conversion of those half-Gentiles and bitter enemies of the Jews, the SAMARITANS, under the preaching and baptism of Philip the evangelist, one of the seven deacons of Jerusalem, and under the confirming instruction of the apostles Peter and and John. The gospel found ready entrance into Samaria, as had been prophetically hinted by the Lord in the conversation at Jacob's well.[1] But there we meet also the first heretical perversion of Christianity by Simon Magus, whose hypocrisy and attempt to degrade the gift of the Holy Spirit received from Peter a terrible rebuke. (Hence the term *simony*, for sordid traffic in church offices and dignities.) This encounter of the prince of the apostles with the arch-heretic was regarded in the ancient church, and fancifully represented, as typifying the relation of ecclesiastical orthodoxy to deceptive heresy.

2. Somewhat later (between 37 and 40) occurred the conversion of the noble centurion, CORNELIUS of Cæsarea, a pious proselyte of the gate, whom Peter, in consequence of a special revelation, received into the communion of the Christian church directly by baptism, without circumcision. This bold step the apostle had to vindicate to the strict Jewish Christians in Jerusalem, who thought circumcision a condition of salvation, and Judaism the only way to Christianity. Thus Peter laid the foundation also of the Gentile-Christian church. The event marked a revolution in Peter's mind, and his emancipation from the narrow prejudices of Judaism.[2]

---

[1] Acts, ch. 8; comp. John, ch. 4.

[2] Acts, chs. 10 and 11. The account which Peter gave to the brethren at Jerusalem was not a mere repetition of the facts related in ch. 10, but an apologetic adaptation to the peculiar wants of the audience. This has been well shown by Dean Howson in his Commentary on those two chapters (in Schaff's *Internat. Com.* vol. II.). Comp. my *Hist. of Ap. Ch.* 217 sqq.

3. Still more important was the rise, at about the same time, of the church at ANTIOCH, the capital of Syria. This congregation, formed under the influence of the Hellenist Barnabas of Cyprus and Paul of Tarsus, seems to have consisted from the first of converted heathens and Jews. It thus became the mother of Gentile Christendom, as Jerusalem was the mother and centre of Jewish. In Antioch, too, the name "Christian" first appeared, which was soon everywhere adopted, as well denoting the nature and mission as the followers of Christ, the divine-human prophet, priest, and king.[1]

The other and older designations were disciples (of Christ the only Master), believers (in Christ as their Saviour), brethren (as members of the same family of the redeemed, bound together by a love which springs not from earth and will never cease), and saints (as those who are purified and consecrated to the service of God and called to perfect holiness).

[1] Acts, 11 : 26 ; comp. 26 : 28, and 1 Pet. 4: 16

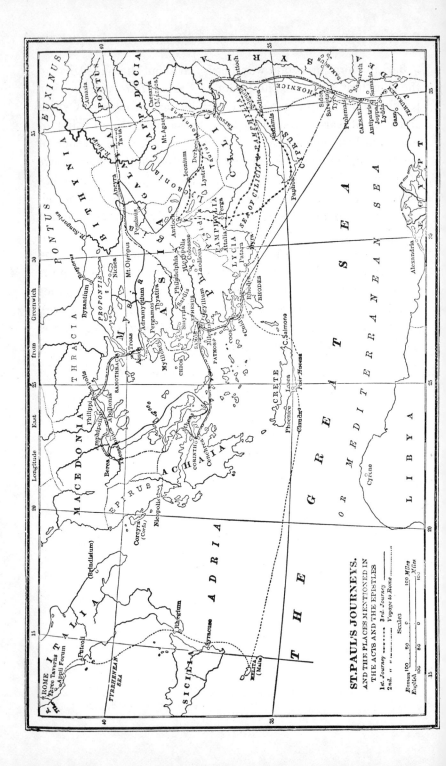

ST. PAUL'S JOURNEYS.

AND THE PLACES MENTIONED IN
THE ACTS AND THE EPISTLES

1st Journey ·········· 3rd Journey ——·——·——
2nd " " ——·——·—— Voyage to Rome ·········

Scales
Roman 100   50   0   100 Miles
English 100   50   0   100 Miles

CHAPTER V

ST. PAUL AND THE CONVERSION OF THE GENTILES.

Χάριτι θεοῦ εἰμὶ ὅ εἰμι, καὶ ἡ χάρις αὐτοῦ ἡ εἰς ἐμὲ οὐ κενὴ ἐγενήθη, ἀλλὰ περισσότερον αὐτῶν πάντων ἐκοπίασα, οὐκ ἐγὼ δὲ, ἀλλὰ ἡ χάρις τοῦ θεοῦ σὺν ἐμοί. —1 Cor. 15 : 10.

Χριστὸς Ἰησοῦς ἦλθεν εἰς τὸν κόσμον ἁμαρτωλοὺς σῶσαι, ὧν πρῶτός εἰμι ἐγώ.— 1 Tim. 1 : 15.

"Paul's mind was naturally and perfectly adapted to take up into itself and to develop the free, universal, and absolute principle of Christianity."— Dr. BAUR (*Paul*, II. 281, English translation).

"Did St. Paul's life end with his own life? . . . . May we not rather believe that in a sense higher than Chrysostom ever dreamt of [when he gave him the glorious name of 'the Heart of the world'], the pulses of that mighty heart are still the pulses of the world's life, still beat in these later ages with even greater force than ever?"—Dean STANLEY (*Sermons and Essays on the Apostolic Age*, p. 166).

§ 29. *Sources and Literature on St. Paul and his Work.*

I. SOURCES.

1. The *authentic* sources :

The EPISTLES OF PAUL, and the ACTS OF THE APOSTLES, ch. 9 : 1–30 ; and chs. 13 to 28. Of the Epistles of Paul the four most important— Galatians, Romans, two Corinthians—are universally acknowledged as genuine even by the most exacting critics ; the Philippians, Philemon, Colossians, and Ephesians are admitted by nearly all critics ; the Pastoral Epistles, especially First Timothy, and Titus, are more or less disputed, but even they bear the stamp of Paul's genius.

On the coincidences between the Acts and the Epistles see the section on the Acts. Comp. also § 22, pp. 213 sqq.

2. The *legendary* and *apocryphal* sources :

ACTA PAULI ET THECLÆ, edition in Greek by *E. Grabe* (from a Bodleian MS. in *Spicileg. SS. PP.*, Oxon. 1698, tom. I. pp. 95–128 ; republished by *Jones*, 1726), and by *Tischendorf* (from three Paris MSS.

in *Acta Apost. Apocrypha*, Lips. 1851); in Syriac, with an English version by *W. Wright* (in *Apocryphal Acts of the Apostles*, Lond. 1871); Engl. transl. by *Alex. Walker* (in Clark's "Ante-Nicene Christian Library," vol. XVI. 279 sqq.). Comp. C. SCHLAU : *Die Acten des Paulus und der Thecla und die ältere Thecla-Legende*, Leipz. 1877. The Acts of Paul and Thecla strongly advocate celibacy. They are probably of Gnostic origin and based on some local tradition. They were originally written, according to Tertullian (*De Bapt.* cap. 17, comp. Jerome, *Catal.* cap. 7), by a presbyter in Asia "out of love to Paul," and in support of the heretical opinion that women have the right to preach and to baptize after the example of Thecla; hence the author was deposed. The book was afterwards purged of its most obnoxious features and extensively used in the Catholic church. (See the patristic quotations in Tischendorf's *Prolegomena*, p. xxiv.) Thecla is represented as a noble virgin of Iconium, in Lycaonia, who was betrothed to Thamyris, converted by Paul in her seventeenth year, consecrated herself to perpetual virginity, was persecuted, carried to the stake, and thrown before wild beasts, but miraculously delivered, and died 90 years old at Seleucia. In the Greek church she is celebrated as the first female martyr. Paul is described at the beginning of this book (Tischend. p. 41) as "little in stature, bald-headed, bow-legged, well built (or vigorous), with knitted eye-brows, rather long-nosed, full of grace, appearing now as a man, and now having the face of an angel." From this description Renan has borrowed in part his fancy-sketch of Paul's personal appearance.

ACTA PAULI (Πράξεις Παύλου), used by Origen and ranked by Euse-bius with the Antilegomena (or νόθα rather). They are, like the *Acta Petri* (Πράξεις, or Περίοδοι Πέτρου), a Gnostic reconstruction of the canonical Acts and ascribed to the authorship of St. Linus. Preserved only in fragments.

ACTA PETRI ET PAULI. A Catholic adaptation of an Ebionite work. The Greek and Latin text was published first in a complete form by *Thilo*, Halle, 1837–'38, the Greek by *Tischendorf* (who collated six MSS.) in his *Acta Apost. Apoc.* 1851, 1–39; English transl. by *Walker* in "Ante-Nicene Libr.," XVI. 256 sqq. This book records the arrival of Paul in Rome, his meeting with Peter and Simon Magus, their trial before the tribunal of Nero, and the martyrdom of Peter by crucifixion, and of Paul by decapitation. The legend of *Domine quo vadis* is here recorded of Peter, and the story of Perpetua is interwoven with the martyrdom of Paul.

The pseudo-CLEMENTINE HOMILIES, of the middle of the second century or later, give a malignant Judaizing caricature of Paul under the disguise of Simon Magus (in part at least), and misrepresent him as an antinomian arch-heretic; while Peter, the proper hero of this romance, is glorified as the apostle of pure, primitive Christianity.

THE CORRESPONDENCE OF PAUL AND SENECA, mentioned by Jerome (*De vir. ill.* c. 12) and Augustin (*Ep. ad Maced.* 153, al. 54), and often copied, though with many variations, edited by Fabricius, *Cod. Apocr. N. T.*, and in several editions of Seneca. It consists of eight letters of Seneca and six of Paul. They are very poor in thought and style, full of errors of chronology and history, and undoubtedly a forgery. They arose from the correspondence of the moral maxims of Seneca with those of Paul, which is more apparent than real, and from the desire to recommend the Stoic philosopher to the esteem of the Christians, or to recommend Christianity to the students of Seneca and the Stoic philosophy. Paul was protected at Corinth by Seneca's brother, Gallio (Acts 18 : 12–16), and *might* have become acquainted with the philosopher who committed suicide at Rome in 65, but there is no trace of such acquaintance. Comp. AMÉDÉE FLEURY : *Saint-Paul et Sénèque* (Paris, 1853, 2 vols.); C. AUBERTIN : *Étude critique sur les rapports supposé entre Sénèque et Saint-Paul* (Par. 1887) ; F. C. BAUR : *Seneca und Paulus*, 1858 and 1876 ; REUSS : art. Seneca in Herzog, vol. XIV. 273 sqq. ; LIGHTFOOT : Excursus in *Com. on Philippians*, pp 268–331 ; art. Paul and Seneca, in "Westminster Review," Lond. 1880, pp. 309 sqq.

II. BIOGRAPHICAL AND CRITICAL.

Bishop PEARSON (d. 1686) : *Annales Paulini.* Lond. 1688. In the various editions of his works, and also separately : *Annals of St. Paul, transl. with geographical and critical notes.* Cambridge, 1825.

Lord LYTTLETON (d. 1773) : *The Conversion and Apostleship of St. Paul.* 3d ed. Lond. 1747. Apologetic as an argument for the truth of Christianity from the personal experience of the author.

Archdeacon WILLIAM PALEY (d. 1805) : *Horæ Paulinæ: or The Truth of the Scripture History of Paul evinced by a comparison of the Epistles which bear his name, with the Acts of the Apostles and with one another.* Lond. 1790 (and subsequent editions). Still valuable for apologetic purposes.

J. HEMSEN : *Der Apostel Paulus.* Gött. 1830.

CARL SCHRADER : *Der Apostel Paulus.* Leipz. 1830–'36 5 Parts. Rationalistic.

F. CHR. BAUR (d. 1860) : *Paulus, der Apostel Jesu Christi.* Tüb. 1845, second ed. by *E. Zeller*, Leipzig, 1866–'67, in 2 vols. Transl. into English by *Allan Menzies.* Lond. (Williams & Norgate) 1873 and '75, 2 vols. This work of the great leader of the philosophico-critical reconstruction of the Apostolic Age (we may call him the modern Marcion) was preceded by several special treatises on the Christ-Party in Corinth (1831), on the Pastoral Epistles (1835), on the

Epistle to the Romans (1836), and a Latin programme on Stephen's address before the Sanhedrin (1829). It marks an epoch in the literature on Paul and opened new avenues of research. It is the standard work of the Tübingen school of critics.

CONYBEARE and HOWSON : *The Life and Epistles of St. Paul.* Lond. 1853, 2 vols., and N. York, 1854 ; 2d ed. Lond. 1856, and later editions; also an abridgment in one vol. A very useful and popular work, especially on the geography of Paul's travels. Comp. also Dean HOWSON : *Character of St. Paul* (Lond. 1862 ; 2d ed. 1864) ; *Scenes from the Life of St. Paul* (1867) ; *Metaphors of St. Paul* (1868) ; *The Companions of St. Paul* (1871). Most of these books were republished in America.

AD. MONOD (d. 1856) : *Saint Paul.* Six sermons. See his *Sermons,* Paris, 1860, vol. II. 121–296. The same in German and English.

W. F. BESSER : *Paulus.* Leipz. 1861. English transl. by *F. Bultmann,* with Introduction by *J. S. Howson.* Lond. and N. York, 1864.

F. BUNGENER : *St. Paul, sa vie, son œuvre et ses épîtres.* Paris, 1865.

A. HAUSRATH : *Der Apostel Paulus.* Heidelb. 1865 ; 2d ed. 1872. Comp. also his *N. T.liche Zeitgeschichte,* Part III.

M. KRENKEL : *Paulus, der Apostel der Heiden.* Leipz. 1869.

ERNEST RENAN : *Saint Paul.* Paris, 1869. Transl. from the French by *J. Lockwood,* N. York, 1869. Very fresh and entertaining, but full of fancies and errors.

THOMAS LEWIN (author of "Fasti Sacri") : *The Life and Epistles of St. Paul,* new ed. Lond. and N. York, 1875, 2 vols. A magnificent work of many years' labor, with 370 illustrations.

Canon F. W. FARRAR : *The Life and Work of St. Paul.* Lond. and N. York, 1879, 2 vols. Learned and eloquent.

W. M. TAYLOR : *Paul as a Missionary.* N. York, 1881.

As biographies, the works of Conybeare and Howson, Lewin, and Farrar are the most complete and instructive.

Also the respective sections in the Histories of the Ap. Age by Neander, Lechler, Thiersch, Lange, Schaff (226–347 and 634–640), Pressensé.

III. CHRONOLOGICAL.

THOMAS LEWIN : *Fasti Sacri, a Key to the Chronology of the New Testament.* London, 1865. Chronological Tables from B.C. 70 to A.D. 70.

WIESELER : *Chronologie des apostolischen Zeitalters.* Göttingen, 1848.

IV. DOCTRINAL AND EXEGETICAL.

L. USTERI : *Entwicklung des Paulinischen Lehrbegriffs.* Zürich, 1824 ; 6th ed. 1851.

A. F. Dähne : *Entwicklung des Paulinischen Lehrbegriffs.* Halle, 1835.
Baur : *Paulus.* See above.

R. A. Lipsius : *Die Paulinische Rechtfertigungslehre.* Leipz. 1853.

C. Holsten : *Zum Evangelium des Paulus und des Petrus.* Rostock, 1868.
This book, contains : 1. An essay on the *Christusvision des Paulus
und die Genesis des paulinischen Evangeliums*, which had previously
appeared in Hilgenfeld's "Zeitschrift," 1861, but is here enlarged
by a reply to Beyschlag ; 2. *Die Messiasvision des Petrus* (new) ;
3. An analysis of the Epistle to the Galatians (1859) ; 4. A discussion
of the meaning of σάρξ in Paul's system (1855). By the same : *Das
Evangelium des Paulus.* Part I. Berlin, 1880.

Th. Simar (R. C.) : *Die Theologie des heil. Paulus.* Freiberg, 1864.

Ernesti : *Die Ethik des Ap. Paulus.* Braunschweig, 1868 ; 3d ed.
1880.

R. Schmidt : *Die Christologie des Ap. Paulus.* Gött., 1870.

Matthew Arnold : *St. Paul and Protestantism.* Lond. 1870 ; 3d ed.
1875.

William I. Irons (Episcop.) : *Christianity as taught by St. Paul.* Eight
Bampton Lectures for 1870. Oxf. and Lond. 1871 ; 2d ed. 1876.

A. Sabatier : *L'apôtre Paul. Esquisse d'une histoire de sa pensée.* Strasb.
and Paris, 1870.

Otto Pfleiderer (Prof. in Berlin) : *Der Paulinismus.* Leipzig, 1873.
Follows Baur and Holsten in developing the doctrinal system of
Paul from his conversion. English translation by *E. Peters.* Lond.
1877, 2 vols. *Lectures on the Influence of the Apostle Paul on the De-
velopment of Christianity* (The Hibbert Lectures). Trsl. by *J. Fr.
Smith.* Lond. and N. Y. 1885. Also his *Urchristenthum*, 1887.

C. Weizsäcker : *D. Apost. Zeitalter* (1886), pp. 68–355.

Fr. Bethge : *Die Paulinischen Reden der Apostelgesch.* Göttingen, 1887.

V. Commentaries.

The *Commentators* on Paul's Epistles (in whole or in part) are so
numerous that we can only mention some of the most important :

1. On *all* the Pauline Epp. : Calvin, Beza, Estius (R. C.), Corn.
a Lapide (R. C.), Grotius, Wetstein, Bengel, Olshausen, De
Wette, Meyer, Lange (Am. ed. enlarged), Ewald, von Hofmann,
Reuss (French), Alford, Wordsworth, Speaker's *Com.*, Ellicott
(*Pop. Com.*), Schaff (*Pop. Com.*, vol. III. 1882). Compare also P.
J. Gloag : *Introduction to the Pauline Epistles.* Edinburgh, 1874.

2. On *single* Epp. : *Romans* by Tholuck (5th ed. 1856), Fritzsche
(3 vols. in Latin), Reiche, Rückert, Philippi (3d ed. 1866, English
transl. by *Banks*, 1878–'79, 2 vols.), Mos. Stuart, Turner, Hodge,
Forbes, Jowett, Shedd (1879), Godet (*L'épitre aux Romains*, 1879
and 1880, 2 vols).—*Corinthians* by Neander, Osiander, Hodge, Stanley, Heinrici, Edwards, Godet, Ellicott.—*Galatians* by Luther,

WINER, WIESELER, HILGENFELD, HOLSTEN, JOWETT, EADIE, ELLICOTT,
LIGHTFOOT.—*Ephesians* by HARLESS, MATTHIES, STIER, HODGE, EADIE,
ELLICOTT, J. L. DAVIES.—Other *minor* Epp. explained by BLEEK
(*Col.*, *Philemon*, and *Eph.*), KOCH (*Thess.*), VAN HENGEL (*Phil.*),
EADIE (*Col.*), ELLICOTT (*Phil.*, *Col.*, *Thess.*, *Philem.*), LIGHTFOOT
(*Phil.*, *Col.*, *Philemon*).—*Pastoral* Epp. by MATTHIES, MACK (R. C.),
BECK (ed. Lindenmeyer, 1879), HOLTZMANN (1880), FAIRBAIRN, ELLI-
COTT, WEISS (1886), KNOKE (1887), KÖLLING (1887).

3. The Commentaries on the second part of *Acts* by DE WETTE,
MEYER, BAUMGARTEN, ALEXANDER, HACKETT, LECHLER, GLOAG,
PLUMPTRE, JACOBSON, LUMBY, HOWSON and SPENCE.

§ 30. *Paul before his Conversion.*

HIS NATURAL OUTFIT.

We now approach the apostle of the Gentiles who decided
the victory of Christianity as a universal religion, who labored
more, both in word and deed, than all his colleagues, and who
stands out, in lonely grandeur, the most remarkable and influential character in history. His youth as well as his closing years
are involved in obscurity, save that he began a persecutor and
ended a martyr, but the midday of his life is better known than
that of any other apostle, and is replete with burning thoughts
and noble deeds that can never die, and gather strength with the
progress of the gospel from age to age and country to country.

Saul or Paul [1] was of strictly Jewish parentage, but was born,
a few years after Christ,[2] in the renowned Grecian commercial

---

[1] "Paul" (Little) is merely the Hellenized or Latinized form for his Hebrew
name "Saul" (Desired), and has nothing whatever to do either with his own
conversion, or with the conversion of Sergius Paulus of Cyprus. There are
many similar instances of double names among the Jews of that time, as
Hillel and Pollio, Cephas and Peter, John and Mark, Barsabbas and Justus,
Simeon and Niger, Silas and Silvanus. Paul may have received his Latin
name in early youth in Tarsus, as a Roman citizen; *Paulus* being the cogno-
men of several distinguished Roman families, as the *gens Æmilia*, *Fabia*,
Julia, *Sergia*. He used it in his intercourse with the Gentiles and in all his
Epistles. See *Hist. Apost. Ch.*, p. 226, and my annotations to Lange on
Romans 1 : 1, pp. 57 and 58.

[2] When Paul wrote to Philemon, A.D. 63, he was an aged man (πρεσβύτης,
ver. 9), that is, about or above sixty. According to Hippocrates a man was
called πρεσβύτης from forty-nine to fifty-six, and after that γέρων, *senex*. In a

and literary city of Tarsus, in the province of Cilicia, and inherited the rights of a Roman citizen. He received a learned
Jewish education at Jerusalem in the school of the Pharisean
Rabbi, Gamaliel, a grandson of Hillel, not remaining an entire
stranger to Greek literature, as his style, his dialectic method,
his allusions to heathen religion and philosophy, and his occasional quotations from heathen poets show. Thus, a "Hebrew
of the Hebrews,"[1] yet at the same time a native Hellenist, and
a Roman citizen, he combined in himself, so to speak, the three
great nationalities of the ancient world, and was endowed with
all the natural qualifications for a universal apostleship. He
could argue with the Pharisees as a son of Abraham, of the
tribe of Benjamin, and as a disciple of the renowned Gamaliel,
surnamed "the Glory of the Law." He could address the
Greeks in their own beautiful tongue and with the convincing
force of their logic. Clothed with the dignity and majesty of
the Roman people, he could travel safely over the whole empire
with the proud watchword: *Civis Romanus sum.*

This providential outfit for his future work made him for a
while the most dangerous enemy of Christianity, but after his
conversion its most useful promoter. The weapons of destruction were turned into weapons of construction. The engine was
reversed, and the direction changed; but it remained the same
engine, and its power was increased under the new inspiration.

---

friendly letter to a younger friend and pupil the expression must not be pressed.
Walter Scott speaks of himself as "an old grey man" at fifty-five. Paul was
still a "youth" (νεανίας, Acts 7 : 58) at the stoning of Stephen, which probably took place in 37; and although this term is likewise vaguely used, yet as
he was then already clothed with a most important mission by the Sanhedrin,
he must have been about or over thirty years of age. Philo extends the limits
of νεανίας from twenty-one to twenty-eight, Xenophon to forty. Comp. Lightfoot on *Philemon*, v. 9 (p. 405), and Farrar, I., 13, 14.

[1] Phil. 3 : 5. A Hebrew by descent and education, though a Hellenist or
Jew of the dispersion by birth, Acts 22 : 3. Probably his parents were Pales-
tinians. This would explain the erroneous tradition preserved by Jerome
(*De vir. ill.* c. 5), that Paul was born at Giscala in Galilee (now El-Jish), and
after the capture of the place by the Romans emigrated with his parents to
Tarsus. But the capture did not take place till A.D. 67.

The intellectual and moral endowment of Saul was of the highest order.   The sharpest thinking was blended with the tenderest feeling, the deepest mind with the strongest will.   He had Semitic fervor, Greek versatility, and Roman energy. Whatever he was, he was with his whole soul.   He was *totus in illis*, a man of one idea and of one purpose, first as a Jew, then as a Christian.   His nature was martial and heroic.   Fear was unknown to him—except the fear of God, which made him fearless of man.   When yet a youth, he had risen to high eminence ; and had he remained a Jew, he might have become a greater Rabbi than even Hillel or Gamaliel, as he surpassed them both in original genius and fertility of thought.

Paul was the only scholar among the apostles.   He never displays his learning, considering it of no account as compared with the excellency of the knowledge of Christ, for whom he suffered the loss of all things,[1] but he could not conceal it, and turned it to the best use after his conversion.   Peter and John had natural genius, but no scholastic education ; Paul had both, and thus became the founder of Christian theology and philosophy.

His Education.

His training was thoroughly Jewish, rooted and grounded in the Scriptures of the Old Covenant, and those traditions of the elders which culminated in the Talmud.[2]   He knew the Hebrew and Greek Bible almost by heart.   In his argumentative epistles, when addressing Jewish converts, he quotes from the Pentateuch, the Prophets, the Psalms, now literally, now freely, sometimes ingeniously combining several passages or verbal reminiscences, or reading between the lines in a manner which betrays the profound student and master of the hidden depths of the word of God, and throws a flood of light on obscure

---

[1] Comp. the sublime passage, Phil. 3 : 8–10, and 1 Cor. 2 : 1, 2.

[2] Gal. 4 : 14 : "I made progress in Judaism beyond many of mine own age in my nation, being more exceedingly zealous for the traditions of my fathers."

passages.[1] He was quite familiar with the typical and allegorical methods of interpretation; and he occasionally and incidentally uses Scriptural arguments, or illustrations rather, which
strike a sober scholar as far-fetched and fanciful, though they
were quite conclusive to a Jewish reader.[2] But he never bases
a truth on such an illustration without an independent argument; he never indulges in the exegetical impositions and frivo-
lities of those "letter-worshipping Rabbis who prided themselves on suspending dogmatic mountains by textual hairs."
Through the revelation of Christ, the Old Testament, instead of
losing itself in the desert of the Talmud or the labyrinth of the
Kabbala, became to him a book of life, full of types and promises
of the great facts and truths of the gospel salvation. In Abraham he saw the father of the faithful, in Habakkuk a preacher
of justification by faith, in the paschal lamb a type of Christ
slain for the sins of the world, in the passage of Israel through
the Red Sea a prefigurement of Christian baptism, and in the
manna of the wilderness a type of the bread of life in the Lord's
Supper.

The Hellenic culture of Paul is a matter of dispute, denied
by some, unduly exalted by others. He no doubt acquired in
the home of his boyhood and early manhood[3] a knowledge of
the Greek language, for Tarsus was at that time the seat of one
of the three universities of the Roman empire, surpassing in
some respects even Athens and Alexandria, and furnished tutors
to the imperial family. His teacher, Gamaliel, was comparatively free from the rabbinical abhorrence and contempt of
heathen literature. After his conversion he devoted his life to
the salvation of the heathen, and lived for years at Tarsus,

---

[1] Scripture references and allusions abound in the Galatians, Romans, and
Corinthians, but are wanting in the Thessalonians, Colossians, and Philemon,
and in his address to the heathen hearers at Athens, whom he referred to
their own poets rather than to Moses and the prophets.

[2] As the reasoning from the singular or rather collective σπέρμα (zera) in
Gal. 3 : 16, the allegorical interpretation of Hagar and Sarah, 4 : 22 sqq., and
the rock in the wilderness, 1 Cor. 10 : 1-4. See the commentaries.

[3] Comp. Gal. 1 : 21; Acts 9 : 30; 11 : 25.

Ephesus, Corinth, and other cities of Greece, and became a
Greek to the Greeks in order to save them.   It is scarcely conceivable that a man of universal human sympathies, and so wide
awake to the deepest problems of thought, as he, should have
under such circumstances taken no notice of the vast treasures
of Greek philosophy, poetry, and history.   He would certainly
do what we expect every missionary to China or India to do
from love to the race which he is to benefit, and from a desire
to extend his usefulness.   Paul very aptly, though only incidentally, quotes three times from Greek poets, not only a proverbial maxim from Menander,[1] and a hexameter from Epimenides,[2] which may have passed into common use, but also a half-
hexameter with a connecting particle, which he must have read
in the tedious astronomical poem of his countryman, Aratus
(about B.C. 270), or in the sublime hymn of Cleanthes to Jupiter, in both of which the passage occurs.[3]   He borrows some of

---

[1] 1 Cor. 15 : 33.   φθείρουσιν ἤδη χρηστὰ ὁμιλίαι κακαί.
   " Evil associations corrupt good manners."

[2] Tit. 1 : 12.   Κρῆτες ἀεὶ ψεῦσται, κακὰ θηρία, γαστέρες ἀργαί.
   " Cretans are liars alway, bad beasts, and indolent gluttons."
As Epimenides was himself a Cretan, this contemptuous depreciation of his
countrymen gave rise to the syllogistic puzzle : " Epimenides calls the Cretans liars ; Epimenides was a Cretan : therefore Epimenides was a liar : therefore the Cretans were not liars : therefore Epimenides was not a liar," etc.

[3] Acts 17 : 28.   Τοῦ [poetic for τούτου] γὰρ καὶ γένος ἐσμέν.
   " For we are also His (God's) offspring."
The passage occurs literally in the *Phænomena* of Aratus, v. 5, in the fol-
lowing connection :

. . . . " We all greatly need Zeus,
For we are his offspring ; full of grace, he grants men
Tokens of favor " . . . .

The Stoic poet, Cleanthes (*Hymn. in Jovem*, 5) uses the same expression in
an address to Jupiter : Ἐκ σοῦ γὰρ γένος ἐσμέν, and in the *Golden Poem*,
θεῖον γὰρ γένος ἐστὶ βροτοῖσιν.   We may also quote a parallel passage of Pindar, *Nem.* VI., which has been overlooked by commentators :

Ἐν ἀνδρῶν, ἓν θεῶν γένος, ἐκ μιᾶς δὲ πνέομεν ματρὸς ἀμφότεροι.
   " One race of men and gods, from one mother breathe we all."

It is evident, however, that all these passages were understood by their
heathen authors in a materialistic and pantheistic sense, which would make
nature or the earth the mother of gods and men.   Paul in his masterly address

his favorite metaphors from the Grecian games; he disputed with Greek philosophers of different schools and addressed them from the Areopagus with consummate wisdom and adaptation to the situation ; some suppose that he alludes even to the terminology of the Stoic philosophy when he speaks of the " rudiments" or " elements of the world." [1] He handles the Greek language, not indeed with classical purity and elegance, yet with an almost creative vigor, transforming it into an obedient organ of new ideas, and pressing into his service the oxymoron, the paronomasia, the litotes, and other rhetorical figures.[2] Yet all this does by no means prove a regular study or extensive knowledge of Greek literature, but is due in part to native genius. His more than Attic urbanity and gentlemanly refinement which breathe in his Epistles to Philemon and the Philippians, must be traced to the influence of Christianity rather than his intercourse with accomplished Greeks. His Hellenic learning seems to have been only casual, incidental, and altogether subordinate to his great aim. In this respect he differed widely from the learned Josephus, who affected Attic purity of style, and from Philo, who allowed the revealed truth of the Mosaic religion to be controlled, obscured, and perverted by Hellenic philosophy. Philo idealized and explained away the Old Testament by allegorical impositions which he substituted for grammatical expositions ; Paul spiritualized the Old Testament and drew out its deepest meaning. Philo's Judaism evaporated in speculative

to the Athenians, without endorsing the error, recognizes the element of truth in pantheism, viz., the divine origin of man and the immanence of God in the world and in humanity.

[1] τὰ στοιχεῖα τοῦ κόσμου, Gal. 4 : 3, 9. So Hilgenfeld, *Einleitung*, p. 223. Thiersch assumes (p. 112) that Paul was familiar with the Nicomachean Ethics of Aristotle, and that his dialectics is classical rather than rabbinical ; but this is scarcely correct. In Romans 5 : 16, 18, he uses the word δικαίωμα in the Aristotelian sense of legal adjustment (*Rechtsausgleichung*). See *Eth. Nicom.* v. 10, and Rothe's monograph on Rom. 5 : 12–21. Baur compares Paul's style with that of Thucydides.

[2] Farrar, I. 629 sq., counts "upwards of fifty specimens of thirty Greek rhetorical figures in St. Paul," which certainly disprove the assertion of Renan that Paul could never have received even elementary lessons in grammar and rhetoric at Tarsus.

abstractions, Paul's Judaism was elevated and transformed into Christian realities.

His Zeal for Judaism.

Saul was a Pharisee of the strictest sect, not indeed of the hypocritical type, so witheringly rebuked by our Saviour, but of the honest, truth-loving and truth-seeking sort, like that of Nico-demus and Gamaliel. His very fanaticism in persecution arose from the intensity of his conviction and his zeal for the religion of his fathers. He persecuted in ignorance, and that diminished, though it did not abolish, his guilt. He probably never saw or heard Jesus until he appeared to him at Damascus. He may have been at Tarsus at the time of the crucifixion and resurrection.[1] But with his Pharisaic education he regarded Jesus of Nazareth, like his teachers, as a false Messiah, a rebel, a blasphemer, who was justly condemned to death. And he acted according to his conviction. He took the most prominent part in the persecution of Stephen and delighted in his death. Not satisfied with this, he procured from the Sanhedrin, which had the oversight of all the synagogues and disciplinary punishments for offences against the law, full power to persecute and arrest the scattered disciples. Thus armed, he set out for Damascus, the capital of Syria, which numbered many synagogues. He was determined to exterminate the dangerous sect from the face of the earth, for the glory of God. But the height of his opposition was the beginning of his devotion to Christianity.

---

[1] 1 Cor. 9 : 1 refers to the vision of Christ at Damascus. In 2 Cor. 5 : 16 : " though we have known Christ after the flesh, yet now henceforth know we him no more," the particles εἰ καί (*quamquam*, even though, *wenn auch*) seem to chronicle a fact, as distinct from καὶ εἰ (*etiam si*, even if, *selbst wenn*), which puts an hypothesis ; but the stress lies on the difference between an external, carnal knowledge of Christ in his humility and earthly relations or a super-ficial acquaintance from hearsay, and a spiritual, experimental knowledge of Christ in his glory. Farrar (I. 73 sqq.), reasons that if Paul had really known and heard Jesus, he would have been converted at once.

His External Relations and Personal Appearance.

On the subordinate questions of Paul's external condition and relations we have no certain information. Being a Roman citizen, he belonged to the respectable class of society, but must have been poor; for he depended for support on a trade which he learned in accordance with rabbinical custom; it was the trade of tent-making, very common in Cilicia, and not profitable except in large cities.[1]

He had a sister living at Jerusalem whose son was instrumental in saving his life.[2]

He was probably never married. Some suppose that he was a widower. Jewish and rabbinical custom, the completeness of his moral character, his ideal conception of marriage as reflecting the mystical union of Christ with his church, his exhortations to conjugal, parental, and filial duties, seem to point to experimental knowledge of domestic life. But as a Christian missionary moving from place to place, and exposed to all sorts of hardship and persecution, he felt it his duty to abide alone.[3]

---

[1] He is called a tent-maker, σκηνοποιός, Acts 18 : 3. Tents were mostly made of the coarse hair of the Cilician goat (Κιλίκιος τράγος, which also denotes a coarse man), and needed by shepherds, travellers, sailors, and soldiers. The same material was also used for mantelets, shoes, and beds. The Cilician origin of this article is perpetuated in the Latin *cilicium* and the French *cilice*, which means hair-cloth. Gamaliel is the author of the maxim that " learning of any kind unaccompanied by a trade ends in nothing and leads to sin."

[2] Acts 23 : 16.

[3] In 1 Cor. 9 : 5 (written in 57) he claims the right to lead a married life, like Peter and the other apostles, and the brethren of the Lord ; but in 1 Cor. 7 : 7, 8 he gives for himself in his peculiar position the preference to single life. Clement of Alexandria, Erasmus, and others supposed that he was married, and understood Syzyge, in Phil. 4 : 3, to be his wife. Ewald regards him as a widower who lost his wife before his conversion (VI. 341). So also Farrar (I. 80) who infers from 1 Cor. 7 : 8 that Paul classed himself with widowers : " I say, therefore, to the *unmarried* [to widowers, for whom there is no special Greek word] and widows, it is good for them if they *abide* even as I." He lays stress on the fact that the Jews in all ages attached great importance to marriage as a moral duty (Gen. 1 : 28), and preferred *early* marriage; he also maintains (I. 169) that Paul, being a member of the Sanhedrin (as he gave his vote for the condemnation of the Christians, Acts

He sacrificed the blessings of home and family to the advance‑
ment of the kingdom of Christ.[1]

His "bodily presence was weak, and his speech contemptible"
(of no value), in the superficial judgment of the Corinthians,
who missed the rhetorical ornaments, yet could not help admit‑
ting that his "letters were weighty and strong."[2]   Some of the
greatest men have been small in size, and some of the purest

26 : 10), must have had, according to the Gemara, a family of his own. Renan
fancies (ch. VI.) that Paul contracted a more than spiritual union with sister
Lydia at Philippi, and addressed *her* in Phil. 4 : 3 as his σύζυγε γνήσιε, that is,
as his true co‑worker or partner (*conjux*), since it is not likely that he would
have omitted her when he mentioned, in the preceding verse, two deaconesses
otherwise unknown, Euodia and Syntyche.   The word σύζυγος, as a noun,
may be either masculine or feminine, and may either mean generally an
associate, a co‑worker ("yoke‑fellow" in the E. V.), or be a proper name.
Several persons have been suggested, Epaphroditus, Timothy, Silas, Luke.
But Paul probably means a man, named Σύζυγος, and plays upon the word :
"Yokefellow by name and yoke‑fellow in deed."   Comp. a similar parono‑
masia in Philem. 10, 11 ('Ονήσιμον, i. e., *Helpful,*—ἄχρηστον, εὔχρηστον, *un‑
profitable, profitable*).   See the notes of Meyer and Lange (Braune and Hackett)
on these passages.

[1] This sublime loneliness of Paul is well expressed in a poem, *Saint Paul,*
by Frederic W. H. Myers (1868), from which we may be permitted to quote a
few lines :

> "Christ ! I am Christ's ! and let the name suffice you ;
>   Aye, for me, too, He greatly hath sufficed ;
> Lo, with no winning words I would entice you ;
>   Paul has no honor and no friend but Christ.

> "Yes, without cheer of sister or of daughter—
>   Yes, without stay of father or of son,
> Lone on the land, and homeless on the water,
>   Pass I in patience till the work be done.

> "Yet not in solitude, if Christ anear me
>   Waketh Him workers for the great employ ;
> Oh, not in solitude, if souls that hear me
>   Catch from my joyance the surprise of joy.

> "Hearts I have won of sister or of brother,
>   Quick on the earth or hidden in the sod ;
> Lo, every heart awaiteth me, another
>   Friend in the blameless family of God."

[2] 2 Cor. 10 : 10 : ἡ παρουσία τοῦ σώματος ἀσθενὴς, καὶ ὁ λόγος ἐξουθενημένος,
or, as Cod. B. reads, ἐξουδενημένος, which has the same meaning. Comp. ver.
1, where he speaks of his "lowly" personal appearance among the Corin‑
thians (κατὰ πρόσωπον ταπεινός). He was little, compared with Barnabas (Acts
14 : 12).

souls forbidding in body. Socrates was the homeliest, and yet the wisest of Greeks. Neander, a converted Jew, like Paul, was short, feeble, and strikingly odd in his whole appearance, but a rare humility, benignity, and heavenly aspiration beamed from his face beneath his dark and bushy eyebrows. So we may well imagine that the expression of Paul's countenance was highly intellectual and spiritual, and that he looked "sometimes like a man and sometimes like an angel." [1]

---

[1] This is from the tradition preserved in the apocryphal *Acts of Thecla*. See the description quoted above, p. 282. Other ancient descriptions of Paul in the *Philopatris* of pseudo-Lucian (of the second, but more probably of the fourth century), Malala of Antioch (sixth century), and Nicephorus (fifteenth century), represent Paul as little in stature, bald, with a prominent aquiline nose, gray hair and thick beard, bright grayish eyes, somewhat bent and stooping, yet pleasant and graceful. See these descriptions in Lewin's *St. Paul*, II. 412. The oldest extant portraiture of Paul, probably from the close of the first or beginning of the second century, was found on a large bronze medallion in the cemetery of Domitilla (one of the Flavian family), and is preserved in the Vatican library. It presents Paul on the left and Peter on the right. Both are far from handsome, but full of character; Paul is the homelier of the two, with apparently diseased eyes, open mouth, bald head and short thick beard, but thoughtful, solemn, and dignified. See a cut in Lewin, II. 211. Chrysostom calls Paul the three-cubit man (ὁ τρίπηχυς ἄνθρωπος, *Serm. in Pet. et Paul.*). Luther imagined: "*St. Paulus war ein armes, dürres Männlein, wie Magister Philippus*" (Melanchthon). A poetic description by J. H. Newman see in Farrar I. 220, and in Plumptre on *Acts*, Appendix, with another (of his own). Renan (*Les Apôtres*, pp. 169 sqq.) gives, partly from Paul's Epistles, partly from apocryphal sources, the following striking picture of the apostle: His behavior was winning, his manners excellent, his letters reveal a man of genius and lofty aspirations, though the style is incorrect. Never did a correspondence display rarer courtesies, tenderer shades, more amiable modesty and reserve. Once or twice we are wounded by his sarcasm (Gal. 5: 12; Phil. 3: 2). But what rapture! What fulness of charming words! What originality! His exterior did not correspond to the greatness of his soul. He was ugly, short, stout, plump, of small head, bald, pale, his face covered with a thick beard, an eagle nose, piercing eyes, dark eyebrows. His speech, embarrassed, faulty, gave a poor idea of his eloquence. With rare tact he turned his external defects to advantage. The Jewish race produces types of the highest beauty and of the most complete homeliness (*des types de la plus grande beauté et de la plus complète laideur*); but the Jewish homeliness is quite unique. The strange faces which provoke laughter at first sight, assume when intellectually enlivened, a peculiar expression of intense brilliancy and majesty (*une sorte d'éclat profond et de majesté*).

He was afflicted with a mysterious, painful, recurrent, and repulsive physical infirmity, which he calls a "thorn in the flesh," and which acted as a check upon spiritual pride and self-exultation over his abundance of revelations.[1] He bore the heavenly treasure in an earthly vessel and his strength was made perfect in weakness.[2] But all the more must we admire the moral heroism which turned weakness itself into an element of strength, and despite pain and trouble and persecution carried the gospel salvation triumphantly from Damascus to Rome.

§ 31. *The Conversion of Paul.*

Εὐδόκησεν ὁ θεός . . . ἀποκαλύψαι τὸν υἱὸν αὐτοῦ ἐν ἐμοί, ἵνα εὐαγγελίζωμαι αὐτὸν ἐν τοῖς ἔθνεσιν.—Gal. 1 : 15, 16.

The conversion of Paul marks not only a turning-point in his personal history, but also an important epoch in the history of the apostolic church, and consequently in the history of mankind. It was the most fruitful event since the miracle of Pentecost, and secured the universal victory of Christianity.

The transformation of the most dangerous persecutor into the most successful promoter of Christianity is nothing less than a miracle of divine grace. It rests on the greater miracle of the

---

[1] 2 Cor. 12 : 7-9 ; Gal. 4 : 13-15. Comp. also 1 Thess. 2 : 18 ; 1 Cor. 2 : 3 ; 2 Cor. 1 : 8, 9 ; 4 : 10. Of the many conjectures only three : sick headache, acute ophthalmia, epilepsy, seem to answer the allusions of Paul which are dark to us at such a distance of time, while they were clear to his personal friends. Tertullian and Jerome, according to an ancient tradition, favor headache ; Lewin, Farrar, and many others, sore eyes, dating the inflammation from the dazzling light which shone around him at Damascus (Acts 9 : 3, 17, 18 ; comp. 22 : 13 ; 23 : 3, 5 ; Gal. 4 . 15)) ; Ewald and Lightfoot, epilepsy, with illustration from the life of King Alfred (Mohammed would be even more to the point). Other conjectures of external, or spiritual trials (persecution, carnal temptations, bad temper, doubt, despondency, blasphemous suggestions of the devil, etc.) are ruled out by à strict exegesis of the two chief passages in 2 Cor. 12 and Gal. 4, which point to a *physical* malady. See an Excursus on Paul's thorn in the flesh, in my *Commentary on Gal.* 4 : 13-15 (*Pop. Com.* vol. III.).

[2] 2 Cor. 4 : 7 ; 12 : 9, 10.

resurrection of Christ. Both are inseparably connected; without the resurrection the conversion would have been impossible, and on the other hand the conversion of such a man and with such results is one of the strongest proofs of the resurrection.

The bold attack of Stephen—the forerunner of Paul—upon the hard, stiff-necked Judaism which had crucified the Messiah, provoked a determined and systematic attempt on the part of the Sanhedrin to crucify Jesus again by destroying his church. In this struggle for life and death Saul the Pharisee, the bravest and strongest of the rising rabbis, was the willing and accepted leader.

After the martyrdom of Stephen and the dispersion of the congregation of Jerusalem, he proceeded to Damascus in pursuit of the fugitive disciples of Jesus, as a commissioner of the Sanhedrin, a sort of inquisitor-general, with full authority and determination to stamp out the Christian rebellion, and to bring all the apostates he could find, whether they were men or women, in chains to the holy city to be condemned by the chief priests.

Damascus is one of the oldest cities in the world, known in the days of Abraham, and bursts upon the traveller like a vision of paradise amidst a burning and barren wilderness of sand; it is watered by the never-failing rivers Abana and Pharpar (which Naaman of old preferred to all the waters of Israel), and embosomed in luxuriant gardens of flowers and groves of tropical fruit trees; hence glorified by Eastern poets as "the Eye of the Desert."

But a far higher vision than this earthly paradise was in store for Saul as he approached the city. A supernatural light from heaven, brighter than the Syrian sun, suddenly flashed around him at midday, and Jesus of Nazareth, whom he persecuted in his humble disciples, appeared to him in his glory as the exalted Messiah, asking him in the Hebrew tongue: "Shaûl, Shaûl, why persecutest thou Me?"[1] It was a question both of rebuke

---

[1] Acts 9 : 4, the Hebrew form Σαούλ, Σαούλ, is used instead of the usual Greek Σαῦλος, vers. 8, 11, 22, 24, etc.

and of love, and it melted his heart. He fell prostrate to the ground. He saw and heard, he trembled and obeyed, he believed and rejoiced. As he rose from the earth he saw no man. Like a helpless child, blinded by the dazzling light, he was led to Damascus, and after three days of blindness and fasting he was cured and baptized—not by Peter or James or John, but—by one of the humble disciples whom he had come to destroy. The haughty, self-righteous, intolerant, raging Pharisee was changed into an humble, penitent, grateful, loving servant of Jesus. He threw away self-righteousness, learning, influence, power, prospects, and cast in his lot with a small, despised sect at the risk of his life. If there ever was an honest, unselfish, radical, and effective change of conviction and conduct, it was that of Saul of Tarsus. He became, by a creative act of the Holy Spirit, a "new creature in Christ Jesus." [1]

We have three full accounts of this event in the Acts, one from Luke, two from Paul himself, with slight variations in detail, which only confirm the essential harmony. [2] Paul also alludes to it five or six times in his Epistles. [3] In all these passages he represents the change as an act brought about by a direct intervention of Jesus, who revealed himself in his glory from heaven, and struck conviction into his mind like lightning at midnight. He compares it to the creative act of God when

---

[1] 2 Cor. 5 : 17 ; Gal. 6 : 15.

[2] Acts, chapters 9, 22, 26. These accounts are by no means mere repetitions, but modifications and adaptations of the same story to the audience under apologetic conditions, and bring out each some interesting feature called forth by the occasion. This has been well shown by Dean Howson in Excursus C on Acts, ch. 26, in his and Canon Spence's *Commentary on Acts.* The discrepancies of the accounts are easily reconciled. They refer chiefly to the effect upon the companions of Paul who saw the light, but not the person of Christ, and heard a voice, but could not understand the words. The vision was not for them any more than the appearance of the risen Lord was for the soldiers who watched the grave. They were probably members of the Levitical temple guard, who were to bind and drag the Christian prisoners to Jerusalem.

[3] Gal. 1 : 15, 16 ; 1 Cor. 15 : 8, 9 ; 9 : 1 ; 2 Cor. 4 : 6 ; Phil. 3 : 6 ; 1 Tim. 1 : 12–14.

He commanded the light to shine out of darkness.[1] He lays great stress on the fact that he was converted and called to the apostolate directly by Christ, without any human agency; that he learned his gospel of free and universal grace by revelation, and not from the older apostles, whom he did not even see till three years after his call.[2]

The conversion, indeed, was not a moral compulsion, but included the responsibility of assent or dissent. God converts nobody by force or by magic. He made man free, and acts upon him as a moral being. Paul *might* have "disobeyed the heavenly vision."[3] He *might* have "kicked against the goads," though it was "hard" (not impossible) to do so.[4] These words imply some psychological preparation, some doubt and misgiving as to his course, some moral conflict between the flesh and the spirit, which he himself described twenty years afterwards from personal experience, and which issues in the cry of despair: "O wretched man that I am! Who shall deliver me from the body of this death?"[5] On his journey from Jerusalem to Damascus, which takes a full week on foot or horseback—the distance being about 140 miles—as he was passing, in the solitude of his own thoughts, through Samaria, Galilee, and across Mount Hermon, he had ample time for reflection, and we may

---

[1] 2 Cor. 4 : 6.

[2] Gal. 1 : 1, 11, 12, 15–18.

[3] This is implied in his words to King Agrippa, Acts 26 : 19.

[4] Acts 26 : 14. Christ said to him : σκληρόν σοι πρὸς κέντρα λακτίζειν. This is a proverbial expression used by Greek writers of refractory oxen in the plough when urged by a sharp-pointed instrument of the driver. The ox may and often does resist, but by doing so he only increases his pain. Resistance is possible, but worse than useless.

[5] Rom. 7 : 7–25. This remarkable section describes the psychological progress of the human heart to Christ from the heathen state of carnal security, when sin is dead because unknown, through the Jewish state of legal conflict, when sin, roused by the stimulus of the divine command, springs into life, and the higher and nobler nature of man strives in vain to overcome this fearful monster, until at last the free grace of God in Christ gains the victory. Some of the profoundest divines—Augustin, Luther, Calvin—transfer this conflict into the regenerate state ; but this is described in the eighth chapter which ends in an exulting song of triumph.

well imagine how the shining face of the martyr Stephen, as he stood like a holy angel before the Sanhedrin, and as in the last moment he prayed for his murderers, was haunting him like a ghost and warning him to stop his mad career.

Yet we must not overrate this preparation or anticipate his riper experience in the three days that intervened between his conversion and his baptism, and during the three years of quiet meditation in Arabia. He was no doubt longing for truth and for righteousness, but there was a thick veil over his mental eye which could only be taken away by a hand from without; access to his heart was barred by an iron door of prejudice which had to be broken in by Jesus himself. On his way to Damascus he was "yet breathing threatening and slaughter against the disciples of the Lord," and thinking he was doing "God service;" he was, to use his own language, "beyond measure" persecuting the church of God and endeavoring to destroy it, "being more exceedingly zealous for the traditions of his fathers" than many of his age, when "it pleased God to reveal his Son in him." Moreover it is only in the light of faith that we see the midnight darkness of our sin, and it is only beneath the cross of Christ that we feel the whole crushing weight of guilt and the unfathomable depth of God's redeeming love. No amount of subjective thought and reflection could have brought about that radical change in so short a time. It was the objective appearance of Jesus that effected it.

This appearance implied the resurrection and the ascension, and this was the irresistible evidence of His Messiahship, God's own seal of approval upon the work of Jesus. And the resurrection again shed a new light upon His death on the cross, disclosing it as an atoning sacrifice for the sins of the world, as the means of procuring pardon and peace consistent with the claims of divine justice. What a revelation! That same Jesus of Nazareth whom he hated and persecuted as a false prophet justly crucified between two robbers, stood before Saul as the risen, ascended, and glorified Messiah! And instead of crushing the persecutor as he deserved, He pardoned him and called him to be His witness before Jews and Gentiles! This revelation was enough for an orthodox Jew waiting for the hope of Israel to make him a Christian, and enough for a Jew of such force of character to make him an earnest and determined Christian. The logic of his intellect and the energy of his will required that he should love and promote the new faith with the same enthusiasm with which he had hated and persecuted it; for hatred is but inverted love, and the intensity of love and hatred depends on the strength of affection and the ardor of temper.

With all the suddenness and radicalness of the transformation there is nevertheless a bond of unity between Saul the Pharisee and Paul the Christian. It was the same person with the same end in view, but in opposite directions. We must remember that he was not a worldly, indifferent, cold-blooded man, but an intensely religious man. While persecuting the church, he was "blameless" as touching the righteousness of the law.[1] He resembled the rich youth who had observed the commandments, yet lacked the one thing needful, and of whom Mark says that Jesus "loved him."[2] He was not converted from infidelity to faith, but from a lower faith to a purer faith, from the religion of Moses to the religion of Christ, from the theology of the law to the theology of the gospel. How shall a sinner be justified before the tribunal of a holy God? That was with him the question of questions before as well as after his conversion; not a scholastic question merely, but even far more a moral and religious question. For righteousness, to the Hebrew mind, is conformity to the will of God as expressed in his revealed law, and implies life eternal as its reward. *The honest and earnest pursuit of righteousness* is the connecting link between the two periods of Paul's life. First he labored to secure it by works of the law, then by obedience of faith. What he had sought in vain by his fanatical zeal for the traditions of Judaism, he found gratuitously and at once by trust in the cross of Christ:

---

[1] Phil 3: 6, κατὰ δικαιοσύνην τὴν ἐν νόμῳ γενόμενος ἄμεμπτος.
[2] Mark 10: 21.

pardon and peace with God. By the discipline of the Mosaic law as a tutor he was led *beyond* its restraints and prepared for manhood and freedom. Through the law he died to the law that he might live unto God. His old self, with its lusts, was crucified with Christ, so that henceforth he lived no longer himself, but Christ lived in him.[1] He was mystically identified with his Saviour and had no separate existence from him. The whole of Christianity, the whole of life, was summed up to him in the one word: Christ. He determined to know nothing save Jesus Christ and Him crucified for our sins, and risen again for our justification.[2]

His experience of justification by faith, his free pardon and acceptance by Christ were to him the strongest stimulus to gratitude and consecration. His great sin of persecution, like Peter's denial, was overruled for his own good: the remembrance of it kept him humble, guarded him against temptation, and intensified his zeal and devotion. "I am the least of the apostles," he said in unfeigned humility, "that am not meet to be called an apostle, because I persecuted the church of God. But by the grace of God I am what I am; and his grace which was bestowed upon me was not in vain; but I labored more abundantly than they all: yet not I, but the grace of God which was with me."[3] This confession contains, in epitome, the whole meaning of his life and work.

The idea of justification by the free grace of God in Christ through a living faith which makes Christ and his merits our own and leads to consecration and holiness, is the central idea of Paul's Epistles. His whole theology, doctrinal, ethical, and practical, lies, like a germ, in his conversion; but it was actually developed by a sharp conflict with Judaizing teachers who con-

---

[1] In his address to Peter at Antioch, Gal. 2 : 11–21, he gives an account of his experience and his gospel, as contrasted with the gospel of the Judaizers. Comp. Gal. 3 : 24; 5 : 24; 6 : 14; Rom. 7 : 6–13; Col. 2 : 20.

[2] 1 Cor. 2 : 2; Gal. 6 : 14; Rom. 4 : 24, 25.

[3] 1 Cor. 15 : 9, 10; comp. Eph. 3 : 8 : "Unto me who am less than the least of all saints, was this grace given;" 1 Tim. 1 : 15, 16 : "to save sinners of whom I am chief," etc.

tinued to trust in the law for righteousness and salvation, and thus virtually frustrated the grace of God and made Christ's death unnecessary and fruitless.

Although Paul broke radically with Judaism and opposed the Pharisaical notion of legal righteousness at every step and with all his might, he was far from opposing the Old Testament or the Jewish people. Herein he shows his great wisdom and moderation, and his infinite superiority over Marcion and other ultra- and pseudo-Pauline reformers. He now expounded the Scriptures as a direct preparation for the gospel, the law as a schoolmaster leading to Christ, Abraham as the father of the faithful. And as to his countrymen after the flesh, he loved them more than ever before. Filled with the amazing love of Christ who had pardoned him, "the chief of sinners," he was ready for the greatest possible sacrifice if thereby he might save them. His startling language in the ninth chapter of the Romans is not rhetorical exaggeration, but the genuine expression of that heroic self-denial and devotion which animated Moses, and which culminated in the sacrifice of the eternal Son of God on the cross of Calvary.[1]

Paul's conversion was at the same time his call to the apostleship, not indeed to a place among the Twelve (for the vacancy of Judas was filled), but to the independent apostleship of the Gentiles.[2] Then followed an uninterrupted activity of more than a quarter of a century, which for interest and for permanent and ever-growing usefulness has no parallel in the annals of history, and affords an unanswerable proof of the sincerity of his conversion and the truth of Christianity.[3]

[1] Rom. 9 : 2, 3; comp. Ex. 32 : 31, 32.

[2] Paul never numbers himself with the Twelve. He distinguishes himself from the apostles of the circumcision, as the apostle of the uncircumcision, but of equal authority with them. Gal. 2 : 7–9. We have no intimation that the election of Matthias (Acts 1 : 26) was a mistake of the hasty Peter; it was ratified by the outpouring of the Holy Spirit immediately following.

[3] On the testimony of Paul to Christianity see above § 22, p. 213. I will add some good remarks of Farrar, I. 202: "It is impossible," he says, "to exaggerate the importance of St. Paul's conversion as one of the evidences of Christianity. . . . . To what does he testify respecting Jesus? To almost

ANALOGOUS CONVERSIONS.

God deals with men according to their peculiar character and condition.   As in Elijah's vision on Mount Horeb, God appears now in the mighty rushing wind that uproots the trees, now in the earthquake that rends the rocks, now in the consuming fire, now in the still small voice.   Some are suddenly converted, and can remember the place and hour; others are gradually and imperceptibly changed in spirit and conduct; still others grow up unconsciously in the Christian faith from the mother's knee and the baptismal font.   The stronger the will the more force it requires to overcome the resistance, and the more thorough and lasting is the change.   Of all sudden and radical conversions that of Saul was the most sudden and the most radical.   In several respects it stands quite alone, as the man himself and his work.   Yet there are faint analogies in history.   The divines who most sympathized with his spirit and system of doctrine, passed through a similar experience, and were much aided by his example and writings.   Among these Augustin, Calvin, and Luther are the most conspicuous.

St. Augustin, the son of a pious mother and a heathen father, was led astray into error and vice and wandered for years through the labyrinth of heresy and scepticism, but his heart was restless and homesick after God.   At last, when he attained to the thirty-third year of his life (Sept., 386), the fermentation

every single primary important fact respecting his incarnation, life, sufferings, betrayal, last supper, trial, crucifixion, resurrection, ascension, and heavenly exaltation. . . The events on which the apostle relied in proof of Christ's divinity, had taken place in the full blaze of contemporary knowledge. He had not to deal with uncertainties of criticism or assaults on authenticity. He could question, not ancient documents, but living men ; he could analyze, not fragmentary records, but existing evidence.   He had thousands of means close at hand whereby to test the reality or unreality of the Resurrection in which, up to this time, he had so passionately and contemptuously disbelieved. In accepting this half-crushed and wholly execrated faith he had everything in the world to lose—he had nothing conceivable to gain ; and yet, in spite of all—overwhelmed by a conviction he felt to be irresistible—Saul, the Pharisee, became a witness of the resurrection, a preacher of the cross."

of his soul culminated in a garden near Milan, far away from his African home, when the Spirit of God, through the combined agencies of the unceasing prayers of Monica, the sermons of Ambrose, the example of St. Anthony, the study of Cicero and Plato, of Isaiah and Paul, brought about a change not indeed as wonderful—for no visible appearance of Christ was vouchsafed to him—but as sincere and lasting as that of the apostle. As he was lying in the dust of repentance and wrestling with God in prayer for deliverance, he suddenly heard a sweet voice as from heaven, calling out again and again: " Take and read, take and read ! " He opened the holy book and read the exhortation of Paul: " Put ye on the Lord Jesus Christ, and make not provision for the flesh, to fulfil the lusts thereof." It was a voice of God ; he obeyed it, he completely changed his course of life, and became the greatest and most useful teacher of his age.

Of Calvin's conversion we know very little, but he himself characterizes it as a sudden change (*subita conversio*) from papal superstition to the evangelical faith. In this respect it resembles that of Paul rather than Augustin. He was no sceptic, no heretic, no immoral man, but as far as we know, a pious Romanist until the brighter life of the Reformation burst on his mind from the Holy Scriptures and showed him a more excellent way. " Only one haven of salvation is left for our souls," he says, " and that is the mercy of God in Christ. We are saved by grace—not by our merits, not by our works." He consulted not with flesh and blood, and burned the bridge after him. He renounced all prospects of a brilliant career, and exposed himself to the danger of persecution and death. He exhorted and strengthened the timid Protestants of France, usually closing with the words of Paul : " If God be for us, who can be against us ? " He prepared in Paris a flaming address on reform, which was ordered to be burned ; he escaped from persecution in a basket from a window, like Paul at Damascus, and wandered for two years as a fugitive evangelist from place to place until he found his sphere of labor in Geneva. With his conversion was born his Pauline theology, which sprang from his brain like Minerva from the head of Jupiter. Paul never had a more logical and theological commentator than John Calvin.[1]

But the most Paul-like man in history is the leader of the German Reformation, who combined in almost equal proportion depth of mind, strength of will, tenderness of heart, and a fiery vehemence of temper, and was the most powerful herald of evangelical freedom; though inferior to Augustin and Calvin (not to say Paul) in self-discipline, consistency, and symmetry of character.[2] Luther's commentary on the Epistle to the Galatians, though not a grammatical or logical exposition, is a fresh reproduction and republication of the Epistle against the self-righteousness and bondage of the papacy. Luther's first conversion took place in his twenty-first year (1505), when, as a student of law at Erfurt, on his return from a visit to his parents, he was so frightened by a fearful thunder-storm and flashes of lightning that he exclaimed: "Help, dear St. Anna, I will become a monk!" But that conversion, although it has often been compared with that of the apostle, had nothing to do with his Paulinism and Protestantism; it made him a pious Catholic, it induced him to flee from the world to the retreat of a convent for the salvation of his soul. And he became one of the most humble, obedient, and self-denying of monks, as Paul was one of the most earnest and zealous of Pharisees. "If ever a monk got to heaven by monkery," says Luther, "I ought to have gotten there." But the more he sought righteousness and peace by ascetic self-denial and penal exercises, the more painfully he felt the weight of sin and the

---

[1] See my *History of the Creeds of Christendom*, I. 426 sqq.

[2] This is fully recognized by Renan, who, however, has little sympathy either with the apostle or the reformer, and fancies that the theology of both is antiquated. "That historical character," he says, "which upon the whole bears most analogy to St. Paul, is Luther. In both there is the same violence in language, the same passion, the same energy, the same noble independence, the same frantic attachment to a thesis embraced as the absolute truth." *St. Paul*, ch. XXII. at the close. And his last note in this book is this: "The work which resembles most in spirit the Epistle to the Galatians is Luther's *De Captivitate Babylonica Ecclesiæ.*"

wrath of God, although unable to mention to his confessor any particular transgression. The discipline of the law drove him to the brink of despair, when by the kind interposition of Staupitz he was directed away from himself to the cross of Christ, as the only source of pardon and peace, and found, by implicit faith in His all-sufficient merits, that righteousness which he had vainly sought in his own strength.[1] This, his second conversion, as we may call it, which occurred several years later (1508), and gradually rather than suddenly, made him an evangelical freeman in Christ and prepared him for the great conflict with Romanism, which began in earnest with the nailing of the ninety-nine theses against the traffic in indulgences (1517). The intervening years may be compared to Paul's sojourn in Arabia and the subordinate labors preceding his first great missionary tour.

FALSE EXPLANATIONS.

Various attempts have been made by ancient heretics and modern rationalists to explain Paul's conversion in a purely natural way, but they have utterly failed, and by their failure they indirectly confirm the true view as given by the apostle himself and as held in all ages by the Christian church.[2]

1. THE THEORY OF FRAUD.—The heretical and malignant faction of the Judaizers was disposed to attribute Paul's conversion to selfish motives, or to the influence of evil spirits.

The Ebionites spread the lie that Paul was of heathen parents, fell in love with the daughter of the high priest in Jerusalem, became a proselyte and submitted to circumcision in order to secure her, but failing in his purpose, he took revenge and attacked the circumcision, the sabbath, and the whole Mosaic law.[3]

In the pseudo-Clementine Homilies, which represent a specu-

---

[1] For particulars of his inner conflicts during his Erfurt period, see Köstlin's *Martin Luther* (1875), I. 40 sqq. and 61 sqq.

[2] Comp. the section on the Resurrection of Christ, pp. 172 sqq.

[3] Reported by Epiphanius, *Hær.* XXX. 16 (ed. Oehler, tom. I. 268 sq.).

lative form of the Judaizing heresy, Paul is assailed under the
disguise of Simon Magus, the arch-heretic, who smuggled antinomian heathenism into the church.   The manifestation of
Christ was either a manifestation of his wrath, or a deliberate
lie.[1]

2. THE RATIONALISTIC THEORY OF THUNDER AND LIGHTNING.
—It attributes the conversion to physical causes, namely, a violent storm and the delirium of a burning Syrian fever, in which
Paul superstitiously mistook the thunder for the voice of God
and the lightning for a heavenly vision.[2]   But the record says

---

[1] In the *Clem. Hom.*, XVII., ch. 19 (p. 351, ed. Dressel), Simon Peter says
to Simon Magus : ``If, then, our Jesus appeared to you in a vision (δι' ὁράματος
ὀφθείς), made himself known to you, and conversed with you, it is as one who
is enraged with an adversary (ὡς ἀντικειμένῳ ὀργιζόμενος).   And this is the
reason why it was through visions and dreams (δι' ὁραμάτων καὶ ἐνυπνίων), or
through revelations that were from without (ἢ καὶ δι' ἀποκαλύψεων ἔξωθεν
οὐσῶν) that He spoke to you.   But can any one be rendered fit for instruction
through apparitions? (δι' ὀπτασίαν) . . . And how are we to believe your
word, when you tell us that He appeared to you ?   And how did He appear
to you, when you entertain opinions contrary to His teaching ?   But if you have
seen and were taught by Him, and became His apostle for a single hour, proclaim His utterances, interpret His sayings, love His apostles, contend not
with me who companied with Him.   For you stand now in direct opposition
to me, who am a firm rock, the foundation of the church (στερεὰν πέτραν,
θεμέλιον ἐκκλησίας, comp. Matt. 16 : 18).   If you were not opposed to me, you
would not accuse me, and revile the truth proclaimed by me, in order that I
may not be believed when I state what I myself have heard with my own
ears from the Lord, as if I were evidently a person that was condemned and
had not stood the test [according to the true reading restored by Lagarde,
ἀδοκίμου ὄντος, instead of ἐνδοκιμοῦντος, 'in good repute'].   But if you say
that I am 'condemned' (εἰ κατεγνωσμένον με λέγεις, comp. Gal. 2 : 11), you
bring an accusation against God, who revealed the Christ to me, and you in-
veigh against Him who pronounced me blessed on account of the revelation
(Matt. 16 : 17).   But if you really wish to be a co-worker, in the cause of
truth, learn first of all from us what we have learned from Him, and, becoming a disciple of the truth, become a fellow-worker with me.''
   The allusions to Paul's Christ-vision and his collision with Peter at Antioch
are unmistakable, and form the chief argument for Baur's identification of
Simon Magus with Paul.   But it is perhaps only an incidental sneer.   Simon
represents all anti-Jewish heresies, as Peter represents all truths.
   [2] This theory was proposed by the so-called ``vulgar '' or deistic rationalists
(as distinct from the more recent speculative or pantheistic rationalists), and
has been revived and rhetorically embellished by Renan in *Les Apôtres* (ch. X.,
pp. 175 sqq.).   ``Every step to Damascus,'' says the distinguished French

nothing about thunderstorm and fever, and both combined could not produce such an effect upon any sensible man, much less upon the history of the world. Who ever heard the thunder speak in Hebrew or in any other articulate language? And had not Paul and Luke eyes and ears and common sense, as well as we, to distinguish an ordinary phenomenon of nature from a supernatural vision?

3. THE VISION-HYPOTHESIS resolves the conversion into a natural psychological process and into an honest self-delusion. It is the favorite theory of modern rationalists, who scorn all other explanations, and profess the highest respect for the intellectual and moral purity and greatness of Paul.[1] It is certainly more

Academicien, "excited in Paul bitter repentance; the shameful task of the hangman was intolerable to him; he felt as if he was kicking against the goads; the fatigue of travel added to his depression; a malignant fever suddenly seized him; the blood rushed to the head; the mind was filled with a picture of midnight darkness broken by lightning flashes; it is probable that one of those sudden storms of Mount Hermon broke out which are unequalled for vehemence, and to the Jew the thunder was the voice of God, the lightning the fire of God. Certain it is that by a fearful stroke the persecutor was thrown on the ground and deprived of his senses; in his feverish delirium he mistook the lightning for a heavenly vision, the voice of thunder for a voice from heaven; inflamed eyes, the beginning of ophthalmia, aided the delusion. Vehement natures suddenly pass from one extreme to another; moments decide for the whole life; dogmatism is the only thing which remains. So Paul changed the object of his fanaticism; by his boldness, his energy, his determination he saved Christianity, which otherwise would have died like Essenism, without leaving a trace of its memory. He is the founder of independent Protestantism. He represents le christianisme conquérant et voyageur. Jesus never dreamed of such disciples; yet it is they who will keep his work alive and secure it eternity." In this work, and more fully in his St. Paul, Renan gives a picture of the great apostle which is as strange a mixture of truth and error, and nearly as incoherent and fanciful, as his romance of Jesus in the Vie de Jésus.

[1] So Strauss (Leben Jesu, § 138, in connection with the resurrection of Christ), Baur (with much more seriousness and force, in his Paul, P. I., ch. 3) and the whole Tübingen School, Holsten, Hilgenfeld, Lipsius, Pfleiderer, Hausrath, and the author of Supernatural Religion (III. 498 sqq.). Baur at last gave up the theory as a failure (1860, see below). But Holsten revived and defended it very elaborately and ingeniously in his essay on the Christusvision des Paulus, in Hilgenfeld's "Zeitschrift" for 1861. W. Beyschlag (of Halle) very ably refuted it in an article: Die Bekehrung des Paulus mit besonderer Rücksicht auf die Erklärungsversuche von Baur und Holsten,

rational and creditable than the second hypothesis, because it ascribes the mighty change not to outward and accidental phenomena which pass away, but to internal causes. It assumes that an intellectual and moral fermentation was going on for some time in the mind of Paul, and resulted at last, by logical necessity, in an entire change of conviction and conduct, without any supernatural influence, the very possibility of which is denied as being inconsistent with the continuity of natural development. The miracle in this case was simply the mythical and symbolical reflection of the commanding presence of Jesus in the thoughts of the apostle.

That Paul saw a vision, he says himself, but he meant, of course, a real, objective, personal appearance of Christ from heaven, which was visible to his eyes and audible to his ears, and at the same time a revelation to his mind through the medium of the senses.[1] The inner spiritual manifestation[2] was more important than the external, but both combined produced conviction. The vision-theory turns the appearance of Christ

---

in the "Studien und Kritiken" for 1864, pp. 197–264. Then Holsten came out with an enlarged edition of his essay in book form, *Zum Evang. des Paulus und des Petrus*, 1868, with a long reply to Beyschlag. Pfleiderer repeated the vision-theory in his *Hibbert Lectures* (1885).

Some English writers have also written on Paul's conversion in opposition to this modern vision-theory, namely, R. MACPHERSON : *The Resurrection of Jesus Christ* (against Strauss), Edinb., 1867, Lect. XIII., pp. 316–360 ; GEO. P. FISHER : *Supernatural Origin of Christianity*, N. York, new ed. 1877, pp. 459–470, comp. his essay on " St. Paul " in *Discussions in History and Theology*, N. Y. 1880, pp. 487–511 ; A. B. BRUCE (of Glasgow) : *Paul's Conversion and the Pauline Gospel*, in the " Presbyt. Review " for Oct. 1880 (against Pfleiderer, whose work on Paulinism Bruce calls " an exegetical justification and a philosophical dissipation of the Reformed interpretation of the Pauline system of doctrine ").

[1] He describes it as an οὐράνιος ὀπτασία, Acts 26 : 19, and says that he *saw* Christ, that Christ *was seen* by him, 1 Cor. 9 : 1 ; 15 : 8. So the vision of the women at the tomb of the risen Lord is called an ὀπτασία τῶν ἀγγέλων, Luke 24 : 23. But even Peter, who was less critical than Paul, well knew how to distinguish between an actual occurrence (an ἀληθῶς γενόμενον) and a merely subjective vision (a ὅραμα), Acts 12 : 9. Objective visions are divine revelations through the senses ; subjective visions are hallucinations and deceptions.

[2] Gal. 1 : 16. ἀποκαλύψαι τὸν υἱὸν αὐτοῦ ἐν ἐμοί, within me, in my inmost soul and consciousness.

into a purely subjective imagination, which the apostle mistook for an objective fact.[1]

[1] Baur was disposed to charge this confusion upon the author of the Acts and to claim for Paul a more correct conception of the Christophany, as being a purely *inner* event or "a spiritual manifestation of Christ to his deeper self-consciousness " (Gal. 1 : 16, ἐν ἐμοί) ; but this is inconsistent with Paul's own language in 1 Cor. 9 : 1 ; 15 : 8.   Holsten admits that, without a full conviction of the *objective* reality of the Christophany, Paul could never have come to the conclusion that the crucified was raised to new life by the almighty power of God.   He states the case from his standpoint clearly in these words (p. 65) : *"Der glaube des Paulus an Jesus als den Christus war folge dessen, dass auch ihm Christus erschienen war* (1 Cor. 15 : 8).   *Diese vision war für das bewusstsein des Paulus das schauen einer objectiv-wirklichen, himmlischen gestalt, die aus ihrer transcendenten unsichtbarkeit sich ihm zur erscheinung gebracht habe.   Aus der wirklichkeit dieser geschauten gestalt, in welcher er den gekreuzigten Jesus erkannte, folgerte auch er, dass der kreuzes-tote zu neuem leben von der allmacht Gottes auferweckt worden, aus der gewiss-heit der auferweckung aber, dass dieser von den toten auferweckte der sohn Gottes und der Messias sei.   Wie also an der wirklichkeit der auferweckung dem Paulus die ganze wahrheit seines evangelium hängt* (vgl. 1 Cor. 15, 12 f.), *so ist es die vision des auferweckten, mit welcher ihm die wahrheit des messias-glaubens aufging, und der umschwung seines bewusstseins sich vollendete.*

"Diese vision war für Paulus der eingriff einer fremden transcendenten macht in sein geistesleben.   Die historische kritik aber unter der herrschaft des gesetzes der immanenten entwicklung des menschlichen geistes aus innerweltlichen causalitäten muss die vision als einen immanenten, psychologischen akt seines eigenen geistes zu begreifen suchen.   Ihr liegt damit eine ihrer schwiezigsten aufgaben vor, eine so schwierige, dass ein meister der historischen kritik, der zugleich so tief in das wesen des paulinischen geistes eingedrungen ist, als Baur, noch eben erklärt hat, dass ' keine, weder psychologische, noch dialektische ana-lyse das innere geheimnis des aktes erforschen könne, in welchem Gott seinen sohn dem Paulus enthüllte.'   Und doch darf sich die kritik von dem versuch, dies geheimnis zu erforschen, nicht abschrecken lassen.   Denn diese vision ist einer der entscheidendsten punkte für ein geschichtliches begreifen des urchristentums. In ihrer genesis ist der keim des paulinischen evangelium gegeben.   So lange der schein nicht aufgehoben ist, dass die empfängnis dieses keims als die wirkung einer transcendenten kraft erfolgt sei, besteht über dem empfangenen fort und fort der schein des transcendenten.   Und die kritik am wenigsten darf sich damit beruhigen, dass eine transcendenz, eine objectivität, wie sie von ihren gegnern für diese vision gefordert wird, von der selbstgewissheit des modernen geistes verworfen sei.   Denn diese selbstgewissheit kann ihre wahrheit nur behaupten, solange und soweit ihre kategorieen als das gesetz der wirklichkeit nachgewiesen sind."   Dr. Pfleiderer moves in the same line with Holsten, and eliminates the supernatural, but it is due to him to say that he admits the purely hypothetical character of this speculative theory, and lays great stress on the *moral* as well as the logical and dialectical process in Paul's mind. *"Darum war,"* he says (*Paulinismus*, p. 16), *" der Prozess der Bekehrung*

It is incredible that a man of sound, clear, and keen mind as that of Paul undoubtedly was, should have made such a radical and far-reaching blunder as to confound subjective reflections with an objective appearance of Jesus whom he persecuted, and to ascribe solely to an act of divine mercy what he must have known to be the result of his own thoughts, if he thought at all.

The advocates of this theory throw the appearances of the risen Lord to the older disciples, the later visions of Peter, Philip, and John in the Apocalypse, into the same category of subjective illusions in the high tide of nervous excitement and religious enthusiasm. It is plausibly maintained that Paul was an enthusiast, fond of visions and revelations,[1] and that he justifies a doubt concerning the realness of the resurrection itself by putting all the appearances of the risen Christ on the same level with his own, although several years elapsed between those of Jerusalem and Galilee, and that on the way to Damascus.

But this, the only possible argument for the vision-hypothesis, is entirely untenable. When Paul says: "*Last* of all, as unto an *untimely* offspring, Christ appeared to me also," he draws a clear line of distinction between the *personal* appearances of Christ and his own *later* visions, and closes the former with the one vouchsafed to him at his conversion.[2]   Once, and

nichts weniger, als eine kalte Denkoperation ; es war vielmehr der tiefsittliche Gehorsamsakt eines zarten Gewissens gegen die sich unwiderstehlich aufdrängende höhere Wahrheit (daher ihm auch der Glaube eine ὑπακοή ist), ein Akt grossartiger Selbstverleugnung, der Hingabe des alten Menschen und seiner ganzen religiösen Welt in den Tod, um fortan keinen Ruhm, ja kein Leben mehr zu haben, als in Christo, dem Gekreuzigten.   Das ist ja der Grundton, den wir aus allen Briefen des Apostels heraustönen hören, wo immer er sein persönliches Verhältniss zum Kreuz Christi schildert ; es ist nie bloss ein Verhältniss objectiver Theorie, sondern immer zugleich und wesentlich das der subjectiven Verbundenheit des innersten Gemüths mit dem Gekreuzigten, eine mystische Gemeinschaft mit dem Kreuzestod und mit dem Auferstehungsleben Christi."

[1] Comp. 2 Cor. 12 : 2 ; Acts 18 : 9 ; 22 : 17.   Some of these modern critics suppose that he was epileptic, like Mohammed and Swedenborg, and therefore all the more open to imaginary visions.

[2] 1 Cor. 15 : 8 : ἔσχατον δὲ πάντων, ὡσπερεὶ τῷ ἐκτρώματι, ὤφθη κἀμοί. Meyer justly remarks *in loc.*: ἔσχατον schliesst die Reihe leibhaftiger Erscheinungen ab, und scheidet damit diese von späteren visionären oder sonst apoka-

once only, he claims to have seen the Lord in visible form and to have heard his voice; last, indeed, and out of due time, yet as truly and really as the older apostles. The only difference is that they saw the *risen* Saviour still abiding on *earth*, while he saw the *ascended* Saviour coming down from *heaven*, as we may expect him to appear to all men on the last day. It is the *greatness* of that vision which leads him to dwell on his personal unworthiness as "the least of the apostles and not worthy to be called an apostle, because he persecuted the church of God." He uses the *realness* of Christ's resurrection as the basis for his wonderful discussion of the future resurrection of believers, which would lose all its force if Christ had not actually been raised from the dead.[1]

Moreover his conversion coincided with his call to the apostleship. If the former was a delusion, the latter must also have been a delusion. He emphasizes his direct call to the apostleship of the Gentiles by the personal appearance of Christ without any human intervention, in opposition to his Judaizing adversaries who tried to undermine his authority.[2]

The whole assumption of a long and deep inward preparation, both intellectual and moral, for a change, is without any evidence, and cannot set aside the fact that Paul was, according to his repeated confession, at that time violently persecuting Christianity in its followers. His conversion can be far less explained from antecedent causes, surrounding circumstances, and personal motives than that of any other disciple. While

---

lyptischen." Similarly Godet (*Com. sur l'épitre aux Romains*, 1879, I. 17):
"*Paul clôt l'énumeration des apparitions de Jésus ressuscité aux apôtres par celle qui lui a été accordée à lui-même ; il lui attribue donc la même réalité qu'à celles-là, et il la distingue ainsi d'une manière tranchée de toutes les visions dont il fut plus tard honoré et que mentionnent le livre des Actes, et les épitres.*"

[1] 1 Cor 15 : 12 sqq. Dean Stanley compares this discussion to the Phædo of Plato and the Tusculan Disputations of Cicero, but it is far more profound and assuring. Heathen philosophy can at best prove only the possibility and probability, but not the certainty, of a future life. Moreover the idea of immortality has no comfort, but terror rather, except for those who believe in Christ, who is "the Resurrection and the Life."

[2] Gal. 1 : 16 ; 1 Cor. 9 : 1; 15 : 8; Acts 22 : 10, 14.

the older apostles were devoted friends of Jesus, Paul was his enemy, bent at the very time of the great change on an errand of cruel persecution, and therefore in a state of mind most unlikely to give birth to a vision so fatal to his present object and his future career. How could a fanatical persecutor of Christianity, "breathing threatenings and slaughter against the disciples of the Lord," stultify and contradict himself by an imaginative conceit which tended to the building up of that very religion which he was laboring to destroy ! [1]

But supposing (with Renan) that his mind was temporarily upset in the delirium of feverish excitement, he certainly soon recovered health and reason, and had every opportunity to correct his error; he was intimate with the murderers of Jesus, who could have produced tangible evidence against the resurrection if it had never occurred; and after a long pause of quiet reflection he went to Jerusalem, spent a fortnight with Peter, and could learn from him and from James, the brother of Christ, their experience, and compare it with his own. Everything in this case is against the mythical and legendary theory which requires a change of environment and the lapse of years for the formation of poetic fancies and fictions.

Finally, the whole life-work of Paul, from his conversion at Damascus to his martyrdom in Rome, is the best possible argument against this hypothesis and for the realness of his conversion, as an act of divine grace. " By their fruits ye shall know them." How could such an effective change proceed from an empty dream ? Can an illusion change the current of history ? By joining the Christian sect Paul sacrificed everything, at last life itself, to the service of Christ. He never wavered in his conviction of the truth as revealed to him, and by his faith in this revelation he has become a benediction to all ages.

The vision-hypothesis denies objective miracles, but ascribes miracles to subjective imaginations, and makes a lie more effective and beneficial than the truth.

---

[1] Acts 9 : 2; comp. Gal. 1 : 13 ; 1 Cor. 15 : 9; Phil. 3 : 6; 1 Tim. 1 : 13

All rationalistic and natural interpretations of the conversion of Paul turn out to be irrational and unnatural ; the supernatural interpretation of Paul himself, after all, is the most rational and natural.

REMARKABLE CONCESSIONS.

Dr. BAUR, the master-spirit of skeptical criticism and the founder of the "Tübingen School," felt constrained, shortly before his death (1860), to abandon the vision-hypothesis and to admit that "no psychological or dialectical analysis can explore the inner mystery of the act in which God revealed his Son in Paul (*keine, weder psychologische noch dialektische Analyse kann das innere Geheimniss des Actes erforschen, in welchem Gott seinen Sohn in ihm enthülte*). In the same connection he says that in "the sudden transformation of Paul from the most violent adversary of Christianity into its most determined herald" he could see "nothing short of a miracle (*Wunder*) ; " and adds that "this miracle appears all the greater when we remember that in this revulsion of his consciousness he broke through the barriers of Judaism and rose out of its particularism into the universalism of Christianity." [1] This frank confession is creditable to the head and heart of the late Tübingen critic, but is fatal to his whole anti-supernaturalistic theory of history. *Si falsus in uno, falsus in omnibus.* If we admit the miracle in one case, the door is opened for all other miracles which rest on equally strong evidence.

The late Dr. KEIM, an independent pupil of Baur, admits at least spiritual manifestations of the ascended Christ *from heaven*, and urges in favor of the objective reality of the Christophanies as reported by Paul, 1 Cor. 15 : 3 sqq., "the whole character of Paul, his sharp understanding which was not weakened by his enthusiasm, the careful, cautious, measured, simple form of his statement, above all the favorable total impression of his narrative and the mighty echo of it in the unanimous, uncontradicted faith of primitive Christendom." [2]

Dr. SCHENKEL, of Heidelberg, in his latest stage of development, says that Paul, with full justice, put his Christophany on a par with the Christophanies of the older apostles ; that all these Christophanies are not simply the result of psychological processes, but "remain in many respects psychologically inconceivable," and point back to the historic background of the person of Jesus ; that Paul was not an ordinary visionary, but carefully distinguished the Christophany at Damascus from his later visions ; that he retained the full possession of his rational mind even in the moments of the highest exaltation ; that his conversion

---

[1] See Baur's *Church History of the First Three Centuries*, Tübingen, 2d ed. p. 45 ; English translation by Allan Menzies, London, 1878, vol. I. 47.

[2] *Geschichte Jesu von Nazara.* Zürich, 1872, vol. III. 532.

was not the sudden effect of nervous excitement, but brought about by the influence of the divine Providence which quietly prepared his soul for the reception of Christ; and that the appearance of Christ vouchsafed to him was "no dream, but reality." [1]

Professor REUSS, of Strasburg, likewise an independent critic of the liberal school, comes to the same conclusion as Baur, that the conversion of Paul, if not an absolute miracle, is at least an unsolved psychological problem. He says : "*La conversion de Paul, après tout ce qui en a été dit de notre temps, reste toujours, si ce n'est un miracle absolu, dans le sens traditionnel de ce mot (c'est-à-dire un événement qui arrête ou change violemment le cours naturel des choses, un effet sans autre cause que l'intervention arbitraire et immédiate de Dieu), du moins un problème psychologique aujourd'hui insoluble. L'explication dite naturelle, qu'elle fasse intervenir un orage ou qu'elle se retranche dans le domaine des hallucinations . . . ne nous donne pas la clef de cette crise elle-même, qui a décidé la métamorphose du pharisien en chrétien.*" [2]

Canon Farrar says (I. 195) : "One fact remains upon any hypothesis—and that is, that the conversion of St. Paul was in the highest sense of the word a miracle, and one of which the spiritual consequences have affected every subsequent age of the history of mankind."

§ 32. *The Work of Paul.*

> "He who can part from country and from kin,
>   And scorn delights, and tread the thorny way,
> A heavenly crown, through toil and pain, to win—
>   He who reviled can tender love repay,
>   And buffeted, for bitter foes can pray—
> He who, upspringing at his Captain's call,
>   Fights the good fight, and when at last the day
>   Of fiery trial comes, can nobly fall—
> Such were a saint—or more—and such the holy Paul!"
>
>   —ANON.

The conversion of Paul was a great intellectual and moral revolution, yet without destroying his identity. His noble gifts and attainments remained, but were purged of selfish motives, inspired by a new principle, and consecrated to a divine end. The love of Christ who saved him, was now his all-absorbing passion, and no sacrifice was too great to manifest his gratitude

---

[1] *Das Christusbild der Apostel.* Leipzig, 1879, pp. 57 sq.
[2] *Les Épitres pauliniennes.* Paris, 1878, vol. I. p. 11.

to Him.   The architect of ruin became an architect of the temple of God.   The same vigor, depth and acuteness of mind, but illuminated by the Holy Spirit; the same strong temper and burning zeal, but cleansed, subdued and controlled by wisdom and moderation; the same energy and boldness, but coupled with gentleness and meekness; and, added to all this, as crowning gifts of grace, a love and humility, a tenderness and delicacy of feeling such as are rarely, if ever, found in a character so proud, manly and heroic.   The little Epistle to Philemon reveals a perfect Christian gentleman, a nobleman of nature, doubly ennobled by grace.   The thirteenth chapter of the first Epistle to the Corinthians could only be conceived by a mind that had ascended on the mystic ladder of faith to the throbbing heart of the God of love; yet without inspiration even Paul could not have penned that seraphic description of the virtue which beareth all things, believeth all things, hopeth all things, endureth all things, which never faileth, but will last for ever, the greatest in the triad of celestial graces: faith, hope, love.

Saul converted became at once Paul the missionary.   Being saved himself, he made it his life-work to save others.   " Straightway " he proclaimed Christ in the synagogues, and confounded the Jews of Damascus, proving that Jesus of Nazareth is the Messiah, the Son of God.[1]   But this was only a preparatory testimony in the fervor of the first love.   The appearance of Christ, and the travails of his soul during the three days and nights of prayer and fasting, when he experienced nothing less than a spiritual death and a spiritual resurrection, had so shaken his physical and mental frame that he felt the need of protracted repose away from the noise and turmoil of the world.   Besides there must have been great danger threatening his life as soon as the astounding news of his conversion became known

---

[1] The εὐθέως of Acts 9 : 20 compels us to put this short testimony during the *few* days (ἡμέρας τινάς) which he spent with the disciples at Damascus, before his departure to Arabia.   About three years afterwards (or after " *many* days," ἡμέραι ἱκαναί, were fulfilled, Acts 9 : 23), he returned to Damascus to renew his testimony (Gal. 1 : 17).

at Jerusalem. He therefore went to the desert of Arabia and
spent there three years,' not in missionary labor (as Chrysostom
thought), but chiefly in prayer, meditation and the study of the
Hebrew Scriptures in the light of their fulfilment through the
person and work of Jesus of Nazareth. This retreat took the
place of the three years' preparation of the Twelve in the
school of Christ. Possibly he may have gone as far as Mount
Sinai, among the wild children of Hagar and Ishmael.² On that
pulpit of the great lawgiver of Israel, and in view of the surrounding panorama of death and desolation which reflects the
terrible majesty of Jehovah, as no other spot on earth, he could
listen with Elijah to the thunder and earthquake, and the still
small voice, and could study the contrast between the killing
letter and the life-giving spirit, between the ministration of
death and the ministration of righteousness.³ The desert, like
the ocean, has its grandeur and sublimity, and leaves the medi-
tating mind alone with God and eternity.

" Paul was a unique man for a unique task." ⁴ His task was
twofold : practical and theoretical. He preached the gospel of
free and universal grace from Damascus to Rome, and secured
its triumph in the Roman empire, which means the civilized
world of that age. At the same time he built up the church
from within by the exposition and defence of the gospel in his
Epistles. He descended to the humblest details of ecclesiastical
administration and discipline, and mounted to the sublimest
heights of theological speculation. Here we have only to do
with his missionary activity ; leaving his theoretical work to be
considered in another chapter.

¹ Gal. 1 : 17, 18. In the Acts (9 : 23) this journey is ignored because it belonged not to the public, but private and inner life of Paul.

² Comp. Gal. 4 : 25, where " Arabia " means the Sinaitic Peninsula.

³ 2 Cor. 3 : 6–9.

⁴ Thus Godet sums up his life (*Romans*, Introd. I. 59). He thinks that Paul
was neither the substitute of Judas, nor of James the son of Zebedee, but a
substitute for a converted Israel, the man who had, single-handed, to execute
the task which properly fell to his whole nation ; and hence the hour of his
call was precisely that when the blood of the two martyrs, Stephen and
James, sealed the hardening of Israel and decided its rejection.

Let us first glance at his missionary spirit and policy.

His inspiring motive was love to Christ and to his fellow-men.
" The love of Christ," he says, " constraineth us ; because we
thus judge, that one died for all, therefore all died : and He
died for all that they who live should no longer live unto themselves, but unto him who for their sakes died and rose again."
He regarded himself as a bondman and ambassador of Christ,
entreating men to be reconciled to God. Animated by this
spirit, he became " as a Jew to the Jews, as a Gentile to the
Gentiles, all things to all men that by all means he might save
some."

He made Antioch, the capital of Syria and the mother church
of Gentile Christendom, his point of departure for, and return
from, his missionary journeys, and at the same time he kept up
his connection with Jerusalem, the mother church of Jewish
Christendom. Although an independent apostle of Christ, he
accepted a solemn commission from Antioch for his first great
missionary tour. He followed the current of history, commerce,
and civilization, from East to West, from Asia to Europe, from
Syria to Asia Minor, Greece, Italy, and perhaps as far as Spain.[1]
In the larger and more influential cities, Antioch, Ephesus, Corinth, Rome, he resided a considerable time. From these salient
points he sent the gospel by his pupils and fellow-laborers into
the surrounding towns and villages. But he always avoided
collision with other apostles, and sought new fields of labor
where Christ was not known before, that he might not build on
any other man's foundation. This is true independence and
missionary courtesy, which is so often, alas ! violated by missionary societies inspired by sectarian rather than Christian zeal.

[1] "Westward the course of empire takes its way." This famous line of
Bishop Berkeley, the philosopher, expresses a general law of history both
civil and religious. Clement of Rome says that Paul came on his missionary
tour "to the extreme west" (ἐπὶ τὸ τέρμα τῆς δύσεως), which means either
Rome or Spain, whither the apostle *intended* to go (Rom. 15 : 24, 28). Some
English historians (Ussher, Stillingfleet, etc.) would extend Paul's travels to
Gaul and Britain, but of this there is no trace either in the New Test., or in
the early tradition. See below.

His chief mission was to the Gentiles, without excluding the Jews, according to the message of Christ delivered through Ananias: "Thou shalt bear my name before the Gentiles, and kings, and the children of Israel." Considering that the Jews had a prior claim in time to the gospel,[1] and that the synagogues in heathen cities were pioneer stations for Christian missions, he very naturally addressed himself first to the Jews and proselytes, taking up the regular lessons of the Old Testament Scriptures, and demonstrating their fulfilment in Jesus of Nazareth. But almost uniformly he found the half-Jews, or "proselytes of the gate," more open to the gospel than his own brethren; they were honest and earnest seekers of the true religion, and formed the natural bridge to the pure heathen, and the nucleus of his congregations, which were generally composed of converts from both religions.

In noble self-denial he earned his subsistence with his own hands, as a tent-maker, that he might not be burthensome to his congregations (mostly belonging to the lower classes), that he might preserve his independence, stop the mouths of his enemies, and testify his gratitude to the infinite mercy of the Lord, who had called him from his headlong, fanatical career of persecution to the office of an apostle of free grace. He never collected money for himself, but for the poor Jewish Christians in Palestine. Only as an exception did he receive gifts from his converts at Philippi, who were peculiarly dear to him. Yet he repeatedly enjoins upon the churches to care for the liberal temporal support of their teachers who break to them the bread of eternal life. The Saviour of the world a carpenter! the greatest preacher of the gospel a tent-maker!

Of the innumerable difficulties, dangers, and sufferings which he encountered with Jews, heathens, and false brethren, we can hardly form an adequate idea; for the book of Acts is only a summary record. He supplements it incidentally. "Of the

---

[1] Rom. 1 : 16, "to the Jews *first*," not on the ground of a superior merit (the Jews, as a people, were most unworthy and ungrateful), but on the ground of God's promise and the historical order (Rom. 15 : 8).

Jews five times received I forty stripes save one. Three times was I beaten with rods, once was I stoned, three times I suffered shipwreck, a night and a day have I been in the deep ; in journeyings often, in perils of rivers, in perils of robbers, in perils from my countrymen, in perils from the heathen, in perils in the city, in perils in the wilderness, in perils in the sea, in perils among false brethren ; in labor and toil, in watchings often, in hunger and thirst, in fastings often, in cold and nakedness. Besides those things that are without, there is that which presseth upon me daily, the anxious care for all the churches. Who is weak, and I am not weak ? Who is offended, and I burn not ?" [1] Thus he wrote reluctantly to the Corinthians, in self-vindication against his calumniators, in the year 57, before his longest and hardest trial in the prisons of Cæsarea and Rome, and at least seven years before his martyrdom. He was "pressed on every side, yet not straitened ; perplexed, yet not in despair ; pursued, yet not forsaken ; smitten down, yet not destroyed." [2] His whole public career was a continuous warfare. He represents the church militant, or "marching and conquering Christianity." He was "*unus versus mundum*," in a far higher sense than this has been said of Athanasius the Great when confronted with the Arian heresy and the imperial heathenism of Julian the Apostate.

Yet he was never unhappy, but full of joy and peace. He exhorted the Philippians from his prison in Rome : " Rejoice in the Lord alway ; again I will say, Rejoice." In all his conflicts with foes from without and foes from within Paul was "more than conqueror" through the grace of God which was sufficient for him. " For I am persuaded," he writes to the Romans in the strain of a sublime ode of triumph, "that neither death, nor life, nor angels, nor principalities, nor things present, nor things to come, nor powers, nor height, nor depth, nor any other creature shall be able to separate us from the love of God, which is in Christ Jesus our Lord." [3] And his dying word is an assur-

[1] 2 Cor. 11 · 24-29.   [2] 2 Cor. 4 : 8, 9.   [3] Rom. 8 : 31-39.

ance of victory: " I have fought the good fight, I have finished
the course, I have kept the faith : henceforth there is laid up
for me the crown of righteousness, which the Lord, the righteous judge, shall give me at that day : and not only to me, but
also to all them that have loved his appearing." [1]

§ 33. *Paul's Missionary Labors.*

The public life of Paul, from the third year after his conversion to his martyrdom, A.D. 40–64, embraces a quarter of a century, three great missionary campaigns with minor expeditions,
five visits to Jerusalem, and at least four years of captivity in
Cæsarea and Rome.   Some extend it to A.D. 67 or 68.   It may
be divided into five or six periods, as follows :

1. A.D. 40–44.   The period of preparatory labors in Syria
and his native Cilicia, partly alone, partly in connection with
Barnabas, his senior fellow-apostle among the Gentiles.

On his return from the Arabian retreat Paul began his public ministry in earnest at Damascus, preaching Christ on the
very spot where he had been converted and called.   His testimony enraged the Jews, who stirred up the deputy of the king
of Arabia against him, but he was saved for future usefulness
and let down by the brethren in a basket through a window in
the wall of the city.[2]   Three years after his conversion he went

---

[1] 2 Tim. 4 : 6–8.   We may add here the somewhat panegyric passage of
Clement of Rome, who apparently exalts Paul above Peter, *Ep. ad Corinth.*
c. 5 : ''Let us set before our eyes the good Apostles.   Peter, who on account
of unrighteous jealousy endured not one or two, but many toils, and thus
having borne his testimony (μαρτυρήσας, or, suffered martyrdom), went to his
appointed place of glory.   By reason of jealousy and strife Paul by his example pointed out the price of patient endurance.   After having been seven
times in bonds, driven into exile, stoned, and after having preached in the
East and in the West, he won the noble reward of his faith, having taught
righteousness unto the whole world and having reached the boundary of the
West; and when he had borne his testimony before the magistrates, he departed from the world and went unto the holy place, having become the
greatest example of patient endurance."

[2] Acts 9 : 23–25 ; comp. 2 Cor. 11: 32, 33.   The window of escape is still
shown in Damascus, as is also the street called Straight, the house of Judas,
and the house of Ananias.   But these local traditions are uncertain.

up to Jerusalem to make the acquaintance of Peter and spent a fortnight with him. Besides him he saw James the brother of the Lord. Barnabas introduced him to the disciples, who at first were afraid of him, but when they heard of his marvellous conversion they "glorified God" that their persecutor was now preaching the faith he had once been laboring to destroy.[1] He did not come to learn the gospel, having received it already by revelation, nor to be confirmed or ordained, having been called "not from men, or through man, but through Jesus Christ." Yet his interview with Peter and James, though barely mentioned, must have been fraught with the deepest interest. Peter, kind-hearted and generous as he was, would naturally receive him with joy and thanksgiving. He had himself once denied the Lord—not malignantly but from weakness—as Paul had persecuted the disciples—ignorantly in unbelief. Both had been mercifully pardoned, both had seen the Lord, both were called to the highest dignity, both could say from the bottom of the heart: "Lord thou knowest all things; thou knowest that I love thee." No doubt they would exchange their experiences and confirm each other in their common faith.

It was probably on this visit that Paul received in a vision in the temple the express command of the Lord to go quickly unto the Gentiles.[2] Had he stayed longer at the seat of the Sanhedrin, he would undoubtedly have met the fate of the martyr Stephen.

He visited Jerusalem a second time during the famine under Claudius, in the year 44, accompanied by Barnabas, on a benevolent mission, bearing a collection of the Christians at Antioch for the relief of the brethren in Judæa.[3] On that occasion he probably saw none of the apostles on account of the persecution in which James was beheaded, and Peter imprisoned.

The greater part of these four years was spent in missionary work at Tarsus and Antioch.

[1] Gal. 1 : 18–24 ; comp. Acts 9 : 26, 27.

[2] Acts 22 : 17–21. It is remarkable that in his prayer he confessed his sin against "Stephen the martyr;" thus making public reparation for a public sin in the city where it was committed.

[3] Acts 11 : 28–30 ; 12 : 25.

2. A.D. 45–50. First missionary journey. In the year 45 Paul entered upon the first great missionary journey, in company with Barnabas and Mark, by the direction of the Holy Spirit through the prophets of the congregation at Antioch. He traversed the island of Cyprus and several provinces of Asia Minor. The conversion of the Roman proconsul, Sergius Paulus, at Paphos; the rebuke and punishment of the Jewish sorcerer, Elymas; the marked success of the gospel in Pisidia, and the bitter opposition of the unbelieving Jews; the miraculous healing of a cripple at Lystra; the idolatrous worship there offered to Paul and Barnabas by the superstitious heathen, and its sudden change into hatred against them as enemies of the gods; the stoning of the missionaries, their escape from death, and their successful return to Antioch, are the leading incidents of this tour, which is fully described in the 13th and 14th chapters of the Acts.

This period closes with the important apostolic conference at Jerusalem, A.D. 50, which will require separate consideration in the next section.

3. From A.D. 51–54. Second missionary journey. After the council at Jerusalem and the temporary adjustment of the difference between the Jewish and Gentile branches of the church, Paul undertook, in the year 51, a second great journey, which decided the Christianization of Greece. He took Silas for his companion. Having first visited his old churches, he proceeded, with the help of Silas and the young convert, Timothy, to establish new ones through the provinces of Phrygia and Galatia, where, notwithstanding his bodily infirmity, he was received with open arms like an angel of God.

From Troas, a few miles south of the Homeric Troy and the entrance to the Hellespont, he crossed over to Greece in answer to the Macedonian cry: "Come over and help us!" He preached the gospel with great success, first in Philippi, where he converted the purple dealer, Lydia, and the jailor, and was imprisoned with Silas, but miraculously delivered and honorably released; then in Thessalonica, where he was persecuted by the

Jews, but left a flourishing church ; in Berœa, where the converts showed exemplary zeal in searching the Scriptures. In
Athens, the metropolis of classical literature, he reasoned with
Stoic and Epicurean philosophers, and unveiled to them on Mars'
Hill (Areopagus), with consummate tact and wisdom, though
without much immediate success, the " unknown God," to whom
the Athenians, in their superstitious anxiety to do justice to all
possible divinities, had unconsciously erected an altar, and Jesus
Christ, through whom God will judge the world in righteousness.[1] In Corinth, the commercial bridge between the East and
the West, a flourishing centre of wealth and culture, but also a
sink of vice and corruption, the apostle spent eighteen months,
and under almost insurmountable difficulties he built up a church,
which exhibited all the virtues and all the faults of the Grecian
character under the influence of the gospel, and which he honored with two of his most important Epistles.[2]

---

[1] "Paul left Athens," says Farrar (I. 550 sq.), " a despised and lonely man.
And yet his visit was not in vain . . . . He founded no church at Athens,
but there—it may be under the fostering charge of the converted Areopagite
—a church grew up. In the next century it furnished to the cause of Christianity its martyr bishops and its eloquent apologists (Publius, Quadratus,
Aristides, Athenagoras). In the third century it flourished in peace and
purity. In the fourth century it was represented at Nicæa, and the noble
rhetoric of the two great Christian friends, St. Basil and St. Gregory of
Nazianzus, was trained in its Christian schools. Nor were many centuries to
elapse ere, unable to confront the pierced hands which held a wooden cross,
its myriads of deities had fled into the dimness of outworn creeds, and its
tutelary goddess, in spite of the flashing eyes which Homer had commemorated, and the mighty spear which had been moulded out of the trophies of
Marathon, resigned her maiden chamber to the honour of that meek Galilæan
maiden who had lived under the roof of the carpenter at Nazareth—the virgin
mother of the Lord." Yet Athens was one of the last cities in the Roman
empire which abandoned idolatry, and it never took a prominent position in
church history. Its religion was the worship of ancient Greek genius rather
than that of Christ. " *Il est bien moins disciple de Jésus et de saint Paul que
de Plutarque et de Julien,*" says Renan, *St. Paul,* p. 208. His chapter on Paul
in Athens is very interesting.

[2] In Corinth Paul wrote that fearful, yet truthful description of pagan depravity in Rom. 1 : 18 sqq. The city was proverbially corrupt, so that
κορινθιάζομαι means *to practise whoredom,* and κορινθιαστής a *whoremonger.*
The great temple of Venus on the acropolis had more than a thousand courte-

In the spring of 54 he returned by way of Ephesus, Cæsarea, and Jerusalem to Antioch.

During this period he composed the two Epistles to the Thessalonians, which are the earliest of his literary remains excepting his missionary addresses preserved in the Acts.

4. A.D. 54–58. Third missionary tour. Towards the close of the year 54 Paul went to Ephesus, and in this renowned capital of proconsular Asia and of the worship of Diana, he fixed for three years the centre of his missionary work. He then revisited his churches in Macedonia and Achaia, and remained three months more in Corinth and the vicinity.

During this period he wrote the great doctrinal Epistles to the Galatians, Corinthians, and Romans, which mark the height of his activity and usefulness.

5. A.D. 58–63. The period of his two imprisonments, with the intervening winter voyage from Cæsarea to Rome. In the spring of 58 he journeyed, for the fifth and last time, to Jerusalem, by way of Philippi, Troas, Miletus (where he delivered his affecting valedictory to the Ephesian presbyter-bishops), Tyre, and Cæsarea, to carry again to the poor brethren in Judæa a contribution from the Christians of Greece, and by this token of gratitude and love to cement the two branches of the apostolic church more firmly together.

But some fanatical Jews, who bitterly hated him as an apostate and a seducer of the people, raised an uproar against him at Pentecost; charged him with profaning the temple, because he had taken into it an uncircumcised Greek, Trophimus; dragged him out of the sanctuary, lest they should defile it with blood, and would undoubtedly have killed him had not Claudius Lysias, the Roman tribune, who lived near by, come promptly with his soldiers to the spot. This officer rescued Paul, out of respect for his Roman citizenship, from the fury of the mob, set him the next day before the Sanhedrin, and after a tumultuous

zans devoted to the service of lust.   With good reason Bengel calls a church of God in Corinth a "*lætum et ingens paradoxon* (in 1 Cor. 1 : 2). See the lively description of Renan, *St. Paul*, ch. VIII. pp. 211 sqq.

and fruitless session of the council, and the discovery of a plot against his life, sent him, with a strong military guard and a certificate of innocence, to the procurator Felix in Cæsarea.

Here the apostle was confined two whole years (58–60), awaiting his trial before the Sanhedrin, uncondemned, occasionally speaking before Felix, apparently treated with comparative mildness, visited by the Christians, and in some way not known to us promoting the kingdom of God.[1]

After the accession of the new and better procurator, Festus, who is known to have succeeded Felix in the year 60, Paul, as a Roman citizen, appealed to the tribunal of Cæsar and thus opened the way to the fulfilment of his long-cherished desire to preach the Saviour of the world in the metropolis of the world. Having once more testified his innocence, and spoken for Christ in a masterly defence before Festus, King Herod Agrippa II. (the last of the Herods), his sister Bernice, and the most distinguished men of Cæsarea, he was sent in the autumn of the year 60 to the emperor. He had a stormy voyage and suffered shipwreck, which detained him over winter at Malta. The voyage is described with singular minuteness and nautical accuracy by Luke as an eye-witness. In the month of March of the year 61, the apostle, with a few faithful companions, reached Rome, a prisoner of Christ, and yet freer and mightier than the emperor on the throne. It was the seventh year of Nero's reign, when he had already shown his infamous character by the murder of Agrippina, his mother, in the previous year, and other acts of cruelty.

In Rome Paul spent at least two years till the spring of 63, in easy confinement, awaiting the decision of his case, and surrounded by friends and fellow-laborers "in his own hired dwelling." He preached the gospel to the soldiers of the imperial

---

[1] Weiss (*Bibl. Theol. des N. T.*, 3d ed. p. 202) is inclined to assign the composition of the Epistles to the Colossians and Ephesians to the period of the imprisonment at Cæsarea. So also Thiersch, Reuss, Schenkel, Meyer, Zöckler, Hausrath. See Meyer *Com. on Eph.* (5th ed. by Woldemar Schmidt, 1878, p. 18), and on the other side, Neander, Wieseler, and Lightfoot (*Philippians*, 3d ed. 1873, p. 29), who date all the Epistles of the captivity from Rome.

body-guard, who attended him; sent letters and messages to his distant churches in Asia Minor and Greece; watched over all their spiritual affairs, and completed in bonds his apostolic fidelity to the Lord and his church.[1]

In the Roman prison he wrote the Epistles to the Colossians, Ephesians, Philippians, and Philemon.

6. A.D. 63 and 64.   With the second year of Paul's imprisonment in Rome the account of Luke breaks off, rather abruptly, yet appropriately and grandly.   Paul's arrival in Rome secured the triumph of Christianity.   In this sense it was true, "*Roma locuta est, causa finita est.*"   And he who spoke at Rome is not dead; he is still "preaching (everywhere) the kingdom of God and teaching the things concerning the Lord Jesus Christ, with all boldness, none forbidding him."[2]

But what became of him after the termination of those two years in the spring of 63?   What was the result of the trial so long delayed?   Was he condemned to death? or was he released by Nero's tribunal, and thus permitted to labor for another season?   This question is still unsettled among scholars. A vague tradition says that Paul was acquitted of the charge of the Sanhedrin, and after travelling again in the East, perhaps also into Spain, was a second time imprisoned in Rome and condemned to death.   The assumption of a second Roman captivity relieves certain difficulties in the Pastoral Epistles; for they seem to require a short period of freedom between the first and a second Roman captivity, and a visit to the East,[3] which is not recorded in the Acts, but which the apostle contemplated

---

[1] Acts 28 : 30, 31.   Comp. the Epistles of the captivity.

[2] Bengel remarks on *Acts* 28 : 31 : "*Paulus Romæ, apex evangelii, Actorum finis: quæ Lucas alioqui* (2 Tim. 4 : 11) *facile potuisset ad exitum Pauli perducere.   Hierosolymis cœpit: Romæ desinit.*"   The abruptness of the close seems not to be accidental, for, as Lightfoot remarks (*Com. on Philippians,* p. 3, note), there is a striking parallelism between the Acts and the Gospel of Luke in their beginning and ending, and there could be no fitter termination of the narrative, since it is the realization of that promise of the universal spread of the gospel which is the starting-point of the Acts.

[3] Namely, to Ephesus, 1 Tim. 1 : 3; 2 Tim. 4 : 13, 20; to Crete, Tit. 1 : 5 and to Nicopolis, Tit. 3 : 12.

in case of his release.[1] A visit to Spain, which he intended,
is possible, though less probable.[2] If he was set at liberty, it
must have been before the terrible persecution in July, 64,
which would not have spared the great leader of the Christian
sect. It is a remarkable coincidence that just about the close
of the second year of Paul's confinement, the celebrated Jewish
historian, Josephus, then in his 27th year, came to Rome (after
a tempestuous voyage and shipwreck), and effected through the
influence of Poppæa (the wife of Nero and a half proselyte of
Judaism) the release of certain Jewish priests who had been
sent to Rome by Felix as prisoners.[3] It is not impossible that
Paul may have reaped the benefit of a general release of Jewish
prisoners.

The martyrdom of Paul under Nero is established by the
unanimous testimony of antiquity. As a Roman citizen, he was
not crucified, like Peter, but put to death by the sword.[4] The
scene of his martyrdom is laid by tradition about three miles
from Rome, near the Ostian way, on a green spot, formerly
called *Aquæ Salviæ*, afterwards *Tre Fontane*, from the three
fountains which are said to have miraculously gushed forth
from the blood of the apostolic martyr. His relics were ultimately removed to the basilica of San Paolo-fuori-le-Mura, built

[1] Phil. 1 : 25; 2 : 24; Philem. ver. 22. These passages, however, are not
conclusive, for the Apostle claims no infallibility in personal matters and
plans; he was wavering between the expectation and desire of speedy martyrdom and further labors for the brethren, Phil. 1 : 20–23; 2 : 17. He may
have been foiled in his contemplated visit to Philippi and Colosse.

[2] Rom. 15 : 24, 28. Renan denies a visit to the Orient, but thinks that the
last labors of Paul were spent in Spain or Gaul, and that he died in Rome by
the sword, A.D. 64 or later (*L'Antechrist*, 106, 190). Dr. Plumptre (in the
Introduction to his *Com. on Luke*, and in an Appendix to his *Com. on Acts*)
ingeniously conjectures some connection between Luke, Paul's companion,
and the famous poet, M. Annæus Lucanus (the author of the *Pharsalia*, and
a nephew of Seneca), who was a native of Corduba (Cordova) in Spain, and
on this basis he accounts for the favorable conduct of J. Annæus Gallio
(Seneca's brother) toward Paul at Corinth, the early tradition of a friendship
between Paul and Seneca, and Paul's journey to Spain. Rather fanciful

[3] Jos. *Vita*, c. 3. Comp. Plumptre, *l.c.*

[4] Tertullian (*De præscr. hæret.* c. 36): "*Romæ Petrus passioni Dominica
adæquatur, Paulus Joannis [Baptistæ] exitu coronatur.*"

by Theodosius and Valentinian in 388, and recently reconstructed. He lies outside of Rome, Peter inside. His memory
is celebrated, together with that of Peter, on the 29th and 30th
of June.[1] As to the year of his death, the views vary from A.D.
64 to 69. The difference of the place and manner of his martyrdom suggests that he was condemned by a regular judicial
trial, either shortly before, or more probably a year or two after
the horrible wholesale massacre of Christians on the Vatican
hill, in which his Roman citizenship would not have been regarded. If he was released in the spring of 63, he had a year
and a half for another visit to the East and to Spain before
the outbreak of the Neronian persecution (after July, 64); but
tradition favors a later date. Prudentius separates the martyrdom of Peter from that of Paul by one year. After that
persecution the Christians were everywhere exposed to danger.[2]

Assuming the release of Paul and another visit to the East,
we must locate the First Epistle to Timothy and the Epistle to
Titus between the first and second Roman captivity, and the
Second Epistle to Timothy in the second captivity. The last
was evidently written in the certain view of approaching martyrdom ; it is the affectionate farewell of the aged apostle to his
beloved Timothy, and his last will and testament to the militant
church below in the bright prospect of the unfading crown in
the church triumphant above.[3]

Thus ended the earthly course of this great teacher of nations,
this apostle of victorious faith, of evangelical freedom, of Christian progress. It was the heroic career of a spiritual conqueror
of immortal souls for Christ, converting them from the service
of sin and Satan to the service of the living God, from the

---

[1] Comp. § 26, pp. 250, 257–259.

[2] Ewald (VI. 631) conjectures that Paul, on hearing of the Neronian persecution, hastened back to Rome of his own accord, to bear testimony to
Christ, and being seized there, was again brought to trial and condemned to
death, A.D. 65. Ewald assumes an intervening visit to Spain, but not to the
East.

[3] 2 Tim. 4 : 6–8. Bengel calls this Epistle *testamentum Pauli et cycnea
cantio.*

bondage of the law to the freedom of the gospel, and leading them to the fountain of life eternal. He labored more abundantly than all the other apostles; and yet, in sincere humility, he considered himself "the least of the apostles," and "not meet to be called an apostle," because he persecuted the church of God; a few years later he confessed: "I am less than the least of all saints," and shortly before his death: "I am the chief of sinners."[1] His humility grew as he experienced God's mercy and ripened for heaven. Paul passed a stranger and pilgrim through this world, hardly observed by the mighty and the wise of his age. And yet how infinitely more noble, beneficial, and enduring was his life and work than the dazzling march of military conquerors, who, prompted by ambition, absorbed millions of treasure and myriads of lives, only to die at last in a drunken fit at Babylon, or of a broken heart on the rocks of St. Helena! Their empires have long since crumbled into dust, but St. Paul still remains one of the foremost benefactors of the human race, and the pulses of his mighty heart are beating with stronger force than ever throughout the Christian world.

NOTE ON THE SECOND ROMAN CAPTIVITY OF PAUL.

The question of a second Roman captivity of Paul is a purely historical and critical problem, and has no doctrinal or ethical bearing, except that it facilitates the defence of the genuineness of the Pastoral Epistles. The best scholars are still divided on the subject. Neander, Gieseler, Bleek, Ewald, Lange, Sabatier, Godet, also Renan (*Saint Paul*, p. 560, and *L'Antechrist*, p. 106), and nearly all English biographers and commentators, as Alford, Wordsworth, Howson, Lewin, Farrar, Plumptre, Ellicott, Lightfoot, defend the second captivity, and thus prolong the labors of Paul for a few years. On the other hand not only radical and skeptical critics, as Baur, Zeller, Schenkel, Reuss, Holtzmann, and all who reject the Pastoral Epistles (except Renan), but also conservative exegetes and historians, as Niedner, Thiersch, Meyer, Wieseler, Ebrard, Otto, Beck, Pressensé, deny the second captivity. I have discussed the problem at length in my *Hist. of the Apost. Church*, § 87, pp. 328–347, and again in my annotations to Lange on *Romans*, pp. 10–12. I will restate

---

[1] 1 Cor. 15 : 9 (A.D. 57); Eph. 3 : 8 (A.D. 62); 1 Tim. 3 : 15 (A.D. 63 or 64 ?).

the chief arguments in favor of a second captivity, partly in rectification of my former opinion.

1. The main argument are the Pastoral Epistles, if genuine, as I hold them to be, notwithstanding all the objections of the opponents from De Wette (1826) and Baur (1835) to Renan (1873) and Holtzmann (1880). It is, indeed, not impossible to assign them to any known period in Paul's life *before* his captivity, as during his three years' sojourn in Ephesus (54–57), or his eighteen months' sojourn in Corinth (52–53), but it is very difficult to do so. The Epistles presuppose journeys of the apostle not mentioned in Acts, and belong apparently to an advanced period in his life, as well as in the history of truth and error in the apostolic church.

2. The release of Timothy from a captivity in Italy, probably in Rome, to which the author of the Epistle to the Hebrews (13 : 23) alludes, may have some connection with the release of Paul, who had probably a share in the inspiration, if not in the composition, of that remarkable production.

3. The oldest post-apostolic witness is Clement of Rome, who wrote about 95 : "Paul . . . . *having come to the limit of the West* (ἐπὶ τὸ τέρμα τῆς δύσεως ἐλθών) and borne witness before the magistrates (μαρτυρήσας ἐπὶ τῶν ἡγουμένων, which others translate, "having suffered martyrdom under the rulers"), departed from the world and went to the holy place, having furnished the sublimest model of endurance" (*Ad Corinth. c. 5*). Considering that Clement wrote in Rome, the most natural interpretation of τέρμα τῆς δύσεως, "the extreme west," is Spain or Britain ; and as Paul *intended* to carry the gospel to Spain, one would first think of that country, which was in constant commercial intercourse with Rome, and had produced distinguished statesmen and writers like Seneca and Lucan. Strabo (II. 1) calls the pillars of Hercules πέρατα τῆς οἰκουμένης ; and Velleius Paterc. calls Spain "*extremus nostri orbis terminus.*" See Lightfoot, *St. Clement*, p. 50. But the inference is weakened by the absence of any trace or tradition of Paul's visit to Spain.[1] Still less can he have suffered martyrdom there, as the logical order of the words would imply. And as Clement wrote to the Corinthians, he *may*, from *their* geographical standpoint, have called the Roman capital the end of the West. At all events the passage is rhetorical (it speaks of *seven* imprisonments, ἑπτάκις δεσμὰ φορέσας), and proves nothing for further labors in the East.[2]

---

[1] A Latin inscription in Spain, which records the success of Nero in extirpating the new superstition, Gruter, *Inscript.*, p. 238, is now commonly abandoned as spurious.

[2] I must here correct an error into which I have fallen with Dr. Wieseler, in my *Hist. of the Ap. Ch.*, p. 342, by reading ὑπὸ τὸ τέρμα, and interpreting it " before the highest tribunal of the West." ἐπί is the reading of the Cod. Alex. (though defectively written), as I have convinced myself by an inspection of the Codex in the British Museum in 1869, in the presence of Mr.

4. An incomplete passage in the fragmentary Muratorian canon (about A.D. 170) : "*Sed profectionem Pauli ab urbe ad Spaniam proficiscentis . . .*" seems to imply a journey of Paul to Spain, which Luke has omitted ; but this is merely a conjecture, as the verb has to be supplied. Comp., however, Westcott, *The Canon of the N. Test.*, p. 189, and Append. C., p. 467, and Renan, *L'Antechrist*, p. 106 sq.

5. Eusebius (d. 340) first clearly asserts that "there is a tradition (λόγος ἔχει) that the apostle, after his defence, again set forth to the ministry of his preaching, and having entered a second time the same city [Rome], was perfected by his martyrdom before him [Nero]." *Hist. Eccl.* II. 22 (comp. ch. 25). But the force of this testimony is weakened first by its late date ; secondly, by the vague expression λόγος ἔχει, "it is said," and the absence of any reference to older authorities (usually quoted by Eusebius) ; thirdly, by his misunderstanding of 2 Tim. 4 : 16, 17, which he explains in the same connection of a deliverance from the first imprisonment (as if ἀπολογία were identical with αἰχμαλωσία) ; and lastly by his chronological mistake as to the time of the first imprisonment which, in his "*Chronicle*," he misdates A.D. 58, that is, three years before the actual arrival of Paul in Rome. On the other hand he puts the conflagration of Rome two years too late, A.D. 66, instead of 64, and the Neronian persecution, and the martyrdom of Paul and Peter, in the year 70.

6. Jerome (d. 419) : "Paul was dismissed by Nero that he might preach Christ's gospel also in the regions of the West (*in Occidentis quoque partibus*)." *De Vir. ill.* sub *Paulus.* This echoes the τέρμα τῆς δύσεως of Clement. Chrysostom (d. 407), Theodoret, and other fathers assert that Paul went to Spain (Rom. 15 : 28), but without adducing any proof.

These post-apostolic testimonies, taken together, make it very probable, but not historically certain, that Paul was released after the spring of 63, and enjoyed an Indian summer of missionary work before his martyrdom. The only remaining monuments, as well as the best proof, of this concluding work are the Pastoral Epistles, if we admit them to be genuine. To my mind the historical difficulties of the Pastoral Epistles are an argument for rather than against their Pauline origin. For why should a forger invent difficulties when he might so easily have fitted his fictions in the frame of the situation known from the Acts and the other Pauline Epistles ? The linguistic and other objections are by no means insurmountable, and are overborne by the evidence of the Pauline spirit which animates these last productions of his pen.

Holmes and the late Dr. Tregelles. The preposition stands at the end of line 17, fol. 159[b], second col., in the IVth vol. of the Codex, and is written in smaller letters from want of space, but by the original hand. The same reading is confirmed by the newly discovered MS. of Bryennios.

§ 34. *The Synod of Jerusalem, and the Compromise between Jewish and Gentile Christianity.*

Literature.

I. Acts, ch. 15, and Gal., ch. 2, and the Commentaries thereon.

II. Besides the general literature already noticed (in §§ 20 and 29), compare the following special discussions on the Conference of the
Apostles, which tend to rectify the extreme view of Baur (*Paulus,*
ch. V.) and Overbeck (in the fourth edition of De Wette's *Com. on
Acts*) on the conflict between Acts 15 and Gal. 2, or between Petrinism and Paulinism, and to establish the true historic view of their
essential unity in diversity.

Bishop Lightfoot: *St. Paul and the Three,* in *Com. on Galat.,*
London, 1866 (second ed.), pp. 283–355. The ablest critical discussion of the problem in the English language.

R. A. Lipsius: *Apostelconvent,* in Schenkel's *Bibel-Lexikon,* I.
(1869), pp. 194–207. A clear and sharp statement of eight apparent
contradictions between Acts 15 and Gal. 2. He admits, however,
some elements of truth in the account of Acts, which he uses to
supplement the account of Paul. Schenkel, in his *Christusbild der
Apostel,* 1879, p. 38, goes further, and says, in opposition to Overbeck, who regards the account of Acts as a *Tendenz- Roman,* or
partisan fiction : "The narrative of Paul is certainly trustworthy, but
one-sided, which was unavoidable, considering his personal apologetic
aim, and passes by in silence what is foreign to that aim. The narrative of Acts follows oral and written traditions which were already
influenced by later views and prejudices, and it is for this reason un-
reliable in part, yet by no means a conscious fiction."

Otto Pfleiderer: *Der Paulinismus.* Leipzig, 1873, pp. 278
sqq. and 500 sqq. He tones down the differences to innocent inaccuracies of the Acts, and rejects the idea of "intentional invention."

C. Weizsäcker (successor of Dr. Baur in Tübingen, but partly
dissenting from him) : *Das Apostelconcil* in the "Jahrbücher für
deutsche Theologie" for 1873, pp. 191–246. And his essay on
Paulus und die Gemeinde in Korinth, ibid., 1876, pp. 603–653. In
the last article he concludes (p. 652) that the real opponents of Paul,
in Corinth as well as in Galatia, were not the primitive apostles (as
asserted by Baur, Schwegler, etc.), but a set of fanatics who abused
the authority of Peter and the name of Christ, and imitated the
agitation of Jewish proselytizers, as described by Roman writers.

K. Schmidt: *Der Apostel-Konvent,* in Herzog and Plitt, *R. E.* I.
(1877), 575–584. Conservative.

Theod. Keim : *Aus dem Urchristenthum.* Zürich, 1879, *Der Apos telkonvent*, pp. 64–89. (Comp. HILGENFELD's review in the "Zeitschrift für wissenschaftl. Theologie," 1879, pp. 100 sqq.) One of the last efforts of the author of the *Leben Jesu von Nazara*. Keim goes a step further than Weizsäcker, strongly maintains the public as well as the private character of the apostolic agreement, and admits the circumcision of Timothy as a fact. He also entirely rejects the view of Baur, Weizsäcker, and Overbeck that the author of Acts derived his information from the Ep. to the Galatians, and perverted it for his irenic purpose.

F. W. FARRAR : *The Life and Work of Paul* (Lond., 1879), chs. XXII.–XXIII. (I. 398–454).

WILIBALD GRIMM : *Der Apostelconvent*, in the "Theol. Studien und Kritiken" (Gotha), for 1880, pp. 405–432. A critical discussion in the right direction. The exegetical essay of WETZEL on Gal. 2 : 14, 21, in the same periodical, pp. 433 sqq., bears in part on the same subject.

F. GODET : *Com. on the Ep. to the Romans*, vol. I. (1879), pp. 37–42, English translation. Able and sound.

KARL WIESELER : *Zur Gesch. der N. T.lichen Schrift und des Urchristenthums.* Leipzig, 1880, pp. 1–53, on the Corinthian parties and their relation to the errorists in the Galatians and the Nicolaitans in the Apocalypse. Learned, acute, and conservati/e.

Comp. above ⸹ 22, pp. 213 sqq. ; my *Hist. of the Apost. Church*, ⸹⸹ 67–70, pp. 245–260 ; and Excursus on the Controversy between Peter and Paul, in my *Com. on the Galat.* (2 : 11–14).

The question of circumcision, or of the terms of admission of the Gentiles to the Christian church, was a burning question of the apostolic age. It involved the wider question of the binding authority of the Mosaic law, yea, the whole relation of Christianity to Judaism. For circumcision was in the synagogue what baptism is in the church, a divinely appointed sign and seal of the covenant of man with God, with all its privileges and responsibilities, and bound the circumcised person to obey the whole law on pain of forfeiting the blessing promised. Upon the decision of this question depended the peace of the church within, and the success of the gospel without. With circumcision, as a necessary condition of church membership, Christianity would forever have been confined to the Jewish race with a small minority of proselytes of the gate, or half-Christians ; while the abrogation of circumcision and the declaration of the

supremacy and sufficiency of faith in Christ ensured the conversion of the heathen and the catholicity of Christianity. The
progress of Paul's mission among the Gentiles forced the question to a solution and resulted in a grand act of emancipation,
yet not without great struggle and temporary reactions.

All the Christians of the first generation were converts from
Judaism or heathenism. It could not be expected that they
should suddenly lose the influence of opposite kinds of religious training and blend at once in unity. Hence the difference between Jewish and Gentile Christianity throughout the
apostolic age, more or less visible in all departments of ecclesiastical life, in missions, doctrine, worship, and government. At
the head of the one division stood Peter, the apostle of the circumcision; at the head of the other, Paul, to whom was intrusted the apostleship of the uncircumcision. In another form
the same difference even yet appears between the different
branches of Christendom. The Catholic church is Jewish-
Christian or Petrine in its character; the Evangelical church is
Gentile or Pauline. And the individual members of these
bodies lean to one or the other of these leading types. Where-
ever there is life and motion in a denomination or sect, there
will be at least two tendencies of thought and action—whether
they be called old and new school, or high church and low
church, or by any other party name. In like manner there is
no free government without parties. It is only stagnant waters
that never run and overflow, and corpses that never move.

The relation between these two fundamental forms of apostolic
Christianity is in general that of authority and freedom, law and
gospel, the conservative and the progressive, the objective and
the subjective. These antithetic elements are not of necessity
mutually exclusive. They are mutually complemental, and for
perfect life they must co-exist and co-operate. But in reality
they often run to extremes, and then of course fall into irreconcilable contradiction. Exclusive Jewish Christianity sinks into
Ebionism; exclusive Gentile Christianity into Gnosticism. And
these heresies were by no means confined to the apostolic and

post-apostolic ages; pseudo-Petrine and pseudo-Pauline errors, in ever-varying phases, run more or less throughout the whole history of the church.

The Jewish converts at first very naturally adhered as closely as possible to the sacred traditions of their fathers. They could not believe that the religion of the Old Testament, revealed by God himself, should pass away. They indeed regarded Jesus as the Saviour of Gentiles as well as Jews; but they thought Judaism the necessary introduction to Christianity, circumcision and the observance of the whole Mosaic law the sole condition of an interest in the Messianic salvation. And, offensive as Judaism was, rather than attractive, to the heathen, this principle would have utterly precluded the conversion of the mass of the Gentile world.[1] The apostles themselves were at first trammelled by this Judaistic prejudice, till taught better by the special revelation to Peter before the conversion of Cornelius.[2]

But even after the baptism of the uncircumcised centurion, and Peter's defence of it before the church of Jerusalem, the old leaven still wrought in some Jewish Christians who had formerly belonged to the rigid and exclusive sect of the Pharisees.[3]

[1] "Circumcision," says Renan (St. Paul, ch. III. p. 67), "was, for adults, a painful ceremony, one not without danger, and disagreeable to the last degree. It was one of the reasons which prevented the Jews from moving freely about among other people, and set them apart as a caste by themselves. At the baths and gymnasiums, those important parts of the ancient cities, circumcision exposed the Jew to all sorts of affronts. Every time that the attention of the Greeks and Romans was directed to this subject, outbursts of jestings followed. The Jews were very sensitive in this regard, and avenged themselves by cruel reprisals. Several of them, in order to escape the ridicule, and wishing to pass themselves off for Greeks, strove to efface the original mark by a surgical operation of which Celsus has preserved us the details. As to the converts who accepted this initiation ceremony, they had only one course to pursue, and that was to hide themselves in order to escape sarcastic taunts. Never did a man of the world place himself in such a position; and this is doubtless the reason why conversions to Judaism were much more numerous among women than among men, the former not being put, at the very outset, to a test, in every respect repulsive and shocking. We have many examples of Jewesses married to heathens, but not a single one of a Jew married to a heathen woman."

[2] Acts, chs. 10 and 11.

[3] Acts 15 : 1, 5 : τινὲς τῶν ἀπὸ τῆς αἱρέσεως τῶν Φαρισαίων πεπιστευκότες.

They came from Judæa to Antioch, and taught the converts of Paul and Barnabas : " Except ye be circumcised after the manner of Moses, ye cannot be saved." They no doubt appealed to the Pentateuch, the universal Jewish tradition, the circumcision of Christ, and the practice of the Jewish apostles, and created a serious disturbance. These ex-Pharisees were the same whom Paul, in the heat of controversy, more severely calls " false brethren insidiously or stealthily foisted in," who intruded themselves into the Christian brotherhood as spies and enemies of Christian liberty.[1] He clearly distinguishes them not only from the apostles, but also from the great majority of the brethren in Judæa who sincerely rejoiced in his conversion and glorified God for it.[2] They were a small, but very active and zealous minority, and full of intrigue. They compassed sea and land to make one proselyte. They were baptized with water, but not with the Holy Spirit. They were Christians in name, but narrow-minded and narrow-hearted Jews in fact. They were scrupulous, pedantic, slavish formalists, ritualists, and traditionalists of the malignant type. Circumcision of the flesh was to them of more importance than circumcision of the heart, or at all events an indispensable condition of salvation.[3] Such men

---

[1] Gal. 2 : 4 : παρείσακτοι (comp. παρεισάξουσιν in 2 Pet. 2 :1) ψευδάδελφοι οἵτινες παρεισῆλθον (who came in sideways, or crept in, sneaked in ; comp. Jude 4, παρεισέδυσαν) κατασκοπῆσαι τὴν ἐλευθερίαν ἡμῶν ἣν ἔχομεν ἐν Χριστῷ Ἰησοῦ, ἵνα ἡμᾶς καταδουλώσουσιν. The emissaries of these Pharisaical Judaizers are ironically called " super-extra-apostles," ὑπερλίαν ἀπόστολοι, 2 Cor. 11 :5 ; 12 : 11. For these are not the real apostles (as Baur and his followers maintained in flat contradiction to the connection of chs. 10 to 12), but identical with the " false apostles, deceitful workers, transforming themselves into apostles of Christ," 2 Cor. 11 : 13. Baur's monstrous misinterpretation has been completely refuted by Weizsäcker (on Paul and the Congregation of Corinth, l. c. p. 640), Keim, Klöpper, Wieseler, and Grimm (l. c. 432). Comp. also Godet, l. c. pp. 49 sq.

[2] Gal. 1 : 22–24.

[3] To what ridiculous extent some Jewish rabbis of the rigid school of Shammai carried the overestimate of circumcision, may be seen from the following deliverances quoted by Farrar (I. 401) : " So great is circumcision that but for it the Holy One, blessed be He, would not have created the world; for it is said (Jer. 33 : 25), ' But for my covenant [circumcision] I would not have made day and night, and the ordinance of heaven and earth.' " " Abraham was not called ' perfect ' till he was circumcised."

could, of course, not understand and appreciate Paul, but hated
and feared him as a dangerous radical and rebel. Envy and
jealousy mixed with their religious prejudice. They got alarmed
at the rapid progress of the gospel among the unclean Gentiles
who threatened to soil the purity of the church. They could
not close their eyes to the fact that the power was fast passing
from Jerusalem to Antioch, and from the Jews to the Gentiles,
but instead of yielding to the course of Providence, they determined to resist it in the name of order and orthodoxy, and to
keep the regulation of missionary operations and the settlement
of the terms of church membership in their own hands at Jerusalem, the holy centre of Christendom and the expected residence of the Messiah on his return.

Whoever has studied the twenty-third chapter of Matthew
and the pages of church history, and knows human nature, will
understand perfectly this class of extra-pious and extra-orthodox
fanatics, whose race is not dead yet and not likely to die out.
They serve, however, the good purpose of involuntarily promoting the cause of evangelical liberty.

The agitation of these Judaizing partisans and zealots brought
the Christian church, twenty years after its founding, to the
brink of a split which would have seriously impeded its progress and endangered its final success.

The Conferences in Jerusalem.

To avert this calamity and to settle this irrepressible conflict,
the churches of Jerusalem and Antioch resolved to hold a private and a public conference at Jerusalem. Antioch sent Paul
and Barnabas as commissioners to represent the Gentile converts. Paul, fully aware of the gravity of the crisis, obeyed at
the same time an inner and higher impulse.[1] He also took with
him Titus, a native Greek, as a living specimen of what the
Spirit of God could accomplish without circumcision. The con-

[1] Paul mentions the subjective motive, Luke the objective call. Both usually unite in important trusts. But Baur and Lipsius make this one of the
irreconcilable contradictions!

ference was held A.D. 50 or 51 (fourteen years after Paul's conversion). It was the first and in some respects the most important council or synod held in the history of Christendom, though differing widely from the councils of later times. It is placed in the middle of the book of Acts as the connecting link between the two sections of the apostolic church and the two epochs of its missionary history.

The object of the Jerusalem consultation was twofold : first, to settle the personal relation between the Jewish and Gentile apostles, and to divide their field of labor; secondly, to decide the question of circumcision, and to define the relation between the Jewish and Gentile Christians. On the first point (as we learn from Paul) it effected a complete and final, on the second point (as we learn from Luke) a partial and temporary settlement. In the nature of the case the public conference in which the whole church took part, was preceded and accompanied by private consultations of the apostles.[1]

1. Apostolic Recognition. The pillars of the Jewish Church, James, Peter, and John [2]—whatever their views may have been

---

[1] Luke reports the former and hints at the latter (comp. ver. 5 and 6) ; Paul reports the private understanding and hints at the public conference, saying (Gal. 2 : 2) : "I laid (ἀνεθέμην) before *them* [the brethren of Jerusalem] the gospel which I preach among the Gentiles, but *privately* before them who were of repute (or, before those in authority)," i. e., the pillar-apostles of the circumcision, James, Cephas, and John, comp. ver. 9. Dr. Baur who denies the *public* conference, mistranslates κατ' ἰδίαν δὲ τοῖς δοκοῦσιν, "*und zwar wandte ich mich speciell* (specially) *an die vorzugsweise Geltenden*," so that τοῖς δοκοῦσιν would be the same as the preceding αὐτοῖς (*Paul*, ch. V. p. 117, in the English translation, I. 122). But this would have been more naturally expressed by τοῖς δοκοῦσιν ἐν αὐτοῖς, and κατ' ἰδίαν, as Grimm, the lexicographer of the N. T., remarks against Baur (l. c., p. 412), does not mean "specially" at all, but *privatim, seorsum,* "apart," "in private," as in Mark 4 : 34, and κατ' ἰδίαν εἰπεῖν, Diod. I. 21.

[2] The order in which they are named by Paul is significant : James first, as the bishop of Jerusalem and the most conservative, John last, as the most liberal of the Jewish apostles. There is no irony in the term οἱ δοκοῦντες and οἱ στῦλοι, certainly not at the expense of the apostles who were pillars in fact as well as in name and repute. If there is any irony in ver. 6, ὁποῖοί ποτε ἦσαν, οὐδέν μοι διαφέρει, it is directed against the Judaizers who overestimated the Jewish apostles to the disparagement of Paul. Even Keim (l. c., p. 74) takes this view : "*Endlich mag man aufhören, von ironischer Bitterkeit des Paulus*

before—were fully convinced by the logic of events in which they recognized the hand of Providence, that Paul as well as Barnabas by the extraordinary success of his labors had proven himself to be divinely called to the apostolate of the Gentiles. They took no exception and made no addition to his gospel. On the contrary, when they saw that God who gave grace and strength to Peter for the apostleship of the circumcision, gave grace and strength to Paul also for the conversion of the uncircumcision, they extended to him and to Barnabas the right hand of fellowship, with the understanding that they would divide as far as practicable the large field of labor, and that Paul should manifest his brotherly love and cement the union by aiding in the support of the poor, often persecuted and famine-stricken brethren of Judæa. This service of charity he had cheerfully done before, and as cheerfully and faithfully did afterward by raising collections among his Greek congregations and carrying the money in person to Jerusalem.[1] Such is the unequivocal testimony of the fraternal understanding among the apostles from the mouth of Paul himself. And the letter of the council officially recognizes this by mentioning "beloved" Barnabas[2] and Paul, as "men who have hazarded their lives for the name of our Lord Jesus Christ." This double testimony of the unity of the apostolic church is quite conclusive against the modern invention of an irreconcilable antagonism between Paul and Peter.[3]

gegenüber den Geltenden zu reden : denn wer gleich nachher den Bundesschluss mit den 'Säulen' feierlich und befriedigt registrirt, der hat seine Abweisung der menschlichen Autoritäten in v. 6 nicht dem Andenken der Apostel gewidmet, sondern dem notorischen Uebermuth der judenchristlichen Parteigänger in Galatien."

[1] Gal. 2 : 7–10 ; comp. Acts 11 : 30 ; 24 : 17 ; 1 Cor. 16 : 1–3 ; 2 Cor. 8 and 9 ; Rom. 15 : 25-27.

[2] Barnabas, as the older disciple, still retained precedence in the Jewish church, and hence is named first. A later forger would have reversed the order.

[3] Dr. Plumptre remarks against the Tübingen critics (on Acts 15 : 7) : " Of all doctrines as to the development of the Christian church, that which sees in Peter, James, and John the leaders of a Judaizing anti-Pauline party is, perhaps, the most baseless and fantastic. The fact that their names were

2. As regards the question of circumcision and the status of the Gentile Christians, there was a sharp conflict of opinions in open debate, under the very shadow of the inspired apostles.[1] There was strong conviction and feeling on both sides, plausible arguments were urged, charges and countercharges made, invidious inferences drawn, fatal consequences threatened. But the Holy Spirit was also present, as he is with every meeting of disciples who come together in the name of Christ, and overruled the infirmities of human nature which will crop out in every ecclesiastical assembly.

The circumcision of Titus, as a test case, was of course strongly demanded by the Pharisaical legalists, but as strongly resisted by Paul, and not enforced.[2] To yield here even for a moment would have been fatal to the cause of Christian liberty, and would have implied a wholesale circumcision of the Gentile converts, which was impossible.

But how could Paul consistently afterwards circumcise Timothy?[3] The answer is that he circumcised Timothy as a Jew, not as a Gentile, and that he did it as a voluntary act of expediency, for the purpose of making Timothy more useful among the Jews, who had a claim on him as the son of a Jewish

---

unscrupulously used by that party, both in their lifetime and, as the pseudo-Clementine *Homilies* and *Recognitions* show, after their death, cannot outweigh their own deliberate words and acts."

[1] This is very evident from the indignant tone of Paul against the Judaizers, and from the remark in Acts 15 : 6 : πολλῆς συζητήσεως γενομένης, comp. ver. 2 : γενομένης στάσεως (factious party spirit, insurrection, Luke 23 : 19 ; Mark 15 : 7) καί ζητήσεως οὐκ ὀλίγης. Such strong terms show that Luke by no means casts the veil of charity over the differences in the apostolic church.

[2] Gal. 2 : 3–5. See the note below.

[3] Acts 16 : 3. The silence of Luke concerning the non-circumcision of Titus has been distorted by the Tübingen critics into a wilful suppression of fact, and the mention of the circumcision of Timothy into a fiction to subserve the catholic unification of Petrinism and Paulinism. What a designing and calculating man this anonymous author of the Acts must have been, and yet not shrewd enough to conceal his literary fraud or to make it more plausible by adapting it to the account in the Galatians, and by mentioning the full understanding between the apostles themselves ! The book of Acts is no more a full history of the church or of the apostles than the Gospels are full biographies of Christ.

mother, and would not have allowed him to teach in a synagogue without this token of membership; while in the case of Titus, a pure Greek, circumcision was demanded as a principle and as a condition of justification and salvation. Paul was inflexible in resisting the demands of *false* brethren, but always willing to accommodate himself to *weak* brethren, and to become as a Jew to the Jews and as a Gentile to the Gentiles in order to save them both.[1] In genuine Christian freedom he cared nothing for circumcision or uncircumcision as a mere rite or external condition, and as compared with the keeping of the commandments of God and the new creature in Christ.[2]

In the debate Peter, of course, as the œcumenical chief of the Jewish apostles, although at that time no more a resident of Jerusalem, took a leading part, and made a noble speech which accords entirely with his previous experience and practice in the house of Cornelius, and with his subsequent endorsement of Paul's doctrine.[3] He was no logician, no rabbinical scholar, but he had admirable good sense and practical tact, and quickly perceived the true line of progress and duty. He spoke in a tone of personal and moral authority, but not of official primacy.[4] He protested against imposing upon the neck of the

[1] Comp. Rom. 14 and 15; 1 Cor. 9 : 19-23 ; Acts 21 : 23-26.

[2] Gal. 5 : 6 ; 6 : 15 ; 1 Cor. 7 : 19. Dr. Plumptre's remarks on the last passage are to the point : " Often those who regard some ceremony as unimportant magnify the very disregard of it into a necessary virtue. The apostle carefully guards against that by expressing the nothingness of both circumcision and uncircumcision (Rom. 2: 25 ; Gal. 5 : 6; 6 : 15). The circumcision of Timothy, and the refusal to circumcise Titus by St. Paul himself, are illustrations at once of the application of the truth here enforced, and of the apostle's scrupulous adherence to the principles of his own teaching. To have refused to circumcise Timothy would have attached some value to non-circumcision. To have circumcised Titus would have attached some value to circumcision."

[3] Acts 15 : 7-11 ; comp. 10 : 28 sqq.; 1 Pet. 1 : 12 ; 5 :12 ; 2 Pet. 3 : 15, 16. The style of Peter is distinctly recognizable, as in the epithet of God, ὁ καρδιογνώστη , Acts 15 :8, comp. 1 : 24. Such minute coincidences go to strengthen the documentary trustworthiness of the Acts.

[4] Like the Popes, who do not attend synods at Jerusalem or elsewhere and make speeches, but expect all doctrinal controversies to be referred to them for their final and infallible decision.

Gentile disciples the unbearable yoke of the ceremonial law, and laid down, as clearly as Paul, the fundamental principle that "Jews as well as Gentiles are saved only by the grace of the Lord Jesus Christ." [1]

After this bold speech, which created a profound silence in the assembly, Barnabas and Paul reported, as the best practical argument, the signal miracles which God had wrought among the Gentiles through their instrumentality.

The last and weightiest speaker was James, the brother of the Lord, the local head of the Jewish Christian church and bishop of Jerusalem, who as such seems to have presided over the council. He represented as it were the extreme right wing of the Jewish church bordering close on the Judaizing faction. It was through his influence chiefly no doubt that the Pharisees were converted who created this disturbance. In a very characteristic speech he endorsed the sentiments of Symeon—he preferred to call Peter by his Jewish name—concerning the conversion of the Gentiles as being in accordance with ancient prophecy and divine foreordination; but he proposed a compromise to the effect that while the Gentile disciples should not be troubled with circumcision, they should yet be exhorted to abstain from certain practices which were particularly offensive to pious Jews, namely, from eating meat offered to idols, from tasting blood, or food of strangled animals, and from every form of carnal uncleanness. As to the Jewish Christians, they knew their duty from the law, and would be expected to continue in their time-honored habits.

The address of James differs considerably from that of Peter, and meant restriction as well as freedom, but after all it conceded the main point at issue—salvation without circumcision. The address entirely accords in spirit and language with his own epistle, which represents the gospel as law, though " the perfect law of freedom," with his later conduct toward Paul in advising him to assume the vow of the Nazarites and thus to

---

[1] Acts 15 : 11 : διὰ τῆς χάριτος τοῦ κυρίου Ἰησοῦ πιστεύομεν σωθῆναι, καθ' ὃν τρόπον κἀκεῖνοι (the heathen). Comp. Rom. 10 : 12, 13.

contradict the prejudices of the myriads of converted Jews, and with the Jewish Christian tradition which represents him as the model of an ascetic saint equally revered by devout Jews and Christians, as the " Rampart of the People " (Obliam), and the intercessor of Israel who prayed in the temple without ceasing for its conversion and for the aversion of the impending doom.[1] He had more the spirit of an ancient prophet or of John the Baptist than the spirit of Jesus (in whom he did not believe till after the resurrection), but for this very reason he had most authority over the Jewish Christians, and could reconcile the majority of them to the progressive spirit of Paul.

The compromise of James was adopted and embodied in the following brief and fraternal pastoral letter to the Gentile churches. It is the oldest literary document of the apostolic age and bears the marks of the style of James:[2]

" The apostles and the elder brethren[3] unto the brethren who are of the Gentiles in Antioch, Syria, and Cilicia, greeting: Forasmuch as we have heard, that some who went out from us have troubled you with words, subverting your souls, to whom we gave no commandment, it seemed good unto us, having come to be of one accord, to choose out men and send them unto you with our beloved Barnabas and Paul, men that have hazarded their lives for the name of our Lord Jesus Christ. We have sent therefore Judas and Silas, who themselves also shall tell you the same things by word of mouth. For it seemed good to the Holy Spirit, and to us, to lay upon you no greater burden than these necessary things: that ye abstain from meats

---

[1] Comp. Acts 15 : 13–21 ; 21 : 18–25 ; James 1 : 25 ; 2 : 12 ; and the account of Hegesippus quoted in § 27, p. 274.

[2] The Gentile form of greeting, χαίρειν, Acts 15 : 23, occurs again in James 1 : 1, but nowhere else in the New Testament, except in the letter of the heathen, Claudius Lysias (Acts 23 : 26) ; the usual form being χάρις καὶ εἰρήνη. This is likewise one of those incidental coincidences and verifications which are beyond the ken of a forger.

[3] According to the oldest reading, οἱ ἀπόστολοι καὶ οἱ πρεσβύτεροι ἀδελφοί, which may also be rendered : " the apostles, and the presbyters, brethren ; " comp. ver. 22. The omission of ἀδελφοί in some MSS. may be due to the later practice, which excluded the laity from synodical deliberations.

sacrificed to idols, and from blood, and from things strangled, and from fornication; from which if ye keep yourselves, it shall be well with you. Farewell." [1]

The decree was delivered by four special messengers, two representing the church at Antioch, Barnabas and Paul, and two from Jerusalem, Judas Barsabbas and Silas (or Silvanus), and read to the Syrian and Cilician churches which were agitated by the controversy.[2] The restrictions remained in full force at least eight years, since James reminded Paul of them on his last visit to Jerusalem in 58.[3] The Jewish Christians observed them no doubt with few exceptions till the downfall of idolatry,[4] and the Oriental church even to this day abstains from blood and things strangled; but the Western church never held itself bound to this part of the decree, or soon abandoned some of its restrictions.

Thus by moderation and mutual concession in the spirit of peace and brotherly love a burning controversy was settled, and a split happily avoided.

ANALYSIS OF THE DECREE.

The decree of the council was a compromise and had two aspects: it was emancipatory, and restrictive.

(1.) It was a decree of emancipation of the Gentile disciples from circumcision and the bondage of the ceremonial law. This was the chief point in dispute, and so far the decree was

---

[1] Acts 15 : 23–29. [2] Acts 16 : 4.

[3] Acts 21 : 15. Comp. also Rev. 2 : 14, 20. But why does Paul never refer to this synodical decree? Because he could take a knowledge of it for granted, or more probably because he did not like altogether its restrictions, which were used by the illiberal constructionists against him and against Peter at Antioch (Gal. 2 : 12). Weizsäcker and Grimm (l. c., p. 423) admit the historic character of some such compromise, but transfer it to a later period (Acts 21 : 25), as a proposition made by James of a *modus vivendi* with Gentile converts, and arbitrarily charge the Acts with an anachronism. But the consultation must have come to a result, the result embodied in a formal action, and the action communicated to the disturbed churches.

[4] Justin Martyr, about the middle of the second century, considered the eating of εἰδωλόθυτα as bad as idolatry. *Dial. c. Tryph. Jud.* 35.

liberal and progressive. It settled the question of *principle* once and forever. Paul had triumphed. Hereafter the Judaizing doctrine of the necessity of circumcision for salvation was a heresy, a false gospel, or a perversion of the true gospel, and is denounced as such by Paul in the Galatians.

(2.) The decree was restrictive and conservative on questions of *expediency* and comparative indifference to the Gentile Christians. Under this aspect it was a wise and necessary measure for the apostolic age, especially in the East, where the Jewish element prevailed, but not intended for universal and permanent use. In Western churches, as already remarked, it was gradually abandoned, as we learn from Augustine. It imposed upon the Gentile Christians abstinence from meat offered to idols, from blood, and from things strangled (as fowls and other animals caught in snares). The last two points amounted to the same thing. These three restrictions had a good foundation in the Jewish abhorrence of idolatry, and every thing connected with it, and in the Levitical prohibition.[1] Without them the churches in Judæa would not have agreed to the compact. But it was almost impossible to carry them out in mixed or in purely Gentile congregations; for it would have compelled the Gentile Christians to give up social intercourse with their unconverted kindred and friends, and to keep separate slaughter-houses, like the Jews, who from fear of contamination with idolatrous associations never bought meat at the public markets. Paul takes a more liberal view of this matter —herein no doubt dissenting somewhat from James—namely,

---

[1] Ex. 34:15; Lev. 17:7 sqq.; Deut. 12:23 sqq. The reason assigned for the prohibition of the taste of blood is that "the *life* of the flesh is in the blood," and the pouring out of blood is the means of "the *atonement* for the soul" (Lev. 17:11). The prohibition of blood as food was traced back to the time of Noah, Gen. 9:4, and seems to have been included in the seven "Noachian commandments" so-called, which were imposed upon the proselytes of the gate, although the Talmud nowhere specifies them very clearly. The Moslems likewise abhor the tasting of blood. But the Greeks and Romans regarded it as a delicacy. It was a stretch of liberality on the part of the Jews that pork was not included among the forbidden articles of food. Bentley proposed to read in Acts 15:20 πορκεία (from πόρκος, *porcus*) for πορνεία, but without a shadow of evidence.

that the eating of meat sacrificed to idols was in itself indifferent, in view of the vanity of idols ; nevertheless he likewise commands the Corinthians to abstain from such meat out of regard
for tender and weak consciences, and lays down the golden rule :
"All things are lawful, but all things are not expedient ; all
things are lawful, but all things edify not.   Let no man seek
his own, but his neighbor's good." [1]

It seems strange to a modern reader that with these ceremonial
prohibitions should be connected the strictly moral prohibition of
fornication. [2]   But it must be remembered that the heathen conscience as to sexual intercourse was exceedingly lax, and looked
upon it as a matter of indifference, like eating and drinking, and
as sinful only in case of adultery where the rights of a husband
are invaded.   No heathen moralist, not even Socrates, or Plato,
or Cicero, condemned fornication absolutely.   It was sanctioned
by the worship of Aphrodite at Corinth and Paphos, and practised to her honor by a host of harlot-priestesses !   Idolatry or
spiritual whoredom is almost inseparable from bodily pollution.
In the case of Solomon polytheism and polygamy went hand in
hand.   Hence the author of the Apocalypse also closely connects the eating of meat offered to idols with fornication, and
denounces them together. [3]   Paul had to struggle against this
laxity in the Corinthian congregation, and condemns all carnal
uncleanness as a violation and profanation of the temple of God. [4]

In this absolute prohibition of sexual impurity we have a
striking evidence of the regenerating and sanctifying influence
of Christianity.   Even the ascetic excesses of the post-apostolic

[1] 1 Cor. 8 : 7–13 ; 10 : 23–33 ; Rom. 14 : 2, 21 ; 1 Tim. 4 : 4.

[2] The word πορνεία, without addition, must be taken in its usual sense, and
cannot mean illegitimate marriages alone, which were forbidden to the Jews,
Ex. 34 ; Lev. 18, although it may include them.

[3] Apoc. 2 : 14, 20.

[4] 1 Cor. 6 : 13–20 ; comp. 5 : 9 ; 1 Thess. 4 : 4, 5 ; Eph. 5 : 3, 5 ; Col. 3 : 5.
What a contrast between these passages and the sentence of Micio in Terence :

"*Non est flagitium, mihi crede, adulescentulum*
Scortari, neque potare."—*Adelph.* i. 2. 21, 22.   (Ed. Fleckeisen, p. 290.)

To which, however, Demea (his more virtuous *married* brother) replies :

"*Pro Juppiter, tu homo adigis me ad insaniam.*
Non est flagitium facere hæc adulescentulum ? "—*Adelph.* i. 2. 31, 32.

writers who denounced the second marriage as "decent adultery" (εὐπρεπὴς μοιχεία), and glorified celibacy as a higher and better state than honorable wedlock, command our respect, as a wholesome and necessary reaction against the opposite excesses of heathen licentiousness.

So far then as the Gentile Christians were concerned the question was settled.

The status of the Jewish Christians was no subject of controversy, and hence the decree is silent about them. They were expected to continue in their ancestral traditions and customs as far as they were at all consistent with loyalty to Christ. They needed no instruction as to their duty, "for," said James, in his address to the Council, "Moses from generations of old has in every city those who preach him, being read in the synagogues every Sabbath." [1] And eight years afterwards he and his elders intimated to Paul that even he, as a Jew, was expected to observe the ceremonial law, and that the exemption was only meant for the Gentiles. [2]

But just here was a point where the decree was deficient. It went far enough for the temporary emergency, and as far as the Jewish church was willing to go, but not far enough for the cause of Christian union and Christian liberty in its legitimate development.

---

[1] Acts 15 : 21 ; comp. 13 : 15 ; 2 Cor. 3 : 14, 15.

[2] Acts 21 : 20–25. Irenæus understood the decree in this sense (*Adv. Hær.* III. 12, 15 : "*Hi qui circa Jacobum apostoli gentibus quidem libere agere permittebant ; ipsi vero . . . . perseverabant in pristinis observationibus . . . . religiose agebant circa dispositionem legis quæ est secundum Mosem.*" Pfleiderer (*l. c.* 284) takes a similar view on this point, which is often overlooked, and yet most important for the proper understanding of the subsequent reaction. He says : "*Die Judenchristen betreffend, wurde dabei stillschweigend als selbstverständliche Voraussetzung angenommen, dass bei diesen Alten bleibe, dass also aus der Gesetzesfreiheit der Heidenchristen keinerlei Consequenzen für die Abrogation des Gesetzes unter den Judenchristen zu ziehen seien ; auf dieser Voraussetzung beruhte die Beschränkung der älteren Apostel auf die Wirksamkeit bei den Juden (da eine Ueberschreitung dieser Schranke ohne Verletzung des Gesetzes nicht möglich war) ; auf dieser Voraussetzung beruhte die Sendung der Leute von Jakobus aus Jerusalem nach Antiochia und beruhte der Einfluss derselben auf Petrus, dessen vorhergegangenes freieres Verhalten dadurch als eine Ausnahme von der Regel gekennzeichnet wird.*"

Notes.

1. The Apostolic Conference at Jerusalem.—This has been one of the chief battle-fields of modern historical criticism. The controversy of circumcision has been fought over again in German, French, Dutch, and English books and essays, and the result is a clearer insight both into the difference and into the harmony of the apostolic church.

We have two accounts of the Conference, one from Paul in the second chapter of the Galatians, and one from his faithful companion, Luke, in the 15th chapter of Acts. For it is now almost universally admitted that they refer to the same event. They must be combined to make up a full history. The Epistle to the Galatians is the true key to the position, the Archimedian ποῦ στῶ.

The accounts agree as to the contending parties—Jerusalem and Antioch—the leaders on both sides, the topic of controversy, the sharp conflict, and the peaceful result.

But in other respects they differ considerably and supplement each other. Paul, in a polemic vindication of his independent apostolic authority against his Judaizing antagonists in Galatia, a few years after the Council (about 56), dwells chiefly on his personal understanding with the other apostles and their recognition of his authority, but he expressly hints also at *public* conferences, which could not be avoided; for it was a controversy between the churches, and an agreement concluded by the leading apostles on both sides was of general authority, even if it was disregarded by a heretical party. Luke, on the other hand, writing after the lapse of at least thirteen years (about 63) a calm and objective history of the primitive church, gives (probably from Jerusalem and Antioch documents, but certainly not from Paul's Epistles) the official action of the public assembly, with an abridgment of the preceding debates, without excluding private conferences; on the contrary he rather includes them; for he reports, 15 : 5, that Paul and Barnabas "were received by the church and the apostles and elders and declared all things that God had done with them," *before* he gives an account of the public consultation, ver. 6. In all assemblies, ecclesiastical and political, the more important business is prepared and matured by committees in private conference for public discussion and action; and there is no reason why the council in Jerusalem should have made an exception. The difference of aim then explains, in part at least, the omissions and minor variations of the two accounts, which we have endeavored to adjust in this section.

The ultra- and pseudo-Pauline hypercriticism of the Tübingen school in several discussions (by Baur, Schwegler, Zeller, Hilgenfeld, Volkmar, Holsten, Overbeck, Lipsius, Hausrath, and Wittichen) has greatly exaggerated these differences, and used Paul's terse polemic allusions as a lever for the overthrow of the credibility of the Acts. But a more conservative critical reaction has recently taken place, partly in the same school (as indicated in the literature above), which tends to harmonize the two accounts and to vindicate the essential consensus of Petrinism and Paulinism.

2. THE CIRCUMCISION OF TITUS.—We hold with most commentators that Titus was *not* circumcised. This is the natural sense of the difficult and much disputed passage, Gal. 2 : 3–5, no matter whether we take δέ in ver. 4 in the explanatory sense (*nempe, and that*), or in the usual adversative sense (*autem, sed, but*). In the former case the sentence is regular, in the latter it is broken, or designedly incomplete, and implies perhaps a slight censure of the other apostles, who may have first *recommended* the circumcision of Titus as a measure of prudence and conciliation out of regard to conservative scruples, but desisted from it on the strong remonstrance of Paul. If we press the ἠναγκάσθη, *compelled*, in ver. 3, such an inference might easily be drawn, but there was in Paul's mind a conflict between the duty of frankness and the duty of courtesy to his older colleagues. So Dr. Lightfoot accounts for the broken grammar of the sentence, "which was wrecked on the hidden rock of the counsels of the apostles of the circumcision."

Quite another view was taken by Tertullian (*Adv. Marc.*, V. 3), and recently by Renan (ch. III. p. 89) and Farrar (I. 415), namely, that Titus *voluntarily* submitted to circumcision for the sake of peace, either in spite of the remonstrance of Paul, or rather with his reluctant consent. Paul *seems* to say that Titus was *not* circumcised, but implies that he *was*. This view is based on the omission of οἷς οὐδέ in ver. 5. The passage then would have to be supplemented in this way : "But not even Titus was *compelled* to be circumcised, but [he submitted to circumcision *voluntarily*] on account of the stealthily introduced false brethren, to whom we yielded by way of submission for an hour [i.e., temporarily]." Renan thus explains the meaning : "If Titus was circumcised, it is not because he was *forced*, but on account of the false brethren, to whom we might yield for a moment without submitting ourselves in principle." He thinks that πρὸς ὥραν is opposed to the following διαμείνῃ. In other words, Paul stooped to conquer. He yielded for a moment by a stretch of charity or a stroke of policy, in order to save Titus from violence, or to bring his case properly before the Council and to achieve a permanent victory of principle. But this view is entirely inconsistent not only with the frankness and firmness of Paul on a question of principle, with the gravity of the crisis, with the uncompromising tone of the Epistle to the Galatians, but also with the addresses of Peter and James, and with the decree of the Council. If Titus was really circumcised, Paul would have said so, and explained his relation to the fact. Moreover, the testimony of Irenæus and Tertullian against οἷς οὐδέ must give way to the authority of the best uncials (א B A C, etc.) and versions in favor of these words. The omission can be better explained from carelessness or dogmatic prejudice than the insertion.

§ 35. *The Conservative Reaction, and the Liberal Victory— Peter and Paul at Antioch.*

The Jerusalem compromise, like every other compromise, was liable to a double construction, and had in it the seed of future troubles. It was an armistice rather than a final settlement. Principles must and will work themselves out, and the one or the other must triumph.

A liberal construction of the spirit of the decree seemed to demand full communion of the Jewish Christians with their uncircumcised Gentile brethren, even at the Lord's table, in the weekly or daily agapæ, on the basis of the common saving faith in Christ, their common Lord and Saviour. But a strict construction of the letter stopped with the recognition of the general Christian character of the Gentile converts, and guarded against ecclesiastical amalgamation on the ground of the continued obligation of the Jewish converts to obey the ceremonial law, including the observance of circumcision, of the Sabbath and new moons, and the various regulations about clean and unclean meats, which virtually forbid social intercourse with unclean Gentiles.[1]

---

[1] Without intending any censure, we may illustrate the position of the strict constructionists of the school of St. James by similar examples of conscientious and scrupulous exclusiveness. Roman Catholics know no church but their own. and refuse all religious fellowship with non Catholics ; yet many of them will admit the action of divine grace and the possibility of salvation outside of the limits of the papacy. Some Lutherans maintain the principle : " Lutheran pulpits for Lutheran ministers only ; Lutheran altars for Lutheran communicants only." Luther himself refused at Marburg the hand of fellowship to Zwingli, who was certainly a Christian, and agreed with him in fourteen out of fifteen articles of doctrine. High church Anglicans recognize no valid ministry without episcopal ordination ; close communion Baptists admit no valid baptism but by immersion; and yet the Episcopalians do not deny the Christian character of non-Episcopalians, nor the Baptists the Christian character of Pedo-Baptists, while they would refuse to sit with them at the Lord's table. There are psalm-singing Presbyterians who would not even worship, and much less commune, with other Presbyterians who sing what they call " uninspired " hymns. In all these cases, whether consistently or not, a distinction is made between Christian fellowship and church fellowship.

The conservative view was orthodox, and must not be confounded with the Judaizing heresy which demanded circumcision from the Gentiles as well as the Jews, and made it a term of church membership and a condition of salvation. This doctrine had been condemned once for all by the Jerusalem agreement, and was held hereafter only by the malignant pharisaical faction of the Judaizers.

The church of Jerusalem, being composed entirely of Jewish converts, would naturally take the conservative view; while the church of Antioch, where the Gentile element prevailed, would as naturally prefer the liberal interpretation, which had the certain prospect of ultimate success. James, who perhaps never went outside of Palestine, far from denying the Christian character of the Gentile converts, would yet keep them at a respectful distance; while Peter, with his impulsive, generous nature, and in keeping with his more general vocation, carried out in practice the conviction he had so boldly professed in Jerusalem, and on a visit to Antioch, shortly after the Jerusalem Council (A.D. 51), openly and habitually communed at table with the Gentile brethren.[1] He had already once before eaten in the house of the uncircumcised Cornelius at Cæsarea, seeing that "God is no respecter of persons, but in every nation he that feareth him and worketh righteousness is acceptable to him."[2]

With reference to all these and other forms of exclusiveness we would say in the spirit of Paul : "In Christ Jesus neither circumcision" (viewed as a mere sign) "availeth anything, nor uncircumcision," neither Catholicism nor Protestantism, neither Lutheranism nor Calvinism, neither Calvinism nor Arminianism, neither episcopacy nor presbytery, neither immersion nor pouring nor sprinkling, nor any other accidental distinction of birth and outward condition, but "a new creature, faith working through love, and the keeping of the commandments of God." Gal. 5 : 6; 6 : 15; 1 Cor. 7 : 19.

[1] The imperfect συνήσθιεν μετὰ τῶν ἐθνῶν, Gal. 2 :12, indicates habit : he *used* to eat with the uncircumcised Christians. This is the best proof from the pen of Paul himself that Peter agreed with him in principle and even in his usual practice. The eating refers, in all probability, not only to common meals, but also to the primitive love-feasts (agapæ) and the holy communion, where brotherly recognition and fellowship is consummated and sealed.

[2] Acts 10 : 27-29, 34, 35; 11 : 3 : "thou wentest in to men uncircumcised and didst eat with them."

But when some delegates of James[1] arrived from Jerusalem and remonstrated with him for his conduct, he timidly withdrew from fellowship with the uncircumcised followers of Christ, and thus virtually disowned them. He unwittingly again denied his Lord from the fear of man, but this time in the persons of his Gentile disciples. The inconsistency is characteristic of his impulsive temper, which made him timid or bold according to the nature of the momentary impression. It is not stated whether these delegates simply carried out the instructions of James or went beyond them. The former is more probable from what we know of him, and explains more easily the conduct of Peter, who would scarcely have been influenced by casual and unofficial visitors. They were perhaps officers in the congregation of Jerusalem; at all events men of weight, not Pharisees exactly, yet extremely conservative and cautious, and afraid of miscellaneous company, which might endanger the purity and orthodoxy of the venerable mother church of Christendom. They did, of course, not demand the circumcision of the Gentile Christians, for this would have been in direct opposition to the synodical decree, but they no doubt reminded Peter of the understanding of the Jerusalem compact concerning the duty of Jewish Christians, which he above all others should scrupulously keep. They represented to him that his conduct was at least very hasty and premature, and calculated to hinder the conversion of the Jewish nation, which was still the object of their dearest hopes and most fervent prayers. The pressure must have been very strong, for even Barnabas, who had stood side by side with Paul at Jerusalem in the defence of the rights of the Gentile Christians, was intimidated and carried away by the example of the chief of the apostles.

The subsequent separation of Paul from Barnabas and Mark, which the author of Acts frankly relates, was no doubt

---

[1] τινὲς ἀπὸ Ἰακώβου, Gal. 2 : 12, seems to imply that they were sent by James (comp. Matt. 26 : 47; Mark 5 : 25; John 3 : 2), and not simply disciples of James or members of his congregation, which would be expressed by τινὲς τῶν ἀπὸ Ἰακώβου. See Grimm, *l. c.*, p. 427.

partly connected with this manifestation of human weakness.[1]

The sin of Peter roused the fiery temper of Paul, and called upon him a sharper rebuke than he had received from his Master. A mere look of pity from Jesus was enough to call forth bitter tears of repentance. Paul was not Jesus. He may have been too severe in the manner of his remonstrance, but he knew Peter better than we, and was right in the matter of dispute, and after all more moderate than some of the greatest and best men have been in personal controversy. Forsaken by the prince of the apostles and by his own faithful ally in the Gentile mission, he felt that nothing but unflinching courage could save the sinking ship of freedom. A vital principle was at stake, and the Christian standing of the Gentile converts must be maintained at all hazards, now or never, if the world was to be saved and Christianity was not to shrink into a narrow corner as a Jewish sect. Whatever might do in Jerusalem, where there was scarcely a heathen convert, this open affront to brethren in Christ could not be tolerated for a moment at Antioch in the church which was of his own planting and full of Hellenists and Gentiles. A public scandal must be publicly corrected. And so Paul confronted Peter and charged him with downright hypocrisy in the face of the whole congregation. He exposed his misconduct by his terse reasoning, to which Peter could make no reply.[2] "If thou," he said to him in substance, "who art a Jew by nationality and training, art eating with the Gentiles in disregard of the ceremonial prohibition,

---

[1] There are not a few examples of successful intimidations of strong and bold men. Luther was so frightened at the prospect of a split of the holy Catholic church, in an interview with the papal legate, Carl von Miltitz, at Altenburg in January, 1519, that he promised to write and did write a most humiliating letter of submission to the Pope, and a warning to the German people against secession. But the irrepressible conflict soon broke out again at the Leipzig disputation in June, 1519.

[2] Gal 2 : 14–21. We take this section to be a brief outline of Paul's address to Peter ; but the historical narrative imperceptibly passes into doctrinal reflections suggested by the occasion and adapted to the case of the Galatians. In the third chapter it naturally expands into a direct attack on the Galatians.

why art thou now, by the moral force of thy example as the chief of the Twelve, constraining the Gentile converts to Judaize or to conform to the ceremonial restraints of the elementary religion ? We who are Jews by birth and not gross sinners like the heathen, know that justification comes not from works of the law, but from faith in Christ. It may be objected that by seeking gratuitous justification instead of legal justification, we make Christ a promoter of sin.[1] Away with this monstrous and blasphemous conclusion! On the contrary, there is sin in returning to the law for justification after we have abandoned it for faith in Christ. I myself stand convicted of transgression if I build up again (as thou doest now) the very law which I pulled down (as thou didst before), and thus condemn my former conduct. For the law itself taught me to exchange it for Christ, to whom it points as its end. Through the Mosaic law as a tutor leading me beyond itself to freedom in Christ, I died to the Mosaic law in order that I might live a new life of obedience and gratitude to God. I have been crucified with Christ, and it is no longer my old self that lives, but it is Christ that lives in me ; and the new life of Christ which I now live in this body after my conversion, I live in the faith of the Son of God who loved me and gave himself for me. I do not frustrate the grace of God ; for if the observance of the law of Moses or any other human work could justify and save, there was no good cause of Christ's death ; his atoning sacrifice on the cross was needless and fruitless."

From such a conclusion Peter's soul shrank back in horror. He never dreamed of denying the necessity and efficacy of the death of Christ for the remission of sins. He and Barnabas stood between two fires on that trying occasion. As Jews they seemed to be bound by the restrictions of the Jerusalem compromise on which the messengers of James insisted ; but by trying to please the Jews they offended the Gentiles, and by going back to Jewish exclusiveness they did violence to their

---

[1] Paul draws, in the form of a question, a *false* conclusion of the Judaizing opponents from *correct* premises of his own, and rejects the conclusion with his usual formula of abhorrence, μὴ γένοιτο, as in Rom. 6 : 2.

better convictions, and felt condemned by their own conscience.[1] They no doubt returned to their more liberal practice.

The alienation of the apostles was merely temporary. They were too noble and too holy to entertain resentment. Paul makes honorable mention afterwards of Peter and Barnabas, and also of Mark, who was a connecting link between the three.[2] Peter in his Epistles endorses the teaching of the "beloved brother Paul," and commends the wisdom of his Epistles, in one of which his own conduct is so severely rebuked, but significantly adds that there are some "things in them hard to be understood, which the ignorant and unsteadfast wrest, as they do also the other Scriptures, to their own destruction."[3]

The scene of Antioch belongs to these things which have been often misunderstood and perverted by prejudice and ignorance in the interest both of heresy and orthodoxy. The memory of it was perpetuated by the tradition which divided the church at Antioch into two parishes with two bishops, Evodius and Ignatius, the one instituted by Peter, the other by Paul. Celsus, Porphyry, and modern enemies of Christianity have used it as an argument against the moral character and inspiration of the apostles. The conduct of Paul left a feeling of intense bitterness and resentment in the Jewish party which manifested itself even a hundred years later in a violent attack of the pseudo-Clementine *Homilies* and *Recognitions* upon Paul, under the disguise of Simon Magus. The conduct of both apostles was so unaccountable to Catholic taste that some of the fathers substituted an unknown Cephas for Peter;[4] while others resolved the scene into a hypocritical farce gotten up by the apostles themselves for dramatic effect upon the ignorant congregation.[5]

---

[1] Gal. 2:11, Peter stood self-condemned and condemned by the Gentiles, κατεγνωσμένος ἦν, not "blameworthy," or "was to be blamed" (E. V.).

[2] Comp. 1 Cor. 9:5, 6; 15:5; Col. 4:10; Philem. 24; 2 Tim. 4:11.

[3] 1 Pet. 5:12; 2 Pet. 3:15, 16.

[4] So Clement of Alexandria, and other fathers, also the Jesuit Harduin.

[5] This monstrous perversion of Scripture was advocated even by such fathers as Origen, Jerome, and Chrysostom. It gave rise to a controversy between Jerome and Augustin, who from a superior moral sense protested against it, and prevailed.

The truth of history requires us to sacrifice the orthodox fiction of moral perfection in the apostolic church. But we gain
more than we lose. The apostles themselves never claimed, but
expressly disowned such perfection.[1] They carried the heavenly
treasure in earthen vessels, and thus brought it nearer to us. The
infirmities of holy men are frankly revealed in the Bible for our
encouragement as well as for our humiliation. The bold attack
of Paul teaches the right and duty of protest even against the
highest ecclesiastical authority, when Christian truth and principle are endangered ; the quiet submission of Peter commends
him to our esteem for his humility and meekness in proportion
to his high standing as the chief among the pillar-apostles ; the
conduct of both explodes the Romish fiction of papal supremacy
and infallibility ; and the whole scene typically foreshadows the
grand historical conflict between Petrine Catholicism and Pauline Protestantism, which, we trust, will end at last in a grand
Johannean reconciliation.

Peter and Paul, as far as we know, never met afterwards till
they both shed their blood for the testimony of Jesus in the
capital of the world.

The fearless remonstrance of Paul had probably a moderating
effect upon James and his elders, but did not alter their practice
in Jerusalem.[2] Still less did it silence the extreme Judaizing
faction ; on the contrary, it enraged them. They were defeated,
but not convinced, and fought again with greater bitterness than
ever. They organized a countermission, and followed Paul into almost every field of his labor, especially to Corinth and
Galatia. They were *a* thorn, if not *the* thorn, in his flesh. He
has them in view in all his Epistles except those to the Thessalonians and to Philemon. We cannot understand his Epistles
in their proper historical sense without this fact. The false
apostles were perhaps those very Pharisees who caused the original trouble, at all events men of like spirit. They boasted of
their personal acquaintance with the Lord in the days of his

---

[1] Comp. 2 Cor. 4: 7; Phil. 3: 12; James 3: 2; 1 John 1: 8; 2: 2.
[2] Comp. Acts 21 : 17–20.

flesh, and with the primitive apostles; hence Paul calls these "false apostles" sarcastically "super-eminent" or "over-extra-apostles."[1] They attacked his apostolate as irregular and spurious, and his gospel as radical and revolutionary. They boldly told his Gentile converts that they must submit to circumcision and keep the ceremonial law; in other words, that they must be Jews as well as Christians in order to *insure* salvation, or at all events to occupy a position of pre-eminence over and above mere proselytes of the gate in the outer court. They appealed, without foundation, to James and Peter, and to Christ himself, and abused their name and authority for their narrow sectarian purposes, just as the Bible itself is made responsible for all sorts of heresies and vagaries. They seduced many of the impulsive and changeable Galatians, who had all the characteristics of the Keltic race. They split the congregation in Corinth into several parties and caused the apostle the deepest anxiety. In Colossæ, and the churches of Phrygia and Asia, legalism assumed the milder form of Essenic mysticism and asceticism. In the Roman church the legalists were weak brethren rather than false brethren, and no personal enemies of Paul, who treats them much more mildly than the Galatian errorists.

This bigoted and most persistent Judaizing reaction was overruled for good. It drew out from the master mind of Paul the most complete and most profound vindication and exposition of the doctrines of sin and grace. Without the intrigues and machinations of these legalists and ritualists we should not have the invaluable Epistles to the Galatians, Corinthians, and Romans. Where error abounded, truth has still more abounded.

At last the victory was won. The terrible persecution under Nero, and the still more terrible destruction of Jerusalem, buried the circumcision controversy in the Christian church. The ceremonial law, which before Christ was " alive but not life-giving,"

---

[1] The E. V. translates ὑπερλίαν ἀπόστολοι, 2 Cor. 11 : 5, " the very chiefest apostles," Plumptre better, "those apostles-extraordinary." They are identical with the ψευδαπόστολοι, ver. 13, and not with the pillar-apostles of the circumcision, Gal. 2 : 9 ; see above, p. 334, note 1.

and which from Christ to the destruction of Jerusalem was "dying but not deadly," became after that destruction "dead and deadly." [1] The Judaizing heresy was indeed continued outside of the Catholic church by the sect of the Ebionites during the second century; and in the church itself the spirit of formalism and bigotry assumed new shapes by substituting Christian rites and ceremonies for the typical shadows of the Mosaic dispensation. But whenever and wherever this tendency manifests itself we have the best antidote in the Epistles of Paul.

§ 36. *Christianity in Rome.*

I. On the general, social, and moral condition of Rome under the Emperors:

> LUDWIG FRIEDLÄNDER : *Sittengeschichte Roms.* Leipzig, 1862, 5th ed. revised and enlarged, 1881, 3 vols.
> ROD. LANCIANI : *Ancient Rome in the Light of Recent Discoveries.* Boston, 1889 (with 100 illustrations).

II. On the Jews in Rome and the allusions of Roman writers to them :

> RENAN : *Les Apôtres*, 287–293 ; MERIVALE : *History of the Romans*, VI., 203 sqq.; FRIEDLÄNDER : *l. c.* III., 505 sqq. ; HAUSRATH : *Neutestamentliche Zeitgeschichte*, III., 383–392 (2d ed.) ; SCHÜRER : *Lehrbuch der Neutestamentlichen Zeitgeschichte*, pp. 624 sq., and *Die Gemeindeverfassung der Juden in Rom in der Kaiserzeit*, Leipz., 1879 ; HUIDEKOPER : *Judaism at Rome*, 1876. Also JOHN GILL : *Notices of the Jews and their Country by the Classic Writers of Antiquity.* 2d ed. London, 1872. On Jewish Roman inscriptions see GARRUCCI (several articles in Italian since 1862), VON ENGESTRÖM (in a Swedish work, Upsala, 1876), and SCHÜRER (1879).

III. On the Christian Congregation in Rome:

> The Histories of the Apostolic Age (see pp. 189 sqq.) ; the Introductions to the Commentaries on *Romans* (mentioned p. 281), and a number of critical essays on the origin and composition of the Church of Rome and the aim of the Epistle to the Romans, by BAUR (*Ueber Zweck und Veranlassung des Römerbriefs*, 1836 ; reproduced in his *Paul*, I., 346 sqq., Engl. transl.), BEYSCHLAG (*Das geschichtliche Problem des Römerbriefs* in the "Studien und Kritiken" for 1867), HILGENFELD (*Einleitung in das N. T.*, 1875, pp. 302 sqq.), C. WEIZSÄCKER (*Ueber die älteste römische Christengemeinde*, 1876, and his *Apost. Zeitalter*, 1886, pp. 415–467).

---

[1] Augustin thus distinguishes three periods in the Mosaic law: 1, *lex viva, sed non vivifica ;* 2, *l. moribunda, sed non mortifera ;* 3, *l. mortua et mortifera.*

W. MANGOLD : *Der Römerbrief und seine gesch. Voraussetzungen,* Marburg, 1884. Defends the Jewish origin and character of the Roman church (against Weizsäcker).

RUD. SEYERLEN : *Entstehung und erste Schicksale der Christengemeinde in Rom.* Tübingen, 1874.

ADOLF HARNACK : *Christianity and Christians at the Court of the Roman Emperors before the Time of Constantine.* In the " Princeton Review," N. York, 1878, pp. 239–280.

J. SPENCER NORTHCOTE and W. R. BROWNLOW (R. C.) : *Roma Sotterranea,* new ed., London, 1879, vol. I., pp. 78–91. Based upon Caval. DE ROSSI'S large Italian work under the same title (*Roma,* 1864–1877, in three vols. fol.). Both important for the remains of early Roman Christianity in the Catacombs.

FORMBY : *Ancient Rome and its Connect. with the Chr. Rel.* Lond., 1880.

KEIM : *Rom. u. das Christenthum.* Berlin, 1881.

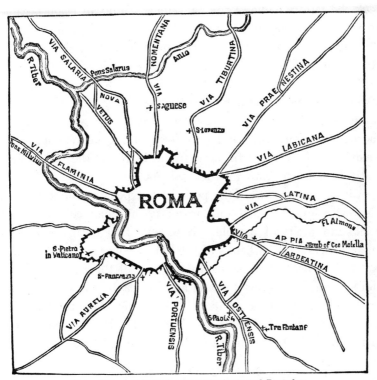

From " Roma Sotterranea," by Northcote and Brownlow.

THE CITY OF ROME.

The city of Rome was to the Roman empire what Paris is to France, what London to Great Britain : the ruling head and the beating heart. It had even a more cosmopolitan character than these modern cities. It was the world in miniature, "*orbis in urbe.*" Rome had conquered nearly all the nationalities of the then civilized world, and drew its population from the East and from the West, from the North and from the South. All languages, religions, and customs of the conquered provinces found a home there. Half the inhabitants spoke Greek, and the natives complained of the preponderance of this foreign tongue which, since Alexander's conquest, had become the language of the Orient and of the civilized world.[1] The palace of the emperor was the chief centre of Oriental and Greek life. Large numbers of the foreigners were freedmen, who generally took the family name of their masters. Many of them became very wealthy, even millionnaires. The rich freedman was in that age the type of the vulgar, impudent, bragging upstart. According to Tacitus, "all things vile and shameful" were sure to flow from all quarters of the empire into Rome as a common sewer. But the same is true of the best elements: the richest products of nature, the rarest treasures of art, were collected there; the enterprising and ambitious youths, the men of genius, learning, and every useful craft found in Rome the widest field and the richest reward for their talents.

With Augustus began the period of expensive building. In his long reign of peace and prosperity he changed the city of bricks into a city of marble. It extended in narrow and irregular streets on both banks of the Tiber, covered the now desolate and feverish Campagna to the base of the Albanian hills, and stretched its arms by land and by sea to the ends of the earth. It was then (as in its ruins it is even now) the most instructive and interesting city in the world. Poets, orators, and historians were lavish in the praises of the *urbs æterna,*

"*qua nihil possis visere majus.*" [2]

---

[1] Friedländer, I. 372 sqq.

[2] See some of these eulogistic descriptions in Friedländer, I. 9, who says that the elements which produced this overwhelming impression were " the enormous, ever changing turmoil of a population from all lands, the confusing and

The estimates of the population of imperial Rome are guess-work, and vary from one to four millions. But in all proba-bility it amounted under Augustus to more than a million, and increased rapidly under the following emperors till it received a check by the fearful epidemic of 79, which for many days de-manded ten thousand victims a day.[1] Afterwards the city grew again and reached the height of its splendor under Hadrian and the Antonines.[2]

THE JEWS IN ROME.

The number of Jews in Rome during the apostolic age is estimated at twenty or thirty thousand souls.[3] They all spoke Hellenistic Greek with a strong Hebrew accent. They had, as far as we know, seven synagogues and three cemeteries, with Greek and a few Latin inscriptions, sometimes with Greek words in Latin letters, or Latin words with Greek letters.[4] They inhabited the fourteenth region, beyond the Tiber (Trastevere),

intoxicating commotion of a truly cosmopolitan intercourse, the number and magnificence of public parks and buildings, and the immeasurable extent of the city.'' Of the Campagna he says, p. 10 : '' *Wo sich jetzt eine ruinener-füllte Einöde gegen das Albanesergebirge hinerstreckt, über der Ficberluft brütet, war damals eine durchaus gesunde, überall angebaute, von Leben wim-melnden Strassen durchschnittene Ebene.*'' See Strabo, v. 3, 12.

[1] Friedländer, I. 54 sqq., by a combination of certain data, comes to the conclusion that Rome numbered under Augustus (A. U. 749) 668,600 people, exclusive of slaves, and 70 or 80 years later from one and a half to two millions.

[2] Friedländer, I. 11 : ''*In dem halben Jahrhundert von Vespasian bis Hadrian erreichte Rom seinen höchsten Glanz, wenn auch unter den Antoninen und später noch vieles zu seiner Verschönerung geschehen ist.*''

[3] By Renan, *L'Antechrist*, p. 7 ; Friedländer, I. 310, 372; and Harnack, *l. c.*, p. 253. But Hausrath, *l. c.*, III. 384, assumes 40,000 Jews in Rome under Augustus, 60,000 under Tiberius. We know from Josephus that 8,000 Roman Jews accompanied a deputation of King Herod to Augustus (*Ant.* XVII. 11, 1), and that 4,000 Jews were banished by Tiberius to the mines of Sardinia (XVIII. 3, 5 ; comp. Tacitus, *Ann.* II. 85). But these data do not justify a very definite calculation.

[4] Friedländer, III. 510 : '' *Die Inschriften sind überwiegend griechisch, aller-dings zum Theil bis zur Unverständlichkeit jargonartig ; daneben finden sich lateinische, aber keine hebräischen.*'' See also Garrucci, *Cimiterio in vigna Rondanini*, and the inscriptions (mostly Greek, some Latin) copied and pub-lished by Schürer, *Die Gemeindeverfassung der Juden*, etc., pp. 33 sqq.

at the base of the Janiculum, probably also the island of the Tiber, and part of the left bank towards the Circus Maximus and the Palatine hill, in the neighborhood of the present Ghetto or Jewry. They were mostly descendants of slaves and captives of Pompey, Cassius, and Antony. They dealt then, as now, in old clothing and broken ware, or rose from poverty to wealth and prominence as bankers, physicians, astrologers, and fortune-tellers. Not a few found their way to the court. Alityrus, a Jewish actor, enjoyed the highest favor of Nero. Thallus, a Samaritan and freedman of Tiberius, was able to lend a million denarii to the Jewish king, Herod Agrippa.[1] The relations between the Herods and the Julian and Claudian emperors were very intimate.

The strange manners and institutions of the Jews, as circumcision, Sabbath observance, abstinence from pork and meat sacrificed to the gods whom they abhorred as evil spirits, excited the mingled amazement, contempt, and ridicule of the Roman historians and satirists. Whatever was sacred to the heathen was profane to the Jews.[2] They were regarded as enemies of the human race. But this, after all, was a superficial judgment. The Jews had also their friends. Their indomitable industry and persistency, their sobriety, earnestness, fidelity, and benevolence, their strict obedience to law, their disregard of death in war, their unshaken trust in God, their hope of a glorious future of humanity, the simplicity and purity of their worship, the sublimity and majesty of the idea of one omnipotent, holy, and merciful God, made a deep impression upon thoughtful and serious persons, and especially upon females (who escaped the odium of circumcision). Hence the large number of proselytes in Rome and elsewhere. Horace, Persius, and Juvenal, as well as Josephus, testify that many Romans abstained from all business on the Sabbath, fasted and prayed, burned

---

[1] Josephus, *Ant.* XVIII. 6, 4. Comp. Harnack, *l. c.*, p. 254.

[2] Tacitus, *Hist.* V. 4 : " *Profana illic omnia quæ apud nos sacra ; rursum concessa apud illos quæ nobis incesta.*" Comp. his whole description of the Jews, which is a strange compound of truth and falsehood.

lamps, studied the Mosaic law, and sent tribute to the temple of Jerusalem. Even the Empress Poppæa was inclined to Judaism after her own fashion, and showed great favor to Josephus, who calls her "devout" or "God-fearing" (though she was a cruel and shameless woman).[1] Seneca, who detested the Jews (calling them *sceleratissima gens*), was constrained to say that this conquered race gave laws to their conquerors.[2]

The Jews were twice expelled from Rome under Tiberius and Claudius, but soon returned to their transtiberine quarter, and continued to enjoy the privileges of a *religio licita*, which were granted to them by heathen emperors, but were afterwards denied them by Christian popes.[3]

---

[1] "Poppæa Sabina, the wife of Otho, was the fairest woman of her time, and with the charms of beauty she combined the address of an accomplished intriguer. Among the dissolute women of imperial Rome she stands preëminent. Originally united to Rufius Crispinus, she allowed herself to be seduced by Otho, and obtained a divorce in order to marry him. Introduced by this new connection to the intimacy of Nero, she soon aimed at a higher elevation. But her husband was jealous and vigilant, and she herself knew how to allure the young emperor by alternate advances and retreats, till, in the violence of his passion, he put his friend out of the way by dismissing him to the government of Lusitania. Poppæa suffered Otho to depart without a sigh. She profited by his absence to make herself more than ever indispensable to her paramour, and aimed, with little disguise, at releasing herself from her union and supplanting Octavia, by divorce or even death." Merivale, *Hist. of the Romans,* VI. 97. Nero accidentally kicked Poppæa to death when in a state of pregnancy (65), and pronounced her eulogy from the rostrum. The senate decreed divine honors to her. Comp. Tac. *Ann.* XIII. 45, 46; XVI. 6; Suet., *Nero,* 35.

[2] "*Victi victoribus leges dederunt.*" Quoted by Augustin (*De Civit. Dei,* VI. 11) from a lost work, *De Superstitionibus.* This word received a singular illustration a few years after Seneca's death, when Berenice, the daughter of King Agrippa, who had heard the story of Paul's conversion at Cæsarea (Acts 25 : 13, 23), became the acknowledged mistress first of Vespasianus and then of his son Titus, and presided in the palace of the Cæsars. Titus promised to marry her, but was obliged, by the pressure of public opinion, to dismiss the incestuous adulteress. "*Dimisit invitus invitam.*" Sueton. *Tit.,* c. 7; Tacit. *Hist.,* II. 81.

[3] The history of the Roman Ghetto (the word is derived from גָּדַע, *cædo,* to cut down, comp. Isa. 10 : 33; 14 : 12; 15 : 2; Jer. 48 : 25, 27, etc., presents a curious and sad chapter in the annals of the papacy. The fanatical Pope Paul IV. (1555–'59) caused it to be walled in and shut out from all intercourse with the Christian world, declaring in the bull *Cum nimis:* "It is most absurd and unsuitable that the Jews, whose own crime has plunged them into everlasting slavery, under the plea that Christian magnanimity allows them, should pre-

When Paul arrived in Rome he invited the rulers of the syna‑
gogues to a conference, that he might show them his good will
and give them the first offer of the gospel, but they replied to
his explanations with shrewd reservation, and affected to know
nothing of Christianity, except that it was a sect everywhere
spoken against. Their best policy was evidently to ignore it as
much as possible. Yet a large number came to hear the apostle
on an appointed day, and some believed, while the majority, as
usual, rejected his testimony.[1]

CHRISTIANITY IN ROME.

From this peculiar people came the first converts to a religion
which proved more than a match for the power of Rome. The
Jews were only an army of defense, the Christians an army of
conquest, though under the despised banner of the cross.

The precise origin of the church of Rome is involved in im‑
penetrable mystery. We are informed of the beginnings of the
church of Jerusalem and most of the churches of Paul, but we
do not know who first preached the gospel at Rome. Chris‑
tianity with its missionary enthusiasm for the conversion of the
world must have found a home in the capital of the world at a
very early day, before the apostles left Palestine. The congre‑
gation at Antioch grew up from emigrant and fugitive disciples
of Jerusalem before it was consolidated and fully organized by
Barnabas and Paul.

It is not impossible, though by no means demonstrable, that

sume to dwell and mix with Christians, not bearing any mark of distinction,
and should have Christian servants, yea even buy houses." Sixtus V. treated
the Jews kindly on the plea that they were "the family from which Christ
came;" but his successors, Clement VIII., Clement XI., and Innocent XIII.,
forbade them all trade except that in old clothes, rags, and iron. Gregory
XIII. (1572–'85), who rejoiced over the massacre of St. Bartholomew, forced
the Jews to hear a sermon every week, and on every Sabbath police agents
were sent to the Ghetto to drive men, women, and children into the church
with scourges, and to lash them if they paid no attention! This custom was only
abolished by Pius IX., who revoked all the oppressive laws against the Jews.
For this and other interesting information about the Ghetto see Augustus J.
C. Hare, *Walks in Rome*, 1873, 165 sqq., and a pamphlet of Dr. Philip, a
Protestant missionary among the Jews in Rome, *On the Ghetto*, Rome, 1874.

[1] Acts 28 : 17–29.

the first tidings of the gospel were brought to Rome soon after the birthday of the church by witnesses of the pentecostal miracle in Jerusalem, among whom were " sojourners from Rome, both Jews and proselytes." [1] In this case Peter, the preacher of the pentecostal sermon, may be said to have had an *indirect* agency in the founding of the church of Rome, which claims him as the rock on which it is built, although the tradition of his early visit (42) and twenty or twenty-five years' residence there is a long exploded fable.[2] Paul greets among the brethren in Rome some kinsmen who had been converted before him, i.e., before 37.[3] Several names in the list of Roman brethren to whom he sends greetings are found in the Jewish cemetery on the Appian Way among the freedmen of the Empress Livia. Christians from Palestine, Syria, Asia Minor, and Greece must have come to the capital for various reasons, either as visitors or settlers.

THE EDICT OF CLAUDIUS.

The first historic trace of Christianity in Rome we have in a notice of the heathen historian Suetonius, confirmed by Luke, that Claudius, about A.D. 52, banished the Jews from Rome because of their insurrectionary disposition and commotion under the instigation of " Chrestus " (misspelt for " Christus "). [4]

---

[1] Acts 2 : 10 : οἱ ἐπιδημοῦντες Ῥωμαῖοι, Ἰουδαῖοί τε καὶ προσήλυτοι. Sojourners are strangers (comp. 17 : 21, οἱ ἐπιδημοῦντες ξένοι), as distinct from inhabitants (κατοικοῦντες, 7 : 48 ; 9 : 22 ; Luke 13 : 4). Among the Hellenistic Jews in Jerusalem who disputed with Stephen were *Libertini*, i.e., emancipated Roman Jews, descendants of those whom Pompey had carried captive to Rome, Acts 6 : 9.

[2] Given up even by Roman Catholic historians in Germany, but still confidently reasserted by Drs. Northcote and Brownlow, *l. c.* I., p. 79, who naïvely state that Peter went to Rome with Cornelius and the Italian band in 42. Comp. on this subject § 26, pp. 254 sqq.

[3] Rom. 16 : 7, " Salute Andronicus and Junias (or Junia), my kinsmen, and my fellow-prisoners who . . . have been in Christ before me." If Junias is masculine, it must be a contraction from Junianus, as Lucas from Lucanus. But Chrysostom, Grotius, Reiche, and others take it as a female, either the wife or sister of Andronicus.

[4] Sueton., *Claud.*, c. 25 : "*Judæos impulsore Chresto assidue tumultuantes Roma expulit.*" The Romans often confounded *Christus* (the *Anointed*) and

This commotion in all probability refers to Messianic controversies between Jews and Christians who were not yet clearly
distinguished at that time.   The preaching of Christ, the true
King of Israel, would naturally produce a great commotion
among the Jews, as it did at Antioch, in Pisidia, in Lystra,
Thessalonica, and Berœa; and the ignorant heathen magistrates
would as naturally infer that Christ was a political pretender
and aspirant to an earthly throne.   The Jews who rejected the
true Messiah looked all the more eagerly for an imaginary
Messiah that would break the yoke of Rome and restore the
theocracy of David in Jerusalem.   Their carnal millennarianism
affected even some Christians, and Paul found it necessary to
warn them against rebellion and revolution.   Among those expelled by the edict of Claudius were Aquila and Priscilla, the

---

Chrestus (from χρηστός, *useful, good*), and called the Christians χρηστιανοί,
Chrestiani.   Compare the French form *chrétien.*   Justin Martyr uses this
etymological error as an argument against the persecution of the Christians
for the sake of their name.   *Apol.* I., c. 4 (I. p. 10, ed. Otto): Χριστιανοὶ εἶναι
κατηγορούμεθα. τὸ δὲ χρηστὸν μισεῖσθαι οὐ δίκαιον.   He knew, however, the true
origin of the name of Christ, I. c. 12 : ᾽Ιησοῦς Χριστός, ἀφ᾽ οὗ καὶ τὸ Χριστιανοὶ
ἐπονομάζεσθαι ἐσχήκαμεν.   Tertullian says that the name *Christus* was almost
invariably mispronounced *Chrestus* by the heathen.   *Apol.,* c. 3 ; *Ad Nat.,* I.
3.   This mistake continued to be made down to the fourth century, Lactantius, *Instit. Div.,* IV. 7, and is found also in Latin inscriptions.   Renan
derives the name *Christianus* from the Latin (like *Herodiani,* Matt. 22 : 16,
Pompejani, Cæsareani), as the derivation from the Greek would require
Χρίστειος (*Les âpotres,* p. 234).   Lightfoot denies this, and refers to Σαρδιανός,
Τραλλιανός (*Philippians,* p. 16, note [1]) ; but Renan would regard these nouns
as Latinisms like ᾽Ασιανός (Acts 20 : 4, Strabo, etc.).   Antioch, where the name
originated (Acts 11 : 26), had long before been Romanized and was famous for
its love of nicknames.   Renan thinks that the term originated with the
Roman authority as an *appellation de police.*   The other two passages of the
N. T. in which it occurs, Acts 26 : 28 ; 1 Pet. 4 : 16, seem to imply contempt
and dislike, and so it is used by Tacitus and Suetonius.   But what was originally meant by the heathen to be a name of derision has become the name of
the highest honor.   For what can be nobler and better than to be a true
Christian, that is, a follower of Christ.   It is a remarkable fact that the name
" Jesuit," which was not in use till the sixteenth century, has become, by the
misconduct of the order which claimed it, a term of reproach even in Roman
Catholic countries; while the term " Christian " embraces proverbially all that
is noble, and good, and Christ-like.

hospitable friends of Paul, who were probably converted before they met him in Corinth.[1]

The Jews, however, soon returned, and the Jewish Christians also, but both under a cloud of suspicion. To this fact Tacitus may refer when he says that the Christian superstition which had been suppressed for a time (by the edict of Claudius) broke out again (under Nero, who ascended the throne in 54).

PAUL'S EPISTLE.

In the early part of Nero's reign (54–68) the Roman congregation was already well known throughout Christendom, had several meeting places and a considerable number of teachers.[2] It was in view of this fact, and in prophetic anticipation of its future importance, that Paul addressed to it from Corinth his most important doctrinal Epistle (A.D. 58), which was to prepare the way for his long desired personal visit. On his journey to Rome three years later he found Christians at Puteoli (the modern Puzzuolo at the bay of Naples), who desired him to tarry with them seven days.[3] Some thirty or forty miles from

---

[1] Acts 18 : 2 ; Rom. 16 : 3. An unconverted Jew would not have taken the apostle under his roof and into partnership. The appellation 'Ιουδαῖος often signifies merely the nationality (comp. Gal. 2 : 13–15). The name Aquila, i.e., Eagle, Adler, is still common among Jews, like other high sounding animal names (Leo, Leopardus, Löwe, Löwenherz, Löwenstein, etc.). The Greek 'Ακύλας was a transliteration of the Latin, and is probably slightly altered in Onkelos, the traditional author of one of the Targums, which the learned Emmanuel Deutsch identifies with Aquila ('Ακύλας, עקרלם in the Talmud), the Greek translator of the Old Testament, a convert to Judaism in the reign of Hadrian, and supposed nephew of the emperor. *Liter. Remains* (N. York, 1874), pp. 337–340. The name of his wife, Priscilla (the diminutive form of Prisca), "probably indicates a connection with the *gens* of the *Prisci*, who appear in the earliest stages of Roman history, and supplied a long series of prætors and consuls." Plumptre on *Acts*, 18 : 2.

[2] Rom. 1 : 8 ; 16 : 5, 14, 15, 19.

[3] Acts 28 : 13. Puteoli was, next after Ostia, the chief harbor of Western Italy and the customary port for the Alexandrian grain ships ; hence the residence of a large number of Jewish and other Oriental merchants and sailors. The whole population turned out when the grain fleet from Alexandria arrived. Sixteen pillars still remain of the mole on which St. Paul landed. See Friedländer, II. 129 sq. ; III. 511, and Howson and Spence on *Acts* 28 : 13.

the city, at Appii Forum and Tres Tabernæ (The Three Taverns), he was met by Roman brethren anxious to see the writer of that marvellous letter, and derived much comfort from this token of affectionate regard.[1]

Paul in Rome.

His arrival in Rome, early in the year 61, which two years later was probably followed by that of Peter, naturally gave a great impulse to the growth of the congregation. He brought with him, as he had promised, " the fulness of the blessing of Christ." His very bonds were overruled for the progress of the gospel, which he was left free to preach under military guard in his own dwelling.[2] He had with him during the whole or a part of the first Roman captivity his faithful pupils and companions: Luke, " the beloved physician " and historian; Timothy, the dearest of his spiritual sons; John Mark, who had deserted him on his first missionary tour, but joined him at Rome and mediated between him and Peter; one Jesus, who is called Justus, a Jewish Christian, who remained faithful to him; Aristarchus, his fellow-prisoner from Thessalonica; Tychicus from Ephesus; Epaphras and Onesimus from Colossæ; Epaphroditus from Philippi; Demas, Pudens, Linus, Eubulus, and others who are honorably mentioned in the Epistles of the captivity.[3] They formed a noble band of evangelists and aided the aged apostle in his labors at Rome and abroad. On the other hand his enemies of the Judaizing party were stimulated to counter-activity, and preached Christ from envy and jealousy;

---

[1] Acts 28: 15. The Forum of Appius (the probable builder of the famous road called after him) is denounced by Horace as a wretched town "filled with sailors and scoundrel tavern-keepers." Tres Tabernæ was a town of more importance, mentioned in Cicero's letters, and probably located on the junction of the road from Antium with the Via Appia, near the modern Cisterna. The distances from Rome southward are given in the Antonine Itinerary as follows: "to Aricia, 16 miles; to Tres Tabernæ, 17 miles; to Appii Forum, 10 miles."

[2] Phil. 1: 12–15; Acts 28: 30.

[3] Col. 4: 7–14; Eph. 6: 21; Philem. 24; Phil. 2: 25–30; 4: 18; comp. also 2 Tim. 4: 10–12.

but in noble self-denial Paul rose above petty sectarianism, and sincerely rejoiced from his lofty standpoint if only Christ was proclaimed and his kingdom promoted. While he fearlessly vindicated Christian freedom against Christian legalism in the Epistle to the Galatians, he preferred even a poor contracted Christianity to the heathenism which abounded in Rome.[1]

The number which were converted through these various agencies, though disappearing in the heathen masses of the metropolis, and no doubt much smaller than the twenty thousand Jews, must have been considerable, for Tacitus speaks of a " vast multitude " of Christians that perished in the Neronian persecution in 64 ; and Clement, referring to the same persecution, likewise mentions a " vast multitude of the elect," who were contemporary with Paul and Peter, and who, " through many indignities and tortures, became a most noble example among ourselves " (that is, the Roman Christians).[2]

COMPOSITION AND CONSOLIDATION OF THE ROMAN CHURCH.

The composition of the church of Rome has been a matter of much learned controversy and speculation. It no doubt was, like most congregations outside of Palestine, of a mixed character, with a preponderance of the Gentile over the Jewish element, but it is impossible to estimate the numerical strength and the precise relation which the two elements sustained to each other.[3]

We have no reason to suppose that it was at once fully or-

---

[1] Phil. 1 : 15–18. Comp. Lightfoot *in loc.*

[2] *Ad Cor.*, ch. 6. The πολὺ πλῆθος ἐκλεκτῶν corresponds precisely to the " *ingens multitudo* " of Tacitus, *Ann.* XV. 44.

[3] Comp. my *Hist. Ap. Ch.*, p. 296 sqq. Dr. Baur attempted to revolutionize the traditional opinion of the preponderance of the Gentile element, and to prove that the Roman church consisted almost exclusively of Jewish converts, and that the Epistle to the Romans is a defense of Pauline universalism against Petrine particularism. He was followed by Schwegler, Reuss, Mangold, Hilgenfeld, Volkmar, Holsten, Holtzmann, and also to some extent by Thiersch and Sabatier. But he was opposed by Olshausen, Tholuck, Philippi, De Wette, Meyer, Schott, Hofmann, in favor of the other view. Beyschlag proposed a compromise to the effect that the majority, in conformity with

ganized and consolidated into one community. The Christians were scattered all over the immense city, and held their devotional meetings in different localities. The Jewish and the Gentile converts may have formed distinct communities, or rather two sections of one Christian community.

Paul and Peter, if they met together in Rome (after 63), would naturally, in accordance with the Jerusalem compact, divide the field of supervision between them as far as practicable, and at the same time promote union and harmony. This may be the truth which underlies the early and general tradition that they were the joint founders of the Roman church. No doubt their presence and martyrdom cemented the Jewish and Gentile sections. But the final consolidation into one organic corporation was probably not effected till after the destruction of Jerusalem.

This consolidation was chiefly the work of Clement, who appears as the first presiding presbyter of the one Roman church. He was admirably qualified to act as mediator between the disciples of Peter and Paul, being himself influenced by both, though more by Paul. His Epistle to the Corinthians combines the distinctive features of the Epistles of Paul, Peter, and James, and has been called "a typical document, reflecting the comprehensive principles and large sympathies which had been impressed upon the united church of Rome." [1]

In the second century we see no more traces of a twofold

Paul's express statements, were Gentile Christians, but mostly ex-proselytes, and hence shared Judaizing convictions. This view has been approved by Schürer and Schultz. Among the latest and ablest discussions are those of Weizsäcker and Godet, who oppose the views both of Baur and Beyschlag. The original nucleus was no doubt Jewish, but the Gentile element soon outgrew it, as is evident from the Epistle itself, from the last chapter of Acts, from the Neronian persecution, and other facts. Paul had a right to regard the Roman congregation as belonging to his own field of labor. The Judaizing tendency was not wanting, as we see from the 14th and 15th chapters, and from allusions in the Philippians and Second Timothy, but it had not the character of a bitter personal antagonism to Paul, as in Galatia, although in the second century we find also a malignant type of Ebionism in Rome, where all heresies congregated.

[1] Lightfoot, *Galat.*, p. 323.

community. But outside of the orthodox church, the heretical schools, both Jewish and Gentile, found likewise an early home in this rendezvous of the world. The fable of Simon Magus in Rome reflects this fact. Valentinus, Marcion, Praxeas, Theodotus, Sabellius, and other arch-heretics taught there. In heathen Rome, Christian heresies and sects enjoyed a toleration which was afterwards denied them by Christian Rome, until, in 1870, it became the capital of united Italy, against the protest of the pope.

LANGUAGE.

The language of the Roman church at that time was the Greek, and continued to be down to the third century. In that language Paul wrote to Rome and from Rome; the names of the converts mentioned in the sixteenth chapter of the Romans, and of the early bishops, are mostly Greek; all the early literature of the Roman church was Greek; even the so-called Apostles' Creed, in the form held by the church of Rome, was originally Greek. The first Latin version of the Bible was not made for Rome, but for the provinces, especially for North Africa. The Greeks and Greek speaking Orientals were at that time the most intelligent, enterprising, and energetic people among the middle classes in Rome. "The successful tradesmen, the skilled artisans, the confidential servants and retainers of noble houses— almost all the activity and enterprise of the common people, whether for good or for evil, were Greek." [1]

SOCIAL CONDITION.

The great majority of the Christians in Rome, even down to the close of the second century, belonged to the lower ranks of society. They were artisans, freedmen, slaves. The proud Roman aristocracy of wealth, power, and knowledge despised the gospel as a vulgar superstition. The contemporary writers

---

[1] Lightfoot, *l. c.*, p. 20. See especially the investigations of Caspari, in his *Quellen zur Geschichte des Taufsymbols*, vol. III. (1875), 267–466. According to Friedländer, I. 142, 481, Greek was the favorite language at the imperial court, and among lovers.

ignored it, or mentioned it only incidentally and with evident contempt. The Christian spirit and the old Roman spirit were sharply and irreconcilably antagonistic, and sooner or later had to meet in deadly conflict. But, as in Athens and Corinth, so there were in Rome also a few honorable exceptions. Paul mentions his success in the prætorian guard and in the imperial household.[1]

It is possible, though not probable, that Paul became passingly acquainted with the Stoic philosopher, Annæus Seneca, the teacher of Nero and friend of Burrus ; for he certainly knew his brother, Annæus Gallio, proconsul at Corinth, then at Rome, and had probably official relations with Burrus, as prefect of the prætorian guard, to which he was committed as prisoner; but the story of the conversion of Seneca, as well as his correspondence with Paul, are no doubt pious fictions, and, if true, would be no credit to Christianity, since Seneca, like Lord Bacon, denied his high moral principles by his avarice and meanness.[2]

Pomponia Græcina, the wife of Aulus Plautius, the conqueror of Britain, who was arraigned for " foreign superstition "

---

[1] Phil. 1 : 13 ; 4 : 22.   The πραιτώριον embraces the officers as well as the soldiers of the imperial regiments ; οἱ ἐκ τῆς καίσαρος οἰκίας may include high functionaries and courtiers as well as slaves and freedmen, but the latter is more probable.   The twenty names of the earlier converts mentioned in Rom. 16 coincide largely with those in the *Columbaria* of the imperial household on the Appian way.   Comp. Lightfoot, *Philipp.*, p. 169 sqq., Plumptre, Excursus to his *Com. on Acts*, and Harnack, *l. c.*, pp. 258 sq.   Harnack makes it appear that the two trusty servants of the Roman church, Claudius Ephebus and Valerius Bito, mentioned in the Epistle of Clement to the Corinthians, c. 63, belonged to the household of the emperor Claudius.

[2] See above, § 29, p. 279, especially the essay of Lightfoot quoted there. Harnack (*l. c.*, p. 260) and Friedländer regard the acquaintance of Paul with Seneca as very improbable, Plumptre as probable.   An epitaph from the third century was found in Ostia which reads: D M. M. ANNEO. PAULO. PETRO. M. ANNEUS. PAULUS. FILIO. CARISSIMO. See De Rossi in the *Bullet. di archeol. christ.*, 1867, pp. 6 sq., and Renan, *L'Antechrist*, p. 12.   Seneca belonged to the *gens Annœa*.   But all that the inscription can be made to prove is that a Christian member of the *gens Annœa* in the third century bore the name of " Paul," and called his son " Paulus Petrus," a combination familiar to Christians, but unknown to the heathen.   Comp. Friedländer, III. 535.

about the year 57 or 58 (though pronounced innocent by her husband), and led a life of continual sorrow till her death in 83, was probably the first Christian lady of the Roman nobility, the predecessor of the ascetic Paula and Eustochium, the companions of Jerome.[1] Claudia and Pudens, from whom Paul sends greetings (2 Tim. 4 : 21), have, by an ingenious conjecture, been identified with the couple of that name, who are respectfully mentioned by Martial in his epigrams; but this is doubtful.[2] A generation later two cousins of the Emperor Domitian (81– 96), T. Flavius Clemens, consul (in 95), and his wife, Flavia Domitilla, were accused of "atheism," that is, of Christianity, and condemned, the husband to death, the wife to exile (A.D. 96).[3] Recent excavations in the catacomb of Domitilla, near that of Callistus, establish the fact that an entire branch of the Flavian family had embraced the Christian faith. Such a change was wrought within fifty or sixty years after Christianity had entered Rome.[4]

[1] Her Christianity has been inferred from the vague description of Tacitus, *Ann.* XIII. 32. See Friedländer III. 534 ; Lightfoot, p. 21 ; Northcote and Brownlow, I. 82 sq. ; Harnack, p. 263. The inference is confirmed by the discovery of the gravestone of a *Pomponius Græcinus* and other members of the same family, in the very ancient crypt of Lucina, near the catacomb of St. Callistus. De Rossi conjectures that Lucina was the Christian name of Pomponia Græcina. But Renan doubts this, *L'Antech.*, p. 4, note 2.

[2] Plumptre, *l. c.* Martial, a Spaniard by birth, came to Rome A.D. 66.

[3] Sueton., *Domit.* 15 ; Dion Cass., 67, 14 ; Euseb., *H. E.* III. 18.

[4] De Rossi, *Bullett.* for 1865, 1874 and 1875; Lightfoot, *St. Clement of Rome*, Append., 257 sq., Harnack, 266–269.

CHAPTER VI.

THE GREAT TRIBULATION. (MATT. 24 : 21.)

§ 37. *The Roman Conflagration and the Neronian Persecution.*

"And I saw the woman drunken with the blood of the saints, and with the blood of the martyrs of Jesus. And when I saw her, I wondered with a great wonder."—Apoc. 17 : 6.

Literature.

I. TACITUS: *Annales,* 1. XV., c. 38–44.

   SUETONIUS : *Nero,* chs. 16 and 38 (very brief).

   SULPICIUS SEVERUS : *Hist. Sacra,* l. II., c. 41.   He gives to the Neronian persecution a more general character.

II. ERNEST RENAN : *L'Antechrist.* Paris, deuxième ed., 1873. Chs. VI.-VIII , pp. 123 sqq. Also his *Hibbert Lectures,* delivered in London, 1880, on Rome and Christianity.

   L. FRIEDLÄNDER : *Sittengeschichte Roms,* I. 6, 27 ; III. 529.

   HERMANN SCHILLER : *Geschichte der röm. Kaiserzeit unter der Regierung des Nero.* Berlin, 1872 (173–179 ; 424 sqq. ; 583 sqq.).

   HAUSRATH : *N. T.liche Zeitgeschichte,* III. 392 sqq. (2d ed., 1875).

   THEOD. KEIM : *Aus dem Urchristenthum.* Zürich, 1878, pp. 171–181.   *Rom u. das Christenthum,* 1881, pp. 132 sqq.

   KARL WIESELER : *Die Christenverfolgungen der Cäsaren.* 1878.

   G. UHLHORN : *The Conflict of Christianity with Heathenism.* Engl. transl. by *Smyth* and *Ropes,* N. Y. 1879, pp. 241–250.

   C. F. ARNOLD : *Die Neron. Christenverfolgung.* Leipz. 1888.

The preaching of Paul and Peter in Rome was an epoch in the history of the church. It gave an impulse to the growth of Christianity. Their martyrdom was even more effective in the end: it cemented the bond of union between the Jewish and Gentile converts, and consecrated the soil of the heathen metropolis. Jerusalem crucified the Lord, Rome beheaded and crucified his chief apostles and plunged the whole Roman church into a baptism of blood. Rome became, for good and for evil, the Jerusalem of Christendom, and the Vatican hill the Golgotha of the West. Peter and Paul, like a new Romulus and Remus, laid the foundation of a spiritual empire vaster and more enduring than that of the Cæsars. The cross was substituted for the sword as the symbol of conquest and power.[1]

But the change was effected at the sacrifice of precious blood. The Roman empire was at first, by its laws of justice, the protector of Christianity, without knowing its true character, and came to the rescue of Paul on several critical occasions, as in Corinth through the Proconsul Annæus Gallio, in Jerusalem through the Captain Lysias, and in Cæsarea through the Procurator Festus. But now it rushed into deadly conflict with the new religion, and opened, in the name of idolatry and patriotism, a series of intermittent persecutions, which ended at last in the triumph of the banner of the cross at the Milvian bridge. Formerly a restraining power that kept back for a while the outbreak of Antichrist,[2] it now openly assumed the character of Antichrist with fire and sword.[3]

---

[1] Lange on *Romans*, p. 29 (Am. ed.): "As the light and darkness of Judaism was centralized in Jerusalem, the theocratic city of God (the holy city, the murderer of the prophets), so was heathen Rome, the humanitarian metropolis of the world, the centre of all the elements of light and darkness prevalent in the heathen world; and so did Christian Rome become the centre of all the elements of vital light, and of all the antichristian darkness in the Christian church. Hence Rome, like Jerusalem, not only possesses a unique *historical* significance, but is a universal picture operative through all ages. Christian Rome, especially, stands forth as a shining light of the nations, which is turned into an idol of magical strength to those who are subject to its rule."

[2] In 2 Thess. 2 : 6, 7, τὸ κατέχον is the Roman empire, ὁ κατέχων the emperor as its representative. This is the patristic interpretation to which some of the best modern commentators have returned. Mediæval sects and many Protestant writers found the great apostacy in the Papacy and the restraining power in the German empire; while papal commentators took revenge by fastening the charge of apostacy on the Reformation which was restrained by the Papacy. I believe in a repeated and growing fulfilment of this and other prophecies on the historic basis of the apostolic age and the old Roman empire.

[3] It is so represented in the Apocalypse (ch. 13–18) after the Neronian persecution.

NERO.

The first of these imperial persecutions with which the martyrdom of Peter and Paul is connected by ecclesiastical tradition, took place in the tenth year of Nero's reign, A.D. 64, and by the instigation of that very emperor to whom Paul, as a Roman citizen, had appealed from the Jewish tribunal. It was, however, not a strictly religious persecution, like those under the later emperors; it originated in a public calamity which was wantonly charged upon the innocent Christians.

A greater contrast can hardly be imagined than that between Paul, one of the purest and noblest of men, and Nero, one of the basest and vilest of tyrants. The glorious first five years of Nero's reign (54–59) under the wise guidance of Seneca and Burrhus, make the other nine (59–68) only more hideous by contrast. We read his life with mingled feelings of contempt for his folly, and horror of his wickedness. The world was to him a comedy and a tragedy, in which he was to be the chief actor. He had an insane passion for popular applause; he played on the lyre; he sung his odes at supper; he drove his chariots in the circus; he appeared as a mimic on the stage, and compelled men of the highest rank to represent in dramas or in tableaux the obscenest of the Greek myths. But the comedian was surpassed by the tragedian. He heaped crime upon crime until he became a proverbial monster of iniquity. The murder of his brother (Britannicus), his mother (Agrippina), his wives (Octavia and Poppæa), his teacher (Seneca), and many eminent Romans, was fitly followed by his suicide in the thirty-second year of his age. With him the family of Julius Cæsar ignominiously perished, and the empire became the prize of successful soldiers and adventurers.[1]

---

[1] Comp. Renan's portraiture of Nero, *l. c.* ch. I. He thinks that there is no parallel to this monster, and calls him *un esprit prodigieusement déclamatoire, une mauvaise nature, hypocrite, légère, vaniteuse ; un composé incroyable d'intelligence fausse, de méchanceté profonde, d'égoïsme atroce et sournois, avec des raffinements inouïs de subtilité."* See also the description of Merivale, ch. LV. (vol. VI. 245 sqq.).

THE CONFLAGRATION IN ROME.

For such a demon in human shape, the murder of a crowd of innocent Christians was pleasant sport. The occasion of the hellish spectacle was a fearful conflagration of Rome, the most destructive and disastrous that ever occurred in history. It broke out in the night between the 18th and 19th of July,[1] among the wooden shops in the south-eastern end of the Great Circus, near the Palatine hill.[2] Lashed by the wind, it defied all exertions of the firemen and soldiers, and raged with unabated fury for seven nights and six days.[3] Then it burst out again in another part, near the field of Mars, and in three days more laid waste two other districts of the city.[4]

The calamity was incalculable. Only four of the fourteen regions into which the city was divided, remained uninjured ; three, including the whole interior city from the Circus to the Esquiline hill, were a shapeless mass of ruins; the remaining

[1] Tacitus (*Ann.* XV. 41) gives the date *quarto decimo* [*ante*] *Kalendas Sextiles . . . quo et Senones captam urbem inflammaverant.* Friedländer, I. 6, wrongly makes it the 17th July. The coincidence with the day when the Gauls had set fire to Rome (July 19, A.U. 364, or 453 years before), was considered a bad omen. It was in the tenth year of Nero's reign, *i.e.*, A.D. 64. See Clinton, *Fasti Romani*, I. Oxon. 1845, pp. 45, 46 ; Friedländer, *l. c.* I. 6 ; Schiller, *l. c.* pp. 173 sq.; Merivale, VI. 131, note. Eusebius, in his *Chronicle*, erroneously puts the fire in the year 66.

[2] For a description of the Circus Maximus see Friedländer, III. 293 sqq. The amphitheatrical rows of seats were eight stadia long, with accommodation for 150,000 persons. After Nero's reconstruction the seats amounted to 250,000 under Vespasianus, and subsequent additions raised the number, in the fourth century, to 385,000. It was surrounded by wooden buildings for shopkeepers (among whom were many Jews), astrologers, caterers, prostitutes, and all sorts of amusements. Nero was most extravagant in his expenditure for the circus and the theatre to gratify the people's passion for *Panem et Circenses*, to use Juvenal's words.

[3] " *Per sex dies septemque noctes,*" Sueton. *Nero*, 38 ; " *sex dies,*" Tacit. *Ann.* XV. 40.

[4] The nine days' duration is proved by an inscription (Gruter, 61. 3). The great fire in London in 1666 lasted only four days and swept an area of 436 acres. Comp. Lambert's *Hist. of London*, II. 91, quoted by Merivale. The fire in Chicago lasted only thirty-six hours, October 8 and 9, 1871, but swept over nearly three and one-third square miles (2,114 square acres), and destroyed 17,450 buildings, the homes of 98,500 people.

seven were more or less destroyed; venerable temples, monu‑
mental buildings of the royal, republican, and imperial times,
the richest creations of Greek art which had been collected for
centuries, were turned into dust and ashes; men and beasts per‑
ished in the flames, and the metropolis of the world assumed
the aspect of a graveyard with a million of mourners over the
loss of irreparable treasures.

This fearful catastrophe must have been before the mind of
St. John in the Apocalypse when he wrote his funeral dirge
of the downfall of imperial Rome (ch. 18).

The cause of the conflagration is involved in mystery. Pub‑
lic rumor traced it to Nero, who wished to enjoy the lurid spec‑
tacle of burning Troy, and to gratify his ambition to rebuild
Rome on a more magnificent scale, and to call it Neropolis.[1]
When the fire broke out he was on the seashore at Antium, his
birthplace; he returned when the devouring element reached
his own palace, and made extraordinary efforts to stay and then
to repair the disaster by a reconstruction which continued till
after his death, not forgetting to replace his partially destroyed
temporary residence (*domus transitoria*) by "the golden house"
(*domus aurea*), as a standing wonder of architectural magnifi‑
cence and extravagance.

THE PERSECUTION OF THE CHRISTIANS.

To divert from himself the general suspicion of incendi‑
arism, and at the same time to furnish new entertainment for
his diabolical cruelty, Nero wickedly cast the blame upon the
hated Christians, who, meanwhile, especially since the public

---

[1] Tacitus XV. 39 : "*Pervaserat rumor ipso tempore flagrantis urbis inisse
eum domesticam scenam et cecinisse Troianum excidium.*" Sueton. c. 38 :
"*Quasi offensus deformitate veterum ædificiorum et angustiis flexurisque vicorum
[Nero] incendit Urbem . . . Hoc incendium e turre Mæcenatiana prospectans,
lætusque 'flammæ,' ut ajebat, 'pulchritudine,' ἅλωσιν Ilii in illo suo scænico
habitu decantavit.*" Robbers and ruffians were seen to thrust blazing brands
into the buildings, and. when seized, they affirmed that they acted under
higher orders. The elder Pliny, Xiphilinus, and the author of the tragedy,
Octavia, likewise charge Nero with incendiarism. But Schiller, *l. c.* 425 sqq.,
labors to relieve him of it.

trial of Paul and his successful labors in Rome, had come to be distinguished from the Jews as a *genus tertium*, or as the most dangerous offshoot from that race. They were certainly despisers of the Roman gods and loyal subjects of a higher king than Cæsar, and they were falsely suspected of secret crimes. The police and people, under the influence of the panic created by the awful calamity, were ready to believe the worst slanders, and demanded victims. What could be expected of the ignorant multitude, when even such cultivated Romans as Tacitus, Suetonius, and Pliny, stigmatized Christianity as a vulgar and pestiferous superstition. It appeared to them even worse than Judaism, which was at least an ancient national religion, while Christianity was novel, detached from any particular nationality, and aiming at universal dominion. Some Christians were arrested, confessed their faith, and were "convicted not so much," says Tacitus, "of the crime of incendiarism as of hating the human race." Their Jewish origin, their indifference to politics and public affairs, their abhorrence of heathen customs, were construed into an "*odium generis humani,*" and this made an attempt on their part to destroy the city sufficiently plausible to justify a verdict of guilty. An infuriated mob does not stop to reason, and is as apt to run mad as an individual.

Under this wanton charge of incendiarism, backed by the equally groundless charge of misanthropy and unnatural vice, there began a carnival of blood such as even heathen Rome never saw before or since.[1] It was the answer of the powers of hell to the mighty preaching of the two chief apostles, which had shaken heathenism to its centre. A "vast multitude" of Christians was put to death in the most shocking manner. Some were crucified, probably in mockery of the punishment of Christ,[2]

---

[1] We do not know the precise date of the massacre. Mosheim fixes it on November, Renan on August, A.D. 64. Several weeks or months at all events must have passed after the fire. If the traditional date of Peter's crucifixion be correct, there would be an interval of nearly a year between the conflagration, July 19, 64, and his martyrdom, June 29th.

[2] "*Crucibus affixi,*" says Tacitus. This would well apply to Peter, to whom our Lord had prophesied such a death, John 21 : 18, 19. Tertullian says:

some sewed up in the skins of wild beasts and exposed to the voracity of mad dogs in the arena. The satanic tragedy reached its climax at night in the imperial gardens on the slope of the Vatican (which embraced, it is supposed, the present site of the place and church of St. Peter): Christian men and women, covered with pitch or oil or resin, and nailed to posts of pine, were lighted and burned as torches for the amusement of the mob ; while Nero, in fantastical dress, figured in a horse race, and displayed his art as charioteer. Burning alive was the ordinary punishment of incendiaries ; but only the cruel ingenuity of this imperial monster, under the inspiration of the devil, could invent such a horrible system of illumination.

This is the account of the greatest heathen historian, the fullest we have—as the best description of the destruction of Jerusalem is from the pen of the learned Jewish historian. Thus enemies bear witness to the truth of Christianity. Tacitus incidentally mentions in this connection the crucifixion of Christ under Pontius Pilate, in the reign of Tiberius. With all his haughty Roman contempt for the Christians whom he knew only from rumor and reading, he was convinced of their innocence of incendiarism, and notwithstanding his cold stoicism, he could not suppress a feeling of pity for them because they were sacrificed not to the public good, but to the ferocity of a wicked tyrant.

Some historians have doubted, not indeed the truth of this

" *Romæ Petrus passioni Dominicæ adæquatur* " (*De Præscript. Hæret.*, c. 36 ; comp. *Adv. Marc.*, IV. 5 ; *Scorpiace*, 15). According to a later tradition he was, at his own request, crucified with his head downwards, deeming himself unworthy to be crucified as was his Lord. This is first mentioned in the *Acta Pauli*, c. 81, by Origen (in Euseb. *H. E.*, III. 1) and more clearly by Jerome (*Catal.* 1) ; but is doubtful, although such cruelties were occasionally practised (see Josephus, *Bell. Jud.*, V. 11, 1). Tradition mentions also the martyrdom of Peter's wife, who was cheered by the apostle on her way to the place of execution and exhorted to remember the Lord on the cross (μέμνησο τοῦ Κυρίου). Clement of Alexandria, *Strom.* VII. 11, quoted by Eusebius, *H. E.*, III. 30. The orderly execution of Paul by the sword indicates a regular legal process before, or more probably at least a year after, the Neronian persecution. in which his Roman citizenship would scarcely have been respected. See p. 326.

terrible persecution, but that the Christians, rather than the Jews, or the Christians alone, were the sufferers.   It seems difficult to understand that the harmless and peaceful Christians, whom the contemporary writers, Seneca, Pliny, Lucan, Persius, ignore, while they notice the Jews, should so soon have become the subjects of popular indignation.   It is supposed that Tacitus and Suetonius, writing some fifty years after the event, confounded the Christians with the Jews, who were generally obnoxious to the Romans, and justified the suspicion of incendiarism by the escape of their transtiberine quarter from the injury of the fire.[1]

But the atrocious act was too public to leave room for such a mistake.   Both Tacitus and Suetonius distinguish the two sects, although they knew very little of either ; and the former expressly derives the name Christians from Christ, as the founder of the new religion.   Moreover Nero, as previously remarked, was not averse to the Jews, and his second wife, Poppæa Sabina, a year before the conflagration, had shown special favor to Josephus, and loaded him with presents.   Josephus speaks of the crimes of Nero, but says not a word of any persecution of his fellow-religionists.[2]   This alone seems to be conclusive.   It is not unlikely that in this (as in all previous persecutions, and often afterwards) the fanatical Jews, enraged by the rapid progress of Christianity, and anxious to avert suspicion from themselves, stirred up the people against the hated Galilæans, and that the heathen Romans fell with double fury on these supposed half Jews, disowned by their own strange brethren.[3]

---

[1] So Gibbon (ch. XVI.), more recently Merivale, *l. c.* ch. 54 (vol. VI. 220, 4th ed.), and Schiller, *l. c.*, pp. 434, 585, followed by Hausrath and Stahr. Merivale and Schiller assume that the persecution was aimed at the Jews and Christians indiscriminately.   Guizot, Milman, Neander, Gieseler, Renan, Lightfoot, Wieseler, and Keim defend or assume the accuracy of Tacitus and Suetonius.

[2] *Ant.* XX. 8. 2, 3.

[3] So Ewald. VI. 627, and Renan, *L'Antechrist*, pp. 159 sqq.   Renan ingeniously conjectures that the " jealousy " to which Clement of Rome (*Ad Cor.* 6) traces the persecution, refers to the divisions among the Jews about the Christian religion.

The Probable Extent of the Persecution.

The heathen historians, if we are to judge from their silence, seem to confine the persecution to the city of Rome, but later Christian writers extend it to the provinces.[1] The example set by the emperor in the capital could hardly be without influence in the provinces, and would justify the outbreak of popular hatred. If the Apocalypse was written under Nero, or shortly after his death, John's exile to Patmos must be connected with this persecution. It mentions imprisonments in Smyrna, the martyrdom of Antipas in Pergamus, and speaks of the murder of prophets and saints and all that have been slain on the earth.[2] The Epistle to the Hebrews which was written in Italy, probably in the year 64, likewise alludes to bloody persecutions, 10 : 32–34, and to the release of Timothy from prison, 13 : 23. And Peter, in his first Epistle, which may be assigned to the same year, immediately after the outbreak of the persecution, and shortly before his death, warns the Christians in Asia Minor of a fiery trial which is to try them, and of sufferings already endured or to be endured, not for any crime, but for the name of "Christians."[3] The name "Babylon" for Rome is most easily explained by the time and circumstances of composition.

Christianity, which had just reached the age of its founder,

---

[1] Orosius (about 400), *Hist.*, VII. 7 : " *Primus Romæ Christianos suppliciis et mortibus adferit* [*Nero*], *ac per omnes provincias pari persecutione excruciari imperavit.*" So also Sulpicius Severus, *Chron.* II. 29. Dodwell (*Dissert. Cypr.* XI., *De paucitate martyrum*, Gibbon, Milman, Merivale, and Schiller (p. 438) deny, but Ewald (VI. 627, and in his *Com. on the Apoc.*) and Renan (p. 183) very decidedly affirm the extension of the persecution beyond Rome. "*L'atrocité commandée par Néron,*" says Renan, "*dut avoir des contre-coups dans les provinces et y exciter une recrudescence de persécution.*" C. L. Roth (*Werke des Tacitus*, VI. 117) and Wieseler (*Christenverfolgungen der Cäsaren*, p. 11) assume that Nero condemned and prohibited Christianity as dangerous to the state. Kiessling and De Rossi have found in an inscription at Pompeii traces of a bloody persecution; but the reading is disputed, see Schiller, p. 438, Friedländer III. 529, and Renan, p. 184.

[2] Ch. 2 : 9, 10, 13 ; 16 : 6 ; 17 : 6 ; 18 : 24.

[3] 1 Pet. 2 : 12, 19, 20 ; 3 : 14–18 ; 4 : 12–19.

[4] At the close, 1 Pet. 5 : 13.

seemed annihilated in Rome. With Peter and Paul the first generation of Christians was buried. Darkness must have overshadowed the trembling disciples, and a despondency seized them almost as deep as on the evening of the crucifixion, thirtyfour years before. But the morning of the resurrection was not far distant, and the very spot of the martyrdom of St. Peter was to become the site of the greatest church in Christendom and the palatial residence of his reputed successors.[1]

THE APOCALYPSE ON THE NERONIAN PERSECUTION.

None of the leading apostles remained to record the horrible massacre, except John. He may have heard of it in Ephesus, or he may have accompanied Peter to Rome and escaped a fearful death in the Neronian gardens, if we are to credit the ancient tradition of his miraculous preservation from being burnt alive with his fellow-Christians in that hellish illumination on the Vatican hill.[2] At all events he was himself a victim of persecu-

---

[1] "Those who survey," says Gibbon (ch. XVI.), "with a curious eye the revolutions of mankind, may observe that the gardens and circus of Nero on the Vatican, which were polluted with the blood of the first Christians, have been rendered still more famous by the triumph and by the abuse of the persecuted religion. On the same spot, a temple, which far surpasses the ancient glories of the capital, has been since erected by the Christian pontiffs, who, deriving their claim of universal dominion from a humble fisherman of Galilee, have succeeded to the throne of the Cæsars, given laws to the barbarian conquerors of Rome, and extended their spiritual jurisdiction from the coast of the Baltic to the shores of the Pacific Ocean." Comp. Renan, *L'Antechr.* p. 177: "*L'orgie de Néron fut le grand baptême de sang qui désigna Rome, comme la ville des martyrs, pour jouer un rôle à part dans l'histoire du christianisme, et en être la seconde ville sainte.   Ce fut la prise de possession de la colline Vaticane par ces triomphateurs d'un genre inconnu jusque-là . . . Rome, rendue responsable de tout le sang versé, devint comme Babylone une sorte de ville sacramentelle et symbolique.*"

[2] Tertullian mentions it in connection with the crucifixion of Peter and the decapitation of Paul as apparently occurring at the same time; *De Præscript. Hær.*, c. 36: "*Ista quam felix ecclesia* (the church of Rome) *cui totam doctrinam apostoli sanguine suo profuderunt, ubi Petrus passioni Dominicæ adæquatur, ubi Paulus Joannis exitu coronatur, ubi* APOSTOLUS JOANNES, POSTEAQUAM IN OLEUM IGNEUM DEMERSUS NIHIL PASSUS EST, IN INSULAM RELEGATUR." Comp. Jerome, *Adv. Jovin.*, 1, 26, and in *Matt.* 22 : 23 ; and Euseb., *H. E.*, VI. 5. Renan (p. 196) conjectures that John was

tion for the name of Jesus, and depicted its horrors, as an exile on the lonely island of Patmos in the vision of the Apocalypse.

This mysterious book—whether written between 68 and 69, or under Domitian in 95—was undoubtedly intended for the church of that age as well as for future ages, and must have been sufficiently adapted to the actual condition and surroundings of its first readers to give them substantial aid and comfort in their fiery trials. Owing to the nearness of events alluded to, they must have understood it even better, for practical purposes, than readers of later generations. John looks, indeed, forward to the final consummation, but he sees the end in the beginning. He takes his standpoint on the historic foundation of the old Roman empire in which he lived, as the visions of the prophets of Israel took their departure from the kingdom of David or the age of the Babylonian captivity. He describes the heathen Rome of his day as "the beast that ascended out of the abyss," as "a beast coming out of the sea, having ten horns and seven heads" (or kings, emperors), as "the great harlot that sitteth among many waters," as a "woman sitting upon a scarlet-colored beast, full of names of blasphemy, having seven heads and ten horns," as "Babylon the great, the mother of the harlots and of the abominations of the earth."[1] The seer must have in view the Neronian persecution, the most cruel that ever occurred, when he calls the woman seated on seven hills, "drunken with the blood of the saints and with the blood of the martyrs of Jesus,"[2] and prophesied her downfall as a matter of rejoicing for the "saints and apostles and prophets."[3]

Recent commentators discover even a direct allusion to Nero, as expressing in Hebrew letters (*Neron Kesar*) the mysterious

---

destined to shine in the illumination of the Neronian gardens, and was actually steeped in oil for the purpose, but saved by an accident or caprice. Thiersch (*Die Kirche im apost. Zeitalter*, p. 227, third edition, 1879) likewise accepts the tradition of Tertullian, but assumes a miraculous deliverance.

[1] Rev. 11 : 7; 13 : 1 ; 17 : 1, 3, 5. Comp. Daniel's description of the fourth (Roman) beast, "dreadful and terrible and strong exceedingly," with "ten horns," Dan. 7 : 7 sqq.

[2] Rev. 17 : 6.   [3] 18 : 20. Comp. also 6 : 9–11.

number 666, and as being the fifth of the seven heads of the beast which was slaughtered, but would return again from the abyss as Antichrist. But this interpretation is uncertain, and in no case can we attribute to John the belief that Nero would literally rise from the dead as Antichrist. He meant only that Nero, the persecutor of the Christian church, was (like Antiochus Epiphanes) the forerunner of Antichrist, who would be inspired by the same bloody spirit from the infernal world. In a similar sense Rome was a second Babylon, and John the Baptist another Elijah.

NOTES.

I. THE ACCOUNTS OF THE NERONIAN PERSECUTION.

1. From heathen historians.

We have chiefly two accounts of the first imperial persecution, from TACITUS, who was born about eight years before the event, and probably survived Trajan (d. 117), and from SUETONIUS, who wrote his *XII. Cæsares* a little later, about A.D. 120. DION CASSIUS (born circa A.D. 155), in his *History of Rome* ('Ρωμαικὴ 'Ιστορία, preserved in fragments, and in the abridgment of the monk Xiphilinus), from the arrival of Æneas to A.D. 229, mentions the conflagration of Rome, but ignores the persecutions of the Christians.

The description of TACITUS is in his terse, pregnant, and graphic style, and beyond suspicion of interpolation, but has some obscurities. We give it in full, from *Annal.*, XV. 44:

"But not all the relief of men, nor the bounties of the emperor, nor the propitiation of the gods, could relieve him [Nero] from the infamy of being believed to have ordered the conflagration. Therefore, in order to suppress the rumor, Nero falsely charged with the guilt, and punished with the most exquisite tortures, those persons who, hated for their crimes, were commonly called *Christians* (*subdidit reos, et quæsitissimis pœnis affecit, quos per flagitia invisos vulgus 'Christianos' appellabat*). The founder of that name, *Christus*, had been put to death (*supplicio affectus erat*) by the procurator of Judæa, Pontius Pilate, in the reign of Tiberius; but the pernicious superstition (*exitiabilis superstitio*), repressed for a time,[1] broke out again, not only through Judæa, the source of this evil, but also through the city [of Rome], whither all things vile and shameful flow from all quarters, and are encouraged (*quo cuncta undique*

---

[1] This refers either to the crucifixion, or more probably to the edict of Claudius, who banished the Jews and Jewish Christians from Rome. See above, p. 363.

atrocia aut pudenda confluunt celebranturque). Accordingly, first, those only were arrested who confessed.[1] Next, on their information, a vast multitude (*multitudo ingens*), were convicted, not so much of the crime of incendiarism as of hatred of the human race (*odio humani generis).*[2] And in their deaths they were made the subjects of sport; for they were wrapped in the hides of wild beasts and torn to pieces by dogs, or nailed to crosses, or set on fire, and when day declined, were burned to serve for nocturnal lights (*in usum nocturni luminis urerentur).* Nero had offered his own gardens [on the Vatican] for this spectacle, and also exhibited a chariot race on the occasion, now mingling in the crowd in the dress of a charioteer, now actually holding the reins. Whence a feeling of compassion arose towards the sufferers, though justly held to be odious, because they seemed not to be cut off for the public good, but as victims to the ferocity of one man."

The account of SUETONIUS, *Nero,* c. 16, is very short and unsatisfactory : "*Afflicti suppliciis Christiani, genus hominum superstitionis novæ ac maleficæ.*" He does not connect the persecution with the conflagration, but with police regulations.

JUVENAL, the satirical poet, alludes, probably as an eye-witness, to the persecution, like Tacitus, with mingled feelings of contempt and pity for the Christian sufferers (*Sat.* I. 155) :

> " Dar'st thou speak of Tigellinus' guilt ?
> Thou too shalt shine like those we saw
> Stand at the stake with throat transfixed
> Smoking and burning."

2. From Christians.

CLEMENT OF ROME, near the close of the first century, must refer to the Neronian persecution when he writes of the " vast multitude of the elect " who suffered "many indignities and tortures, being the victims of jealousy ; " and of Christian women who were made to personate " Danaides " and " Dirces," *Ad Corinth.,* c. 6. I have made no use of this passage in the text. Renan amplifies and weaves it into his graphic description of the persecution (*L'Antechrist,* pp. 163 sqq., almost literally repeated in his *Hibbert Lectures*). According to the legend, Dirce was bound to a raging bull and dragged to death. The scene is represented in the famous

---

[1] Confessed what ? Probably the Christian religion, which was already regarded as a sort of crime. If they confessed to be guilty of incendiarism, they must have been either weak neophytes who could not stand the pain of the torture, or hired scoundrels.

[2] This is to be understood in the active sense of the reputed enmity to mankind, with which Tacitus charges the Jews also in almost the same terms ("*Adversus omnes alios hostile odium,*" *Hist.* V. 5). But Thiersch and others explain it of the hatred of mankind towards the Christians (comp. Matt. 10 : 22, " Ye shall be hated of all men for my name's sake ").

marble group in the museum at Naples. But the Danaides can furnish
no suitable parallel to Christian martyrs, unless, as Renan suggests, Nero
had the sufferings of the Tartarus represented. Lightfoot, following
the bold emendation of Wordsworth (on Theocritus, XXVI. 1), rejects
the reading Δαναΐδες καὶ Δίρκαι (which is retained in all editions, including that of Gebhardt and Harnack), and substitutes for it νεανίδες, παιδίσ-
και, so that Clement would say : " Matrons (γυναῖκες), maidens, slave-girls,
being persecuted, after suffering cruel and unholy insults, safely reached
the goal in the race of faith, and received a noble reward, feeble though
they were in body."

TERTULLIAN (d. about 220) thus alludes to the Neronian persecution,
Ad Nationes, I. ch. 7 : " This name of ours took its rise in the reign of
Augustus ; under Tiberius it was taught with all clearness and publicity ;
under Nero it was ruthlessly condemned (sub Nerone damnatio invaluit),
and you may weigh its worth and character even from the person of its
persecutor. If that prince was a pious man, then the Christians are
impious ; if he was just, if he was pure, then the Christians are unjust
and impure ; if he was not a public enemy, we are enemies of our country : what sort of men we are, our persecutor himself shows, since he of
course punished what produced hostility to himself. Now, although
every other institution which existed under Nero has been destroyed,
yet this of ours has firmly remained—righteous, it would seem, as being
unlike the author [of its persecution]."

SULPICIUS SEVERUS, *Chron.* II. 28, 29, gives a pretty full account, but
mostly from Tacitus. He and OROSIUS (*Hist.* VII. 7) first clearly assert
that Nero extended the persecution to the provinces.

II. NERO'S RETURN AS ANTICHRIST.

Nero, owing to his youth, beauty, dash, and prodigality, and the startling novelty of his wickedness (Tacitus calls him *" incredibilium cupitor,"*
Ann. XV. 42), enjoyed a certain popularity with the vulgar democracy of
Rome. Hence, after his suicide, a rumor spread among the heathen
that he was not actually dead, but had fled to the Parthians, and would
return to Rome with an army and destroy the city. Three impostors
under his name used this belief and found support during the reigns of
Otho, Titus, and Domitian. Even thirty years later Domitian trembled
at the name of Nero. Tacit., *Hist.* I. 2 ; II. 8, 9 ; Sueton., *Ner.* 57 ; Dio
Cassius, LXIV. 9 ; Schiller, *l. c.*, p. 288.

Among the Christians the rumor assumed a form hostile to Nero.
Lactantius (*De Mort. Persecut.*, c. 2) mentions the Sibylline saying that,
as Nero was the first persecutor, he would also be the last, and precede
the advent of Antichrist. Augustin (*De Civit. Dei*, XX. 19) mentions
that at his time two opinions were still current in the church about Nero :
some supposed that he would rise from the dead as Antichrist, others

that he was not dead, but concealed, and would live until he should be revealed and restored to his kingdom. The former is the Christian, the latter the heathen belief. Augustin rejects both. Sulpicius Severus (*Chron.*, II. 29) also mentions the belief (*unde creditur*) that Nero, whose deadly wound was healed, would return at the end of the world to work out "the mystery of lawlessness" predicted by Paul (2 Thess. 2 : 7).

Some commentators make the Apocalypse responsible for this absurd rumor and false belief, while others hold that the writer shared it with his heathen contemporaries. The passages adduced are ch. 17 : 8 : "The beast was, and is not, and is about to come up out of the abyss and to go into perdition" . . . "the beast was, and is not, and shall be present" (καὶ πάρεσται, not καίπερ ἐστίν, "and yet is," as the E. V. reads with the text. rec.) ; 17 : 11 : "And the beast that was, and is not, is himself also an eighth, and is of the seven ; and he goeth into perdition ;" and 13 : 3 : "And I saw one of his heads as though it had been smitten unto death ; and his death-stroke was healed : and the whole world wondered after the beast."

But this is said of the beast, i. e., the Roman empire, which is throughout clearly distinguished from the seven heads, *i. e.*, the emperors. In Daniel, too, the beast is collective. Moreover, a distinction must be made between the death of one ruler (Nero) and the deadly wound which thereby was inflicted on the beast or the empire, but from which it recovered (under Vespasian).

§ 38. *The Jewish War and the Destruction of Jerusalem.*

A.D. 70.

"And as He went forth out of the temple, one of his disciples saith unto Him, Master, behold, what manner of stones and what manner of buildings ! And Jesus said unto him, Seest thou these great buildings? *There shall not be left here one stone upon another, which shall not be thrown down.*"—Mark 13 : 1, 2.

Sources.

Josephus : *Bell. Jud.*, in 7 books ; and *Vita*, c. 4–74. The history of the Jewish war was written by him as eye-witness about A.D. 75. English translations by W. Whiston, in *Works of Jos.*, and by Rob. Traill, ed. by Isaac Taylor, new ed., Lond., 1862. German translations by Gfrörer and W. Hoffmann, Stuttgart, 1836 ; and Paret, Stuttg., 1855 ; French translations by Arnauld d'Andilly, 1667, Joachim Gillet, 1756, and Abbé Glaire, 1846.

Rabbinical traditions in Derenbourg : *Histoire de la Palestine depuis Cyrus jusqu'à Adrien.* Paris, 1867 (first part of his *L'Histoire et la géographie de la Palestine d'après les Thalmuds et les autres sources rabbiniques*), pp. 255–295.

TACITUS : *Hist.*, II. 4 ; V. 1–13. A mere fragment, full of errors and insults towards the vanquished Jews. The fifth book, except this
fragment, is lost. While Josephus, the Jew, is filled with admiration
for the power and greatness of Rome, Tacitus, the heathen, treats
Jews and Christians with scorn and contempt, and prefers to derive
his information from hostile Egyptians and popular prejudice rather
than from the Scriptures, and Philo, and Josephus.
SULPICIUS SEVERUS : *Chronicon,* II. 30 (p. 84, ed. Halm). Short.

Literature.

MILMAN : *The History of the Jews,* Books XIV.–XVII. (New York ed.,
vol. II., 219 sqq.).
EWALD : *Geschichte des Volkes Israel,* VI. 705–753 (second ed.).
GRÄTZ : *Geschichte der Juden,* III. 336–414.
HITZIG : *Geschichte des Volkes Israel,* II. 594–629.
LEWIN : *The Siege of Jerusalem by Titus. With the Journal of a recent
Visit in the Holy City, and a general Sketch of the Topography of Jeru-
salem from the Earliest Times down to the Siege.* London, 1863.
COUNT DE CHAMPAGNY : *Rome et la Judée au temps de la chute de Néron
(ans 66–72 après Jésus-Christ),* 2. éd., Paris, 1865. T. I., pp. 195–
254 ; T. II., pp. 55–200.
CHARLES MERIVALE : *History of the Romans under the Empire,* ch. LIX.
(vol. VI., 415 sqq., 4th ed., New York, 1866).
DE SAULCY : *Les derniers jours de Jérusalem.* Paris, 1866.
E. RENAN : *L'Antechrist* (ch. X.–XX., pp. 226–551). Paris, second ed.,
1873.
EMIL SCHÜRER : *Lehrbuch der Neutestamentlichen Zeitgeschichte* (Leipzig,
1874), pp. 323–350. He also gives the literature.
A. HAUSRATH : *Neutestamentliche Zeitgeschichte,* Part III., second ed.,
Heidelberg, 1875, pp. 424–487.
ALFRED J. CHURCH : *The Story of the Last Days of Jerusalem, from Jose-
phus.* With illustrations. London, 1880.

There is scarcely another period in history so full of vice,
corruption, and disaster as the six years between the Neronian
persecution and the destruction of Jerusalem. The prophetic
description of the last days by our Lord began to be fulfilled
before the generation to which he spoke had passed away, and
the day of judgment seemed to be close at hand. So the Christians believed and had good reason to believe. Even to earnest
heathen minds that period looked as dark as midnight. We
have elsewhere quoted Seneca's picture of the frightful moral

depravity and decay under the reign of Nero, his pupil and murderer. Tacitus begins his history of Rome after the death of Nero with these words: "I proceed to a work rich in disasters, full of atrocious battles, of discord and rebellion, yea, horrible even in peace. Four princes [Galba, Otho, Vitellius, Domitian] killed by the sword; three civil wars, several foreign wars; and mostly raging at the same time. Favorable events in the East [the subjugation of the Jews], unfortunate ones in the West. Illyria disturbed, Gaul uneasy; Britain conquered and soon relinquished; the nations of Sarmatia and Suevia rising against us; the Parthians excited by the deception of a pseudo-Nero. Italy also weighed down by new or oft-repeated calamities; cities swallowed up or buried in ruins; Rome laid waste by conflagrations, the old temples burned up, even the capitol set on fire by citizens; sanctuaries desecrated; adultery rampant in high places. The sea filled with exiles; the rocky islands contaminated with murder. Still more horrible the fury in the city. Nobility, riches, places of honor, whether declined or occupied, counted as crimes, and virtue sure of destruction." [1]

The Approaching Doom.

The most unfortunate country in that period was Palestine, where an ancient and venerable nation brought upon itself unspeakable suffering and destruction. The tragedy of Jerusalem prefigures in miniature the final judgment, and in this light it is represented in the eschatological discourses of Christ, who foresaw the end from the beginning.

The forbearance of God with his covenant people, who had crucified their own Saviour, reached at last its limit. As many as could be saved in the usual way, were rescued. The mass of the people had obstinately set themselves against all improvement. James the Just, the man who was fitted, if any could be, to reconcile the Jews to the Christian religion, had been stoned by his hardened brethren, for whom he daily interceded

[1] *Hist.* I. c. 2.

in the temple; and with him the Christian community in Jerusalem had lost its importance for that city. The hour of the "great tribulation" and fearful judgment drew near. The prophecy of the Lord approached its literal fulfilment: Jerusalem was razed to the ground, the temple burned, and not one stone was left upon another.[1]

Not long before the outbreak of the Jewish war, seven years before the siege of Jerusalem (A.D. 63), a peasant by the name of Joshua, or Jesus, appeared in the city at the Feast of Tabernacles, and in a tone of prophetic ecstasy cried day and night on the street among the people: "A voice from the morning, a voice from the evening! A voice from the four winds! A voice of ruin against Jerusalem and the Temple! A voice against the bridegrooms and the brides! A voice against the whole people! Woe, woe to Jerusalem!" The magistrates, terrified by this woe, had the prophet of evil taken up and scourged. He offered no resistance, and continued to cry his "Woe." Being brought before the procurator, Albinus, he was scourged till his bones could be seen, but interposed not a word for himself; uttered no curse on his enemies; simply exclaimed at every blow in a mournful tone: "Woe, woe to Jerusalem!" To the governor's question, who and whence he was, he answered nothing. Finally they let him go, as a madman. But he continued for seven years and five months, till the outbreak of the war, especially at the three great feasts, to proclaim the approaching fall of Jerusalem. During the siege he was singing his dirge, for the last time, from the wall. Suddenly he added: "Woe, woe also to me!"—and a stone of the Romans hurled at his head put an end to his prophetic lamentation.[2]

THE JEWISH REBELLION.

Under the last governors, Felix, Festus, Albinus, and Florus, moral corruption and the dissolution of all social ties, but at the same time the oppressiveness of the Roman yoke, increased every

---

[1] Matt. 24 : 1, 2 ; Mark 13 : 1 ; Luke 19 : 43, 44 ; 21 : 6.
[2] Jos , B. Jud., VI. 5, 3 sqq.

year. After the accession of Felix, assassins, called "Sicari-
ans" (from *sica*, a dagger), armed with daggers and purchasable
for any crime, endangering safety in city and country, roamed
over Palestine. Besides this, the party spirit among the Jews
themselves, and their hatred of their heathen oppressors, rose
to the most insolent political and religious fanaticism, and was
continually inflamed by false prophets and Messiahs, one of
whom, for example, according to Josephus, drew after him thirty
thousand men. Thus came to pass what our Lord had predicted :
"There shall arise false Christs, and false prophets, and shall
lead many astray."

At last, in the month of May, A.D. 66, under the last procurator, Gessius Florus (from 65 onward), a wicked and cruel
tyrant who, as Josephus says, was placed as a hangman over
evil-doers, an organized rebellion broke out against the Romans,
but at the same time a terrible civil war also between different
parties of the revolters themselves, especially between the Zealots and the Moderates, or the Radicals and Conservatives. The
ferocious party of the Zealots had all the fire and energy which
religious and patriotic fanaticism could inspire ; they have been
justly compared with the Montagnards of the French Revolution. They gained the ascendancy in the progress of the war,
took forcible possession of the city and the temple and introduced a reign of terror. They kept up the Messianic expectations of the people and hailed every step towards destruction as
a step towards deliverance. Reports of comets, meteors, and
all sorts of fearful omens and prodigies were interpreted as
signs of the coming of the Messiah and his reign over the heathen. The Romans recognized the Messiah in Vespasian and
Titus.

To defy Rome in that age, without a single ally, was to defy
the world in arms ; but religious fanaticism, inspired by the recollection of the heroic achievements of the Maccabees, blinded
the Jews against the inevitable failure of this mad and desperate
revolt.

The Roman Invasion.

The emperor Nero, informed of the rebellion, sent his most
famous general, Vespasian, with a large force to Palestine

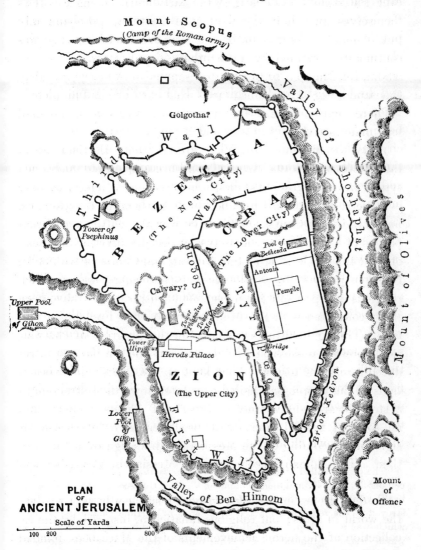

PLAN
OF
ANCIENT JERUSALEM
Scale of Yards

100 200   800

Vespasian opened the campaign in the year 67 from the Syrian
port-town, Ptolemais (Acco), and against a stout resistance over-
ran Galilee with an army of sixty thousand men. But events

in Rome hindered him from completing the victory, and required him to return thither.   Nero had killed himself.   The
emperors, Galba, Otho, and Vitellius followed one another in
rapid succession.   The latter was taken out of a dog's kennel in
Rome while drunk, dragged through the streets, and shamefully
put to death.   Vespasian, in the year 69, was universally proclaimed emperor, and restored order and prosperity.

His son, Titus, who himself ten years after became emperor,
and highly distinguished himself by his mildness and philanthropy,[1] then undertook the prosecution of the Jewish war, and
became the instrument in the hand of God of destroying the holy
city and the temple.   He had an army of not less than eighty
thousand trained soldiers, and planted his camp on Mount Scopus
and the adjoining Mount Olivet, in full view of the city and the
temple, which from this height show to the best advantage.   The
valley of the Kedron divided the besiegers from the besieged.

In April, A.D. 70, immediately after the Passover, when Jerusalem was filled with strangers, the siege began.   The zealots rejected, with sneering defiance, the repeated proposals of Titus
and the prayers of Josephus, who accompanied him as interpreter
and mediator ; and they struck down every one who spoke of surrender.   They made sorties down the valley of the Kedron and
up the mountain, and inflicted great loss on the Romans.   As
the difficulties multiplied their courage increased.   The crucifixion of hundreds of prisoners (as many as five hundred a day)
only enraged them the more.   Even the famine which began
to rage and sweep away thousands daily, and forced a woman
to roast her own child,[2] the cries of mothers and babes, the most

---

[1] The people called him *Amor et Deliciæ generis humani*.   He was born December 30, A.D. 40, and died September 13, 81.   He ascended the throne 79,
in the year when the towns of Herculaneum, Stabiæ, and Pompeii were destroyed.   His reign was marked by a series of terrible calamities, among
which was a conflagration in Rome which lasted three days, and a plague
which destroyed thousands of victims daily.   He made earnest efforts to
repair the injuries, and used to say, when a day passed without an act of
philanthropy, "*Amici, diem perdidi.*"   See Suetonius, *Titus*.

[2] Josephus, VI. 3, 4, gives a full account of this horrible and most unnatural incident.

pitiable scenes of misery around them, could not move the crazy fanatics. History records no other instance of such obstinate resistance, such desperate bravery and contempt of death. The Jews fought, not only for civil liberty, life, and their native land, but for that which constituted their national pride and glory, and gave their whole history its significance—for their religion, which, even in this state of horrible degeneracy, infused into them an almost superhuman power of endurance.

THE DESTRUCTION OF THE CITY AND THE TEMPLE.

At last, in July, the castle of Antonia was surprised and taken by night. This prepared the way for the destruction of the Temple in which the tragedy culminated. The daily sacrifices ceased July 17th, because the hands were all needed for defence. The last and the bloodiest sacrifice at the altar of burnt offerings was the slaughter of thousands of Jews who had crowded around it.

Titus (according to Josephus) intended at first to save that magnificent work of architecture, as a trophy of victory, and perhaps from some superstitious fear; and when the flames threatened to reach the Holy of Holies he forced his way through flame and smoke, over the dead and dying, to arrest the fire.[1] But the destruction was determined by a higher decree. His own soldiers, roused to madness by the stubborn resistance, and greedy of the golden treasures, could not be restrained from the work of destruction. At first the halls around the

---

[1] Josephus is, however, not quite consistent ; he says first that Titus, perceiving that his endeavors to spare a foreign temple turned to the damage of his soldiers, commanded the gates to be set on fire (VI. 4, 1) ; and then, that on the next day he gave orders to extinguish it (§ 3, 6, and 37). Sulpicius Severus (II. 30) makes Titus responsible for the destruction, who thought that it would make an end both to the Jewish and the Christian religion. This is defended by Stange, *De Titi imperatoris vita*, P. I., 1870, pp. 39–43, but doubted by Schürer, *l. c.* p. 346. Renan (511 sqq.), following Bernays, *Ueber die Chronik des Sulpicius Sev.*, 1861, p. 48, believes that Sulpicius drew his account from the lost portion of the *Histories* of Tacitus, and that Titus neither ordered nor forbade the burning of the Temple, but left it to its fate, with a prudent reservation of his motives. So also Thiersch, p. 224.

temple were set on fire.   Then a firebrand was hurled through
the golden gate.   When the flames arose the Jews raised a
hideous yell and tried to put out the fire ; while others, clinging
with a last convulsive grasp to their Messianic hopes, rested in
the declaration of a false prophet, that God in the midst of the
conflagration of the Temple would give a signal for the deliverance of his people.   The legions vied with each other in feeding the flames, and made the unhappy people feel the full force
of their unchained rage.   Soon the whole prodigious structure
was in a blaze and illuminated the skies.   It was burned on the
tenth of August, A.D. 70, the same day of the year on which,
according to tradition, the first temple was destroyed by Nebuchadnezzar.   " No one," says Josephus, " can conceive a louder,
more terrible shriek than arose from all sides during the burning of the temple.   The shout of victory and the jubilee of the
legions sounded through the wailings of the people, now surrounded with fire and sword, upon the mountain, and throughout
the city.   The echo from all the mountains around, even to
Peræa (?), increased the deafening roar.   Yet the misery itself
was more terrible than this disorder.   The hill on which the
temple stood was seething hot, and seemed enveloped to its base
in one sheet of flame.   The blood was larger in quantity than
the fire, and those that were slain more in number than those
that slew them.   The ground was nowhere visible.   All was
covered with corpses ; over these heaps the soldiers pursued the
fugitives." [1]

The Romans planted their eagles on the shapeless ruins, over
against the eastern gate, offered their sacrifices to them, and
proclaimed Titus *Imperator* with the greatest acclamations of
joy.   Thus was fulfilled the prophecy concerning the abomination of desolation standing in the holy place." [2]

Jerusalem was razed to the ground ; only three towers of the
palace of Herod—Hippicus (still standing), Phasael, and Mari-

---

[1] *B. J.*, VI. 5, 1.

[2] Daniel, 9 : 27 ; Matt. 24 : 15 ; comp. Luke 21 : 20 ; Josephus, *B. Jud.*, VI.
6, 1.

amne—together with a portion of the western wall, were left as monuments of the strength of the conquered city, once the centre of the Jewish theocracy and the cradle of the Christian Church.

Even the heathen Titus is reported to have publicly declared that God, by a special providence, aided the Romans and drove the Jews from their impregnable strongholds.[1] Josephus, who went through the war himself from beginning to end, at first as governor of Galilee and general of the Jewish army, then as a prisoner of Vespasian, finally as a companion of Titus and mediator between the Romans and Jews, recognized in this tragical event a divine judgment and admitted of his degenerate countrymen, to whom he was otherwise sincerely attached : " I will not hesitate to say what gives me pain : I believe that, had the Romans delayed their punishment of these villains, the city would have been swallowed up by the earth, or overwhelmed with a flood, or, like Sodom, consumed with fire from heaven. For the generation which was in it was far more ungodly than the men on whom these punishments had in former times fallen. By their madness the whole nation came to be ruined." [2]

Thus, therefore, must one of the best Roman emperors execute the long threatened judgment of God, and the most learned Jew of his time describe it, and thereby, without willing or knowing it, bear testimony to the truth of the prophecy and the divinity of the mission of Jesus Christ, the rejection of whom brought all this and the subsequent misfortune upon the apostate race.

The destruction of Jerusalem would be a worthy theme for the genius of a Christian Homer. It has been called "the most soul-stirring struggle of all ancient history." [3] But there was no Jeremiah to sing the funeral dirge of the city of David and Solomon. The Apocalypse was already written, and had predicted that the heathen "shall tread the holy city under foot

---

[1] *B. Jud.*, VI. 9, 1.   Titus is said to have approved such passages (Jos. *Vita*, 65).

[2] *B. Jud.*, V. 13, 6.   [3] Merivale, *l. c.*, p. 445.

forty and two months." [1] One of the master artists of modern
times, Kaulbach, has made it the subject of one of his greatest
paintings in the museum at Berlin. It represents the burning
temple : in the foreground, the high-priest burying his sword in
his breast ; around him, the scenes of heart-rending suffering ;
above, the ancient prophets beholding the fulfilment of their
oracles ; beneath them, Titus with the Roman army as the unconscious executor of the Divine wrath ; below, to the left,
Ahasuerus, the Wandering Jew of the mediæval legend, driven
by furies into the undying future ; and to the right the group of
Christians departing in peace from the scene of destruction, and
Jewish children imploring their protection.

The Fate of the Survivors, and the Triumph in Rome.

After a siege of five months the entire city was in the hands
of the victors. The number of the Jews slain during the siege,
including all those who had crowded into the city from the
country, is stated by Josephus at the enormous and probably
exaggerated figure of one million and one hundred thousand.
Eleven thousand perished from starvation shortly after the close
of the siege. Ninety-seven thousand were carried captive and
sold into slavery, or sent to the mines, or sacrificed in the gladia-
torial shows at Cæsarea, Berytus, Antioch, and other cities. The
strongest and handsomest men were selected for the triumphal
procession in Rome, among them the chief defenders and leaders
of the revolt, Simon Bar-Giora and John of Gischala. [2]

Vespasian and Titus celebrated the dearly bought victory together (71). No expense was spared for the pageant. Crowned
with laurel, and clothed in purple garments, the two conquerors

---

[1] Apoc. 11 : 2 ; comp. Luke, 21 : 24. In Dan. 7 : 25 ; 9 : 27 ; 12 : 7, the
duration of the oppression of the Jewish people is given as seven half-years
(= 42 months).

[2] B. Jud. VI. 9, 2–4. Milman (II. 388) sums up the scattered statements
of Josephus, and makes out the total number of killed, from the beginning to
the close of the war, to be 1,356,460, and the total number of prisoners
101,700.

rcde slowly in separate chariots, Domitian on a splendid charger, to the temple of Jupiter Capitolinus, amid the shouts of the people and the aristocracy. They were preceded by the soldiers in festive attire and seven hundred Jewish captives. The images of the gods, and the sacred furniture of the temple—the table of show-bread, the seven-armed candlestick, the trumpets which announced the year of jubilee, the vessel of incense, and the rolls of the Law—were borne along in the procession and deposited in the newly built Temple of Peace,[1] except the Law and the purple veils of the holy place, which Vespasian reserved for his palace. Simon Bar-Giora was thrown down from the Tarpeian Rock; John of Gischala doomed to perpetual imprisonment. Coins were cast with the legend *Judæa capta, Judæa devicta.* But neither Vespasian nor Titus assumed the victorious epithet *Judæus;* they despised a people which had lost its fatherland.

Josephus saw the pompous spectacle of the humiliation and wholesale crucifixion of his nation, and described it without a tear.[2] The thoughtful Christian, looking at the representation of the temple furniture borne by captive Jews on the triumphal arch of Titus, still standing between the Colosseum and the Forum, is filled with awe at the fulfilment of divine prophecy.

The conquest of Palestine involved the destruction of the Jewish commonwealth. Vespasian retained the land as his private property or distributed it among his veterans. The people were by the five years' war reduced to extreme poverty, and left

---

[1] The Temple of Peace was afterwards burned under Commodus, and it is not known what became of the sacred furniture.

[2] *B. Jud.*, VII. 5, 5–7. Josephus was richly rewarded for his treachery. Vespasian gave him a house in Rome, an annual pension, the Roman citizenship, and large possessions in Judæa. Titus and Domitian continued the favors. But his countrymen embittered his life and cursed his memory. Jost and other Jewish historians speak of him with great contempt. King Agrippa. the last of the Idumæan sovereigns, lived and died an humble and contented vassal of Rome, in the third year of Trajan, A.D. 100. His licentious sister, Berenice, narrowly escaped the fate of a second Cleopatra. The conquering Titus was conquered by her sensual charms, and desired to raise her to the imperial throne, but the public dissatisfaction forced him to dismiss her, "*invitus invitam.*" Suet., *Tit.* 7. Comp. Schürer, *l. c.* 321, 322.

without a magistrate (in the Jewish sense), without a temple, without a country. The renewal of the revolt under the false Messiah, Bar-Cocheba, led only to a still more complete destruction of Jerusalem and devastation of Palestine by the army of Hadrian (132–135). But the Jews still had the law and the prophets and the sacred traditions, to which they cling to this day with indestructible tenacity and with the hope of a great future. Scattered over the earth, at home everywhere and nowhere; refusing to mingle their blood with any other race, dwelling in distinct communities, marked as a peculiar people in every feature of the countenance, in every rite of religion; patient, sober, and industrious; successful in every enterprise, prosperous in spite of oppression, ridiculed yet feared, robbed yet wealthy, massacred yet springing up again, they have outlived the persecution of centuries and are likely to continue to live to the end of time: the object of the mingled contempt, admiration, and wonder of the world.

§ 39. *Effects of the Destruction of Jerusalem on the Christian Church.*

The Christians of Jerusalem, remembering the Lord's admonition, forsook the doomed city in good time and fled to the town of Pella in the Decapolis, beyond the Jordan, in the north of Peræa, where king Herod Agrippa II., before whom Paul once stood, opened to them a safe asylum. An old tradition says that a divine voice or angel revealed to their leaders the duty of flight.[1] There, in the midst of a population chiefly Gentile, the church of the circumcision was reconstructed. Unfortunately, its history is hidden from us. But it never recovered its former importance. When Jerusalem was rebuilt as a Christian city, its bishop was raised to the dignity of one of the four patriarchs of the East, but it was a patriarchate of honor,

---

[1] In Eusebius, *H. E.*, III. 5 : κατά τινα χρησμὸν τοῖς αὐτόθι δοκίμοις δι' ἀποκα-λύψεως ἐκδοθέντα. Comp. Epiphanius, *De pond. et mens.* c. 15, and the warning of Christ, Matt. 24: 15 sq. Eusebius puts the flight to Pella before the war (πρὸ τοῦ πολέμου), or four years before the destruction of Jerusalem.

not of power, and sank to a mere shadow after the Mohammedan invasion.

The awful catastrophe of the destruction of the Jewish theocracy must have produced the profoundest sensation among the
Christians, of which we now, in the absence of all particular information respecting it, can hardly form a true conception.[1] It
was the greatest calamity of Judaism and a great benefit to
Christianity; a refutation of the one, a vindication and emancipation of the other. It not only gave a mighty impulse to faith,
but at the same time formed a proper epoch in the history of
the relation between the two religious bodies. It separated them
forever. It is true the apostle Paul had before now inwardly
completed this separation by the Christian universality of his
whole system of doctrine; but outwardly he had in various ways
accommodated himself to Judaism, and had more than once
religiously visited the temple. He wished not to appear as a
revolutionist, nor to anticipate the natural course of history,
the ways of Providence.[2] But now the rupture was also outwardly consummated by the thunderbolt of divine omnipotence.
God himself destroyed the house, in which he had thus far dwelt,
in which Jesus had taught, in which the apostles had prayed; he
rejected his peculiar people for their obstinate rejection of the
Messiah; he demolished the whole fabric of the Mosaic theocracy,
whose system of worship was, in its very nature, associated exclusively with the tabernacle at first and afterwards with the temple; but in so doing he cut the cords which had hitherto bound,
and according to the law of organic development necessarily bound
the infant church to the outward economy of the old covenant,
and to Jerusalem as its centre. Henceforth the heathen could
no longer look upon Christianity as a mere sect of Judaism, but
must regard and treat it as a new, peculiar religion. The destruction of Jerusalem, therefore, marks that momentous crisis
at which the Christian church as a whole burst forth forever
from the chrysalis of Judaism, awoke to a sense of its maturity,

[1] It is alluded to in the Ep. of Barnabas, cap. 16.
[2] Comp. 1 Cor. 7 : 18 sqq. ; Acts 21 : 26 sqq.

and in government and worship at once took its independent stand before the world.[1]

This breaking away from hardened Judaism and its religious forms, however, involved no departure from the spirit of the Old Testament revelation. The church, on the contrary, entered into the inheritance of Israel. The Christians appeared as genuine Jews, as spiritual children of Abraham, who, following the inward current of the Mosaic religion, had found Him, who was the fulfilment of the law and the prophets; the perfect fruit of the old covenant and the living germ of the new; the beginning and the principle of a new moral creation.

It now only remained to complete the consolidation of the church in this altered state of things; to combine the premises in their results; to take up the conservative tendency of Peter and the progressive tendency of Paul, as embodied respectively in the Jewish-Christian and the Gentile-Christian churches, and to fuse them into a third and higher tendency in a permanent organism; to set forth alike the unity of the two Testaments in diversity, and their diversity in unity; and in this way to wind up the history of the apostolic church.

This was the work of John, the apostle of completion.

---

[1] Dr. Richard Rothe (*Die Anfänge der Christl. Kirche*, p. 341 sqq.), Thiersch (p. 225), Ewald (VII. 26), Renan (*L'Antechr.*, p. 545), and Lightfoot (*Gal.*, p. 301) ascribe the same significance to the destruction of Jerusalem. Ewald says: "As by one great irrevocable stroke the Christian congregation was separated from the Jewish, to which it had heretofore clung as a new, vigorous offshoot to the root of the old tree and as the daughter to the mother." He also quotes the newly discovered letter of Serapion, written about 75, as showing the effect which the destruction of Jerusalem exerted on thoughtful minds. See above, p. 171.

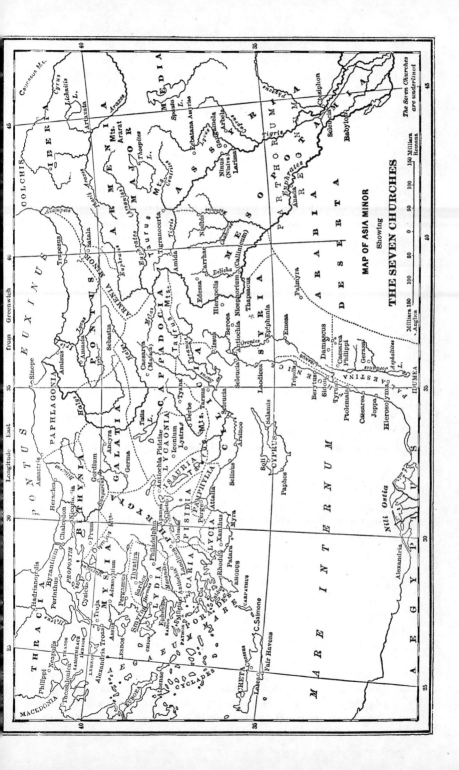

MAP OF ASIA MINOR

Showing

THE SEVEN CHURCHES

Milliara 150   100   50   0   50   100   150 Milliara
Anglica.   Romana.

The Seven Churches
are underlined

CHAPTER VII.

**ST. JOHN, AND THE LAST STADIUM OF THE APOSTOLIC PERIOD.
THE CONSOLIDATION OF JEWISH AND GENTILE CHRISTIANITY.**

Καὶ ὁ λόγος σὰρξ ἐγένετο καὶ ἐσκήνωσεν ἐν ἡμῖν, καὶ ἐθεασάμεθα τὴν δόξαν αὐτοῦ.
—John 1 : 14.

§ 40.   *The Johannean Literature.*

I. Sources.

1. The *Gospel, Epistles*, and *Revelation* of John.   The notices of John in
the Synoptical Gospels, in the Acts, and in Gal. 2 : 9.   (See the
passages in Young's *Analytical Concordance*.)
2. Patristic traditions.   Irenæus: *Adv. Haer.* II. 22, 5 (John lived to
the age of Trajan) ; III. 1, 1 (John at Ephesus) ; III. 3, 4 (John and
Cerinthus) ; V. 30, 3 (John and the Apocalypse).   Clemens Alex. :
Quis dives salvus, c. 42 (John and the young robber).   Polycrates
of Ephesus in Eus. *Hist. Eccl.*, III. 31 ; V. 24 (John, one of the μεγάλα
στοιχεῖα, and a ἱερεὺς τὸ πέταλον πεφορηκώς).   Tertullian : *De praescr.
haer.*, c. 36 (the legend of John's martyrdom in Rome by being
steeped in oil, and his miraculous preservation).   Eusebius : *Hist.
Eccl.*, III. chs. 18, 23, 31 ; IV. 14 ; V. 24 (the paschal controversy).
Jerome : *Ad Gal.* 6 : 10 (the last words of John) ; *De vir. ill.*, c. 9.
Augustin : *Tract.* 124 *in Evang. Joann.* (*Opera* III. 1970, ed. Migne).
Nicephorus Cal. : *Hist. Eccl.*, II. 42.

II. Apocryphal Traditions.

Acta Johannis, ed. Const. Tischendorf, in his *Acta Apost. Apocr.*, Lips.,
1851, pp. 266–276.   Comp. Prolegg. LXXIII. sqq., where the
patristic testimonies on the apocryphal Acts of John are collected.
*Acta Joannis, unter Benutzung von C. v. Tischendorf's Nachlass bear-
beitet* von Theod. Zahn.   Erlangen, 1880 (264 pages and clxxii. pages
of Introd.).

The " Acta " contain the πράξεις τοῦ . . . 'Ιωάννου τοῦ θεολόγου by
Prochorus, who professes to be one of the Seventy Disciples, one of
the Seven Deacons of Jerusalem (Acts 6 : 5), and a pupil of St.
John ; and fragments of the περίοδοι 'Ιωάννου, " the Wanderings of

John," by LEUCIUS CHARINUS, a friend and pupil of John. The former work is a religious romance, written about 400 years after the death of John; the latter is assigned by Zahn to an author in Asia Minor before 160, and probably before 140; it uses the fourth as well as the Synoptical Gospels, and so far has some apologetic value. See p. cxlviii.

Max Bonnet, the French philologist, promises a new critical edition of the Acts of John. See E. Leroux's " Revue critique," 1880, p. 449.

Apocalypsis Johannis, in TISCHENDORF'S *Apocalypses Apocryphæ Mosis, Esdræ, Pauli, Johannis, item Mariæ Dormitio.* Lips., 1866, pp. 70–94.

This pseudo-Johannean Apocalypse purports to have been written shortly after the ascension of Christ, by St. John, on Mount Tabor. It exists in MS. from the ninth century, and was first edited by A. Birch, 1804.

On the legends of St. John comp. Mrs. JAMESON : *Sacred and Legendary Art*, I. 157–172, fifth edition.

III. BIOGRAPHICAL AND CRITICAL.

FRANCIS TRENCH : *Life and Character of St. John the Evangelist.* London, 1850.

DEAN STANLEY (d. 1881) : *Sermons and Essays on the Apostolic Age.* Oxford and London, 1847, third ed., 1874, pp. 234–281.

MAX KRENKEL : *Der Apostel Johannes.* Leipzig, 1871.

JAMES M. MACDONALD : *The Life and Writings of St. John. With Introduction by Dean Howson.* New York, 1877 (new ed. 1880).

WEIZSÄCKER : *Das Apost. Zeitalter.* 1886, pp. 493–559.

Comp. the biographical sketches in the works on the Apostolic Church, mentioned ℐ 20 (p. 189); and the Introductions to the Commentaries of LÜCKE, MEYER, LANGE, LUTHARDT, GODET, WESTCOTT PLUMMER.

IV. DOCTRINAL.

The Johannean type of doctrine is expounded by NEANDER (in his work on the Apost. Age, 4th ed., 1847; E. transl. by Robinson, N. York, 1865, pp. 508–531); FROMMANN (*Der Johanneische Lehrbegriff*, Leipz., 1839); C. REINH. KÖSTLIN (*Der Lehrbegriff des Ev. und der Briefe Johannis, Berlin*, 1843); REUSS (*Die johann. Theologie*, in the Strasburg "Beiträge zu den theol. Wissenschaften," 1847, in *La Théologie johannique*, Paris, 1879, and in his *Theology of the Apost. Age*, 2d ed. 1860, translated from the third French ed. by ANNIE HARWOOD, Lond. 1872–74, 2 vols.); SCHMID (in his *Bibl. Theol. des N. T.*, Stuttg. 1853); BAUR (in *Vorlesungen über N. T. Theol.*, Leipz. 1864);

HILGENFELD (1849 and 1863) ; B. WEISS (*Der Johanneische Lehrbegriff*, Berlin, 1862, and in his *Bibl. Theol. des N. T.*, 4th ed. 1884). There are also special treatises on John's Logos-doctrine and Christology by WEIZSÄCKER (1862), BEYSCHLAG (1866), and others.

V. COMMENTARIES ON THE GOSPEL OF JOHN.

The Literature on the Gospel of John and its genuineness, from 1792 to 1875 (from Evanson to Luthardt), is given with unusual fulness and accuracy by Dr. CASPAR RENÉ GREGORY (an American scholar), in an appendix to his translation of LUTHARDT's *St. John, the Author of the Fourth Gospel.* Edinb. 1875, pp. 283–360. Comp. also the very careful lists of Dr. EZRA ABBOT (down to 1869) in the article *John, Gospel of,* in the Am. ed. of Smith's "Dict. of the Bible," I. 1437–1439.

ORIGEN (d. 254) ; CHRYSOSTOM (407) ; AUGUSTIN (430) ; CYRIL OF ALEXANDRIA (444) ; CALVIN (1564) ; LAMPE (1724, 3 vols.) ; BENGEL (*Gnomon*, 1752) ; LÜCKE (1820, 3d ed. 1843) ; OLSHAUSEN (1832, 4th ed. by EBRARD, 1861) ; THOLUCK (1827, 7th ed. 1857) ; HENGSTENBERG (1863, 2d ed. 1867 ; Eng. transl. 1865) ; LUTHARDT (1852, 2d ed. entirely rewritten 1875 ; Eng. transl. by GREGORY, in 2 vols., and a special volume on the Authorship of the Fourth Gospel, 1875) ; DE WETTE-BRÜCKNER (5th ed. 1863) ; MEYER (5th and last ed. of Meyer, 1869 ; 6th ed. by WEISS, 1880) ; EWALD (1861) ; ALFORD (6th ed. 1868 ; WORDSWORTH (5th ed. 1866), GODET (1865, 2 vols., 2d ed. 1877, Eng. transl. in 3 vols. ; 3d edition, Paris, 1881, trsl. by T. DWIGHT, 1886) ; LANGE (as translated and enlarged by SCHAFF, N. Y. and Edinb. 1871) ; WATKINS (in Ellicott's " N. T. Com. for English Readers," 1878) ; WESTCOTT (in "Speaker's Commentary," 1879, and separately) ; MILLIGAN and MOULTON (in "Schaff's Popul. Com.," 1880) ; KEIL (1881) ; PLUMMER (1881) ; THOMA (*Die Genesis des Joh.-Evangeliums*, 1882) ; PAUL SCHANZ (Tübingen, 1885).

VI. SPECIAL TREATISES ON THE GENUINENESS AND CREDIBILITY OF THE FOURTH GOSPEL.

We have no room to give all the titles of books, or the pages in the introductions to Commentaries, and refer to the lists of Abbot and Gregory.

a. Writers against the Genuineness :

E. EVANSON (*The Dissonance of the Four generally received Evangelists*, Gloucester, 1792). K. G. BRETSCHNEIDER (*Probabilia de Ev. et Ep. Joh. Ap. Indole et Origine*, Leips. 1820, refuted by Schott, Eichhorn, Lücke, and others ; retracted by the author himself in 1828). D. F. STRAUSS (in his *Leben Jesu*, 1835 ; withdrawn in the 3d ed. 1838, but renewed in the 4th, 1840 ; and in his *Leben Jesu für das deutsche*

Volk, 1864) ; LÜTZELBERGER (1840) ; BRUNO BAUER (1840).—F. CHR.
BAUR (first in a very acute and ingenious analysis of the Gospel, in the
"Theol. Jahrbücher," of Tübingen, 1844, and again in 1847, 1848,
1853, 1855, 1859). He represents the fourth Gospel as the ripe result
of a literary development, or evolution, which proceeded, according
to the Hegelian method, from thesis to antithesis and synthesis, or
from Judaizing Petrinism to anti-Jewish Paulinism and (pseudo-)
Johannean reconciliation. He was followed by the whole Tübingen
School; ZELLER (1845, 1847, 1853) ; SCHWEGLER (1846); HILGENFELD
(1849, 1854, 1855, 1875) ; VOLKMAR (1870, 1876) ; SCHENKEL (1864 and
1873) ; HOLTZMANN (in Schenkel's "Bibellexikon," 1871, and *Einleitung*, 1886).—KEIM (*Gesch. Jesu v. Nazara*, since 1867, vol. I.,
146 sqq. ; 167 sqq., and in the 3d ed. of his abridgement, 1875, p. 40) ;
HAUSRATH (1874) ; MANGOLD (in the 4th ed. of Bleek's *Introd.*, 1886) ;
THOMA (1882). In Holland, SCHOLTEN (Leyden, 1865, and again
1871). In England, J. J. TAYLER (London, 1867) ; SAMUEL DAVIDSON
(in the new ed. of his *Introduction to the N. T.*, 1868, II. 323 sqq.
and 357 sqq.) ; the anonymous author of *Supernatural Religion* (vol.
II. 251 sqq., of the 6th ed., London, 1875) ; and E. A. A. (Edwin
A. Abbott, D.D., of London, in art. *Gospels*, "Encycl. Brit.," vol.
X., 1879, pp. 818–843).

The dates assigned to the composition of the Fourth Gospel by
these opponents vary from 110 to 170, but the best scholars among
them are more and more forced to retreat from 170 (Baur's date) to
130 (Keim), or to the very beginning of the second century (110).
This is fatal to their theory; for at that time many of the personal
friends and pupils of John must have been still living to prevent a
literary fiction from being generally accepted in the church as a
genuine work of the apostle.

REUSS (in his *Théologie johannique*, 1879, in the sixth part of his
great work, "La Bible" and in the sixth edition of his *Geschichte
der heil. Schriften N. T.*, 1887, pp. 249 sqq.) leaves the question
undecided, though inclining against the Johannean authorship.
SABATIER, who had formerly defended the authenticity (in his *Essai
sur les sources de la vie de Jésus*, 1866), follows the steps of Reuss,
and comes to a negative conclusion (in his art. *Jean* in Lichtenberger's "Encycl. des Sciences Relig.," Tom. VII., Paris, 1880, pp.
173 sqq.).

WEISSE (1836), SCHWEIZER (1841), WEIZSÄCKER (1857, 1859, 1862,
1886), HASE (in his *Geschichte Jesu*, 1875, while in his earlier writings he had defended the genuineness), and RENAN (1863, 1867, and
1879) admit genuine portions in the Fourth Gospel, but differ
among themselves as to the extent. Some defend the genuineness
of the discourses, but reject the miracles. Renan, on the contrary,
favors the historical portions, but rejects the discourses of Christ, in

a special discussion in the 13th ed. of his *Vie de Jésus*, pp. 477 sqq.
He changed his view again in his *L'église chrétienne*, 1879, pp. 47
sqq. "*Ce qui paraît le plus probable,*" he says, "*c'est qu'un disciple
de l'apôtre, dépositaire de plusieurs de ses souvenirs, se crut autorisé à
parler en son nom et à écrire, vingt-cinq ou trente ans après sa mort, ce
que l'on regrettait qu'il n'eût pas lui-même fixé de son vivant.*" He is
disposed to ascribe the composition to the "Presbyter John"
(whose very existence is doubtful) and to Aristion, two Ephesian
disciples of John the Apostle. In characterizing the discourses in
the Gospel of John he shows his utter incapacity of appreciating
its spirit. MATTHEW ARNOLD (*God and the Bible*, p. 248) conjectures
that the Ephesian presbyters composed the Gospel with the aid of
materials furnished by John.

It should be remarked that Baur and his followers, and Renan,
while they reject the authenticity of the Fourth Gospel, strongly
defend the Johannean origin of the Apocalypse, as one of the certain
documents of the apostolic age. But Keim, by denying the whole
tradition of John's sojourn at Ephesus, destroys the foundation of
Baur's theory.

b. The genuineness has been defended by the following writers :

Jos. PRIESTLEY (Unitarian, against Evanson, 1793). SCHLEIER-
MACHER and his school, especially LÜCKE (1820 and 1840), BLEEK
(1846 and 1862), and DE WETTE (after some hesitation, 1837, 5th ed.,
by *Brückner*, 1863). CREDNER (1836) ; NEANDER (*Leben Jesu*, 1837) ;
THOLUCK (in *Glaubwürdigkeit der evang. Geschichte*, against Strauss,
1837) ; ANDREWS NORTON (Unitarian, in *Evidences of the Genuine-
ness of the Gospels*, 1837–1844, 3 vols., 2d ed. 1846, abridged ed.,
Boston, 1875) ; EBRARD (1845, against Baur ; again 1861, 1868,
and 1880, in Herzog's "Encykl.") ; THIERSCH (1845, against Baur) ;
SCHNEIDER (1854) ; HENGSTENBERG (1863) ; ASTIÉ (1863) ; HOFSTEDE DE
GROOT (*Basilides*, 1863 ; Germ. transl. 1868) ; VAN OOSTERZEE (against
Scholten, Germ. ed. 1867 ; Engl. transl. by Hurst) ; TISCHENDORF
(*Wann wurden unsere Evangelien verfasst?* 1865, 4th ed. 1866 ; also
translated into English, but very poorly) ; RIGGENBACH (1866, against
Volkmar). MEYER (*Com.*, 5th ed. 1869) ; WEISS (6th ed. of Meyer,
1880) ; LANGE (in his *Leben Jesu*, and in his *Com.*, 3d ed. 1868, translated and enlarged by Schaff, 1871) ; SANDAY (*Authorship and Historical Character of the Fourth Gospel*, London, 1872) ; BEYSCHLAG
(in the "Studien und Kritiken" for 1874 and 1875) ; LUTHARDT
(2d ed. 1875) ; LIGHTFOOT (in the "Contemporary Review," 1875–
1877, against *Supernatural Religion*) ; GEO. P. FISHER (*Beginnings
of Christianity*, 1877, ch. X., and art. *The Fourth Gospel*, in "The
Princeton Review" for July, 1881, pp. 51–84) ; GODET (*Commentaire
sur l'Évangile de Saint Jean*, 2d ed. 1878 ; 3d ed. "*complètement
revue,*" vol. I., *Introduction historique et critique*, Paris, 1881, 376

pages) ; WESTCOTT (*Introd. to the Gospels*, 1862, 1875, and *Com.* 1879) ;
McCLELLAN (*The Four Gospels*, 1875) ; MILLIGAN (in several articles
in the "Contemp. Review" for 1867, 1868, 1871, and in his and
MOULTON's *Com.*, 1880) ; EZRA ABBOT (*The Authorship of the Fourth
Gospel*, Boston, 1880 ; republished in his *Critical Essays*, Boston,
1888 ; conclusive on the external evidences, especially the important
testimony of Justin Martyr) ; GEORGE SALMON (*Historical Introd. to
the N. T.*, London, 1886 ; third ed. 1888, pp. 210 sqq.). See also A.
H. FRANKE: *Das Alte Test. bei Johannes*, Göttingen, 1885.

VIII. COMMENTARIES ON THE EPISTLES OF JOHN.

OECUMENIUS (1000) ; THEOPHYLACT (1071) ; LUTHER ; CALVIN ; BULLIN-
GER ; LÜCKE (3d ed. 1856) ; DE WETTE (1837, 5th ed. by BRÜCKNER,
1863) ; NEANDER (1851, Engl. transl. by Mrs. *Conant*, 1852) ; DÜS-
TERDIECK 1852-1856, 2 vols.) ; HUTHER (in Meyer's *Com.*, 1855, 4th
ed. 1880) ; F. D. MAURICE (1857) ; EBRARD (in Olshausen's *Com.*,
1859, transl. by *W. B. Pope*, Edinb. 1860) ; EWALD (1861) ; BRAUNE
(in Lange's *Com.*, 1865, Engl. ed. by *Mombert*, 1867) ; CANDLISH
(1866) ; ERICH HAUPT (1869, Engl. transl. by *W. B. Pope*, Edinb.,
1879) ; R. ROTHE (posthumous ed. by *K. Mühlhäuser*, 1879) ; W. B.
POPE (in Schaff's *Pop. Com.*, 1883) ; WESTCOTT (1883).

IX. COMMENTARIES ON THE APOCALYPSE OF JOHN.

BULLINGER (1535, 6th ed. 1604) ; GROTIUS (1644) ; Jos. MEDE (*Clavis
Apocalyptica*, 1682) ; BOSSUET (R. C., 1689) ; VITRINGA (1719) ; BEN-
GEL (1740, 1746, and new ed. 1834) ; HERDER (1779) ; EICHHORN
(1791) ; E. P. ELLIOTT (*Horæ Apocalypticæ, or, a Com. on the Apoc.*,
5th ed., Lond., 1862, 4 vols.) ; LÜCKE (1852) ; EWALD (1828 and
1862) ; ZÜLLIG (1834 and 1840) ; MOSES STUART (1845, 2 vols.) ; DE
WETTE (1848, 3d ed. 1862) ; ALFORD (3d ed. 1866) ; HENGSTENBERG
(1849 and 1861) ; EBRARD (1853) ; AUBERLEN (*Der Prophet Daniel
und die Offenbarung Johannis*, 1854 ; Engl. transl. by Ad. Saphir,
1856, 2d Germ. ed. 1857) ; DÜSTERDIECK (1859, 3d ed. 1877) ; BLEEK
(1820 and 1862) ; LUTHARDT (1861) ; VOLKMAR (1862) ; KIENLEN
(1870) ; LANGE (1871, Am. ed., with large additions by CRAVEN,
1874) ; COWLES (1871) ; GEBHARDT (*Der Lehrbegriff der Apocalypse*,
1873 ; Engl. transl., *The Doctrine of the Apocalypse*, by J. Jefferson,
1878) ; KLIEFOTH (1874) ; LEE (1882) ; MILLIGAN (in Schaff's *Internat.
Com.*, 1883, and in *Lectures on the Revel.*, 1886) ; SPITTA (1889). VÖL-
TER (1882) and VISCHER (1886) deny the unity of the book. Vischer
makes it a Jewish Apocalypse worked over by a Christian, in spite
of the warning, 22 : 18, 19, which refutes this hypothesis.

§ 41. *Life and Character of John.*

" Volat avis sine meta,
Quo nec vates nec propheta
Evolavit altius :
Tam implenda quam impleta,
Numquam vidit tot secreta
Purus homo purius."

(Adam of St. Victor.)

The Mission of John.

Peter, the Jewish apostle of authority, and Paul, the Gentile apostle of freedom, had done their work on earth before the destruction of Jerusalem—had done it for their age and for all ages to come; had done it, and by the influence of their writings are doing it still, in a manner that can never be superseded. Both were master-builders, the one in laying the foundation, the other in rearing the superstructure, of the church of Christ, against which the gates of Hades can never prevail.

But there remained a most important additional work to be done, a work of union and consolidation. This was reserved for the apostle of love, the bosom-friend of Jesus, who had become his most perfect reflection so far as any human being can reflect the ideal of divine-human purity and holiness. John was not a missionary or a man of action, like Peter and Paul. He did little, so far as we know, for the outward spread of Christianity, but all the more for the inner life and growth of Christianity where it was already established. He has nothing to say about the government, the forms, and rites of the visible church (even the name does not occur in his Gospel and first Epistle), but all the more about the spiritual substance of the church —the vital union of believers with Christ and the brotherly communion of believers among themselves. He is at once the apostle, the evangelist, and the seer, of the new covenant. He lived to the close of the first century, that he might erect on the foundation and superstructure of the apostolic age the majestic dome gilded by the light of the new heaven.

He had to wait in silent meditation till the church was ripe for his sublime teaching. This is intimated by the mysterious word of our Lord to Peter with reference to John: "If I will that he tarry till I come, what is that to thee?"[1] No doubt the Lord did come in the terrible judgment of Jerusalem. John outlived it personally, and his type of doctrine and character will outlive the earlier stages of church history (anticipated and typified by Peter and Paul) till the final coming of the Lord. In that wider sense he tarries even till now, and his writings, with their unexplored depths and heights still wait for the proper interpreter. The best comes last. In the vision of Elijah on Mount Horeb, the strong wind that rent the mountains and brake in pieces the rocks, and the earthquake, and the fire preceded the still small voice of Jehovah.[2] The owl of Minerva, the goddess of wisdom, begins its flight at twilight. The storm of battle prepares the way for the feast of peace. The great warrior of the apostolic age already sounded the keynote of love which was to harmonize the two sections of Christendom; and John only responded to Paul when he revealed the inmost heart of the supreme being by the profoundest of all definitions: "God is love."[3]

JOHN IN THE GOSPELS.

John was a son (probably the younger son) of Zebedee and Salome, and a brother of the elder James, who became the protomartyr of the apostles.[4] He may have been about ten years

---

[1] John 21 : 22, 23. Milligan and Moulton *in loc.* : " The point of contrast between the words spoken respectively to Peter and John, is not that between a violent death by martyrdom and a peaceful departure; but that between impetuous and struggling apostleship, ending in a violent death, and quiet, thoughtful, meditative waiting for the Second Coming of Jesus, ending in a peaceful transition to the heavenly repose. Neither Peter nor himself is to the Evangelist a mere individual. Each is a type of one aspect of apostolic working—of Christian witnessing for Jesus to the very end of time."

[2] 1 Kings 19 : 11, 12.

[3] 1 Cor., ch. 13 ; 1 John 4 : 8, 16.

[4] The name *John*, from the Hebrew יְהוֹחָנָן, or יוֹחָנָן, i.e., *Jehovah is gracious* (comp. the German *Gotthold*), implied to his mind a prophecy of his

younger than Jesus, and as, according to the unanimous testimony of antiquity, he lived till the reign of Trajan, *i.e.*, till after
98, he must have attained an age of over ninety years. He
was a fisherman by trade, probably of Bethsaida in Galilee (like
Peter, Andrew, and Philip). His parents seem to have been in
comfortable circumstances. His father kept hired servants ; his
mother belonged to the noble band of women who followed Jesus
and supported him with their means, who purchased spices to
embalm him, who were the last at the cross and the first at the
open tomb. John himself was acquainted with the high priest,
and owned a house in Jerusalem or Galilee. into which he received the mother of our Lord.[1]

He was a cousin of Jesus, according to the flesh, from his
mother, a sister of Mary.[2] This relationship, together with the
enthusiasm of youth and the fervor of his emotional nature,
formed the basis of his intimacy with the Lord.

He had no rabbinical training, like Paul, and in the eyes of
the Jewish scholars he was, like Peter and the other Galilæan
disciples, an " unlearned and ignorant man."[3] But he passed
through the preparatory school of John the Baptist who summed
up his prophetic mission in the testimony to Jesus as the "Lamb
of God that taketh away the sin of the world," a testimony
which he afterwards expanded in his own writings. It was this
testimony which led him to Jesus on the banks of the Jordan
in that memorable interview of which, half a century after-

relation to Jesus, the incarnate Jehovah (comp. 12 : 41 with Isa. 6 : 1), and is
equivalent to " the disciple whom Jesus loved," 13 : 23 ; 19 : 26 ; 20 : 2 ; 21 : 7,
20. The Greek fathers call John ὁ ἐπιστήθιος, the leaner on the bosom, or,
as we would say, the bosom-friend (of Jesus).

[1] Mark 1 : 20 ; 15 : 40 sq. ; Luke 8 : 3 ; John 19 : 27.   Godet (I. 37) thinks
that his home was on the lake of Gennesareth, and accounts thus for his
absence in Jerusalem at Paul's first visit (Gal. 1 : 18, 19).

[2] According to the correct interpretation of John 19 : 25, that four women
(not three) are meant there, as Wieseler, Ewald, Meyer. Lange, and other
commentators now hold. The writer of the Fourth Gospel, from peculiar
delicacy, never mentions his own name, nor the name of his mother, nor
the name of the mother of our Lord ; yet his mother was certainly at the
cross, according to the Synoptists, and he would not omit her.

[3] Acts 4 : 13, ἄνθρωποι ἀγράμματοι καὶ ἰδιῶται.

wards, he remembered the very hour.[1] He was not only one of
the Twelve, but the chosen of the chosen Three. Peter stood
out more prominently before the public as the friend of the
Messiah ; John was known in the private circle as the friend of
Jesus.[2] Peter always looked at the official character of Christ,
and asked what he and the other apostles should do ; John gazed
steadily at the person of Jesus, and was intent to learn what the
Master said. They differed as the busy Martha, anxious to
serve, and the pensive Mary, contented to learn. John alone,
with Peter and his brother James, witnessed the scene of the
transfiguration and of Gethsemane—the highest exaltation and
the deepest humiliation in the earthly life of our Lord. He
leaned on his breast at the last Supper and treasured those wonderful farewell discourses in his heart for future use. He followed him to the court of Caiaphas. He alone of all the disciples was present at the crucifixion, and was intrusted by the
departing Saviour with the care of his mother. This was a
scene of unique delicacy and tenderness : the *Mater dolorosa*
and the beloved disciple gazing at the cross, the dying Son
and Lord uniting them in maternal and filial love. It furnishes
the type of those heaven-born spiritual relationships, which are
deeper and stronger than those of blood and interest. As John
was the last at the cross, so he was also, next to Mary Magdalene, the first of the disciples who, outrunning even Peter,
looked into the open tomb on the resurrection morning ; and he
first recognized the risen Lord when he appeared to the disciples on the shore of the lake of Galilee.[3]

He seems to have been the youngest of the apostles, as he long
outlived them all ; he certainly was the most gifted and the
most favored. He had a religious genius of the highest order
—not indeed for planting, but for watering; not for outward

---

[1] John 1 : 35–40. The commentators are agreed that the unnamed of the
two disciples is John. See my notes in Lange on the passage.

[2] The well-known distinction made by Grotius between φιλόχριστος and
φιλιησοῦς.

[3] John 20 : 4 ; 21 : 7.

action and aggressive work, but for inward contemplation and insight into the mystery of Christ's person and of eternal life in him. Purity and simplicity of character, depth and ardor of affection, and a rare faculty of spiritual perception and intuition, were his leading traits, which became ennobled and consecrated by divine grace.

There are no violent changes reported in John's history; he grew silently and imperceptibly into the communion of his Lord and conformity to his example ; he was in this respect the anti-pode of Paul. He heard more and saw more, but spoke less, than the other disciples. He absorbed his deepest sayings, which escaped the attention of others ; and although he himself did not understand them at first, he pondered them in his heart till the Holy Spirit illuminated them. His intimacy with Mary must also have aided him in gaining an interior view of the mind and heart of his Lord. He appears throughout as the beloved disciple, in closest intimacy and in fullest sympathy with the Lord.[1]

The Son of Thunder and the Beloved Disciple.

There is an apparent contradiction between the Synoptic and the Johannean picture of John, as there is between the Apoca-lypse and the fourth Gospel ; but on closer inspection it is only the twofold aspect of one and the same character. We have a parallel in the Peter of the Gospels and the Peter of his Epis-tles : the first youthful, impulsive, hasty, changeable, the other matured, subdued, mellowed, refined by divine grace.

In the Gospel of Mark, John appears as a Son of Thunder (Boanerges).[2] This surname, given to him and to his elder

---

[1] For an ingenious comparison between John and Salome, John and James, John and Andrew, John and Peter, John and Paul, see Lange's *Com on John,* pp. 4–10 (Am. ed.).

[2] Mark 3 : 17. Βοανηργές (as Lachmann, Tischendorf, and Tregelles read, in-stead of Βοανεργές), *i.e.,* υἱοὶ βροντῆς. The word is usually derived from בְּנֵי רֶגֶשׁ (as pronounced in the broad Galilean dialect). רֶגֶשׁ means a *noisy crowd of men,* but may have had the significance of *thunder* in Syriac

brother by our Saviour, was undoubtedly an epithet of honor and foreshadowed his future mission, like the name Peter given to Simon. Thunder to the Hebrews was the voice of God.[1] It conveys the idea of ardent temper, great strength and vehemence of character whether for good or for evil, according to the motive and aim. The same thunder which terrifies does also purify the air and fructify the earth with its accompanying showers of rain. Fiery temper under the control of reason and in the service of truth is as great a power of construction as the same temper, uncontrolled and misdirected, is a power of destruction. John's burning zeal and devotion needed only discipline and discretion to become a benediction and inspiration to the church in all ages.

In their early history the sons of Zebedee misunderstood the difference between the law and the gospel, when, in an outburst of holy indignation against a Samaritan village which refused to receive Jesus, they were ready, like Elijah of old, to call consuming fire from heaven.[2] But when, some years afterwards, John went to Samaria to confirm the new converts, he called down upon them the fire of divine life and light, the gift of the Holy Spirit.[3] The same mistaken zeal for his Master was at the bottom of his intolerance towards those who performed a good work in the name of Christ, but outside of the apostolic circle.[4] The desire of the two brothers, in which their mother shared,

---

Robinson derives it from רָגַן, which means *tumult, alarm*, and is used of the roaring noise of thunder, Job 37 : 2. The usual Hebrew word for thunder is רַעַם (Ps. 77 : 19 ; 81 : 8 ; Job 26 : 14). This name completely dispels the popular notion of John. " *Nichts*," says Hilgenfeld (*Einleit.*, p. 393), "*stimmt zu den synoptischen Evangelien weniger als jenes mädchenhafte Johannesbild, welches unter uns gangbar geworden ist.*" Comp. Godet's remarks at the close of this section.

[1] " The Lord thundered with a great thunder ; " "The Lord shall send thunder and rain." See Ex. 9 : 23 ; 1 Sam. 7 : 10 ; 12 : 17, 18 ; Job 26 : 14 ; Ps. 77 : 18 ; 81 : 7 ; 104 : 7 ; Isa. 29 : 6, etc.

[2] Luke 9 : 54–56. Some commentators think that this incident suggested the giving of the name Boanerges ; but that would make it an epithet of censure, which the Lord would certainly not fasten upon his beloved disciple.

[3] Acts 8 : 14–17.

[4] Mark 9 : 38–40 ; comp. Luke 9 : 49, 50.

for the highest positions in the Messianic kingdom, likewise reveals both their strength and their weakness, a noble ambition
to be near Christ, though it be near the fire and the sword, yet
an ambition that was not free from selfishness and pride, which
deserved the rebuke of our Lord, who held up before them the
prospect of the baptism of blood.[1]

All this is quite consistent with the writings of John. He
appears there by no means as a soft and sentimental, but as a
positive and decided character. He had no doubt a sweet and
lovely disposition, but at the same time a delicate sensibility,
ardent feelings, and strong convictions. These traits are by no
means incompatible. He knew no compromise, no division of
loyalty. A holy fire burned within him, though he was moved
in the deep rather than on the surface. In the Apocalypse,
the thunder rolls loud and mighty against the enemies of
Christ and his kingdom, while on the other hand there are
in the same book episodes of rest and anthems of peace and
joy, and a description of the heavenly Jerusalem, which could
have proceeded only from the beloved disciple. In the Gospel
and the Epistles of John, we feel the same power, only subdued and restrained. He reports the severest as well as the
sweetest discourses of the Saviour, according as he speaks to the
enemies of the truth, or in the circle of the disciples. No
other evangelist gives us such a profound inside-view of the antagonism between Christ and the Jewish hierarchy, and of the
growing intensity of that hatred which culminated in the bloody
counsel; no apostle draws a sharper line of demarcation between
light and darkness, truth and falsehood, Christ and Antichrist,
than John. His Gospel and Epistles move in these irreconcilable antagonisms. He knows no compromise between God and
Baal. With what holy horror does he speak of the traitor, and
the rising rage of the Pharisees against their Messiah! How
severely does he, in the words of the Lord, attack the unbelieving Jews with their murderous designs, as children of the devil!
And, in his Epistles, he terms every one who dishonors his

[1] Matt. 20: 20–24; comp. Mark 10: 35–41.

Christian profession a liar; every one who hates his brother a murderer; every one who wilfully sins a child of the devil; and he earnestly warns against teachers who deny the mystery of the incarnation, as Antichrists, and he forbids even to salute them.[1] The measure of his love of Christ was the measure of his hatred of Antichrist. For hatred is inverted love. Love and hatred are one and the same passion, only revealed in opposite directions. The same sun gives light and heat to the living, and hastens the decay of the dead.

Christian art has so far well understood the double aspect of John by representing him with a face of womanly purity and tenderness, but not weakness, and giving him for his symbol a bold eagle soaring with outspread wings above the clouds.[2]

The Apocalypse and the Fourth Gospel.

A proper appreciation of John's character as thus set forth removes the chief difficulty of ascribing the Apocalypse and the fourth Gospel to one and the same writer.[3] The temper is the same in both: a noble, enthusiastic nature, capable of intense emotions of love and hatred, but with the difference between vigorous manhood and ripe old age, between the roar of battle and the repose of peace. The theology is the same, including the most characteristic features of Christology and soteriology.[4]

---

[1] John 8:44; 1 John 1:6, 8, 10; 2:18 sqq.; 3:8, 15; 4:1 sqq.; 2 John vers. 10 and 11.

[2] Jerome (*Com. ad Matth.*, *Proœm.*, *Opera*, ed. Migne, Tom. vii. 19): *Quarta* [*facies*] *Joannem evangelistam* [*significat*], *qui assumptis pennis aquilæ, et ad altiora festinans, de Verbo Dei disputat.* An old epigram says of John :

"*More volans aquilæ verbo petit astra Joannes.*"

[3] The author of *Supernat. Relig.*, II. 400, says : "Instead of the fierce and intolerant spirit of the Son of Thunder, we find [in the Fourth Gospel] a spirit breathing forth nothing but gentleness and love." How superficial this judgment is appears from our text.

[4] This is well shown in Gebhardt's *Doctrine of the Apocalypse*, and is substantially even acknowledged by those who deny the Johannean origin of either the Apocalypse (the Schleiermacher School), or of the Gospel (the Tübingen School). "*Es ist nicht blos,*" says Baur (in his *Church History*, vol. I. p. 147), "*eine äussere Anlehnung an einen vielgefeierten Namen, es fehlt auch*

By no other apostle is Christ called the Logos. The Gospel is "the Apocalypse spiritualized," or idealized. Even the difference of style, which is startling at first sight, disappears on closer inspection. The Greek of the Apocalypse is the most Hebraizing of all the books of the New Testament, as may be expected from its close affinity with Hebrew prophecy to which the classical Greek furnished no parallel, while the Greek of the fourth Gospel is pure, and free from irregularities; yet after all John the Evangelist also shows the greatest familiarity with, and the deepest insight into, the Hebrew religion, and preserves its purest and noblest elements ; and his style has all the childlike simplicity and sententious brevity of the Old Testament ; it is only a Greek body inspired by a Hebrew soul.[1]

In accounting for the difference between the Apocalypse and the other writings of John, we must also take into consideration the necessary difference between prophetic composition under direct inspiration, and historical and didactic composition, and the intervening time of about twenty years ; the Apocalypse being written before the destruction of Jerusalem, the fourth Gospel towards the close of the first century, in extreme old age, when his youth was renewed like the eagle's, as in the case of some of the greatest poets, Homer, Sophocles, Milton, and Goethe.

nicht an innern Berührungspunkten zwischen dem Evangelium und der Apokalypse, und man kann nur die tiefe Genialität und feine Kunst bewundern, mit welcher der Evangelist die Elemente, welche vom Standpunkt der Apokalypse auf den freiern und höhern des Evangeliums hinüberleiteten, in sich aufgenommen hat, um die Apokalypse zum Evangelium zu vergeistigen. Nur vom Standpunkt des Evangeliums aus lässt sich das Verhältniss, in das sich der Verfasser desselben zu der Apokalypse setzte, richtig begreifen."   Schwegler and Köstlin make similar concessions. See my *Hist. of the Apost. Ch.*, p. 425.

[1] In this way the opposite views of two eminent Hebrew scholars and judges of style may be reconciled. While Renan, looking at the surface, says of the fourth Gospel : "John's style has nothing Hebrew, nothing Jewish, nothing Talmudic," Ewald, on the contrary, penetrating to the core, remarks : "In its true spirit and afflatus, no language can be more genuinely Hebrew than that of John." Godet agrees with Ewald when he says : "The dress only is Greek, the body is Hebrew."

NOTES.

I. THE SON OF THUNDER AND THE APOSTLE OF LOVE.

I quote some excellent remarks on the character of John from my friend, Dr. GODET (*Com.* I. 35, English translation by Crombie and Cusin): " How are we to explain two features of character apparently so opposite? There exist profound receptive natures which are accustomed to shut up their impressions within themselves, and this all the more that these impressions are keen and thrilling. But if it happens that these persons once cease to be masters of themselves, their long-restrained emotions then burst forth in sudden explosions, which fill the persons around them with amazement. Does not the character of John belong to this order? And when Jesus gave to him and his brother the surname of Boanerges, sons of thunder (Mark 3 : 17), could he have described them better? I cannot think that, by that surname, Jesus intended, as all the old writers have believed, to signalize the eloquence which distinguished them. Neither can I allow that he desired by that surname to perpetuate the recollection of their anger in one of the cases indicated. We are led by what precedes to a more natural explanation, and one more worthy of Jesus himself. As electricity is stored up by degrees in the cloud until it bursts forth suddenly in the lightning and thunderbolt, so in those two loving and passionate natures impressions silently accumulated till the moment when the heart overflowed, and they took an unexpected and violent flight. We love to represent St. John to ourselves as of a gentle rather than of an energetic nature, tender even to weakness. Do not his writings insist before and above all else upon love? Were not the last sermons of the old man 'Love one another?' That is true; but we forget other features of a different kind, during the first and last periods of his life, which reveal something decisive, sharp, absolute, even violent in his disposition. If we take all the facts stated into consideration, we shall recognize in him one of those sensitive, ardent souls, worshippers of an ideal, who attach themselves at first sight, and without reservation, to that being who seems to them to realize that of which they have dreamt, and whose devotion easily becomes exclusive and intolerant. They feel themselves repelled by everything which is not in sympathy with their enthusiasm. They no longer understand a division of heart which they themselves know not how to practice. All for all! such is their motto. Where that all is not, there is in their eyes nothing. Such affections do not subsist without including an alloy of impure egoism. A divine work is needed, in order that the true devotion, which constitutes the basis of such, may shine forth at the last in all its sublimity. Such was, if we are not deceived, the inmost history of John." Comp. the third French ed. of Godet's *Com.*, I. p. 50.

Dr. WESTCOTT (in his *Com.*, p. xxxiii.) : "John knew that to be with Christ was life, to reject Christ was death ; and he did not shrink from expressing the thought in the spirit of the old dispensation. He learned from the Lord, as time went on, a more faithful patience, but he did not unlearn the burning devotion which consumed him. To the last, words of awful warning, like the thunderings about the throne, reveal the presence of that secret fire. Every page of the Apocalypse is inspired with the cry of the souls beneath the altar, 'How long' (Rev. 6 : 10) ; and nowhere is error as to the person of Christ denounced more sternly than in his Epistles (2 John 10 ; 1 John 4 : 1 ff.)." Similar passages in Stanley.

II. THE MISSION OF JOHN.

Dean STANLEY (*Sermons and Essays on the Apost. Age*, p. 249 sq., 3d ed.) : "Above all, John spoke of the union of the soul with God, but it was by no mere process of oriental contemplation, or mystic absorption ; it was by that word which now for the first time took its proper place in the order of the world—by LOVE. It has been reserved for St. Paul to proclaim that the deepest principle in the heart of man was Faith ; it was reserved for St. John to proclaim that the essential attribute of God is Love. It had been taught by the Old Testament that 'the beginning of wisdom was the fear of God ;' it remained to be taught by the last apostle of the New Testament that 'the end of wisdom was the love of God.' It had been taught of old time by Jew and by heathen, by Greek philosophy and Eastern religion, that the Divinity was well pleased with the sacrifices, the speculations, the tortures of man ; it was to St. John that it was left to teach in all its fulness that the one sign of God's children is 'the love of the brethren.' And as it is Love that pervades our whole conception of his teaching, so also it pervades our whole conception of his character. We see him—it surely is no unwarranted fancy—we see him declining with the declining century ; every sense and faculty waxing feebler, but that one divinest faculty of all burning more and more brightly ; we see it breathing through every look and gesture ; the one animating principle of the atmosphere in which he lives and moves ; earth and heaven, the past, the present, and the future alike echoing to him that dying strain of his latest words, 'We love Him because He loved us.' And when at last he disappears from our view in the last pages of the sacred volume, ecclesiastical tradition still lingers in the close : and in that touching story, not the less impressive because so familiar to us, we see the aged apostle borne in the arms of his disciples into the Ephesian assembly, and there repeating over and over again the same saying, 'Little children, love one another ;' till, when asked why he said this and nothing else, he replied in those well known words, fit indeed to be the farewell speech of the Beloved Disciple, 'Because this is our Lord's command, and if you fulfil this, nothing else is needed.' "

§ 42. *Apostolic Labors of John.*

JOHN IN THE ACTS.

In the first stadium of Apostolic Christianity John figures as one of the three pillars of the church of the circumcision, together with Peter and James the brother of the Lord ; while Paul and Barnabas represented the Gentile church.[1] This seems to imply that at that time he had not yet risen to the full apprehension of the universalism and freedom of the gospel. But he was the most liberal of the three, standing between James and Peter on the one hand, and Paul on the other, and looking already towards a reconciliation of Jewish and Gentile Christianity. The Judaizers never appealed to him as they did to James, or to Peter.[2] There is no trace of a Johannean party, as there is of a Cephas party and a party of James. He stood above strife and division.

In the earlier chapters of the Acts he appears, next to Peter, as the chief apostle of the new religion ; he heals with him the cripple at the gate of the temple ; he was brought with him before the Sanhedrin to bear witness to Christ ; he is sent with him by the apostles from Jerusalem to Samaria to confirm the Christian converts by imparting to them the Holy Spirit ; he returned with him to Jerusalem.[3] But Peter is always named first and takes the lead in word and act ; John follows in mysterious silence and makes the impression of a reserved force which will manifest itself at some future time. He must have been present at the conference of the apostles in Jerusalem, A.D. 50, but he made no speech and took no active part in the great discussion about circumcision and the terms of church membership.[4] All this is in entire keeping with the character of modest and silent prominence given to him in the Gospels.

[1] Gal. 2 : 9, Ἰάκωβος, καὶ Κηφᾶς καὶ Ἰωάννης, οἱ δοκοῦντες στῦλοι εἶναι . . . . αὐτοὶ εἰς τὴν περιτομήν. They are named in the order of their conservatism.

[2] Gal. 2 : 12, τινὲς ἀπὸ Ἰακώβου. 1 Cor. 1 : 12, ἐγώ εἰμι Κηφᾶ.

[3] Acts 3 : 1 sqq.; 4 : 1, 13, 19, 20 ; 5 : 19, 20, 41, 42 ; 8 : 14–17, 25.

[4] He is included among the "apostles," assembled in Jerusalem on that occasion, Acts 15 : 6, 22, 23, and is expressly mentioned as one of the three pillar-apostles by Paul in the second chapter of the Galatians, which refers to the same conference.

After the year 50 he seems to have left Jerusalem. The Acts no more mention him nor Peter. When Paul made his fifth and last visit to the holy city (A.D. 58) he met James, but none of the apostles.[1]

JOHN AT EPHESUS.

The later and most important labors of John are contained in his writings, which we shall fully consider in another chapter. They exhibit to us a history that is almost exclusively inward and spiritual, but of immeasurable reach and import. They make no allusion to the time and place of residence and composition. But the Apocalypse implies that he stood at the head of the churches of Asia Minor.[2] This is confirmed by the unanimous testimony of antiquity, which is above all reasonable doubt, and assigns Ephesus to him as the residence of his latter years.[3] He died there in extreme old age during the reign of Trajan, which began in 98. His grave also was shown there in the second century.

We do not know when he removed to Asia Minor, but he

---

[1] Acts 21 : 18. John may have been, however, still in Palestine, perhaps in Galilee, among the scenes of his youth. According to tradition he remained in Jerusalem till the death of the Holy Virgin, about A.D. 48.

[2] Rev. 1 : 4, 9, 11, 20 ; chs. 2 and 3. It is very evident that only an apostle could occupy such a position, and not an obscure presbyter of that name, whose very existence is doubtful.

[3] Irenæus, the disciple of Polycarp (a personal pupil of John), *Adv. Hær.* III. 1, 1 ; 3, 4 ; II. 22, 5, etc., and in his letter to Florinus (in Eusebius, *H. E.* V. 20); Clemens Alex., *Quis dives salvetur*, c. 42 ; Apollonius and Polycrates, at the close of the second century, in Euseb. *H. E.* III. 31 ; V. 18, 24 ; Origen, Tertullian, Eusebius, Jerome, etc. Leucius, also, the reputed author of the Acts of John about 130, in the fragments recently published by Zahn, bears witness to the residence of John in Ephesus and Patmos, and transfers his martyrdom from Rome to Ephesus. Lützelberger, Keim (*Leben Jesu v. Nazara*, I. 161 sq.), Holtzmann, Scholten, the author of *Supernatural Religion* (II. 410), and other opponents of the Gospel of John, have dared to remove him out of Asia Minor with negative arguments from the silence of the Acts, the Ephesians, Colossians, Papias, Ignatius, and Polycarp, arguments which either prove nothing at all, or only that John was not in Ephesus before 63. But the old tradition has been conclusively defended not only by Ewald, Grimm, Steitz, Riggenbach, Luthardt, Godet, Weiss, but even by Krenkel, Hilgenfeld (*Einleitung*, pp. 395 sqq.), and Weizsäcker (498 sqq.), of the Tübingen school.

cannot have done so before the year 63. For in his valedictory address to the Ephesian elders, and in his Epistles to the Ephesians and Colossians and the second to Timothy, Paul makes no allusion to John, and speaks with the authority of a superintendent of the churches of Asia Minor. It was probably the martyrdom of Peter and Paul that induced John to take charge of the orphan churches, exposed to serious dangers and trials.[1]

Ephesus, the capital of proconsular Asia, was a centre of Grecian culture, commerce, and religion; famous of old for the songs of Homer, Anacreon, and Mimnermus, the philosophy of Thales, Anaximenes, and Anaximander, the worship and wonderful temple of Diana. There Paul had labored three years (54–57) and established an influential church, a beacon-light in the surrounding darkness of heathenism. From there he could best commune with the numerous churches he had planted in the provinces. There he experienced peculiar joys and trials, and foresaw great dangers of heresies that should spring up from within.[2] All the forces of orthodox and heretical Christianity were collected there. Jerusalem was approaching its downfall; Rome was not yet a second Jerusalem. Ephesus, by the labors of Paul and of John, became the chief theatre of church history in the second half of the first and during the greater part of the second century. Polycarp, the patriarchal martyr, and Irenæus, the leading theologian in the conflict with Gnosticism, best represent the spirit of John and bear testimony to his influence. He alone could complete the work of Paul and Peter, and give the church that compact unity which she

---

[1] " The maintenance of evangelical truth," says Godet (I. 42), "demanded at that moment powerful aid. It is not surprising then that John, one of the last survivors amongst the apostles, should feel himself called upon to supply in those countries the place of the apostle of the Gentiles, and to water, as Apollos had formerly done in Greece, that which Paul had planted." Pressensé (*Apost. Era*, p. 424): "No city could have been better chosen as a centre from which to watch over the churches, and follow closely the progress of heresy. At Ephesus John was in the centre of Paul's mission field, and not far from Greece."

[2] See his farewell address at Miletus, Acts 20 : 29, 30, and the Epistles to Timothy.

needed for her self-preservation against persecution from without and heresy and corruption from within.

If it were not for the writings of John the last thirty years
of the first century would be almost an entire blank. They resemble that mysterious period of forty days between the resurrection and the ascension, when the Lord hovered, as it were,
between heaven and earth, barely touching the earth beneath,
and appearing to the disciples like a spirit from the other world.
But the theology of the second and third centuries evidently
presupposes the writings of John, and starts from his Christology
rather than from Paul's anthropology and soteriology, which
were almost buried out of sight until Augustin, in Africa, re
vived them.

JOHN AT PATMOS.

John was banished to the solitary, rocky, and barren island
of Patmos (now Patmo or Palmosa), in the Ægean sea, south-
west of Ephesus. This rests on the testimony of the Apocalypse, 1 : 9, as usually understood: " I John, your brother and
partaker with you in the tribulation and kingdom and patience
in Jesus, was in the isle that is called Patmos, for (on account
of) the word of God and the testimony of Jesus." [1]   There he
received, while " in the spirit, on the Lord's day," those wonderful revelations concerning the struggles and victories of Christianity.

The fact of his banishment to Patmos is confirmed by the
unanimous testimony of antiquity.[2] It is perpetuated in the
traditions of the island, which has no other significance.   " John
—that is the thought of Patmos; the island belongs to him; it

---

[1] Bleek understands διά of the object: John was carried (in a vision) to
Patmos *for the purpose* of receiving there the revelation of Christ. He derives
the whole tradition of John's banishment to Patmos from a misunderstanding of this passage. So also Lücke, De Wette, Reuss, and Düsterdieck. But
the traditional exegesis is confirmed by the mention of the θλίψις, βασιλεία and
ὑπομονή in the same verse, by the natural meaning of μαρτυρία, and by the
parallel passages 6 : 9 and 20 : 4, where διά likewise indicates the occasion or
reason of suffering.

[2] Irenæus, Clement of Alexandria, Origen, Tertullian, Eusebius, Jerome, etc.

is his sanctuary. Its stones preach of him, and in every heart he lives." [1]

The time of the exile is uncertain, and depends upon the disputed question of the date of the Apocalypse. External evidence points to the reign of Domitian, A.D. 95 ; internal evidence to the reign of Nero, or soon after his death, A.D. 68.

The prevailing—we may say the only distinct tradition, beginning with so respectable a witness as Irenæus about 170, assigns the exile to the end of the reign of Domitian, who ruled from 81 to 96.[2] He was the second Roman emperor who persecuted Christianity, and banishment was one of his favorite modes of punishment.[3] Both facts give support to this tradition. After a promising beginning he became as cruel and bloodthirsty as Nero, and surpassed him in hypocrisy and blasphemous self-deification. He began his letters : " Our Lord and God commands," and required his subjects to address him so.[4] He ordered gold and silver statues of himself to be placed in the holiest place of the temples. When he seemed most friendly, he was most dangerous. He spared neither senators nor consuls when they fell under his dark suspicion, or stood in

[1] Tischendorf, *Reise in's Morgenland*, II. 257 sq. A grotto on a hill in the southern part of the island is still pointed out as the place of the apocalyptic vision, and on the summit of the mountain is the monastery of St. John, with a library of about 250 manuscripts.

[2] Irenæus, *Adv. Hær.*, V. 30. says that the Apocalypse was seen πρὸς τῷ τέλει τῆς Δομετιανοῦ ἀρχῆς. So also Eusebius, *H. E.* III. 18, 20, 33 ; *Chron.* ad ann. 14 Domitiani ; and Jerome, *De vir. illustr.*, c. 9. This view has prevailed among commentators and historians till quite recently, and is advocated by Hengstenberg, Lange, Ebrard (and by myself in the *Hist. of the Ap. Ch.*, § 101, pp. 400 sqq.). It is indeed difficult to set aside the clear testimony of Irenæus, who, through Polycarp, was connected with the very age of John. But we must remember that he was mistaken even on more important points of history, as the age of Jesus, which he asserts, with an appeal to tradition, to have been above fifty years.

[3] Tacitus congratulates Agricola (*Vita Agr.*, c. 44) that he did not live to see under this emperor " *tot consularium cædes, tot nobilissimarum feminarum exilia et fugas.*" Agricola, whose daughter Tacitus married, died in 93, two years before Domitian.

[4] Suetonius, *Domit.*, c. 13 : " *Dominus et Deus noster hoc fieri jubet. Unde institutum posthac, ut ne scripto quidem ac sermone cujusquam appellaretur aliter.*"

the way of his ambition. He searched for the descendants of David and the kinsmen of Jesus, fearing their aspirations, but found that they were poor and innocent persons.[1] Many Christians suffered martyrdom under his reign, on the charge of atheism—among them his own cousin, Flavius Clemens, of consular dignity, who was put to death, and his wife Domitilla, who was banished to the island of Pandateria, near Naples.[2] In favor of the traditional date may also be urged an intrinsic propriety that the book which closes the canon, and treats of the last things till the final consummation, should have been written last.

Nevertheless, the internal evidence of the Apocalypse itself, and a comparison with the fourth Gospel, favor an earlier date, before the destruction of Jerusalem, and during the interregnum which followed the death of Nero (68), when the beast, that is the Roman empire, was wounded, but was soon to be revived (by the accession of Vespasian). If there is some foundation for the early tradition of the intended oil-martyrdom of John at Rome, or at Ephesus, it would naturally point to the Neronian persecution, in which Christians were covered with inflammable material and burned as torches. The unmistakable allusions to imperial persecutions apply much better to Nero than to Domitian. The difference between the Hebrew coloring and fiery vigor of the Apocalypse and the pure Greek and calm repose of the fourth Gospel, to which we have already alluded, are more easily explained if the former was written some twenty years earlier. This view has some slight support in ancient tradition,[3] and has been adopted

---

[1] Hegesippus in Eusebius, *Hist. Eccl.*, III., 19, 20. Hegesippus, however, is silent about the banishment of John, and this silence has been used by Bleek as an argument against the fact.

[2] Dion Cassius in the abridgment of Xiphilinus, 67, 14.

[3] So the title of the Syriac translation of the Apocalypse (which, however, is of much later date than the Peshitto, which omits the Apocalypse): "*Revelatio quam Deus Joanni Evangelistæ in Patmo insula dedit, in quam a Nerone Cæsare relegatus fuerat.*" Clement of Alexandria (*Quis dives salv.*, c. 42, and quoted by Eusebius, III., 23) says indefinitely that John returned from Patmos to Ephesus after the death of "the tyrant" (τοῦ τυράννου τελευτήσαντος), which

by the majority of modern critical historians and commentators.[1]

We hold, then, as the most probable view, that John was exiled to Patmos under Nero, wrote the Apocalypse soon after Nero's death, A.D. 68 or 69, returned to Ephesus, completed his Gospel and Epistles several (perhaps twenty) years later, and fell asleep in peace during the year of Trajan, after A.D. 98.

The faithful record of the historical Christ in the whole fulness of his divine-human person, as the embodiment and source of life eternal to all believers, with the accompanying epistle of practical application, was the last message of the Beloved Disciple at the threshold of the second century, at the golden sunset of the apostolic age.   The recollections of his youth, ripened by long experience, transfigured by the Holy Spirit, and radiant with heavenly light of truth and holiness, are the most precious legacy of the last of the apostles to all future generations of the church.

§ 43.   *Traditions Respecting John.*[2]

The memory of John sank deep into the heart of the church, and not a few incidents more or less characteristic and probable have been preserved by the early fathers.

Clement of Alexandria, towards the close of the second century, represents John as a faithful and devoted pastor when, in his old age, on a tour of visitation, he lovingly pursued one of

---

may apply to Nero as well as to Domitian.   Origen mentions simply a Roman βασιλεύς.   Tertullian's legend of the Roman oil-martyrdom of John seems to point to Nero rather than to any other emperor, and was so understood by Jerome (*Adv. Jovin.* I. 26), although Tertullian does not say so, and Jerome himself assigns the exile and the composition of the Apocalypse to the reign of Domitian (*De vir. ill.*, c. 9).   Epiphanius (*Hær.* LI. 33) puts the banishment back to the reign of Claudius (A.D. 41–53), which is evidently much too early.

[1] Neander, Gieseler, Baur, Ewald, Lücke, Bleek, De Wette, Reuss, Düsterdieck, Weiss, Renan, Stanley, Lightfoot, Westcott.

[2] These traditions are reproduced in a pleasing manner by Dean Stanley, in his *Sermons and Essays on the Apost. Age*, pp. 266–281 (3d ed.).   Comp. also my *Hist. of the Ap. Ch.*, pp. 404 sqq.

his former converts who had become a robber, and reclaimed him to the church.

Irenæus bears testimony to his character as "the Son of Thunder" when he relates, as from the lips of Polycarp, that, on meeting in a public bath at Ephesus the Gnostic heretic Cerinthus,[1] who denied the incarnation of our Lord, John refused to remain under the same roof, lest it might fall down. This reminds one of the incident recorded in Luke 9 : 49, and the apostle's severe warning in 2 John 10 and 11. The story exemplifies the possibility of uniting the deepest love of truth with the sternest denunciation of error and moral evil.[2]

Jerome pictures him as the disciple of love, who in his extreme old age was carried to the meeting-place on the arms of his disciples, and repeated again and again the exhortation, "Little children, love one another," adding: "This is the Lord's command, and if this alone be done, it is enough." This, of all the traditions of John, is the most credible and the most useful.

In the Greek church John bears the epithet "the theologian" (θεολόγος), for teaching most clearly the divinity of Christ (τὴν θεότητα τοῦ λόγου). He is also called "the virgin" (παρθένος),[3] for his chastity and supposed celibacy. Augustin says that the singular chastity of John from his early youth was supposed by some to be the ground of his intimacy with Jesus.[4]

The story of John and the huntsman, related by Cassian, a

---

[1] Or Ebion, according to Epiphanius, *Hær.*, xxx. 25.

[2] Stanley mentions, as an illustration of the magnifying influence of fancy, that Jeremy Taylor, in relating this story, adds that "immediately upon the retreat of the apostle the bath fell down and crushed Cerinthus in the ruins" (*Life of Christ*, Sect. xii. 2).

[3] παρθένος usually means a virgin (Matt. 1 : 23 ; Luke 1 : 27 ; Acts 21 : 9 ; 1 Cor. 7 : 25, 28, 34), but is applied also to men who never touched women, Apoc. 14 : 4, and in patristic writers.

[4] Augustin, *Tract.* 124 *in Joh. Evang.* (*Opera* III. 1976, ed. Migne) : "*Sunt qui senserint . . . . a Christo Joannem apostolum propterea plus amatum quod neque uxorem duxerit, et ab ineunte pueritia castissimus vixerit.*" He quotes Jerome, *Contr. Jovin.* l. c., but adds : "*Hoc quidem in Scripturis non evidenter apparet.*" According to Ambrosiaster, *Ad 2 Cor.* 11 : 2, all the apostles were married except John and Paul. Tertullian calls John *Christi spado.*

monk of the fifth century, represents him as gently playing with
a partridge in his hand, and saying to a huntsman, who was surprised at it: " Let not this brief and slight relaxation of my
mind offend thee, without which the spirit would flag from
over-exertion and not be able to respond to the call of duty
when need required." Childlike simplicity and playfulness are
often combined with true greatness of mind.

Polycrates, bishop of Ephesus, at the close of the second century, relates (according to Eusebius) that John introduced in
Asia Minor the Jewish practice of observing Easter on the 14th
of Nisan, irrespective of Sunday. This fact entered largely
into the paschal controversies of the second century, and into
the modern controversy about the genuineness of the Gospel of
John.

The same Polycrates of Ephesus describes John as wearing
the plate, or diadem of the Jewish high-priest (Ex. 28 : 36, 37 ;
39 : 30, 31). It is probably a figurative expression of priestly
holiness which John attaches to all true believers (comp. Rev.
2 : 17), but in which he excelled as the patriarch.[1]

From a misunderstanding of the enigmatical word of Jesus,
John 21 : 22, arose the legend that John was only asleep in his
grave, gently moving the mound as he breathed, and awaiting
the final advent of the Lord. According to another form of the
legend he died, but was immediately raised and translated to
heaven, like Elijah, to return with him as the herald of the
second advent of Christ.[2]

---

[1] In Euseb. *H. E.* III. 31, 3 ; V. 24, 3 : Ἰωάννης . . . . ὃς ἐγεννήθη ἱερεὺς τὸ
πέταλον πεφορηκὼς καὶ μάρτυς καὶ διδάσκαλος οὗτος ἐν Εφέσῳ κεκοίμηται.   Epiphanius reports (no doubt from Hegesippus) the same, with some ascetic
features, of James the brother of the Lord. See Stanley's remarks, pp. 276–
278, and Lightfoot on *Galat.*, p. 345 note, and *Philipp.* p. 252. " As a figurative expression," says Lightfoot, " or as a literal fact, the notice points to St.
John as the veteran teacher, the chief representative, of a pontifical race.
On the other hand, it is possible that this was not the sense which Polycrates
himself attached to the figure or the fact ; and if so, we have here perhaps
the earliest passage in any extant Christian writing where the sacerdotal
view of the ministry is distinctly put forward." But in the *Didache* (ch. 13)
the Christian prophets are called " high priests."

[2] Augustin mentions the legend, but contradicts it, *Tract.* 224 *in Ev. Joann.*

CHAPTER VIII.

CHRISTIAN LIFE IN THE APOSTOLIC CHURCH.

Sources.

The teaching and example of Christ as exhibited in the *Gospels*, and of the apostles in the *Acts* and *Epistles;* compared and contrasted with the rabbinical ethics and the state of Jewish society, and with the Greek systems of philosophy and the moral condition of the Roman empire, as described in the writings of Seneca, Tacitus, the Roman satirists, etc.

Literature.

I. The respective sections in the *Histories of the Apost. Church* by NEANDER : I. 229–283 (Germ. ed.) ; SCHAFF : §§ 109–123 (pp. 433–492) ; LANGE : II. 495–534 ; WEIZSÄCKER : 647–698.

II. The works on the *Theology of the Apostolic Age*, by SCHMID, REUSS, BAUR, WEISS, etc.

III. The Systems of *Christian Ethics* by SCHLEIERMACHER, ROTHE, NEANDER, SCHMID, WUTTKE, HARLESS, MARTENSEN, LUTHARDT, and LECKY'S *History of European Morals* (1869), vol. I. 357 sqq.

IV. A. THOMA (pastor in Mannheim) : *Geschichte der christlichen Sittenlehre in der Zeit des Neuen Testamentes*, Haarlem, 1879 (380 pp.). A crowned prize-essay of the Teyler Theol. Society. The first attempt of a separate critical history of N. T. ethics, but written from the negative standpoint of the Tübingen school, and hence very unsatisfactory. It is divided in three parts : I. The Ethics of Jesus ; II. The Ethics of Paul ; III. The Ethics of the Congregation.

V. Works which treat of Christian life in the post-apostolic age (CAVE, ARNOLD, SCHMIDT, CHASTEL, PRESSENSÉ, etc.) will be noticed in the second period.

§ 44. *The Spiritual Power of Christianity.*

Practical Christianity is the manifestation of a new life ; a spiritual (as distinct from intellectual and moral) life ; a supernatural (as distinct from natural) life ; it is a life of holiness and peace; a life of union and communion with God the Father, the Son, and the Spirit; it is eternal life, beginning with regeneration and culminating in the resurrection. It lays hold of the inmost centre of man's personality, emancipates him from the dominion of sin, and brings him into vital union with God in Christ; from this centre it acts as a purifying, ennobling, and regulating force upon all the faculties of man—the emotions, the will, and the intellect—and transforms even the body into a temple of the Holy Spirit.

Christianity rises far above all other religions in the theory and practice of virtue and piety. It sets forth the highest standard of love to God and to man; and this not merely as an abstract doctrine, or an object of effort and hope, but as a living fact in the person of Jesus Christ, whose life and example have more power and influence than all the maxims and precepts of sages and legislators. Deeds speak louder than words. *Præcepta docent, exempla trahunt.* The finest systems of moral philosophy have not been able to regenerate and conquer the world. The gospel of Christ has done it and is doing it constantly. The wisest men of Greece and Rome sanctioned slavery, polygamy, concubinage, oppression, revenge, infanticide; or they belied their purer maxims by their conduct. The ethical standard of the Jews was much higher; yet none of their patriarchs, kings, or prophets claimed perfection, and the Bible honestly reports the infirmities and sins, as well as the virtues, of Abraham, Jacob, Moses, David, and Solomon.

But the character of Christ from the manger to the cross is without spot or blemish; he is above reproach or suspicion, and acknowledged by friend and foe to be the purest as well as the wisest being that ever appeared on earth. He is the nearest approach which God can make to man, and which man can make to God; he represents the fullest imaginable and attainable harmony of the ideal and real, of the divine and human. The Christian church may degenerate in the hands of sinful men, but the doctrine and life of her founder are a never-failing fountain of purification.

The perfect life of harmony with God and devotion to the welfare of the human race, is to pass from Christ to his followers. Christian life is an imitation of the life of Christ. From his word and spirit, living and ruling in the church, an unbroken stream of redeeming, sanctifying, and glorifying power has been flowing forth upon individuals, families, and nations for these eighteen centuries, and will continue to flow till the world is transformed into the kingdom of heaven, and God becomes all in all.

One of the strongest proofs of the supernatural origin of Christianity, is its elevation above the natural culture and moral standard of its first professors. The most perfect doctrine and life described by unschooled fishermen of Galilee, who never before had been outside of Palestine, and were scarcely able to read and to write! And the profoundest mysteries of the kingdom of heaven, the incarnation, redemption, regeneration, resurrection, taught by the apostles to congregations of poor and illiterate peasants, slaves and freedmen! For "not many wise after the flesh, not many mighty, not many noble" were called, " but God chose the foolish things of the world, that he might put to shame them that are wise ; and God chose the weak things of the world, that he might put to shame the things that are strong ; and the base things of the world, and the things that are despised, did God choose, yea, and the things that are not, that he might bring to naught the things that are : that no flesh should glory before God. But of him are ye in Christ Jesus, who was made unto us wisdom from God, and righteousness and sanctification and redemption : that, according as it is written, he that glorieth, let him glory in the Lord." [1]

If we compare the moral atmosphere of the apostolic churches with the actual condition of surrounding Judaism and heathenism, the contrast is as startling as that between a green oasis with living fountains and lofty palm trees, and a barren desert of sand and stone. Judaism in its highest judicatory committed the crime of crimes, the crucifixion of the Saviour of the world,

[1] 1 Cor. 2 : 26–31.

and hastened to its doom. Heathenism was fitly represented by such imperial monsters as Tiberius, Caligula, Nero, and Domitian, and exhibited a picture of hopeless corruption and decay, as described in the darkest colors not only by St. Paul, but by his heathen contemporary, the wisest Stoic moralist, the teacher and victim of Nero.[1]

NOTES.

The rationalistic author of *Supernatural Religion* (vol. II. 487) makes the following remarkable concession: "The teaching of Jesus carried morality to the sublimest point attained, or even attainable, by humanity. The influence of his spiritual religion has been rendered doubly great by the unparalleled purity and elevation of his character. Surpassing in his sublime simplicity and earnestness the moral grandeur of Sâkya Muni, and putting to the blush the sometimes sullied, though generally admirable, teaching of Socrates and Plato, and the whole round of Greek philosophers, he presented the rare spectacle of a life, so far as we can estimate it, uniformly noble and consistent with his own lofty principles, so that the 'imitation of Christ' has become almost the final word in the preaching of his religion, and must continue to be one of the most powerful elements of its permanence."

LECKY, likewise a rationalistic writer and historian of great ability and fairness, makes this weighty remark in his *History of European Morals* (vol. II. 9) : "It was reserved for Christianity to present to the world an ideal character, which through all the changes of eighteen centuries has inspired the hearts of men with an impassioned love ; has shown itself capable of acting on all ages, nations, temperaments, and conditions; has been not only the highest pattern of virtue, but the strongest incen-

---

[1] Comp. the well known passage of Seneca, *De Ira*, II. 8 : *Omnia sceleribus ac vitiis plena sunt ; plus committitur, quam quod possit coërcitione sanari. Certatur ingenti quodam nequitiæ certamine : maior quotidie peccandi cupiditas, minor verecundia est. Expulso melioris æquiorisque respectu, quocunque visum est, libido se impingit ; nec furtiva jam scelera sunt, præter oculos eunt. Adeoque in publicum missa nequitia est, et in omnium pectoribus evaluit, ut innocentia non rara, sed nulla sit. Numquid enim singuli aut pauci rupere legem ; undique, velut signo dato, ad fas nefasque miscendum coörti sunt.*" Similar passages might be gathered from Thucydides, Aristophanes, Sallust, Horace, Juvenal, Persius, Tacitus, Suetonius. It is true that almost every heathen vice still exists in Christian countries, but they exist in spite of the Christian religion, while the heathen immorality was the legitimate result of idolatry, and was sanctioned by the example of the heathen gods, and the apotheosis of the worst Roman emperors.

tive to its practice, and has exercised so deep an influence that it may be truly said that the simple record of three short years of active life has done more to regenerate and to soften mankind than all the disquisitions of philosophers and all the exhortations of moralists. This has, indeed, been the wellspring of whatever is best and purest in Christian life. Amid all the sins and failings, amid all the priestcraft and persecution and fanaticism that have defaced the Church, it has preserved, in the character and example of its Founder, an enduring principle of regeneration."

To this we may add the testimony of the atheistic philosopher, JOHN STUART MILL, from his essay on *Theism*, written shortly before his death (1873), and published, 1874, in *Three Essays on Religion* (Am. ed., p. 253) : "Above all, the most valuable part of the effect on the character which Christianity has produced, by holding up in a divine person a standard of excellence and a model for imitation, is available even to the absolute unbeliever, and can never more be lost to humanity. For it is Christ rather than God whom Christianity has held up to believers as the pattern of perfection for humanity. It is the God incarnate more than the God of the Jews, or of nature, who, being idealized, has taken so great and salutary a hold on the modern mind. And whatever else may be taken away from us by rational criticism, Christ is still left ; a unique figure, not more unlike all his precursors than all his followers, even those who had the direct benefit of his personal teaching. It is of no use to say that Christ, as exhibited in the Gospels, is not historical, and that we know not how much of what is admirable has been superadded by the tradition of his followers. The tradition of followers suffices to insert any number of marvels, and may have inserted all the miracles which he is reputed to have wrought. But who among his disciples, or among their proselytes, was capable of inventing the sayings ascribed to Jesus, or of imagining the life and character revealed in the Gospels? Certainly not the fishermen of Galilee ; as certainly not St. Paul, whose character and idiosyncrasies were of a totally different sort ; still less the early Christian writers, in whom nothing is more evident than that the good which was in them was all derived, as they always professed that it was derived, from the higher source."

§ 45. *The Spiritual Gifts.*

Comp. the Commentaries on Rom. 12 : 3–9, and 1 Cor., chs. 12–14.

The apostolic church was endowed from the day of Pentecost with all the needful spiritual gifts for the moral regeneration of the world. They formed, as it were, her bridal garment and her panoply against Jewish and Gentile opposition. They are called charisms[1] or gifts of grace, as distinguished from, though not opposed to, natural endowments. They are certain special energies and manifestations of the Holy Spirit in believers for the common good.[2] They are supernatural, therefore, in their origin; but they correspond to natural virtues, and in operation they follow all the mental and moral faculties of man, raising them to higher activity, and consecrating them to the service of Christ. They all rest on faith, that "gift of gifts."

The spiritual gifts may be divided into three classes: first, *intellectual gifts* of knowledge, mainly theoretical in their character, and concerned primarily with doctrine and theology; secondly, *emotional* gifts of feeling, appearing chiefly in divine worship and for immediate edification; and thirdly, *practical* gifts of will, devoted to the organization, government, and discipline of the church. They are not, however, abstractly separate, but work together harmoniously for the common purpose of edifying the body of Christ. In the New Testament ten charisms are specially mentioned; the first four have to do chiefly, though not exclusively, with doctrine, the next two with worship, and the remaining four with government and practical affairs.

1. The gift of WISDOM and KNOWLEDGE,[3] or of deep insight into the nature and system of the divine word and the doctrines of the Christian salvation.

2. The gift of TEACHING,[4] or of practically applying the gift of knowledge; the power of clearly expounding the Scriptures for the instruction and edification of the people.

3. The gift of PROPHECY,[5] akin to the two preceding, but addressed rather to pious feeling than to speculative reflection, and employing commonly the language of higher inspiration, rather than that of logical exposition and demonstration. It is by no means confined to the prediction of future events, but consists in disclosing the hidden counsel of God, the deeper sense of the Scriptures, the secret state of the heart, the abyss

---

[1] χαρίσματα. [2] Comp. 1 Cor. 12 : 7; 14 : 12.
[3] σοφία and γνῶσις. [4] διδασκαλία. [5] προφητεία.

of sin, and the glory of redeeming grace. It appears particu-larly in creative periods, times of mighty revival; while the gift of teaching suits better a quiet state of natural growth in the church. Both act not only in the sphere of doctrine and theology, but also in worship, and might in this view be reck-oned also among the gifts of feeling.

4. The gift of DISCERNING SPIRITS,[1] serves mainly as a guide to the third gift, by discriminating between true prophets and false, between divine inspiration and a merely human or satanic enthusiasm. In a wider sense it is a deep discernment in sepa-rating truth and error, and in judging of moral and religious character ; a holy criticism still ever necessary to the purity of Christian doctrine and the administration of the discipline of the church.

5. The gift of TONGUES,[2] or of an utterance proceeding from a state of unconscious ecstasy in the speaker, and unintelligible to the hearer unless interpreted—thus differing from prophecy, which requires a self-conscious though highly elevated state of feeling, serves directly to profit the congregation, and is therefore preferred by Paul.[3] The speaking with tongues is an involun-tary psalm-like prayer or song, uttered from a spiritual trance, and in a peculiar language inspired by the Holy Spirit. The soul is almost entirely passive, an instrument on which the Spirit plays his heavenly melodies. This gift has, therefore, properly, nothing to do with the spread of the church among foreign peoples and in foreign languages, but is purely an act of worship, for the edification primarily of the speaker himself, and indirectly, through interpretation, for the hearers. It ap-peared, first, indeed, on the day of Pentecost, but *before* Peter's address to the people, which was the proper mission-sermon ; and we meet with it afterwards in the house of Cornelius and in the Corinthian congregation, as a means of edification for believers, and not, at least not directly, for unbelieving hearers,

---

[1] διακρίσεις πνευμάτων.

[2] καιναῖς or ἑτέραις γλώσσαις λαλεῖν, or simply, γλώσσαις, sometimes γλώσσῃ λαλεῖν. See § 24, p. 234.   [3] 1 Cor. 14 : 1–5.

although it served to them as a significant sign,[1] arresting their attention to the supernatural power in the church.

6. The gift of INTERPRETATION[2] is the supplement of the glossolalia, and makes that gift profitable to the congregation by translating the prayers and songs from the language of the spirit and of ecstasy[3] into that of the understanding and of sober self-consciousness.[4] The preponderance of reflection here puts this gift as properly in the first class as in the second.

7. The gift of MINISTRY and HELP,[5] that is, of special qualification primarily for the office of deacon and deaconess, or for the regular ecclesiastical care of the poor and the sick, and, in the wide sense, for all labors of Christian charity and philanthropy.

8. The gift of church GOVERNMENT and the CARE OF SOULS,[6] indispensable to all pastors and rulers of the church, above all to the apostles and apostolic men, in proportion to the extent of their respective fields of labor. Peter warns his co-presbyters against the temptation to hierarchical arrogance and tyranny over conscience, of which so many priests, bishops, patriarchs, and popes have since been guilty; and points them to the sublime example of the great Shepherd and Archbishop, who, in infinite love, laid down his life for the sheep.[7]

9. The gift of MIRACLES[8] is the power possessed by the apostles and apostolic men, like Stephen, to heal all sorts of physical maladies, to cast out demons, to raise the dead, and perform other similar works, in virtue of an extraordinary energy or faith, by word, prayer, and the laying on of hands in the name of Jesus, and for his glory. These miracles were outward credentials and seals of the divine mission of the apostles in a time and among a people which required such sensible helps to faith. But as Christianity became established in the world, it could point to its continued moral effects as the best evidence of its truth, and the necessity for outward physical miracles ceased.

---

[1] σημεῖον. 1 Cor. 14 : 22.   [2] ἑρμηνεία γλωσσῶν.
[3] Of the πνεῦμα.   [4] Of the νοῦς.
[5] διακονία, ἀντιλήψεις.   [6] κυβερνήσεις, gubernationes.
[7] 1 Pet. 5 : 1–4.   [8] χάρισμα ἰαμάτων, δύναμις σημείων καὶ τεράτων.

10. Finally, the gift of LOVE, the greatest, most precious,
most useful, most needful, and most enduring of all, described
and extolled by St. Paul in the thirteenth chapter of 1 Corinthians with the pen of an angel in the vision and enjoyment of
the God of infinite love himself.[1] Love is natural kindness and
affection sanctified and raised to the spiritual sphere, or rather a
new heavenly affection created in the soul by the experience of
the saving love of God in Christ. As faith lies at the bottom
of all charisms, so love is not properly a separate gift, but the
soul of all the gifts, guarding them from abuse for selfish and
ambitious purposes, making them available for the common
good, ruling, uniting, and completing them. It alone gives
them their true value, and without love even the speaking with
tongues of angels, and a faith which removes mountains, are
nothing before God. It holds heaven and earth in its embrace.
It "believeth all things," and when faith fails, it "hopeth all
things," and when hope fails, it "endureth all things," but it
"never fails." As love is the most needful of all the gifts on
earth, so it will also outlast all the others, and be the ornament
and joy of the saints in heaven. For love is the inmost essence,
the heart, as it were, of God, the ground of all his attributes,
and the motive of all his works. It is the beginning and the
end of creation, redemption, and sanctification—the link which
unites us with the triune God, the cardinal virtue of Christianity, the fulfilling of the law, the bond of perfectness, and
the fountain of bliss.

---

[1] The Revision of 1881 has substituted, in 1 Cor. ch. 13, "love" (with
Tyndale, Cranmer, and Geneva Vers.) for " charity " (which came into James's
Version from the Vulgate through the Rheims Vers.). This change has given
great offence among conservative people. It may indeed involve a loss of
rhythm in that wonderful chapter, but it was necessitated by the restricted
meaning which charity has assumed in modern usage, being identical with
practical benevolence, so that Paul might seem to contradict himself in verses
3 and 8. The Saxon word love is just as strong, as musical, and as sacred as
the Latin charity, and its meaning is far more comprehensive and enduring,
embracing both God's love to man and man's love to God, and to his neighbor,
both here and hereafter.

§ 46. *Christianity in Individuals.*

The transforming spiritual power of Christianity appears first in the lives of individuals. The apostles and primitive Christians rose to a morality and piety far above that of the heroes of heathen virtue and even that of the Jewish saints. Their daily walk was a living union with Christ, ever seeking the glory of God and the salvation of men. Many of the cardinal virtues, humility, for example, and love for enemies, were unknown before the Christian day.

Peter, Paul, and John represent the various leading forms or types of Christian piety, as well as of theology. They were not without defect, indeed they themselves acknowledged only one sinless being, their Lord and Master, and they confessed their own shortcomings;[1] yet they were as nearly perfect as it is possible to be in a sinful world; and the moral influence of their lives and writings on all generations of the church is absolutely immeasurable. Each exhibits the spirit and life of Christ in a peculiar way. For the gospel does not destroy, but redeems and sanctifies the natural talents and tempers of men. It consecrates the fire of a Peter, the energy of a Paul, and the pensiveness of a John to the same service of God. It most strikingly displays its new creating power in the sudden conversion of the apostle of the Gentiles from a most dangerous foe to a most efficient friend of the church. Upon Paul the Spirit of God came as an overwhelming storm; upon John, as a gentle, refreshing breeze. But in all dwelt the same new, supernatural, divine principle of life. All are living apologies for Christianity, whose force no truth-loving heart can resist.

Notice, too, the moral effects of the gospel in the female characters of the New Testament. Christianity raises woman from the slavish position which she held both in Judaism and in heathendom, to her true moral dignity and importance; makes

---

[1] Comp. Phil. 3 : 12–14; 2 Cor. 4 : 7 sqq. ; 12 : 7 ; 1 Cor. 9 : 27; Jas. 3 : 2 ; 1 John 1 : 8, 9 ; Gal. 2 : 11 ; Acts 15 : 36–39 ; 23 : 3 sqq.

her an heir of the same salvation with man,[1] and opens to her a field for the noblest and loveliest virtues, without thrusting her, after the manner of modern pseudo-philanthropic schemes of emancipation, out of her appropriate sphere of private, domestic life, and thus stripping her of her fairest ornament and peculiar charm.

The Virgin Mary marks the turning point in the history of the female sex. As the mother of Christ, the second Adam, she corresponds to Eve, and is, in a spiritual sense, the mother of all living.[2] In her, the "blessed among women," the whole sex was blessed, and the curse removed which had hung over the era of the fall. She was not, indeed, free from actual and native sin, as is now taught, without the slightest ground in Scripture, by the Roman church since the 8th of December, 1854. On the contrary, as a daughter of Adam, she needed, like all men, redemption and sanctification through Christ, the sole author of sinless holiness, and she herself expressly calls God her Saviour.[3] But in the mother and educator of the Saviour of the world we no doubt may and should revere, though not worship, the model of female Christian virtue, of purity, tenderness, simplicity, humility, perfect obedience to God, and unreserved surrender to Christ. Next to her we have a lovely group of female disciples and friends around the Lord: Mary, the wife of Clopas; Salome, the mother of James and John; Mary of Bethany, who sat at Jesus' feet; her busy and hospitable sister, Martha; Mary of Magdala, whom the Lord healed of a demoniacal possession; the sinner, who washed his feet with her tears of penitence and wiped them with her hair; and all the noble women, who ministered to the Son of man in his earthly poverty with the gifts of their love,[4] lingered last around his cross,[5] and were the first at his open sepulchre on the morning of the resurrection.[6]

[1] 1 Pet. 3 : 7; Gal. 3 : 28.

[2] Gen. 3 : 20. This parallel was first drawn by Irenæus, but overdrawn and abused by later fathers in the service of Mariolatry.

[3] Luke 1 : 47 ἐπὶ τῷ θεῷ τῷ σωτῆρί μου.   [4] Luke 8 : 3; Matt. 27:55; Mark 15 : 41.

[5] John 19 : 15.   [6] Matt. 28 : 1 ; John 20 : 1.

Henceforth we find woman no longer a slave of man and tool of lust, but the pride and joy of her husband, the fond mother training her children to virtue and godliness, the ornament and treasure of the family, the faithful sister, the zealous servant of the congregation in every work of Christian charity, the sister of mercy, the martyr with superhuman courage, the guardian angel of peace, the example of purity, humility, gentleness, patience, love, and fidelity unto death. Such women were unknown before. The heathen Libanius, the enthusiastic eulogist of old Grecian culture, pronounced an involuntary eulogy on Christianity when he exclaimed, as he looked at the mother of Chrysostom : " What women the Christians have ! "

§ 47. *Christianity and the Family.*

H. GREGOIRE : *De l'influence du christianisme sur la condition des femmes.* Paris, 1821.

F. MÜNTER : *Die Christin im heidnischen Hause vor den Zeiten Constantin's des Grossen.* Kopenhagen, 1828.

JULIA KAVANAGH : *Women of Christianity, Exemplary for Acts of Piety and Charity.* Lond., 1851 ; N. York, 1866.

Thus raising the female sex to its true freedom and dignity, Christianity transforms and sanctifies the entire family life. It abolishes polygamy, and makes monogamy the proper form of marriage ; it condemns concubinage with all forms of unchastity and impurity. It presents the mutual duties of husband and wife, and of parents and children, in their true light, and exhibits marriage as a copy of the mystical union of Christ with his bride, the church ; thus imparting to it a holy character and a heavenly end.[1]

Henceforth the family, though still rooted, as before, in the soil of nature, in the mystery of sexual love, is spiritualized. and becomes a nursery of the purest and noblest virtues, a miniature church, where the father, as shepherd, daily leads his household into the pastures of the divine word, and, as priest,

[1] Comp. Eph. 5 : 22-23 ; 6 : 1-9 ; Col. 3 : 18-25.

offers to the Lord the sacrifice of their common petition, intercession, thanksgiving, and praise.

With the married state, the single also, as an exception to the
rule, is consecrated by the gospel to the service of the kingdom
of God ; as we see in a Paul, a Barnabas, and a John,[1] and in
the history of missions and of ascetic piety. The enthusiasm
for celibacy, which spread so soon throughout the ancient church,
must be regarded as a one-sided, though natural and, upon the
whole, beneficial reaction against the rotten condition and misery
of family life among the heathen.

§ 48. *Christianity and Slavery.*

Literature.

H. WALLON (Prof. of Modern History in Paris) : *Histoire de l'esclavage
dans l'antiquité*, Par. 1879, 3 vols., treats very thoroughly of Slavery
in the Orient, among the Greeks and the Romans, with an Introduction on modern negro slavery in the Colonies.

AUGUSTIN COCHIN (ancien maire et conseiller municipal de la ville de
Paris) : *L'abolition de l'esclavage*, Paris, 1862, 2 vols. This work
treats not only of the modern abolition of slavery, but includes in
vol. II., p. 348–470, an able discussion of the relation of Christianity and slavery.

MÖHLER (R. C., d. 1848) : *Bruchstücke aus der Geschichte der Aufhebung
der Sklaverei*, 1834. (" Vermischte Schriften," vol. II., p. 54.)

H. WISKEMANN : *Die Sklaverei.* Leiden, 1866. A crowned prize-essay.

P. ALLARD : *Les esclaves chrétiens depuis les premiers temps de l'église jusqu'
à la fin de la domination romaine en Occident.* Paris, 1876 (480 pp.).

G. V. LECHLER : *Sklaverei und Christenthum.* Leipz. 1877–78.

PH. SCHAFF : *Slavery and the Bible*, in his " Christ and Christianity,"
N. York and London, 1885, pp. 184–212.

Compare the Commentaries on the Epistle of Paul to Philemon, especially BRAUNE, and LIGHTFOOT (in *Colossians and Philemon*, 1875).

The numerous American works on slavery by Channing, Parker, Hodge,
Barnes, Wilson, Cheever, Bledsoe, and others, relate to the question
of negro slavery, now providentially abolished by the civil war of
1861–65.

---

[1] Comp. Matt. 19 : 10–12 ; 1 Cor. 7 : 7 sqq. ; Rev. 14 : 4.

To Christianity we owe the gradual extinction of slavery.

This evil has rested as a curse on all nations, and at the time of Christ the greater part of the existing race was bound in beastly degradation—even in civilized Greece and Rome the slaves being more numerous than the free-born and the freed-men. The greatest philosophers of antiquity vindicated slavery as a natural and necessary institution; and Aristotle declared all barbarians to be slaves by birth, fit for nothing but obedience. According to the Roman law, "slaves had no head in the State, no name, no title, no register"; they had no rights of matrimony, and no protection against adultery; they could be bought and sold, or given away, as personal property; they might be tortured for evidence, or even put to death, at the discretion of their master. In the language of a distinguished writer on civil law, the slaves in the Roman empire "were in a much worse state than any cattle whatsoever." Cato the elder expelled his old and sick slaves out of house and home. Hadrian, one of the most humane of the emperors, wilfully destroyed the eye of one of his slaves with a pencil. Roman ladies punished their maids with sharp iron instruments for the most trifling offences, while attending, half-naked, on their toilet. Such legal degradation and cruel treatment had the worst effect upon the character of the slaves. They are described by the ancient writers as mean, cowardly, abject, false, voracious, intemperate, voluptuous, also as hard and cruel when placed over others. A proverb prevailed in the Roman empire: "As many slaves, so many enemies." Hence the constant danger of servile insurrections, which more than once brought the republic to the brink of ruin, and seemed to justify the severest measures in self-defence.

Judaism, indeed, stood on higher ground than this; yet it tolerated slavery, though with wise precautions against maltreatment, and with the significant ordinance, that in the year of jubilee, which prefigured the renovation of the theocracy, all Hebrew slaves should go free.[1]

---

[1] Lev. 25: 10: "Ye shall hallow the fiftieth year, and proclaim *liberty* throughout the land unto *all the inhabitants* thereof." Comp. Isa. 41 :1 ; Luke 4 19.

This system of permanent oppression and moral degradation the gospel opposes rather by its whole spirit than by any special law. It nowhere recommends outward violence and revolutionary measures, which in those times would have been worse than useless, but provides an internal radical cure, which first mitigates the evil, takes away its sting, and effects at last its entire abolition. Christianity aims, first of all, to redeem man, without regard to rank or condition, from that worst bondage, the curse of sin, and to give him true spiritual freedom; it confirms the original unity of all men in the image of God, and teaches the common redemption and spiritual equality of all before God in Christ;[1] it insists on love as the highest duty and virtue, which itself inwardly levels social distinctions; and it addresses the comfort and consolation of the gospel particularly to all the poor, the persecuted, and the oppressed. Paul sent back to his earthly master the fugitive slave, Onesimus, whom he had converted to Christ and to his duty, that he might restore his character where he had lost it; but he expressly charged Philemon to receive and treat the bondman hereafter as a beloved brother in Christ, yea, as the apostle's own heart. It is impossible to conceive of a more radical cure of the evil in those times and within the limits of established laws and customs. And it is impossible to find in ancient literature a parallel to the little Epistle to Philemon for gentlemanly courtesy and delicacy, as well as for tender sympathy with a poor slave.

This Christian spirit of love, humanity, justice, and freedom, as it pervades the whole New Testament, has also, in fact, gradually abolished the institution of slavery in almost all civilized nations, and will not rest till all the chains of sin and misery are broken, till the personal and eternal dignity of man redeemed by Christ is universally acknowledged, and the evangelical freedom and brotherhood of men are perfectly attained.

[1] Gal. 3:28; Col. 3:11.

NOTE ON THE NUMBER AND CONDITION OF SLAVES IN GREECE AND ROME.

Attica numbered, according to Ctesicles, under the governorship of Demetrius the Phalerian (309 B.C.), 400,000 slaves, 10,000 foreigners, and only 21,000 free citizens. In Sparta the disproportion was still greater.

As to the Roman empire, Gibbon estimates the number of slaves under the reign of Claudius at no less than one half of the entire population, i.e., about sixty millions (I. 52, ed. Milman, N. Y., 1850). According to Robertson there were twice as many slaves as free citizens, and Blair (in his work on Roman slavery, Edinb. 1833, p. 15) estimates over three slaves to one freeman between the conquest of Greece (146 B.C.) and the reign of Alexander Severus (A.D. 222–235). The proportion was of course very different in the cities and in the rural districts. The majority of the *plebs urbana* were poor and unable to keep slaves ; and the support of slaves in the city was much more expensive than in the country. Marquardt assumes the proportion of slaves to freemen in Rome to have been three to two. Friedländer (*Sittengeschichte Roms.* I. 55, fourth ed.) thinks it impossible to make a correct general estimate, as we do not know the number of wealthy families. But we know that Rome A.D. 24 was thrown into consternation by the fear of a slave insurrection (Tacit. *Ann.* IV. 27). Athenæus, as quoted by Gibbon (I. 51) boldly asserts that he knew very many (πάμπολλοι) Romans who possessed, not for use, but ostentation, ten and even twenty thousand slaves. In a single palace at Rome, that of Pedanius Secundus, then prefect of the city, four hundred slaves were maintained, and were all executed for not preventing their master's murder (Tacit. *Ann.* XIV. 42, 43).

The legal condition of the slaves is thus described by Taylor on *Civil Law*, as quoted in Cooper's *Justinian*, p. 411: "Slaves were held *pro nullis, pro mortuis, pro quadrupedibus ;* nay, were in a much worse state than any cattle whatsoever. They had no head in the state, no name, no title, or register ; they were not capable of being injured ; nor could they take by purchase or descent ; they had no heirs, and therefore could make no will ; they were not entitled to the rights and considerations of matrimony, and therefore had no relief in case of adultery ; nor were they proper objects of cognation or affinity, but of quasi-cognation only ; they could be sold, transferred, or pawned, as goods or personal estate, for goods they were, and as such they were esteemed ; they might be tortured for evidence, punished at the discretion of their lord, and even put to death by his authority ; together with many other civil incapacities which I have no room to enumerate." Gibbon (I. 48) thinks that "against such internal enemies, whose desperate insurrections had more than once reduced the republic to the brink of destruction, the most severe regulations and the most cruel treatment seemed almost justifiable by the great law of self-preservation."

The individual treatment of slaves depended on the character of the master. As a rule it was harsh and cruel. The bloody spectacles of the amphitheatre stupefied the finer sensibilities even in women. Juvenal describes a Roman mistress who ordered her female slaves to be unmercifully lashed in her presence till the whippers were worn out; Ovid warns the ladies not to scratch the face or stick needles into the naked arms of the servants who adorned them; and before Hadrian a mistress could condemn a slave to the death of crucifixion without assigning a reason. See the references in Friedländer, I. 466. It is but just to remark that the philosophers of the first and second century, Seneca, Pliny, and Plutarch, entertained much milder views on this subject than the older writers, and commend a humane treatment of the slaves; also that the Antonines improved their condition to some extent, and took the oft abused jurisdiction of life and death over the slaves out of private hands and vested it in the magistrates. But at that time Christian principles and sentiments already freely circulated throughout the empire, and exerted a silent influence even over the educated heathen. This unconscious atmospheric influence, so to speak, is continually exerted by Christianity over the surrounding world, which without this would be far worse than it actually is.

§ 49. *Christianity and Society.*

Christianity enters with its leaven-like virtue the whole civil and social life of a people, and leads it on the path of progress in all genuine civilization. It nowhere prescribes, indeed, a particular form of government, and carefully abstains from all improper interference with political and secular affairs. It accommodates itself to monarchical and republican institutions, and can flourish even under oppression and persecution from the State, as the history of the first three centuries sufficiently shows. But it teaches the true nature and aim of all government, and the duties of rulers and subjects; it promotes the abolition of bad laws and institutions, and the establishment of good; it is in principle opposed alike to despotism and anarchy; it tends, under every form of government, towards order, propriety, justice, humanity, and peace; it fills the ruler with a sense of responsibility to the supreme king and judge, and the ruled with the spirit of loyalty, virtue, and piety.

Finally, the Gospel reforms the international relations by breaking down the partition walls of prejudice and hatred among the different nations and races. It unites in brotherly fellowship and harmony around the same communion table even the Jews and the Gentiles, once so bitterly separate and hostile. The spirit of Christianity, truly catholic or universal, rises above all national distinctions. Like the congregation at Jerusalem, the whole apostolic church was of "one heart and of one soul." [1] It had its occasional troubles, indeed, temporary collisions between a Peter and a Paul, between Jewish and Gentile Christians; but instead of wondering at these, we must admire the constant victory of the spirit of harmony and love over the remaining forces of the old nature and of a former state of things. The poor Gentile Christians of Paul's churches in Greece sent their charities to the poor Jewish Christians in Palestine, and thus proved their gratitude for the gospel and its fellowship, which they had received from that mother church. [2] The Christians all felt themselves to be "brethren," were constantly impressed with their common origin and their common destiny, and considered it their sacred duty to "keep the unity of the spirit in the bond of peace." [3] While the Jews, in their spiritual pride and "*odium generis humani*" abhorred all Gentiles; while the Greeks despised all barbarians as only half men; and while the Romans, with all their might and policy, could bring their conquered nations only into a mechanical conglomeration, a giant body without a soul; Christianity, by purely moral means, founded a universal spiritual empire and a communion of saints, which stands unshaken to this day, and will spread till it embraces all the nations of the earth as its living members, and reconciles all to God.

[1] Acts 4 : 32.
[2] Gal. 2 : 10; 2 Cor. 9 : 12–15; Rom. 15 : 25–27.
[3] Gal. 3 : 28; Eph. 4 : 3.

§ 50. *Spiritual Condition of the Congregations.—The Seven Churches in Asia.*

We must not suppose that the high standard of holiness set up in doctrine and example by the evangelists and apostles was fully realized in their congregations. The dream of the spotless purity and perfection of the apostolic church finds no support in the apostolic writings, except as an ideal which is constantly held up before our vision to stimulate our energies. If the inspired apostles themselves disclaimed perfection, much less can we expect it from their converts, who had just come from the errors and corruptions of Jewish and heathen society, and could not be transformed at once without a miracle in violation of the ordinary laws of moral growth.

We find, in fact, that every Epistle meets some particular difficulty and danger. No letter of Paul can be understood without the admission of the actual imperfection of his congregations. He found it necessary to warn them even against the vulgar sins of the flesh as well as against the refined sins of the spirit. He cheerfully and thankfully commended their virtues, and as frankly and fearlessly condemned their errors and vices.

The same is true of the churches addressed in the Catholic Epistles, and in the Revelation of John.[1]

The seven Epistles in the second and third chapters of the Apocalypse give us a glimpse of the church in its light and shade in the last stage of the apostolic age—primarily in Asia Minor, but through it also in other lands. These letters are all very much alike in their plan, and present a beautiful order, which has been well pointed out by Bengel. They contain (1) a command of Christ to write to the "angel" of the congregation. (2) A designation of Jesus by some imposing title, which generally refers to his majestic appearance (1:13 sqq.), and serves

---

[1] The remainder of this paragraph is taken in part from my *Hist. of the Apost. Church* (§ 108, pp. 427 sqq.), where it is connected with the life and labors of St. John. Comp. also the monographs of Trench and Plumptre on the Seven Churches, and Lange's Com. on Rev. chs. 2 and 3.

as the basis and warrant of the subsequent promises and threatenings. (3) The address to the angel, or the responsible head of the congregation, be it a single bishop or the college of pastors and teachers. The angels are, at all events, the representatives of the people committed to their charge, and what was said to them applies at the same time to the churches. This address, or the epistle proper, consists always of (*a*) a short sketch of the present moral condition of the congregation—both its virtues and defects—with commendation or censure as the case may be; (*b*) an exhortation either to repentance or to faithfulness and patience, according to the prevailing character of the church addressed; (*c*) a promise to him who overcomes, together with the admonition: "He that hath an ear, let him hear what the Spirit saith unto the churches," or the same in the reverse order, as in the first three epistles. This latter variation divides the seven churches into two groups, one comprising the first three, the other the remaining four, just as the seven seals, the seven trumpets, and the seven vials are divided. The ever-recurring admonition: "He that hath an ear," etc., consists of ten words. This is no unmeaning play, but an application of the Old Testament system of symbolical numbers, in which three was the symbol of the Godhead; four of the world or humanity; the indivisible number seven, the sum of three and four (as also twelve, their product), the symbol of the indissoluble covenant between God and man; and ten (seven and three), the round number, the symbol of fulness and completion.

As to their moral and religious condition, the churches and the representatives fall, according to the Epistles, into three classes:

1. Those which were *predominantly good and pure*, viz., those of Smyrna and Philadelphia. Hence, in the messages to these two churches we find no exhortation to repentance in the strict sense of the word, but only an encouragement to be steadfast, patient, and joyful under suffering.

The church of Smyrna (a very ancient, still flourishing com-

mercial city in Ionia, beautifully located on the bay of Smyrna)
was externally poor and persecuted, and had still greater tribulation in view, but is cheered with the prospect of the crown of
life. It was in the second century ruled by Polycarp, a pupil of
John, and a faithful martyr.

Philadelphia (a city built by king Attalus Philadelphus, and
named after him, now Ala-Schär), in the province of Lydia, a
rich wine region, but subject to earthquakes, was the seat of a
church likewise poor and small outwardly, but very faithful and
spiritually flourishing—a church which was to have all the tribu-
lations and hostility it met with on earth abundantly rewarded
in heaven.

2. Churches which were in a *predominantly evil and critical condition*, viz., those of Sardis and Laodicea. Here accordingly we find severe censure and earnest exhortation to repentance.

The church at Sardis (till the time of Crœsus the flourishing
capital of the Lydian empire, but now a miserable hamlet of
shepherds) had indeed the name and outward form of Christianity, but not its inward power of faith and life. Hence it was
on the brink of spiritual death. Yet the Epistle, 3 : 4 sq., distinguishes from the corrupt mass a few souls which had kept
their walk undefiled, without, however, breaking away from the
congregation as separatists, and setting up an opposition sect
for themselves.

The church of Laodicea (a wealthy commercial city of Phrygia, not far from Colosse and Hierapolis, where now stands only
a desolate village by the name of Eski-Hissar) proudly fancied
itself spiritually rich and faultless, but was in truth poor and
blind and naked, and in that most dangerous state of indifference and lukewarmness from which it is more difficult to return
to the former decision and ardor, than it was to pass at first
from the natural coldness to faith. Hence the fearful threatening: " I will spew thee out of my mouth." (Lukewarm water
produces vomiting.) Yet even the Laodiceans are not driven to
despair. The Lord, in love, knocks at their door and promises

them, on condition of thorough repentance, a part in the mar-
riage-supper of the lamb (3 : 20).

3. Churches of a *mixed* character, viz., those of Ephesus,
Pergamum, and Thyatira. In these cases commendation and
censure, promise and threatening are united.

Ephesus, then the metropolis of the Asian church, had with-
stood, indeed, the Gnostic errorists predicted by Paul, and
faithfully maintained the purity of the doctrine delivered to it ;
but it had lost the ardor of its first love, and it is, therefore,
earnestly exhorted to repent. It thus represents to us that state
of dead, petrified orthodoxy, into which various churches oftentimes fall. Zeal for pure doctrine is, indeed, of the highest importance, but worthless without living piety and active love.
The Epistle to the angel of the church of Ephesus is peculiarly
applicable to the later Greek church as a whole.

Pergamum in Mysia (the northernmost of these seven cities,
formerly the residence of the kings of Asia of the Attalian
dynasty, and renowned for its large library of 200,000 volumes
and the manufacture of parchment; hence the name *charta
Pergamena ;*—now Bergamo, a village inhabited by Turks,
Greeks, and Armenians) was the seat of a church, which under
trying circumstances had shown great fidelity, but tolerated in
her bosom those who held dangerous Gnostic errors.   For this
want of rigid discipline she also is called on to repent.

The church of Thyatira (a flourishing manufacturing and
commercial city in Lydia, on the site of which now stands a
considerable Turkish town called Ak-Hissar, or "the White
Castle," with nine mosques and one Greek church) was very
favorably distinguished for self-denying, active love and patience, but was likewise too indulgent towards errors which cor-
rupted Christianity with heathen principles and practices.

The last two churches, especially that of Thyatira, form thus
the exact counterpart to that of Ephesus, and are the representatives of a zealous practical piety in union with theoretical lati-
tudinarianism.   As doctrine always has more or less influence
on practice, this also is a dangerous state.   That church alone

is truly sound and flourishing in which purity of doctrine and purity of life, theoretical orthodoxy and practical piety are harmoniously united and promote one another.

With good reason have theologians in all ages regarded these seven churches of Asia Minor as a miniature of the whole Christian church. " There is no condition, good, bad, or mixed, of which these epistles do not present a sample, and for which they do not give suitable and wholesome direction."   Here, as everywhere, the word of God and the history of the apostolic church evince their applicability to all times and circumstances, and their inexhaustible fulness of instruction, warning, and encouragement for all states and stages of religious life.

CHAPTER IX.

WORSHIP IN THE APOSTOLIC AGE.

Literature.

TH. HARNACK: *Der christliche Gemeindegottesdienst im apost. und altkathol. Zeitalter.* Erlangen, 1854. The same: *Prakt. Theol.*, I. 1877.

F. PROBST (R. C.) : *Liturgie der drei ersten Jahrhunderte.* Tüb., 1870.

W. L. VOLZ: *Anfänge des christl. Gottesdienstes,* in "Stud. und Krit." 1872.

H. JACOBY : *Die constitutiven Factoren des apost. Gottesdienstes,* in "Jahrb. für deutsche Theol." for 1873.

C. WEIZSÄCKER : *Die Versammlungen der ältesten Christengemeinden,* 1876 ; and *Das Apost. Zeitalter,* 1886, pp. 566 sqq.

TH. ZAHN : *Gesch. des Sonntags in der alten Kirche.* Hann., 1878.

SCHAFF : *Hist. of the Apost. Ch.,* pp. 545–586.

Comp. the Lit. on Ch. X., and on the *Didache,* vol. II. 184.

§ 51. *The Synagogue.*

CAMPEG. VITRINGA (d. at Franeker, 1722) : *De Synagoga Vetere libri tres.* Franeker, 1696. 2 vols. (also Weissenfels, 1726). A standard work, full of biblical and rabbinical learning. A condensed translation by J. L. BERNARD : *The Synagogue and the Church.* London, 1842.

C. BORNITIUS : *De Synagogis veterum Hebræorum.* Vitemb., 1650. And in UGOLINUS : *Thesaurus Antiquitatum sacrarum* (Venet., 1744–69), vol. XXI. 495–539.

ANT. TH. HARTMANN : *Die enge Verbindung des A. Testaments mit dem Neuen.* Hamburg, 1831 (pp. 225–376).

ZUNZ (a Jewish Rabbi) : *Die gottesdienstlichen Vorträge der Juden.* Berlin, 1832.

The *Histories of the Jews,* by JOST, HERZFELD, and MILMAN.

The *Histories of N. T. Times,* by HAUSRATH (I. 73 sqq. 2d ed.) and SCHÜRER (463–475, and the literature there given).

Art. "Synag.," by GINSBURG in " Kitto "; PLUMPTRE in "Smith" (with additions by Hackett, IV. 3133, Am. ed.) ; LEYRER in "Herzog" (XV. 299, first ed.) ; KNEUKER in "Schenkel" (V. 443).

As the Christian Church rests historically on the Jewish Church, so Christian worship and the congregational organization rest on that of the synagogue, and cannot be well understood without it.

The synagogue was and is still an institution of immense conservative power. It was the local centre of the religious and social life of the Jews, as the temple of Jerusalem was the centre of their national life. It was a school as well as a church, and the nursery and guardian of all that is peculiar in this peculiar people. It dates probably from the age of the captivity and of Ezra.[1] It was fully organized at the time of Christ and the apostles, and used by them as a basis of their public instruction.[2] It survived the temple, and continues to this day unaltered in its essential features, the chief nursery and protection of the Jewish nationality and religion.[3]

The term "synagogue" (like our word church) signifies first the congregation, then also the building where the congregation meet for public worship.[4] Every town, however small, had a synagogue, or at least a place of prayer in a private house or in the open air (usually near a river or the sea-shore, on account of the ceremonial washings). Ten men were sufficient to constitute a religious assembly. "Moses from generations of old hath

---

[1] The Jewish tradition traces it back to the schools of the prophets, and even to patriarchal times, by far-fetched interpretations of Gen. 25 : 27 ; Judg. 5 : 9 ; Isa. 1 : 13, etc.

[2] Comp. § 17, p. 152.

[3] "*Bei dem Untergang aller Institutionen,*" says Dr. Zunz (*l. c.* p. 1), "*blieb die Synagoge als einziger Träger ihrer Nationalität ; dorthin floh ihr Glauben und von dorther empfingen sie Belehrung für ihren irdischen Wandel, Kraft zur Ausdauer in unerhörten Leiden und Hoffnung auf eine künftige Morgenröthe der Freiheit. Der öffentliche Gottesdienst der Synagoge ward das Panier jüdischer Nationalität, die Aegide des jüdischen Glaubens.*"

[4] συναγωγή, often in the Septuagint (130 times as translation of עֵדָה, 25 times for קָהָל) ; in the Greek Test. (Matt. 4 : 23 ; Mark 1 : 21 ; Luke 4 : 15 ; 12 : 11 ; Acts 9 : 2 ; 13 : 43, etc. ; of a Christian congregation, James 2 : 2) ; also in Philo and Josephus ; sometimes συναγώγιον (Philo), σαββατεῖον (Josephus), προσευκτήριον (Philo), προσευχή, house of prayer, oratory (Acts 16 : 13 and Josephus) ; also ἐκκλησία. Hebrew designations : חֶבֶר, צִבּוּר, קָהָל, עֵדָה ; בֵּית הַכְּנֶסֶת, בֵּית תְּפִלָּה, בֵּית וַעַד.

in every city them that preach him, being read in the synagogues every Sabbath." [1] To erect a synagogue was considered a work of piety and public usefulness.[2] In large cities, as Alexandria and Rome, there were many; in Jerusalem, about four hundred for the various sects and the Hellenists from different countries.[3]

1. The *building* was a plain, rectangular hall of no peculiar style of architecture, and in its inner arrangement somewhat resembling the Tabernacle and the Temple. It had benches, the higher ones ("the uppermost seats") for the elders and richer members,[4] a reading-desk or pulpit, and a wooden ark or closet for the sacred rolls (called "Copheret" or Mercy Seat, also "Aaron"). The last corresponded to the Holy of Holies in the Tabernacle and the Temple. A sacred light was kept burning as a symbol of the divine law, in imitation of the light in the Temple, but there is no mention made of it in the Talmud. Other lamps were brought in by devout worshippers at the beginning of the Sabbath (Friday evening). Alms-boxes were provided near the door, as in the Temple, one for the poor in Jerusalem, another for local charities. Paul imitated the example by collecting alms for the poor Christians in Jerusalem.

There was no artistic (except vegetable) ornamentation; for the second commandment strictly forbids all images of the Deity as idolatrous. In this, as in many other respects, the Mohammedan mosque, with its severe iconoclastic simplicity, is a second edition of the synagogue. The building was erected on the most elevated spot of the neighborhood, and no house was allowed to overtop it. In the absence of a commanding site, a tall pole from the roof rendered it conspicuous.[5]

---

[1] Acts 15 : 21.   [2] Luke 7 : 5.

[3] Acts 6 : 9. The number of synagogues in Jerusalem is variously stated from 394 to 480.

[4] Matt. 23 : 6 ; comp. James 2 : 2, 3. In the synagogue of Alexandria there were seventy-one golden chairs, according to the number of members of the Sanhedrin. The πρωτοκαθεδρίαι were near the ark, the place of honor.

[5] Ruins of eleven or more ancient synagogues still exist in Palestine (all in Galilee) at Tell-Hum (Capernaum), Kerazeh (Chorazin), Meiron, Irbid (Arbela), Kasyun, Umm el-'Amud, Nebratein, two at Kefr-Birim, two at el-Jish (Giscala). See *Palest. Explor. Quart. Statement* for July, 1878.

2. *Organization.*—Every synagogue had a president,[1] a number of elders (*Zekenim*) equal in rank,[2] a reader and interpreter,[3]
one or more envoys or clerks, called "messengers" (*Sheliach*),[4]
and a sexton or beadle (*Chazzan*) for the humbler mechanical
services.[5] There were also deacons (*Gabae zedaka*) for the
collection of alms in money and produce. Ten or more wealthy
men at leisure, called *Batlanim*, represented the congregation at
every service. Each synagogue formed an independent republic,
but kept up a regular correspondence with other synagogues.
It was also a civil and religious court, and had power to excommunicate and to scourge offenders.[6]

3. *Worship.*—It was simple, but rather long, and embraced
three elements, devotional, didactic, and ritualistic. It included
prayer, song, reading, and exposition of the Scripture, the rite
of circumcision, and ceremonial washings. The bloody sacrifices were confined to the temple and ceased with its destruction; they were fulfilled in the eternal sacrifice on the cross.
The prayers and songs were chiefly taken from the Psalter,
which may be called the first liturgy and hymn book.

The opening prayer was called the *Shema* or *Keriath Shema*,
and consisted of two introductory benedictions, the reading of
the Ten Commandments (afterward abandoned) and several
sections of the Pentateuch, namely, Deut. 6 : 4–9 ; 11 : 13–21 ;
Num. 15 : 37–41. Then followed the eighteen prayers and

---

[1] The ἀρχισυνάγωγος (הַכְּנֶסֶת רֹאשׁ), Luke 8 : 49 ; 13 : 14 ; Mark 5 : 36, 33 ;
Acts 18 : 8, 17 ; or ἄρχων τῆς συναγωγῆς, Luke 8 : 41 ; or ἄρχων, Matt. 9 : 18.
He was simply *primus inter pares ;* hence, several ἀρχισυνάγωγοι appear in
one and the same synagogue, Luke 13 : 14 ; Mark 5 : 22 ; Acts 13 : 15 ; 18 : 17.
In smaller towns there was but one.

[2] πρεσβύτεροι (זְקֵנִים).

[3] After the Babylonian captivity an interpreter (*Methurgeman*) was usually
employed to translate the Hebrew lesson into the Chaldee or Greek, or other
vernacular languages.

[4] ἀπόστολοι, ἄγγελοι (שָׁלִיחַ צִבּוּר).   Not to be confounded with the angels
in the Apocalypse.

[5] ὑπηρέτης (חַזָּן), Luke 4 : 20.

[6] Matt. 10 : 17 ; 23 : 34 ; Luke 12 : 11 ; 21 : 12 ; John 9 : 34 ; 16 : 2 ; Acts
22 : 19 ; 26 : 11. The Chazzan had to administer the corporal punishment.

benedictions (*Berachoth*). This is one of them : "Bestow peace, happiness, blessing, grace, mercy, and compassion upon us and upon the whole of Israel, thy people. Our Father, bless us all unitedly with the light of thy countenance, for in the light of thy countenance didst thou give to us, O Lord our God, the law of life, lovingkindness, justice, blessing, compassion, life, and peace. May it please thee to bless thy people Israel at all times, and in every moment, with peace. Blessed art thou, O Lord, who blessest thy people Israel with peace." These benedictions are traced in the Mishna to the one hundred and twenty elders of the Great Synagogue. They were no doubt of gradual growth, some dating from the Maccabean struggles, some from the Roman ascendancy. The prayers were offered by a reader, and the congregation responded "Amen." This custom passed into the Christian church.[1]

The didactic and homiletical part of worship was based on the Hebrew Scriptures. A lesson from the Law (called *parasha*),[2] and one from the Prophets (*haphthara*) were read in the original,[3] and followed by a paraphrase or commentary and homily (*midrash*) in the vernacular Aramaic or Greek. A benediction and the "Amen" of the people closed the service.

As there was no proper priesthood outside of Jerusalem, any Jew of age might get up to read the lessons, offer prayer, and address the congregation. Jesus and the apostles availed themselves of this democratic privilege to preach the gospel, as the fulfilment of the law and the prophets.[4] The strong didactic element which distinguished this service from all heathen forms of worship, had the effect of familiarizing the Jews of all grades,

---

[1] 1 Cor. 14 : 16. The responsive element is the popular feature in a liturgy, and has been wisely preserved in the Anglican Church.

[2] The Thorah was divided into 154 sections, and read through in three years, afterwards in 54 sections for one year.

[3] The ἀνάγνωσις τοῦ νόμου καὶ τῶν προφητῶν, Acts 13 : 15.

[4] Luke 4 : 17–20 ; 13 : 54 ; John 18 : 20 ; Acts 13 : 5, 15, 44 ; 14 : 1 ; 17 : 2–4, 10, 17 ; 18 : 4, 26 ; 19 : 8. Paul and Barnabas were requested by the rulers of the synagogue at Antioch in Pisidia to speak after the reading of the law and the prophets (Acts 13 : 15).

even down to the servant-girls, with their religion, and raising them far above the heathen. At the same time it attracted proselytes who longed for a purer and more spiritual worship.

The days of public service were the Sabbath, Monday, and Thursday; the hours of prayer the third (9 A.M.), the sixth (noon), and the ninth (3 P.M.).[1]

The sexes were divided by a low wall or screen, the men on the one side, the women on the other, as they are still in the East (and in some parts of Europe). The people stood during prayer with their faces turned to Jerusalem.

§ 52. *Christian Worship.*

Christian worship, or cultus, is the public adoration of God in the name of Christ; the celebration of the communion of believers as a congregation with their heavenly Head, for the glory of the Lord, and for the promotion and enjoyment of spiritual life. While it aims primarily at the devotion and edification of the church itself, it has at the same time a missionary character, and attracts the outside world. This was the case on the Day of Pentecost when Christian worship in its distinctive character first appeared.

As our Lord himself in his youth and manhood worshipped in the synagogue and the temple, so did his early disciples as long as they were tolerated. Even Paul preached Christ in the synagogues of Damascus, Cyprus, Antioch in Pisidia, Amphipolis, Berœa, Athens, Corinth, Ephesus. He "reasoned with the Jews every sabbath in the synagogue," which furnished him a pulpit and an audience.

The Jewish Christians, at least in Palestine, conformed as closely as possible to the venerable forms of the cultus of their fathers, which in truth were divinely ordained, and were an expressive type of the Christian worship. So far as we know, they scrupulously observed the Sabbath, the annual Jewish

---

[1] Comp. Ps. 55 : 18; Dan. 7 : 11 ; Acts 2 : 15 ; 3 : 1 ; 10 : 30. These hours of devotion are respectively called *Shacharith, Minchah,* and *'Arabith.*

feasts, the hours of daily prayer, and the whole Mosaic ritual, and celebrated, in addition to these, the Christian Sunday, the death and the resurrection of the Lord, and the holy Supper. But this union was gradually weakened by the stubborn opposition of the Jews, and was at last entirely broken by the destruction of the temple, except among the Ebionites and Nazarenes.

In the Gentile-Christian congregations founded by Paul, the worship took from the beginning a more independent form. The essential elements of the Old Testament service were transferred, indeed, but divested of their national legal character, and transformed by the spirit of the gospel. Thus the Jewish Sabbath passed into the Christian Sunday; the typical Passover and Pentecost became feasts of the death and resurrection of Christ, and of the outpouring of the Holy Spirit; the bloody sacrifices gave place to the thankful remembrance and appropriation of the one, all-sufficient, and eternal sacrifice of Christ on the cross, and to the personal offering of prayer, intercession, and entire self-consecration to the service of the Redeemer; on the ruins of the temple made without hands arose the never-ceasing worship of the omnipresent God in spirit and in truth.'

So early as the close of the apostolic period this more free and spiritual cultus of Christianity had no doubt become well nigh universal; yet many Jewish elements, especially in the Eastern church, remain to this day.

§ 53. *The Several Parts of Worship.*

The several parts of public worship in the time of the apostles were as follows :

1. The PREACHING of the gospel. This appears in the first period mostly in the form of a missionary address to the unconverted ; that is, a simple, living presentation of the main facts of the life of Jesus, with practical exhortation to repentance and conversion. Christ crucified and risen was the luminous centre, whence a sanctifying light was shed on all the relations of life.

Comp. John 2 : 19 ; 4 : 23, 24.

Gushing forth from a full heart, this preaching went to the heart ; and springing from an inward life, it kindled life—a new, divine life—in the susceptible hearers. It was revival preaching in the purest sense. Of this primitive Christian testimony several examples from Peter and Paul are preserved in the Acts of the Apostles.

The Epistles also may be regarded in the wider sense as sermons, addressed, however, to believers, and designed to nourish the Christian life already planted.

2. The READING of portions of the Old Testament,[1] with practical exposition and application ; transferred from the Jewish synagogue into the Christian church.[2] To these were added in due time lessons from the New Testament ; that is, from the canonical Gospels and the apostolic Epistles, most of which were addressed to whole congregations and originally intended for public use.[3] After the death of the apostles their writings became doubly important to the church, as a substitute for their oral instruction and exhortation, and were much more used in worship than the Old Testament.

3. PRAYER, in its various forms of petition, intercession, and thanksgiving. This descended likewise from Judaism, and in fact belongs essentially even to all heathen religions ; but now it began to be offered in childlike confidence to a reconciled Father in the name of Jesus, and for all classes and conditions, even for enemies and persecutors. The first Christians accompanied every important act of their public and private life with this holy rite, and Paul exhorts his readers to "pray without ceasing." On solemn occasions they joined fasting with prayer, as a help to devotion, though it is nowhere directly enjoined in the New Testament.[4] They prayed freely from the heart, as they were moved by the Spirit, according to special needs and circumstances. We have an example in the fourth chapter of

---

[1] The Parashioth and Haphtaroth, as they were called.
[2] Comp. Acts 13 : 15 ; 15 : 21.
[3] 1 Thess. 5 : 27 ; Col. 4 : 16.
[4] Comp. Matt. 9 : 15; Acts 13 : 3 ; 14 : 23; 1 Cor. 7 : 5.

Acts. There is no trace of a uniform and exclusive liturgy; it would be inconsistent with the vitality and liberty of the apostolic churches. At the same time the frequent use of psalms and short forms of devotion, as the Lord's Prayer, may be inferred with certainty from the Jewish custom, from the Lord's direction respecting his model prayer,[1] from the strong sense of fellowship among the first Christians, and finally from the liturgical spirit of the ancient church, which could not have so generally prevailed both in the East and the West without some apostolic and post-apostolic precedent. The oldest forms are the eucharistic prayers of the *Didache*, and the petition for rulers in the first Epistle of Clement, which contrasts most beautifully with the cruel hostility of Nero and Domitian.[2]

4. The SONG, a form of prayer, in the festive dress of poetry and the elevated language of inspiration, raising the congregation to the highest pitch of devotion, and giving it a part in the heavenly harmonies of the saints. This passed immediately, with the psalms of the Old Testament, those inexhaustible treasures of spiritual experience, edification, and comfort, from the temple and the synagogue into the Christian church. The Lord himself inaugurated psalmody into the new covenant at the institution of the holy Supper,[3] and Paul expressly enjoined the singing of "psalms and hymns and spiritual songs," as a means of social edification.[4] But to this precious inheritance from the past, whose full value was now for the first time understood in the light of the New Testament revelation, the church, in the enthusiasm of her first love, added original, specifically Christian psalms, hymns, doxologies, and benedictions, which afforded the richest material for sacred poetry and music in succeeding centuries; the song of the heavenly hosts, for example, at the birth of the Saviour;[5] the "Nunc dimittis" of Simeon;[6] the "Magnificat" of the Virgin Mary;[7] the "Benedictus" of

---

[1] Matt. 6 : 9; Luke 11 : 1, 2. The *Didache*, ch. 8, gives the Lord's Prayer from Matthew, with a brief doxology (comp. 1 Cor. 29 : 11), and the direction to pray it three times a day. See Schaff on the *Did.*, p. 188 sq.

[2] *Didache*, chs. 8–10; Clement, *Ad Cor.*, chs. 59–61. See vol. II. 226.

[3] Comp. Matt. 26 : 30; Mark 14 : 26.   [4] Eph. 5 : 19; Col. 3 : 16.

[5] The "Gloria," Luke 2 : 14.   [6] Luke 2 : 29,   [7] Luke 1 : 46 sqq.

Zacharias;[1] the thanksgiving of Peter after his miraculous de‹
liverance;[2] the speaking with tongues in the apostolic churches,
which, whether song or prayer, was always in the elevated language of enthusiasm; the fragments of hymns scattered through
the Epistles;[3] and the lyrical and liturgical passages, the doxologies and antiphonies of the Apocalypse.[4]

5. CONFESSION OF FAITH. All the above-mentioned acts of
worship are also acts of faith. The first express confession of
faith is the testimony of Peter, that Jesus was the Christ, the
Son of the living God. The next is the trinitarian baptismal
formula. Out of this gradually grew the so-called Apostles'
Creed, which is also trinitarian in structure, but gives the confession of Christ the central and largest place. Though not

---

[1] Luke 1 : 68 sqq.   [2] Acts 4 : 24–30.   Comp. Ps. 2.
[3] Eph. 5 : 14 ; 1 Tim. 3 : 16; 2 Tim. 2 : 11–13; 1 Pet. 3 : 10–12.   The quotation is introduced by διὸ λέγει and πιστὸς ὁ λόγος. The rhythmical arrangement and adjustment in these passages, especially the first two, is obvious,
and Westcott and Hort have marked it in their Greek Testament as follows :

Ἔγειρε, ὁ καθεύδων,
καὶ ἀνάστα ἐκ τῶν νεκρῶν,
καὶ ἐπιφαύσει σοι ὁ χριστός.
                        —Eph. 5 : 14.

Ὃς ἐφανερώθη ἐν σαρκί,
ἐδικαιώθη ἐν πνεύματι,
ὤφθη ἀγγέλοις,
ἐκηρύχθη ἐν ἔθνεσιν,
ἐπιστεύθη ἐν κόσμῳ,
ἀνελήμφθη ἐν δόξῃ.
                        —1 Tim. 3 : 16.

The last passage is undoubtedly a quotation. The received reading, θεός, is
justly rejected by critical editors and exchanged for ὅς, which refers to God or
Christ. Some manuscripts read the neuter ὅ, which would refer to μυστήριον.
1 Pet. 3 : 10–12, which reads like a psalm, is likewise metrically arranged by
Westcott and Hort. James 1 : 17, though probably not a quotation, is a complete hexameter :

πᾶσα δόσις ἀγαθὴ καὶ πᾶν δώρημα τελεῖον.

Liddon (Lectures on the *Divinity of Christ*, p. 328) adds to the hymnological
fragments the passage Tit. 3 : 4–7, as " a hymn on the way of salvation,"
and several other passages which seem to me doubtful.
[4] Apoc. 1 : 5–8 ; 3 : 7, 14; 5 : 9, 12, 13; 11 : 15, 17, 19 ; 15 : 4 ; 19 : 6–8,
and other passages. They lack the Hebrew parallelism, but are nevertheless
poetical, and are printed in uncial type by Westcott and Hort.

traceable in its present shape above the fourth century, and
found in the second and third in different longer or shorter
forms, it is in substance altogether apostolic, and exhibits an
incomparable summary of the leading facts in the revelation of
the triune God from the creation of the world to the resurrection of the body; and that in a form intelligible to all, and
admirably suited for public worship and catechetical use. We
shall return to it more fully in the second period.

6. Finally, the administration of the SACRAMENTS, or sacred
rites instituted by Christ, by which, under appropriate symbols
and visible signs, spiritual gifts and invisible grace are represented, sealed, and applied to the worthy participators.

The two sacraments of Baptism and the Lord's Supper, the
antitypes of circumcision and the passover under the Old Testament, were instituted by Christ as efficacious signs, pledges, and
means of the grace of the new covenant. They are related to
each other as regeneration and sanctification, or as the beginning
and the growth of the Christian life. The other religious rites
mentioned in the New Testament, as confirmation and ordination, cannot be ranked in dignity with the sacraments, as they
are not commanded by Christ.

§ 54. *Baptism.*

Literature.

The commentaries on Matt. 28 : 19; Mark 16 : 16; John 3 : 5; Acts 2 : 38;
8 : 13, 16, 18, 37; Rom. 6 : 4; Gal. 3 : 27; Tit. 3 : 5; 1 Pet. 3 : 21.

G. J. VOSSIUS : *De Baptismo Disputationes XX.* Amsterdam, 1648.

W. WALL (Episcopalian) : *The History of Infant Baptism* (a very learned
work), first published in London, 1705, 2 vols., best edition by H.
Cotton, Oxford, 1836, 4 vols., and 1862, 2 vols., together with *Gale's*
(Baptist) *Reflections and Wall's Defense.* A Latin translation by
Schlosser appeared, vol. I., at Bremen, 1743, and vol. II. at Ham-
burg, 1753.

F. BRENNER (R. Cath.) : *Geschichtliche Darstellung der Verrichtung der
Taufe von Christus bis auf unsere Zeiten.* Bamberg, 1818.

MOSES STUART (Congregat.) : *Mode of Christian Baptism Prescribed in the
New Testament.* Andover, 1833 (reprinted 1876).

HÖFLING (Lutheran) : *Das Sacrament der Taufe.* Erlangen, 1846 and 1848, 2 vols.

SAMUEL MILLER (Presbyterian) : *Infant Baptism Scriptural and Reasonable ; and Baptism by Sprinkling or Affusion, the most Suitable and Edifying Mode.* Philadelphia, 1840.

ALEX. CARSON (Baptist) : *Baptism in its Mode and Subjects.* London, 1844 ; 5th Amer. ed., Philadelphia, 1850.

ALEX. CAMPBELL (founder of the Church of the Disciples, who teach that baptism by immersion is regeneration) : *Christian Baptism, with its Antecedents and Consequents.* Bethany, 1848, and Cincinnati, 1876.

T. J. CONANT (Baptist) : *The Meaning and Use of Baptism Philologically and Historically Investigated for the American* (Baptist) *Bible Union.* New York, 1861.

JAMES W. DALE (Presbyterian, d. 1881) : *Classic Baptism. An inquiry into the meaning of the word baptizo.* Philadelphia, 1867. *Judaic Baptism,* 1871. *Johannic Baptism,* 1872. *Christic and Patristic Baptism,* 1874. In all, 4 vols. Against the immersion theory.

R. INGHAM (Baptist) : *A Handbook on Christian Baptism,* in 2 parts. London, 1868.

D. B. FORD (Baptist) : *Studies on Baptism.* New York, 1879. (Against Dale.)

G. D. ARMSTRONG (Presbyterian minister at Norfolk, Va.) : *The Sacraments of the New Testament, as Instituted by Christ.* New York, 1880. (Popular.)

DEAN STANLEY : *Christian Institutions.* London and New York, 1881. Chap. I.

On the (post-apostolic) archæology of baptism see the archæological works of MARTENE (*De Antiquis Eccles. Ritibus*), GOAR (*Euchologion Græcorum*), BINGHAM, AUGUSTI, BINTERIM, SIEGEL, MARTIGNY, and SMITH and CHEETHAM (*Dict. of Christ. Ant.,* I., 155 sqq.).

On the baptismal pictures in the catacombs see the works of DE ROSSI, GARRUCCI, and SCHAFF on the *Didache,* pp. 36 sqq.

1. The IDEA of Baptism. It was solemnly instituted by Christ, shortly before his ascension, to be performed in the name of the Father, the Son, and the Holy Spirit. It took the place of circumcision as a sign and seal of church membership. It is the outward mark of Christian discipleship, the rite of initiation into the covenant of grace. It is the sacrament of repentance (conversion), of remission of sins, and of regeneration by the power of the Holy Spirit.[1] In the nature of the case it is to

---

[1] Mark 1 : 4 (βάπτισμα μετανοίας εἰς ἄφεσιν ἁμαρτιῶν, said of John's baptism), ver. 8, where John distinguishes his baptism, as a baptism by water (ὕδατι),

be received but once. It incorporates the penitent sinner in the visible church, and entitles him to all the privileges, and binds him to all the duties of this communion. Where the condition of repentance and faith is wanting, the blessing (as in the case of the holy Supper, and the preaching of the Word) is turned into a curse, and what God designs as a savor of life unto life becomes, by the unfaithfulness of man, a savor of death unto death.

The necessity of baptism for salvation has been inferred from John 3 : 5 and Mark 16 : 16; but while we are bound to God's ordinances, God himself is free and can save whomsoever and by whatsoever means he pleases. The church has always held the principle that the mere want of the sacrament does not condemn, but only the contempt. Otherwise all unbaptized infants that die in infancy would be lost. This horrible doctrine was indeed inferred by St. Augustin and the Roman church, from the supposed absolute necessity of baptism, but is in direct conflict with the spirit of the gospel and Christ's treatment of children, to whom belongs the kingdom of heaven.

The first administration of this sacrament in its full Christian sense took place on the birthday of the church, after the first independent preaching of the apostles. The baptism of John was more of a negative sort, and only preparatory to the baptism with the Holy Spirit. In theory, Christian baptism is pre-

---

from the baptism of Christ, as a baptism by the *Holy Spirit* (πνεύματι ἁγίῳ); Matt. 3 : 11; Luke 3 : 16; John 1 : 33 (ὁ βαπτίζων ἐν πνεύματι ἁγίῳ); Acts 2 : 38 (the first instance of Christian baptism, when Peter called on his hearers : Μετανοήσατε, καὶ βαπτισθήτω ἕκαστος ὑμῶν ἐν τῷ ὀνόματι Ἰησοῦ Χρ. εἰς ἄφεσιν τῶν ἁμαρτιῶν ὑμῶν, καὶ λήμψεσθε τὴν δωρεὰν τοῦ ἁγίου πνεύματος); 8 : 13; 11 : 16; 18 : 8 (ἐπίστευον καὶ ἐβαπτίζοντο); Rom. 6 : 4 (βάπτισμα εἰς τὸν θάνατον); Gal. 3 : 27 (εἰς Χριστὸν ἐβαπτίσθητε). The μετάνοια was the connecting link between the baptism of John and that of Christ. The English rendering, "repentance" (retained in the Revision of 1881), is inaccurate (after the Latin *pœnitentia*). The Greek means a change of mind, νοῦς (a *transmentation*, as Coleridge proposed to call it), *i.e.*, an entire reformation and transformation of the inner life of man, with a corresponding outward change. It was the burden of the preaching of John the Baptist, and Christ himself, who began with the enlarged exhortation : Μετανοεῖτε καὶ πιστεύετε ἐν τῷ εὐαγγελίῳ, Mark 1 : 15.

ceded by conversion, that is the human act of turning from sin
to God in repentance and faith, and followed by regeneration,
that is the divine act of forgiveness of sin and inward cleansing and renewal. Yet in practice the outward sign and inward state and effect do not always coincide; in Simon Magus
we have an example of the baptism of water without that of the
Spirit, and in Cornelius an example of the communication of
the Spirit before the application of the water. In the case of
infants, conversion, as a conscious act of the will, is impossible
and unnecessary. In adults the solemn ordinance was preceded
by the preaching of the gospel, or a brief instruction in its main
facts, and then followed by more thorough inculcation of the
apostolic doctrine. Later, when great caution became necessary
in receiving proselytes, the period of catechetical instruction and
probation was considerably lengthened.

2. The usual FORM of baptism was immersion. This is inferred from the original meaning of the Greek βαπτίζειν and
βαπτισμός;[1] from the analogy of John's baptism in the Jordan; from the apostles' comparison of the sacred rite with the
miraculous passage of the Red Sea, with the escape of the ark
from the flood, with a cleansing and refreshing bath, and with
burial and resurrection; finally, from the general custom of the
ancient church, which prevails in the East to this day.[2] But

---

[1] Comp. the German *taufen*, the English *dip*. Grimm defines βαπτίζω (the
frequentative of βάπτω): ' *immergo, submergo;* ' Liddell and Scott: '*to dip in* or
under the water.' But in the Sept. and the New Test. it has also a wider
meaning. Hence Robinson defines it: '*to wash, to lave, to cleanse by washing.*' See below.

[2] The Oriental and the orthodox Russian churches require even a *threefold*
immersion, in the name of the Trinity, and deny the validity of any other.
They look down upon the Pope of Rome as an unbaptized heretic, and
would not recognize the *single* immersion of the Baptists. The Longer Russian Catechism thus defines baptism : " A sacrament in which a man who
believes, having his body *thrice plunged* in water in the name of God, the
Father, the Son, and the Holy Ghost, dies to the carnal life of sin, and is
born again of the Holy Ghost to a life spiritual and holy." Marriott (in
Smith and Cheetham, I., 161) says : " *Triple immersion*, that is thrice dip-
ping the head while standing in the water, was the all but universal rule
of the church in early times," and quotes in proof Tertullian, Cyril of
Jerusalem, Chrysostom, Jerome, Leo I., etc. But he admits, on page 168 sq.,

sprinkling, also, or copious pouring rather, was practised at an early day with sick and dying persons, and in all such cases where total or partial immersion was impracticable. Some writers suppose that this was the case even in the first baptism of the three thousand on the day of Pentecost; for Jerusalem was poorly supplied with water and private baths; the Kedron is a small creek and dry in summer; but there are a number of pools and cisterns there. Hellenistic usage allows to the relevant expressions sometimes the wider sense of washing, bathing, sprinkling, and ceremonial cleansing.[1] Unquestionably, immersion expresses the idea of baptism, as a purification and renovation of the whole man, more completely than pouring or sprinkling, but it is not in keeping with the genius of the gospel to limit the operation of the Holy Spirit by the quantity or the quality of the water or the mode of its application. Water is absolutely necessary to baptism, as an appropriate symbol of the purifying and regenerating energy of the Holy Spirit; but whether the water be in large quantity or small, cold or warm, fresh or salt, from river, cistern, or spring, is relatively immaterial, and cannot affect the validity of the ordinance.

3. As to the SUBJECTS of baptism: the apostolic origin of *infant* baptism is denied not only by the Baptists, but also by many pædobaptist divines. The Baptists assert that infant

---

that *affusion* and *aspersion* were exceptionally also used, especially in clinical baptism, the validity of which Cyprian defended (*Ep.* 76 or 69 *ad Magnum*). This mode is already mentioned in the *Didache* (ch. 7) as valid ; see my book on the *Did.*, third ed., 1889, pp. 29 sqq.

[1] 2 Kings 5 : 14 (Sept.) ; Luke 11 : 38 ; Mark 7 : 4 ($\beta a\pi\tau\iota\sigma\mu\sigma\dot{\upsilon}s$ $\pi\sigma\tau\eta\rho\dot{\iota}\omega\nu$, etc.) ; Heb. 6 : 2 ($\beta a\pi\tau\iota\sigma\mu\hat{\omega}\nu$ $\delta\iota\delta a\chi\dot{\eta}$) ; 9 : 10 ($\delta\iota a\phi\dot{\delta}\rho\sigma\iota s$ $\beta a\pi\tau\iota\sigma\mu\hat{\sigma}\hat{\iota}s$). Observe also the remarkable variation of reading in Matt. 7 : 4 : $\dot{\epsilon}\dot{a}\nu$ $\mu\dot{\eta}$ $\beta a\pi\tau\dot{\iota}\sigma\omega\nu\tau a\iota$ (except they *bathe themselves*), and $\dot{\rho}a\nu\tau\dot{\iota}\sigma\omega\nu\tau a\iota$ (*sprinkle themselves*). Westcott and Hort adopt the latter in the text, the former in the margin. The Revision of 1881 reverses the order. The 'divers baptisms' in Heb. 9 : 10 (in the Revision " washings ") probably include all the ceremonial purifications of the Jews, whether by bathing (Lev. 11 : 25 ; 14 : 9 ; Num. 19 : 7), or washing (Num. 19 : 7 ; Mark 7 : 8), or sprinkling (Lev. 14 : 7 ; Num. 19 : 19). In the figurative phrase $\beta a\pi\tau\dot{\iota}\zeta\epsilon\iota\nu$ $\dot{\epsilon}\nu$ $\pi\nu\epsilon\dot{\upsilon}\mu a\tau\iota$ $\dot{a}\gamma\dot{\iota}\psi$, to overwhelm, plentifully to endow with the Holy Spirit (Matt. 3 : 11 ; Luke 3 : 16 ; Mark 1 : 8 ; John 1 : 33 ; Acts 1 : 5 ; 11 : 16), the idea of immersion is scarcely admissible since the Holy Spirit is *poured* out. See my *Hist. of the Apost. Ch.*, p. 569.

baptism is contrary to the idea of the sacrament itself, and, accordingly, an unscriptural corruption. For baptism, say they, necessarily presupposes the preaching of the gospel on the part of the church, and repentance and faith on the part of the candidate for the ordinance ; and as infants can neither understand preaching, nor repent and believe, they are not proper subjects for baptism, which is intended only for adult converts. It is true, the apostolic church was a missionary church, and had first to establish a mother community, in the bosom of which alone the grace of baptism can be improved by a Christian education. So even under the old covenant circumcision was first performed on the adult Abraham ; and so all Christian missionaries in heathen lands now begin with preaching, and baptizing adults. True, the New Testament contains no express command to baptize infants ; such a command would not agree with the free spirit of the gospel. Nor was there any compulsory or general infant baptism before the union of church and state ; Constantine, the first Christian emperor, delayed his baptism till his death-bed (as many now delay their repentance) ; and even after Constantine there were examples of eminent teachers, as Gregory Nazianzen, Augustin, Chrysostom, who were not baptized before their conversion in early manhood, although they had Christian mothers.

But still less does the New Testament *forbid* infant baptism ; as it might be expected to do in view of the universal custom of the Jews, to admit their children by circumcision on the eighth day after birth into the fellowship of the old covenant.

On the contrary, we have presumptive and positive arguments for the apostolic origin and character of infant baptism, first, in the fact that circumcision as truly prefigured baptism, as the passover the holy Supper ; then in the organic relation between Christian parents and children ; in the nature of the new covenant, which is even more comprehensive than the old ; in the universal virtue of Christ, as the Redeemer of all sexes, classes, and ages, and especially in the import of his own infancy, which has redeemed and sanctified the infantile age ; in his express invitation to children, whom he assures of a title to the kingdom of heaven, and whom, therefore, he certainly would not leave without the sign and seal of such membership; in the words of institution, which plainly look to the Christianizing, not merely of individuals, but of whole nations, including, of course, the children; in the express declaration of Peter at the first administration of the ordinance, that this promise of forgiveness of sins and of the Holy Spirit was to the Jews "and to their children;" in the five instances in the New Testament of the baptism of whole families, where the presence of children in most of the cases is far more probable than the absence of children in all; and finally, in the universal practice of the early church, against which the isolated protest of Tertullian proves no more, than his other eccentricities and Montanistic peculiarities; on the contrary, his violent protest implies the prevailing practice of infant baptism. He advised delay of baptism as a measure of prudence, lest the baptized by sinning again might forever forfeit the benefit of this ordinance; but he nowhere denies the apostolic origin or right of early baptism.

We must add, however, that infant baptism is unmeaning, and its practice a profanation, except on the condition of Christian parentage or guardianship, and under the guarantee of a Christian education. And it needs to be completed by an act of personal consecration, in which the child, after due instruction in the gospel, intelligently and freely confesses Christ, devotes himself to his service, and is thereupon solemnly admitted to the full communion of the church and to the sacrament of the holy Supper. The earliest traces of confirmation are supposed to be found in the apostolic practice of laying on hands, or symbolically imparting the Holy Spirit, after baptism.[1]

§ 55. *The Lord's Supper.*

The commentaries on Matt. 26 : 26 sqq., and the parallel passages in Mark and Luke; 1 Cor. 10 : 16, 17; 11 : 23 sqq.; John 6 : 47–58; 63.

[1] Acts 8 : 15 ; 19 : 6 ; Heb. 6 : 2.

D. WATERLAND (Episcopal., d. 1740) : *A Review of the Doctrine of the Eucharist*, a new edition, 1868 (*Works*, vols. IV. and V.).

J. DÖLLINGER : *Die Lehre von der Eucharistie in den drei ersten Jahrhunderten.* Mainz, 1826. (Rom. Cath.)

EBRARD : *Das Dogma vom heil. Abendmahl u. seine Geschichte.* Frankf. a. M., 1845, 2 vols., vol. I., pp. 1–231. (Reformed.)

J. W. NEVIN : *The Mystical Presence. A Vindication of the Reformed or Calvinistic Doctrine of the Holy Eucharist.* Philadelphia, 1846, pp. 199–256. (Reformed.)

KAHNIS : *Die Lehre vom heil. Abendmahl.* Leipz., 1851. (Lutheran.)

ROBERT WILBERFORCE : *The Doctrine of the Holy Eucharist.* London, 1853. (Anglican, or rather Tractarian or Romanizing.)

L. IMM. RÜCKERT : *Das Abendmahl. Sein Wesen und seine Geschichte in der alten Kirche.* Leipz., 1856. (Rationalistic.)

E. B. PUSEY : *The Doctrine of the Real Presence, as contained in the Fathers, from St. John to the Fourth General Council.* Oxford, 1855. (Anglo-Catholic.)

PHILIP FREEMAN : *The Principles of Divine Service.* London, 1855–1862, in two parts. (Anglican, contains much historical investigation on the subject of eucharistic worship in the ancient Catholic church.)

THOS. S. L. VOGAN : *The True Doctrine of the Eucharist.* London, 1871. (Anglican.)

JOHN HARRISON : *An Answer to Dr. Pusey's Challenge respecting the Doctrine of the Real Presence.* London, 1871, 2 vols. (Anglican, Low Church. Includes the doctrine of the Scripture and the first eight centuries.)

Dean STANLEY : *Christian Institutions*, London and New York, 1881, chs. IV., V., and VI. (He adopts the Zwinglian view, and says of the Marburg Conference of 1529 : "Everything which could be said on behalf of the dogmatic, coarse, literal interpretation of the institution was urged with the utmost vigor of word and gesture by the stubborn Saxon. Everything which could be said on behalf of the rational, refined, spiritual construction was urged with a union of the utmost acuteness and gentleness by the sober-minded Swiss.")

L. GUDE (Danish Lutheran) : *Den hellige Nadvere.* Copenhagen, 1887, 2 vols. Exegetical and historical. Reviewed in Luthardt's "Theol. Literaturblatt.," 1889, Nos. 14 sqq.

The sacrament of the holy Supper was instituted by Christ under the most solemn circumstances, when he was about to offer himself a sacrifice for the salvation of the world. It is the feast of the thankful remembrance and appropriation of his atoning death, and of the living union of believers with him, and their communion among themselves. As the Passover kept in

lively remembrance the miraculous deliverance from the land of
bondage, and at the same time pointed forward to the Lamb of
God; so the eucharist represents, seals, and applies the now
accomplished redemption from sin and death until the end of
time.   Here the deepest mystery of Christianity is embodied
ever anew, and the story of the cross reproduced before us.
Here the miraculous feeding of the five thousand is spiritually
perpetuated.   Here Christ, who sits at the right hand of God,
and is yet truly present in his church to the end of the world,
gives his own body and blood, sacrificed for us, that is, his very
self, his life and the virtue of his atoning death, as spiritual
food, as the true bread from heaven, to all who, with due self-
examination, come hungering and thirsting to the heavenly feast.
The communion has therefore been always regarded as the inmost sanctuary of Christian worship.

In the apostolic period the eucharist was celebrated daily in
connection with a simple meal of brotherly love (*agape*), in which
the Christians, in communion with their common Redeemer,
forgot all distinctions of rank, wealth, and culture, and felt
themselves to be members of one family of God.   But this
childlike exhibition of brotherly unity became more and more
difficult as the church increased, and led to all sorts of abuses,
such as we find rebuked in the Corinthians by Paul.   The love-
feasts, therefore, which indeed were no more enjoined by law
than the community of goods at Jerusalem, were gradually
severed from the eucharist, and in the course of the second and
third centuries gradually disappeared.

The apostle requires the Christians[1] to prepare themselves
for the Lord's Supper by self-examination, or earnest inquiry
whether they have repentance and faith, without which they
cannot receive the blessing from the sacrament, but rather provoke judgment from God.   This caution gave rise to the appropriate custom of holding special preparatory exercises for the
holy communion.

In the course of time this holy feast of love has become the

[1] 1 Cor. 11 : 28.

subject of bitter controversy, like the sacrament of baptism, and even the Person of Christ himself. Three conflicting theories—transubstantiation, consubstantiation, and spiritual presence of Christ—have been deduced from as many interpretations of the simple words of institution ("This is my body," etc.), which could hardly have been misunderstood by the apostles in the personal presence of their Lord, and in remembrance of his warning against carnal misconception of his discourse on the eating of his flesh.[1] The eucharistic controversies in the middle ages and during the sixteenth century are among the most unedifying and barren in the history of Christianity. And yet they cannot have been in vain. The different theories represent elements of truth which have become obscured or perverted by scholastic subtleties, but may be purified and combined. The Lord's Supper is: (1) a commemorative ordinance, a memorial of Christ's atoning sacrifice on the cross; (2) a feast of living union of believers with the Saviour, whereby they truly, that is spiritually and by faith, receive Christ, with all his benefits, and are nourished with his life unto life eternal; (3) a communion of believers with one another as members of the same mystical body of Christ; (4) a eucharist or thankoffering of our persons and services to Christ, who died for us that we might live for him.

Fortunately, the blessing of the holy communion does not depend upon the scholastic interpretation and understanding of the words of institution, but upon the promise of the Lord and upon childlike faith in him. And therefore, even now, Christians of different denominations and holding different opinions can unite around the table of their common Lord and Saviour, and feel one with him and in him.

[1] John 6 : 63 : "It is the spirit that quickeneth; the flesh profiteth nothing; the words that I have spoken unto you are spirit, and are life." This passage furnishes the key for the understanding of the previous discourse, whether it refers to the Lord's Supper, directly or indirectly, or not at all. That the ἐστί in the words of institution *may* indicate a figurative or symbolical (as well as a real) relation, is now admitted by all critical exegetes; that it *must* be so understood in that connection is admitted by those who are not under the control of a doctrinal bias. See my annotations to Lange's *Com. on Matthew,* 26 : 26, pp. 470 sqq.

§ 56. *Sacred Places.*

Although, as the omnipresent Spirit, God may be worshipped in all places of the universe, which is his temple,[1] yet our finite, sensuous nature, and the need of united devotion, require special localities or sanctuaries consecrated to his worship. The first Christians, after the example of the Lord, frequented the temple at Jerusalem and the synagogues, so long as their relation to the Mosaic economy allowed. But besides this, they assembled also from the first in private houses, especially for the communion and the love feast. The church itself was founded, on the day of Pentecost, in the upper room of an humble dwelling.

The prominent members and first converts, as Mary, the mother of John Mark in Jerusalem, Cornelius in Cæsarea, Lydia in Philippi, Jason in Thessalonica, Justus in Corinth, Priscilla in Ephesus, Philemon in Colosse, gladly opened their houses for social worship. In larger cities, as in Rome, the Christian community divided itself into several such assemblies at private houses,[2] which, however, are always addressed in the epistles as a unit.

That the Christians in the apostolic age erected special houses of worship is out of the question, even on account of their persecution by Jews and Gentiles, to say nothing of their general poverty; and the transition of a whole synagogue to the new faith was no doubt very rare. As the Saviour of the world was born in a stable, and ascended to heaven from a mountain, so his apostles and their successors down to the third century, preached in the streets, the markets, on mountains, in ships, sepulchres, caves, and deserts, and in the homes of their converts. But how many thousands of costly churches and chapels have since been built and are constantly being built in all parts of the world to the honor of the crucified Redeemer, who in the days of his humiliation had no place of his own to rest his head![3]

[1] Comp. John 4 : 24.

[2] ἐκκλησίαι κατ᾽ οἶκον, Rom. 16 : 5 ; 1 Cor. 16 : 19.   [3] Luke 9 : 58.

§ 57. *Sacred Times—The Lord's Day.*

Literature.

GEORGE HOLDEN : *The Christian Sabbath.* London, 1825. (See ch. V.)
W. HENGSTENBERG : *The Lord's Day.* Transl. from the German by *James Martin*, London, 1853. (Purely exegetical; defends the continental view, but advocates a better practical observance.)
JOHN T. BAYLEE : *History of the Sabbath.* London, 1857. (See chs. X.-XIII.)
JAMES AUG. HESSEY : *Sunday: Its Origin, History, and Present Obligation. Bampton Lectures, preached before the University of Oxford,* London, 1860. (Defends the Dominican and moderate Anglican, as distinct both from the Continental latitudinarian, and from the Puritanic Sabbatarian, view of Sunday, with proofs from the church fathers.)
JAMES GILFILLAN : *The Sabbath viewed in the Light of Reason, Revelation, and History, with Sketches of its Literature.* Edinb. 1861, republished and widely circulated by the Am. Tract Society and the "New York Sabbath Committee," New York, 1862. (The fullest and ablest defence of the Puritan and Scotch Presbyterian theory of the Christian Sabbath, especially in its practical aspects.)
ROBERT COX (F. S. A.) : *Sabbath Laws and Sabbath Duties.* Edinb. 1853. By the same : *The Literature of the Sabbath Question.* Edinb. 1865, 2 vols. (Historical, literary, and liberal.)
TH. ZAHN : *Geschichte des Sonntags in der alten Kirche.* Hannover, 1878.
There is a very large Sabbath literature in the English language, of a popular and practical character. For the Anglo-American theory and history of the Christian Sabbath, compare the author's essay, *The Anglo-American Sabbath,* New York, 1863 (in English and German), the publications of the *New York Sabbath Committee* from 1857–1886, the *Sabbath Essays,* ed. by *Will. C. Wood,* Boston (Congreg. Publ. Soc.), 1879 ; and A. E. WAFFLE : *The Lord's Day,* Philad. 1886.

As every place, so is every day and hour alike sacred to God, who fills all space and all time, and can be worshipped everywhere and always. But, from the necessary limitations of our earthly life, as well as from the nature of social and public worship, springs the use of sacred seasons. The apostolic church followed in general the Jewish usage, but purged it from superstition and filled it with the spirit of faith and freedom.

1. Accordingly, the Jewish HOURS of *daily* prayer, particularly

in the morning and evening, were observed as a matter of habit, besides the strictly private devotions which are bound to no time.

2. The LORD'S DAY took the place of the Jewish Sabbath as the *weekly* day of public worship. The substance remained, the form was changed. The institution of a periodical weekly day of rest for the body and the soul is rooted in our physical and moral nature, and is as old as man, dating, like marriage, from paradise.[1] This is implied in the profound saying of our Lord : "The Sabbath is made for man."

It is incorporated in the Decalogue, the moral law, which Christ did not come to destroy, but to fulfil, and which cannot be robbed of one commandment without injury to all the rest.

At the same time the Jewish Sabbath was hedged around by many national and ceremonial restrictions, which were not intended to be permanent, but were gradually made so prominent as to overshadow its great moral aim, and to make man subservient to the sabbath instead of the sabbath to man. After the exile and in the hands of the Pharisees it became a legal bondage rather than a privilege and benediction. Christ as the Lord of the Sabbath opposed this mechanical ceremonialism and restored the true spirit and benevolent aim of the institu-

---

[1] Gen. 2 : 3. This passage is sometimes explained in a proleptic sense ; but religious rest-days, *dies feriati*, are found among most ancient nations, and recent Assyrian and Babylonian discoveries confirm the pre-Mosaic origin of the weekly Sabbath. See Sayce's revision of George Smith's *Chaldean Account of Genesis,* Lond. and N. York, 1881, p. 89 : "If references to the Fall are few and obscure, there can be no doubt that the Sabbath was an Accadian [primitive Chaldæan] institution, intimately connected with the worship of the seven planets. The astronomical tablets have shown that the seven-day week was of Accadian origin, each day of it being dedicated to the sun, moon, and five planets, and the word Sabbath itself, under the form of *Sabattu,* was known to the Assyrians, and explained by them as 'a day of rest for the heart.' A calendar of Saints' days for the month of the intercalary Elul makes the 7th, 14th, 19th, 21st, and 28th days of the lunar months, Sabbaths on which no work was allowed to be done. The Accadian words by which the idea of Sabbath is denoted, literally mean : 'a day on which work is unlawful,' and are interpreted in the bilingual tablets as signifying ' a day of peace or completion of labors.' " Smith then gives the rigid injunctions which the calendar lays down to the king for each of these sabbaths. Comp. also *Transactions of Soc. for Bibl. Archœol.*, vol. V., 427.

tion.[1] When the slavish, superstitious, and self-righteous sab-batarianism of the Pharisees crept into the Galatian churches and was made a condition of justification, Paul rebuked it as a relapse into Judaism.[2]

The day was transferred from the seventh to the first day of the week, not on the ground of a particular command, but by the free spirit of the gospel and by the power of certain great facts which lie at the foundation of the Christian church. It was on that day that Christ rose from the dead; that he appeared to Mary, the disciples of Emmaus, and the assembled apostles; that he poured out his Spirit and founded the church;[3] and that he revealed to his beloved disciple the mysteries of the future. Hence, the first day was already in the apostolic age honorably designated as "the Lord's Day." On that day Paul met with the disciples at Troas and preached till midnight. On that day he ordered the Galatian and Corinthian Christians to make, no doubt in connection with divine service, their weekly contributions to charitable objects according to their ability. It appears, therefore, from the New Testament itself, that Sunday was observed as a day of worship, and in special commemoration of the Resurrection, whereby the work of redemption was finished.[4]

The universal and uncontradicted Sunday observance in the

---

[1] Matt. 12 : 1 sqq., 10 sqq., and the parallel passages in Mark and Luke; also John 5 : 8 sqq.; 6 : 23; 9 : 14, 16.

[2] Gal. 4 : 10; comp. Rom. 14 : 5; Col. 2 : 16. The spirit of the pharisaical sabbatarianism with which Christ and St. Paul had to deal may be inferred from the fact that even Gamaliel, Paul's teacher, and one of the wisest and most liberal Rabbis, let his ass die on the sabbath because he thought it a sin to unload him; and this was praised as an act of piety. Other Rabbis prohibited the saving of an ass from a ditch on the sabbath, but allowed a plank to be laid so as to give the beast a chance to save himself. One great controversy between the schools of Shammai and Hillel turned around the mighty question whether it was lawful to eat an egg which was laid on the sabbath day, and the wise Hillel denied it! Then it would be still more sinful to eat a chicken that had the misfortune to be born, or to be killed, on a sabbath.

[3] The day of Pentecost (whether Saturday or Sunday) is disputed, but the church always celebrated it on a Sunday. See § 24, p. 241.

[4] John 20 : 19, 26; Acts 20 : 7; 1 Cor. 16 : 2; Rev. 1 : 10.

second century can only be explained by the fact that it had its roots in apostolic practice. Such observance is the more to be appreciated as it had no support in civil legislation before the age of Constantine, and must have been connected with many inconveniences, considering the lowly social condition of the majority of Christians and their dependence upon their heathen masters and employers. Sunday thus became, by an easy and natural transformation, the Christian Sabbath or weekly day of rest, at once answering the typical import of the Jewish Sabbath, and itself forming in turn a type of the eternal rest of the people of God in the heavenly Canaan.[1] In the gospel dispensation the Sabbath is not a degradation, but an elevation, of the week days to a higher plane, looking to the consecration of all time and all work. It is not a legal ceremonial bondage, but rather a precious gift of grace, a privilege, a holy rest in God in the midst of the unrest of the world, a day of spiritual refreshing in communion with God and in the fellowship of the saints, a foretaste and pledge of the never-ending Sabbath in heaven.

The due observance of it, in which the churches of England, Scotland, and America, to their incalculable advantage, excel the churches of the European continent, is a wholesome school of discipline, a means of grace for the people, a safeguard of public morality and religion, a bulwark against infidelity, and a source of immeasurable blessing to the church, the state, and the family. Next to the Church and the Bible, the Lord's Day is the chief pillar of Christian society.

Besides the Christian Sunday, the Jewish Christians observed their ancient Sabbath also, till Jerusalem was destroyed. After that event, the Jewish habit continued only among the Ebionites and Nazarenes.

As Sunday was devoted to the commemoration of the Saviour's resurrection, and observed as a day of thanksgiving and joy, so, at least as early as the second century, if not sooner,

---

[1] Comp. Heb. 4 : 1–11 ; Rev. 4 : 13.

Friday came to be observed as a day of repentance, with prayer and fasting, in commemoration of the sufferings and death of Christ.

3. ANNUAL festivals. There is no injunction for their observance, direct or indirect, in the apostolic writings, as there is no basis for them in the Decalogue. But Christ observed them, and two of the festivals, the Passover and Pentecost, admitted of an easy transformation similar to that of the Jewish into the Christian Sabbath. From some hints in the Epistles,[1] viewed in the light of the universal and uncontradicted practice of the church in the second century, it may be inferred that the annual celebration of the death and the resurrection of Christ, and of the outpouring of the Holy Spirit, originated in the apostolic age. In truth, Christ crucified, risen, and living in the church, was the one absorbing thought of the early Christians; and as this thought expressed itself in the weekly observance of Sunday, so it would also very naturally transform the two great typical feasts of the Old Testament into the Christian Easter- and Whit-Sunday. The Paschal controversies of the second century related not to the fact, but to the time of the Easter festival, and Polycarp of Smyrna and Anicet of Rome traced their customs to an unimportant difference in the practice of the apostles themselves.

Of other annual festivals, the New Testament contains not the faintest trace. Christmas came in during the fourth century by a natural development of the idea of a church year, as a sort of chronological creed of the people The festivals of Mary, the Apostles, Saints, and Martyrs, followed gradually, as the worship of saints spread in the Nicene and post-Nicene age, until almost every day was turned first into a holy day and then into a holiday. As the saints overshadowed the Lord, the saints' days overshadowed the Lord's Day.

---

[1] 1 Cor. 5 : 7, 8 ; 16 : 8 ; Acts 18 : 21 ; 20 : 6, 16.

CHAPTER X.

ORGANIZATION OF THE APOSTOLIC CHURCH.

§ 58. *Literature.*

I. SOURCES.

The *Acts* represent the first, the *Pastoral Epistles* the second stage of the apostolic church polity. BAUR (*Die sogenannten Pastoralbriefe des Ap. Paulus*, 1835), HOLTZMANN (*Die Pastoralbriefe*, 1880, pp. 190 sqq.), and others, who deny the Pauline authorship of the Epistles to Timothy and Titus, date the organization laid down there from the post-apostolic age, but it belongs to the period from A.D. 60–70. The Epistles to the *Corinthians* (1 Cor. 12 : 28) and to the *Ephesians* (4 : 11), and the *Apocalyptic Epistles* (Rev. chs. 2 and 3) contain important hints on the church offices. Comp. the *Didache*, and the Epp. of CLEMENT and IGNATIUS.

II. GENERAL WORKS.

Comp. in part the works quoted in ch. IX. (especially VITRINGA), and the respective sections in the " Histories of the Apostolic Age " by NEANDER, THIERSCH (pp. 73, 150, 281), LECHLER, LANGE, and SCHAFF (Amer. ed., pp. 495–545).

III. SEPARATE WORKS.

Episcopal and Presbyterian writers during the seventeenth century, and more recently, have paid most attention to this chapter, generally with a view of defending their theory of church polity.

RICHARD HOOKER (called "the Judicious," moderate Anglican, d. 1600): *Ecclesiastical Polity*, 1594, and often since, best edition by *Keble*, 1836, in 4 vols. A standard work for Episcopal churchmen.

JOS. BINGHAM (Anglican, d. 1668): *Origines Ecclesiasticæ ; or, The Antiquities of the Christian Church*, first published 1710–22, in 10 vols. 8vo, and often since, Books II.–IV. Still an important work.

THOMAS CARTWRIGHT (the father of English Presbyterianism, d. 1603): *Directory of Church Government anciently contended for*, written in 1583, published by authority of the Long Parliament in 1644.

In the controversy during the Long Parliament and the Westminster Assembly, Bishop HALL and Archbishop USSHER were the most learned champions of episcopacy; while the five SMECTYMNIANS (so called from their famous tract *Smectymnuus*, 1641, in reply to Hall), i.e., Stephen Marshall, Edmund Calamy, Thomas Young, Matthew Newcomen, and William Spurstow, were the most prominent Presbyterians trying to "demonstrate the parity of bishops and presbyters in Scripture, and the antiquity of ruling elders." See also *A Vindication of the Presbyterian Government and Ministry*, London, 1650, and *Jus Divinum Ministerii Evangelici, or the Divine Right of the Gospel Ministry*, London, 1654, both published by the Provincial Assembly of London.   These books have only historical interest.

SAMUEL MILLER (Presbyterian d. 1850): *Letters concerning the Constitution and Order of the Christian Ministry*, 2d ed., Philadelphia, 1830.

JAMES P. WILSON (Presbyterian): *The Primitive Government of Christian Churches.*   Philadelphia, 1833 (a learned and able work).

JOH. ADAM MÖHLER (Rom. Cath., d. 1848): *Die Einheit der Kirche, oder das Princip des Katholicismus, dargestellt im Geiste der Kirchenväter der drei ersten Jahrhunderte.*   Tübingen, 1825 (new ed. 1844).   More important for the post-apostolic age.

RICH. ROTHE (d. 1866): *Die Anfänge der christlichen Kirche u. ihrer Verfassung*, vol. I.   Wittenb., 1837, pp. 141 sqq.   A Protestant counterpart of Möhler's treatise, exceedingly able, learned, and acute, but wrong on the question of church and state, and partly also on the origin of the episcopate, which he traces back to the apostolic age.

F. CHR. BAUR: *Ueber den Ursprung des Episcopates in der christl. Kirche.*   Tübingen, 1838.   Against Rothe.

WILLIAM PALMER (Anglo-Catholic): *A Treatise on the Church of Christ.*   London, 1838, 2 vols., 3d ed., 1841.   Amer. ed., with notes, by Bishop *Whittingham*, New York, 1841.

W. LÖHE (Luth.): *Die N. T. lichen Aemter u. ihr Verhältniss zur Gemeinde.*   Nürnb. 1848.   Also: *Drei Bücher von der Kirche*, 1845.

FR. DELITZSCH (Luth.): *Vier Bücher von der Kirche.*   Leipz., 1847.

J. KÖSTLIN (Luth.): *Das Wesen der Kirche nach Lehre und Geschichte des N. T.*, Gotha, 1854; 2d ed. 1872.

SAMUEL DAVIDSON (Independent): *The Ecclesiastical Polity of the New Testament.*   London, 1848; 2d ed. 1854.

RALPH WARDLAW (Independent): *Congregational Independency, in contradistinction to Episcopacy and Presbyterianism, the Church Polity of the New Testament.*   London, 1848.

ALBERT BARNES (Presbyterian, d. 1870): *Organization and Government of the Apostolic Church.*   Philadelphia, 1855.

CHARLES HODGE (Presbyterian, d. 1878) and others: *Essays on the Primitive Church Offices*, reprinted from the "Princeton Review," N. York,

1858. Also Ch. Hodge: *Discussions in Church Polity.* Selected from the "Princeton Review," and arranged by *W. Durant.* New York, 1878.

Bishop Kaye (Episc.): *Account of the External Discipline and Government of the Church of Christ in the First Three Centuries.* London, 1855.

K. Lechler (Luth.): *Die N. Testamentliche Lehre vom heil. Amte.* Stuttgart, 1857.

Albrecht Ritschl: *Die Entstehung der altkatholischen Kirche,* 2d ed., thoroughly revised, Bonn, 1857 (605 pp.). Purely historical and critical.

James Bannerman (Presbyterian): *The Church of Christ. A Treatise on the Nature, Powers, Ordinances, Discipline, and Government of the Christian Church.* Edinburgh, 1868, 2 vols.

John J. McElhinney (Episc.): *The Doctrine of the Church. A Historical Monograph.* Philadelphia, 1871. It begins *after* the apostolic age, but has a useful list of works on the doctrine of the Church from A.D. 100 to 1870.

G. A. Jacob (Low Church Episc.): *Ecclesiastical Polity of the New Testament: Study for the Present Crisis in the Church of England.* London, 1871; 5th Amer. ed., New York (Whittaker), 1879.

J. B. Lightfoot (Evangelical Broad Church Episcop., Bishop of Durham, very learned, able, and fair): *The Christian Ministry.* Excursus to his *Commentary on Philippians.* London, 1868, 3d ed. London, 1873, pp. 179-267; also separately printed in New York (without notes), 1879.

Charles Wordsworth (High Church Episcop., Bishop of St. Andrews): *The Outlines of the Christian Ministry.* London, 1872.

Henry Cotterill (Bishop of Edinburgh): *The Genesis of the Church.* Edinburgh and London, 1872.

W. Beyschlag: *Die christliche Gemeindeverfassung im Zeitalter des N. Testaments* (Crowned prize essay). Harlem, 1876.

C. Weizsäcker: *Die Versammlungen der ältesten Christengemeinden.* In the "Jahrbücher für Deutsche Theologie," Gotha, 1876, pp. 474-530. His *Apost. Zeitalter* (1886), pp. 606-645.

Henry M. Dexter (Congregationalist): *Congregationalism.* 4th ed. Boston, 1876.

E. Mellor: *Priesthood in the Light of the New Testament.* Lond., 1876.

J. B. Paton: *The Origin of the Priesthood in the Christian Church.* London, 1877.

H. Weingarten: *Die Umwandlung der ursprünglichen christl. Gemeindeorganisation zur katholischen Kirche,* in Sybel's "Histor. Zeitschrift" for 1881, pp. 441-467.

Edwin Hatch (Broad Church Episcop.): *The Organization of the Early Christian Churches.* Bampton Lectures for 1880. Oxford and

Cambridge, 1881.—Discusses the post-apostolic organization (Bishops, Deacons, Presbyters, Clergy and Laity, Councils, etc.). A learned and independent work, which endeavors to show that the development of the organization of the church was gradual; that the elements of which it was composed were already existing in human society; that the form was originally a democracy and became by circumstances a monarchy; and that the Christian church has shown its vitality and its divinity by readjusting its form in successive ages. German translation by AD. HARNACK, Giessen, 1883.

ARTHUR P. STANLEY (Broad Church Episc., d. 1881): *Christian Institutions*, London and New York, 1881. Ch. X. on the Clergy.

CH. GORE: *The Ministry of the Church*, London, 1889 (Anglo-Catholic).

Articles on the *Christian Ministry* by SANDAY, HARNACK, MILLIGAN, GORE, SIMCOX, SALMON, and others, in "The Expositor," London, 1887 and 1888.

§ 59. *The Christian Ministry, and its Relation to the Christian Community.*

Christianity exists not merely as a power or principle in this world, but also in an institutional and organized form which is intended to preserve and protect (not to obstruct) it. Christ established a visible church with apostles, as authorized teachers and rulers, and with two sacred rites, baptism and the holy communion, to be observed to the end of the world.[1]

At the same time he laid down no minute arrangements, but only the simple and necessary elements of an organization, wisely leaving the details to be shaped by the growing and changing wants of the church in different ages and countries. In this respect Christianity, as a dispensation of the Spirit, differs widely from the Mosaic theocracy, as a dispensation of the letter.

The ministerial office was instituted by the Lord before his ascension, and solemnly inaugurated on the first Christian Pentecost by the outpouring of the Holy Ghost, to be the regular organ of the kingly power of Christ on earth in founding, maintaining, and extending the church. It appears in the New Testa-

[1] Comp. Matt. 16 : 18; 18 : 18; 28 : 18–20; Mark 16 : 15; Luke 22 : 19; John 20 : 21–23; Eph. 2 : 20 ff.; 4 : 11 ff.

ment under different names, descriptive of its various functions:
—the "ministry of the word," "of the Spirit," "of righteousness," "of reconciliation." It includes the preaching of the
gospel, the administration of the sacraments, and church discipline or the power of the keys, the power to open and shut the
gates of the kingdom of heaven, in other words, to declare to
the penitent the forgiveness of sins, and to the unworthy excommunication in the name and by the authority of Christ.
The ministers of the gospel are, in an eminent sense, servants
of God, and, as such, servants of the churches in the noble
spirit of self-denying love according to the example of Christ,
for the eternal salvation of the souls intrusted to their charge.
They are called—not exclusively, but emphatically—the light of
the world, the salt of the earth, fellow-workers with God,
stewards of the mysteries of God, ambassadors for Christ. And
this unspeakable dignity brings with it corresponding responsibility. Even a Paul, contemplating the glory of an office,
which is a savor of life unto life to believers, and of death unto
death to the impenitent, exclaims: "Who is sufficient for these
things?"[1] and ascribes all his sufficiency and success to the un-
merited grace of God.

The internal call to the sacred office and the moral qualification for it must come from the Holy Spirit,[2] and be recognized
and ratified by the church through her proper organs. The
apostles were called, indeed, immediately by Christ to the work
of founding the church; but so soon as a community of believers
arose, the congregation took an active part also in all religious
affairs. The persons thus inwardly and outwardly designated
by the voice of Christ and his church, were solemnly set apart
and inducted into their ministerial functions by the symbolical
act of ordination; that is, by prayer and the laying on of the
hands of the apostles or their representatives, conferring or
authoritatively confirming and sealing the appropriate spiritual
gifts.[3]

---

[1] 2 Cor. 2 : 16. [2] Acts 20 : 28.
[3] Acts 6 : 6; 1 Tim. 4 : 14; 5 : 22; 2 Tim. 1 : 6.

Yet, high as the sacred office is in its divine origin and import, it was separated by no impassable chasm from the body of believers. The Jewish and later Catholic antithesis of clergy and laity has no place in the apostolic age. The ministers, on the one part, are as sinful and as dependent on redeeming grace as the members of the congregation; and those members, on the other, share equally with the ministers in the blessings of the gospel, enjoy equal freedom of access to the throne of grace, and are called to the same direct communion with Christ, the head of the whole body. The very mission of the church is, to reconcile all men with God, and make them true followers of Christ. And though this glorious end can be attained only through a long process of history, yet regeneration itself contains the germ and the pledge of the final perfection. The New Testament, looking at the principle of the new life and the high calling of the Christian, styles all believers " brethren," " saints," a " spiritual temple," a " peculiar people," a " holy and royal priesthood." It is remarkable, that Peter in particular should present the idea of the priesthood as the destiny of all, and apply the term *clerus* not to the ministerial order as distinct from the laity, but to the community; thus regarding every Christian congregation as a spiritual tribe of Levi, a peculiar people, holy to the Lord.[1]

The temporal organization of the empirical church is to be a means (and not a hindrance, as it often is) for the actualization of the ideal republic of God when all Christians shall be prophets, priests, and kings, and fill all time and all space with his praise.

NOTES.

1. Bishop Lightfoot begins his valuable discussion on the Christian ministry (p. 179) with this broad and liberal statement : " The kingdom of Christ, not being a kingdom of this world, is not limited by the re-

---

[1] 1 Pet. 2 : 5, 9 ; 5 : 3 ; comp. Rev. 1 : 6 ; 5 : 10 ; 20 : 6. The English " priest " (the German *Priester*) is etymologically a harmless contraction of " presbyter " (*i. e.*, elder), but has become a synonyme for the Latin *sacerdos* (ἱερεύς, כֹּהֵן), meaning an offerer of sacrifices and a mediator between God and the people Milton said rather sarcastically, " presbyter is priest writ large."

strictions which fetter other societies, political or religious. It is in the fullest sense free, comprehensive, universal. It displays this character, not only in the acceptance of all comers who seek admission, irrespective of race or caste or sex, but also in the instruction and treatment of those who are already its members. It has no sacred days or seasons, no special sanctuaries, because every time and every place alike are holy. Above all it has no sacerdotal system. It interposes no sacrificial tribe or class between God and man, by whose intervention alone God is reconciled and man forgiven. Each individual member holds personal communion with the Divine Head. To Him immediately he is responsible, and from Him directly he obtains pardon and draws strength."

But he immediately proceeds to qualify this statement, and says that this is simply the ideal view—" a holy season extending the whole year round, a temple confined only by the limits of the habitable world, a priesthood co-extensive with the race "—and that the Church of Christ can no more hold together without officers, rules, and institutions than any other society of men. " As appointed days and set places are indispensable to her efficiency, so also the Church could not fulfil the purposes for which she exists without rulers and teachers, without a ministry of reconciliation, in short, without an order of men who may in some sense be designated a priesthood. In this respect the ethics of Christianity present an analogy to the politics. Here also the ideal conception and the actual realization are incommensurate and in a manner contradictory."

2. Nearly all denominations appeal for their church polity to the New Testament, with about equal right and equal wrong : the Romanists to the primacy of Peter ; the Irvingites to the apostles and prophets and evangelists, and the miraculous gifts ; the Episcopalians to the bishops, the angels, and James of Jerusalem ; the Presbyterians to the presbyters and their identity with the bishops ; the Congregationalists to the independence of the local congregations and the absence of centralization. The most that can be said is, that the apostolic age contains fruitful germs for various ecclesiastical organizations subsequently developed, but none of them can claim divine authority except for the gospel ministry, which is common to all. Dean Stanley asserts that no existing church can find any pattern or platform of its government in the first century, and thus strongly contrasts the apostolic and post-apostolic organizations (l.c.) : " It is certain that the officers of the apostolical or of any subsequent church, were not part of the original institution of the Founder of our religion ; that of Bishop, Presbyter, and Deacon ; of Metropolitan, Patriarch, and Pope, there is not the shadow of a trace in the four Gospels. It is certain that they arose gradually out of the pre-existing institutions either of the Jewish synagogue, or of the Roman empire, or of the Greek municipalities, or under the pressure of local

emergencies. It is certain that throughout the first century, and for the first years of the second, that is, through the later chapters of the Acts, the Apostolical Epistles, and the writings of Clement and Hermas, Bishop and Presbyter were convertible terms, and that the body of men so-called were the rulers—so far as any permanent rulers existed—of the early church. It is certain that, as the necessities of the time demanded, first at Jerusalem, then in Asia Minor, the elevation of one Presbyter above the rest by the almost universal law, which even in republics engenders a monarchial element, the word 'Bishop' gradually changed its meaning, and by the middle of the second century became restricted to the chief Presbyter of the locality. It is certain that in no instance were the apostles called 'Bishops' in any other sense than they were equally called 'Presbyters' and 'Deacons.' It is certain that in no instance before the beginning of the third century the title or function of the Pagan or Jewish priesthood is applied to the Christian pastors. . . . . It is as sure that nothing like modern Episcopacy existed before the close of the first century as it is that nothing like modern Presbyterianism existed after the beginning of the second. That which was once the Gordian knot of theologians has at least in this instance been untied, not by the sword of persecution, but by the patient unravelment of scholarship."

§ 60. *Apostles, Prophets, Evangelists.*

The ministry originally coincided with the apostolate; as the church was at first identical with the congregation of Jerusalem. No other officers are mentioned in the Gospels and the first five chapters of the Acts. But when the believers began to number thousands, the apostles could not possibly perform all the functions of teaching, conducting worship, and administering discipline; they were obliged to create new offices for the ordinary wants of the congregations, while they devoted themselves to the general supervision and the further extension of the gospel. Thus arose gradually, out of the needs of the Christian church, though partly at the suggestion of the existing organization of the Jewish synagogue, the various general and congregational offices in the church. As these all have their common root in the apostolate, so they partake also, in different degrees, of its divine origin, authority, privileges, and responsibilities.

We notice first, those offices which were not limited to any one congregation, but extended over the whole church, or at least over a great part of it. These are apostles, prophets, and evangelists. Paul mentions them together in this order.[1] But the prophecy was a gift and function rather than an office, and the evangelists were temporary officers charged with a particular mission under the direction of the apostles. All three are usually regarded as extraordinary officers and confined to the apostolic age; but from time to time God raises extraordinary missionaries (as Patrick, Columba, Boniface, Ansgar), divines (as Augustin, Anselm, Thomas Aquinas, Luther, Melancthon, Calvin), and revival preachers (as Bernard, Knox, Baxter, Wesley, Whitefield), who may well be called apostles, prophets, and evangelists of their age and nation.[2]

1. APOSTLES. These were originally twelve in number, answering to the twelve tribes of Israel. In place of the traitor, Judas, Matthias was chosen by lot, between the ascension and Pentecost.[3] After the outpouring of the Holy Spirit, Paul was

---

[1] In Eph. 4 : 11, he adds "pastors and teachers." In 1 Cor. 12 : 28 he enumerates first, apostles ; secondly, prophets ; thirdly, teachers ; then powers, then gifts of healing, helps, governments, kinds of tongues. Neither list is intended to be strictly methodical and exhaustive.

[2] So Calvin, *Inst.* IV. ch. 3, § 4 : "*Secundum hanc interpretationem (quæ mihi et verbis et sententiæ Pauli consentanea videtur) tres illæ functiones [Apostoli, Prophetæ, Evangelistæ] non ideo institutæ in ecclesia fuerunt, ut perpetuæ forent, sed ad id modo tempus quo erigendæ erant ecclesiæ, ubi nullæ ante fuerant, vel certe a Mose ad Christum traducendæ. Quanquam non nego quin Apostolos postea quoque, vel saltem eorum loco Evangelistas interdum excitarit Deus, ut nostro tempore factum est.*" Most Protestant historians hold substantially the same view. The followers of the " Catholic Apostolic Church," usually called " Irvingites," claim to have apostles, prophets, evangelists raised up by the Lord himself in these last days preparatory to his Advent; but these "apostles" died one by one, and their places remain vacant. See my *Hist. of the Ap. Church,* pp. 516 sqq., and *Creeds of Christendom,* I. 905 sqq. In a very substantial sense the original apostles survive in their teaching, and need and can have no successors or substitutes.

[3] Some commentators wrongly hold that the election of Matthias, made before the pentecostal illumination, was a hasty and invalid act of Peter, and that Christ alone could fill the vacancy by a direct call, which was intended for Paul. But Paul never represents himself as belonging to the Twelve and distinguishes himself from them as their equal. See Gal., chs. 1 and 2.

added as the thirteenth by the direct call of the exalted Saviour. He was the independent apostle of the Gentiles, and afterward gathered several subordinate helpers around him. Besides these there were apostolic men, like Barnabas, and James the brother of the Lord, whose standing and influence were almost equal to that of the proper apostles. The Twelve (excepting Matthias, who, however, was an eye-witness of the resurrection) and Paul were called directly by Christ, without human intervention, to be his representatives on earth, the inspired organs of the Holy Spirit, the founders and pillars of the whole church. Their office was universal, and their writings are to this day the un-erring rule of faith and practice for all Christendom. But they never exercised their divine authority in arbitrary and despotic style. They always paid tender regard to the rights, freedom, and dignity of the immortal souls under their care. In every believer, even in a poor slave like Onesimus, they recognized a member of the same body with themselves, a partaker of their redemption, a beloved brother in Christ. Their government of the church was a labor of meekness and love, of self-denial and unreserved devotion to the eternal welfare of the people. Peter, the prince of the apostles, humbly calls himself a "fellow-pres-byter," and raises his prophetic warning against the hierarchical spirit which so easily takes hold of church dignitaries and alien-ates them from the people.

2. PROPHETS. These were inspired and inspiring teachers and preachers of the mysteries of God. They appear to have had special influence on the choice of officers, designating the persons who were pointed out to them by the Spirit of God in their prayer and fasting, as peculiarly fitted for missionary labor or any other service in the church. Of the prophets the book of Acts names Agabus, Barnabas, Symeon, Lucius, Manaen, and Saul of Tarsus, Judas and Silas.[1] The gift of prophecy in the wider sense dwelt in all the apostles, pre-eminently in John, the seer of the new covenant and author of the Revela-tion. It was a function rather than an office.

[1] Acts 11 : 28 ; 21 : 19 ; 13 : 1 ; 15 : 32.

3. EVANGELISTS, itinerant preachers, delegates, and fellow-
laborers of the apostles—such men as Mark, Luke, Timothy,
Titus, Silas, Epaphras, Trophimus, and Apollos.[1]   They may
be compared to modern missionaries.   They were apostolic
commissioners for a special work.   "It is the conception of a
later age which represents Timothy as bishop of Ephesus, and
Titus as bishop of Crete.   St. Paul's own language implies that
the position which they held was temporary.   In both cases
their term of office is drawing to a close when the apostle
writes."[2]

§ 61.   *Presbyters or Bishops.   The Angels of the Seven
Churches.   James of Jerusalem.*

We proceed to the officers of local congregations who were
charged with carrying forward in particular places the work
begun by the apostles and their delegates.   These were of two
kinds, Presbyters or Bishops, and Deacons or Helpers.   They
multiplied in proportion as Christianity extended, while the
number of the apostles diminished by death, and could, in the
nature of the case, not be filled up by witnesses of the life and
resurrection of Christ.   The extraordinary officers were necessary for the founding and being of the church, the ordinary
officers for its preservation and well-being.

The terms PRESBYTER (or Elder)[3] and BISHOP (or Overseer,

---

[1] 1 Tim. 1 : 3 ; 3 : 14 ; 2 Tim. 4 : 9, 21 ; Tit. 1 : 5 ; 3 : 12 ; 1 **Pet.** 5 : 12.
Calvin takes the same view of the Evangelists, *Inst.* IV., ch. 3, § 4 : "*Per
Evangelistas eos intelligo, qui quum dignitate essent Apostolis minores, officio
tamen proximi erant, adeoque vices eorum gerebant.   Quales fuerunt, Lucas,
Timotheus, Titus, et reliqui similes: ac fortassis etiam septuaginta discipuli,
quos secundo ab Apostolis loco Christus designavit* (Luc. 10 . 1)."

[2] Lightfoot, p. 197.   Other Episcopal writers, accepting the later tradition
(Euseb., *H. E.* III. 4 ; *Const. Apost.,* VII. 46), regard Timothy and Titus
as apostolic types of diocesan bishops.   So Bishop Chr. Wordsworth : *A
Church History to the Council of Nicæa* (1880, p. 42), and the writer of the
article "Bishop," in Smith and Cheetham (I. 211).

[3] The πρεσβύτεροι correspond to the Jewish *zekenim ;* see above, § 51.   It
was originally a term of age, and then of dignity, like *Senators, Senatus,*
γερουσία (comp. our "Senate," "Aldermen"), for the members of the govern-

Superintendent)¹ denote in the New Testament one and the
same office, with this difference only, that the first is borrowed
from the Synagogue, the second from the Greek communities;
and that the one signifies the dignity, the other the duty.²

1. The *identity* of these officers is very evident from the following facts:

ing body of a municipality or state. Aged and experienced men were generally chosen for office, but not without exceptions. Timothy was comparatively young when he was ordained (1 Tim. 4 : 12). The Roman Senate
consisted originally of venerable men, but after the time of Augustus the
ætas senatoria was reduced to twenty-five. The use of presbyter in the sense
of *sacerdos*, ἱερεύς, *priest*, dates from the time of Cyprian, and became common from the fifth century onward to the Reformation. In the New Test.
there is no trace of any special sacerdotal office or caste.

¹ The term ἐπίσκοπος occurs about a dozen times in the Septuagint for
various Hebrew words meaning "inspector," "taskmaster," "captain,"
"president" (see Trommius, *Concord. Gr. LXX. Interpr.* sub verbo, and also
sub ἐπισκοπή and ἐπισκοπέω). It was used in Egypt of the officers of a temple,
in Greece of overseers or guardians in general, or of municipal and financial
officers. In Athens the commissioners to regulate colonies and subject states
were called ἐπίσκοποι. The Spartans sent ἐπιμεληταί in the same capacity.
The term was not only applied to permanent officers, but also to the governing body, or a committee of the governing body. The feminine ἐπισκοπή is
not classical, but passed from the Sept. into the Greek Test. (Acts 1 : 20 ;
1 Tim. 3 : 1) and patristic usage with the meaning : the work or office of a
bishop (*inspectio, visitatio*). See Lightfoot, *Philippians*, 93 sqq., Gebhardt and
Harnack, *Patr. Apost. Op.* p. 5 ; Hatch, *l. c.*, 37 sqq., and Hatch, art. "Priest"
in Smith and Cheetham, II. 1698 sqq.

The distinction between them, as two separate orders of ministers, dates
from the second century, and is made a dogma in the Greek and Roman
churches. The Council of Trent (*Sess.* XXIII., cap. 4, and can. vii. *de sacra-
mento ordinis*) declares bishops to be successors of the apostles, and pronounces the anathema on those who affirm "that bishops are not superior to
priests (presbyters)." Yet there are Roman Catholic historians who are
learned and candid enough to admit the original identity. So Probst, *Sacra-
mente*, p. 215; Döllinger (before his secession), *First Age of the Church*,
Engl. transl. II. 111 ; and Kraus, *Real-Encykl. der christl. Alterthümer* (1880),
I. 62. Kraus says : "*Anfangs werden beide Termini* [ἐπίσκοπος and πρεσβύτερος]
vielfach mit demselben Werthe angewendet (Act 20 : 17, 28 ; Tit. 1 : 5 ; Clem.
ad Cor. I. 42, 44, 47). *Noch im zweiten Jahrh. findet man die Bischöfe auch
πρεσβύτεροι genannt, nicht aber umgekehrt. Sofort fixirt sich dann der Sprachgebrauch : der B. ist der Vorsteher der παροικία, διοίκησις, als Nachfolger der
Apostel ; ihm unterstehen Volk und Geistlichkeit ; ihm wohnt die Fülle der
priesterlichen Gewalt inne.*" The sacerdotal idea, however, does not synchro-
nize with the elevation of the episcopate, but came in a little later.

a. They appear always as a plurality or as a college in one and the same congregation, even in smaller cities, as Philippi.[1]

b. The same officers of the church of Ephesus are alternately called presbyters[2] and bishops.

c. Paul sends greetings to the "bishops" and "deacons" of Philippi, but omits the presbyters because they were included in the first term; as also the plural indicates.[3]

d. In the Pastoral Epistles, where Paul intends to give the qualifications for *all* church officers, he again mentions only two, bishops and deacons, but uses the term presbyter afterwards for bishop.[4]

Peter urges the "presbyters" to "tend the flock of God," and to "fulfil the office of bishops" with disinterested devotion and without "lording it over the charge allotted to them."[5]

e. The interchange of terms continued in use to the close of the first century, as is evident from the Epistle of Clement of Rome (about 95), and the *Didache*, and still lingered towards the close of the second.[6]

---

[1] The only apparent exceptions are 1 Tim. 3 : 2 ; Tit. 1 : 7, but there the definite article before ἐπίσκοπος is generic.

[2] Acts 20 : 17 (presbyters), 28 (bishops). In the English version the argument of the identity is obscured by the exceptional translation "overseers," instead of the usual "bishops." The Revised Version of 1881 has mended this defect by adopting "elders " and "bishops" in the text, and "presbyters" and "overseers" in the margin. The perversion of the passage, under the unconscious influence of a later distinction, began with Irenæus, who says (*Adv. Hær.* III. 14, 2): "The bishops *and* presbyters were called together (*convocatis episcopis et presbyteris*) at Miletus from Ephesus, *and the other neighboring cities* (*et a reliquis proximis civitatibus*)." The last addition was necessary to justify the plurality of bishops as distinct from presbyters. The latter alone are mentioned, Acts 20 : 17.

[3] Phil. 1 : 1 : πᾶσιν τοῖς ἁγίοις . . . σὺν ἐπισκόποις καὶ διακόνοις.

[4] 1 Tim. 3 : 1–13 ; 5 : 17–19 ; Tit. 1 : 5–7.

[5] 1 Pet. 5 : 1, 2 : πρεσβυτέρους . . . παρακαλῶ ὁ συνπρεσβύτερος · ποιμάνατε τὸ ἐν ὑμῖν ποίμνιον τοῦ θεοῦ, ἐπισκοποῦντες . . . The last word is omitted by ℵ and B. Tischendorf (8th ed.), Westcott and Hort, but ποιμάνατε implies the episcopal function, the oversight of the flock.

[6] Clem., *Ad Cor.* c. 42 (" bishops and deacons "), c. 44 (" bishopric . . . the presbyters "). The *Didache* (ch. 15) knows only bishops and deacons, as local officers, the former being identical with presbyters. Irenæus still occasionally calls the bishops "presbyters," and uses *successiones episcoporum* and *successiones presbyterorum* synonymously, but he evidently recognized the episcopal constitution. The higher office includes the lower, but not conversely.

With the beginning of the second century, from Ignatius onward, the two terms are distinguished and designate two offices ; the bishop being regarded first as the head of a congregation surrounded by a council of presbyters, and afterwards as the head of a diocese and successor of the apostles. The episcopate grew out of the presidency of the presbytery, or, as Bishop Lightfoot well expresses it : " The episcopate was formed, not out of the apostolic order by localization, but out of the presbyteral by elevation ; and the title, which originally was common to all, came at length to be appropriated to the chief among them." [1] Nevertheless, a recollection of the original identity was preserved by the best biblical scholars among the fathers, such as Jerome (who taught that the episcopate rose from the presbyterate as a safeguard against schism), Chrysostom, and Theodoret. [2]

The reason why the title bishop (and not presbyter) was given afterwards to the superior officer, may be explained from the

---

[1] *L. c.*, p. 194. He illustrates this usage by a parallel instance from the Athenian institutions. Neander has the same view of the origin of the episcopate. It dates, in fact, from Jerome.

[2] See the patristic quotations in my *Hist. of the Ap. Ch.* pp. 524 sq. Even Pope Urban II. (A.D. 1091) says that the primitive church knew only two orders, the deaconate and the presbyterate. The original identity of presbyter and bishop is not only insisted on by Presbyterians, Lutherans, and Congregationalists, but freely conceded also by Episcopal commentators, as Whitby, Bloomfield, Conybeare and Howson, Alford, Ellicott, Lightfoot, Stanley, and others. It is also conceded by purely critical historians, as Rothe, Ritschl, Baur (*K. Gesch.* I. 270), and Renan (*Les Évangiles*, p. 332). Renan calls the history of the ecclesiastical hierarchy the history of a triple abdication : first the community of believers committed their power to the presbyters, then the corps of presbyters abdicated to the bishop, and, last, the bishops to the pope (in the Vatican council). " *La création de l'épiscopat est l'œuvre du IIe siècle. L'absorption de l'Église par les 'presbyteri' est un fait accompli avant la fin du premier. Dans l'épître de Clément Romain, etc., ce n'est pas encore l'épiscopat, c'est le presbytérat qui est en cause. On n'y trouve pas trace d'un 'presbyteros' supérieur aux autres et devant détrôner les autres. Mais l'auteur proclame hautement que le presbytérat, le clergé, est antérieur au peuple.*" Comp. also Renan's *Saint Paul*, 238 sq., and *L'Église Chrétienne*, ch. VI. p. 85 sqq. This subject then may be regarded as finally settled among scholars. At the same time it should in all fairness be admitted that the *tendency* toward an episcopal concentration of presbyteral power may be traced to the close of the apostolic age.

fact that it signified, according to monumental inscriptions recently discovered, financial officers of the temples, and that the
bishops had the charge of all the funds of the churches, which
were largely charitable institutions for the support of widows
and orphans, strangers and travellers, aged and infirm people in
an age of extreme riches and extreme poverty.[1]

2. The *origin* of the presbytero-episcopal office is not recorded in the New Testament, but when it is first mentioned in
the congregation at Jerusalem, A.D. 44, it appears already as a
settled institution.[2] As every Jewish synagogue was ruled by
elders, it was very natural that every Jewish Christian congregation should at once adopt this form of government; this may be
the reason why the writer of the Acts finds it unnecessary to
give an account of the origin; while he reports the origin of
the deaconate which arose from a special emergency and had no
precise analogy in the organization of the synagogue. The
Gentile churches followed the example, choosing the already
familiar term bishop. The first thing which Paul and Barnabas did after preaching the gospel in Asia Minor was to organ-
ize churches by the appointment of elders.[3]

3. The office of the presbyter-bishops was to teach and to
rule the particular congregation committed to their charge.
They were the regular "pastors and teachers."[4] To them be-

[1] See Hatch, *Organiz.* Lect. II. and IV., and his art. "*Priest*" in Smith and
Cheetham, II. 1700. Hatch makes large use of the inscriptions found at
Salkhad, in the Haurân, at Thera, and elsewhere. He advances the new
theory that the bishops were originally a higher order of deacons and supreme
almoners of the sovereign congregation, while the presbyters had charge of
the discipline. He admits that bishops and presbyters were equals in rank,
and their names interchangeable, but that their relations differed in different
churches during the first two centuries, and that the chief function of the
bishop originally was the care and disposition of the charitable funds. Hence
the stress laid by Paul on the necessity of a bishop being ἀφιλάργυρος and
φιλόξενος. In the long series of ecclesiastical canons and imperial edicts, the
bishops are represented especially in the light of trustees of church property.

[2] Acts 11 : 30, at the time of the famine when the church of Antioch sent a
collection to the elders for their brethren in Judæa.

[3] Acts 14 : 23 ; comp. Tit. 1 : 5.

[4] ποιμένες καὶ διδάσκαλοι, Eph. 4 : 11.

longed the direction of public worship, the administration of discipline, the care of souls, and the management of church property. They were usually chosen from the first converts, and appointed by the apostles or their delegates, with the approval of the congregation, or by the congregation itself, which supported them by voluntary contributions. They were solemnly introduced into their office by the apostles or by their fellow presbyters through prayers and the laying on of hands.[1]

The presbyters always formed a college or corporation, a presbytery; as at Jerusalem, at Ephesus, at Philippi, and at the ordination of Timothy.[2] They no doubt maintained a relation of fraternal equality. The New Testament gives us no information about the division of labor among them, or the nature and term of a presidency. It is quite probable that the members of the presbyteral college distributed the various duties of their office among themselves according to their respective talents, tastes, experience, and convenience. Possibly, too, the president, whether temporary or permanent, was styled distinctively the bishop; and from this the subsequent separation of the episcopate from the presbyterate may easily have arisen. But so long as the general government of the church was in the hands of the apostles and their delegates, the bishops were limited in their jurisdiction either to one congregation or to a small circle of congregations.

The distinction of "teaching presbyters" or ministers proper, and "ruling presbyters" or lay-elders, is a convenient arrangement of Reformed churches, but can hardly claim apostolic sanction, since the one passage on which it rests only speaks of two functions in the same office.[3] Whatever may have been the distribution and rotation of duties, Paul expressly mentions

---

[1] Acts 14 : 23 ; Tit. 1 : 5 ; 1 Tim. 5 : 22 ; 4 : 14 ; 2 Tim. 1 : 6.   On the election, ordination and support of ministers, see my *Hist. Ap. Ch.* pp. 500–506.

[2] Acts 11 : 30 ; 14 : 23 ; 15 : 2, 4, 6, 23 ; 16 : 4 ; 20 : 17, 28 ; 21 : 18 ; Phil. 1 : 1 ; 1 Tim. 4 : 14 ; James 5 : 14 ; 1 Pet. 5 : 1.

[3] 1 Tim. 5 : 17 :   "Let the elders that rule well (οἱ καλῶς προεστῶτες πρεσβύτεροι) be counted of double honor (διπλῆς τιμῆς), especially those who labor in the word and in teaching (ἐν λόγῳ καὶ διδασκαλίᾳ)."   Some commen-

ability to teach among the regular requisites for the episcopal
or presbyteral office.[1]

4. The ANGELS of the Seven Churches in Asia Minor must
be regarded as identical with the presbyter-bishops or local pastors. They represent the presiding presbyters, or the corps of
regular officers, as the responsible messengers of God to the
congregation.[2] At the death of Paul and Peter, under Nero,
the congregations were ruled by a college of elders, and if the
Apocalypse, as the majority of critical commentators now hold,

tators emphasize καλῶς, some refer the "double honor" to higher rank and
position, others to better remuneration, still others to both.

[1] 1 Tim. 3 : 2 : "The bishop must be . . . . apt to teach (διδακτικόν)." The
same is implied in Tit. 1 : 9 ; Acts 20 : 28 ; and Heb. 13 : 17. Lightfoot takes
the right view (p. 192): "Though government was probably the first conception of the office, yet the work of *teaching* must have fallen to the presbyters
from the very first and have assumed greater prominence as time went on."
On the question of teaching and ruling elders, compare, besides other treatises,
Peter Colin Campbell : *The Theory of Ruling Eldership* (Edinb. and London,
1866), and two able articles by Dr. R. D. Hitchcock and Dr. E. F. Hatfield (both
Presbyterians) in the "American Presbyterian Review" for April and October,
1868. All these writers dissent from Calvin's interpretation of 1 Tim. 5 : 17,
as teaching two kinds of presbyters : (1) those who both taught and ruled, and
(2) those who ruled only ; but Campbell pleads from 1 Cor. 12 : 28 ; Rom.
12 : 8 ; and Acts 15 : 22, 25 for what he calls "Lay Assessors." Dr. Hitchcock
holds that the primitive presbyters were empowered and expected both to
teach and to rule. Dr. Hatfield tries to prove that the Christian presbyters,
like the Jewish elders, were only to rule ; the office of teaching having been
committed to the apostles, evangelists, and other missionaries. The last was
also the view of Dr. Thornwell, of South Carolina (on *Ruling Elders*), and is
advocated in a modified form by an Oxford scholar of great ability, Vice-Prin-
cipal Hatch (*l.c.* Lecture III. pp. 35 sqq., and art. "Priest" in Smith and
Cheetham, II. 1700). He holds that the Christian presbyters, like the Jewish,
were at first *chiefly* officers of *discipline*, not of worship, and that the fitness
for teaching and soundness in the faith were altogether subordinate to the
moral qualities which are necessary to a governor. He also remarks (p. 1707)
that neither Clement nor Ignatius makes any mention of presbyters in connection with teaching, and that teaching was a delegated function committed to
the wiser presbyters.

[2] Other interpretations of the apocalyptic angels : 1. Heavenly messengers,
guardian angels of the several churches. Origen. Jerome, De Wette, Alford,
Bishop Lightfoot. 2. Deputies or clerks of the churches, corresponding to
the *shelichai* of the synagogues. Vitringa, John Lightfoot, Bengel, Winer.
3. Figurative personifications of the churches. Arethas, Salmasius. 4.
Bishops proper. See my *Hist. of the Ap Ch.* pp. 537 sqq.

was written before the year 70, there was too little time for a radical change of the organization from a republican to a monarchical form. Even if we regard the " angels " as single persons, they were evidently confined to a single church, and subject to St. John; hence, not successors of the apostles, as the latter diocesan bishops claim to be. The most that can be said is that the angels were congregational, as distinct from diocesan bishops, and mark one step from the primitive presbyters to the Ignatian bishops, who were likewise congregational officers, but in a monarchical sense as the heads of the presbytery, bearing a patriarchal relation to the congregation and being eminently responsible for its spiritual condition.[1]

5. The nearest approach to the idea of the ancient catholic episcopate may be found in the unique position of James, the Brother of the Lord. Unlike the apostles, he confined his labors to the mother church of Jerusalem. In the Jewish Christian traditions of the second century he appears both as bishop and pope of the church universal.[2] But in fact he was only *primus inter pares*. In his last visit to Jerusalem, Paul was received by the body of the presbyters, and to them he gave an account of his missionary labors.[3] Moreover, this authority of James, who was not an apostle, was exceptional and due chiefly to his close relationship with the Lord, and his personal sanctity, which won the respect even of the unconverted Jews.

The institution of episcopacy proper cannot be traced to the apostolic age, so far as documentary evidence goes, but is very apparent and well-nigh universal about the middle of the second century. Its origin and growth will claim our attention in the next period.

---

[1] Rothe, Bunsen, Thiersch, and Bishop Lightfoot trace the institution of episcopacy to the Gentile churches in Asia Minor, and claim for it some sanction of the surviving apostle John during the mysterious period between A.D. 70 and 100. Neander, Baur, and Ritschl opposed Rothe's theory (which created considerable sensation in learned circles at the time). Rothe was not an Episcopalian, but regarded episcopacy as a temporary historical necessity in the ancient church.

[2] See § 27, pp. 264 sqq. [3] Acts 21 : 18 ; comp, 11 : 30 ; 12 : 17 ; and ch. 15.

§ 62. *Deacons and Deaconesses.*

DEACONS,[1] or helpers, appear first in the church of Jerusalem, seven in number. The author of the Acts (ch. 6) gives us an account of the origin of this office, which is mentioned before that of the presbyters. It had a precedent in the officers of the synagogue who had charge of the collection and distribution of alms.[2] It was the first relief of the heavy burden that rested on the shoulders of the apostles, who wished to devote themselves exclusively to prayer and the ministry of the word. It was occasioned by a complaint of the Hellenistic Christians against the Hebrew or Palestinian brethren, that their widows were neglected in the daily distribution of food (and perhaps money). In the exercise of a truly fraternal spirit the congregation elected seven Hellenists instead of Hebrews, if we are to judge from their Greek names, although they were not uncommon among the Jews in that age. After the popular election they were ordained by the apostles.

The example of the mother church was followed in all other congregations, though without particular regard to the number. The church of Rome, however, perpetuated even the number seven for several generations.[3] In Philippi the deacons took their rank after the presbyters, and are addressed with them in Paul's Epistle.

The office of these deacons, according to the narrative in Acts, was to minister at the table in the daily love-feasts and to attend to the wants of the poor and the sick. The primitive churches were charitable societies, taking care of the widows

---

[1] διάκονος, *diaconus*, in later usage also διάκων, *diacones* (in Cyprian's works and in synodical decrees).

[2] Lightfoot (*Hor. Hebr.* in Act. 6 : 3) says : " *Tralatum erat officium Diaconatus . . . in Ecclesiam Evangelicam ex Judaica. Erant enim in unaquaque Synagoga* פרנסים 'ג, *tres Diaconi quibus incubuit ista cura (pauperum).*"

[3] According to a letter of Cornelius, the Roman Church in 251 had forty-six presbyters, but only seven deacons, Euseb., *H. E.*, VI. 43. The places were filled by *sub*-deacons. In Constantinople, Justinian authorized the appointment of a hundred deacons.

and orphans, dispensing hospitality to strangers, and relieving the needs of the poor. The presbyters were the custodians, the deacons the collectors and distributors, of the charitable funds. To this work a kind of pastoral care of souls very naturally attached itself, since poverty and sickness afford the best occasions and the most urgent demand for edifying instruction and consolation. Hence, living faith and exemplary conduct were necessary qualifications for the office of deacon.[1]

Two of the Jerusalem deacons, Stephen and Philip, labored also as preachers and evangelists, but in the exercise of a personal gift rather than of official duty.

In post-apostolic times, when the bishop was raised above the presbyter and the presbyter became priest, the deacon was regarded as Levite, and his primary function of care of the poor was lost in the function of assisting the priest in the subordinate parts of public worship and the administration of the sacraments. The diaconate became the first of the three orders of the ministry and a stepping-stone to the priesthood. At the same time the deacon, by his intimacy with the bishop as his agent and messenger, acquired an advantage over the priest.

DEACONESSES,[2] or female helpers, had a similar charge of the poor and sick in the female portion of the church. This office was the more needful on account of the rigid separation of the sexes at that day, especially among the Greeks and Orientals. It opened to pious women and virgins, and chiefly to widows, a most suitable field for the regular official exercise of their peculiar gifts of self-denying charity and devotion to the welfare of the church. Through it they could carry the light and comfort of the gospel into the most private and delicate relations of domestic life, without at all overstepping their natural sphere. Paul mentions Phœbe as a deaconess of the church of Cenchreæ, the port of Corinth, and it is more than probable that Prisca (Priscilla), Mary, Tryphæna, Tryphosa, and Persis, whom he

---

[1] Acts 6 : 3 ; 1 Tim. 3 : 8 sqq.

[2] ἡ διάκονος, afterwards also διακόνισσα, diaconissa, diacona.

commends for their labor in the Lord, served in the same capacity at Rome.[1]

The deaconesses were usually chosen from elderly widows. In the Eastern churches the office continued to the end of the twelfth century.[2]

§ 63. *Church Discipline.*

Holiness, like unity and catholicity or universality, is an essential mark of the Church of Christ, who is himself the one, holy Saviour of all men; but it has never yet been perfectly actualized in her membership on earth, and is subject to gradual growth with many obstructions and lapses. The church militant, as a body, like every individual Christian, has to pass through a long process of sanctification, which cannot be complete till the second coming of the Lord.

Even the apostles, far as they tower above ordinary Christians, and infallible as they are in giving all the instruction necessary to salvation, never during their earthly life claimed sinless perfection of character, but felt themselves oppressed with manifold infirmities, and in constant need of forgiveness and purification.

Still less can we expect perfect moral purity in their churches. In fact, all the Epistles of the New Testament contain exhortations to progress in virtue and piety, warnings against unfaithfulness and apostasy, and reproofs respecting corrupt practices among the believers. The old leaven of Judaism and heathenism could not be purged away at once, and to many of the blackest sins the converts were for the first time fully exposed

---

[1] Rom. 16 : 1, where Phœbe is called (ἡ) διάκονος τῆς ἐκκλησίας τῆς ἐν Κεγχρεαῖς. Comp. 16 : 3, 6, 12. On the question whether the widows mentioned 1 Tim. 3 : 11 ; 5 : 9–15, were deaconesses, see my *Hist. of the Ap. Ch.*, p. 536.

[2] In the Roman Church, sisterhoods for charitable work have supplanted congregational deaconesses ; and similar institutions (without the vow of celibacy) were established among the Moravians, in the Lutheran, Episcopal, and other churches. The Roman Catholic Sisters of Charity, and the Evangelical Deaconesses of Kaiserswerth are worthy of special honor. See art. *Deacon, Deaconess,* and *Deaconesses* in Schaff's *Rel. Cyclop.*, vol. I. (1882), pp. 613 sqq.

after their regeneration by water and the Spirit. In the churches of Galatia many fell back from grace and from the freedom of the gospel to the legal bondage of Judaism and the "rudiments of the world." In the church of Corinth, Paul had to rebuke the carnal spirit of sect, the morbid desire for wisdom, participation in the idolatrous feasts of the heathen, the tendency to uncleanness, and a scandalous profanation of the holy Supper or the love-feasts connected with it. Most of the churches of Asia Minor, according to the Epistles of Paul and the Apocalypse, were so infected with theoretical errors or practical abuses, as to call for the earnest warnings and reproofs of the Holy Spirit through the apostles.[1]

These facts show how needful discipline is, both for the church herself and for the offenders. For the church it is a process of self-purification, and the assertion of the holiness and moral dignity which essentially belong to her. To the offender it is at once a merited punishment and a means of repentance and reform. For the ultimate end of the agency of Christ and his church is the salvation of souls; and Paul styles the severest form of church discipline the delivering of the back-slider "to Satan for the destruction of the flesh, that the spirit may be saved in the day of the Lord Jesus."[2]

The means of discipline are of various degrees of severity; first, private admonition, then public correction, and, finally, when these prove fruitless, excommunication, or temporary exclusion from all the means of grace and from Christian intercourse.[3] Upon sincere repentance, the fallen one is restored to the communion of the church. The act of discipline is that of the whole congregation in the name of Christ; and Paul himself, though personally absent, excommunicated the fornicator at Corinth with the concurrence of the congregation, and as being in spirit united with it. In one of the only two passages where our Lord uses the term *ecclesia*, he speaks of it as a court which, like the Jewish synagogue, has authority to decide dis-

---

[1] Comp. § 50, p. 450.   [2] 1 Cor. 5 : 5.
[3] Comp. Matt. 18 : 15–18 ; Tit. 3 : 10 ; 1 Cor. 5 : 5.

putes and to exercise discipline.[1] In the synagogue, the college
of presbyters formed the local court for judicial as well as administrative purposes, but acted in the name of the whole
congregation.

The two severest cases of discipline in the apostolic church
were the fearful punishment of Ananias and Sapphira by Peter
for falsehood and hypocrisy in the church of Jerusalem in the
days of her first love,[2] and the excommunication of a member
of the Corinthian congregation by Paul for adultery and incest.[3]
The latter case affords also an instance of restoration.[4]

§ 64. *The Council at Jerusalem.*

(Comp. § 34, pp. 335 sqq. and 346 sq.)

The most complete outward representation of the apostolic
church as a teaching and legislative body was the council con-
vened at Jerusalem in the year 50, to decide as to the authority
of the law of Moses, and adjust the difference between Jewish
and Gentile Christianity.[5]

We notice it here simply in its connection with the organization of the church.

It consisted not of the apostles alone, but of apostles, elders,
and brethren. We know that Peter, Paul, John, Barnabas, and
Titus were present, perhaps all the other apostles. James—not
one of the Twelve—presided as the local bishop, and proposed
the compromise which was adopted. The transactions were
public, before the congregation; the brethren took part in the
deliberations; there was a sharp discussion, but the spirit of
love prevailed over the pride of opinion; the apostles passed
and framed the decree not without, but with the elders and
"with the whole church;" and sent the circular letter not in
their own name only, but also in the name of "the brother

---

[1] Matt. 18 : 17. The words: "Tell it to the church," cannot apply to the
church universal, as ἐκκλησία does in Matt. 16 : 18.

[2] Acts 5 : 1–10.   [3] 1 Cor. 5 : 1 sqq.

[4] 2 Cor. 2 : 5–10.   [5] Acts, ch. 15, and Galatians, ch. 2.

elders " or " elder brethren " to " the brethren " of the congregations disturbed by the question of circumcision.[1]

All of which plainly proves the right of Christian people to
take part in some way in the government of the church, as they
do in the acts of worship. The spirit and practice of the apostles favored a certain kind of popular self-government, and the
harmonious, fraternal co-operation of the different elements of
the church. It countenanced no abstract distinction of clergy
and laity. All believers are called to the prophetic, priestly,
and kingly offices in Christ. The bearers of authority and
discipline should therefore never forget that their great work is
to train the governed to freedom and independence, and by the
various spiritual offices to build them up unto the unity of faith
and knowledge, and to the perfect manhood of Christ.

The Greek and Roman churches gradually departed from the
apostolic polity and excluded not only the laity, but also the
lower clergy from all participation in the legislative councils.

The conference of Jerusalem, though not a binding precedent,
is a significant example, giving the apostolic sanction to the
synodical form of government, in which all classes of the Christian community are represented in the management of public
affairs and in settling controversies respecting faith and discipline. The decree which it passed and the pastoral letter which
it sent, are the first in the long line of decrees and canons and
encyclicals which issued from ecclesiastical authorities. But it
is significant that this first decree, though adopted undoubtedly
under the guidance of the Holy Spirit, and wisely adapted to
the times and circumstances of the mixed churches of Jewish
and Gentile converts, was after all merely " a temporary expedient for a temporary emergency," and cannot be quoted as a
precedent for infallible decrees of permanent force. The spirit
of fraternal concession and harmony which dictated the Jerusalem compromise, is more important than the letter of the decree itself. The kingdom of Christ is not a dispensation of law,
but of spirit and of life.

[1] Acts 15 : 6, 12, 22, 23. See Notes.

NOTES.

I. There is an interesting *difference of reading* in Acts 15 : 23 (see the
critical editions), but it does not affect the composition of the conference, at least as far as the elders are concerned. The textus receptus
reads : οἱ ἀπόστολοι, καὶ οἱ πρεσβύτεροι, κ α ὶ ο ἱ ἀδελφοί (א‫', H, L, P,
Syr., etc.), "The apostles, and the elders, *and the* brethren send greeting unto the brethren," etc. So the E. V., except that it omits the
article twice. The Revised V., following the better attested reading : οἱ
ἀπόστολοι, καὶ οἱ πρεσβύτεροι ἀδελφοί, renders in the text : "The apostles,
and the elders, brethren," and in the margin : "The apostles and the
elder brethren" (omitting the comma). But it may also be translated :
"The apostles, and brother-elders," considering that Peter addresses the
elders as συμπρεσβύτερος, or "fellow-elder" (1 Pet. 5 : 1). The textus
rec. agrees better with ver. 22, and the omission of καὶ οἱ may possibly
have arisen from a desire to conform the text to the later practice which
excluded the laity from synods, but it is strongly supported by א*, A, B,
C, D, the Vulg. and Irenæus, and adopted by Tischendorf (ed. VIII.)
and Westcott and Hort.

Bellarmin and other Roman Catholic and certain Episcopal divines
get over the fact of the participation of the elders and brethren in a
legislative council by allowing the elders and brethren simply a silent
consent. So Secker (as quoted by Bishop Jacobson, in Speaker's Commentary on Acts 15 : 22) : "The apostles join the elders and brethren
with themselves . . . not to allow them equal authoity, but merely to
express their concurrence." Very different is the view of Dr. Plumptre
on Acts 15 : 22 : "The latter words ['with the whole church'] are important as showing the position occupied by the laity. If they concurred in the latter, it must have been submitted to their approval, and
the right to approve involves the power to reject and probably to
modify." Bishop Cotterill (*Genesis of the Church*, p. 379) expresses the
same view. "It was manifestly," he says, "a free council, and not a
mere private meeting of some office-bearers. It was in fact much what
the *Agora* was in archaic times, as described in Homer : in which the
council of the nobles governed the decisions, but the people were present and freely expressed their opinion. And it must be remembered
that the power of free speech in the councils of the church is the true
test of the character of these assemblies. Free discussion, and arbitrary
government, either by one person or by a privileged class, have been
found, in all ages and under all polities, to be incompatible with each
other. Again, not only were the multitude present, but we are expressly
told that the whole church concurred in the decision and in the action
taken upon it."

II. The *authority* of the Jerusalem conference as a precedent for
regular legislative councils and synods has been often overrated. On

the other hand, Canon Farrar (*Life and Work of St. Paul*, I. 431) greatly underrates it when he says : "It is only by an unwarrantable extension of terms that the meeting of the church of Jerusalem can be called a 'council,' and the word connotes a totally different order of conceptions to those that were prevalent at that early time. The so-called Council of Jerusalem in no way resembled the General Councils of the Church, either in its history, its constitution, or its object. It was not a convention of ordained delegates, but a meeting of the entire church of Jerusalem to receive a deputation from the church of Antioch. Even Paul and Barnabas seem to have had no vote in the decision, though the votes of a promiscuous body could certainly not be more enlightened than theirs, nor was their allegiance due in any way to James. The church of Jerusalem might out of respect be consulted, but it had no claim to superiority, no abstract prerogative to bind its decisions on the free church of God. The 'decree' of the 'council' was little more than the wise recommendation of a single synod, addressed to a particular district, and possessing only a temporary validity. It was, in fact, a local *concordat*. Little or no attention has been paid by the universal church to two of its restrictions ; a third, not many years after, was twice discussed and settled by Paul, on the same general principles, but with a by no means identical conclusion. The concession which it made to the Gentiles, in not insisting on the necessity of circumcision, was equally treated as a dead letter by the Judaizing party, and cost Paul the severest battle of his lifetime to maintain. If this circular letter is to be regarded as a binding and final decree, and if the meeting of a single church, not by delegates, but in the person of all its members, is to be regarded as a council, never was the decision of a council less appealed to, and never was a decree regarded as so entirely inoperative alike by those who repudiated the validity of its concessions, and by those who discussed, as though they were still an open question, no less than three of its four restrictions."

§ 65. *The Church and the Kingdom of Christ.*

Thus the apostolic church appears as a free, independent, and complete organism, a system of supernatural, divine life in a human body. It contains in itself all the offices and energies required for its purposes. It produces the supply of its outward wants from its own free spirit. It is a self-supporting and self-governing institution, within the state, but not of the state. Of a union with the state, either in the way of hierarchical supremacy or of Erastian subordination, the first three centuries afford no trace. The apostles honor the civil authority as a divine institution for the protection of life and property, for the reward of the good and the punishment of the evil-doer; and they enjoin, even under the reign of a Claudius and a Nero, strict obedience to it in all civil concerns; as, indeed, their heavenly Master himself submitted in temporal matters to Herod and to Pilate, and rendered unto Cæsar the things that were Cæsar's. But in their spiritual calling they allowed nothing to be prescribed or forbidden to them by the authorities of the state. Their principle was, to "obey God rather than men." For this principle, for their allegiance to the King of kings, they were always ready to suffer imprisonment, insult, persecution, and death, but never to resort to carnal weapons, or stir up rebellion and revolution. "The weapons of our warfare," says Paul, "are not carnal, but mighty through God." Martyrdom is a far nobler heroism than resistance with fire and sword, and leads with greater certainty at last to a thorough and permanent victory.

The apostolic church, as to its membership, was not free from impurities, the after-workings of Judaism and heathenism and the natural man. But in virtue of an inherent authority it exercised rigid discipline, and thus steadily asserted its dignity and holiness. It was not perfect; but it earnestly strove after the perfection of manhood in Christ, and longed and hoped for the reappearance of the Lord in glory, to the exaltation of his people. It was as yet not actually universal, but a little flock compared with the hostile hosts of the heathen and Jewish world; yet it carried in itself the principle of true catholicity, the power and pledge of its victory over all other religions, and its final prevalence among all nations of the earth and in all classes of society.

Paul defines the church as the body of Jesus Christ.[1] He thus represents it as an organic living system of various members, powers, and functions, and at the same time as the abode of Christ and the organ of his redeeming and sanctifying influ-

---

[1] Rom. 12 : 5 ; 1 Cor. 6 : 15 ; 10 : 17 ; 12 : 27 ; Eph. 1 : 23 ; 4 : 12 ; 5 : 23, 30; Col. 1 : 18, 24 ; 2 : 17.

ence upon the world. Christ is, in one view, the ruling head, in another the all-pervading soul, of this body. Christ without the church were a head without a body, a fountain without a stream, a king without subjects, a captain without soldiers, a bridegroom without a bride. The church without Christ were a body without soul or spirit—a lifeless corpse. The church lives only as Christ lives and moves and works in her. At every moment of her existence she is dependent on him, as the body on the soul, or the branches on the vine. But on his part he perpetually bestows upon her his heavenly gifts and supernatural powers, continually reveals himself in her, and uses her as his organ for the spread of his kingdom and the christianizing of the world, till all principalities and powers shall yield free obedience to him, and adore him as the eternal Prophet, Priest, and King of the regenerate race. This work must be a gradual process of history. The idea of a body, and of all organic life, includes that of development, of expansion and consolidation. And hence the same Paul speaks also of the growth and edification of the body of Christ, "till we all attain unto the unity of the faith, and of the knowledge of the Son of God, unto a full-grown man, unto the measure of the stature of the fulness of Christ." [1]

This sublime idea of the church, as developed in the First Epistle to the Corinthians, and especially in the Epistle to the Ephesians, when Paul was a prisoner chained to a heathen soldier, soars high above the actual condition of the little flocks of peasants, freedmen, slaves, and lowly, uncultured people that composed the apostolic congregations. It has no parallel in the social ideals of ancient philosophers and statesmen. It can only be traced to divine inspiration.

We must not confound this lofty conception of the church as the body of Christ with any particular ecclesiastical organization, which at best is only a part of the whole, and an imperfect approach to the ideal. Nor must we identify it with the still higher idea of the kingdom of God or the kingdom of heaven.

[1] Eph. 4 : 13.

A vast amount of presumption, bigotry, and intolerance has grown out of such confusion. It is remarkable that Christ speaks only once of the church in the organic or universal sense.[1] But he very often speaks of the kingdom, and nearly all his parables illustrate this grand idea. The two conceptions are closely related, yet distinct. In many passages we could not possibly substitute the one for the other without manifest impropriety.[2] The church is external, visible, manifold, temporal; the kingdom of heaven is internal, spiritual, one, and everlasting. The kingdom is older and more comprehensive; it embraces all the true children of God on earth and in heaven, before Christ and after Christ, inside and outside of the churches and sects. The historical church with its various ramifications is a pædagogic institution or training-school for the kingdom of heaven, and will pass away as to its outward form when its mission is fulfilled. The kingdom has come in Christ, is continually coming, and will finally come in its full grown strength and beauty when the King will visibly appear in his glory.

The coming of this kingdom in and through the visible churches, with varying conflicts and victories, is the proper object of church history. It is a slow, but sure and steady progress, with many obstructions, delays, circuitous turns and windings, but constant manifestations of the presence of him who sits at the helm of the ship and directs it through rain, storm, and sunshine to the harbor of the other and better world.

[1] Matt. 16 : 18. In the other passage where he speaks of the ἐκκλησία, Matt. 18 : 17, it denotes a local congregation (a synagogue), as in very many passages of the Acts and Epistles. We use the word church in two additional senses in which it never occurs in the New Test., because the thing did not exist then, namely, of church buildings and of denominations (as the Roman Church, Anglican Church, Lutheran Church).

[2] We could not say "Thy *church* come" (Matt. 6 : 9); "to such (children) belongeth the church" (Mark 10 : 14); "the *church* cometh not with observation" (Luke 17 : 21); "neither fornicators, etc. . . . . shall inherit the *church*" (1 Cor. 6 : 10); "the *church* is not eating and drinking, but righteousness and peace and joy in the Holy Spirit" (Rom. 15 : 17). On the other hand, it would be improper to call the kingdom of God "the body of Christ" or "the bride of the Lamb."

CHAPTER XI.

THEOLOGY OF THE APOSTOLIC CHURCH.

§ 66. *Literature.*

I. Works on the Theology of the whole New Testament.

AUGUST NEANDER (d. 1850): *Geschichte der Pflanzung und Leitung der christl. Kirche durch die Apostel.* Hamburg, 1832; 4th ed., 1847, 2 vols. (in the second vol.); Engl. transl. by *J. A. Ryland,* Edinb., 1842; revised and corrected by *E. G. Robinson,* New York, 1865. Neander and Schmid take the lead in a historical analysis of the different types of Apostolic doctrine (James, Peter, Paul, John).

SAM. LUTZ: *Biblische Dogmatik, herausgeg.* von *R. Rüetschi.* Pforzheim, 1847.

CHRIST. FRIEDR. SCHMID (an independent co-laborer of Neander, d. 1852): *Biblische Theologie des Neuen Testaments.* Ed. by Weizsäcker. Stuttg., 1853, 2d ed. 1859. 2 vols. (The Engl. translation by G. H. Venables, Edinb., 1870, is merely an abridgment.)

EDWARD REUSS (Prof. in Strassburg): *Histoire de la théologie chrétienne au siècle apostolique.* Strassb., 1852. 3d ed., Paris, 1864. 2 vols. English translation from the third French ed. by *Annie Harwood.* London, 1872. 2 vols.

LUTTERBECK (a liberal Rom. Cath.): *Die N. T.lichen Lehrbegriffe, oder Untersuchungen über das Zeitalter der Religionswende.* Mainz, 1852. 2 vols.

G. L. HAHN: *Die Theologie des Neuen Testaments.* Bd. I. Leipzig, 1854.

H. MESSNER: *Die Lehre der Apostel.* Leipz., 1856. Follows in the path of Neander.

F. CHR. BAUR (d. 1860): *Vorlesungen über neutestamentliche Theologie.* Leipz., 1864. Published after his death, by his son. Sums up the bold critical speculations of the founder of the Tübingen School. The most important part is the section on the system of Paul.

W. BEYSCHLAG: *Die Christologie des Neuen Testaments.* Berlin, 1866 (260 pages).

THOMAS DEHANEY BERNARD: *Progress of Doctrine in the New Testament.* Lectures on the Bampton Foundation. London and Boston, 1867.

H. EWALD: *Die Lehre der Bibel von Gott oder die Theologie des alten und neuen Bundes.* Leipzig, 1871–76. 4 vols. (More important for the Old Test. than for the New.)

A. IMMER: *Theologie des neuen Testaments.* Bern, 1877.

J. J. VAN OOSTERZEE: *Biblische Theol. des N. T.* (translated from the Dutch). Elberf., 1868. Engl. transl. by Prof. *G. E. Day.* New Haven, 1870. Another English translation by *Maurice J. Evans: The Theology of the New Test.*, etc. London, 1870.

BERNH. WEISS: *Bibl. Theologie des Neuen Testaments.* Berlin, 1868; 4th ed., 1884. Engl. translation, Edinb., 1883, 2 vols.

II. Separate works on the doctrinal types of the several apostles, by W. G. SCHMIDT, and BEYSCHLAG, on James; by MAYERHOFF, WEISS, and MORICH, on Peter; by USTERI, PFLEIDERER, HOLSTEN, LEATHES, IRONS, on Paul; by RIEHM, on Hebrews; by FROMMANN, KÖSTLIN, WEISS, LEATHES, on John—quoted in previous sections.

III. The doctrinal sections in the Histories of the Apostolic Church by LANGE, LECHLER, THIERSCH, STANLEY, and SCHAFF (pp. 614–679), besides NEANDER already mentioned. Comp. also CHARLES A. BRIGGS: *The idea, history and importance of Biblical Theology,* in the "Presbyterian Review," New York, July, 1882.

IV. For the contrast between the apostolic and the rabbinical theology, see FERD. WEBER (a missionary among the Jews, d. 1879): *System der altsynagogalen palästinsichen Theologie, aus Targum, Midrasch, und Talmud dargestellt. Nach des Verf. Tode herausgeg. von Frz. Delitzsch und G. Schnedermann.* Leipz., 1880.

§ 67. *Unity of Apostolic Teaching.*

Christianity is primarily not merely doctrine, but life, a new moral creation, a saving fact, first personally embodied in Jesus Christ, the incarnate Word, the God-man, to spread from him and embrace gradually the whole body of the race, and bring it into saving fellowship with God. The same is true of Christianity as it exists subjectively in single individuals. It begins not with religious views and notions simply; though it includes these, at least in germ. It comes as a new life; as regeneration, conversion, and sanctification; as a creative fact in experience, taking up the whole man with all his faculties and capacities, releasing him from the guilt and the power of sin, and reconciling him with God, restoring harmony and peace to the soul, and at last glorifying the body itself. Thus, the life of Christ is mirrored in his people, rising gradually, through the use of the means of grace and the continued exercise of faith and love, to its maturity in the resurrection.

But the new life necessarily contains the element of doctrine, or knowledge of the truth. Christ calls himself "the way, the truth, and the life." He is himself the personal revelation of saving truth, and of the normal relation of man to God. Yet this element of doctrine itself appears in the New Testament, not in the form of an abstract theory, the product of speculation, a scientific system of ideas subject to logical and mathematical demonstration; but as the fresh, immediate utterance of the supernatural, divine life, a life-giving power, equally practical and theoretical, coming with divine authority to the heart, the will, and the conscience, as well as to the mind, and irresistibly drawing them to itself. The knowledge of God in Christ, as it meets us here, is at the same time eternal life.[1] We must not confound truth with dogma. Truth is the divine substance, doctrine or dogma is the human apprehension and statement of it; truth is a living and life-giving power, dogma a logical formula; truth is infinite, unchanging, and eternal; dogma is finite, changeable, and perfectible.

The Bible, therefore, is not only, nor principally, a book for the learned, but a book of life for every one, an epistle written by the Holy Spirit to mankind. In the words of Christ and his apostles there breathes the highest and holiest spiritual power, the vivifying breath of God, piercing bone and marrow, thrilling through the heart and conscience, and quickening the dead. The life, the eternal life, which was from the beginning with the Father, and is manifested to us, there comes upon us, as it were, sensibly, now as the mighty tornado, now as the gentle zephyr; now overwhelming and casting us down in the dust of humility and penitence, now reviving and raising us to the joy of faith and peace; but always bringing forth a new creature, like the word of power, which said at the first creation, "Let there be light!" Here verily is holy ground. Here is the door of eternity, the true ladder to heaven, on which the angels of God are

---

[1] John 17 : 3.

ascending and descending in unbroken line. No number of systems of Christian faith and morals, therefore, indispensable as
they are to the scientific purposes of the church and of theology,
can ever fill the place of the Bible, whose words are spirit and
life.

When we say the New Testament is no logically arranged
system of doctrines and precepts, we are far from meaning that
it has no internal order and consistency. On the contrary, it
exhibits the most beautiful harmony, like the external creation, and like a true work of art. It is the very task of the historian, and especially of the theologian, to bring this hidden living order to view, and present it in logical and scientific forms.
For this work Paul, the only one of the apostles who received a
learned education, himself furnishes the first fruitful suggestions,
especially in his epistle to the Romans. This epistle follows a
logical arrangement even in form, and approaches as nearly to
a scientific treatise as it could consistently with the fervent,
direct, practical, popular spirit and style essential to the Holy
Scriptures and inseparable from their great mission for all
Christendom.

The substance of all the apostolic teaching is the witness of
Christ, the gospel, and the free message of that divine love and
salvation, which appeared in the person of Christ, was secured
to mankind by his work, is gradually realized in the kingdom of
God on earth, and will be completed with the second coming of
Christ in glory. This salvation also comes in close connection
with Judaism, as the fulfilment of the law and the prophets,
the substance of all the Old Testament types and shadows. The
several doctrines entering essentially into this apostolic preaching are most beautifully and simply arranged and presented in
what is called the Apostles' Creed, which, though not in its precise form, yet, as regards its matter, certainly dates from the
primitive age of Christianity. On all the leading points, the
person of Jesus as the promised Messiah, his holy life, his atoning death, his triumphant resurrection and exaltation at the
right hand of God, and his second coming to judge the world,

the establishment of the church as a divine institution, the communion of believers, the word of God, and the sacraments of baptism and the Lord's supper, the work of the Holy Spirit, the necessity of repentance and conversion, of regeneration and sanctification, the final completion of salvation in the day of Jesus Christ, the resurrection of the body, and the life everlasting—on all these points the apostles are perfectly unanimous, so far as their writings have come down to us.

The apostles all drew their doctrine in common from personal contact with the divine-human history of the crucified and risen Saviour, and from the inward illumination of the Holy Spirit, revealing the person and the work of Christ in them, and opening to them the understanding of his words and acts. This divine enlightenment is inspiration, governing not only the composition of the sacred writings, but also the oral instructions of their authors; not merely an act, but a permanent state. The apostles lived and moved continually in the element of truth. They spoke, wrote, and acted from the spirit of truth; and this, not as passive instruments, but as conscious and free organs. For the Holy Spirit does not supersede the gifts and peculiarities of nature, which are ordained by God; it sanctifies them to the service of his kingdom. Inspiration, however, is concerned only with moral and religious truths, and the communication of what is necessary to salvation. Incidental matters of geography, history, archæology, and of mere personal interest, can be regarded as directed by inspiration only so far as they really affect religious truth.

The revelation of the body of Christian truth essential to salvation coincides in extent with the received canon of the New Testament. There is indeed constant growth and development in the Christian church, which progresses outwardly and inwardly in proportion to the degree of its vitality and zeal, but it is a progress of apprehension and appropriation by man, not of communication or revelation by God. We may speak of a *secondary* inspiration of extraordinary men whom God raises from time to time, but their writings must be measured by the only infallible standard, the teaching of Christ and his apostles. Every true advance in Christian knowledge and life is conditioned by a deeper descent into the mind and spirit of Christ, who declared the whole counsel of God and the way of salvation, first in person, and then through his apostles.

The New Testament is thus but one book, the teaching of one mind, the mind of Christ. He gave to his disciples the words of life which the Father gave him, and inspired them with the spirit of truth to reveal his glory to them. Herein consists the unity and harmony of the twenty-seven writings which constitute the New Testament, for all emergencies and for perpetual use, until the written and printed word shall be superseded by the reappearance of the personal Word, and the beatific vision of saints in light.

§ 68. *Different Types of Apostolic Teaching.*

With all this harmony, the Christian doctrine appears in the New Testament in different forms according to the peculiar character, education, and sphere of the several sacred writers. The truth of the gospel, in itself infinite, can adapt itself to every class, to every temperament, every order of talent, and every habit of thought. Like the light of the sun, it breaks into various colors according to the nature of the bodies on which it falls; like the jewel, it emits a new radiance at every turn.

Irenæus speaks of a fourfold "Gospel." [1] In like manner we may distinguish a fourfold "Apostle," [2] or four corresponding types of apostolic doctrine. [3] The Epistle of James corresponds to the Gospel of Matthew; the Epistles of Peter and his addresses in the Acts to that of Mark; the Epistles of Paul to the Gospel of Luke and his Acts; and the Epistles of John to the Gospel of the same apostle.

---

[1] εὐαγγέλιον τετράμορφον. [2] ἀπόστολος.

[3] Comp. τύπος διδαχῆς, Rom. 6 : 17, and the remarks of Weiss *in loc.* (6th ed. of Meyer's *Com.*, 1881), who takes the word in specific application to the Pauline doctrine of Christianity ; while others refer it to the Christian system in general. Similar terms in Plato, τύποι παιδείας, τύπος τῆς διδασκαλίας, etc.

This division, however, both as regards the Gospels and the Epistles, is subordinate to a broader difference between Jewish and Gentile Christianity, which runs through the entire history of the apostolic period and affects even the doctrine, the polity, the worship, and the practical life of the church. The difference rests on the great religious division of the world, before and at the time of Christ, and continued until a native Christian race took the place of the first generation of converts. The Jews naturally took the Christian faith into intimate association with the divinely revealed religion of the old covenant, and adhered as far as possible to their sacred institutions and rites; while the heathen converts, not having known the law of Moses, passed at once from the state of nature to the state of grace. The former represented the historical, traditional, conservative principle; the latter, the principle of freedom, independence, and progress.

Accordingly we have two classes of teachers: apostles of the Jews or of the circumcision, and apostles of the Gentiles or of the uncircumcision. That this distinction extends farther than the mere missionary field, and enters into all the doctrinal views and practical life of the parties, we see from the accounts of the apostolic council which was held for the express purpose of adjusting the difference respecting the authority of the Mosaic law.

But the opposition was only relative, though it caused collisions at times, and even temporary alienation, as between Paul and Peter at Antioch.[1] As the two forms of Christianity had a common root in the full life of Christ, the Saviour of both Gentiles and Jews, so they gradually grew together into the unity of the catholic church. And as Peter represents the Jewish church, and Paul the Gentile, so John, at the close of the apostolic age, embodies the higher union of the two.

With this difference of standpoint are connected subordinate differences, as of temperament, style, method. James has been distinguished as the apostle of the law or of works; Peter, as the

---

[1] Gal. 2 : 11 sqq. See § 35, pp. 352 sqq.

apostle of hope; Paul, as the apostle of faith; and John, as
the apostle of love.   To the first has been assigned the phleg-
matic (?) temperament, in its sanctified Christian state, to the
second the sanguine, to the third the choleric, and to the fourth
the melancholic; a distribution, however, only admissible in a
very limited sense.   The four gospels also present similar differences; the first having close affinity to the position of James,
the second to that of Peter, the third to that of Paul, and the
fourth representing in its doctrinal element the spirit of John.

If we make the difference between Jewish and Gentile Christianity the basis of classification, we may reduce the books of
the New Testament to three types of doctrine: the Jewish
Christian, the Gentile Christian, and the ideal or unionistic
Christian.   The first is chiefly represented by Peter, the second
by Paul, the third by John.   As to James, he must be ranked
under the first type as the local head of the Jerusalem wing of
the conservative school, while Peter was the œcumenical head
of the whole church of the circumcision.[1]

§ 69. *The Jewish Christian Theology—I. James and the Gospel of Law.*

(Comp. § 27, and the Lit. given there.)

The Jewish Christian type embraces the Epistles of James,
Peter, and Jude, the Gospels of Matthew and Mark, and to
some extent the Revelation of John; for John is placed by
Paul among the "pillars" of the church of the circumcision,
though in his later writings he took an independent position

---

[1] Schelling's great idea of the three ages in the history of Christianity, the
Petrine (catholic), the Pauline (protestant), and the Johannean (future), is
well known.   I saw the aged philosopher shortly before his death, in a hotel
at Ragatz, Switzerland (August, 1854), and found him lying on his bed, as
pale as a corpse, but with clear mind and brilliant eyes.   When I asked him
whether he still held to that construction of church history, he emphatically
replied in the affirmative, but added that he had, on further reflection, made
room for *James* as the representative of the *Greek* church, in distinction from
the Roman or Petrine church.   I mention this as an interesting modification
of his theory, not made known before, and as containing a grain of truth.

above the distinction of Jew and Gentile. In these books, originally designed mainly, though not exclusively, for Jewish Christian readers, Christianity is exhibited in its unity with the Old Testament, as the fulfilment of the same. They unfold the fundamental idea of the Sermon on the Mount (Matt. 5 : 17), that Christ did not come to destroy the law or the prophets, but to "fulfil." The Gospels, especially that of Matthew, show historically that Jesus is the Messiah, the lawgiver, the prophet, priest, and king of Israel.

On this historical basis James and Peter build their practical exhortations, with this difference, that the former shows chiefly the agreement of the gospel with the law, the latter with the prophets.

JAMES, the brother of the Lord, in keeping with his life-long labors in Jerusalem, his speech at the Council, and the letter of the Council—which he probably wrote himself—holds most closely to the Mosaic religion, and represents the gospel itself as *law*, yet as the "*perfect* law of *liberty*." [1] Herein lies the difference as well as the unity of the two dispensations. The "law" points to the harmony, the qualifying "perfect" and "liberty" to the superiority of Christianity, and intimates that Judaism was *imperfect* and a law of *bondage*, from which Christ has set us free. Paul, on the contrary, distinguishes the gospel as freedom from the law, as a system of slavery; [2] but he re-establishes the law on the basis of freedom, and sums up the whole Christian life in the fulfilment of the law of love to God and to our neighbor; therein meeting James from the opposite starting-point. [3]

James, the Christian legalist, lays great stress on good *works* which the law requires, but he demands works which are the fruit of *faith* in Him, whom he, as his servant, reverently calls "the Lord of glory," and whose words as reported by Matthew are the basis of his exhortations. [4] Such faith, moreover, is the

---

[1] James 1 : 25 : εἰς νόμον τέλειον τὸν τῆς ἐλευθερίας.   [2] Gal. 5 : 1 ; 2 Cor. 3 : 6
[3] Comp. Gal. 6 : 2 (the law of Christ) ; Rom. 13 : 8 sqq. ; 3 : 22   8 : 2.
[4] Ch. 1 : 1 ; 2 : 1 : τὴν πίστιν τοῦ Κυρίου ἡμῶν 'Ιησοῦ Χριστοῦ τῆς δόξης.

result of a new birth, which he traces to "the will of God" through the agency of "the word of truth," that is, the gospel.[1] As to the relation between faith and works and their connection with justification at the tribunal of God, he seems to teach the doctrine of justification by faith *and works;* while Paul teaches the doctrine of justification by *faith alone,* to be followed by good works, as the necessary *evidence* of faith. The two views as thus stated are embodied in the Roman Catholic and the evangelical Protestant confessions, and form one of the chief topics of controversy. But the contradiction between James and Paul is verbal rather than logical and doctrinal, and admits of a reconciliation which lies in the inseparable connection of a living faith and good works, or of justification and sanctification, so that they supplement and confirm each other, the one laying the true foundation in character, the other insisting on the practical manifestation. James wrote probably long before he had seen any of Paul's Epistles, certainly with no view to refute his doctrine or even to guard it against antinomian abuse; for this was quite unnecessary, as Paul did it clearly enough himself, and it would have been quite useless for Jewish Christian readers who were exposed to the danger of a barren legalism, but not of a pseudo-Pauline liberalism and antinomianism. They cannot, indeed, be made to say precisely the same thing, only using one or more of the three terms, "to justify," "faith," "works" in different senses; but they wrote from different standpoints and opposed different errors, and thus presented two distinct aspects of the same truth. James says: Faith is dead without works. Paul says: Works are dead without faith. The one insists on a working faith, the other on faithful works. Both are right: James in opposition to the dead Jewish orthodoxy, Paul in opposition to self-righteous legalism. James does not demand works without faith, but works prompted by faith;[2] while Paul, on the other hand, likewise

[1] Ch. 1 : 18 : βουληθεὶς ἀπεκύησεν ἡμᾶς λόγῳ ἀληθείας.
[2] Ch. 2 : 22 : ἡ πίστις συνήργει τοῖς ἔργοις αὐτοῦ καὶ ἐκ τῶν ἔργων ἡ πίστις ἐτελειώθη.

declares a faith worthless which is without love, though it remove mountains,[1] and would never have attributed a justifying
power to the mere belief in the existence of God, which James
calls the trembling faith of demons.[2] But James mainly looks
at the fruit, Paul at the root; the one is concerned for the evidence, the other for the principle; the one takes the practical
and experimental view, and reasons from the effect to the cause,
the other goes deeper to the inmost springs of action, but comes
to the same result: a holy life of love and obedience as the
necessary evidence of true faith. And this, after all, is the
ultimate standard of judgment according to Paul as well as
James.[3] Paul puts the solution of the difficulty in one sentence:
"faith working through love." This is the Irenicon of contending apostles and contending churches.[4]

The Epistle of James stands at the head of the Catholic Epistles, so called, and represents the first and lowest stage of
Christian knowledge. It is doctrinally very meagre, but emi-

---

[1] 1 Cor. 13 : 2.   [2] Ch. 2 : 19.

[3] See Rom. 2 : 6 (ὃς ἀποδώσει ἑκάστῳ κατὰ τὰ ἔργα αὐτοῦ); 2 Cor. 5 : 10 ;
Gal. 6 : 7; comp. Matt. 12 : 37 ; 25 : 35 sqq. The solution of the apparent
contradiction between the doctrines of justification by faith and judgment by
works lies in the character of the works as being the evidence of faith.

[4] Gal. 5 : 6 : πίστις δἰ ἀγάπης ἐνεργουμένη, is operative (in the middle sense,
as always in the New Test.). "These words," says Bishop Lightfoot (in loc.),
"bridge the gulf which seems to separate the language of St. Paul and St.
James. Both assert a principle of practical energy, as opposed to a barren
inactive theory." To quote from my own commentary on the passage (1882):
"The sentence 'faith working through love' reconciles the doctrine of Paul
with that of James; comp. 6 : 15 ; 1 Thess. 1 : 3 ; 1 Cor. ch. 13 ; 1 Tim. 1 : 5 ;
James 2 : 22. Here is the basis for a final settlement of the controversy on
the doctrine of justification. Romanism (following exclusively the language
of James) teaches justification by faith *and works;* Protestantism (on the authority of Paul), justification by faith *alone;* Paul and James combined:
justification and salvation by *faith working through love.* Man is justified
by faith alone, but faith remains not alone : it is the fruitful mother of
good works, which are summed up in love to God and love to men. Faith and
love are as inseparable as light and heat in the sun. Christ's merits are the
objective and *meritorious ground* of justification ; faith (as the organ of appropriation) is the *subjective condition;* love or good works are the necessary *evidence;* without love faith is dead, according to James, or no faith at all,
according to Paul. A great deal of misunderstanding in this and other theological controversies has arisen from the different use of terms."

nently practical and popular.   It enjoins a simple, earnest, and devout style of piety that visits the orphans and widows, and keeps itself unspotted from the world.[1]

The close connection between the Epistle of James and the Gospel of Matthew arises naturally from their common Jewish Christian and Palestinian origin.

NOTES.

I. JAMES and PAUL.   The apparent contradiction in the doctrine of justification appears in James 2 : 14–26, as compared with Rom. 3 : 20 sqq. ; 4 : 1 sqq. ; Gal. 2 : 16 sqq.   Paul says (Rom. 3 : 28) : "Man is justified by faith apart from works of law" (πίστει χωρὶς ἔργων νόμου), comp. Gal. 2 : 16 (οὐ δικαιοῦται ἄνϑρωπος ἐξ ἔργων νόμου ἐὰν μὴ διὰ πίστεως Χριστοῦ Ἰησοῦ), and appeals to the example of Abraham, who was justified by faith *before* he was circumcised (Gen. 17 : 10).   James says (2 : 24) : "By works a man is justified, and not only by faith" (ἐξ ἔργων δικαιοῦται ἄνϑρωπος καὶ οὐκ ἐκ πίστεως μόνον), and appeals to the example of the same Abraham who showed his true faith in God by offering up his son Isaac upon the altar (Gen. 22 : 9, 12).   Luther makes the contradiction worse by unnecessarily inserting the word *allein* (*sola fide*) in Rom. 3 : 28, though not without precedent (see my note on the passage in the Am. ed. of Lange on *Romans*, p. 136).   The great Reformer could not reconcile the two apostles, and rashly called the Epistle of James an "epistle of straw" (*eine recht ströherne Epistel*, Pref. to the New Test., 1524).

Baur, from a purely critical point of view, comes to the same conclusion ; he regards the Epistle of James as a direct attack upon the very heart of the doctrine of Paul, and treats all attempts at reconciliation as vain. (*Vorles. über neutestam. Theol.*, p. 277).   So also Renan and Weiffenbach. Renan (*St. Paul*, ch. 10) asserts without proof that James organized a Jewish counter-mission to undermine Paul.   But in this case, James, as a sensible and practical man, ought to have written to Gentile Christians, not to "the twelve tribes," who needed no warning against Paul and his doctrine.   His Epistle represents simply an earlier and lower form of Christianity ignorant of the higher, yet preparatory to it, as the preaching of John the Baptist prepared the way for that of Christ.   It was written without any reference to Paul, probably before the Council of Jerusalem and before the circumcision controversy, in the earliest stage of the apostolic church as it is described in the first chapters of the Acts, when the Christians were not yet clearly distinguished and finally separated from the Jews.   This view of the early origin of the Epistle is maintained by some of the ablest historians and commentators, as

[1] Ch. 1 : 27 ; comp. 5 : 13 sqq., and the concluding verse.

Neander, Schneckenburger, Theile, Thiersch, Beyschlag, Alford, Bassett, Plumptre, Stanley. Weiss also says very confidently (*Bibl. Theol.*, 3d ed., p. 120) : "*Der Brief gehört der vorpaulinischen Zeit an und steht jeden-falls zeitlich wie inhaltlich dem ersten Brief Petri am nächsten.*" He there-fore treats both James and Peter on their own merits, without regard to Paul's teaching. Comp. his *Einleitung in d. N. T.* (1886), p. 400.

II. JAMES and MATTHEW. The correspondence has often been fully pointed out by Theile and other commentators. James contains more reminiscences of the words of Christ than any other Epistle, especially from the Sermon on the Mount. Comp. James 1 : 2 with Matt. 5 : 10–12 ; James 1 : 4 with Matt. 5 : 48 ; James 1 : 17 with Matt. 7 : 11 ; James 1 : 20 with Matt. 5 : 22 ; James 1 : 22 sqq. with Matt. 7 : 21 sq. ; James 1 : 23 with Matt. 7 : 26 ; James 2 : 13 with Matt. 6 : 14 sq. ; James 2 : 14 with Matt. 7 : 21–23 ; James 3 : 2 with Matt. 12 : 36, 37 ; James 3 : 17, 18 with Matt. 5 : 9 ; James 4 : 3 with Matt. 7 : 7 ; James 4 : 4 with Matt. 6 : 24 ; James 5 : 12 with Matt. 5 : 34. According to a notice in the pseudo-Athanasian Synopsis, James "the Bishop of Jerusalem" translated the Gospel of Matthew from the Aramaic into the Greek. But there are also parallelisms between James and the first Epistle of Peter, and even be-tween James and the apocryphal books of Ecclesiasticus and the Wisdom of Solomon. See Plumptre, *Com. on James*, pp. 32 sq.

§ 70. II. *Peter and the Gospel of Hope.*

(Comp. the Lit. in §§ 25 and 26.)

PETER stands between James and Paul, and forms the transi-tion from the extreme conservatism of the one to the progres-sive liberalism of the other. The germ of his doctrinal system is contained in his great confession that Jesus is the Messiah, the Son of the living God.[1] A short creed indeed, with only one article, but a fundamental and all-comprehensive article, the corner-stone of the Christian church. His system, therefore, is christological, and supplements the anthropological type of James. His addresses in the Acts and his Epistles are full of the fresh impressions which the personal intercourse with Christ made upon his noble, enthusiastic, and impulsive nature. Chris-tianity is the fulfilment of all the Messianic prophecies ; but it is at the same time itself a prophecy of the glorious return of the Lord. This future glorious manifestation is so certain that it is

[1] Matt. 16 : 16 ; comp. John 6 : 68, 69.

already anticipated here in blessed joy by a lively hope which
stimulates to a holy life of preparation for the end. Hence,
Peter eminently deserves to be called "the Apostle of hope." [1]

I. Peter began his testimony with the announcement of the
historical facts of the resurrection of Jesus and the outpouring of
the Holy Spirit, and represents these facts as the divine seal of
his Messiahship, according to the prophets of old, who bear
witness to him that through his name every one that believes
shall receive remission of sins. The same Jesus whom God
raised from the dead and exalted to his right hand as Lord and
Saviour, will come again to judge his people and to bring in
seasons of refreshing from his presence and the *apokatastasis*
or restitution of all things to their normal and perfect state,
thus completely fulfilling the Messianic prophecies. There is
no salvation out of the Lord Jesus Christ. The condition of
this salvation is the acknowledgment of his Messiahship and
the change of mind and conduct from the service of sin to
holiness.[2]

These views are so simple, primitive, and appropriate that we
cannot conceive how Peter could have preached differently and
more effectively in that early stage of Christianity. We need
not wonder at the conversion of three thousand souls in consequence of his pentecostal sermon. His knowledge gradually
widened and deepened with the expansion of Christianity and
the conversion of Cornelius. A special revelation enlightened
him on the question of circumcision and brought him to the
conviction that "in every nation he that fears God and works
righteousness, is acceptable to him," and that Jews and Gentiles
are saved alike by the grace of Christ through faith, without
the unbearable yoke of the ceremonial law.[3]

---

[1] Weiss (p. 172) : "*Die Hoffnung bildet in der Anschauung des Petrus den
eigentlichen Mittelpunkt des Christenlebens. Sie erscheint bei ihm in der höchsten Energie, wonach die gehoffte Vollendung bereits unmittelbar nahe gerückt
erscheint.*"

[2] See his pentecostal sermon, Acts 2 : 14 sqq. ; his addresses to the people,
3 : 12 sqq. ; before the Sanhedrin, 4 : 8 sqq. ; 5 : 29 sqq. ; to Cornelius,
10 : 34 sqq.   [3] Acts 10 : 35 ; 15 : 7–11.

II. The Epistles of Peter represent this riper stage of knowl edge. They agree substantially with the teaching of Paul. The leading idea is the same as that presented in his addresses in the Acts : Christ the fulfiller of the Messianic prophecies, and the hope of the Christian. Peter's christology is free of all speculative elements, and simply derived from the impression of the historical and risen Jesus. He emphasizes in the first Epistle, as in his earlier addresses, the resurrection whereby God "begat us again unto a lively hope, unto an inheritance incorruptible, and undefiled, and that fadeth not away, reserved in heaven," when " the chief shepherd shall be manifested," and we "shall receive the crown of glory." And in the second Epistle he points forward to "new heavens and a new earth, wherein dwelleth righteousness." [1] He thus connects tne resurrection of Christ with the final consummation of which it is the sure pledge. But, besides the resurrection, he brings out also the atoning efficacy of the death of Christ almost as strongly and clearly as Paul. Christ " suffered for sins once, the righteous for the unrighteous, that he might bring us to God; " he himself "bare our sins in his body upon the tree, that we, having died unto sins, might live unto righteousness ; " he redeemed us " with precious blood, as of a lamb without blemish and without spot." [2] Christ is to him the only Saviour, the Lord, the Prince of life, the Judge of the world. He assigns him a majestic position far above all other men, and brings him into the closest contact with the eternal Jehovah, though in subordination to him. The doctrine of the pre-existence seems to be intimated and implied, if not expressly stated, when Christ is spoken of as being " foreknown before the foundation of the world " and " manifested at the end of the time," and his Spirit as dwelling in the prophets of old and pointing them to his future sufferings and glory. [3]

---

[1] 1 Pet. 1 : 3–5 ; 5 : 4 ; 2 Pet. 3 : 13.   [2] 1 Pet. 1 : 18 sqq. ; 2 : 24 ; 3 : 18 sqq.

[3] 1 Pet. 1 : 20 : Χριστοῦ προεγνωσμένου μὲν πρὸ καταβολῆς κόσμου, φανερωθέντος δέ, κ. τ. λ. ; 1 : 11 : τὸ ἐν αὐτοῖς (τοῖς προφήταις) πνεῦμα Χριστοῦ προμαρτυρόμενον, κ. τ. λ. Schmid, Lechler, Gess, and others understand these passages as teaching a *real* pre-existence ; Beyschlag (l.c., p. 121)

III. Peter extends the preaching, judging, and saving activity of Christ to the realm of the departed spirits in Hades during the mysterious triduum between the crucifixion and the resurrection.[1] The descent into Hades is also taught by Paul (Eph. 4 : 9, 10).

IV. With this theory correspond the practical exhortations. Subjective Christianity is represented as faith in the historical Christ and as a lively hope in his glorious reappearance, which should make the Christians rejoice even amidst trials and perse- cution, after the example of their Lord and Saviour.

§ 71. *The Gentile Christian Theology. Paul and the Gospel of Faith.*

(See the Lit. in § 29, pp. 280 sqq.)

The Gentile Christian type of the gospel is embodied in the writings of Paul and Luke, and in the anonymous Epistle to the Hebrews.

The sources of Paul's theology are his discourses in the Acts (especially the speech on the Areopagus) and his thirteen Epis- tles, namely, the Epistles to the Thessalonians—the earliest, but chiefly practical; the four great Epistles to the Corinthians, Galatians, and Romans, which are the mature result of his con-

---

finds in them only an *ideal* pre-existence in the foreknowledge of God, and emphasizes the ἐποίησεν in Acts 2 : 36. He refers the πνεῦμα Χριστοῦ to the Holy Spirit, which was afterwards given in full measure to Christ at his bap- tism. So also Weiss (p. 161). But in this case Peter would have said τὸ πνεῦμα ἅγιον, as he did 1 Pet. 1 : 12 ; 2 Pet. 1 : 21 ; Acts 2 : 33, 38.

[1] 1 Pet. 3 : 19; 4 : 6 ; comp. Acts 2 : 27. The reference of the first passage to a preaching of Christ through Noah at the time of the flood is artificial, breaks the historic connection (ἀπέθανεν . . . θανατωθείς . . . ζωοποιηθείς πνεύματι . . . ἐκήρυξεν . . . πορευθείς εἰς οὐρανόν), and is set aside by ch. 4 : 6, which explains and generalizes the statement of the former passage. Baur (p. 291) understands the πνεύματα ἐν φυλακῇ to be the fallen angels (comp. 2 Pet. 2 : 4; Gen. 6 : 1), and the preaching of Christ an announcement of the judgment. But in this case we should have to distinguish between the ἐκήρυξεν, 1 Pet. 3 : 9, and the εὐηγγελίσθη in 4 : 6. The latter always means preaching the gospel, which is a savor of life unto life to believers, and a savor of death unto death to unbelievers.

flict with the Judaizing tendency; the four Epistles of the captivity; and the Pastoral Epistles. These groups present as
many phases of development of his system and discuss different
questions with appropriate variations of style, but they are animated by the same spirit, and bear the marks of the same profound and comprehensive genius.

Paul is the pioneer of Christian theology. He alone among
the apostles had received a learned rabbinical education and
was skilled in logical and dialectical argument. But his logic is
vitalized and set on fire. His theology springs from his heart
as well as from his brain; it is the result of his conversion, and
all aglow with the love of Christ; his scholasticism is warmed
and deepened by mysticism, and his mysticism is regulated and
sobered by scholasticism; the religious and moral elements,
dogmatics, and ethics, are blended into a harmonious whole.
Out of the depths of his personal experience, and in conflict
with the Judaizing contraction and the Gnostic evaporation of
the gospel he elaborated the fullest scheme of Christian doctrine
which we possess from apostolic pens. It is essentially soteriological, or a system of the way of salvation. It goes far beyond
the teaching of James and Peter, and yet is only a consistent
development of the teaching of Jesus in the Gospels.[1]

The Central Idea.

Paul's personal experience embraced intense fanaticism for
Judaism, and a more intense enthusiasm for Christianity. It
was first an unavailing struggle of legalism towards human
righteousness by works of the law, and then the apprehension

---

[1] Dr. Baur, who was formerly disposed to make Paul the founder of Christian universalism, admits in his last elaboration of the Pauline system (*N.
T.liche Theol.*, p. 128), that "Paul only expressed to the consciousness what in
itself, in principle and actually, or by implication, was contained already in the
doctrine of Jesus (*was an sich, principiell und thatsächlich, oder implicite schon
in der Lehre Jesu enthalten war*)." Pressensé misstates here Baur's position,
but himself correctly calls Paul's doctrine "as a whole and in all its parts, the
logical deduction and development of the teaching of the Master" (*Apost. Era,*
p. 255).

of divine righteousness by faith in Christ. This dualism is reflected in his theology. The idea of righteousness or conformity to God's holy will is the connecting link between the Jewish Saul and the Christian Paul. Law and works, was the motto of the self-righteous pupil of Moses; gospel and faith, the motto of the humble disciple of Jesus. He is the emancipator of the Christian consciousness from the oppressive bondage of legalism and bigotry, and the champion of freedom and catholicity. Paul's gospel is emphatically the gospel of saving faith, the gospel of evangelical freedom, the gospel of universalism, centring in the person and work of Christ and conditioned by union with Christ. He determined to know nothing but Christ and him crucified; but this included all it is the soul of his theology. The Christ who died is the Christ who was raised again and ever lives as Lord and Saviour, and was made unto us wisdom from God, and righteousness, and sanctification, and redemption.[1] A dead Christ would be the grave of all our hopes, and the gospel of a dead Saviour a wretched delusion. "If Christ has not been raised then is our preaching vain, your faith also is vain."[2] His death becomes available only through his resurrection. Paul puts the two facts together in the comprehensive statement: "Christ delivered up for our trespasses, and raised for our justification."[3] He is a conditional universalist; he teaches the universal need of salvation, and the divine intention and provision for a universal salvation, but the actual salvation of each man depends upon his faith or personal acceptance and appropriation of Christ. His doctrinal system, then, turns on the great antithesis of sin and grace. Before Christ and out of Christ is the reign of sin and death; after Christ and in Christ is the reign of righteousness and life.

We now proceed to an outline of the leading features of his theology as set forth in the order of the Epistle to the Romans, the most methodical and complete of his writings. Its central

[1] 1 Cor. 1 : 30; 2 : 2. [2] 1 Cor. 15 : 13.
[3] Rom. 4 : 23. The first δίδ is retrospective, the second prospective : for the destruction of sin and for the procurement of righteousness.

thought is: *The Gospel of Christ, a power of God for the salvation of all men, Jew and Gentile.*[1]

I. THE UNIVERSAL NEED OF SALVATION.—It arises from the fall of Adam and the whole human race, which was included in him as the tree is included in the seed, so that his one act of disobedience brought sin and death upon the whole posterity. Paul proves the depravity of Gentiles and Jews without exception to the extent that they are absolutely unable to attain to righteousness and to save themselves. "There is none righteous, no, not one." They are all under the dominion of sin and under the sentence of condemnation.[2] He recognizes indeed, even among the heathen, the remaining good elements of reason and conscience,[3] which are the connecting links for the regenerating work of divine grace; but for this very reason they are inexcusable, as they sin against better knowledge. There is a conflict between the higher and the lower nature in man (the νοῦς, which tends to God who gave it, and the σάρξ, which tends to sin), and this conflict is stimulated and brought to a crisis by the law of God; but this conflict, owing to the weakness of our carnal, fallen, depraved nature, ends in defeat and despair till the renewing grace of Christ emancipates us from the curse and bondage of sin and gives us liberty and victory. In the seventh chapter of the Romans, Paul gives from his personal experience a most remarkable and truthful description of the religious history of man from the natural or heathen state of carnal security (without the law, ver. 7–9) to the Jewish state under the law which calls out sin from its hidden recess, reveals its true character, and awakens the sense of the wretchedness of slavery under sin (ver. 10–25), but in this very way prepares the way for the Christian state of freedom (ver. 24 and ch. 8).[4]

---

[1] 1 : 17 : δύναμις θεοῦ εἰς σωτηρίαν παντὶ τῷ πιστεύοντι, Ἰουδαίῳ τε [πρῶτον] καὶ Ἕλληνι. Other pregnant passages in which Paul summarizes his dogmatics and ethics, are Rom. 1 : 16, 17 : 3 : 21-26 ; 4 : 25 ; 11 : 32 ; 1 Cor. 15 : 22 ; Gal. 3 : 22 ; Tit. 3 : 3-7.

[2] Rom. 1 : 18 ; 3 : 20.   First the depravity of the heathen, then that of the Jews (2 : 1, comp. ver. 17).

[3] Rom. 1 : 18-21 ; 2 : 14-16 ; comp. Acts 17 : 28.

[4] The Augustinian application of this conflict to the *regenerate* state, in-

II. The Divine Intention and Provision of Universal Salvation.—God sincerely wills (θέλει) that all men, even the greatest of sinners, should be saved, and come to the knowledge of
truth through Christ, who gave himself a ransom for all.[1] The
extent of Christ's righteousness and life is as universal as the
extent of Adam's sin and death, and its intensive power is even
greater.   The first and the second Adam are perfectly parallel
by contrast in their representative character, but Christ is much
stronger and remains victor of the field, having slain sin and death,
and living for ever as the prince of life.   Where sin abounds
there grace superabounds.   As through the first Adam sin (as
a pervading force) entered into the world, and death through
sin, and thus death passed unto all men, inasmuch as they all
sinned (in Adam generically and potentially, and by actual transgression individually) ; so much more through Christ, the second
Adam, righteousness entered into the world and life through
righteousness, and thus righteousness passed unto all men on
condition of faith by which we partake of his righteousness.[2]

volves the seventh chapter in contradiction with chapters 6 and 8, and obliterates the distinction between the regenerate and the unregenerate state.
Augustine understood that chapter better in his earlier years, before the
Pelagian controversy drove him to such an extreme view of total depravity as
destroys all freedom and responsibility.   We see here the difference between
an inspired apostle and an enlightened theologian.   The chief object of
chapter 7 is to show that the law cannot sanctify any more than it can justify
(ch. 3), and that the legal conflict with the sinful flesh ends in total failure.
Paul always uses here νοῦς for the higher principle in man (including reason
and conscience) ; while in chapter 8. where he speaks of the regenerate man,
he uses πνεῦμα, which is the νοῦς sanctified and enlightened by the Holy
Spirit.   In verse 25 he indeed alludes to the regenerate state by way of anticipation and as an immediate answer to the preceding cry for redemption ; but
from this expression of thanks he once more points back with ἄρα οὖν to the
previous state of bondage before he enters more fully with ἄρα νῦν into the
state of freedom.

[1] 1 Tim. 1 : 15 ; 2 : 4, 6 ; Tit. 2 : 11.   Particularistic restrictions of "all" in
these passages are arbitrary.   The same doctrine is taught 2 Pet. 3 : 9, and
John 3 : 16 ; 1 John 2 : 2.   The last passage is as clear as the sun : "Christ
is the propitiation (ἱλασμός) for our sins ; and not for ours only, *but also for
the whole world*" (οὐ μόνον . . . ἀλλὰ καὶ περὶ ὅλου τοῦ κόσμου).

[2] Rom. 5 : 12–21 ; 1 Cor. 15 : 21, 22.   The πάντες and the οἱ πολλοί (which
is equivalent to πάντες and opposed, not to a *few*, but to the *one*) in the second
clause referring to the second Adam, is as comprehensive and unlimited as in

God shut up all men in disobedience, that he might have mercy upon all that believe.[1]

(1.) The PREPARATION for this salvation was the promise and the law of the Old dispensation. The promise given to Abraham and the patriarchs is prior to the law, and not set aside by the law; it contained the germ and the pledge of salvation, and Abraham stands out as the father of the faithful, who was justified by faith even before he received circumcision as a sign and seal. The law came in besides, or between the promise and the gospel in order to develop the disease of sin, to reveal its true character as a transgression of the divine will, and thus to excite the sense of the need of salvation. The law is in itself holy and good, but cannot give life; it commands and threatens, but gives no power to fulfil; it cannot renew the flesh, that is, the depraved, sinful nature of man; it can neither justify nor sanctify, but it brings the knowledge of sin, and by its discipline it prepares men for the freedom of Christ, as a schoolmaster prepares children for independent manhood.[2]

(2.) The SALVATION itself is comprehended in the person and work of CHRIST. It was accomplished in the fulness of the time by the sinless life, the atoning death, and the glorious resurrection and exaltation of Christ, the eternal Son of God, who appeared in the likeness of the flesh of sin and as an offering for sin, and thus procured for us pardon, peace, and reconciliation. " God spared not his own Son, but delivered him up for us all." This is the greatest gift of the eternal love of the Father for his creatures. The Son of God, prompted by the same infinite love,

---

the first clause. The English Version weakens the force of οἱ πολλοί, and limits the number by omitting the article. The πολλῷ μᾶλλον (Rom. 5 : 15, 17) predicated of Christ's saving grace, is not a numerical, nor a logical, but a dynamic *plus*, indicating a higher degree of efficacy, inasmuch as Christ brought far greater blessings than we lost in Adam.

[1] Rom. 11 : 32; Gal. 3 : 22. These passages contain the briefest statement of the sad mystery of the fall cleared up by the blessed mystery of redemption. In the first passage the masculine is used (τοὺς πάντας), in the second the neuter (τὰ πάντα), and the application is confined to believers (τοῖς πιστεύουσιν).

[2] Rom. chs. 3–7 ; Gal. chs. 2–4 ; especially Rom. 3 : 20 ; 5 : 20 ; Gal. 3 : 24.

laid aside his divine glory and mode of existence, emptied himself, exchanged the form of God for the form of a servant, humbled himself and became obedient, even unto the death of the cross. Though he was rich, being equal with God, yet for our sakes he became poor, that we through his poverty might become rich. In reward for his active and passive obedience God exalted him and gave him a name above every name, that in the name of Jesus every knee should bow and every tongue confess that he is Lord.[1]

Formerly the cross of Christ had been to the carnal Messianic expectations and self-righteousness of Paul, as well as of other Jews, the greatest stumbling-block, as it was the height of folly to the worldly wisdom of the heathen mind.[2] But the heavenly vision of the glory of Jesus at Damascus unlocked the key for the understanding of this mystery, and it was confirmed by the primitive apostolic tradition,[3] and by his personal experience of the failure of the law and the power of the gospel to give peace to his troubled conscience. The death of Christ appeared to him now as the divinely appointed means for procuring righteousness. It is the device of infinite wisdom and love to reconcile the conflicting claims of justice and mercy whereby God could justify the sinner and yet remain just himself.[4] Christ, who knew no sin, became sin for us that we might become righteousness of God in him. He died in the place and for the benefit ($\acute{v}\pi\acute{e}\rho$, $\pi\epsilon\rho\acute{\iota}$) of sinners and enemies, so that his death has a universal significance. If one died for all, they all died.[5] He offered his spotless and holy life as a ransom

---

[1] Rom. 8 : 3, 32 ; Phil. 2 : 6–11 ; 2 Cor. 8 : 9. On the Christology of Paul, see the Notes at the end of this section.

[2] Gal. 5 : 11 ; 6 : 12. 1 Cor. 1 : 23.

[3] 1 Cor. 15 : 3 : " I delivered unto you first of all that which I also *received*, that *Christ died for our sins* according to the Scriptures."

[4] Rom. 3 : 26 : εἰς τὸ εἶναι αὐτὸν δίκαιον καὶ δικαιοῦντα τὸν ἐκ πίστεως Χριστοῦ. Bengel calls this " *summum paradoxon evangelicum*."

[5] 2 Cor. 5 : 15 : ὅτι εἷς ὑπὲρ πάντων ἀπέθανεν, ἄρα οἱ πάντες ἀπέθανον. Mark the aorist. The prepositions ὑπέρ (used of persons) and περί (of things, but also of persons) express the idea of benefit, but often in close connection with the idea of vicariousness (ἀντί). Comp. Gal. 1 : 4 ; 3 : 13 ; Rom. 4 : 25 ; 5 : 6, etc.

(λύτρον) or price (τιμή) for our sins, and thus effected our redemption (ἀπολύτρωσις), as prisoners of war are redeemed by
the payment of an equivalent. His death, therefore, is a vi-
carious sacrifice, an atonement, an expiation or propitiation
(ἱλασμός, ἱλαστήριον, sacrificium expiatorium) for the sins of
the whole world, and secured full and final remission (ἄφεσις)
and reconciliation between God and man (καταλλαγή). This
the Mosaic law and sacrifices could not accomplish. They could
only keep alive and deepen the sense of the necessity of an
atonement. If righteousness came by the law, Christ's death
would be needless and fruitless. His death removes not only
the guilt of sin, but it destroyed also its power and dominion.
Hence the great stress Paul laid on the preaching of the cross
(ὁ λόγος τοῦ σταυροῦ), in which alone he would glory.[1]

This rich doctrine of the atonement which pervades the
Pauline Epistles is only a legitimate expansion of the word of
Christ that he would give his life as a ransom for sinners and
shed his blood for the remission of sins.

(3.) While Christ accomplished the salvation, the HOLY SPIRIT
appropriates it to the believer. The Spirit is the religious and
moral principle of the new life. Emanating from God, he
dwells in the Christian as a renewing, sanctifying, comforting
energy, as the higher conscience, as a divine guide and monitor.
He mediates between Christ and the church as Christ mediates between God and the world ; he is the divine revealer of
Christ to the individual consciousness and the source of all
graces (χαρίσματα) through which the new life manifests itself.

---

[1] Rom. 3 : 21–26 ; 5 : 6–10 ; 8 : 32 ; 1 Cor. 1 : 17, 18 ; 2 : 2 ; 6 : 20 ; 7 : 23 ;
11 : 24 ; 15 : 3 ; 2 Cor. 5 : 15, 18, 19, 21 ; Gal. 1 : 4 ; 2 : 11 sqq. ; 3 : 13 ; 6 : 14,
etc. Comp. Weiss, p. 302 ; Pfleiderer, p. 7 ; Baur (*N. T. Theol.*, p. 156),
Holsten and Pfleiderer (in his able introduction) regard the atoning death of
Christ as the kernel of Paul's theology, and Holsten promises to develop the
whole system from this idea in his new work, *Das Evangelium des Paulus*,
of which the first part appeared in 1880. But they deny the *objective* character of the revelation at Damascus, and resolve it into a subjective moral
struggle and a dialectical process of reflection and reasoning. Luther passed
through a similar moral conflict and reached the same conclusion, but on the
basis of the Scriptures and with the aid of the divine Spirit.

"Christ in us" is equivalent to having the "Spirit of Christ." It is only by the inward revelation of the Spirit that we can call Christ our Lord and Saviour, and God our Father; by the Spirit the love of God is shed abroad in our hearts; the Spirit works in us faith and all virtues; it is the Spirit who transforms even the body of the believer into a holy temple; those who are led by the Spirit are the sons of God and heirs of salvation; it is by the law of the Spirit of life in Christ Jesus that we are made free from the law of sin and death and are able to walk in newness of life. Where the Spirit of God is there is true liberty.[1]

(4.) There is, then, a threefold cause of our salvation: the Father who sends his Son, the Son who procures salvation, and the Holy Spirit who applies it to the believer. This threefold agency is set forth in the benediction, which comprehends all divine blessings: "the grace ($\chi\acute{a}\rho\iota\varsigma$) of the Lord Jesus Christ, and the love ($\dot{a}\gamma\acute{a}\pi\eta$) of God, and the communion ($\kappa o\iota\nu\omega\nu\acute{\iota}a$) of the Holy Spirit."[2] This is Paul's practical view of the Holy Trinity as revealed in the gospel. The grace of Christ is mentioned first because in it is exhibited to us the love of the Father in its highest aspect as a saving power; to the Holy Spirit is ascribed the communion because he is the bond of union between the Father and the Son, between Christ and the believer, and between the believers as members of one brotherhood of the redeemed.

To this divine trinity corresponds, we may say, the human trinity of Christian graces: faith, hope, love.[3]

---

[1] The passages in which the Holy Spirit is mentioned are very numerous, especially in the Thessalonians, Romans, Corinthians, Galatians, and Ephesians. Comp. Rom. 5 : 5; 7 : 6; 8 : 2, 5, 9, 11, 14, 15, 16, 26; 1 Cor. 2 : 4 sqq.; 3 : 16; 6 : 11, 17, 19; 12 : 3–16; 2 Cor. 1 : 12; 2 : 7; Gal. 4 : 6; 5 : 16, 22, 25; Eph. 1 : 17; 2 : 2; 4 : 23, 30; 5 : 18; 1 Thess. 1 : 5, 6; 4 : 8; 5 : 19, 23; 2 Thess. 2 : 2, 8, 13; 2 Tim. 1 : 7, 14; Tit. 3 : 5.

[2] The concluding verse in the second Epistle to the Corinthians; comp. Eph. 2 : 18, 22; 4 : 4–6, where God the Father, the Lord Jesus Christ, and the Holy Spirit are mentioned as distinct personalities, if we may use this unsatisfactory yet indispensable term.

[3] 1 Cor. 13 : 13.

III. The Order of Salvation.—(1.) Salvation has its roots
in the eternal counsel of God, his FOREKNOWLEDGE (πρόγνωσις),
and his FOREORDINATION (προορισμός, πρόθεσις); the former an
act of his omniscient intellect, the latter of his omnipotent
will. Logically, foreknowledge precedes foreordination, but
in reality both coincide and are simultaneous in the divine
mind, in which there is no before nor after.[1]

Paul undoubtedly teaches an eternal *election* by the sovereign
grace of God, that is an unconditioned and unchangeable predestination of his children to holiness and salvation in and through
his Son Jesus Christ.[2] He thus cuts off all human merit, and
plants the salvation upon an immovable rock. But he does
not thereby exclude human freedom and responsibility; on the
contrary, he includes them as elements in the divine plan, and
boldly puts them together.[3] Hence he exhorts and warns men
as if salvation might be gained or lost by their effort. Those
who are lost, are lost by their own unbelief. Perdition is the
righteous judgment for sin unrepented of and persisted in. It
is a strange misunderstanding to make Paul either a fatalist or a
particularist; he is the strongest opponent of blind necessity and
of Jewish particularism, even in the ninth chapter of Romans.
But he aims at no philosophical solution of a problem which
the finite understanding of man cannot settle; he contents
himself with asserting its divine and human aspects, the reli-

---

[1] Rom. 8 : 29 : "Whom he *foreknew* (οὓς προέγνω), he also *foreordained*
(προώρισεν), to be conformed to the image of his Son." The verb προγινώσκω
occurs in the New Test. five times (Rom. 8 : 29 ; 11 : 1, 2 ; Acts 26 : 5 ; 1 Pet.
1 : 20), the noun πρόγνωσις twice (Acts 2 : 23 ; 1 Pet. 1 : 2), always, as in classical Greek, in the sense of previous knowledge (not election). The verb
προορίζω occurs six times, and means always to foreordain, to determine before. The words ἐκλέγω and ἐκλέγομαι, ἐκλογή, ἐκλεκτός occur much more
frequently, mostly with reference to eternal choice or election. See note
below.

[2] Eph. 1 : 4 : "Even as he chose us in Christ (ἐξελέξατο ἡμᾶς ἐν αὐτῷ) before the foundation of the world, that we should be holy and without blemish
before him in love : having foreordained us unto adoption as sons (προορίσας
ἡμᾶς εἰς υἱοθεσίαν) through Jesus Christ unto himself, according to the good
pleasure of his will."

[3] Phil. 2 : 12, 13.   Comp. the ninth chapter of Romans with the tenth.

gious and ethical view, the absolute sovereignty of God and the relative freedom of man, the free gift of salvation and the just punishment for neglecting it. Christian experience includes both truths, and we find no contradiction in praying as if all depended on God, and in working as if all depended on man. This is Pauline theology and practice.

Foreknowledge and foreordination are the eternal background of salvation: call, justification, sanctification, and glorification mark the progressive steps in the time of execution, and of the personal application of salvation.[1]

(2.) The CALL (κλῆσις) proceeds from God the Father through the preaching of the gospel salvation which is sincerely offered to all. Faith comes from preaching, preaching from preachers, and the preachers from God who sends them.[2]

The human act which corresponds to the divine call is the *conversion* (μετάνοια) of the sinner; and this includes repentance or turning away from sin, and faith or turning to Christ, under the influence of the Holy Spirit who acts through the word.[3] The Holy Spirit is the objective principle of the new life of the Christian. Faith is the free gift of God, and at the same time the highest act of man. It is unbounded trust in Christ, and the organ by which we apprehend him, his very life and benefits, and become as it were identified with him, or mystically incorporated with him.[4]

---

[1] Rom. 8 : 30 : "Whom he foreordained them he also *called* (ἐκάλεσεν) : and whom he called them he also *justified* (ἐδικαίωσεν, which is also the beginning of *sanctification*). and whom he justified. them he also *glorified* (ἐδόξασεν)." The proleptic aorist is used for the future to indicate the absolute certainty that God will carry out his gracious design to the glorious consummation.

[2] Rom. 10 : 14, 15. A chain of abridged syllogisms (*sorites*) by which Paul reasons back from effect to cause till he reaches the first link in the chain. On the κλῆσις (*vocatio*) see Rom. 11 : 29 ; 1 Cor. 1 : 26 ; 7 : 20 ; Gal. 1 : 6 ; Eph. 1 : 18 ; 4 : 14 ; Phil. 3 : 14, etc. The verb καλέω is of very frequent occurrence in the Gospels and Epistles.

[3] Rom. 2 : 4 ; 2 Cor 7 : 9, 10 ; 2 Tim. 2 : 25.

[4] Baur (p. 154) distinguishes five conceptions of πίστις (from πείθειν): 1st, conviction in general, a theoretical belief or assent. In this sense it does not occur in Paul, but in James 1 : 17. 2d, conviction of the invisible and supernatural ; 2 Cor. 5 : 7, πίστις as distinct from εἶδος. 3d, religious conviction,

(3.) JUSTIFICATION (δικαίωσις) is the next step. This is a vital doctrine in Paul's system and forms the connecting link as well as the division line between the Jewish and the Christian period of his life. It was with him always a burning life-question. As a Jew he sought righteousness by works of the law, honestly and earnestly, but in vain ; as a Christian he found it, as a free gift of grace, by faith in Christ. Righteousness (δικαιοσύνη), as applied to man, is the normal relation of man to the holy will of God as expressed in his revealed law, which requires supreme love to God and love to our neighbor ; it is the moral and religious ideal, and carries in itself the divine favor and the highest happiness. It is the very end for which man was made ; he is to be conformed to God who is absolutely holy and righteous. To be god-like is the highest conception of human perfection and bliss.

But there are two kinds of righteousness, or rather two ways of seeking it : one of the law, and sought by works of the law ; but this is imaginary, at best very defective, and cannot stand before God ; and the righteousness of Christ, or the righteousness of faith, which is freely communicated to the believer and accepted by God. Justification is the act of God by which he puts the repenting sinner in possession of the righteousness of Christ. It is the reverse of condemnation ; it implies the remission of sins and the imputation of Christ's righteousness. It is based upon the atoning sacrifice of Christ and conditioned by faith, as the subjective organ of apprehending and appropriating Christ with all his benefits. We are therefore justified by grace alone through faith alone ; yet faith remains not alone, but is ever fruitful of good works.

The result of justification is peace (εἰρήνη) with God, and the

1 Cor. 2 : 5 ; 2 Cor. 1 : 24, etc. 4th, trust in God, Rom. 4 : 17–21. 5th, trust in Christ, or the specific Christian faith, Rom. 3 : 22 ; 1 Cor. 15 : 14 ; Gal. 1 : 23, and always where justifying faith is meant. Weiss (p. 316) defines the Pauline idea of justifying faith as "the very opposite of all the works required by the law ; it is no human performance, but, on the contrary, an abandonment of all work of our own, an unconditional reliance on God who justifies, or on Christ as the Mediator of salvation." But this is only the receptive side of faith, it has an active side as well, πίστις is ἐνεργουμένη δι' ἀγάπης. See below.

state of adoption (υἱοθεσία), and this implies also the heirship (κληρονομία) of eternal life. "The Spirit itself beareth witness with our spirit that we are children of God: and if children, then heirs; heirs of God, and joint-heirs with Christ; if so be that we suffer with him, that we may be also glorified with him." [1] The root of Paul's theory of justification is found in the teaching of Christ: he requires from his disciples a far better righteousness than the legal righteousness of the Scribes and Pharisees, as a condition of entering the kingdom of heaven, namely, the righteousness of God; he holds up this righteousness of God as the first object to be sought; and teaches that it can only be obtained by faith, which he everywhere presents as the one and only condition of salvation on the part of man. [2]

(4.) SANCTIFICATION (ἁγιασμός). [3] The divine act of justification is inseparable from the conversion and renewal of the sinner. It affects the will and conduct as well as the feeling. Although gratuitous, it is not unconditional. It is of necessity the beginning of sanctification, the birth into a new life which is to grow unto full manhood. We are not justified outside of Christ, but only in Christ by a living faith, which unites us with him in his death unto sin and resurrection unto holiness. Faith is operative in love and must produce good works as the inevitable proof of its existence. Without love, the greatest of Christian graces, even the strongest faith would be but "sounding brass or clanging cymbal." [4]

[1] Rom. 5 : 1; 8 : 15-17; Gal. 4 : 5-7. If we read in Rom. 5 : 1 (with the oldest authorities) the hortative subjunctive ἔχωμεν, "let us have" (instead of the indicative ἔχομεν, "we have"), peace is represented as a blessing which we should grasp and fully enjoy—an exhortation well suited for Judaizing and gloomy Christians who groan under legal bondage. On justification see the notes below.

[2] Matt. 5 : 20; 6 : 33; 9 : 22, 29; 17 : 20; Mark 11 : 22; 16 : 16; Luke 5 : 50; 18 : 10-14; John 3 : 16, 17; 6 : 47, etc.

[3] Comp. Rom. 6 : 19, 22; 1 Cor. 1 : 30; 1 Thess. 4 : 3, 4, 7; 2 Thess. 2 : 13.

[4] 1 Cor. 13: 1, 2. Luther's famous description of faith (in his Preface to Romans), as "a lively, busy, mighty thing that waits not for work, but is ever working, and is as inseparable from love as light is from heat," is in the very spirit of Paul, and a sufficient reply to the slander brought against the doctrine of justification by faith as being antinomian in its tendency.

Sanctification is not a single act, like justification, but a pro
cess. It is a continuous growth of the whole inner man in holiness from the moment of conversion and justification to the
reappearance of Jesus Christ in glory.[1] On the part of God it
is insured, for he is faithful and will perfect the good work
which he began; on the part of man it involves constant watch-
fulness, lest he stumble and fall. In one view it depends all on
the grace of God, in another view it depends all on the exertion
of man. There is a mysterious co-operation between the two
agencies, which is expressed in the profound paradox: "Work
out your own salvation with fear and trembling; for it is God
who worketh in you both to will and to work, for his good
pleasure."[2] The believer is mystically identified with Christ
from the moment of his conversion (sealed by baptism). He
died with Christ unto sin so as to sin no more; and he rose with
him to a new life unto God so as to live for God; he is crucified to the world and the world to him; he is a new creature in
Christ; the old man of sin is dead and buried, the new man
lives in holiness and righteousness. "It is no longer I (my own
sinful self) that lives, but it is Christ that lives in me: and that
life which I now live in the flesh, I live in faith in the Son of
God, who loved me and gave himself up for me."[3] Here is the
whole doctrine of Christian life: it is *Christ in us, and we in*

---

[1] 1 Thess. 5 : 23: "The God of peace sanctify you wholly; and may your
spirit and soul and body be preserved entire, without blame at the coming
(παρουσία) of our Lord Jesus Christ. Faithful is he that calleth you, who will
also do it." Comp. the 6th, 7th, and 8th chs. of Romans, which treat most
fully of sanctification, also chs. 12–15, and all the ethical or hortatory portions
of his other epistles.

[2] Phil. 2 : 12, 13. The apostle emphatically uses the same verb, ἐνεργῶν and
ἐνεργεῖν, while the E. V., with its usual love for variation, renders "worketh"
and "to do." Augustin (*De dono persev.* 33): "*Nos ergo volumus, sed Deus
in nobis operatur et velle; nos ergo operamur, sed Deus in nobis operatur et
operari.*" Ver. 13 "supplies at once the stimulus to, and the corrective of the
precept in the preceding verse: 'Work, for God works with you;' and 'The
good is not yours but God's.'" Lightfoot, *in loc.* Comp. also Calvin, Alford,
and Braune, *in loc.*

[3] Gal. 2 : 20. This passage is obscured in the E V. by the omission of
οὐκέτι, "no longer," and the insertion of "nevertheless."

Christ. It consists in a vital union with Christ, the crucified and risen Redeemer, who is the indwelling, all-pervading, and controlling life of the believer; but the union is no pantheistic confusion or absorption; the believer continues to live as a self-conscious and distinct personality. For the believer "to live is Christ, and to die is gain." "Whether we live, we live unto the Lord; whether we die, we die unto the Lord: whether we live therefore, or die, we are the Lord's." [1]

In the twelfth chapter of Romans, Paul sums up his ethics in the idea of gratitude which manifests itself in a cheerful sacrifice of our persons and services to the God of our salvation. [2]

(5.) GLORIFICATION ($\delta o \xi \acute{a} \zeta \epsilon \iota \nu$). This is the final completion of the work of grace in the believer and will appear at the parousia of our Lord. It cannot be hindered by any power present or future, visible or invisible, for God and Christ are stronger than all our enemies and will enable us to come out more than conquerors from the conflict of faith.

This lofty conviction of final victory finds most eloquent expression in the triumphal ode which closes the eighth chapter of Romans. [3]

IV. THE HISTORICAL PROGRESS of the gospel of salvation from Jews to Gentiles and back again to the Jews. [4] Salvation

---

[1] Gal. 3 : 27; Eph. 5 : 30; 1 Cor. 1 : 9; 2 Cor. 1 : 3, 5; 5 : 17; 13 : 4; Col. 3 : 4; Phil. 1 : 21; Rom. 6 : 4–8; 14 : 8; 1 Thess. 5 : 10. Comp. those numerous passages where Paul uses the significant phrase ἐν Χριστῷ, living and moving and acting in Him, as the element of our spiritual existence.

[2] Hence the Heidelberg Catechism, following the order of the Ep. to the Romans, represents Christian life, in the third and last part, under the head: "Thankfulness."

[3] Erasmus justly regarded the conclusion of Rom. 8 : 31–39 as unsurpassed for genuine eloquence: "*Quid unquam Cicero dixit grandiloquentius?*" It is only equalled by the ode on love in 1 Cor. 13.

[4] This is the subject of Rom. 9–11. These three chapters contain a theodicy and an outline of the philosophy of church history. They are neither the chief part of Romans (Baur), nor a mere episode or appendix (De Wette), but an essential part of the Epistle in exposition of the concluding clause of the theme, ch. 1 : 17 . . . "to the Jew first, and also to the Greek" (or Gentile). Ch. 9 treats of divine sovereignty; ch. 10 (which should begin

was first intended for and offered to the Jews, who were for centuries prepared for it by the law and the promise, and among whom the Saviour was born, lived, died, and rose again. But the Jews as a nation rejected Christ and his apostles, and hardened their hearts in unbelief. This fact filled the apostle with unutterable sadness, and made him willing to sacrifice even his own salvation (if it were possible) for the salvation of his kinsmen.

But he sees light in this dark mystery. First of all, God has a sovereign right over all his creatures and manifests both his mercy and his righteousness in the successive stages of the historical execution of his wise designs. His promise has not failed, for it was not given to all the carnal descendants of Abraham and Isaac, but only to the spiritual descendants, the true Israelites who have the faith of Abraham, and they have been saved, as individual Jews are saved to this day. And even in his relation to the vessels of wrath who by unbelief and ingratitude have fitted themselves for destruction, he shows his longsuffering.

In the next place, the real cause of the rejection of the body of the Jews is their own rejection of Christ. They sought their own righteousness by works of the law instead of accepting the righteousness of God by faith.

Finally, the rejection of the Jews is only temporary and incidental in the great drama of history. It is overruled for the speedier conversion of the Gentiles, and the conversion of the full number or the organic totality of the Gentiles (not all individual Gentiles) will lead ultimately to the conversion of Israel. " A hardening in part has befallen Israel, until the fulness of the Gentiles be come in ; and so all Israel shall be saved."

With this hopeful prophecy, which seems yet far off, but

at ch. 9 : 30) treats of human responsibility ; ch. 11 of the future solution of this great problem. They must be taken together as a unit. Ch. 9 alone may be and has been made to prove Calvinism and even extreme supralapsarianism ; ch. 10 Arminianism ; and ch. 11 Universalism. But Paul is neither a Calvinist nor an Arminian nor a Universalist in the dogmatic sense. See the doctrinal expositions in Lange on *Romans*, much enlarged in the translation, pp. 327–334.

which is steadily approaching fulfilment, and will be realized in
God's own time and way, the apostle closes the doctrinal part of
the Epistle to the Romans. "God has shut up all men (τοὺς
πάντας) unto disobedience that he might have mercy upon all
men. O the depth of the riches both of the wisdom and the
knowledge of God! how unsearchable are his judgments, and
his ways past tracing out! . . . For of Him (ἐξ αὐτοῦ) and
through Him (δι 'αὐτοῦ), and unto Him (εἰς αὐτόν) are all
things. To Him be the glory forever. Amen."[1]

Before this glorious consummation, however, there will be a
terrible conflict with Antichrist or "the man of sin," and the
full revelation of the mystery of lawlessness now held in check.
Then the Lord will appear as the conqueror in the field, raise
the dead, judge the world, destroy the last enemy, and restore
the kingdom to the Father that God may be all in all (τὰ πάντα
ἐν πᾶσιν).[2]

NOTES.

I. The PAULINE SYSTEM OF DOCTRINE has been more frequently explained than any other.

Among the earlier writers Neander, Usteri, and Schmid take the lead,
and are still valuable. Neander and Schmid are in full sympathy with
the spirit and views of Paul. Usteri adapted them somewhat to Schleiermacher's system, to which he adhered.

Next to them the Tübingen school, first the master, Baur (twice, in his
Paul, and in his *New Test. Theology*), and then his pupils, Pfleiderer and
Holsten, have done most for a critical reproduction. They rise far
above the older rationalism in an earnest and intelligent appreciation of
the sublime theology of Paul, and leave the impression that he was a
most profound, bold, acute, and consistent thinker on the highest
themes. But they ignore the supernatural element of inspiration, they
lack *spiritual* sympathy with the faith of the apostle, overstrain his antagonism to Judaism (as did Marcion of old), and confine the authentic
sources to the four anti-Judaic Epistles to the Galatians, Romans, and
Corinthians, although recognizing in the minor Epistles the "*paulinische Grundlage.*" The more moderate followers of Baur, however, now
admit the genuineness of from seven to ten Pauline Epistles, leaving
only the three Pastoral Epistles and Ephesians in serious doubt.

The *Paulinismus* of Weiss (in the third ed. of his *Bibl. Theol.*, 1881,

---

[1] Rom. 11 : 32, 33, 36.   [2] 2 Thess. 2 : 3–12 ; 1 Cor. 15 : 28.

pp. 194–472) is based upon a very careful philological exegesis in detail, and is in this respect the most valuable of all attempts to reproduce Paul's theology. He divides it into three sections: 1st, the system of the four great doctrinal and polemical Epistles; 2d, the further development of Paulinism in the Epistles of the captivity; 3d, the doctrine of the Pastoral Epistles. He doubts only the genuineness of the last group, but admits a progress from the first to the second.

Of French writers, Reuss, Pressensé, and Sabatier give the best expositions of the Pauline system, more or less in imitation of German labors. Reuss, of Strasburg, who writes in German as well, is the most independent and learned; Pressensé is more in sympathy with Paul's belief, but gives only a meagre summary; Sabatier leans to the Tübingen school. Reuss discusses Paul's system (in vol. II., 17–220) very fully under these heads: righteousness; sin; the law; the gospel; God; the person of Christ; the work of Christ; typical relation of the old and new covenant; faith; election; calling and the Holy Spirit; regeneration; redemption; justification and reconciliation; church; hope and trial; last times; kingdom of God. Sabatier (*L'apôtre Paul*, pp. 249–318, second ed., 1881) more briefly but clearly develops the Pauline theology from the Christological point of view (*la personne de Christ principe générateur de la conscience chrétienne*) under three heads: 1st, the Christian principle in the psychological sphere (anthropology); 2d, in the social and historical sphere (religious philosophy of history); 3d, in the metaphysical sphere (theology), which culminates in the θεὸς τὰ πάντα ἐν πᾶσιν "*Ainsi naît et.grandit cet arbre magnifique de la pensée de Paul, dont les racines plongent dans le sol de la conscience chrétienne et dont la cime est dans les cieux.*"

Renan, who professes so much sentimental admiration for the poetry and wisdom of Jesus, "the charming Galilæan peasant," has no organ for the theology of Paul any more than Voltaire had for the poetry of Shakespeare. He regards him as a bold and vigorous, but uncouth and semi-barbarous genius, full of rabbinical subtleties, useless speculations, and polemical intolerance even against good old Peter at Antioch.

Several doctrines of Paul have been specially discussed by German scholars, as Tischendorf: *Doctrina Pauli apostoli de Vi Mortis Christi Satisfactoria* (Leipz., 1837); Räbiger: *De Christologia Paulina* (Breslau, 1852); Lipsius: *Die paulinische Rechtfertigungslehre* (Leipz., 1853); Ernesti: *Vom Ursprung der Sünde nach paulinischem Lehrgehalt* (Wolfenbüttel, 1855); *Die Ethik des Paulus* (Braunschweig, 1868; 3d ed., 1881); W. Beyschlag: *Die paulinische Theodicee* (Berlin, 1868); R. Schmidt: *Die Christologie des Ap. Paulus* (Gött., 1870); A. Dietzsch: *Adam und Christus* (Bonn, 1871); H. Lüdemann: *Die Anthropologie des Ap. Paulus* (Kiel, 1872); R. Stähelin: *Zur paulinischen Eschatologie* (1874); A. Schumann: *Der weltgeschichtl. Entwickelungsprocess nach dem Lehrsystem des Ap. Paulus* (Crefeld, 1875); Fr. Köstlin: *Die Lehre des Paulus von der Auferstehung* (1877) ; H. H. WENDT: *Die Begriffe Fleisch und Geist im biblischen Sprachgebrauch* (Gotha, 1878).

II. THE CHRISTOLOGY OF PAUL is closely interwoven with his soteriology. In Romans and Galatians the soteriological aspect prevails, in Philippians and Colossians the christological. His christology is very rich, and with that of the Epistle to the Hebrews prepares the way for the christology of John. It is even more fully developed than John's, only less prominent in the system.

The chief passages on the person of Christ are : Rom. 1 : 3, 4 (ἐκ σπέρματος Δαυεὶδ κατὰ σάρκα . . υἱὸς Ͽεοῦ κατὰ πνεῦμα ἁγιωσύνης) ; 8 : 3 (ὁ Ͽεὸς τὸν ἑαυτοῦ υἱὸν πέμψας ἐν ὁμοιώματι σαρκὸς ἁμαρτίας), ver. 32 (ὃς τοῦ ἰδίου υἱοῦ οὐκ ἐφείσατο) ; 9 : 5 (ἐξ ὧν ὁ Χριστὸς τὸ κατὰ σάρκα, ὁ ὢν ἐπὶ πάντων, Ͽεὸς εὐλογητὸς εἰς τοὺς αἰῶνας—but the punctuation and consequently the application of the doxology—whether to God or to Christ—are disputed) ; 1 Cor. 1 : 19 (ὁ κύριος ἡμῶν, a very frequent designation) ; 2 Cor. 5 : 21 (τὸν μὴ γνόντα ἁμαρτίαν) ; 8 : 9 (ἐπτώχευσεν πλούσιος ὤν, ἵνα ὑμεῖς τῇ ἐκείνου πτωχείᾳ πλουτήσητε) ; Phil. 2 : 5–11 (the famous passage about the κένωσις) ; Col. 1 : 15–18 (ὅς ἐστιν εἰκὼν τοῦ Ͽεοῦ τοῦ ἀοράτου πρωτότοκος πάσης κτίσεως, ὅτι ἐν αὐτῷ ἐκτίσϿη τὰ πάντα . . . τὰ πάντα δι' αὐτοῦ καὶ εἰς αὐτὸν ἔκτισται . . .) ; 2 : 9 (ἐν αὐτῷ κατοικεῖ πᾶν τὸ πλήρωμα τῆς Ͽεότητος σωματικῶς) ; 1 Tim. 3 : 16 (ὃς ἐφανερώϿη ἐν σαρκί . . .) ; Tit. 2 : 13 (τοῦ μεγάλου Ͽεοῦ καὶ σωτῆρος ἡμῶν Χριστοῦ Ἰησοῦ, where, however, commentators differ in the construction, as in Rom. 9 : 5).

From these and other passages the following doctrinal points may be inferred :

1. The eternal *pre-existence* of Christ as to his divine nature. The pre-existence generally is implied in Rom. 8 : 3, 32 ; 2 Cor. 5 : 21 ; Phil. 2 : 5 ; the pre-existence *before the creation* is expressly asserted, Col. 1 : 15 ; the *eternity* of this pre-existence is a metaphysical inference from the nature of the case, since an existence *before* all creation must be an uncreated, therefore a divine or eternal existence which has no beginning as well as no end. (John carefully distinguishes between the eternal ἦν of the pre-existent Logos, and the temporal ἐγένετο of the incarnate Logos, John 1 : 1, 14 ; comp. 8 : 58.) This is not inconsistent with the designation of Christ as "the *first-born* of all creation," Col. 1 : 15 ; for πρωτότοκος is different from πρωτόκτιστος (*first-created*), as the Nicene fathers already remarked, in opposition to Arius, who inferred from the passage that Christ was the first *creature* of God and the *creator* of all other creatures. The word *first-born* corresponds to the Johannean μονογενής, *only-begotten*. "Both express," as Lightfoot says (*Com. on Col.*) "the same eternal fact; but while μονογενής states it in itself, πρωτότοκος places it in relation to the universe." We may also compare the πρωτόγονος, *first-begotten*, which Philo applies to the Logos, as including the original archetypal idea of the created world. "The first-born," used absolutely (πρωτότοκος, בְּכוֹר, Ps. 89 : 28), became a recognized title of the Mes-

siah. Moreover, the genitive πάσης κτίσεως is not the partitive, but the comparative genitive : the first-born as compared with, that is, *before*, every creature. So Justin Martyr (πρὸ πάντων τῶν κτισμάτων), Meyer, and Bp. Lightfoot, *in loc.;* also Weiss, *Bibl. Theol. d. N. T.*, p. 431 (who refutes the opposite view of Usteri, Reuss, and Baur, and says : " *Da πάσης κτίσεως jede einzelne Creatur bezeichnet, so kann der Genit. nur comparativ genommen werden, und nur besagen, dass er im Vergleich mit jedei Creatur der Erstgeborne war* "). The words immediately following, ver. 16, 17, exclude the possibility of regarding Christ himself as a creature. Lightfoot, in his masterly Comm. (p. 212 sq.), very fully explains the term as teaching the absolute pre-existence of the Son, his priority to and sovereignty over all creation.

The recent attempt of Dr. Beyschlag (*Christologie des N. T.*, pp. 149 sqq., 242 sqq.) to resolve the pre-existent Christ of Paul and John into an *ideal principle*, instead of a real personality, is an exegetical failure, like the similar attempts of the Socinians, and is as far from the mark as the interpretation of some of the Nicene fathers (*e. g.*, Marcellus) who, in order to escape the Arian argument, understood *prototokos* of the *incarnate* Logos as the head of the new spiritual creation.

2. Christ is the *mediator* and the *end* of creation. " All things were created *in him*, in the heavens and upon the earth, things visible and things invisible . . . ; all things have been created *through him* (δι' αὐτοῦ) and *unto him* (εἰς αὐτόν) ; and he is *before* all things, and *in him* all things consist," Col. 1 : 15–18. The same doctrine is taught in 1 Cor. 8 : 6 ("Jesus Christ, *through whom* are all things "); 10 ; 9 ; 15 : 47; as well as in the Ep. to the Hebrews (1 : 2 : " through whom he also made the worlds " or " ages "), and in John 1 : 3.

3. The *divinity* of Christ is clearly implied in the constant co-ordination of Christ with the Father as the author of " grace and peace," in the salutations of the Epistles, and in such expressions as " the image of the invisible God " (Col. 1 : 15) ; " in him dwells the fulness of the God-head bodily " (2 : 9) : " existing in the form of God," and " being on an equality with God " (Phil. 2 : 6). In two passages he is, according to the usual interpretation, even called " God " (ꙅεός), but, as already remarked, the exegetes are still divided on the reference of ꙅεός in Rom. ꙅ : 5 and Tit. 2 : 13. Meyer admits that Paul, according to his christolɔgy, could call Christ " God" (as predicate, without the article, ꙅεός, not ὁ ꙅεός) ; and Weiss, in the 6th edition of Meyer on Romans (1881), adopts the prevailing orthodox punctuation and interpretation in ch. 9 : 5 as the most natural, on purely exegetical grounds (the necessity of a supplement to κατὰ σάρκα, and the position of εὐλόγητος *after* ꙅεός) : " Christ as concerning the flesh, who [at the same time according to his higher nature] is over all, even God blessed for ever." Westcott and Hort are not quite agreed on the punctuation. See their note in *Greek Test., Introd. and Appendix*, p. 109.

4. The *incarnation*. This is designated by the terms "God *sent* his own Son (Rom. 8 : 3, comp. 32) ; Christ " emptied himself, taking the form of a servant, being made in the likeness of men " (Phil. 2 : 7). Without entering here into the Kenosis controversy (the older one between Giessen and Tübingen, 1620–1630, and the recent one which began with Thomasius, 1845), it is enough to say that the Kenosis, or self-exinanition, refers not to the incarnate, but to the pre-existent Son of God, and implies a certain kind of self-limitation or temporary surrender of the divine mode of existence during the state of humiliation. This humiliation was followed by exaltation as a reward for his obedience unto death (ver. 9–11) ; hence he is now " the Lord of glory " (1 Cor. 2 : 8). To define the limits of the Kenosis, and to adjust it to the immutability of the Godhead and the intertrinitarian process, lies beyond the sphere of exegesis and belongs to speculative dogmatics.

5. The true, but *sinless humanity* of Christ. He appeared " in the likeness of the flesh of sin" (Rom. 8 : 3) ; he is a son of David "according to the flesh" (1 : 3), which includes the whole human nature, body, soul, and spirit (as in John 1 : 14) ; he is called a man (ἄνθρωπος) in the full sense of the term (1 Cor. 15 : 21 ; Rom. 5 : 15 ; Acts 17 : 31). He was "born of a woman, born under the law" (Gal. 4 : 4) ; he was " found in fashion as a man " and became " obedient even unto death " (Phil. 2 : 8), and he truly suffered and died, like other men. But he " knew no sin" (2 Cor. 5 : 21). He could, of course, not be the Saviour of sinners if he himself were a sinner and in need of salvation.

Of the events of Christ's life, Paul mentions especially and frequently his death and resurrection, on which our salvation depends. He also reports the institution of the Lord's Supper, which perpetuates the memory and the blessing of the atoning sacrifice on the cross (1 Cor. 11 : 23–30). He presupposes, of course, a general knowledge of the historical Christ, as his Epistles are all addressed to believing converts ; but he incidentally preserves a gem of Christ's sayings not reported by the Evangelists, which shines like a lone star on the firmament of uncertain traditions : " It is more blessed to give than to receive " (Acts 20 : 35).

III. PAUL'S DOCTRINE OF PREDESTINATION.—Eternal *foreknowledge* of all persons and things is necessarily included in God's omniscience, and is uniformly taught in the Bible ; eternal *foreordination* or predestination is included in his almighty power and sovereignty, but must be so conceived as to leave room for free agency and responsibility, and to exclude God from the authorship of sin. Self-limitation is a part of freedom even in man, and may be exercised by the sovereign God for holy purposes and from love to his creatures ; in fact it is necessary, if salvation is to be a moral process, and not a physical or mechanical necessity. Religion is worth nothing except as the expression of free conviction and voluntary devotion. Paul represents sometimes the

divine sovereignty, sometimes the human responsibility, sometimes, as
in Phil. 2 : 12, 13, he combines both sides, without an attempt to solve
the insolvable problem which really lies beyond the present capacity of
the human mind. " He does not deal with speculative extremes ; and
in whatever way the question be speculatively adjusted, absolute dependence and moral self-determination are *both* involved in the immediate Christian self-consciousness," Baur, *Paul*, II. 249. " Practical
teaching," says Reuss (II. 532) to the same effect, " will always be constrained to insist upon the fact that man's salvation is a free gift of
God, and that his condemnation is only the just punishment of sin."
Comp. also Farrar, *St. Paul*, II. 243, 590 ; Weiss, p. 356 sqq. ; Beyschlag, *Die paulinische Theodicee* (Berlin, 1868). Weiss thus sums up
Paul's doctrine of predestination : " *An sich hat Gott das absolute Recht,
die Menschen von vornherein zum Heil oder zum Verderben zu erschaffen
und durch freie Machtwirkung diesem Ziele zuzuführen ; aber er hat sich in
Betreff des christlichen Heils dieses Rechtes nur insofern bedient, als er un-
abhängig von allem menschlichen Thun und Verdienen nach seinem unbe-
schränkten Willen bestimmt, an welche Bedingung er seine Gnade knüpfen
will. Die Bedingung, an welche er seine Erwählung gebunden hat, ist nun
nichts anders als die Liebe zu ihm, welche er an den empfänglichen Seelen
vorhererkennt. Die Erwählten aber werden berufen, indem Gott durch das
Evangelium in ihnen den Glauben wirkt.*"

There can be no doubt that Paul teaches an eternal election to eternal salvation by free grace, an election which is to be actualized by faith
in Christ and a holy life of obedience. But he does not teach a decree
of reprobation or a predestination to sin and perdition (which would
indeed be a " *decretum horribile,*" if *verum*). This is a logical invention
of supralapsarian theologians who deem it to be the necessary counterpart of the decree of election. But man's logic is not God's logic. A
decree of reprobation is nowhere mentioned. The term ἀδόκιμος, *disap-
proved, worthless, reprobate*, is used five times only as a description of
character (twice of things). The ninth chapter of Romans is the Gibraltar of supralapsarianism, but it must be explained in connection with
chapters 10 and 11, which present the other aspects. The strongest
passage is Rom. 9 : 22, where Paul speaks of σκεύη ὀργῆς κατηρτισμένα
εἰς ἀπώλειαν. But he significantly uses here the passive : "*fitted*
unto destruction," or rather (as many of the best commentators from
Chrysostom to Weiss take it) the middle : " who *fitted themselves* for
destruction," and so deserved it ; while of the vessels of mercy he says
that God " *before prepared* " them unto glory (σκεύη ἐλέους ἃ προητοίμασεν,
ver. 23). He studiously avoids to say of the vessels of wrath : ἃ κατήρ-
τισεν, which would have corresponded to ἃ προητοίμασεν, and thus he
exempts God from a direct and efficient agency in sin and destruction.
When in the same chapter, ver. 17, he says of Pharaoh, that God *raised
him up* for the very purpose (εἰς αὐτὸ τοῦτό ἐξήγειρά σε) that he might

show in him His power, he does not mean that God created him or called him into existence (which would require a different verb), but, according to the Hebrew (Ex. 9 : 16, the hiphil of עָמַד), that "he caused him to stand forth" as actor in the scene; and when he says with reference to the same history that God "hardens whom he will" (ver. 18. ὃν δέ ϑέλει σκληρύνει), it must be remembered that Pharaoh had already repeatedly hardened his own heart (Ex.. 8 : 15, 32 ; 9 : 34, 35), so that God punished him for his sin and abandoned him to its consequences. God does not cause evil, but he bends, guides, and overrules it and often punishes sin with sin. "Das ist der Fluch der bösen That, dass sie, fortzeugend, immer Böses muss gebären." (Schiller.)

In this mysterious problem of predestination Paul likewise faithfully carries out the teaching of his Master. For in the sublime description of the final judgment, Christ says to the "blessed of my Father:" "Inherit the kingdom prepared for you from the foundation of the world" (Matt. 25 : 34), but to those on the left hand he says, "Depart from me, ye cursed, into the eternal fire which is prepared for the devil and his angels" (ver. 41). The omission of the words "of my Father," after "ye cursed," and of the words "for you," and "from the foundation of the world," is very significant, and implies that while the inheritance of the kingdom is traced to the eternal favor of God, the damnation is due to the guilt of man.

IV. The doctrine of JUSTIFICATION. This occupies a prominent space in Paul's system, though by no means to the disparagement of his doctrine of sanctification, which is treated with the same fulness even in Romans (comp. chs. 6–8 and 12–15). Luther, in conflict with Judaizing Rome, overstated the importance of justification by faith when he called it the articulus stantis vel cadentis ecclesiæ. This can only be said of Christ (comp. Matt. 16 : 16 ; 1 Cor. 3 : 11 ; 1 John 4 : 2, 3). It is not even the theme of the Epistle to the Romans, as often stated (e.g., by Farrar, St. Paul, II. 181) ; for it is there subordinated by γάρ to the broader idea of salvation (σωτηρία), which is the theme (1 : 16, 17). Justification by faith is the way by which salvation can be obtained.

The doctrine of justification may be thus illustrated :

Δικαιοσύνη

(צְדָקָה, צֶדֶק)

Δικαιοσύνη τοῦ νόμου	Δικαιοσύνη τοῦ θεοῦ
ἐξ ἔργων	ἐκ θεοῦ
ἰδία.	τῆς πίστεως
	ἐκ τῆς πίστεως
	διὰ πίστεως Χριστοῦ.

The cognate words are δικαίωσις, δικαίωμα, δίκαιος, δικαιόω. The Pauline idea of righteousness is derived from the Old Testament, and is inseparable from the conception of the holy will of God and his revealed law. But the classical usage is quite consistent with it, and illustrates the biblical usage from a lower plane. The Greek words are derived from δίκη, *jus*, *right*, and further back from δίχα, or δίς, *two-fold*, *in two parts* (according to Aristotle, *Eth. Nic.*, v. 2) ; hence they indicate a well-proportioned relation between parts or persons where each has his due. It may when apply to the relation between God and man, or to the relation between man and man, or to both at once. To the Greeks a righteous man was one who fulfils his obligations to God and man. It was a Greek proverb : " In righteousness all virtue is contained."

Δικαιοσύνη (צְדָקָה, צֶדֶק) is an attribute of God, and a corresponding moral condition of man, *i.e.*, man's conformity to the will of God as expressed in his holy law. It is therefore identical with true religion, with piety and virtue, as required by God, and insures his favor and blessing. The word occurs (according to Bruder's *Concord.*) sixty times in all the Pauline Epistles, namely : thirty-six times in Romans, four times in Galatians, seven times in 2 Corinthians, once in 1 Corinthians, four times in Philippians, three times in Ephesians, three times in 2 Timothy, once in 1 Timothy, and once in Titus.

Δίκαιος (צַדִּיק), *righteous* (*rechtbeschaffen*), is one who fulfils his duties to God and men, and is therefore well pleasing to God. It is used seventeen times by Paul (seven times in Romans), and often elsewhere in the New Testament.

Δικαίωσις occurs only twice in the New Test. (Rom. 4 : 25 ; 5 : 18). It signifies *justification*, or the act of God by which he puts the sinner into the possession of righteousness.

Δικαίωμα, which is found Rom. 1 : 32 ; 2 : 26 ; 5 : 16, 18 ; 8 : 4, means a *righteous decree*, or *judgment*. Aristotle (*Eth. Nicom.*, v. 10) defines it as τὸ ἐπανόρθωμα τοῦ ἀδικήματος, *the amendment of an evil deed*, or a legal adjustment ; and this would suit the passage in Rom. 5 : 16, 18.

The verb δικαιόω (צָדֵק, 'הִצְדִּיק) occurs twenty-seven times in Paul, mostly in Romans, several times in the Synoptical Gospels, once in Acts, and three times in James (2 : 21, 24, 25). It may mean, etymologically, *to make just, justificare* (for the verbs in όω, derived from adjectives of the second declension, indicate the making of what the adjective denotes, *e.g.*, δηλόω, *to make clear*, φανερόω, *to reveal*, τυφλόω, *to blind*) ; but in the Septuagint and the Greek Testament it hardly ever has this meaning ("*hæc significatio*," says Grimm, " *admodum rara, nisi prorsus dubia est*"), and is used in a forensic or judicial sense : *to declare one righteous* (*aliquem justum declarare, judicare*). This justification of the sinner is, of course, not a legal fiction, but perfectly true, for it is based on the real righteousness of Christ which the sinner makes his own by faith, and must prove his own by a life of holy obedience, or good works. For further expositions, see my annotations to Lange on *Romans*, pp. 74, 130, 136, 138 ;

and my *Com. on Gal.* 2 : 16, 17. On the imputation controversies see my essay in Lange on *Romans* 5 : 12, pp. 190–195. On the relation of Paul's doctrine of justification to that of James, see ¾ 69, p. 521.

V. Paul's doctrine of the CHURCH has been stated in ¾ 65, p. 506. But it requires more than one book to do anything like justice to the won‐ derful theology of this wonderful man.

§ 72. *John and the Gospel of Love.*

(See the Lit. in § 40, p. 405.)

GENERAL CHARACTER.

The unity of Jewish Christian and Gentile Christian theology meets us in the writings of John, who, in the closing decades of the first century, summed up the final results of the preceding struggles of the apostolic age and transmitted them to posterity. Paul had fought out the great conflict with Judaism and secured the recognition of the freedom and universality of the gospel for all time to come. John disposes of this question with one sentence : "The law was given through Moses ; grace and truth came through Jesus Christ." [1] His theology marks the culmi‐ nating height of divine knowledge in the apostolic age. It is im‐ possible to soar higher than the eagle, which is his proper symbol. [2]

His views are so much identified with the words of his Lord, to whom he stood more closely related than any other disciple, that it is difficult to separate them ; but the prologue to his Gospel contains his leading ideas, and his first Epistle the prac‐ tical application. The theology of the Apocalypse is also es‐ sentially the same, and this goes far to confirm the identity of authorship. [3]

---

[1] John 1 : 17.

[2] Herein Baur agrees with Neander and Schmid. He says of the Johannean type (*l.c.*, p. 351) : "*In ihm erreicht die neutestamentliche Theologie ihre höchste Stufe und ihre vollendetste Form.*" This admission makes it all the more impossible to attribute the fourth Gospel to a literary forger of the second century. See also some excellent remarks of Weiss, pp. 605 sqq., and the concluding chapter of Reuss on Paul and John.

[3] For the theology of the Apocalypse as compared with that of the Gospel and Epistles of John, see especially Gebhardt, *The Doctrine of the Apoc.*, transl. by Jefferson, Edinb., 1878.

John was not a logician, but a seer; not a reasoner, but a mystic; he does not argue, but assert; he arrives at conclusions with one bound, as by direct intuition. He speaks from personal experience and testifies of that which his eyes have seen and his ears heard and his hands have handled, of the glory of the Only-Begotten of the Father full of grace and truth.[1]

John's theology is marked by artless simplicity and spiritual depth. The highest art conceals art. As in poetry, so in religion, the most natural is the most perfect. He moves in a small circle of ideas as compared with Paul, but these ideas are fundamental and all-comprehensive. He goes back to first principles and sees the strong point without looking sideways or taking note of exceptions. Christ and Antichrist, believers and unbelievers, children of God and children of the devil, truth and falsehood, light and darkness, love and hatred, life and death: these are the great contrasts under which he views the religious world. These he sets forth again and again with majestic simplicity.

John and Paul.

John's type of doctrine is less developed and fortified than Paul's, but more ideal. His mind was neither so rich nor so strong, but it soared higher and anticipated the beatific vision. Although Paul was far superior to him as a scholar (and practical worker), yet the ancient Greek church saw in John the ideal theologian.[2] John's spirit and style may be compared to a calm, clear mountain-lake which reflects the image of the sun, moon, and stars, while Paul resembles the mountain-torrent that rushes over precipices and carries everything before it; yet there are trumpets of war in John, and anthems of peace in Paul. The one begins from the summit, with God and the Logos, the other from the depths of man's sin and misery; but both meet in the God-man who brings God down to man and lifts man up to God.

---

[1] John 1 : 14 (ἐθεασάμεθα τὴν δόξαν αὐτοῦ) ; 1 John 1 : 1–3.

[2] In the strictest sense of θεολόγος, as the chief champion of the eternal *deity* of the *Logos:* John 1 : 1 : θεος ἦν ὁ λόγος. So in the superscription of the Apocalypse in several cursive MSS.

John is contemplative and serene, Paul is aggressive and polemical; but both unite in the victory of faith and the never-ending dominion of love. John's theology is christological, Paul's soteriological; John starts from the person of Christ, Paul from his work; but their christology and soteriology are essentially agreed. John's ideal is life eternal, Paul's ideal is righteousness; but both derive it from the same source, the union with Christ, and find in this the highest happiness of man. John represents the church triumphant, Paul the church militant of his day and of our day, but with the full assurance of final victory even over the last enemy.

The Central Idea.

John's Christianity centres in the idea of love and life, which in their last root are identical. His dogmatics are summed up in the word: God first loved us; his ethics in the exhortation: Therefore let us love Him and the brethren. He is justly called the apostle of love. Only we must not understand this word in a sentimental, but in the highest and purest moral sense. God's love is his self-communication to man; man's love is a holy self-consecration to God. We may recognize—in rising stages of transformation—the same fiery spirit in the Son of Thunder who called vengeance from heaven; in the Apocalyptic seer who poured out the vials of wrath against the enemies of Christ; and in the beloved disciple who knew no middle ground, but demanded undivided loyalty and whole-souled devotion to his Master. In him the highest knowledge and the highest love coincide: knowledge is the eye of love, love the heart of knowledge; both constitute eternal life, and eternal life is the fulness of happiness.[1]

The central truth of John and the central fact in Christianity itself is the incarnation of the eternal Logos as the highest manifestation of God's love to the world. The denial of this truth is the criterion of Antichrist.[2]

---

[1] John 17 : 3; 15 : 11; 16 : 24; 1 John 1 : 4.
[2] Comp. John 1 : 14; 3 : 16; 1 John 4 : 1–3.

The Principal Doctrines.

I. The doctrine of God. He is spirit ($\pi\nu\epsilon\hat{\upsilon}\mu a$), he is light ($\phi\hat{\omega}\varsigma$), he is love ($\dot{a}\gamma\dot{a}\pi\eta$).[1] These are the briefest and yet the profoundest definitions which can be given of the infinite Being of all beings. The first is put into the mouth of Christ, the second and third are from the pen of John. The first sets forth God's metaphysical, the second his intellectual, the third his moral perfection; but they are blended in one.

God is spirit, all spirit, absolute spirit (in opposition to every materialistic conception and limitation); hence omnipresent, all-pervading, and should be worshipped, whether in Jerusalem or Gerizim or anywhere else, in spirit and in truth.

God is light, all light without a spot of darkness, and the fountain of all light, that is of truth, purity, and holiness.

God is love; this John repeats twice, looking upon love as the inmost moral essence of God, which animates, directs, and holds together all other attributes; it is the motive power of his revelations or self-communications, the beginning and the end of his ways and works, the core of his manifestation in Christ.

II. The doctrine of Christ's Person. He is the eternal and the incarnate Logos or Revealer of God. No man has ever yet seen God ($\vartheta\epsilon\acute{o}\nu$, without the article, God's nature, or God as God); the only-begotten Son (or God only-begotten),[2] who is in

---

[1] John 4 : 24 ; 1 John 1 : 5 ; 4 : 8, 16. The first definition or oracle is from Christ's dialogue with the woman of Samaria, who could, of course, not grasp the full meaning, but understood sufficiently its immediate practical application to the question of dispute between the Samaritans and the Jews concerning the worship on Gerizim or Jerusalem.

[2] There is a remarkable variation of reading in John 1 : 18 between μονογενὴς θ ε ό s, *one who is God only-begotten*, and ὁ μονογενής υ ἱ ό s, *the only-begotten Son*. (A third reading : ὁ μονογενὴς θεός, "*the* only-begotten God," found in ℵ′ and 33, arose simply from a combination of the two readings, the article being improperly transferred from the second to the first.) The two readings are of equal antiquity ; θεός is supported by the oldest Greek MSS., nearly all Alexandrian or Egyptian (ℵ* BC*L, also the Peshitto Syr.) ; υἱός by the oldest versions (Itala Vulg., Curet. Syr., also the secondary uncials and all known cursives except 33). The usual abbreviations in the uncial MS., $\overline{\Theta C}$ for θεός and $\overline{\Upsilon C}$ for υἱός, may easily be confounded. The connection of μονογενής with

the bosom [1] of the Father, he and he alone (ἐκεῖνος) declared
him and brought to light, once and forever, the hidden mystery
of his being.[2]

This perfect knowledge of the Father, Christ claims himself
in that remarkable passage in Matthew (11 : 27) which strikingly confirms the essential harmony of the Johannean and
Synoptical representations of Christ.

John (and he alone) calls Christ the "Logos" of God, i.e., the
embodiment of God and the organ of all his revelations.[3] As

Θεός is less natural than with υἱός, although John undoubtedly could call the
Son Θεός (not ὁ Θεός), and did so in ver. 1. Μονογενὴς Θεός simply combines
the two attributes of the Logos, Θεός, ver. 1, and μονογενής, ver. 14. For a
learned and ingenious defence of Θεός see Hort's *Dissertations* (Cambridge,
1877), Westcott on *St. John* (p. 71), and Westcott and Hort's *Gr. Test. Introd.
and Append.*, p. 74. Tischendorf and nearly all the German commentators
(except Weiss) adopt υἱός, and Dr. Abbot, of Cambridge, Mass., has written
two very able papers in favor of this reading, one in the *Bibliotheca Sacra* for
1861, pp. 840–872, and another in the "Unitarian Review" for June, 1875. The
Westminster Revision first adopted "God" in the text, but afterwards put it
on the margin. Both readings are intrinsically unobjectionable, and the sense
is essentially the same. Μονογενής does not necessarily convey the Nicene idea
of eternal generation, but simply the unique character and superiority of the
eternal and uncreated sonship of Christ over the sonship of believers which is
a gift of grace. It shows his intimate relation to the Father, as the Pauline
πρωτότοκος his sovereign relation to the world.

[1] Lit. "towards the bosom" (εἰς τὸν κόλπον), i.e., leaning on, and moving
to the bosom. It expresses the union of motion and rest and the closest and
tenderest intimacy, as between mother and child, like the German term
Schoosskind, bosom-child. Comp. πρὸς τὸν Θεόν in ver. 1 and Prov. 8 : 30, where
Wisdom (the Logos) says : "I was near Him as one brought up with Him,
and I was daily his delight, rejoicing always before him."

[2] With this sentence the Prologue returns to the beginning and suggests the
best reason why Christ is called Logos. He is the Exegete, the Expounder,
the Interpreter of the hidden being of God. "The word ἐξηγήσατο is used by
classical writers of the interpretation of divine mysteries. The absence of
the object in the original is remarkable. Thus the literal rendering is simply,
he made declaration (Vulg. *ipse enarravit*). Comp. Acts 15 : 14. Westcott,
in loc. See the classical parallels in Wetstein.

[3] John 1 : 1, 14 : 1 John 1 : 1 ; Rev. 19 : 13. The Logos theory of John
is the fruitful germ of the speculations of the Greek church on the mysteries
of the incarnation and the trinity. See my ed. of Lange's *Com. on John,*
pp. 51 and 55 sqq., where also the literature is given. On the latest discussions see Weiss in the sixth ed. of Meyer's *Com. on John* (1880), pp. 49 sqq.
Λόγος means both *ratio* and *oratio*, reason and speech, which are inseparably

the human reason or thought is expressed in word, and as the word is the medium of making our thoughts known to others, so God is known to himself and to the world in and through Christ as the personal Word. While "Logos" designates the metaphysical and intellectual relation, the term "Son" designates the moral relation of Christ to God, as a relation of love, and the epithet "only-begotten" or "only-born" (μονογενής) raises his sonship as entirely unique above every other sonship, which is only a reflection of it. It is a blessed relation of infinite knowledge and infinite love. The Logos is eternal, he is personal, he is divine.[1] He was in the beginning before creation or from eternity. He is, on the one hand, distinct from God and in the closest communion with him (πρὸς τὸν θεόν); on the other hand he is himself essentially divine, and therefore called "God" (θεός, but not ὁ θεός).[2]

connected. "Logos," being masculine in Greek, is better fitted as a designation of Christ than our neuter "Word." Hence Ewald, in defiance of German grammar, renders it "der Wort." On the apocalyptic designation ὁ λόγος τοῦ θεοῦ and on the christology of the Apocalypse, see Gebhardt, l. c., 94 and 333 sqq. On Philo's idea of the Logos I refer to Schürer, Neutestam. Zeitgeschichte, pp. 648 sqq., and the works of Gfrörer, Zeller, Frankel, etc., there quoted.

[1] These three ideas are contained in the first verse of the Gospel, which has stimulated and puzzled the profoundest minds from Origen and Augustin to Schelling and Goethe. Mark the unique union of transparent simplicity and inexhaustible depth, and the symmetry of the three clauses. The subject (λόγος) and the verb (ἦν) are three times repeated. "The three clauses contain all that it is possible for man to realize as to the essential nature of the Word in relation to time and mode of being and character : He was (1) in the beginning : He was (2) with God : He was (3) God. At the same time these three clauses answer to the three great moments of the Incarnation of the Word declared in ver. 14. He who 'was God,' became flesh : He who 'was with God,' tabernacled among us (comp. 1 John 1 : 2) : He who 'was in the beginning,' became (in time)." Westcott (in Speaker's Com.). A similar interpretation is given by Lange. The personality of the Logos is denied by Beyschlag. See Notes.

[2] Here we have the germ (but the germ only) of the orthodox distinction between unity of essence and trinity of persons or hypostases ; also of the distinction between an immanent, eternal trinity, and an economical trinity which is revealed in time (in the works of creation, redemption, and sanctification). A Hebrew monotheist could not conceive of an eternal and independent being of a different essence (ἑτεροούσις) existing besides the one God. This would be dualism.

This pre-existent Logos is the agent of the creation of all things visible and invisible.[1] He is the fulness and fountain of life (ἡ ζωή, the true, immortal life, as distinct from βίος, the natural, mortal life), and light (τὸ φῶς, which includes intellectual and moral truth, reason and conscience) to all men. Whatever elements of truth, goodness, and beauty may be found shining like stars and meteors in the darkness of heathendom, must be traced to the Logos, the universal Life-giver and Illuminator.

Here Paul and John meet again; both teach the agency of Christ in the creation, but John more clearly connects him with all the preparatory revelations before the incarnation. This extension of the Logos revelation explains the high estimate which some of the Greek fathers (Justin Martyr, Clement of Alexandria, Origen) put upon the Hellenic, especially the Platonic philosophy, as a training-school of the heathen mind for Christ.

The Logos revealed himself to every man, but in a special manner to his own chosen people; and this revelation culminated in John the Baptist, who summed up in himself the meaning of the law and the prophets, and pointed to Jesus of Nazareth as "the Lamb of God that taketh away the sin of the world."

At last the Logos became flesh.[2] He completed his revela-

---

[1] 1 : 3, with a probable allusion to Gen. 1 : 3, "God *said*," as ἐν ἀρχῇ refers to *bereshith*, Gen. 1 : 1. The negative repetition οὐδὲ ἕν, *prorsus nihil, not even one thing* (stronger than οὐδέν, *nihil*), excludes every form of dualism (against the Gnostics), and makes the πάντα absolutely unlimited. The Socinian interpretation, which confines it to the *moral* creation, is grammatically impossible.

[2] 1 : 14 : ὁ λόγος σὰρξ ἐγένετο, a sentence of immeasurable import, the leading idea not only of the Prologue, but of the Christian religion and of the history of mankind. It marks the close of the preparation for Christianity and the beginning of its introduction into the human race. Bengel calls attention to the threefold antithetic correspondence between vers. 1 and 14 :

The Logos

| was (ἦν) in the beginning God, with God. | became (ἐγένετο) flesh, and dwelt among us. |

tion by uniting himself with man once and forever in all things, except sin.¹ The Hebraizing term "flesh" best expresses his condescension to our fallen condition and the complete reality of his humanity as an object of sense, visible and tangible, in strong contrast with his immaterial divinity. It includes not only the body (σῶμα), but also a human soul (ψυχή) and a rational spirit (νοῦς, πνεῦμα); for John ascribes them all to Christ. To use a later terminology, the incarnation (ἐνσάρκωσις, *incarnatio*) is only a stronger term for the assumption of humanity (ἐνανθρώπησις, *Menschwerdung*). The Logos became man—not partially but totally, not apparently but really, not transiently but permanently, not by ceasing to be divine, nor by being changed into a man, but by an abiding, personal union with man. He is henceforth the Godman. He tabernacled on earth as the true Shekinah, and manifested to his disciples the glory of the only begotten which shone from the veil of his humanity.² This is the divine-human glory in the state of humiliation as distinct from the divine glory in his pre-existent state, and from the final and perfect manifestation of his glory in the state of exaltation in which his disciples shall share.³

The fourth Gospel is a commentary on the ideas of the Prologue. It was written for the purpose that the readers may believe "that Jesus is the Christ (the promised Messiah), the Son of God (in the sense of the only begotten and eternal Son), and that believing they may have life in his name."⁴

III. The Work of Christ (Soteriology). This implies the conquest over sin and Satan, and the procurement of eternal life. Christ appeared without sin, to the end that he might destroy the works of the devil, who was a liar and murderer from

---

¹ Paul expresses the same idea : God sent his Son "in the likeness of the flesh of sin," Rom. 8 : 3 ; comp. Heb. 2 : 17 ; 4 : 15. See the note at the close of the section.

² 1 : 14 : ἐσκήνωσεν ἐν ἡμῖν, in allusion to the indwelling of Jehovah in the holy of holies of the tabernacle (σκηνή) and the temple. The humanity of Christ is now the true tabernacle of God, and the believers are the spectators of that glory. Comp. Rev. 7 : 15 ; 21 : 3.

³ John 17 : 5, 24 ; 1 John 3 : 2.   ⁴ John 20 : 31.

the beginning of history, who first fell away from the truth and then brought sin and death into mankind.[1] Christ laid down his life and shed his blood for his sheep. By this self-consecration in death he became the propitiation (ἱλασμός) for the sins of believers and for the sins of the whole world.[2] His blood cleanses from all the guilt and contamination of sin. He is (in the language of the Baptist) the Lamb of God that bears and takes away the sin of the world; and (in the unconscious prophecy of Caiaphas) he died for the people.[3] He was priest and sacrifice in one person. And he continues his priestly functions, being our Advocate in Heaven and ready to forgive us when we sin and come to him in true repentance.[4]

This is the negative part of Christ's work, the removal of the obstruction which separated us from God. The positive part consists in the revelation of the Father, and in the communication of eternal life, which includes eternal happiness. He is himself the Life and the Light of the world. He calls himself the Way, the Truth, and the Life. In him the true, the eternal life, which was from the beginning with the Father, appeared personally in human form. He came to communicate it to men. He is the bread of life from heaven, and feeds the believers everywhere spiritually without diminishing, as He fed the five thousand physically with five loaves. That miracle is

---

[1] 1 John 3 : 5, 8; comp. the words of Christ, John 8 : 44.

[2] John 6 : 52–58 ; 10 : 11, 15 ; 1 John 2 : 2 : αὐτὸς ἱλασμός ἐστιν περὶ τῶν ἁμαρτιῶν ἡμῶν, οὐ περὶ τῶν ἡμετέρων δὲ μόνον, ἀλλὰ καὶ περὶ ὅλου τοῦ κόσμου. The universality of the atonement could not be more clearly expressed ; but there is a difference between universal sufficiency and universal efficiency.

[3] 1 John 1 : 10 ; John 1 : 29 ; 11 : 50 ; comp. 18 : 14.

[4] 1 John 2 : 1 : ἐάν τις ἁμάρτῃ, παράκλητον ἔχομεν πρὸς τὸν πατέρα Ἰησοῦν Χριστὸν δίκαιον.

[5] 1 John 1 : 2 : ἡ ζωὴ ἐφανερώθη, καὶ ἑωράκαμεν καὶ μαρτυροῦμεν καὶ ἀπαγγέλλομεν ὑμῖν τὴν ζωὴν τὴν αἰώνιον ἥτις ἦν πρὸς τὸν πατέρα καὶ ἐφανερώθη ἡμῖν. Comp. John 1 : 4 ; 5 : 26 ; 14 : 6. The passage 1 John 5 : 20 : οὗτός ἐστιν ὁ ἀληθινὸς θεὸς καὶ ζωὴ αἰώνιος, is of doubtful application. The natural connection of οὗτος with the immediately preceding Ἰησοῦ Χριστῷ, and the parallel passages where Christ is called "life," favor the reference to Christ ; while the words ὁ ἀληθινὸς θεός suit better for the Father. See Braune, Huther, Ebrard, Haupt, Rothe, in loc.

continued in the mystical self-communication of Christ to his people. Whosoever believes in him has eternal life, which begins here in the new birth and will be completed in the resurrection of the body.[1] Herein also the Apocalypse well agrees with the Gospel and Epistles of John. Christ is represented as the victor of the devil.[2] He is the conquering Lion of the tribe of Judah, but also the suffering Lamb slain for us. The figure of the lamb, whether it be referred to the paschal lamb, or to the lamb in the Messianic passage of Isaiah 53 : 7, expresses the idea of atoning sacrifice which is fully realized in the death of Christ. He " washed " (or, according to another reading, he " loosed ") " us from our sins by his blood ; " he redeemed men " of every tribe, and tongue, and people, and nation, and made them to be unto our God a kingdom and priests." The countless multitude of the redeemed " washed their robes and made them white (bright and shining) in the blood of the Lamb." This implies both purification and sanctification ; white garments being the symbols of holiness.[3] Love was the motive which prompted him to give his life for his people.[4] Great stress is laid on the resurrection, as in the Gospel, where he is called the Resurrection and the Life. The exalted Logos-Messiah has the keys of death and Hades.[5] He is a sharer in the universal government of God ; he is the mediatorial ruler of the world, " the Prince of the kings of the earth," " King of kings and Lord of lords." [6] The apocalyptic seer likewise brings in the

---

[1] John 6 : 47; and the whole mysterious discourse which explains the spiritual meaning of the preceding miracle.

[2] Apoc. 12 : 1–12; 20 : 2. Comp. with 1 John 3 : 8; John 8 : 44; 12 : 31 , 13 : 2, 27; 14 : 30; 16 : 11.

[3] Apoc. 1 : 6; 5 : 6, 9, 12, 13; 7 : 14, etc. Comp. John 1 : 29 ; 17 : 19; 19 : 36 ; 1 John 1 : 7 ; 2 : 2 ; 5 : 6. The apocalyptic diminutive ἀρνίον (agnellus, lamb-kin, pet-lamb) for ἀμνός is used to sharpen the contrast with the Lion. Paul Gerhardt has reproduced it in his beautiful passion hymn : " Ein LÄMMLEIN geht und trägt die Schuld. "

[4] Apoc. 1 : 5 : " Unto him that loveth us," etc.; comp. John 15 : 13 ; 1 John 3 : 16.

[5] Apoc. 1 : 5, 17, 18; 2 : 8; comp. John 5 : 21, 25 ; 6 : 39, 40 · 11 : 25.

[6] Apoc. 1 : 5; 3 : 21; 17 : 14; 19 : 16.

idea of life in its highest sense as a reward of faith in Christ. To those who overcome and are faithful unto death, Christ will give " a crown of life," and a seat on his throne. He " shall guide them unto fountains of waters of life; and God shall wipe away every tear from their eyes." [1]

IV. The Doctrine of the Holy Spirit (Pneumatology). This is most fully set forth in the farewell discourses of our Lord, which are reported by John exclusively. The Spirit whom Christ promised to send after his return to the Father, is called the *Paraclete*, *i.e.*, the Advocate or Counsellor, Helper, who pleads the cause of the believers, directs, supports, and comforts them.[2] He is "another Advocate" (ἄλλος παράκλητος), Christ himself being the first Advocate who intercedes for believers at the throne of the Father, as their eternal High priest. The Spirit proceeds (eternally) from the Father, and was sent by the Father and the Son on the day of Pentecost.[3] He reveals

---

[1] Apoc. 2 : 10 ; 3 : 21 ; 7 : 17 ; 14 : 1–5 ; 21 : 6, 7 ; 22 : 1–5. Comp. Gebhardt, *l. c.*, 106–128, 343–353.

[2] John 14 : 16, 26 ; 15 : 26; 16 : 7. Comp. also 1 John 2 : 1, where Christ is likewise called παράκλητος. He is our Advocate objectively at the throne of the Father, the Holy Spirit is our Advocate subjectively in our spiritual experience. The E. V. renders the word in all these passages, except the last, by "Comforter" (*Consolator*), which rests on a confusion of the passive παράκλητος with the active παρακλήτωρ. See my notes in Lange's *Com. on John*, pp. 440 sqq., 468 sqq.

[3] There is a distinction between the eternal procession (ἐκπόρευσις) of the Spirit from the Father (παρὰ τοῦ Πατρὸς ἐ κ π ο ρ ε ύ ε τ α ι, *procedit*, John 15 : 26), and the temporal mission (πέμψις) of the Spirit from the Father and the Son (15 : 26, where Christ says of the Spirit : ὃν ἐγὼ π έ μ ψ ω, and 14 : 26, where he says: ὃ π έ μ ψ ε ι ὁ πατὴρ ἐν τῷ ὀνόματί μου). The Greek church to this day strongly insists on this distinction, and teaches an *eternal procession* of the Spirit from *the Father alone*, and a *temporal mission* of the Spirit by *the Father and the Son*. The difference between the present ἐκπορεύεται and the future πέμψω seems to favor such a distinction, but the exclusive *alone* (μόνον) in regard to the procession is an addition of the Greek church as much as the *Filioque* is an addition of the Latin church to the original Nicene Creed. It is doubtful whether John meant to make a *metaphysical* distinction between procession and mission. But the distinction between the eternal trinity of the divine being and the temporal trinity of the divine revelation has an exegetical basis in the *pre-existence* of the Logos and the Spirit. The trinitarian revelation reflects the trinitarian essence ; in other words, God reveals himself as he is, as Father, Son, and Spirit. We have a right to reason from the

Christ to the heart and glorifies him (ἐμὲ δοξάσει); he bears
witness to him (μαρτυρήσει περὶ ἐμοῦ); he calls to remembrance
and explains his teaching (ὑμᾶς διδάξει πάντα καὶ ὑπομνήσει
ὑμᾶς πάντα ἃ εἶπον ὑμῖν ἐγώ); he leads the disciples into the
whole truth (ὁδηγήσει ὑμᾶς εἰς τὴν ἀλήθειαν πᾶσαν); he takes
out of the fulness of Christ and shows it to them (ἐκ τοῦ ἐμοῦ
λαμβάνει καὶ ἀναγγελεῖ ὑμῖν). The Holy Spirit is the Mediator and Intercessor between Christ and the believer, as Christ
is the Mediator between God and the world. He is the Spirit
of truth and of holiness. He convicts (ἐλέγχει) the world, that
is, all men who come under his influence, in respect of sin (περὶ
ἁμαρτίας), of righteousness (δικαιοσύνης), and of judgment (κρί-
σεως); and this conviction will result either in the conversion,
or in the impenitence of the sinner. The operation of the
Spirit accompanies the preaching of the word, and is always
internal in the sphere of the heart and conscience. He is one
of the three witnesses and gives efficacy to the other two witnesses of Christ on earth, the baptism (τὸ ὕδωρ), and the atoning
death (τὸ αἷμα) of Christ.[1]

V. CHRISTIAN LIFE. It begins with a new birth from above
or from the Holy Spirit. Believers are children of God who
are "born, not of blood, nor of the will of the flesh, nor of the
will of man, but of God."[2] It is a "new" birth compared

revelation of God to his nature, but with proper reverence and modesty; for
who can exhaust the ocean of the Deity!

[1] 1 John 5 : 8. There are different interpretations of water and blood :
1st, reference to the miraculous flow of blood and water from the wounded
side of Christ, John 19 : 34 ; 2d, Christ's baptism, and Christ's atoning death ;
3d, the two sacraments which he instituted as perpetual memorials. I would
adopt the last view, if it were not for τὸ αἷμα, which nowhere designates the
sacrament of the Lord's Supper, and more naturally refers to the blood of
Christ shed for the remission of sins. The passage on the three *heavenly*
witnesses in ver. 7, formerly quoted as a proof text for the doctrine of the
trinity, is now generally given up as a mediæval interpolation, and must be
rejected on internal as well as external grounds ; for John would never have
written : "the Father, the *Word*, and the Spirit," but either "the Father,
the *Son*, and the Spirit," or "*God*, the Word (Logos), and the Spirit."

[2] John 1 : 13 : τέκνα θεοῦ . . . ἐκ θεοῦ ἐγεννήθησαν. The classical section
on the new birth is Christ's discourse with Nicodemus, ch. 3 : 1–15. The
terms γεννηθῆναι ἄνωθεν, *to be born anew, afresh,* or *from above, i.e.,* from

with the old, a birth " from God," as compared with that from
man, a birth from the Holy " Spirit," in distinction from carnal birth, a birth "from heaven," as opposed to earthly birth.
The life of the believer does not descend through the channels
of fallen nature, but requires a creative act of the Holy Spirit
through the preaching of the gospel. The life of the regenerate
is free from the principle and power of sin. " Whosoever is
begotten of God doeth no sin, because his seed abideth in him ;
and he cannot sin because he is begotten of God." [1] Over him
the devil has no power.[2]

The new life is the life of Christ in the soul. It is eternal intrinsically and as to duration. Eternal life in man consists in the
knowledge of the only true God and of Jesus Christ—a knowledge which implies full sympathy and communion of love.[3] It begins here in faith; hence the oft-repeated declaration that he who
believes in Christ *has* (ἔχει) eternal life.[4] But it will not appear
in its full development till the time of his glorious manifestation,

heaven, comp. 3 : 31 ; 19 : 11 (the reference is not to a repetition, *again, a
second time*, πάλιν, δεύτερον, but to an analogous process) ; 3 : 6, 7 ; γεννηθῆναι
ἐξ ὕδατος καὶ πνεύματος, *of water* (baptism) *and spirit*, ver. 5 ; ἐκ θεοῦ, *of God*,
ἐκ τοῦ οὐρανοῦ, *from heaven*, are equivalent. John himself most frequently
uses ἐκ θεοῦ, 1 : 13 ; 1 John 2 : 29 ; 3 : 9 ; 4 : 7; 5 : 1, 4, 18. He does not use
ἀναγεννάομαι, *to be begotten* or *born again* (but it occurs in Justin Martyr's
quotation, *Apol.* I. 61; also in 1 Pet. 1 : 23, ἀναγεγεννημένοι . . διὰ λόγου
ζῶντος θεοῦ, and 1 Pet. 1 : 3, ἀναγεννήσας ἡμᾶς εἰς ἐλπίδα), and the noun
ἀναγέννησις, *regeneration*, is not found at all in the Greek Test. (though often
in the Greek fathers); but the analogous παλιγγενεσία occurs once in connection with baptism, Tit. 3 : 5 (ἔσωσεν ἡμᾶς διὰ λουτροῦ παλιγγενεσίας καὶ ἀνακαι-
νώσεως πνεύματος ἁγίου), and once in a more comprehensive sense of the final
restitution and consummation of all things, Matt. 19 : 18. Paul speaks of the
new creature in Christ (καινὴ κτίσις, 2 Cor. 5 : 17) and of the *new man* (καινὸς
ἄνθρωπος, Eph. 4 : 24). In the Rabbinical theology regeneration meant simply
the change of the external status of a proselyte to Judaism.

[1] 1 John 3 : 9; comp. 5 : 18. But ch. 5 : 16 implies that a "brother" may
sin, though not "unto death," and ch. 1 : 10 also excludes the idea of *absolute* freedom from sin in the present state.

[2] 1 John 5 : 18 : ὁ πονηρὸς οὐχ ἅπτεται αὐτοῦ.

[3] John 17 : 3, words of our Lord in the sacerdotal prayer.

[4] 1 John 5 : 12, 13 : ὁ ἔχων τὸν υἱὸν ἔχει τὴν ζωήν . . . ζωὴν ἔχετε αἰώνιον.
Comp. the words of Christ, John 3 : 36; 5 : 24 ; 6 : 47, 54 ; and of the Evangelist, 20 : 31.

when we shall be like him and see him even as he is.[1] Faith is the medium of communication, the bond of union with Christ. Faith is the victory over the world, already here in principle.[2]

John's idea of life eternal takes the place of Paul's idea of righteousness, but both agree in the high conception of faith as the one indispensable condition of securing it by uniting us to Christ, who is both righteousness and life eternal.[3]

The life of the Christian, moreover, is a communion with Christ and with the Father in the Holy Spirit. Our Lord prayed before his passion that the believers of that and all future ages might be one with him, even as he is one with the Father, and that they may enjoy his glory. John writes his first Epistle for the purpose that his readers may have "fellowship with the Father, and with his Son Jesus Christ, and that thus their joy may be made full."[4] This fellowship is only another word for love, and love to God is inseparable from love to the brethren. "If God so loved us, we also ought to love one another." "God is love; and he that abideth in love abideth in God and God abideth in him." Love to the brethren is the true test of practical Christianity.[5] This brotherly fellowship is the true essence of the Church, which is nowhere even mentioned in John's Gospel and First Epistle.[6]

Love to God and to the brethren is no mere sentiment, but an active power, and manifests itself in the keeping of God's commandments.[7]

---

[1] 1 John 3 : 2: οἴδαμεν ὅτι ἐὰν φανερωθῇ (he, or it), ὅμοιοι αὐτῷ ἐσόμεθα, ὅτι ὀψόμεθα αὐτὸν καθώς ἐστιν.

[2] 1 John 5 : 4: αὕτη ἐστὶν ἡ νίκη ἡ νικήσασα τὸν κόσμον, ἡ πίστις ἡμῶν.

[3] John uses the term δικαιοσύνη, but never δικαίωσις or δικαιόω. A striking example of religious agreement and theological difference.

[4] John 17 : 22–24 ; 1 John 1 : 3, 4.

[5] 1 John 3 : 11, 23 ; 4 : 7, 11 ; comp. John 13 : 34, 35 ; 15 : 12, 17.

[6] The word ἐκκλησία occurs in the third Epistle, but in the sense of a local congregation. Of the external organization of the church John is silent ; he does not even report the institution of the sacraments, though he speaks of the *spiritual* meaning of baptism (John 3 : 5), and indirectly of the *spiritual* meaning of the Lord's Supper (6 : 53–56).

[7] 1 John 2 : 3, 4 ; 3 : 22, 24 ; 4 : 7, 11 ; 5 : 2, 3 ; 2 John ver. 6 ; comp. the Gospel, 14 : 15, 21 : "If ye love me, ye will keep my commandments," etc.

Here again John and Paul meet in the idea of love, as the highest of the Christian graces which abides forever when faith shall have passed into sight, and hope into fruition.[1]

NOTES.

The INCARNATION is expressed by John briefly and tersely in the phrase "*The Word became flesh*" (1 : 14).

I. The meaning of σάρξ Apollinaris confined "flesh" to the body, including the *animal* soul, and taught that the Logos occupied the place of the *rational* soul or spirit (νοῦς, πνεῦμα) in Christ ; that consequently he was not a full man, but a sort of middle being between God and man, half divine and half human, not wholly divine and wholly human. This view was condemned as heretical by the Nicene church, but renewed substantially by the Tübingen school, as being the doctrine of John. According to Baur (*l. c.*, p. 363) σὰρξ ἐγένετο is not equivalent to ἄνθρωπος ἐγένετο, but means that the Logos assumed a human body and continued otherwise the same. The incarnation was only an incidental phenomenon in the unchanging personality of the Logos. Moreover the flesh of Christ was not like that of other men, but almost immaterial, so as to be able to walk on the lake (John 6 : 16 ; comp. 7 : 10, 15 ; 8 : 59 ; 10 : 39). To this exegesis we object :

1. John expressly ascribes to Christ a *soul*, 10 : 11, 15, 17 ; 12 : 27 (ἡ ψυχή μου τετάρακται), and a *spirit*, 11 : 33 (ἐνεβριμήσατο τῷ πνεύματι) ; 13 : 21 (ἐταράχθη τῷ πνεύματι) ; 19 : 30 (παρέδωκεν τὸ πνεῦμα). It may be said that πνεῦμα is here nothing more than the *animal* soul, because the same affection is attributed to both, and because it was surrendered in death. But Christ calls himself in John frequently "the Son of man" (1 : 52, etc.), and once "a man" (ἄνθρωπος, 8 : 40), which certainly must include the more important intellectual and spiritual part as well as the body.

2. "Flesh" is often used in the Old and New Testament for the *whole* man, as in the phrase "all flesh" (πᾶσα σάρξ, every mortal man), or μία σάρξ (John 17 : 2 ; Rom. 3 : 20 ; 1 Cor. 1 : 29 ; Gal. 2 : 16). In this passage it suited John's idea better than ἄνθρωπος, because it more strongly expresses the condescension of the Logos to the human nature in its present condition, with its weakness, trials, temptations, and sufferings. He completely identified himself with our earthly lot, and became homogeneous with us, even to the likeness, though not the essence, of sin (Rom. 8 : 3 ; comp. Heb. 2 : 14 ; 5 : 8, 9). "Flesh" then, when ascribed to Christ, has the same comprehensive meaning in John as it has in Paul (comp. also 1 Tim. 3 : 16). It is animated flesh, and the soul of that flesh contains the spiritual as well as the physical life.

[1] Rom. 13 : 7-10 ; 1 Cor. 13 : 1-13.

II. Another difficulty is presented by the verb ἐγένετο. The champions of the modern Kenosis theory (Thomasius, Gess, Ebrard, Godet,
etc.), while differing from the Apollinarian substitution of the Logos for
a rational human soul in Christ, assert that the Logos himself *became*
a human soul by voluntary transformation; and so they explain ἐγένετο
and the famous Pauline phrase ἑαυτὸν ἐκένωσεν, μορφὴν δούλου λαβών
(Phil. 2 : 7). As the water was changed into wine at Cana (2 : 9: τὸ ὕδωρ
οἶνον γεγενημένον), so the Logos in infinite self-denial changed his divine
being into a human being during the state of his humiliation, and thus
led a single life, not a double life (as the Chalcedonian theory of two
complete natures simultaneously coexisting in the same person from
the manger to the cross seems to imply). But

1. The verb ἐγένετο must be understood in agreement with the parallel
passages : "he *came* in the flesh," 1 John 4 : 2 (ἐν σαρκὶ ἐληλυθότα) ;
2 John 7 (ἐρχόμενον ἐν σαρκί), with this difference, that "became" indicates the realness of Christ's manhood, "came" the continuance of his
godhood. Compare also Paul's expression, ἐφανερώθη ἐν σαρκί, 1 Tim.
3 : 16.

2. Whatever may be the objections to the Chalcedonian dyophysitism,
they cannot be removed by running the Kenosis to the extent of a self-
suspension of the Logos or an actual surrender of his essential attributes; for this is a metaphysical impossibility, and inconsistent with
the unchangeableness of God and the intertrinitarian process. The
Logos did not cease to be God when he entered into the human state of
existence, nor did he cease to be man when he returned to the state of
divine glory which he had with the Father before the foundation of the
world.

III. Beyschlag (*Die Christologie des N. T.*, p. 168) denies the identity
of the Logos with Christ, and resolves the Logos into a divine *principle*,
instead of a person. "*Der Logos ist nicht die Person Christi . . . sondern
er ist das gottheitliche Princip dieser menschlichen Persönlichkeit.*" He
assumes a gradual unfolding of the Logos principle in the human person of Christ. But the personality of the Logos is taught in vers. 1–3,
and ἐγένετο denotes a completed act. We must remember, however, that
personality in the trinity and personality of the Logos are different from
personality of man. Human speech is inadequate to express the distinction.

§ 73. *Heretical Perversions of the Apostolic Teaching.*

(Comp. my *Hist. of the Ap. Ch.*, pp. 649–674.)

The three types of doctrine which we have briefly unfolded,
exhibit Christianity in the whole fulness of its life; and they
form the theme for the variations of the succeeding ages of the

church. Christ is the key-note, harmonizing all the discords and resolving all the mysteries of the history of his kingdom.

But this heavenly body of apostolic truth is confronted with the ghost of heresy; as were the divine miracles of Moses with the satanic juggleries of the Egyptians, and as Christ was with demoniacal possessions. The more mightily the spirit of truth rises, the more active becomes the spirit of falsehood. "Where God builds a church the devil builds a chapel close by." But in the hands of Providence all errors must redound to the unfolding and the final victory of the truth. They stimulate inquiry and compel defence. Satan himself is that " power which constantly *wills* the bad, and *works* the good." Heresies in a disordered world are relatively necessary and negatively justifiable; though the teachers of them are, of course, not the less guilty. " It must needs be, that scandals come; but woe to that man by whom the scandal cometh." [1]

The heresies of the apostolic age are, respectively, the caricatures of the several types of the true doctrine. Accordingly we distinguish three fundamental forms of heresy, which reappear, with various modifications, in almost every subsequent period. In this respect, as in others, the apostolic period stands as the type of the whole future; and the exhortations and warnings of the New Testament against false doctrine have force for every age.

1. The JUDAIZING tendency is the heretical counterpart of Jewish Christianity. It so insists on the unity of Christianity with Judaism, as to sink the former to the level of the latter, and to make the gospel no more than an improvement or a perfected law. It regards Christ as a mere prophet, a second Moses; and denies, or at least wholly overlooks, his divine nature and his priestly and kingly offices. The Judaizers were Jews in fact, and Christians only in appearance and in name. They held circumcision and the whole moral and ceremonial

---

[1] Matt. 18 : 7; 1 Cor. 11 : 19 : "There must be also heresies (factions) among you, that they who are approved may be made manifest among you." Comp. Acts 20 : 30 ; 1 Tim. 4 : 1 ; 2 Pet. 2 : 1-3.

law of Moses to be still binding, and the observance of them
necessary to salvation. Of Christianity as a new, free, and universal religion, they had no conception. Hence they hated Paul,
the liberal apostle of the Gentiles, as a dangerous apostate and
revolutionist, impugned his motives, and everywhere, especially
in Galatia and Corinth, labored to undermine his authority in
the churches. The epistles of Paul, especially that to the Galatians, can never be properly understood, unless their opposition
to this false Judaizing Christianity be continually kept in view.

The same heresy, more fully developed, appears in the second
century under the name of Ebionism.

2. The opposite extreme is a false Gentile Christianity, which
may be called the PAGANIZING or GNOSTIC heresy. It is as radical and revolutionary as the other is contracted and reactionary.
It violently breaks away from the past, while the Judaizing
heresies tenaciously and stubbornly cling to it as permanently
binding. It exaggerates the Pauline view of the distinction of
Christianity from Judaism, sunders Christianity from its historical basis, resolves the real humanity of the Saviour into a
Doketistic illusion, and perverts the freedom of the gospel into
antinomian licentiousness. The author, or first representative
of this baptized heathenism, according to the uniform testimony
of Christian antiquity, is Simon Magus, who unquestionably
adulterated Christianity with pagan ideas and practices, and
gave himself out, in pantheistic style, for an emanation of God.[1]
Plain traces of this error appear in the later epistles of Paul (to
the Colossians, to Timothy, and to Titus), the second epistle of
Peter, the first two epistles of John, the epistle of Jude, and
the messages of the Apocalypse to the seven churches.

This heresy, in the second century, spread over the whole
church, east and west, in the various schools of Gnosticism.

3. As attempts had already been made, before Christ, by
Philo, by the Therapeutæ and the Essenes, etc., to blend the
Jewish religion with heathen philosophy, especially that of
Pythagoras and Plato, so now, under the Christian name, there

---

[1] Acts 8 : 10 : ἡ Δύναμις τοῦ θεοῦ ἡ καλουμένη Μεγάλη.

appeared confused combinations of these opposite systems, forming either a PAGANIZING JUDAISM, *i.e.*, Gnostic Ebionism, or a JUDAIZING PAGANISM, *i.e.*, Ebionistic Gnosticism, according as the Jewish or the heathen element prevailed. This SYNCRETISTIC heresy was the caricature of John's theology, which truly reconciled Jewish and Gentile Christianity in the highest conception of the person and work of Christ. The errors combated in the later books of the New Testament are almost all more or less of this mixed sort, and it is often doubtful whether they come from Judaism or from heathenism. They were usually shrouded in a shadowy mysticism and surrounded by the halo of a self-made ascetic holiness, but sometimes degenerated into the opposite extreme of antinomian licentiousness.

Whatever their differences, however, all these three fundamental heresies amount at last to a more or less distinct denial of the central truth of the gospel—the incarnation of the Son of God for the salvation of the world. They make Christ either a mere man, or a mere superhuman phantom; they allow, at all events, no real and abiding union of the divine and human in the person of the Redeemer. This is just what John gives as the mark of antichrist, which existed even in his day in various forms.[1] It plainly undermines the foundation of the church. For if Christ be not God-man, neither is he mediator between God and men; Christianity sinks back into heathenism or Judaism. All turns at last on the answer to that fundamental question: "What think ye of Christ?" The true solution of this question is the radical refutation of every error.

NOTES.

"It has often been remarked that truth and error keep pace with each other. Error is the shadow cast by truth, truth the bright side brought out by error. Such is the relation between the heresies and the apostolical teaching of the first century. The Gospels indeed, as in other respects, so in this, rise almost entirely above the circumstances of the time, but the Epistles are, humanly speaking, the result of the very

[1] 1 John 2 : 23 ; 4 : 1–3.

conflict between the good and the evil elements which existed togethel in the bosom of the early Christian society. As they exhibit the principles afterward to be unfolded into all truth and goodness, so the heresies which they attack exhibit the principles which were afterward to grow up into all the various forms of error, falsehood and wickedness. The energy, the freshness, nay, even the preternatural power which belonged to the one belonged also to the other. Neither the truths in the writings of the Apostles, nor the errors in the opinions of their opponents, can be said to exhibit the dogmatical form of any subsequent age. It is a higher and more universal good which is aimed at in the former; it is a deeper and more universal principle of evil which is attacked in the latter. Christ Himself, and no subordinate truths or speculations concerning Him, is reflected in the one; Antichrist, and not any of the particular outward manifestations of error which have since appeared, was justly regarded by the Apostles as foreshadowed in the other." —Dean STANLEY (*Apostolic Age*, p. 182).

LITERATURE.—The heresies of the Apostolic Age have been thoroughly investigated by Neander and Baur in connection with the history of Ebionism and Gnosticism (see next vol.), and separately in the introductions to critical commentaries on the Colossians and Pastoral Epistles; also by Thiersch, Lipsius, Hilgenfeld. Among English writers we mention BURTON: *Inquiry into the Heresies of the Apostolic Age*, in eight Sermons (Bampton Lectures). Oxford, 1829. Dean STANLEY: *Sermons and Essays on the Apostolic Age*, pp. 182–233, 3d ed. Oxford, 1874. Bishop LIGHTFOOT: *Com. on St. Paul's Ep. to the Colossians and to Philemon*, pp. 73–113 (on the Colossian heresy and its connection with Essenism). London, 1875. Comp. also HILGENFELD: *Die Ketzergeschichte des Urchristenthums*. Leipzig, 1884 (642 pages).

CHAPTER XII.

THE NEW TESTAMENT.

§ 74. *Literature.*

Comp. the Lit. on the Life of Christ, § 14, and on the Apostolic Age, § 20.

I. The CRITICAL EDITIONS of the *Greek Testament* by LACHMANN (1842-50, 2 vols.) ; TISCHENDORF (ed. octava critica major, 1869-72, 2 vols., with *Prolegomena* by C. R. GREGORY, Part I., Leipz., 1884) ; TREGELLES (1857-79) ; WESTCOTT and HORT (1881, with a vol. of Introd. and Appendix. Cambridge and New York, revised ed. 1888).

Lachmann laid the foundation ; Tischendorf and Tregelles greatly enlarged and carefully sifted the critical apparatus ; Westcott and Hort restored the cleanest text from the oldest attainable sources ; all substantially agree in principle and result, and give us the ancient uncial instead of the mediæval cursive text.

Two bilingual editions also deserve special mention in connection with the recent revision of Luther's and King James's versions. OSKAR VON GEBHARDT : *Novum Testamentum Græce et Germanice*, Lips., 1881, gives the last text of Tischendorf (with the readings of Tregelles, and Westcott and Hort below) and the revised translation of Luther. His Greek text is also separately issued with an "Adnotatio critica," not contained in the diglott edition. *The Greek-English New Testament, containing Westcott and Hort's Greek Text and the Revised English Version on opposite pages,* with introduction by *Schaff.* New York (Harper & Brothers), 1882, revised ed. 1888.

II. The historico-critical INTRODUCTIONS, or literary HISTORIES of the New Testament by HUG, DE WETTE, CREDNER, GUERICKE, HORNE, DAVIDSON, TREGELLES, GRAU, HILGENFELD, ABERLE (R. Cath.), BLEEK (4th ed. by MANGOLD, 1886), REUSS (6th ed. 1887), HOLTZMANN (2d ed. 1886), WEISS (1886), SALMON (3d ed. 1888).

III. THIERSCH : *Herstellung des historischen Standpunktes für die Kritik der neutestamentl. Schriften.* Erlangen, 1845. (Against Baur and the Tübingen School.)—EDWARD C. MITCHELL : *Critical Handbook to the New Test.* (on Authenticity, Canon, etc.). Lond. and Andover, 1880 ; French translation, Paris, 1882.—J. P. LANGE : *Grundriss der Bibelkunde.* Heidelberg, 1881.—PHILIP SCHAFF : *Companion to the Greek Testament and the English Version.* N. Y. and Lond., 1883, 3d ed. revised 1888.—G. D. LADD : *The Doctrine of Sacred Scripture,* N. York, 1883, 2 vols. The same, abridged, 1888.

IV. The works quoted below on the *Gospels* and *Epistles*.

V. On the CANON of the New Test., the works of KIRCHHOFER (*Quellen-sammlung*, etc. Zürich, 1844, Engl. transl. enlarged by CHARTERIS : *Canonicity*, etc. Edinb., 1881) ; CREDNER (*Zur Gesch. des Kanon.* Halle, 1847 ; *Geschichte des Neutest. Kanon, herausg. von Volkmar.* Berlin, 1860)) ; GAUSSEN (Engl. transl., London, 1862 ; abridged transl. by *Kirk*, Boston, 1862) ; TREGELLES (*Canon Muratorianus.* Oxford, 1867) ; SAM. DAVIDSON (Lond., 1878, 3d ed., 1880) ; WEST-COTT (Cambridge and London, 1855 ; 6th ed., 1889) ; REUSS (*Histoire du canon des S. Écritures.* Strasb., 2d ed., 1864) ; AD. HARNACK (*Das muratorische Fragment und die Entstehung einer Sammlung apost.-katholischer Schriften*, in Brieger's "Zeitschrift f. Kirchenge-schichte," 1879, III., 358 sqq. ; comp. 595 sqq.) ; F. OVERBECK (*Zur Geschichte des Kanons.* Chemnitz, 1880) ; RÉVILLE (French, 1881) ; THEOD. ZAHN (*Forschungen zur Geschichte des neutestamentl. Kanons*, Part I.–III., 1881–84 ; and *Geschichte des Kanons d. N. T., Leipz.,* 1888 sqq., 3 vols). Comp. HARNACK : *Das N. T. um das Jahr.* 200, Freiburg, 1889 (against Zahn), and Zahn's reply, Leipz., 1889.

§ 75. *Rise of the Apostolic Literature.*

Christ is the book of life to be read by all. His religion is not an outward letter of command, like the law of Moses, but free, quickening spirit ; not a literary production, but a moral creation ; not a new system of theology or philosophy for the learned, but a communication of the divine life for the redemption of the whole world. Christ is the personal Word of God, the eternal Logos, who became flesh and dwelt upon earth as the true Shekinah, in the veiled glory of the only begotten from the Father, full of grace and truth. He spoke ; and all the words of his mouth were, and still are, spirit and life. The human heart craves not a learned, letter-writing, literary Christ, but a wonder-working, cross-bearing, atoning Redeemer, risen, enthroned in heaven, and ruling the world ; furnishing, at the same time, to men and angels an unending theme for meditation, discourse, and praise.

So, too, the Lord chose none of his apostles, with the single exception of Paul, from the ranks of the learned ; he did not train them to literary authorship, nor give them, throughout his earthly life, a single express command to labor in that way.

Plain fishermen of Galilee, unskilled in the wisdom of this world, but filled with the Holy Spirit of truth and the powers of the world to come, were commissioned to preach the glad tidings of salvation to all nations in the strength and in the name of their glorified Master, who sits on the right hand of God the Father Almighty, and has promised to be with them to the end of time.

The gospel, accordingly, was first propagated and the church founded by the personal oral teaching and exhortation, the "preaching," "testimony," "word," "tradition," of the apostles and their disciples; as, in fact, to this day the living word is the indispensable or, at least, the principal means of promoting the Christian religion. Nearly all the books of the New Testament were written between the years 50 and 70, at least twenty years after the resurrection of Christ, and the founding of the church; and the Gospel and Epistles of John still later.

As the apostles' field of labor expanded, it became too large for their personal attention, and required epistolary correspondence. The vital interests of Christianity and the wants of coming generations demanded a faithful record of the life and teaching of Christ by perfectly reliable witnesses. For oral tradition, among fallible men, is liable to so many accidental changes, that it loses in certainty and credibility as its distance from the fountain-head increases, till at last it can no longer be clearly distinguished from the additions and corruptions collected upon it. There was great danger, too, of a wilful distortion of the history and doctrine of Christianity by Judaizing and paganizing errorists, who had already raised their heads during the lifetime of the apostles. An authentic written record of the words and acts of Jesus and his disciples was therefore absolutely indispensable, not indeed to originate the church, but to keep it from corruption and to furnish it with a pure standard of faith and discipline.

Hence seven and twenty books by apostles and apostolic men, written under the special influence and direction of the Holy Spirit. These afford us a truthful picture of the history, the faith, and the practice of primitive Christianity, "for teaching, for reproof, for correction, for instruction in righteousness." [1]

The collection of these writings into a canon, in distinction both from apocryphal or pseudo-apostolic works, and from orthodox yet merely human productions, was the work of the early church; and in performing it she was likewise guided by the Spirit of God and by a sound sense of truth. It was not finished to the satisfaction of all till the end of the fourth century, down to which time seven New Testament books (the "Antilegomena" of Eusebius), the second Epistle of Peter, the second and third Epistles of John, the anonymous Epistle to the Hebrews, the Epistles of James and Jude, and in a certain sense also the Apocalypse of John, were by some considered of doubtful authorship or value. But the collection was no doubt begun, on the model of the Old Testament canon, in the first century; [2] and the principal books, the Gospels, the Acts, the thirteen Epistles of Paul, the first Epistle of Peter, and the first of John, in a body, were in general use after the middle of the second century, and were read, either entire or by sections, in public worship, after the manner of the Jewish synagogue, for the edification of the people.

The external testimony of tradition alone cannot (for the Protestant Christian) decide the apostolic origin and canonical character of a book; it must be confirmed by the internal testimony of the book itself. But this is not wanting, and the general voice of Christendom for these eighteen hundred years has recognized in the little volume, which we call the New Testament, a book altogether unique in spiritual power and influence over the mind and heart of man, and of more interest and value than all the ancient and modern classics combined. If ever God spoke and still speaks to man, it is in this book.

---

[1] 2 Tim. 3:16. It applies to "every Scripture inspired of God," more immediately to the Old Test., but *a fortiori* still more to the New.

[2] Comp. 2 Pet. 3:16, where a collection of Paul's Epistles is implied.

§ 76. *Character of the New Testament.*

In these inspired writings we have, not indeed an equivalent, but a reliable substitute for the personal presence and the oral instruction of Christ and his apostles. The written word differs from the spoken only in form; the substance is the same, and has therefore the same authority and quickening power for us as it had for those who heard it first. Although these books were called forth apparently by special and accidental occasions, and were primarily addressed to particular circles of readers and adapted to peculiar circumstances, yet, as they present the eternal and unchangeable truth in living forms, they suit all circumstances and conditions. Tracts for the times, they are tracts for all times; intended for Jews and Greeks of the first century, they have the same interest for Englishmen and Americans of the nineteenth century. They are to this day not only the sole reliable and pure fountain of primitive Christianity, but also the infallible rule of Christian faith and practice. From this fountain the church has drunk the water of life for more than fifty generations, and will drink it till the end of time. In this rule she has a perpetual corrective for all her faults, and a protective against all error. Theological systems come and go, and draw from that treasury their larger or smaller additions to the stock of our knowledge of the truth; but they can never equal that infallible word of God, which abideth forever.

> " Our little systems have their day,
>   They have their day and cease to be :
>   They are but broken lights of Thee,
>   And Thou, O God, art more than they."

The New Testament evinces its universal design in its very style, which alone distinguishes it from all the literary productions of earlier and later times. It has a Greek body, a Hebrew soul, and a Christian spirit which rules both. The language is the Hellenistic idiom; that is, the Macedonian Greek as spoken by the Jews of the dispersion in the time of Christ; uniting, in a regenerated Christian form, the two great antagonistic nation-alities and religions of the ancient world. The most beautiful language of heathendom and the venerable language of the Hebrews are here combined, and baptized with the spirit of Christianity, and made the picture of silver for the golden apple of the eternal truth of the gospel. The style of the Bible in general is singularly adapted to men of every class and grade of culture, affording the child the simple nourishment for its religious wants, and the profoundest thinker inexhaustible mat-ter of study. The Bible is not simply a popular book, but a book of all nations, and for all societies, classes, and conditions of men. It is more than a book, it is an institution which rules the Christian world.

The New Testament presents, in its way, the same union of the divine and human as the person of Christ. In this sense also "the word became flesh, and dwells among us." As Christ was like us in body, soul, and spirit, sin only excepted, so the Scriptures, which "bear witness of him," are thoroughly human (though without doctrinal and ethical error) in con-tents and form, in the mode of their rise, their compilation, their preservation, and transmission; yet at the same time they are thoroughly divine both in thoughts and words, in origin, vitality, energy, and effect, and beneath the human servant-form of the letter, the eye of faith discerns the glory of "the only begotten from the Father, full of grace and truth."

The apostolic writings are of three kinds: historical, didactic, and prophetic. To the first class belong the Gospels and Acts; to the second, the Epistles; to the third, the Revelation. They are related to each other as regeneration, sanctification, and glori-fication; as foundation, house, and dome. Jesus Christ is the beginning, the middle, and the end of all. In the Gospels he walks in human form upon the earth, and accomplishes the work of redemption. In the Acts and Epistles he founds the church, and fills and guides it by his Spirit. And at last, in the visions of the Apocalypse, he comes again in glory, and with his bride, the church of the saints, reigns forever upon the new earth in the city of God.

This order corresponds with the natural progress of the Christian revelation and was universally adopted by the church, with the exception of a difference in the arrangement of the Epistles. The New Testament was not given in the form of a finished volume, but the several books grew together by recognition and use according to the law of internal fitness. Most of the ancient Manuscripts, Versions, and Catalogues arrange the books in the following order: Gospels, Acts, Catholic Epistles, Pauline Epistles, Apocalypse.[1] Some put the Pauline Epistles before the Catholic Epistles.[2] Our English Bible follows the order of the Latin Vulgate.[3]

§ 77. *Literature on the Gospels.*

I. HARMONIES OF THE GOSPELS.

They begin with TATIAN's *Diatessaron*, A.D. 170. See lists of older works in Fabricius, *Bibl. Gr.*, III. 212; Hase, *Leben Jesu*, pp. 22–31 (fifth ed.); Robinson, *Harmony*, pp. v. and vi.; Darling, *Cyclopædia Bibliog.* (I. Subjects, cols. 761–767); and McClintock and Strong (*Cyclop.*, IV. 81). We give the chief works from Griesbach to Rushbrooke.

GRIESBACH (*Synopsis*, Halle, 1774, etc., 1822); NEWCOME (Dublin, 1778 and often; also Andover, 1834); Jos. PRIESTLEY (in Greek, London, 1778; in English, 1780); Jos. WHITE (*Diatessaron*, Oxford, 1799, 1803); DE WETTE and LÜCKE (1818, 1842); RÖDIGER (1829, 1839); GRESWELL (*Harmonia Evangelica*, 1830, 5th ed. Oxford, 1856; *Dissertations upon an Harmony*, etc., 2d ed., Oxford, 1837, 4 vols.); MACBRIDE (*Diatessaron*, Oxford, 1837); WIESELER (*Chronolog. Synopse*, Hamb., 1843); KRAFFT (d. 1845; *Chronologie u. Harmonie der 4 Evang.*

---

[1] This order is restored in the critical editions of Lachmann, Tischendorf, Tregelles, Westcott and Hort.

[2] The Codex Sinaiticus puts the Pauline Epistles before the Acts, and the Hebrews between 2 Thessalonians and 1 Timothy.

[3] This order agrees with the Muratorian Fragment, the catalogue of Eusebius (*H. E.*, III. 25), that of the Synod of Carthage (A.D. 397), and the Codex Basiliensis. Luther took the liberty of disconnecting the Hebrews (which he ascribed to Apollos) from the Pauline Epistles, and putting it and the Epistle of James (which he disliked) at the end of the Catholic Epistles (except Jude).

Erlangen, 1848; edit. by Burger); TISCHENDORF (*Synopsis Evang.*
Lips., 1851, 1854; 4th ed., 1878); RUD. ANGER (Lips., 1852);
STROUD (comprising a Synopsis and a Diatessaron, London, 1853);
E. ROBINSON (*A Harmony of the Four Gospels in Greek, according to
the text of Hahn*, Boston, 1845, 1851; revised ed., 1862; in English,
1846); JAMES STRONG (in English, New York, 1852; in Greek, 1854);
R. MIMPRISS (London, 1855); DOUGLAS (1859); SEVIN (Wiesbaden,
1866); FR. GARDINER (*A Harmony of the Four Gospels in Greek,
according to the text of Tischendorf, with a Collation of the Textus Receptus*, etc. Andover, 1876; also his *Diatessaron, The Life of our
Lord in the Words of the Gospels*, Andover, 1871); J. R. GILMORE
and LYMAN ABBOTT (*The Gospel History: being a Complete Chronological Narrative of the Life of our Lord*, New York, 1881); W. G.
RUSHBROOKE (*Synopticon: an Exposition of the Common Matter in the
Synoptic Gospels*, Cambridge, 1880–81, 2 parts; the Greek text of
Tischendorf, corrected from Westcott and Hort). The last work is
unique and superbly printed. It marks the differences of the narratives by different types and color, namely, the matter common to all
Evangelists in red type, the matter common to each pair in black
spaced type or capitals, the matter peculiar to each in ordinary
black type. It furnishes the best basis for a detailed comparison
and critical analysis.

II. CRITICAL DISCUSSIONS.

NATHANIEL LARDNER (1684–1768, a dissenting minister of great learning):
The Credibility of the Gospel History. First published in 17 vols.
8vo, London, 1727–1757, and in his collected *Works*, ed. by A.
Kippis, London, 1788 (in 11 vols.), vols. I.–V. Unsurpassed for
honest and solid learning, and still valuable.

J. G. EICHHORN (d. 1827): *Allgem. Bibliothek der bibl. Liter.*, vol. V.
(1794), pp. 759 sqq. *Einleitung in das N. Testament.*, 1804, vol. I., 2d
ed., 1820. Here he brought out his new idea of an *Urevangelium.*

HERBERT MARSH (Bishop of Peterborough, d. 1839): *An Illustration of
the Hypothesis proposed in the Dissertation on the Origin and Composition of our Three First Canonical Gospels.* Cambridge, 1803. Also
his translation of J. D. Michaelis: *Introduction to the New Test., with
a Dissertation on the Origin and Composition of the Three First Gospels.* London, 1802. A modification of Eichhorn's hypothesis.

FR. SCHLEIERMACHER: *Kritischer Versuch über die Schriften des Lucas.*
Berlin, 1817 (*Werke* I. 2, pp. 1–220); trans. by Thirlwall, Lond.,
1825. Comp. his *Einleitung in das N. Testament.* (posthumous).

J. C. L. GIESELER: *Historisch-kritischer Versuch über die Entstehung und
die frühesten Schicksale der schriftlichen Evangelien.* Leipz., 1818.

ANDREWS NORTON (a conservative Unitarian, died at Cambridge, 1853):

The Evidences of the Genuineness of the Gospels. Boston, 1837 ; 2d ed., Cambridge, Mass., 1846–1848, 3 vols. Abridged ed. in 1 vol., Boston (Am. Unitar. Assoc.), 1867 and 1875. By the same : *Internal Evidences of the Genuineness of the Gospels* (posthumous). Boston, 1855. With special reference to Strauss.

FR. BLEEK (d. 1859) : *Beiträge zur Evangelien-Kritik.* Berlin, 1846.

F. CHR. BAUR (d. 1860) : *Kritische Untersuchungen über die kanonischen Evangelien.* 1847. Comp. the first volume of his *Church History* (Germ. ed., pp. 22 sqq., 148 sqq.).

ISAAC DA COSTA : *The Four Witnesses : being a Harmony of the Gospels on a New Principle.* Transl. (from the Dutch) by *David Scott,* 1851; New York ed., 1855. Against Strauss.

AD. HILGENFELD (Tübingen School) : *Die Evangelien nach ihrer Entstehung und geschichtl. Bedeutung.* Leipz., 1854. His *Einleitung,* 1875.

CANON WESTCOTT : *Introduction to the Study of the Gospels.* London and Boston, 1860 ; 7th ed., London, 1888. Very useful.

CONST. TISCHENDORF (d. 1874) : *Wann wurden unsere Evangelien verfasst?* Leipz., 4th ed., 1866 (Engl. transl. by *W. L. Gage,* Boston, 1868).

H. JUL. HOLTZMANN : *Die synoptischen Evangelien, ihr Ursprung und geschichtl. Charakter.* Leipz., 1863. See also his art. *Evangelien* in Schenkel's " Bibel-Lex.," II. 207, and two articles on the Synoptic Question in the " Jahrbücher für Protest. Theol.," 1878, pp. 145 sqq. and 533 sqq.; but especially his *Einleitung in das N. T.,* 2d ed., 1886.

C. WEIZSÄCKER (successor of Dr. Baur, but less radical) : *Untersuchungen über die evang. Gesch., ihre Quellen,* etc. Gotha, 1864.

GUSTAVE D'EICHTHAL : *Les Évangiles.* Paris, 1863. 2 vols.

L. A. SABATIER : *Essai sur les sources de la vie de Jésus.* Paris, 1866.

ANDREW JUKES : *The Characteristic Differences of the Four Gospels.* London, 1867.

EDWARD A. THOMSON : *The Four Evangelists ; with the Distinctive Characteristics of their Gospels.* Edinburgh, 1868.

C. A. ROW : *The Historical Character of the Gospels Tested by an Examination of their Contents.* 1865–67. *The Jesus of the Evangelists.* London, 1868.

KARL WIESELER : *Beiträge zur richtigen Würdigung der Evangelien und der evangel. Geschichte.* Gotha, 1869.

Supernatural Religion (anonymous). London, 1873, 7th ed., 1879, vol. I., Part II., pp. 212 sqq., and vol. II. Comp. the careful review and refutation of this work by Bishop LIGHTFOOT in a series of articles in the " Contemporary Review," 1875, sqq.

F. GODET : *The Origin of the Four Gospels.* In his " Studies on the New Test.," 1873. Engl. transl. by *W. H. Lyttelton.* London, 1876. See also his *Commentary on the Gospel of St. Luke,* Introd. and Appendix, Eng. trans. from 2d French ed. Edinb., 1875.

W. SANDAY : *The Gospels in the Second Century.* London, 1876.

BERNHARD WEISS (Professor in Berlin) : *Das Marcusevangelium und seine synoptischen Parallelen.* Berlin, 1872. *Das Matthäusevangelium und seine Lucas-Parallelen erklärt.* Halle, 1876. Two very thorough critical works. Comp. also his reply to Holtzmann in the " Jahrbücher für Protest. Theologie," 1878 ; and his *Einleitung in's N. T.*, 1886.

D. S. GREGORY : *Why Four Gospels ? or, the Gospels for all the World.* New York, 1877.

E. RENAN : *Les évangiles et la seconde génération Chrétienne.* Paris, 1877.

GEO. P. FISHER (Professor in New Haven) : *The Beginnings of Christianity.* New York, 1877. Chs. VIII.–XII. Also several articles on the Gospels in the " Princeton Review " for 1881.

WM. THOMSON (Archbishop of York) : *The Gospels.* General Introduction to Speaker's *" Com. on the New Test.,"* vol. I., pp. xiii.–lxxv. London and New York, 1878.

EDWIN A. ABBOTT (Head Master, City of London School) : *Gospels,* in the ninth edition of the *"Encyclopædia Britannica,"* vol. X., pp. 789–843. Edinburgh and New York, 1879.

FRED. HUIDEKOPER (Unitar. Theol. Seminary, Meadville, Pa.) : *Indirect Testimony of History to the Genuineness of the Gospels.* New York, 2d ed., 1879.

JOHN KENNEDY (D.D.) : *The Four Gospels : their Age and Authorship. Traced from the Fourth Century into the First.* London ; Am. ed., with an introduction by Edwin W. Rice. Philadelphia, 1880 (Am. Sunday School Union).

J. H. SCHOLTEN : *Das Paulinische Evangelium.* Transl. from the Dutch by E. R. Redepenning. Elberfeld, 1881.

C. HOLSTEN : *Die drei ursprünglichen, noch ungeschriebenen Evangelien.* Leipzig, 1883 (79 pages). A modification of Baur's tendency-hypothesis. Holsten assumes three forms of the original oral Gospel—the Pauline, the Petrine, and the Judaistic.

Norton, Tischendorf, Wieseler, Ebrard, Da Costa, Westcott, Lightfoot, Sanday, Kennedy, Thomson, Godet, Ezra Abbot, and Fisher are conservative and constructive, yet critical ; Baur, Hilgenfeld, Holtzmann, Keim, Renan, Scholten, Davidson, and the author of "Supernatural Religion " are radical, but stimulating and negatively helpful, especially Baur, Keim, and Renan. Bleek, Ewald, Reuss, Meyer, and Weiss occupy independent middle ground, but all defend the genuineness of John except Reuss, who hesitates.

III. COMMENTARIES.

1. Ancient Works : ORIGEN (*in Math., Luc.,* etc., fragmentary) ; CHRYSOSTOM (*Hom. in Matth.,* ed. Fr. Field, 1839) ; JEROME (in *Matth. ;* in *Luc.*) ; AUGUSTIN (*Quæstionum Evangeliorum libri* II.) ; THEOPHYLACT (*Comment. in* 4 *Evang., Gr. et Lat.*) ; EUTHYMIUS ZIGABENUS (*Com. in* 4 *Evang., Gr. et Lat.*) ; THOMAS AQUINAS (*Catena aurea in Evang. ;* English edition by Pusey, Keble, and Newman. Oxford, 1841–45, 4 vols.).

2. Since the Reformation: CALVIN (*Harmonia*, and *Ev. Joa.*, 1553; Engl. ed., Edinb., 1846, 3 vols.); MALDONATUS (R. Cath., *Com. in quatuor Evang.*, 1615); PASQUIER QUESNEL (Jansenist; *The Four Gospels*, French and English, several editions); JOHN LIGHTFOOT (*Horæ Hebraicæ et Talmudicæ in quatuor Evangelistas*, and *Harmonia quatuor Evangelistarum tum inter se, tum cum Veteri Testamento*, in his *Opera*. London, 1684; also Leipz., 1675; Rotterdam, 1686; London, 1825); J. MACKNIGHT (*Harm. of the Four Gospels, with Paraphrase and Notes*. London, 1756; 5th ed., 1819, 2 vols.); GEORGE CAMPBELL (d. 1796; *The Four Gospels, with Dissertations and Notes*. Aberdeen, 1814, 4 vols.; Andover, 1837, 2 vols.).

3. In the nineteenth century: OLSHAUSEN (d. 1839; 3d ed., 1837 sqq.; revised and completed by Ebrard and others; Engl. transl., Edinb. and New York); DE WETTE (d. 1849; *Exeget. Handbuch zum N. T.*, 1837; 5th ed. by Brückner and others, 1863 sqq.); BLEEK (d. 1859; *Synopt. Erklärung der 3 ersten Evang.*, 1862, 2 vols.); MEYER (d. 1874; 6th ed., 1876–80, Matthew by MEYER, Mark, Luke and John revised by WEISS); LANGE (Am. ed. enlarged, New York and Edinb., 1864 sqq., 3 vols.); ALFORD (d. 1871; 6th ed., 1868; new ed., 1877); WORDSWORTH (5th ed., 1866); Jos. A. ALEXANDER (d. 1859; *Mark* and *Matthew*, the latter unfinished); McCLELLAN (*The Four Gospels, with the Chronological and Analytical Harmony*. London, 1875); KEIL (*Matthew, Mark, Luke*, and *John*, 1877–1881); MORISON (*Matthew* and *Mark*, the latter in a third ed., 1882); GODET (*Luke* and *John*, French and English), STRACK and ZÖCKLER (1888). For English readers: SPEAKER'S *Com.*, ELLICOTT'S *Com.*, SCHAFF'S *Revision Com.*, 1882, etc. Comp. a list of Com. on the Gospels in the English transl. of Meyer on *Matthew* (Edinb., 1877, pp. xxiv.–xliii.).

§ 78. *The Four Gospels.*

GENERAL CHARACTER AND AIM OF THE GOSPELS.

Christianity is a cheerful religion and brings joy and peace from heaven to earth. The New Testament opens with the gospel, that is with the authentic record of the history of all histories, the glad tidings of salvation through the life, death, and resurrection of Jesus Christ.[1] The four canonical Gospels

---

[1] The Greek word εὐαγγέλιον which passed into the Latin *evangelium*, and through this into modern languages (French, German, Italian, etc.), means 1st, reward for good news to the messenger (in Homer); 2d, good news, glad tidings; 3d, glad tidings of Christ and his salvation (so in the New Test.); 4th, the record of these glad tidings (so in the headings of the Gospels and in ecclesiastical usage). The Saxon "gospel," *i.e.*, God's spell or good spell (from *spellian*, to tell), is the nearest idiomatic equivalent for εὐαγγέλιον.

are only variations of the same theme, a fourfold representation
of one and the same gospel, animated by the same spirit.[1] They
are not full biographies,[2] but only memoirs or a selection of
characteristic features of Christ's life and work as they struck
each Evangelist and best suited his purpose and his class of
readers.[3] They are not photographs which give only the momentary image in a single attitude, but living pictures from
repeated sittings, and reproduce the varied expressions and
aspects of Christ's person.

The style is natural, unadorned, straightforward, and objective. Their artless and naïve simplicity resembles the earliest
historic records in the Old Testament, and has its peculiar
and abiding charm for all classes of people and all degrees of
culture. The authors, in noble modesty and self-forgetfulness,
suppress their personal views and feelings, retire in worshipful
silence before their great subject, and strive to set it forth in all
its own unaided power.

The first and fourth Gospels were composed by apostles and
eye-witnesses, Matthew and John; the second and third, under
the influence of Peter and Paul, and by their disciples Mark
and Luke, so as to be indirectly likewise of apostolic origin and
canonical authority. Hence Mark is often called the Gospel of
Peter, and Luke the Gospel of Paul.

The common practical aim of the Evangelists is to lead the
reader to a saving faith in Jesus of Nazareth as the promised
Messiah and Redeemer of the world.[4]

---

[1] Irenæus very properly calls them τετράμορφον τὸ εὐαγγέλιον, ἐνὶ πνεύματι
συνεχόμενον, *quadriforme evangelium quod uno spiritu continetur. Adv. Hær.*
III. 11, § 8.

[2] This is expressly disclaimed in John 20 : 30; comp. 21 : 25.

[3] Hence Justin Martyr, in his two "Apologies" (written about 146), calls
the Gospels "Memoirs" or "Memorabilia" (Ἀπομνημονεύματα) of Christ or of
the Apostles, in imitation no doubt of the Memorabilia of Socrates by Xenophon. That Justin means no other books but our canonical Gospels by these
"Memoirs," which he says were read in public worship on Sunday, there can
be no reasonable doubt. See especially Dr. Abbot's *Authorship of the Fourth
Gospel*, 1880.

[4] John 20 : 30, 31 : ταῦτα δὲ γέγραπται ἵνα πιστεύητε ὅτι Ἰησοῦς ἐστὶν
Χριστός, ὁ υἱὸς τοῦ θεοῦ, καὶ ἵνα πιστεύοντες ζωὴν ἔχητε ἐν τῷ ὀνόματι αὐτοῦ.

COMMON ORIGIN.

The Gospels have their common source in the personal intercourse of two of the writers with Christ, and in the oral tradition of the apostles and other eye-witnesses. Plain fishermen of Galilee could not have drawn such a portrait of Jesus if he had not sat for it. It would take more than a Jesus to invent a Jesus. They did not create the divine original, but they faithfully preserved and reproduced it.

The gospel story, being constantly repeated in public preaching and in private circles, assumed a fixed, stereotyped form; the more readily, on account of the reverence of the first disciples for every word of their divine Master. Hence the striking agreement of the first three, or synoptical Gospels, which, in matter and form, are only variations of the same theme. Luke used, according to his own statement, besides the oral tradition, written documents on certain parts of the life of Jesus, which doubtless appeared early among the first disciples. The Gospel of Mark, the confidant of Peter, is a faithful copy of the gospel preached and otherwise communicated by this apostle; with the use, perhaps, of Hebrew records which Peter may have made from time to time under the fresh impression of the events themselves.

INDIVIDUAL CHARACTERISTICS.

But with all their similarity in matter and style, each of the Gospels, above all the fourth, has its peculiarities, answering to the personal character of its author, his special design, and the circumstances of his readers. The several evangelists present the infinite fulness of the life and person of Jesus in different aspects and different relations to mankind; and they complete one another. The symbolical poesy of the church compares them with the four rivers of Paradise, and with the four cherubic representatives of the creation, assigning the man to Matthew, the lion to Mark, the ox to Luke, and the eagle to John.

The apparent contradictions of these narratives, when closely examined, sufficiently solve themselves, in all essential points, and serve only to attest the honesty, impartiality, and credibility of the authors. At the same time the striking combination of resemblances and differences stimulates close observation and minute comparison, and thus impresses the events of the life of Christ more vividly and deeply upon the mind and heart of the reader than a single narrative could do. The immense labor of late years in bringing out the comparative characteristics of the Gospels and in harmonizing their discrepancies has not been in vain, and has left a stronger conviction of their independent worth and mutual completeness.

Matthew wrote for Jews, Mark for Romans, Luke for Greeks, John for advanced Christians; but all are suited for Christians in every age and nation.[1] The first Gospel exhibits Jesus of Nazareth as the Messiah and Lawgiver of the kingdom of heaven who challenges our obedience; the second Gospel as the mighty conqueror and worker of miracles who excites our astonishment; the third Gospel as the sympathizing Friend and Saviour of men who commands our confidence; the fourth Gospel as the eternal Son of God who became flesh for our salvation and claims our adoration and worship, that by believing in him we may have eternal life. The presiding mind which planned this fourfold gospel and employed the agents without a formal agreement and in conformity to their talents, tastes, and spheres of usefulness, is the Spirit of that Lord who is both the Son of Man and the Son of God, the Saviour of us all.

TIME OF COMPOSITION.

As to the time of composition, external testimony and internal evidence which modern critical speculations have not been able to invalidate, point to the seventh decade of the first cen-

---

[1] This characterization is very old, and goes back to Gregory Nazianzen, *Carmen* 33, where he enumerates the books of the New Test., and says:

Ματθαῖος μὲν ἔγραψεν Ἑβραίοις θαύματα Χριστοῦ,
Μάρκος δ᾽ Ἰταλίῃ, Λουκᾶς Ἀχαΐδι,
Πᾶσι δ᾽ Ἰωάννης κῆρυξ μέγας, οὐρανοφοίτης.

tury for the Synoptic Gospels, and to the ninth decade for the
Gospel of John.

The Synoptic Gospels were certainly written before A.D. 70;
for they describe the destruction of Jerusalem as an event still
future, though nigh at hand, and connect it immediately with
the glorious appearing of our Lord, which it was thought might
take place within the generation then living, although no precise
date is fixed anywhere, the Lord himself declaring it to be unknown even to him.   Had the Evangelists written after that
terrible catastrophe, they would naturally have made some allusion to it, or so arranged the eschatological discourses of our
Lord (Matt. 24; Mark 13; Luke 21) as to enable the reader
clearly to discriminate between the judgment of Jerusalem and
the final judgment of the world, as typically foreshadowed by
the former.[1]

On the other hand, a considerable number of years must have
elapsed after the resurrection.   This is indicated by the fact
that several imperfect attempts at a gospel history had previously been made (Luke 1 : 1), and by such a phrase as:
" *until this day* " (Matt. 27 : 8; 28 : 15).

But it is quite impossible to fix the precise year of composition.   The silence of the Epistles is no conclusive argument
that the Synoptists wrote *after* the death of James, Peter, and
Paul; for there is the same silence in the Acts concerning the
Epistles of Paul, and in the Epistles concerning the Acts.   The
apostles did not quote each other's writings; the only exception is the reference of Peter to the Epistles of Paul.   In the
multiplicity of their labors the Evangelists may have been engaged for several years in preparing their works until they
assumed their present shape.   The composition of a life of
Christ now may well employ many years of the profoundest
study.

The Hebrew Matthew was probably composed first; then
Mark; the Greek Matthew and Luke cannot be far apart.

---

[1] See on this subject Fisher's *Beginnings of Christianity*, ch. XI. : " Water
marks of Age in the New Test. Histories," pp. 363 sqq., especially p. 371.

If the Acts, which suddenly break off with Paul's imprisonment in Rome (61–63), were written before the death of the
apostle, the third Gospel, which is referred to as "the first
treatise" (Acts 1 : 1), must have been composed before A.D. 65
or 64, perhaps, in Cæsarea, where Luke had the best opportunity
to gather his material during Paul's imprisonment between 58
and 60; but it was probably not published till a few years afterwards. Whether the later Synoptists knew and used the earlier
will be discussed in the next section.

John, according to the universal testimony of antiquity, which
is confirmed by internal evidence, wrote his Gospel last, after
the fall of Jerusalem and after the final separation of the Christians from the Jews. He evidently presupposes the Synoptic
Gospels (although he never refers to them), and omits the eschatological and many other discourses and miracles, even the
institution of the sacraments, because they were already sufficiently known throughout the church. But in this case too it
is impossible to fix the year of composition. John carried his
Gospel in his heart and memory for many years and gradually
reduced it to writing in his old age, between A.D. 80 and 100;
for he lived to the close of the first century and, perhaps, saw the
dawn of the second.

CREDIBILITY.

The Gospels make upon every unsophisticated reader the impression of absolute honesty. They tell the story without rhetorical embellishment, without any exclamation of surprise or
admiration, without note and comment. They frankly record
the weaknesses and failings of the disciples, including themselves, the rebukes which their Master administered to them
for their carnal misunderstandings and want of faith, their
cowardice and desertion in the most trying hour, their utter
despondency after the crucifixion, the ambitious request of John
and James, the denial of Peter, the treason of Judas. They
dwell even with circumstantial minuteness upon the great sin of

the leader of the Twelve, especially the Gospel of Mark, who derived his details no doubt from Peter's own lips.   They conceal nothing, they apologize for nothing, they exaggerate nothing.   Their authors are utterly unconcerned about their own fame, and withhold their own name; their sole object is to tell the story of Jesus, which carries its own irresistible force and charm to the heart of every truth-loving reader.   The very discrepancies in minor details increase confidence and exclude the suspicion of collusion; for it is a generally acknowledged principle in legal evidence that circumstantial variation in the testimony of witnesses confirms their substantial agreement.   There is no historical work of ancient times which carries on its very face such a seal of truthfulness as these Gospels.

The credibility of the canonical Gospels receives also negative confirmation from the numerous apocryphal Gospels which by their immeasurable inferiority and childishness prove the utter inability of the human imagination, whether orthodox or heterodox, to produce such a character as the historical Jesus of Nazareth.

No post-apostolic writers could have composed the canonical Gospels, and the apostles themselves could not have composed them without the inspiration of the spirit of Christ.

Notes.

I. The Symbolism of the Gospels.   This belongs to the history of Christian poetry and art, but also to the history of exegesis, and may be briefly mentioned here.   It presents the limited recognition of the individuality of the Gospels among the fathers and throughout the middle ages.

The symbolic attributes of the Evangelists were suggested by Ezekiel's vision of the four cherubim which represent the creation and carry the throne of God (Ez. 1 : 15 sqq. ; 10 : 1 sqq. ; 11 : 22), and by the four "living creatures" (ζῶα, not ϑηρία, "beasts," with which the E. V. confounds them) in the Apocalypse (Rev. 4 : 6–9 ; 5 : 6, 8, 11, 14 ; 6 : 1, 3, 5, 6, 7 ; 7 : 11 ; 14 : 3 ; 15 : 7 ; 19 : 4).

(1.) The theological use.   The cherubic figures which the prophet saw in his exile on the banks of the Chebar, symbolize the divine attributes of majesty and strength reflected in the animal creation; and

the winged bulls and lions and the eagle-headed men of Assyrian monuments have a similar significance. But the cherubim were interpreted
as prophetic types of the four Gospels as early as the second century,
with some difference in the application.

Irenæus (about 170) regards the faces of the cherubim (man, lion, ox,
eagle) as "images of the life and work of the Son of God," and assigns
the man to Matthew, and the ox to Luke, but the *eagle to Mark* and the
lion to John (*Adv. Hær.*, III. 11, 8, ed. Stieren I. 469 sq.). Afterwards
the signs of Mark and John were properly exchanged. So by Jerome (d.
419) in his Com. on Ezekiel and other passages. I quote from the Pro-
logus to his *Comment. in Ev. Matthæi* (*Opera*, vol. VII., p. 19, ed. Migne):
"*Hæc igitur quatuor Evangelia multo ante prædicta, Ezechielis quoque
volumen probat, in quo prima visio ita contexitur : ' Et in medio sicut simi-
litudo quatuor animalium : et vultus eorum facies hominis, et facies leonis,
et facies vituli, et facies aquilæ' (Ezech.* 1 : 5 *et* 10). *Prima hominis facies
Matthæum significat, qui quasi de homine exorsus est scribere : ' Liber gen-
erationis Jesu Christi, filii David, filii Abraham' (Matth.* 1). *Secunda,
Marcum, in quo [al. qua] vox leonis in eremo rugientis auditur : ' Vox cla-
mantis in deserto [al. eremo], Parate viam Domini, rectas facite semitas
ejus' (Marc.* 1 : 3). *Tertia, vituli, quæ evangelistam Lucam a Zacharia
sacerdote sumpsisse initium præfigurat. Quarta, Joannem evangelistam,
qui assumptis pennis aquilæ, et ad altiora festinans, de Verbo Dei disputat.*"

Augustin (*De Consens. Evang.*, Lib. I., c. 6, in Migne's ed. of the *Opera*,
tom. III., 1046) assigns the lion to Matthew, the man to Mark (whom he
wrongly regarded as an abbreviator of Matthew), the ox to Luke, and
the eagle to John, because "he soars as an eagle above the clouds of
human infirmity, and gazes on the light of immutable truth with most
keen and steady eyes of the heart." In another place (*Tract. XXXVI.
in Joh. Ev.*, c. 8, § 1) Augustin says : "The other three Evangelists
walked as it were on earth with our Lord as man (*tamquam cum homine
Domino in terra ambulabant*) and said but little of his divinity. But
John, as if he found it oppressive to walk on earth, opened his treatise,
so to speak, with a peal of thunder. . . . To the sublimity of this beginning all the rest corresponds, and he speaks of our Lord's divinity as
no other." He calls the evangelic quaternion "the fourfold car of the
Lord, upon which he rides throughout the world and subdues the
nations to his easy yoke." Pseudo-Athanasius (*Synopsis Script.*) assigns
the man to Matthew, the ox to Mark, the lion to Luke. These variations in the application of the emblems reveal the defects of the analogy. The man might as well (with Lange) be assigned to Luke's Gospel of humanity as the sacrificial ox. But Jerome's distribution of the
symbols prevailed and was represented in poetry by Sedulius in the
fifth century.

Among recent divines, Bishop Wordsworth, of Lincoln, who is in full sympathy with the fathers and all their pious exegetical fancies, has thus eloquently reproduced the cherubic symbolism (in his *Com. on the New Test.*, vol. I., p. xli) : "The Christian church, looking at the origin of the Four Gospels, and the attributes which God has in rich measure been pleased to bestow upon them by his Holy Spirit, found a prophetic picture of them in the four living cherubim, named from heavenly knowledge, seen by the prophet Ezekiel at the river of Chebar. Like them the Gospels are four in number; like them they are the chariot of God, *who sitteth between the cherubim;* like them they bear him on a winged throne into all lands; like them they move wherever the Spirit guides them; like them they are marvellously joined together, intertwined with coincidences and differences : wing interwoven with wing, and wheel interwoven with wheel; like them they are full of eyes, and sparkle with heavenly light; like them they sweep from heaven to earth, and from earth to heaven, and fly with lightning's speed and with the noise of many waters. *Their sound is gone out into all lands, and their words to the end of the world."* Among German divines, Dr. Lange is the most ingenious expounder of this symbolism, but he exchanges the symbols of Matthew and Luke. See his *Leben Jesu*, I., 156 sqq., and his *Bibelkunde* (1881), p. 176.

(2.) The pictorial representations of the four Evangelists, from the rude beginnings in the catacombs and the mosaics of the basilicas at Rome and Ravenna to modern times, have been well described by Mrs. Jameson, *Sacred and Legendary Art*, vol. I., 132–175 (Boston ed., 1865). She distinguishes seven steps in the progress of Christian art : 1st, the mere *fact*, the four scrolls, or books of the Evangelists ; 2d, the *idea*, the four rivers of salvation flowing from on high to fertilize the whole earth ; 3d, the *prophetic* symbol, the winged cherub of fourfold aspect ; 4th, the *Christian* symbol, the four "beasts" (better, "living creatures") in the Apocalypse, with or without the angel-wings ; 5th, the combination of the *emblematical animal* with the *human* form ; 6th, the *human* personages, each of venerable or inspired aspect, as becomes the teacher and witness, and each attended by the scriptural emblem—no longer an emblem, but an attribute—marking his individual vocation and character ; 7th, the *human* being *only*, holding his Gospel, *i.e.*, his version of the teaching and example of Christ.

(3.) Religious poetry gives expression to the same idea. We find it in Juvencus and Sedulius, and in its perfection in Adam of St. Victor, the greatest Latin poet of the middle ages (about 1172). He made the Evangelists the subject of two musical poems : "*Plausu chorus lœtabundo*," and "*Jocundare plebs fidelis.*" Both are found in Gautier's edition (1858), and with a good English translation by Digby S. Wrangham in *The Liturgical Poetry of Adam of St. Victor*, London, 1881, vol. II., pp. 156–169. The first has been well reproduced in English by Dr. Plumptre (in his *Com. on the Synoptists*, in Ellicott's series, but with the omission of the first three stanzas).   I will quote the third stanza of the first (with Wrangham's version):

"Circa thema generale,
Habet quisque speciale
Styli privilegium :
Quod præsignat in propheta
Forma pictus sub discreta
Vultus animalium."

"Though one set of facts is stated,
They by each one are related
In a manner all his own :
This the prophet by four creatures,
Each of different form and features,
Pictures for us, one by one."

In the second poem the following stanzas are the best :

Formam viri dant Matthæo,
Quia scripsit sic de Deo,
Sicut descendit ab eo,
Quem plasmavit, homine.
Lucas bos est in figura
Ut præmonstrat in Scriptura,
Hostiarum tangens jura
Legis sub velamine.

Matthew as the man is treated,
Since 'tis he, who hath related,
How from man, by God created,
God did, as a man, descend.
Luke the ox's semblance weareth,
Since his Gospel first declareth,
As he thence the Law's veil teareth,
Sacrifices' aim and end.

Marcus, leo per desertum
Clamans, rugit in apertum :
Iter fiat Deo certum,
Mundum cor a crimine.
Sed Johannes, ala bina
Charitatis, aquilina
Forma, fertur in divina
Puriori lumine.

Mark, the lion, his voice upraises,
Crying out in desert places :
"Cleanse your hearts from all sin's traces,
For our God a way prepare !"
John, the eagle's feature having,
Earth on love's twain pinions leaving,
Soars aloft, God's truth perceiving
In light's purer atmosphere.

Ecce forma bestialis,
Quam Scriptura prophetalis
Notat, sed materialis
Hæc est impositio.
Currunt rotis, volant alis ;
Inest sensus spiritalis ;
Rota gressus est æqualis,
Ala contemplatio.

Thus the forms of brute creation
Prophets in their revelation
Use ; but in their application
All their sacred lessons bring.
Mystic meaning underlieth
Wheels that run, or wing that flieth
One consent the first implieth,
Contemplation means the wing.

Quatuor describunt isti
Quadriformes actus Christi :
Et figurant, ut audisti,
Quisque sua formula.
Natus homo declaratur,
Vitulus sacrificatur,
Leo mortem deprædatur,
Et ascendit aquila.

These four writers, in portraying
Christ, his fourfold acts displaying,
Show him—thou hast heard the saying—
Each of them distinctively :
Man—of woman generated ;
Ox—in offering dedicated ;
Lion—having death defeated ;
Eagle—mounting to the sky.

Paradisus his rigatur,
Viret, floret, fœcundatur,
His abundat, his lætatur
Quatuor fluminibus :

These four streams, through Eden flowing,
Moisture, verdure, still bestowing,
Make the flowers and fruit there growing
In rich plenty laugh and sing

Fons est Christus, hi sunt rivi,
Fons est altus, hi proclivi,
Ut saporem fontis vivi
    Ministrent fidelibus.

Christ the source, these streams forth
    sending;
High the source, these downward trend-
    ing;
That they thus a taste transcending
    Of life's fount to saints may bring.

Horum rivo debriatis
Sitis crescat caritatis,
Ut de fonte pietatis
    Satiemur plenius.
Horum trahat nos doctrina
Vitiorum de sentinâ,
Sicque ducat ad divina
    Ab imo superius.

At their stream inebriated,
Be our love's thirst aggravated,
More completely to be sated
    At a holier love's full fount!
May the doctrine they provide us
Draw us from sin's slough beside us,
And to things divine thus guide us,
    As from earth we upward mount!

II. The CREDIBILITY of the Gospels would never have been denied if it were not for the philosophical and dogmatic skepticism which desires to get rid of the supernatural and miraculous at any price. It impresses itself upon men of the highest culture as well as upon the unlearned reader. The striking testimony of Rousseau is well known and need not be repeated. I will quote only from two great writers who were by no means biased in favor of orthodoxy. Dr. W. E. CHANNING, the distinguished leader of American Unitarianism, says (with reference to the Strauss and Parker skepticism): "I know no histories to be compared with the Gospels in marks of truth, in pregnancy of meaning, in quickening power." . . . "As to his [Christ's] biographers, they speak for themselves. Never were more simple and honest ones. They show us that none in connection with Christ would give any aid to his conception, for they do not receive it. . . . The Gospels are to me their own evidence. They are the simple records of a being who could not have been invented, and the miraculous and more common parts of his life so hang together, are so permeated by the same spirit, are so plainly outgoings of one and the same man, that I see not how we can admit one without the other." See Channing's *Memoir* by his nephew, tenth ed., Boston, 1874, vol. II., pp. 431, 434, 436. The testimony of GOETHE will have with many still greater weight. He recognized in the Gospels the highest manifestation of the Divine which ever appeared in this world, and the summit of moral culture beyond which the human mind can never rise, however much it may progress in any other direction. " *Ich halte die Evangelien*," he says, "*für durchaus ächt; denn es ist in ihnen der Abglanz einer Hoheit wirksam, die von der Person Christi ausging: die ist göttlicher Art, wie nur je auf Erden das Göttliche erschienen ist.*" (*Gespräche mit Eckermann*, III., 371.) Shortly before his death he said to the same friend: "*Wir wissen gar nicht, was wir Luther'n und der Reformation zu danken haben. Mag die geistige Cultur immer fortschreiten, mögen die Naturwissenschaften in immer breiterer Ausdehnung und Tiefe wachsen und der menschliche Geist sich erweitern wie er will: über die*

Hoheit und sittliche Cultur des Christenthums, wie es in den Evangelien leuchtet, wird er nicht hinauskommen." And such Gospels Strauss and Renan would fain make us believe to be poetic fictions of illiterate Galilæans! This would be the most incredible miracle of all.

§ 79. *The Synoptists.*

(See the Lit. in § 78.)

THE SYNOPTIC PROBLEM.

The fourth Gospel stands by itself and differs widely from the others in contents and style, as well as in distance of time of composition. There can be no doubt that the author, writing towards the close of the first century, must have known the three older ones.

But the first three Gospels present the unique phenomenon of a most striking agreement and an equally striking disagreement both in matter and style, such as is not found among any three writers on the same subject. Hence they are called the *Synoptic* or Synoptical Gospels, and the three Evangelists, *Synoptists.*[1] This fact makes a harmony of the Gospels possible in all essentials, and yet impossible in many minor details. The agreement is often literal, and the disagreement often borders on contradiction, but without invalidating the essential harmony.

The interrelationship between Matthew, Mark, and Luke is, perhaps, the most complicated and perplexing critical problem in the history of literature. The problem derives great importance from its close connection with the life of Christ, and has therefore tried to the utmost the learning, acumen, and ingenuity of modern scholars for nearly a century. The range of

---

[1] *Synopsis (conspectus)*, from σύν, *together*, and ὄψις, *view*, is applied since Griesbach (though used before him) to a parallel arrangement of the Gospels so as to exhibit a general view of the whole and to facilitate a comparison. In some sections the fourth Gospel furnishes parallels, especially in the history of the passion and resurrection. The first three Evangelists should not be called Synop*tics* (as is done by the author of *Supernatural Religion*, vol. I., 213, and Dr. Davidson), but Synop*tists*. The former is a Germanism (*Synoptiker*).

hypotheses has been almost exhausted, and yet no harmonious conclusion reached.

THE RELATIONSHIP.

The general agreement of the Synoptists consists:

1. In the harmonious delineation of the character of Christ. The physiognomy is the same, only under three somewhat different aspects. All represent him as the Son of man and as the Son of God, as the promised Messiah and Saviour, teaching the purest doctrine, living a spotless life, performing mighty miracles, suffering and dying for the sins of the world, and rising in triumph to establish his kingdom of truth and righteousness. Such unity in the unique character of the hero of the three narratives has no parallel in secular or sacred histories or biographies, and is the best guarantee of the truthfulness of the picture.

2. In the plan and arrangement of the evangelical history, yet with striking peculiarities.

(*a.*) Matthew, ch. 1 and 2, and Luke, ch. 1 and 2, and 3 : 23–38, begin with the genealogy and infancy of Christ, but with different facts drawn from different sources. Mark opens at once with the preaching of the Baptist; while the fourth Evangelist goes back to the eternal pre-existence of the Logos. About the thirty years of Christ's private life and his quiet training for the great work they are all silent, with the exception of Luke, who gives us a glimpse of his early youth in the temple (2 : 42–52).

(*b.*) The preaching and baptism of John which prepared the way for the public ministry of Christ, is related by all the Synoptists in parallel sections: Matt. 3 : 1–12; Mark 1 : 1–8; Luke 3 : 1–18.

(*c.*) Christ's baptism and temptation, the Messianic inauguration and Messianic trial: Matt. 3 : 13–17; 4 : 1–11; Mark 1 : 9–11; ver. 12 and 13 (very brief); Luke 3 : 21–23; 4 : 1–13. The variations here between Matthew and Luke are very slight, as in the order of the second and third temptation. John gives the testimony of the Baptist to Christ, and alludes to his baptism (1 : 32–34), but differs from the Synoptists.

(*d.*) The public ministry of Christ in Galilee: Matt., chs 4 : 12–18 : 35; Mark 1 : 14–9 : 50; Luke 4 : 14–9 : 50. But Matthew 14 : 22–16 : 12, and Mark 6 : 45–8 : 26, narrate a series of events connected with the Galilæan ministry, which are wanting in Luke; while Luke 9 : 51–18 : 14, has another series of events and parables connected with the last journey to Jerusalem which are peculiar to him.

(*e.*) The journey to Jerusalem: Matt., chs. 19 : 1–20 : 34; Mark 10 : 1–52; Luke 18 : 15–19 : 28.

(*f.*) The entry into Jerusalem and activity there during the week before the last passover: Matt., chs. 21–25; Mark, chs. 11–13; Luke 19 : 29–21 : 38.

(*g.*) The passion, crucifixion, and resurrection in parallel sections, but with considerable minor divergences, especially in the denial of Peter and the history of the resurrection: Matt., chs. 26–28; Mark, chs. 14–16; Luke, chs. 22–24.

The events of the last week, from the entry to the resurrection (from Palm Sunday to Easter), occupy in all the largest space, about one-fourth of the whole narrative.

3. In the selection of the same material and in verbal coincidences, as in the eschatological discourses of Christ, with an almost equal number of little differences. Thus the three accounts of the healing of the paralytic (Matt. 9 : 1–8, and parallel passages), the feeding of the five thousand, the transfiguration, almost verbally agree. Occasionally the Synoptists concur in rare and difficult words and forms in the same connection, as ἐπιούσιος (in the Lord's Prayer), the diminutive ὠτίον, *little ear* (of Malchus, Matt. 26 : 51, and parallel passages), δυσκόλως, *hard* (for a rich man to enter into the kingdom, Matt. 19 : 23, etc.). These coincidences are the more striking since our Lord spoke usually in Aramaic; but those words may have been Palestinian provincialisms.[1]

---

[1] Holtzmann (p. 12) and others include also among the verbal coincidences the irregular ἀφέωνται (the Doric form of pass. perf., 3 pers., plur.), Matt.

The largest portion of verbal agreement, to the extent of about seven-eighths, is found in the words of others, especially of Christ; and the largest portion of disagreement in the narratives of the writers.[1]   This fact bears against the theory of interdependence, and proves, on the one hand, the reverent

9 : 2, 5 ; Mark 2 : 5, 9 ; Luke 5 : 20, 23, and the double augment in ἀπεκα-τεστάϑη, Matt. 12 : 13 ; Mark 3 : 5 ; Luke 6 : 10. But the former is ruled out by the better reading ἀφίενται, which is adopted by Lachmann, Tischendorf, Tregelles, and Westcott and Hort, in Matt. 9 : 2, 5, and in Mark 2 : 5. Moreover, the Doric form is not confined to the New Test., but somewhat widely diffused ; see Moulton's Winer, p. 97, note. And as to the double augment, it occurs also in the Sept. (see Trommius' Concord., I., 163, sub ἀποκαϑίστημι) ; comp. also ἀπεκατέστη in Mark 8 : 25. Ebrard (Wiss. Krit., p. 1054) quotes a passage from Pseudo-Lucian (Philopatr., c. 27) where ἀπεκατέστησε occurs.

[1] Mr. Norton brings out this fact very fully in his Evidences of the Genuineness of the Gospels (Boston, ed. of 1875, p. 464 sq.). I give his results : " In Matthew's Gospel, the passages verbally coincident with one or both of the other two Gospels amount to less than a sixth part of its contents ; and of this about seven-eighths occur in the recital of the words of others, and only about one-eighth in what, by way of distinction, I may call mere narrative, in which the evangelist, speaking in his own person, was unrestrained in the choice of his expressions. In Mark, the proportion of coincident passages to the whole contents of the Gospel is about one-sixth, of which not one-fifth occurs in the narrative.   Luke has still less agreement of expression with the other evangelists. The passages in which it is found amount only to about a tenth part of his Gospel ; and but an inconsiderable portion of it appears in the narrative, in which there are few instances of its existence for more than half a dozen words together.   In the narrative, it may be computed as less than a twentieth part. These definite proportions are important, as showing distinctly in how small a part of each Gospel there is any verbal coincidence with either of the other two ; and to how great a degree such coincidence is confined to passages in which the evangelists professedly give the words of others, particularly of Jesus.—The proportions should, however, be further compared with those which the narrative part of each Gospel bears to that in which the words of others are professedly repeated.   Matthew's narrative occupies about one-fourth of his Gospel, Mark's about one-half, and Luke's about one-third. It may easily be computed, therefore, that the proportion of verbal coincidence found in the narrative part of each Gospel, compared with what exists in the other part, is about in the following ratios : in Matthew as one to somewhat more than two, in Mark as one to four, and in Luke as one to ten. . . . We cannot explain this phenomenon by the supposition that the Gospels were transcribed either one from another, or all from common documents; for, if such transcription had been the cause, it would not have produced results so unequal in the different portions into which the Gospels naturally divide themselves."

loyalty of all the Synoptists to the teaching of the great Master, but also, on the other hand, their freedom and independence of observation and judgment in the narration of facts. Words can be accurately reported only in one form, as they were spoken; while events may be correctly narrated in different words.

Numerical Estimates of the Harmony and Variation.

The extent of the coincidences and divergences admits of an approximate calculation by sections, verses, and words. In every case the difference of size must be kept in mind: Luke is the largest, with 72 pages (in Westcott and Hort's Greek Testament); Matthew comes next, with 68 pages; Mark last, with 42 pages. (John has 55 pages.)

1. *Estimate by Sections.*

Matthew has in all 78, Mark, 67, Luke, 93 sections.
Dividing the Synoptic text into 124 sections, with Dr. Reuss,[1]

All Evangelists have in common...............	47 sections.
Matthew and Mark alone have.................	12 "
Matthew and Luke " "	2 "
Mark and Luke " "	6 "
Sections peculiar to Matthew.................	17
" " " Mark.....................	2
" " " Luke	38

Another arrangement by sections has been made by Norton, Stroud, and Westcott.[2] If the total contents of the Gospels be represented by 100, the following result is obtained:

Mark has	7 peculiarities and 93 coincidences.			
Matthew has 42	"	" 58	"
Luke has 59	"	" 41	"
[John has.............. 92	"	" 8	"]

---

[1] *Geschichte der heil. Schriften N. Test.*, I., p. 175 (5th ed., 1874). See also his *Histoire Evangelique*, Paris, 1876 (*Nouveau Testament, I. partie*).
[2] See Westcott, *Introd. to the Gospels*, p. 191, fifth ed.

If the extent of all the coincidences be represented by 100, their proportion is:

Matthew, Mark, and Luke have............. 53 coincidences.
Matthew and Luke have.................. 21 "
Matthew and Mark have.................. 20 "
Mark and Luke have..................... 6 "

"In St. Mark," says Westcott, "there are not more than twenty-four verses to which no parallel exists in St. Matthew and St. Luke, though St. Mark exhibits everywhere traits of vivid detail which are peculiar to his narrative."

2. *Estimate by Verses.*

According to the calculation of Reuss,[1]

Matthew contains............... 330 verses peculiar to him.
Mark contains.................. 68 " " "
Luke contains.................. 541 " " "
Matthew and Mark have from 170 to 180 verses in common, but not found in Luke.
Matthew and Luke have from 230 to 240 verses in common, but not found in Mark.
Mark and Luke have about 50 verses in common, but not found in Matthew.

The total number of verses common to all three Synoptists is only from 330 to 370. But, as the verses in the second Gospel are generally shorter, it is impossible to make an exact mathematical calculation by verses.

3. *Estimate by Words.*

A still more accurate test can be furnished by the number of words. This has not yet been made as far as I know, but a basis of calculation is furnished by Rushbrooke in his admirably printed *Synopticon* (1880), where the words common to the three Synoptists, the words common to each pair, and the words

---

[1] *Gesch.*, etc., I., p. 175, followed by Archbishop Thomson in Speaker's *Com. New Test.*, vol. I., p. viii.

peculiar to each, are distinguished by different type and color. The words found in all constitute the "triple tradition," and the nearest approximation to the common Greek source from which all have directly or indirectly drawn.

On the basis of this *Synopticon* the following calculations have been made : [2]

A.—Number of words in		Words common to all.	Per cent. of words in common.
Matthew	18,222	2,651, or	.14⅓
Mark	11,158	2,651, or	.23¾
Luke	19,209	2,651, or	.13¾
	48,589 [3]	7,953	.16⅓

B.—Additional words in common.   Whole per cent. in common

Matthew.... } 2,793 (or in all 5,444) { with Mark.........29 +
Mark.......   { " Matthew......48 +

Matthew.... } 2,415 (or in all 5,066) { " Luke.........27 +
Luke.......   { " Matthew......26 +

Mark.......   } 1,174 (or in all 3,825) { " Luke.........34 +
Luke.......   { " Mark.........20 −

[1] See the Literature above. Dr. Edwin A. Abbott, of London, suggested the work, and quotes a specimen (though all in black type) in his art. "Gospels" in the "Encycl. Brit." He draws from it a conclusion favorable to the priority of Mark, from whom, he thinks, Matthew and Luke have borrowed. The specimen is the parable of the wicked husbandmen, Matt. 21 : 33–44; Luke 20 : 9–18; Mark 12 : 1–11.

[2] With the aid of my son (Rev. D. S. S.). The method by which the estimate was made deals with the root forms of the words *only*, and ignores all inflexions—as, for instance, tenses of verbs and cases of nouns. The result is *approximately*, though not exactly, true.

[3] This includes 172 words of the disputed section, Mark 16 : 9–20 (bracketed by Westcott and Hort, and set apart in the English Revision). Deducting these, the total number of words in Mark is 10,986, and the total number of words in the three Synoptists, 48,417.

The number of words in the English Version is of course much larger, but has no bearing upon the argument. I merely present as an item of interest the calculation of Rev. Rufus Wendell, in the "Student's Edition of the (Revised) New Testament" (N. Y., 1882). He gives the following results :

	Whole number of words in the Revised Version. 1881.
Matthew	23,407
Mark....................................	14,854
Luke....................................	25,654
John....................................	19,007

c.—Words peculiar to Matthew....... 10,363, or 56 + per cent.

    "   "   " Mark.......... 4,540, or 40 +   "

    "   "   " Luke.......... 12,969, or 67 +   "

                           27,872

D.—These figures give the following results:

(*a.*) The proportion of words peculiar to the Synoptic Gos‧ pels is 28,000 out of 48,000, more than one half.

In Matthew.......... 56 words out of every 100 are peculiar.
In Mark............. 40   "   "   " 100   "
In Luke............. 67   "   "   " 100   "

(*b.*) The number of coincidences common to all three is less than the number of the divergences.

Matthew agrees with the other two Gospels in 1 word out of 7.
Mark   "   "   "   "   " 1 "   " 4½.
Luke   "   "   "   "   " 1 "   " 8.

(*c.*) But, comparing the Gospels *two by two*, it is evident that Matthew and Mark have most in common, and Matthew and Luke are most divergent.

One-half of Mark is found in Matthew.
One fourth of Luke is found in Matthew.
One-third of Mark is found in Luke.[1]

(*d.*) The general conclusion from these figures is that all three Gospels widely diverge from the common matter, or triple tradition, Mark the least so and Luke the most (almost twice as much as Mark). On the other hand, both Matthew and Luke are nearer Mark than Luke and Matthew are to each other.

THE SOLUTION OF THE PROBLEM.

Three ways open themselves for a solution of the Synoptic problem: either the Synoptists depend on one another; or they

---

[1] The following lines, representing the relative lengths of the three Gospels, show the extent of their verbal coincidence and divergence. The dots divide the lines in half, and the marks into thirds:

Luke,
Mark,
Matthew,

all depend on older sources; or the dependence is of both kinds. Each of these hypotheses admits again of several modifications.[1]

A satisfactory solution of the problem must account for the differences as well as for the coincidences. If this test be applied, the first and the third hypotheses with their various modifications must be ruled out as unsatisfactory, and we are shut up to the second as at least the most probable.

The Canonical Gospels Independent of One Another.

There is no direct evidence that any of the three Synoptists saw and used the work of the others; nor is the agreement of such a character that it may not be as easily and better explained from antecedent sources. The advocates of the theory of interdependency, or the "borrowing" hypothesis,[2] differ widely among themselves: some make Matthew, others Mark, others Luke, the source of the other two or at least of one of them; while still others go back from the Synoptists in their *present* form to a *proto-*Mark (*Urmarkus*), or *proto-*Matthew (*Urmatthæus*), or *proto-*Luke (*Urlukas*), or other fictitious antecanonical documents; thereby confessing the insufficiency of the borrowing hypothesis pure and simple.

There is no allusion in any of the Synoptists to the others; and yet Luke expressly refers to many earlier attempts to write the gospel history. Papias, Irenæus, and other ancient writers assume that they wrote independently.[3] The first who made Mark a copyist of Matthew is Augustin, and his view has been completely reversed by modern research. The whole theory degrades one or two Synoptists to the position of slavish and yet arbitrary compilers, not to say plagiarists; it assumes a strange

---

[1] German scholars have convenient terms for these various hypotheses, as *Benützungshypothese* (" borrowing " hypothesis), *Urevangeliumshypothese, Traditionshypothese, Tendenzhypothese, Combinationshypothese, Diegesentheorie, Markushypothese, Urmarkushypothese*, etc.   See the Notes below.

[2] Used by recent English writers as a rendering for *Benützungshypothese.*

[3] Clement of Alexandria makes no exception, for he merely states (in Euseb. *H. E.*, VI. 14) that those Gospels which contain the genealogies (Matthew and Luke) were written first, Mark next, and John last.

mixture of dependence and affected originality; it weakens the independent value of their history; and it does not account for the omissions of most important matter, and for many differences in common matter. For the Synoptists often differ just where we should most expect them to agree. Why should Mark be silent about the history of the infancy, the whole sermon on the Mount (the Magna Charta of Christ's kingdom), the Lord's Prayer, and important parables, if he had Matthew, chs. 1 and 2, chs. 5–7, and ch. 13, before him? Why should he, a pupil of Peter, record the Lord's severe rebuke to Peter (8 : 27–33), but fail to mention from Matthew (16 : 16–23) the preceding remarkable laudation: "Thou art Rock, and upon this rock I will build my church?" Why should Luke omit the greater part of the sermon on the Mount, and all the appearances of the risen Lord in Galilee? Why should he ignore the touching anointing scene in Bethany, and thus neglect to aid in fulfilling the Lord's prediction that this act of devotion should be spoken of as a memorial of Mary "wheresoever this gospel shall be preached in the whole world" (Matt. 26 : 13; Mark 14 : 9)? Why should he, the pupil and companion of Paul, fail to record the adoration of the Magi, the story of the woman of Canaan, and the command to evangelize the Gentiles, so clearly related by Matthew, the Evangelist of the Jews (2 : 1–12; 15 : 21–28; 24 : 14; 28 : 19)? Why should Luke and Matthew give different genealogies of Christ, and even different reports of the model prayer of our Lord, Luke omitting (beside the doxology, which is also wanting in the best MSS. of Matthew) the petition, "Thy will be done, as in heaven, so on earth," and the concluding petition, "but deliver us from evil" (or "the evil one"), and substituting "sins" for "debts," and "Father" for "Our Father who art in heaven"? Why should all three Synoptists differ even in the brief and official title on the Cross, and in the words of institution of the Lord's Supper, where Paul, writing in 57, agrees with Luke, referring to a revelation from the Lord (1 Cor. 11 : 23)? Had the Synoptists seen the work of the others, they could easily have harmonized these discrepancies and avoided the appearance of contradiction. To suppose that they purposely varied to conceal plagiarism is a moral impossibility. We can conceive no reasonable motive of adding a third Gospel to two already known to the writer, except on the ground of serious defects, which do not exist (certainly not in Matthew and Luke as compared with Mark), or on the ground of a presumption which is inconsistent with the modest tone and the omission of the very name of the writers.

These difficulties are felt by the ablest advocates of the borrowing hypothesis, and hence they call to aid one or several pre-canonical Gospels which are to account for the startling discrepancies and signs of independence, whether in omissions or additions or arrangement. But these pre-canonical Gospels, with the exception of the lost Hebrew Matthew, are as fictitious as the Syro-Chaldaic *Urevangelium* of Eichhorn, and have been compared to the epicycles of the old astronomers, which were invented to sustain the tottering hypothesis of cycles.

As to Luke, we have shown that he departs most from the triple tradition, although he is supposed to have written last, and it is now almost universally agreed that he did *not* use the *canonical* Matthew.[1] Whether he used the *Hebrew* Matthew and the Greek Mark or a lost proto-Mark, is disputed, and at least very doubtful.[2] He follows a plan of his own ; he ignores

---

[1] So Weisse, Ewald, Reuss, Ritschl, Thiersch, Plitt, Meyer, Holtzmann, Weizsäcker, Mangold, Godet, Weiss. See Meyer on *Matthew*, p. 34 (6th ed.), and on *Luke*, p. 238 (6th ed. by Weiss, 1878). Only the Tübingen "tendency critics" maintain the contrary, and this is almost necessary in order to maintain the late date which they assign to Luke. Had he written in the second or even at the end of the first century, he could not possibly have been ignorant of Matthew. But his very independence proves his early date.

[2] For the use of Mark by Luke are Reuss, Weiss, and most of the advocates of the Urmarkushypothese. Against such use are Weizsäcker, Godet, and all those who (with Griesbach) make Mark an epitomizer of Matthew and Luke. Farrar also, in his *Com. on Luke*, p. 9, very decidedly maintains the independence of Luke both on Matthew and Mark : "It may be regarded as certain," he says, "that among these 'attempts' Luke did *not* class the Gospels of St. Matthew and St. Mark. The inference that he was either unaware of the existence of those Gospels, or made no direct use of them, suggests

a whole cycle of events in Mark from ch. 6 : 45 to ch. 8 : 26 ; he omits in the common sections the graphic touches of Mark, for which he has others equally graphic ; and with a far better knowledge of Greek he has yet more Hebraisms than Mark, because he drew largely on Hebrew sources. As to Matthew, he makes the impression of primitive antiquity, and his originality and completeness have found able advocates from Augustin down to Griesbach and Keim. And as to Mark, his apparent abridgments, far from being the work of a copyist, are simply rapid statements of an original writer, with many fresh and lively details which abundantly prove his independence. On the other hand, in several narratives he is more full and minute than either Matthew or Luke.[1] His independence has been successfully proven by the most laborious and minute investigations and comparisons.[2] Hence many regard him as the primitive Evangelist made use of by both Matthew and Luke, but disagree among themselves as to whether it was the canonical Mark or a proto-Mark.[3] In either case Matthew and

itself with the utmost force when we place side by side any of the events which they narrate in common, and mark the minute and inexplicable differences which incessantly occur even amid general similarity."

[1] Compare the healing of the paralytic, ch. 2 : 3-12, with Matt. 9 : 2-8 ; the murder of John the Baptist, ch. 6 : 14-29, with Matt. 14 : 1-13 ; Luke 9 : 7-9 ; the healing of the demoniac boy, ch. 9 : 14-29, with Matt. 17 : 14-21 and Luke 9 : 37-43 ; also the accounts of Peter's denial.

[2] I mean especially the works of Wilke (*Der Urevangelist*, 1838), Holtzmann (*Die Synopt. Evang.*, 1863), and Weiss (*Das Marcusevangelium und seine synoptischen Parallelen*, 1872 ; comp. his *Matthäusevangelium*, etc., 1876). Weiss deserves all the more a hearing as he strenuously advocates the genuineness of John. See notes below. Dr. Fisher thinks that "the independence of Mark as related to the other Gospels is one of the most assured and most valuable results of recent criticism." *The Beginnings of Christianity*, p. 275. Dr. Davidson in the "revised and improved edition" of his *Introduction*, vol. I., 551-563, still adheres to the old Tübingen position of the dependence of Mark upon both Matthew and Luke, and ignores the works of Wilke, Holtzmann, Weiss, Renan, and the article of his own countryman, Abbott, in the "Encycl. Brit."

[3] Holtzmann, Mangold, E. A. Abbott, and others go back to a fictitious *Urmarkus ;* while Ewald, Meyer, and Weiss make our *canonical* Mark the basis of Matthew and Luke, yet with the important addition that Mark himself used, besides the oral tradition of Peter, the lost Hebrew Matthew, or rather

Luke would be guilty of plagiarism. What should we think of an historian of our day who would plunder another historian of one-third or one-half of the contents of his book without a word of acknowledgment direct or indirect? Let us give the Evangelists at least the credit of common honesty, which is the basis of all morality.

APOSTOLIC TEACHING THE PRIMARY SOURCE OF ALL THE SYNOPTISTS.

The only certain basis for the solution of the problem is given to us in the preface of Luke. He mentions two sources of his own Gospel—but not necessarily of the two other Synoptic Gospels—namely, the oral tradition or deliverance of original "eye-witnesses and ministers of the word" (apostles, evangelists, and other primitive disciples), and a number of written "narratives," drawn up by "many," but evidently incomplete and fragmentary, so as to induce him to prepare, after accurate investigation, a regular history of "those matters which have been fulfilled among us." Besides this important hint, we may be aided by the well-known statements of Papias about the Hebrew Gospel of Matthew and the Greek Mark, whom he represents as the interpreter of Peter.

The chief and common source from which the Synoptists derived their Gospels was undoubtedly the living apostolic tradition or teaching which is mentioned by Luke in the first order. This teaching was nothing more or less than a faithful report of the words and deeds of Christ himself by honest and intelligent eye-witnesses.[1] He told his disciples to preach, not to write, the gospel, although the writing was, of course, not forbidden, but became necessary for the *preservation* of the gospel

a Greek translation of it, which was more than a mere collection of discourses (σύνταξις τῶν λογίων) and embraced also brief narratives. But if Mark had the rich collection of our Lord's discourses before him, his meagreness in that department is all the more difficult to account for.

[1] Luke 1 : 2 : καθὼς παρέδοσαν (handed down by the living word) ἡμῖν οἱ ἀπ' ἀρχῆς (i. e., from the beginning of the public ministry of Christ; comp. Acts 1 : 21 sq.; John 15 : 27) αὐτόπται καὶ ὑπηρέται γενόμενοι τοῦ λόγου (the same persons).

in its purity. They had at first only "hearers;" while the law and the prophets had readers.[1]

Among the Jews and Arabs the memory was specially trained in the accurate repetition and perpetuation of sacred words and facts.[2] The Mishna was not reduced to writing for two or three hundred years. In the East everything is more settled and stationary than in the West, and the traveller feels himself as by magic transferred back to manners and habits as well as the surroundings of apostolic and patriarchal times. The memory is strongest where it depends most on itself and least upon books.[3]

The apostolic tradition or preaching was chiefly historical, a recital of the wonderful public life of Jesus of Nazareth, and centred in the crowning facts of the crucifixion and resurrection. This is evident from the specimens of sermons in the Acts. The story was repeated in public and in private from day to day and sabbath to sabbath. The apostles and primitive evangelists adhered closely and reverently to what they saw and heard from their divine Master, and their disciples faithfully reproduced their testimony. "They continued steadfastly in

[1] Hearers and hearing of the gospel are spoken of in many passages, as Matt. 13 : 14 ; Luke 7 : 1 ; John 12 : 38 ; Acts 17 : 20 ; Rom. 2 : 13 ; 1 Thess. 2 : 13 ; James 1 : 22, 23, 25. The reading (ἀναγινώσκειν) is mostly used of the Old Testament : Matt. 12 : 3, 5 ; 21 : 16, 42 ; 24 : 15 ; Mark 2 : 25; 12 : 10, 26; 13 : 14 ; Luke 4 : 16 ; 6 : 3 ; 10 : 26 ; Acts 8 : 28, 30, 32 ; 13 : 27 ; 15 : 21, etc. ; of the Epistles of Paul : Eph. 3 : 4; Col. 4 : 16 ; 1 Thess. 6 : 27; of the book of Revelation : Rev. 1 : 3 ; 5 : 4.

[2] The rabbinical rule (in *Shabb.* f. 15, 1) was : "*Verba præceptoris sine ulla immutatione, ut prolata ab illo fuerunt, erant recitanda, ne diversa illi affingeretur sententia.*"

[3] Renan, *Les Évangiles,* p. 96 : "*La tradition vivante* (ζῶσα φωνὴ καὶ μένουσα, Papias) *était le grand réservoir où tous puisaient. . . . Le même phénomène se retrouve, du reste, dans presque toutes les littératures sacrées. Les Védas ont traversé des siècles sans être écrits ; un homme qui se respectait devait les savoir par cœur. Celui qui avait besoin d'un manuscrit pour réciter ces hymnes antiques faisait un aveu d'ignorance ; aussi les copies n'en ont-elles jamais été estimées. Citer de mémoire la Bible, le Coran, est encore de nos jours un point d'honneur pour les Orientaux.*" Renan thinks that most of the Old Testament quotations in the New Test. are from memory. My own observations, and those of friends residing in the East, confirm the uniformity of oral tradition and the remarkable strength of memory among the Arabs.

the apostles' teaching" (Acts 2 : 42). Reverence would forbid them to vary from it; and yet no single individual, not even Peter or John, could take in the whole fulness of Christ. One recollected this, another another part of the gospel story; one had a better memory for words, another for facts. These differences, according to varying capacities and recollections, would naturally appear, and the common tradition adapted itself, without any essential alteration, to particular classes of hearers who were first Hebrews in Palestine, then Greek Jews, proselytes, and Gentiles.

The Gospels are nothing more than comprehensive summaries of this apostolic preaching and teaching. Mark represents it in its simplest and briefest form, and agrees nearest with the preaching of Peter as far as we know it from the Acts; it is the oldest in essence, though not necessarily in composition. Matthew and Luke contain the same tradition in its expanded and more matured form, the one the Hebrew or Jewish Christian, the other the Hellenistic and Pauline type, with a corresponding selection of details. Mark gives a graphic account of the main facts of the public life of Christ "beginning from the baptism of John unto the day that he was received up," as they would naturally be first presented to an audience (Acts 1 : 22). Matthew and Luke add the history of the infancy and many discourses, facts, and details which would usually be presented in a fuller course of instruction.

WRITTEN DOCUMENTS.

It is very natural that parts of the tradition were reduced to writing during the thirty years which intervened between the events and the composition of the canonical Gospels. One evangelist would record for his own use a sketch of the chief events, another the sermon on the Mount, another the parables, another the history of the crucifixion and resurrection, still another would gather from the lips of Mary the history of the infancy and the genealogies. Possibly some of the first hearers noted down certain words and events under the fresh impressions of the moment. The apostles were indeed unlearned, but not illiterate men, they could read and write and had sufficient rudimentary education for ordinary composition. These early memoranda were numerous, but have all disappeared, they were not intended for publication, or if published they were superseded by the canonical Gospels. Hence there is room here for much speculation and conjectural criticism.[1] "*Many*," says Luke, "have taken in hand to draw up a narrative concerning those matters which have been fulfilled among us."[2] He cannot mean the apocryphal Gospels which were not yet written, nor the canonical Gospels of Matthew and Mark which would have spared him much trouble and which he would not have dared to supersede by an improved work of his own without a word of acknowledgment, but pre-canonical records, now lost, which emanated from "eye-witnesses and ministers of the word," yet were so fragmentary and incomplete as to justify his own attempt to furnish a more satisfactory and connected history. He had the best opportunity to gather such documents in Palestine, Antioch, Greece, and Rome. Matthew, being himself an eye-witness, and Mark, being the companion of Peter, had less need of previous documents, and could rely chiefly on their own memory and the living tradition in its primitive freshness. They may have written sketches or memoranda for their own use long before they completed their Gospels; for such important works cannot be prepared without long continued labor and care. The best books grow gradually and silently like trees.

CONCLUSION.

We conclude, then, that the Synoptists prepared their Gospels independently, during the same period (say between A.D. 60 and 69), in different places, chiefly from the living teaching

---

[1] In such conjectures Eichhorn, Marsh, Schleiermacher, Ewald, Volkmar, Wittichen, and Renan have shown great ingenuity, and accumulated a vast amount of *docta ignorantia*.

[2] Luke 1 : 1 : πολλοὶ ἐπεχείρησαν (indicating the difficulty of the undertaking and probably also the insufficiency of the execution) ἀνατάξασθαι διήγησιν περὶ τῶν πεπληροφορημένων ἐν ἡμῖν πραγμάτων.

of Christ and the first disciples, and partly from earlier frag·
mentary documents. They bear independent testimony to the
truth of the gospel. Their agreement and disagreement are
not the result of design, but of the unity, richness, and variety of
the original story as received, understood, digested, and applied
by different minds to different conditions and classes of hearers
and readers.[1]

THE TRADITIONAL ORDER.

There is no good reason to doubt that the canonical arrange·
ment which is supported by the prevailing oldest tradition,
correctly represents the order of composition.[2] Matthew, the

[1] In this conclusion (which I stated thirty years ago in the first edition of
my *Hist. of the Ap. Ch.*) some of the ablest investigators of the Synoptic
problem independently agree, as Lange, Ebrard (*Wissenschaftliche Kritik der
ev. Gesch.*, third ed., pp. 1044 sqq.), Norton, Alford, Godet, Westcott, Farrar.
"The Synoptic Gospels," says Alford (in his *Proleg.* to vol. I., p. 11, 6th ed.),
"contain the substance of the Apostles' testimony, collected principally from
their oral teaching current in the church, partly also from written documents
embodying portions of that teaching : there is, however, no reason, from their
internal structure, to believe, but every reason to disbelieve that any one of
the three evangelists had access to either of the other two gospels in its present form." Godet concludes his discussion (*Com. on Luke*, 2d ed., p. 556, Am.
ed.) with these words : "It is impossible to conceive anything more capricious
and less reverential than the part which we make the author of any one whatever of our Synoptic Gospels play with the history and sayings of Jesus, supposing that he had before him the other two, or one of them. Such an
explanation will only be allowable when we are brought absolutely to despair
of finding any other. And even then it were better still to say, *Non liquet*.
For this explanation involves a moral contradiction. Most of our present
critics are so well aware of this that they have recourse to middle terms."

[2] Irenæus, III. 1, 1; Origen in Euseb., *H. E.*, VI. 25; Tertullian, and
others. Irenæus gives this order with the approximate data : "Matthew
issued a written Gospel among the Hebrews in their own dialect, while Peter
and Paul were preaching at Rome and laying the foundations of the church.
After their departure, Mark, the disciple and interpreter of Peter, did also hand
down to us in writing what had been preached by Peter. Luke also, the companion of Paul, recorded in a book the gospel preached by him. Afterwards,
John, the disciple of the Lord, who also had leaned upon His breast, did himself publish a Gospel during his residence at Ephesus in Asia." Clement of
Alexandria differs by putting Mark *after* Matthew and Luke, and yet *before*
the death of Peter ; for he says (in Eus., *H. E.*, VI. 14), that when Peter proclaimed the gospel at Rome, Mark was requested by the hearers to reduce it
to writing, which he did, Peter neither hindering nor encouraging it. According to this view all the Synoptists would have written before 64.

apostle, wrote first in Aramaic and in Palestine, from his personal observation and experience with the aid of tradition; Mark next, in Rome, faithfully reproducing Peter's preaching; Luke last, from tradition and sundry reliable but fragmentary documents. But all wrote under a higher inspiration, and are equally honest and equally trustworthy; all wrote within the lifetime of many of the primitive witnesses, before the first generation of Christians had passed away, and before there was any chance for mythical and legendary accretions. They wrote not too late to insure faithfulness, nor too early to prevent corruption. They represent not the turbid stream of apocryphal afterthoughts and fictions, but the pure fountain of historic truth.

The gospel story, being once fixed in this completed shape, remained unchanged for all time to come. Nothing was lost, nothing added. The earlier sketches or pre-canonical gospel fragments disappeared, and the four canonical records of the one gospel, no more nor less, sufficient for all purposes, monopolized the field from which neither apocryphal caricatures nor sceptical speculations have been able to drive them.

Exoteric and Esoteric Tradition.

Besides the common Galilæan tradition for the people at large which is embodied in the Synoptic Gospels, there was an esoteric tradition of Christ's ministry in Judæa and his private relation to the select circle of the apostles and his mysterious relation to the Father. The bearer of this tradition was the beloved disciple who leaned on the beating heart of his Master and absorbed his deepest words. He treasured them up in his memory, and at last when the church was ripe for this higher revelation he embodied it in the fourth Gospel.

Notes.

The problem of the RELATIONSHIP OF THE SYNOPTISTS was first seriously discussed by Augustin (d. 430), in his three books *De Consensu Evangelistarum* (*Opera*, Tom. III., 1041–1230, ed. Migne). He defends the order in our canon, first Matthew, last John, and the two apostolic disciples in the middle (*in loco medio constituti tamquam filii amplectendi,*

I., 2), but wrongly makes Mark dependent on Matthew (see below, sub. I. 1). His view prevailed during the middle ages and down to the close of the eighteenth century. The verbal inspiration theory checked critical investigation.

The problem was resumed with Protestant freedom by Storr (1786), more elaborately by Eichhorn (1794), and Marsh (1803), and again by Hug (a liberal Roman Catholic scholar, 1808), Schleiermacher (1817), Gieseler (1818), De Wette (1826), Credner (1836), and others. It received a new impulse and importance by the *Leben Jesu* of Strauss (1836), and the Tübingen school, and has been carried forward by Baur (1847), Hilgenfeld, Bleek, Reuss, Holtzmann, Ewald, Meyer, Keim, Weiss, and others mentioned in the Literature (p. 577). Starting in Germany, the investigation was prosecuted also in France, Holland, England, and the United States.

It is not easy to find a way through the labyrinth of the Synoptic question, with all its by-ways and cross-ways, turns and windings, which at first make the impression :

> " *Mir wird von alle dem so dumm,*
> *Als ging mir ein Mühlrad im Kopf herum.*"

Holtzmann gives a brief history of opinions (in his able work, *Die Synopt. Evang.*) down to 1863, and Hilgenfeld (*Hist. Krit. Einl. in das N. T.*, pp. 173–210) down to 1874. Comp. also Reuss (*Gesch. der heil. Schr. N. T.*, I., §§ 165–198, 6th ed., 1887), Holtzmann, *Einleitung*, 351 sqq., and Weiss, *Einl.*, 473 sqq. The following classification of theories is tolerably complete, but several overlap each other, or are combined.

I. The INSPIRATION hypothesis cuts the gordian knot by tracing the agreement of the Synoptists directly and solely to the Holy Spirit. But this explains nothing, and makes God responsible for all the discrepancies and possible inaccuracies of the Evangelists. No inspiration theory can stand for a moment which does not leave room for the personal agency and individual peculiarities of the sacred authors and the exercise of their natural faculties in writing. Luke expressly states in the preface his own agency in composing his Gospel and the use he made of his means of information.

II. The INTERDEPENDENCY hypothesis, or BORROWING hypothesis (*Benützungshypothese*) holds that one or two Evangelists borrowed from the other. This admits of as many modifications as the order in which they may be placed.

1. *Matthew, Mark, Luke.* This is the traditional order defended by Augustin, who called Mark, rather disrespectfully, a "footman and abbreviator of Matthew" (*tamquam pedissequus et breviator Matthæi*, II., 3), Grotius, Mill, Bengel, Wetstein, Hug (1808), Hilgenfeld, Klostermann, Keil. Among English writers Townson and Greswell.

Many scholars besides those just mentioned hold to this order *without admitting an interdependence*, and this I think is the correct view, in connection with the tradition hypothesis. See below, sub V. and the text.

2. *Matthew, Luke, Mark.* So first Clement of Alexandria (Eus., *H. E.*, VI. 14), but, without intimating a dependence of Mark except on Peter. Griesbach (in two Programs, 1789) renewed this order and made Mark an extract from both Matthew and Luke. So Theile (1825), Fritzsche (1830), Sieffert (1832), De Wette, Bleek, Anger, Strauss, Baur, Keim. The Tübingen school utilized this order for the tendency theory (see below). Keim puts Matthew A.D. 66, Luke, 90, Mark, 100.

Bleek is the most considerate advocate of this order (*Einleitung in das N. T.*, 2d ed., 1866, 91 sqq., 245 sqq.), but Mangold changed it (in the third ed. of Bleek, 1875, pp. 388 sqq.) in favor of the priority of a proto-Mark.

3. *Mark, Matthew, Luke.* The originality and priority of Mark was first suggested by Koppe (1782) and Storr (1786 and 1794). The same view was renewed by Lachmann (1835), elaborately carried out by Weisse (1838, 1856 ; Hilgenfeld calls him the " *Urheber der conservativen Markus-hypothese* "), and still more minutely in all details by Wilke (*Der Urevangelist*, 1838 ; but he assumes numerous interpolations in the present Mark and goes back to a proto-Mark), and by B. Weiss (*Das Marcus-evangelium*, 1872). It is maintained in various ways by Hitzig (*Johannes Markus*, 1843), Ewald (1850, but with various prior sources), Ritschl (1851), Reuss, Thiersch, Tobler, Réville (1862), Eichthal (1863), Schenkel, Wittichen, Holtzmann (1863), Weizsäcker (1864), Scholten (1869), Meyer (Com. on *Matt.*, 6th ed., 1876, p. 35), Renan (*Les Évangiles*, 1877, pp. 113, but the Greek Mark was preceded by the lost Hebrew Matthew, p. 93 sqq.). Among English writers, James Smith, of Jordan Hill (*Dissertat. on the Origin of the Gospels*, etc., Edinb., 1853), G. P. Fisher (*Beginnings of Christianity*, New York, 1877, p. 275), and E. A. Abbott (in " Encyclop. Brit.," vol. X., 1879, art. " Gospels ") adopt the same view.

The priority of Mark is now the prevailing theory among German critics, notwithstanding the protest of Baur and Keim, who had almost a personal animosity against the second Evangelist. One of the last utterances of Keim was a passionate protest against the *Präkonisation des Markus* (*Aus dem Urchristenthum*, 1878, pp. 28–45). But the advocates of this theory are divided on the question whether the canonical Mark or a lost proto-Mark was the primitive evangelist. The one is called the *Markushypothese*, the other the *Urmarkushypothese*. We admit the originality of Mark, but this does not necessarily imply priority of composition. Matthew and Luke have too much original matter to be dependent on Mark, and are far more valuable, as a whole, though Mark is indispensable for particulars.

4. *Mark, Luke, Matthew.* Herder (1796), Volkmar (1866 and 1870).

5. *Luke, Matthew, Mark.* Büsching (1776), Evanson (1792).

6. *Luke, Mark, Matthew.* Vogel (1804), Schneckenburger (1832).

The conflicting variety of these modifications shakes the whole borrowing theory. It makes the omissions of most important sections, as
Matt., chs. 12–17; 14 : 22–16 : 12 ; and Luke, chs. 10–18 : 14, and the
discrepancies in the common sections entirely inexplicable. See text.

III. The hypothesis of a PRIMITIVE GOSPEL (*Urevangelium*) written
before those of the Synoptists and used by them as their common source,
but now lost.

1. A lost *Hebrew* or *Syro-Chaldaic Gospel* of official character, written
very early, about 35, in Palestine by the apostles as a manual for the
travelling preachers. This is the famous *Urevangeliumshypothese* of the
learned Professor Eichhorn (1794, 1804, 1820), adopted and modified by
Bishop Herbert Marsh (1803), Gratz (1809); and Bertholdt (who, as
Baur says, was devoted to it with "carnal self-security").

But there is no trace of such an important Gospel, either Hebrew or
Greek. Luke knows nothing about it, although he speaks of several
attempts to write portions of the history. To carry out his hypothesis,
Eichhorn was forced to assume four altered copies or recensions of the
original document, and afterwards he added also Greek recensions.
Marsh, outgermanizing the German critic, increased the number of recensions to eight, including a Greek translation of the Hebrew original.
Thus a new recension might be invented for every new set of facts *ad
infinitum*. If the original Gospel was an apostolic composition, it needed
no alterations and would have been preserved ; or if it was so defective,
it was of small account and unfit to be used as a basis of the canonical
Gospels. Eichhorn's hypothesis is now generally abandoned, but in
modified shape it has been renewed by Ewald and others. See below.

2. The Gospel "*according to the Hebrews*," of which some fragments
still remain. Lessing (1784, in a book published three years after his
death), Semler (who, however, changed his view repeatedly), Weber
(1791), Paulus (1799). But this was a heretical or Ebionitic corruption
of Matthew, and the remaining fragments differ widely from the canonical Gospels.

3. The *Hebrew Matthew* (*Urmatthäus*). It is supposed in this case that
the famous *Logia*, which Matthew is reported by Papias to have written
in Hebrew, consisted not only of a collection of discourses of our Lord
(as Schleiermacher, Ewald, Reuss, I., 183, explained the term), but also
of his deeds : "things said *and done*." But in any case the Hebrew
Matthew is lost and cannot form a safe basis for conclusions. Hug and
Roberts deny that it ever existed. See next section.

4. The *canonical Mark*.

5. A pre-canonical *proto-Mark* (*Urmarkus*). The last two hypotheses
have already been mentioned under the second general head (II. 3).

IV. The theory of a number of *fragmentary documents* (the *Diegesentheorie*), or *different recensions*. It is based on the remark of Luke that
"*many* have taken in hand to draw up a *narrative* (διήγησιν) concerning

those matters which have been fulfilled among us" (1 : 1). Schleier-macher (1817) assumed a large number of such written documents, or detached narratives, and dealt very freely with the Synoptists, resting his faith chiefly on John.

Ewald (1850) independently carried out a similar view in fierce oppo-sition to the "beastly wildness" of the Tübingen school. He informs us with his usual oracular self-assurance that Philip, the evangelist (Acts, ch. 8), first wrote a historical sketch in Hebrew, and then Mat-thew a collection of discourses (the λόγια of Papias), also in Hebrew, of which several Greek translations were made ; that Mark was the third, Matthew the fifth, and Luke the ninth in this series of Gospels, repre-senting the "Höhebilder, die himmlische Fortbewegung der Geschichte," which at last assumed their most perfect shape in John.

Köstlin, Wittichen, and Scholten likewise assume a number of pre-canonical Gospels which exist only in their critical fancy.

Renan (Les Évang., Introd., p. vi.) distinguishes three sets of Gos-pels : (1) original Gospels of the first hand, taken from the oral tradi-tion without a previous written text : the Hebrew Matthew and the Greek proto-Mark ; (2) Gospels partly original and partly second-handed : our canonical Gospels falsely attributed to Matthew, Mark, and Luke ; (3) Gospels of the second and third hand : Marcion's and the Apocryphal Gospels.

V. The theory of a common ORAL TRADITION (Traditionshypothese). Herder (1796), Gieseler (who first fully developed it, 1818), Schulz (1829), Credner, Lange, Ebrard (1868), Thiersch (1845, 1852), Norton, Alford, Westcott (1860, 6th ed., 1881), Godet (1873), Keil (1877), and others. The Gospel story by constant repetition assumed or rather had from the beginning a uniform shape, even in minute particulars, espe-cially in the words of Christ. True, as far as it goes, but must be supple-mented, at least in the case of Luke, by pre-canonical, fragmentary documents or memoranda (διηγήσεις). See the text.

VI. The TENDENCY hypothesis (Tendenzhypothese), or the theory of DOCTRINAL ADAPTATION. Baur (1847) and the Tübingen school (Schwe-gler, Ritschl, Volkmar, Hilgenfeld, Köstlin), followed in England by Samuel Davidson (in his Introd. to the New Test., 1868, revised ed., 1882). Each Evangelist modified the Gospel history in the interest of the religious school or party to which he belonged. Matthew represents the Jewish Christian, Luke the Pauline or Gentile Christian tendency, Mark obliterates the difference, or prepares the way from the first to the second. Every individual trait or characteristic feature of a Gospel is connected with the dogmatic antithesis between Petrinism and Paulinism. Baur regarded Matthew as relatively the most primitive and credible Gospel, but it is itself a free reproduction of a still older Aramaic Gos-pel "according to the Hebrews." He was followed by an Urlukas, a purely Pauline tendency Gospel. Mark is compiled from our Matthew and the *Urlukas* in the interest of neutrality. Then followed the present Luke with an irenical Catholic tendency. Baur overstrained the difference between Petrinism and Paulinism far beyond the limits of historic truth, transformed the sacred writers into a set of partisans and fighting theologians after modern fashion, set aside the fourth Gospel as a purely ideal fiction, and put all the Gospels about seventy years too far down (130–170), when they were already generally used in the Christian church—according to the concurrent testimonies of Justin Martyr, Tatian, Irenæus, and Tertullian. Volkmar went even beyond Baur in reckless radicalism, although he qualified it in other respects, as regards the priority of Mark, the originality of Luke (as compared with Marcion), and the date of Matthew which he put back to about 110. See a summary of his views in Hilgenfeld's *Einleitung*, pp. 199-202. But Ritschl and Hilgenfeld have considerably moderated the Tübingen extravagancies. Ritschl puts Mark first, and herein Volkmar agrees. Hilgenfeld assigns the composition of Matthew to the sixth decade of the first century (though he thinks it was somewhat changed soon after the destruction of Jerusalem), then followed Mark and paved the way from Petrinism to Paulinism, and Luke wrote last before the close of the first century. He ably maintained his theory in a five years' conflict with the Tübingen master (1850–1855) and reasserts it in his *Einleitung* (1875). So he brings us back to the traditional order. As to the time of composition, the internal evidence strongly supports the historical tradition that the Synoptists wrote *before* the destruction of Jerusalem.

§ 80. *Matthew.*

Critical.

BERNH. WEISS : *Das Matthäusevangelium und seine Lucas-Parallelen erklärt.* Halle, 1876. Exceedingly elaborate.

EDW. BYRON NICHOLSON : *The Gospel according to the Hebrews. Its Fragments translated and annotated.* Lond., 1879.

Exegetical.

Commentaries on Matthew by ORIGEN, JEROME, CHRYSOSTOM, MELANCHTHON (1523), FRITZSCHE, DE WETTE, ALFORD, WORDSWORTH, SCHEGG (R. Cath., 1856–58, 3 vols.), J. A. ALEXANDER, LANGE (trsl. and enlarged by SCHAFF, N. Y., 1864, etc.), JAMES MORISON (of Glasgow, Lond., 1870), MEYER (6th ed., 1876), WICHELHAUS (Halle, 1876), KEIL (Leipz., 1877), PLUMPTRE (Lond., 1878), CARR (Cambr., 1879), NICHOLSON (Lond., 1881), SCHAFF (N. Y., 1882).

LIFE OF MATTHEW.

MATTHEW,[1] formerly called LEVI, one of the twelve apostles, was originally a publican or taxgatherer [2] at Capernaum, and hence well acquainted with Greek and Hebrew in bilingual Galilee, and accustomed to keep accounts. This occupation prepared him for writing a Gospel in topical order in both languages. In the three Synoptic lists of the apostles he is associated with Thomas, and forms with him the fourth pair; in Mark and Luke he precedes Thomas, in his own Gospel he is placed after him (perhaps from modesty).[3] Hence the conjecture that he was a twin brother of Thomas (Didymus, *i. e.*, Twin), or associated with him in work. Thomas was an honest and earnest doubter, of a melancholy disposition, yet fully convinced at last when he saw the risen Lord; Matthew was a strong and resolute believer.

Of his apostolic labors we have no certain information. Palestine, Ethiopia, Macedonia, the country of the Euphrates, Persia, and Media are variously assigned to him as missionary fields. He died a natural death according to the oldest tradition, while later accounts make him a martyr.[4]

[1] Ματθαῖος, Matt. 9 : 9 (according to the spelling of א B* D, adopted by Lachmann, Tischendorf, Tregelles, Westcott and Hort), or Ματθαῖος (as spelled in the *text. rec.*), like *Matthias* and *Mattathias*, means *Gift of Jehovah* (מַתַּי, מַתָּא, מַתַּנְיָה, מַתִּתְיָה), and corresponds to the Greek *Theodore.* He perhaps took this name after his call; his former name being *Levi*, Λευΐς, Λευείς (לֵוִי, a joining), according to Mark 2 : 12; Luke 5 : 27, 29. The new name overshadowed the old, as the names of Peter and Paul replaced Simon and Saul. The identity is evident from the fact that the call of Matthew or Levi is related by the three Synoptists in the same terms and followed by the same discourse. Nicholson (*Com. on Matt.* 9 : 9) disputes the identity, as Grotius and Sieffert did before, but on insufficient grounds. Mark calls Peter also before 3 : 16 by his former name Simon (1 : 16, 29, 30, 36), and thereby shows his historical tact.

[2] Hence called Ματθαῖος ὁ τελώνης, Matt. 10 : 3. He inserts his previous employment to intimate the power of divine grace in his conversion.

[3] Matt. 10 : 3, compared with Mark 3 : 18; Luke 6 : 15. But in the list in Acts 1 : 13 he is associated with Bartholomew, and Thomas with Philip.

[4] Clement of Alexandria represents him as a strict Jewish Christian who abstained from the use of flesh. This would make him one of the weak

The first Gospel is his imperishable work, well worthy a long life, yea many lives. Matthew the publican occupies as to time the first place in the order of the Evangelists, as Mary Magdalene, from whom Christ expelled many demons, first proclaimed the glad tidings of the resurrection. Not that it is on that account the best or most important—the best comes last,—but it naturally precedes the other, as the basis precedes the superstructure.[1]

In his written Gospel he still fulfils the great commission to bring all nations to the school of Christ (28 : 19).

The scanty information of the person and life of Matthew in connection with his Gospel suggests the following probable inferences:

1. Matthew was a Hebrew of the Hebrews, yet comparatively liberal, being a publican who came in frequent contact with merchants from Damascus. This occupation was indeed disreputable in the eyes of the Jews, and scarcely consistent with the national Messianic aspirations; but Capernaum belonged to the tetrarchy of Herod Antipas, and the Herodian family, which, with all its subserviency to heathen Rome, was yet to a certain extent identified with the Jewish nation.

2. He was a man of some means and good social position. His office was lucrative, he owned a house, and gave a farewell banquet to "a great multitude" of his old associates, at which Jesus presided.[2] It was at the same time his farewell to the world, its wealth, its pleasures and honors. "We may conceive

brethren whom Paul (Rom. 14 : 1 sqq.) charitably judges. But there is nothing in the first Gospel to justify this tradition.

[1] The priority and relative superiority of Matthew are maintained not only by Augustin and the catholic tradition, but also by moderately liberal critics from Griesbach to Bleek, and even by the radical critics of the Tübingen school (Baur, Strauss, Schwegler, Zeller, Hilgenfeld, Davidson), and especially by Keim.

[2] So Luke 5 : 29. Mark 2 : 15 ("*many* publicans and sinners sat down with Jesus and his disciples") and Matt. 9 : 10 ("*many* publicans and sinners") agree; but Matthew modestly omits his own name in connection with that feast. Some commentators understand "the house" to be the house of Jesus. but Jesus had no house and gave no dinner parties. Luke says expressly that it was the house of Levi.

what a joyous banquet that was for Matthew, when he marked
the words and acts of Jesus, and stored within his memory the
scene and the conversation which he was inspired to write according to his clerkly ability for the instruction of the church in
all after ages." [1] It was on that occasion that Jesus spoke that
word which was especially applicable to Matthew and especially
offensive to the Pharisees present: "I came not to call the
righteous, but sinners." It is remarkable that the first post-
apostolic quotation from the Gospel of Matthew is this very
passage, and one similar to it (see below).

3. He was a man of decision of character and capable of
great sacrifice to his conviction. When called, while sitting in
Oriental fashion at his toll-booth, to follow Jesus, he "forsook
all, rose up, and followed Him," whom he at once recognized
and trusted as the true king of Israel.[2] No one can do more
than leave his "all," no matter how much or how little this may
be; and no one can do better than to "follow Christ."

CHARACTER AND AIM OF THE GOSPEL.

The first Gospel makes the impression of primitive antiquity.
The city of Jerusalem, the temple, the priesthood and sacrifices,
the entire religious and political fabric of Judaism are supposed
to be still standing, but with an intimation of their speedy downfall.[3] It alone reports the words of Christ that he came not to
destroy but to fulfil the law and the prophets, and that he was
only sent to the lost sheep of the house of Israel.[4] Hence the
best critics put the composition several years before the destruction of Jerusalem.[5]

[1] Carr, *Com.*, p. 6. [2] Luke 5 : 28 ; Mark 2 : 14 ; Matt. 9 : 9.
[3] Ch. 5 : 35 ("Jerusalem is the city of the great king"); 23 : 1 ("sit on
Moses' seat"); 23 : 16 ("swear by the temple"); 16 : 28; 24 : 15 ("in the
holy place;" "let him that readeth understand"), and the whole twenty-
fourth chapter.
[4] 5 : 17 ; 15 : 24; comp. 10 : 6.
[5] Hug, Bleek, Olshausen, Ebrard, Meyer, Keim, Lange, and most commentators fix the date between 60 and 69, other writers as early as 37–45 (but
in conflict with ch. 27 : 8 ; 28 : 15). Baur's view, which brings the Greek
Matthew down to the second destruction of Jerusalem under Hadrian, 130–

Matthew's Gospel was evidently written for Hebrews and Hebrew Christians with the aim to prove that Jesus of Nazareth is the promised Messiah, the last and greatest prophet, priest, and king of Israel. It presupposes a knowledge of Jewish customs and Palestinian localities (which are explained in other Gospels).[1] It is the connecting link between the Old and the New Covenant. It is, as has been well said,[2] "the *ultimatum* of Jehovah to his ancient people: Believe, or prepare to perish! Recognize Jesus as the Messiah, or await Him as your Judge!" Hence he so often points out the fulfilment of Messianic prophecy in the evangelical history with his peculiar formula: "that it might be fulfilled," or "then was fulfilled."[3]

In accordance with this plan, Matthew begins with the genealogy of Jesus, showing him to be the son and heir of David the king, and of Abraham the father, of the Jewish race, to whom the promises were given. The wise men of the East come from a distance to adore the new-born king of the Jews. The dark suspicion and jealousy of Herod is roused, and foreshadows the future persecution of the Messiah. The flight to Egypt and the return from that land both of refuge and bondage are a fulfilment of the typical history of Israel. John the

---

134, is exploded. Even Volkmar puts it much earlier (105 to 115), Hilgenfeld (*Einleitung in das N. T.*, p. 497) immediately after the destruction of Jerusalem, Keim A.D. 66. Dr. Samuel Davidson, in the second ed. of his *Introd. to the N. T.* (London, 1882, vol. I. 413–416), assigns the present Greek Matthew with Volkmar to 105, but assumes an Aramæan original and Greek paraphrases of the same which were written before the destruction of Jerusalem. He thinks that "the eschatological discourses which connect the fall of Jerusalem, the destruction of the temple and the end of the world, have been falsified by history" (?); that consequently Jesus did not utter them as they are recorded, but they were revised and altered by writers who incorporated with them Jewish ideas and expressions (I. 403).

[1] Comp. Matt. 15 : 2 with Mark 7 : 3, 4. The translation of the exclamation on the cross, Matt. 27 : 46, is intended for Greek Jews.

[2] By Godet, *Studies on the New Testament*, p. 23.

[3] ἵνα (or ὅπως) πληρωθῇ τὸ ῥηθέν, or τότε ἐπληρώθη τὸ ῥηθέν. This formula occurs twelve times in Matthew (1 : 22 ; 2 : 15, 17, 23 ; 4 : 14 ; 8 : 17 ; 12 : 17 ; 13 : 35 ; 21 : 4 ; 26 : 56 ; 27 : 9, 35), six times in John, but nowhere in Luke nor in Mark ; for Mark 15 : 28 (καὶ ἐπληρώθη ἡ γραφή, κ. τ. λ.) in the text. rec. is spurious and probably inserted from Luke 22 : 37.

Baptist completes the mission of prophecy in preparing the way for Christ. After the Messianic inauguration and trial Jesus opens his public ministry with the Sermon on the Mount, which is the counterpart of the Sinaitic legislation, and contains the fundamental law of his kingdom. The key-note of this sermon and of the whole Gospel is that Christ came to fulfil the law and the prophets, which implies both the harmony of the two religions and the transcendent superiority of Christianity. His mission assumes an organized institutional form in the kingdom of heaven which he came to establish in the world. Matthew uses this term (ἡ βασιλεία τῶν οὐρανῶν) no less than thirty-two times, while the other Evangelists and Paul speak of the "kingdom of God" (ἡ βασιλεία τοῦ Θεοῦ). No other Evangelist has so fully developed the idea that Christ and his kingdom are the fulfilment of all the hopes and aspirations of Israel, and so vividly set forth the awful solemnity of the crisis at this turning point in its history.

But while Matthew wrote from the Jewish Christian point of view, he is far from being Judaizing or contracted. He takes the widest range of prophecy. He is the most national and yet the most universal, the most retrospective and yet the most prospective, of Evangelists. At the very cradle of the infant Jesus he introduces the adoring Magi from the far East, as the forerunners of a multitude of believing Gentiles who "shall come from the east and the west, and shall sit down with Abraham, Isaac, and Jacob, in the kingdom of heaven;" while "the sons of the kingdom shall be cast forth into the outer darkness." The heathen centurion, and the heathen woman of Canaan exhibit a faith the like of which Jesus did not find in Israel. The Messiah is rejected and persecuted by his own people in Galilee and Judæa. He upbraids Chorazin, Bethsaida, and Capernaum, wherein his mighty works were done, because they repented not; He sheds tears over Jerusalem because she would not come to Him; He pronounces his woe over the Jewish hierarchy, and utters the fearful prophecies of the destruction of the theocracy. All this is most fully recorded by

Matthew, and he most appropriately and sublimely concludes with the command of the universal evangelization of all nations, and the promise of the unbroken presence of Christ with his people to the end of the world.[1]

TOPICAL ARRANGEMENT.

The mode of arrangement is clear and orderly. It is topical rather than chronological. It far surpasses Mark and Luke in the fulness of the discourses of Christ, while it has to be supplemented from them in regard to the succession of events. Matthew groups together the kindred words and works with special reference to Christ's teaching; hence it was properly called by Papias a collection of the Oracles of the Lord. It is emphatically the didactic Gospel.

The first didactic group is the Sermon on the Mount of Beatitudes, which contains the legislation of the kingdom of Christ and an invitation to the whole people to enter, holding out the richest promises to the poor in spirit and the pure in heart (chs. 5–7). The second group is the instruction to the disciples in their missionary work (ch. 10). The third is the collection of the parables on the kingdom of God, illustrating its growth, conflict, value, and consummation (ch. 13). The fourth, the denunciation of the Pharisees (ch. 23), and the fifth, the prophecy of the destruction of Jerusalem and the end of the world (chs. 24 and 25).

Between these chief groups are inserted smaller discourses of Christ, on his relation to John the Baptist (11 : 1–19) ; the woe on the unrepenting cities of Galilee (11 : 20–24) ; the thanksgiving for the revelation to those of a childlike spirit (11 : 25–27) ; the invitation to the weary and heavy laden (11 : 28–30) ; on the observance of the Sabbath and warning to the Pharisees who were on the way to commit the unpardonable sin by tracing his miracles to Satanic powers (ch. 12) ; the attack on the traditions of the elders and the hypocrisy of the Pharisees (chs. 15

---

[1] Comp. ch. 2 : 1–12 ; 8 : 11, 12 ; 11 : 21 ; 12 : 41 ; 15 : 21–28 ; ch. 23 and 24 ; 28 : 19, 20.

and 16); the prophecy of the founding of the church after the great confession of Peter, with the prediction of his passion as the way to victory (ch. 16); the discourse on the little children with their lesson of simplicity and humility against the temptations of hierarchial pride ; the duty of forgiveness in the kingdom and the parable of the unforgiving servant (ch. 18); the discourse about divorce, against the Pharisees ; the blessing of little children; the warning against the danger of riches; the parable of the Laborers in the Vineyard and the nature of the future rewards (chs. 19 and 20); the victorious replies of the Lord to the tempting questions of the Pharisees and Sadducees (ch. 22).

These discourses are connected with narratives of the great miracles of Christ and the events in his life. The miracles are likewise grouped together (as in chs. 8 and 9), or briefly summed up (as in 4 : 23-25). The transfiguration (ch. 17) forms the turning-point between the active and the passive life; it was a manifestation of heaven on earth, an anticipation of Christ's future glory, a pledge of the resurrection, and it fortified Jesus and his three chosen disciples for the coming crisis, which culminated in the crucifixion and ended in the resurrection.[1]

PECULIAR SECTIONS.

Matthew has a number of original sections :

1. Ten Discourses of our Lord, namely, the greater part of the Sermon on the Mount (ch. 5-7); the thanksgiving for the

---

[1] For a full analysis see the critical monograph of Weiss, and Lange's *Matth.*, pp. 43-46. Keim, who builds his *Geschichte Jesu*—the ablest and least objectionable of the purely critical biographies of Christ—chiefly on Matthew, praises its plan as *sorgfältig, einfach und einleuchtend, durchsichtig und sehr wohl durchgeführt* (I. 52). He divides it into two chief sections : the entry upon the public ministry with the *Bussruf* and *Reichspredigt* (4 : 17 : ἀπὸ τότε ἤρξατο ὁ Ἰησοῦς κηρύσσειν, κ. τ. λ.), and the entry upon the path of death with the *Leidensruf* and the *Zukunftspredigt* (16 : 21 : ἀπὸ τότε ἤρξατο ὁ Ἰησ., κ. τ. λ.). He also finds an ingenious symmetry of numbers in the collocation of 10 miracles, 8 [7] beatitudes, 7 woes, 4 and 3 parables, 3 temptations, etc.

revelation to babes (11 : 25–27); the touching invitation to the heavy laden (11 : 28–30), which is equal to anything in John; the warning against idle words (12 : 36, 37); the blessing pronounced upon Peter and the prophecy of founding the church (16 : 17–19); the greater part of the discourse on humility and forgiveness (ch. 18); the rejection of the Jews (21 : 43); the denunciation of the scribes and Pharisees (ch. 23); the description of the final judgment (25 : 31–46); the great commission and the promise of Christ's presence to the end of time (28 : 18–20).

2. Ten Parables: the tares; the hidden treasure; the pearl of great price; the draw-net (13 : 24–50); the unmerciful servant (18 : 23–35); the laborers in the vineyard (20 : 1–16); the two sons (21 : 28–32); the marriage of the king's son (22 : 1–14); the ten virgins (25 : 1–13); the talents (25 : 14–30).

3. Two Miracles: the cure of two blind men (9 : 27–31); the stater in the fish's mouth (17 : 24–27).

4. Facts and Incidents: the adoration of the Magi; the massacre of the innocents; the flight into Egypt; the return from Egypt to Nazareth (all in ch. 2); the coming of the Pharisees and Sadducees to John's baptism (3 : 7); Peter's attempt to walk on the sea (14 : 28–31); the payment of the temple tax (17 : 24–27); the bargain of Judas, his remorse, and suicide (26 : 14–16; 27 : 3–10); the dream of Pilate's wife (27 : 19); the appearance of departed saints in Jerusalem (27 : 52); the watch at the sepulchre (27 : 62–66); the lie of the Sanhedrin and the bribing of the soldiers (28 : 11–15); the earthquake on the resurrection morning (28 : 2, a repetition of the shock described in 27 : 51, and connected with the rolling away of the stone from the sepulchre).

The Style.

The style of Matthew is simple, unadorned, calm, dignified, even majestic; less vivid and picturesque than that of Mark; more even and uniform than Luke's, because not dependent on written sources. He is Hebraizing, but less so than Mark, and not so much as Luke in his first two chapters. He omits some minor details which escaped his observation, but which Mark heard from Peter, and which Luke learned from eye-witnesses or found in his fragmentary documents. Among his peculiar expressions, besides the constant use of " kingdom of *heaven*," is the designation of God as " our heavenly Father," and of Jerusalem as " the holy city " and " the city of the Great King." In the fulness of the teaching of Christ he surpasses all except John. Nothing can be more solemn and impressive than his reports of those words of life and power, which will outlast heaven and earth (24 : 34). Sentence follows sentence with overwhelming force, like a succession of lightning flashes from the upper world.[1]

PATRISTIC NOTICES OF MATTHEW.

The first Gospel was well known to the author of the " Didache of the Apostles," who wrote between 80 and 100, and made large use of it, especially the Sermon on the Mount.[2]

The next clear allusion to this Gospel is made in the Epistle of Barnabas, who quotes two passages from the *Greek* Matthew, one from ch. 22 : 14 : " Many are called, but few chosen," with the significant formula used only of inspired writings · " It is written."[3] This shows clearly that early in the second century, if not before, it was an acknowledged authority in the church. The Gospel of John also indirectly presupposes, by its numerous omissions, the existence of all the Synoptical Gospels.

---

[1] For particulars on the style of Matthew and the other Evangelists see my *Companion to the Study of the Greek Testament* (third ed., 1888), pp. 43 sqq.

[2] See my book on the *Didache* (N. York, third ed., 1889), pp. 61–88.

[3] Ep. Barn., c. 4, at the close : προσέχωμεν, μήποτε, ὡς γέγραπται, πολλοὶ κλητοί, ὀλίγοι δὲ ἐκλεκτοὶ εὑρεθῶμεν. Since the discovery of the entire Greek text of this Epistle in the Codex Sinaiticus (1859), where it follows the Apocalypse, there can be no doubt any more about the formula γέγραπται (*scriptum est*). The other passage quoted in ch. 5 is from Matt. 9 : 13 : οὐκ ἦλθεν καλέσαι δικαίους ἀλλὰ ἁμαρτωλούς. The Ep. of Barnabas dates from the close of the first or the beginning of the second century. Some place it as early as A.D. 70, others as late as 120. The *Didache* is older.

THE HEBREW MATTHEW.

Next we hear of a *Hebrew* Matthew from Papias, bishop of Hierapolis, " a hearer of John and a companion of Polycarp." [1] He collected from apostles and their disciples a variety of apostolic traditions in his " Exposition of Oracles of the Lord," in five books (λογίων κυριακῶν ἐξήγησις). In a fragment of this lost work preserved by Eusebius, he says distinctly that " Matthew composed the *oracles* [of the Lord] in the *Hebrew* tongue, and everyone interpreted them as best he could." [2]

Unfortunately the Hebrew Matthew, if it ever existed, has disappeared, and consequently there is much difference of opinion about this famous passage, both as regards the proper meaning of " oracles " (λόγια) and the truth of the whole report.

1. The " oracles " are understood by some to mean only the discourses of our Lord ; [3] by others to include also the narrative

---

[1] Euseb., *H. E.*, III. 39 : Ἰωάννου μὲν ἀκουστής, Πολυκάρπου δὲ ἑταῖρος γεγονώς. Whether this " John " is the apostle or the mysterious " Presbyter John," is a matter of dispute which will be discussed in the second volume in the section on Papias. Eusebius himself clearly distinguishes two Johns. The date of Papias must be set back several years with that of Polycarp, his ··companion," who suffered martyrdom in 155 (not 164). The *Chronicon Paschale* which represents Papias as martyred at Pergamum about the same time, mistook ΠΑΠΥΛΟΣ in Eusebius, *H. E.*, IV. 15 (at the close), for ΠΑΠΙΑΣ. See Lightfoot, "Contemp. Review" for August, 1875, p. 381 sqq.

[2] Eus., *Hist. Eccl.*, III. 39 : Ματθαῖος μὲν οὖν Ἑβραΐδι διαλέκτῳ τὰ λόγια συνετάξατο (or, according to the reading of Heinichen, I. 150, συνεγράψατο), ἡρμήνευσε δ᾽ αὐτὰ ὡς ἦν δυνατὸς ἕκαστος. This testimony has been thoroughly discussed by Schleiermacher (in the "Studien und Kritiken," 1832), Holtzmann (*Synopt. Evang.*, 248 sqq.), Weizsäcker (*Untersuchungen üb. d. ev. Gesch.*, 27 sqq.), Ewald (*Jahrbücher*, VI., 55 sqq.), Zahn (in "Stud. u. Kritiken," 1866, 649 sqq.), Steitz (*ibid.*, 1868, 63 sqq.), Keim (*Gesch. Jesu v. Naz.*, I., 56 sqq.), Meyer (*Com. Evang. Matth.*, 6th ed. (1876), 4 sqq.), Lightfoot (in "Contemp. Review" for August, 1875, pp. 396–403), and Weiss (*Das Matthäusevang.*, 1876, 1 sqq.).

[3] So Schleiermacher who first critically examined this passage (1832), Schneckenburger (1834), Lachmann (1835), Credner, Wieseler, Ewald, Reuss, Weizsäcker, Holtzmann, Meyer (p. 11). It is supposed that Matthew's Hebrew Gospel was similar to the lost work of Papias, with this difference that the former was simply a collection (σύνταξις or συγγραφή), the latter an interpretation (ἐξήγησις), of the Lord's discourses (τῶν λογίων κυριακῶν).

portions.[1] But in any case the Hebrew Matthew must have been *chiefly* an orderly collection of discourses. This agrees best with the natural and usual meaning of *Logia*, and the actual preponderance of the doctrinal element in our canonical Matthew, as compared with our Mark. *A parte potiori fit denominatio.*

2. The report of a Hebrew original has been set aside altogether as a sheer mistake of Papias, who confounded it with the Ebionite " Gospel according to the Hebrews," known to us from a number of fragments.[2] It is said that Papias was a credulous and weak-minded, though pious man.[3] But this does not impair his veracity or invalidate a simple historical notice. It is also said that the universal spread of the Greek language made a Hebrew Gospel superfluous. But the Aramaic was still the vernacular and prevailing language in Palestine (comp. Acts 21 : 40 ; 22 : 2) and in the countries of the Euphrates.

There is an intrinsic probability of a Hebrew Gospel for the

[1] So Lücke (1833), Kern, Hug, Harless, Anger, Bleek, Baur, Hilgenfeld, Lange, Ebrard, Thiersch, Keim, Zahn, Lightfoot, Thomson, Keil, Weiss (but the last with a limitation to a meagre thread of narrative). The chief arguments are : 1, that all early writers, from Irenæus onward, who speak of a Hebrew Matthew mean a regular Gospel corresponding to our Greek Matthew ; 2, the parallel passage of Papias concerning the Gospel of Mark (Eus., III. 39), where apparently " the Lord's discourses" (λόγοι κυριακοί) includes actions as well as words. τὰ ὑπὸ τοῦ Χριστοῦ ἢ λεχθέντα ἢ πραχθέντα. But it is said, somewhat disparagingly, that Mark (as compared with Matthew) did *not* give " an orderly arrangement of the Lord's words " (οὐχ ὥσπερ σύνταξιν τῶν κυριακῶν ποιούμενος λόγων). The wider meaning of λόγια is supported by Rom. 3 : 1, where τὰ λόγια τοῦ θεοῦ, with which the Jews were intrusted, includes the whole Old Testament Scriptures ; and Hebr. 5 : 12, " the first principles of the oracles of God " (τὰ στοιχεῖα τῆς ἀρχῆς τῶν λογίων τοῦ θεοῦ). Lightfoot quotes also passages from Philo, Clement of Rome, Polycarp, and Origen (*l. c.*, p. 400 sq.).

[2] So Wetstein, Hug, De Wette, Bleek, Ewald, Ritschl, Holtzmann, Keim, Delitzsch, Keil. Some of these writers assume that the Gospel according to the Hebrews was an Ebionite translation and recension of the Greek Matthew. So Delitzsch and Keil (*Com.*, p. 23). Keim is mistaken when he asserts (I. 54) that scarcely anybody nowadays believes in a Hebrew Matthew. The contrary opinion is defended by Meyer, Weiss, and others, and prevails among English divines.

[3] Eusebius (III. 39) calls him σφόδρα σμικρὸς τὸν νοῦν, " very narrow-minded," but on account of his millenarianism, as the context shows. In another place he calls him a man of comprehensive learning and great knowledge of the Scriptures (III. 39 : τὰ πάντα μάλιστα λογιώτατος καὶ τῆς γραφῆς εἰδήμων).

early stage of Christianity. And the existence of a Hebrew Matthew rests by no means merely on Papias. It is confirmed by the independent testimonies of most respectable fathers, as Irenæus,[1] Pantænus,[2] Origen,[3] Eusebius,[4] Cyril of Jerusalem,[5] Epiphanius,[6] and Jerome.[7] This Hebrew Matthew must not be identified with the Judaizing " Gospel according to the Hebrews," the best among the apocryphal Gospels, of which in all thirty-three fragments remain. Jerome and other fathers clearly distinguish the two. The latter was probably an adaptation of the former to the use of the Ebionites and Nazarenes.[8] Truth always precedes heresy,

[1] *Adv. Hær.*, III. 1, 1: ὁ μὲν δὴ Ματθαῖος ἐν τοῖς Ἑβραίοις τῇ ἰδίᾳ διαλέκτῳ αὐτῶν καὶ γραφὴν ἐξήνεγκεν εὐαγγελίου, τοῦ Πέτρου καὶ Παύλου ἐν Ῥώμῃ εὐαγγελιζομένων καὶ θεμελιούντων τὴν ἐκκλησίαν. The chronological reference is so far inaccurate, as neither Peter nor Paul were personally the founders of the church of Rome, yet it was founded through their influence and their pupils, and consolidated by their presence and martyrdom.

[2] He is reported by Eus., *H. E.*, V. 10, to have found in India (probably in Southern Arabia) the Gospel according to Matthew in Hebrew (Ἑβραίων γράμμασι), which had been left there by Bartholomew, one of the apostles. This testimony is certainly independent of Papias. But it may be questioned whether a Hebrew original, or a Hebrew translation, is meant.

[3] In Eus., *H. E.*, VI. 25. Origen, however, drew his report of a Hebrew Matthew not from personal knowledge, but from tradition (ὡς ἐν παραδόσει μαθών).

[4] *H. E.*, III. 24 : Ματθαῖος μὲν γὰρ πρότερον Ἑβραίοις κηρύξας, ὡς ἔμελλε καὶ ἐφ᾿ ἑτέρους ἰέναι, πατρίῳ γλώττῃ γραφῇ παραδοὺς τὸ κατ᾿ αὐτὸν εὐαγγέλιον, τὸ λεῖπον τῇ αὐτοῦ παρουσίᾳ τούτοις, ἀφ᾿ ὧν ἐστέλλετο, διὰ τῆς γραφῆς ἀπεπλήρου. "M., having first preached the Gospel in Hebrew, when on the point of going also to other nations, committed it to writing in his native tongue, and thus supplied the want of his presence to them by his book."

[5] *Catech.* 14 : Ματθ. ὁ γράψας τὸ εὐαγγέλιον Ἑβραΐδι γλώσσῃ.

[6] *Hær.*, XXX. 3 ; comp. LI. 5.

[7] *Præf. in Matth.* ; on Matt. 12 : 13 ; *Dial. c Pelag.*, III., c. 2 ; *De Vir. illustr.*, c. 2 and 3. Jerome's testimony is somewhat conflicting. He received a copy of the Hebrew M. from the Nazarenes in Berœa in Syria for *transcription* (392). But afterward (415) he seems to have found out that the supposed Hebrew Matthew in the library of Pamphilus at Cæsarea was "the Gospel according to the Hebrews" (*Evangelium juxta*, or *secundum Hebræos*), which he *translated* both into Greek and Latin (*De vir. ill.*, c. 2). This would have been useless, if the Hebrew Gospel had been only the original of the canonical Matthew. See Weiss, *l. c.*, pp. 7 sq.

[8] The fragments of this Gospel ("*quo utuntur Nazareni et Ebionitae,*" Jerome) were collected by Credner, *Beiträge*, I. 380 sqq. ; Hilgenfeld, *Nov. Test. extra can. rec.*, IV., and especially by Nicholson in the work quoted

as the genuine coin precedes the counterfeit, and the real portrait the caricature. Cureton and Tregelles maintain that the Curetonian Syriac fragment is virtually a translation of the Hebrew Matthew, and antedates the Peshito version. But Ewald has proven that it is derived from our Greek Matthew.[1]

Papias says that everybody "interpreted" the Hebrew Matthew as well as he could. He refers no doubt to the use of the Gospel in public discourses before Greek hearers, not to a number of written translations of which we know nothing. The past tense ($\dot{\eta}\rho\mu\dot{\eta}\nu\epsilon\upsilon\sigma\epsilon$) moreover seems to imply that such necessity existed no longer at the time when he wrote; in other words, that the authentic Greek Matthew had since appeared and superseded the Aramaic predecessor which was probably less complete.[2] Papias accordingly is an indirect witness of the Greek Matthew in his own age; that is, the early part of the second century (about A.D. 130). At all events the Greek Matthew was in public use even before that time, as is evident from the quotations in the *Didache*, and the Epistle of Barnabas (which were written before 120, probably before 100).

THE GREEK MATTHEW.

The Greek Matthew, as we have it now, is not a close translation from the Hebrew and bears the marks of an original composition. This appears from genuine Greek words and

---

above. It is far superior to the other apocryphal Gospels, and was so much like the Hebrew Matthew that many confounded it with the same, as Jerome observes, ad Matth. 12 : 13 (" *quod vocatur a plerisque Matthæi authenticum*") and *C. Pelag.*, III. 2. The Tübingen view (Baur, Schwegler, Hilgenfeld) reverses the natural order and makes this heretical gospel the *Urmatthæus* (proto-Matthew), of which our Greek Matthew is an orthodox transformation made as late as 130 ; but Keim (I., 29 sqq.), Meyer (p 19), and Weiss (pp. 8 and 9) have sufficiently refuted this hypothesis. Nicholson modifies the Tübingen theory by assuming that Matthew wrote at different times the canonical Gospel and those portions of the Gospel according to the Hebrews, which run parallel with it.

[1] See Holtzmann, p. 269, and Ewald's "Jahrbücher," IX. 69 sqq.

[2] So Meyer (p. 12, against Holtzmann), and Lightfoot (p. 397, against the author of "Supern. Rel."). Schleiermacher was wrong in referring $\dot{\eta}\rho\mu\dot{\eta}\nu\epsilon\upsilon\sigma\epsilon$ to narrative *additions*.

phrases to which there is no parallel in Hebrew, as the truly
classical "Those wretches he will wretchedly destroy," [1] and
from the discrimination in Old Testament quotations which are
freely taken from the Septuagint in the course of the narrative,
but conformed to the Hebrew when they convey Messianic
prophecies, and are introduced by the solemn formula: "that
there might be fulfilled," or "then was fulfilled." [2]

If then we credit the well nigh unanimous tradition of the
ancient church concerning a prior Hebrew Matthew, we must
either ascribe the Greek Matthew to some unknown translator
who took certain liberties with the original, [3] or, what seems
most probable, we must assume that Matthew himself at different periods of his life wrote his Gospel first in Hebrew in
Palestine, and afterward in Greek. [4] In doing so, he would not
literally translate his own book, but like other historians freely
reproduce and improve it. Josephus did the same with his history of the Jewish war, of which only the Greek remains. When
the Greek Matthew once was current in the church, it naturally
superseded the Hebrew, especially if it was more complete.

Objections are raised to Matthew's authorship of the first
canonical Gospel, from real or supposed inaccuracies in the

---

[1] 21 : 41 : κακοὺς κακῶς ἀπολέσει, pessimos pessime (or malos male) perdet.
The E. Revision reproduces the paronomasia (which is obliterated in the
E. V.) thus : "He will miserably destroy those miserable men." Other plays
on words : Πέτρος and πέτρα, 16 : 18 ; βαττολογεῖν and πολυλογία, 6 : 7 ; ἀφανίζ-
ουσιν ὅπως φανῶσι, "they make their faces unappearable (disfigure them), that
they may appear," 6 : 16; comp. 24 : 7. Weiss derives the originality of the
Greek Matthew from the use of the Greek Mark ; but this would not account
for these and similar passages.

[2] Jerome first observed that Matthew follows not Septuaginta transla-
torum auctoritatem, sed Hebraicam (De vir. illustr., c. 3). Credner and Bleek
brought out this important difference more fully, and Holtzmann (Die Syn.
Evang., p. 259), Ritschl, Köstlin, Keim (I., 59 sqq), Meyer (p. 9), and Weiss
(p. 44) confirm it. But Hilgenfeld and Keim unnecessarily see in this fact an
indication of a later editor, who exists only in their critical fancy.

[3] Jerome acknowledges the uncertainty of the translator, De vir. ill., c. 3 :
"Quis postea in Graecum transtulerit [the Hebrew Matthew], non satis cer-
tum est." It has been variously traced to James. the brother of the Lord
Synops. Pseudo-Athan.), to a disciple of Matthew, or to another disciple.

[4] So Bengel, Guericke, Schott, Olshausen, Thiersch.

narrative, but they are at best very trifling and easily explained by the fact that Matthew paid most attention to the words of Christ, and probably had a better memory for thoughts than for facts.[1]

But whatever be the view we take of the precise origin of the first canonical Gospel, it was universally received in the ancient church as the work of Matthew. It was our Matthew who is often, though freely, quoted by Justin Martyr as early as A.D. 146 among the "Gospel Memoirs;" it was one of the four Gospels of which his pupil Tatian compiled a connected "Diatessaron;" and it was the only Matthew used by Irenæus and all the fathers that follow.

§ 81. *Mark.*

Commentaries.

GEORGE PETTER (the largest Com. on M., London, 1661, 2 vols. fol.); C. FR. A. FRITZSCHE (*Evangelium Marci*, Lips., 1830); A. KLOSTER-MANN (*Das Marcusevangelium nach seinem Quellenwerthe für die evang. Gesch.*, Göttingen, 1867); B. WEISS (*Das Marcusevangelium und seine synopt. Parallelen*, Berlin, 1872); MEYER (6th ed. by WEISS, Gött., 1878); JOSEPH A. ALEXANDER (New York, 1858, and London, 1866); HARVEY GOODWIN (London, 1860); JOHN H. GODWIN (London, 1869); JAMES MORISON (*Mark's Memoir of Jesus Christ*, London and Glasgow, 1873, second ed., 1876, third ed., 1881, one of the very best Com., learned, reverential, and sensible); C. F. MACLEAR (Cambridge, 1877); Canon COOK (London, 1878); EDWIN W. RICE (Philad., 1881); MATTHEW B. RIDDLE (New York, 1881).

---

[1] Meyer and Weiss regard the reports of the resurrection of the dead at the crucifixion and the story of the watch, ch. 27 : 52, 62-66, as post-apostolic legends ; but the former is not more difficult than the resurrection of Lazarus, and the latter has all the marks of intrinsic probability. Meyer also gratuitously assumes that Matthew must be corrected from John on the date of the crucifixion ; but there is no real contradiction between the Synoptic and the Johannean date. See p. 133. Meyer's opinion is that Matthew wrote only a Hebrew collection of the discourses of our Lord, that an unknown hand at an early date added the narrative portions, and another anonymous writer, before the year 70, made the Greek translation which was universally and justly, as far as substance is concerned, regarded as Matthew's work (pp. 14, 23). But these are all pure conjectures.

LIFE OF MARK.

The second Evangelist combines in his name, as well as in his mission, the Hebrew and the Roman, and is a connecting link between Peter and Paul, but more especially a pupil and companion of the former, so that his Gospel may properly be called the Gospel of Peter. His original name was John or Johanan (*i. e.*, Jehovah is gracious, *Gotthold*), his surname was Mark (*i. e.*, Mallet).[1] The surname supplanted the Hebrew name in his later life, as Peter supplanted Simon, and Paul supplanted Saul. The change marked the transition of Christianity from the Jews to the Gentiles. He is frequently mentioned in the Acts and the Epistles.[2]

He was the son of a certain Mary who lived at Jerusalem and offered her house, at great risk no doubt in that critical period of persecution, to the Christian disciples for devotional meetings. Peter repaired to that house after his deliverance from prison (A.D. 44). This accounts for the close intimacy of Mark with Peter; he was probably converted through him, and hence called his spiritual "son" (1 Pet. 5 : 13).[3] He may have had a superficial acquaintance with Christ; for he is probably identical with that unnamed "young man" who, according to his own report, left his "linen cloth and fled naked" from Gethsemane in the night of betrayal (14 : 51). He would hardly have mentioned such a trifling incident, unless it had a special significance for him as the turning-point in his life. Lange ingeniously conjectures that his mother owned the garden of Gethsemane or a house close by.

Mark accompanied Paul and Barnabas as their minister (ὑπηρέτης) on their first great missionary journey; but left

---

[1] *Marcus*, and the diminutive *Marcellus* (Little Mallet), are well known Roman names. Marcus Tullius Cicero wrote an oration *pro Marco Marcello*.

[2] Acts 12 : 12, 25; 13 : 5, 13; 15 : 37; Col. 4 : 10; 2 Tim. 4 : 11; Philem. 24; 1 Pet. 5 : 13.

[3] There is no good reason for taking "son" here literally (with Credner), when the figurative meaning so fully harmonizes with Scripture usage and with what we otherwise certainly know of Mark's intimate relations to Peter both from the Acts and from tradition. A daughter of Peter (Petronilla) is mentioned by tradition, but not a son. Clement of Alexandria says that "Peter and Philip begat children."

them half-way, being discouraged, it seems, by the arduous work, and returned to his mother in Jerusalem. For this reason Paul refused to take him on his next tour, while Barnabas was willing to overlook his temporary weakness (Acts 15 : 38). There was a " sharp contention " on that occasion between these good men, probably in connection with the more serious collision between Paul and Peter at Antioch (Gal. 2 : 11 sqq.). Paul was moved by a stern sense of duty ; Barnabas by a kindly feeling for his cousin.[1] But the alienation was only temporary. For about ten years afterwards (63) Paul speaks of Mark at Rome as one of his few " fellow-workers unto the kingdom of God," who had been " a comfort " to him in his imprisonment ; and he commends him to the brethren in Asia Minor on his intended visit (Col. 4 : 10, 11 ; Philem. 24). In his last Epistle he charges Timothy to bring Mark with him to Rome on the ground that he was " useful to him for ministering " (2 Tim. 4 : 11). We find him again in company with Peter at " Babylon," whether that be on the Euphrates, or, more probably, at Rome (1 Pet. 5 : 13).

These are the last notices of him in the New Testament. The tradition of the church adds two important facts, that he wrote his Gospel in Rome as the interpreter of Peter, and that afterwards he founded the church of Alexandria. The Coptic patriarch claims to be his successor. The legends of his martyrdom in the eighth year of Nero (this date is given by Jerome) are worthless. In 827 his relics were removed from Egypt to Venice, which built him a magnificent five-domed cathedral on the Place of St. Mark, near the Doge's palace, and chose him with his symbol, the Lion, for the patron saint of the republic.

His Relation to Peter.

Though not an apostle, Mark had the best opportunity in his mother's house and his personal connection with Peter, Paul, Barnabas, and other prominent disciples for gathering the most authentic information concerning the gospel history.

---

[1] ἀνεψιός, Col. 4 : 10.

The earliest notice of his Gospel we have from Papias of Hierapolis in the first half of the second century. He reports among the primitive traditions which he collected, that "Mark, having become the interpreter of Peter (ἑρμηνευτὴς Πέτρου γενόμενος), wrote down accurately (ἀκριβῶς ἔγραψεν) whatever he remembered,[1] without, however, recording in order (τάξει) what was either said or done by Christ. For neither did he hear the Lord, nor did he follow Him; but afterwards, as I said, [he followed] Peter, who adapted his instructions to the needs [of his hearers], but not in the way of giving a connected account of the Lord's discourses.[2] So then Mark committed no error in thus writing down such details as he remembered; for he made it his one forethought not to omit or to misrepresent any details that he had heard."[3]

In what sense was Mark an "interpreter" of Peter? Not as the translator of a written Aramaic Gospel of Peter into the Greek, for of such an Aramaic original there is no trace, and Peter (to judge from his Epistles) wrote better Greek; nor as the translator of his discourses into Latin, for we know not whether he understood that language, and it was scarcely needed even in Rome among Jews and Orientals who spoke Greek;[4] nor in the wider sense, as a mere clerk or amanuensis, who wrote down what Peter dictated; but as the literary editor and publisher of

---

[1] ἐμνημόνευσε. It is so translated by Valois, Lardner, Meyer, Weiss, Lightfoot. The rendering " recorded," which is preferred by Crusé and Morison, makes it tautological with the preceding ἔγραψεν. The "he" may be referred to Mark or to Peter, probably to the former.

[2] ἀλλ' οὐχ ὥσπερ σύνταξιν τῶν κυριακῶν ποιούμενος λόγων (or λογίων, oracles).

[3] Euseb., Hist. Eccl., III. 39. For a critical discussion of this important testimony see Weiss and Morison, also Lightfoot in the "Contemp. Rev.," vol. XXVI. (1875), pp. 393 sqq. There is not the slightest evidence for referring this description to a fictitious pre-canonical Mark, as is still done by Davidson (new ed., I. 539).

[4] The Latin was provincial, the Greek universal in the Roman empire. Cicero (Pro Arch., 10) : " Græca leguntur in omnibus fere gentibus ; Latina suis finibus, exiguis sane, continentur." The tradition that Mark wrote his Gospel first in Latin is too late to deserve any credit. Baronius defends it in the interest of the Vulgate, and puts the composition back to the year 45. The supposed Latin autograph of Mark's Gospel at Venice is a fragment of the Vulgate.

the oral Gospel of his spiritual father and teacher. So Mercury was called the interpreter of the gods, because he communicated to mortals the messages of the gods. It is quite probable, however, that Peter sketched down some of the chief events under the first impression, in his vernacular tongue, and that such brief memoirs, if they existed, would naturally be made use of by Mark.[1]

We learn, then, from Papias that Mark wrote his Gospel from the personal reminiscences of Peter's discourses, which were adapted to the immediate wants of his hearers; that it was not complete (especially in the didactic part, as compared with Matthew or John), nor strictly chronological.

Clement of Alexandria informs us that the people of Rome were so much pleased with the preaching of Peter that they requested Mark, his attendant, to put it down in writing, which Peter neither encouraged nor hindered. Other ancient fathers emphasize the close intimacy of Mark with Peter, and call his Gospel the Gospel of Peter.[2]

THE GOSPEL.

This tradition is confirmed by the book: it is derived from the apostolic preaching of Peter, but is the briefest and so far the least complete of all the Gospels, yet replete with significant details. It reflects the sanguine and impulsive temperament, rapid movement, and vigorous action of Peter. In this respect its favorite particle "straightway" is exceedingly characteristic. The break-down of Mark in Pamphylia, which provoked the censure of Paul, has a parallel in the denial and inconsistency of Peter; but, like him, he soon rallied, was ready to accompany Paul on his next mission, and persevered faithfully to the end.

---

[1] Justin Martyr (*Dial. c. Tryph.*, c. 106) actually quotes from the "Memoirs (ἀπομνημονεύματα) of Peter" the designation of the sons of Zebedee, "Boanerges" or "Sons of Thunder;" but he evidently refers to the written Gospel of Mark, who alone mentions this fact, 3 : 17.

[2] See the testimonies of Jerome, Eusebius, Origen, Tertullian, Clement of Alexandria, Irenæus, Justin Martyr, and Papias, well presented in Kirchhofer (ed. Charteris) on *Canonicity*, pp. 141–150, and in Morison's *Com.*, pp. xx-xxxiv.

He betrays, by omissions and additions, the direct influence of Peter. He informs us that the house of Peter was "the house of Simon *and Andrew*" (1 : 29). He begins the public ministry of Christ with the calling of these two brothers (1 : 16), and ends the undoubted part of the Gospel with a message to Peter (16 : 7), and the supplement almost in the very words of Peter.[1] He tells us that Peter on the Mount of Transfiguration, when he proposed to erect three tabernacles, "knew not what to say" (9 : 6). He gives the most minute account of Peter's denial, and—alone among the Evangelists—records the fact that he warmed himself "in the light" of the fire so that he could be distinctly seen (14 : 54), and that the cock crew *twice*, giving him a second warning (14 : 72). No one would be more likely to remember and report the fact as a stimulus to humility and gratitude than Peter himself.

On the other hand, Mark omits the laudatory words of Jesus to Peter: "Thou art Rock, and upon this rock I will build my church;" while yet he records the succeeding rebuke: "Get thee behind me, Satan."[2] The humility of the apostle, who himself warns so earnestly against the hierarchical abuse of the former passage, offers the most natural explanation of this conspicuous omission. "It is likely," says Eusebius, "that Peter maintained silence on these points; hence the silence of Mark."[3]

CHARACTER AND AIM OF MARK.

The second Gospel was—according to the unanimous voice of the ancient church, which is sustained by internal evidence—written at Rome and primarily for Roman readers, probably

---

[1] 16 : 19 : "The Lord Jesus . . . was received up into heaven, and sat down at the right hand of God;" comp. 1 Pet. 3 : 22: "who is on the right hand of God, having gone into heaven."

[2] Ch. 8 : 27-33 ; compared with Matt. 16 : 13-33.

[3] *Dem. Evang.*, III. 5, quoted by Morison, p. xxxv. In view of the facts quoted above the reader may judge of Dr. Davidson's assertion (*Introd.*, 1882, vol. I., 541) : "That Mark was not the writer of the canonical Gospel may be inferred from the fact that it is not specially remarkable in particulars relative to Peter."

before the death of Peter, at all events before the destruction of Jerusalem.[1]

It is a faithful record of Peter's preaching, which Mark must have heard again and again.   It is an historical sermon on the text of Peter when addressing the Roman soldier Cornelius: "God anointed Jesus of Nazareth with the Holy Spirit and with power: who went about doing good, and healing all that were oppressed of the devil; for God was with him."[2]   It omits the history of the infancy, and rushes at once into the public ministry of our Lord, beginning, like Peter, with the baptism of John, and ending with the ascension.   It represents Christ in the fulness of his living energy, as the Son of God and the mighty wonder-worker who excited amazement and carried the people irresistibly before him as a spiritual conqueror.   This aspect would most impress the martial mind of the Romans, who were born to conquer and to rule.   The teacher is lost in the founder of a kingdom.   The heroic element prevails over the prophetic.   The victory over Satanic powers in the healing of demoniacs is made very prominent.   It is the gospel of divine force manifested in Christ.   The symbol of the lion is not inappropriate to the Evangelist who describes Jesus as the Lion of the tribe of Judah.[3]

---

[1] Irenæus (*Adv. Hær.*, III. 1) says "*after* the departure" of Peter and Paul, "*post horum excessum*," or in the original Greek preserved by Eusebius (*H. E.*, V. 8, ed. Heinichen, I. 224), μετὰ τὴν τούτων ἔξοδον. This must mean "after their decease," not "after their departure from Rome" (Grabe). But Clement of Alexandria, Origen, Epiphanius, Eusebius, Jerome, and other fathers assign the composition to a time *before* the martyrdom of Peter. Christophorson (in his Latin Version of the Church History of Eusebius, publ. 1570, as quoted by Stieren in Iren. *Op.*, I. 423, note 4) suggested a different reading, μετὰ τὴν ἔκδοσιν, *i. e.*, after the publication of Matthew's Hebrew Gospel, as spoken of in the preceding sentence, and Morison (p. xxv) seems inclined to accept this conjecture.   Very unlikely; all the MSS., Rufinus and the Latin translator of Irenæus read ἔξοδον.   See Stieren, *in loc.* The conflicting statements can be easily harmonized by a distinction between the composition before, and the publication after, the death of Peter.   By publication in those days was meant the copying and distribution of a book.

[2] Acts 10 : 38.   The sermon of Peter to Cornelius is the Gospel of Mark in a nutshell.

[3] Lange (*Com.*, p. 2) : "Mark delineates Christ as, from first to last, preeminently the victorious conqueror of all Satanic powers.   He has left us a

Mark gives us a Gospel of facts, while Matthew's is a Gospel of divine oracles. He reports few discourses, but many miracles. He unrolls the short public life of our Lord in a series of brief life-pictures in rapid succession. He takes no time to explain and to reveal the inside. He dwells on the outward aspect of that wonderful personality as it struck the multitude. Compared with Matthew and especially with John, he is superficial, but not on that account incorrect or less useful and necessary. He takes the theocratic view of Christ, like Matthew; while Luke and John take the universal view; but while Matthew for his Jewish readers begins with the descent of Christ from David the King and often directs attention to the fulfilment of prophecy, Mark, writing for Gentiles, begins with "the Son of God" in his independent personality.[1] He rarely quotes prophecy; but, on the other hand, he translates for his Roman readers Aramaic words and Jewish customs and opinions.[2] He exhibits the Son of God in his mighty power and expects the reader to submit to his authority.

Two miracles are peculiar to him, the healing of the deaf and dumb man in Decapolis, which astonished the people "beyond measure" and made them exclaim: "He hath done all things well: he maketh even the deaf to hear, and the dumb to speak" (7 : 31–37). The other miracle is a remarkable specimen of a

record of the manifestation of Christ's power when that great Lion seized upon the ancient world, and of his brief but decisive victory, after which only the ruins of the ancient world are left, which in turn furnish the materials for the new one." Thomson (Speaker's *Com., Introd. to Gospels*, p. xxxv): "The wonder-working Son of God sweeps over his kingdom, swiftly and meteor-like : and men are to wonder and adore. His course is sometimes represented as abrupt, mysterious, awful to the disciples : He leaves them at night ; conceals himself from them on a journey. The disciples are amazed and afraid (10 : 24, 32). And the Evangelist means the same impression of awe to be imparted to the reader."

[1] The reading of the textus rec. υἱοῦ (τοῦ) θεοῦ in Mark 1 : 1 is sustained by א^a ABDL, nearly all the cursives, and retained by Lachmann and Tregelles in the text, by Westcott and Hort in the margin. Tischendorf omitted it in his 8th ed. on the strength of his favorite א* (in its original form), and Origen. Irenæus has both readings. The term occurs seven times in Mark, and is especially appropriate at the beginning of his Gospel and a part of its very title

[2] 3 : 17; 5 : 41; 7 : 1–4; 12 : 18; 15 : 6, 35.

gradual cure, the healing of the blind man at Bethsaida, who upon the first touch of Christ saw the men around him walking, but indistinctly as trees, and then after the second laying on of hands upon his eyes "saw all things clearly" (8 : 22–26). He omits important parables, but alone gives the interesting parable of the seed growing secretly and bearing first the blade, then the ear, then the full grain in the ear (4 : 26–29).

It is an interesting feature to which Dr. Lange first has directed attention, that Mark lays emphasis on the periods of pause and rest which "rhythmically intervene between the several great victories achieved by Christ." He came out from his obscure abode in Nazareth; each fresh advance in his public life is preceded by a retirement, and each retirement is followed by a new and greater victory. The contrast between the contemplative rest and the vigorous action is striking and explains the overpowering effect by revealing its secret spring in the communion with God and with himself. Thus we have after his baptism a retirement to the wilderness in Judæa before he preached in Galilee (1 : 12); a retirement to the ship (3 : 7); to the desert on the eastern shore of the lake of Galilee (6 : 31); to a mountain (6 : 46); to the border land of Tyre and Sidon (7 : 24); to Decapolis (7 : 31); to a high mountain (9 : 2); to Bethany (11 : 1); to Gethsemane (14 : 34); his rest in the grave before the resurrection; and his withdrawal from the world and his reappearance in the victories of the gospel preached by his disciples. "The ascension of the Lord forms his last withdrawal, which is to be followed by his final onset and absolute victory." [1]

Doctrinal Position.

Mark has no distinct doctrinal type, but is catholic, irenic, unsectarian, and neutral as regards the party questions within the apostolic church. But this is not the result of calculation

---

[1] See Lange's Analysis of Mark, *Com.*, pp. 12–14; also his *Bibelkunde*, pp. 185–187. Lange discovered many characteristic features of the Gospels, which have passed without acknowledgment into many other books.

or of a tendency to obliterate and conciliate existing differences.[1] Mark simply represents the primitive form of Christianity itself before the circumcision controversy broke out which occasioned the apostolic conference at Jerusalem twenty years after the founding of the church. His Gospel is Petrine without being anti-Pauline, and Pauline without being anti-Petrine. Its doctrinal tone is the same as that of the sermons of Peter in the Acts. It is thoroughly practical. Its preaches Christianity, not theology.

The same is true of the other Gospels, with this difference, however, that Matthew has a special reference to Jewish, Luke to Gentile readers, and that both make their selection accordingly under the guidance of the Spirit and in accordance with their peculiar charisma and aim, but without altering or coloring the facts. Mark stands properly between them just as Peter stood between James and Paul.

THE STYLE.

The style of Mark is unclassical, inelegant, provincial, homely, poor and repetitious in vocabulary, but original, fresh, and picturesque, and enlivened by interesting touches and flickers.[2]

---

[1] As asserted by Baur, Schwegler, Köstlin, and quite recently again by Dr. Davidson, who says. (I. 505) : " The colorless neutrality of the Gospel was an important factor in conciliating antagonistic parties." Dr. Morison (p. xlvi) well remarks against this Tübingen tendency criticism : "There is not so much as a straw of evidence that the Gospel of Mark occupied a position of mediation, or irenic neutrality, in relation to the other two Synoptic Gospels. It is in the mere wantonness of a creative imagination that its penman is depicted as warily steering his critical bark between some Scylla in St. Matthew's representations and some Charybdis in St. Luke's. There is no Scylla in the representations of St. Matthew. It must be invented if suspected. There is no Charybdis in the representations of St. Luke. Neither is there any indication in St. Mark of wary steering, or of some latent aim of destination kept, like sealed orders, under lock and key. There is, in all the Gospels, perfect transparency and simplicity, 'the simplicity that is in Christ.' "

[2] Ewald characterizes Mark's style as the *Schmelz der frischen Blume*, as the *volle, reine Leben der Stoffe*, Kahnis as *drastisch* and *frappant*, Meyer as *malerisch anschaulich*. Lange speaks of the "enthusiasm and vividness of realization which accounts for the brevity, rapidity, and somewhat dramatic tone of the narrative, and the introduction of details which give life to the scene."

He was a stranger to the arts of rhetoric and unskilled in literary composition, but an attentive listener, a close observer, and
faithful recorder of actual events. He is strongly Hebraizing,
and uses often the Hebrew *and*, but seldom the argumentative
for. He inserts a number of Latin words, though most of these
occur also in Matthew and Luke, and in the Talmud.[1] He uses
the particle " forthwith " or " straightway " more frequently
than all the other Evangelists combined.[2] It is his pet word,
and well expresses his haste and rapid transition from event
to event, from conquest to conquest. He quotes names and
phrases in the original Aramaic, as " Abba," " Boanerges,"
" Talitha, kum," " Corban," " Ephphathah," and " Eloi, Eloi,"
with a Greek translation.[3] He is fond of the historical present,[4]
of the direct instead of the indirect mode of speech,[5] of pic-
torical participles,[6] and of affectionate diminutives.[7] He observes time and place of important events.[8] He has a number
of peculiar expressions not found elsewhere in the New Testament.[9]

---

[1] κῆνσος (*census*), κεντυρίων (*centurio*), ξέστης (*sextarius*), σπεκουλάτωρ (*specu-
lator*), and the Latinizing phrases τὸ ἱκανὸν ποιεῖν (*satisfacere*, 15 : 15), ἐσχάτως
ἔχειν (*in extremis esse*), συμβούλιον διδόναι (*consilium dare*). Mark even uses
the Roman names of coins instead of the Greek, κοδράντης (*quadrans*,
12 : 42).

[2] εὐθέως or εὐθύς occurs (according to Bruder's *Concord.*) forty-one times in the
Gospel of Mark, nearly as often as in all other New Test. writings combined.
But there are some variations in reading. Codex D omits it in several passages. The English Version, by its inexcusable love of variations, obliterates
many characteristic features of the sacred writers. This very particle is
translated in no less than seven different ways : straightway, immediately,
forthwith, as soon as, by and by, shortly, and anon.

[3] 3 : 17 ; 5 : 41 ; 7 : 11, 34 ; 14 : 36 ; 15 : 34.

[4] 1 : 21, 40, 44 ; 2 : 3, 10, 17 ; 11 : 1 ; 14 : 43, 66.

[5] 4 : 39 ; 5 : 8, 9, 12 ; 6 : 23, 31 ; 9 : 25 ; 12 : 6.

[6] Such as ἀναβλέψαι, ἐμβλέψας, περιβλεψάμενος, ἀναπηδήσας, κύψας, ἐμβριμησά-
μενος, ἐπιστραφείς, ἀποστενάξας.

[7] As παιδίον, κοράσιον, κυνάριον, θυγάτριον, ἰχθύδιον, ὠτάριον.

[8] Time : 1 : 35 ; 2 : 1 ; 4 : 35 ; 6 : 2 ; 11 : 11, 19 ; 15 : 25 ; 16 : 2. Place :
2 : 13 ; 5 : 20 ; 7 : 31 ; 12 : 41 ; 13 : 3 ; 14 : 68 ; 15 : 39 ; 16 : 5.

[9] As ἀγρεύειν, ἄλαλος, ἀλεκτοροφωνία, γναφεύς, ἐκθαμβεῖσθαι, ἐναγκαλίζεσθαι,
ἐξάπινα, ἐνειλέω, ἐξουδενόω, ἔννυχον, μογιλάλος, πρασιαὶ πρασιαί, προσάββατον,
προμεριμνᾶν, προσορμιζεσθαι, συνθλίβειν, τηλαυγῶς, ὑπολήνιον, and others.

Characteristic Details.

Mark inserts many delicate tints and interesting incidents of persons and events which he must have heard from primitive witnesses. They are not the touches of fancy or the reflections of an historian, but the reminiscences of the first impressions. They occur in every chapter. He makes some little contribution to almost every narrative he has in common with Matthew and Luke. He notices the overpowering impression of awe and wonder, joy and delight, which the words and miracles of Jesus and his very appearance made upon the people and the disciples;[1] the actions of the multitude as they were rushing and thronging and pressing upon Him that He might touch and heal them, so that there was scarcely standing room, or time to eat.[2] On one occasion his kinsmen were about forcibly to remove Him from the throng. He directs attention to the human emotions and passions of our Lord, how he was stirred by pity, wonder, grief, anger and indignation.[3] He notices his attitudes, looks and gestures,[4] his sleep and hunger.[5]

He informs us that Jesus, "looking upon" the rich young ruler, "loved him," and that the ruler's "countenance fell" when he was told to sell all he had and to follow Jesus. Mark, or Peter rather, must have watched the eye of our Lord and read in his face the expression of special interest in that man who notwithstanding his self-righteousness and worldliness had some lovely qualities and was not very far from the kingdom.[6]

---

[1] 1 : 22, 27; 2 : 12 ; 4 : 41 ; 6 : 2, 51 ; 10 : 24, 26, 32.

[2] 3 : 10, 20, 32 ; 4 : 1 ; 5 : 21, 31; 6 : 31, 33.

[3] 6 : 34 : "he had compassion on them; " 6 : 6 : "he marvelled because of their unbelief" (as he marvelled also at the great faith of the heathen centurion, Matt. 8 : 10 ; Luke 7 : 8); 3 : 5 : "when he had looked round about them with anger, being grieved at the hardening of their heart ;" 8 : 12 : "he sighed deeply in his spirit ;" 10 : 14 : "he was moved with indignation," or "was much displeased" with the conduct of the disciples.

[4] 1 : 31 ; 3 : 5, 34 ; 5 : 32 ; 7 : 33, 34 ; 8 : 12, 33 ("but he, turning about, and seeing his disciples, rebuked Peter "); 9 : 35 ; 10 : 23, 32 ; 11 : 11.

[5] 4 : 38 ; 6 : 31 ; 11 : 12.

[6] 10 : 21, 22: ἐμβλέψας αὐτῷ ἠγάπησεν αὐτόν. This must be taken in its natural meaning and not weakened into "kissed him," or "spoke kindly to

The cure of the demoniac and epileptic at the foot of the mount of transfiguration is narrated with greater circumstantiality and dramatic vividness by Mark than by the other Synoptists. He supplies the touching conversation of Jesus with the father of the sufferer, which drew out his weak and struggling faith with the earnest prayer for strong and victorious faith: "I believe; help Thou mine unbelief."[1] We can imagine how eagerly Peter, the confessor, caught this prayer, and how often he repeated it in his preaching, mindful of his own weakness and trials.

All the Synoptists relate on two distinct occasions Christ's love for little children, but Mark alone tells us that He "took little children into his arms, and laid his hands upon them."[2]

Many minor details not found in the other Gospels, however insignificant in themselves, are yet most significant as marks of the autopticity of the narrator (Peter). Such are the notices that Jesus entered the house of "Simon and Andrew, with James and John" (1 : 29); that the Pharisees took counsel "with the Herodians" (3 : 6); that the raiment of Jesus at the transfiguration became exceeding white as snow "so as no fuller on earth can whiten them" (9 : 3); that blind Bartimæus when called, "casting away his garment, leaped up" (10 : 50), and came to Jesus; that "Peter and James and John and Andrew asked him privately" on the Mount of Olives about the coming events (13 : 3); that the five thousand sat down "in ranks, by hundreds and fifties" (6 : 40); that the Simon who carried the cross of Christ (15 : 21) was a "Cyrenian" and "the father of Alexander and Rufus" (no doubt, two well-known disciples, perhaps at Rome, comp. Rom. 16 : 13).

---

him," or "pitied him." Our Saviour, says Morison, *in l.*, "would discern in the young man not a little that was really amiable, the result of the partial reception and reflection of gracious Divine influences. There was ingenuousness, for instance, and moral earnestness. There was restraint of the animal passions, and an aspiration of the spirit toward the things of the world to come."

[1] 9 : 21–25. Comp. Matt. 17 : 14–18 ; Luke 9 : 37–42.
[2] 9 : 36 ; 10 : 16 ; comp. with Matt. 18 : 2 ; 19 : 13 ; and Luke 9 : 48 ; 18 : 16.

We may add, as peculiar to Mark and "bewraying" Peter, the designation of Christ as "the carpenter" (6 : 3); the name of the blind beggar at Jericho, "Bartimæus" (10 : 46); the "cushion" in the boat on which Jesus slept (4 : 38); the "green grass" on the hill side in spring time (4 : 39); the "one loaf" in the ship (8 : 14); the colt "tied at the door without in the open street" (11 : 4); the address to the daughter of Jairus in her mother tongue (5 : 41); the bilingual "Abba, Father," in the prayer at Gethsemane (14 : 36; comp. Rom. 8 : 15; Gal. 4 : 6).

CONCLUSION.

The natural conclusion from all these peculiarities is that Mark's Gospel, far from being an extract from Matthew or Luke or both, as formerly held,[1] is a thoroughly independent and original work, as has been proven by minute investigations of critics of different schools and aims.[2] It is in all its essential parts a fresh, life-like, and trustworthy record of the persons and events of the gospel history from the lips of honest old Peter and from the pen of his constant attendant and pupil. Jerome hit it in the fourth century, and unbiassed critics in the nineteenth century confirm it: Peter was the narrator, Mark the writer, of the second Gospel.[3]

Some have gone further and maintain that Mark, "the interpreter of Peter," simply translated a Hebrew Gospel of his teacher;[4] but tradition knows nothing of a Hebrew Peter,

---

[1] By Augustin, Griesbach, De Wette, Bleek, Baur, Davidson.

[2] As C. H. Weisse, Wilke, Ewald, Lange, Holtzmann, Bernhard Weiss, Westcott, Abbott, Morison. See § 79, p. 609.

[3] Jerome wrote to Hedibia, a pious lady in Gaul (Ep. CXX. c. 10, in *Opera*, ed. Migne, I. 1002): "*Habebat ergo [Paulus] Titum interpretem; sicut et beatus Petrus Marcum, cuius evangelium Petro narrante* (not *dictante*), *et illo [Marco] scribente, compositum est.*" This letter was written in 406 or 407, from Bethlehem. Morison (p. xxxvii): "If we assume the patristic tradition regarding St. Peter's relation to St. Mark, we find the contents and texture of the Gospel to be without a jar at any point, in perfect accord with the idea."

[4] So James Smith in his *Dissertation on the Origin and Connection of the Gospels*, and again in the *Dissertation on the Life and Writings of St. Luke,*

while it speaks of a Hebrew Matthew; and a book is called after its author, not after its translator. It is enough to say, Peter was the preacher, Mark the reporter and editor.

The bearing of this fact upon the reliableness of the Synop tic record of the life of Christ is self-evident. It leaves no room for the mythical or legendary hypothesis.[1]

INTEGRITY OF THE GOSPEL.

The Gospel closes (16 : 9–20) with a rapid sketch of the wonders of the resurrection and ascension, and the continued manifestations of power that attend the messengers of Christ in preaching the gospel to the whole creation. This close is upon the whole characteristic of Mark and presents the gospel as a divine power pervading and transforming the world, but it contains some peculiar features, namely : (1) one of the three *distinct* narratives of Christ's ascension (ver. 19, " he was received up into heaven ; " the other two being those of Luke 24 : 51 and Acts 1 : 9–11), with the additional statement that he " sat down at the right hand of God " (comp. the similar statement, 1 Pet. 3 : 22) ; (2) an emphatic declaration of the necessity of baptism for salvation ("he that believeth and is *baptized* shall be saved"), with the negative clause that unbelief (*i. e.*, the rejection of the gospel offer of salvation) condemns (" he that disbelieveth shall be condemned ") ;[2] (3) the fact that the apostles disbelieved

prefixed to the fourth ed. of his *Voyage and Shipwreck of St. Paul* (1880), pp. 29 sqq.

[1] " In substance and style and treatment, the Gospel of St. Mark is essentially a transcript from life. The course and the issue of facts are imaged in it with the clearest outline. If all other arguments against the mythic origin of the Evangelic narratives were wanting, this vivid and simple record, stamped with the most distinct impress of independence and originality,—totally unconnected with the symbolism of the Old Dispensation, totally independent of the deeper reasonings of the New,—would be sufficient to refute a theory subversive of all faith in history. The details which were originally addressed to the vigorous intelligence of Roman hearers are still pregnant with instruction for us. The teaching which 'met their wants' in the first age, finds a corresponding field for its action now." Westcott, *l. c.*, 369 (Am. ed.).

[2] Ver. 16 : ὁ πιστεύσας καὶ βαπτισθεὶς σωθήσεται, ὁ δὲ ἀπιστήσας κατακριθήσεται. This declaration takes the place of the command to baptize, Matt. 28 : 19. It

the report of Mary Magdalene until the risen Lord appeared to them personally (vers. 11–14; but John intimates the same, 20 : 8, 9, especially in regard to Thomas, ver. 25, and Matthew mentions that some doubted, 28 : 17; comp. Luke 24 : 37–41); (4) an authoritative promise of supernatural powers and signs which shall accompany the believers (vers. 17, 18). Among these is mentioned the pentecostal glossolalia under the unique name of speaking with *new* tongues.[1]

The genuineness of this closing section is hotly contested, and presents one of the most difficult problems of textual criticism. The arguments are almost equally strong on both sides, but although the section cannot be *proven* to be a part of the original Gospel, it seems clear: (1) that it belongs to primitive tradition (like the disputed section of the adulteress in John, ch. 8); and (2) that Mark cannot have closed his Gospel with ver. 8 (γάρ) without intending a more appropriate conclusion.

applies only to converted believers (ὁ πιστεύσας), not to children who are incapable of an act of faith or unbelief, and yet are included in the covenant blessing of Christian parents (comp. 1 Cor. 7 : 14). Hence it is only positive unbelief which condemns, whether with or without baptism; while faith saves with baptism, ordinarily, but exceptionally also without baptism. Else we should have to condemn the penitent thief, the Quakers, and all unbaptized infants. St. Augustin derived from this passage and from John 3 : 5 (ἐξ ὕδατος) the doctrine of the absolute and universal necessity of water-baptism for salvation; and hence the further (logical, but not theological) inference drawn by the great and good bishop of Hippo, with reluctant heart, that all *unbaptized* infants dying in infancy are forever damned (or, at least, excluded from heaven), simply on account of Adam's sin, before they were capable of committing an actual transgression. This is the doctrine of the Roman Church to this day. Some Calvinistic divines in the seventeenth century held the same view with regard to *reprobate* infants (if there be such), but allowed an indefinite extension of the number of *elect* infants beyond the confines of Christendom. Zwingli held that *all* infants dying in infancy are saved. Fortunately the Saviour of mankind has condemned the *dogma horribile* of infant damnation by his own conduct toward (unbaptized) children, and his express declaration that to them belongs the kingdom of heaven, and that our heavenly Father does not wish any of them to perish. Matt. 18 : 2–6; 19 : 13–15; Mark 10 : 13–16; Luke 18 : 15–17. In the light of these passages we must explain John 3 : 5 and Mark 16 : 16, which have been so grossly misunderstood.

[1] γλώσσαις λαλήσουσιν καιναῖς. Tischendorf retains καιναῖς; Tregelles, Westcott and Hort put it in the margin, as it is omitted in several uncials and ancient versions.

The result does not affect the character and credibility of the Gospel. The section may be authentic or correct in its statements, without being genuine or written by Mark. There is nothing in it which, properly understood, does not harmonize with apostolic teaching.

NOTE ON THE DISPUTED CLOSE OF MARK, CH. 16 : 9–20.

I. Reasons against the genuineness :

1. The section is wanting altogether in the two oldest and most valuable uncial manuscripts, the Sinaitic ($\aleph$) and the Vatican (B). The latter, it is true, after ending the Gospel with ver. 8 and the subscription KATA MAPKON, leaves the remaining third column blank, which is sufficient space for the twelve verses. Much account is made of this fact by Drs. Burgon and Scrivener ; but in the same MS. I find, on examination of the fac-simile edition, blank spaces from a few lines up to two-thirds and three-fourths of a column, at the end of Matthew, John, Acts, 1 Pet. (fol. 200), 1 John (fol. 208), Jude (fol. 210), Rom. (fol. 227), Eph. (fol. 262), Col. (fol. 272). In the Old Testament of B, as Dr. Abbot has first noted (in 1872), there are two blank columns at the end of Nehemiah, and a blank column and a half at the end of Tobit. In any case the omission indicates an objection of the copyist of B to the section, or its absence in the earlier manuscript he used.

I add the following private note from Dr. Abbot : "In the Alexandrian MS. a column and a third are left blank at the end of Mark, half a page at the end of John, and a whole page at the end of the Pauline Epistles. (Contrast the ending of Matthew and Acts.) In the Old Testament, note especially in this MS. Leviticus, Isaiah, and the Ep. of Jeremiah, at the end of each of which half a page or more is left blank ; contrast Jeremiah, Baruch, Lamentations. There are similar blanks at the end of Ruth, 2 Samuel, and Daniel, but the last leaf of those books ends a quaternion or quire in the MS. In the Sinaitic MS. more than two columns with the whole following page are left blank at the end of the Pauline Epistles, though the two next leaves belong to the same quaternion ; so at the end of the Acts a column and two-thirds with the whole of the following page ; and at the end of Barnabas a column and a half. These examples show that the matter in question depended largely on the whim of the copyist ; and that we can not infer with confidence that the scribe of B knew of any other ending of the Gospel."

There is also a shorter conclusion, unquestionably spurious, which in L and several MSS. of the Æthiopic version *immediately follows* ver. 8, and appears also in the margin of 274, the Harclean Syriac, and the best

Coptic MS. of the Gospel, while in k of the Old Latin it takes the place
of the longer ending. For details, see Westcott and Hort, II., *Append.*,
pp. 30, 38, 44 sq.

2. Eusebius and Jerome state expressly that the section was wanting
in almost all the Greek copies of the Gospels. It was not in the copy
used by Victor of Antioch. There is also negative patristic evidence
against it, particularly strong in the case of Cyril of Jerusalem, Tertullian, and Cyprian, who had special occasion to quote it (see Westcott
and Hort, II., *Append.*, pp. 30–38). Jerome's statement, however, is
weakened by the fact that he seems to depend upon Eusebius, and that
he himself translated the passage in his Vulgate.

3. It is wanting in the important MS. k representing the African
text of the Old Latin version, which has a different conclusion (like that
in L), also in some of the best MSS. of the Armenian version, while in
others it *follows* the usual subscription. It is also wanting in an unpub-
lished Arabic version (made from the Greek) in the Vatican Library,
which is likewise noteworthy for reading ὅς in 1 Tim. 3 : 16.

4. The way in which the section begins, and in which it refers to
Mary Magdalene, give it the air of a conclusion derived from some ex-
traneous source. It does not record the fulfilment of the promise in
ver. 7. It uses (ver. 9) πρώτῃ ϛαββάτου for the Hebraistic τῇ μιᾷ τῶν
σαββάτων of 16 : 2. It has many words or phrases (*e.g.*, πορεύομαι used
three times) not elsewhere found in Mark, which strengthen the impression that we are dealing with a different writer, and it lacks Mark's
usual graphic detail. But the argument from difference of style and
vocabulary has been overstrained, and can not be regarded as in itself
decisive.

II. Arguments in favor of the genuineness :

1. The section is found in most of the uncial MSS., A C D X Γ Δ Σ,
in all the late uncials (in L as a secondary reading), and in all the
cursive MSS., including 1, 33, 69, etc. ; though a number of the cursives
either mark it with an asterisk or note its omission in older copies.
Hence the statements of Eusebius and Jerome seem to need some
qualification. In 22 (as Dr. Burgon has first pointed out) the liturgical
word τέλος, denoting the end of a reading lesson, is inserted after both
ver. 8 and ver. 20, while no such word is placed at the end of the other
Gospels. This shows that there were two endings of Mark in different
copies.

2. Also in most of the ancient versions, the Itala (with the exception
of " k," or the codex Bobbiensis, used by Columban), the Vulgate, the
Curetonian Syriac (last part), the Peshito, the Philoxenian, the Coptic,
the Gothic (first part), and the Æthiopic, but in several MSS. only
after the spurious shorter conclusion. Of these versions the Itala, the
Curetonian and Peshito Syriac, and the Coptic, are older than any of
our Greek codices, but the *MSS.* of the Coptic are not older than the

twelfth or tenth century, and may have undergone changes as well as the Greek MSS.; and the MSS. of the Æthiopic are all modern. The best MSS. of the old Latin are mutilated here. The only extant fragment of Mark in the Curetonian Syriac is vv. 17–20, so that we cannot tell whether vv. 9–20 immediately followed ver. 8, or appeared as they do in cod. L. But Aphraates quotes it.

3. In all the existing Greek and Syriac lectionaries or evangeliaries and synaxaries, as far as examined, which contain the Scripture reading lessons for the churches. Dr. Burgon lays great stress on their testimony (ch. X.), but he overrates their antiquity. The lection-systems cannot be traced beyond the middle of the fourth century when great liturgical changes took place. At that time the disputed verses were widely circulated and eagerly seized as a suitable resurrection and ascension lesson.

4. Irenæus of Lyons, in the second half of the second century, long before Eusebius, expressly quotes verse 19 as a part of the Gospel of Mark (Adv. Hær., III. 10, 6). The still earlier testimony of Justin Martyr (Apol., I. 45) is doubtful. (The quotation of vers. 17 and 18 in lib. viii., c. 1 of the Apostolic Constitutions is wrongly ascribed to Hippolytus.) Marinus, Macarius Magnes (or at least the heathen writer whom he cites), Didymus, Chrysostom (??), Epiphanius, Nestorius, the apocryphal Gesta Pilati, Ambrose, Augustin, and other later fathers quote from the section.

5. A strong intrinsic argument is derived from the fact that Mark cannot *intentionally* have concluded his Gospel with the words ἐφοβοῦντο γάρ (16 : 8). He must either have himself written the last verses or some other conclusion, which was accidently lost before the book was multiplied by transcription ; or he was unexpectedly prevented from finishing his book, and the conclusion was supplied by a friendly hand from oral tradition or some written source.

In view of these facts the critics and exegetes are very much divided. The passage is defended as genuine by Simon, Mill, Bengel, Storr, Matthæi, Hug, Schleiermacher, De Wette, Bleek, Olshausen, Lange, Ebrard, Hilgenfeld, Broadus ("Bapt. Quarterly," Philad., 1869), Burgon (1871), Scrivener, Wordsworth, McClellan, Cook, Morison (1882). It is rejected or questioned by the critical editors, Griesbach, Lachmann, Tischendorf, Tregelles, Alford, Westcott and Hort (though retained by all in the text with or without brackets), and by such critics and commentators as Fritzsche, Credner, Reuss, Wieseler, Holtzmann, Keim, Scholten, Klostermann, Ewald, Meyer, Weiss, Norton, Davidson. Some of these opponents, however, while denying the composition of the section by Mark, regard the contents as a part of the apostolic tradition. Michelsen surrenders only vers. 9–14, and saves vers. 15–20. Ewald and Holtzmann conjecture the original conclusion from vers. 9, 10, and 16–20 ; Volkmar invents one from elements of all the Synoptists.

III. Solutions of the problem. All mere conjectures; certainty is impossible in this case.

1. Mark himself added the section in a later edition, issued perhaps in Alexandria, having been interrupted in Rome just as he came to 16 : 8, either by Peter's imprisonment and martyrdom, or by sickness, or some accident. Incomplete copies got into circulation before he was able to finish the book. So Michaelis, Hug, and others.

2. The original conclusion of Mark was lost by some accident, most probably from the original autograph (where it may have occupied a separate leaf), and the present paragraph was substituted by an anonymous editor or collector in the second century. So Griesbach, Schulthess, David Schulz.

3. Luke wrote the section. So Hitzig (*Johannes Marcus*, p. 187).

4. Godet (in his *Com. on Luke*, p. 8 and p. 513, Engl. transl.) modifies this hypothesis by assuming that a third hand supplied the close, partly from Luke's Gospel, which had appeared in the mean time, and partly (vers. 17 and 18) from another source. He supposes that Mark was interrupted by the unexpected outbreak of the Neronian persecution in 64 and precipitously fled from the capital, leaving his unfinished Gospel behind, which was afterward completed when Luke's Gospel appeared. In this way Godet accounts for the fact that up to Mark 16 : 8 Luke had no influence on Mark, while such influence is apparent in the concluding section.

5. It was the end of one of the lost Gospel fragments used by Luke (1 : 1), and appended to Mark's by the last redactor. Ewald.

6. The section is from the pen of Mark, but was purposely omitted by some scribe in the third century from hierarchical prejudice, because it represents the apostles in an unfavorable light after the resurrection, so that the Lord "upbraided them with their unbelief and hardness of heart" (ver. 14). Lange (*Leben Jesu*, I. 166). Unlikely.

7. The passage is genuine, but was omitted in some valuable copy by a misunderstanding of the word τέλος, which often is found after ver. 8 in cursives. So Burgon. "According to the Western order," he says (in the "Quarterly Review" for Oct., 1881), "S. Mark occupies *the last* place. From the earliest period it had been customary to write τέλος (THE END) after the 8th verse of his last chapter, in token that *there* a famous ecclesiastical lection comes to a close. Let the last leaf of one very ancient archetypal copy have begun at ver. 9, and let that last leaf have perished;—and all is plain. A faithful copyist will have ended the Gospel perforce—as B and ℵ have done—at S. Mark 16 : 8." But this liturgical mark is not old enough to explain the omission in ℵ, B, and the MSS. of Eusebius and Jerome ; and a reading lesson would close as abruptly with γάρ as the Gospel itself.

8. The passage cannot claim any apostolic authority ; but it is doubtless founded on some tradition of the apostolic age. Its authorship and

precise date must remain unknown, but it is apparently older than the time when the canonical Gospels were generally received; for although it has points of contact with them all, it contains no attempt to harmonize their various representations of the course of events. So Dr. Hort (II., *Appendix*, 51). A similar view was held by Dean Alford.

For full information we refer to the critical apparatus of Tischendorf and Tregelles, to the monograph of Weiss on *Mark* (*Das Marcusevang.*, pp. 512–515), and especially to the exhaustive discussion of Westcott and Hort in the second volume (*Append.*, pp. 29–51). The most elaborate vindication of the genuineness is by Dean Burgon : *The Last Twelve Verses of the Gospel according to S. Mark Vindicated against Recent Critical Objections and Established* (Oxford and Lond., 1871, 334 pages), a very learned book, but marred by its over-confident tone and unreasonable hostility to the oldest uncial MSS. (ℵ and B) and the most meritorious textual critics (Lachmann, Tischendorf, Tregelles). For other able defences see Dr. Scrivener (*Introd. to the Criticism of the New Test.*, 3d ed., 1883, pp. 583–590), Dr. Morison (*Com. on Mark*, pp. 446 and 463 sqq.), and Canon Cook (in Speaker's *Com. on Mark*, pp. 301–308).

Lachmann gives the disputed section, according to his principle to furnish the text as found in the fourth century, but did not consider it genuine (see his article in "Studien und Kritiken" for 1830, p. 843). Tischendorf and Tregelles set the twelve verses apart. Alford incloses them in single brackets, Westcott and Hort in double brackets, as an early interpolation; the Revised Version of 1881 retains them with a marginal note, and with a space between vers. 8 and 9. Dean Burgon ("Quarterly Rev." for Oct., 1881) holds this note of the Revision (which simply states an acknowledged fact) to be "the gravest blot of all," and triumphantly refers the critical editors and Revisionists to his "separate treatise extending over 300 pages, which for the best of reasons has never yet been answered," and in which he has "demonstrated," as he assures us, that the last twelve verses in Mark are "as trustworthy as any other verses which can be named." The infallible organ in the Vatican seems to have a formidable rival in Chichester, but they are in irreconcilable conflict on the true reading of the angelic anthem (Luke 2 : 14) : the Pope chanting with the Vulgate the genitive (εὐδοκίας, *bonæ voluntatis*), the Dean, in the same article, denouncing this as a "grievous perversion of the truth of Scripture," and holding the evidence for the nominative (εὐδοκία) to be "absolutely decisive," as if the combined testimony of ℵ* A B D, Irenæus, Origen (lat.), Jerome, all the Latin MSS., and the Latin *Gloria in Excelsis* were of no account, as compared with his judgment or preference.

§ 82. *Luke.*

" Lucas, Evangelii et medicinæ munera pandens ;
Artibus hinc, illinc religione, valet :
Utilis ille labor, per quem vixere tot ægri ;
Utilior, per quem tot didicere mori ! "

Critical and Biographical.

SCHLEIERMACHER : *Ueber die Schriften des Lukas.* Berlin, 1817. Reprinted in the second vol. of his *Sämmtliche Werke*, Berlin, 1836 (pp. 1–220). Translated by Bishop THIRLWALL, London, 1825.

JAMES SMITH (of Jordanhill, d. 1867) : *Dissertation on the Life and Writings of St. Luke*, prefixed to his *Voyage and Shipwreck of St. Paul* (1848), 4th ed., revised by Walter E. Smith, London, 1880 (pp. 293). A most important monograph, especially for the historical accuracy and credibility of the Acts, by an expert in navigation and an able scholar.

E. RENAN : *Les Évangiles.* Paris, 1877. Ch. XIX., pp. 435–448.

TH. KEIM : *Aus dem Urchristenthum.* Zürich, 1878, *Josephus im N. T.*, pp. 1–27. An unsuccessful attempt to prove that Luke used Josephus in his chronological statement, 3 : 1, 2. Keim assumes that the third Gospel was written after the "Jewish war" of Josephus (about 75–78), and *possibly* after his "Antiquities" (A.D. 94), though in his *Geschichte Jesu* (I. 71) he assigns the composition of Luke to A.D. 90.

SCHOLTEN : *Das Paulinische Evangelium*, transl. from the Dutch by Redepenning. Elberf., 1881.

The Ancient Testimonies on the Genuineness of Luke, see in CHARTERIS (Kirchhofer) : *Canonicity*, Edinb., 1880, pp. 154–166.

On the relation of Luke to Marcion, see especially VOLKMAR : *Das Evangelium Marcions*, Leipz., 1852, and SANDAY : *The Gospels in the Second Century*, London, 1876 (and his article in the "Fortnightly Review" for June, 1875).

Exegetical.

Commentaries by ORIGEN (in Jerome's Latin translation, with a few Greek fragments), EUSEBIUS (fragments), CYRIL OF ALEXANDRIA (Syriac Version with translation, ed. by Dean Smith, Oxf., 1858 and 1859), EUTHYMIUS ZIGABENUS, THEOPHYLACT.—Modern Com. : BORNEMANN (*Scholia in Luc. Ev.*, 1830), DE WETTE (*Mark and Luke*, 3d ed., 1846), MEYER (*Mark and Luke*, 6th ed., revised by B. WEISS, 1878), JAMES THOMSON (Edinb., 1851, 3 vols.), J. J. VAN OOSTERZEE (in Lange, 3d ed., 1867, Engl. ed. by Schaff and Starbuck, N. Y., 1866), FR. GODET (one of the very best, 2d French ed., 1870, Engl. transl.

by Shalders and Cusin, Edinb., 1875, 2 vols., reprinted in N. Y., 1881), Bishop W. B. JONES (in *Speaker's Com.*, Lond. and N. Y., 1878), E. H. PLUMPTRE (in Bp. Ellicott's *Com. for English Readers*, Lond., 1879), FREDERICK W. FARRAR (Cambridge, 1880), MATTHEW B. RIDDLE (1882).

LIFE OF LUKE.

As Mark is inseparably associated with Peter, so is Luke with Paul. There was, in both cases, a foreordained correspondence and congeniality between the apostle and the historian or co-laborer. We find such holy and useful friendships in the great formative epochs of the church, notably so in the time of the Reformation, between Luther and Melanchthon, Zwingli and Oecolampadius, Calvin and Beza, Cranmer, Latimer and Ridley; and at a later period between the two Wesleys and Whitefield. Mark, the Hebrew Roman "interpreter" of the Galilæan fisherman, gave us the shortest, freshest, but least elegant and literary of the Gospels; Luke, the educated Greek, "the beloved physician," and faithful companion of Saul of Tarsus, composed the longest and most literary Gospel, and connected it with the great events in secular history under the reigns of Augustus and his successors. If the former was called the Gospel of Peter by the ancients, the latter, in a less direct sense, may be called the Gospel of Paul, for its agreement in spirit with the teaching of the Apostle of the Gentiles. In their accounts of the institution of the Lord's Supper there is even a verbal agreement which points to the same source of information. No doubt there was frequent conference between the two, but no allusion is made to each other's writings, which tends to prove that they were composed independently during the same period, or not far apart.[1]

Luke nowhere mentions his name in the two books which are

[1] Origen, Eusebius, and Jerome erroneously supposed that Paul meant the written Gospel of Luke when he speaks of "my gospel," Rom. 2 : 16; 16 : 25; 2 Tim. 2 : 8. The word gospel is not used in the New Test. in the sense of a written record, except in the titles which are of post-apostolic date ; and the preface of Luke is inconsistent with the idea that he composed his work under the direction of any one man.

by the unanimous consent of antiquity ascribed to him, and bear
all the marks of the same authorship; but he is modestly concealed under the "we" of a great portion of the Acts, which is
but a continuation of the third Gospel.[1] He is honorably and
affectionately mentioned three times by Paul during his imprisonment, as "the beloved physician" (Col. 4 : 14), as one of
his "fellow-laborers" (Philem. 24), and as the most faithful
friend who remained with him when friend after friend had
deserted him (2 Tim. 4 : 11). His medical profession, although
carried on frequently by superior slaves, implies some degree
of education and accounts for the accuracy of his medical terms
and description of diseases.[2] It gave him access to many families of social position, especially in the East, where physicians
are rare. It made him all the more useful to Paul in the infirmities of his flesh and his exhausting labors.[3]

He was a Gentile by birth,[4] though he may have become a
proselyte of the gate. His nationality and antecedents are unknown. He was probably a Syrian of Antioch, and one of the
earliest converts in that mother church of Gentile Christianity.[5]
This conjecture is confirmed by the fact that he gives us much

---

[1] The name Λουκᾶς, *Lucas*, is abridged from Λουκανός, *Lucanus* or *Lucilius*
(as Apollos from Apollonius, Silas from Silvanus). It is not to be confounded
with *Lucius*, Acts 13 : 1 ; Rom. 16 : 21. The name was not common, but con-
tractions in *as* were frequent in the names of slaves, as Lobeck observes. Dr.
Plumptre (in his *Com.*) ingeniously conjectures that Luke was from the region
of Lucania in Southern Italy, and called after the famous poet, M. Annæus
Lucanus, as his freedman. In this way he accounts for Luke's familiarity
with Italian localities (Acts 28 : 13–15), the favor of the uncle of Lucanus,
J. Annæus Gallio, shown to Paul (18 : 14–17), the tradition of the friendship
between Paul and Seneca (a brother of Gallio), and the intended journey of
Paul to Spain (Rom. 15 : 28), where Seneca and Lucanus were born (at Corduba). But the chronology is against this hypothesis. Lucanus was born
A.D. 39, when Luke must have been already about thirty years of age, as he
cannot have been much younger than Paul.

[2] Jerome (*Ep. ad Paulinum*) says of Luke : "*Fuit medicus, et pariter omnia
verba illius animæ languentis sunt medicinæ.*"

[3] Comp. Gal. 4 : 13 ; 2 Cor. 1 : 9 ; 4 : 10, 12, 16 ; 12 : 7.

[4] He is distinguished from "those of the circumcision," Col. 4 : 14 ; comp. 11.

[5] Eusebius, III. 4 : Λουκᾶς τὸ μὲν γένος ὢν τῶν ἀπ' Ἀντιοχείας, τὴν ἐπιστήμην
δὲ ἰατρός, κ. τ. λ. Jerome, *De vir. ill.*, 7 : "*Lucas medicus Antiochensis . .
sectator apostoli Pauli, et omnis peregrinationis ejus comes.*"

information about the church in Antioch (Acts 11 : 19–30 ;
13 : 1–3 ; 15 : 1–3, 22–35), that he traces the origin of the name
"Christians" to that city (11 : 19), and that in enumerating the
seven deacons of Jerusalem he informs us of the Antiochian
origin of Nicolas (6 : 5), without mentioning the nationality of
any of the others.[1]

We meet Luke first as a companion of Paul at Troas, when,
after the Macedonian call, "Come over and help us," he was
about to carry the gospel to Greece on his second great missionary tour. For from that important epoch Luke uses the first
personal pronoun in the plural: "When he [Paul] had seen
the vision, straightway *we* sought to go forth into Macedonia,
concluding that God had called *us* to preach the gospel unto
them" (Acts 16 : 10). He accompanied him to Philippi and
seems to have remained there after the departure of Paul and
Silas for Corinth (A.D. 51), in charge of the infant church ; for
the "we" is suddenly replaced by "they" (17 : 1). Seven years
later (A.D. 58) he joined the apostle again, when he passed through
Philippi on his last journey to Jerusalem, stopping a week at
Troas (Acts 20 : 5, 6) ; for from that moment Luke resumes the
"we" of the narrative. He was with Paul or near him at
Jerusalem and two years at Cæsarea, accompanied him on his
perilous voyage to Rome, of which he gives a most accurate
account, and remained with him to the end of his first Roman
captivity, with which he closes his record (A.D. 63). He may,
however, have been temporarily absent on mission work during
the four years of Paul's imprisonment. Whether he accompanied him on his intended visit to Spain and to the East, after
the year 63, we do not know. The last allusion to him is the
word of Paul when on the point of martyrdom: "Only Luke is
with me" (2 Tim. 4 : 11).

The Bible leaves Luke at the height of his usefulness in the

---

[1] James Smith (*l.c.*, p. 4) illustrates the argumentative bearing of this notice
by the fact that of eight accounts of the Russian campaign of 1812, three by
French, three by English, and two by Scotch authors (Scott and Alison), the
last two only make mention of the Scotch extraction of the Russian General
Barclay de Tolly.

best company, with Paul preaching the gospel in the metropolis of the world.

Post-apostolic tradition, always far below the healthy and certain tone of the New Testament, mostly vague and often contradictory, never reliable, adds that he lived to the age of eighty-four, labored in several countries, was a painter of portraits of Jesus, of the Virgin, and the apostles, and that he was crucified on an olive-tree at Elæa in Greece. His real or supposed remains, together with those of Andrew the apostle, were transferred from Patræ in Achaia to the Church of the Apostles in Constantinople.[1]

The symbolic poetry of the Church assigns to him the sacrificial ox; but the symbol of man is more appropriate; for his Gospel is *par excellence* the Gospel of the Son of Man.

SOURCES OF INFORMATION.

According to his own confession in the preface, Luke was no eye-witness of the gospel history,[2] but derived his information from oral reports of primitive disciples, and from numerous fragmentary documents then already in circulation. He wrote the Gospel from what he had heard and read, the Acts from what he had seen and heard. He traced the origin of Christianity "accurately from the beginning."

His opportunities were the very best. He visited the principal apostolic churches between Jerusalem and Rome, and came in personal contact with the founders and leaders. He met Peter, Mark, and Barnabas at Antioch, James and his elders at Jerusalem (on Paul's last visit), Philip and his daughters at Cæsarea, the early converts in Greece and Rome; and he enjoyed, besides, the benefit of all the information which Paul himself had received by revelation or collected from personal intercourse with his fellow-apostles and other primitive disciples.

---

[1] Jerome, *De vir. ill.*, 7 : "*Sepultus est Constantinopoli, ad quam urbem vicesimo Constantii anno ossa ejus cum reliquiis Andreæ apostoli translata sunt.*"

[2] Hence the ancient tradition that he was one of the Seventy Disciples, or one of the two disciples of Emmaus, cannot be true.

The sources for the history of the infancy were Jewish-Christian and Aramæan (hence the strongly Hebraizing coloring of
the first two chapters); his information of the activity of
Christ in Samaria was probably derived from Philip, who
labored there as an evangelist and afterwards in Cæsarea. But
a man of Luke's historic instinct and conscientiousness would
be led to visit also in person the localities in Galilee which
are immortalized by the ministry of Christ. From Jerusalem
or Cæsarea he could reach them all in three or four days.

The question whether Luke also used one or both of the other
Synoptic Gospels has already been discussed in a previous section. It is improbable that he included them among his evidently fragmentary sources alluded to in the preface. It is
certain that he had no knowledge of our Greek Matthew; on
the use of a lost Hebrew Matthew and of Mark the opinion
of good scholars is divided, but the resemblance with Mark,
though very striking in some sections,[1] is not of such a character that it cannot as well, and even better, be explained from
prior oral tradition or autoptical memoirs, especially if we consider that the resemblances are neutralized by unaccountable
differences and omissions. The matter is not helped by a reference to a proto-Mark, either Hebrew or Greek, of which we
know nothing.

Luke has a great deal of original and most valuable matter,
which proves his independence and the variety of his sources.
He adds much to our knowledge of the Saviour, and surpasses
Matthew and Mark in fulness, accuracy, and chronological order
—three points which, with all modesty, he claims to have aimed
at in his preface.[2] Sometimes he gives special fitness and

---

[1] As the account of the stilling of the tempest, Luke 8 : 22–25, compared
with Mark 4 : 35–41 ; and the parable of the wicked husbandmen, Luke 20 : 9–
19, compared with Mark 12 : 1–12.

[2] 1 : 3 : πᾶσιν—ἀκριβῶς—καθεξῆς. Says Godet : "Matthew groups together
doctrinal teachings in the form of great discourses ; he is a preacher. Mark
narrates events as they occur to his mind ; he is a chronicler. Luke reproduces the external and internal development of events ; he is the historian,
properly so called."

beauty to a word of Christ by inserting it in its proper place in the narrative, and connecting it with a particular occasion. But there are some exceptions, where Matthew is fuller, and where Mark is more chronological. Considering the fact that about thirty years had elapsed since the occurrence of the events, we need not wonder that some facts and words were dislocated, and that Luke, with all his honest zeal, did not always succeed in giving the original order.

The peculiar sections of Luke are in keeping with the rest. They have not the most remote affinity with apocryphal marvels and fables, nor even with the orthodox traditions and legends of the post-apostolic age, but are in full harmony with the picture of Christ as it shines from the other Gospels and from the Epistles. His accuracy has been put to the severest test, especially in the Acts, where he frequently alludes to secular rulers and events; but while a few chronological difficulties, as that of the census of Quirinius, are not yet satisfactorily removed, he has upon the whole, even in minute particulars, been proven to be a faithful, reliable, and well informed historian.

He is the proper father of Christian church history, and a model well worthy of imitation for his study of the sources, his conscientious accuracy, his modesty and his lofty aim to instruct and confirm in the truth.

Dedication and Object.

The third Gospel, as well as the Acts of the Apostles, is dedicated to a certain Theophilus (*i.e.*, Friend of God), a man of social distinction, perhaps in the service of the government, as appears from his title "honorable" or "most noble." [1] He was

---

[1] Luke 1 : 4 : κράτιστε Θεόφιλε. In Acts 1 : 1 the epithet is omitted. Bengel infers from this omission that when Luke wrote the Acts he was on more familiar terms with Theophilus. The same title is applied to Governors Felix and Festus, Acts 23 : 26; 24 : 3; 26 : 25. The A. V. varies between "most excellent" and "most noble;" the R. V. uniformly renders "most excellent," which is apt to be applied to moral character rather than social position. "Honorable" or "most noble" would be preferable. Occasionally, however, the term is used also towards a personal friend (see passages in Wetstein).

either a convert or at least a catechumen in preparation for church membership, and willing to become sponsor and patron of these books. The custom of dedicating books to princes and rich friends of literature was formerly very frequent, and has not died out yet. As to his race and residence we can only conjecture that Theophilus was a Greek of Antioch, where Luke, himself probably an Antiochean, may have previously known him either as his freedman or physician. The pseudo-Clementine Recognitions mention a certain nobleman of that name at Antioch who was converted by Peter and changed his palace into a church and residence of the apostle.[1]

The object of Luke was to confirm Theophilus and through him all his readers in the faith in which he had already been orally instructed, and to lead him to the conviction of the irrefragable certainty of the facts on which Christianity rests.[2]

Luke wrote for Gentile Christians, especially Greeks, as Matthew wrote for Jews, Mark for Romans, John for advanced believers without distinction of nationality. He briefly explains for Gentile readers the position of Palestinian towns, as Nazareth, Capernaum, Arimathæa, and the distance of Mount Olivet and Emmaus from Jerusalem.[3] He does not, like Matthew, look back to the past and point out the fulfilment of ancient prophecy with a view to prove that Jesus of Nazareth is the promised Messiah, but takes a universal view of Christ as the Saviour of all men and fulfiller of the aspirations of every human heart. He brings him in contact with the events of secular history in the vast empire of Augustus, and with the whole human race by tracing his ancestry back to Adam.

These features would suit Gentile readers generally, Romans as well as Greeks. But the long residence of Luke in Greece, and the ancient tradition that he labored and died there, give

---

[1] For other conjectures on Theophilus, which locate him at Alexandria or at Rome or somewhere in Greece, see the *Bible Dicts.* of Winer and Smith *sub* Theophilus. Some have fancied that he was merely an ideal name for every right-minded reader of the Gospel, as a lover of truth.

[2] 1 : 4 : ἵνα ἐπιγνῷς περὶ ὧν κατηχήθης τὴν ἀσφάλειαν.

[3] 1 : 26 ; 4 : 31 ; 23 : 51 ; 24 : 13 (Acts 1 : 12).

strength to the view that he had before his mind chiefly readers of that country. According to Jerome the Gospel was written (completed) in Achaia and Bœotia. The whole book is undoubtedly admirably suited to Greek taste. It at once captivates the refined Hellenic ear by a historic prologue of classic construction, resembling the prologues of Herodotus and Thucydides. It is not without interest to compare them.

LUKE begins: "Forasmuch as many have taken in hand to draw up a narrative concerning those matters which have been fulfilled among us, even as they delivered them unto us, which from the beginning were eyewitnesses and ministers of the word : it seemed good to me also, having traced the course of all things accurately from the first, to write unto thee in order, most noble Theophilus ; that thou mightest know the certainty concerning the things wherein thou wast instructed."

HERODOTUS : "These are the researches of Herodotus of Halicarnassus, which he publishes, in order to preserve from oblivion the remembrance of former deeds of men, and to secure a just tribute of glory to the great and wonderful actions of the Greeks and the barbarians; and withal to put on record what were their grounds of feud."

THUCYDIDES : "Thucydides, an Athenian, wrote the history of the war in which the Peloponnesians and the Athenians fought against one another. He began to write when they first took up arms, believing that it would be great and memorable above any previous war. For he argued that both States were then at the full height of their military power, and he saw the rest of the Hellenes either siding or intending to side with one or other of them. No movement ever stirred Hellas more deeply than this ; it was shared by many of the barbarians, and might be said even to affect the world at large." (Jowett's translation.)

These prefaces excel alike in brevity, taste, and tact, but with this characteristic difference : the Evangelist modestly withholds his name and writes in the pure interest of truth a record of the gospel of peace for the spiritual welfare of all men ; while the great pagan historians are inspired by love of glory, and aim to immortalize the destructive wars and feuds of Greeks and barbarians.

CONTENTS OF THE GOSPEL OF LUKE.

After a historiographic preface, Luke gives us first a history of the birth and infancy of John the Baptist and Jesus, from Hebrew sources, with an incident from the boyhood of the

Saviour (chs. 1 and 2). Then he unfolds the history of the
public ministry in chronological order from the baptism in the
Jordan to the resurrection and ascension. We need only point
out those facts and discourses which are not found in the other
Gospels and which complete the Synoptic history at the beginning, middle, and end of the life of our Lord.[1]

Luke supplies the following sections:

I. In the history of the INFANCY of John and Christ:

The appearance of the angel of the Lord to Zacharias
in the temple announcing the birth of John, 1 : 5–25.

The annunciation of the birth of Christ to the Virgin
Mary, 1 : 26–38.

The visit of the Virgin Mary to Elizabeth; the salutation of Elizabeth, 1 : 39–45.

The Magnificat of the Virgin Mary, 1 : 46–56.

The birth of John the Baptist, 1 : 57–66.

The Benedictus of Zacharias, 1 : 67–80.

The birth of Jesus in Bethlehem, 2 : 1–7.

The appearance of the angels to the shepherds of
Bethlehem, and the "Gloria in excelsis," 2 : 8–20.

The circumcision of Jesus, and his presentation in the
Temple, 2 : 21–38.

The visit of Jesus in his twelfth year to the passover
in Jerusalem, and his conversation with the Jewish
doctors in the Temple, 2 : 41–52.

To this must be added the genealogy of Christ from
Abraham up to Adam; while Matthew begins, in
the inverse order, with Abraham, and presents in
the parallel section several differences which show
their mutual independence, Luke 3 : 23–38; comp.
Matt. 1 : 1–17.

II. In the PUBLIC LIFE of our Lord a whole group of important events, discourses, and incidents which occurred

---

[1] For a full analysis of contents see Van Oosterzee, *Com.*, 8–10; Westcott,
Introd. to the G., 370–372 (Am. ed.); McClellan, *Com. on N. T.*, I. 425–438;
Farrar, *Com.*, 31–36; Lange, *Bibelkunde*, 187–193.

at different periods, but mostly on a circuitous journey
from Capernaum to Jerusalem through Samaria and
Peræa (9 : 51–18 : 14).   This section includes—

1. The following *miracles* and *incidents:*

The miraculous draught of fishes, 5 : 4–11.

The raising of the widow's son at Nain, 7 : 11–18.

The pardoning of the sinful woman who wept
at the feet of Jesus, 7 : 36–50.

The support of Christ by devout women who
are named, 8 : 2, 3.

The rebuke of the Sons of Thunder in a Samaritan village, 9 : 51–56.

The Mission and Instruction of the Seventy,
10 : 1–6.

Entertainment at the house of Martha and
Mary ; the one thing needful, 10 : 38–42.

The woman who exclaimed : "Blessed is the
womb that bare thee," 11 : 27.

The man with the dropsy, 14 : 1–6.

The ten lepers, 17 : 11–19.

The visit to Zacchæus, 19 : 1–10.

The tears of Jesus over Jerusalem, 19 : 41–44.

The sifting of Peter, 22 : 31, 32.

The healing of Malchus, 22 : 50, 51.

2. Original *Parables:*

The two Debtors, 7 : 41–43.

The good Samaritan, 10 : 25–37.

The importunate Friend, 11 : 5–8.

The rich Fool, 12 : 16–21.

The barren Fig-tree, 13 : 6–9.

The lost Drachma, 15 : 8–10.

The prodigal Son, 15 : 11–32.

The unjust Steward, 16 : 1–13.

Dives and Lazarus, 16 : 19–31.

The importunate Widow, and the unjust Judge,
18 : 1–8.

The Pharisee and the Publican, 18 : 10–14.

The ten Pounds, 19 : 11–28 (not to be identified
with the Parable of the Talents in Matt.
25 : 14–30).

III. In the history of the CRUCIFIXION and RESURRECTION:

The lament of the women on the way to the cross,
23 : 27–30.

The prayer of Christ for his murderers, 23 : 34.

His conversation with the penitent malefactor and
promise of a place in paradise, 23 : 39–43.

The appearance of the risen Lord to the two Disciples
on the way to Emmaus, 24 : 13–25 ; briefly mentioned also in the disputed conclusion of Mark,
16 : 12, 13.

The account of the ascension, 24 : 50–53 ; comp. Mark
16 : 19, 20 ; and Acts 1 : 3–12.

CHARACTERISTIC FEATURES OF LUKE.

The third Gospel is the Gospel of free salvation to all men.[1]
This corresponds to the two cardinal points in the doctrinal system of Paul: gratuitousness and universalness of salvation.

1. It is eminently the Gospel of *free salvation* by grace
through faith. Its motto is: Christ came to save sinners.
"Saviour" and "salvation" are the most prominent ideas.[2]
Mary, anticipating the birth of her Son, rejoices in God her
"Saviour" (1 : 47); and an angel announces to the shepherds of

---

[1] Lange (*Leben Jesu*, I. 258) gives as the theme of Luke : "the revelation
of divine mercy ;" Godet (*Com.*) : "the manifestation of divine philanthropy"
(Tit. 3 : 4) ; McClellan (I. 436) : "salvation of sinners, by God's grace, through
faith in Jesus Christ, and him crucified ; " Farrar (p. 17) : "who went about
doing good and healing all that were oppressed of the devil" (Acts 10 : 38,
better suited for Mark) ; Van Oosterzee : "as Paul led the people of the Lord
out of the bondage of the law into the enjoyment of gospel liberty, so did
Luke raise sacred history from the standpoint of the Israelitish *nationality*
to the higher and holier ground of universal *humanity*."

[2] The term σωτήρ occurs, 1 : 47 ; 2 : 11 ; John 4 : 42, and often in the Acts
and the Epistles of Paul, but neither in Matthew nor Mark ; σωτηρία occurs,
Luke 1 : 69, 77 ; 19 : 9 ; John 4 : 22, and repeatedly in the Acts and the Epistles ; σωτήριος, Luke 2 : 30 ; 3 : 6 ; Acts 28 : 28 ; Eph. 6 : 17 ; Tit. 2 : 11.

Bethlehem " good tidings of great joy which shall be to all the people " (2 : 10), namely, the birth of Jesus as the " Saviour " of men (not only as the Christ of the Jews). He is throughout represented as the merciful friend of sinners, as the healer of the sick, as the comforter of the broken-hearted, as the shepherd of the lost sheep. The parables peculiar to Luke—of the prodigal son, of the lost piece of money, of the publican in the temple, of the good Samaritan—exhibit this great truth which Paul so fully sets forth in his Epistles. The parable of the Pharisee and the publican plucks up self-righteousness by the root, and is the foundation of the doctrine of justification by faith. The paralytic and the woman that was a sinner received pardon by faith alone. Luke alone relates the prayer of Christ on the cross for his murderers, and the promise of paradise to the penitent robber, and he ends with a picture of the ascending Saviour lifting up his hands and blessing his disciples.

The other Evangelists do not neglect this aspect of Christ ; nothing can be more sweet and comforting than his invitation to sinners in the eleventh chapter of Matthew, or his farewell to the disciples in John ; but Luke dwells on it with peculiar delight. He is the painter of CHRISTUS SALVATOR and CHRISTUS CONSOLATOR.

2. It is the Gospel of *universal* salvation. It is emphatically the Gospel for the Gentiles. Hence the genealogy of Christ is traced back not only to Abraham (as in Matthew), but to Adam, the son of God and the father of all men (3 : 38). Christ is the second Adam from heaven, the representative Head of redeemed humanity—an idea further developed by Paul. The infant Saviour is greeted by Simeon as a " Light for revelation to the Gentiles, and the glory of his people Israel " (2 : 32). The Baptist, in applying the prophecy of Isaiah concerning the voice in the wilderness (ch. 40), adds the words (from Isa. 52 : 10) : " All flesh shall see the salvation of God " (3 : 6). Luke alone records the mission of the Seventy Disciples who represent the Gentile nations, as the Twelve represent the twelve tribes of Israel. He alone mentions the mission of Elijah to the heathen widow in

Sarepta, and the cleansing of Naaman the Syrian by Elisha
(4 : 26, 27). He contrasts the gratitude of the leprous Samaritan with the ingratitude of the nine Jewish lepers (17 : 12-18).
He selects discourses and parables, which exhibit God's mercy
to Samaritans and Gentiles.¹ Yet there is no contradiction, for
some of the strongest passages which exhibit Christ's mercy to
the Gentiles and humble the Jewish pride are found in Matthew, the Jewish Evangelist.² The assertion that the third
Gospel is a glorification of the Gentile (Pauline) apostolate, and
a covert attack on the Twelve, especially Peter, is a pure fiction
of modern hypercriticism.

3. It is the Gospel of the genuine and full *humanity of Christ*.³
It gives us the key-note for the construction of a real history of
Jesus from infancy to boyhood and manhood. Luke represents
him as the purest and fairest among the children of men, who
became like unto us in all things except sin and error. He follows him through the stages of his growth. He alone tells us
that the child Jesus " grew and waxed strong," not only physically, but also in "wisdom" (2 : 40); he alone reports the remarkable scene in the temple, informing us that Jesus, when
twelve years old, sat as a learner "in the midst of the doctors,
both hearing them and asking questions;" and that, even after
that time, He "advanced in wisdom and stature, and in favor
with God and men" (2 : 46, 52). All the Synoptists narrate
the temptation in the wilderness, and Mark adds horror to the
scene by the remark that Christ was "with the wild beasts "
(1 : 12, μετὰ τῶν θηρίων); but Luke has the peculiar notice
that the devil departed from Jesus only "for a season." He
alone mentions the tears of Jesus over Jerusalem, and "the
bloody sweat " and the strengthening angel in the agony of
Gethsemane. As he brings out the gradual growth of Jesus,
and the progress of the gospel from Nazareth to Capernaum,

---

¹ 4 : 25-27; 9 : 52-56; 10 : 33; 15 : 11 sqq. ; 17 : 19 ; 18 : 10 ; 19 : 5.
² See § 80, p. 617.
³ Lange (*Bibelkunde*, p. 187) calls it "*das Evangelium des Menschensohnes,
der Humanität Christi, der Verklärung aller Humanität.*"

from Capernaum to Jerusalem, so afterwards, in the Acts, he traces the growth of the church from Jerusalem to Antioch, from Antioch to Ephesus and Corinth, from Greece to Rome. His is the Gospel of historical development. To him we are indebted for nearly all the hints that link the gospel facts with the contemporary history of the world.

4. It is the Gospel of *universal humanity*. It breathes the genuine spirit of charity, liberty, equality, which emanate from the Saviour of mankind, but are so often counterfeited by his great antagonist, the devil. It touches the tenderest chords of human sympathy. It delights in recording Christ's love and compassion for the sick, the lowly, the despised, even the harlot and the prodigal. It mentions the beatitudes pronounced on the poor and the hungry, his invitation to the maimed, the halt, and the blind, his prayer on the cross for pardon of the wicked murderers, his promise to the dying robber. It rebukes the spirit of bigotry and intolerance of the Jews against Samaritans, in the parable of the good Samaritan. It reminds the Sons of Thunder when they were about to call fire from heaven upon a Samaritan village that He came not to destroy but to save. It tells us that "he who is not against Christ is for Christ," no matter what sectarian or unsectarian name he may bear.

5. It is the Gospel for *woman*. It weaves the purest types of womanhood into the gospel story: Elizabeth, who saluted the Saviour before his birth; the Virgin, whom all generations call blessed; the aged prophetess Anna, who departed not from the temple; Martha, the busy, hospitable housekeeper, with her quiet, contemplative sister Mary of Bethany; and that noble band of female disciples who ministered of their substance to the temporal wants of the Son of God and his apostles.

It reveals the tender compassion of Christ for all the suffering daughters of Eve: the widow at Nain mourning at the bier of her only son; for the fallen sinner who bathed his feet with her tears; for the poor sick woman, who had wasted all her living upon physicians, and whom he addressed as "Daughter;" and

for the "daughters of Jerusalem" who followed him weeping to
Calvary. If anywhere we may behold the divine humanity of
Christ and the perfect union of purity and love, dignity and
tender compassion, it is in the conduct of Jesus towards women
and children. "The scribes and Pharisees gathered up their
robes in the streets and synagogues lest they should touch a
woman, and held it a crime to look on an unveiled woman in
public; our Lord suffered a woman to minister to him out of
whom he had cast seven devils."

6. It is the Gospel for *children*, and all who are of a childlike
spirit. It sheds a sacred halo and celestial charm over infancy,
as perpetuating the paradise of innocence in a sinful world. It
alone relates the birth and growth of John, the particulars of
the birth of Christ, his circumcision and presentation in the
temple, his obedience to parents, his growth from infancy to
boyhood, from boyhood to manhood. The first two chapters
will always be the favorite chapters for children and all who
delight to gather around the manger of Bethlehem and to rejoice with shepherds on the field and angels in heaven.

7. It is the Gospel of *poetry*.[1] We mean the poetry of religion,
the poetry of worship, the poetry of prayer and thanksgiving,
a poetry resting not on fiction, but on facts and eternal truth.
In such poetry there is more truth than in every-day prose. The
whole book is full of dramatic vivacity and interest. It begins
and ends with thanksgiving and praise. The first two chapters
are overflowing with festive joy and gladness; they are a paradise of fragrant flowers, and the air is resonant with the sweet
melodies of Hebrew psalmody and Christian hymnody. The
Salute of Elizabeth ("Ave Maria"), the "Magnificat" of Mary,
the "Benedictus" of Zacharias, the "Gloria in Excelsis" of the
Angels, the "Nunc Dimittis" of Simeon, sound from genera-

[1] Farrar (p. 23) calls Luke "the first Christian hymnologist" (better hym-
nist), and quotes the lines from Keble:

"Thou hast an ear for angel songs,
A breath the gospel trump to fill,
And taught by thee the Church prolongs
Her hymns of high thanksgiving still."

tion to generation in every tongue, and are a perpetual inspira
tion for new hymns of praise to the glory of Christ.

No wonder that the third Gospel has been pronounced, from
a purely literary and humanitarian standpoint, to be the most
beautiful book ever written.[1]

THE STYLE.

Luke is the best Greek writer among the Evangelists.[2] His
style shows his general culture. It is free from solecisms, rich
in vocabulary, rhythmical in construction. But as a careful and
conscientious historian he varies considerably with the subject
and according to the nature of his documents.

Matthew begins characteristically with " Book of generation "
or "Genealogy" (βίβλος γενέσεως), which looks back to the
Hebrew *Sepher toledoth* (comp. Gen. 5:1; 2:4); Mark with
" Beginning of the gospel " (ἀρχὴ τοῦ εὐαγγελίου), which
introduces the reader at once to the scene of present action;
Luke with a historiographic prologue of classical ring, and unsurpassed for brevity, modesty, and dignity. But when he
enters upon the history of the infancy, which he derived no
doubt from Aramaic traditions or documents, his language has

---

[1] This is the judgment of Renan, which is worth preserving in full.
" *L'Évangile de Luc*," he says (in *Les Évangiles*, p. 282 and 283), " *est le plus
littéraire des évangiles. Tout y révèle un esprit large et doux, sage, modéré,
sobre et raisonnable dans l'irrationnel. Ses exagérations, ses invraisemblances,
ses inconséquences tiennent à la nature même de la parabole et en font le charme.
Matthieu arrondit les contours un peu secs de Marc. Luc fait bien plus ; il écrit,
il montre une vraie entente de la composition. Son livre est un beau récit bien
suivi, à la fois hébraïque et hellénique, joignant l'émotion du drame à la sérénité
de l'idylle. Tout y rit, tout y pleure, tout y chante ; partout des larmes et des
cantiques ; c'est l'hymne du peuple nouveau,* L'HOSANNA *des petits et des humbles
introduits dans le royaume de Dieu. Un esprit de sainte enfance, de joie, de fer-
veur, le sentiment évangélique dans son originalité première répandent sur toute
la légende une teinte d'une incomparable douceur. On ne fut jamais moins sec-
taire. Pas un reproche, pas un mot dur pour le vieux peuple exclu ; son exclusion ne le punit-elle pas assez ? C'est le plus beau livre qu'il y ait. Le plaisir
que l'auteur dut avoir à l'écrire ne sera jamais suffisamment compris.*"

[2] Jerome, who had a great genius for language, says, *Epist. ad Dam.*, 20
(145) : " *Lucas qui inter omnes evangelistas Græci sermonis eruditissimus fuit,
quippe et medicus, et qui Evangelium Græcis scripserit.*" In another passage
he says that Luke's " *sermo sæcularem redolet eloquentiam.*"

a stronger Hebrew coloring than any other portion of the New Testament. The songs of Zacharias, Elizabeth, Mary, and Simeon, and the anthem of the angelic host, are the last of Hebrew psalms as well as the first of Christian hymns. They can be literally translated back into the Hebrew, without losing their beauty.[1] The same variation in style characterizes the Acts; the first part is Hebrew Greek, the second genuine Greek.

His vocabulary considerably exceeds that of the other Evangelists: he has about 180 terms which occur in his Gospel alone and nowhere else in the New Testament; while Matthew has only about 70, Mark 44, and John 50 peculiar words. Luke's Gospel has 55, the Acts 135 ἅπαξ λεγόμενα, and among them many verbal compounds and rare technical terms.

The medical training and practice of Luke, "the beloved physician," familiarized him with medical terms, which appear quite naturally, without any ostentation of professional knowledge, in his descriptions of diseases and miracles of healing, and they agree with the vocabulary of ancient medical writers. Thus he speaks of the "*great* fever" of Peter's mother-in-law, with reference to the distinction made between great and small fevers (according to Galen);[2] and of "*fevers* and dysentery," of which the father of Publius at Melita was healed (as Hippocrates uses fever in the plural).[3]

---

[1] See the Version of Delitzsch in his Hebrew New Testament, published by the Brit. and For. Bible Society.

[2] 4 : 38 : ἦν συνεχομένη πυρετῷ μεγάλῳ. συνεχομένη is likewise a medical term.

[3] Acts. 28 : 8 : πυρετοῖς καὶ δυσεντερίῳ συνεχόμενον. Other instances of medical knowledge are found in Luke 8 : 46; 22 : 44; Acts 3 : 7; 9 : 18; 10 : 9, 10. Dr. Plumptre even traces several expressions of Paul, such as "*healthy* doctrine" (1 Tim. 1 : 10; 6 : 3), "gangrene" or "cancer" (2 Tim. 2 : 17), the conscience "seared," or rather "cauterized" (1 Tim. 4 : 2), and the recommendation of a little wine for the stomach's sake (1 Tim. 5 : 23), to the influence of "the beloved physician," who administered to him in his peculiar physical infirmities. Rather fanciful. Rev. W. K. Hobart, of Trinity College, Dublin, published a work (1882) on *The Medical Language of St. Luke*, in which he furnished the proof from internal evidence that the Gospel of Luke and the Acts of the Apostles were written by the same person, and that the writer was a medical man. He has compared over four hundred peculiar words and phrases of these books with the use of the same words in Hippocrates, Aretæus, Dioscorides, and Galen.

He was equally familiar with navigation, not indeed as a professional seaman, but as an experienced traveller and accurate observer. He uses no less than seventeen nautical terms with perfect accuracy.[1] His description of the Voyage and Shipwreck of Paul in the last two chapters of Acts, as explained and confirmed by a scholarly seaman, furnishes an irrefragable argument for the ability and credibility of the author of that book.[2] Luke is fond of words of joy and gladness.[3] He often mentions the Holy Spirit, and he is the only writer who gives us an account of the pentecostal miracle.[4] Minor peculiarities are the use of the more correct λίμνη of the lake of Galilee for θάλασσα, νομικός and νομοδιδάσκαλος for γραμματεύς, τὸ εἰρημένον in quotations for ῥηθέν, νῦν for ἄρτι, ἑσπέρα for ὀψία, the frequency of attraction of the relative pronoun and participial construction.

There is a striking resemblance between the style of Luke and Paul, which corresponds to their spiritual sympathy and long intimacy.[5] They agree in the report of the institution of

---

[1] Among these are seven compounds of πλέω, describing the motion and management of a ship, as follows : πλέω, to sail, Luke 8 : 23 ; Acts 21 : 3 ; 27 : 6, 24. ἀποπλέω, to sail from, Acts 13 : 4 ; 14 : 26 ; 20 : 15 ; 27 : 1. βραδυπλοέω (from βραδύς, slow), to sail slowly, Acts 27 : 7. διαπλέω, to sail through (not "over," as in the A. V.), Acts 27 : 5. ἐκπλέω, to sail away, Acts 15 : 39 ; 18 : 18 ; 20 : 6. καταπλέω, to arrive, Luke 8 : 26. ὑποπλέω, to sail under the lee, Acts 27 : 4, 7. παραπλέω, to sail by, Acts 20 : 16. Add to these the following nautical terms : ἀνάγομαι, to get under way, to put to sea, Acts 27 : 4. διαπεράω, to sail over, Acts 21 : 2. διαφέρομαι, to be driven to and fro, Acts 27 : 27. ἐπικέλλω, to run the ship ashore, Acts 27 : 41. εὐθυδρομέω, to make a straight course, Acts 16 : 11 ; 21 : 1. παραλέγομαι (middle), to sail by, Acts 27 : 8, 13. ὑποτρέχω (aor. 2, ὑπέδραμον), to run under the lee, Acts 27 : 16. φέρομαι (pass.), to be driven, Acts 27 : 15, 17. Also, ἐκβολὴν ἐποιοῦντο, Acts 27 : 18, and ἐκούφιζον τὸ πλοῖον, 27 : 38, which are technical terms for lightening the ship by throwing cargo overboard.

[2] See James Smith, l.c., and Schaff's *Companion to the Gr. Test.*, pp. 57–61.

[3] As χαρά, Luke 1 : 14 ; 2 : 10 ; 8 : 13 ; 10 : 17 ; 15 : 7, 10 ; 24 : 41, 51.

[4] πνεῦμα ἅγιον or πνεῦμα alone, 1 : 15, 34, 35, 41, 67 ; 2 : 25, 26, 27 ; 3 : 16, 22 , 4 : 1, 14, 18 ; 12 : 10, 12 ; and still more frequently in the Acts, which is the Gospel of the Holy Spirit.

[5] See Holtzmann, *Syn. Evang.*, pp. 316–324, copied in part (without acknowledgment) by Davidson, *Introd.*, I. 437 sqq. Holtzmann enumerates about two hundred expressions or phrases common to Luke and Paul, and more or less foreign to the other writers of the New Testament.

the Lord's Supper, which is the oldest we have (from A.D. 57);
both substitute: "This cup is the new covenant in My blood,"
for "This is My blood of the (new) covenant," and add: "This
do in remembrance of Me" (Luke 22 : 19, 20 ; 1 Cor. 11 : 24,
25). They are equally fond of words which characterize the
freedom and universal destination of the gospel salvation.¹
They have many terms in common which occur nowhere else in
the New Testament.² And they often meet in thought and expression in a way that shows both the close intimacy and the
mutual independence of the two writers.³

---

¹ As χάρις, ἔλεος, πίστις, δικαιοσύνη, δίκαιος, πνεῦμα ἅγιον, γνῶσις, δύναμις κυρίου.

² As ἀγνοεῖν, ἀδικία, ἀθετεῖν, αἰχμαλωτίζειν, ἀναπέμπειν, ἀνταποκρίνεσθαι, ἀντι-
κείμενος, ἀντιλαμβάνεσθαι, ἀπελπίζειν, ἀπολογεῖσθαι, ἀτενίζειν, ἐκδιώκειν, ἐπιφαίνειν,
εὐγενής, ἠχεῖν, καταργεῖν, κινδυνεύειν, κυριεύειν, πανοπλία, παράδεισος, συγχαίρειν,
συνευδοκεῖν, ὑστέρημα, χαρίζεσθαι, ψαλμός, and others, also the particles ἀλλ'
οὐδέ, εἰ καί, εἰ μήτι, τίς οὖν. The word κύριος as a substitute for Jesus occurs
fourteen times in Luke and often in the Epistles, but only once in the Synoptists (the closing verses of Mark, 16 : 19, 20).

³ Take the following specimens of striking parallelism (quoted by Holtzmann, 322):

LUKE.	PAUL.
6 : 48: ἔθηκεν θεμέλιον ἐπὶ τὴν πέτραν.	1 Cor. 3 : 10: ὡς σοφὸς ἀρχιτέκτων θεμέλιον ἔθηκα.
8 : 15: καρποφοροῦσιν ὑπομονῇ.	Col. 1 : 10, 11: καρποφοροῦντες καὶ αὐξανό- μενοι εἰς πᾶσαν ὑπομονήν.
9 : 56: οὐκ ἦλθε ψυχὰς ἀνθρώπων ἀπολέσαι, ἀλλὰ σῶσαι.	2 Cor. 10 : 8: ἔδωκεν εἰς οἰκοδομὴν καὶ οὐκ εἰς καθαίρεσιν. 13 : 10.
10 : 8: ἐσθίετε τὰ παρατιθέμενα ὑμῖν.	1 Cor. 10 : 27: πᾶν τὸ παρατιθέμενον ὑμῖν ἐσθίετε.
10 : 20: τὰ ὀνόματα ὑμῶν ἐγράφη ἐν τοῖς οὐρανοῖς.	Phil. 4 : 3: ὧν τὰ ὀνόματα ἐν βίβλῳ ζωῆς.
10 : 21: ἀπέκρυψας ταῦτα ἀπὸ σοφῶν καὶ συνε- τῶν καὶ ἀπεκάλυψας αὐτὰ νηπίοις.	1 Cor. 1 : 19: ἀπολῶ τὴν σοφίαν τῶν σοφῶν καὶ τὴν σύνεσιν τῶν συνετῶν ἀθετήσω. 27: τὰ μωρὰ τοῦ κόσμου ἐξελέξατο ὁ θεὸς ἵνα καται- σχύνῃ τοὺς σοφούς.
11 : 41: πάντα καθαρὰ ὑμῖν ἐστιν.	Tit. 1 : 15: πάντα μὲν καθαρὰ τοῖς καθαροῖς.
11 : 49: ἀποστελῶ εἰς αὐτοὺς προφήτας καὶ ἀποστόλους καὶ ἐξ αὐτῶν ἀποκτενοῦσι καὶ ἐκδιώξουσιν·	1 Thess. 2 : 15: τῶν καὶ τὸν κύριον ἀποκτει- νάντων Ἰησοῦν καὶ τοὺς προφήτας καὶ ἡμᾶς ἐκδιωξάντων.
12 : 35: ἔστωσαν ὑμῶν αἱ ὀσφύες περιεζω- σμέναι.	Eph. 6 : 14: στῆτε οὖν περιζωσάμενοι τ' ὀσφὺν ὑμῶν ἐν ἀληθείᾳ.
18 : 1: δεῖν πάντοτε προσεύχεσθαι καὶ μὴ ἐκκακεῖν.	2 Thess. 1 : 11: εἰς ὃ καὶ προσευχόμεθα πάν- τοτε. Col. 4 : 12: πάντοτε ἀγωνιζόμενος ὑπὲρ ὑμῶν ἐν ταῖς προσευχαῖς. Comp. 1 Thess. 5 : 1, 7 ; Rom. 1 : 10.
20 : 16: μὴ γένοιτο. 20 : 38: πάντες γὰρ αὐτῷ ζῶσιν.	Rom. 9 : 14; 11 : 11; Gal. 3 : 21. Rom. 14 : 7, 8: ἐάν τε γὰρ ζῶμεν, τῷ κυρίῳ ζῶμεν. Comp. 2 Cor. 5 : 15.
21 : 24: καὶ Ἱερουσαλὴμ ἔσται πατουμένη ὑπὸ ἐθνῶν ἄχρι πληρωθῶσι καιροὶ ἐθνῶν.	Rom. 11 : 25: ὅτι πώρωσις τῷ Ἰσραὴλ γέγονεν ἄχρις οὗ τὸ πλήρωμα τῶν ἐθνῶν εἰσέλθῃ.

♦ Genuineness.[1]

The genuineness of Luke is above reasonable doubt. character of the Gospel agrees perfectly with what we might expect from the author as far as we know him from the Acts and the Epistles. No other writer answers the description. The external evidence is not so old and clear as that in favor of Matthew and Mark. Papias makes no mention of Luke. Perhaps he thought it unnecessary, because Luke himself in the preface gives an account of the origin and aim of his book. The allusions in Barnabas, Clement of Rome, and Hermas are vague and uncertain. But other testimonies are sufficient for the purpose. Irenæus in Gaul says: "Luke, the companion of Paul, committed to writing the gospel preached by the latter." The Muratori fragment which contains the Italian traditions of the canon, mentions the Gospel of "Luke, the physician, whom Paul had associated with himself as one zealous for righteousness, to be his companion, who had not seen the Lord in the flesh, but having carried his inquiries as far back as possible, began his history with the birth of John." Justin Martyr makes several quotations from Luke, though he does not name him.[2] This brings us up to the year 140 or 130. The Gospel is found in all ancient manuscripts and translations.

The heretical testimony of Marcion from the year 140 is likewise conclusive. It was always supposed that his Gospel, the only one he recognized, was a mutilation of Luke, and this view is now confirmed and finally established by the investigations and concessions of the very school which for a short time had endeavored to reverse the order by making Marcion's caricature the original of Luke.[3] The pseudo-Clementine Homilies and

---

[1] See the ancient testimonies in Charteris's Kirchhofer, *l.c.*, 154 sqq.

[2] Freely admitted by Zeller, Davidson (I. 444), and others of that school.

[3] Even the author of "Supernatural Religion" was forced at last to surrender to the arguments of Dr. Sanday, in 1875, after the question had already been settled years before in Germany by Hilgenfeld (1850) and Volkmar (1852). Davidson also (*Introd.*, new ed., I. 446) admits: "There is no doubt that Marcion had the Gospel of Luke, which he adapted to his own ideas by arbi-

Recognitions quote from Luke. Basilides and Valentinus and
followers used all the four Gospels, and are reported to
have quoted Luke 1 : 35 for their purpose.

Celsus must have had Luke in view when he referred to the
genealogy of Christ as being traced to Adam.

CREDIBILITY.

The credibility of Luke has been assailed on the ground that
he shaped the history by his motive and aim to harmonize the
Petrine and Pauline, or the Jewish-Christian and the Gentile-
Christian parties of the church. But the same critics contradict
themselves by discovering, on the other hand, strongly Judaizing
and even Ebionitic elements in Luke, and thus make it an incoherent mosaic or clumsy patchwork of moderate Paulinism and
Ebionism, or they arbitrarily assume different revisions through
which it passed without being unified in plan.

Against this misrepresentation we have to say : (1) An irenic
spirit, such as we may freely admit in the writings of Luke, does
not imply an alteration or invention of facts. On the contrary,
it is simply an unsectarian, catholic spirit which aims at the
truth and nothing but the truth, and which is the first duty and
virtue of an historian. (2) Luke certainly did not invent those
marvellous parables and discourses which have been twisted into
subserviency to the tendency hypothesis ; else Luke would have
had a creative genius of the highest order, equal to that of Jesus
himself, while he modestly professes to be simply a faithful
collector of actual facts. (3) Paul himself did not invent his
type of doctrine, but received it, according to his own solemn
asseveration, by revelation from Jesus Christ, who called him to
the apostleship of the Gentiles. (4) It is now generally admitted that the Tübingen hypothesis of the difference between
the two types and parties in the apostolic church is greatly overstrained and set aside by Paul's own testimony in the Galatians,
which is as irenic and conciliatory to the pillar-apostles as it is

trary treatment. He lived before Justin, about A.D. 140, and is the earliest
writer from whom we learn the existence of the Gospel."

uncompromisingly polemic against the "false" brethren or the heretical Judaizers. (5) Some of the strongest anti-Jewish and pro-Gentile testimonies of Christ are found in Matthew and omitted by Luke.[1]

The accuracy of Luke has already been spoken of, and has been well vindicated by Godet against Renan in several minor details. "While remaining quite independent of the other three, the Gospel of Luke is confirmed and supported by them all."

TIME OF COMPOSITION.

There are strong indications that the third Gospel was composed (not published) between 58 and 63, before the close of Paul's Roman captivity. No doubt it took several years to collect and digest the material; and the book was probably not published, *i.e.*, copied and distributed, till after the death of Paul, at the same time with the Acts, which forms the second part and is dedicated to the same patron. In this way the conflicting accounts of Clement of Alexandria and Irenæus may be harmonized.[2]

[1] Davidson still adheres to this exploded Tübingen view in his new edition (I. 467): "Luke wished to bring Judaism [sic!] and Paulinism together in the sphere of comprehensive Christianity, where the former would merge into the latter. In conformity with this purpose, he describes the irreconcilable opposition between Jesus and his opponents." As if Matthew and Mark and John did not precisely the same thing. He even repeats the absurd fiction of Baur, which was refuted long ago, not only by Godet, but even in part at least by Zeller, Holtzmann, and Keim, that Luke had "the obvious tendency to depreciate the twelve, in comparison with the seventy" (p. 469). Baur derived the chief proof of an alleged hostility of Luke to Peter from his omission of the famous passage, "Thou art Rock;" but Mark omits it likewise; and Luke, on the other hand, is the only Evangelist who records the word of Christ to Peter, ch. 22 : 32, on which the Romanists base the dogma of papal infallibility.

[2] The critics differ widely as to the date of composition : (1) For a date prior to A.D. 70 are all the older divines, also Lange, Ebrard, Guericke, van Oosterzee, Godet (60–67), Thiersch (58–60), Alford (58), Riddle (60). (2) For a date between 70 and 90: De Wette, Bleek, Reuss, Holtzmann, Güder, Meyer, Weiss (70–80), Keim, Abbott (80–90). (3) For A.D. 100 and later : Hilgenfeld and Volkmar (100), Zeller and Davidson (100–110). The date of Baur, A.D. 140, is perfectly wild and made impossible by the clear testimonies of Justin

1. Luke had the best leisure for literary composition during the four years of Paul's imprisonment at Cæsarea and Rome. In Cæsarea he was within easy reach of the surviving eye-witnesses and classical spots of the gospel history, and we cannot suppose that he neglected the opportunity.

2. The Gospel was written before the book of Acts, which expressly refers to it as the first treatise inscribed to the same Theophilus (1 : 1). As the Acts come down to the second year of Paul's captivity in Rome, they cannot have been finished before A.D. 63 ; but as they abruptly break off without any mention of Paul's release or martyrdom, it seems quite probable that they were concluded before the fate of the apostle was decided one way or the other, unless the writer was, like Mark, prevented by some event, perhaps the Neronian persecution, from giving his book the natural conclusion. In its present shape it excites in the reader the greatest curiosity, which could have been gratified with a few words, either that the apostle sealed his testimony with his blood, or that he entered upon new missionary tours East and West until at last he finished his course after a second captivity in Rome. I may add that the entire absence of any allusion in the Acts to any of Paul's Epistles can be easily explained by the assumption of a nearly contemporaneous composition, while it seems almost unaccountable if we assume an interval of ten or twenty years.

3. Luke's ignorance of Matthew and probably also of Mark points likewise to an early date of composition. A careful investigator, like Luke, writing after the year 70, could hardly have overlooked, among his many written sources, such an important document as Matthew which the best critics put before A.D. 70.

4. Clement of Alexandria has preserved a tradition that the Gospels containing the genealogies, i.e., Matthew and Luke, were written first. Irenæus, it is true, puts the third Gospel

Martyr and Marcion. Hence he was unwilling to retract in toto his former view about the priority of Marcion's Gospel, though he felt obliged to do it in part (Kirchengesch., I. 75 and 78).

after Matthew and Mark and after the death of Peter and Paul, that is, after 64 (though certainly not after 70). If the Synoptic Gospels were written nearly simultaneously, we can easily account for these differences in the tradition. Irenæus was no better informed on dates than Clement, and was evidently mistaken about the age of Christ and the date of the Apocalypse. But he may have had in view the time of publication, which must not be confounded with the date of composition. Many books nowadays are withheld from the market for some reason months or years after they have passed through the hands of the printer.

The objections raised against such an early date are not well founded.[1]

The prior existence of a number of fragmentary Gospels implied in 1 : 1 need not surprise us; for such a story as that of Jesus of Nazareth must have set many pens in motion at a very early time. "Though the art of writing had not existed," says Lange, "it would have been invented for such a theme."

---

[1] Dr. Abbott, of London (in "Enc. Brit.," X. 813, of the ninth ed., 1879), discovers no less than ten reasons for the later date of Luke, eight of them in the preface alone : "(1) the pre-existence and implied failure of many 'attempts' to set forth continuous narratives of the things 'surely believed;' (2) the mention of 'tradition' of the eye-witnesses and ministers of the word as past, not as present ($\pi\alpha\rho\acute{\epsilon}\delta\sigma\sigma\alpha\nu$, 1 : 2); (3) the dedication of the Gospel to a man of rank (fictitious or otherwise), who is supposed to have been 'catechized' in Christian truth ; (4) the attempt at literary style and at improvement of the 'usus ecclesiasticus' of the common tradition ; (5) the composition of something like a commencement of a Christian hymnology; (6) the development of the genealogy and the higher tone of the narrative of the incarnation ; (7) the insertion of many passages mentioning our Lord as $\acute{o}$ $\kappa\acute{\upsilon}\rho\iota os$, not in address, but in narrative; (8) the distinction, more sharply drawn, between the fall of Jerusalem and the final coming ; (9) the detailed prediction of the fall of Jerusalem, implying reminiscences of its fulfilment; (10) the very great development of the manifestations of Jesus after the resurrection. The inference from all this evidence would be that Luke was not written till about A.D. 80 at earliest. If it could be further demonstrated that Luke used any Apocryphal book (Judith, for example), and if it could be shown that the book in question was written after a certain date (Renan suggests A.D. 80 for the date of the book of Judith), it might be necessary to place Luke much later ; but no such demonstration has been hitherto produced." But most of these arguments are set aside by the $\acute{\eta}\mu\hat{\iota}\nu$ in 1 : 2, which includes

Of more weight is the objection that Luke seems to have
shaped the eschatological prophecies of Christ so as to suit the
fulfilment by bringing in the besieging (Roman) army, and by
interposing " the times of the Gentiles " between the destruction of Jerusalem and the end of the world (19 : 43, 44 ; 21 : 20--
24). This would put the composition *after* the destruction of
Jerusalem, say between 70 and 80, if not later.[1] But such an
intentional change of the words of our Lord is inconsistent with
the unquestionable honesty of the historian and his reverence
for the words of the Divine teacher.[2] Moreover, it is not borne
out by the facts. For the other Synoptists likewise speak of
wars and the abomination of desolation in the holy place, which
refers to the Jewish wars and the Roman eagles (Matt. 24 : 15 ;
Mark 13 : 14). Luke makes the Lord say : " Jerusalem shall be
trodden down by the Gentiles till the times of the Gentiles be
fulfilled " (21 : 24). But Matthew does the same when he

the writer among those who heard the gospel story from the eye-witnesses of
the life of Christ. It is also evident from the Acts that the writer, who is
identical with the third Evangelist, was an intimate companion of Paul, and
hence belonged to the first generation of disciples, which includes all the
converts of the apostles from the day of Pentecost down to the destruction of
Jerusalem.

[1] Keim (I. 70) thus eloquently magnifies this little difference : " *Anders als
dem Matthæus steht diesem Schriftsteller* [Lukas] *das Wirklichkeitsbild der Katastrophe der heiligen Stadt in seiner ganzen schrecklichen Grösse vor der Seele,
die langwierige und kunstvolle Belagerung des Feindes, die Heere, die befestigten
Lager, der Ring der Absperrung, die tausend Bedrängnisse, die Blutarbeit des
Schwerts, die Gefangenführung des Volks, der Tempel, die Stadt dem Boden
gleich, Alles unter dem ernsten Gesichtspunkt eines Strafgerichtes Gottes für
die Ermordung des Gesandten. Ja über die Katastrophe hinaus, die äusserste
Perspektive des ersten Evangelisten, dehnt sich dem neuen Geschichtschreiber
eine neue unbestimmbar grosse Periode der Trümmerlage Jerusalems unter dem
ehernen Tritt der Heiden und heidnischer Weltzeiten, innerhalb deren er selber
schreibt. Unter solchen Umständen hat die grosse Zukunftsrede Jesu bei aller
Sorgfalt, die wesentlichen Züge, sogar die Wiederkunft in diesem 'Geschlecht' zu
halten, die mannigfaltigsten Aenderungen erlitten.*" The same argument is
urged more soberly by Holtzmann (*Syn. Evang.*, 406 sq.), and even by Güder
(in Herzog, IX. 19) and Weiss (in Meyer, 6th ed., p. 243), but they assume
that Luke wrote only a few years after Matthew.

[2] " It is psychologically impossible," says Godet (p. 543), "that Luke should
have indulged in manipulating at pleasure the sayings of that Being on whom
his faith was fixed, whom he regarded as the Son of God."

reports that Christ predicted and commanded the preaching of
the gospel of the kingdom in all parts of the world before the
end can come (Matt. 24 : 14 ; 28 : 19 ; comp. Mark 16 : 15).
And even Paul said, almost in the same words as Luke, twelve
years before the destruction of Jerusalem : " Blindness is happened to Israel until the fulness of the Gentiles be come in "
(Rom. 11 : 25). Must we therefore put the composition of
Romans after A.D. 70 ? On the other hand, Luke reports as
clearly as Matthew and Mark the words of Christ, that " this
generation shall not pass away till all things " (the preceding
prophecies) " shall be fulfilled " (21 : 32). Why did he not omit
this passage if he intended to interpose a larger space of time
between the destruction of Jerusalem and the end of the
world ?

The eschatological discourses of our Lord, then, are essentially
the same in all the Synoptists, and present the same difficulties,
which can only be removed by assuming : (1) that they refer
both to the destruction of Jerusalem and the end of the world,
two analogous events, the former being typical of the latter ;
(2) that the two events, widely distant in time, are represented
in close proximity of space after the manner of prophetic vision
in a panoramic picture. We must also remember that the precise date of the end of the world was expressly disclaimed even
by the Son of God in the days of his humiliation (Matt. 24 : 36 ;
Mark 13 : 32), and is consequently beyond the reach of human
knowledge and calculation. The only difference is that Luke
more clearly distinguishes the two events by dividing the prophetical discourses and assigning them to different occasions
(17 : 20–37 and 21 : 5–33) ; and here, as in other cases, he is
probably more exact and in harmony with several hints of our
Lord that a considerable interval must elapse between the catastrophe of Jerusalem and the final catastrophe of the world.

PLACE OF COMPOSITION.

The third Gospel gives no hint as to the place of composition.
Ancient tradition is uncertain, and modern critics are divided

between Greece,[1] Alexandria,[2] Ephesus,[3] Cæsarea,[4] Rome.[5] It was probably written in sections during the longer residence of the author at Philippi, Cæsarea, and Rome, but we cannot tell where it was completed and published.[6]

§ 83. *John.*

See Literature on John, § 40, pp. 405 sqq. ; Life and Character of John, §§ 41–43, pp. 411 sqq. ; Theology of John, § 72, pp. 549 sqq.

The best comes last. The fourth Gospel is the Gospel of Gospels, the holy of holies in the New Testament. The favorite disciple and bosom friend of Christ, the protector of his mother, the survivor of the apostolic age was pre-eminently qualified by nature and grace to give to the church the inside view of that most wonderful person that ever walked on earth. In his early youth he had absorbed the deepest words of his Master, and treasured them in a faithful heart; in extreme old age, yet with the fire and vigor of manhood, he reproduced them under the influence of the Holy Spirit who dwelt in him and led him, as well as the other disciples, into "the whole truth."

His Gospel is the golden sunset of the age of inspiration, and sheds its lustre into the second and all succeeding centuries of the church. It was written at Ephesus when Jerusalem lay in ruins, when the church had finally separated from the synagogue, when "the Jews" and the Christians were two distinct races, when Jewish and Gentile believers had melted into a homogeneous Christian community, a little band in a hostile

---

[1] Jerome : Achaia and Bœotia ; Hilgenfeld (in 1858) : Achaia or Macedonia ; Godet (in his first ed.) : Corinth, in the house of Gaius (Rom. 16 : 23), but more indefinitely in the second ed. : Achaia.

[2] The Peshito, which gives the title : "Gospel of Luke the Evangelist, which he published and preached in Greek in Alexandria the Great." Köstlin and Overbeck, also Hilgenfeld in 1875 (*Einleit.*, p. 612).

[4] Michaelis, Kuinöl, Schott, Thiersch, and others.

[5] Hug, Ewald, Zeller, Holtzmann, Keim, Davidson.

[6] Weiss, in the sixth ed. of Meyer (p. 244) : "*Wo das Evang. geschrieben sei, ist völlig unbekannt.*"

world, yet strong in faith, full of hope and joy, and certain of victory.

For a satisfactory discussion of the difficult problems involved in this Gospel and its striking contrast with the Synoptic Gospels, we must keep in view the fact that Christ communed with the apostles after as well as before his visible departure, and spoke to them through that " other Advocate " whom he sent to them from the Father, and who brought to remembrance all things he had said unto them.[1] Here lies the guarantee of the truthfulness of a picture which no human artist could have drawn without divine inspiration. Under any other view the fourth Gospel, and indeed the whole New Testament, becomes the strangest enigma in the history of literature and incapable of any rational solution.

John and the Synoptists.

If John wrote long after the Synoptists, we could, of course, not expect from him a repetition of the story already so well told by three independent witnesses. But what is surprising is the fact that, coming last, he should produce the most original of all the Gospels.

The transition from Matthew to Mark, and from Mark to Luke is easy and natural; but in passing from any of the Synoptists to the fourth Gospel we breathe a different atmosphere, and feel as if we were suddenly translated from a fertile valley to the height of a mountain with a boundless vision over new scenes of beauty and grandeur. We look in vain for a genealogy of Jesus, for an account of his birth, for the sermons of the Baptist, for the history of the temptation in the wilderness, the baptism in the Jordan, and the transfiguration on the Mount, for a list of the Twelve, for the miraculous cures of demoniacs. John says nothing of the institution of the church and the sacraments ; though he is full of the mystical union and communion which is the essence of the church, and presents the spiritual meaning of baptism and the Lord's Supper (ch. 3 and 6).

[1] John 14 : 26 ; 16 : 13. Comp. Matt. 10 : 19, 20 ; Luke 12 : 12 ; Acts 4 : 8.

He omits the ascension, though it is promised through Mary Magdalene (20 : 17). He has not a word of the Sermon on the Mount, and the Lord's Prayer, none of the inimitable parables about the kingdom of heaven, none of those telling answers to the entangling questions of the Pharisees. He omits the prophecies of the downfall of Jerusalem and the end of the world, and most of those proverbial, moral sentences and maxims of surpassing wisdom which are strung together by the Synoptists like so many sparkling diamonds.

But in the place of these Synoptical records John gives us an abundance of new matter of equal, if not greater, interest and importance. Right at the threshold we are startled, as by a peal of thunder from the depths of eternity : " In the beginning was the Word." And as we proceed we hear about the creation of the world, the shining of the true light in darkness, the preparatory revelations, the incarnation of the Logos, the testimony of the Baptist to the Lamb of God. We listen with increasing wonder to those mysterious discourses about the new birth of the Spirit, the water of life, the bread of life from heaven, about the relation of the eternal and only-begotten Son to the Father, to the world, and to believers, the mission of the Holy Spirit, the promise of the many mansions in heaven, the farewell to the disciples, and at last that sacerdotal prayer which brings us nearest to the throne and the beating heart of God. John alone reports the interviews with Nicodemus, the woman of Samaria, and the Greek foreigners. He records six miracles not mentioned by the Synoptists, and among them the two greatest—the changing of water into wine and the raising of Lazarus from the grave. And where he meets the Synoptists, as in the feeding of the five thousand, he adds the mysterious discourse on the spiritual feeding of believers by the bread of life which has been going on ever since. He makes the nearest approach to his predecessors in the closing chapters on the betrayal, the denial of Peter, the trial before the ecclesiastical and civil tribunals, the crucifixion and resurrection, but even here he is more exact and circumstantial, and adds interesting details which bear the unmistakable marks of personal observation.

He fills out the ministry of Christ in Judæa, among the hierarchy and the people of Jerusalem, and extends it over three years; while the Synoptists seem to confine it to one year and dwell chiefly on his labors among the peasantry of Galilee. But on close inspection John leaves ample room for the Galilæan, and the Synoptists for the Judæan ministry. None of the Gospels is a complete biography. John expressly disclaims this (20 : 31). Matthew implies repeated visits to the holy city when he makes Christ exclaim : " O Jerusalem, Jerusalem . . . *how often* would I have gathered thy children together " (23 : 37 ; comp. 27 : 57). On the other hand John records several miracles in Cana, evidently only as typical examples of many (2 : 1 sqq. ; 4 : 47 sqq. ; 6 : 1 sqq.). But in Jerusalem the great conflict between light and darkness, belief and unbelief, was most fully developed and matured to the final crisis ; and this it was one of his chief objects to describe.

The differences between John and the Synoptists are many and great, but there are no contradictions.

The Occasion.

Irenæus, who, as a native of Asia Minor and a spiritual grand-pupil of John, is entitled to special consideration, says : " Afterward " [*i.e.*, after Matthew, Mark, and Luke] " John, the disciple of the Lord, who also had leaned upon his breast, did himself publish a Gospel during his residence at Ephesus in Asia." [1] In another place he makes the rise of the Gnostic heresy the prompting occasion of the composition. [2]

A curious tradition, which probably contains a grain of truth, traces the composition to a request of John's fellow-disciples and elders of Ephesus. " Fast with me," said John, according to the Muratorian fragment (170), "for three days from this time " [when the request was made], "and whatever shall be revealed to each of us " [concerning my composing the Gospel],

---

[1] *Adv. Hær.*, III., cap. 1, § 2.   [2] *Ibid.*, III. 11, 1.

" let us relate it to one another.   On the same night it was revealed to Andrew, one of the apostles, that John should relate
all things in his own name, aided by the revision of all.[1] . . .
What wonder is it then that John brings forward every detail
with so much emphasis, even in his Epistles, saying of himself,
What we have seen with our eyes, and heard with our ears, and
our hands have handled, these things have we written unto you.
For so he professes that he was not only an eye-witness, but
also a hearer, and moreover a writer of all the wonderful works
of the Lord in their historical order." [2]

The mention of Andrew in this fragment is remarkable, for
he was associated with John as a pupil of the Baptist and as the
first called to the school of Christ (John 1 : 35–40).   He was
also prominent in other ways and stood next to the beloved
three, or even next to his brother Peter in the catalogues of the
apostles.[3]

Victorinus of Pettau (d. about 304), in the Scholia on the
Apocalypse, says that John wrote the Gospel after the Apoca·
lypse, in consequence of the spread of the Gnostic heresy and
at the request of "all the bishops from the neighboring provinces." [4]

Jerome, on the basis of a similar tradition, reports that John,
being constrained by his brethren to write, consented to do so if
all joined in a fast and prayer to God, and after this fast, being
saturated with revelation (*revelatione saturatus*), he indited the
heaven-sent preface: "In the beginning was the Word." [5]

---

[1] " *Ut recognoscentibus omnibus, Joannes suo nomine cuncta describeret.*"

[2] " *Sic enim non solum visorem, sed et auditorem, sed et scriptorem omnium
mirabilium Domini per ordinem profitetur.*"   See the Latin text as published
by Tregelles, also in Charteris, *l.c.*, p. 3, and the translation of Westcott, *History of the Canon*, p. 187.

[3] Matt. 10 : 2 ; Luke 6 : 14; Mark 3 : 16 ; 13 : 3 ; John 1 : 41 ; 12 : 22 ; Acts
1 : 13.

[4] Quoted by Westcott and Hilgenfeld.   I will add the original from Migne,
Patrol., V. 333 : " *Cum enim essent Valentinus et Cerinthus, et Ebion, et cæteri
scholæ satanæ diffusi per orbem, convenerunt ad illum de finitimis provinciis
omnes episcopi, et compulerunt eum, ut et ipse testimonium conscriberet.*"

[5] Preface to *Com. in Matt.*

Possibly those fellow-disciples and pupils who prompted John to write his Gospel, were the same who afterward added their testimony to the genuineness of the book, speaking in the plural (" *we* know that *his* witness is true," 21 : 24), one of them acting as scribe (" *I* suppose," ver. 25).

The outward occasion does not exclude, of course, the inward prompting by the Holy Spirit, which is in fact implied in this tradition, but it shows how far the ancient church was from such a mechanical theory of inspiration as ignores or denies the human and natural factors in the composition of the apostolic writings. The preface of Luke proves the same.

THE OBJECT.

The fourth Gospel does not aim at a complete biography of Christ, but distinctly declares that Jesus wrought " many other signs in the presence of the disciples which are not written in this book " (20 : 30 ; comp. 21 : 25).

The author plainly states his object, to which all other objects must be subordinate as merely incidental, namely, to lead his readers to the faith " that Jesus is *the Christ, the Son of God ;* and that believing they may have life in his name" (20 : 31). This includes three points: (1) the Messiahship of Jesus, which was of prime importance to the Jews, and was the sole or at least the chief aim of Matthew, the Jewish Evangelist; (2) the Divine Sonship of Jesus, which was the point to be gained with the Gentiles, and which Luke, the Gentile Evangelist, had also in view; (3) the practical benefit of such faith, to gain true, spiritual, eternal life in Him and through Him who is the personal embodiment and source of eternal life.

To this historico-didactic object all others which have been mentioned must be subordinated. The book is neither polemic and apologetic, nor supplementary, nor irenic, except incidentally and unintentionally, as it serves all these purposes. The writer wrote in full view of the condition and needs of the church at the close of the first century, and shaped his record accordingly, taking for granted a general knowledge of the older Gospels, and refuting indirectly, by the statement of facts and truths, the errors of the day. Hence there is some measure of truth in those theories which have made an incidental aim the chief or only aim of the book.

1. The anti-heretical theory was started by Irenæus. Being himself absorbed in the controversy with Gnosticism and finding the strongest weapons in John, he thought that John's motive was to root out the error of Cerinthus and of the Nicolaitans by showing that "there is one God who made all things by his word; and not, as they say, one who made the world, and another, the Father of the Lord."[1] Jerome adds the opposite error of Ebionism, Ewald that of the disciples of the Baptist.

No doubt the fourth Gospel, by the positive statement of the truth, is the most effective refutation of Gnostic dualism and doketism, which began to raise its head in Asia Minor toward the close of the first century. It shows the harmony of the ideal Christ of faith and the real Christ of history, which the ancient and modern schools of Gnosticism are unable to unite in one individual. But it is not on this account a polemical treatise, and it even had by its profound speculation a special attraction for Gnostics and philosophical rationalists, from Basilides down to Baur. The ancient Gnostics made the first use of it and quoted freely from the prologue, e.g., the passage: "The true light, which enlighteneth every man, was coming into the world" (1 : 9).[2]

The polemical aim is more apparent in the first Epistle of John, which directly warns against the anti-Christian errors then threatening the church, and may be called a doctrinal and practical postscript to the Gospel.

2. The supplementary theory. Clement of Alexandria (about 200) states, on the authority of "presbyters of an earlier generation," that John, at the request of his friends and the prompting of the divine Spirit, added a *spiritual* Gospel to the older

[1] *Adv. Hær.*, III. 11, 1.   [2] Basilides in Hippolytus, *Ref. Hær.*, VII. 22.

bodily Gospels which set forth the outward facts.[1] The distinction is ingenious.   John is more spiritual and ideal than the
Synoptists, and he represents as it were the esoteric tradition as
distinct from the exoteric tradition of the church.   Eusebius records also as a current opinion that John intended to supply an
account of the earlier period of Christ's ministry which was
omitted by the other Evangelists.[2]   John is undoubtedly a most
welcome supplementer both in matter and spirit, and furnishes
in part the key for the full understanding of the Synoptists,
yet he repeats many important events, especially in the closing
chapters, and his Gospel is as complete as any.[3]

3. The Irenic tendency-theory is a modern Tübingen invention.   It is assumed that the fourth Gospel is purely speculative
or theological, the last and crowning literary production which
completed the process of unifying Jewish and Gentile Christianity and melting them into the one Catholic church of the
second century.

No doubt it is an Irenicon of the church in the highest and
best sense of the term, and a prophecy of the church of the
future, when all discords of Christendom past and present will
be harmonized in the perfect union of Christians with Christ,
which is the last object of his sacerdotal prayer.   But it is not
an Irenicon at the expense of truth and facts.

[1] In Eusebius, *H. E.*, VI. 14 (quoting from the *Hypotyposes*): τὸν Ἰωάννην
ἔσχατον συνιδόντα ὅτι τὰ σωματικὰ ἐν τοῖς εὐαγγελίοις δεδήλωται προτραπέντα ὑπὸ
τῶν γνωρίμων [*i.e.*, either *well known* friends, or *distinguished, notable men*],
πνεύματι θεοφορηθέντα, πνευματικὸν ποιῆσαι εὐαγγέλιον.   Origen had a similar
view, namely, that John alone among the Evangelists clearly teaches the
divinity of Christ.   Tom. 1 : 6 *in Joan.* (*Opp.*, IV. 6).

[2] *H. E.*, III. 24.   Jerome repeats this view and connects it with the anti-
heretical aim, *De vir. illustr.*, c. 9, comp. *Com. in Matt. Proœm.*   Theodore
of Mopsuestia thought that John intended to supplement the Synoptists chiefly
by the discourses on the divinity of Christ.   See Fritzsche's ed. of fragments
of his Commentaries on the New Test., Turici, p. 19 sq. (quoted by Hilgenfeld, *Einleitung*, p. 696).

[3] Godet expresses the same view (I. 362) : " *Cette intention de compléter les
récits antérieurs, soit au point de vue historique, comme l'a pensé Eusèbe, soit
sous un rapport plus spirituel, comme l'a déclaré Clément d'Alexandrie, est donc
parfaitement fondée en fait ; nous la constatons comme un but secondaire et,
pour mieux dire, comme moyen servant au but principal.*"

In carrying out their hypothesis the Tübingen critics have resorted to the wildest fictions.   It is said that the author depreciated the Mosaic dispensation and displayed jealousy of Peter. How in the world could this promote peace?   It would rather have defeated the object.   But there is no shadow of proof for such an assertion.   While the author opposes the unbelieving Jews, he shows the highest reverence for the Old Testament, and derives salvation from the Jews.   Instead of showing jealousy of Peter, he introduces his new name at the first interview with Jesus (1 : 42), reports his great confession even more fully than Matthew (6 : 68, 69), puts him at the head of the list of the apostles (21 : 2), and gives him his due prominence throughout down to the last interview when the risen Lord committed to him the feeding of his sheep (21 : 15–19).   This misrepresentation is of a piece with the other Tübingen myth adopted by Renan, that the real John in the Apocalypse pursues a polemical aim against Paul and deliberately excludes him from the rank of the twelve Apostles.   And yet Paul himself, in the acknowledged Epistle to the Galatians, represents John as one of the three pillar-apostles who recognized his peculiar gift for the apostolate of the Gentiles and extended to him the right hand of fellowship.

Analysis.

The object of John determined the selection and arrangement of the material.   His plan is more clear and systematic than that of the Synoptists.   It brings out the growing conflict between belief and unbelief, between light and darkness, and leads step by step to the great crisis of the cross, and to the concluding exclamation of Thomas, "My Lord and my God."

In the following analysis the sections peculiar to John are marked by a star.

*I. The Prologue.   The theme of the Gospel: the Logos, the eternal Revealer of God:

(1.) In relation to God, 1 : 1, 2.

(2.) In relation to the world.   General revelation, 1 : 3–5.

(3.) In relation to John the Baptist and the Jews Particular revelation, 1 : 6–13.

(4.) The incarnation of the Logos, and its effect upon the disciples, 1 : 14–18.

II. THE PUBLIC MANIFESTATION OF THE INCARNATE LOGOS IN ACTIVE WORD AND WORK, 1 : 19 to 12 : 50.

*(1.) The preparatory testimony of John the Baptist pointing to Jesus as the promised and expected Messiah, and as the Lamb of God that beareth the sin of the world, 1 : 19–37.

*(2.) The gathering of the first disciples, 1 : 38–51.

*(3.) The first sign : the changing of water into wine at Cana in Galilee, 2 : 1–11. First sojourn in Capernaum, 2 : 12. First Passover and journey to Jerusalem during the public ministry, 2 : 13.

*(4.) The reformatory cleansing of the Temple, 2 : 14–22. (Recorded also by the Synoptists, but at the close of the public ministry.) Labors among the Jews in Jerusalem, 2 : 23–25.

*(5.) Conversation with Nicodemus, representing the timid disciples, the higher classes among the Jews. Regeneration the condition of entering into the kingdom of God, 3 : 1–15. The love of God in the sending of his Son to save the world, 3 : 16–21. (Jerusalem.)

*(6.) Labors of Jesus in Judæa. The testimony of John the Baptist : He must increase, but I must decrease, 3 : 22–36. (Departure of Jesus into Galilee after John's imprisonment, 4 : 1–3 ; comp. Matt. 4 : 12 ; Mark 1 : 14 ; Luke 4 : 14.)

*(7.) Labors in Samaria on the journey from Judæa to Galilee. The woman of Samaria ; Jacob's well ; the water of life ; the worship of God

the Spirit in spirit and in truth; the fields ripening for the harvest, 4 : 1–42.

Jesus teaches publicly in Galilee, 4 : 43–45 (comp. Matt. 4 : 17; Mark 1 : 14, 15; Luke 4 : 14, 15).

*(8.) Jesus again visits Cana in Galilee and heals a nobleman's son at Capernaum, 4 : 46–54.

*(9.) Second journey to Jerusalem at a feast (the second Passover ?). The healing of the infirm man at the pool of Bethesda on the Sabbath, 5 : 1–18. Beginning of the hostility of the Jews. Discourse of Christ on his relation to the Father, and his authority to judge the world, 5 : 19–47.

(10.) The feeding of the five thousand, 6 : 1–14. The stilling of the tempest, 6 : 15–21.

* The mysterious discourse in Capernaum on the bread of life ; the sifting of the disciples; the confession of Peter : " To whom shall we go," etc. ; the hinting at the treason of Judas, 6 : 22–71.

*(11.) Third visit to Jerusalem, at the feast of the Tabernacles. The hasty request of the brethren of Jesus who did not believe on him. His discourse in the Temple with opposite effect. Rising hostility of the Jews, and vain efforts of the hierarchy to seize him as a false teacher misleading the people, 7 : 1–52.

[*(12ª.) The woman taken in adultery and pardoned by Jesus, 7 : 53 to 8 : 11. Jerusalem. Probably an interpolation from oral tradition, authentic and true, but not from the pen of John. Also found at the end, and at Luke 21.]

*(12ᵇ.) Discourse on the light of the world. The children of God and the children of the

devil.   Attempts to stone Jesus, 8 : 12–59.

*(13.) The healing of the man born blind, on a Sabbath, and his testimony before the Pharisees, 9 : 1–41.

*(14.) The parable of the good shepherd, 10 : 1–21. Speech at the feast of Dedication in Solomon's porch, 10 : 22–39.   Departure to the country beyond the Jordan, 10 : 40–42.

*(15.) The resurrection of Lazarus at Bethany, and its effect upon hastening the crisis.   The counsel of Caiaphas.   Jesus retires from Jerusalem to Ephraim, 11 : 1–57.

(16.) The anointing by Mary in Bethany, 12 : 1–8. The counsel of the chief priests, 12 : 9–11.

(17.) The entry into Jerusalem, 12 : 12–19. (Comp. Matt. 21 : 1–17 ; Mark 11 : 1–11 ; Luke 19 : 29–44.)

*(18.) Visit of the Greeks.   Discourse of Jesus on the grain of wheat which must die to bear fruit; the voice from heaven; the attraction of the cross; the opposite effect; reflection of the Evangelist; summary of the speeches of Jesus, 12 : 20–50.

III. The Private Manifestation of Christ in the Circle of his Disciples.   During the fourth and last Passover week.   Jerusalem, 13 : 1 to 17 : 26.

*(1.) Jesus washes the feet of the disciples before the Passover meal, 13 : 1–20.

(2.) He announces the traitor, 13 : 21–27.   The departure of Judas, 13 : 27–30.

*(3.) The new commandment of love, 13 : 31–35. (Here is the best place for the institution of the Lord's Supper, omitted by John, but reported by all the Synoptists and by Paul.)

(4.) Prophecy of Peter's denial, 13 : 36–38.

*(5.) The farewell discourses to the disciples; the promise of the Paraclete, and of Christ's return, 14 : 1 to 16 : 33.

*(4.) The Sacerdotal Prayer, 17 : 1–26.

IV. The Glorification of Christ in the Crucifixion and Resurrection, 18 : 1 to 20 : 31.

(1.) The passage over the Kedron, and the betrayal, 18 : 1–11.

(2.) Jesus before the high priests, Annas and Caiaphas, 18 : 12–14, 19–24.

(3.) Peter's denial, 18 : 15–18, 25–27.

(4.) Jesus before the Roman governor, Pontius Pilate, 18 : 28 to 19 : 16. Original in part (19 : 4–16).

(5.) The crucifixion, 19 : 17–37.

(6.) The burial of Jesus. 19 : 38–42.

(7.) The resurrection. Mary Magdalene, Peter and John visit the empty tomb, 20 : 1–10.

(8.) Christ appears to Mary Magdalene, 20 : 11–18.

*(9.) Christ appears to the apostles, except Thomas, on the evening of the resurrection day, 20 : 19–23.

*(10.) Christ appears to the apostles, including Thomas, on the following Lord's Day, 20 : 26–29.

*(11.) Object of the Gospel, 20 : 30, 31.

*V. The Appendix and Epilogue, 21 : 1–25.

(1.) Christ appears to seven disciples on the lake of Galilee. The third manifestation to the disciples, 21 : 1–14.

(2.) The dialogue with Simon Peter: "Lovest thou Me?" "Feed My sheep." "Follow Me," 21 : 15–19.

(3.) The mysterious word about the beloved disciple, 21 : 21–23.

(4.) The attestation of the authorship of the Gospel by the pupils of John, 21 : 24, 25.

CHARACTERISTICS OF THE FOURTH GOSPEL.

The Gospel of John is the most original, the most important, the most influential book in all literature. The great Origen called it the crown of the Gospels, as the Gospels are the crown of all sacred writings.[1] It is pre-eminently the spiritual and ideal, though at the same time a most real Gospel, the truest transcript of the original. It lifts the veil from the holy of holies and reveals the glory of the Only Begotten from the Father, full of grace and truth. It unites in harmony the deepest knowledge and the purest love of Christ. We hear as it were his beating heart; we lay our hands in his wound-prints and exclaim with doubting Thomas: "My Lord and my God." No book is so plain and yet so deep, so natural and yet so full of mystery. It is simple as a child and sublime as a seraph, gentle as a lamb and bold as an eagle, deep as the sea and high as the heavens.

It has been praised as "the unique, tender, genuine Gospel," "written by the hand of an angel," as "the heart of Christ," as "God's love-letter to the world," or "Christ's love-letter to the church." It has exerted an irresistible charm on many of the strongest and noblest minds in Christendom, as Origen in Egypt, Chrysostom in Asia, Augustin in Africa, the German Luther, the French Calvin, the poetic Herder, the critical Schleiermacher, and a multitude of less famous writers of all schools and shades of thought. Even many of those who doubt or deny the apostolic authorship cannot help admiring its more than earthly beauties.[2]

---

[1] *Opera*, IV. 6: τολμητέον τοίνυν εἰπεῖν ἀπαρχὴν μὲν πασῶν γραφῶν εἶναι τὰ εὐαγγέλια, τῶν δὲ εὐαγγελίων ἀπαρχὴν τὸ κατὰ Ἰωάννην.

[2] DeWette says that the discourses of Christ in John shine with more than earthly brilliancy (*sie strahlen in mehr als irdischem Brillantfeuer, Exeg. Handbuch*, I. 3, p. 7). Holtzmann: "The fundamental ideas of the fourth Gospel lie far beyond the horizon of the church in the second century, and indeed of the whole Christian church down to the present day" (in Schenkel's "Bibel-Lexik.," II. 234). Baur and Keim (I. 133) give the Gospel the highest praise as a philosophy of religion, but deny its historical value.

But there are other sceptics who find the Johannean discourses monotonous, tedious, nebulous, unmeaning, hard, and feel as much offended by them as the original hearers.[1]

Let us point out the chief characteristics of this book which distinguish it from the Synoptical Gospels.

1. The fourth Gospel is the Gospel of the INCARNATION, that is, of the perfect union of the divine and human in the person of Jesus of Nazareth, who for this very reason is the Saviour of the world and the fountain of eternal life. " The Word became flesh." This is the theoretical theme. The writer begins with the eternal pre-existence of the Logos, and ends with the adoration of his incarnate divinity in the exclamation of the sceptical Thomas. " My Lord and my God!" Luke's preface is historiographic and simply points to his sources of information ; John's prologue is metaphysical and dogmatic, and sounds the keynote of the subsequent history. The Synoptists begin with the man Jesus and rise up to the recognition of his Messiahship and divine Sonship ; John descends from the pre-existent Son of God through the preparatory revelations to his incarnation and crucifixion till he resumes the glory which he had before the world began. The former give us the history of a divine man,

---

[1] Renan and John Stuart Mill have confessed a strong antipathy to these discourses. Renan's last judgment on the Gospel of John (in *L'église chrét.*, 1879, p. 51) is as follows : " *On l'a trop admiré. Il a de la chaleur, parfois une sorte de sublimité, mais quelque chose d'enflé, de faux, d'obsur. La naïveté manque tout à fait. L'auteur ne raconte pas ; il démontre. Rien de plus fatigant que ses longs récits de miracles et que ces discussions, roulant sur des malentendus, où les adversaires de Jésus jouent le rôle d'idiots. Combien à ce pathos verbeux nous préférons le doux style, tout hébreu encore, du Discours sur la montagne, et cette limpidité de narration qui fait le charme des évangélistes primitifs ! Ceux-ci n'ont pas besoin de répéter sans cesse que ce qu'ils racontent est vrai. Leur sincérité, inconsciente de l'objection, n'a pas cette soif fébrile d'attestations répétées qui montre que l'incrédulité, le doute, ont déjà commencé. Au ton légèrement excité de ce nouveau narrateur, on dirait qu'il a peur de n'être pas cru, et qu'il cherche à surprendre la religion de son lecteur par des affirmations pleines d'emphase.*" John Stuart Mill (*Three Essays on Religion,* p. 253) irreverently calls the discourses in John " poor stuff," imported from Philo and the Alexandrian Platonists, and imagines that a multitude of Oriental Gnostics might have manufactured such a book. But why did they not do it?

the latter the history of a human God. Not that he identifies him with the Godhead (ὁ θεός); on the contrary, he clearly distinguishes the Son and the Father and makes him inferior in dignity ("the Father is greater than I"); but he declares that the Son is "God" (θεός), that is, of divine essence or nature.

And yet there is no contradiction here between the Evangelists except for those who deem a union of the Divine and human in one person an impossibility. The Christian Church has always felt that the Synoptic and the Johannean Christ are one and the same, only represented from different points of view. And in this judgment the greatest scholars and keenest critics, from Origen down to the present time, have concurred.

For, on the one hand, John's Christ is just as real and truly human as that of the Synoptists. He calls himself the Son of man and "a man" (8 : 40); he "groaned in the spirit" (11 : 33), he "wept" at the grave of a friend (11 : 35), and his "soul" was "troubled" in the prospect of the dark hour of crucifixion (12 : 27) and the crime of the traitor (13 : 1). The Evangelist attests with solemn emphasis from what he saw with his own eyes that Jesus truly suffered and died (19 : 33–35).[1]

The Synoptic Christ, on the other hand, is as truly elevated above ordinary mortals as the Johannean. It is true, he does not in so many words declare his pre-existence as in John (1 : 1; 6 : 62; 8 : 58; 17 : 5, 24), but it is implied, or follows as a legitimate consequence. He is conceived without sin, a descendant of David, and yet the Lord of David (Matt. 22 : 41); he claims authority to forgive sins, for which he is accused of blasphemy by the Jews (quite consistently from their standpoint of unbelief); he gives his life a ransom for the redemption of the world; he will come in his glory and judge all nations; yea, in the very Sermon on the Mount, which all schools of Rationalists accept

---

[1] Notwithstanding such passages Dr. Davidson asserts (II. 278) : "In uniting the only-begotten Son of God with the historical Jesus, the evangelist implies the absence of full humanity. The personality consists essentially of the Logos, the flesh being only a temporary thing. Body, soul, and spirit do not belong to Jesus Christ ; he is the Logos incarnate for a time, who soon returns to the original state of oneness with the Father."

as his genuine teaching, He declares himself to be the judge of the world (Matt. 7 : 21–23 ; comp. 25 : 31–46), and in the baptismal formula He associates himself and the Holy Spirit with the eternal Father, as the connecting link between the two, thus assuming a place on the very throne of the Deity (28 : 19). It is impossible to rise higher. Hence Matthew, the Jewish Evangelist, does not hesitate to apply to Him the name Immanuel, that is, "God with us" (1 : 23). Mark gives us the Gospel of Peter, the first who confessed that Jesus is not only "the Christ" in his official character, but also "the Son of the living God." This is far more than *a* son ; it designates his unique personal relation to God and forms the eternal basis of his historical Messiahship (Matt. 16 : 16 ; comp. 26 : 63). The two titles are distinct, and the high priest's charge of blasphemy (26 : 65) could only apply to the latter. A false Messiah would be an impostor, not a blasphemer. We could not substitute the Messiah for the Son in the baptismal formula. Peter, Mark, and Matthew were brought up in the most orthodox monotheism, with an instinctive horror of the least approach to idolatry, and yet they looked up to their Master with feelings of adoration. And, as for Luke, he delights in representing Jesus throughout as the sinless Saviour of sinners, and is in full sympathy with the theology of his elder brother Paul, who certainly taught the pre-existence and divine nature of Christ several years before the Gospels were written or published (Rom. 1 : 3, 4 ; 9 : 5 ; 2 Cor. 8 : 9 ; Col. 1 : 15–17 ; Phil. 2 : 6–11).

2. It is the Gospel of LOVE. Its practical motto is : "God is love." In the incarnation of the eternal Word, in the historic mission of his Son, God has given the greatest possible proof of his love to mankind. In the fourth Gospel alone we read that precious sentence which contains the very essence of Christianity : "God so loved the world, that he gave his only begotten Son, that whosoever believeth on him should not perish, but have eternal life" (3 : 16). It is the Gospel of the Good Shepherd who laid down his life for the sheep (10 : 11) ; the Gospel of the new commandment : "Love one another" (13 : 34). And

this was the last exhortation of the aged disciple "whom Jesus loved."

But for this very reason that Christ is the greatest gift of God to the world, unbelief is the greatest sin and blackest ingratitude, which carries in it its own condemnation. The guilt of unbelief, the contrast between faith and unbelief is nowhere set forth in such strong light as in the fourth Gospel. It is a consuming fire to all enemies of Christ.

3. It is the Gospel of MYSTIC SYMBOLISM.[1] The eight miracles it records are significant "signs" ($\sigma\eta\mu\epsilon\hat{\iota}a$) which symbolize the character and mission of Christ, and manifest his glory. They are simply his "works" ($\check{\epsilon}\rho\gamma a$), the natural manifestations of his marvellous person performed with the same ease as men perform their ordinary works. The turning of water into wine illustrates his transforming power, and fitly introduces his public ministry; the miraculous feeding of the five thousand set him forth as the Bread of life for the spiritual nourishment of countless believers; the healing of the man born blind, as the Light of the world; the raising of Lazarus, as the Resurrection and the Life. The miraculous draught of fishes shows the disciples to be fishers of men, and insures the abundant results of Christian labor to the end of time. The serpent in the wilderness prefigured the cross. The Baptist points to him as the Lamb of God which taketh away the sin of the world. He represents himself under the significant figures of the Door, the good Shepherd, the Vine; and these figures have inspired Christian art and poetry, and guided the meditations of the church ever since.

The whole Old Testament is a type and prophecy of the New. "The law was given by Moses; grace and truth came by Jesus Christ" (1 : 17). Herein lies the vast superiority of Christianity, and yet the great importance of Judaism as an essential part in the scheme of redemption. Clearly and strongly as John brings out the opposition to the unbelieving Jews, he is yet far from going to the Gnostic extreme of rejecting or depreciating the

[1] Lange, Westcott, Milligan and Moulton dwell at length on this feature.

Old Testament; on the contrary "salvation comes from the Jews" (says Christ to the Samaritan woman, 4 : 22); and turning the Scripture argument against the scribes and Pharisees who searched the letter of the Scriptures, but ignored the spirit, Christ confronts them with the authority of Moses on whom they fixed their hope. "If ye believed Moses, ye would believe me; for he wrote of me. But ye believe not his writings, how shall ye believe my words?" (5 : 46). John sees Christ everywhere in those ancient Scriptures which cannot be broken. He unfolds the true Messianic idea in conflict with the carnal perversion of it among the Jews under the guidance of the hier archy.

The Johannean and Synoptic Discourses of Christ.

4. John gives prominence to the transcendent Discourses about the person of Christ and his relation to the Father, to the world, and the disciples. His words are testimonies, revealing the inner glory of his person; they are spirit and they are life.

Matthew's Gospel is likewise didactic; but there is a marked difference between the contents and style of the Synoptic and the Johannean discourses of Jesus. The former discuss the nature of the Messianic kingdom, the fulfilment of the law, the duty of holy obedience, and are popular, practical, brief, pointed, sententious, parabolic, and proverbial ; the latter touch the deepest mysteries of theology and Christology, are metaphysical, lengthy, liable to carnal misunderstanding, and scarcely discernible from John's own style in the prologue and the first Epistle, and from that used by the Baptist. The transition is almost imperceptible in 3 : 16 and 3 : 31.

Here we reach the chief difficulty in the Johannean problem. Here is the strong point of sceptical criticism. We must freely admit at the outset that John so reproduced the words of his Master as to mould them unconsciously into his own type of thought and expression. He revolved them again and again in his heart, they were his daily food, and the burden of his teaching to the churches from Sunday to Sunday; yet he had to translate, to condense, to expand, and to apply them; and in this process it was unavoidable that his own reflections should more or less mingle with his recollections. With all the tenacity of his memory it was impossible that at such a great interval of time (fifty or sixty years after the events) he should be able to record literally every discourse just as it was spoken; and he makes no such claim, but intimates that he selects and summarizes.

This is the natural view of the case, and the same concession is now made by all the champions of the Johannean authorship who do not hold to a magical inspiration theory and turn the sacred writers into unthinking machines, contrary to their own express statements, as in the Preface of Luke. But we deny that this concession involves any sacrifice of the truth of history or of any lineament from the physiognomy of Christ. The difficulty here presented is usually overstated by the critics, and becomes less and less, the higher we rise in our estimation of Christ, and the closer we examine the differences in their proper connection. The following reflections will aid the student:

(1) In the first place we must remember the marvellous heighth and depth and breadth of Christ's intellect as it appears in the Synoptists as well as in John. He commanded the whole domain of religious and moral truth; he spake as never man spake, and the people were astonished at his teaching (Matt. 7:28, 29; Mark 1:22; 6:2; Luke 4:32; John 7:46). He addressed not only his own generation, but through it all ages and classes of men. No wonder that his hearers often misunderstood him. The Synoptists give examples of such misunderstanding as well as John (comp. Mark 8:16). But who will set limits to his power and pædagogic wisdom in the matter and form of his teaching? Must he not necessarily have varied his style when he addressed the common people in Galilee, as in the Synoptists, and the educated, proud, hierarchy of Jerusalem, as in John? Or when he spoke on the mountain, invit-

ing the multitude to the Messianic Kingdom at the opening of his ministry, and when he took farewell from his disciples in the chamber, in view of the great sacrifice? Socrates appears very different in Xenophon and in Plato, yet we can see him in both. But here is a far greater than Socrates.[1]

(2) John's mind, at a period when it was most pliable and plastic, had been so conformed to the mind of Christ that his own thoughts and words faithfully reflected the teaching of his Master. If there ever was spiritual sympathy and congeniality between two minds, it was between Jesus and the disciple whom he loved and whom he intrusted with the care of his mother. John stood nearer to his Lord than any Christian or any of the Synoptists. "Why should not John have been formed upon the model of Jesus rather than the Jesus of his Gospel be the reflected image of himself? Surely it may be left to all candid minds to say whether, to adopt only the lowest supposition, the creative intellect of Jesus was not far more likely to mould His disciple to a conformity with itself, than the receptive spirit of the disciple to give birth by its own efforts to that conception of a Redeemer which so infinitely surpasses the loftiest image of man's own creation." [2]

(3) John reproduced the discourses from the fulness of the spirit of Christ that dwelt in him, and therefore without any departure from the ideas. The whole gospel history assumes that Christ did not finish, but only began his work while on earth, that he carries it on in heaven through his chosen organs,

---

[1] Hase (*Geschichte Jesu*, p. 61) makes some striking remarks on this parallel: "*Der Sokrates des Xenophon ist ein anderer als der des Plato, jeder hat diejenige Seite aufgefasst, die ihm die nächste und liebste war; erst aus beiden. Darstellungen erkennen wir den rechten Sokrates. Xenophons anschauliche Einfachheit trägt das volle Gepräge der Wahrheit dessen, was er erzählt. Dennoch dieser Sokrates, der sich im engen Kreise sittlicher und politischer Vorstellungen herumdreht, ist nicht der ganze Sokrates, der weiseste in Griechenland, der die grosse Revolution in den Geistern seines Volks hervorgerufen hat. Dagegen der platonische Sokrates sich weit mehr zum Schöpfer der neuen Periode griechischer Philosophie eignet und darnach aussieht, als habe er die Weisheit vom Himmel zur Erde gebracht, der attische Logos.*"

[2] Milligan and Moulton, in their excellent Commentary on *John*, Introd., p. xxxiii.

to whom he promised mouth and wisdom (Luke 21 : 15 ; Matt.
10 : 19) and his constant presence (Matt. 19 : 20 ; 28 : 20). The
disciples became more and more convinced of the superhuman
character of Christ by the irresistible logic of fact and thought.
His earthly life appeared to them as a transient state of humiliation which was preceded by a pre-existent state of glory with
the Father, as it was followed by a permanent state of glory
after the resurrection and ascension to heaven. He withheld
from them "many things" because they could not bear them
before his glorification (John 16 : 12). "What I do," he said
to Peter, "thou knowest not now, but thou shalt come to know
hereafter" (13 : 7). Some of his deepest sayings, which they
had at first misunderstood, were illuminated by the resurrection
(2 : 22 ; 12 : 16), and then by the outpouring of the Spirit, who
took things out of the fulness of Christ and declared them to the
disciples (16 : 13, 14). Hence the farewell discourses are so full
of the promises of the Spirit of truth who would glorify Christ
in their hearts. Under such guidance we may be perfectly sure
of the substantial faithfulness of John's record.

(4) Beneath the surface of the similarity there is a considerable difference between the language of Christ and the language
of his disciple. John never attributes to Christ the designation
Logos, which he uses so prominently in the Prologue and the
first Epistle. This is very significant, and shows his conscientious care. He distinguished his own theology from the teaching of his Master, no matter whether he borrowed the term
Logos from Philo (which cannot be proven), or coined it himself from his reflections on Old Testament distinctions between
the hidden and the revealed God and Christ's own testimonies
concerning his relation to the Father. The first Epistle of John
is an echo of his Gospel, but with original matter of his own
and polemical references to the anti-Christian errors of his day.
"The phrases of the Gospel," says Westcott, "have a definite
historic connection : they belong to circumstances which explain
them. The phrases in the Epistle are in part generalizations,
and in part interpretations of the earlier language in view of

Christ's completed work and of the experience of the Christian church."

As to the speeches of the Baptist, in the fourth Gospel, they keep, as the same writer remarks, strictly within the limits suggested by the Old Testament.   "What he says spontaneously of Christ is summed up in the two figures of the 'Lamb' and the 'Bridegroom,' which together give a comprehensive view of the suffering and joy, the redemptive and the completive work of Messiah under prophetic imagery.   Both figures appear again in the Apocalypse; but it is very significant that they do not occur in the Lord's teaching in the fourth Gospel or in St. John's Epistles."

(5) There are not wanting striking resemblances in thought and style between the discourses in John and in the Synoptists, especially Matthew, which are sufficient to refute the assertion that the two types of teaching are irreconcilable.[1]   The Synoptists were not quite unfamiliar with the other type of teaching. They occasionally rise to the spiritual height of John and record briefer sayings of Jesus which could be inserted without a discord in his Gospel.   Take the prayer of thanksgiving and the touching invitation to all that labor and are heavy laden, in Matt. 11 : 25-30.   The sublime declaration recorded by Luke (10 : 22) and Matthew (11 : 27): "No one knoweth the Son, save the Father; neither doth any know the Father, save the Son, and he to whomsoever the Son willeth to reveal him," is thoroughly Christ-like according to John's conception, and is the basis of his own declaration in the prologue: "No man hath seen God at any time; the only begotten Son, who is in the bosom of the Father, he hath declared him" (1 : 18).   Jesus makes no higher claim in John than he does in Matthew when he proclaims: "All authority hath been given unto me in heaven and on earth" (28 : 19).   In almost the same words Jesus says in John (17 : 2) : "Thou hast given him power over all flesh."

On the other hand, John gives us not a few specimens of

---

[1] " *Si Jésus*," says Renan, "*parlait comme le veut Matthieu, il n'a pu parler comme le veut Jean.*"

those short, pithy maxims of oriental wisdom which characterize the Synoptic discourses.[1]

[1] John 1 : 26, 43 ; 2 : 19 ; 4 : 44 ; 6 : 20, 35, 37 ; 12 : 13, 25, 27 ; 13 : 16, 20 ; 20 : 19, 23. See the lists in Godet, I. 197 sq., and Westcott, p lxxxii sq. The following are the principal parallel passages :

John 2 : 19: Jesus answered and said unto them, Destroy this temple, and in three days I will raise it up.

Matt. 26 : 61: This man said, I am able to destroy the temple of God, and to build it in three days. Cf. Mark 14 : 58 ; 15 : 29.

3 : 18: He that believeth on him is not judged : he that believeth not hath been judged already.

Mark 16 : 16: He that believeth and is baptized shall be saved ; but he that disbelieveth shall be condemned.

4 : 44: For Jesus himself testified, that a prophet hath no honor in his own country.

Matt. 13 : 57: But Jesus said unto them, A prophet is not without honor, save in his own country, and in his own house. Cf. Mark 6 : 4 ; Luke 4 : 24.

5 : 8: Jesus saith unto him, Arise, take up thy bed, and walk.

6 : 20: It is I, be not afraid.

Matt. 9 : 6: Arise, and take up thy bed, and go unto thy house. Cf. Mark 2 : 9 ; Luke 5 : 24.

Matt. 14 : 27 : It is I, be not afraid. Cf. Mark 6 : 50.

6 : 35: He that cometh to me shall not hunger, and he that believeth on me shall never thirst.

Matt. 5 : 6 ; Luke 6 : 21 : Blessed are they that hunger and thirst after righteousness ; for they shall be filled.

6 : 37: All that which the Father giveth me shall come unto me ; and him that cometh unto me I will in no wise cast out.

Matt. 11 : 28, 29: Come unto me, all ye that labor and are heavy laden, . . . and ye shall find rest unto your souls.

6 : 46: Not that any man hath seen the Father, save he which is from God, he hath seen the Father. Cf. 1 : 18: No man hath seen God at any time ; the only begotten Son, who is in the bosom of the Father, he hath declared him.

Matt. 11 : 27: And no one knoweth the Son, save the Father, neither doth any know the Father, save the Son, and he to whomsoever the Son willeth to reveal him.

12 : 8: For the poor ye have always with you ; but me ye have not always.

Matt. 26 : 11: For ye have the poor always with you ; but me ye have not always. Cf. Mark 14 : 7.

12 : 25: He that loveth his life loseth it ; and he that hateth his life in this world shall keep it unto life eternal.

Matt. 10 : 39: He that findeth his life shall lose it ; and he that loseth his life for my sake shall find it. Cf. 16 : 25 ; Mark 8 : 35 ; Luke 9 : 24 ; 17 : 33.

12 : 27: Now is my soul troubled ; and what shall I say ? Father, save me from this hour. But for this cause came I unto this hour.

Matt. 26 : 38: Then saith he unto them, My soul is exceeding sorrowful, even unto death. Cf. Mark 14 : 34.

13 : 3: Jesus knowing that the Father had given all things into his hands. . . .

13 : 16: Verily, verily I say unto you, A servant is not greater than his lord.

Matt. 11 : 27: All things have been delivered unto me of my Father.

Matt. 10 : 24: A disciple is not above his master, nor a servant above his lord. Cf. Luke 6 : 40.

13 : 20: He that receiveth whomsoever I send receiveth me ; and he that receiveth me receiveth him that sent me.

Matt. 10 : 40: He that receiveth you receiveth me, and he that receiveth me receiveth him that sent me.

14 : 18: I will not leave you desolate ; I come unto you. Cf. v. 23: We will . . . make our abode with him.

Matt. 28 : 20: I am with you alway, even unto the end of the world.

15 : 21: But all these things will they do unto you for my name's sake.

Matt. 10 : 22: And ye shall be hated of all men for my name's sake.

17 : 2: Even as thou gavest him authority over all flesh.

ιatt. 28 : 18: All authority hath been given unto me in heaven and on earth.

20 : 23: Whosesoever sins ye forgive, they are forgiven unto them.

Matt. 18 : 18: What things soever ye shall loose on earth shall be loosed in heaven.

THE STYLE OF THE GOSPEL OF JOHN.

The style of the fourth Gospel differs widely from the ecclesiastical writers of the second century, and belongs to the apostolic age. It has none of the technical theological terms of post-apostolic controversies, no allusions to the state of the church, its government and worship, but moves in the atmosphere of the first Christian generation; yet differs widely from the style of the Synoptists and is altogether unique in the history of secular and religious literature, a fit expression of the genius of John: clear and deep, simple as a child, and mature as a saint, sad and yet serene, and basking in the sunshine of eternal life and love. The fourth Gospel is pure Greek in vocabulary and grammar, but thoroughly Hebrew in temper and spirit, even more so than any other book, and can be almost literally translated into Hebrew without losing its force or beauty. It has the childlike simplicity, the artlessness, the imaginativeness, the directness, the circumstantiality, and the rhythmical parallelism which characterize the writings of the Old Testament. The sentences are short and weighty, co-ordinated, not subordinated. The construction is exceedingly simple: no involved periods, no connecting links, no logical argumentation, but a succession of self-evident truths declared as from immediate intuition. The parallelism of Hebrew poetry is very apparent in such double sentences as: "Peace I leave with you; my peace I give unto you;" "A servant is not greater than his lord; neither one that is sent greater than he that sent him;" "All things were made by him, and without him was not anything made that hath been made." Examples of antithetic parallelism are also frequent: "The light shineth in the darkness, and the darkness comprehended it not;" "He was in the world, and the world knew him not;" "He confessed, and denied not;" "I give unto them eternal life, and they shall never perish."

The author has a limited vocabulary, but loves emphatic repetition, and his very monotony is solemn and impressive.

He uses certain key-words of the profoundest import, as Word, life, light, truth, love, glory, testimony, name, sign, work, to know, to behold, to believe. These are not abstract conceptions but concrete realities. He views the world under comprehensive contrasts, as life and death, light and darkness, truth and falsehood, love and hatred, God and the devil, and (in the first Epistle) Christ and Antichrist.

He avoids the optative, and all argumentative particles, but uses very frequently the simple particles καί, δέ, οὖν, ἵνα. His most characteristic particle in the narrative portions is "therefore" (οὖν), which is with him not syllogistic (like ἄρα and its compounds), but indicative simply of continuation and retrospect (like "so" and "then" or the German "nun"), yet with the idea that nothing happens without a cause; while the particle "in order that" (ἵνα) indicates that nothing happens without a purpose. He avoids the relative pronoun and prefers the connecting "and" with the repetition of the noun, as "In the beginning was the Word, and the Word was with God, and the Word was God. . . . In him was life, and the life was the light of men." The "and" sometimes takes the place of "but," as "The light shineth in the darkness, and the darkness comprehended it not" (1 : 5).

We look in vain for such important words as church, gospel, repentance (μετάνοια), but the substance is there in different forms. He does not even use the noun "faith" (πίστις), which frequently occurs in the Synoptists and in Paul, but he uses the verb "to believe" (πιστεύειν) ninety-eight times, about twice as often as all three Synoptists together.

He applies the significant term Logos (ratio and oratio) to Christ as the Revealer and the Interpreter of God (1 : 18), but only in the Prologue, and such figurative designations as "the Light of the world," "the Bread of life," "the Good Shepherd," "the Vine," "the Way," "the Truth," and "the Life." He alone uses the double "Verily" in the discourses of the Saviour. He calls the Holy Spirit the "Paraclete" or "Advocate" of believers, who pleads their cause here on earth, as Christ pleads it on the throne in heaven. There breathes through this book an air of calmness and serenity, of peace and repose, that seems to come from the eternal mansions of heaven.[1]

Is such a style compatible with the hypothesis of a post- and pseudo-apostolic fiction? We have a large number of fictitious Gospels, but they differ as much from the fourth canonical Gospel as midnight darkness from noonday brightness.

AUTHORSHIP.

For nearly eighteen centuries the Christian church of all denominations has enjoyed the fourth Gospel without a shadow of doubt that it was the work of John the Apostle. But in the nineteenth century the citadel was assailed with increasing force, and the conflict between the besiegers and defenders is still raging among scholars of the highest ability. It is a question of life and death between constructive and destructive criticism. The vindication of the fourth Gospel as a genuine product of John, the beloved disciple, is the death-blow of the mythical and legendary reconstruction and destruction of the life of Christ and the apostolic history. The ultimate result cannot be doubtful. The opponents have been forced gradually to retreat from the year 170 to the very beginning of the second century, as the time when the fourth Gospel was already known and used in the church, that is to the lifetime of many pupils and friends of John and other eye-witnesses of the life of Christ.[2]

I. The EXTERNAL PROOF of the Johannean authorship is as strong, yea stronger than that of the genuineness of any classical writer of antiquity, and goes up to the very beginning of the

---

[1] For further particulars of John's style see my *Companion to the Study of the Greek Test.*, pp. 66–75, where the opinions of Renan, Ewald, Luthardt, Keim, Godet, Westcott, Hase, and Weiss are given on the subject.

[2] See the literary notices on p. 405 sqq. To the able vindications of the genuineness of John there mentioned must now be added the masterly discussion of Dr. Weiss in his *Leben Jesu* (vol. I., 1882, pp. 84–124), which has just come to hand.

second century, within hailing distance of the living John.   It includes catholic writers, heretics, and heathen enemies.   There is but one dissenting voice, hardly audible, that of the insignificant sect of the Alogi who opposed the Johannean doctrine of the Logos (hence their name, with the double meaning of unreasonable, and anti-Logos heretics) and absurdly ascribed both the Gospel of John and the Apocalypse to his enemy, the Gnostic Cerinthus.[1]   Let us briefly sum up the chief testimonies.

1. *Catholic* testimonies.   We begin at the fourth century and gradually rise up to the age of John.   All the ancient Greek manuscripts of the New Testament, including the Sinaitic and the Vatican, which date from the age of Constantine and are based upon older copies of the second century, and all the ancient versions, including the Syriac and old Latin from the third and second centuries, contain without exception the Gospel of John, though the Peshito omits his second and third Epistles and the Apocalypse.   These manuscripts and versions represent the universal voice of the churches.

Then we have the admitted individual testimonies of all the Greek and Latin fathers up to the middle of the second century, without a dissenting voice or doubt: Jerome (d. 419) and Eusebius (d. 340), who had the whole ante-Nicene literature before them; Origen in Egypt (d. 254), the greatest scholar of his age and a commentator on John; Tertullian of North Africa (about 200), a Catholic in doctrine, a Montanist in discipline, and a zealous advocate of the dispensation of the Paraclete announced by John; Clement of Alexandria (about 190), a cultivated philosopher who had travelled in Greece, Italy, Syria, and Palestine, seeking religious instruction everywhere; Irenæus, a native of Asia Minor and from 178 bishop of Lyons, a pupil of Polycarp and a grand-pupil of John himself, who derived his chief ammunition against the Gnostic heresy from the fourth Gospel, and represents the four canonical Gospels—no more and no less—as universally accepted by the churches of his time; Theophilus of Antioch (180), who expressly quotes from the fourth Gospel

---

[1] Recently renewed in part by Renan (1879).   See below.

under the name of John;[1] the Muratorian Canon (170), which
reports the occasion of the composition of John's Gospel by
urgent request of his friends and disciples; Tatian of Syria
(155–170), who in his "Address to the Greeks" repeatedly
quotes the fourth Gospel, though without naming the author,
and who began his "Diatessaron"—once widely spread in the
church notwithstanding the somewhat Gnostic leanings of the
author, and commented on by Ephraem of Syria—with the prologue of John.[2] From him we have but one step to his teacher,
Justin Martyr, a native of Palestine (103–166), and a bold and
noble-minded defender of the faith in the reigns of Hadrian
and the Antonines. In his two Apologies and his Dialogue
with Trypho the Jew, he often quotes freely from the four
Gospels under the name of Apostolic "Memoirs" or "Memorabilia of the Apostles," which were read at his time in public
worship.[3] He made most use of Matthew, but once at least he
quotes a passage on regeneration[4] from Christ's dialogue with

[1] His quotation is considered the earliest by *name;* but Irenæus, who wrote
between 177 and 192, represents an older tradition, and proves to his satisfaction that there must be just four Gospels to answer the four cherubim in
Ezekiel's vision. *Adv. Hær.*, III. 1, 1 ; 11, 8 ; V. 36, 2.

[2] The Commentary of Ephraem Syrus on the Diatessaron (375) has recently
been discovered and published from an Armenian translation, at Venice, in
1876. Comp. Zahn, *Tatian's Diatessaron*, Erlangen, 1881, and Harnack, *Die
Ueberlieferung der griechischen Apologeten des zwei ten Jahrh.*, Leipzig, 1882,
pp. 213 sqq.

[3] The use of the Gospel of John by Justin Martyr was doubted by Baur and
most of his followers, but is admitted by Hilgenfeld and Keim. It was again
denied by the anonymous author of "Supernatural Religion," and by Edwin
A. Abbott (in the art. *Gospels*, "Enc. Brit.," vol. X. 821), and again conclusively proven by Sanday in England, and Ezra Abbot in America.

[4] The quotation is not literal but from memory, like most of his quotations :

Justin, *Apol.*, I. 61: "For Christ also said,
Except *ye* be *born again* [ἀναγεννηθῆτε, comp.
1 Pet. 3 : 23], ye shall in no wise *enter* [εἰσέλθητε,
but comp. the same word in John 3 : 5 and 7]
into the kingdom of *heaven* [the phrase of
Matthew]. Now that it is impossible for those
who have once been born to re-enter the wombs
of those that bare them is manifest to all."

John 3 : 3, 4: "Jesus answered and said to
him [Nicodemus], Verily, verily, I say unto
thee, Except a man be *born anew* [or *from
above*, γεννηθῇ ἄνωθεν], he cannot *see* [ἰδεῖν,
ver. 5, *enter into*] the kingdom of *God*. Nicodemus saith unto him, How can a man be born
when he is old? can he enter a second time
into his mother's womb and be born?"

Much account has been made by the Tübingen critics of the slight differences in the quotation (ἀναγεννηθῆτε for γεννηθῇ ἄνωθεν, εἰσελθεῖν for ἰδεῖν and
βασιλεία τῶν οὐρανῶν for βασ. τοῦ θεοῦ) to disprove the connection, or, as this is

Nicodemus which is recorded only by John. Several other allusions of Justin to John are unmistakable, and his whole doctrine
of the pre-existent Logos who sowed precious seeds of truth
among Jews and Gentiles before his incarnation, is unquestionably derived from John. To reverse the case is to derive the
sunlight from the moon, or the fountain from one of its streams.

But we can go still farther back. The scanty writings of the
Apostolic Fathers, so called, have very few allusions to the New
Testament, and breathe the atmosphere of the primitive oral tradition. The author of the "Didache" was well acquainted with
Matthew. The first Epistle of Clement has strong affinity with
Paul. The shorter Epistles of Ignatius show the influence of
John's Christology.[1] Polycarp (d. A.D. 155 in extreme old age), a
personal pupil of John, used the First Epistle of John, and thus
furnishes an *indirect* testimony to the Gospel, since both these
books must stand or fall together.[2] The same is true of Papias
(died about 150), who studied with Polycarp, and probably was
likewise a hearer of John. He "used testimonies from the

impossible, to prove the dependence of John on Justin! But Dr. Abbot, a
most accurate and conscientious scholar, who moreover as a Unitarian cannot
be charged with an orthodox bias, has produced many parallel cases of free
quotations of the same passage not only from patristic writers, but even from
modern divines, including no less than nine quotations of the passage by
Jeremy Taylor, only two of which are alike. I think he has conclusively
proven his case for every reasonable mind. See his invaluable monograph on
The Authorship of the Fourth Gospel, pp. 28 sqq. and 91 sqq. Comp. also
Weiss, *Leben Jesu*, I. 83, who sees in Justin Martyr not only " an unquestionable allusion to the Nicodemus story of the fourth Gospel," but other isolated
reminiscences.

[1] Comp. such expressions as "I desire bread of God, which is the flesh of
Jesus Christ . . . and I desire as drink His blood, which is love imperishable."
Ad Rom., ch. 7, with John 6 : 47 sqq.; "living water," *Ad Rom.*, 7, with John
4 : 10, 11 ; "being Himself the Door of the Father." *Ad Philad.*, 9, with John
10 : 9 ; [the Spirit] "knows whence it cometh and whither it goeth," *Ad
Philad.*, 7, with John 3 : 8. I quoted from the text of Zahn. See the able art.
of Lightfoot in "Contemp. Rev." for February, 1875, and his *S. Ignatius*, 1885.

[2] Polyc., *Ad Phil.*, ch. 7 : "Every one that doth not confess that Jesus
Christ hath come in the flesh is Antichrist ; and whosoever doth not confess
the mystery of the cross is of the devil." Comp. 1 John 4 : 3. On the testimony of Polycarp see Lightfoot in the "Contemp. Rev." for May, 1875.
Westcott, p. xxx, says : "A testimony to one" (the Gospel or the first Ep.)
"is necessarily by inference a testimony to the other."

former Epistle of John." [1] In enumerating the apostles whose living words he collected in his youth, he places John out of his regular order of precedence, along with Matthew, his fellow-Evangelist, and "Andrew, Peter, and Philip" in the same order as John (1 : 40–43) ; from which it has also been inferred that he knew the fourth Gospel. There is some reason to suppose that the disputed section on the woman taken in adultery was recorded by him in illustration of John 8 : 15 ; for, according to Eusebius, he mentioned a similar story in his lost work. [2] These facts combined, make it at least extremely probable that Papias was familiar with John. [3] The joint testimony of Polycarp and Papias represents the school of John in the very field of his later labors, and the succession was continued through Polycrates at Ephesus, through Melito at Sardis, through Claudius Apollinaris at Hieropolis, and Pothinus and Irenæus in Southern Gaul. It is simply incredible that a spurious Gospel should have been smuggled into the churches under the name of their revered spiritual father and grandfather.

Finally, the concluding verse of the appendix, ch. 21 : 24, is a still older testimony of a number of personal friends and pupils

[1] According to Eusebius, III. 39. See Lightfoot in the "Contemp. Rev." for August and October, 1875.

[2] Eusebius, *H. E.*, III. 39, closes his account of Papias with the notice : "He has likewise set forth another narrative [in his *Exposition of the Lord's Oracles*] concerning a woman who was maliciously accused before the Lord touching many sins, which is contained in the Gospel according to the Hebrews."

[3] In a tradition too late (ninth century) to be of any critical weight, Papias is even made the amanuensis of John in the preparation of his Gospel. A Vatican Codex (of Queen Christina of Sweden) has this marginal gloss : "*Evangelium Johannis manifestatum et datum est ecclesiis ab Johanne adhuc in corpore constituto ; sicut Papias, nomine Hieropolitanus discipulus Johannis carus, in exotericis [exegeticis], id est in extremis, quinque libris retulit* [referring no doubt to the five books of Λογίων Κυριακῶν ἐξηγήσεις]. *Descripsit vero evangelium dictante Johanne recte.*" This was hailed as a direct testimony of Papias for John by Prof. Aberle (Rom. Cath.) in the "Tübing. Quartalschrift," 1864, No. 1, but set aside by Hilgenfeld *versus* Aberle, in his "Zeitschrift," 1865, pp. 77 sqq., and Hase, *l.c* , p. 35. If Eusebius had found this notice in the work of Papias, he would have probably mentioned it in connection with his testimonies on the Gospels of Matthew and Mark. But see Westcott, *Canon*, 5th ed., p. 77, note 1.

of John, perhaps the very persons who, according to ancient tradition, urged him to write the Gospel. The book probably closed with the sentence: " This is the disciple who beareth witness of these things, and wrote these things." To this the elders add their attestation in the plural : " And *we* know that *his* witness is true." A literary fiction would not have been benefited by an anonymous postscript. The words as they stand are either a false testimony of the pseudo-John, or the true testimony of the friends of the real John who first received his book and published it before or after his death.

The voice of the whole Catholic church, so far as it is heard on the subject at all, is in favor of the authorship of John. There is not a shadow of proof to the contrary opinion except one, and that is purely negative and inconclusive. Baur to the very last laid the greatest stress on the entangled paschal controversy of the second century as a proof that John could not have written the fourth Gospel because he was quoted as an authority for the celebration of the Lord's Supper on the 14th of Nisan ; while the fourth Gospel, in flat contradiction to the Synoptists, puts the crucifixion on that day (instead of the 15th), and represents Christ as the true paschal lamb slain at the very time when the typical Jewish passover was slain. But, in the first place, some of the ablest scholars know how to reconcile John with the Synoptic date of the crucifixion on the 15th of Nisan ; and, secondly, there is no evidence at all that the apostle John celebrated Easter with the Quartodecimans on the 14th of Nisan in commemoration of the day of the *Lord's Supper*. The controversy was between conforming the celebration of the Christian Passover to the day of the *month*, that is to Jewish chronology, or to the day of the *week* on which Christ died. The former would have made Easter, more conveniently, a fixed festival like the Jewish Passover, the latter or Roman practice made it a movable feast, and this practice triumphed at the Council of Nicæa.[1]

[1] See Schürer's Latin dissertation *De controversiis paschalibus*, etc., Leipz., 1869, and the German translation in the " Zeitschrift für hist. Theol." for 1870, pp. 182–284.

2. *Heretical* testimonies. They are all the more important in view of their dissent from Catholic doctrine. It is remarkable that the heretics seem to have used and commented on the fourth Gospel even before the Catholic writers. The Clementine Homilies, besides several allusions, very clearly quote from the story of the man born blind, John 9 : 2, 3.[1] The Gnostics of the second century, especially the Valentinians and Basilidians, made abundant use of the fourth Gospel, which alternately offended them by its historical realism, and attracted them by its idealism and mysticism. Heracleon, a pupil of Valentinus, wrote a commentary on it, of which Origen has preserved large extracts; Valentinus himself (according to Tertullian) tried either to explain it away, or he put his own meaning into it. Basilides, who flourished about A.D. 125, quoted from the Gospel of John such passages as the "true light, which enlighteneth every man, was coming into the world" (1 : 9), and "my hour is not yet come" (2 : 4).[2]

These heretical testimonies are almost decisive by themselves. The Gnostics would rather have rejected the fourth Gospel altogether, as Marcion actually did, from doctrinal objection. They certainly would not have received it from the Catholic church, as little as the church would have received it from the Gnostics. The concurrent reception of the Gospel by both at so early a date is conclusive evidence of its genuineness. "The Gnostics of that date," says Dr. Abbot,[3] "received it because they could not help it. They would not have admitted the authority of a book which could be reconciled with their doctrines only by the most forced interpretation, if they could have destroyed its authority by denying its genuineness. Its genuineness could then be easily ascertained. Ephesus was one of the

---

[1] In the last portion of the book, discovered and first published by Dressel (XIX. 22). This discovery has induced Hilgenfeld to retract his former denial of the quotations in the earlier books, *Einleit. in d. N. T.*, p. 43 sq., note.

[2] See the *Philosophumena* of Hippolytus, VII. 22, 27 ; Hofstede de Groot, *Basilides*, trans. from the Dutch, Leipz., 1868 ; Hort, *Basilides*, in Smith and Wace, I. 271 ; Abbot, *l.c.*, 85 sqq.

[3] *L.c.*, p. 89.

principal cities of the Eastern world, the centre of extensive commerce, the metropolis of Asia Minor. Hundreds, if not thousands, of people were living who had known the apostle John. The question whether he, the beloved disciple, had committed to writing his recollections of his Master's life and teaching, was one of the greatest interest. The fact of the reception of the fourth Gospel as his work at so early a date, by parties so violently opposed to each other, proves that the evidence of its genuineness was decisive. This argument is further confirmed by the use of the Gospel by the opposing parties in the later Montanistic controversy, and in the disputes about the time of celebrating Easter."

3. *Heathen* testimony. Celsus, in his book against Christianity, which was written about A.D. 178 (according to Keim, who reconstructed it from the fragments preserved in the refutation of Origen), derives his matter for attack from the four Gospels, though he does not name their authors, and he refers to several details which are peculiar to John, as, among others, the blood which flowed from the body of Jesus at his crucifixion (John 19 : 34), and the fact that Christ "after his death arose and showed the marks of his punishment, and how his hands had been pierced" (20 : 25, 27).[1]

The radical assertion of Baur that no distinct trace of the fourth Gospel can be found before the last quarter of the second century has utterly broken down, and his own best pupils have been forced to make one concession after another as the successive discoveries of the many Gnostic quotations in the Philosophumena, the last book of the pseudo-Clementine Homilies, the Syrian Commentary on Tatian's Diatessaron, revealed the stubborn fact of the use and abuse of the Gospel before the middle and up to the very beginning of the second century, that is, to a time when it was simply impossible to mistake a pseudo-apostolic fiction for a genuine production of the patriarch of the apostolic age.

---

[1] See Keim, *Celsus' Wahres Wort*, 1873, pp. 223–230, besides the older investigations of Lardner, Norton, Tholuck, and the recent one of Dr. Abbot, *l.c.*, 58 sq.

II. INTERNAL EVIDENCE. This is even still stronger, and leaves at last no alternative but truth or fraud.

1. To begin with the *style* of the fourth Gospel, we have already seen that it is altogether unique and without a parallel in post-apostolic literature, betraying a Hebrew of the Hebrews, impregnated with the genius of the Old Testament, in mode of thought and expression, in imagery and symbolism, in the symmetrical structure of sentences, in the simplicity and circumstantiality of narration; yet familiar with pure Greek, from long residence among Greeks. This is just what we should expect from John at Ephesus. Though not a rabbinical scholar, like Paul, he was acquainted with the Hebrew Scriptures and not dependent on the Septuagint. He has in all fourteen quotations from the Old Testament.[1] Four of these agree with the Hebrew *and* the Septuagint; three agree with the Hebrew *against* the Septuagint (6 : 45; 13 : 18; 19 : 37), the rest are neutral, either agreeing with both or differing from both, or being free adaptations rather than citations; but none of them agrees with the Septuagint *against* the Hebrew.[2]

Among the post-apostolic writers there is no converted Jew, unless it be Hegesippus; none who could read the Hebrew and write Hebraistic Greek. After the destruction of Jerusalem the church finally separated from the synagogue and both assumed an attitude of uncompromising hostility.

2. The author was a *Jew of Palestine.* He gives, incidentally and without effort, unmistakable evidence of minute familiarity with the Holy Land and its inhabitants before the destruction of Jerusalem. He is at home in the localities of the holy city and the neighborhood. He describes Bethesda as "a pool by the sheep gate, having five porches" (5 : 2), Siloam as "a pool which is by interpretation Sent" (9 : 7), Solomon's porch as being "in the Temple" (10 : 23), the brook Kedron "where was a garden" (18 : 1); he knows the location of the prætorium (18 : 28),

---

[1] John 1 : 23; 2 : 17; 6 : 31, 45; 7 : 38; 10 : 34; 12 : 14, 38, 40; 13 : 18; 15 : 25; 19 : 24, 36, 37.

[2] See the careful analysis of the passages by Westcott, *Intr.*, pp. xiii sqq.

the meaning of Gabbatha (19 : 13), and Golgotha (19 : 17), the distance of Bethany from Jerusalem "about fifteen furlongs off" (11 : 18), and he distinguishes it from Bethany beyond Jordan (1 : 28). He gives the date when the Herodian reconstruction of the temple began (2 : 19). He is equally familiar with other parts of Palestine and makes no mistakes such as are so often made by foreigners. He locates Cana in Galilee (2 : 1; 4 : 26; 21 : 2), to distinguish it from another Cana; Aenon "near to Salim," where there are "many waters" (3 : 23); Sychar in Samaria near "Jacob's well," and in view of Mount Gerizim (4 : 5). He knows the extent of the Lake of Tiberias (6 : 19); he describes Bethsaida as "the city of Andrew and Peter" (1 : 44), as distinct from Bethsaida Julias on the eastern bank of the Jordan; he represents Nazareth as a place of proverbial insignificance (1 : 46).

He is well acquainted with the confused politico-ecclesiastical Messianic ideas and expectations of the Jews (1 : 19–28, 45–49; 4 : 25; 6 : 14, 15; 7 : 26; 12 : 34, and other passages); with the hostility between Jews and Samaritans (4 : 9, 20, 22; 8 : 48); with Jewish usages and observances, as baptism (1 : 25; 3 : 22, 23; 4 : 2), purification (2 : 6; 3 : 25, etc.), ceremonial pollution (18 : 28), feasts (2 : 13, 23; 5 : 1; 7 : 37, etc.), circumcision, and the Sabbath (7 : 22, 23). He is also acquainted with the marriage and burial rites (2 : 1–10; 11 : 17–44), with the character of the Pharisees and their influence in the Sanhedrin, the relationship between Annas and Caiaphas. The objection of Bretschneider that he represents the office of the high-priest as an *annual* office arose from a misunderstanding of the phrase "that year" (11 : 49, 51; 18 : 13), by which he means that *memorable* year in which Christ died for the sins of the people.

3. The author was an *eye-witness* of most of the events narrated. This appears from his life-like familiarity with the acting persons, the Baptist, Peter, Andrew, Philip, Nathanael, Thomas, Judas Iscariot, Pilate, Caiaphas, Annas, Nicodemus, Martha and Mary, Mary Magdalene, the woman of Samaria, the man born blind; and from the minute traits and vivid de-

tails which betray autopticity. He incidentally notices what the Synoptists omit, that the traitor was "the son of Simon" (6 : 71 ; 12 : 4; 13 : 2, 26), that Thomas was called "Didymus" (11 : 16 ; 20 : 24; 21 : 2); while, on the other hand, he calls the Baptist simply "John" (he himself being the other John), without adding to it the distinctive title as the Synoptists do more than a dozen times to distinguish him from the son of Zebedee.[1] He indicates the days and hours of certain events,[2] and the exact or approximate number of persons and objects mentioned.[3] He was privy to the thoughts of the disciples on certain occasions, their ignorance and misunderstanding of the words of the Master,[4] and even to the motives and feelings of the Lord.[5]

No literary artist could have invented the conversation of Christ with Nicodemus on the mystery of spiritual regeneration (ch. 3), or the conversation with the woman of Samaria (ch. 4), or the characteristic details of the catechization of the man born blind, which brings out so naturally the proud and heartless bigotry of the Jewish hierarchy and the rough, outspoken honesty and common sense of the blind man and his parents (9 : 13–34). The scene at Jacob's well, described in the fourth chapter, presents a most graphic, and yet unartificial picture of nature and human life as it still remains, though in decay, at the foot of Gerizim and Ebal : there is the well of Jacob in a

---

[1] "*Johannes als der Erzählende, in seinem Selbstbewusstsein, bedarf für den anderen Johannes des Beinamens nicht, ihm liegt die Verwechslung ganz fern.*" Hase, *Geschichte Jesu*, p. 48. The former belief of the venerable historian of Jena in the full Johannean authorship of the fourth Gospel was unfortunately shaken in his conflict with the Tübingen giant, but he declares the objections of Baur after all inconclusive, and seeks an escape from the dilemma by the untenable compromise that the oral teaching of John a few years after his death was committed to writing and somewhat mystified by an able pupil. "*Die Botschaft hört er wohl, allein ihm fehlt der Glaube.*"

[2] 1 : 29, 35, 39, 43; 2 : 1; 4 : 6, 40, 43, 52 ; 6 : 22; 7 : 14, 37 ; 11 · 6, 17, 39 ; 12 : 1, 12 ; 13 : 30; 18 : 28 ; 19 : 31 ; 20 : 1, 19, 26 ; 21 : 4.

[3] 1 : 35 ; 2 : 6; 4 : 18; 6 : 9, 10. 19; 19 : 23, 39 ; 21 : 8, 11.

[4] 2 : 17, 22 ; 4 : 27 ; 6 : 60 ; 12 : 16 ; 13 : 22, 28 ; 20 : 9 ; 21 : 12.

[5] 2 : 24, 25 ; 4 : 1–3; 5 : 6; 6 : 6, 15; 7 : 1 ; 11 : 33, 38 ; 13 : 1, 3, 11, 21 ; 16 : 19; 18 : 4; 19 : 28.

fertile, well-watered valley, there the Samaritan sanctuary on the top of Mount Gerizim, there the waving grain-fields ripening for the harvest; we are confronted with the historic antagonism of Jews and Samaritans which survives in the Nablus of to-day; there we see the genuine humanity of Jesus, as he sat down "wearied with his journey," though not weary of his work, his elevation above the rabbinical prejudice of conversing with a woman, his superhuman knowledge and dignity; there is the curiosity and quick-wittedness of the Samaritan Magdalene; and how natural is the transition from the water of Jacob's well to the water of life, and from the hot dispute of the place of worship to the highest conception of God as an omnipresent spirit, and his true worship in spirit and in truth.[1]

4. The writer represents *himself* expressly as an *eye-witness* of the life of Christ. He differs from the Synoptists, who never use the first person nor mix their subjective feelings with the narrative. "*We* beheld his glory," he says, in the name of all the apostles and primitive disciples, in stating the general impression made upon them by the incarnate Logos dwelling.[2] And in the parallel passage of the first Epistle, which is an inseparable companion of the fourth Gospel, he asserts with solemn emphasis his personal knowledge of the incarnate Word of life whom he heard with his ears and saw with his eyes and handled

---

[1] "How often has this fourth chapter been read since by Christian pilgrims on the very spot where the Saviour rested, with the irresistible impression that every word is true and adapted to the time and place, yet applicable to all times and places. Jacob's well is now in ruins and no more used, but the living spring of water which the Saviour first opened there to a poor, sinful, yet penitent woman is as deep and fresh as ever, and will quench the thirst of souls to the end of time." So I wrote in 1871 for the English edition of Lange's *Com. on John*, p. 151. Six years afterward I fully realized my anticipations, when with a company of friends I sat down on Jacob's well and read the fourth chapter of John as I never read it before. Palestine, even in "the imploring beauty of decay," is indeed a "fifth Gospel" which sheds more light on the four than many a commentary brimful of learning and critical conjectures.

[2] 1 : 14 : ἐθεασάμεθα τὴν δόξαν.-θεάομαι is richer than ὁράω, and means to behold or contemplate with admiration and delight. The plural adds force to the statement, as in 21 : 24 ; 1 John 1 : 1 ; 2 Pet. 1 : 16.

with his hands (1 John 1 : 1–3).   This assertion is general, and
covers the whole public life of our Lord.   But he makes it also
in particular a case of special interest for the realness of Christ's
humanity ; in recording the flow of blood and water from the
wounded side, he adds emphatically : " He that *hath seen* hath
borne witness, and his witness is true : and he knoweth that he
saith things that are true, that ye also may believe " (19 : 35).
Here we are driven to the alternative : either the writer was a
true witness of what he relates, or he was a false witness who
wrote down a deliberate lie.

5. Finally, the writer intimates that he is one of the *Twelve*,
that he is one of the favorite *three*, that he is not Peter, nor
James, that he is none other than the beloved *John* who leaned
on the Master's bosom.   He never names himself, nor his brother
James, nor his mother Salome, but he has a very modest, delicate, and altogether unique way of indirect self-designation.
He stands behind his Gospel like a mysterious figure with a
thin veil over his face without ever lifting the veil.   He leaves
the reader to infer the name by combination.   He is undoubtedly
that unnamed disciple who, with Andrew, was led to Jesus by
the testimony of the Baptist on the banks of the Jordan (1 : 35–
40), the disciple who at the last Supper " was reclining at the
table in Jesus' bosom " (13 : 23–25), that " other disciple " who,
with Peter, followed Jesus into the court of the high-priest
(18 : 15, 16), who stood by the cross and was intrusted by the
dying Lord with the care of His mother (19 : 26, 27), and that
" other disciple whom Jesus loved," who went with Peter to the
empty sepulchre on the resurrection morning and was convinced
of the great fact by the sight of the grave-cloths, and the head-
cover rolled up in a place by itself (20 : 2–8).   All these narratives are interwoven with autobiographic details.   He calls
himself " the disciple whom Jesus loved," not from vanity (as
has been most strangely asserted by some critics), but in blessed
and thankful remembrance of the infinite mercy of his divine
Master who thus fulfilled the prophecy of his name *Johanan*,
i.e., Jehovah is gracious.   In that peculiar love of his all-beloved

Lord was summed up for him the whole significance of his life.

With this mode of self-designation corresponds the designation of members of his family: his mother is probably meant by the unnamed "sister of the mother" of Jesus, who stood by the cross (John 19 : 25), for Salome was there, according to the Synoptists, and John would hardly omit this fact; and in the list of the disciples to whom Jesus appeared at the Lake of Galilee, "the sons of Zebedee" are put last (21 : 2), when yet in all the Synoptic lists of the apostles they are, with Peter and Andrew, placed at the head of the Twelve. This difference can only be explained from motives of delicacy and modesty.

What a contrast the author presents to those pseudonymous literary forgers of the second and third centuries, who unscrupulously put their writings into the mouth of the apostles or other honored names to lend them a fictitious charm and authority; and yet who cannot conceal the fraud which leaks out on every page.

Conclusion.

A review of this array of testimonies, external and internal, drives us to the irresistible conclusion that the fourth Gospel is the work of John, the apostle. This view is clear, self-consistent, and in full harmony with the character of the book and the whole history of the apostolic age; while the hypothesis of a literary fiction and pious fraud is contradictory, absurd, and self-condemned. No writer in the second century could have produced such a marvellous book, which towers high above all the books of Justin Martyr and Irenæus and Tertullian and Clement and Origen, or any other father or schoolman or reformer. No writer in the first century could have written it but an apostle, and no apostle but John, and John himself could not have written it without divine inspiration.

§ 84. *Critical Review of the Johannean Problem.*

See the Liter. in ¿ 40, pp. 408 sqq., and the history of the controversy by HOLTZMANN, in Bunsen's *Bibelwerk*, VIII. 56 sqq. ; REUSS, *Gesch. der heil. Schriften N. T.'s* (6th ed.), I. 248 sqq. ; GODET, *Com.* (3d ed.), I. 32 sqq. ; HOLTZMANN, *Einleitung* (2d ed.), 423 sqq. ; WEISS, *Einleitung* (1886), 609 sqq.

The importance of the subject justifies a special section on the opposition to the fourth Gospel, after we have presented our own view on the subject with constant reference to the recent objections.

THE PROBLEM STATED.

The Johannean problem is the burning question of modern criticism on the soil of the New Testament. It arises from the difference between John and the Synoptists on the one hand, and the difference between the fourth Gospel and the Apocalypse on the other.

I. The *Synoptic* aspect of the problem includes the differences between the first three Evangelists and the fourth concerning the theatre and length of Christ's ministry, the picture of Christ, the nature and extent of his discourses, and a number of minor details. It admits the following possibilities:

(1.) Both the Synoptists and John are historical, and represent only different aspects of the same person and work of Christ, supplementing and confirming each other in every essential point. This is the faith of the Church and the conviction of nearly all conservative critics and commentators.

(2.) The fourth Gospel is the work of John, and, owing to his intimacy with Christ, it is more accurate and reliable than the Synoptists, who contain some legendary embellishments and even errors, derived from oral tradition, and must be rectified by John. This is the view of Schleiermacher, Lücke, Bleek, Ewald, Meyer, Weiss, and a considerable number of liberal critics and exegetes who yet accept the substance of the whole gospel history as true, and Christ as the Lord and Saviour of the race. The difference between these scholars and the church tradition is not fundamental, and admits of adjustment.

(3.) The Synoptists represent (in the main) the Christ of history, the fourth Gospel the ideal Christ of faith and fiction. So Baur and the Tübingen school (Schwegler, Zeller, Köstlin, Hilgenfeld, Volkmar, Holtzmann, Hausrath, Schenkel, Mangold, Keim, Thoma), with their followers and sympathizers in France (Nicolas, d'Eichthal, Renan, Réville, Sabatier), Holland (Scholten and the Leyden school), and England (the anonymous author of "Supernatural Religion," Sam. Davidson, Edwin A. Abbott). But these critics eliminate the miraculous even from the Synoptic Christ, at least as far as possible, and approach the fourth hypothesis.

(4.) The Synoptic and Johannean Gospels are alike fictitious, and resolve themselves into myths and legends or pious frauds. This is the position of the extreme left wing of modern criticism represented chiefly by Strauss. It is the legitimate result of the denial of the supernatural and miraculous, which is as inseparable from the Synoptic as it is from the Johannean Christ; but it is also subversive of all history and cannot be seriously maintained in the face of overwhelming facts and results. Hence there has been a considerable reaction among the radical critics in favor of a more historical position. Keim's "History of Jesus of Nazara" is a very great advance upon Strauss's "Leben Jesu," though equally critical and more learned, and meets the orthodox view half way on the ground of the Synoptic tradition, as represented in the Gospel of Matthew, which he dates back to A.D. 66.

II. The *Apocalyptic* aspect of the Johannean problem belongs properly to the consideration of the Apocalypse, but it has of late been inseparably interwoven with the Gospel question. It admits likewise of four distinct views:

(1.) The fourth Gospel and the Apocalypse are both from the pen of the apostle John, but separated by the nature of the subject, the condition of the writer, and an interval of at least twenty or thirty years, to account for the striking differences of temper and style. When he met Paul at Jerusalem, A.D. 50, he was one of the three "pillar-apostles" of Jewish Christianity (Gal. 2 : 9), but probably less than forty years of age, remarkably silent with his reserved force, and sufficiently in sympathy with Paul to give him the right hand of fellowship; when he wrote the Apocalypse, between A.D. 68 and 70, he was not yet sixty, and when he wrote the Gospel he was over eighty years of age. Moreover, the differences between the two books are more than counterbalanced by an underlying harmony. This has been acknowledged even by the head of the Tübingen critics, who calls the fourth Gospel an Apocalypse spiritualized or a transfiguration of the Apocalypse.[1]

(2.) John wrote the Gospel, but not the Apocalypse. Many critics of the moderate school are disposed to surrender the Apocalypse and to assign it to the somewhat doubtful and mysterious "Presbyter John," a contemporary of the Apostle John. So Schleiermacher, Lücke, Bleek, Neander, Ewald, Düsterdieck, etc. If we are to choose between the two books, the Gospel has no doubt stronger claims upon our acceptance.

(3.) John wrote the Apocalypse, but for this very reason he cannot have written the fourth Gospel. So Baur, Renan, Davidson, Abbott, and nearly all the radical critics (except Keim).

(4.) The fourth Gospel and the Apocalypse are both spurious and the work of the Gnostic Cerinthus (as the Alogi held), or of some anonymous forger. This view is so preposterous and unsound that no critic of any reputation for learning and judgment dares to defend it.

There is a correspondence between the four possible attitudes on both aspects of the Johannean question, and the parties advocating them.

The result of the conflict will be the substantial triumph of the faith of the church which accepts, on new grounds of evidence, all the four Gospels as genuine and historical, and the Apocalypse and the fourth Gospel as the works of John.

[1] See p. 419 sq., and my *Companion to the Greek Testament*, pp. 76 sqq.

The Assaults on the Fourth Gospel.

Criticism has completely shifted its attitude on both parts of the problem. The change is very remarkable. When the first serious assault was made upon the genuineness of the fourth Gospel by the learned General Superintendent Bretschneider (in 1820), he was met with such overwhelming opposition, not only from evangelical divines like Olshausen and Tholuck, but also from Schleiermacher, Lücke, Credner, and Schott, that he honestly confessed his defeat a few years afterward (1824 and 1828).[1] And when Dr. Strauss, in his *Leben Jesu* (1835), renewed the denial, a host of old and new defenders arose with such powerful arguments that he himself (as he confessed in the third edition of 1838) was shaken in his doubt, especially by the weight and candor of Neander, although he felt compelled, in self-defence, to reaffirm his doubt as essential to the mythical hypothesis (in the fourth edition, 1840, and afterward in his popular *Leben Jesu*, 1864).

But in the meantime his teacher, Dr. Baur, the coryphæus of the Tübingen school, was preparing his heavy ammunition, and led the second, the boldest, the most vigorous and effective assault upon the Johannean fort (since 1844).[2] He was followed in the main question, though with considerable modifications in detail, by a number of able and acute critics in Germany and other countries. He represented the fourth Gospel as a purely ideal work which grew out of the Gnostic, Monta-

---

[1] Before him Edward Evanson, an ex-clergyman of the Church of England, had attacked John and all other Gospels except Luke, in *The Dissonance of the Four generally received Evangelists*, 1792. He was refuted by the Unitarian, Dr. Priestley, who came to the conclusion that the Gospel of John "bears more internal and unequivocal marks of being written by an eye-witness than any other writings whatever, sacred or profane." See his *Letters to a Young Man* (*Works*, vol. XX. 430).

[2] *Ueber die Composition und den Charakter des joh. Evangeliums*, an essay in the "Theol. Jahrbücher" of Zeller, Tübingen, 1844 ; again in his *Krit. Untersuchungen über die kanon. Evang.*, Tüb., 1847. and in his *Kirchengesch.*, 1853 (vol. I., pp. 146 sqq., 166 sqq., third ed.). Godet (I. 17) calls the first dissertation of Baur justly " one of the most ingenious and brilliant compositions which theological science ever produced."

nistic, and paschal controversies after the middle of the second century, and adjusted the various elements of the Catholic faith with consummate skill and art. It was not intended to be a history, but a system of theology in the garb of history. This "tendency" hypothesis was virtually a death-blow to the mythical theory of Strauss, which excludes conscious design.

The third great assault inspired by Baur, yet with independent learning and judgment, was made by Dr. Keim (in his *Geschichte Jesu von Nazara*, 1867). He went beyond Baur in one point: he denied the whole tradition of John's sojourn in Ephesus as a mistake of Irenæus; he thus removed even the foundation for the defence of the Apocalypse as a Johannean production, and neutralized the force of the Tübingen assault derived from that book. On the other hand, he approached the traditional view by tracing the composition back from 170 (Baur) to the reign of Trajan, *i.e.*, to within a few years after the death of the apostle. In his denial of the Ephesus tradition he met with little favor,[1] but strong opposition from the Tübingen critics, who see the fatal bearing of this denial upon the genuineness of the Apocalypse.[2] The effect of Keim's movement therefore tended rather to divide and demoralize the besieging force.

Nevertheless the effect of these persistent attacks was so great that three eminent scholars, Hase of Jena (1876), Reuss of Strassburg, and Sabatier of Paris (1879), deserted from the camp of the defenders to the army of the besiegers. Renan, too, who had in the thirteenth edition of his *Vie de Jesus* (1867) defended the fourth Gospel at least in part, has now (since 1879, in his *L'Église chrétienne*) given it up entirely.[3]

---

[1] From Wittichen and Scholten.

[2] Especially from Hilgenfeld. The tradition of the Ephesian sojourn of John is one of the strongest and most constant in the ancient church, and goes back to Polycrates, Irenæus, Polycarp, and Papias, the very pupils and grandpupils of John, who could not possibly be mistaken on such a simple fact as this.

[3] Dr. Weiss (*Leben Jesu*, I. 106) accords to Dr. Baur the merit of having penetrated deeper into the peculiar character of the fourth Gospel and done more for the promotion of its understanding than the mechanical old exegesis,

THE DEFENCE OF THE FOURTH GOSPEL.

The incisive criticism of Baur and his school compelled a thorough reinvestigation of the whole problem, and in this way has been of very great service to the cause of truth. We owe to it the ablest defences of the Johannean authorship of the fourth Gospel and the precious history which it represents. Prominent among these defenders against the latest attacks were Bleek, Lange, Ebrard, Thiersch, Schneider, Tischendorf, Riggenbach, Ewald, Steitz, Aberle, Meyer, Luthardt, Wieseler, Beyschlag, Weiss, among the Germans; Godet, Pressensé, Astié, among the French; Niermeyer, Van Oosterzee, Hofstede de Groot, among the Dutch; Alford, Milligan, Lightfoot, Westcott, Sanday, Plummer, among the English; Fisher, and Abbot among the Americans.[1]

It is significant that the school of negative criticism has produced no learned commentary on John. All the recent commentators on the fourth Gospel (Lücke, Ewald, Lange, Hengstenberg, Luthardt, Meyer, Weiss, Alford, Wordsworth, Godet, Westcott, Milligan, Moulton, Plummer, etc.) favor its genuineness.

which had no conception of the difference and looked only for *dicta probantia ;* but he justly adds that Baur's criticism is "sicklied all over with the pale cast" of modern philosophical construction (*von der Blässe moderner philosophischer Construction angekränkelt*). We are prepared to say the same of Dr. Keim, a proud, but noble and earnest spirit who died of overwork in elaborating his History of Jesus of Nazara. The most scholarly, high-toned, and singularly able argument in the English language against the Johannean authorship of the fourth Gospel is the article "Gospels" in the "Encycl. Brit.," 9th ed., vol. X. 818–843 (1879), from the pen of Dr. Edwin A. Abbott, head-master of the City of London School.

[1] Without detracting from the merits of the many worthy champions of the cause of truth, I venture to give the palm to Dr. Godet, of Neuchâtel, in the introductory volume to his *third* and thoroughly revised Commentary on John (*Introduction historique et critique*, Paris, 1881, 376 pages), and to Dr. Weiss, of Berlin, in his very able *Leben Jesu*, Berlin, 1882, vol. I. 84–198. In England the battle has been fought chiefly by Bishop Lightfoot, Canon Westcott, Prof. Milligan, and Dr. Sanday. In America, Dr. Ezra Abbott (1880) is equal to any of them in the accurate and effective presentation of the historical argument for the Johannean authorship of the fourth Gospel. His treatise has been reprinted in his *Critical Essays*, Boston, 1888 (pp. 9–107).

The Difficulties of the Anti-Johannean Theory.

The prevailing theory of the negative critics is this: They accept the Synoptic Gospels, with the exception of the miracles, as genuine history, but for this very reason they reject John; and they accept the Apocalypse as the genuine work of the apostle John, who is represented by the Synoptists as a Son of Thunder, and by Paul (Gal. 2) as one of the three pillars of conservative Jewish Christianity, but for this very reason they deny that he can have written the Gospel, which in style and spirit differs so widely from the Apocalypse. For this position they appeal to the fact that the Synoptists and the Apocalypse are equally well, and even better supported by internal and external evidence, and represent a tradition which is at least twenty years older.

But what then becomes of the fourth Gospel? It is incredible that the real John should have falsified the history of his Master; consequently the Gospel which bears his name is a post-apostolic fiction, a religious poem, or a romance on the theme of the incarnate Logos. It is the Gospel of Christian Gnosticism, strongly influenced by the Alexandrian philosophy of Philo. Yet it is no fraud any more than other literary fictions. The unknown author dealt with the historical Jesus of the Synoptists, as Plato dealt with Socrates, making him simply the base for his own sublime speculations, and putting speeches into his mouth which he never uttered.

Who was that Christian Plato? No critic can tell, or even conjecture, except Renan, who revived, as possible at least, the absurd view of the Alogi, that the Gnostic heretic, Cerinthus, the enemy of John, wrote the fourth Gospel![1] Such a conjec-

---

[1] "*Tout est possible*," says Renan (*L'Église chrét.*, p. 54), " *à ces époques ténébreuses ; et, si l'Église, en vénérant le quatrième Évangile comme l'œuvre de Jean, est dupe de celui qu'elle regarde comme un de ses plus dangereux ennemis, cela n'est pas en somme plus étrange que tant d'autres malentendus qui composent la trame de l'histoire religieuse de l'humanité. Ce qu'il y a de sûr, c'est que l'auteur est à la fois le père et l'adversaire du gnosticisme, l'ennemi de ceux qui laissaient s'évaporer dans un docétisme nuageux l'humanité réelle de Jésus et le*

ture requires an extraordinary stretch of imagination and an amazing amount of credulity. The more sober among the critics suppose that the author was a highly gifted Ephesian disciple of John, who freely reproduced and modified his oral teaching after he was removed by death. But how could his name be utterly unknown, when the names of Polycarp and Papias and other disciples of John, far less important, have come down to us? "The great unknown" is a mystery indeed. Some critics, half in sympathy with Tübingen, are willing to admit that John himself wrote a part of the book, either the historic narratives or the discourses, but neither of these compromises will do: the book is a unit, and is either wholly genuine or wholly a fiction.

Nor are the negative critics agreed as to the time of composition. Under tne increasing pressure of argument and evidence they have been forced to retreat, step by step, from the last quarter of the second century to the first, even within a few years of John's death, and within the lifetime of hundreds of his hearers, when it was impossible for a pseudo-Johannean book to pass into general currency without the discovery of the fraud. Dr. Baur and Schwegler assigned the composition to A.D. 170 or 160; Volkmar to 155; Zeller to 150; Scholten to 140; Hilgenfeld to about 130; Renan to about 125; Schenkel to 120 or 115; until Keim (in 1867) went up as high as 110 or even 100, but having reached such an early date, he felt compelled (1875)[1] in self-defence to advance again to 130, and this notwithstanding the conceded testimonies of Justin Martyr and the early Gnostics. These vacillations of criticism reveal the impossibility of locating the Gospel in the second century.

If we surrender the fourth Gospel, what shall we gain in its place? Fiction for fact, stone for bread, a Gnostic dream for the most glorious truth.

---

complice de ceux qui le reléguaient dans l'abstraction divine." He thinks it more probable, however (p. 47), that two Ephesian disciples of John (John the Presbyter and Aristion) wrote the Gospel twenty or thirty years after his death.

[1] In the last edition of his abridged Geschichte Jesu.

Fortunately the whole anti-Johannean hypothesis breaks down at every point. It suffers shipwreck on innumerable details which do not fit at all into the supposed dogmatic scheme, but rest on hard facts of historical recollections.[1]

And instead of removing any difficulties it creates greater difficulties in their place. There are certain contradictions which no ingenuity can solve. If "the great unknown" was the creative artist of his ideal Christ, and the inventor of those sublime discourses, the like of which were never heard before or since, he must have been a mightier genius than Dante or Shakespeare, yea greater than his own hero, that is greater than the greatest: this is a psychological impossibility and a logical absurdity. Moreover, if he was not John and yet wanted to be known as John, he was a deceiver and a liar:[2] this is a moral impossibility. The case of Plato is very different, and his relation to Socrates is generally understood. The Synoptic Gospels are anonymous, but do not deceive the reader. Luke and the author of the Epistle to the Hebrews honestly make themselves known as mere disciples of the apostles. The real parallel would be the apocryphal Gospels and the pseudo-Clementine productions, where the fraud is unmistakable, but the contents are so far below the fourth Gospel that a comparison is out of the question. Literary fictions were not uncommon in the ancient church, but men had common sense and moral sense then as well as now to distinguish between fact and fiction, truth and lie. It is simply incredible that the ancient church should have been duped into a unanimous acceptance of such an important book as the work of the beloved disciple almost from the very date of his death, and that the whole Christian church, Greek, Latin,

---

[1] As Weiss (I. 109) admirably expresses it : "*Ueberall im Einzelnen, wie in der Gesammtgestaltung des Lebens Jesu stossen wir auf das harte Gestein geschichtlicher Erinnerung, welches dem kritischen Auflösungsprozess, der es in ideelle Bildungen verwandeln will, unüberwindlichen Widerstand leistet.*"

[2] "*Als die Dichtung eines halbgnostischen Philosophen aus dem zweiten Jahrhundert ist es* [the fourth Gospel] *ein trügerisches Irrlicht, ja in Wahrheit eine grosse Lüge,*" Weiss, I. 124. Renan admits the alternative, only in milder terms : "*Il y a là un petit artifice littéraire, du genre de ceux qu'affectionne Platon,*" l.c., p. 52.

Protestant, including an innumerable army of scholars, should
have been under a radical delusion for eighteen hundred years,
mistaking a Gnostic dream for the genuine history of the
Saviour of mankind, and drinking the water of life from the
muddy source of fraud.[1]

In the meantime the fourth Gospel continues and will continue to shine, like the sun in heaven, its own best evidence, and
will shine all the brighter when the clouds, great and small, shall
have passed away.

§ 85. *The Acts of the Apostles.*

Comp. § 82.

1. *Critical Treatises.*

M. Schneckenburger : *Zweck der Apostelgeschichte.* Bern, 1841.
Schwanbeck : *Quellen der Ap. Gesch.* Darmstadt, 1847.
Ed. Zeller : *Contents and Origin of the Acts of the Apostles.* Stuttg.,
1854 ; trsl. by *Jos. Dare,* 1875–76, London, 2 vols.
Lekebusch : *Composition u. Entstehung der Ap. Gesch.* Gotha, 1854.
Klostermann : *Vindiciæ Lucanæ.* Göttingen, 1866.
Arthur König (R. C.) : *Die Aechtheit der Ap. Gesch.* Breslau, 1867.
J. R. Oertel : *Paulus in der Ap. Gesch. Der histor. Char. dieser Schrift,*
etc. Halle, 1868.
J. B. Lightfoot : *Illustrations of the Acts from recent Discoveries,* in the
"Contemporary Review" for May, 1878, pp. 288–296.
Dean Howson : *Bohlen Lectures on the Evidential Value of the Acts of the
Apostles,* delivered in Philadelphia, 1880. London and New York,
1880.
Friedr. Zimmer : *Galaterbrief und Apostelgeschichte.* Hildburghausen,
1882.
Comp. also, in part, J. H. Scholten : *Das Paulinische Evangelium,* trsl.
from the Dutch by *Redepenning,* Elberf., 1881. A critical essay on
the writings of Luke (pp. 254 sqq.).

---

[1] This absurdity is strikingly characterized in the lines of the Swabian poet,
Gustav Schwab, which he gave me when I was a student at Tübingen shortly
after the appearance of Strauss's *Leben Jesu :*

> " *Hat dieses Buch, das ew'ge Wahrheit ist,*
> *Ein lügenhafter Gnostiker geschrieben,*
> *So hat seit tausend Jahren Jesus Christ*
> *Den Teufel durch Beelzebub vertrieben.*"

2. *Commentaries on Acts.*

By CHRYSOSTOM ; JEROME ; CALVIN ; OLSHAUSEN ; DE WETTE (4th ed., revised by *Overbeck*, 1870) ; MEYER (4th ed., 1870 ; 5th ed., revised by *Wendt*, 1880) ; BAUMGARTEN (in 2 parts, 1852, Engl. transl. in 3 vols., Edinburgh, 1856) ; Jos. A. ALEXANDER ; H. B. HACKETT (2d ed., 1858 ; 3d ed., 1877) ; EWALD (1872) ; LECHLER-GEROK (in Lange's *Bibelwerk*, transl. by *Schœffer*, N. Y., 1866) ; F. C. COOK (Lond., 1866) ; ALFORD ; WORDSWORTH ; GLOAG ; PLUMPTRE (in Ellicott's Com.) ; JACOBSON (in the "Speaker's Com.," 1880) ; LUMBY (in the "Cambridge Bible for Schools," 1880) ; HOWSON and SPENCE (in Schaff's "Popul. Com.," 1880 ; revised for "Revision Com.," N. Y., 1882) ; K. SCHMIDT (*Die Apostelgesch. unter dem Hauptgesichtspunkt ihrer Glaubwürdigkeit kritisch exegetisch bearbeitet*. Erlangen, 1882, 2 vols.) ; NÖSGEN (Leipz. 1882), BETHGE (1887).

THE ACTS AND THE THIRD GOSPEL.

The book of Acts, though placed by the ancient ecclesiastical division not in the " Gospel," but in the " Apostle," is a direct continuation of the third Gospel, by the same author, and addressed to the same Theophilus, probably a Christian convert of distinguished social position. In the former he reports what he heard and read, in the latter what he heard and saw. The one records the life and work of Christ, the other the work of the Holy Spirit, who is recognized at every step. The word Spirit, or Holy Spirit, occurs more frequently in the Acts than in any other book of the New Testament. It might properly be called " the Gospel of the Holy Spirit."

The universal testimony of the ancient church traces the two books to the same author. This is confirmed by internal evidence of identity of style, continuity of narrative, and correspondence of plan. About fifty words not found elsewhere in the New Testament are common to both books.[1]

---

[1] See the conclusive proof in Zeller, pp. 414–452 (Engl. transl. by Dare, vol. II. 213–254). Holtzmann (*Syn. Evang.*, p. 375) : " *Als ausgemacht darf man heutzutage wohl annehmen, dass der Verfasser der Apostelgeschichte und des dritten Evangeliums ein und dieselbe Person sind.*" Renan speaks in the same confident tone (*Les Apôtres*, pp. x. and xi.) : " *Une chose hors de doute, c'est que les Actes ont eut le même auteur que le troisième évangile et sont une continuation de cet évangile. . . . La parfaite ressemblance du style et des idées*

OBJECT AND CONTENTS.

The Acts is a cheerful and encouraging book, like the third Gospel ; it is full of missionary zeal and hope ; it records progress after progress, conquest after conquest, and turns even persecution and martyrdom into an occasion of joy and thanksgiving. It is the first church history. It begins in Jerusalem and ends in Rome. An additional chapter would probably have recorded the terrible persecution of Nero and the heroic martyrdom of Paul and Peter. But this would have made the book a tragedy ; instead of that it ends as cheerfully and triumphantly as it begins.

It represents the origin and progress of Christianity from the capital of Judaism to the capital of heathenism. It is a history of the planting of the church among the Jews by Peter, and among the Gentiles by Paul. Its theme is expressed in the promise of the risen Christ to his disciples (1 : 8) : " Ye shall receive power, when the Holy Spirit is come upon you (ch. 2) : and ye shall be my witnesses both in Jerusalem (chs. 3–7), and in all Judæa and Samaria (chs. 8–12), and unto the uttermost part of the earth " (chs. 13–28). The Gospel of Luke, which is the Pauline Gospel, laid the foundation by showing how salvation, coming from the Jews and opposed by the Jews, was intended for all men, Samaritans and Gentiles. The Acts exhibits the progress of the church from and among the Jews to the Gentiles by the ministry of Peter, then of Stephen, then of Philip in Samaria, then of Peter again in the conversion of Cornelius, and at last by the labors of Paul and his companions.[1]

---

fournissent à cet égard d'abondantes démonstrations. . . . *Les deux livres réunis font un ensemble absolument du même style, présentant les mêmes locutions favorites et la même façon de citer l'écriture.*" Scholten dissents from this view and vainly tries to show that while both books originated in the school of Paul, the third evangelist elevates Paulinism above Jewish Christianity, and the author of Acts recommends Paul to the Jewish-Christian party. The Gospel is polemical, the Acts apologetic. *Das Paulinische Evangelium,* etc., transl. from the Dutch by Redepenning, Elberf., 1881, p. 315.

[1] The history of the Reformation furnishes a parallel ; namely, the further progress of Christianity from Rome (the Christian Jerusalem) to Wittenberg,

The Acts begins with the ascension of Christ, or his accession to his throne, and the founding of his kingdom by the outpouring of the Holy Spirit; it closes with the joyful preaching of the Apostle of the Gentiles in the capital of the then known world.

The objective representation of the progress of the church is the chief aim of the work, and the subjective and biographical features are altogether subordinate. Before Peter, the hero of the first or Jewish-Christian division, and Paul, the hero of the second or Gentile-Christian part, the other apostles retire and are only once named, except John, the elder James, Stephen, and James, the brother of the Lord. Even the lives of the pillar-apostles appear in the history only so far as they are connected with the missionary work. In this view the long-received title of the book, added by some other hand than the author's, is not altogether correct, though in keeping with ancient usage (as in the apocryphal literature, which includes "Acts of Pilate," "Acts of Peter and Paul," "Acts of Philip," etc.). More than three-fifths of it are devoted to Paul, and especially to his later labors and journeys, in which the author could speak from personal knowledge. The book is simply a selection of biographical memoirs of Peter and Paul connected with the planting of Christianity or the beginnings of the church (*Origines Ecclesiæ*).

Sources.

Luke, the faithful pupil and companion of Paul, was eminently fitted to produce the history of the primitive church. For the first part he had the aid not only of oral tradition, but also of Palestinian documents, as he had in preparing his Gospel. Hence the Hebrew coloring in the earlier chapters of Acts; while afterward he writes as pure Greek, as in the classical prologue of his Gospel. Most of the events in the second part came under his personal observation. Hence he often speaks

Geneva, Oxford and Edinburgh, through the labors of Luther, Calvin, Cranmer and Knox.

in the plural number, modestly including himself.[1]   The " we "
sections begin ch. 16 : 10, when Paul started from Troas to
Macedonia (A.D. 51); they break off when he leaves Philippi
for Corinth (17 : 1); they are resumed (20 : 5, 6) when he visits
Macedonia again seven years later (58), and then continue to
the close of the narrative (A.D. 63).   Luke probably remained
several years at Philippi, engaged in missionary labors, until
Paul's return.   He was in the company of Paul, including the
interruptions, at least twelve years.   He was again with Paul
in his last captivity, shortly before his martyrdom, his most
faithful and devoted companion (2 Tim. 4 : 11).

Time of Composition.

Luke probably began the book of Acts or a preliminary diary
during his missionary journeys with Paul in Greece, especially
in Philippi, where he seems to have tarried several years; he
continued it in Cæsarea, where he had the best opportunity to
gather reliable information of the earlier history, from Jerusalem, and such living witnesses as Cornelius and his friends,
from Philip and his daughters, who resided in Cæsarea; and
he finished it soon after Paul's first imprisonment in Rome,
before the terrible persecution in the summer of 64, which he
could hardly have left unnoticed.

We look in vain for any allusion to this persecution and the
martyrdom of Paul or Peter, or to any of their Epistles, or to
the destruction of Jerusalem, or to the later organization of the
church, or the superiority of the bishop over the presbyter
(Comp. 20 : 17, 28), or the Gnostic heresies, except by way of
prophetic warning (20 : 30).   This silence in a historical work

---

[1] Ewald, in his Commentary on Acts (1872). pp. 35 sqq., infers from the use
of the little word *we* and its connection with the other portions that the whole
work is from one and the same author, who is none other than Luke of Antioch, the " beloved " friend and colaborer of Paul.   Renan says (*Les apôtres*,
p. xiv.) : " *Je persiste à croire que le dernier rédacteur des Actes est bien le disciple de Paul qui dit ' nous' aux derniers chapitres*," but he puts the composition down to A.D. 71 or 72 (p. xx.), and in his *Les Évangiles*, ch. xix., pp. 435
sqq., still later, to the age of Domitian.

like this seems inexplicable on the assumption that the book was written *after* A.D. 70, or even after 64. But if we place the composition *before* the martyrdom of Paul, then the last verse is after all an appropriate conclusion of a missionary history of Christianity from Jerusalem to Rome. For the bold and free testimony of the Apostle of the Gentiles in the very heart of the civilized world was the sign and pledge of victory.

THE ACTS AND THE GOSPELS.

The Acts is the connecting link between the Gospels and Epistles. It presupposes and confirms the leading events in the life of Christ, on which the church is built. The fact of the resurrection, whereof the apostles were witnesses, sends a thrill of joy and an air of victory through the whole book. God raised Jesus from the dead and mightily proclaimed him to be the Messiah, the prince of life and a Saviour in Israel; this is the burden of the sermons of Peter, who shortly before had denied his Master. He boldly bears witness to it before the people, in his pentecostal sermon, before the Sanhedrin, and before Cornelius. Paul likewise, in his addresses at Antioch in Pisidia, at Thessalonica, on the Areopagus before the Athenian philosophers, and at Cæsarea before Festus and Agrippa, emphasizes the resurrection without which his own conversion never could have taken place.

THE ACTS AND THE EPISTLES.

The Acts gives us the external history of the apostolic church; the Epistles present the internal life of the same. Both mutually supplement and confirm each other by a series of coincidences in all essential points. These coincidences are all the more conclusive as they are undesigned and accompanied by slight discrepancies in minor details. Archdeacon Paley made them the subject of a discussion in his *Horæ Paulinæ*,[1] which will retain its place among classical monographs alongside of

---

[1] First published in 1790, and often since. See also the list of parallel passages in Dr. Plumptre's *Com. on Acts*, pp. x. and xi.

James Smith's *Voyage and Shipwreck of St. Paul.* Arguments such as are furnished in these two books are sufficient to
silence most of the critical objections against the credibility of
Acts for readers of sound common sense and unbiased judgment. There is not the slightest trace that Luke had read
any of the thirteen Epistles of Paul, nor that Paul had read a
line of Acts. The writings were contemporaneous and independent, yet animated by the same spirit. Luke omits, it is
true, Paul's journey to Arabia, his collision with Peter at
Antioch, and many of his trials and persecutions; but he did
not aim at a full biography. The following are a few examples of these conspicuously undesigned coincidences in the
chronological order:

PAUL'S CONVERSION.

Comp. Acts chs. 9; 22 and 26; three accounts which differ only in minor details.	Gal. 1 : 15–17; 1 Cor. 15 : 8; 1 Tim. 1 : 13–16.

PAUL'S PERSECUTION AND ESCAPE AT DAMASCUS.

Acts 9 : 23–25. The Jews took counsel together to kill him . . . but his disciples took him by night, and let him down through the wall, lowering him in a basket.	2 Cor. 11:32, 33. In Damascus the governor under Aretas the king guarded the city of the Damascenes, in order to take me; and through a window was I let down in a basket by the wall, and escaped his hands.

PAUL'S VISITS TO JERUSALEM.

9 : 26, 27. And when he was come to Jerusalem . . . Barnabas took him, and brought him to the apostles.	Gal. 1 : 18. Then after three years [counting from his conversion] I went up to Jerusalem to visit Cephas, and tarried with him fifteen days.
15 : 2. They appointed that Paul and Barnabas, and certain other of them, should go up to Jerusalem unto the apostles and elders [to the apostolic conference to settle the question about circumcision].	Gal. 2 : 1. Then after the space of fourteen years I went up again to Jerusalem with Barnabas, taking Titus also with me. And I went up by revelation. [This inner motive does, of course, not exclude the church appointment mentioned by Luke.]

PAUL LEFT AT ATHENS ALONE.

17 : 16. Now while Paul waited for them [Silas and Timothy] at Athens.	1 Thess. 3 : 1. We thought it good to be left behind at Athens alone ; and sent Timothy, etc. Comp. ver. 7.

PAUL WORKING AT HIS TRADE.

18 : 3. And because he [Aquila] was of the same trade, he abode with them, and they wrought; for by their trade they were tent makers. Comp. 20 : 34.	1 Thess. 2 : 9. Ye remember, brethren, our labor and travail: working night and day, that we might not burden any of you. Comp. 1 Cor. 4 : 11, 12.

PAUL'S TWO VISITS TO CORINTH.

18 : 1; 20 : 2. | 1 Cor. 2 : 1; 4 : 19; 16 : 5.

WORK OF APOLLOS AT CORINTH.

18 : 27, 28. | 1 Cor. 1 : 12; 3 : 6.

PAUL BECOMING A JEW TO THE JEWS.

16 : 3; 18 : 18; 21 : 23–26. | 1 Cor. 9 : 20.

BAPTISM OF CRISPUS AND GAIUS.

18 : 8. | 1 Cor. 1 : 14–17.

COLLECTION FOR THE POOR BRETHREN.

18 : 23. | 1 Cor. 16 : 1.

PAUL'S LAST JOURNEY TO JERUSALEM.

20 : 6; 24 : 17. | Rom. 15 : 25, 26.

HIS DESIRE TO VISIT ROME.

19 : 21. | Rom. 1 : 13; 15 : 23.

PAUL AN AMBASSADOR IN BONDS.

28 : 16–20. | Eph. 6 : 19, 20.

THE ACTS AND SECULAR HISTORY.

The Acts brings Christianity in contact with the surrounding world and makes many allusions to various places, secular persons and events, though only incidentally and as far as its object required it. These allusions are—with a single exception, that of Theudas—in full harmony with the history of the

age as known from Josephus and heathen writers, and establish
Luke's claim to be considered a well-informed, honest, and
credible historian. Bishop Lightfoot asserts that no ancient
work affords so many tests of veracity, because no other has
such numerous points of contact in all directions with contemporary history, politics, and typography, whether Jewish or
Greek or Roman. The description of persons introduced in
the Acts, such as Gamaliel, Herod, Agrippa I., Bernice, Felix,
Festus, Gallio, agrees as far as it goes entirely with what we
know from contemporary sources. The allusions to countries,
cities, islands, in Syria, Asia Minor, Greece, and Italy are without exception correct and reveal an experienced traveller. We
mention the chief points, some of which are crucial tests.

1. The rebellion of Theudas, 5 : 36, alluded to in the speech
of Gamaliel, which was delivered about A.D. 33. Here is, apparently, a conflict with Josephus, who places this event in the
reign of Claudius, and under the procuratorship of Cuspius
Fadus, A.D. 44, ten or twelve years after Gamaliel's speech.[1]
But he mentions no less than three insurrections which took
place shortly after the death of Herod the Great, one under
the lead of Judas (who may have been Theudas or Thaddæus,
the two names being interchangeable, comp. Matt. 10 : 3 ; Luke
6 : 16), and he adds that besides these there were many highway robbers and murderers who pretended to the name of king.[2]
At all events, we should hesitate to charge Luke with an anachronism. He was as well informed as Josephus, and more credible.
This is the only case of a conflict between the two, except the
case of the census in Luke 2 : 2, and here the discovery of a
double governorship of Quirinius has brought the chronological
difficulty within the reach of solution.[3]

2. The rebellion of Judas of Galilee, mentioned in the same
speech, 5 : 37, as having occurred in the days of the enrolment
(the census of Quirinius), is confirmed by Josephus.[4] The in-

---

[1] *Ant.* XX. 5, § 1.   [2] *Ant.* XVII. 10.   [3] See above, p. 122.
[4] *Ant.* XVIII. 1 ; XX. 5, § 2 ; *War*, II. 8, § 1. In the first passage Josephus calls Judas a Gaulonite (*i.e.*, from the country east of Galilee), but in

surrection of this Judas was the most vigorous attempt to throw off the Roman yoke before the great war.

3. Candace, Queen of the Ethiopians, 8 : 27. Strabo mentions a queen of Meroè in Ethiopia, under that name, which was probably, like Pharaoh, a dynastic title.[1]

4. The famine under Claudius, 11 : 28. This reign (A.D. 41–54) was disturbed by frequent famines, one of which, according to Josephus, severely affected Judæa and Syria, and caused great distress in Jerusalem, under the procuratorship of Cuspius Fadus, A.D. 45.[2]

5. The death of King Herod Agrippa I. (grandson of Herod the Great), 12 : 20–23. Josephus says nothing about the preceding persecution of the church, but reports in substantial agreement with Luke that the king died of a loathsome disease in the seventh year of his reign (A.D. 44), five days after he had received, at the theatre of Cæsarea, divine honors, being hailed, in heathen fashion, as a god by his courtiers.[3]

6. The proconsular (as distinct from the proprætorian) status of Cyprus, under Sergius Paulus, 13 : 7 (σὺν τῷ ἀνθυπάτῳ Σεργίῳ Παύλῳ). Here Luke was for a long time considered inaccurate, even by Grotius, but has been strikingly confirmed by modern research. When Augustus assumed the supreme power (B.C. 27), he divided the government of the provinces with the Senate, and called the ruler of the imperatorial provinces, which needed direct military control under the emperor as commander of the legions, proprætor (ἀντιστράτηγος) or legate (πρεσβύτης), the ruler of a senatorial province, proconsul (ἀνθύπατος). Formerly these terms had signified that the holder of the office had previously been prætor (στρατηγός or ἡγεμών) or consul (ὕπατος); now they signified the administrative heads of the provinces. But this subdivision underwent frequent changes, so that only a well-informed person could tell

the other passage he is described as a Galilæan. He may have been a native of Gaulonitis and a resident of Galilee.

[1] Strabo, XVII., p. 820 ; comp. Pliny IV. 35; Dion Cass., LIV. 5.
[2] Josephus, *Ant.* XX. 5 ; comp. Tacitus, *Ann.* XII. 43 ; Sueton., *Claud.* 28.
[3] *Ant.* XVIII. 8.

the distinction at any time. Cyprus was in the original distribution (B.C. 27) assigned to the emperor,[1] but since B.C. 22, and
at the time of Paul's visit under Claudius, it was a senatorial
province;[2] and hence Sergius Paulus is rightly called proconsul.
Coins have been found from the reign of Claudius which confirm this statement.[3] Yea, the very name of (Sergius) Paulus
has been discovered by General di Cesnola at Soli (which, next
to Salamis, was the most important city of the island), in a
mutilated inscription, which reads: "in the proconsulship of
Paulus."[4] Under Hadrian the island was governed by a proprætor; under Severus, again by a proconsul.

7. The proconsular status of Achaia under Gallio, ch. 18 : 12
(Γαλλίωνος ἀνθυπάτου ὄντος τῆς Ἀχαίας). Achaia, which included the whole of Greece lying south of Macedonia, was
originally a senatorial province, then an imperatorial province
under Tiberius, and again a senatorial province under Claudius.[5]
In the year 53–54, when Paul was at Corinth, M. Annæus
Novatus Gallio, the brother of the philosopher L. Annæus Seneca, was proconsul of Achaia, and popularly esteemed for his
mild temper as "dulcis Gallio."

8. Paul and Barnabas mistaken for Zeus and Hermes in
Lycaonia, 14 : 11. According to the myth described by Ovid,[6]
the gods Jupiter and Mercury (Zeus and Hermes) had appeared

---

[1] Strabo, XIV., at the close.   [2] Dio Cassius, LIII. 12.
[3] Akerman, *Numismatic Illustrations*, pp. 39–42.
[4] ΤΩΝ ΕΠΙ · ΠΑΥΛΟΥ · [ΑΝΘ]ΥΠΑΤΟΥ. See Louis Palma di Cesnola's
Cyprus: Its Ancient Cities, Tombs, and Temples, New York, 1878, p. 424 sq.
He says : "The Proconsul Paulus may be the Sergius Paulus of the Acts of
the Apostles (ch. 13), as instances of the suppression of one or two names are
not rare." Bishop Lightfoot ("Cont. Review" for 1876, p. 290 sq.) satisfactorily accounts for the omission of Sergius, and identifies also the name
Sergius Paulus from the elder Pliny, who mentions him twice as a Latin
author in the first book of his *Natural History*, and as his chief authority for
the facts in the second and eighteenth books, two of these facts being especially connected with Cyprus. The Consul L. Sergius Paulus, whom Galen
the physician met at Rome A.D. 151, and whom he mentions repeatedly, first
under his full name and then simply as Paulus, may have been a descendant
of the convert of the apostle.
[5] Tacitus, *Ann.* I. 76 ; Sueton., *Claudius*, c. 25.   [6] *Metam.*, VIII. 625–724.

to the Lycaonians in the likeness of men, and been received by Baucis and Philemon, to whom they left tokens of that favor. The place where they had dwelt was visited by devout pilgrims and adorned with votive offerings. How natural, therefore, was it for these idolaters, astonished by the miracle, to mistake the eloquent Paul for Hermes, and Barnabas who may have been of a more imposing figure, for Zeus.

9. The colonial dignity of the city of Philippi, in Macedonia, 16 : 12 ("a *Roman* colony," κολώνια ; comp. ver. 21, "being Romans"). Augustus had sent a colony to the famous battle-field where Brutus and the Republic expired, and conferred on the place new importance and the privileges of Italian or Roman citizenship (*jus Italicum*).[1]

10. "Lydia, a seller of purple, of the city of Thyatira," 16 : 14. Thyatira (now Akhissar), in the valley of Lycus in Asia Minor, was famous for its dying works, especially for purple or crimson.[2]

11. The "politarchs" of Thessalonica, 17 : 6, 8.[3] This was a very rare title for magistrates, and might easily be confounded with the more usual designation "*poliarchs.*" But Luke's accuracy has been confirmed by an inscription still legible on an archway in Thessalonica, giving the names of seven "politarchs" who governed before the visit of Paul.[4]

12. The description of Athens, the Areopagus, the schools of philosophy, the idle curiosity and inquisitiveness of the Athenians (mentioned also by Demosthenes), the altar of an un-

---

[1] Dion Cass., LI. 4 ; Pliny, *Nat. Hist.* IV. 11.

[2] Strabo, XIII. 4, § 14. Inscriptions found in the place attest the existence of a guild of purple-dealers, with which Lydia was probably connected.

[3] τοὺς πολιτάρχας, *i.e.*, τοὺς ἄρχοντας τῶν πολιτῶν, *præfectos civitatis*, the rulers of the city. Grimm says: "*Usitatius Græcis erat,* πολίαρχος."

[4] The Thessalonian inscription in Greek letters is given by Boeckh, Leake, and Howson (in Conybeare and Howson's *Life and Letters of St. Paul*, ch. IX., large Lond. ed., I. 360). Three of the names are identical with those of Paul's friends in that region—Sopater of Beræa (Acts 20 : 4), Gaius of Macedonia (19 : 29), and Secundus of Thessalonica (20 : 4). I will only give the first line :

ΠΟΛΕΙΤΑΡΧΟΥΝΤΩΝ ΣΩΣΙΠΑΤΡΟΥ ΤΟΥ ΚΛΕΟ.

known God, and the quotation from Aratus or Cleanthes, in ch. 17, are fully borne out by classical authorities.[1]

13. The account of Ephesus in the nineteenth chapter has been verified as minutely accurate by the remarkable discoveries of John T. Wood, made between 1863 and 1874, with the aid of the English Government. The excessive worship of Diana, " the great goddess of Artemis," the temple-warden, the theatre (capable of holding twenty-five thousand people) often used for public assemblies, the distinct officers of the city, the Roman proconsul (ἀνϑύπατος), the recorder or " town-clerk " (γραμμα-τεύς), and the Asiarchs ('Ασιαρχαί) or presidents of the games and the religious ceremonials, have all reappeared in ruins and on inscriptions, which may now be studied in the British Museum. " With these facts in view," says Lightfoot, " we are justified in saying that ancient literature has preserved no picture of the Ephesus of imperial times—the Ephesus which has been unearthed by the sagacity and perseverance of Mr. Wood —comparable for its life-like truthfulness to the narrative of St. Paul's sojourn there in the Acts." [2]

14. The voyage and shipwreck of Paul in ch. 27. This chapter contains more information about ancient navigation than any work of Greek or Roman literature, and betrays the minute accuracy of an intelligent eye-witness, who, though not a professional seaman, was very familiar with nautical terms from close observation. He uses no less than sixteen technical terms, some of them rare, to describe the motion and management of a ship, and all of them most appropriately; and he is strictly correct in the description of the localities at Crete, Sal-

[1] See the commentaries on Acts 17 : 16, 18, 21, 22, 23, 28. The singular Θεῷ in ver. 23 creates some difficulty ; for Pausanias (I. 1–4) mentions "altars to unknown *gods*" which were set up in the harbor and streets of Athens; and Diogenes Laërtius (*Epimen.*, c. 3) speaks of "altars without name" in many parts of Athens. It is supposed that Paul meant one of these altars, or that he ingeniously adapted the polytheistic inscription to his argument. In the dialogue *Philopatris*, which is erroneously ascribed to Lucian, one of the speakers swears "by the unknown god of Athens."

[2] See Wood : *Discoveries at Ephesus*, and Lightfoot's article above quoted, p. 295. Lightfoot aided Mr. Wood in explaining the inscriptions.

mone, Fair Havens, Cauda, Lasea and Phœnix (two small places recently identified), and Melita (Malta), as well as the motions and effects of the tempestuous northeast wind called Euraquilo (A. V. Euroclydon) in the Mediterranean. All this has been thoroughly tested by an expert seaman and scholar, James Smith, of Scotland, who has published the results of his examination in the classical monograph already mentioned.[1] Monumental and scientific evidence outweighs critical conjectures, and is an irresistible vindication of the historical accuracy and credibility of Luke.

The Acts an Irenicum.

But some critics have charged the Acts with an intentional falsification of history in the interest of peace between the Petrine and Pauline sections of the church. The work is said to be a Catholic Irenicum, based probably on a narrative of Luke, but not completed before the close of the first century, for the purpose of harmonizing the Jewish and Gentile sections of the church by conforming the two leading apostles, *i.e.*, by raising Peter to the Pauline and lowering Paul to the Petrine plane, and thus making both subservient to a compromise between Judaizing bigotry and Gentile freedom.[2]

The chief arguments on which this hypothesis is based are the suppression of the collision between Paul and Peter at Antioch, and the friendly relation into which Paul is brought to James, especially at the last interview. The fifteenth chapter of Acts is supposed to be in irreconcilable conflict with the second chapter of the Galatians. But a reaction has taken

[1] Comp. § 82, p. 666, and my *Companion to the Greek Test.*, p. 61.

[2] This view was first broached by Baur (1836, 1838, and 1845), then carried out by Schneckenburger (1841), more fully by Zeller (1854), and by Hilgenfeld (1872, and in his *Einleitung*, 1875). Renan also presents substantially the same view, though somewhat modified. "*Les Actes*" (*Les Apôtres*, p. xxix.) "*sont une histoire dogmatique, arrangée pour appuyer les doctrines orthodoxes du temps ou inculquer les idées qui souriaient le plus à la piété de l'auteur.*" He thinks, it could not be otherwise, as we know the history of religions only from the reports of believers ; "*il n'y a que le sceptique qui écrive l'histoire* ad narrandum.*"

place in the Tübingen school, and it is admitted now by some of the ablest critics that the antagonism between Paulinism and Petrinism has been greatly exaggerated by Baur, and that Acts is a far more trustworthy account than he was willing to admit. The Epistle to the Galatians itself is the best vindica-- tion of the Acts, for it expressly speaks of a cordial agreement between Paul and the Jewish pillar-apostles. As to the omis- sion of the collision between Peter and Paul at Antioch, it was merely a passing incident, perhaps unknown to Luke, or omitted because it had no bearing on the course of events recorded by him. On the other hand, he mentions the "sharp contention" between Paul and Barnabas, because it resulted in a division of the missionary work, Paul and Silas going to Syria and Cilicia, Barnabas and Mark sailing away to Cyprus (15 : 39–41). Of this Paul says nothing, because it had no bearing on his argu- ment with the Galatians. Paul's conciliatory course toward James and the Jews, as represented in the Acts, is confirmed by his own Epistles, in which he says that he became a Jew to the Jews, as well as a Gentile to the Gentiles, in order to gain them both, and expresses his readiness to make the greatest possible sacrifice for the salvation of his brethren after the flesh (1 Cor. 9 : 20; Rom. 9 : 3).

THE TRUTHFULNESS OF THE ACTS.

The book of Acts is, indeed, like every impartial history, an Irenicum, but a truthful Irenicum, conceived in the very spirit of the Conference at Jerusalem and the concordat concluded by the leading apostles, according to Paul's own testimony in the polemical Epistle to the Galatians. The principle of selection required, of course, the omission of a large number of facts and incidents. But the selection was made with fairness and jus- tice to all sides. The impartiality and truthfulness of Luke is very manifest in his honest record of the imperfections of the apostolic church. He does not conceal the hypocrisy and mean selfishness of Ananias and Sapphira, which threatened to poison Christianity in its cradle (5 : 1 sqq.); he informs us that the in-

stitution of the diaconate arose from a complaint of the Grecian
Jews against their Hebrew brethren for neglecting their widows
in the daily ministration (6 : 1 sqq.) ; he represents Paul and
Barnabas as "men of like passions" with other men (14 : 15),
and gives us some specimens of weak human nature in Mark
when he became discouraged by the hardship of missionary life
and returned to his mother in Jerusalem (13 : 13), and in Paul and
Barnabas when they fell out for a season on account of this very
Mark, who was a cousin of Barnabas (15 : 39); nor does he pass
in silence the outburst of Paul's violent temper when in righteous indignation he called the high-priest a "whited wall" (23 :
3) ; and he speaks of serious controversies and compromises even
among the apostles under the guidance of the Holy Spirit—all
for our humiliation and warning as well as comfort and encouragement.

Examine and compare the secular historians from Herodotus
to Macaulay, and the church historians from Eusebius to Neander, and Luke need not fear a comparison. No history of thirty
years has ever been written so truthful and impartial, so important and interesting, so healthy in tone and hopeful in spirit, so
aggressive and yet so genial, so cheering and inspiring, so replete with lessons of wisdom and encouragement for work in
spreading the gospel of truth and peace, and yet withal so simple and modest, as the Acts of the Apostles. It is the best as
well as the first manual of church history.

§ 86. *The Epistles.*

The sermons of Stephen and the apostles in Acts (excepting the farewell of Paul to the Ephesian Elders) are missionary addresses to outsiders, with a view to convert them to
the Christian faith. The Epistles are addressed to baptized
converts, and aim to strengthen them in their faith, and, by
brotherly instruction, exhortation, rebuke, and consolation, to
build up the church in all Christian graces on the historical
foundation of the teaching and example of Christ. The

prophets of the Old Testament delivered divine oracles to the people; the apostles of the New Testament wrote letters to the brethren, who shared with them the same faith and hope as members of Christ.

The readers are supposed to be already " in Christ," saved and sanctified " in Christ," and holding all their social and domestic relations and discharging their duties "in Christ." They are "grown together" [1] with Christ, sharing in his death, burial, and resurrection, and destined to reign and rule with him in glory forever. On the basis of this new relation, constituted by a creative act of divine grace, and sealed by baptism, they are warned against every sin and exhorted to every virtue. Every departure from their profession and calling implies double guilt and double danger of final ruin.

Occasions and calls for correspondence were abundant, and increased with the spread of Christianity over the Roman empire. The apostles could not be omnipresent, and had to send messengers and letters to distant churches. They probably wrote many more letters than we possess, although we have good reason to suppose that the most important and permanently valuable are preserved. A former letter of Paul to the Corinthians is implied in 1 Cor. 5 : 9 : " I wrote to you in my epistle ; " [2] and traces of further correspondence are found in 1 Cor. 16 : 3 ; 2 Cor. 10 : 9 ; Eph. 3 : 3. The letter "from Laodicea," referred to in Col. 4 : 16, is probably the encyclical Epistle to the Ephesians.

The Epistles of the New Testament are without a parallel in ancient literature, and yield in importance only to the Gospels, which stand higher, as Christ himself rises above the apostles. They are pastoral letters to congregations or individuals, beginning with an inscription and salutation, consisting of doctrinal expositions and practical exhortations and consolations, and con-

---

[1] σύμφυτοι, Rom. 6 : 5 ; not " planted together " (as in the A. V. and the Vulgate) ; the word being derived from φύω, to cause to grow, not from φυτεύω, to plant.

[2] The so-called Epistle of the Corinthians to Paul and his answer, preserved in Armenian, are spurious and worthless.

cluding with personal intelligence, greetings, and benediction. They presuppose throughout the Gospel history, and often allude to the death and resurrection of Christ as the foundation of the church and the Christian hope. They were composed amidst incessant missionary labors and cares, under trial and persecution, some of them from prison, and yet they abound in joy and thanksgiving. They were mostly called forth by special emergencies, yet they suit all occasions. Tracts for the times, they are tracts for all times. Children of the fleeting moment, they contain truths of infinite moment. They compress more ideas in fewer words than any other writings, human or divine, excepting the Gospels. They discuss the highest themes which can challenge an immortal mind—God, Christ, and the Spirit, sin and redemption, incarnation, atonement, regeneration, repentance, faith and good works, holy living and dying, the conversion of the world, the general judgment, eternal glory and bliss. And all this before humble little societies of poor, uncultured artisans, freedmen and slaves! And yet they are of more real and general value to the church than all the systems of theology from Origen to Schleiermacher—yea, than all the confessions of faith. For eighteen hundred years they have nourished the faith of Christendom, and will continue to do so to the end of time. This is the best evidence of their divine inspiration.

The Epistles are divided into two groups, Catholic and Pauline. The first is more general; the second bears the strong imprint of the intense personality of the Apostle of the Gentiles.

§ 87. *The Catholic Epistles.*

I. STORR: *De Catholicarum Epp. Occasione et Consilio.* Tüb. 1789. STÆUDLIN: *De Fontibus Epp. Cath.* Gott. 1790. J. D. SCHULZE: *Der schriftstellerische Charakter und Werth des Petrus, Jacobus und Judas.* Leipz. 1802. *Der schriftsteller. Ch. des Johannes.* 1803.

II. Commentaries on all the Catholic Epistles by GOEPFERT (1780), SCHLEGEL (1783), CARPZOV (1790), AUGUSTI (1801), GRASHOF (1830), JACHMANN (1838), SUMNER (1840), DE WETTE (3d ed. by BRÜCKNER.

1865), Meyer (the Cath. Epp. by Huther, Düsterdieck, Beyschlag), Lange (Eng. transl. with additions by Mombert, 1872), John T. Demarest (N. York, 1879); also the relevant parts in the "Speaker's Com.," in Ellicott's Com., the *Cambridge Bible for Schools* (ed. by Dean Perowne), and in the *International Revision Com.* (ed. by Schaff), etc. P. I. Gloag : *Introduction to the Catholic Epp.*, Edinb., 1887.

The seven Epistles of James, 1st and 2d Peter, 1st, 2d, and 3d John, and Jude usually follow in the old manuscripts the Acts of the Apostles, and precede the Pauline Epistles, perhaps as being the works of the older apostles, and representing, in part at least, the Jewish type of Christianity. They are of a more general character, and addressed not to individuals or single congregations, as those of Paul, but to a larger number of Christians scattered through a district or over the world. Hence they are called, from the time of Origen and Eusebius, Catholic. This does not mean in this connection anti-heretical (still less, of course, Greek Catholic or Roman Catholic), but *encyclical* or *circular.* The designation, however, is not strictly correct, and applies only to five of them. The second and third Epistles of John are addressed to individuals. On the other hand the Epistle to the Hebrews is encyclical, and ought to be numbered with the Catholic Epistles, but is usually appended to those of Paul. The Epistle to the Ephesians is likewise intended for more than one congregation. The first Christian document of an encyclical character is the pastoral letter of the apostolic Conference at Jerusalem (A.D. 50) to the Gentile brethren in Syria and Cilicia (Acts 15 : 23–29).[1]

The Catholic Epistles are distinct from the Pauline by their more general contents and the absence of personal and local references. They represent different, though essentially harmonious, types of doctrine and Christian life. The individuality of James, Peter, and John stand out very prominently in these brief remains of their correspondence. They do not enter into theological discussions like those of Paul, the learned

---

[1] Hence Origen calls it an ἐπιστολὴ καθολική.

Rabbi, and give simpler statements of truth, but protest against the rising ascetic and Antinomian errors, as Paul does in the Colossians and Pastoral Epistles. Each has a distinct character and purpose, and none could well be spared from the New Testament without marring the beauty and completeness of the whole.

The time of composition cannot be fixed with certainty, but is probably as follows : James before A.D. 50 ; 1st Peter (probably also 2d Peter and Jude) before A.D. 67 ; John between A.D. 80 and 100.

Only two of these Epistles, the 1st of Peter and the 1st of John, belong to the Eusebian *Homologumena*, which were universally accepted by the ancient church as inspired and canonical. About the other five there was more or less doubt as to their origin down to the close of the fourth century, when all controversy on the extent of the canon went to sleep till the time of the Reformation. Yet they bear the general imprint of the apostolic age, and the absence of stronger traditional evidence is due in part to their small size and limited use.

JAMES.

Comp. on the lit., biography, and doctrine of James, §§ 27 and 69.

The Epistle of JAMES the Brother of the Lord was written, no doubt, from Jerusalem, the metropolis of the ancient theocracy and Jewish Christianity, where the author labored and died a martyr at the head of the mother church of Christendom and as the last connecting link between the old and the new dispensation. It is addressed to the Jews and Jewish Christians of the dispersion before the final doom in the year 70.

It strongly resembles the Gospel of Matthew, and echoes the Sermon on the Mount in the fresh, vigorous, pithy, proverbial, and sententious style of oriental wisdom. It exhorts the readers to good works of faith, warns them against dead orthodoxy, covetousness, pride, and worldliness, and comforts them in view of present and future trials and persecutions. It is eminently

practical and free from subtle theological questions. It preaches
a religion of good works which commends itself to the approval
of God and all good men. It represents the primary stage of
Christian doctrine. It takes no notice of the circumcision controversy, the Jerusalem compromise, and the later conflicts of
the apostolic age. Its doctrine of justification is no protest
against that of Paul, but prior to it, and presents the subject
from a less developed, yet eminently practical aspect, and against
the error of a barren monotheism rather than Pharisaical legalism, which Paul had in view. It is probably the oldest of the
New Testament books, meagre in doctrine, but rich in comfort
and lessons of holy living based on faith in Jesus Christ, "the
Lord of glory." It contains more reminiscences of the words
of Christ than any other epistle.[1] Its leading idea is "the perfect law of freedom," or the law of love revealed in Christ.

Luther's harsh, unjust, and unwise judgment of this Epistle
has been condemned by his own church, and reveals a defect in
his conception of the doctrine of justification which was the
natural result of his radical war with the Romish error.

PETER.

See on the lit., biography, and theology of Peter, §§ 25, 26, and 70.

The FIRST Epistle of PETER, dated from Babylon,[2] belongs to
the later life of the apostle, when his ardent natural temper was

---

[1] Reuss (*Gesch. d. heil. Schriften N. Testaments*, 5th ed., I. 138): "*Thatsache ist, dass die Ep. Jacobi für sich allein mehr wörtliche Reminiscenzen aus
den Reden Jesu enthält als alle übrigen apost. Schriften zusammen. . . .
Insofern dieselben offenbar nicht aus schriftlichen Quellen geflossen sind, mögen
sie mit das höhere Alter des Briefs verbürgen.*" Beyschlag (in the new ed.
of Huther in Meyer, 1881) and Erdmann (1881), the most recent commentators of James, agree with Schneckenburger, Neander, and Thiersch in assigning the Epistle to the earliest date of Christian literature, against the Tübingen
school, which makes it a polemical treatise against Paul. Reuss occupies a
middle position. The undeveloped state of Christian doctrine, the use of
συναγωγή for a Christian assembly (2 : 2), the want of a clear distinction between Jews and Jewish Christians, who are addressed as "the twelve tribes,"
and the expectation of the approaching parousia (5 : 8), concur as signs of the
high antiquity.

[2] Commentators are divided on the meaning of Babylon, 5 : 13, whether it
be the mystic Babylon of the Apocalypse, *i.e.*, heathen Rome, as a persecuting

deeply humbled, softened, and sanctified by the work of grace. It was written to churches in several provinces of Asia Minor, composed of Jewish and Gentile Christians together, and planted mainly by Paul and his fellow-laborers ; and was sent by the hands of Silvanus, a former companion of Paul. It consists of precious consolations, and exhortations to a holy walk after the example of Christ, to joyful hope of the heavenly inheritance, to patience under the persecutions already raging or impending. It gives us the fruit of a rich spiritual experience, and is altogether worthy of Peter and his mission to tend the flock of God under Christ, the chief shepherd of souls.[1]

It attests also the essential agreement of Peter with the doctrine of the Gentile apostle, in which the readers had been before instructed (5 : 12). This accords with the principle of Peter professed at the Council in Jerusalem (Acts 15 : 11) that we are saved without the yoke of the law, "through the grace of the Lord Jesus." His doctrinal system, however, precedes that

power (the fathers, Roman Catholic divines, also Thiersch, Baur, Renan), or Babylon on the Euphrates, or Babylon in Egypt (old Cairo). The question is connected with Peter's presence in Rome, which has been discussed in § 26. On the date of composition commentators are likewise divided, as they differ in their views on the relation of Peter's Epistle to Romans, Ephesians, and James, and on the character of the persecution alluded to in the Epistle. Weiss, who denies that Peter used the Epistles of Paul, dates it back as far as 54 ; the Tübingen critics bring it down to the age of Trajan (Volkmar even to 140 !), but most critics assign it to the time between 63 and 67, Renan to 63, shortly before the Neronian persecution. For once I agree with him. See Huther (in the Meyer series), 4th ed., pp. 30 sqq. ; Weiss, *Die Petrinische Frage* (1865) ; Renan, *L'Antechrist*, p. vi and 110 ; and, on the part of the Tübingen school, Pfleiderer, *Paulinismus*, pp. 417 sqq.; Hilgenfeld, *Einleitung*, pp. 625 sqq.; Holtzmann, *Einleitung*, pp. 514 sqq. (2d ed.).

[1] "This excellent Epistle," says Archbishop Leighton, whose *Practical Commentary upon the First Epistle General of St. Peter* is still unsurpassed for spirituality and unction, "is a brief and yet very clear summary both of the consolations and instructions needful for the encouragement and direction of a Christian in his journey to heaven, elevating his thoughts and desires to that happiness, and strengthening him against all opposition in the way, both that of corruption within and temptations and afflictions from without." Bengel : "*Mirabilis est gravitas et alacritas Petrini sermonis, lectorem suavissime retinens.*" Alford : "There is no Epistle in the sacred canon, the language and spirit of which come more directly home to the personal trials and wants and weaknesses of the Christian life."

of Paul and is independent of it, standing between James and Paul. Peculiar to him is the doctrine of the descent of Christ into Hades (3 : 18; 4 : 6; comp. Acts 2 : 32), which contains the important truth of the universal intent of the atonement. Christ died for all men, for those who lived before as well as after his coming, and he revealed himself to the spirits in the realm of Hades. Peter also warns against hierarchical ambition in prophetic anticipation of the abuse of his name and his primacy among the apostles.

The SECOND Epistle of PETER is addressed, shortly before the author's death, as a sort of last will and testament, to the same churches as the first. It contains a renewed assurance of his agreement with his "beloved brother Paul," to whose Epistles he respectfully refers, yet with the significant remark (true in itself, yet often abused by Romanists) that there are in them "some things hard to be understood" (3 : 15, 16). As Peter himself receives in one of these Epistles (Gal. 2 : 11) a sharp rebuke for his inconsistency at Antioch (which may be included in the hard things), this affectionate allusion proves how thoroughly the Spirit of Christ had, through experience, trained him to humility, meekness, and self-denial. The Epistle exhorts the readers to diligence, virtue, temperance, patience, godliness, brotherly love, and brotherly kindness; refers to the Transfiguration on the Mount, where the author witnessed the majesty of Christ, and to the prophetic word inspired by the Holy Spirit; warns against antinomian errors; corrects a mistake concerning the second coming; exhorts them to prepare for the day of the Lord by holy living, looking for new heavens and a new earth wherein dwelleth righteousness; and closes with the words: "Grow in the grace and knowledge of our Lord and Saviour Jesus Christ, to whom be glory both now and forever."

The second Epistle is reckoned by Eusebius among the seven *Antilegomena*, and its Petrine authorship is doubted or denied, in whole or in part, by many eminent divines,[1] but defended by

[1] Erasmus, Calvin, Grotius, Neander, De Wette, Huther, and all the Tübingen critics.

competent critics.[1] The chief objections are: the want of early attestation, the reference to a collection of the Pauline Epistles, the polemic against Gnostic errors, some peculiarities of style, and especially the apparent dependence of the second chapter on the Epistle of Jude.

On the other hand, the Epistle, at least the first and third chapters, contains nothing which Peter might not have written, and the allusion to the scene of transfiguration admits only the alternative: either Peter, or a forger. It seems morally impossible that a forger should have produced a letter so full of spiritual beauty and unction, and expressly denouncing all cunning fabrications. It may have been enlarged by the editor after Peter's death. But the whole breathes an apostolic spirit, and could not well be spared from the New Testament. It is a worthy valedictory of the aged apostle awaiting his martyrdom, and with its still valid warnings against internal dangers from false Christianity, it forms a suitable complement to the first Epistle, which comforts the Christians amidst external dangers from heathen and Jewish persecutors.

Jude.

The Epistle of Jude, a "brother of James" (the Just),[2] is very short, and strongly resembles the second chapter of the second Epistle of Peter, but differs from it by an allusion to the remarkable apocryphal book of Enoch and the legend of the dispute of Michael with the devil about the body of Moses. It seems to be addressed to the same churches and directed against the same Gnostic heretics. It is a solemn warning against the antinomian and licentious tendencies which revealed themselves between A.D. 60 and 70. Origen remarks that it is "of few

---

[1] Weiss, Thiersch, Fronmüller, Alford, and especially Fr. Spitta in his *Der Zweite Brief des Petrus und der Brief des Judas* (Halle, 1885, 544 pages).

[2] Clement of Alexandria, Origen (in Greek), and Epiphanius distinguish him from the Apostles. He is mentioned with James as one of the brothers of Jesus, Matt. 13 : 55; Mark 6 : 3. Comp. on this whole question the discussion in § 27.

lines, but rich in words of heavenly wisdom." The style is
fresh and vigorous.

The Epistle of Jude belongs likewise to the Eusebian *Antilegomena*, and has signs of post-apostolic origin, yet may have
been written by Jude, who was not one of the Twelve, though
closely connected with apostolic circles. A forger would hardly
have written under the name of a "brother of James" rather
than a brother of Christ or an apostle.

The time and place of composition are unknown. The Tübingen critics put it down to the reign of Trajan; Renan, on the
contrary, as far back as 54, wrongly supposing it to have been
intended, together with the Epistle of James, as a counter-
manifesto against Paul's doctrine of free grace. But Paul condemned antinomianism as severely as James and Jude (comp.
Rom. 6, and in fact all his Epistles). It is safest to say, with
Bleek, that it was written shortly before the destruction of
Jerusalem, which is not alluded to (comp. vers. 14, 15).

The Epistles of John.

Comp. §§ 40–43, 83 and 84.

The First Epistle of John betrays throughout, in thought
and style, the author of the fourth Gospel. It is a postscript to
it, or a practical application of the lessons of the life of Christ
to the wants of the church at the close of the first century. It
is a circular letter of the venerable apostle to his beloved children in Asia Minor, exhorting them to a holy life of faith and
love in Christ, and earnestly warning them against the Gnostic
"antichrists," already existing or to come, who deny the mystery of the incarnation, sunder religion from morality, and run
into Antinomian practices.

The Second and Third Epistles of John are, like the Epistle
of Paul to Philemon, short private letters, one to a Christian
woman by the name of Cyria, the other to one Gaius, probably an
officer of a congregation in Asia Minor. They belong to the seven
Antilegomena, and have been ascribed by some to the "Presbyter John," a contemporary of the apostle, though of disputed

existence.   But the second Epistle resembles the first, almost to
verbal repetition,[1] and such repetition well agrees with the familiar tradition of Jerome concerning the apostle of love, ever exhorting the congregation, in his advanced age, to love one another.
The difference of opinion in the ancient church respecting them
may have risen partly from their private nature and their brevity,
and partly from the fact that the author styles himself, somewhat remarkably, the " elder," the "presbyter." This term,
however, is probably to be taken, not in the official sense, but
in the original, signifying age and dignity ; for at that time
John was in fact a venerable father in Christ, and must have
been revered and loved as a patriarch among his "little children."

§ 88.   *The Epistles of Paul.*

Παῦλος γενόμενος μέγιστος ὑπογραμμός.   (Clement of Rome.)

Comp. §§ 29–36 and 71.

GENERAL CHARACTER.

Paul was the greatest worker among the apostles, not only as
a missionary, but also as a writer.   He "labored more than
all."   And we may well include in this " all " the whole body
of theologians who came after him ; for where shall we find an
equal wealth of the profoundest thoughts on the highest themes
as in Paul ?   We have from him thirteen Epistles ; how many
more were lost, we cannot even conjecture.   The four most important of them are admitted to be genuine even by the most
exacting and sceptical critics.   They are so stamped with the
individuality of Paul, and so replete with tokens of his age and
surroundings, that no sane man can mistake the authorship.
We might as well doubt the genuineness of Luther's work on
the Babylonian captivity, or his small catechism.   The heretic
Marcion, in the first half of the second century, accepted ten,
excluding only the three Pastoral Epistles which did not suit
his notions.

[1] Comp. 2 John 4–7 with 1 John 2 : 7, 8 ; 4, 2, 3.

The Pauline Epistles are pastoral addresses to congregations of his own founding (except that of Rome, and probably also that of Colossæ, which were founded by his pupils), or to individuals (Timothy, Titus, Philemon).   Several of them hail from prison, but breathe the same spirit of faith, hope, and joy as the others, and the last ends with a shout of victory.   They proceeded from profound agitation, and yet are calm and serene.   They were occasioned by the trials, dangers, and errors incident to every new congregation, and the care and anxiety of the apostle for their spiritual welfare.   He had led them from the darkness of heathen idolatry and Jewish bigotry to the light of Christian truth and freedom, and raised them from the slime of depravity to the pure height of saving grace and holy living.   He had no family ties, and threw the whole strength of his affections into his converts, whom he loved as tenderly as a mother can love her offspring.[1]   This love to his spiritual children was inspired by his love to Christ, as his love to Christ was the response to Christ's love for him.   Nor was his love confined to the brethren : he was ready to make the greatest sacrifice for his unbelieving and persecuting fellow-Jews, as Christ himself sacrificed his life for his enemies.

His Epistles touch on every important truth and duty of the Christian religion, and illuminate them from the heights of knowledge and experience, without pretending to exhaust them. They furnish the best material for a system of dogmatics and ethics.   Paul looks back to the remotest beginning before the creation, and looks out into the farthest future beyond death and the resurrection.   He writes with the authority of a commissioned apostle and inspired teacher, yet, on questions of expediency, he distinguishes between the command of the Lord and his private judgment.   He seems to have written rapidly and under great pressure, without correcting his first draft.   If

---

[1] As he writes himself to the Thessalonians (1 Thess. 2 : 7) : "We were gentle in the midst of you, as when a nurse cherisheth her own children." And to the ungrateful and unsteady Galatians he writes (4 : 9) : " My little children, of whom I am again in travail until Christ be formed in you."

we find, with Peter, in his letters, "some things hard to be understood," even in this nineteenth century, we must remember that Paul himself bowed in reverence before the boundless ocean of God's truth, and humbly professed to know only in part, and to see through a mirror darkly. All knowledge in this world "ends in mystery."[1]   Our best systems of theology are but dim reflections of the sunlight of revelation. Infinite truths transcend our finite minds, and cannot be compressed into the pigeon-holes of logical formulas. But every good commentary adds to the understanding and strengthens the estimate of the paramount value of these Epistles.

THE CHRONOLOGICAL ORDER.

Paul's Epistles were written within a period of about twelve years, between A.D. 52 or 53 and 64 or 67, when he stood at the height of his power and influence. None was composed before the Council of Jerusalem. From the date of his conversion to his second missionary journey (A.D. 37 to 52) we have no documents of his pen. The chronology of his letters can be better ascertained than that of the Gospels or Catholic Epistles, by combining internal indications with the Acts and contemporary events, such as the dates of the proconsulship of Gallio in Achaia, and the procuratorship of Felix and Festus in Judæa. As to the Romans, we can determine the place, the year, and the season of composition : he sends greetings from persons in Corinth (16 : 23), commends Phœbe, a deaconess of Kenchreæ, the port of Corinth, and the bearer of the letter (16 : 1); he had not yet been in Rome (1 : 13), but hoped to get there after another visit to Jerusalem, on which he was about to enter, with collections from Macedonia and Achaia for the poor brethren in Judæa (15 : 22–29 ; comp. 2 Cor. 8 : 1–3); and from Acts we learn that on his last visit to Achaia he abode three months in Corinth, and returned to Syria between the Passover and Pentecost (Acts 20 : 3, 6, 16).   This was his fifth

---

[1] " *Das ist das Ende der Philosophie : zu wissen, dass wir glauben müssen.*"— (Geibel.)

and last journey to Jerusalem, where he was taken prisoner and sent to Felix in Cæsarea, two years before he was followed by Festus. All these indications lead us to the spring of A.D. 58.

The chronological order is this: Thessalonians were written first, A.D. 52 or 53; then Galatians, Corinthians, and Romans, between 56 and 58; then the Epistles of the captivity: Colossians, Ephesians, Philemon, Philippians, between 61 and 63; last, the Pastoral Epistles, but their date is uncertain, except that the second Epistle to Timothy is his farewell letter on the eve of his martyrdom.

It is instructive to study the Epistles in their chronological order with the aid of the Acts, and so to accompany the apostle in his missionary career from Damascus to Rome, and to trace the growth of his doctrinal system from the documentary truths in Thessalonians to the height of maturity in Romans; then through the ramifications of particular topics in Colossians, Ephesians, Philippians, and the farewell counsels in the Pastoral Epistles.

Doctrinal Arrangement.

More important than the chronological order is the topical order, according to the prevailing object and central idea. This gives us the following groups:

1. Anthropological and Soteriological: Galatians and Romans.
2. Ethical and Ecclesiastical: First and Second Corinthians.
3. Christological: Colossians and Philippians.
4. Ecclesiological: Ephesians (in part also Corinthians).
5. Eschatological: Thessalonians.
6. Pastoral: Timothy and Titus.
7. Social and Personal: Philemon.

The Style.

"The style is the man." This applies with peculiar force to Paul. His style has been called "the most personal that ever existed." [1] It fitly represents the force and fire of his mind and the tender affections of his heart. He disclaims classical elegance and calls himself " rude in speech," though by no means " in knowledge." He carried the heavenly treasure in earthen vessels. But the defects are more than made up by excellences. In his very weakness the strength of Christ was perfected. We are not lost in the admiration of the mere form, but are kept mindful of the paramount importance of the contents and the hidden depths of truth which lie behind the words and defy the power of expression.

Paul's style is manly, bold, heroic, aggressive, and warlike; yet at times tender, delicate, gentle, and winning. It is involved, irregular, and rugged, but always forcible and expressive, and not seldom rises to more than poetic beauty, as in the triumphant pæan at the end of the eighth chapter of Romans, and in the ode on love (1 Cor. 13). His intense earnestness and overflowing fulness of ideas break through the ordinary rules of grammar. His logic is set on fire. He abounds in skilful arguments, bold antitheses, impetuous assaults, abrupt transitions, sudden turns, zigzag flashes, startling questions and exclamations. He is dialectical and argumentative; he likes logical particles, paradoxical phrases, and plays on words. He reasons from Scripture, from premises, from conclusions; he drives the opponent to the wall without mercy and reduces him *ad absurdum*, but without ever indulging in personalities. He is familiar with the sharp weapons of ridicule, irony, and sarcasm, but holds them in check and uses them rarely. He varies the argument by touching appeals to the heart and bursts of seraphic eloquence. He is never dry or dull, and never wastes words; he is brief, terse, and hits the nail on the head. His terseness makes him at times obscure, as is the case with the somewhat similar style of Thucydides, Tacitus, and Tertullian. His words are as many warriors marching on to victory and peace; they are like a mountain torrent rushing in foaming rapids over pre-

---

[1] By Renan, who, notwithstanding his fastidious French taste and antipathy to Paul's theology, cannot help admiring his lofty genius.

cipices, and then calmly flowing over green meadows, or like a thunderstorm ending in a refreshing shower and bright sunshine.

Paul created the vocabulary of scientific theology and put a profounder meaning into religious and moral terms than they ever had before. We cannot speak of sin, flesh, grace, mercy, peace, redemption, atonement, justification, glorification, church, faith, love, without bearing testimony to the ineffaceable effect which that greatest of Jewish rabbis and Christian teachers has had upon the language of Christendom.

NOTES.

CHRYSOSTOM justly compares the Epistles of Paul to metals more precious than gold and to unfailing fountains which flow the more abundantly the more we drink of them.

BEZA: "When I more closely consider the whole genius and character of Paul's style, I must confess that I have found no such sublimity of speaking in Plato himself . . . no exquisiteness of vehemence in Demosthenes equal to his."

EWALD begins his Commentary on the Pauline Epistles (Göttingen, 1857) with these striking and truthful remarks: "Considering these Epistles for themselves only, and apart from the general significance of the great Apostle of the Gentiles, we must still admit that, in the whole history of all centuries and of all nations, there is no other set of writings of similar extent, which, as creations of the fugitive moment, have proceeded from such severe troubles of the age, and such profound pains and sufferings of the author himself, and yet contain such an amount of healthfulness, serenity, and vigor of immortal genius, and touch with such clearness and certainty on the very highest truths of human aspiration and action. . . . The smallest as well as the greatest of these Epistles seem to have proceeded from the fleeting moments of this earthly life only to enchain all eternity; they were born of anxiety and bitterness of human strife, to set forth in brighter lustre and with higher certainty their superhuman grace and beauty. The divine assurance and firmness of the old prophets of Israel, the all-transcending glory and immediate spiritual presence of the Eternal King and Lord, who had just ascended to heaven, and all the art and culture of a ripe and wonderfully excited age, seem to have joined, as it were, in bringing forth the new creation of these Epistles of the times which were destined to last for all times."

On the *style* of Paul, see my *Companion*, etc., pp. 62 sqq. To the testimonies there given I add the judgment of REUSS (*Geschichte der h.*

Schr. N. T., I. 67) : " Still more [than the method] is the style of all these Epistles the true expression of the personality of the author. The defect of classical correctness and rhetorical finish is more than compensated by the riches of language and the fulness of expression. The condensation of construction demands not reading simply, but studying. Broken sentences, ellipses, parentheses, leaps in the argumentation, allegories, rhetorical figures express inimitably all the moods of a wide-awake and cultured mind, all the affections of a rich and deep heart, and betray everywhere a pen at once bold, and yet too slow for the thought. Antitheses, climaxes, exclamations, questions keep up the attention, and touching effusions win the heart of the reader."

§ 89. *The Epistles to the Thessalonians.*

Thessalonica,[1] a large and wealthy commercial city of Macedonia, the capital of " Macedonia secunda," the seat of a Roman proconsul and quæstor, and inhabited by many Jews, was visited by Paul on his second missionary tour, A.D. 52 or 53, and in a few weeks he succeeded, amid much persecution, in founding a flourishing church composed chiefly of Gentiles. From this centre Christianity spread throughout the neighborhood, and during the middle ages Thessalonica was, till its capture by the Turks (A.D. 1430), a bulwark of the Byzantine empire and Oriental Christendom, and largely instrumental in the conversion of the Slavonians and Bulgarians ; hence it received the designation of " the Orthodox City." It numbered many learned archbishops, and still has more remains of ecclesiastical antiquity than any other city in Greece, although its cathedral is turned into a mosque.

To this church Paul, as its spiritual father, full of affection for his inexperienced children, wrote in familiar conversational style two letters from Corinth, during his first sojourn in that city, to comfort them in their trials and to correct certain misapprehensions of his preaching concerning the glorious return of Christ, and the preceding development of " the man of sin " or Antichrist, and " the mystery of lawlessness," then already at work, but checked by a restraining power. The hope of the

[1] Strabo calls it Θεσσαλονίκεια. Its present name is Salonichi.

near advent had degenerated into an enthusiastic adventism
which demoralized the every-day life.   He now taught them
that the Lord will not come so soon as they expected, that it
was not a matter of mathematical calculation, and that in no
case should the expectation check industry and zeal, but rather
stimulate them.   Hence his exhortations to a sober, orderly,
diligent, and prayerful life.

It is remarkable that the first Epistles of Paul should treat of
the last topic in the theological system and anticipate the end
at the beginning.   But the hope of Christ's speedy coming was,
before the destruction of Jerusalem, the greatest source of consolation to the infant church amid trial and persecution, and the
church at Thessalonica was severely tried in its infancy, and
Paul driven away.   It is also remarkable that to a young church
in Greece rather than to that in Rome should have first been
revealed the beginning of that mystery of anti-Christian lawlessness which was then still restrained, but was to break out in its
full force in Rome.[1]

The objections of Baur to the genuineness of these Epistles,
especially the second, are futile in the judgment of the best
critics.[2]

---

[1] The difficult passage, 2 Thess. 2 : 1–12, must be explained in connection
with the prophecies of Daniel (the fourth empire) and the Apocalypse.   See
the commentaries of Lünemann, Lange (Riggenbach, translated by Lillie),
Ellicott, Jowett, Marcus Dods, and the Excursus of Farrar on the Man of Sin
(*St. Paul*, II. 583–587).   Many modern exegetes adopt the patristic interpreta-
tion that "the restraining power" ($\tau\grave{o}$ $\kappa\alpha\tau\acute{e}\chi o\nu$) is the Roman empire, "the
restrainer" ($\acute{o}$ $\kappa\alpha\tau\acute{e}\chi\omega\nu$) the then reigning emperor (Claudius), and "the man of
sin " his successor, Nero.   But the last is very doubtful.   The whole passage
must have a prophetic sweep far beyond the time of the old Roman empire.
There are " many antichrists " and many restraining forces and persons in the
successive ages, and the end is yet apparently afar off.   " Obviously, whatever
the words signify, they must mean something which has existed from Paul's day
to our own, something which, during that whole period, has had the effect of
restraining wickedness."   (Dods, in Schaff's *Com. on the N. T.*, III 535.)

[2] Grimm, Lünemann, Reuss, Lipsius, and others have refuted the arguments of Baur.   The first Epistle is conceded to be genuine also by Hilgenfeld,
who declares (*Einleit.*, p 246) : " *In dem ganzen Brief erkennt man die
Sprache des Paulus.   Es ist kein Grund vorhanden, denselben dem Paulus
abzusprechen.   Nicht so bedeutsam, wie andere Briefe, ist derselbe eines Paulus*

The Theoretical Theme: The parousia of Christ. The Practical Theme: Christian hope in the midst of persecution.

Leading Thoughts: This is the will of God, even your sanctification (1 Thess. 4 : 3). Sorrow not as the rest who have no hope (4 : 13). The Lord will descend from heaven, and so shall we ever be with the Lord (4 : 16, 17). The day of the Lord so cometh as a thief in the night (5 : 2). Let us watch and be sober (5 : 6). Put on the breastplate of faith and love, and for a helmet, the hope of salvation (5 : 8). Rejoice always; pray without ceasing; in everything give thanks (5 : 16). Prove all things; hold fast that which is good; abstain from every form of evil (5 : 21, 22). The Lord will come to be glorified in his saints (2 Thess. 1 : 10). But the falling away must come first, and the man of sin be revealed, the son of perdition (2 : 3, 4). The mystery of lawlessness doth already work, but is restrained for the time (2 : 7). Stand fast and hold the traditions which ye were taught, whether by word, or by epistle of ours (2 : 15). If any will not work, neither let him eat (3 : 10). Be not weary in well-doing (3 : 13). The God of peace sanctify you wholly; and may your spirit and soul and body be preserved entire, without blame at the coming (ἐν τῇ παρουσίᾳ) of our Lord Jesus Christ (1 Thess. 5 : 23).

§ 90. *The Epistles to the Corinthians.*

Corinth was the metropolis of Achaia, on the bridge of two seas, an emporium of trade between the East and the West—wealthy, luxurious, art-loving, devoted to the worship of Aphrodite. Here Paul established the most important church in Greece, and labored, first eighteen months, then three months, with, perhaps, a short visit between (2 Cor. 12 : 14; 13 : 1). The church presented all the lights and shades of the Greek nationality under the influence of the Gospel. It was rich in "all utterance and all knowledge," "coming behind in no gift," but troubled by the spirit of sect and party, infected with a

keineswegs unwürdig, vielmehr ein liebenswürdiges Denkmal väterlicher Für-sorge des Apostels für eine junge Christengemeinde." But the second Ep. to the Thess. Hilgenfeld assigns to the age of Trajan, as a sort of Pauline Apocalypse; thus reversing the view of Baur, who regarded the First Ep. as an imitation of the second. Grotius and Ewald put the Second Ep. likewise first (especially on account of 1 Thess. 1 : 7, 8, which seems to imply that the congregation had already become famous throughout Greece), but they regarded both as genuine.

morbid desire for worldly wisdom and brilliant eloquence, with
scepticism and moral levity—nay, to some extent polluted with
gross vices, so that even the Lord's table and love feasts were
desecrated by excesses, and that the apostle, in his absence,
found himself compelled to excommunicate a particularly offensive member who disgraced the Christian profession.[1] It was
distracted by Judaizers and other troublers, who abused the
names of Cephas, James, Apollos, and even of Christ (as *extra*-
Christians), for sectarian ends.[2] A number of questions of
morality and casuistry arose in that lively, speculative, and ex-
citable community, which the apostle had to answer from a
distance before his second (or third) and last visit.

Hence, these Epistles abound in variety of topics, and show
the extraordinary versatility of the mind of the writer, and his
practical wisdom in dealing with delicate and complicated
questions and unscrupulous opponents. For every aberration
he has a word of severe censure, for every danger a word of
warning, for every weakness a word of cheer and sympathy,
for every returning offender a word of pardon and encouragement. The Epistles lack the unity of design which characterizes
Galatians and Romans. They are ethical, ecclesiastical, pastoral, and personal, rather than dogmatic and theological, although some most important doctrines, as that on the resurrection, are treated more fully than elsewhere.

I. The First Epistle to the Corinthians was composed in
Ephesus shortly before Paul's departure for Greece, in the spring

---

[1] Such scandals would be almost incredible in a Christian church if the
apostle did not tell us so. As to the case of incest, 1 Cor. 5 : 1 sqq., we should
remember that Corinth was the most licentious city in all Greece, and that in
the splendid temple of her patron-goddess on the Acropolis there were kept
more than a thousand sacred female slaves (ἱερόδουλοι) for the pleasure of
strangers. Κορινθία κόρη was the name for a courtesan. Chastity was therefore one of the most difficult virtues to practice there ; and hence the apostle's
advice of a radical cure by absolute abstinence under the peculiar circumstances
of the time.

[2] The question of the Corinthian parties (with special reference to the Christ
party) I have discussed at length in my *Hist. of the Ap. Church*, pp. 285–291.
Baur's essay on this subject (1831) was the opening chapter in the development of the Tübingen theory.

of A.D. 57.[1] It had been preceded by another one, now lost
(5 : 9). It was an answer to perplexing questions concerning
various disputes and evils which disturbed the peace and spotted
the purity of the congregation. The apostle contrasts the foolish
wisdom of the gospel with the wise folly of human philosophy;
rebukes sectarianism; unfolds the spiritual unity and harmonious variety of the church of Christ, her offices and gifts of
grace, chief among which is love; warns against carnal impurity
as a violation of the temple of God; gives advice concerning
marriage and celibacy without binding the conscience (having
"no commandment of the Lord," 7 : 25); discusses the question
of meat sacrificed to idols, on which Jewish and Gentile Christians, scrupulous and liberal brethren, were divided; enjoins
the temporal support of the ministry as a Christian duty of
gratitude for greater spiritual mercies received; guards against
improprieties of dress; explains the design and corrects the
abuses of the Lord's Supper; and gives the fullest exposition
of the doctrine of the resurrection on the basis of the resurrection of Christ and his personal manifestations to the disciples,
and last, to himself at his conversion. Dean Stanley says of
this Epistle that it "gives a clearer insight than any other portion of the New Testament into the institutions, feelings, and
opinions of the church of the earlier period of the apostolic age.
It is in every sense the earliest chapter of the history of the
Christian church." The last, however, is not quite correct.
The Corinthian chapter was preceded by the Jerusalem and
Antioch chapters.

LEADING THOUGHTS : Is Christ divided? Was Paul crucified for you
(1 : 13)? It was God's pleasure through the foolishness of the preaching
[not through foolish preaching] to save them that believe (1 : 21). We
preach Christ crucified, unto the Jews a stumbling block, and unto Gentiles
foolishness, but unto them that are called, both Jews and Greeks, Christ
the power of God, and the wisdom of God (1 : 24). I determined not
to know anything among you, save Jesus, and him crucified (2 : 2). The
natural man receiveth not the things of the Spirit of God (2 : 14). Other
foundation can no man lay than that which is laid, which is Jesus

[1] Comp. 1 Cor. 16 : 5, 8 ; 5 : 7, 8 ; Acts 19 : 10, 21 ; 20 : 31.

Christ (3 : 11). Know ye not that ye are a temple of God, and that the Spirit of God dwelleth in you? If any man destroy the temple of God, him shall God destroy (3 : 16, 17). Let a man so account of ourselves as of ministers of Christ, and stewards of the mysteries of God (4 : 1). The kingdom of God is not in word, but in power (4 : 20). Purge out the old leaven (5 : 7). All things are lawful for me ; but not all things are expedient (6 : 12). Know ye not that your bodies are members of Christ (6 : 15)? Flee fornication (6 : 18). Glorify God in your body (6 : 20). Circumcision is nothing, and uncircumcision is nothing; but the keeping of the commandments of God (7 : 19). Let each man abide in that calling wherein he was called (7 : 20). Ye were bought with a price ; become not bondservants of men (7 : 23). Take heed lest this liberty of yours become a stumbling block to the weak (8 : 9). If meat [or wine] maketh my brother to stumble, I will eat no flesh [and drink no wine] for evermore, that I make not my brother to stumble (8 : 13). They who proclaim the gospel shall live of the gospel (9 : 14). Woe is unto me if I preach not the gospel (9 : 16). I am become all things to all men, that I may by all means save some (9 : 22). Let him that thinketh he standeth take heed lest he fall (10 : 12). All things are lawful, but all things are not expedient. Let no man seek his own, but each his neighbor's good (10 : 23). Whosoever shall eat the bread or drink the cup of the Lord in an unworthy manner, shall be guilty of the body and the blood of the Lord . . . He that eateth and drinketh eateth and drinketh judgment unto himself if he discern (discriminate) not the body (11 : 27–29). There are diversities of gifts, but the same Spirit (12 : 4). Now abideth faith, hope, love, these three ; and the greatest of these is love (13 : 13). Follow after love (14 : 1). Let all things be done unto edifying (14 : 26). By the grace of God I am what I am (15 : 9). If Christ hath not been raised, your faith is vain ; ye are yet in your sins (15 : 17). As in Adam all die, so also in Christ shall all be made alive (15 : 22). God shall be all in all (15 : 28). If there is a natural body, there is also a spiritual body (15 : 44). This corruptible must put on incorruption, and this mortal must put on immortality (15 : 54). Be ye steadfast, immovable, always abounding in the work of the Lord (15 : 58). Upon the first day in the week let each one of you lay by him in store, as he may prosper (16 : 2). Watch ye, stand fast in the faith, quit you like men, be strong. Let all that ye do be done in love (16 : 13, 14.).

II. THE SECOND EPISTLE TO THE CORINTHIANS was written in the summer or autumn of the same year, 57, from some place in Macedonia, shortly before the author's intended personal visit to the metropolis of Achaia.[1] It evidently proceeded

---

[1] 2 Cor. 7 : 5 ; 8 : 1 ; 9 : 2. Some ancient MSS. date the second Epistle from Philippi.

from profound agitation, and opens to us very freely the personal character and feelings, the official trials and joys, the noble pride and deep humility, the holy earnestness and fervent love, of the apostle. It gives us the deepest insight into his heart, and is almost an autobiography. He had, in the meantime, heard fuller news, through Titus, of the state of the church, the effects produced by his first Epistle, and the intrigues of the emissaries of the Judaizing party, who followed him everywhere and tried to undermine his work. This unchristian opposition compelled him, in self-defence, to speak of his ministry and his personal experience with overpowering eloquence. He also urges again upon the congregation the duty of charitable collections for the poor. The Epistle is a mine of pastoral wisdom.

LEADING THOUGHTS : As the sufferings of Christ abound unto us, even so our comfort also aboundeth through Christ (1 : 5). As ye are partakers of the sufferings, so also are ye of the comfort (1 : 7). Not that we have lordship over your faith, but are helpers of your joy (1 : 24). Who is sufficient for these things (2 : 16) ? Ye are our epistle, written in our hearts, known and read of all men (3 : 2). Not that we are sufficient of ourselves, but our sufficiency is from God (3 : 5). The letter killeth, but the spirit giveth life (3 : 6). The Lord is the Spirit : and where the Spirit of the Lord is, *there* is liberty (3 : 17). We preach not ourselves, but Christ Jesus as Lord, and ourselves as your servants for Jesus' sake (4 : 5). We have this treasure in earthen vessels, that the exceeding greatness of the power may be of God, and not from ourselves (4 : 7). Our light affliction, which is for the moment, worketh for us more and more exceedingly an eternal weight of glory (4 : 17). We know that if the earthly house of our tabernacle be dissolved, we have a building from God, a house not made with hands, eternal, in the heavens (5 : 1). We walk by faith, not by sight (5 : 7). We must all be made manifest before the judgment seat of Christ (5 : 10). The love of Christ constraineth us, because we thus judge, that one died for all, therefore all died (5 : 14). And he died for all, that they who live should no longer live unto themselves, but unto him who for their sakes died and rose again (5 : 15). If any man is in Christ, he is a new creature : the old things are passed away ; behold, they are become new (5 : 17). God was in Christ, reconciling the world unto himself, not reckoning unto them their trespasses, and having committed unto us the word of reconciliation (5 : 19). We beseech you on behalf of Christ, be ye reconciled to God (5 : 20). Him who knew no sin he made to be sin in our behalf; that we might become the righteousness of God in him (5 : 21). Be not unequally yoked with unbelievers (6 : 14). I am filled with comfort, I overflow with joy in all our affliction (7 : 4). Godly sorrow worketh repentance unto salvation, but the sorrow of the world worketh death (7 : 10). Ye know the grace of our Lord Jesus Christ, that, though he was rich, yet for your sakes he became poor, that ye through his poverty might become rich (8 : 9). He that soweth sparingly shall reap also sparingly ; and he that soweth bountifully shall reap also bountifully (9 : 6). God loveth a cheerful giver (9 : 7). He that glorieth, let him glory in the Lord (10 : 17). Not he that commendeth himself is approved, but whom the Lord commendeth (10 : 18). My grace is sufficient for thee ; for my power is made perfect in weakness (12 : 9). We can do nothing against the truth, but for the truth (13 : 8). The grace of the Lord Jesus Christ, and the love of God, and the communion of the Holy Spirit, be with you all (13 : 14).

§ 91. *The Epistle to the Galatians.*

Comp. the introduction to my *Com. on Gal.* (1882).

Galatians and Romans discuss the doctrines of sin and redemption, and the relation of the law and the gospel. They teach salvation by free grace and justification by faith, Christian universalism in opposition to Jewish particularism, evangelical freedom versus legalistic bondage. But Galatians is a rapid sketch and the child of deep emotion, Romans an elaborate treatise and the mature product of calm reflexion. The former Epistle is polemical against foreign intruders and seducers, the latter is irenical and composed in a serene frame of mind. The one rushes along like a mountain torrent and foaming cataract, the other flows like a majestic river through a boundless prairie ; and yet it is the same river, like the Nile at the Rapids and below Cairo, or the Rhine in the Grisons and the lowlands of Germany and Holland, or the St. Lawrence at Niagara Falls and below Montreal and Quebec where it majestically branches out into the ocean.

It is a remarkable fact that the two races represented by the readers of these Epistles—the Celtic and the Latin—have far departed from the doctrines taught in them and exchanged the gospel freedom for legal bondage ; thus repeating the apostasy of the sanguine, generous, impressible, mercurial, fickle-minded Galatians. The Pauline gospel was for centuries ignored, misunderstood, and (in spite of St. Augustin) cast out at last by Rome, as Christianity itself was cast out by Jerusalem of old. But the overruling wisdom of God made the rule of the papacy a training-school of the Teutonic races of the North and West for freedom; as it had turned the unbelief of the Jews to the conversion of the Gentiles. Those Epistles, more than any book of the New Testament, inspired the Reformation of the sixteenth century, and are to this day the Gibraltar of evangelical Protestantism. Luther, under a secondary inspiration, reproduced Galatians in his war against the " Babylonian captivity of the church;" the battle for Christian freedom was won once more, and its fruits are enjoyed by nations of which neither Paul nor Luther ever heard.

The Epistle to the GALATIANS (Gauls, originally from the borders of the Rhine and Moselle, who had migrated to Asia Minor) was written after Paul's second visit to them, either during his long residence in Ephesus (A.D. 54–57), or shortly afterwards on his second journey to Corinth, possibly from Corinth, certainly before the Epistle to the Romans. It was occasioned by the machinations of the Judaizing teachers who undermined his apostolic authority and misled his converts into an apostasy from the gospel of free grace to a false gospel of legal bondage, requiring circumcision as a condition of justification and full membership of the church. It is an " Apologia pro vita sua," a personal and doctrinal self-vindication. He defends his independent apostleship (1 : 1 to 2 : 14), and his teaching (2 : 15 to 4 : 31), and closes with exhortations to hold fast to Christian freedom without abusing it, and to show the fruits of faith by holy living (chs. 5 and 6).

The Epistle reveals, in clear, strong colors, both the difference and the harmony among the Jewish and Gentile apostles—a difference ignored by the old orthodoxy, which sees only the harmony, and exaggerated by modern scepticism, which sees only the difference. It anticipates, in grand fundamental outlines, a conflict which is renewed from time to time in the history of different churches, and, on the largest scale, in the conflict between Petrine Romanism and Pauline Protestantism. The temporary collision of the two leading apostles in Antioch is typical of the battle of the Reformation.

At the same time Galatians is an Irenicon and sounds the key-note of a final adjustment of all doctrinal and ritualistic controversies. "In Christ Jesus neither circumcision availeth anything, nor uncircumcision, but *faith working through love*" (5 : 6). "And as many as shall walk by this rule, peace be upon them, and mercy, and upon the Israel of God" (6 : 16).

CENTRAL IDEA : Evangelical freedom.

KEY-WORDS : For freedom Christ set us free : stand fast therefore, and be not entangled again in the yoke of bondage (5 : 1). A man is not justified by works of the law, but only through faith in Jesus Christ (2 : 16). I have been crucified with Christ, and it is no longer I that live but Christ liveth in me (2 : 20). Christ redeemed us from the curse of the law, having become a curse for us (3 : 13). Ye were called for freedom, only use not your freedom for an occasion to the flesh, but through love be servants one to another (5 : 13). Walk by the Spirit, and ye shall not fulfil the lust of the flesh (5 : 16).

§ 92. *The Epistle to the Romans.*

On the church in Rome, see § 36 (pp. 360 sqq.) ; on the theology of the Ep. to the Rom., § 71 (pp. 525 sqq.).

A few weeks before his fifth and last journey to Jerusalem, Paul sent, as a forerunner of his intended personal visit, a letter to the Christians in the capital of the world, which was intended by Providence to become the Jerusalem of Christendom. Foreseeing its future importance, the apostle chose for his theme : The gospel the power of God unto salvation to every believer, the Jew first, and also the Gentile (1 : 16, 17). Writing to the philosophical Greeks, he contrasts the *wisdom* of God with the wisdom of man. To the world-ruling Romans he represents Christianity as the *power* of God which by spiritual weapons will conquer even conquering Rome. Such a bold idea must have struck a Roman statesman as the wild dream of a visionary or madman, but it was fulfilled in the ultimate conversion of the empire after three centuries of persecution, and is still in the process of ever-growing fulfilment.

In the exposition of his theme the apostle shows: (1) that all men are in need of salvation, being under the power of sin and exposed to the judgment of the righteous God, the Gentiles not only (1 : 18–32), but also the Jews, who are still more guilty, having sinned against the written law and extraordinary privileges (2 : 1 to 3 : 20); (2) that salvation is accomplished by Jesus Christ, his atoning death and triumphant resurrection, freely offered to all on the sole condition of faith, and applied in the successive acts of justification, sanctification, and glorification (3 : 21 to end of chapter 8); (3) that salvation was offered first to the Jews, and, being rejected by them in unbelief, passed on to the Gentiles, but will return again to the Jews after the fulness of the Gentiles shall have come in (chs. 9–11); (4) that we should show our gratitude for so great a salvation by surrendering ourselves to the service of God, which is true freedom (chs. 12 to 16).

The salutations in the last chapter, the remarkable variations of the manuscripts in 15 : 33; 16 : 20, 24, 27, and the omission of the words "in Rome," 1 : 7, 15, in Codex G, are best explained by the conjecture that copies of the letter were also sent to Ephesus (where Aquila and Priscilla were at that time, 1 Cor. 16 : 19, and again, some years afterwards, 2 Tim. 4 : 19), and perhaps to other churches with appropriate conclusions, all of which are preserved in the present form.[1]

This letter stands justly at the head of the Pauline Epistles.

---

[1] On the textual variations, see Westcott and Hort, *Appendix*, pp. 110–114. Reuss, Ewald, Farrar suppose that ch. 16 (or 16 : 3–20) was addressed to Ephesus. Renan conjectures that an editor has combined four copies of the same encyclical letter of Paul, each addressed to a different church and having a different ending. Both these views are preferable to Baur's rejection of the last two chapters as spurious; though they are full of the Pauline spirit. Hilgenfeld (*Einleit.*, p. 323) and Pfleiderer (*Paulinismus*, p. 314) maintain, against Baur, the genuineness of chs. 15 and 16. On the names in ch. 16 see the instructive discussion of Lightfoot in his *Com. on Philippians*, pp. 172–176.

It is more comprehensive and systematic than the others, and admirably adapted to the mistress of the world, which was to become also the mistress of Western Christendom. It is the most remarkable production of the most remarkable man. It is his heart. It contains his theology, theoretical and practical, for which he lived and died. It gives the clearest and fullest exposition of the doctrines of sin and grace and the best possible solution of the universal dominion of sin and death in the universal redemption by the second Adam. Without this redemption the fall is indeed the darkest enigma and irreconcilable with the idea of divine justice and goodness. Paul reverently lifts the veil from the mysteries of eternal foreknowledge and foreordination and God's gracious designs in the winding course of history which will end at last in the triumph of his wisdom and mercy and the greatest good to mankind. Luther calls Romans "the chief book of the New Testament and the purest Gospel," Coleridge: "the profoundest book in existence," Meyer: "the greatest and richest of all the apostolic works," Godet (best of all): "the cathedral of the Christian faith."

THEME: Christianity the power of free and universal salvation, on condition of faith.

LEADING THOUGHTS: They are all under sin (3 : 9). Through the law cometh the knowledge of sin (3 : 20). Man is justified by faith apart from works of the law (3 : 28). Being justified by faith we have ($\check{\epsilon}\chi o\mu\epsilon\nu$, or, let us have, $\check{\epsilon}\chi\omega\mu\epsilon\nu$) peace with God through our Lord Jesus Christ (5 : 1). As through one man sin entered into the world, and death through sin, and so death passed unto all men, for that all sinned (5 : 12) [so through one man righteousness entered into the world, and life through righteousness, and so life passed unto all men on condition that they believe in Christ and by faith become partakers of his righteousness]. Where sin abounded, grace did abound much more exceedingly: that as sin reigned in death, even so might grace reign through righteousness unto eternal life through Jesus Christ our Lord (5 : 20, 21). Reckon yourselves to be dead unto sin, but alive unto God in Christ Jesus (6 : 11). There is no condemnation to them that are in Christ Jesus (8 : 1). To them that love God all things work together for good (8 : 28). Whom he foreknew, he also foreordained to be conformed to the image of his Son . . . and whom he foreordained them he also called : and whom he called, them he also justified : and whom he justified, them he also glorified (8 : 29, 30). If God is for us, who is against us (8 : 31)? Who shall separate us from the love of Christ (8 : 35)? Hardening in part hath befallen Israel, until the fulness of the Gentiles be come in ; and so all Israel shall be saved (11 : 25). God hath shut up all unto disobedience, that he might have mercy upon all (11 : 32). Of Him, and through Him, and unto Him are all things (11 : 36). Present your bodies a living sacrifice, holy, acceptable to God, which is your reasonable service (12 : 1).

§ 93. *The Epistles of the Captivity.*

During his confinement in Rome, from A.D. 61 to 63, while waiting the issue of his trial on the charge of being "a mover of insurrections among all the Jews throughout the world, and a ringleader of the sect of the Nazarenes" (Acts 24 : 5), the aged apostle composed four Epistles, to the COLOSSIANS, EPHESIANS, PHILEMON, and PHILIPPIANS. He thus turned the prison into a pulpit, sent inspiration and comfort to his distant congregations, and rendered a greater service to future ages than he could have done by active labor. He gloried in being a "prisoner of Christ." He experienced the blessedness of persecution for righteousness' sake (Matt. 5 : 10), and "the peace of God which passeth all understanding" (Phil. 4 : 7). He often refers to his bonds, and the coupling chain or hand-cuff ($\ddot{a}\lambda\nu\sigma\iota\varsigma$) by which, according to Roman custom, he was with his right wrist fettered day and night to a soldier; one relieving the other and being in turn chained to the apostle, so that his imprisonment became a means for the spread of the gospel "throughout the whole prætorian guard." [1] He had the privilege of living in his own hired lodging (probably in the neighborhood of the prætorian camp, outside of the walls, to the northeast of Rome), and of free intercourse with his companions and distant congregations.

Paul does not mention the place of his captivity, which extended through four years and a half (two at Cæsarea, two at Rome, and six months spent on the stormy voyage and at Malta).

[1] Phil. 1 : 7, 13, 14, 17 ; Eph. 3 : 1 ("the prisoner of Christ Jesus in behalf of you Gentiles"); 4 : 1 ("the prisoner in the Lord"); Col. 4 : 3, 18 ("remember my bonds"); Philem. vers. 10, 13; comp. Acts 28 : 17, 30.

The traditional view dates the four Epistles from the Roman captivity, and there is no good reason to depart from it. Several modern critics assign one or more to Cæsarea, where he cannot be supposed to have been idle, and where he was nearer to his congregations in Asia Minor.[1] But in Cæsarea Paul looked forward to Rome and to Spain; while in the Epistles of the captivity he expresses the hope of soon visiting Colossæ and Philippi. In Rome he had the best opportunity of correspondence with his distant friends, and enjoyed a degree of freedom which may have been denied him in Cæsarea. In Philippians he sends greetings from converts in " Cæsar's household " (4 : 22), which naturally points to Rome; and the circumstances and surroundings of the other Epistles are very much alike.

Ephesians, Colossians, and Philemon were composed about the same time and sent by the same messengers (Tychicus and Onesimus) to Asia Minor, probably toward the close of the Roman captivity, for in Philemon, ver. 22, he engaged a lodging in Colossæ in the prospect of a speedy release and visit to the East.

Philippians we place last in the order of composition, or, at all events, in the second year of the Roman captivity; for some time must have elapsed after Paul's arrival in Rome before the gospel could spread " throughout the whole prætorian guard " (Phil. 1 : 13), and before the Philippians, at a distance of seven hundred miles from Rome (a full month's journey in those days), could receive news from him and send him contributions through Epaphroditus, besides other communications which seem to have preceded the Epistle.[2]

On the other hand, the priority of the composition of Philippians has been recently urged on purely internal evidence, namely, its doctrinal affinity with the preceding anti-Judaic Epistles; while Colossians and Ephesians presuppose the rise of

---

[1] So Böttger, Thiersch, Reuss, Meyer, Weiss. Thiersch dates even Second Timothy from Cæsarea, but denies the second Roman captivity.

[2] This is the prevailing view among critics. I have discussed the order in the *History of the Apost. Ch.* (1853), pp. 322 sqq.

the Gnostic heresy and thus form the connecting link between them and the Pastoral Epistles, in which the same heresy appears in a more matured form.[1] But Ephesians has likewise striking affinities in thought and language with Romans in the doctrine of justification (comp. Eph. 2 : 8), and with Romans (ch. 12) and First Corinthians (12 and 14) in the doctrine of the church. As to the heresy, Paul had predicted its rise in Asia Minor several years before in his farewell to the Ephesian elders. And, finally, the grateful and joyful tone of Philippians falls in most naturally with the lofty and glorious conception of the church of Christ as presented in Ephesians.

§ 94. *The Epistle to the Colossians.*

THE CHURCHES IN PHRYGIA.

The cities of Colossæ, Laodicea, and Hierapolis are mentioned together as seats of Christian churches in the closing chapter of Colossians, and the Epistle may be considered as being addressed to all, for the apostle directs that it be read also in the churches of the Laodiceans (4 : 13–16). They were situated within a few miles of each other in the valley of the Lycus (a tributary of the Mæander) in Phrygia on the borders of Lydia, and belonged, under the Roman rule, to the proconsular province of Asia Minor.

Laodicea was the most important of the three, and enjoyed metropolitan rank; she was destroyed by a disastrous earthquake A.D. 61 or 65, but rebuilt from her own resources without the customary aid from Rome.[2] The church of Laodicea is the last of the seven churches addressed in the Apocalypse (3 : 14–

---

[1] So Lightfoot (p. 31), followed by Farrar (II. 417). Ewald likewise puts Philippians before Colossians, but denies the genuineness of Ephesians. Bleek regards the data as insufficient to decide the chronological order. See his *Einleitung*, p. 461, and his posthumous *Lectures on Colossians, Philemon, and Ephesians*, published 1865, p. 7.

[2] The earthquake took place, according to Tacitus (*Ann.*, XIV. 27), in the seventh, according to Eusebius (*Chron.*, Ol. 210, 4), in the tenth year of Nero's reign, and extended also to Hierapolis and Colossæ.

22), and is described as rich and proud and lukewarm. It har-bored in the middle of the fourth century (after 344) a council which passed an important act on the canon, forbidding the public reading of any but "the canonical books of the New and Old Testaments" (the list of these books is a later addition), a prohibition which was confirmed and adopted by later councils in the East and the West.

Hierapolis was a famous watering-place, surrounded by beautiful scenery,[1] and the birthplace of the lame slave Epictetus, who, with Seneca and Marcus Aurelius, ranks among the first heathen moralists, and so closely resembles the lofty maxims of the New Testament that some writers have assumed, though without historic foundation, a passing acquaintance between him and Paul or his pupil Epaphras of Colossæ.[2] The church of Hierapolis figures in the post-apostolic age as the bishopric of Papias (a friend of Polycarp) and Apollinaris.

Colossæ,[3] once likewise famous, was at the time of Paul the smallest of the three neighboring cities, and has almost disap-

---

[1] In a Greek inscription, published by Boeckh and quoted by Lightfoot, Hierapolis is thus apostrophized :

> "Hail, fairest soil in all broad Asia's realm ;
> Hail, golden city, nymph divine, bedeck'd
> With flowing rills, thy jewels."

[2] Epictetus (Ἐπίκτητος), a slave and then a freedman of Epaphroditus (who was himself a freedman of Nero), was considerably younger than Paul, and taught first at Rome, and, after the expulsion of the philosophers by Domitian, at Nicopolis in Epirus, where his discourses (*Enchiridion*) were taken down by Arrian. For, like Socrates, he himself wrote nothing. A meeting with Paul or Epaphras would "solve more than one riddle," as Lightfoot says. But he shows no trace of a knowledge of Christianity any more than Seneca, whose correspondence with Paul is spurious, though both lived at Rome under Nero. Marcus Aurelius, a century later, persecuted the Christians and alludes to them only once in his *Meditations* (XI. 3), where he traces their heroic zeal for martyrdom to sheer obstinacy. The self-reliant, stoic morality of these philosophers, sublime as it is, would have hindered rather than facilitated their acceptance of Christianity, which is based on repentance and humility.

[3] Κολοσσαί, *Colossæ*, is the correct reading of the oldest MSS. against the later Κολασσαί, *Colassæ*. Herodotus calls it πόλις μεγάλη, and Xenophon εὐδαίμων καὶ μεγάλη. In the middle ages it was called Χῶναι. There are few remains of it left two miles north of the present town of Chonos, which is inhabited by Christians and Turks.

peared from the earth; while magnificent ruins of temples, theatres, baths, aqueducts, gymnasia, and sepulchres still testify to the former wealth and prosperity of Laodicea and Hierapolis. The church of Colossæ was the least important of the churches to which Paul addressed an Epistle, and it is scarcely mentioned in post-apostolic times; but it gave rise to a heresy which shook the church in the second century, and this Epistle furnished the best remedy against it.

There was a large Jewish population in Phrygia, since Antiochus the Great had despotically transplanted two thousand Jewish families from Babylonia and Mesopotamia to that region. It thus became, in connection with the sensuous and mystic tendency of the Phrygian character, a nursery of religious syncretism and various forms of fanaticism.

PAUL AND THE COLOSSIANS.

Paul passed twice through Phrygia, on his second and third missionary tours,[1] but probably not through the valley of the Lycus. Luke does not say that he established churches there, and Paul himself seems to include the Colossians and Laodiceans among those who had not seen his face in the flesh.[2] He names Epaphras, of Colossæ, his "dear fellow-servant" and "fellow-prisoner," as the teacher and faithful minister of the Christians in that place.[3] But during his long residence in Ephesus (A.D. 54-57) and from his imprisonment he exercised a general supervision over all the churches in Asia. After his death they passed under the care of John, and in the second century they figure prominently in the Gnostic, Paschal, Chiliastic, and Montanistic controversies.

Paul heard of the condition of the church at Colossæ through Epaphras, his pupil, and Onesimus, a runaway slave. He sent

---

[1] Acts 16 : 6 (τὴν Φρυγίαν καὶ Γαλατικὴν χώραν); 18 : 23.

[2] Col. 2 : 1; comp. 1 : 4, 8, 9; and Lightfoot, *Com.*, pp. 23 sqq. and 238.

[3] Col. 1 : 7; 4 : 12; comp. Philem., ver. 23. Hilgenfeld (p. 663) thinks that Paul founded those churches, and uses this as an argument against the genuineness of the Epistle which implies the contrary. But how easily could a forger have avoided such an apparent contradiction.

through Tychicus (4 : 7) a letter to the church, which was also intended for the Laodiceans (4 : 16); at the same time he sent through Onesimus a private letter of commendation to his master, Philemon, a member of the church of Colossæ. He also directed the Colossians to procure and read "the letter from Laodicea," which is most probably the evangelical Epistle to the Ephesians which was likewise transmitted through Tychicus.‧ He had special reasons for writing to the Colossians and to Philemon, and a general reason for writing to all the churches in the region of Ephesus; and he took advantage of the mission of Tychicus to secure both ends. In this way the three Epistles are closely connected in time and aim. They would mutually explain and confirm one another.

THE COLOSSIAN HERESY.

The special reason which prompted Paul to write to the Colossians was the rise of a new heresy among them which soon afterward swelled into a mighty and dangerous movement in the ancient church, as rationalism has done in modern times. It differed from the Judaizing heresy which he opposed in Galatians and Corinthians, as Essenism differed from Phariseeism, or as legalism differs from mysticism. The Colossian heresy was an Essenic and ascetic type of Gnosticism; it derived its ritualistic and practical elements from Judaism, its speculative elements from heathenism; it retained circumcision, the observance of Sabbaths and new moons, and the distinction of meats and drinks; but it mixed with it elements of oriental mysticism and theosophy, the heathen notion of an evil principle, the worship of subordinate spirits, and an ascetic struggle for emancipation from the dominion of matter. It taught an antagonism between God and matter and interposed between them a series of angelic mediators as objects of worship. It thus contained the essential features of Gnosticism, but in its in-

---

[1] Col. 4 : 16 : τὴν ἐκ Λαοδικείας ἵνα καὶ ὑμεῖς ἀναγνῶτε. An abridged expression for "the letter left at Laodicea which you will procure thence." So Bleek and Lightfoot, *in loco*.

cipient and rudimental form, or a Christian Essenism in its transition to Gnosticism. In its ascetic tendency it resembles that of the weak brethren in the Roman congregation (Rom. 14 : 5, 6, 21). Cerinthus, in the age of John, represents a more developed stage and forms the link between the Colossian heresy and the post-apostolic Gnosticism.[1]

THE REFUTATION.

Paul refutes this false philosophy calmly and respectfully by the true doctrine of the Person of Christ, as the one Mediator between God and men, in whom dwells all the fulness of the Godhead bodily. And he meets the false asceticism based upon the dualistic principle with the doctrine of the purification of the heart by faith and love as the effectual cure of all moral evil.

THE GNOSTIC AND THE PAULINE PLEROMA.

"Pleroma" or "fulness" is an important term in Colossians and Ephesians.[2] Paul uses it in common with the Gnostics,

---

[1] On the Colossian heresy I refer chiefly to Neander (I. 319 sqq.), the lectures of Bleek (pp. 11–19), and the valuable Excursus of Lightfoot, *Com.*, pp. 73–113, who agrees with Neander and Bleek, but is more full. Lightfoot refutes the view of Hilgenfeld (*Der Gnosticismus u. das N. Test.*, in the "Zeitschrift für wissensch. Theol.," vol. XIII. 233 sqq.), who maintains that the Ep. opposes two different heresies, pure Gnosticism (2 : 8–10) and pure Judaism (2 : 16–23). Comp. his *Einleitung*, pp. 665 sqq. The two passages are connected by τὰ στοιχεῖα τοῦ κόσμου (vers. 8 and 20), and the later history of Gnosticism shows, in a more developed form, the same strange mixture of Judaizing and paganizing elements. See the chapter on Gnosticism in the second volume.

[2] The word πλήρωμα, from πληροῦν, to fill, to complete, occurs eighteen times in the New Test., thirteen times in the Epistles of Paul (see Bruder). It designates the result of the action implied in the verb, *i.e.*, complement, completeness, plenitude, perfection; and, in a wider sense (as in John 1 : 16; Col. 1 : 19; 2 : 9), fulness, abundance. Like other substantives ending in —μα, it has an active sense : the filling substance, that which fills (*id quod implet*, or *id quo res impletur*). So it is often used by the classics, *e.g.*, πλήρωμα πόλεως, the population of a city ; in the Septuagint, for the Hebrew מְלֹא, abundance, *e.g.*, τὸ πλήρωμα τῆς γῆς, or τὸ πλήρωμα τῆς θαλάσσης, that which fills the earth, or the sea ; and in the New Test., *e.g.*, Mark 6 : 43 (κοφίνων πληρώματα); 8 : 20 (σπυρίδων πλ.). The passive sense is rare : that

and this has been made an argument for the post-apostolic origin of the two Epistles. He did, of course, not borrow it from the Gnostics; for he employs it repeatedly in his other Epistles with slight variations. It must have had a fixed theological meaning, as it is not explained. It cannot be traced to Philo, who, however, uses "Logos" in a somewhat similar sense for the plenitude of Divine powers.

Paul speaks of "the pleroma of the earth," *i.e.*, all that fills the earth or is contained in it (1 Cor. 10 : 26, 28, in a quotation from Ps. 24 : 1) ; "the pleroma," *i.e.*, the fulfilment or accomplishment, "of the law," which is love (Rom. 13 : 10 [1]); "the pleroma," *i.e.*, the fulness or abundance, "of the blessing of Christ" (Rom. 15 : 29); "the pleroma," or full measure, "of the time" (Gal. 4 : 4 ; comp. Eph. 1 : 10; Mark 1 : 15 ; Luke 21 : 24); "the pleroma of the Gentiles," meaning their full number, or whole body, but not necessarily all individuals (Rom. 11 : 25); "the pleroma of the Godhead," *i.e.*, the fulness or plenitude of all Divine attributes and energies (Col. 1 : 19 ; 2 : 9); "the pleroma of Christ," which is the church as the body of Christ (Eph. 1 : 23; comp. 3 : 19; 4 : 13).

In the Gnostic systems, especially that of Valentinus, "pleroma" signifies the intellectual and spiritual world, including all Divine powers or æons, in opposition to the "kenoma," *i.e.*, the void, the emptiness, the material world. The distinction was based on the dualistic principle of an eternal antagonism between spirit and matter, which led the more earnest Gnostics to an extravagant asceticism, the frivolous ones to wild antinomianism. They included in the pleroma a succession of emanations from the Divine abyss, which form the links between the infinite and the finite; and they lowered the dignity of Christ by making him simply the highest of those intermediate æons. The burden of the Gnostic speculation was always

---

which is filled (*id quod impletur* or *impletum est*), the filled receptacle. Comp. Grimm and Robinson. *sub verbo*, and especially Fritzsche, *Ad Rom.* II. 469 sqq., and Lightfoot. *Coloss.* 323 sqq.

[1] In this passage it is equivalent to πλήρωσις, *legis observatio*.

the question: Whence is the world? and whence is evil? It sought the solution in a dualism between mind and matter, the pleroma and the kenoma; but this is no solution at all.

In opposition to this error, Paul teaches, on a thoroughly monotheistic basis, that Christ is " the image of the invisible God " (εἰκὼν τοῦ Θεοῦ τοῦ ἀοράτου, 1 : 15 ; comp. 2 Cor. 4 : 4 —an expression often used by Philo as a description of the Logos, and of the personified Wisdom, in Wisd. 7 : 26); that he is the preëxistent and incarnate pleroma or plenitude of Divine powers and attributes; that in him the whole fulness of the Godhead, that is, of the Divine nature itself,[1] dwells bodily-wise or corporeally (σωματικῶς), as the soul dwells in the human body ; and that he is the one universal and all-sufficient Mediator, through whom the whole universe of things, visible and invisible, were made, in whom all things hold together (or cohere, συνέστηκεν), and through whom the Father is pleased to reconcile all things to himself.

The Christology of Colossians approaches very closely to the Christology of John ; for he represents Christ as the incarnate " Logos " or Revealer of God, who dwelt among us " full (πλήρης) of grace and truth," and out of whose Divine " fulness " (ἐκ τοῦ πληρώματος αὐτοῦ) we all have received grace for grace (John 1 : 1, 14, 16). Paul and John fully agree in teaching the eternal preëxistence of Christ, and his agency in the creation and preservation of the world (Col. 1 : 15–17 ; John 1 : 3). According to Paul, He is " the *first-born* or *first-begotten*" of all creation (πρωτότοκος πάσης κτίσεως, Col. 1 : 15, distinct from πρωτόκτιστος, first-*created*), *i.e.*, prior and superior to the whole created world, or eternal ; according to John He is " the *only-begotten* Son " of the Father (ὁ μονογενὴς υἱός,[2] John 1 : 14, 18 ; comp. 3 : 16, 18 ; 1 John 4 : 9), before and above all created children of God. The former term denotes

---

[1] 2 : 9 τὸ πλήρωμα τῆς Θεότητος, *deitas, Deity,* not Θειότητος, *divinitas, divinity.* Bengel remarks : " *Non modo divinæ virtutes, sed ipsa divina natura.*" So also Lightfoot.

[2] Or, according to the other reading, which is equally well supported, μονο· γενὴς Θεός, one who is only-begotten *God.*

Christ's unique relation to the world, the latter his unique relation to the Father.

The Pauline authorship of the Epistle to the Colossians will
be discussed in the next section in connection with the Epistle
to the Ephesians.

THEME : Christ all in all. The true gnosis and the false gnosis. True
and false asceticism.

LEADING THOUGHTS : Christ is the image of the invisible God, the
first-begotten of all creation (1 : 15).—In Christ are hidden all the treasures of wisdom and knowledge (2 : 3).—In him dwelleth all the fulness
(τὸ πλήρωμα) of the Godhead bodily (2 : 9).—If ye were raised together
with Christ, seek the things that are above, where Christ is, seated on
the right hand of God (3 : 1).—When Christ, who is our life, shall be
manifested, then shall ye also with him be manifested in glory (3 : 4).—
Christ is all, and in all (3 : 11).—Above all things put on love, which is
the bond of perfectness (3 : 14).—Whatsoever ye do, in word or in deed,
do all in the name of the Lord Jesus (3 : 17).

§ 95.   *The Epistle to the Ephesians.*

CONTENTS.

When Paul took leave of the Ephesian Elders at Miletus, in
the spring of the year 58, he earnestly and affectionately exhorted them, in view of threatening disturbances from within,
to take heed unto themselves and to feed " the church of the
Lord, which he acquired with his own blood." [1]

This strikes the key-note of the Epistle to the Ephesians. It
is a doctrinal and practical exposition of the idea of the church,
as the house of God (2 : 20–22), the spotless bride of Christ
(5 : 25–27), the mystical body of Christ (4 : 12–16), " the fulness

---

[1] Acts 20 : 28. Some of the best authorities (א, B, Vulg., etc.) read "church
of *God.*" So also Westcott and Hort, and the English Revision; but the
American Committee prefers, with Tischendorf, the reading τοῦ κυρίου, which
is supported by A, C*, D, E, etc., and suits better in this connection. Paul
often speaks of " the *church* of God," but nowhere of " the *blood* of God."
Possibly, as Dr. Hort suggests, υἱοῦ may have dropped out in a very early copy
after τοῦ ἰδίου. See a full discussion by Dr. Abbot, in "Bibl. Sacra" for
1876, pp. 313 sqq. (for κυρίου), and by Westcott and Hort, *Greek Test.*, II.,
Notes, pp. 98 sqq. (for ϑεοῦ).

of Him that filleth all in all" (1 : 23). The pleroma of the Godhead resides in Christ corporeally; so the pleroma of Christ, the plenitude of his graces and energies, resides in the church, as his body. Christ's fulness is God's fulness; the church's fulness is Christ's fulness. God is reflected in Christ, Christ is reflected in the church.

This is an ideal conception, a celestial vision, as it were, of the church in its future state of perfection. Paul himself represents the present church militant as a gradual growth unto the complete stature of Christ's fulness (4 : 13–16). We look in vain for an actual church which is free from spot or wrinkle or blemish (5 : 27). Even the apostolic church was full of defects, as we may learn from every Epistle of the New Testament. The church consists of individual Christians, and cannot be complete till they are complete. The body grows and matures with its several members. " It is not yet made manifest what we shall be " (1 John 3 : 2).

Nevertheless, Paul's church is not a speculation or fiction, like Plato's Republic or Sir Thomas More's Utopia. It is a reality in Christ, who is absolutely holy, and is spiritually and dynamically present in his church always, as the soul is present in the members of the body. And it sets before us the high standard and aim to be kept constantly in view; as Christ exhorts every one individually to be perfect, even as our heavenly Father is perfect (Matt. 5 : 48).

With this conception of the church is closely connected Paul's profound and most fruitful idea of the family. He calls the relation of Christ to his church a great mystery (5 : 32), and represents it as the archetype of the marriage relation, whereby one man and one woman become one flesh. He therefore bases the family on new and holy ground, and makes it a miniature of the church, or the household of God. Accordingly, husbands are to love their wives even as Christ loved the church, his bride, and gave himself up for her; wives are to obey their husbands as the church is subject to Christ, the head; parents are to love their children as Christ and the church love the in-

dividual Christians; children are to love their parents as individual Christians are to love Christ and the church. The full
and general realization of this domestic ideal would be heaven
on earth. But how few families come up to this standard.[1]

EPHESIANS AND THE WRITINGS OF JOHN.

Paul emphasizes the person of Christ in Colossians, the person and agency of the Holy Spirit in Ephesians. For the Holy
Spirit carries on the work of Christ in the church. Christians
are sealed with the Holy Spirit of promise unto the day of redemption (1 : 13 ; 4 : 30). The spirit of wisdom and revelation
imparts the knowledge of Christ (1 : 17 ; 3 : 16). Christians
should be filled with the Spirit (5 : 18), take the sword of the
Spirit, which is the word of God, and pray in the Spirit at all
seasons (6 : 17, 18).

The pneumatology of Ephesians resembles that of John, as
the christology of Colossians resembles the christology of John.
It is the Spirit who takes out of the " fulness " of Christ, and
shows it to the believer, who glorifies the Son and guides into
the truth (John 14 : 17 ; 15 : 26 ; 16 : 13–15, etc.). Great prominence is given to the Spirit also in Romans, Galatians, Corinthians, and the Acts of the Apostles.

John does not speak of the church and its outward organization (except in the Apocalypse), but he brings Christ in as close
and vital a contact with the individual disciples as Paul with
the whole body. Both teach the unity of the church as a
fact, and as an aim to be realized more and more by the effort
of Christians, and both put the centre of unity in the Holy
Spirit.

[1] For a fine analysis of the Epistle, I refer to Braune's *Com.* in the Lange
Series (translated by Dr. Riddle). He adopts a twofold, Stier and Alford a
threefold (trinitarian) division. See also Dr. Riddle's clear analysis in Schaff's
Popular Com. on the New Test., III. (1882). p. 355. I. Doctrinal Part, chs. 1–3 :
The church, the mystical body of Christ, chosen, redeemed, and united in
Christ. II. Practical Part. chs. 4–6 : Therefore, let all the members of the
church walk in unity, in love, in newness of life, in the armor of God. But
we should remember that the Epistle is not strictly systematic, and the doctrinal expositions and practical exhortations interlace each other.

ENCYCLICAL INTENT.

Ephesians was intended not only for the church at Ephesus, the metropolis of Asia Minor, but for all the leading churches of that district. Hence the omission of the words " in Ephesus" (1 : 1) in some of the oldest and best MSS.[1] Hence, also, the absence of personal and local intelligence. The encyclical destination may be inferred also from the reference in Col. 4 : 16 to the Epistle to the church of Laodicea, which the Colossians were to procure and to read, and which is probably identical with our canonical Epistle to the Ephesians." [2]

CHARACTER AND VALUE OF THE EPISTLE.

Ephesians is the most churchly book of the New Testament. But it presupposes Colossians, the most Christly of Paul's Epistles. Its churchliness is rooted and grounded in Christliness, and has no sense whatever if separated from this root. A church without Christ would be, at best, a praying corpse (and there are such churches). Paul was at once the highest of high churchmen, the most evangelical of evangelicals, and the broadest of the broad, because most comprehensive in his grasp and furthest removed from all pedantry and bigotry of sect or party.

Ephesians is, in some respects, the most profound and diffi-

---

[1] ἐν Ἐφέσῳ is omitted in the Sinaitic and Vatican MSS. Marcion retained the Epistle under the title " To the Laodicenes," as Tertullian reports. Dr. Hort says : " Transcriptional evidence strongly supports the testimony of documents against ἐν Ἐφέσῳ." The arguments of Meyer and of Woldemar Schmidt (in the fifth ed. of Meyer *on Ephesians*) in favor of the words are not conclusive.

[2] This was already the view of Marcion in the second century. Meyer, however, *in loc.*, insists that another letter is meant, which was lost, like one to the Corinthians The apocryphal Ep. to the Laodiceans (in Fabricius, *Cod. Apocr. N. T.*, I. 873 sqq.), consisting of twenty verses, is a mere fabrication from the other Epistles of Paul. It was forbidden by the Second Council of Nicæa (787).

[3] But the very reverse of *churchy*. Nothing can be further removed from the genius of Paul than that narrow, mechanical, and pedantic *churchiness* which sticks to the shell of outward forms and ceremonies, and mistakes them for the kernel within.

cult (though not the most important) of his Epistles. It certainly
is the most spiritual and devout, composed in an exalted and
transcendent state of mind, where theology rises into worship,
and meditation into oration. It is the Epistle of the Heaven-
lies (τὰ ἐπουράνια), a solemn liturgy, an ode to Christ and his
spotless bride, the Song of Songs in the New Testament. The
aged apostle soared high above all earthly things to the invis
ible and eternal realities in heaven. From his gloomy confinement he ascended for a season to the mount of transfiguration.
The prisoner of Christ, chained to a heathen soldier, was transformed into a conqueror, clad in the panoply of God, and singing a pæan of victory.

The style has a corresponding rhythmical flow and overflow,
and sounds at times like the swell of a majestic organ.[1] It is
very involved and presents unusual combinations, but this is
owing to the pressure and grandeur of ideas; besides, we must
remember that it was written in Greek, which admits of long
periods and parentheses.   In ch. 1 : 3–14 we have one sentence
with no less than seven relative clauses, which rise like a thick
cloud of incense higher and higher to the very throne of God.[2]

----

[1] Ch. 5 : 14 may be a part of a primitive hymn after the type of Hebrew
parallelism :

"Awake thou that sleepest,
Arise thou from the dead :
And Christ will shine upon thee."

[2] In literal English translation such a sentence is unquestionably heavy and
cumbrous.   Unsympathetic critics, like De Wette, Baur, Renan, Holtzmann,
characterize the style of Ephesians as verbose, diffuse, overloaded, monotonous, and repetitious.   But Grotius, a first-class classical scholar, describes it
(in his Preface) as "*rerum sublimitatem adæquans verbis sublimioribus quam
ulla habuit unquam lingua humana.*" Harless asserts that not a single word
in the Epistle is superfluous, and has proved it in his very able commentary.
Alford (III. 25) remarks : "As the wonderful effect of the Spirit of inspiration on the mind of man is nowhere in Scripture more evident than in this
Epistle, so, to discern those things of the Spirit, is the spiritual mind here
more than anywhere required."   He contrasts, under this view, the commentaries of DeWette and Stier, putting rather too high an estimate on the latter.
Maurice (*Unity of the N. T.*, p. 535) : "Every one must be conscious of an
overflowing fulness in the style of this Epistle, as if the apostle's mind could
not contain the thoughts that were at work in him, as if each one that he
uttered had a luminous train before it and behind it, from which it could not

Luther reckoned Ephesians among "the best and noblest books of the New Testament." Witsius characterized it as a divine Epistle glowing with the flame of Christian love and the splendor of holy light. Braune says: "The exalted significance of the Epistle for all time lies in its fundamental idea: the church of Jesus Christ a creation of the Father through the Son in the Holy Spirit, decreed from eternity, destined for eternity; it is the ethical cosmos; the family of God gathered in the world and in history and still further to be gathered, the object of his nurture and care in time and in eternity."

These are Continental judgments. English divines are equally strong in praise of this Epistle. Coleridge calls it "the sublimest composition of man;" Alford: "the greatest and most heavenly work of one whose very imagination is peopled with things in the heavens;" Farrar: "the Epistle of the Ascension, the most sublime, the most profound, and the most advanced and final utterance of that mystery of the gospel which it was given to St. Paul for the first time to proclaim in all its fulness to the Gentile world."

THEME: The church of Christ, the family of God, the fulness of Christ.

LEADING THOUGHTS: God chose us in Christ before the foundation of the world that we should be holy and without blemish before him in love (1:4). In him we have our redemption through his blood, the forgiveness of our trespasses, according to the riches of his grace (1:7). He purposed to sum up all things in Christ, the things in the heavens, and the things upon the earth (1:10). God gave him to be head over all things to the church, which is his body, the fulness of him that filleth all in all (1:23). God, being rich in mercy, quickened us together with Christ and raised us up with him, and made us to sit with him in the heavenly *places*, in Christ Jesus (2:4-6). By grace have ye been saved through faith; and that not of yourselves: *it is* the gift of God: not of works, that no man should glory (2:8, 9).

disengage itself." Bishop Ellicott says that the difficulties of the first chapter are "so great and so deep that the most exact language and the most discriminating analysis are too poor and too weak to convey the force or connection of expressions so august, and thoughts so unspeakably profound." Dr. Riddle: "It is the greatness of the Epistle which makes it so difficult; the thought seems to struggle with the words, which seem insufficient to convey the transcendent idea."

Christ is our peace, who made both one, and broke down the middle wall of partition (2 : 14). Ye are no more strangers and sojourners, but ye are fellow-citizens with the saints, and of the household of God, being built upon the foundation of the apostles and prophets, Christ Jesus himself being the chief corner stone (2 : 19, 20). Unto me, who am less than the least of all saints, was this grace given, to preach unto the Gentiles the unsearchable riches of Christ (3 : 8). That Christ may dwell in your hearts through faith ; to the end that ye, being rooted and grounded in love, may be strong to apprehend with all the saints what is the breadth and length and height and depth, and to know the love of Christ which passeth knowledge, that ye may be filled unto all the fulness of God (3 : 17–19). Give diligence to keep the unity of the Spirit in the bond of peace (4 : 3). *There is* one body, and one Spirit, one Lord, one faith, one baptism, one God and Father of all, who is over all, and through all, and in all (4 : 6). He gave some *to be* apostles ; and some, prophets ; and some, pastors and teachers for the perfecting of the saints (4 : 11, 12). Speak the truth in love (4 : 15). Put on the new man, which after God hath been created in righteousness and holiness of truth (4 : 24). Be ye therefore imitators of God, as beloved children, and walk in love, even as Christ also loved you, and gave himself up for us, an offering and a sacrifice to God for an odor of a sweet smell (5 : 1, 2). Wives, *be in subjection* unto your own husbands, as unto the Lord (5 : 22). Husbands, love your wives, even as Christ also loved the church, and gave himself up for it (5 : 25). This mystery is great; but I speak in regard of Christ and of the church (5 : 32). Children, obey your parents in the Lord (6 : 1). Put on the whole armor of God, that ye may be able to stand against the wiles of the devil (6 : 11).

§ 96. *Colossians and Ephesians Compared and Vindicated.*

Comparison.

The Epistles to the Colossians and Ephesians were written about the same time and transmitted through the same messenger, Tychicus. They are as closely related to each other as the Epistles to the Galatians and to the Romans. They handle the same theme, Christ and his church ; as Galatians and Romans discuss the same doctrines of salvation by free grace and justification by faith.

But Colossians, like Galatians, arose from a specific emergency, and is brief, terse, polemical; while Ephesians, like Romans, is expanded, calm, irenical. Colossians is directed against the incipient Gnostic (paganizing) heresy, as Galatians is directed against the Judaizing heresy. The former is anti-Essenic and anti-ascetic, the latter is anti-Pharisaic and anti-legalistic; the one deals with a speculative expansion and fantastic evaporation, the latter, with a bigoted contraction, of Christianity; yet both these tendencies, like all extremes, have points of contact and admit of strange amalgamations; and in fact the Colossian and Galatian errorists united in their cere-monial observance of circumcision and the Sabbath. Ephesians, like Romans, is an independent exposition of the positive truth, of which the heresy opposed in the other Epistles is a perversion or caricature.

Again, Colossians and Ephesians differ from each other in the modification and application of their common theme: Colos-sians is christological and represents Christ as the true *pleroma* or plenitude of the Godhead, the totality of divine attributes and powers; Ephesians is ecclesiological and exhibits the ideal church as the body of Christ, as the reflected *pleroma* of Christ, "the fulness of Him who filleth all in all." Christology natur-ally precedes ecclesiology in the order of the system, as Christ precedes the church; and Colossians preceded Ephesians most probably also in the order of composition, as the outline pre-cedes the full picture; but they were not far apart, and arose from the same train of meditation.[1]

This relationship of resemblance and contrast can be satisfac-torily explained only on the assumption of the same authorship, the same time of composition, and the same group of churches

---

[1] Lardner, Credner, Mayerhoff, Hofmann, and Reuss reverse the order on the ground of Col. 4 : 16, which refers to "the Epistle from Laodicea," as-suming that this is the encyclical Epistle to the Ephesians. But Paul may have done that by anticipation. On the other hand, the καὶ ὑμεῖς (that *ye also as well as those* to whom I have just written) in Eph. 6 : 21, as compared with Col. 4 : 7, justifies the opposite conclusion (as Harless shows, *Com.*, p. lix). Reuss thinks that in writing two letters on the same topic the second is apt to be the shorter. But the reverse is more frequent, as a second edition of a book is usually larger than the first. DeWette, Baur, Hilgenfeld, and Holtz-mann regard Ephesians as an enlarged recasting (*Umarbeitung* and *Ueberar-beitung*) of Colossians by a pupil of Paul.

endangered by the same heretical modes of thought. With Paul as the author of both everything is clear ; without that assumption everything is dark and uncertain. *" Non est cuius- vis hominis,"* says Erasmus, *" Paulinum pectus effingere ; tonat, fulgurat, meras flammas loquitur Paulus."* [1]

AUTHORSHIP.

The genuineness of the two cognate Epistles has recently been doubted and denied, but the negative critics are by no means agreed ; some surrender Ephesians but retain Colossians, others reverse the case ; while Baur, always bolder and more consistent than his predecessors, rejects both.[2]

[1] *Annot. ad Col.* 4 : 16.

[2] DeWette first attacked Ephesians as a verbose expansion (*wortreiche Er- weiterung*) of the genuine Colossians by a pupil of Paul.   See his *Introd. to the New Test.* (1826, 6th ed. by Messner and Lünemann, 1860, pp. 313 sqq., and es- pecially his *Com.* on Eph., 1843 and 1847). He based his doubts chiefly on the apparent dependence of Ephesians on Colossians, and could not appreciate the originality and depth of Ephesians. Mayerhoff first attacked Colossians (1838) as a post-Pauline abridgment of Ephesians which he regarded as genuine. Baur attacked both (1845), as his pupil Schwegler did (1846), and assigned them to an anti-Gnostic writer of the later Pauline school. He was followed by Hilgen- feld (1870, 1873, and 1875). Hitzig proposed a middle view (1870), that a genuine Epistle of Paul to the Colossians was enlarged and adapted by the same author who wrote Ephesians, and this view was elaborately carried out by Holtzmann with an attempt to reconstruct the Pauline original (*Kritik der Epheser- und Kolosserbriefe*, Leipzig, 1872). But the assumption of another Epistle of Paul to the Colossians is a pure critical fiction. History knows only of one such Epistle. Pfleiderer (1873, *Paulinismus*, p. 370 sq. and 434) substan- tially agrees with Holtzmann, but assumes two different authors for the two Epistles. He regards Ephesians as an advance from old Paulinism to the Johannean theology. Renan and Ewald admit Colossians to be genuine, but surrender Ephesians, assigning it, however, to an earlier date than the Tübingen critics (Ewald to A.D. 75 or 80). On the other hand, the genuine- ness of both Epistles has been ably defended by Bleek, Meyer, Woldemar Schmidt, Braune, Weiss, Alford, Farrar. Bishop Lightfoot, in his *Com. on Col.*, promises to take the question of genuineness up in the *Com. on Ephes.*, which, however, has not yet appeared. Dr. Samuel Davidson, in the revised edition of his *Introduction to the Study of the New Test.* (1882, vol. II. 176 sqq. and 205 sqq.), reproduces the objections of the Tübingen critics, and adds some new ones which are not very creditable to his judgment, *e.g.*, Paul could not warn the Ephesians to steal no more (4 : 28), and not to be drunk (5 : 18), because "the Christians of Asia Minor had no tendency to drunken excesses, but rather to ascetic abstinence from wine ; and the advice

They must stand or fall together. But they will stand. They represent, indeed, an advanced state of christological and ecclesiological knowledge in the apostolic age, but they have their roots in the older Epistles of Paul, and are brimful of his spirit. They were called forth by a new phase of error, and brought out new statements of truth with new words and phrases adapted to the case. They contain nothing that Paul could not have written consistently with his older Epistles, and there is no known pupil of Paul who could have forged such highly intellectual and spiritual letters in his name and equalled, if not out-Pauled Paul.[1] The external testimonies are unanimous in favor of the Pauline authorship, and go as far back as Justin Martyr, Polycarp, Ignatius, and the heretical Marcion (about 140), who included both Epistles in his mutilated canon.[2]

The difficulties which have been urged against their Pauline origin, especially of Ephesians, are as follows:

1. The striking resemblance of the two Epistles, and the apparent repetitiousness and dependence of Ephesians on Colossians, which seem to be unworthy of such an original thinker as Paul.[3] But this resemblance, which is more striking in the practical than in the doctrinal part, is not the resemblance between an author and an imitator, but of two compositions of

given to Timothy might perhaps have been more suitable : 'Drink a little wine' " (p. 213). But what then becomes of the Epistle to the Corinthians who tolerated an incestuous person in their midst and disgraced the love feasts by intemperance? What of the Epistle to the Romans, which contains a similar warning against drunkenness (13 : 13)? And what could induce a pseudo-Paul to slander the church at Ephesus, if it was exceptionally pure?

[1] Farrar (II. 602) : "We might well be amazed if the first hundred years after the death of Christ produced a totally unknown writer who, assuming the name of Paul, treats the mystery which it was given him to reveal with a masterly power which the apostle himself rarely equalled, and most certainly never surpassed. Let any one study the remains of the Apostolic Fathers, and he may well be surprised at the facility with which writers of the Tübingen school, and their successors, assume the existence of Pauls who lived unheard of and died unknown, though they were intellectually and spiritually the equals, if not the superiors, of St. Paul himself !"

[2] See the quotations in Charteris's *Canonicity*, pp. 237 sqq and 247 sqq.

[3] This is DeWette's chief argument. See his table of parallel passages in *Einleitung*, § 146a (pp. 313–318 of the sixth ed.).

the same author, written about the same time on two closely connected topics; and it is accompanied by an equally marked variety in thought and language.

2. The absence of personal and local references in Ephesians. This is, as already remarked, sufficiently explained by the encyclical character of that Epistle.

3. A number of peculiar words not found elsewhere in the Pauline Epistles.[1] But they are admirably adapted to the new ideas, and must be expected from a mind so rich as Paul's. Every Epistle contains some *hapaxlegomena*. The only thing which is somewhat startling is that an apostle should speak of "*holy* apostles and prophets" (Eph. 3 : 5), but the term "holy" (ἅγιοι) is applied in the New Testament to all Christians, as being consecrated to God (ἁγιασμένοι, John 17 : 17), and not in the later ecclesiastical sense of a spiritual nobility. It implies no contradiction to Eph. 3 : 8, where the author calls himself "the least of all saints" (comp. 1 Cor. 15 : 9, "I am the least of the apostles").

4. The only argument of any weight is the alleged post-Pauline rise of the Gnostic heresy, which is undoubtedly opposed in Colossians (not in Ephesians, at least not directly). But why should this heresy not have arisen in the apostolic age as well as the Judaizing heresy which sprung up before A.D. 50, and followed Paul everywhere? The tares spring up almost simultaneously with the wheat. Error is the shadow of truth. Simon Magus, the contemporary of Peter, and the Gnostic Cerinthus, the contemporary of John, are certainly historic persons. Paul speaks (1 Cor. 8 : 1) of a "gnosis which puffeth

---

[1] Such as αἰσχρολογία (Col. 3 : 8), ἀνταναπληρόω (1 : 24), εἰρηνοποιέω (1 : 20), ἐθελοθρησκεία (2 : 23), πιθανολογία (2 : 4); τὰ ἐπουράνια (Eph. 1 : 3, 20 ; 2 : 6; 3 : 10 ; 6 : 12), τὰ πνευματικά (6 : 12), κοσμοκράτορες (6 : 12), πολυποίκιλος σοφία (3 : 10). Even the word ἄφεσις (Col. 1 : 14 and Eph. 1 : 7) for πάρεσις (Rom. 3 : 25) has been counted among the strange terms, as if Paul had not known before of the remission of sins. Holtzmann has most carefully elaborated the philological argument. But the veteran Reuss (I. 112) treats it as futile, and even Davidson must admit (II. 219) that "the sentiments (of Ephesians) are generally Pauline, as well as the diction," though he adds that "both betray marks of another writer."

up," and warned the Ephesian elders, as early as 58, of the rising of disturbing errorists from their own midst; and the Apocalypse, which the Tübingen critics assign to the year 68, certainly opposes the antinomian type of Gnosticism, the error of the Nicolaitans (2 : 6, 15, 20), which the early Fathers derived from one of the first seven deacons of Jerusalem. All the elements of Gnosticism—Ebionism, Platonism, Philoism, syncretism, asceticism, antinomianism — were extant before Christ, and it needed only a spark of Christian truth to set the inflammable material on fire. The universal sentiment of the Fathers, as far as we can trace it up to Irenæus, Justin Martyr, and Polycarp found the origin of Gnosticism in the apostolic age, and called Simon Magus its father or grandfather.

Against their testimony, the isolated passage of Hegesippus, so often quoted by the negative critics,[1] has not the weight of a feather. This credulous, inaccurate, and narrow-minded Jewish Christian writer said, according to Eusebius, that the church enjoyed profound peace, and was "a pure and uncorrupted virgin," governed by brothers and relations of Jesus, until the age of Trajan, when, after the death of the apostles, "the knowledge falsely so called" (ψευδώνυμος γνῶσις, comp. 1 Tim. 6 : 20), openly raised its head.[2] But he speaks of the church in Palestine, not in Asia Minor; and he was certainly mistaken in this dream of an age of absolute purity and peace. The Tübingen school itself maintains the very opposite view. Every

---

[1] Baur, Schwegler, and Hilgenfeld (*Einleit.*, 652 sq.).

[2] Eus., *H. E.*, III. 32 : " The same author [Hegesippus], relating the events of the times, also says that ' the church continued until then as a pure and uncorrupt virgin (παρθένος καθαρὰ καὶ ἀδιάφθορος ἔμενεν ἡ ἐκκλησία); whilst if there were any at all that attempted to pervert the sound doctrine of the saving gospel, they were yet skulking in darkness (ἐν ἀδήλῳ που σκότει); but when the sacred choir of the apostles became extinct, and the generation of those that had been privileged to hear their inspired wisdom had passed away, then also arose the combination of godless error through the fraud of false teachers. These also, as there was none of the apostles left, henceforth attempted, without shame (γυμνῇ λοιπὸν ἤδη τῇ κεφαλῇ), to preach their falsely so-called gnosis against the gospel of truth.' Such is the statement of Hegesippus." Comp. the notes on the passage by Heinichen in his ed. of Euseb., Tome III., pp. 100–103.

Epistle, as well as the Acts, bears testimony to the profound agitations, parties, and evils of the church, including Jerusalem, where the first great theological controversy was fought out by the apostles themselves. But Hegesippus corrects himself, and makes a distinction between the *secret working* and the *open* and *shameless manifestation* of heresy. The former began, he intimates, in the apostolic age; the latter showed itself afterward.[1] Gnosticism, like modern Rationalism,[2] had a growth of a hundred years before it came to full maturity. A post-apostolic writer would have dealt very differently with the fully developed systems of Basilides, Valentinus, and Marcion. And yet the two short Epistles to the Colossians and Ephesians strike at the roots of this error, and teach the positive truth with an originality, vigor, and depth that makes them more valuable, even as a refutation, than the five books of Irenæus against Gnosticism, and the ten books of the Philosophumena of Hippolytus; and this patent fact is the best proof of their apostolic origin.

§ 97. *The Epistle to the Philippians.*

The Church at Philippi.

Philippi was a city of Macedonia, founded by and called after Philip, the father of Alexander the Great, in a fertile region, with contiguous gold and silver mines, on the banks of a small river and the highway between Asia and Europe, ten miles from the seacoast. It acquired immortal fame by the battle between Brutus and Mark Antony (B.C. 42), in which the

---

[1] The same Hegesippus, in Eus., IV. 22, places the rise of the heresies in the Palestinian church immediately after the death of James, and traces some of them back to Simon Magus. He was evidently familiar with the Pastoral Epistles, and borrowed from them the terms ψευδώνυμος γνῶσις, ἑτεροδιδάσκαλοι, ὑγιὴς κανών.

[2] The critical school of Rationalism began in Germany with Semler of Halle (1725–1791), in the middle of the eighteenth century, and culminated in the Tübingen School of our own age.

Roman republic died and the empire was born. After that event it had the rank of a Roman military colony, with the high-sounding title, " Colonia Augusta Julia Philippensis." [1] Hence its mixed population, the Greeks, of course, prevailing, next the Roman colonists and magistrates, and last a limited number of Jews, who had a place of prayer on the riverside. It was visited by Paul, in company with Silas, Timothy, and Luke, on his second missionary tour, in the year 52, and became the seat of the first Christian congregation on the classical soil of Greece. Lydia, the purple dealer of Thyatira and a half proselyte to Judaism, a native slave-girl with a divining spirit, which was used by her masters as a means of gain among the superstitious heathen, and a Roman jailer, were the first converts, and fitly represent the three nationalities (Jew, Greek, and Roman) and the classes of society which were especially benefited by Christianity. " In the history of the gospel at Philippi, as in the history of the church at large, is reflected the great maxim of Christianity, the central truth of the apostle's teaching, that here is ' neither Jew nor Greek, neither bond nor free, neither male nor female, but all are one in Christ Jesus.' " [2] Here, also, are the first re-corded instances of whole households (of Lydia and the jailer) being baptized and gathered into the church, of which the family is the chief nursery. The congregation was fully organ-ized, with bishops (presbyters) and deacons at the head (Phil. 1 : 1).

Here the apostle was severely persecuted and marvellously delivered. Here he had his most loyal and devoted converts, who were his " joy and crown." For them he felt the strongest personal attachment ; from them alone he would receive contri-butions for his support. In the autumn of the year 57, after

---

[1] Augustus conferred upon Philippi the special privilege of the "jus Itali-cum," which made it a miniature likeness of the Roman people, with " præ-tors " and " lictors," and the other titles of the Roman magistrates. Under this character the city appears in the narrative of the Acts (16 : 12 sqq.), where "the pride and privilege of Roman citizenship confront us at every turn." See Lightfoot, pp. 50 sqq., Braune, and Lumby.

[2] Lightfoot, l. c., p. 53.

five years' absence, he paid a second visit to Philippi, having in the meantime kept up constant intercourse with the congregation through living messengers; and on his last journey to Jerusalem, in the spring of the following year, he stopped at Philippi to keep the paschal feast with his beloved brethren. They had liberally contributed out of their poverty to the relief of the churches in Judæa. When they heard of his arrival at Rome, they again sent him timely assistance through Epaphroditus, who also offered his personal services to the prisoner of the Lord, at the sacrifice of his health and almost his life. It was through this faithful fellow-worker that Paul sent his letter of thanks to the Philippians, hoping, after his release, to visit them in person once more.

The Epistle.

The Epistle reflects, in familiar ease, his relations to this beloved flock, which rested on the love of Christ. It is not systematic, not polemic, nor apologetic, but personal and autobiographic, resembling in this respect the First Epistle to the Thessalonians, and to some extent, also, the Second Epistle to the Corinthians. It is the free outflow of tender love and gratitude, and full of joy and cheerfulness in the face of life and death. It is like his midnight hymn of praise in the dungeon of Philippi. "Rejoice in the Lord alway; again I will say, Rejoice" (4 : 4).[1] This is the key-note of the letter.[2] It proves that a healthy Christian faith, far from depressing and saddening the heart, makes truly happy and contented even in prison. It is an important contribution to our knowledge of

[1] χαίρετε "combines a parting benediction with an exhortation to cheerfulness. It is neither 'farewell' alone, nor 'rejoice' alone" (Lightfoot).

[2] Bengel : " Summa Epistolæ: Gaudeo, gaudete." Farrar (II. 423): "If any one compare the spirit of the best-known classic writers in their adversity with that which was habitual to the far deeper wrongs and far deadlier sufferings of St. Paul—if he will compare the Epistle to the Philippians with the ʻTristiaʼ of Ovid, the letters of Cicero from exile, or the treatise which Seneca dedicated to Polybius from his banishment in Corsica—he may see, if he will, the difference which Christianity has made in the happiness of man."

the character of the apostle. In acknowledging the gift of the Philippians, he gracefully and delicately mingles manly independence and gratitude. He had no doctrinal error, nor practical vice to rebuke, as in Galatians and Corinthians.

The only discordant tone is the warning against "the dogs of the concision" (κατατομή, 3 : 2), as he sarcastically calls the champions of circumcision (περιτομή), who everywhere sowed tares in his wheat fields, and at that very time tried to check his usefulness in Rome by substituting the righteousness of the law for the righteousness of faith. But he guards the readers with equal earnestness against the opposite extreme of antinomian license (3 : 12–21). In opposition to the spirit of personal and social rivalry and contention which manifested itself among the Philippians, Paul reminds them of the self-denying example of Christ, who was the highest of all, and yet became the lowliest of all by divesting himself of his divine majesty and humbling himself, even to the death on the cross, and who, in reward for his obedience, was exalted above every name (2 : 1–11).

This is the most important doctrinal passage of the letter, and contains (together with 2 Cor. 8 : 9) the fruitful germ of the speculations on the nature and extent of the *kenosis*, which figures so prominently in the history of christology.[1] It is a striking example of the apparently accidental occasion of some of the deepest utterances of the apostle. "With passages full of elegant negligence (1 : 29), like Plato's dialogues and Cicero's letters, it has passages of wonderful eloquence, and proceeds from outward relations and special circumstances to wide-reaching thoughts and grand conceptions."[2]

The objections against the genuineness raised by a few hypercritics are not worthy of a serious refutation.[3]

---

[1] The kenosis controversy between the Lutherans of Giessen and Tübingen in the early part of the seventeenth century, and the more extensive kenosis literature in the nineteenth century (Thomasius, Liebner, Gess, Godet, etc.).

[2] Dr. Braune, in Lange's *Com.*, p. 4.

[3] The arguments of Baur and Schwegler have been set aside by Lünemann (1847), Brückner (1848), Resch (1850), Hilgenfeld (1871), and Reuss (1875); those of Holsten (1875 and 1876) by P. W. Schmidt, *Neutestam. Hyperkritik*, 1880. Comp. Holzmann in Hilgenfeld's "Zeitschrift für wiss. Theol.," 1881, 98 sqq.

The Later History.

The subsequent history of the church at Philippi is rather disappointing, like that of the other apostolic churches in the East. It appears again in the letters of Ignatius, who passed through the place on his way to his martyrdom in Rome, and was kindly entertained and escorted by the brethren, and in the Epistle of Polycarp to the Philippians, who expressed his joy that "the sturdy root of their faith, famous from the earliest days, still survives and bears fruit unto our Lord Jesus Christ," and alludes to the labors of "the blessed and glorious Paul" among them. Tertullian appeals to the Philippian church as still maintaining the apostle's doctrine and reading his Epistle publicly. The name of its bishop is mentioned here and there in the records of councils, but that is all. During the middle ages the city was turned into a wretched village, and the bishopric into a mere shadow. At present there is not even a village on the site, but only a caravansary, a mile or more from the ruins, which consist of a theatre, broken marble columns, two lofty gateways, and a portion of the city wall.[1] "Of the church which stood foremost among all the apostolic communities in faith and love, it may literally be said that not one stone stands upon another. Its whole career is a signal monument of the inscrutable counsels of God. Born into the world with the brightest promise, the church of Philippi has lived without a history and perished without a memorial."[2]

But in Paul's Epistle that noble little band of Christians still lives and blesses the church in distant countries.

---

[1] Dr. H. B. Hackett, who visited the spot, corrects the false statement of Meyer and other commentators that there is still a village (Felibah, or Filibidjek, as Farrar says) on the former site. See his translation of Braune on *Phil.*, p. 6.

[2] Lightfoot, p. 64. But almost the same sad tale may be told of the churches of Palestine, Syria, and Asia Minor, under the withering rule of the Mohammedan Turks. Even Ephesus, where both Paul and John labored so successfully, is little more than a heap of ruins.

THEME : Theological : The self-humiliation (κένωσις) of Christ for our salvation (2 : 5–11). Practical : Christian cheerfulness.

LEADING THOUGHTS : He who began a good work in you will perfect it (1 : 6). If only Christ is preached, I rejoice (1 : 13). To me to live is Christ, and to die is gain (1 : 21). Have this mind in you, which was also in Christ Jesus : who emptied himself, etc. (2 : 5 sqq.). God worketh in you both to will and to work (2 : 13). Rejoice in the Lord alway ; again I will say, Rejoice (3 : 1 ; 4 : 1). I count all things to be loss for the excellency of the knowledge of Christ (3 : 8). I press on toward the goal unto the prize of the high calling of God in Christ Jesus (3 : 14). Whatsoever things are true, whatsoever things are honorable, whatsoever things are just, whatsoever things are pure, whatsoever things are lovely, whatsoever things are of good report ; if there be any virtue, and if there be any praise, think on these things (4 : 8). The peace of God passeth all understanding (4 : 7).

§ 98. *The Epistle to Philemon.*

Of the many private letters of introduction and recommendation which Paul must have written during his long life, only one is left to us, very brief but very weighty. It is addressed to Philemon, a zealous Christian at Colossæ, a convert of Paul and apparently a layman, who lent his house for the religious meetings of the brethren.[1] The name recalls the touching mythological legend of the faithful old couple, Philemon and Baucis, who, in the same province of Phrygia, entertained gods unawares and were rewarded for their simple hospitality and conjugal love. The letter was written and transmitted at the same time as that to the Colossians. It may be regarded as a personal postscript to it.

It was a letter of recommendation of Onesimus (*i.e.*, Profitable),[2] a slave of Philemon, who had run away from his master on account of some offence (probably theft, a very common sin

---

[1] A worthless tradition makes him bishop of Colossæ and a martyr in the Neronian persecution. So Onesimus and almost every important man in the apostolic church was turned into a bishop and martyr. On the names in the Epistle, see Lightfoot's *Com. on Col. and Philem.*, pp. 372 sqq.

[2] Hence the good-humored play on the meaning of the word, ver. 11, ἄχρηστος, εὔχρηστος, "unprofitable to thee, but now profitable to thee and to me ;" and the play on the name, ver. 20, ὀναίμην, "let me have comfort in thee."

of slaves),[1] fell in with Paul at Rome, of whom he may have
heard in the weekly meetings at Colossæ, or through Epaphras,
his fellow-townsman, was converted by him to the Christian
faith, and now desired to return, as a penitent, in company with
Tychicus, the bearer of the Epistle to the Colossians (Col. 4 : 9).

PAUL AND SLAVERY.

The Epistle is purely personal, yet most significant. Paul
omits his official title, and substitutes the touching designation,
"a prisoner of Christ Jesus," thereby going directly to the
heart of his friend. The letter introduces us into a Christian
household, consisting of father (Philemon), mother (Apphia),
son (Archippus, who was at the same time a "fellow-soldier," a
Christian minister), and a slave (Onesimus). It shows the effect
of Christianity upon society at a crucial point, where heathenism
was utterly helpless. It touches on the institution of slavery,
which lay like an incubus upon the whole heathen world and was
interwoven with the whole structure of domestic and public life.

The effect of Christianity upon this gigantic social evil is
that of a peaceful and gradual cure from within, by teaching
the common origin and equality of men, their common redemption and Christian brotherhood, by emancipating them from
slavery unto spiritual freedom, equality, and brotherhood in
Christ, in whom there is neither Jew nor Greek, neither bond
nor free, neither male nor female, but all are one moral person
(Gal. 3 : 28). This principle and the corresponding practice
wrought first an amelioration, and ultimately the abolition of
slavery. The process was very slow and retarded by the counter-
acting influence of the love of gain and power, and all the sinful
passions of men; but it was sure and is now almost complete
throughout the Christian world; while paganism and Mohammedanism regard slavery as a normal state of society, and hence

---

[1] Ver. 18 seems to describe the actual offence, though the case is stated
hypothetically, εἰ δέ τι . . ὀφείλει (a mild word for ἔκλεψεν, stole). The apostle would not wound the feelings of the slave, nor irritate the master, and
offers himself to discharge the debt.

do not even make an attempt to remove it. It was the only wise way for the apostles to follow in dealing with the subject. A proclamation of emancipation from them would have been a mere *brutum fulmen*, or, if effectual, would have resulted in a bloody revolution of society in which Christianity itself would have been buried.

Paul accordingly sent back Onesimus to his rightful master, yet under a new character, no more a contemptible thief and runaway, but a regenerate man and a "beloved brother," with the touching request that Philemon might receive him as kindly as he would the apostle himself, yea as his own heart (vers. 16, 17). Such advice took the sting out of slavery ; the form remained, the thing itself was gone. What a contrast! In the eyes of the heathen philosophers (even Aristotle) Onesimus, like every other slave, was but a live chattel ; in the eyes of Paul a redeemed child of God and heir of eternal life, which is far better than freedom.[1]

The New Testament is silent about the effect of the letter. We cannot doubt that Philemon forgave Onesimus and treated him with Christian kindness. In all probability he went beyond the letter of the request and complied with its spirit, which hints at emancipation. Tradition relates that Onesimus received his freedom and became bishop of Berœa in Macedonia ; sometimes he is confounded with his namesake, a bishop of Ephesus in the second century, or made a missionary in Spain and a martyr in Rome, or at Puteoli.[2]

---

[1] "The Gospel," says Lightfoot (p. 389), "never directly attacks slavery as an institution : the apostles never command the liberation of slaves as an absolute duty. It is a remarkable fact that St. Paul in this Epistle stops short of any positive injunction. The word 'emancipation' seems to be trembling on his lips, and yet he does not once utter it. He charges Philemon to take the runaway slave Onesimus into his confidence again ; to receive him with all affection ; to regard him no more as a slave, but as a brother ; to treat him with the same consideration, the same love, which he entertains for the apostle himself to whom he owes everything. In fact he tells him to do very much more than emancipate his slave, but this one thing he does not directly enjoin. St. Paul's treatment of this individual case is an apt illustration of the attitude of Christianity toward slavery in general."

[2] For these conflicting legends, see the *Acta Sanctorum Boll.*, XVI. Febr., II. 857 sqq.

PAUL AND PHILEMON.

The Epistle is at the same time an invaluable contribution to our knowledge of Paul. It reveals him to us as a perfect Christian gentleman. It is a model of courtesy, delicacy, and tenderness of feeling. Shut up in a prison, the aged apostle had a heart full of love and sympathy for a poor runaway slave, made him a freeman in Christ Jesus, and recommended him as if he were his own self.

PAUL AND PLINY.

Grotius and other commentators [1] quote the famous letter of Pliny the Consul to his friend Sabinianus in behalf of a runaway slave. It is very creditable to Pliny, who was born in the year when Paul arrived as a prisoner in Rome, and shows that the natural feelings of kindness and generosity could not be extinguished even by that inhuman institution. Pliny was a Roman gentleman of high culture and noble instincts, although he ignorantly despised Christianity and persecuted its innocent professors while Proconsul in Asia. The letters present striking points of resemblance: in both, a fugitive slave, guilty, but reformed, and desirous to return to duty; in both, a polite, delicate, and earnest plea for pardon and restoration, dictated by sentiments of disinterested kindness. But they differ as Christian charity differs from natural philanthropy, as a Christian gentleman differs from a heathen gentleman. The one could appeal only to the amiable temper and pride of his friend, the other to the love of Christ and the sense of duty and gratitude; the one was concerned for the temporal comfort of his client, the other even more for his eternal welfare; the one could at best remand him to his former condition as a slave, the other raised him to the high dignity of a Christian brother, sitting with his master at the same communion table of a common Lord and Saviour. "For polished speech the Roman

---

[1] As Hackett (in Lange), Lightfoot, Lumby, and others.

may bear the palm, but for nobleness of tone and warmth of heart he falls far short of the imprisoned apostle."

The Epistle was poorly understood in the ancient church when slavery ruled supreme in the Roman empire. A strong prejudice prevailed against it in the fourth century, as if it were wholly unworthy of an apostle. Jerome, Chrysostom, and other commentators, who themselves had no clear idea of its ultimate social bearing, apologized to their readers that Paul, instead of teaching metaphysical dogmas and enforcing ecclesiastical discipline, should take so much interest in a poor runaway slave.[1] But since the Reformation full justice has been done to it. Erasmus says: "Cicero never wrote with greater elegance." Luther and Calvin speak of it in high terms, especially Luther, who fully appreciated its noble, Christ-like sentiments. Bengel: "*mire ἀστεῖος*." Ewald: "Nowhere can the sensibility and warmth of a tender friendship blend more beautifully with the loftier feeling of a commanding spirit than in this letter, at once so brief, and yet so surpassingly full and significant." Meyer: "A precious relic of a great character, and, viewed merely as a specimen of Attic elegance and urbanity, it takes rank among the epistolary masterpieces of antiquity." Baur rejects it with trifling arguments as post-apostolic, but confesses that it "makes an agreeable impression by its attractive form," and breathes "the noblest Christian spirit."[2] Holtzmann calls it "a model of tact, refinement, and amiability." Reuss: "a model of tact and humanity, and an expression of a fine appreciation of Christian duty and genial, amiable humor." Renan, with his keen eye on the literary and æsthetic merits or defects, praises it as "a verit-

---

[1] See Lightfoot, p. 383, and the Speaker's *Com. New Test.*, III. 829.

[2] "*Es wird hier,*" he says (*Paulus*, II. 88, second ed.), "*im Christenthum die schöne Idee aufgefasst, dass die durch dasselbe mit einander Verbundenen in einer wahren Wesensgemeinschaft mit einander stehen, so dass der Eine in dem Anderen sein eigenes Selbst erkennt, sich mit ihm völlig Eins weiss und einer für alle Ewigkeit dauernden Vereinigung angehört.*" Hilgenfeld admits the genuineness, saying (p. 331): "*Der ganze Brief trägt das Gepräge der einfachen Wahrheit an sich und verräth auch in den Wortspielen, vers. 11, 20, die Schreibart des Paulus.*"

able little *chef-d'œuvre* of the art of letter-writing." And Light-foot, while estimating still higher its moral significance on the question of slavery, remarks of its literary excellency: "As an expression of simple dignity, of refined courtesy, of large sympathy, of warm personal affection, the Epistle to Philemon stands unrivalled. And its pre-eminence is the more remarkable because in style it is exceptionally loose. It owes nothing to the graces of rhetoric; its effect is due solely to the spirit of the writer."

§ 99. *The Pastoral Epistles.*

Comp. § 33, pp. 327–329.

Contents.

The three Pastoral Epistles, two to Timothy and one to Titus, form a group by themselves, and represent the last stage of the apostle's life and labors, with his parting counsels to his beloved disciples and fellow-workers. They show us the transition of the apostolic church from primitive simplicity to a more definite system of doctrine and form of government. This is just what we might expect from the probable time of their composition *after* the first Roman captivity of Paul, and *before* the composition of the Apocalypse.

They are addressed not to congregations, but to individuals, and hence more personal and confidential in their character. This fact helps us to understand many peculiarities. Timothy, the son of a heathen father and a Jewish mother, and Titus, a converted Greek, were among the dearest of Paul's pupils.[1] They were, at the same time, his delegates and commissioners on special occasions, and appear under this official character in the Epistles, which, for this reason, bear the name "Pastoral."

The Epistles contain Paul's pastoral theology and his theory of church government. They give directions for founding, training, and governing churches, and for the proper treatment of

---

[1] For biographical details, see the Bible Dictionaries and Commentaries.

individual members, old and young, widows and virgins, back-sliders and heretics. They are rich in practical wisdom and full of encouragement, as every pastor knows.

The Second Epistle to Timothy is more personal in its contents than the other two, and has the additional importance of concluding the autobiography of Paul. It is his last will and testament to all future ministers and soldiers of Christ.

THE PAULINE AUTHORSHIP.

There never was a serious doubt as to the Pauline authorship of these Epistles till the nineteenth century, except among a few Gnostics in the second century. They were always reckoned among the *Homologumena*, as distinct from the seven *Antilegomena*, or disputed books of the New Testament. As far as external evidence is concerned, they stand on as firm a foundation as any other Epistle. They are quoted as canonical by Eusebius, Tertullian, Clement of Alexandria, and Irenæus. Reminiscences from them, in some cases with verbal agreement, are found in several of the Apostolic Fathers. They are included in the ancient MSS. and Versions, and in the list of the Muratorian canon. Marcion (about 140), it is true, excluded them from his canon of ten Pauline Epistles, but he excluded also the Gospels (except a mutilated Luke), the Catholic Epistles, and the Apocalypse.[1]

But there are certain internal difficulties which have induced a number of modern critics to assign them all, or at least First Timothy, to a post-Pauline or pseudo-Pauline writer, who either changed and adapted Pauline originals to a later state of the

---

[1] See the testimonies in Kirchhofer's *Quellensammlung*, as translated and enlarged by Charteris, *Canonicity*, 255–268. Renan admits the resemblance between the First Epistle of Clemens Romanus (c. 44) and Second Timothy (*e.g.*, in the use of the word ἀνάλυσις for death), but assumes that both borrowed from a common source, the favorite language of the church of Rome, and also that the forger of the Pastoral Epistles probably made use of some authentic letters of Paul. *L'Église chrét.*, p. 95 : " *Quelques passages de ces trois épîtres sont d'ailleurs si beaux, qu'on peut se demander si le faussaire n'avait pas entre les mains quelques billets authentiques de Paul.*"

church, or fabricated the whole in the interest of Catholic orthodoxy. In either case, the writer is credited with the best
intentions, and must not be judged according to the modern
standard of literary honesty and literary property. Doctrinally,
the Pastoral Epistles are made the connecting link between
genuine Paulinism and the Johannean Logos-philosophy; eccle-
siastically, the link between primitive Presbyterianism and
Catholic Episcopacy; in both respects, a necessary element in
the formation process of the orthodox Catholic church of the
second century.

The objections against the Pauline authorship deserve serious
consideration, and are as follows: (1) The impossibility of locating these Epistles in the recorded life of Paul; (2) the Gnostic heresy opposed; (3) the ecclesiastical organization implied;
(4) the peculiarities of style and temper. If they are not genuine, Second Timothy must be the oldest, as it is least liable to
these objections, and First Timothy and Titus are supposed to
represent a later development.[1]

THE TIME OF COMPOSITION.

The chronology of the Pastoral Epistles is uncertain, and has
been made an objection to their genuineness. It is closely connected with the hypothesis of a second Roman captivity, which
we have discussed in another place.

The Second Epistle to Timothy, whether genuine or not,
hails from a Roman prison, and appears to be the last of Paul's
Epistles; for he was then hourly expecting the close of his fight
of faith, and the crown of righteousness from his Lord and
Master (2 Tim. 4 : 7, 8). Those who deny the second imprisonment, and yet accept Second Timothy as Pauline, make it the
last of the first imprisonment.

---

[1] Baur and Hilgenfeld (*Einleit.*, p. 764) bring them down to 150 (after Marcion, 140), and date them from Rome. But this is impossible, and rests on a
false exegesis. Pfleiderer, of the same Tübingen school, puts Second Timothy
in the age of Trajan, the other two in the age of Hadrian. He, moreover,
regards the passages 2 Tim 1 : 15–18 and 4 : 9–21 as fragments of a genuine
Epistle of Paul. Comp. also Holtzmann, p. 271.

As to First Timothy and Titus, it is evident from their contents that they were written while Paul was free, and after he had made some journeys, which are *not recorded* in the Acts. Here lies the difficulty. Two ways are open:

1. The two Epistles were written in 56 and 57. Paul may, during his three years' sojourn in Ephesus, A.D. 54–57 (see Acts 19 : 8–10 ; 20 : 31), easily have made a second journey to Macedonia, leaving Ephesus in charge of Timothy (1 Tim. 1 : 3); and also crossed over to the island of Crete, where he left Titus behind to take care of the churches (Tit. 1 : 5). Considering the incompleteness of the record of Acts, and the probable allusions in 2 Cor. 2 : 1 ; 12 : 13, 14, 21 ; 13 : 1, to a second visit to Corinth, not mentioned in the Acts, these two journeys are within the reach of possibility.[1] But such an early date leaves the other difficulties unexplained.

2. The tradition of the second Roman captivity, which can be raised at least to a high degree of probability, removes the difficulty by giving us room for new journeys and labors of Paul between his release in the spring of 63 and the Neronian persecution in July, 64 (according to Tacitus), or three or four years later (according to Eusebius and Jerome), as well as for the development of the Gnostic heresy and the ecclesiastical organization of the church which is implied in these Epistles. Hence, most writers who hold to the genuineness place First Timothy and Titus between the first and second Roman captivities.[2]

Paul certainly *intended* to make a journey from Rome to Spain (Rom. 15 : 24), and also one to the East (Philem. 22 ; Phil. 1 : 25, 26 ; 2 : 24), and he had ample time to carry out his intention even before the Neronian persecution, if we insist upon confining this to the date of Tacitus.[3]

---

[1] So Schrader, Wieseler, Reythmayr, formerly also Reuss (in his *Gesch.*, etc., 5th ed., 1875, but withdrawn in his French Com. on the Pauline Epp., 1878).

[2] So Theophylact, Oecumenius, Ussher, Pearson, Tillemont, Neander, Bleek, Ruffet, Lange, Farrar, Plumptre, Lightfoot, etc.

[3] A release of Paul from the first Roman captivity and a visit to Spain is also asserted by such critics as Ewald and Renan.

Those who press the chronological difficulty should not forget that a forger could have very easily fitted the Epistles into the narrative of the Acts, and was not likely to invent a series of journeys, circumstances, and incidents, such as the bringing of the cloak, the books, and the parchments which Paul, in the hurry of travel, had left at Troas (2 Tim. 4 : 13).

THE GNOSTIC HERESY.

The Pastoral Epistles, like Colossians, oppose the Gnostic heresy (γνῶσις ψευδώνυμος, 1 Tim. 6 : 20) which arose in Asia Minor during his first Roman captivity, and appears more fully developed in Cerinthus, the contemporary of John. This was acknowledged by the early Fathers, Irenæus and Tertullian, who used these very Epistles as Pauline testimonies against the Gnosticism of their day.

The question arises, which of the many types of this many-sided error is opposed? Evidently the *Judaizing* type, which resembled that at Colossæ, but was more advanced and malignant, and hence is more sternly denounced. The heretics were of "the circumcision" (Tit. 1 : 10); they are called "teachers of the law" (νομοδιδάσκαλοι, 1 Tim. 1 : 7, the very reverse of antinomians), "given to *Jewish* fables" (Ἰουδαϊκοί μῦθοι, Tit. 1 : 14), and "disputes connected with the law" (μάχαι νομικαί, Tit. 3 : 9), and fond of foolish and ignorant questionings (2 Tim. 2 : 23). They were, moreover, extravagant ascetics, like the Essenes, forbidding to marry and abstaining from meat (1 Tim. 4 : 3, 8; Tit. 1 : 14, 15). They denied the resurrection and " overthrew the faith of some " (2 Tim. 2 : 18).

Baur turned these heretics into *anti-Jewish* and *antinomian* Gnostics of the school of Marcion (about 140), and then, by consequence, put the Epistles down to the middle of the second century. He finds in the "genealogies" (1 Tim. 1 : 4; Tit. 3 : 9) the emanations of the Gnostic æons, and in the "antitheses" (1 Tim. 6 : 20), or anti-evangelical assertions of the heretical teachers, an allusion to Marcion's "antitheses" (antilogies), by which he set forth the supposed contradictions between the Old and New Testaments.[1] But this is a radical misinterpretation, and the more recent opponents of the genuineness are forced to admit the Judaizing character of those errorists; they identify them with Cerinthus, the Ophites, and Saturninus, who preceded Marcion by several decades.[2]

As to the origin of the Gnostic heresy, which the Tübingen school would put down to the age of Hadrian, we have already seen that, like its counterpart, the Ebionite heresy, it dates from the apostolic age, according to the united testimony of the later Pauline Epistles, the Epistles of Peter, John, and Jude, the Apocalypse, and the patristic tradition.[3]

ECCLESIASTICAL ORGANIZATION.

The Pastoral Epistles seem to presuppose a more fully developed ecclesiastical organization than the other Pauline Epistles, and to belong to an age of transition from apostolic simplicity, or Christo-democracy—if we may use such a term—to the episcopal hierarchy of the second century. The church, in proportion as it lost, after the destruction of Jerusalem, its faith in the speedy advent of Christ, began to settle down in this world, and to make preparations for a permanent home by a fixed creed and a compact organization, which gave it unity and strength against heathen persecution and heretical corruption. This organization, at once simple and elastic, was episcopacy, with its subordinate offices of the presbyterate and deaconate, and charitable institutions for widows and orphans. Such an organization we have, it is said, in the Pastoral Epistles, which

---

[1] The ἀντιθέσεις τῆς ψευδωνύμου γνώσεως ("oppositions" in the E. V. and Revision) are understood by the best exegetes to mean simply the doctrinal theses which the heretics opposed to the sound doctrine (comp. 2 Tim. 2 : 23; Tit. 1 : 9). So DeWette, Matthies, and Wiesinger. Hofmann and Huther identify them with κενοφωνίαι and λογομαχίαι (1 Tim. 5 : 4). Holtzmann (p. 131) likewise rejects Baur's interpretation.

[2] Holtzmann, l.c., p. 127; also Lipsius, Schenkel, Pfleiderer.

[3] See above, § 96, pp. 786 sqq.

were written in the name of Paul, to give the weight of his authority to the incipient hierarchy.[1]

But, on closer inspection, there is a very marked difference between the ecclesiastical constitution of the Pastoral Epistles and that of the second century.   There is not a word said about the divine origin of episcopacy ; not a trace of a congregational episcopate, such as we find in the Ignatian epistles, still less of a diocesan episcopate of the time of Irenæus and Tertullian. Bishops and presbyters are still identical as they are in the Acts (20 : 17, 28), and in the undoubtedly genuine Epistle to the Philippians (1 : 1).   Even Timothy and Titus appear simply as delegates of the apostle for a specific mission.[2]   The qualifications and functions required of the bishop are aptness to teach and a blameless character ; and their authority is made to depend upon their moral character rather than their office. They are supposed to be married, and to set a good example in governing their own household.   The ordination which Timothy received (1 Tim. 4 : 14 ; 5 : 22) need not differ from the ordination of deacons and elders mentioned in the early part of the Acts

[1] Such is the ingenious reasoning of Baur and Renan (*L'Egl. chrét.*, pp. 85 and 94 sqq.).   Comp. the discussion of details by Holtzmann, *l.c.*, ch. XI., pp. 190 sqq.

[2] 1 Tim. 1 : 3 ; 3 : 14 ; 2 Tim. 4 : 9, 21 ; Tit. 1 : 5 ; 3 : 12.   See above, § 61, pp. 491 sqq.   The fact is acknowledged by impartial episcopal writers. as Dean Alford, Bishop Lightfoot, Dean Stanley, and Dean Plumptre (in Schaff's *Com. N. T.*, III. 552).   I will quote from Canon Farrar (*St. Paul.* II. 417) · "If the Pastoral Epistles contained a clear defence of the Episcopal system of the second century, this alone would be sufficient to prove their spuriousness ; but the total absence of anything resembling it is one of the strongest proofs that they belong to the apostolic age.   Bishop and presbyter are still synonymous, as they are throughout the New Testament.   .   .   .   Timothy and Titus exercise functions which would be now called episcopal ; but they are not called 'bishops.'   Their functions were temporary, and they simply act as authoritative delegates of the Apostle of the Gentiles.   Nor is there any trace of exalted pretensions in the overseers whom they appoint.   The qualifications required of them are almost exclusively moral."   Comp. also some good remarks of Prof. Wace, in the Speaker's *Com. on the New Test.*, III. 764, where it is justly said that the church polity in the Pastoral Epistles represents an intermediate stage between the Presbyterian episcopacy of the earlier apostolic period and the post-apostolic episcopacy.

(6 : 6 ; 8 : 17 ; comp. 14 : 23 ; 19 : 6). " Few features," says Dr.
Plumptre, himself an Episcopalian, " are more striking in these
Epistles than the absence of any high hierarchical system." The
Apocalypse, which these very critics so confidently assign to
the year 68, shows a nearer approach to episcopal unity in the
" angels " of the seven churches. But even from the " angels "
of the Apocalypse there was a long way to the Ignatian and
pseudo-Clementine bishops, who are set up as living oracles and
hierarchical idols.

The Style.

The language of the Pastoral Epistles shows an unusual
number of un-Pauline words and phrases, especially rare compounds, some of them nowhere found in the whole New Testament, or even in Greek literature.[1]

But, in the first place, the number of words peculiar to each
one of the three epistles is much greater than the number of
peculiar words common to all three; consequently, if the argument proves anything, it leads to the conclusion of three different authors, which the assailants will not admit, in view of the
general unity of the Epistles. In the next place, every one of
Paul's Epistles has a number of peculiar words, even the little
Epistle of Philemon.[2] The most characteristic words were re-

---

[1] This philological argument was begun by Schleiermacher, but confined to
First Timothy, and was carried out, with reference to all three Epistles, by
Holtzmann, *l.c.*, ch. VI., pp. 84–118. I will give his results. The Pastoral
Epistles have, in all, 897 words. Of these there are 169 *Hapaxlegomena* not
found in the New Testament, namely :

(*a*) 74 in First Timothy, such as ἀγαθοεργεῖν, ἁγνεία, ἀδηλότης, ἀνδραποδιστής,
ἀνδροφόνος, ἑτεροδιδασκαλεῖν, θεοσέβεια, καταστολή, πλέγμα, πορισμός, φιλαργυρία,
ψευδολόγος, ψευδώνυμος.

(*b*) 46 in Second Timothy, *e.g.*, ἀγωγή, ἀθλεῖν, βέλτιον, μεμβράνα, ὀρθοτομεῖν,
πραγματεία, φιλόθεος.

(*c*) 28 in Titus, *e.g.*, αἱρετικός, ἀκατάγνωστος, ἀφθορία, ἀψευδής, καλοδιδάσκαλος,
ματαιολόγος, πρεσβύτις, σωτήριος, φιλάγαθος, φίλανδρος (παλινγενεσία, Tit. 3 : 5,
occurs also Matt. 19 : 28, but in a different sense).

(*d*) 21 common to two or three Past. Epp., *e.g* , διάβολος (as adjective),
ἀνόσιος, διδακτικός, κενοφωνία, νουίμως, παραθήκη, γενεαλογία, εὐσεβῶς.

[2] Farrar (II. 611) affirms that there are no less than 111 peculiar terms
in Romans, 186 in Corinthians, 57 in Galatians, 54 in Philippians, 6 in Phil-

quired by the nature of the new topics handled and the heresy combated, such as "knowledge falsely so called" (ψευδώνυμος γνῶσις, 1 Tim. 6 : 20); "healthful doctrine" (ὑγιαίνουσα διδασκαλία, 1 Tim. 1 : 10); "Jewish myths" (Tit. 1 : 14); "genealogies" (Tit. 3 : 9); "profane babblings" (2 Tim. 2 : 16). Paul's mind was uncommonly fertile and capable of adapting itself to varying conditions, and had to create in some measure the Christian idiom. The Tübingen critics profess the highest admiration for his genius, and yet would contract his vocabulary to a very small compass. Finally, the peculiarities of style are counterbalanced by stronger resemblances and unmistakable evidences of Pauline authorship. "There are flashes of the deepest feeling, outbursts of the most intense expression. There is rhythmic movement and excellent majesty in the doxologies, and the ideal of a Christian pastor drawn not only with an unfaltering hand, but with a beauty, fulness, and simplicity which a thousand years of subsequent experience have enabled no one to equal, much less to surpass." [1]

On the other hand, we may well ask the opponents to give a good reason why a forger should have chosen so many new words when he might have so easily confined himself to the vocabulary of the other Epistles of Paul; why he should have added "mercy" to the salutation instead of the usual form; why he should have called Paul "the chief of sinners" (1 Tim. 1 : 15), and affected a tone of humility rather than a tone of high apostolic authority?

OTHER OBJECTIONS.

The Epistles have been charged with want of logical connection, with abruptness, monotony, and repetitiousness, unworthy of such an original thinker and writer as Paul. But this feature is only the easy, familiar, we may say careless, style which

---

emon. Luke's peculiar vocabulary is especially rich; he uses, as Holtzmann observes (p. 96), 34 words in common with the Pastoral Epistles; and has, besides, 82 words not found in Paul.

[1] Farrar, II. 611.

forms the charm as well as the defect of personal correspondence. Moreover, every great author varies more or less at different periods of life, and under different conditions and moods.

It would be a more serious objection if the theology of these Epistles could be made to appear in conflict with that of his acknowledged works.[1] But this is not the case. It is said that greater stress is laid on sound doctrine and good works. But in Galatians, Paul condemns most solemnly every departure from the genuine gospel (1 : 8, 9), and in all his Epistles he enjoins holiness as the indispensable evidence of faith; while salvation is just as clearly traced to divine grace alone, in the Pastoral Epistles (1 Tim. 1 : 9; Tit. 3 : 5), as in Romans.

In conclusion, while we cannot be blind to certain difficulties, and may not be able, from want of knowledge of the precise situation of the writer, satisfactorily to explain them, we must insist that the prevailing evidence is in favor of the genuineness of these Epistles. They agree with Paul's doctrinal system; they are illuminated with flashes of his genius; they bear the marks of his intense personality; they contain rare gems of inspired truth, and most wholesome admonition and advice, which makes them to-day far more valuable than any number of works on pastoral theology and church government. There are not a few passages in them which, for doctrine or practice, are equal to the best he ever wrote, and are deeply lodged in the experience and affection of Christendom.[2]

And what could be a more fitting, as well as more sublime and beautiful, finale of such a hero of faith than the last words of his last Epistle, written in the very face of martyrdom: " I

---

[1] Pfleiderer (*Protestanten-Bibel*, p. 834) says: " *Die kirchliche Lehrrichtung der Hirtenbriefe ist eine von der altpaulinischen sehr weit verschiedene. Von den eigenthümlich paulinischen Lehren über Gesetz und Evangelium, über Werke und Glauben finden sich in unseren Briefen nur abgeblasste Reste, die fast wie feststehende überlieferte Formeln klingen, während das Glaubensbewusstsein ein anderes geworden ist.*" In this harsh and unjust judgment the fact is overlooked that the three Epistles are pastoral and not doctrinal Epistles.

[2] Such passages as 1 Tim. 1 : 15, 17; 2 : 1, 4–6, 8; 3 : 2, 16; 4 : 1, 4, 7, 10, 15; 5 : 8, 17, 18, 22; 6 : 6, 9–12; 2 Tim. 1 : 6; 2 : 11, 12, 19, 22; 3 : 12, 16, 17; 4 : 2, 6–8; Tit. 1 : 7, 15; 2 : 11; 3 : 5, 6.

am already being offered, and the time of my departure is
come.   I have fought the good fight, I have finished the course,
I have kept the faith : henceforth there is laid up for me the
crown of righteousness, which the Lord, the righteous judge,
shall give to me at that day : and not only to me, but also to all
them that have loved his appearing."

NOTE.

Schleiermacher led the way, in 1807, with his attack on 1 Timothy,
urging very keenly historical, philological, and other objections, but
assuming 2 Timothy and Titus to be the genuine originals from which
the first was compiled.   DeWette followed in his *Introduction*.   Baur
left both behind and rejected all, in his epoch-making treatise, *Die
sogenannten Pastoralbriefe*, 1835.   He was followed by Schwegler (1846),
Hilgenfeld (1875), Mangold, Schenkel, Hausrath, Pfleiderer (both in his
Paulinismus and in his Commentary in the *Protestanten-Bibel*, 1874),
Holtzmann ; also by Ewald, Renan (*L'Église chrétienne*, pp. 85 sqq.), and
Sam. Davidson (*Introd.*, revised ed., II. 21 sqq.).   The most elaborate
book against the genuineness is Holtzmann's *Die Pastoralbriefe kritisch
und exeg. behandelt*, Leipzig, 1880 (504 pp.) ; comp. his *Einleitung* (1886).
Reuss (*Les épitres Pauliniennes*, 1878, II. 243 sq., 307 sq., and *Gesch.
des N. T.*, 1887, p. 257 sqq.) rejects 1 Timothy and Titus, but admits 2
Timothy, assigning it to the *first* Roman captivity.   He thinks that 2 Timothy would never have been doubted except for its suspicious companionship.   Some of the opponents, as Pfleiderer and Renan, feel forced to
admit some scraps of genuine Pauline Epistles or notes, and thus they
break the force of the opposition.   The three Epistles must stand or fall
together, either as wholly Pauline, or as wholly pseudo-Pauline.

The genuineness has been ably vindicated by Guericke, Thiersch,
Huther, Wiesinger, Otto, Wieseler, Van Oosterzee, Lange, Herzog, von
Hofmann, Beck, Alford, Gloag, Fairbairn (*Past. Ep.*, 1874), Farrar (*St.
Paul*, II. 607 sqq.), Wace (in the Speaker's *Com. New Test.*, III., 1881,
749 sqq.), Plumptre (in Schaff's *Com. on the New Test.*, III., 1882, pp.
550 sqq.), Kölling (*Der erste Br. a. Tim.* 1882), Salmon (1885), and
Weiss (1886).

§ 100.   The Epistle to the Hebrews.

I. *Commentaries on Hebrews* by CHRYSOSTOM (d. 407, ἑρμηνεία, in 34 Hom-
ilies publ. after his death by an Antioch. presbyter, Constantinus) ;
THEODORET (d. 457) ; ŒCUMENIUS (10th cent.) ; THEOPHYLACT (11th
cent.) ; THOMAS AQUINAS (d. 1274) ; ERASMUS (d. 1536, *Annotationes in
N. T.*, with his Greek Test., 1516 and often, and *Paraphrasis in N.
T.*, 1522 and often) ; Card. CAJETANUS (*Epistolæ Pauli*, etc., 1531) ;

CALVIN (d. 1564, *Com. in omnes P. Ep. atque etiam in Ep. ad Hebræos*, 1539 and often, also Halle, 1831) ; BEZA (d. 1605, transl. and
notes, 1557 and often ; had much influence on King James' Version) ;
HYPERIUS (at Marburg, d. 1564) ; DAV. PAREUS (d. 1615, *Com. in Ep.
ad Hebr.*) ; CORN. A LAPIDE (Jesuit, d. 1637, *Com. in omnes Pauli
Epp.*, 1627 and often) ; GUIL. ESTIUS (R. C. Prof. at Douai, 1614,
etc.) ; JAC. CAPPELLUS (Sedan, 1624) ; LUD. CAPPELLUS (Geneva,
1632) ; GROTIUS (d. 1645, Arminian, a great classical and general
scholar) ; JOH. GERHARD (d. 1637) ; JOHN OWEN (the great Puritan
divine, d. 1683, *Exercitations on the Epistle to the Hebrews*, London,
1668–80, in 4 vols. fol., Lat. transl., Amsterd., 1700 [new Engl. ed.
in 7 vols., in his *Works*, Lond., 1826, 21 vols. ; Edinb. ed. of *Works*
by W. H. Goold, 1850–55 ; 24 vols., Philad. reprint, 1869], "a work
of gigantic strength as well as gigantic size," as Chalmers called it,
and containing a whole system of Puritan theology) ; JAC. PEIRCE
(Non-conformist, d. 1726) ; SYKES (d. 1756) ; CARPZOV (d. 1803,
Exercitat., etc., 1750) ; J. D. MICHAELIS (2d ed., 1780–86, 2 vols.) ;
ROSENMÜLLER (1793) ; STORR (d. 1805 ; Tüb., 1789) ; BÖHME (Lips.,
1825) ; Mos. STUART (Andover, 1827, 2 vols., 4th ed., abridged and
revised by Robbins, 1860) ; KÜHNÖL (1831) ; FRIEDRICH BLEEK (Prof.
in Bonn., d. 1859 ; the large Com. in 3 vols., Berlin, 1836–40, an
exegetical masterpiece, most learned, critical, candid, judicious, and
reverential, though free ; his *Lectures on Hebrews* were ed., after his
death, by Windrath, 1868) ; THOLUCK (Hamburg, 1836, dedicated to
Bunsen, 3d ed., 1850, transl. by James Hamilton, Edinb., 1852) ;
STIER (1842) ; DEWETTE (1847, 2d ed.) ; EBRARD (1850, in Olshau-
sen's *Com.*, vol. v. ; Engl. transl., Edinb., 1853) ; TURNER (new ed..
N. Y., 1855) ; SAMPSON (ed. by Dabney, N. Y., 1856) ; LÜNEMANN (in
Meyer's *Com.*, 1857, 4th ed., 1878) ; DELITZSCH (1857, transl. by TH. L.
KINGSBURY, Edinb., 1868, 2 vols.) ; JOHN BROWN (Edinb., 1862, 2 vols.);
REUSS (in French, 1862) ; LINDSAY (Edinb., 1867, 2 vols.) ; MOLL
(in Lange's *Com.*, translated and enlarged by Kendrick, 1868) ; RIP-
LEY (1868) ; KURTZ (1869) ; EWALD (1870) ; HOFMANN (1873) ; BIESEN-
THAL (1878) ; BLOOMFIELD ; ALFORD ; WORDSWORTH ; W. KAY (in the
Speaker's *Com. N. T.*, vol. iv., 1882) ; MOULTON (in Ellicott's *Com.
for Engl. Readers*) ; A. B. DAVIDSON (of the New College, Edinburgh.
1882) ; ANGUS (1883) ; SAM. T. LOWRIE (1884) ; WEISS (1888).

II. The *doctrinal system* of the Ep. has been most fully expounded
by RIEHM (d. 1888 in Halle) : *Der Lehrbegriff des Hebräerbriefs*,
Basel und Ludwigsburg, 1858–59, 2 vols. ; new ed., 1867, in 1 vol.
(899 pages). Comp. the expositions of NEANDER, MESSNER, BAUR,
REUSS, and WEISS. On the use of the O. T., see THOLUCK : *Das A.
T. im N.*, Hamb., 3d ed., 1849 ; on the Christology of the Epistle,
BEYSCHLAG : *Christologie des N. T.* (1866), 176 sqq. ; on the Melchise-
dek priesthood, AUBERLEN, in "Studien und Kritiken" for 1857, pp.

453 sqq. PFLEIDERER, in his *Paulinismus* (pp. 324–366), treats of Hebrews, together with Colossians and the Epistle of Barnabas, as representing Paulinism under the influence of Alexandrinism.

III. On the *introductory* questions, comp. NORTON in the "Christian Examiner" (Boston), 1827–29 ; OLSHAUSEN : *De auctore Ep. ad Hebræos* (in *Opusc. theol.*, 1834) ; WIESELER : *Untersuchung über den Hebräerbrief*, Kiel, 1861 ; J. H. THAYER : *Authorship and Canonicity of the Ep. to the Hebrews*, in the "Bibliotheca Sacra," Andover, 1867 ; ZAHN, in Herzog's "Encykl.," vol. v. (1879), pp. 656–671 ; and articles in "Bible Dictionaries," and in "Encycl. Brit.," 9th ed., vol. xi., 602 sqq.

The anonymous Epistle "to the Hebrews," like the Book of Job, belongs to the order of Melchizedek, combining priestly unction and royal dignity, but being "without father, without mother, without pedigree, having neither beginning of days nor end of life" (7 : 1–3). Obscure in its origin, it is clear and deep in its knowledge of Christ. Hailing from the second generation of Christians (2 : 3), it is full of pentecostal inspiration. Traceable to no apostle, it teaches, exhorts, and warns with apostolic authority and power. Though not of Paul's pen, it has, somehow, the impress of his genius and influence, and is altogether worthy to occupy a place in the canon, *after* his Epistles, or *between* them and the Catholic Epistles. Pauline in spirit, it is catholic or encyclical in its aim.[1]

CONTENTS.

The Epistle to the Hebrews is not an ordinary letter. It has, indeed, the direct personal appeals, closing messages, and salutations of a letter ; but it is more, it is a homily, or rather a theological discourse, aiming to strengthen the readers in their Christian faith, and to protect them against the danger of apostasy from Christianity. It is a profound argument for the superiority of Christ over the angels, over Moses, and over the Levitical priesthood, and for the finality of the second covenant. It unfolds far more fully than any other book the great idea of the eternal priesthood and sacrifice of Christ, offered once and

---

[1] See notes at the end of the section.

forever for the redemption of the world, as distinct from the
national and transient character of the Mosaic priesthood and
the ever-repeated sacrifices of the Tabernacle and the Temple.
The author draws his arguments from the Old Testament itself,
showing that, by its whole character and express declarations,
it is a preparatory dispensation for the gospel salvation, a significant type and prophecy of Christianity, and hence destined
to pass away like a transient shadow of the abiding substance.
He implies that the Mosaic œconomy was still existing, with its
priests and daily sacrifices, but in process of decay, and looks
forward to the fearful judgment which a few years afterward
destroyed the Temple forever.[1]   He interweaves pathetic ad-
monitions and precious consolations with doctrinal expositions,
and every exhortation leads him to a new exposition.   Paul
puts the hortatory part usually at the end.

The author undoubtedly belonged to the Pauline school,
which emphasized the great distinction between the Old and
the New Covenant; while yet fully acknowledging the divine
origin and pædagogic use of the former.   But he brings out
the superiority of Christ's priesthood and sacrifice to the Mosaic
priesthood and sacrifice; while Paul dwells mainly on the distinction between the law and the gospel.   He lays chief stress
on faith, but he presents it in its general aspect as trust in God,
in its prospective reference to the future and invisible, and
in its connection with hope and perseverance under suffering;
while Paul describes faith, in its specific evangelical character,
as a hearty trust in Christ and his atoning merits, and in its
justifying effect, in opposition to legalistic reliance on works.
Faith is defined, or at least described, as "assurance (ὑπόστασις)
of things hoped for, a conviction (ἔλεγχος) of things not seen"
(11 : 1).   This applies to the Old Testament as well as the New,

---

[1] 9 : 9, "while as the first tabernacle is yet standing" (τῆς πρώτης σκηνῆς
ἐχούσης στάσιν); vers. 6, "the priests *go in* continually" (εἰσίασιν, not
went in, as in the E. V.); 8 : 4; 13 : 10; 6 : 8; 8 : 13; 10 : 25, 27; 12 : 27.
Those who assign the composition to a time *after* the destruction of Jerusalem, deprive the present tenses of their natural import and proper effect.

and hence appropriately opens the catalogue of patriarchs and prophets, who encourage Christian believers in their conflict; but they are to look still more to Jesus as "the author and perfecter of our faith" (12 : 2), who is, after all, the unchanging object of our faith, "the same yesterday, and to-day, and for ever" (13 : 8).

The Epistle is eminently Christological. It resembles in this respect Colossians and Philippians, and forms a stepping-stone to the Christology of John. From the sublime description of the exaltation and majesty of Christ in ch. 1 : 1–4 (comp. Col. 1 : 15–20), there is only one step to the prologue of the fourth Gospel. The exposition of the high priesthood of Christ reminds one of the sacerdotal prayer (John 17).

The use of proof-texts from the Old Testament seems at times contrary to the obvious historical import of the passage, but is always ingenious, and was, no doubt, convincing to Jewish readers. The writer does not distinguish between typical and direct prophecies. He recognizes the typical, or rather antitypical, character of the Tabernacle and its services, as reflecting the archetype seen by Moses in the mount, but all the Messianic prophecies are explained as direct (1 : 5–14; 2 : 11–13; 10 : 5–10). He betrays throughout a high order of Greek culture, profound knowledge of the Greek Scriptures, and the symbolical import of the Mosaic worship.[1] He was also familiar with the Alexandrian theosophy of Philo,[2] but he never introduces foreign ideas into the Scriptures, as Philo did by his

---

[1] The charge of partial ignorance of the Jewish ritual is unfounded, and can therefore not be made an argument either for or against the Pauline authorship. In the genuine text of 10 : 11, the *high* priest is not mentioned, but the priest (ἱερεύς), and in 7 : 27 the high priest is not asserted to offer *daily sacrifice*, but to need *daily repentance*. The altar of incense is placed in the holy of holies, 9 : 4; but this seems to have been a current opinion, which is also mentioned in the Apocalypse of Baruch. See Harnack in "Studien und Kritiken" for 1876, p. 572, and W. R. Smith in "Enc. Brit.," xi., 606.

[2] See Carpzov, *Sacræ Exercitationes in Ep. ad Heb. ex Philone Alex.* (Helmstadii, 1750); Riehm, *l.c.*, pp. 9 sqq.; Hilgenfeld, *Einleit.*, p. 384; and Pfleiderer, *Paulinismus.*

allegorical interpretation. His exhortations and warnings go to the quick of the moral sensibility ; and yet his tone is also cheering and encouraging. He had the charisma of exhortation and consolation in the highest degree.[1] Altogether, he was a man full of faith and the Holy Spirit, and gifted with a tongue of fire.

THE STYLE.

Hebrews is written in purer Greek than any book of the New Testament, except those portions of Luke where he is independent of prior documents. The Epistle begins, like the third Gospel, with a rich and elegant period of classic construction. The description of the heroes of faith in the eleventh chapter is one of the most eloquent and sublime in the entire history of religious literature. He often reasons *a minori ad majus* (εἰ . . . πόσῳ μᾶλλον). He uses a number of rare and choice terms which occur nowhere else in the New Testament.[2]

As compared with the undoubted Epistles of Paul, the style of Hebrews is less fiery and forcible, but smoother, more correct, rhetorical, rhythmical, and free from anacolutha and solecisms. There is not that rush and vehemence which bursts through ordinary rules, but a calm and regular flow of speech. The sentences are skilfully constructed and well rounded. Paul is bent exclusively on the thought ; the author of Hebrews evidently paid great attention to the form. Though not strictly classical, his style is as pure as the Hellenistic dialect and the close affinity with the Septuagint permit.

All these considerations exclude the idea of a translation from a supposed Hebrew original.

THE READERS.

The Epistle is addressed to the Hebrew Christians, that is, according to the usual distinction between Hebrews and Hellenists (Acts 6 : 1 ; 9 : 27), to the converted Jews in Palestine,

---

[1] The Epistle is called a λόγος παρακλήσεως, 13 : 22 ; comp. 12 : 5 ; 6 : 18.
[2] See note II. at the close.

chiefly to those in Jerusalem. To them it is especially adapted. They lived in sight of the Temple, and were exposed to the persecution of the hierarchy and the temptation of apostasy. This has been the prevailing view from the time of Chrysostom to Bleek.[1] The objection that the Epistle quotes the Old Testament uniformly after the Septuagint is not conclusive, since the Septuagint was undoubtedly used in Palestine alongside with the Hebrew original.

Other views more or less improbable need only be mentioned : (1) All the Christian Jews as distinct from the Gentiles;[2] (2) the Jews of Jerusalem alone;[3] (3) the Jews of Alexandria;[4] (4) the Jews of Antioch;[5] (5) the Jews of Rome;[6] (6) some community of the dispersion in the East (but not Jerusalem).[7]

Occasion and Aim.

The Epistle was prompted by the desire to strengthen and comfort the readers in their trials and persecutions (10 : 32–39 ; ch. 11 and 12), but especially to warn them against the danger of apostasy to Judaism (2 : 2, 3 ; 3 : 6, 14 ; 4 : 1, 14 ; 6 : 1–8 ; 10 : 23, 26–31). And this could be done best by showing the infinite superiority of Christianity, and the awful guilt of neglecting so great a salvation.

Strange that but thirty years after the resurrection and the

---

[1] So also DeWette, Tholuck, Thiersch, Delitzsch, Lünemann, Riehm, Moll (in Lange's *Com.*), Langen, Weiss.

[2] So Œcumenius, Lightfoot, Lange ; also Grimm (*sub verbo*) : " *Omnes de Judæis sive aramaice sive græce loquentibus Christiani.*"

[3] Ebrard. Moulton, on the contrary, thinks that some other church in Palestine is addressed, and that Jerusalem is excluded by ch. 2 : 3.

[4] Wieseler (who adds an unlikely reference to the temple of Onias in Leontopolis), Credner, Baur, Hilgenfeld, Köstlin, Reuss, Bunsen, Conybeare and Howson, and Plumptre.

[5] Von Hofmann.

[6] Wetstein, Alford, Holtzmann, Kurtz, Zahn ; also Renan, who thinks (*L'Antechrist*, p. 211) that the Ep. was written by Barnabas in Ephesus, and addressed to the church in Rome ; hence it was first known in Rome.

[7] A. B. Davidson (*Ep. to the Hebr.*, 1882, p. 18).

pentecostal effusion of the Spirit, there should have been such a danger of apostasy in the very mother church of Christendom. And yet not strange, if we realize the condition of things between 60 and 70. The Christians in Jerusalem were the most conservative of all believers, and adhered as closely as possible to the traditions of their fathers. They were contented with the elementary doctrines, and needed to be pressed on "unto perfection" (5 : 12 ; 6 : 1–4). The Epistle of James represents their doctrinal stand-point. The strange advice which he gave to his brother Paul, on his last visit, reflects their timidity and narrowness. Although numbered by "myriads," they made no attempt in that critical moment to rescue the great apostle from the hands of the fanatical Jews ; they were "all zealous for the law," and afraid of the radicalism of Paul on hearing that he was teaching the Jews of the Dispersion "to forsake Moses, telling them not to circumcise their children, neither to walk after the customs" (Acts 21 : 20, 21).

They hoped against hope for the conversion of their people. When that hope vanished more and more, when some of their teachers had suffered martyrdom (13 : 7), when James, their revered leader, was stoned by the Jews (62), and when the patriotic movement for the deliverance of Palestine from the hated yoke of the heathen Romans rose higher and higher, till it burst out at last in open rebellion (66), it was very natural that those timid Christians should feel strongly tempted to apostatize from the poor, persecuted sect to the national religion, which they at heart still believed to be the best part of Christianity. The solemn services of the Temple, the ritual pomp and splendor of the Aaronic priesthood, the daily sacrifices, and all the sacred associations of the past had still a great charm for them, and allured them to their embrace. The danger was very strong, and the warning of the Epistle fearfully solemn.

Similar dangers have occurred again and again in critical periods of history.

TIME AND PLACE OF COMPOSITION.

The Epistle hails and sends greetings from some place in Italy, at a time when Timothy, Paul's disciple, was set at liberty, and the writer was on the point of paying, with Timothy, a visit to his readers (13 : 23, 24). The passage, "Remember them that are in bonds, as bound with them" (13 : 3), does not necessarily imply that he himself was in prison, indeed verse 23 seems to imply his freedom. These notices naturally suggest the close of Paul's first Roman imprisonment, in the spring of the year 63, or soon after; for Timothy and Luke were with him there, and the writer himself evidently belonged to the circle of his friends and fellow-workers.

There is further internal evidence that the letter was written before the destruction of Jerusalem (70), before the outbreak of the Jewish war (66), before the Neronian persecution (in July, 64), and before Paul's martyrdom. None of these important events are even alluded to;[1] on the contrary, as already remarked, the Temple was still standing, with its daily sacrifices regularly going on, and the doom of the theocracy was still in the future, though "nigh unto a curse," "becoming old and ready to vanish away;" it was "shaken" and about to be removed; the day of the fearful judgment was drawing nigh.[2]

The place of composition was either Rome or some place in

---

[1] Zahn refers 10 : 32–34 to the Neronian persecution; but this is excluded by 12 : 4, "Ye have not yet resisted unto blood" (μέχρι αἵματος). Harnack finds also traces of the Domitian persecution. Still more unlikely.

[2] Lardner, Thiersch, Lindsay, Bullock (in Smith's *B. Dict.*, Am. ed., II., 1028), and others, assign the Epistle to A.D. 63 ; DeWette, Moll, and Lange to between 62 and 66 (between the death of James and the outbreak of the Jewish war) ; Ebrard to 62 ; Wieseler (*Chronol. des Ap. Zeitalters*, p. 519) to July, 64 ; Stuart and Tholuck to about 64 ; Weiss to 65 ("*bald nach der Mitte der sechsziger Jahre*") ; Hilgenfeld to between 64 and 66 ; Davidson (*Introd.*, revised ed., I. 222) to 66 ; Ewald to 67 ; Renan and Kay to 65. On the other hand, Zahn gives as the date A.D. 80, Holtzmann and Harnack about 90, Volkmar and Keim, 116–118. These late dates are simply impossible, not only for intrinsic reasons and the allusion to Timothy, but also because Clement of Rome, who wrote about 95, shows a perfect familiarity with Hebrews.

Southern Italy, if we assume that the writer had already started on his journey to the East.[1] Others assign it to Alexandria, or Antioch, or Ephesus.[2]

AUTHORSHIP.

This is still a matter of dispute, and will probably never be decided with absolute certainty. The obscurity of its origin is the reason why the Epistle to the Hebrews was ranked among the seven *Antilegomena* of the ante-Nicene church. The controversy ceased after the adoption of the traditional canon in 397, but revived again at the time of the Reformation. The different theories may be arranged under three heads: (1) sole authorship of Paul; (2) sole authorship of one of his pupils; (3) joint authorship of Paul and one of his pupils. Among the pupils again the views are subdivided between Luke, Barnabas, Clement of Rome, Silvanus, and Apollos.[3]

1. The PAULINE AUTHORSHIP was the prevailing opinion of the church from the fourth century to the eighteenth, with the exception of the Reformers, and was once almost an article of

---

[1] The inference of the place from οἱ ἀπὸ τῆς Ἰταλίας, 13 : 24, is uncertain, since in the epistolary style it may imply that the writer was at that time *out of* Italy, or *in* Italy (which would be more distinctly expressed by ἐν Ἰταλίᾳ or οἱ ἐξ). The brethren may have been fugitives from Italy (so Bleek). But the latter view seems more natural, and is defended by Theodoret, who knew Greek as his mother tongue. Tholuck and Ebrard quote the phrases οἱ ἀπὸ γῆς and οἱ ἀπὸ θαλάσσης, travellers by land and sea, and from Polybius, οἱ ἀπὸ τῆς Ἀλεξανδρείας βασιλεῖς, the Alexandrian kings. Still more to the point is Pseudo-Ignatius *Ad Her.* 8, quoted by Zahn (see his ed. of Ign., p. 270, 12) : ἀσπάζονταί σε . . . . πάντες οἱ ἀπὸ Φιλίππων ἐν χριστῷ, ὅτεν καὶ ἐπέστειλά σοι.

[2] The Sinaitic MS. and C have the subscription " to the Hebrews," A adds "from Rome," K " from Italy." Sam. Davidson dates it from Alexandria, Renan from Ephesus, where he thinks Barnabas was at that time with some fugitive Italians, while Timothy was imprisoned perhaps at Corinth (*L'Antechrist.* p. 210).

[3] For the patristic testimonies, I refer to the collection in Charteris, *Canonicity*, pp. 272–288; for a candid and exhaustive discussion of the whole question, to Bleek's large *Com.*, I., 82–272 ; also to Alford's *Com.*, vol. iv., Part I., pp. 1–62.

faith, but has now very few defenders among scholars.[1] It
rests on the following arguments :

(*a*) The unanimous tradition of the Eastern church, to which
the letter was in all probability directed ; yet with the important qualification which weakens the force of this testimony,
that there was a widely prevailing perception of a difference of
style, and consequent supposition of a Hebrew original, of which
there is no historic basis whatever. Clement of Alexandria
ascribed the Greek composition to Luke.[2] Origen observes the
greater purity of the Greek style,[3] and mentions Luke and Clement, besides Paul, as possible authors, but confesses his own
ignorance.[4]

(*b*) The mention of Timothy and the reference to a release
from captivity (13 : 23) point to Paul. Not necessarily, but only
to the circle of Paul. The alleged reference to Paul's own captiv-
ity in 10 : 34 rests on a false reading ($\delta\epsilon\sigma\mu o\hat{\iota}s\ \mu ov$, E. V., "in *my*
bonds," instead of the one now generally adopted, $\tauo\hat{\iota}s\ \delta\epsilon\sigma\mu io\iota s$,
"those that were in bonds "). Nor does the request, ch. 13 : 18,
19, imply that the writer was a prisoner at the time of composition; for v. 23 rather points to his freedom, as he expected
shortly to see his readers in company with Timothy.

(*c*) The agreement of the Epistle with Paul's system of doctrine, the tone of apostolic authority, and the depth and unction
which raises the Epistle to a par with his genuine writings.
But all that can be said in praise of this wonderful Epistle at

---

[1] Von Hofmann (of Erlangen) is almost the only one in Germany ; Bishop
Wordsworth and Dr. Kay in England. Among the older defenders of the
Pauline authorship we mention Owen (1668), Mill (1707), Carpzov (1750),
Bengel (1752), Sykes (1755), Andr. Cramer (1757), Storr (1789), and especially
the learned and acute Roman Catholic scholar, Hug, in his *Einleitung.*

[2] Dr. Biesenthal has, by a retranslation of the Ep. into Hebrew, endeavored
to prove this theory in "*Das Trostschreiben des Ap. Paulus an die Hebräer,*"
Leipz., 1878. But, of course, this is no argument any more than Delitzsch's
Hebrew translation of the entire New Testament. Such happy phrases as
$\pi o\lambda v\mu\epsilon\rho\hat{\omega}s\ \kappa a\grave{\iota}\ \pi o\lambda v\tau\rho\delta\pi\omega s$ (1 : 1) and $\check{\epsilon}\mu a\vartheta\epsilon\nu\ \dot{a}\phi'\ \hat{\omega}\nu\ \check{\epsilon}\pi a\vartheta\epsilon\nu\ \tau\grave{\eta}\nu\ \dot{v}\pi a\kappa o\acute{\eta}\nu$ (5 : 8)
cannot be reproduced in Hebrew at all.

[3] $\sigma v\nu\vartheta\acute{\epsilon}\sigma\epsilon\iota\ \tau\hat{\eta}s\ \lambda\acute{\epsilon}\xi\epsilon\omega s\ \dot{\epsilon}\lambda\lambda\eta\nu\iota\kappa\omega\tau\acute{\epsilon}\rho a.$ *Ap.* Euseb. *H. E.* VI. 25.

[4] $\tau\acute{\iota}s\ \delta\grave{\epsilon}\ \dot{o}\ \gamma\rho\acute{a}\psi as\ \tau\grave{\eta}\nu\ \dot{\epsilon}\pi\iota\sigma\tauo\lambda\acute{\eta}\nu,\ \tau\grave{o}\ \mu\grave{\epsilon}\nu\ \dot{a}\lambda\eta\vartheta\grave{\epsilon}s\ \vartheta\epsilon\grave{o}s\ o\hat{\iota}\delta\epsilon\nu.$

best proves only its inspiration and canonicity, which must be extended beyond the circle of the apostles so as to embrace the writings of Luke, Mark, James, and Jude.

2. The NON-PAULINE AUTHORSHIP is supported by the following arguments:

(a) The Western tradition, both Roman and North African, down to the time of Augustin, is decidedly against the Pauline authorship. This has all the more weight from the fact that the earliest traces of the Epistle to the Hebrews are found in the Roman church, where it was known before the close of the first century. Clement of Rome makes very extensive use of it, but nowhere under the name of Paul. The Muratorian Canon enumerates only thirteen Epistles of Paul and omits Hebrews. So does Gaius, a Roman presbyter, at the beginning of the third century. Tertullian ascribed the Epistle to Barnabas. According to the testimony of Eusebius, the Roman church did not regard the Epistle as Pauline at his day (he died 340). Philastrius of Brescia (d. about 387) mentions that some denied the Pauline authorship, because the passage 6:4–6 favored the heresy and excessive disciplinary rigor of the Novatians, but he himself believed it to be Paul's, and so did Ambrose of Milan. Jerome (d. 419) can be quoted on both sides. He wavered in his own view, but expressly says: "The Latin custom (*Latina consuetudo*) does *not* receive it among the canonical Scriptures;" and in another place: "All the Greeks receive the Epistle to the Hebrews, and *some* Latins (*et nonnulli Latinorum*)." Augustin, a profound divine, but neither linguist nor critic, likewise wavered, but leaned strongly toward the Pauline origin. The prevailing opinion in the West ascribed only thirteen Epistles to Paul. The Synod of Hippo (393) and the third Synod of Carthage (397), under the commanding influence of Augustin, marked a transition of opinion in favor of fourteen.[1] This opinion prevailed until Erasmus and the Reformers revived the doubts of the early Fathers. The Council of Trent sanctioned it.

[1] "*Pauli Apostoli epistolæ tredecim, ejusdem ad Hebræos una.*"

(*b*) The absence of the customary name and salutation. This has been explained from modesty, as Paul was sent to the Gentiles rather than the Jews (Pantænus), or from prudence and the desire to secure a better hearing from Jews who were strongly prejudiced against Paul (Clement of Alexandria). Very unsatisfactory and set aside by the authoritative tone of the Epistle.

(*c*) In ch. 2 : 3 the writer expressly distinguishes himself from the apostles, and reckons himself with the second genera· tion of Christians, to whom the word of the Lord was "confirmed by them that heard" it at the first from the Lord. Paul, on the contrary, puts himself on a par with the other apostles, and derives his doctrine directly from Christ, without any human intervention (Gal. 1 : 1, 12, 15, 16). This passage alone is conclusive, and decided Luther, Calvin, and Beza against the Pauline authorship.[1]

(*d*) The difference, not in the substance, but in the form and method of teaching and arguing.[2]

(*e*) The difference of style (which has already been discussed). This argument does not rest on the number of peculiar words, for such are found in every book of the New Testament, but in the superior purity, correctness, and rhetorical finish of style.

(*f*) The difference in the quotations from the Old Testament. The author of Hebrews follows uniformly the Septuagint, even with its departures from the Hebrew; while Paul is more independent, and often corrects the Septuagint from the Hebrew. Bleek has also discovered the important fact that the

---

[1] Calvin : "*Scriptor unum se ex apostolorum discipulis profitetur, quod est a Paulina consuetudine longe alienum.*" And on 2 : 3, "*Hic locus indicio est, epistolam a Paulo non fuisse compositam,*" etc.

[2] As Calvin expresses it : "*Ipsa docendi ratio et stilus alium quam Paulum esse satis testantur.*" On this point, see especially Riehm's valuable *Lehrbegriff*, etc., and the respective sections in the works on the N. T. Theology ; also Kurtz's *Com.*, pp. 24 sqq. The parallelisms which Dr. Kay sets against this argument in the Speaker's *Com.*, pp. 14 sqq., only prove what nobody denies. the *essential* agreement of Hebrews with the Pauline Epistles.

former used the text of Codex Alexandrinus, the latter the text of Codex Vaticanus.[1] It is incredible that Paul, writing to the church of Jerusalem, should not have made use of his Hebrew and rabbinical learning in quoting the Scriptures.

3 CONJECTURES concerning the probable author. Four Pauline disciples and co-workers have been proposed, either as sole or as joint authors with Paul, three with some support in tradition—Barnabas, Luke, and Clement—one without any—Apollos. Silvanus also has a few advocates.[2]

(a) Barnabas.[3] He has in his favor the tradition of the African church (at least Tertullian), his Levitical training, his intimacy with Paul, his close relation to the church in Jerusalem, and his almost apostolic authority. As the $\upsilon\grave{\iota}\grave{o}\varsigma$ $\pi\alpha\rho\alpha\kappa\lambda\acute{\eta}\sigma\epsilon\omega\varsigma$ (Acts 4 : 36), he may have written the $\lambda\acute{o}\gamma\sigma\varsigma$ $\pi\alpha\rho\alpha\kappa\lambda\acute{\eta}\sigma\epsilon\omega\varsigma$ (Heb. 13 : 22). But in this case he cannot be the author of the Epistle which goes by his name, and which, although belonging to the Pauline and strongly anti-Judaizing tendency, is yet far inferior to Hebrews in spirit and wisdom. Moreover, Barnabas was a primitive disciple, and cannot be included in the second generation (2 : 3).

(b) Luke.[4] He answers the description of 2 : 3, writes pure Greek, and has many affinities in style.[5] But against him is

---

[1] See the proof in Bleek, vol. I. 338–375. Conveniently ignored in the Speaker's *Com.*, p. 13.

[2] Of the other friends of Paul, Timothy is excluded by the reference to him in ch. 13 : 23. Mark, Demas, Titus, Tychicus, Epaphroditus, Epaphras, Aristarchus, Aquila, Jesus Justus have never been brought forward as candidates. Silvanus, or Silas, is favorably mentioned by Böhme, Mynster, and Riehm (890 sqq.), on account of his prominent position, Acts 15 : 22, 27, 34, 40; 16 : 19; 1 Pet. 5 : 12.

[3] Tertullian, Ullmann, Wieseler, Thiersch, Ritschl, Renan, Zahn. W. R. Smith (in the "Enc. Brit.") likewise leans to the Barnabas hypothesis.

[4] Clement of Alexandria (who, however, regarded Luke only, and wrongly, as translator), Calvin, Grotius, Crell, Ebrard, Delitzsch, Döllinger. Ebrard supposes that Luke wrote the Epistle at the request and in the name of Paul, who suggested the general plan and leading ideas. This is the most plausible form of the Luke hypothesis, but does not account for the doctrinal differences.

[5] This linguistic argument has been overdone by Delitzsch and weakened by fanciful or far-fetched analogies. See the strictures of Lünemann, pp. 24–31.

the fact that the author of Hebrews was, no doubt, a native Jew, while Luke was a Gentile (Col. 4 : 11, 14). This objection, however, ceases in a measure if Luke wrote in the name and under the instruction of Paul.

(c) Clemens Romanus.[1] He makes thorough use of Hebrews and interweaves passages from the Epistle with his own ideas, but evidently as an imitator, far inferior in originality and force.

(d) Apollos.[2] A happy guess of the genius of Luther, suggested by the description given of Apollos in the Acts (18 : 24–28), and by Paul (1 Cor. 1 : 12; 3 : 4–6, 22; 4 : 6; 16 : 12; Tit. 3 : 13). Apollos was a Jew of Alexandria, mighty in the Scriptures, fervent in spirit, eloquent in speech, powerfully confuting the Jews, a friend of Paul, and independently working with him in the same cause at Ephesus, Corinth, Crete. So far everything seems to fit. But this hypothesis has not a shadow of support in tradition, which could hardly have omitted Apollos in silence among the three or four probable authors. Clement names him once,[3] but not as the author of the Epistle which he so freely uses. Nor is there any trace of his ever having been in Rome, and having stood in so close a relationship to the Hebrew Christians in Palestine.

The learned discussion of modern divines has led to no certain and unanimous conclusion, but is, nevertheless, very valuable, and sheds light in different directions. The following points may be regarded as made certain, or at least in the highest degree probable : the author of Hebrews was a Jew by

---

[1] Mentioned as a subjective conjecture by Origen (Κλήμης ὁ γενόμενος ἐπίσκοπος 'Ρωμαίων ἔγραψε τὴν ἐπιστολήν) alongside with Luke. Renewed by Erasmus and Bisping.

[2] Luther, Osiander, Norton, Semler, Bleek, Tholuck, Credner, Reuss, Bunsen, Hilgenfeld, Lange, Moll, Kendrick, Alford, Lünemann, Kurtz, Samuel Davidson, A. B. Davidson. The Apollos hypothesis has been the most popular until, within the last few years, Renan, Zahn, and W. Robertson Smith have turned the current again in favor of the Barnabas hypothesis. Riehm, after a full and judicious discussion, wavers between Apollos and Silvanus, but ends with Origen's modest confession of ignorance (p. 894).

[3] Ep. ad Cor., c. 47.

birth; a Hellenist, not a Palestinian; thoroughly at home in the Greek Scriptures (less so, if at all, in the Hebrew original); familiar with the Alexandrian Jewish theology (less so, if at all, with the rabbinical learning of Palestine); a pupil of the apostles (not himself an apostle); an independent disciple and co-worker of Paul; a friend of Timothy; in close relation with the Hebrew Christians of Palestine, and, when he wrote, on the point of visiting them; an inspired man of apostolic insight, power, and authority, and hence worthy of a position in the canon as "the great unknown."

Beyond these marks we cannot go with safety. The writer purposely withholds his name. The arguments for Barnabas, Luke, and Apollos, as well as the objections against them, are equally strong, and we have no data to decide between them, not to mention other less known workers of the apostolic age. We must still confess with Origen that God only knows the author of the Epistle to the Hebrews.

NOTES.

I.—The POSITION of Hebrews in the New Testament. In the old Greek MSS. (אֹ, B, C, D) the Epistle to the Hebrews stands *before* the Pastoral Epistles, as being an acknowledged letter of Paul. This order has, perhaps, a chronological value, and is followed in the critical editions (Lachmann, Tischendorf, Tregelles, Westcott and Hort), although Westcott and Hort regard the Pastoral Epistles as Pauline, and the Ep. to the Hebrews as un-Pauline. See their *Gr. Test.*, vol. II., 321.

But in the Latin and English Bibles, Hebrews stands more appropriately at the *close* of the Pauline Epistles, and immediately precedes the Catholic Epistles.

Luther, who had some doctrinal objections to Hebrews and James, took the liberty of putting them after the Epistles of Peter and John, and making them the last Epistles except Jude. He misunderstood Heb. 6 : 4–6; 10 : 26, 27; 12 : 17, as excluding the possibility of a second repentance and pardon after baptism, and called these passages "hard knots" that run counter to all the Gospels and Epistles of Paul; but, apart from this, he declared Hebrews to be "an Epistle of exquisite beauty, discussing from Scripture, with masterly skill and thoroughness, the priesthood of Christ, and interpreting on this point the Old Testament with great richness and acuteness."

The English Revisers retained, without any documentary evidence,

the traditional title, "The Epistle *of Paul the Apostle* to the Hebrews."
This gives sanction to a particular theory, and is properly objected to
by the American Revisers. The Pauline authorship is, to say the least,
an open question, and should have been left open by the Revisers. The
ancient authorities entitle the letter simply, Πρὸς Ἑβραίους, and even
this was probably added by the hand of an early transcriber. Still less
is the subscription "Written to the Hebrews from Italy by Timothy"
to be relied on as original, and was probably a mere inference from the
contents (13 : 23, 24).

II.—The HAPAXLEGOMENA of the Epistle. ἀγενεαλόγητος, without
pedigree (said of Melchizedek), 7 : 3. ἀμήτωρ, motherless, 7 : 3. ἀπάτωρ,
fatherless, 7 : 3. ἀπαύγασμα, effulgence (said of Christ in relation to
God), 1 : 2. αἰσθητήριον, sense, 5 : 14. ἀκροθίνιον, spoils, 7 : 4. εὐπερίσ-
τατος (from εὖ and περιΐστημι, to place round), a difficult word of uncertain interpretation, easily besetting, closely clinging to (E. R. on
the margin : admired by many), 12 : 1. κριτικός, quick to discern, 4 : 12.
ἡ μέλλουσα οἰκουμένη. the future world, 2 : 5. μεσιτεύειν, to interpose
one's self, to mediate, 6 : 17. μετριοπαθεῖν, to have compassion on, to
bear gently with, 5 : 2 (said of Christ). ὁρκωμοσία, oath, 7 : 20, 21, 28.
παραπικραίνειν, to provoke, 3 : 16. παραπικρασμός, provocation, 3 : 8, 15.
πολυμερῶς, by divers portions, 1 : 1. πολυτρόπως, in divers manners, 1 : 1.
πρόδρομος, forerunner, 6 : 20 (of Christ). συνεπιμαρτυρεῖν, to bear witness
with, 2 : 4. τραχηλίζειν, to open, 4 : 13 (τετραχηλισμένα, laid open).
ὑπόστασις, substance (or person), 1 : 3 (of God) ; confidence, 3 : 14 ;
assurance, 11 : 1. This word, however, occurs also in 2 Cor. 11 : 17, in
the sense of confidence. χαρακτήρ, express image (Christ, the very image
of the essence of God), 1 : 3.

On the other hand, the Ep. to the Hebrews has a number of rare
words in common with Paul which are not elsewhere found in the New
Testament or the Septuagint, as αἰδώς (12 : 13 ; 1 Tim. 2 : 9), ἀναθεωρέω
(13 : 7 ; Acts 17 : 23), ἀνυπότακτος (2 : 8 ; 1 Tim. 1 : 9 ; Tit. 1 : 6, 10), ἀπεί-
θεια (4 : 6, 11 ; Rom. 11 : 30, 32 ; Eph. 2 : 2 ; Col. 3 : 5), ἀπόλαυσις (11 : 25 ;
1 Tim. 6 : 17), ἀφιλάργυρος (13 : 5 ; 1 Tim. 3 : 3), ἔνδικος (2 : 1 ; Rom. 3 : 8),
ἐνεργής (4 : 12 ; 1 Cor. 16 : 9 ; Philem. 6), ἐφάπαξ (7 : 27 ; 10 : 10 ; Rom.
6 : 10 ; 1 Cor. 15 : 6), κοσμικός (9 : 11 ; Tit. 2 : 12), μιμητής (6 : 12 ; 1 Cor.
4 : 16, etc.), νεκρόω (11 : 12 ; Rom. 4 : 19 ; Col. 3 : 5), ὀρέγομαι (11 : 16 ; 1
Tim. 3 : 1 ; 6 : 10), παρακοή (2 : 2 ; Rom. 5 : 10 ; 2 Cor. 10 : 6), πληροφορία
(6 : 11 ; 10 : 22 ; Col. 2 : 2 ; 1 Thess. 1 : 5), φιχοξενία (13 : 2 ; Rom. 12 : 13).

On the linguistic peculiarities of Hebrews, see Bleek, I. 315–338 ;
Lünemann, *Com.*, pp. 12 and 24 sqq. (4th ed., 1878) ; Davidson, *Introd.*,
I. 209 sqq. (revised ed., 1882) ; and the Speaker's *Com. N. T.*, IV. 7–16.

§ 101. *The Apocalypse.*

On the lit. and life of John, see §§ 40 and 41 (pp. 406 sqq.) ; on the authorship of the Apoc. and the time of composition, § 37 (pp. 385–390) ; § 41 (pp. 416–422) ; and § 84 (pp. 716 sq.).

1. MODERN CRITICAL works of GERMAN and FRENCH scholars on the Apocalypse : LÜCKE (*Voltständige Einleitung*, etc., 2d ed., 1852 ; 1,074 pages of introductory matter, critical and historical ; compare with it the review of BLEEK in the " Studien and Kritiken " for 1854 and 1855) ; DEWETTE (*Com.*, 1848, with a remarkable preface, 3d ed. by Mœller, 1862) ; BLEEK (Posthumous Lectures, ed. by Hossbach, 1862) ; EWALD (*Die Johann. Schriften*, vol. II., 1862 ; besides his older Latin Com., 1828) ; DÜSTERDIECK (in Meyer's *Com.*, 3d ed., 1877) ; RENAN (*L'Antechrist*, 1873) ; REUSS (1878). A. SABATIER, in Lichtenberger's " Encyclopédie," I. 396–407. E. VISCHER : *Die Offenb. Joh. eine Jüd. Apok. in christl. Bearbeitung*, Leipz., 1886. F. SPITTA : *Die Offenb. Joh. untersucht*, Halle, 1889.

2. For DOCTRINAL and PRACTICAL exposition, the Commentaries of HENGSTENBERG (1849, spoiled by false prophecies and arbitrary fancies) ; AUBERLEN (on *Daniel* and *Revelation*, 2d ed., 1854) ; GAUSSEN (*Daniel le prophète*, 1850) ; EBRARD (in Olshausen's *Com.*, 1853) ; LUTHARDT (1861) ; J. C. K. HOFMANN (1844 and 1862) ; J. L. FÜLLER (follows Hofmann, 1874) ; LANGE (1871, Am. ed. enlarged by Craven, 1874) ; GEBHARDT (*Lehrbegriff der Apok.*, 1873) ; KLIEFOTH (1874). Comp. also ROUGEMONT : *La Révélation de St. Jean expliquant l'histoire* (1866). GODET : *Essay upon the Apoc.*, in his *Studies on the N. T.*, translated from the French by W. H. Lyttleton, London, 1876, 294–398.

3. ENGLISH Com. : E. H. ELLIOTT (d. 1875, *Horæ Apoc.*, 5th ed., 1862, 4 vols.) ; WORDSWORTH (4th ed., 1866) ; ALFORD (3d ed., 1866) ; C. J. VAUGHAN (3d ed., 1870, practical) ; WILLIAM LEE (Archdeacon in Dublin, in the " Speaker's " *Com. N. T.*, vol. iv., 1881, pp. 405–844) ; E. HUNTINGFORD (Lond., 1882) ; MILLIGAN (1883 and 1886 the best).— TRENCH : *The Epistles to the Seven Churches* (2d ed., 1861), and PLUMPTRE : *Expos. of the Epp. to the Seven Ch.* (Lond. and N. Y.,1877).

4. AMERICAN Com. by MOSES STUART (1845, 2 vols., new ed., 1864, with an Excursus on the Number of the Beast, II. 452) ; COWLES (1871).

5. Of OLDER Commentaries, the most important and valuable are the following :

(a) *Greek:* ANDREAS of Cæsarea in Cappadocia (5th cent. ; the first continuous Com. on the Apoc., publ. 1596, also in the works of Chrysostom ; see Lücke, p. 983) ; ARETHAS of Cæs. in Cappad. (not of the 6th cent., as stated by Lücke, p. 990, and others, but of the 10th, according to Otto, and Harnack, in *Altchristl. Liter.*, 1882, pp.

36 sqq. ; his *σύνοψις σχολική*, ed. by J. A. Cramer, in his *Catenæ Græc. Patr. in N. T.*, Oxon., 1840, vol. VIII. ; and in the works of Oecumenius) ; OECUMENIUS (10th cent., see Lücke, p. 991).

(b) *Rom. Cath.:* LUD. AB ALCASAR (a Jesuit, 1614) ; CORNELIUS A LAPIDE (1662) ; BOSSUET (1690, and in *Oeuvres*, vol. III., 1819) ; BISPING (1876).

(c) *Protestant:* JOS. MEDE (*Clavis Apocalyptica*, Cambr., 1632 ; Engl. transl. by More, 1643 ; a new transl. by R. B. Cooper, Lond., 1833) ; HUGO GROTIUS (first, 1644) ; VITRINGA (1705, 1719, 1721) ; BENGEL (1740) ; Bishop THOMAS NEWTON (in *Dissertations on the Prophecies*, 3 vols., 1758).

This list is a small selection. The literature on the Apocalypse, especially in English, is immense, but mostly impository rather than expository, and hence worthless or even mischievous, because confounding and misleading. Darling's list of English works on the Apocalypse contains nearly fifty-four columns (I., 1732–1786).

GENERAL CHARACTER OF THE APOCALYPSE.

"The Revelation" of John, or rather "of Jesus Christ" through John,[1] appropriately closes the New Testament. It is the one and only prophetic book, but based upon the discourses of our Lord on the destruction of Jerusalem and the end of the world, and his second advent (Matt. ch. 24). It has one face turned back to the prophecies of old, the other gazing into the future. It combines the beginning and the end in Him who is "the Alpha and the Omega." It reminds one of the mysterious sphinx keeping ceaseless watch, with staring eyes, at the base of the Great Pyramid. "As many words as many mysteries," says Jerome ; "Nobody knows what is in it," adds Luther.[2] No book has been more misunderstood and abused ; none calls for greater modesty and reserve in interpretation.[3]

---

[1] *'Αποκάλυψις 'Ιησοῦ Χριστοῦ*, 1 : 1. The oldest inscription in Cod. ℵ is *αποκαλυψις ιωανου*. Later MSS. add *τοῦ ἁγίου* and *τοῦ θεολόγου*, etc.

[2] " *Tot verba, tot mysteria.*"—" *Niemand weiss, was darinnen steht.*" Zwingli would take no doctrinal proof-text from Revelation.

[3] The amount of nonsense, false chronology, and prophecy which has been put into the Apocalypse is amazing, and explains the sarcastic saying of the Calvinistic, yet vehemently anti-Puritanic preacher, Robert South (*Serm.* XXIII., vol. I., 377, Philad. ed., 1844), that "the book called the Revelation, the more it is studied, the less it is understood, as generally either finding a

The opening and closing chapters are as clear and dazzling as sunlight, and furnish spiritual nourishment and encouragement to the plainest Christian; but the intervening visions are, to most readers, as dark as midnight, yet with many stars and the full moon illuminating the darkness.   The Epistles to the Seven Churches, the description of the heavenly Jerusalem, and the anthems and doxologies [1] which are interspersed through the mysterious visions, and glister like brilliant jewels on a canopy of richest black, are among the most beautiful, sublime, edifying, and inspiring portions of the Bible, and they ought to guard us against a hasty judgment of those chapters which we may be unable to understand.   The Old Testament prophets were not clearly understood until the fulfilment cast its light upon them, and yet they served a most useful purpose as books of warning, comfort, and hope for the coming Messiah. The Revelation will be fully revealed when the new heavens and the new earth appear—not before. [2]

"A prophet" (says the sceptical DeWette in his Commentary on Revelation, which was his last work) "is essentially an inspired man, an interpreter of God, who announces the Word of God to men in accordance with, and within the limits of, the divine truth already revealed through Moses in the Old Testament, through Christ in the New (the ἀποκάλυψις μυστηρίου, Rom. 16 : 25.   Prophecy rests on faith in a continuous providence of God ruling over the whole world, and with peculiar efficacy over Israel and the congregation of Christ, according to the moral laws revealed through Moses and Christ, especially the laws of retribution.   According to the secular view,

man cracked, or making him so.''   The remark is sometimes falsely attributed to Calvin, but he had great respect for the book, and quotes it freely for doctrinal purposes, though he modestly or wisely abstained from writing a commentary on it.

[1] Chs. 4 : 11; 5 : 8–14; 7 : 12–17; 11 : 15; 14 : 13; 15 : 3; 19 : 1, 2, 6, 7.

[2] Herder: " How many passages in the prophets are obscure in their primary historical references, and yet these passages, containing divine truth, doctrine, and consolation, are manna for all hearts and all ages.   Should it not be so with the book which is an abstract of almost all prophets and apostles ? "

all changes .n human affairs proceed partly from man's powei and prudence, partly from accident and the hidden stubbornness of fate; but according to the prophetic view, everything happens through the agency of God and in harmony with his counsels of eternal and unchangeable justice, and man is the maker of his own fortunes by obeying or resisting the will of God." [1]

The prophecy of the Bible meets the natural desire to know the future, and this desire is most intense in great critical periods that are pregnant with fears and hopes. But it widely differs from the oracles of the heathen, and the conjectures of far-seeing men. It rests on revelation, not on human sagacity and guesses; it gives certainty, not mere probability; it is general, not specific; it does not gratify curiosity, but is intended to edify and improve. The prophets are not merely revealers of secrets, but also preachers of repentance, revivalists, comforters, rebuking sin, strengthening faith, encouraging hope.

The Apocalypse is in the New Testament what the Book of Daniel is in the Old, and differs from it as the New Testament differs from the Old. Both are prophetic utterances of the will of God concerning the future of his kingdom on earth. Both are books of the church militant, and engage heaven and earth, divine, human, and satanic powers, in a conflict for life and death. They march on as " a terrible army with banners." They reverberate with thunderings and reflect the lightning flashes from the throne. But while Daniel looks to the first advent of the Messiah as the heir of the preceding world-monarchies, John looks to the second advent of Christ and the new heavens and the new earth. He gathers up all the former prophecies and sends them enriched to the future. He assures us of the final fulfilment of the prophecy of the serpent-bruiser, which was given to our first parents immediately after the fall as a guiding star of hope in the dark night of sin. He blends the glories of creation and redemption in the finale of the new Jerusalem from heaven.

---

[1] *Zur Einleit. in die Offenb. Joh.*, p. 1. The translation is condensed.

The Apocalypse, as to its style of composition, is written in prose, like Daniel, but belongs to prophetic poetry, which is peculiar to the Bible and takes there the place of the epic poetry of the Greeks; God himself being the hero, as it were, who rules over the destinies of man.   It is an inspired work of art, and requires for its understanding a poetic imagination, which is seldom found among commentators and critics; but the imagination must be under the restraint of sober judgment, or it is apt to run into fantastic comments which themselves need a commentary.   The apocalyptic vision is the last and most complete form of the prophetic poetry of the Bible.   The strong resemblance between the Revelation and Daniel, Ezekiel and Zechariah is admitted, and without them it cannot be understood.

But we may compare it also, as to its poetic form and arrangement, with the book of Job.   Both present a conflict on earth, controlled by invisible powers in heaven.   In Job it is the struggle of an individual servant of God with Satan, the arch-slanderer and persecutor of man, who, with the permission of God, uses temporal losses, bodily sufferings, mental anguish, harassing doubt, domestic affliction, false and unfeeling friends to secure his ruin.   In the Apocalypse it is the conflict of Christ and his church with the anti-Christian world.   In both the scene begins in heaven; in both the war ends in victory; but in Job long life and temporal prosperity of the individual sufferer is the price, in the Apocalypse redeemed humanity in the new heavens and the new earth.   Both are arranged in three parts: a prologue, the battle with successive encounters, and an epilogue.   In both the invisible power presiding over the action is the divine counsel of wisdom and mercy, in the place of the dark impersonal fate of the Greek drama.[1]

---

[1] Prof. Godet compares the Apocalypse with the Song of Songs, viewed as a *dramatic* poem, and calls it "the Canticle of the New Testament," as the Song of Songs is "the Apocalypse of the Old."   But I cannot see the aptness of this comparison.   Eichhorn treated the Apocalypse as a regular drama with a prologue, three acts, and an epilogue.

A comparison between the Apocalypse and the pseudo-apocalyptic Jewish and Christian literature—the Fourth Book of Esdras, the Book of Enoch, the Testaments of the Twelve Patriarchs, the Apocalypse of Baruch, the Sibylline Oracles, etc.—opens a wide field on which we cannot enter without passing far beyond the limits of this work. We may only say that the relation is the same as that between the canonical Gospels and the apocryphal pseudo-Gospels, between real history and the dreamland of fable, between the truth of God and the fiction of man.[1]

The theme of the Apocalypse is: "I come quickly," and the proper attitude of the church toward it is the holy longing of a bride for her spouse, as expressed in the response (22 : 20): "Amen: come, Lord Jesus." It gives us the assurance that Christ is coming in every great event, and rules and overrules all things for the ultimate triumph of his kingdom; that the state of the church on earth is one of continual conflict with hostile powers, but that she is continually gaining victories and will at last completely and finally triumph over all her foes and enjoy unspeakable bliss in communion with her Lord. From the concluding chapters Christian poetry has drawn rich inspiration, and the choicest hymns on the heavenly home of the saints are echoes of John's description of the new Jerusalem. The whole atmosphere of the book is bracing, and makes one feel fearless and hopeful in the face of the devil and the beasts from the abyss. The Gospels lay the foundation in faith, the Acts and Epistles build upon it a holy life; the Apocalypse is the book of hope to the struggling Christian and the militant church, and insures final victory and rest. This has been its mission; this will be its mission till the Lord come in his own good time.[2]

---

[1] See Lücke, pp. 66–345; Lange, pp. 6 sqq. ; Hilgenfeld, *Die jüdische Apokalyptik* (1857); Schürer, *N. T'liche Zeitgeschichte* (1874), pp. 511–563.

[2] Godet (p. 297) : "The Apocalypse is the precious vessel in which the treasure of Christian hope has been deposited for all ages of the church, but especially for the church under the cross." Dr. Chambers (p. 15) : "The scope of this mysterious book is not to convince unbelievers, nor to illustrate the

Analysis of Contents.

The Apocalypse consists of a Prologue, the Revelation proper, and an Epilogue. We may compare this arrangement to that of the Fourth Gospel, where ch. 1 : 1–18 forms the Prologue, ch. 21 the Epilogue, and the intervening chapters contain the evangelical history from the gathering of the disciples to the Resurrection.

I. The Prologue and the Epistles to the Seven Churches, chs. 1–3. The introductory notice; John's salutation and dedication to the Seven Churches in Asia; the vision of Christ in his glory, and the Seven Churches; the Seven Epistles addressed to them and through them to the whole church, in its various states.[1]

II. The Revelation proper or the Prophetic Vision of the Church of the Future, 4 : 1 to 22 : 5. It consists chiefly of seven Visions, which are again subdivided according to a symmetrical plan in which the numbers seven, three, four, and twelve are used with symbolic significance. There are intervening scenes of rest and triumph. Sometimes the vision goes back to the beginning and takes a new departure.

(1) The Prelude in heaven, chs. 4 and 5. (*a*) The appearance of the throne of God (ch. 4). (*b*) The appearance of the Lamb who takes and opens the sealed book (ch. 5).

(2) The vision of the seven seals, with two episodes between the sixth and seventh seals, 6 : 1 to 8 : 1.

(3) The vision of the seven trumpets of vengeance, 8 : 2 to 11 : 19.

(4) The vision of the woman (the church) and her three ene-

---

divine prescience, nor to minister to men's prurient desire to peer into the future, but to edify the disciples of Christ in every age by unfolding the nature and character of earth's conflicts, by preparing them for trial as not a strange thing, by consoling them with the prospect of victory, by assuring them of God's sovereign control over all persons and things, and by pointing them to the ultimate issue when they shall pass through the gates of pearl never more to go out."

[1] Comp. § 50, pp. 450–454.

mies, 12 : 1 to 13 : 18.   The three enemies are the dragon
(12 : 3–17), the beast from the sea (12 : 18 to 13 : 10), and the
beast from the earth, or the false prophet (13 : 11–18).

(5) The group of visions in ch. 14: (*a*) the vision of the
Lamb on Mount Zion (vers. 1–5); (*b*) of the three angels of
judgment (vers. 6–11), followed by an episode (12, 13); (*c*) the
vision of the harvest and the vintage of the earth (vers. 14–20).

(6) The vision of the seven vials of wrath, 15 : 1 to 16 : 21.

(7) The vision of the final triumph, 17 : 1 to 22 : 5: (*a*) the
fall of Babylon (17 : 1 to 19 : 10); (*b*) the overthrow of Satan
(19 : 11 to 20 : 10), with the millennial reign intervening (20 : 1–
6); (*c*) the universal judgment (20 : 11–15); (*d*) the new hea‑
vens and the new earth, and the glories of the heavenly Jerusa
lem (21 : 1 to 22 : 5).

III. The Epilogue, 22 : 6–21.   The divine attestation, threats,
and promises.

Authorship and Canonicity.

The question of authorship has already been discussed in con‑
nection with John's Gospel.   The Apocalypse professes to be
the work of John, who assumes a commanding position over the
churches of Asia.   History knows only one such character, the
Apostle and Evangelist, and to him it is ascribed by the earliest
and most trustworthy witnesses, going back to the lifetime of
many friends and pupils of the author.   It is one of the best
authenticated books of the New Testament.[1]

And yet, owing to its enigmatical obscurity, it is the most
disputed of the seven *Antilegomena ;* and this internal diffi‑
culty has suggested the hypothesis of the authorship of " Pres‑
byter John," whose very existence is doubtful (being based on
a somewhat obscure passage of Papias), and who at all events
could not occupy a rival position of superintendency over
the churches in Asia during the lifetime of the great John.
The Apocalypse was a stumbling-block to the spiritualism of

[1] See the testimonies in Charteris, *Canonicity,* pp. 336–357; also Lücke (pp.
419–887), Alford (iv. 198–229), Lee (pp. 405–442), and other commentators.

the Alexandrian fathers, and to the realism of the Reformers (at least Luther and Zwingli), and to not a few of eminent modern divines; and yet it has attracted again and again the most intense curiosity and engaged the most patient study of devout scholars; while humble Christians of every age are cheered by its heroic tone and magnificent close in their pilgrimage to the heavenly Jerusalem. Rejected by many as unapostolic and uncanonical, and assigned to a mythical Presbyter John, it is now recognized by the severest school of critics as an undoubted production of the historical Apostle John.[1]

If so, it challenges for this reason alone our profound reverence. For who was better fitted to be the historian of the past and the seer of the future than the bosom friend of our Lord and Saviour? Able scholars, rationalistic as well as orthodox, have by thorough and patient investigation discovered or fully confirmed its poetic beauty and grandeur, the consummate art in its plan and execution. They have indeed not been able to clear up all the mysteries of this book, but have strengthened rather than weakened its claim to the position which it has ever occupied in the canon of the New Testament.

It is true, the sceptical critics who so confidently vindicate the apostolic origin of the Apocalypse, derive from this very fact their strongest weapon against the apostolic origin of the fourth Gospel. But the differences of language and spirit which have been urged are by no means irreconcilable, and are overruled by stronger resemblances in the theology and christology and even in the style of the two books. A proper estimate of John's character enables us to see that he was not only able, but eminently fitted to write both; especially if we take into consideration the intervening distance of twenty or thirty years, the difference of the subject (prospective prophecy in one, and retrospective history in the other), and the difference of the state of mind, now borne along in ecstacy ($\grave{\epsilon}\nu$ $\pi\nu\epsilon\acute{\nu}\mu\alpha\tau\iota$) from vision to vision and recording what the Spirit dictated, now

[1] This is the almost unanimous opinion of the Tübingen critics and their sympathizers on the Continent and in England.

calmly collecting his reminiscences in full, clear self-conscious ness (ἐν νοῖ).[1]

THE TIME OF COMPOSITION.

The traditional date of composition at the end of Domitian's reign (95 or 96) rests on the clear and weighty testimony of Irenæus, is confirmed by Eusebius and Jerome, and has still its learned defenders,[2] but the internal evidence strongly favors an earlier date between the death of Nero (June 9, 68) and the destruction of Jerusalem (August 10, 70).[3] This helps us at the same time more easily to explain the difference between the fiery energy of the Apocalypse and the calm repose of the fourth Gospel, which was composed in extreme old age. The Apocalypse forms the natural transition from the Synoptic Gospels to the fourth Gospel. The condition of the Seven Churches was indeed different from that which existed a few years before when Paul wrote to the Ephesians; but the movement in the apostolic age was very rapid. Six or seven years intervened to account for the changes. The Epistle to the Hebrews implies a similar spiritual decline among its readers in 63 or 64. Great revivals of religion are very apt to be quickly followed by a re-action of worldliness or indifference.

[1] Comp. Rev. 1 : 10 ; 1 Cor. 14: 15. See, besides the references mentioned at the head of the section, the testimony of Dr. Weiss, who, in his *Leben Jesu* (1882), I. 97–101, ably discusses the differences between the two books, and comes to the conclusion that they are both from the same Apostle John. "Yes" (he says, with reference to a significant concession of Dr. Baur), "the fourth Gospel is 'the spiritualized Apocalypse,' but not because an intellectual hero of the second century followed the seer of the Apocalypse, but because the Son of Thunder of the Apocalypse had been matured and transfigured by the Spirit and the divine guidance into a mystic, and the flames of his youth had burnt down into the glow of a holy love."

[2] The great majority of older commentators, and among the recent ones Elliott, Alford, Hengstenberg, Ebrard, Lange, Hofmann, Godet, Lee, Milligan, and Warfield (in Schaff's "Encycl." III. 2035). I myself formerly advocated the later date, in the *Hist. of the Ap. Church* (1853), pp. 418 sqq.

[3] The early date is advocated or accepted by Neander, Lücke, Bleek, Ewald, DeWette, Baur, Hilgenfeld, Reuss, Düsterdieck, Renan, Aubé, Stuart, Davidson, Cowles, Bishop Lightfoot, Westcott, Holtzmann, Weiss ; and among earlier writers by Alcasar, Grotius, Hammond, Abauzit, and John Lightfoot.

The arguments for the early date are the following:

1. Jerusalem was still standing, and the seer was directed to measure the Temple and the altar (11 : 1), but the destruction is predicted as approaching. The Gentiles "shall tread ($\pi\alpha\tau\dot{\eta}\sigma o\upsilon$-$\sigma\iota\nu$) the holy city under foot forty and two months" (11 : 2; comp. Luke 21 : 24), and the "dead bodies shall lie in the street of the great city, which spiritually is called Sodom and Egypt, where also their Lord was crucified" (ver. 8). The existence of the twelve tribes seems also to be assumed in ch. 7 : 4–8. The advocates of the traditional date understand these passages in a figurative sense. But the allusion to the crucifixion compels us to think of the historical Jerusalem.

2. The book was written not long after the death of the fifth Roman emperor, that is, Nero, when the empire had received a deadly wound (comp. 13 : 3, 12, 14). This is the natural interpretation of ch. 17 : 10, where it is stated that the seven heads of the scarlet-colored beast, i.e., heathen Rome, "are seven kings; the five are fallen, the one is, the other is not yet come, and when he cometh, he must continue a little while." The first five emperors were Augustus, Tiberius, Caligula, Claudius, and Nero, with whom the gens Julia ingloriously perished. Next came Galba, a mere usurper (seventy-three years old), who ruled but a short time, from June, 68, to January, 69, and was followed by two other usurpers, Otho and Vitellius, till Vespasian, in 70, restored the empire after an interregnum of two years, and left the completion of the conquest of the Jews and the destruction of Jerusalem to his son Titus.[1] Vespasian may therefore be regarded as the sixth head, the three rebels not being counted; and thus the composition of the Apocalypse would fall in the spring (perhaps Easter) of the year 70. This is confirmed by 13 : 3, 12, 14, where the deadly wound of the beast is represented as being already healed.[2] But if the usurpers

---

[1] Suetonius, Vespas. c. 1: "Rebellione trium principum et caede incertum diu et quasi vagum imperium suscepit firmavitque tandem gens Flavia."

[2] So Bleek (p. 121), Lücke (in the second ed.), Böhmer, Weiss, Düsterdieck (Introd. pp. 55 sqq. and Com. on 13 : 3, and 17 : 7–14).

are counted, Galba is the sixth head, and the Revelation was written in 68. In either case Julius Cæsar must be excluded from the series of emperors (contrary to Josephus).

Several critics refer the seventh head to Nero, and ascribe to the seer the silly expectation of the return of Nero as Antichrist.[1] In this way they understand the passage 17 : 11 : "The beast that was, and is not, is himself also an eighth and is of the seven." But John makes a clear distinction between the heads of the beast, of whom Nero was one, and the beast itself, which is the Roman empire. I consider it simply impossible that John could have shared in the heathen delusion of Nero redivivus, which would deprive him of all credit as an inspired prophet. He may have regarded Nero as a fit type and forerunner of Antichrist, but only in the figurative sense in which Babylon of old was the type of heathen Rome.

3. The early date is best suited for the nature and object of the Apocalypse, and facilitates its historical understanding. Christ pointed in his eschatological discourses to the destruction of Jerusalem and the preceding tribulation as the great crisis in the history of the theocracy and the type of the judgment of the world. And there never was a more alarming state of society. The horrors of the French Revolution were confined to one country, but the tribulation of the six years preceding the destruction of Jerusalem extended over the whole Roman empire and embraced wars and rebellions, frequent and unusual conflagrations, earthquakes and famines and plagues, and all sorts of public calamities and miseries untold. It seemed, indeed, that the world, shaken to its very centre, was coming to a close, and every Christian must have felt that the prophecies of Christ were being fulfilled before his eyes.[2]

It was at this unique juncture in the history of mankind that

---

[1] So Ewald, Reuss, Baur, etc. See below, p. 846.

[2] Comp. ch. vi., pp. 376–402, and especially the most graphic description of those terrible years by Renan, in *L'Antechrist*, ch. xiv., pp. 320–339, which I would like to transcribe if space permitted. His facts are well supported by heathen and Jewish testimonies, especially Tacitus, Suetonius, Strabo, Pliny, Josephus, etc.

St. John, with the consuming fire in Rome and the infernal spectacle of the Neronian persecution behind him, the terrors of the Jewish war and the Roman interregnum around him, and the catastrophe of Jerusalem and the Jewish theocracy before him, received those wonderful visions of the impending conflicts and final triumphs of the Christian church. His was truly a book of the times and for the times, and administered to the persecuted brethren the one but allsufficient consolation: *Maran atha!* *Maran atha!*

INTERPRETATION.

The different interpretations are reduced by English writers to three systems according as the fulfilment of the prophecy is found in the past, present, or future.[1]

1. The PRETERIST system applies the Revelation to the destruction of Jerusalem and heathen Rome. So among Roman Catholics: Alcasar (1614), Bossuet (1690). Among Protestants: Hugo Grotius (1644), Hammond (1653), Clericus (1698), Wetstein (1752), Abauzit, Herder, Eichhorn, Ewald, Lücke, Bleek, DeWette, Reuss, Renan, F. D. Maurice, Samuel Davidson, Moses Stuart, Cowles, Desprez, etc. Some[2] refer it chiefly to the overthrow of the Jewish theocracy, others chiefly to the conflict with the Roman empire, still others to both.

But there is a radical difference between those Preterists who

---

[1] See Alford, Com. iv., 245 sqq.; Elliott, 4th vol.; Sam. Davidson, *Introd. to the N. T.*, first ed. III. 619, revised ed., vol. II. 297, and Lee, *Com.* p. 488. Davidson adds a fourth class of " extreme," as distinguished from simple " Futurists," who refer the entire book, including chs. 2 and 3, to the last times. Lee substitutes with Lücke the term " Historical " for " Continuous," but Historical applies better to the first class called " Preterists." Lee adds (491), as a fourth system, the " Spiritual system," and names Augustin (his "City of God," as the first philosophy of history), J. C. K. von Hofmann, Hengstenberg, Auberlen, Ebrard as its chief defenders. It is the same with what Auberlen calls the *reichsgeschichtliche Auslegung.*

[2] So Herder, in his suggestive book *ΜΑΡΑΝ ΑΘΑ, das Buch von der Zukunft des Herrn, des N. Testaments Siegel*, Riga, 1779. He was preceded in the anti-Jewish explication by Abauzit of Geneva (1730), who assigned the book to the reign of Nero, and Wetstein (1752), and followed by Hartwig (1780) and Züllig. The last, in a learned work on the Apocalypse (Stuttgart, 1834, 2 vols., 1840), refers it exclusively to the Jewish state.

acknowledge a real prophecy and permanent truth in the book, and the rationalistic Preterists who regard it as a dream of a visionary which was falsified by events, inasmuch as Jerusalem, instead of becoming the habitation of saints, remained a heap of ruins, while Rome, after the overthrow of heathenism, became the metropolis of Latin Christendom. This view rests on a literal misunderstanding of Jerusalem.

2. The CONTINUOUS (or HISTORICAL) system: The Apocalypse is a prophetic compend of church history and covers all Christian centuries to the final consummation. It speaks of things past, present, and future ; some of its prophecies are fulfilled, some are now being fulfilled, and others await fulfilment in the yet unknown future. Here belong the great majority of orthodox Protestant commentators and polemics who apply the beast and the mystic Babylon and the mother of harlots drunken with the blood of saints to the church of Rome, either exclusively or chiefly. But they differ widely among themselves in chronology and the application of details. Luther, Bullinger, Collado, Pareus, Brightman, Mede, Robert Fleming, Whiston, Vitringa, Bengel, Isaac Newton, Bishop Newton, Faber, Woodhouse, Elliott, Birks, Gaussen, Auberlen, Hengstenberg, Alford, Wordsworth, Lee.

3. The FUTURIST system: The events of the Apocalypse from ch. 4 to the close lie beyond the second advent of Christ. This scheme usually adopts a literal interpretation of Israel, the Temple, and the numbers (the $3\frac{1}{2}$ times, 42 months, 1260 days, $3\frac{1}{2}$ years). So Ribera (a Jesuit, 1592), Lacunza (another Jesuit, who wrote under the name of Ben-Ezra "On the coming of Messiah in glory and majesty," and taught the premillennial advent, the literal restoration of the ancient Zion, and the future apostasy of the clergy of the Roman church to the camp of Antichrist), S. R. Maitland, De Burgh, Todd, Isaac Williams, W. Kelly.

Another important division of historical interpreters is into POST-MILLENNARIANS and PRE-MILLENNARIANS, according as the millennium predicted in ch. 20 is regarded as past or future.

Augustin committed the radical error of dating the millennium from the time of the Apocalypse or the beginning of the Christian era (although the seer mentioned it near the end of his book), and his view had great influence; hence the wide expectation of the end of the world at the close of the first millennium of the Christian church. Other post-millennarian interpreters date the millennium from the triumph of Christianity over paganism in Rome at the accession of Constantine the Great (311); still others (as Hengstenberg) from the conversion of the Germanic nations or the age of Charlemagne. All these calculations are refuted by events. The millennium of the Apocalypse must lie in the future, and is still an article of hope.

The grammatical and historical interpretation of the Apocalypse, as well as of any other book, is the only safe foundation for all legitimate spiritual and practical application. Much has been done in this direction by the learned commentators of recent times. We must explain it from the standpoint of the author and in view of his surroundings. He wrote out of his time and for his time of things which must shortly come to pass (1 : 1, 3 ; 22 : 20), and he wished to be read and understood by his contemporaries (1 : 3). Otherwise he would have written in vain, and the solemn warning at the close (22 : 18, 19) would be unintelligible. In some respects they could understand him better than we; for they were fellow-sufferers of the fiery persecutions and witnesses of the fearful judgments described. Undoubtedly he had in view primarily the overthrow of Jerusalem and heathen Rome, the two great foes of Christianity at that time. He could not possibly ignore that great conflict.

But his vision was not confined to these momentous events. It extends even to the remotest future when death and Hades shall be no more, and a new heaven and a new earth shall appear. And although the fulfilment is predicted as being near at hand, he puts a millennium and a short intervening conflict before the final overthrow of Satan, the beast, and the false prophet. We have an analogy in the prophecy of the Old

Testament and the eschatalogical discourses of our Lord, which furnish the key for the understanding of the Apocalypse. He describes the destruction of Jerusalem and the general judgment in close proximity, as if they were one continuous event. He sees the end from the beginning. The first catastrophe is painted with colors borrowed from the last, and the last appears as a repetition of the first on a grand and universal scale. It is the manner of prophetic vision to bring distant events into close proximity, as in a panorama. To God a thousand years are as one day. Every true prophecy, moreover, admits of an expanding fulfilment. History ever repeats itself, though never in the same way. There is nothing old under the sun, and, in another sense, there is nothing new under the sun.

In the historical interpretation of details we must guard against arbitrary and fanciful schemes, and mathematical calculations, which minister to idle curiosity, belittle the book, and create distrust in sober minds. The Apocalypse is not a prophetical manual of church history and chronology in the sense of a prediction of particular persons, dates, and events. This would have made it useless to the first readers, and would make it useless now to the great mass of Christians. It gives under symbolic figures and for popular edification an outline of the general *principles* of divine government and the leading *forces* in the conflict between Christ's kingdom and his foes, which is still going on under ever-varying forms. In this way it teaches, like all the prophetic utterances of the Gospels and Epistles, lessons of warning and encouragement to every age. We must distinguish between the spiritual coming of Christ and his personal arrival or *parousia*. The former is progressive, the latter instantaneous. The coming began with his ascension to heaven (comp. Matt. 26 : 64: "*Henceforth* ye shall see the Son of man sitting at the right hand of power, and coming on the clouds of heaven"), and goes on in unbroken succession of judgments and blessings (for "the history of the world is a judgment of the world"); hence the alternation of action and repose, of scenes of terror and scenes of joy, of battles and victories. The arrival of the Bridegroom is still in the unknown future, and may be accelerated or delayed by the free action of the church, but it is as certain as the first advent of Christ The hope of the church will not be disappointed, for it rests on the promise of Him who is called "the Amen, the faithful and true witness" (3 : 14).

NOTES.

THE NUMBER 666.

The historical understanding of the Apocalypse turns, according to its own statement, chiefly on the solution of the numerical riddle in the thirteenth chapter, which has tried the wits of commentators from the time of Irenæus in the second century to the present day, and is still under dispute. The history of its solution is a history of the interpretation of the whole book. Hence I present here a summary of the most important views. First some preliminary remarks.

1. The *text*, Apoc. 13 : 18 : "Here is wisdom : he that hath understanding, let him count the number of the beast ; for it is the number of a man ($\dot{a}\rho\iota\vardelta\mu\dot{o}s$ $\gamma\dot{a}\rho$ $\dot{a}\nu\vardelta\rho\dot{\omega}\pi\sigma\nu$ $\dot{\epsilon}\sigma\tau\dot{\iota}\nu$), and the number is six hundred and sixty-six" ($\chi\xi\varsigma'$, or $\dot{\epsilon}\xi\alpha\kappa\dot{o}\sigma\iota\sigma\iota$ $\dot{\epsilon}\xi\dot{\eta}\kappa\sigma\nu\tau\alpha$ $\dot{\epsilon}\xi$).

This is the correct reading in the Greek text (supported by Codd. ℵ, A, B (2), P (2), Origen, Primasius, and Versions), and is adopted by the best editors. Irenæus (*Adv. Hær.* v. 30, quoted also in full by Tischendorf in his edition VIII. critica major) found it "in all the most approved and ancient copies" ($\dot{\epsilon}\nu$ $\pi\hat{a}\sigma\iota$ $\tauο\hat{\iota}s$ $\sigma\pi\sigma\nu\delta\alpha\dot{\iota}\sigma\iota s$ $\kappa\alpha\dot{\iota}$ $\dot{a}\rho\chi\alpha\dot{\iota}\sigma\iota s$ $\dot{a}\nu\tau\iota\gamma\rho\dot{a}$-$\phi\sigma\iota s$), and "attested by those who had themselves seen John face to face." There was, however, in his day, a very remarkable variation, sustained by Cod. C, and "some" copies, known to, but not approved by, Irenæus, namely, 616 ($\chi\iota\varsigma'$, *i.e.*, $\dot{\epsilon}\xi\alpha\kappa\dot{o}\sigma\iota\sigma\iota$ $\delta\dot{\epsilon}\kappa\alpha$ $\dot{\epsilon}\xi$). In the Anglo-American revision this reading is noted in the margin.

2. "The number of a *man*" may mean either the number of an individual, or of a corporate person, or a human number (*Menschenzahl*), *i.e.*, a number according to ordinary human reckoning (so Bleek, who compares $\mu\dot{\epsilon}\tau\rho\sigma\nu$ $\dot{a}\nu\vardelta\rho\dot{\omega}\pi\sigma\nu$, "the measure of a man," 21 : 17, and Isa. 8 : 1). Just because the number may be counted in the customary way, the writer could expect the reader to find it out. He made the solution difficult indeed, but not impossible. Dr. Lee (p. 687) deems it not inconsistent with a proper view of inspiration that John himself did not know the meaning of the number. But how could he then ask his less knowing readers to count the number ?

3. The *mystic use of numbers* (the rabbinical *Ghematria*, $\gamma\epsilon\omega\mu\epsilon\tau\rho\dot{\iota}a$) was familiar to the Jews in Babylon, and passed from them to the Greeks in

Asia. It occurs in the Cabbala, in the Sibylline Books (I. 324–331), in the Epistle of Barnabas, and was very common also among the Gnostic sects (e g., the *Abrasax* or *Abraxas*, which signified the unbegotten Father, and the three hundred and sixty-five heavens, corresponding to the number of days in the year).[1] It arose from the employment of the letters of the Hebrew and Greek alphabets for the designation of numbers. The Hebrew *Aleph* counts 1, *Beth* 2, etc., *Yodh* 10 ; but *Kaph* (the eleventh letter) counts 20, *Resh* (the twentieth letter) 200, etc. The Greek letters, with the addition of an acute accent (as ε′, β′), have the same numerical value in their order down to *Sigma*, which counts 200 ; except that ς′ (*st*) is used for 6, and ϙ′ (an antiquated letter *Koppa* between π and ρ) for 90. The Hebrew alphabet ends with *Tav* = 400, the Greek with *Omega* = 800. To express thousands an accent is put beneath the letter, as ͵α = 1,000 ; ͵β, = 2,000 ; ͵ι, = 10,000.

4. On this fact most interpretations of the Apocalyptic puzzle are based. It is urged by Bleek, DeWette, Wieseler, and others, that the number 666 must be deciphered from the *Greek* alphabet, since the book was written in Greek and for Greek readers, and uses the Greek letters *Alpha* and *Omega* repeatedly as a designation of Christ, the Beginning and the End (1 : 8 ; 21 : 6; 22 : 13). On the other hand, Ewald and Renan, and all who favor the Nero-hypothesis, appeal against this argument to the strongly Hebraistic spirit and coloring of the Apocalypse and the familiarity of its Jewish Christian readers with the Hebrew alphabet. The writer, moreover, may have preferred this for the purpose of partial concealment ; just as he substituted Babylon for Rome (comp. 1 Pet. 5 : 13). But after all, the former view is much more natural. John wrote to churches of Asia Minor, chiefly gathered from Gentile converts who knew no Hebrew. Had he addressed Christians in Palestine, the case might be different.

5. The number 666 (three sixes) must, in itself, be a significant number, if we keep in view the symbolism of numbers which runs through the whole Apocalypse. It is remarkable that the numerical value of the name *Jesus* is 888 (three eights), and exceeds the trinity of the sacred number (777) as much as the number of the beast falls below it.[2]

6. The "*beast*" coming out of the sea and having seven heads and ten horns (ch. 13 : 1–10) is the anti-Christian world-power at war with the church of Christ. It is, as in Daniel, an apt image of the brutal nature of the pagan state. It is, when in conflict with the church, the secular

---

[1] α = 1, β = 2, ρ = 100, α = 1, ξ = 60, α = 1, s = 200 ; total, 365. A vast number of engraved stones, called "Abraxas-gems," are still extant. The origin of Abraxas is usually ascribed to Basilides or his followers.

[2] I = 10 + η = 8 + σ = 200 + ο = 70 + υ = 400 + σ = 200 ; total Ιησουσ = 888. Comp. Barnabas, *Ep.* c. 9 ; and the Sibylline Books, I. 324–331.

or political Antichrist; while "the false prophet," who works signs and deceives the worshippers of the beast (16 : 13; 19 : 20; 20 : 10), is the intellectual and spiritual Antichrist, in close alliance with the former, his high-priest and minister of cultus, so to say, and represents the idolatrous religion which animates and supports the secular imperialism. In wider application, the false prophet may be taken as the personification of all false doctrine and heresy by which the world is led astray. For as there are "many Antichrists," so there are also many false prophets. The name "Antichrist," however, never occurs in the Apocalypse, but only in the Epistles of John (five times), and there in the plural, in the sense of "false prophets" or heretical teachers, who deny that Jesus Christ is come in the flesh (1 John 4 : 1–3). Paul designates the Antichrist as "the man of sin," "the son of perdition who opposeth and exalteth himself against all that is called God or that is worshipped; so that he sitteth in the temple of God, setting himself forth as God" (2 Thess. 2 : 3, 4). But he seems to look upon the Roman empire as a restraining power which, for a time at least, prevented the full outbreak of the "mystery of lawlessness," then already at work (ver. 6–8). He thus wrote a year or two before the accession of Nero, and sixteen years or more before the composition of the Apocalypse.

The beast must refer to heathen Rome and the seven heads to seven emperors. This is evident from the allusion to the "seven mountains," that is, the seven-hilled city (*urbs septicollis*) on which the woman sits, 17 : 9. But not a few commentators give it a wider meaning, and understand by the heads as many world-monarchies, including those of Daniel, before Christ, and extending to the last times. So Auberlen, Gaussen, Hengstenberg, Von Hofmann, Godet, and many English divines.

7. The numerous *interpretations* of the mystic number of the beast may be reduced to three classes :

(a) The figures 666 represent the letters composing the name of a historical power, or of a single man, in conflict with Christ and his church. Here belong the explanations : Latinus, Cæsar-Augustus, Nero, and other Roman emperors down to Diocletian. Even such names as Julian the Apostate, Genseric, Mohammed (*Maometis*), Luther (*Martinus Lauterus*), Joannes Calvinus, Beza Antitheos, Louis XIV., Napoleon Bonaparte, the Duke of Reichstadt (called "King of Rome"), Napoleon III., have been discovered in the three sixes by a strange kind of imposition.[1]

[1] These pious absurdities are surpassed by the rationalistic absurdity of Volkmar, who (in his *Com. on the Apoc.*, 1862, p. 197) carries the imaginary hostility of John to Paul so far as to refer "the false prophet" (16 : 13 ; 19 : 20) to the Apostle of the Gentiles, because he taught (Rom. 13) that every soul should be subject to the then reigning Nero (*i. e.*, the beast) ! Even Hilgenfeld (*Einleit.* p. 436) and Samuel Davidson (I. 291), while agreeing with Volkmar in the Nero-hypothesis, protest against such impious nonsense.

(b) The number is chronological, and designates the duration of the life of the beast, whether it be heathenism, or Mohammedanism, or popery.

(c) The number is symbolical of Antichrist and the anti-Christian power.

We now proceed to the principal interpretations.

LATINUS OR THE ROMAN EMPIRE.

LATEINOS (Λατεῖνος for Λατῖνος, *Latinus*), i.e., the Latin or Roman empire. This is the numerical value of 666 in Greek: λ = 30 + α = 1 + τ = 300 + ε = 5 + ι = 10 + ν = 50 + o = 70 + σ = 200 = total 666. The Greek form Λατεῖνος is no valid objection; for ει often represents the Latin long i, as in Ἀντονεῖνος, Παυλεῖνος, Παπεῖρος, Σαβεῖνος, Φαυστεῖνος. J. E. Clarke shows that ἡ Λατινὴ βασιλεία, "the Latin empire," likewise gives the number 666.[1]

This interpretation is the oldest we know of, and is already mentioned by Irenæus, the first among the Fathers who investigated the problem, and who, as a pupil of Polycarp in Smyrna (d. 155), the personal friend of John, deserves special consideration as a witness of traditions from the school of the beloved disciple. He mentions three interpretations, all based on the Greek alphabet, namely Εὐανϑας (which is of no account), Λατεινος (which he deems possible), and Τειταν, i.e., *Titus* (which he, upon the whole, prefers), but he abstains from a positive decision, for the reason that the Holy Scripture does not clearly proclaim the name of the beast or Antichrist.[2]

The interpretation *Latinus* is the only sensible one among the three, and adopted by Hippolytus, Bellarmin, Eichhorn, Bleek, DeWette, Ebrard, Düsterdieck, Alford, Wordsworth, Lee, and others.

Latinus was the name of a king of Latium, but not of any Roman emperor. Hence it must here be taken in a generic sense, and applied to the whole heathen Roman empire.

Here the Roman Catholic divines stop.[3] But many Protestant com-

---

[1] See Lee, *Com.* p. 687. Adam Clarke regarded this unanswerable.

[2] *Adv. Hær.*, v. 30, §§ 3 and 4. Josephus, from prudential regard to his patrons, the Flavian emperors, withheld the interpretation of the fourth beast and the stone cut out of the mountain in Daniel's vision. *Ant.* x. 10, § 4. On which Havercamp remarks : "Nor is this to be wondered at that he would not now meddle with things future ; for he had no mind to provoke the Romans by speaking of the destruction of that city, which they called the *eternal city.*"

[3] If they go further, they discover the anti-Christian beast in the mediæval German (the so-called "Holy Roman") empire in conflict with the papacy, in the Napoleonic imperialism, the Russian Czarism, the modern German empire (the anti-papal *Cultur-Kampf*), in fact in every secular power which is hostile to the interests of the Roman hierarchy and will "not go to Canossa." This would be the very reverse of the old Protestant interpretation.

mentators apply it also, in a secondary sense, to the Latin or papal church as far as it repeated in its persecuting spirit the sins of heathen Rome. The second beast which is described, ch. 13 : 11–17, as coming out of the earth, and having two horns like unto a lamb, and speaking as a dragon, and exercising all the authority of the first beast in his sight, is referred to the papacy. The false prophet receives a similar application. So Luther, Vitringa, Bengel, Auberlen, Hengstenberg, Ebrard, and many English divines.

Dean Alford advocates this double application in his Commentary. "This name," he says, "describes the common character of the rulers of the former Pagan Roman Empire — '*Latini sunt qui nunc regnant*,' Iren.: and, which Irenæus could not foresee, unites under itself the character of the later Papal Roman Empire also, as revived and kept up by the agency of its false prophet, the priesthood. The Latin Empire, the Latin Church, Latin Christianity, have ever been its commonly current appellations : its language, civil and ecclesiastical, has ever been Latin : its public services, in defiance of the most obvious requisite for public worship, have ever been throughout the world conducted in Latin ; there is no one word which could so completely describe its character, and at the same time unite the ancient and modern attributes of the two beasts, as this. Short of saying absolutely that this *was* the word in St. John's mind, I have the strongest persuasion that no other can be found approaching so near to a complete solution." Bishop Wordsworth gives the same anti-papal interpretation to the beast, and indulges in a variety of pious and far-fetched fancies. See his *Com.* on ch. 13 : 18, and his special work on the Apocalypse.

NERO.

The Apocalypse is a Christian counterblast against the Neronian persecution, and Nero is represented as the beast of the abyss who will return as Antichrist. The number 666 signifies the very name of this imperial monster in Hebrew letters, נרון קסר, NERON KÆSAR, as follows : ‎נ (n) = 50, ‎ר (r) = 200, ‎ו (o) = 6, ‎נ (n) = 50, ‎ק (k) = 100, ‎ס (s) = 60, ‎ר (r) = 200 ; in all 666. The Neronian coins of Asia bear the inscription : Νερων Καισαρ. But the omission of the ‎ר (which would add 10 to 666) from ‎קיסר = Καῖσαρ, has been explained by Ewald (*Johanneische Schriften*, II. 263) from the Syriac in which it is omitted, and this view is confirmed by the testimony of inscriptions of Palmyra from the third century ; see Renan (*L'Antechrist*, p. 415).

The coincidence, therefore, must be admitted, and is at any rate most remarkable, since Nero was the first, as well as the most wicked, of all imperial persecutors of Christianity, and eminently worthy of being characterized as the beast from the abyss, and being regarded as the type and forerunner of Antichrist.

This interpretation, moreover, has the advantage of giving the num‹ ber of a man or a particular person (which is not the case with Lateinos), and affords a satisfactory explanation of the *varians lectio* 616; for this number precisely corresponds to the Latin form, NERO CÆSAR, and was probably substituted by a Latin copyist, who in his calculation dropped the final *Nun* (=50), from Neron (666 less 50=616).

The series of Roman emperors (excluding Julius Cæsar), according to this explanation, is counted thus : Augustus, Tiberius, Caligula, Claudius, Nero, Galba. This makes Nero (who died June 9, 68) the fifth, and Galba the sixth, and seems to fit precisely the passage ch. 17 : 10 : "Five [of the seven heads of the beast] are fallen, the one [Galba] is, the other [the seventh] is not yet come ; and when he cometh he must continue a little while." This leads to the conclusion that the Apocalypse was written during the short reign of Galba, between June 9, 68, and January 15, 69. It is further inferred from ver. 11 ("the beast that was, and is not, is himself also an eighth, and is of the seven ; and he goeth into perdition"), that, in the opinion of the seer and in agreement with a popular rumor, Nero, one of the seven emperors, would return as the eighth in the character of Antichrist, but shortly perish.

This plausible solution of the enigma was almost simultaneously and independently discovered, between 1831 and 1837, by several German scholars, each claiming the credit of originality, viz. : C. F. A. Fritzsche (in the "Annalen der gesammten theol. Liter.," I. 3, Leipzig, 1831) ; F. Benary (in the "Zeitschrift für specul. Theol.," Berlin, 1836) ; F. Hitzig (in *Ostern und Pfingsten*, Heidelb., 1837) ; E. Reuss (in the "Hallesche Allg. Lit.-Zeitung" for Sept., 1837) ; and Ewald, who claims to have made the discovery before 1831, but did not publish it till 1862. It has been adopted by Baur, Zeller, Hilgenfeld, Volkmar, Hausrath, Krenkel, Gebhardt, Renan, Aubé, Réville, Sabatier, Sam. Davidson (I. 291) ; and among American commentators by Stuart and Cowles. It is just now the most popular interpretation, and regarded by its champions as absolutely conclusive.

But, as already stated in the text, there are serious objections to the Nero-hypothesis :

(1) The language and readers of the Apocalypse suggest a Greek rather than a Hebrew explanation of the numerical riddle.

(2) The seer clearly distinguishes the beast, as a collective name for the Roman empire (so used also by Daniel), from the seven heads, *i.e.*, kings (βασιλεῖς) or emperors. Nero is one of the five heads who ruled before the date of the Apocalypse. He was "slain" (committed suicide), and the empire fell into anarchy for two years, until Vespasian restored it, and so the death-stroke was healed (13 : 3). The three emperors between Nero and Vespasian (Galba, Otho, and Vitellius) were usurpers, and represent an interregnum and the deadly wound of the beast. This at least is a more worthy interpretation and consistent with the actual facts.

It should be noticed, however, that Josephus, *Ant.* XVIII. 2, 2 ; 6, 10, very distinctly includes Julius Cæsar among the emperors, and calls Augustus the *second*, Tiberius the *third*, Caius Caligula the *fourth* Roman emperor.   Suetonius begins his *Lives of the Twelve Cæsars* with Julius and ends with Domitian, including the lives of Galba, Otho, and Vitellius. This fact tends at all events to weaken the foundation of the Nero-hypothesis.

(3) It is difficult to conceive of a reasonable motive for concealing the detested name of Nero after his death.   For this reason Cowles makes Nero the sixth emperor (by beginning the series with Julius Cæsar) and assigns the composition to his persecuting reign.   But this does not explain the wound of the beast and the statement that "it was and *is not.*"

(4) A radical error, such as the belief in the absurd heathen fable of the return of Nero, is altogether incompatible with the lofty character and profound wisdom of the Apocalypse, and would destroy all confidence in its prophecy.   If John, as these writers maintain, composed it in 68, he lived long enough to be undeceived, and would have corrected the fatal blunder or withheld the book from circulation.

(5) It seems incredible that such an easy solution of the problem should have remained unknown for eighteen centuries and been reserved for the wits of half a dozen rival rationalists in Germany.   Truth is truth, and must be thankfully accepted from any quarter and at any time ; yet as the Apocalypse was written for the benefit of contemporaries of Nero, one should think that such a solution would not altogether have escaped them.   Irenæus makes no mention of it.

The Emperor of Rome.

Cæsar Romæ, from קיסר רום.   So Ewald formerly (in his first commentary, published in 1828).   But this gives the number 616, which is rejected by the best critics in favor of 666.   In his later work, Ewald adopts the Nero-hypothesis (*Die Johanneischen Schriften*, Bd. II., 1862, p. 202 sq.).

Caligula.

From Γάϊος Καῖσαρ.   But this counts likewise 616.

Titus.

The Greek Τεῖταν.   Irenæus considers this the most probable interpretation, because the word is composed of six letters, and belongs to a royal tyrant.   If we omit the final ν (n), we get the other reading (616).   The objection is that Titus, the destroyer of Jerusalem, was one of the best emperors, and not a persecutor of Christians.

Vespasian, Titus, and Domitian.

Wetstein refers the letters to Titus Flavius Vespasianus, father and sons (Titus and Domitian).   He thinks that John used both numbers,

616 in the first, 666 in the second edition of his book. "*Eleganter,*" he says in his notes, "*et apposite Joannes Titum Flavium Vespasianum patrem et filios hoc nomine designat . . . Convenit secundo nomen* Τειτάν *prænomini ipsorum* Titus. *Res ipsa etiam convenit. Titanes fuerunt* 3εομάχοι, *tales etiam Vespasiani.*" *Nov. Test.,* II., p. 806 ; comp. his critical note on p. 805.

DIOCLETIAN.

DIOCLETIAN, Emperor, in Roman characters, DIOCLES AUGUSTUS, counting only some of the letters, namely : DIo CLes aVg Vst Vs.[1] Diocletian was the last of the persecuting emperors (d. 313). So Bossuet. To his worthless guess the Huguenots opposed the name of the "grand monarch" and persecutor of Protestants, Louis XIV., which yields the same result (LVDo VICVs).

THE ROMAN EMPERORS FROM AUGUSTUS TO VESPASIAN.

Märcker (in the "Studien und Kritiken" for 1868, p. 699) has found out that the initial letters of the first ten Roman emperors from Octavianus (Augustus) to Titus, including the three usurpers Galba, Otho, and Vitellius, yield the numerical value of 666. Düsterdieck (p. 467) calls this "*eine frappante Spielerei.*"

CÆSAR AUGUSTUS.

Καισαρσεβαστον (for — ς, suited to the neuter 3ηρίον), *i.e.,* the "Cæsar Augustan" beast.[2] The official designation of the Roman emperors was Καισαρ Σεβαστός (CÆSAR AUGUSTUS), in which their blasphemous apotheosis culminates. In support of it may be quoted "the names of blasphemy on the heads of the beast," 13 : 1.

This is the conjecture proposed by Dr. Wieseler in his book : *Zur Geschichte der Neutest. Schrift und des Urchristenthums,* 1880, p. 169. It is certainly ingenious and more consistent with the character of the Apocalypse than the Nero-hypothesis. It substantially agrees with the interpretation *Lateinos.* But the substitution of a final ν for σ is an objection, though not more serious than the omission of the yodh from קרסר.

THE CHRONOLOGICAL SOLUTIONS.—THE DURATION OF ANTICHRIST.

The number 666 signifies the duration of the beast or anti-Christian world power, and the false prophet associated with the beast.

(1) The duration of HEATHENISM. But heathen Rome, which persecuted the church, was christianized after the conversion of Constantine,

---

[1] $D = 500 + I = 1 + C = 100 + L = 50 + V = 5 + V = 5 = 666.$

[2] The numerical value of Καισαρσεβαστον is $= 20 + 1 + 10 + 200 + 1 + 100 + 200 + 5 + 2 + 1 + 6 + 70 + 50$, in all 666.

A.D. 311. The other forms and subsequent history of heathenism lie outside of the apocalyptic vision.

(2) MOHAMMEDANISM. Pope Innocent III., when rousing Western Europe to a new crusade, declared the Saracens to be the beast, and Mohammed the false prophet whose power would last six hundred and sixty-six years. See his bull of 1213, in which he summoned the fourth Lateran Council, in Hardouin, *Conc.*, Tom. VII. 3. But six hundred and sixty-six years have passed since the Hegira (622), and even since the fourth Lateran Council (1215); yet Islam still sits on the throne in Constantinople, and rules over one hundred and sixty million of consciences.

(3). The anti-Christian PAPACY. This interpretation was suggested by mediæval sects hostile to Rome, and was matured by orthodox Protestant divines of the sixteenth and seventeenth centuries under the fresh impression of the fearful persecutions which were directly instigated or approved by the papacy, and which surpass in cruelty and extent the persecutions of heathen Rome. It is asserted that the terrible Duke of Alva alone put more Protestants to death in the Netherlands within a few years than all the heathen emperors from Nero to Diocletian; and that the victims of the Spanish Inquisition (105,000 persons in eighteen years under Torquemada's administration) outnumber the ancient martyrs. It became almost a Protestant article of faith that the mystical Babylon, the mother of harlots, riding on the beast, the woman drunken with the blood of the saints, and with the blood of the martyrs of Jesus (Apoc. 17:5 sqq.), is none other than the pseudo-Christian and anti-Christian church of Rome, and this view is still widely prevalent, especially in Great Britain and North America.

Luther struck the key-note of this anti-popery exegesis. He had at first a very low opinion of the Apocalypse, and would not recognize it as apostolic or prophetic (1522), but afterward he utilized it for polemic purposes (in a preface to his edition of the N. T. of 1530). He dated the one thousand years (20:7) with Augustin from the composition of the book, and the six hundred and sixty-six years from Gregory VII., as the supposed founder of the papacy, and understood Gog and Magog to mean the unspeakable Turks and the Jews. As Gregory VII. was elected pope 1073, the anti-Christian era ought to have come to an end A.D. 1739; but that year passed off without any change in the history of the papacy.

Luther was followed by Chytræus (1563), Selnecker (1567), Hoe v. Honegg (1610 and 1640), and other Lutheran commentators. Calvin and Beza wisely abstained from prophetic exposition, but other Reformed divines carried out the anti-popery scheme with much learning, as Bibliander (1549 and 1559), Bullinger (1557), David Pareus (1618), Joseph Mede (the founder of the ingenious system of synchronism, in his *Clavis Apocalyptica*, 1627), Coccejus (1696), Vitringa (a very learned and useful commentator, 1705, 3d ed. 1721), and Joh. Albrecht Bengel (in his *Gnomon*, his *Ordo Temporum*, 1741, and especially his *Erklärte Offenbarung Johannis*, 1740, new ed. 1834). This truly great and good man elaborated a learned scheme of chronological interpretation, and fixed the end of the anti-Christian (papal) reign at the year 1836, and many pious people among his admirers in Würtemburg were in anxious expectation of the millennium during that year. But it passed away without any serious change, and this failure, according to Bengel's own correct prediction, indicates a serious error in his scheme. Later writers have again and again predicted the fall of the papacy and the beginning of the millennium, advancing the date as times progress; but the years 1848 and 1870 have passed away, and the Pope still lives, enjoying a green old age, with the additional honor of infallibility, which the Fathers never heard of, which even St. Peter never claimed, and St. Paul effectually disputed at Antioch. All mathematical calculations about the second advent are doomed to disappointment, and those who want to know more than our blessed Lord knew in the days of his flesh deserve to be disappointed. "It is not for you to know times or seasons, which the Father hath set within his own authority" (Acts 1 : 7). This settles the question.

MYSTICAL AND SYMBOLICAL INTERPRETATIONS.

The number is neither alphabetical nor chronological, but the mystical or symbolical name of Antichrist, who is yet to come. Here we meet again with different views.

Primasius, the African commentator of the Apocalypse (a pupil of Augustin), mentions two names as giving the general characteristics of Antichrist : 'Αντεμος and ἀρνουμε, the former *honori contrarius*, the other from ἀρνέομαι, *to deny*, by which the Antichrist is justly described, "*utpote per duas partes orationis, nominis scilicet et verbi, et personæ qualitas et operis insinuatur asperitas.*" Utterly worthless. See Lücke, p. 997. Züllig finds in the figure the name of *Bileam*. Not much better is Hengstenberg's explanation : *Adonikam, i.e.,* "The Lord arises," a good name for Antichrist (2 Thess. 2 : 4)! He bases it on Ezra 2 : 13 : "The children of Adonikam, six hundred and sixty-six." Ezra gives a list of the children of Israel who returned from the captivity under Zerubbabel. What this has to do with Antichrist is difficult to see.

Von Hofmann and Füller think that the number implies the *personal* name of Antichrist.

Another view is this : the number is symbolical, like all other numbers in the Apocalypse, and signifies the *anti-Christian world-power* in all its successive forms from heathen Rome down to the end. Hence it admits of many applications, as there are "many Antichrists." The number six is the number of human work and toil (six days of the week), as seven is the number of divine rest. Or, six is the half of twelve—the number of the church—and indicates the divided condition of the temporal power. Three sixes signify worldliness (worldly glory, worldly wisdom, worldly civilization) at the height of power, which with all vaunted strength is but weakness and folly, and falls short of the divine perfection symbolized by the numbers seven and twelve. Such or similar views were suggested by Herder, Auberlen, Rösch, Hengstenberg, Burger, Maurice, Wordsworth, Vaughan, Carpenter, etc.

THE MESSIAH OF SATAN.

To the class of mystical interpretation belongs the recent view of Professor Godet, of Neuchatel, which deserves special mention. This eminent commentator sees in 666 the emblematic name of THE MESSIAH OF SATAN in opposition to the divine Messiah. The number was originally represented by the three letters $\chi \xi \varsigma'$. The first and the last letters are an abridgment of the name of Christ, and have the value of 606 ($\chi = 600 + \varsigma = 6$); the middle ξ is, in virtue of its form and of the sibilant sound, the emblem of Satan, and as a cipher has the value of 60. Satan is called in the Apocalypse the *old serpent* in allusion to the history of the temptation (Gen. 3). This explanation was first suggested by Heumann and Herder, and is made by Godet the basis of an original theory, namely, that Antichrist or the man of sin will be a *Jew* who will set up a carnal Israel in opposition to the true Messiah, and worship the prince of this world in order to gain universal empire.[1] *Corruptio optimi pessima.* Renan says: "Nothing can equal in wickedness the wickedness of Jews : at the same time the best of men have been Jews ; you may say of this race whatever good or evil you please, without danger of overstepping the truth." In blasphemy, as well as in adoration, the Jew is the foremost of mankind. Only an apostate can blaspheme with all his heart. Our Gentile Voltaires are but lambs as compared with Jews in reviling Christ and his church. None but Israel could give birth to Judas, none but apostate Israel can give birth to Antichrist. Israel answers precisely to the description of the apocalyptic beast, which *was* and *is not* and *shall be* (17 : 11), which was *wounded to death*, and is to be miraculously *healed*, in order to play, as the eighth head, the part of Antichrist. Godet refers to the rising power of the Jews in wealth, politics, and literature, and especially their command of the anti-Christian press in Christian countries, as indications of the approach of the fulfilment of this prophecy.

Godet holds to the late date of the Apocalypse under Domitian, and rejects the application of the seven heads of the beast to Roman emperors. He applies them, like Auberlen, Hengstenberg, and others, to as many empires, before and after Christ, but brings in, as a new feature, the Herodian dynasty, which was subject to the Roman power.

[1] In the essay above quoted, p. 388, and in the article *Revelation* in Johnson's " Cyclopædia," III. 1606 sqq.

According to his view, the first head is ancient Egypt trying to destroy Israel in its cradle ; the second is the Assyro-Babylonian empire which destroyed the kingdom of the ten tribes, and then Jerusalem ; the third is the Persian empire, which held restored Israel under its authority ; the fourth is the Greek monarchy under Antiochus Epiphanes (the little horn of Daniel, ch. 8, the Antichrist of the Old Testament), who attempted to suppress the worship of God in Israel, and to substitute that of Zeus ; the fifth is the Jewish state under the Herods and the pontificates of Annas and Caiaphas, who crucified the Saviour and then tried to destroy his church ; the sixth is the Roman empire, which is supposed to embrace all political power in Europe to this day ; the seventh head is that power of short duration which shall destroy the whole political system of Europe, and prepare it for the arrival of Antichrist from the bosom of infidel Judaism. In this way Godet harmonizes the Apocalypse with the teaching of Paul concerning the restraining effect of the Roman empire, which will be overthrown in order to give way to the full sway of Antichrist. The eighth head is Israel restored, with a carnal Messiah at its head, who will preach the worship of humanity and overthrow Rome, the old enemy of the Jews (Apoc. 18), but be overthrown in turn by Christ (ch. 19 and 2 Thess. 2 : 8). Then follows the millennium, the sabbath of humanity on earth after its long week of work, not necessarily a visible reign of Christ, but a reign by his Spirit. At the end of this period, Satan, who as yet is only bound, shall try once more to destroy the work of God, but shall only prepare his final defeat, and give the signal for the universal judgment (ch. 20). The terrestrial state founded on the day of creation now gives place to the new heavens and the new earth (ch. 21), in which God shall be all in all. Anticipating the sight of this admirable spectacle, John prostrates himself and invites all the faithful to cry with the Spirit and the spouse, "Lord, come—come soon " (ch. 22). What a vast drama ! What a magnificent conclusion to the Scriptures opening with Genesis ! The first creation made man free ; the second shall make him holy, and then the work of God is accomplished.

Conclusion.

A very ingenious interpretation, with much valuable truth, but not the last word yet on this mysterious book, and very doubtful in its solution of the numerical riddle. The primary meaning of the beast, as already remarked, is heathen Rome, as represented by that monster tyrant and persecutor, Nero, the very incarnation of satanic wickedness. The oldest interpretation (*Lateinos*), known already to a grand-pupil of St. John, is also the best, and it is all the more plausible because the other interpretations which give us the alphabetical value of 666, namely, *Nero* and *Cæsar Augustus*, likewise point to the same Roman power which kept up a bloody crusade of three hundred years against Christianity. But the political beast, and its intellectual ally, the false prophet, appear again and again in history, and make war upon the church and the truth of Christ, within and without the circle of the old Roman empire. Many more wonders of exegetical ability and historical learning will yet be performed before the mysteries of Revelation are solved, if they ever will be solved before the final fulfilment. In the meantime, the book will continue to accomplish its practical mission of comfort and encouragement to every Christian in the conflict of faith for the crown of life.

§ 102. *Concluding Reflections. Faith and Criticism.*

There is no necessary conflict between faith and criticism any more than between revelation and reason or between faith and philosophy. God is the author of both, and he cannot contradict himself. There is an uncritical faith and a faithless criticism, as there is a genuine philosophy and a philosophy falsely so called; but this is no argument either against faith or criticism; for the best gifts are liable to abuse and perversion; and the noblest works of art may be caricatured. The apostle of faith directs us to "prove all things," and to "hold fast that which is good." We believe in order to understand, and true faith is the mother of knowledge. A rational faith in Christianity, as the best and final religion which God gave to mankind, owes it to itself to examine the foundation on which it rests; and it is urged by an irresistible impulse to vindicate the truth against every form of error. Christianity needs no apology. Conscious of its supernatural strength, it can boldly meet every foe and convert him into an ally.

Looking back upon the history of the apostolic age, it appears to us as a vast battle-field of opposite tendencies and schools. Every inch of ground is disputed and has to be reconquered; every fact, as well as every doctrine of revelation, is called in question; every hypothesis is tried; all the resources of learning, acumen, and ingenuity are arrayed against the citadel of the Christian faith. The citadel is impregnable, and victory is certain, but not to those who ignorantly or superciliously

underrate the strength of the besieging army. In the sixteenth
century the contest was between Roman Catholicism and Evangelical Protestantism ; in the nineteenth century the question
is Christianity or infidelity. Then both parties believed in the
inspiration of the New Testament and the extent of the canon,
differing only in the interpretation ; now inspiration is denied,
and the apostolicity of all but four or five books is assailed.
Then the Word of God, with or without tradition, was the final
arbiter of religious controversies ; now human reason is the ultimate tribunal.

We live in an age of discovery, invention, research, and
doubt. Scepticism is well nigh omnipresent in the thinking
world. It impregnates the atmosphere. We can no more ignore it than the ancient Fathers could ignore the Gnostic speculations of their day. Nothing is taken for granted ; nothing
believed on mere authority ; everything must be supported by
adequate proof, everything explained in its natural growth from
the seed to the fruit. Roman Catholics believe in an infallible
oracle in the Vatican ; but whatever the oracle may decree,
the earth moves and will continue to move around the sun.
Protestants, having safely crossed the Red Sea, cannot go back
to the flesh-pots of the land of bondage, but must look forward
to the land of promise. In the night, says a proverb, all cattle
are black, but the daylight reveals the different colors.

Why did Christ not write the New Testament, as Mohammed
wrote the Koran ? Writing was not beneath his dignity ; he
did write once in the sand, though we know not what. God
himself wrote the Ten Commandments on two tables of stone.
But Moses broke them to pieces when he saw that the people of
Israel worshipped the golden calf before the thunders from Sinai
had ceased to reverberate in their ears. They might have
turned those tables into idols. God buried the great law-giver
out of sight and out of the reach of idolatry. The gospel was
still less intended to be a dumb idol than the law. It is not a
killing letter but a lifegiving spirit. It is the spirit that quickeneth ; the flesh profiteth nothing ; the words of Christ

"are spirit and are life." A book written by his own unerring hand, unless protected by a perpetual miracle, would have been subject to the same changes and corruptions in the hands of fallible transcribers and printers as the books of his disciples, and the original autograph would have perished with the brittle papyrus. Nor would it have escaped the unmerciful assaults of sceptical and infidel critics, and misinterpretations of commentators and preachers. He himself was crucified by the hierarchy of his own people, whom he came to save. What better fate could have awaited his book? Of course, it would have risen from the dead, in spite of the doubts and conjectures and falsehoods of unbelieving men; but the same is true of the writings of the apostles, though thousands of copies have been burned by heathens and false Christians. Thomas might put his hand into the wound-prints of his risen Lord; but "Blessed are they that have not seen and yet have believed."

We must believe in the Holy Spirit who lives and moves in the Church and is the invisible power behind the written and printed word.

The form in which the authentic records of Christianity have come down to us, with their variations and difficulties, is a constant stimulus to study and research and calls into exercise all the intellectual and moral faculties of men. Every one must strive after the best understanding of the truth with a faithful use of his opportunities and privileges, which are multiplying with every generation.

The New Testament is a revelation of spiritual and eternal truth to faith, and faith is the work of the Holy Spirit, though rooted in the deepest wants and aspirations of man. It has to fight its way through an unbelieving world, and the conflict waxes hotter and hotter as the victory comes nearer. For the last half century the apostolic writings have been passing through the purgatory of the most scorching criticism to which a book can be subjected. The opposition is itself a powerful testimony to their vitality and importance.

There are two kinds of scepticism: one represented by

Thomas, honest, earnest, seeking and at last finding the truth;
the other represented by Sadducees and Pontius Pilate, superficial, worldly, frivolous, indifferent to truth and ending in despair. With the latter " even the gods reason in vain." When
it takes the trouble to assail the Bible, it deals in sneers and
ridicule which admit of no serious answer. The roots of infidelity lie in the heart and will rather than in the reason and intellect, and wilful opposition to the truth is deaf to any argument. But honest, truth-loving scepticism always deserves regard and sympathy and demands a patient investigation of the
real or imaginary difficulties which are involved in the problem of the origin of Christianity. It may be more useful
to the church than an unthinking and unreasoning orthodoxy.
One of the ablest and purest sceptical critics of the century
(DeWette) made the sad, but honorable confession:

> "I lived in times of doubt and strife,
>   When childlike faith was forced to yield ;
> I struggled to the end of life,
>   Alas ! I did not gain the field."

But he did gain the field, after all, at last ; for a few months
before his death he wrote and published this significant sentence : " I know that in no other name can salvation be found,
than in the name of Jesus Christ the Crucified, and there is
nothing higher for mankind than the divine humanity (*Gott-
menschheit*) realized in him, and the kingdom of God planted by
him." Blessed are those that seek the truth, for they shall find it.

The critical and historical rationalism which was born and
matured in this century in the land of Luther, and has spread in
Switzerland, France, Holland, England, Scotland, and America,
surpasses in depth and breadth of learning, as well as in earnestness of spirit, all older forms of infidelity and heresy. It is not
superficial and frivolous, as the rationalism of the eighteenth
century ; it is not indifferent to truth, but intensely interested in
ascertaining the real facts, and tracing the origin and development of Christianity, as a great historical phenomenon   But it

arrogantly claims to be the criticism *par excellence*, as the Gnosticism of the ancient church pretended to have the monopoly of knowledge. There is a historical, conservative, and constructive criticism, as well as an unhistorical, radical, and destructive criticism ; and the former must win the fight as sure as God's truth will outlast all error. So there is a believing and Christian Gnosticism as well as an unbelieving and anti- (or pseudo-) Christian Gnosticism.

The negative criticism of the present generation has concentrated its forces upon the life of Christ and the apostolic age, and spent an astonishing amount of patient research upon the minutest details of its history. And its labors have not been in vain ; on the contrary, it has done a vast amount of good, as well as evil. Its strength lies in the investigation of the human and literary aspect of the Bible ; its weakness in the ignoring of its divine and spiritual character. It forms thus the very antipode of the older orthodoxy, which so overstrained the theory of inspiration as to reduce the human agency to the mechanism of the pen. We must look at both aspects. The Bible is the Word of God and the word of holy men of old. It is a revelation of man, as well as of God. It reveals man in all his phases of development—innocence, fall, redemption—in all the varieties of character, from heavenly purity to satanic wickedness, with all his virtues and vices, in all his states of experience, and is an ever-flowing spring of inspiration to the poet, the artist, the historian, and divine. It reflects and perpetuates the mystery of the incarnation. It is the word of him who proclaimed himself the Son of Man, as well as the Son of God. "*Men* spake from God, being moved by the *Holy Spirit*." Here all is divine and all is human.

No doubt the New Testament is the result of a gradual growth and conflict of different forces, which were included in the original idea of Christianity and were drawn out as it passed from Christ to his disciples, from the Jews to the Gentiles, from Jerusalem to Antioch and Rome, and as it matured in the mind of the leading apostles. No doubt the Gospels and Epistles were written by certain men, at a certain time, in a certain place, under certain surroundings, and for definite ends ; and all these questions are legitimate objects of inquiry and eminently deserving of ever-renewed investigation.   Many obscure points have been cleared up, thanks, in part, to these very critics, who intended to destroy, and helped to build up.

The literary history of the apostolic age, like its missionary progress, was guided by a special providence.   Christ only finished a part of his work while on earth.   He pointed his disciples to greater works, which they would accomplish in his name and by his power, after his resurrection.   He promised them his unbroken presence, and the gift of the Holy Spirit, who, as the other Advocate, should lead them into the whole truth and open to them the understanding of all his words.   The Acts of the Apostles are a history of the Holy Spirit, or of the post-resurrection work of Christ in establishing his kingdom on earth. Filled with that Spirit, the apostles and evangelists went forth into a hostile world and converted it to Christ by their living word, and they continue their conquering march by their written word.

Unbelieving criticism sees only the outside surface of the greatest movement in history, and is blind to the spiritual forces working from within or refuses to acknowledge them as truly divine.   In like manner, the materialistic and atheistic scientists of the age conceive of nature's laws without a lawgiver ; of a creature without a creator ; and stop with the effect, without rising to the cause, which alone affords a rational explanation of the effect.

And here we touch upon the deepest spring of all forms of rationalism, and upon the gulf which inseparably divides it from supernaturalism.   It is the opposition to the supernatural and the miraculous.   It denies God in nature and God in history, and, in its ultimate consequences, it denies the very existence of God. Deism and atheism have no place for a miracle ; but belief in the existence of an Almighty Maker of all things visible and invisible, as the ultimate and allsufficient cause of all phenomena in nature and in history, implies the possibility of miracle at any time ; not, indeed, as a violation of his own laws, but as a manifestation of his lawgiving and creative power over and above (not against) the regular order of events. The reality of the miracle, in any particular case, then, becomes a matter of historical investigation. It cannot be disposed of by a simple denial from *à priori* philosophical prejudice; but must be fairly examined, and, if sufficiently corroborated by external and internal evidence, it must be admitted.

Now, the miracles of Christ cannot be separated from his person and his teachings. His words are as marvellous as his deeds; both form a harmonious whole, and they stand or fall together. His person is the great miracle, and his miracles are simply his natural works. He is as much elevated above other men as his words and deeds are above ordinary words and deeds. He is separated from all mortals by his absolute freedom from sin. He, himself, claims superhuman origin and supernatural powers; and to deny them is to make him a liar and impostor. It is impossible to maintain his human perfection, which all respectable rationalists admit and even emphasize, and yet to refuse his testimony concerning himself. The Christ of Strauss and of Renan is the most contradictory of all characters; the most incredible of all enigmas. There is no possible scientific mediation between a purely humanitarian conception of Christ, no matter how high he may be raised in the scale of beings, and the faith in Christ as the Son of God, whom Christendom has adored from the beginning and still adores as the Lord and Saviour of the world.

Nor can we eliminate the supernatural element from the Apostolic Church without destroying its very life and resolving it into a gigantic illusion. What becomes of Paul if we deny his conversion, and how shall we account for his conversion without the Resurrection and Ascension? The greatest of modern sceptics paused at the problem, and felt almost forced to admit an actual miracle, as the only rational solution of that conversion. The Holy Spirit was the inspiring and propelling power of the apostolic age, and made the fishers of Galilee fishers of men.

A Christian, who has experienced the power of the gospel in his heart, can have no difficulty with the supernatural. He is as sure of the regenerating and converting agency of the Spirit of God and the saving efficacy of Christ as he is of his own natural existence. He has tasted the medicine and has been healed. He may say with the man who was born blind and made to see : " One thing I do know, that, whereas I was blind, now I see." This is a short creed ; but stronger than any argument. The fortress of personal experience is impregnable ; the logic of stubborn facts is more cogent than the logic of reason. Every genuine conversion from sin to holiness is a psychological miracle, as much so as the conversion of Saul of Tarsus.

The secret or open hostility to the supernatural is the moving spring of infidel criticism. We may freely admit that certain difficulties about the time and place of composition and other minor details of the Gospels and Epistles are not, and perhaps never can be, satisfactorily solved ; but it is, nevertheless, true that they are far better authenticated by internal and external evidence than any books of the great Greek and Roman classics, or of Philo and Josephus, which are accepted by scholars without a doubt. As early as the middle of the second century, that is, fifty years after the death of the Apostle John, when yet many of his personal pupils and friends must have been living, the four Canonical Gospels, no more and no less, were recognized and read in public worship as sacred books, in the churches of Syria, Asia Minor, Egypt, Italy, and Gaul ; and such universal acceptance and authority in the face of Jewish and heathen hostility and heretical perversion can only be explained on the ground that they were known and used long before. Some of them, Matthew and John, were quoted and used in the first quarter of the second century by Orthodox and Gnostic writers. Every new discovery, as the last book of the pseudo-" Clementine Homilies," the " Philosophumena " of Hippolytus, the " Diatessaron " of Tatian, and every deeper investigation of the " Gospel Memoirs " of Justin Martyr, and the " Gospel " of Marcion in its relation to Luke, have strengthened the cause of historical and conservative criticism and inflicted bleeding wounds on destructive criticism. If quotations from the end of the first and the beginning of the second century are very rare, we must remember that we have only a handful of literary documents from that period, and that the second generation of Christians was not a race of scholars and scribes and critics, but of humble, illiterate confessors and martyrs, who still breathed the bracing air of the living teaching, and personal reminiscences of the apostles and evangelists.

But the Synoptical Gospels bear the strongest internal marks of having been composed before the destruction of Jerusalem (A.D. 70), which is therein prophesied by Christ as a future event and as the sign of the fast approaching judgment of the world, in a manner that is consistent only with such early composition. The Epistle to the Hebrews, likewise, was written when the Temple was still standing, and sacrifices were offered from day to day. Yet, as this early date is not conceded by all, we will leave the Epistle out of view. The Apocalypse of John is very confidently assigned to the year 68 or 69 by Baur, Renan, and others, who would put the Gospels down to a much later date. They also concede the Pauline authorship of the great anti-Judaic Epistles to the Galatians, Romans, and Corinthians, and make them the very basis of their assaults upon the minor Pauline Epistles and the Acts of the Apostles, on the ground of exaggerated or purely imaginary differences. Those Epistles of Paul were written twelve or fourteen years before the destruction of Jerusalem. This brings us within less than thirty years of the resurrection of Christ and the birthday of the church.

Now, if we confine ourselves to these five books, which the most exacting and rigorous criticism admits to be apostolic— the four Pauline Epistles and the Apocalypse—they alone are sufficient to establish the foundation of historical faith; for they confirm by direct statement or allusion every important fact and doctrine in the gospel history, without referring to the written Gospels. The memory and personal experience of the writers—Paul and John—goes back to the vision of Damascus, to the scenes of the Resurrection and Crucifixion, and the first call of the disciples on the banks of the Jordan and the shores of the Lake of Galilee. Criticism must first reason Paul and John out of history, or deny that they ever wrote a line, before it can expect sensible men to surrender a single chapter of the Gospels.

Strong as the external evidence is, the internal evidence of the truth and credibility of the apostolic writings is still stronger, and may be felt to this day by the unlearned as well as the scholar. They widely differ in style and spirit from all post-apostolic productions, and occupy a conspicuous isolation even among the best of books. This position they have occupied for eighteen centuries among the most civilized nations of the globe; and from this position they are not likely to be deposed.

We must interpret persons and events not only by themselves, but also in the light of subsequent history. "By their fruits ye shall know them." Christianity can stand this test better than any other religion, and better than any system of philosophy.

Taking our position at the close of the apostolic age, and looking back to its fountain-head and forward to succeeding generations, we cannot but be amazed at the magnitude of the effects produced by the brief public ministry of Jesus of Nazareth, which sends its blessings through centuries as an unbroken and ever-expanding river of life. There is absolutely nothing like it in the annals of the race. The Roman empire embraced, at the birth of Christ, over one hundred millions of men, conquered by force, and, after having persecuted his religion for three hundred years, it died away without the possibility of a resurrection. The Christian church now numbers four hundred millions, conquered by the love of Christ, and is constantly increasing. The first century is the life and light of history and the turning point of the ages. If ever God revealed himself to man, if ever heaven appeared on earth, it was in the person and work of Jesus of Nazareth. He is, beyond any shadow of doubt, and by the reluctant consent of sceptics and infidels, the wisest of the wise, the purest of the pure, and the mightiest of the mighty. His Cross has become the tree of life to all nations; his teaching is still the highest standard of religious truth; his example the unsurpassed ideal of holiness; the Gospels and Epistles of his Galilean disciples are still the book of books, more powerful than all the classics of human wisdom and genius. No book has attracted so much attention, provoked so much opposition, outlived so many persecutions, called forth so much reverence and gratitude, inspired so many noble thoughts and deeds, administered so much comfort and peace from the cradle to the grave to all classes and conditions of men. It is more than a book; it is an institution, an all-pervading omnipresent force, a converting, sanctifying, transforming agency; it rules from the pulpit and the chair; it presides at the family altar; it is the sacred ark of every household, the written conscience of every Christian man, the pillar of cloud by day, the pillar of light by night in the pilgrimage of life. Mankind is bad enough, and human life dark enough with it; but how much worse and how much darker would they be without it? Christianity might live without the letter of the New Testament, but not without the facts and truths which it records and teaches. Were it possible to banish them from the world, the sun of our civilization would be extinguished, and mankind left to midnight darkness, with the dreary prospect of a dreamless and endless Nirvana.

But no power on earth or in hell can extinguish that sun. There it shines on the horizon, the king of day, obscured at times by clouds great or small, but breaking through again and again, and shedding light and life from east to west, until the darkest corners of the globe shall be illuminated. The past is secure; God will take care of the future.

MAGNA EST VERITAS ET PRÆVALEBIT.

ALPHABETICAL INDEX